FINANCIAL SERVICES LAW

FINANCIAL SERVICES LAW

SECOND EDITION

Edited by

MICHAEL BLAIR QC
of 3 Verulam Buildings,
Gray's Inn, London

GEORGE WALKER
Centre for Commercial Law Studies,
London

ROBERT PURVES
(Deputy Editor)
of 3 Verulam Buildings,
Gray's Inn, London

OXFORD
UNIVERSITY PRESS

OXFORD

UNIVERSITY PRESS

Great Clarendon Street, Oxford ox2 6DP

Oxford University Press is a department of the University of Oxford.
It furthers the University's objective of excellence in research, scholarship,
and education by publishing worldwide in

Oxford New York

Auckland Cape Town Dar es Salaam Hong Kong Karachi
Kuala Lumpur Madrid Melbourne Mexico City Nairobi
New Delhi Shanghai Taipei Toronto

With offices in

Argentina Austria Brazil Chile Czech Republic France Greece
Guatemala Hungary Italy Japan Poland Portugal Singapore
South Korea Switzerland Thailand Turkey Ukraine Vietnam

Oxford is a registered trade mark of Oxford University Press
in the UK and in certain other countries

Published in the United States
by Oxford University Press Inc., New York

British Library Cataloguing in Publication Data

Data available

Library of Congress Cataloging in Publication Data

Data available

Typeset by Cepha Imaging Private Ltd, Bangalore, India
Printed in Great Britain
on acid-free paper by
CPI Antony Rowe

ISBN 978–0–19–956418–7

1 3 5 7 9 10 8 6 4 2

CONTENTS—SUMMARY

III FINANCIAL SECTORS AND ACTIVITIES

CONTENTS

II FINANCIAL SERVICES REGULATION

5. FSA Handbook and High-Level Standards

11. Integrated Prudential Regulation

III FINANCIAL SECTORS AND ACTIVITIES

Contents

15. Home Finance Transactions

TABLE OF CASES

TABLES OF LEGISLATION

Statutory Instruments

TABLES OF EUROPEAN LEGISLATION

TABLE OF TREATIES AND CONVENTIONS

LIST OF ABBREVIATIONS

1MLD	First Money Laundering Directive (Directive 91/308/EEC [1991] OJ L166/77)
2MLD	Second Money Laundering Directive (Directive 2001/97/EC [2001] OJ L344/76)
3MLD	Third Money Laundering Directive (Directive 2005/60/EC [2005] OJ L309/15)
3NLD	The Three Non-life Directives/the 3rd Non-life Directive
AAOIFI	Accounting and Auditing Organisation for Islamic Financial Institutions
ABI	Association of British Insurers
ABCP	asset-backed commercial paper
ABTA	Association of British Travel Agents
ACD	authorised corporate director
ACPO	Association of Chief Police Officers of England & Wales
AFTA	ASEAN Free Trade Area
AICPA	American Institute of Certified Public Accountants
AIG	Accord Implementation Group
AIM	Alternative Investment Market
AISG	Accountants International Study Group
AMA	advanced measurement approach
AMF	Autorité des Marchés Financiers
AML	anti-money laundering
APEC	Asia Pacific Economic Cooperation
APER	Statements of Principle and Code of Practice for Approved Persons
APG	Asia/Pacific Group on Money Laundering
ARA	Assets Recovery Agency
ARROW	Advanced Risk-Responsive Operating Framework
ASEAN	Association of Southeast Asian Nations
AUT	Authorised Unit Trust
AUTH	Authorisation Manual
BAC	Banking Advisory Committee
BAFTA	Baltic Free-Trade Area
BANGKOK	Bangkok Agreement
BBA	British Bankers' Association
BCBS	Basel Committee on Banking Supervision

BCD	Directive (EC) 2006/48 relating to the taking up and pursuit of the business of credit institutions
BCRR	base capital resources requirement
BERR	Department for Business, Enterprise & Regulatory Reform
BIBA	British Insurance Brokers' Association
BIFCOM	Banks and Investment Firms Commodity Standing Group
BIPRU	Prudential Sourcebook for Banks, Building Societies and Investment Firms
BIS	Bank for International Settlements
BRAP	Better Regulation Action Plan
BRE	Better Regulation Executive
BSOG	Building Societies Regulatory Guide
BSCB	Banking Code Standards Board
CACM	Central American Common Market
CAD I	Capital Adequacy Directive 1993
CAD II	Capital Adequacy Directive 1998
CAMEL	capital, assets, management, earnings, and liquidity
CAN	Andean Community
CARD	Consolidated Admissions and Reporting Directive
CARICOM	Caribbean Community
CASS	Client Assets Sourcebook
CBB	Central Bank of Bahrain
CBSG	Covered Bond Standing Group
CDCF	Community Development Carbon Fund
CDD	customer due diligence
CDO	collateralised debt obligations
CEBS	Committee of European Banking Supervisors
CEFTA	Central European Free Trade Agreement
CEIOPS	Committee of European Insurance and Occupational Pension Supervisors
CEMAC	Economic and Monetary Community of Central Africa
CEO	Chief Executive Officer
CER	Closer Trade Relations Trade Agreement
CESR	Committee of European Securities Regulators
CFATF	Caribbean Financial Action Task Force
CFD	contract for differences
CFTC	Commodities Futures Trading Commission
CGAP	Consultative Group to Assist the Poor
CGFS	Committee on the Global Financial System
CGIAR	Consultative Group on International Agricultural Research
CGSG	Capital and Groups Standing Group
CICA	Canadian Institute of Chartered Accountants
CIDD	combined initial disclosure document

CIS	collective investment scheme
CIS	Commonwealth of Independent States
CIU	collective investment undertakings
CJA	Criminal Justice Act 1993
CLD	Consolidated Life Directive
CLN	credit-linked note
CMR	Client Money Rules contained in the Client Money Sourcebook
CNCOM	concentration risk capital component
COAF	Complaints against the FSA
COBS	Conduct of Business Sourcebook
COLLG	Collective Investment Scheme Information Guide
COM	controls, organisation, and management
COMC	Code of Market Conduct
COMESA	Common Market for Eastern and Southern Africa
COMP	Compensation Sourcebook
COMSG	Commodity Standing Group
COND	Threshold Conditions Sourcebook
CPS	Crown Prosecution Service
CPSS	Committee on Payment and Settlement Systems
CR	capital resources
CRA	credit rating agency
CRD	Capital Requirements Directive
CRED	Credit Unions Sourcebook
CRM	credit risk mitigation
CRMSG	Credit Risk Mitigation Standing Group
CRR	capital resources requirement
CRSG	Credit Risk Standing Group
CTFs	child trust funds
CTI	connected travel insurance
CTS	Council for Trade in Services
CTSA	Consumer and Trading Standards Agency
DDA	Doha Development Agenda
DEC	Decision Making Manual
DEPP	Decision Procedure and Penalties manual
DFSA	Dubai Financial Services Authority
DGD	Deposit Guarantee Directive
DIFC	Dubai International Financial Centre
DISP	Dispute Resolution: Complaints Sourcebook
DMD	Distance Marketing Directive (Council Directive 02/65/EC on distance marketing of consumer financial services [2002] OJ L271/16)
DPP	Director of Public Prosecutions
DR	disclosure rules

DR–CAFTA	Dominican Republic–Central America Free Trade Agreement
DSU	Understanding on Rules and Procedures Governing the Settlement of Disputes
DTI	Department of Trade and Industry
DTR	Disclosure and Transparency Rules
DVP	delivery versus payment
EAD	exposure at default
EAG	Eurasian Group
EBC	European Banking Committee
EC	European Commission
ECAI	external credit assessment institution
ECB	European Central Bank
ECBS	European Committee of Banking Supervisors
ECD	Electronic Commerce Directive (Directive 2000/31/EC [2000] OJ L178/1)
ECHR	European Convention on Human Rights
ECJ	European Court of Justice
ECO	Electronic Commerce Directive Sourcebook
ECOFIN	Economic and Financial Affairs Council (EU)
ECRGI	Enhanced capital requirement for general insurance
ECRLT	Enhanced Capital Requirement for long-term business
ECtHR	European Court of Human Rights
EEA	European Economic Area
EG	Enforcement Guide
EGMONT	Egmont Group of Financial Intelligence Units
EIOPC	European Insurance and Occupational Pensions Committee
ELAS	Equitable Life Assurance Society Limited
ELM	Electronic Money Sourcebook
EMEAP	Executives' Meeting of East Asia and Pacific Central Banks
EMPS	Energy Market Participants
ENF	Enforcement Manual
EPU	European Payments Union
ESAAMLG	Eastern and Southern Africa Anti-Money Laundering Group
ESC	European Securities Committee
ESME	European Securities Markets Expert Group
EU	European Union
EZPUT	Enterprise Zone Property Unit Trust
FAF	Financial Accounting Foundation
FAO	Food and Agriculture Organisation
FASAC	Financial Accounting Standards Council
FASB	Financial Accounting Standards Board
FATF	Financial Action Task Force

FBD	First Banking Directive (EEC) 77/780 on the co-ordination of laws, regulations and administrative provisions relating to the taking up and pursuit of the business of credit institutions
FCD	Financial Conglomerates Directive (EC) 02/87 on the supplementary supervision of credit institutions, insurance undertakings and investment firms in a financial conglomerate
FESCO	Federation of European Securities Commissions
FGD	Financial Groups Directive (EC) 02/87 on the supplementary supervision of credit institutions, insurance undertakings and investment firms in a financial conglomerate
FHC	financial holding company
FIMBRA	Financial Intermediaries and Brokers Regulatory Association
FISMOU	financial information sharing agreements
FIT	fit and proper test for approved persons
FIU	financial intelligence unit
FMRF	Financial Management Reporting Framework
FOS	Financial Ombudsman Service
FPO	Financial Services and Markets Act 2000 (Financial Promotion) Order 2005 (SI 2005/1529)
FPRU	Friendly Societies Prudential Sourcebook
FREN	small friendly societies
FSA	Financial Services Authority
FSA 1986	Financial Services Act 1986
FSA Handbook	FSA Handbook of rules and regulations
FSAP	Financial Services Action Plan
FSAVC	free standing additional voluntary contributions
FSCS	Financial Services Compensation Scheme
FSF	Financial Stability Forum
FSI	Financial Stability Institute
FSMA	Financial Services and Markets Act 2000
FSMT	Financial Services and Markets Tribunal
FTAA	Free Trade Area of the Americas
GAAP	generally accepted accounting principles
GAB	general arrangements to borrow
GABRIEL	GAthering Better Regulatory Information Electronically
GAFISUD	Financial Action Task Force on Money Laundering in South America
GASB	Government Accounting Standards Board
GATS	General Agreement on Trade in Services
GATT	General Agreement on Tariffs and Trade
GCC	Gulf Co-operation Council
GCR	group capital resources
GCRR	group capital resources requirement
GDR	Global depository receipts
GEN	General Provisions Sourcebook

GENPRU	General Prudential Sourcebook
GICR	general insurance capital requirement
GIGI	Insurance Intermediaries
GISC	General Insurance Standards Council
HIPC	Heavily Indebted Poor Countries
HPP	home purchase plan
HRA	Human Rights Act
IAA	internal assessment approach
IADI	International Association of Deposit Insurers
IAIS	International Association of Insurance Supervisors
IAS	International Accounting Standards
IASB	International Accounting Standards Board
IASC	International Accounting Standards Committee
IBAs	insurance bank accounts
IBB	Islamic Bank of Britain
IBRA	Insurance Brokers (Registration) Act 1997
IBRC	Insurance Brokers Registration Council
IBRD	International Bank for Reconstruction and Development
ICA	individual capital assessment
ICA	Insurance Companies Act 1982
ICAAP	Internal Capital Adequacy Assessment Process
ICAEW	Institute of Chartered Accountants in England and Wales
ICD	Investor Compensation Directive
ICG	individual capital guidance
ICMA	International Capital Market Association
ICOB	Insurance: Conduct of Business Sourcebook
ICSID	International Centre for Settlement of Investment Disputes
ICTA	Income and Corporation Taxes Act 1988
ICVC	investment company with variable capital
IDA	International Development Association
IDD	initial disclosure document
IDD	Insider Dealing Directive (EEC) 89/592
IDO	Insider Dealing (Securities and Regulated Markets) Order 1994
IETA	International Emissions Trading Association
IFAs	independent financial advisers
IFC	International Finance Corporation
IFF	Islamic Finance Firm
IFRS	international financial reporting standards
IFSB	Islamic Financial Services Board
IFSB (CAS)	IFSB Capital Adequacy Standard for Institutions (Other than Insurance Institutions) Offering Only Islamic Financial Services, 2005

IGD	Insurance Groups Directive (Council Directive (EC) 98/78 on the supplementary supervision of insurance undertakings in an insurance group (1998) OJ L330)
IIB	Institute of Insurance Brokers
IMD	Insurance Mediation Directive (Council Directive (EC) 02/92 on insurance mediation (2002) OJ L9/3)
IMF	International Monetary Fund
IMFC	International Monetary and Financial Committee
IMRO	Investment Management Regulatory Organisation
INSPRU	Prudential Sourcebook for Insurers
INVPRU	Prudential Sourcebook for Investment Business
IOB	Insurance Ombudsman Bureau
IOSCO	International Organisation of Securities Commissions
IOSCO MOU	Multilateral Memorandum Concerning Consultation and Cooperation and the Exchange of Information
IPMA	International Primary Market Association (merged with ISMA on 1 July 2005 to form ICMA)
IPO	initial public offering
IPRU(BANK)	Interim Prudential Sourcebook for banks
IPRU(BSOC)	Interim Prudential Sourcebook for building societies
IPRU(FSOC)	Interim Prudential Sourcebook for friendly societies
IPRU(INS)	Interim Prudential Sourcebook for insurers
IPRU(INV)	Interim Prudential Sourcebook for investment and securities firms
IRB	internal ratings based approaches
IRR	integrated regulatory reporting
ISA	individual savings account
ISD	Investment Services Directive (EEC) 22/93 on investment services in the securities field
ISDA	International Swaps and Derivatives Association
ISMA	International Securities Market Association (merged with IPMA on 1 July 2005 to form ICMA)
ISPRU	Prudential Sourcebook for insurers
ISPV	insurance special purpose vehicle
ISSRO	international securities self-regulating organisation
ITC	International Trade Centre
JAC	Joint Associations Committee
JMLSG	Joint Money Laundering Steering Group
KII	Key investor information
KYC	know your customer
LAAC	Listing Authority Advisory Committee
LARC	Listing Authority Review Committee

LAUTRO	Life Assurance and Unit Trust Regulatory Organisation
LECB	large exposures capital base
LGD	loss given default
LIBA	London Investment Banking Association
LLD	Lloyd's Sourcebook
LLR	lender of last resort
Lloyd's	Lloyd's of London
LMBC	London Market Insurance Brokers' Committee
LR	Listing Rules
LSF	Loi de Sécurité Financière
LTICR	long term insurance capital requirement
M&GI	Mortgage and General Insurance
MAD	Market Abuse Directive (EC) 2003/6
MAR	Market Conduct Sourcebook
MARD	Making A Real Difference
MCOB	Mortgage advice and arranging: Conduct of Business Sourcebook
MCR	minimum capital requirement
MEAFs	mortgage exit administration fees
MENAFATF	Middle East and North Africa Financial Action Task Force
MGF	Minimum Guarantee Fund
MiFID	Markets in Financial Instruments Directive (Council Directive (EC) 39/2004 on markets in financial instruments)
MIG	Guide for Small Mortgage and Insurance Intermediaries
MIGA	Multilateral Investment Guarantee Agency
MIGI	Small Mortgage and Insurance Intermediaries General Rules
MIPRU	Prudential Sourcebook for Mortgage and Home Finance Firm and Insurance Intermediaries/the prudential requirements for mortgage and home finance firms and insurance intermediaties
ML	Money Laundering Sourcebook
MLRO	money laundering reporting officer
MOGI	Mortgage Intermediaries General Rules
MONEYVAL	Council of Europe Select Committee of Experts on the Evaluation of Anti-Money Laundering Measures
MOU	Memoranda/Memorandum of Understanding
MPBR	more principles-based regulation
MPC	Monetary Policy Committee
MRTSG	Market Risk and Trading Books Standing Group
MTF	multi-lateral trading facility
MTM	mark-to-market
N1	1 June 1998
N2	1 December 2001—ie the date on which FSA assumed its powers under the Financial Services and Markets Act 2000

N3	October 2004 and January 2005
NAB	new arrangements to borrow
NAFTA	North American Free Trade Agreement
NAO	National Audit Office
NATO	North Atlantic Treaty Organisation
NCCT	Non-co-operative Countries and Territories
NCIS	National Criminal Intelligence Service
NGI	14 January 2005—ie the date on which FSA started to regulate the sale and administration of general insurance and pure protection products
OECD	Organization for Economic Co-operation and Development
OEEC	Organization for European Economic Cooperation
OEIC	open-ended investment companies
OFAR	overall financial adequacy rule
OFT	Office of Fair Trading
OMO	open market operation
OMPS	Oil Market Participants
OPR	outcome performance report
ORA	Ongoing Regulatory Activities
ORCR	operational risk capital requirement
ORD	Own Funds Directive
ORSA	own risk and solvency assessment
ORSG	Operational Risk Standing Group
OTC	over the counter
PBR	principles-based regulation
PCAOB	Public Companies Accounting Oversight Board
PD	Prospectus Directive (EC) 2003/71
PD	probability of default
PDMR	person discharging managerial responsibility
PEP	politically exposed persons
PEP	private equity plan
PERG	Perimeter Guidance Manual
PFA	Prevention of Fraud (Investments) Act 1939
PFE	potential future exposure
PIA	Personal Investment Authority
PII	professional indemnity insurance
PMI	private medical insurance
PMO	Financial Services and Markets Act 2000 (Prescribed Markets and Qualifying Investments) Order 2001
POCA	Proceeds of Crime Act 2002
POSR	The Public Offers of Securities Regulations 1995 (SI 1995/1537)
PPA	Policyholders Protection Act 1975

PPFM	principles and practices of financial management
PPI	payment protection insurance
PPS	Public Prosecution Service (Northern Ireland)
PR	prospectus rules
PRA	position risk addition
PRIN	Principles for Businesses Sourcebook
PROF	Professional Firms Sourcebook
PRU	Integrated Prudential Sourcebook
PSIA	profit sharing investment account
PSM	professional securities market
PTSG	Pillar Two Standing Group
QCS	qualitative consolidated supervision
QIS	qualified investor scheme/quantitative impact studies
RAO	The Financial Services and Markets Act 2000 (Regulated Activities) Order 2001 (SI 2001/544)
RBA	ratings-based approach
RCB	regulated covered bonds
RCR	resilience capital requirement
RDC	Regulatory Decisions Committee
RDR	retail distribution review
REC	Recognised Investment Exchanges and Clearing Houses Sourcebook
RID	Council Directive (EC) 05/68 on reinsurance
RINGA	relevant information not generally available
RIS	regulatory information service
RMAR	retail mediation activities return
RMM	required minimum margin
RMP	risk mitigation programme
RPB	recognised professional body
RPPD	responsibilities of providers and distributors for the fair treatment of customers
RTO	reception and transmission of orders
SBD	Second Banking Directive (EEC) 89/646 on the co-ordination of laws, regulations and administrative provisions relating to the taking up and pursuit of the business of credit institutions
SCR	solvency capital requirement
SD	securitised derivative
SDR	special drawing rights
SEC	US Securities and Exchange Commission
SEP	Supervisory Enhancement Programme
SETS	The LSE order book for the most liquid equities
SERV	service companies
SF	supervisory formula

SFA	Securities and Futures Authority
SFO	Serious Fraud Office
SFT	securities financing transaction
SIB	Securities and Investments Board
SIFA	small IFA firms
SIFMA	Securities Industry and Financial Markets Association
SIPP	self invested personal pension scheme
SLS	special liquidity scheme
SLS	special lending scheme
SOCA	Serious Organised Crime Authority
SOCPA	Serious Organised Crime and Police Act 2005
SPE	special purpose entity
SPP	Security and Prosperity Partnership of North America
SPV	special purpose vehicle
SRD	Solvency Ratio Directive
SREP	supervisory review and evaluation process
SRP	supervisory review process
SRO	self regulating organisation
SRR	special resolution regime
SSB	*Shari'a* Supervisory Board
SSG	Securitisation Standing Group
STR	suspicious transaction report
SUP	supervision manual
SWIFT	Society for Worldwide Interbank Financial Telecommunication
SYSC	Senior Management Arrangements, Systems and Controls Sourcebook
TAF	term auction facility
TARP	Troubled Asset Recovery Programme
TC	training and competence
TCF	treating customers fairly
TD	Transparency Directive (EC) 2004/109
Third Parties Act	Contracts (Rights of Third Parties) Act 1999
TOBA	Terms of Business Agreement
Training & Competence	Interim Prudential Sourcebook for training and competence
TRIPS	Agreement on Trade-Related Aspects of Intellectual Property Rights
TSLF	Term Securities Lending Facility
UCITS	undertakings for collective investment in transferable securities
UK	United Kingdom
UKLA	UK Listing Authority
UNCTAD	United Nations Conference on Trade and Development
UNDP	United Nations Development Programme
UNFCOG	The Unfair Contract Terms Regulatory Guide

UNIDROIT	International Institution for the Unification of Private Law
UPRU	Prudential Sourcebook for UCITS firms
US	United States of America
VaR	value at risk
VAR	value at risk
WIG	wider integrated group
WTO	World Trade Organisation

EDITORS AND CONTRIBUTORS

EDITORS

Michael Blair QC
3 Verulam Buildings

Professor George Walker
Centre for Commercial Law Studies

Dr Robert Purves
(Deputy Editor)
3 Verulam Buildings

CONTRIBUTORS

Richard Brearley
Investec Bank (UK) Limited

Margaret Chamberlain
Travers Smith LLP

Paul Edmondson
CMS Cameron McKenna LLP

Andrew Henderson
Clifford Chance LLP

Jonathan Herbst
Norton Rose LLP

Shaun Karpelowsky
Investec Bank (UK) Limited

Etay Katz
Allen & Overy LLP

Paul Kennedy
Financial Reporting Council

Alex Kuczynski
Financial Services Compensation Scheme

Professor Eva Lomnicka
Four New Square and King's College London

Professor Gerard McMeel
University of Bristol, Guildhall Chambers and Quadrant Chambers

Jonathan Melrose
Simmons & Simmons

John Virgo
*Guildhall Chambers and 5 Stone
Buildings*

Deborah A Sabalot
*Solicitor, Professional Associate, Outer
Temple Chambers, London*

Jane Welch
*British Institute of International and
Comparative Law*

Peter Snowdon
Norton Rose LLP

INTRODUCTION

In the Introduction to the first edition of this work, published in 2005, the editors wrote:

> much has happened in the four years since the Financial Services and Markets Act 2000 (FSMA) came into force to clarify and develop the UK approach to financial regulation. . . . The technological development and financial innovation that have occurred in recent years have created enormous new levels and types of financial risk and exposure. With this, the dangers of financial crisis and collapse have grown significantly. Modern financial markets are now characterized by significant, and indeed still increasing, complexity and interdependence both within and across national borders. All of this has, in turn, placed new pressures on national regulatory systems for consequent financial review and reform.
>
> These pressures for financial revision have been accompanied by continuing, if not heightened, risks of general financial crisis at the domestic, regional, and international levels, and by the more limited but still serious risks of specific losses and damage to reputation or confidence caused by misconduct or neglect in particular markets, product, or service areas.

The intervening four years (and in particular the unfolding banking crisis in 2008) have demonstrated both the validity of that comment and (we hope) the value of this book in bringing together in one volume the insights of experienced practitioners, academics and commentators into the UK regulation of financial services as a whole.

The basic structure of this edition is unchanged, but much of the material in individual chapters has been re-worked to reflect changes in the landscape of financial services regulation. These include:

- Developments in the FSA's regulatory approach and philosophy, epitomised by the drive to 'principle-based regulation' as a substitute for regulation on the basis of detailed, prescriptive rules. That drive reflects external pressures on the FSA (particularly the Government's 'better regulation' initiative and the passage of the Legislative and Regulatory Reform Act 2006); but it also reflects internal pressures for the FSA to act more effectively and efficiently and to focus its efforts to achieve 'outcomes that matter'. Without doubt, the banking crisis of 2008 will result in renewed scrutiny of the FSA and of the content of its rules. In some areas (notably, for example, prudential regulation and valuation) there is likely to be pressure for more prescriptive rules. At the time of writing, however, the FSA has maintained its stance in favour of principle-based regulation, not least because it believes that high-level rules offer the best opportunity for firms and the regulator to respond rapidly and flexibly to changing circumstances. The FSA has also emphasised that 'regulation on the cheap' is at an end, and that the number and quality of FSA staff will need to increase if future crises are to be handled effectively. Perhaps paradoxically, that may ultimately be the making of principle-based regulation: in a regulatory system built on principles, the quality of the regulator's judgement is the biggest source of risk for firms and the regulator alike. The better the FSA's people, the lower that risk should be.

- The FSA reviewed its enforcement procedures in 2005 in response to the shared perception of the FSA, regulated firms and industry commentators that (for a range of rather different reasons) the FSA enforcement process was inefficient and ineffective. The intervening years have shown the beneficial consequences of the FSA's implementation of many of the recommendations of that review.

- The implementation and entry into force in the UK of a very substantial volume of European legislation, not least the Capital Requirements Directive (the re-cast Banking Consolidation Directive and the re-cast Capital Adequacy Directive, reflecting the European interpretation of the Basel II Accords); the Markets in Financial Instruments Directive; and the Reinsurance Directive. MiFID and CRD have impinged heavily on the shape of the FSA Conduct of Business and Prudential requirements. On the prudential front, the FSA has largely succeeded; it seems, in maintaining the integrity of its risk-based supervision model. But there are new pressures, not least a fresh emphasis on supervisory cooperation across Europe and on the output of Lamfalussy 'Level 3 committees' of regulators as the progenitors of regulatory standards and approaches for the future. Along the way it seems the FSA has finally laid to rest the ideal of a single prudential rulebook, opting in the end for a set of CRD-compliant common prudential standards for most firms (in the PRU sourcebook of the FSA's Handbook of Rules and Guidance), supplemented by additional sectoral sourcebooks for different types of firms. There will be further developments on the prudential front as the Solvency II Directive on the prudential regulation of insurance business takes effect (which at the time of writing is expected to happen in 2012).

- Ongoing work in support of the FSA's consumer protection objective. In particular the development of a substantial body of material, both inside and outside the Handbook, on the meaning, content, measurement, and enforcement of firms' obligations under FSA Principle for Business 6, to pay due regard to their customers' interests and treat their customers fairly. In parallel the FSA embarked on a substantial review of retail distribution and commission disclosure, but without, as yet, producing concrete proposals for reform.

- The increasing importance of Islamic financial products and financial services in the UK and international market, which brings not only opportunities for the UK financial services industry but also challenges for regulators and practitioners alike. To accommodate this development, this edition includes a new chapter on Islamic Financial Services, a topic previously touched on in part of the chapter on Islamic Securities Exchanges in the first edition of the companion work *Financial Markets and Exchanges*.[1]

- The final report of the Parliamentary and Health Service Ombudsman into the regulation of Equitable Life. The report includes 10 determinations of maladministration on the part of the former Department of Trade and Industry, the Government Actuary's Department, and the Financial Services Authority, in relation to their regulation of Equitable in the period before 1 December 2001. The report calls on the Government to apologise to Equitable Life policyholders and to establish and fund a compensation scheme for those policyholders damaged by the maladministration the Ombudsman has identified.

- The failure of Northern Rock and the FSA's subsequent internal report, which indicated, broadly, that FSA supervision had failed to deliver the 'outcomes that mattered' in that case: in particular that the FSA had failed sufficiently to prioritise and follow up on the risks posed to Northern Rock by its strategy of funding consumer mortgage lending with capital market borrowing, and its consequent acute exposure to the severe restrictions in the availability of funds that followed the exposure of the sub-prime lending crisis in the United States. In the FSA's defence, however, one might remark that it was by no means the only actor in the Northern Rock drama to be surprised by the impact of the sub-prime crisis on bank to bank lending and that its forthright assessment of its own performance is the mark of an increasingly mature and robust organisation.

We are very grateful to all the contributors for their informed and expert revision and updating of their work, produced to a tight timetable. The law is stated as the contributors believe it to be at September 2008. We could not have completed the work at all without the support of Oxford University Press and our Development Editor Sophie Barham who was always efficient, persistent when necessary, and unfailingly charming under pressure.

Michael Blair QC
Professor George Walker
Dr Robert Purves
London, September 2008

---

[1] Blair M., Walker G. (eds), *Financial Markets and Exchanges Law*, (Oxford University Press, 2007).

PART I

FINANCIAL SERVICES AND MARKETS

1

FINANCIAL SERVICES AUTHORITY

A complex system of financial regulation has been set up in the UK under the   **1.01**
Financial Services and Markets Act 2000 ('FSMA'). This provides for the establishment of a single integrated regulatory system for all financial services and markets administered by a single body, the Financial Services Authority ('FSA'), which replaces all of the earlier sector agencies that previously operated within the UK. The FSA was not set up under FSMA directly although the Act does provide for its statutory recognition and contains a number of important constitutional directions. The FSA is a private as opposed to public corporation although it does carry out public duties. FSMA defines the legal powers and functions of the FSA and establishes an extended support or oversight regime to ensure that it exercises its statutory authority properly and discharges its assigned duties effectively.

The FSA is given specific authority to issue rules and supporting guidance under   **1.02**
FSMA. The particular regulatory obligations with which financial institutions have to comply are not set out in the Act directly but in the Handbook of Rules and Guidance issued by the FSA under the authority conferred in the Act. This has the advantages of flexibility and speed of revision in response to rapid changes in financial markets and practices, as well as of transparency and easier and cheaper access and availability. The earlier traditional advantages of industry and practitioner involvement have nevertheless been retained through the use of consultation panels, although now within a more formal statutory framework.

The new regulatory regime set up in the UK is also significant in that provides for   **1.03**
both the establishment of a single regulator with the FSA as well as the creation of a single set of supporting regulatory provisions with the Handbook of Rules and Guidance. The new framework accordingly provides for both institutional or agency integration and rules or regulatory integration. This distinguishes the UK system from many other similar overseas experiments. This institutional and regulatory integration also operates within a more general single marketplace not broken up by any formal legal restrictions on cross-sector activities such as in the

US and certain other countries.[1] Financial innovation is then protected and promoted at the same time as depositor and consumer interests are safeguarded.

1.04 The statutory duties and responsibilities of the FSA have also been extended under FSMA beyond more traditional prudential conduct of business matters to include consumer education, public awareness, and financial crime in addition to market confidence. This again distinguishes the new UK regime from other countries. The range and type of financial institutions for which it is responsible have also been increased since the enactment of FSMA to include, in particular, mortgage advice and general insurance sales as well as personal pension schemes, travel insurance, and payment services. This has then created a considerably more sophisticated and complex regulatory environment than could have been anticipated even before the reform process began.

1.05 The system of regulation set up under FSMA has nevertheless not been static nor fixed and has progressed and evolved over time. Many of the changes made have been necessitated through EU implementation. A number of the other revisions have then either been internal policy-based or scandal or crisis driven such as with regard to pensions mis-selling, Equitable Life, split capital investment trusts, soft commissions, and the more recent forced rescue of Northern Rock. Key continuing FSA policy initiatives include the further move to more principles-based regulation ('MPBR'), the better regulation agenda, Handbook simplification, and other initiatives on financial capability, treating customers fairly ('TCF'), and the retail distribution review ('RDR') and enforcement reviews conducted. Creating a regulatory regime that is capable of responding to continuing changes in market conditions and market practices is a dynamic process that has to be constantly adjusted and extended over time as necessary.

1.06 The purpose of this chapter is to consider the regulatory background to the creation of the FSA and the principal sections of FSMA that apply with regard to its structure and operation. The immediate circumstances surrounding the enactment of FSMA and the creation of the FSA are outlined. More specific historical discussion in connection with particular sectors is provided in later chapters. The main sections of FSMA governing the FSA's constitutional design and statutory duties and functions are then considered in further detail. The oversight or accountability regime established under FSMA is examined. Changes adopted with regard to internal organisation and some of the FSA's key continuing regulatory policy initiatives are reviewed. The most recent institutional reforms announced to the structure and operation of financial stability management in the UK following the crisis at Northern Rock are also examined.

---

[1] GA Walker, 'United Kingdom Regulatory Reform: A New Beginning in Policy and Programme Construction' in D Arner and JJ Lin, *Financial Regulation—A Guide to Structural Reform* (2003), ch 7.

UK Financial Reform

The FSA was set up at its formal launch on 27 October 1997. The FSA's precursor **1.07**
was the Securities and Investments Board ('SIB') which was responsible for the
regulation of securities and investment business in the UK under the Financial
Services Act 1986 ('FSA 1986'). The SIB had been a private limited company to
which statutory functions had been delegated by the Secretary of State under the
FSA 1986. Following a series of subsequent scandals and crises in the financial
services area, the Labour Government, which came into power in May 1997,
announced that the earlier regulatory system operating under the 1986 Act would
be abolished and a new single regulatory system established. The proposed regulatory agency was initially referred to as NewRO (for New Regulatory Organisation)
until it was renamed the Financial Services Authority at its formal launch in
October 1997.[2]

Regulatory function

The FSA was originally to be responsible for the regulation of investment services **1.08**
and securities markets in the UK under the FSA 1986 following its establishment
in 1997. It became responsible for bank supervision following transfer of this
function from the Bank of England under section 21(1) of the Bank of England
Act 1998 in summer 1998 ('N1').

Assumption of responsibility for banking supervision was considered necessary **1.09**
following the Barings crisis in February 1995 which revealed the potential difficulty of having the Bank of England continue to be responsible for both bank
supervision and monetary policy. In the event of a banking crisis, the effective
discharge of the central bank's monetary policy function may be undermined or
otherwise adversely affected. Following the conferral of full policy and operational autonomy in connection with monetary policy on the Bank of England in
May 1997, it was decided that it was necessary to remove bank supervision to a
separate regulatory agency.[3]

It was then confirmed through a series of subsequent Government announcements **1.10**
that the FSA would become responsible for the regulation of other sectors including building societies, insurance companies, friendly societies, and Lloyd's of
London. The FSA assumed formal responsibility for all financial services and markets with the coming into effect of FSMA on 1 December 2001 ('N2'). The FSA

---

[2] The current Memorandum of Association of the FSA is set out in n 15 below.
[3] HM Treasury News Release, 'The Chancellor's Statement to the House of Commons on Bank
of England', 49/97, 20 May 1997, para 13.

also became responsible for mortgage advice and general insurance sales in October 2004 and January 2005 ('N3') and then personal pension schemes, travel insurance and payment services, and an extended money laundering function.[4]

Financial Services and Markets Act

1.11   FSMA was enacted on 14 June 2000 after an extended consultation period. The Chancellor of the Exchequer had originally announced on 20 May 1997 that the structure of financial regulation within the UK would be revised. The then chairman of the SIB, Sir Andrew Large, was invited to take this work forward and subsequently produced a report which was presented to the Chancellor on 29 July 1997.[5] A further report was produced at the time of the FSA's launch in October 1997 with an initial plan and budget being produced in February 1998.[6]

1.12   The necessary draft legislation was produced in July 1998 in the form of a package of Consultation Papers issued by HM Treasury which included an outline Bill and Explanatory Notes. Lord Burns, former Permanent Secretary to the Treasury, was asked to chair a joint committee of both Houses of Parliament to consider a number of key aspects of the Bill during the consultation and examination process. A first report was produced on 29 April 1999 and a second on 20 May 1999.

1.13   The Financial Services and Markets Bill was formally introduced to the House of Commons on 17 June 1999.[7] It went into Committee stage in July 1999 and was carried over from one Parliamentary session to the next and began its Report stage in January 2000. 2,750 amendments were considered with 1,500 being adopted during over 200 hours of Parliamentary debate. The Act finally received Royal Assent on 14 June 2000.

Regulatory transfer

1.14   Until the coming into effect of FSMA on N2, investment services regulation continued to be carried out by the Self-Regulating Organisations ('SROs') appointed

---

[4] Para 1.113. The commencement date for the regulation of general insurance sales on 14 January 2005 was referred to as 'GI Day'. 'A Day' was the date the new pension tax simplification rules came into effect on 6 April 2006.

[5] Letter from the Chancellor to Sir Andrew Large, Reform of Financial Regulation, 20 May 1997; and HM Treasury News Release, 'The Chancellor's Statement to the House of Commons on Bank of England', 49/97 (20 May 1997); and SIB, 'Report to the Chancellor on the Reform of the Financial Regulatory System' (July 1997).

[6] FSA, 'Financial Services Authority: an Outline' (October 1997); and FSA, 'Plan & Budget 1998–99' (February 1998).

[7] HM Treasury, 'Financial Services and Markets Act 2000: Regulated Activities—Second Consultation Document' (October 2000).

under the FSA 1986 including the Securities and Futures Authority ('SFA'), the Investment Management Regulatory Organisation ('IMRO'), and the Personal Investment Authority ('PIA') (which replaced the earlier Life Assurance and Unit Trust Regulatory Organisation ('LAUTRO')), and Financial Intermediaries and Brokers Regulatory Association ('FIMBRA').

All of these bodies were formally abolished under FSMA with the Building Societies **1.15** Commission and Friendly Societies Commission, and the closure of the Insurance Department of the then Department of Trade and Industry. The Bank of England staff involved with bank supervision had been relocated to the new FSA headquarters in Canary Wharf in anticipation of the coming into effect of the Bank of England Act 1998 in June 1998. Responsibility for listed money market institutions (under section 43 of the FSA 1986 and the Investment Services Regulations 1995) was also transferred at that time with the listing of persons providing settlement arrangements (under section 171 of the Companies Act 1989).

The main parts of the new regulatory regime set up under FSMA came into effect **1.16** on N2 at the beginning of December 2001. This then represented the key date in the creation of a single integrated regulatory system in the UK although responsibility for general insurance sales and mortgage advice would only take effect in 2004 and 2005, while construction of an integrated single prudential sourcebook would have to be postponed until the coming into effect of revised European and international capital standards in 2008 and then further revised.[8]

Statutory framework

FSMA establishes the basic framework for financial regulation within the UK. **1.17** This includes designation of the functions and conferral of powers on the FSA and the other main supporting agencies created including the Financial Services and Markets Tribunal ('FSMT'), the Financial Ombudsman Service ('FOS'), and the Financial Services Compensation Scheme ('FSCS').

FSMA provides for the creation of a dual authorisation and permission regime **1.18** (FSMA, sections 19 and 20) and the introduction of a new definition of regulated activities (FSMA, section 22). It contains revised restrictions on financial promotion (section 21), the creation of an extended approved persons regime (section 59), and extended measures on recognised investment exchanges and clearing houses (Part 18). The introduction of a new market abuse offence (section 118) is provided for, and a prohibition imposed in connection with misleading statements and practices (section 397). The FSA is given power to issue rules and guidance (sections 132 and 157), and significant information gathering and enforcement

---

[8] Chapters 3 and 11, and 14, paras 14.141–14.183, 14.184–14.190, and 14.191–14.219.

powers including the issuance of penalties or public and private censure notices as well as to apply for restitution, injunction, and bankruptcy orders (Parts 24, 25, and 27).[9]

1.19 FSMA contains further provisions with regard to Official Listing (under Part 6 with the FSA subsequently being appointed the UK Listing Authority ('UKLA')) and new provisions concerning banking and insurance business transfers (Part 7). There are restated statutory provisions governing collective investment schemes (Part 17), new rules concerning Lloyd's of London (Part 19), the provision of financial services by the professions (Part 20) and mutual societies (Part 21). Restated measures governing auditors and actuaries (Part 22) as well as records, disclosure, and cooperation rules (Part 23) and notices (Part 26) are also included with other miscellaneous and supplemental measures (Parts 28, 29, and 30).

Rules and guidance

1.20 The detailed regulatory rules that apply to financial institutions are not set out in FSMA as such. This would have made the statute excessively long and operationally inflexible requiring costly and protracted legislative amendment in response to even minor changes in market and financial practice. The new regulatory regime is rules–based rather than exclusively statute-based, with the FSA being granted power to issue rules and guidance (sections 138 and 157) in accordance with a simplified adoption procedure subject to public consultation, impact assessments, and Treasury oversight. As well as securing a necessary degree of flexibility in the development of the new regulatory regime, this allows the detailed provisions to be made as transparent and easy to follow as possible. This then further assists accessibility and comprehensibility, with the new measures being made available on the FSA's website (the Handbook Online) and in a CD-ROM format as well as in hard copy without the need to purchase revised statutory documentation every time a relevant amendment is agreed and adopted.

1.21 The main regulatory obligations are now set out in the Handbook of Rules and Guidance issued by the FSA under FSMA.[10] This is made up of a number of blocks consisting of Glossary and High-Level Standards in Block 1 (including the Principles for Businesses ('PRIN'), Senior Management Arrangements, Systems and Controls ('SYSC'), Threshold Conditions ('COND'), Statements of Principle and Code of Practice for Approved Persons ('APER'), Fit and Proper Test for Approved Persons ('FIT'), General Provisions ('GEN'), and FEES). The new

---

[9] Paras 1.72–1.78.

[10] The Handbook has been extended and restructured on various occasions. On the earlier provisions, see GA Walker 'Financial Services Authority' in M Blair and GA Walker, *Financial Services Law* (Oxford: OUP, 2006), ch 1, paras 1.21–1.22. See generally ch 5.

Block 2 Prudential Standards consist of the General Prudential Sourcebook ('GENPRU') and the Prudential Sourcebook for Banks, Building Societies and Investment Firms ('BIPRU') which replaces the earlier interim prudential sourcebooks for banks ('IPRU(BANK)'), building societies ('IPRU(BSOC)'), and securities firms ('IPRU(INV)'). The earlier interim prudential sourcebook for insurance companies ('IPRU(INS)') has been replaced by INSPRU with a new sourcebook for UCITS firms ('UPRU') and for mortgage and home finance firms and insurance intermediaries ('MIPRU').[11] The Business Standards have now been moved from the old Block 2 to a new Block 3 and include the revised Conduct of Business Sourcebook ('COBS'), the Market Conduct Sourcebook ('MAR'), Training and Competence ('TC'), the Client Assets Sourcebook ('CASS'), as well as the new Insurance Conduct of Business Sourcebook ('ICOB') and Mortgages and Home Finance Conduct of Business Sourcebook ('MCOB').

The Block 4 Regulatory processes used to consist of the Authorisation Manual ('AUTH'), the Supervision Manual ('SUP'), and the Enforcement Manual ('ENF') with a revised Decision Procedure and Penalties Manual ('DEPP') although AUTH and ENF have since been replaced by alternative provisions including the inclusion of a new Enforcement Guide ('EG') in Block 9.[12] Block 6 Redress consists of the Dispute Resolution and Complaints Sourcebook ('DISP'), Compensation ('COMP'), and Complaints against the FSA ('COAF'). The Handbook includes a number of specialist sourcebooks in Block 6 (including revised requirements for Collective Investment Schemes ('COLL' replacing 'CIS'), Professional firms ('PROF'), Lloyd's of London ('LLD'), Recognised investment exchanges and clearing houses ('REC'), Credit Unions ('CRED'), the Electronic Commerce Directive ('ECO'), Electronic Money ('ELM') and Regulated Covered Bonds ('RCB'), as well as other special Handbook guides in Block 8 (including Energy Market Participants ('EMPS'), Oil Market Participants ('OMPS'), Small Friendly Societies ('FREN'), Service Companies ('SERV'), Overview for small IFA firms ('SIFA') and Small Mortgage and Insurance Intermediaries ('MIGI', 'MOGI', and 'GIGI'). The restructured Handbook also contains Listing, Prospectus and Disclosure in Block 7 (Listing Rules ('LR'), Prospectus Rules ('PR'), and Disclosure Rules and Transparency Rules ('DRT')) and revised and extended Regulatory Guides in Block 10 (The Building Societies Regulatory Guide ('BSOC'), The Collective Investment Scheme Information Guide ('COLLG'), The Enforcement Guide ('EG'), The Perimeter Guidance Manual ('PERG'), The Responsibilities of

1.22

---

[11] Limited provisions have been retained within the Interim Prudential Sourcebook for Building Societies (IPRU(BSCO)), Interim Prudential Sourcebook for Investment Businesses (IPRU(INV)), Interim Prudential Sourcebook for Insurers (IPRU(INS)), and Interim Prudential Sourcebook for Friendly Societies (IPRU(FSOC)), as well as IPRU(BANK).

[12] Chapter 6.

Providers and Distributors for the Fair Treatment of Customers ('RPPD'), and The Unfair Contract Terms Regulatory Guide ('UNFCOG')).

1.23 A new core statutory framework for the regulation of financial services and markets has accordingly been set up under FSMA with the more detailed regulatory obligations to be imposed on financial firms and markets being set out in the separate Handbook of Rules and Guidance issued by the FSA under the Act.[13]

Financial Services Authority

1.24 The FSA is to have the functions conferred on it by the Act.[14] The FSA is not established under FSMA although its existence is given statutory recognition and its general duties defined.[15] Its more specific functions and supporting statutory powers are then expanded in other parts of the Act.

Constitution

1.25 FSMA contains a number of core constitutional provisions concerning the governance and operation of the FSA. The FSA is expressly required to comply with the constitutional requirements set out in Schedule 1.[16]

---

[13] Chapters 2 and 5 and Chapter 14, paras 14.30–14.67 and 14.68–14.84.

[14] FSMA, s 1(1).

[15] ibid, s 2. The Memorandum of Association of the FSA provides that: (1) the name of the company is 'The Financial Services Authority' (the 'Authority'); (2) the registered office of the Authority will be situated in England; (3) the Authority's objects are—(a) to carry out any functions conferred on the Authority by or under any provision of any legislation, as amended from time to time, and to carry out such other functions or exercise such powers as, from time to time, may be carried out or exercisable by the Authority; (b) to carry out any other function or exercise any other power as may, in the Authority's view, assist or enable it to carry out the functions and powers referred to above or which the Authority considers incidental, desirable or expedient; (4)(a) the income of the Authority shall be applied in promoting its objects; (b) no dividends may be paid to members of the Authority; (c) on a winding up of the Authority all assets which would otherwise be available to its members generally shall be transferred either to another body with objects similar to those of the Authority or to another body the objects of which are the promotion of charity and anything incidental or conducive thereto; (5) the liability of the members is limited; and (6) every member of the Authority undertakes to contribute to the assets of the Authority in the event of the same being wound up while he is a member, or within one year after he ceases to be a member, for payment of the debts and liabilities of the Authority contracted before he ceases to be a member, and of the costs, charges and expenses of winding up, and for the adjustment of the rights of the contributories among themselves, such amounts as may be required not exceeding one pound.

[16] ibid, s 1(2).

Officers

The FSA is to have a chairman and a governing body.[17] The governing body is **1.26** to include the chairman (para 2(2)) with the chairman and other members of the governing board being appointed and liable for removal by the Treasury (para 2(3)).[18] Howard Davies had originally been appointed chairman and Chief Executive Officer ('CEO'), although these functions were subsequently divided with Sir Callum McCarthy and John Tiner being appointed chairman and CEO respectively in summer 2003 following concerns that the two principal governance roles should be separated. Hector Sants replaced John Tiner in 2006 and Lord Adair Turner replaced Callum McCarthy in autumn 2008.

Members of the House of Commons and the Northern Ireland Assembly are **1.27** disqualified from acting as members of the governing body (paras 20 and 21). The validity of any act of the FSA is nevertheless not affected by any vacancy in the office of chairman or defect in the appointment of a member of the governing body or the chairman (para 2(4)).

The FSA is to ensure that a majority of the members of its governing body are **1.28** non-executive members and that a non-executive committee is set up and maintained (para 3(1)).[19] Members of the non-executive committee are to be appointed by the FSA with its chairman being appointed from within its members by the Treasury (paras 3(2) and (3)).

The functions of the non-executive committee are to keep under review whether **1.29** the FSA is using its resources in the most efficient and economic way in discharging its functions in accordance with the decisions of its governing body. The committee is also to assess whether the FSA's internal financial controls secure the proper conduct of its financial affairs and determine the remuneration of its chairman and the executive members of the governing body (para 4(3)).

Reviewing financial controls and determining remuneration may be delegated **1.30** to a sub-committee (para 4(4)). Any sub-committees must be chaired by the chairmen of the committee but may include other non-committee members (para 4(5)). The non-executive committee is to prepare a report on the discharge of its functions to be included in the FSA's annual report to the Treasury which must relate to the same period covered (para 4(6) and (7)).

---

[17] FSMA, Sched 1, para 2(1). On operations, paras 1.100–1.112.

[18] A list of the current members of the board is available on the FSA website, <http://www.fsa.gov.uk/pages/about/who/board/>.

[19] The committee of non-executive directors is referred to as NEDCo. Para 1.111. A corporate governance statement and remuneration statement are included in each annual report. Paras 1.30 and 1.38. See, for example, FSA Annual Report 2007/2008 (June 2007) section 5.

Sub-committees

1.31 The FSA may make arrangements for any of its functions to be discharged by a committee, sub-committee, officer, or member of staff of the FSA (para 5(1)). The FSA must nevertheless carry out its legislative functions directly through its governing body with non-executive functions not being delegated except as otherwise provided (para 5(2) and (3)).

Monitoring and enforcement

1.32 The FSA must maintain necessary arrangements to be able to determine whether persons are complying with any requirements imposed on them by or under the Act (para 6(1)). These functions may be carried on by any other body or a person competent to perform them (para 6(2)). The FSA must maintain arrangements for enforcing FSMA or any provisions made under the Act (para 6(3)).

Complaints

1.33 The FSA must maintain arrangements for the investigation of complaints in connection with the exercise of its functions (other than legislative functions) and appoint an independent person to be responsible for such investigations under the complaints scheme set up under FSMA (para 7(1)). The current arrangements are set out under the COAF section of the Handbook of Rules and Guidance.[20] The complaints scheme must allow for complaints to be investigated as quickly as reasonably practicable (para 7(2)). Treasury approval is required for the appointment or dismissal of the investigator appointed with the terms and conditions of appointment ensuring that the investigator is free to act independently of the FSA and with complaints being investigated without favour (para 7(3) and (4)).

1.34 The FSA is required to consult on the establishment of the complaints scheme and take into account any representations made. Any changes are subject to consultation (para 7(5)–(9) and (14)). Up-to-date details are to be published including the power to conduct investigations and to make recommendations for corrective action with the Treasury being provided with a copy (para 7(10) and (12)). The FSA may make a reasonable charge for consultation documents and scheme details (para 7(13)).

1.35 The complaints scheme is to provide for the reference to the investigator of any complaint being considered by the FSA. The FSA is not required to investigate all complaints where this can be dealt with more appropriately through alternative

---

[20] Chapter 7. A summary of the complaints made and copy of the FSA's response to the Complaints Commissioner's Annual Report is included with the FSA annual report. See, for example, FSA, Annual Report 2007/2008 (June 2007), appendices 3 and 4.

means including before the Financial Services and Markets Tribunal ('FSMT') or the courts (para 8(1) and (2)(a)). Investigations may be conducted by persons appointed by the investigator other than officers or employees of the FSA (para 8(8) and (9)). In the event of a reference being made, the scheme must require the investigator to conduct a full investigation of the complaint, report on the investigation, and publish the results either in whole or in part where this is considered to be in the public interest (para 8(1)(b)).

The FSA is to notify the investigator where a complaint is not to be investigated **1.36** although the investigator may still proceed to consider the matter if appropriate (para 8(3) and (4)). The investigator may require the FSA to make a compensatory payment or otherwise remedy the matter complained of (para 8(5)). The FSA must advise the investigator and complainant of the action taken with the investigator being able to require the response to be published in whole or in part (para 8(6) and (7)).

Records

The FSA is required to maintain satisfactory arrangements for recording decisions **1.37** made in the exercise of its functions and the safekeeping of those records which it considers ought to be preserved (para 9(a) and (b)).[21]

Annual report

The FSA is to make a report to the Treasury on the discharge of its functions, the **1.38** extent to which its regulatory objectives have been secured and supervisory principles complied with and on any other matters the Treasury may require (para 10(1)).[22] The report is to be accompanied by the non-executive committee report and any other reports or information that the Treasury may direct (para 10(2)). The Treasury is to place a copy of the report before Parliament (para 10(3)).

Annual general meeting

The FSA is to hold an annual meeting within three months of its annual report **1.39** (para 11(1)). The purpose of the meeting is to discuss the contents of the report and to provide a reasonable opportunity for those attending to question the FSA on the discharge (or failure to discharge) its functions (para 11(2)).

---

[21] On operation of Data Protection Act 1998 and access to electronic and hard copy FSA records, see *Michael John Durant v FSA* [2003] EWCA Civ 1746. The need to prepare and retain proper records in connection with the supervision of individual institutions was highlighted by the action by former depositors in BCCI against the Bank of England, which case was abandoned in November 2005. Paras 1.44 (nn 25 and 26) and 1.99.

[22] Copies of the FSA's annual reports are available on its website (n 215).

Reasonable notice is to be provided and the meeting organised and conducted in such manner as the FSA considers appropriate (para 11(3) and (4)). The notice is to be published in an appropriate manner and include details of time and place, agenda, duration, and attendance arrangements (para 11(5)). Notice of any changes are to be provided separately (para 11(6)). The FSA is to publish a report on the proceedings of the meeting within one month (para 12).

Status

1.40 The FSA is a private corporation and is not to be regarded as acting on behalf of the Crown, and its members, officers, and staff are not to be regarded as Crown agents in relation to any of their functions (para 13(1)). The FSA is exempt from the need to include the term limited within its name (para 14) subject to subsequent Treasury direction (para 15).[23]

Penalties

1.41 The FSA is not to take into account expenses incurred in discharging its functions in determining its policy on penalties (para 16(1)). The FSA is to ensure that penalties are applied for the benefit of authorised persons with the relevant scheme details making separate provisions with regard to different classes of authorised person (para 16(2) and (3)). The initial provisions were subject to consultation and representation with the Treasury being provided with a copy (para 16(6)–(11)). Up-to-date scheme details must be made available to the public and published in an appropriate manner although a reasonable fee may be charged for consultation documents or copy details (para 16(4), (5), and (12)).

Fees

1.42 The FSA may make rules providing for the payment of fees in connection with the discharge of its functions to cover expenses incurred and to repay principal or interest on any money borrowed in connection with its assumption of responsibility for bank supervision under the Bank of England Act 1988 (para 17(1)(a) and (b)). The fees are also to be used to maintain adequate reserves (para 17(1)(c)). In so doing, the FSA is not to take into account any amounts received by way of penalty or fine (para 17(2)). Any amounts due may be recovered as a debt due (para 17(3)), although no fees may be charged in connection with Treaty or passport rights (under Schedules 3 or 4, FSMA) or the approved persons regime (under section 59, FSMA) (para 17(4)).

---

[23] On the FSA's Memorandum of Association (n 15).

Immunity

Neither the FSA nor any person acting as a member, officer, or member of staff is **1.43** to be liable in damages for anything done or omitted in the discharge (or purported discharge) of the FSA's functions (para 19(1)). This continues the earlier statutory exceptions provided for in connection with the discharge of supervisory and regulatory functions, in particular, under the Banking Act 1987 and the FSA 1986. This is also extended to apply to investigators or their appointees in connection with the investigation of any complaints against the FSA (para 19(2)). This exemption from liability is not, however, available against acts or omissions in bad faith or acts or omissions unlawful under section 6(1) of the Human Rights Act 1998 (para 19(3)).

The restated statutory exemption provided for under para 19, Schedule 1 of FSMA **1.44** will generally only apply to acts carried out in good faith or negligence.[24] Liability may nevertheless still arise for acts (or omissions) carried out in bad faith as well as under the tort of misfeasance in public office. Misfeasance includes either targeted or untargeted malice. A public power has to be exercised for an improper purpose with the specific intention of injuring a person or persons or a public officer has to act in the knowledge that he has no power to do the act complained of and that it would probably injure the claimant. The availability of this remedy was confirmed by the House of Lords in an action by the former depositors of BCCI against the Bank of England following the collapse of BCCI in July 1991. Two separate rulings were issued confirming the availability and content of the tort and allowing the action to proceed to trial.[25] The formal trial hearings began in January 2004 before the then Mr Justice Tomlinson and were expected to last for up to two years. The action was subsequently abandoned on 2 November 2005 after the

---

[24] The allegation of bad faith on the part of the SIB in connection with the disclosure of information under s 179 of the FSA 1986 was struck out in *Melton Medes Ltd and another v SIB* Ch D (Lightman J) 2 July 1994. Bad faith was to be construed in the context of s 187(3) of the 1986 Act as meaning either (a) malice in the sense of personal spite or a desire to injure for improper reasons or (b) knowledge of absence of power to make the decision in question. See *Administrative Law* (6th edn, 1988), 782, citing *Bourgoin SA v Ministry of Agriculture Fisheries and Food* [1985] 3 All ER 585, [1986] QB 716. The SIB's disclosure of non-restricted information was considered to have accorded with the aim of the 1986 Act and the role of the SIB to protect the interests of investors and customers of financial services and there was no evidence that the SIB had acted in bad faith but believed itself to be acting properly and within its powers with the aim of assisting in the maintenance of proper standards of integrity and fair dealing.

[25] *Three Rivers v Bank of England* [2000] 2 WLR 1220 of 18 May 2000 before Lord Steyn, Lord Hope of Craighead, Lord Hutton, Lord Hobhouse of Woodborough, and Lord Millett. See also *Three Rivers v Bank of England* [2001] UKHL 16 in which the case was allowed to proceed to trial. For comment, see GA Walker, 'Regulatory Comment' and 'Three Rivers v Bank of England' in *Farrer's Financial Services Quarterly Bulletin* (Summer 2001).

Chancellor of the High Court ruled that it would no longer be in the interests of creditors to continue.[26]

General duties

1.45 The duties of the FSA are defined in terms of its general functions and regulatory objectives.[27] In discharging its general functions, the FSA is insofar as possible to act in a way that is compatible with and most appropriate to meet its regulatory objectives as set out under section 2(2).[28] The general functions of the FSA are to make rules (under sections 138–156), prepare and issue codes (section 140), provide general guidance (under sections 157–158), and determine the general policy and principles to govern the performance of particular functions.[29] General guidance means guidance given to persons generally (including regulated persons or a class of regulated persons) intended to have continuing effect and provided in a written or other legible form.[30]

1.46 In discharging its general functions, the FSA is also to have regard to certain further requirements generally referred to as supervisory principles.[31] The FSA's general duties are accordingly defined in terms of the discharge of its general functions (of issuing rules and guidance, codes, and general policy and principles) all of which are to be understood in accordance with the regulatory objectives and supervisory principles set under FSMA.[32]

---

[26] Mr Justice Tomlinson was highly critical of the action taken by the claimants in his final judgment on 12 April 2006. *Three Rivers District Council and others and the Bank of Credit and Commerce International SA (in liquidation) v the Governor and Company of the Bank of England* [2006] EWHC 816 (Comm). For comment, GA Walker, 'BCCI Closure but Not Without Cost' in *Financial Regulation International* (Informa) January 2006, 1. The difficulties that arose with complex civil litigation such as the *Three Rivers* and the *Equitable Life* cases were considered separately by Mr Justice Richard Aikens who produced a Report and Recommendations to the Long Trials Working Party in December 2007. This was adopted by the Commercial Court Judges and the Committee of Users of the Commercial Court in November 2007 and came into effect on a trial basis on 1 February 2008. The revisions include limitations on the length of Statements of Case and the early creation of a judicially settled List of Issues to manage the disclosure of documents and the content of witness statements and expert reports. The greater use of summary judgment is also encouraged in appropriate cases with striking out procedures and limits on the length of written and oral arguments at trial.

[27] FSMA, s 2. Chapter 2.

[28] FSMA, s 2(1).

[29] ibid, s 2(4).

[30] ibid, s 158(5).

[31] ibid, s 2(3). Paras 1.54–1.55.

[32] Paras 1.47–1.53 and paras 1.54–1.55.

Statutory objectives

The regulatory objectives to which the FSA is to have regard are expressed in terms **1.47**
of market confidence, public awareness, consumer protection, and combating
financial crime.[33] This represents the first time that a clearly articulated set of
statutory objectives has been imposed on a financial regulator in the UK.

Market confidence is concerned with maintaining confidence in the financial **1.48**
system with the financial system including the UK financial markets and exchanges,
regulated activities, and any other activities connected with financial market and
exchanges.[34] Public awareness is concerned with promoting public understanding
of the financial system and, in particular, includes increasing awareness of the
benefits and risks associated with the different kinds of investments or other financial dealings, and the provision of appropriate information and advice.[35] The protection of consumers is concerned with securing an appropriate degree of consumer
protection having regard to the differing degrees of risk involved in different
investments or transactions, differing degrees of expertise and experience that
consumers have, and the need for accurate advice and information to be given to
consumers subject to the general principle that consumers are responsible for
their own decisions.[36] Consumers include any persons who use, have used, or may
contemplate using the services provided by authorised persons or appointed
representatives, who have rights or interests derived from or attributable to the use
of such services, or who have rights or interests that may otherwise be adversely
affected by the use of such services by persons acting on their behalf or in a
fiduciary capacity.[37]

Reduction of financial crime is concerned with limiting the extent to which finan- **1.49**
cial businesses may be used for purposes connected with financial crime.[38] In
considering this objective, the FSA is to have regard to the desirability of regulated
persons being aware of the risk of their business being used for the purposes of
committing financial crime, taking appropriate measures to prevent financial
crime, facilitating its detection and monitoring its incidence (including in administration and employment practices and the conduct of transactions), and devoting adequate resources to such matters.[39] Financial crime means any offence
involving fraud or dishonesty, misconduct, or misuse of information relating to
financial markets or handling the proceeds of crime and an offence includes any

---

[33] FSMA, s 2(2).
[34] ibid, s 3(1) and (2).
[35] ibid, s 4(1) and (2).
[36] ibid, s 5(1) and (2).
[37] ibid, ss 5(3) and 138(7).
[38] ibid, s 3(1).
[39] ibid, s 6(2).

act or omission which would be an offence if committed in the UK.[40] In addition to fraud or dishonesty, financial crime will include such other specific acts as making misleading statements and practices[41] and money laundering, although market abuse[42] is not strictly an offence for the purposes of the Act. The provisions with regard to market abuse and misleading statements are developed in the MAR section of the FSA's Handbook. The earlier Money Laundering ('ML') source-book has since been deleted and replaced by high-level standards in SYSC.[43]

1.50 The statutory defined regulatory objectives of the FSA are accordingly based on confidence, awareness (or information), consumer protection, and financial crime. Market confidence, awareness, and financial crime are all more immediately con-cerned with customer protection rather than with market stability as such. All of these could also be considered to fall within consumer protection more generally (under section 2(2)(c)). It could be claimed that the effect of this is to transform the FSA principally into a consumer protection rather than a market stability agency. While this is not objectionable from a public interest perspective, it could be argued that this does not reflect the traditional core theoretical or operational purposes of financial regulation which are principally concerned with market and systems stability as well as possibly market efficiency. Against this, it could be claimed that market confidence is simply a statutory analogue for market stability with stability also necessarily being implied in confidence. The reason for the particular drafting solution adopted is nevertheless still unclear.

1.51 The particular difficulty that arose in drafting the regulatory objectives of the FSA was that while the Treasury is nominally responsible for financial system stability within the UK more generally, this function is mainly carried on in practice through the Bank of England as the national central bank. The Bank of England has since the 1990s been divided into two main wings or divisions consisting of monetary stability and financial stability. It may then have been considered impos-sible to include market stability as a primary objective of the FSA within the defi-nition of core statutory objectives. Despite this, the FSA has subsequently stated that it interprets market confidence to include stability.[44] It is also, in practice, closely involved with the operational maintenance of financial stability within the UK, in particular, under the Memoranda of Understanding (MOU) entered into between the FSA, the Bank of England, and the Treasury at the time of its launch

---

[40] ibid, s 6(3) and (4). On territorial scope, Chapter 2, paras 2.56–2.61.
[41] FSMA, s 397.
[42] Under FSMA, s 118.
[43] Chapter 10. See also GA Walker, 'Money Laundering' in *Encyclopaedia of Banking Law* (Butterworths, 6 Volumes Looseleaf) Division A.
[44] FSA, 'A new regulator for the new millennium' (January 2000); FSA, 'Building the New Regulator—Progress Report 1' (December 2000); and FSA, 'Building the New Regulator—Progress Report 2' (February 2002).

in 1998 and revised in 2006.[45] The particular drafting of statutory objectives adopted can then be, at least partly, understood in terms of the desire to extend the core functions of the FSA to include consumer as well as market protection issues but also to reflect the complex relations that exist between the main bodies responsible for the regulation of financial markets in the UK. This issue has had to be reconsidered following the Northern Rock crisis with the Treasury confirming that the Bank of England will be given an express statutory function with regard to financial stability although it remained unclear whether the statutory objectives of the FSA would also be revised.[46]

The practical or operational importance of the regulatory objectives can separately be questioned in terms of the degree of specific compliance required. The FSA is stated only to act in a way that is 'compatible with' (rather than actually secure) the objectives stated, and then only insofar 'as reasonably possible'.[47] The FSA is further entitled to act in any way that it 'considers most appropriate' for the purpose of achieving those objectives and with no indication as to relative priority being provided.[48] The standard imposed is then subjective rather than objective, with the FSA being freely entitled to select between and across the objectives set. No formal sanction is included in the event of breach. The FSA is only required to explain the extent to which (in its opinion) the regulatory objectives have been met in the annual report to be provided to the Treasury.[49]   **1.52**

The inclusion of formal statutory objectives for the FSA is an interesting and novel feature within the new regime set up under FSMA although their formal or legal significance and relevance may be more limited in practice. The FSA does nevertheless have continuing regard to the regulatory objectives and makes frequent reference to them in its consultation documents, impact studies, and annual reports and other policy statements. The statutory objectives accordingly remain of considerable practical and operational importance, and especially having regard to their public relations, public information, and public awareness relevance despite their more limited legal or formal validity and enforceability as such.   **1.53**

Supervisory principles

The FSA is also to have regard to certain further considerations in discharging its general functions.[50] These include using its resources in the most efficient and   **1.54**

---

[45] Paras 1.134–1.147.
[46] See generally paras 1.160–1.180.
[47] FSMA, s 2(1)(a).
[48] ibid, s 2(1)(b).
[49] ibid, para 10(1)(b) Sched 1. Para 1.38.
[50] ibid, s 2(3).

economic manner, recognising the responsibilities of those who manage the affairs of authorised persons, ensuring that burdens or restrictions are proportionate, and facilitating innovation.[51] These are then essentially concerned with efficiency, management responsibility (or subsidiarity), proportionality, and efficiency. These are supported by three further specific competition objectives having regard to the general position of the UK, minimising adverse effects on competition, and facilitating competition between regulated persons and entities.[52]

1.55 The effect of this is generally to include a further five supervisory principles (of efficiency, subsidiarity, proportionality, innovation, and competition) within the matters to be taken into account by the FSA in discharging its general functions (in issuing rules and guidance, codes, and general policy and principles). No formal use or application is nevertheless required, with the FSA only being required to 'have regard to' these additional statutory directions or considerations. These are again of importance in terms of FSA policy development, although, as with the statutory objectives, their formal legal relevance is limited. The difference between them is reflected in the fact that the FSA is not subject to the same transparency and reporting obligations as required with regard to the formal statutory objectives imposed under section 2(1) and (2).[53]

Rules

1.56 The FSA's general functions principally include issuing rules.[54] A number of distinct types of rules are provided for under FSMA. These include general rules, specific rules, and endorsing rules.

General rules

1.57 The FSA is given a general rule-making power.[55] This applies with regard to such obligations as may be imposed on authorised persons in connection with the carrying on of regulated (and non-regulated) activities, and considered necessary to protect the interests of consumers. These are referred to as general rules.[56] General rules may be applied to all authorised persons even if no relationship exists between the persons covered and the persons to be protected,[57] and contain obligations

---

51 FSMA, s 2(3)(a), (b), (c), and (d).
52 ibid, s 2(e), (f) and (g).
53 Paras 1.47–1.53.
54 FSMA, s 2(1) and (4)(a).
55 ibid, s 138(1).
56 ibid, s 138(2).
57 ibid, s 138(4) and (5).

taking into account group relationships.[58] They may not be used to limit the rights available to EEA firms exercising directive (passport) rights or to impose additional obligations that fall within the authority of the home State authority.[59] For the purposes of FSMA, particular types of general rules may be issued including client money rules,[60] authorised unit trust rules,[61] insurance business rules,[62] and asset identification rules.[63]

Specific and endorsing rules

The FSA may issue other specific rules which include price stabilising rules,[64]   **1.58** financial promotion rules,[65] money laundering rules,[66] and control of information rules.[67] Separate endorsing rules may also be issued with regard to the City Code on Takeovers and Mergers issued by the Takeover Panel and the rules governing substantial acquisitions of shares issued by the Panel.[68]

Procedure

The FSA is required to provide the Treasury with a copy of any made rules with   **1.59** details of any alterations or revocations.[69] Rule-making powers are only exercisable in writing with rule-making instruments being required to specify the statutory provision under which the rules are issued, failing which they are made void and unenforceable.[70] Rule-making instruments must be published subject to a reasonable fee being charged for copies.[71]

Where new rules are to be issued, a draft must be published accompanied by a cost   **1.60** benefit analysis, an explanation of their purpose and compatibility with the FSA's general duties (under section 2), and a notice of representations.[72] Representations must be considered and published with the FSA's response.[73] Any significant amendments must be published separately and an additional cost–benefit

---

58 ibid, s 138(5).
59 ibid, s 138(6).
60 ibid, s 139.
61 ibid, s 140.
62 ibid, s 141.
63 ibid, s 142(2).
64 ibid, s 144.
65 ibid, s 145.
66 ibid, s 146. Chapter 10 and Walker (n 43).
67 ibid, s 147.
68 ibid, s 143.
69 ibid, s 152(1)–(3).
70 ibid, s 153(1)–(3) and (6).
71 ibid, s 153(4)–(5).
72 ibid, s 155(1) and (2).
73 ibid, s 155(4) and (5).

analysis conducted.[74] The FSA may dispense with the statutory consultation procedure where the delay may be considered prejudicial to the interests of consumers.[75] Rules may make different provisions with regard to distinct types of authorised person, their activities, or investments and include such incidental, supplemental, consequential, or transitional provisions as the FSA may consider appropriate.[76]

1.61 A certified copy of a rule-making instrument is to be treated as sufficient evidence of its content. This must be signed by a member of the FSA staff and include a (required) statement that the instrument was made by the FSA, that it is a true copy, and that it was published on a specified date.[77]

Modification or waiver

1.62 FSMA contains further provisions with regard to the modification or waiver of particular rules. The FSA may direct that all or any listed rules may not apply to authorised persons or only apply subject to such modification as may be specified.[78] Applications for modification or waiver are to be made in such manner as may be specified and will only be granted where the FSA is satisfied that compliance would be unduly burdensome or would not achieve the purpose for which the rule was made, and that no undue risk would result for the persons intended to be protected.[79] Directions may be conditional and must be published unless it is considered inappropriate or unnecessary to do so.[80] Modification or waiver applies with regard to general rules, auditors' and actuaries' rules, control of information rules, financial promotion rules, insurance business rules, money laundering rules, and price stabilising rules.

Breach

1.63 Rules may provide that contravention does not trigger any of the statutory consequences provided for under FSMA.[81] Contravention of a rule is generally actionable by a private person suffering loss subject to the defences and other incidents applicable to actions for breach of statutory duty.[82] Availability of an action for damages may nevertheless be excluded under particular rules or rules extended to

---

[74] ibid, s 155(6).
[75] ibid, s 155(7).
[76] ibid, s 156.
[77] ibid, s 154(1) and (2).
[78] ibid, s 148(1).
[79] ibid, s 148(3) and (4).
[80] ibid, s 148(5) and (6).
[81] ibid, s 150(5).
[82] ibid, s 150(1). A more limited provision was included within FSA 1986, s 62 although no corresponding right was available in the banking or insurance areas. See Freshfields Bruckhaus Deringer, *Financial Services Investigations and Enforcement* (2001), paras 10.23–10.24 and 10.27–10.48. See also Chapters 6 and 7.

include actions by non-private persons.[83] These remedies are generally not available with regard to breach of the Listing Rules or requirements with regard to financial resources.[84] A private person is as specified.[85] A person does not commit an offence only by reason of breach of an FSA rule with contravention not making the transaction void or unenforceable.[86]

Guidance

The FSA may issue guidance consisting of such information and advice as it con- **1.64** siders appropriate.[87] This may apply with regard to the operation of FSMA or rules made under it, to any matters relating to the functions of the FSA, to its regulatory objectives, or with respect to any other matter that the FSA considers desirable to give information or advice on. Guidance includes any recommendation made by the FSA to persons, generally, regulated persons, or any class of regulated persons. Significant parts of the Handbook including some whole sections only consist of guidance rather than rules. This is still considered appropriate to clarify the meaning or content of particular provisions and assist regulated persons understand and comply with relevant obligations. The FSA may provide financial or other assistance to persons giving information or advice under FSMA.[88]

The provision of guidance is generally subject to the same consultation require- **1.65** ments as apply with regard to issuing rules. The FSA may publish its guidance, offer copies for sale at a reasonable price, and make a reasonable charge for guidance provided in response to a particular request.[89]

A copy of any general guidance issued must be provided to the Treasury.[90] A copy **1.66** of any alterations and details of the alteration must be provided as well as a notice of any revocations.[91]

Competition compliance

Regulating provisions issued by the FSA and its practices are subject to competi- **1.67** tion scrutiny by the Office of Fair Trading ('OFT') (formerly the Director General of Fair Trading) and the Competition Commission. Regulating provisions include rules, general guidance, the approved persons code of conduct, and market

---

[83] FSMA, s 150(2) and (3).
[84] ibid, s 150(4).
[85] ibid, s 150(5).
[86] ibid, s 151(1) and (2).
[87] ibid, s 157(1).
[88] ibid, s 157(2).
[89] ibid, s 157(5).
[90] ibid, s 158(1).
[91] ibid, s 158(2)–(4).

abuse code. Practices mean any practices adopted by the FSA in the exercise of its functions under the Act.[92]

1.68 The OFT is required to keep the regulating provisions and the FSA's practices under review.[93] Where any regulating provision or practice (or two or more provisions or practices) are considered to have a significantly adverse effect on competition, the OFT is to make a report which includes details of the adverse effect involved.[94] Provisions or practices will have a significantly adverse effect on competition if they have (or are intended or likely to have) the effect of requiring or encouraging behaviour which has (or is intended or likely to have) a significantly adverse effect on competition.[95] This will include the effect of requiring or encouraging the exploitation of the strength of a market or dominant position.[96]

1.69 The OFT may require the provision of documentation or other information before issuing a report.[97] A report of an adverse effect on competition must be copied to the Treasury, the Competition Commission, and the FSA, and be published.[98] The OFT has a discretionary power to issue a report where it considers that a regulating provision does not have a significantly adverse effect on competition.[99]

1.70 The Competition Commission is required to consider any report of an adverse effect on competition or a request to consider a report that an adverse effect does not arise.[100] The Commission will issue its own report unless no useful purpose would be served following a change in circumstances. The Commission's report is to state whether an adverse effect on competition is established and whether that effect is justified or not justified and what further action should be taken.[101] Where an adverse effect on competition is established that is not justified, the Treasury is to issue a direction to the FSA requiring it to take such action as may be specified[102] unless appropriate action has since been taken or it is otherwise inappropriate or unnecessary to do so.[103]

1.71 The Competition Act 1998 is generally disapplied with regard to agreements entered into by authorised persons under regulating provisions or practices subject to regulating provisions issued by the FSA.[104]

---

[92] ibid, s 159(1).
[93] ibid, s 160(1).
[94] ibid, s 160(2) and (4).
[95] ibid, s 159(2).
[96] ibid, s 159(3).
[97] ibid, s 161.
[98] ibid, s 160(5).
[99] ibid, s 160(2).
[100] ibid, s 162(1).
[101] ibid, s 162(4) and (5).
[102] ibid, s 163(1) and (2).
[103] ibid, s 163(3).
[104] ibid, s 164(1).

Enforcement

The rules issued by the FSA under FSMA were supported by the extended enforce- **1.72**
ment powers conferred as expanded in the Enforcement Manual ('ENF') within
the old Block 3 of the Handbook.[105] These have since been replaced by a new
Enforcement Guide ('EG') in the new final Block.[106] FSMA enforcement measures include information gathering and investigations (Part 11), disciplinary measures (Part 14), intervention in connection with incoming firms (Part 18),
injunctions[107] and restitution (Part 25),[108] and general offences (Part 27). A number of other more specific offences are included with regard to contravention of
the general prohibition (section 23(1)), making false claims as to authorisation or
exemption (section 24(1)), financial promotions (section 25(1)), and making
false or misleading statements or practices (section 397(2) and (3)). Separate prohibitions apply with regard to market abuse (sections 118 and 123(1)). The FSA can
issue a prohibition order against an individual (section 56(2)), or impose a financial
penalty or issue a statement of misconduct (section 66(1) and (3)).[109] The FSA can
withdraw authorisation (section 33) or restrict or cancel permission (section 44) as
well as apply for a bankruptcy or winding up order (sections 367 and 372).[110]

The powers of information collection and sanction conferred on the FSA under **1.73**
FSMA are developed in Enforcement Guide ('EG') which replaced the
Enforcement Manual ('ENF'). ENF contains provisions concerning the FSA's
approach to enforcement (Chapter 2), information gathering and investigation
(Chapter 3), conduct of investigations (Chapter 4), settlement (Chapter 5), and
publicity (Chapter 6). Specific provisions are included with regard to penalties
and censures (Chapter 7), variation and cancellation of permission (Chapter 8),
and prohibition orders and withdrawal of approval (Chapter 9). The FSA may

---

[105] Chapter 6.

[106] Para 1.22 and Chapter 6.

[107] An order can be issued under s 37 of the Supreme Court Act 1981 and s 380(3) FSMA
freezing the bank accounts of investors over which an authorised person has a power of attorney.
An order was granted in *FSA v Fitt* [2004] All ER (D) 229 Ch D (Lewison J). The application to
discharge a freezing order by the FSA was adjourned with liberty to restore in the event that the
bankruptcy order was not made in *FSA v Bartholomew-White* [2004] All ER (D) 117.

[108] The validity of restitution orders was upheld by the Court of Appeal in *FSA v Martin and
another* [2006] 2 BCLC 193. See also *FSA v Matthews (t/a William's Life Pension Mortgage &
Insurance Services) and another* [2004] All ER (D) 334. Compensation may be awarded under FSMA,
s 382 on a top-up rather than reinstatement basis in respect of the loss suffered on the transfer of
an occupational pension scheme. *FSA v William Matthews and Patricia Janet Matthews* (Ch D, 21
December 2004), (Peter Smith J).

[109] On the difference between ss 56 and 66 and issuance of relevant notices, see *R v FSA, ex parte
Vivian John Davis, Rawdon Quentin Vevers and Colin Mark Gamwells* [2003] EWCA Civ 1128.

[110] It was held in *FSA v Foster* [2005] All ER (D) 55 that the particular scheme was a pyramid
scheme and it was in the public interest that a trustee in bankruptcy should be permitted to investigate as it would have greater powers than the supervisor with the application for an interim order
being denied.

apply for injunctions or for restitution orders (Chapters 10 and 11). Criminal proceedings initiated (Chapter 12) and insolvency proceedings commenced and orders against their avoidance applied for (Chapter 13). EG contained further provisions with regard to disciplinary action in relation to collective investment schemes, auditors and actuaries or professionals and incoming ECA providers as well as cancellation of sponsor approval (Chapters 14, 15, 16, 17, and 18).

1.74 One of the difficulties that arose in setting up the new regulatory regime under FSMA was determining whether all of the powers of intervention would be civil or criminal in nature. If specific provisions are classified as being criminal in nature, a number of additional protections would have to be provided under the European Convention on Human Rights and UK Human Rights Act 1998.[111] The presumption of innocence would, for example, apply with privilege against self-incrimination. Disciplinary proceedings would have to be conducted by an independent and impartial court with a fair trial being ensured and a right to proper legal assistance provided to the extent necessary.

1.75 The nature of the market abuse regime had, in particular, been considered by the Joint Parliamentary Committee under Lord Burns.[112] The Government had also taken legal advice from Sir Sidney Kentridge, QC and James Eadie. While the general opinion was that the proceedings would not be criminal in nature, a number of safeguards were introduced in connection with the market abuse offences, in particular, to ensure that appropriate protections were made available to parties to proceedings commenced by the FSA.

1.76 The FSA also decided to set up a separate Regulatory Decisions Committee ('RDC') to attempt to ensure impartiality of decisions within enforcement proceedings. FSMA had also provided for the establishment of a separate Financial Services and Markets Tribunal (Part 9, FSMA).[113] The Tribunal is fully independent of the FSA and is administered by the Ministry of Justice. Following a reference, the Tribunal is to determine the appropriate action to be taken by the FSA with decisions being remitted back for further action. The FSA is required to act in accordance with any direction given[114] with a further right of appeal being available to the courts on a point of law.[115]

---

[111] A declaration that a bookmaker receiving deposits was carrying on an unauthorised activity under ss 22(3) and 35 of the Banking Act 1987 would not affect any potential subsequent criminal proceedings and was in the public interest. *FSA v John Edward Rouke* (Ch D 19 October 2001 (Neuberger J)) .

[112] Para 1.12.

[113] Paras 1.95–1.97; and Chapter 6, para 6.2. For a review of the decisions of the FSMT see J Bagge, C Evans, and K Stephen (eds), *Financial Services Decisions Digest: FSA Final Notices and FSMT Decisions* (London: Lexis Nexis Butterworths, 2007).

[114] FSMA, s 133(10).

[115] ibid, s 137.

Despite the safeguards included within the enforcement regime, the FSA's policies **1.77** and practices in this area have been subject to continuing criticism in response to which the FSA has conducted a number of reviews. This included an investigation by David Strachan, Director of Retail Firms, which reported in July 2005.[116] The review considered the processes followed by supervisors, enforcement staff, and decision-makers in considering possible statutory or regulatory breaches. It looked at the role and involvement of senior FSA management within these processes, the options for a fair procedure, and the accountability of decision-takers to the FSA Board. The review attempted to ensure that there had been a clear articulation of the FSA's overall approach to enforcement, sufficient checks and controls during investigations to ensure balance and fairness, and proper transparency and clarity of the separation of investigation and decision-taking functions. The review nevertheless accepted that the FSA could not transfer its decision-making responsibilities to a wholly independent body. Decision-taking remained an administrative process that could not be made to replicate court or tribunal proceedings.

The final Report confirmed that no general change was required with regard to **1.78** the FSA's risk-based approach to financial regulation and enforcement. The FSA should continue with its prioritisation of investigatory and enforcement proceedings. The current structure and operation of the RDC should be maintained and the FSA continue not to attempt to intervene or influence its decisions. The RDC should nevertheless be provided with independent legal advice rather than depend on enforcement staff. Proceedings should be more interactive and transparent with the separation of function applying with regard to both decided and settled cases. A discount of 30 per cent should also be considered on financial penalties subject to early settlement. The FSA should obtain feedback on enforcement cases and publish an annual performance report on enforcement. It was hoped that with all of these recommendations, the enforcement process could be made more efficient and accountable.

Accountability

One of the particular dangers that arises with the creation of a single regulator is **1.79** that a significant amount of administrative and enforcement power is concentrated in one agency.[117] This can create potential difficulties in terms of the inefficient regulation of a particular sector as well as more general abuse of power

---

[116] The FSA had decided to review its enforcement process following the criticisms made in *Legal & General Assurance Society Ltd* 27 May 2005 [App 2.150]. See also *Legal & General Assurance Society Ltd v FSA* [2005] All ER (D) 154.

[117] M Taylor, 'Accountability and Objectives of the FSA' in M Blair et al, *Financial Services and Markets Act 2000* (Blackstone, 2001), ch 2.

within the agency itself. It was for this reason that a number of extended account-ability measures were incorporated within the new regulatory regime set up under FSMA. These include a number of internal and external mechanisms to ensure that the FSA operates in a transparent, fair, and efficient manner and within the proper scope of the legal authority conferred.

1.80 The accountability regime set up is principally based on Treasury oversight which includes Treasury reporting and appointment with express powers being con-ferred on the Treasury to conduct formal statutory reviews and inquiries. Annual FSA reports are to be published, laid before Parliament, and followed by an annual public meeting. In addition to full public consultation being carried on all new rules and guidance, the FSA is required to take opinions from specially established practitioner and consumer panels. Its regulating provisions are subject to compe-tition scrutiny by the OFT and the Competition Commission. A formal com-plaints scheme is also to be maintained.

1.81 Further internal mechanisms include maintaining a governing body with a majority of non-executive members and a non-executive committee with assigned gover-nance functions. A general good governance requirement is imposed with enforce-ment actions now being decided on by the separate RDC. The major decisions of the FSA (including the issuance of warning, decision, and supervisory notices) are subject to reference to the FSMT with a further right of appeal on a point of law to the courts. The activities of regulatory agencies are subject to judicial review and potential tortious liability for misfeasance in public office. Each of these is considered in further detail below.

Treasury oversight and appointment

1.82 The FSA is required to prepare an annual report to the Treasury on the discharge of its functions, the achievement of its regulatory objectives and supervisory prin-ciples, and any other matters required (FSMA, Schedule 1 para 10(1)). The annual report is to include the non-executive committee report (under para 4(6)) and any other reports or information required.[118]

1.83 The chairman and other members of the governing body of the FSA are appointed and liable to removal from office by the Treasury (para 2(3)). The chairman of the non-executive committee is also appointed by the Treasury (para 3(2)). Legitimate grounds for removal would presumably include the failure to carry out the FSA's functions.

---

[118] Paras 1.28–1.30 and 1.38.

Treasury review

The Treasury may appoint an independent person to conduct a review of the **1.84**
economy, efficiency, and effectiveness with which the FSA uses its resources in the
discharge of its functions.[119] This may be limited to specific functions although it
cannot cover the FSA's general policy or principles used in securing its regulatory
objectives or its functions in connection with Official Listing.[120] The person conducting the review may ask for copies of all such documents in the custody or
control of the FSA as may reasonably be required, or ask any person for such information or explanation as may be reasonably necessary.[121] Inquiry requests are
enforceable by injunction or specific performance.[122] A written report is to be provided to the Treasury setting out the results of the review and making any such
recommendations as may be considered appropriate.[123] A copy of the report is to
be laid before each House of Parliament and published in such manner as the
Treasury considers appropriate.[124] Review expenses are to be covered by the Treasury
out of money made available by Parliament.[125] The Treasury commissioned a
review under section 12, FSMA by the National Audit Office ('NAO') into the
FSA's economy, efficiency, and effectiveness which reported in June 2007.[126]

Treasury inquiries

The Treasury may appoint such person as may be considered appropriate to con- **1.85**
duct a separate independent inquiry into specified events and circumstances
where this is considered in the public interest.[127] An inquiry may be requested
where a grave risk has occurred (or could have occurred) to the financial system
or could cause significant damage to the interests of consumers as a result of a
serious failure in the regulatory system set up under FSMA or the operation of

---

[119] FSMA, s 12(1).
[120] ibid, s 12(2) and (3).
[121] ibid, s 13(1) and (2).
[122] ibid, s 13(3).
[123] ibid, s 12(4).
[124] ibid, s 13(1).
[125] ibid, s 13(6).
[126] The NAO report confirmed that the FSA was a well-established regulator with an impressive
set of processes and structures to deal with high risk organisations and markets. The review had
considered FSA performance management, relations with other domestic regulators, international
influence and representation, financial crime, and financial capability. The FSA should nevertheless enhance its control on cost management and streamline the operation of its new Outcomes
Performance Reports with non-executive directors continuing to monitor economy and efficiency
although this remains the responsibility of the FSA Board as a whole. NAO, 'The Financial Services
Authority—A review under section 12 of the Financial Services and Markets Act 2000' (April 2007)
available <http://www.nao.org.uk/publications/nao_reports/06-07/0607500.pdf>.
[127] ibid, s 13(1) and (4).

that system.[128] The event must either have related to a person carrying on a regulated activity (whether or not authorised to do so) or a collective investment scheme. An inquiry may also be set up where events have occurred in relation to listed securities or an issuer of securities and significant damage was caused or threatened to investors as a result of a serious failure in the listing system.[129]

1.86 The Treasury may control the scope and duration of the inquiry as well as its conduct and the making of reports by direction.[130] Directions may, in particular, limit or extend the inquiry, discontinue it, or require other steps to be taken. Interim reports may be required.[131] The person conducting the inquiry may obtain such information and make such inquiries as considered fit and determine the procedure to be followed in the conduct of the inquiry.[132] Information or documents may be requested with the person conducting the inquiry having the same powers as a court in respect of the attendance and examination of witnesses and the production of documents.[133]

1.87 A written report is to be prepared for the Treasury setting out the results of the inquiry and containing any recommendations as considered appropriate.[134] This may be published in whole or in part and in such manner as the Treasury may consider appropriate with copies being laid before each House of Parliament. Sensitive information may be removed which may seriously prejudice the interests of a particular person or where this may be incompatible with an international obligation of the UK.[135] Expenses are to be covered by the Treasury out of money made available by Parliament.[136] Failure to comply with requests made under an inquiry or obstructing an inquiry are subject to contempt.[137]

Public meetings

1.88 An annual public meeting is to be held within three months of the FSA's annual report to discuss the report and manner in which the FSA has discharged (or failed) to discharge its functions (para 11(1)).[138] Proper notice of time and place, agenda, duration, and attendance arrangements are to be provided. A separate report on the proceedings of the meeting is to be provided within one month (para 12).[139]

---

[128] ibid, s 14(2)(a) and (b).
[129] ibid, s 14(3)(a) and (b).
[130] ibid, s 15(2).
[131] ibid, s 15(3).
[132] ibid, s 16(1) and (2).
[133] ibid, s 17(2) and (3).
[134] ibid, s 17(1).
[135] ibid, s 17(3) and (4).
[136] ibid, s 17(6).
[137] ibid, s 18.
[138] Paras 1.38–1.39 and 1.45–1.46.
[139] Para 1.39.

Practitioner Panel

The FSA is required to maintain effective arrangements for the consultation of **1.89**
practitioners and consumers on the extent to which its general policies and practices are consistent with its general duties as set out under section 2, FSMA.[140]
A Practitioner Panel was established to represent the interests of financial market
practitioners including authorised persons and recognised investment exchanges
and clearing houses.[141] The FSA appoints the chairman with the chairman's
appointment or dismissal being subject to Treasury approval.[142] The FSA is
required to consider the representations made by the Practitioner Panel[143] and
provide the Panel with a written statement if it disagrees with the views or proposals made.[144] The Practitioner Panel was set up in 2000 and reports and papers are
available on its own website.[145] The FSA has also established a separate Smaller
Businesses Practitioner Panel in 1999 to represent the interests of small regulated
firms. Its purpose is to provide input on the impact and effect on small firms of
regulatory policy and operation. It also monitors the FSA's performance more
generally in the context of its treatment of small firms.[146]

Consumer Panel

The FSA is required to set up and maintain a separate Consumer Panel as part of **1.90**
its general duty to consult.[147] The Panel is made up of consumers or persons representing the interests of consumers and includes a fair proportion of retail rather
than business representatives.[148] The chairman's appointment is made by the FSA
with selection and dismissal again subject to Treasury approval.[149] The FSA is
required to consider the representations made and explain in writing any disagree-
ment on the views or proposals made.[150] Collecting opinions and discussing issues
with the Consumer Panel is particularly important in allowing the FSA to discharge
effectively its consumer-related obligations as set out in the regulatory objectives
in section 2(2) of FSMA. The Consumer Panel's terms of reference and reports
and papers are available on its own website.[151]

---

[140] FSMA, s 8.
[141] ibid, s 9(1) and (5)
[142] ibid, s 9(2) and (3)
[143] ibid, ss 9(4) and 11(2).
[144] ibid, s 11(3).
[145] <http://www.fs-pp.org.uk/>.
[146] <http://www.fsa.gov.uk/Pages/About/Who/Accountability/Business/index.shtml>.
[147] FSMA, ss 8 and 10(1).
[148] ibid, s 10(5) and (6).
[149] ibid, s 10(2) and (3).
[150] ibid, ss 10(4) and 11(2) and (3).
[151] <http://www.fs-cp.org.uk/ct_about_panel.html>.

Board and committee structure

1.91 The main constitutional obligations imposed on the FSA under FSMA in connection with the appointment of its chairman (and CEO) and governing body have already been referred to.[152] The FSA's constitution is to provide for the appointment of a chairman and a governing body with all relevant persons being subject to Treasury appointment and removal.[153] The governing body is to include a majority of non-executive members and a non-executive committee to review the discharge of the FSA's functions, its internal financial controls, and the remuneration of the chairman and executive members of the governing board (paras 3(1) and 4(3)).[154] The FSA may delegate certain functions to other committees, sub-committees, officers, or members of staff although this does not apply to its legislative functions which must be carried out by the board (para 5(1) and (2)).

Complaints

1.92 The FSA is required to maintain a complaints scheme for the investigation of complaints arising in connection with the discharge of its functions with an independent investigator being appointed to consider such complaints.[155] The investigator is to be appointed and removed by the Treasury (para 7(3)). Complaints may either be considered through the complaints scheme, by the Financial Services and Markets Tribunal, or through legal proceedings (para 8(1)). Where complaints are considered under the scheme, these must be referred to the investigator to conduct a full investigation and report, with the investigator being able to require that the FSA makes compensatory payments or takes such other action as may be required to remedy the matter complained of (para 8(2) and (5)). The FSA is required to respond to any recommendations made which the investigator may require to be published in whole or in part (para 8(6) and (7)). This is distinct from the more general complaints scheme maintained under DISP within the FSA Handbook which provides for grievances by clients against authorised institutions to be referred to the Financial Ombudsman Service ('FOS').[156]

---

[152] Paras 1.26–1.30.

[153] FSMA, Sched 1, para 2(1), (2), and (3).

[154] Paras 1.26–1.30 and (nn 18 and 19) and para 1.111.

[155] FSMA, Sched, para 7(1). Paras 1.33–1.36.

[156] Chapter 7. Section 228, FSMA does not require the FOS to determine complaints in accordance with the common law. *R (on the application of Heather Moor & Edgecomb Ltd) v Financial Ombudsman Service and Simon Lodge* [2008] EWCA Civ 642.

Good governance

The FSA is under a general statutory obligation to have regard to such accepted **1.93** principles of good corporate governance as it is reasonable to regard as being applicable to its activities.[157] This is a general obligation in addition to the other more specific requirements imposed such as with regard to regulatory objectives and principles, corporate structure and operation, non-executive directors and committee functions, internal controls, records, complaints, and monitoring and enforcement.

Corporate governance has become an important issue especially following Enron **1.94** and WorldCom and other such scandals. UK corporate governance is generally considered in accordance with the Financial Reporting Council Combined Report referred to in the Listing Rules and the more recent Hutton Report. All of these requirements will not be directly applicable to the FSA as such as it does not maintain a large independent shareholder base. It will nevertheless be expected to comply with all of the other obligations to the extent appropriate.

Tribunal

FSMA provides for the establishment of a separate Financial Services and Markets **1.95** Tribunal which is to discharge the functions conferred on it under the Act.[158] This applies with regard to enforcement actions taken including, in particular, the issuance of supervisory, warning, and decision notices.[159] References to the Tribunal are to be made within 28 days of a decision or supervisory notice having been given or such other time as may be required under the rules to be issued by the Lord Chancellor.[160]

The Tribunal may consider any evidence relating to the subject matter of the **1.96** reference whether or not available to the FSA at the time.[161] The burden of proof in enforcement cases is generally on the FSA although this may be reversed where, for example, an applicant wishes to establish that he satisfies the threshold

---

[157] FSMA, s 7.

[158] ibid, s 132(1) and (2). The rules of the FSMT were set out in the Financial Services and Markets Tribunal Rules 2001 (SI 2001/2476) as amended. On the decisions of the FSMT, *'Financial Services Decisions Digest: FSA Final Notices and FSMT Decisions'* (n 113).

[159] ibid, ss 387 and 388.

[160] ibid, ss 132(3) and 133(1).

[161] ibid, s 133(3). The FSMT does not evaluate the evidence with a view to determining the merits of the opposing cases but to undertake a balancing exercise between the protection of the public and the need to avoid imposing an undue burden on the applicant. *Theophilus Folagbade Sonaike (trading as FT Insurance Services)* (19 August 2005) [App 2.19].

conditions and that he is fit and proper.[162] The standard of proof is the ordinary civil standard of the balance of probability.[163] The Tribunal is to determine what (if any) is the appropriate action for the FSA to take in relation to the matter considered.[164] The Tribunal must remit the matter to the FSA with such directions as the Tribunal considers appropriate subject to the FSA not being required to take any action that it would not otherwise have power to take.[165] The FSA is required to act in accordance with the determination of or any direction issued by the Tribunal.[166] Tribunal orders may be enforced as orders of the County Court or the Court of Session in Scotland.

1.97 Legal assistance is available in connection with proceedings before the Tribunal subject to regulations issued by the Lord Chancellor.[167] Recipients must be individuals who have referred the matter to the Tribunal and who satisfy such other criteria as may be prescribed by the Lord Chancellor.[168] The legal assistance scheme is to contain provisions with regard to the types of assistance available, eligibility, applications, decisions, appeals, revocation or variation of decisions, and administration and enforcement.[169] The FSA is required to pay to the Lord Chancellor such sums as may be determined in respect of the anticipated or actual costs of the legal assistance provided in connection with proceedings before the Tribunal under the scheme.[170] The FSA is to issue corresponding rules requiring the payment by authorised persons (or classes of authorised persons) of such amount as may be specified to cover the scheme's costs.[171] Sums received by the Lord Chancellor are to be paid into the Consolidated Fund with the Lord Chancellor covering the costs of legal assistance from money provided by Parliament.[172]

---

[162] *Norman Deakin, Gwynneth Roe, Ivan Harrison, Ridings GB, Glenbow Financial Management* 8 February 2005 [App 2.14].

[163] In *Hoodless and Blackwell,* the Tribunal endorsed the approach followed *Re Dellow's Will Trusts, Lloyds Bank Ltd v Institute of Cancer Research* [1964] 1 All ER 771 at 773. A more flexible approach may nevertheless be followed in market abuse cases. See *Paul Anthony Davidson and Ashley Tatham* 16 May 2006 [App 2.31]. On market abuse, see for example *ABN AMRO Equities (UK) Ltd* 15 April 2003 [App 1.20]; *Hoodless Brennan & Partners Plc* 17 December 2003 [App 1.33]; *Philippe Jabré & GLC Partners LP* 1 August 2006 [App 1.116], *James Parker* 18 August 2006, and *Sean Julian Pignatelli* 20 November 2006 [App 1.137].

[164] FSMA, s 133(5).

[165] ibid, s 133(5) and (6). In determining an appropriate penalty, the Tribunal will consider sanctions imposed by the FSA in previous cases. See *Legal & General Assurance Society Ltd* 27 May 2005 [App 2.11].

[166] ibid, s 133(10).

[167] ibid, s 134(1).

[168] ibid, s 134(2) and (3).

[169] ibid, s 135(1).

[170] ibid, s 136(1).

[171] ibid, s 136(2).

[172] ibid, s 136(3) and (4).

Appeal

A further right of appeal on a point of law is available to the courts.[173] A party to a **1.98** reference to the Tribunal may with permission appeal to the Court of Appeal or the Court of Session in Scotland on a point of law arising from a decision of the Tribunal disposing of the reference.[174] The court may remit the matter to the Tribunal for rehearing and determination or make a determination itself in the event that it considers that the decision was wrong in law.[175] A further appeal is only available on leave of the Court of Appeal or the House of Lords or the Court of Session in Scotland.[176]

Judicial review

Judicial review is available against the decisions or activities of the FSA under **1.99** general administrative law. A separate right of action for misfeasance in public office may also be available where a party has suffered loss as a result of the FSA's conduct or through its failure to act in a particular case. The availability of this action was confirmed by the House of Lords in the decision in *Three Rivers District Council v Bank of England* in 2000.[177] This applies where either the officers or personnel of a regulatory agency have acted with targeted or untargeted malice and loss has arisen. This is not subject to the statutory immunity from liability in damages provided under para 19(1) of Schedule 1, FSMA as this does not cover any acts or omission shown to have been in bad faith. A high standard of proof is nevertheless required to establish all of the constituent elements of the tort. The trial by the former depositors in BCCI against the Bank of England began in January 2004 following leave by the House of Lords in 2001, although the action was subsequently abandoned in November 2005.[178]

Operations

The FSA has a number of separate divisions or directorates. No specific operational **1.100** structure or direction is provided for under FSMA with the FSA being able to determine the most appropriate framework within which to carry out its functions.

---

[173] The FSA announced that it would appeal the decision of the FSMT to the Court of Appeal following its decision in *Fox Hayes* of 5 to 14 June 2007 in light of the importance of the issues raised. The decision was concerned with the approval of non-real time financial promotions for unauthorised overseas persons.

[174] FSMA, s 137(1).

[175] ibid, s 137(2).

[176] ibid, s 137(4) and (5).

[177] Para 1.44 and (nn 25 and 26).

[178] (n 26).

The FSA decided at an early stage to adopt a model based on regulatory function rather than regulated group or activity. This reflected the more general supervision by risk approach adopted with regard to financial regulation.

1.101 The original functions identified included policy formation and review, authorisation of firms and the approval and registration of individuals, investigations, enforcement and discipline, relations with consumers and the public, and supervision of prudential and conduct of business supervision. The original organisational structure adopted was based on four directorates consisting of (a) Consumer, Investment and Insurance, (b) Deposit Takers and Markets, (c) Regulatory Processes and Risk, and (d) Operations with a number of additional separate functions reporting directly to the chairman.

Restructuring

1.102 The original organisational structure was revised in 2003 following the appointment of Callum McCarthy as chairman in April 2003 and John Tiner as Chief Executive Officer in July 2003. The decision was taken to restructure the internal management organisation of the FSA in 2004 although this has been revised again subsequently.[179] The purpose of the restructurings have been to align the organisation with the FSA's strategic priorities and to facilitate a shift in emphasis from policy development to policy implementation and enforcement. The FSA identified the three business priorities of promoting efficient, orderly, and fair markets, ensuring that retail consumers achieve a fair deal, and improving its own business capability effectiveness as part of its restructuring.[180]

1.103 The FSA Board now consists of the chairman and deputy chairman with the chief executive, the directors of Retail Markets, Wholesale & Institutional Markets, seven non-executive directors, the Managing Governor (Financial Stability) of the Bank of England, the company secretary, and the general counsel. Below the chairman and chief executive officer, the main operations of the FSA are currently divided into three distinct business units consisting of Retail Markets, Wholesale & Institutional Markets, and Operations.

- Retail Markets consists of Major Retail Groups, Retail Firms, Small Firms & Contact, Retail Policy & Themes, Financial Capability, Treating Customers Fairly, and Permissions, Decisions & Reporting Services.

---

[179] On the earlier structure and functions, GA Walker 'Financial Services Authority' in M Blair and GA Walker, *Financial Services Law* (Oxford: OUP, 2006), ch 1 paras 103–110.

[180] FSA, Annual Report 2003/04 (June 2004), sections 1, 2, and 3.

- Wholesale and Institutional Markets is divided into Prudential Risk, Markets, Wholesale Firms, Wholesale & Prudential Policy, and Financial Crime & Intelligence.
- Operations (previously Regulatory Services) includes HR, Finance & Planning & MI, Information Systems, and FSA Facilities.

Eight separate sector leaders have been appointed who act as staff directors in respect of cross-FSA functions within defined sectors or key issue areas. The purpose of the sectoral teams is to ensure that issues relevant to a particular financial area are identified and resolved as quickly as possible, develop the depth and breadth of sector specific and cross-sector expertise, and represent the FSA on external committees and bodies and in external relations. The main current cross-sector teams consist of Auditing & Accounting, Asset Management, Banking, Capital Markets, Consumers, Financial Crime, Financial Stability, Insurance, and Retail Intermediaries & Mortgage. **1.104**

The responsibilities of the chairman are to establish and develop an effective Board, lead the Board as a team, plan and manage the Board's business, establish priorities for the FSA, and maintain and develop productive relationships with the FSA CEO. The chairman is to communicate FSA policies with external constituencies, represent the FSA on national and international financial institutions, establish and maintain high-level contacts with the most important financial institutions globally, and act as an accountability focus for the FSA (including chairing the annual public meeting, providing evidence to select committees, and writing to the Chancellor as appropriate). The chairman also represents the FSA in the senior meetings with the Tripartite Standing Committee including the Chancellor of the Exchequer and the Governor of the Bank of England.[181] **1.105**

The main functions of the CEO are to report regularly to the Board with appropriate, timely, and quality information to allow it to discharge its responsibilities effectively. The CEO is to inform and consult the chairman on all matters of significance to the Board, develop, and deliver the strategic objectives agreed with the Board, recommend significant operational changes and major capital expenditures to the Board as appropriate, assign responsibilities to senior management and oversee the establishment of effective risk management and control systems, recruit, develop, and retain personnel, communicate strategic objectives and values within the FSA, cooperate with the chairman and other senior management in communicating the FSA's policies externally, and represent the FSA on selected international financial institutions. **1.106**

---

[181] <http://fsa/gov/uk/pages/about/who/management/who/chairman/index.shtml>.

1.107 Retail Markets is responsible for assisting retail consumers achieve a fair deal. In so doing, it regulates the major firms involved in the retail markets (including high street banks, insurance companies, and other financial institutions). It regulates retail banks, building societies, insurers, mortgage lenders, asset managers, and retail financial services intermediaries. It assists in the design and development of a proportionate and cost-effective regime for firms carrying on mortgage and general insurance business, and overseas 25,000 smaller firms involved with mortgage advice, insurance broking, and investment advice.

1.108 Wholesale & Institutional Markets is responsible for the regulation of firms and markets of a wholesale or institutional nature and generally involving professional counterparties. It supervises all regulated markets, related infrastructure (including clearing and settlement), and the operation of the UK Listing Rules. It supervises firms conducting wholesale business including investment banks, specialist deposit takers, Lloyd's of London, market insurers, re-insurers, corporate finance firms, venture capital firms, and institutional asset managers. It is also responsible for the maintenance and development of relevant prudential policies that apply to regulated firms and conduct of business standards for wholesale and institutional markets.

1.109 Operations provides a range of services to consumers, firms, and the FSA itself. It is divided into a number of divisions including HR, Finance & Planning & MI, Information Systems, and FSA Facilities. The function of Operations is to assist in making the FSA a more effective organisation through the provision of various support services to firms, consumers, and other stakeholders. This includes processing applications for waivers and guidance, handling calls to consumer help lines, and receiving and processing regulatory returns. Operations also manages other FSA facilities including IT systems and working capital.

1.110 The functions reporting directly to the CEO consist of Strategy and Risk (including Regulatory Transparency, Regulatory Strategy, Economics of Financial Regulation, Risk and International Strategy and Policy Coordination), and Communications (including Press Office, Public Affairs, Accountability, and Events). There is also a separate General Counsel's division with separate Chief Counsel offices for European Law & Prudential Policy, Markets & Wholesale Firms, Retail Markets, and Perimeter, Insurance & Regulatory Services) as well as the Enforcement Division (which is divided into Retail 1, Retail 2, Retail 3, Wholesale, Wholesale and Legal). The chairman of the RDC reports directly the FSA chairman with the company secretary. The head of the new Supervisory Enhancement Programme ('SEP') following Northern Rock reports directly to the CEO with the heads of the Banking Sector and Financial Stability and Internal Audit. A separate function has been set up on Banking & Compensation Reform following Northern Rock which reports to the Head of the Banking Sector.

The Board has two main committees with the Audit Committee ('AuditCo') and **1.111** the Risk Committee ('RiskCo'). AuditCo advises the Board on the strength of the FSA's financial management and the adequacy and effectiveness of the internal controls used by the executive to manage the organisation's operational risks which includes appointing the external auditors. RiskCo assists in reviewing exposures to the statutory objectives with reference to the larger environment within which the FSA operates rather than day-to-day risks or individual firm risks. There is also a special Committee of the Non-Executive Directors ('NEDCo') which reviews reports on the efficient and economic use of the FSA's resources and receives other reports, in particular, from AuditCo and the Remuneration Committee ('RemCo'). The FSA also has two listing committees made up of external practitioners with the Listing Authority Advisory Committee ('LAAC') and the Listing Authority Review Committee ('LARC') to assist the Board and review its function as competence authority for listing. The RDC is also appointed by the Board with the Board receiving quarterly reports.

Costs and staff

Net costs of Ongoing Regulatory Activities ('ORA') are around £300m.[182] The **1.112** total staff of the FSA is between 2,500 and 3,000. The FSA is responsible for the oversight of the activities of 10,000 regulated institutions including 7,500 investment firms, 660 banks, 70 building societies, 1,000 insurance companies and friendly societies, 700 credit unions, and Lloyd's of London. The FSA is also responsible for 180,000 approved persons and since the beginning of 2005, 14,400 mortgage advisers and general insurance salesmen The FSA operates a Making A Real Difference ('MARD') agenda to attempt to attract recruits and retain good staff. The FSA has expanded its supervisory team further following the Northern Rock crisis. It also operates a programme of external secondments to regulated firms and trade bodies.

Functions

The responsibilities of the FSA have been further extended to cover all personal **1.113** pension schemes including self-invested personal pensions ('SIPPS') from April 2007. The FSA has also been responsible for supervising the anti-money laundering controls of leasing companies, commercial finance providers, safe custody services, and other businesses from December 2007 following implementation of the EU Third Money Laundering Directive. The FSA also regulates connected

---

[182] Net costs of ORA and expenditure on ORA for 2008/09 were £298.1m. FSA, Annual Report 2007/08 (June 2008). Fees for 2007/08 were £303.3m.

travel insurance ('CTI') which is sold with holiday or other related travel firms and holiday providers from 1 January 2009. The FSA has become the competent authority for the provision of payment services under the Payment Services Directive from 1 November 2009.

Agency relations

1.114 In addition to the MOU entered into with the Treasury and the Bank of England,[183] the FSA works with other institutions such as the Pensions Regulatory Authority, the OFT on consumer credit, consumer protection, and competition issues, the Department for Business, Enterprise and Regulatory Reform ('BERR') on company and insolvency matters, and the Serious Fraud Office ('SFO') and Serious Organised Crime Agency ('SOCA') on financial crime. The FSA also cooperates with other national financial regulators and law agencies and has representatives on all of the major international committees including the Basel Committee on Banking Supervision, the International Securities Regulatory Commission ('IOSCO'), the International Association of Insurance Supervisors ('IAIS'), the Financial Stability Forum ('FSF'), the Joint Forum on Financial Conglomerates, as well as the Committee on Payment and Settlement Systems ('CPSS'), the Committee on the Global Financial System ('CGFS'), and the Financial Action Task Force ('FATF').[184]

Policy Development

1.115 The FSA carries out its specific supervisory and regulatory functions through the main divisions within its organisational structure. In addition to these daily operational activities, the FSA undertakes a number of more general policy development initiatives either in particular sector areas or on a cross-sector basis and at the national, European, or international levels. Progress in the adoption and application of these policy initiatives is reported on a continuous basis in the FSA's annual publications as well as in other more specific consultation, discussion, feedback, or other papers.

Policy base

1.116 FSA activities are generally either EU implementation, internal policy, or scandal or crisis driven. A significant amount of recent work has been created in recent years with the need to implement major EU directives including, for example, MiFID

---

[183] Paras 1.134–1.147.
[184] See generally Chapter 4.

and the CRD with further work required on Solvency II in the insurance area. A large number of Handbook rules and guidance revisions have been EU directive-based. A number of reforms have also been reactionary to the extent that they are scandal or crisis driven such as in connection with mortgage endowments or split capital investment trusts. Considerably more activity is nevertheless based on continuing internal FSA policy initiatives.

Many of the FSA's continuing core policy initiatives are not directly FSMA-based **1.117** to the extent that they have no specific statutory origin, definition, or direction. Many are nevertheless related to or intended to secure the FSA's core statutory objectives as set out in section 2(2), FSMA of market confidence, public awareness, consumer protection, and combating financial crime as supported by the supervisory principles in section 2(3), FSMA.[185] While some of these are given effect to through particular rules or guidance as set out in the Handbook, many are issued in the form of more general documents based only on particular principles within PRIN or other High-Level Standards.[186]

Such initiatives can be of particular value to the extent that they are not more **1.118** traditional sector or market-based but intended to secure larger common regulatory objectives or targets not dealt with under previous institutionally specific regulatory regimes. While this can have advantage in terms of flexibility and the development of a more general culture of compliance as opposed to the adoption of a simple formalistic approach to compliance within firms, this has raised concerns with regard to legal certainty and possibly excessive discretion on enforcement. The challenge for the FSA has then been to balance this flexibility and support with sufficient legal certainty and proper due process. The development and implementation of these policy initiatives are among the most unique and defining characteristics of the new UK regime as well as its underlying integrated single market, single regulated, and single regulation basis.[187] These allow a new complexity and sophistication in terms of market control and regulation.

Such key policy initiatives include Financial Stability as part of the larger National **1.119** Strategy for Financial Capability,[188] Treating Customers Fairly ('TCF'), the Retail Distribution Review ('RDR'),[189] Listing Review,[190] Mortgage Effectiveness

---

[185] Paras.1.47–1.53 and 1.54–1.55.

[186] Chapter 5 and Ch 14, paras 14.76 and 14.77–14.84.

[187] Walker (n 1).

[188] For a review of Financial Capability performance, FSA, Annual Report 2007/08, Appendix 6.

[189] The FSA published an interim report on the Retail Distribution Review ('RDR') following its discussion paper DP/07/1 in June 2007. A separate paper was issued on 'Platforms: The Role of Wraps and Fund Supermarkets' (DP 07/2).

[190] See, for example, FSA CP 06/21, 'Investment Entities Listing Review—Further consultation and feedback' in December 2006 following original consultation paper 04/6 in March 2006 on 'Implementation of the Transparency Directive/Investment Entities Listing Review'.

Review and mortgage exit administration fees ('MEAFs') and Transparency,[191] Payment Protection Insurance ('PPI') sales practices and with-profits funds sales, as well as such other matters as a review of inside information and short selling. Many of these are considered in other parts of this book. Some of the other main programmes relevant to the FSA's continuing activities may nevertheless be referred to in outline at this stage.

Risk-based regulation

1.120   The regulatory approach adopted by the FSA is risk-based. This originated in the post-Barings reforms adopted by the Bank of England with the development of a risk-based approach to bank supervision assessed in terms of individual bank compliance with a range of specific risk factors (capital, assets, management, earnings, and liquidity ('CAMEL') as against the firm's controls, organisation, and management ('COM')).[192] This was then extended post FSMA to constitute an assessment of all of the main risks to the FSA's statutory objectives.

1.121   The original regulatory approach was developed in early FSA papers[193] and later in its ARROW and ARROW II supervisory framework from 2000 onwards.[194] Risk by risk refers to the aggregation of risks across different sectors rather than within a specific sector. The core risks identified under the PRU before the separate sub-sourcebooks were produced were credit risk, market risk, interest rate risk, liquidity risk, insurance risk, and group risk.[195]

---

[191] FSA issued a discussion paper on 'Transparency as a regulatory tool' DP 08/3 with a separate consultation paper on changes to its Decision Procedure and Penalties ('DEPP') manual and Enforcement Guide ('EG') (CP 08/10).

[192] GA Walker, 'Deposit Taking and Banking Supervision' in Blair, Allison, Morton, Richards-Carpenter, Walker, and Walmsley, *Banking and Financial Services Regulation* (Butterworths, 3rd edn, 2002) ch 6, paras 6.4 and 6.84–6.100.

[193] See, for example, FSA, 'New regulator for the new millennium' (January 2000). See also FSA, 'Building the New Regulator—Progress Report 1' (December 2000); and FSA, 'Building the New Regulator—Progress Report 2' (February 2002) (n 44); and FSA, 'The FSA's Risk-Based Approach' (November 2006). Chapter 14, paras 14.94–14.103.

[194] FSA, 'The FSA's Risk-Based Approach' (November 2008), Table 2. Under the FSA's revised probability model, the FSA considers Business Risks (including Environmental Risk and Business Model Risks (customers, products and markets, business processes, and prudential), Controls (customer, product and market controls; financial and operating controls; and prudential risk controls), and Oversight and Governance (including both control functions and management governance and culture) with other mitigants being considered (made up of excess capital and liquidity). Risks are then assessed horizontally under three groups of Business, Controls, and Oversight and Governance risks. These are aggregated into three net probability scores based on Customer Treatment and Market Conduct, Operating, and Financial Soundness. The FSA then prepares a Risk Mitigation Programme ('RMP') for the firm following an onsite visit and risk evaluation.

[195] On the development and components of the FSA Integrated Sourcebook, Chapter 11 and Chapter 14, paras 14.171–14.183.

ARROW and ARROW II

The FSA's operating framework is referred to as ARROW (Advance, Risk-Responsive **1.122**
Operating frameWork). ARROW is used to link statutory objectives and regulatory activities with an identification of the FSA's core statutory purposes, an assessment and prioritisation of the applicable risks and determination as to the most
appropriate regulatory response to be adopted using the regulatory tools available.[196]
Risk management is then based on an assessment of the impact of a risk as against
its probability of occurring.[197] The ARROW framework allows for risk identification, risk measurement, risk mitigation[198] and risk monitoring and reporting.[199]
Firms are then divided into medium and high impact firms ('Full ARROW') and
low impact firms ('ARROW Light')[200] in terms of supervisory treatment. Under
ARROW II from 2006, the FSA has adopted an 'ARROW Firms' approach (to
assess risks within individual firms on a vertical supervision basis) and an 'ARROW
Themes' approach (to assess cross-firm or sector risks on a horizontal basis).

The FSA has also been issuing 'Milestones' against which to measure the progress **1.123**
achieved in securing its objectives.[201] These are generally organised into its strategies
of promoting efficient, orderly, and fair markets, helping retail consumers achieve
a fair deal, and improving business capability and effectiveness. The FSA has a
separate programme for Integrated Regulatory Reporting ('IRR') and is developing a new reporting system GABRIEL (GAthering Better Regulatory Information
Electronically) which was intended to come into effect from August 2008.

Principles-based regulation

The FSA has moved in recent years to a more principles-based regulation ('MPBR') **1.124**
approach.[202] Principles-based regulation is concerned with shifting the focus of
regulatory attention and resources as well as firm compliance activities to focusing
on principles and high-level rules rather than more detailed prescriptive rules.

---

[196] This is achieved through an assessment of risk indicators, risk assessment and prioritisation, decision on regulatory response, resource allocation, decision on relevant regulatory tools, and
performance evaluation. This is generally expressed in the form of a table available at <http://www.
fsa.gov.uk/pages/About/What/Approach/Framework/>. See also FSA, 'The FSA's Risk-Assessment
Framework' (August 2006) and also (n 194).

[197] FSA, 'The FSA's Risk-Assessment Framework' (August 2006) para 3.1 and Figure 2.

[198] Under a Risk Mitigation Programme (RMP). FSA, 'The FSA's Risk-Assessment Framework'
(August 2006) Appendix 2.

[199] FSA, 'The FSA's Risk-Assessment Framework' (August 2006) para 2.6 and Figure 1.

[200] ARROW Light applies with regard to 3% of firms with Full ARROW for 2% and 0.33%.
The FSA has also developed a separate ARROW Small Firms categorisation for 95% of regulated
institutions. FSA, 'The FSA's Risk-Based Approach' (November 2006).

[201] The milestones for 2008/9 were set out in its Business Plan 2009/08 (February 2008) with
a review of previous Performance against Business Plan milestones in its Annual Report 2007/08,
Appendix 6.

[202] FSA, 'Principles-Based Regulation—Focusing on the Outcomes that Matter' (April 2007).

This is stated to complement the risk and evidence-based models otherwise used by the FSA.[203] The emphasis is then on principles and 'outcome focused' rules. The FSA has stated that it will invest in necessary personnel resources and capabilities to allow staff to acquire the necessary experience, expertise, judgement, and communication skills as well as extend the advice and support provided to firms. Reforms are also measured against a new Outcome Performance Report ('OPR') to be integrated into the FSA's operations and governance.

1.125   While FSMA represented a shift from prescriptive law-based regulation to a rules-based model with the FSA being given a delegated power to issue its own rules with the same legal effect as statutory instruments,[204] the FSA has moved more recently to focus on principles and general (outcome focused) rules. There has then been a shift from a law to a delegated rules and then from a rules to a combined principles and general rules-based model. This emphasis on expertise, judgement, and communication reflects the earlier discretion and personal relationship-based nature of bank supervision previously conducted by the Bank of England under its earlier 'moral suasion' approach.[205] Moral suasion referred to the control that the Bank was able to exercise over individual banks and the financial system more generally solely based on its authority in the markets rather than specific statutory power.[206] There has then been a larger shift from supervisory discretion and judgement to law and then rules back to discretion through principles although within a more complex and sophisticated integrated regime operated by the FSA under FSMA.

1.126   The main advantages of principles-based regulation can be considered to include allowing firms greater flexibility in designing and operating their own internal compliance systems, a higher and wider level of compliance with the establishment of more general compliance cultures, consequent increased consumer protection and arguably lower costs of compliance, and closer and better relations with the regulator. Significant difficulties nevertheless arise in terms of loss of regulatory certainty, increased regulatory burden and regulatory cost, as well as perceived more arbitrary enforcement and consequent increased liability. The FSA also recognises that the European Commission has already moved towards a more rules-based approach which is more detailed and prescriptive than the new FSA principles-based model. European directive implementation then requires a significant minimum level of regulatory prescription. Difficulties may also arise in ensuring consistency between the FSA's action and the decisions of the Financial Ombudsman Service and Financial Services and Markets Tribunal. The FSA has

---

[203] FSA, 'Principles-Based Regulation—Focusing on the Outcomes that Matter' 2 and 4.
[204] Para 1.20.
[205] Chapter 14, paras 14.9–14.11
[206] Chapter 14, para 14.11.

already begun to simplify its Handbook[207] and has produced a new Enforcement Guide to assist firms although difficulties will remain in balancing firm and FSA flexibility with sufficient legal and regulatory certainty in practice.

Better Regulation Action Plan ('BRAP')

Better Regulation is concerned with ensuring that the overall benefits of regula- **1.127** tion outweigh the costs and that the benefits generated are maximised. The FSA had set out its original Better Regulation Action Plan ('BRAP') in December 2005[208] with other special studies being commissioned.[209] Various update reports have been published subsequently.[210] Better regulation in the UK is now managed more generally through the Better Regulation Executive ('BRE') under the Department for Business Enterprise & Regulatory Reform ('BERR').[211] Better regulation can be considered to be more procedural than substantive although it does assist in determining whether regulation should be adopted and the content of the regulation in place. The Hampton Review of effective inspection and enforcement in 2005 had identified the FSA as an example of a consolidated regulator with a strong risk-based approach.[212]

The Better Regulation agenda requires that new regulation is only introduced **1.128** where there has been a demonstrable failure of the market and where the cost of regulation can be shown to be less than that of allowing the market failure to persist. Better Regulation can then be considered in terms of five key requirements of cost–benefit analysis, consultation, consideration of non-legislative responses

---

[207] The main areas affected by the adoption of a more principles-based approach and relevant consultation documents are summarised in the table on p 24 of FSA, 'Principles-Based Regulation— Focusing on the Outcomes that Matter' (April 2007).

[208] FSA, 'Better Regulation Action Plan' (December 2005). This follows the Government's more general better regulation initiative and Legislative and Regulatory Reform Act 2006 which replaced the earlier Regulatory Reform Act 2001. Part 2 of the Act gives effect to the recommendations of the Hampton Review on 'Reducing administrative burdens: effective inspection and enforcement' (March 2005) (n 212). The Act includes the principles that regulatory activities should be carried out in a way that is transparent, accountable, proportionate, and consistent and that regulatory activities should be targeted only at cases in which action is needed. It also provides for the production of a supporting Code of Conduct.

[209] Deloitte, 'The Cost of Regulation Study' (2006); Real Assurance Risk Management, 'Estimation of FSA Administrative Burdens' (June 2006), and Oxera, 'A Framework for Assessing the Benefits of Financial Regulation' (September 2006).

[210] FSA, 'Better Regulation Action Plan Progress Report' (June 2006); and FSA and the Office of Fair Trading, 'Delivering Better Regulatory Outcomes—May 2008 Update' (May 2008).

[211] <http://www.betterregulation.gov.uk/>.

[212] The Hampton review had been commissioned to consider the scope for reducing administrative burdens by promoting more efficient approaches to regulatory inspection and enforcement, without compromising regulatory standards or outcomes (n 208). P Hampton, *Reducing Administrative Burdens: Effective Inspection and Enforcement* (March 2005) available <http://www.hm-treasury.gov.uk/media/7/F/bud05hamptonv1.pdf>. See also FSA, 'Response to the Hampton Implementation Review of the Financial Services Authority' (March 2008).

(such as using competition or codes of conduct), or occasional or one-off regulatory responses (such as through thematic or catalytic work) and subsequent evaluation. In applying Better Regulation, the FSA examines whether there has been a material market failure, why that creates a threat to its statutory objectives, and the reasons for the absence of any appropriate alternative market solution. The costs of intervention are then assessed against the benefits generated through impact assessments. The process is fully transparent with maximum consultation and subsequent review and evaluation to determine whether the intended outcomes have been achieved or whether further legislative or other regulatory revision is required.

Handbook simplification

1.129 The FSA has been attempting to streamline its rules as part of a larger Handbook review. The FSA announced its original Simplification Plan in December 2006 following the earlier publications in 2006 on Better Regulation.[213] An update was published in December 2007 with continuing progress work referred to in the FSA's *Annual Report* and *Business Plan*.[214]

1.130 This generally assesses whether specific requirements are more restrictive than needed to achieve the FSA's objectives, where benefits do not justify their costs or where they are not consistent with the FSA's emphasis on senior management responsibility. Changes are made where they have a real impact and where the benefits are clear. Opportunities to streamline the Handbook are also taken on a continuing basis as they arise such as with MiFID implementation. High-level standards are used in preference to more detailed rules although firms are also to be provided with sufficient guidance. The FSA also attempts not to introduce any changes where rules have recently been introduced, avoid increasing regulatory costs, deliver an appropriate level of consumer protection, ensure that the Handbook remains easy to understand and navigate, and avoid any 'super-equivalence' in EU implementation without independent justification.

1.131 Simplification has already involved replacing 57 pages of the earlier Money Laundering Sourcebook with two pages of high-level principles (with an estimated cost saving of over £250m) and deletion of the requirement for small firms to have an external auditor (with £30m in savings) and annual reporting requirements for Approved Persons (saving £2.2m). The earlier COB was substantially revised as part of the MiFID implementation process to create the new COBS. The FSA 'Handbook online' facility now allows firms to construct their own

---

[213] FSA, 'Simplification Plan' (December 2006) available <http://www.fsa.gov.uk/pubs/other/simplifybaselineplan.pds>.
[214] FSA, 'Simplification Plan Update' (December 2007). On the update of the FSA Simplification Plan, FSA, 'Annual Report 2007/08' (June 20078) Appendix 7.

Handbook on a customised basis following the completion of 10 test questions. Fourteen tailored Handbooks are available which only contain the relevant parts that affect the activities of the particular category of firm. These generally contain less than 10 per cent of the full Handbook and apply to approximately 70 per cent of firms.

Policy publications

More general policy work is reported on by the FSA through its *Annual Reports* which it is required to publish (under FSMA, Schedule 1 para 11).[215] These include information on the manner in which the FSA has discharged its functions and the extent to which it has secured its regulatory objectives during the previous year. The FSA also publishes a separate *Business Plan* which includes its priorities for the year ahead and more recent 'Milestones' against which to measure the progress achieved in securing its objectives.[216] It has also been conducting studies on particular regulatory issues such as its review into the costs of regulation and the extent to which they could be reduced over time. The FSA conducts its annual review on the basis of a Financial Management Reporting Framework ('FMRF') which is updated in its Business Plan.

1.132

The FSA produces a separate *Financial Risk Outline* which identifies underlying exposures or vulnerabilities within the financial sector against which its regulatory priorities are set. The *Financial Risk Outlook* considers general economic and financial conditions including alternative scenarios as well as priority risks and industry focus.[217] The FSA has also more recently produced a new *International Regulatory Outlook* which examines international developments and their potential impact on the FSA's work over the following year. The *International Regulatory Outlook* contains highlights on new rules, standards, and guidance in international supervision, a section on sector messages, a summary of better regulation developments, an EU 'legislation information bank' and a directory of EU and international committees.[218]

1.133

---

[215] Para 1.38. Annual Reports are available at <http://www.fsa.gov.uk/Pages/Library/Corporate/Annual/index.shtml>.

[216] Para 1.123. Business Plans are available at <http://www.fsa.gov.uk/Pages/Library/Corporate/Plan/index.shtml>.

[217] FSA, 'Financial Risk Outlook' (2008). Copies are available at <http://www.fsa.gov.uk/Pages/Library/Corporate/Outlook/index.shtml>.

[218] FSA, 'International Regulatory Outlook' (December 2006). Copies are available at <http://www.fsa.gov.uk/Pages/Library/Corporate/iro/index.shtml>.

Memoranda of Understanding

1.134 The FSA is party to the Memorandum of Understanding (MOU) which was originally entered into with the Treasury and the Bank of England on 28 October 1997
with a revised and updated MOU being executed on 22 March 2006.[219] This sets
out the terms of the relationship between the three principal agencies responsible
for the operation and oversight of financial markets in the UK. A separate MOU
was entered into between the FSA, the Bank of England, and the US Securities and
Exchange Commission (SEC) and Commodities Futures Trading Commission
(CFTC) at the time of the FSA launch in October 1997. The FSA has also entered
into a large number of bilateral and multilateral MOUs subsequently with other
banking and financial regulators within the EU and across the world.[220]

Financial stability

1.135 The Treasury, the Bank of England, and the FSA are parties to the reissued MOU
in August 2006 which sets out the terms of the relations between them and replaces
the earlier 1997 MOU. It is expected that a further MOU will be issued following
the Northern Rock crisis and the other institutional reforms announced.[221]

1.136 The revised MOU sets out the updated framework for monitoring, assessing, and
coordinating the three authorities' responses to financial stability risks including
business continuity concerns. The MOU contains a revised definition of the role
and function of each agency. The Bank of England is generally to continue to
contribute to the maintenance of the stability of the financial system as a whole
based on its macroeconomic and financial analysis and its operational involvement in the markets, payment systems, and market infrastructure. The FSA is
primarily responsible for the authorisation and supervision of financial institutions, supervising financial markets and securities clearing and settlement systems, and for relevant regulatory policy. The Treasury is responsible for the overall
institutional structure of regulation and the legislation governing it in the UK.

1.137 Cooperation is managed through a Tripartite Standing Committee made up of
the Chancellor of the Exchequer, the Governor of the Bank of England, and the
chairman of the FSA. The Committee meets at deputy's level on a monthly basis
with principals' meetings being conducted as necessary. The purpose is to review

---

[219] See GA Walker, 'Revised Memorandum of Understanding on UK Financial Stability' (2006)
Bankers' Law, Vol 2 No.
[220] Paras 1.148–1.150.
[221] Para 1.179.

key systemic issues concerning UK financial markets and to coordinate responses and contingency planning.

The division of responsibilities is based on four guiding principles consisting of **1.138** clear accountability, transparency, avoidance of duplication, and regulatory information exchange (para 1). Each party is accountable for its actions based on unambiguous and well-defined responsibilities. Parliament, the markets, and the public have to know which agency is responsible for which functions. Each authority must have a clearly defined role to avoid uncertainty, inefficiency, and unnecessary duplication. Each is to discharge its responsibilities as efficiently and effectively as possible.

The Bank is to continue to contribute to the maintenance of the stability of the **1.139** financial system as a whole (para 2). Four specific sub-functions are then identified. The Bank is responsible for ensuring the stability of the monetary system as part of its monetary policy function, overseeing systemically significant financial system infrastructure, maintaining an overview of the system as a whole and undertaking official financial operations in exceptional circumstances in accordance with the procedures set out in paras 13 and 14 of the MOU. Financial system infrastructure includes the payments system with the Bank advising the Chancellor on any major problems that arise as well as developing and improving infrastructure arrangements and strengthening the ability of the system to reduce systemic risk over time. Its oversight role includes identifying potential problems and advising on financial stability consequences of changes in domestic and international markets and payment system. The Bank is principally then responsible for monetary stability although it also contributes to financial stability including oversight of systems infrastructure and providing exceptional assistance in the form of lender-of-last-resort ('LLR') support.

The powers and responsibilities of the FSA are as set out in the Financial Services **1.140** and Markets Act 2000 (FSMA). The MOU identifies four specific functions including the authorisation and prudential supervision of financial institutions, supervision of financial markets, securities listing and of clearing and settlement systems, emergency operations, and regulatory policy. The FSA's involvement with emergency operations is nevertheless limited to assisting in problem cases affecting firms, markets, and clearing and settlement systems where this falls within the scope of the MOU (paras 13 and 14) but not within the responsibilities of the Bank. In such cases, the FSA may impose additional capital or other regulatory requirements and assist facilitate market solutions. This is important in clarifying the degree and nature of the FSA's possible intervention in a crisis situation. This will generally include managing regulatory or market-based responses with more general LLR support being provided by the Bank of England.

1.141   The Treasury is responsible for the overall institutional structure of financial regulation and supporting legislation (para 4). This will include negotiating relevant EU directives. The Treasury is also to inform and be accountable to Parliament for the management of serious financial system problems and response measures. It is also to account for financial sector resilience to operational disruption within government. This essentially includes continuity planning within government departments and agencies.

1.142   The Treasury is to have no operational responsibility for the activities of the FSA and the Bank (para 5). The FSA and the Bank are nevertheless to advise the Treasury of potential difficulties in advance. This may include serious problems that could have caused wider financial or economic disruption, require a support operation, involve diplomatic or foreign relations issues, require law reform, or involve questions being referred to Ministers in Parliament. The FSA and the Bank are responsible for determining whether the Treasury is to be informed in each case.

1.143   The MOU attempts to clarify the procedures governing information collection by the FSA and the Bank for their separate statutory purposes (para 6). The FSA and the Bank are to work together to avoid duplication in the collection of financial data (para 7). Where the same information is required by both, they are to agree who is to be responsible for its collection and subsequent exchange.

1.144   The MOU contains separate additional provisions concerning financial crisis management and operational crisis management. The financial crisis management is defined in terms of operations going beyond the Bank's published framework for its normal activities in the money market. This is only to be considered where there is a genuine threat to the stability of the financial system that is necessary to avoid a serious disturbance to the UK economy (para 14). A double stability and disturbance test is accordingly adopted although both conditions would presumably be satisfied in most serious emergency situations. Individual cases of significance had been considered by a joint Standing Committee of representatives of the Treasury, the Bank, and the FSA which meets on a monthly basis or as required.[222]

---

[222] HM Treasury, the Bank of England, and the FSA make up the UK's Tripartite Standing Committee which examines financial stability issues. The Standing Committee meets monthly at deputy's level although additional meetings may be called at short notice if necessary. A sub-group was also convened monthly to consider work on contingency planning for operational disruption and financial sector resilience. This followed the earlier Treasury consultation on the 'Financial System and Major Operational Disruption' (February 2003) and the Report of the Task Force chaired by Sir Andrew Large. See 'Report of the Taskforce on major disruption to the financial system'. (December 2003). See also Financial Markets Law Committee, 'Emergency Powers Legislation' (November 2003); and the Financial Sector Business Continuity Progress Report available on the UK Financial Sector Continuity website <http://www.fsc.gov.uk/>. The Tripartite Group also steered the UK's work on the IMF's Financial Sector Assessment Programme ('FSAP') assessment of the UK financial system in 2003. See IMF, 'United Kingdom—Financial System Stability Assessment' (February 2003). (December 2003). See also Financial Markets Law Committee, 'Emergency Powers

The Bank or the FSA may identify situations in which support operations are **1.145** necessary. In such cases, they are required to inform each other immediately and act in accordance with the revised coordination framework provided for under the MOU (paras 14 and 16). The Treasury is to be informed concerning any developing situation with the Chancellor having ultimate responsibility to determine whether any support operation should continue. In the event of a crisis arising, the objective must be to reduce the risk of a problem causing wider financial or economic damage (para 15). In so doing, the authorities are to seek to minimise private sector moral hazard and financial risk to the taxpayer from the provision of any support operation. The three authorities are to maintain an appropriate framework for the coordination of activity in the management of a financial crisis (para 16).

The authorities are to maintain a separate new framework for the management of **1.146** coordination in the event of an operational as opposed to financial crisis (para 17). An operational crisis is not defined although this presumably applies to systems failure and continuity planning including technological failures or terrorist attacks.

This is an important and necessary revision. The original 1997 MOU was charac- **1.147** terised by its almost calculated brevity and vagueness especially concerning relevant emergency responses. The drafting read as if the deliberate intention had been to be as unspecific as possible to allow maximum operational flexibility. Whether it would have achieved this result in practice must be questioned. The new MOU is a considerably clearer and well structured document that expands on the lessons learned concerning financial crisis and operational crisis management and contingency planning especially post-9/11. A further revision is neverthless expected following the institutional reforms to be adopted after the Northern Rock crisis.[223]

UK Memoranda of Understanding

The FSA has entered into a number of other bilateral MOUs with other UK author- **1.148** ities in connection with a range of regulatory matters.[224] These include with the Financial Ombudsman Service ('FOS'), Financial Services Compensation Scheme ('FSCS'), the Banking Code Standards Board ('BCSB'), the Institute of Chartered

---

Legislation' (November 2003); and the Financial Sector Business Continuity Progress Report available on the UK Financial Sector Continuity website <http://www.fsc.gov.uk/>.

[223] Paras 1.151–1.180.
[224] <http://www.fsa.gov.uk/Pages/Library/corporate/Memorandums/UK/index.shtml>.

Accountants in England and Wales, the Institute of Chartered Accountants in Scotland, the Institute of Chartered Accountants in Ireland, the Association of Chartered Certified Accountants, the Institute of Actuaries, the Law Society of England and Wales, the Law Society of Scotland, the Law Society of Northern Ireland, the Pensions Regulator, the Financial Reporting Review Panel, the Inland Revenue, the Office of the Scottish Charity Regulator, the Association of Chief Police Officers England & Wales, the Skills Council, and the Housing Corporation.

Bilateral and multilateral Memoranda of Understanding

1.149 The FSA has also entered into other bilateral and multilateral MOUs with authorities in overseas jurisdictions in all the main sector areas.[225] The FSA entered into a first MOU with the SEC, the CFTC, and the Bank of England in October 1997. A protocol was signed with the SEC and Financial Reporting Council in 25 April 2007 and separate MOU with the SEC in 14 March 2006. The purpose of the 1997 MOU was to enhance the ability of the bodies concerned to exchange information concerning the activities of US and UK internationally active firms including on internal controls and management systems. The MOU established procedures to ensure cooperation in connection with potentially significant market events experienced by US or UK securities or banking firms. It was hoped that the MOU would improve relations between the national authorities more generally and the effectiveness of financial supervision on both a cross-border and cross-sector basis.

1.150 MOUs and shorter FISMOUs (financial information sharing agreements) were originally developed in the securities area between national authorities on a bilateral basis. IOSCO produced a model set of principles for MOUs in 1992[226] which were used as the basis for many securities related MOUs subsequently. IOSCO has issued a multilateral standard form MOU in May 2002 which has since become the industry model. This provides for the exchange of relevant information and cooperation as well as coordination of action in emergency situations. The list of signatory institutions is provided on IOSCO's website.[227] This is a highly useful document in establishing clear contact channels and operational

---

[225] <http://www.fsa.gov.uk/Pages/Library/Corporate/Memorandums/international/index.shtml>.

[226] See Working Party No 4 of the Technical Committee of IOSCO 'Principles for Memorandum of Understanding', Documents of the XVI Annual Conference IOSCO, No 5, September 1991 (IOSCO Principles). In connection with information sharing, see J Michau, Workshop No 4, 'Information Sharing Between Securities Regulators (Market Surveillance and Insider Trading)', XVth Annual Conference, November 1990. See also GA Walker, *International Banking Regulation— Law, Policy and Practice* (2001), ch 4; and GA Walker, 'International Supervisory Co-operation' in W Blair et al, *Bank Regulation* (3rd edn, 2002), ch 21, paras 21.6–21.17.

[227] IOSCO, 'Multilateral Memorandum of Understanding Concerning Consultation and Cooperation and the Exchange of Information' (May 2002) available at <http://www.iosco.org/library/index.cfm?section=mou_siglist>. See also Chapter 4.

procedures between national supervisory and regulatory agencies. MOUs are nevertheless legally unenforceable and generally subject to a public interest exemption. Their main operational effectiveness is to a significant extent dependent on the goodwill and cooperation of the authorities and individual regulatory staff involved in any particular case.[228]

Financial Stability

The structure and operation of the system of financial stability management **1.151** in the UK have been revised most recently following the circumstances surrounding the provision of emergency liquidity assistance to Northern Rock bank in September 2007 and its subsequent public acquisition in February 2008.[229] A number of early papers were issued by the FSA, HM Treasury, and Bank of England as the core tripartite regulatory authorities.[230] The main recommendations were contained in a July 2008 consultation document on *Financial Stability and Depositor Protection*.[231] Proposed implementing legislation was expected in autumn 2008 with a new Banking Bill. These are an important set of revisions as they give effect to the most substantial set of amendments made to the new integrated regulatory system set up under FSMA since its inauguration in 2000 and readjusts and strengthens the institutional support arrangements underlying this system. While some of the changes made are more minor or predictable, other more substantial elements are involved. These accordingly constitute an important and welcome adjustment and refinement to the integrated regulated model created. This regulatory work was then taken forward further with the subsequent market support announcements made as the global credit crisis heightened. The Government confirmed on 8 October 2008 that it would provide up to £50bn to recapitalise the main UK banks with the Bank of England's Special Lending

---

[228] GA Walker, 'International Supervisory Co-operation' (n 226) para 21.16.

[229] GA Walker, 'Northern Rock Falls' (2008) *Bankers' Law* Vol 2 No 2, 4–12. See also GA Walker, 'The Deconstruction of Financial Risk' (October 2008) *Palgrave Journal of Banking Regulation*, 1, 2; and GA Walker, 'Credit Crisis—Regulatory and Financial Systems Reform' *Butterworths JIBL* (November 2007) 567–72; and GA Walker, 'Sub-prime Loans, Inter-Bank Markets and Financial Support' (November 2007) *The Company Lawyer*, 22–5. See also Walker, 'Credit Contraction, Financial Collapse and Global Recession' *Butterworths JIBL* (January 2009) 5–10; and Walker, 'Credit Crisis, Bretton Woods II and A New Global Response' *Butterworths JIBL* (February 2009). See also Chapter 14, paras 14.22–14.24 and paras 14.220–14.240.

[230] HM Treasury, the Bank of England, and the FSA, 'Banking Reform—Protecting Depositors: a Discussion Paper' (October 2007); and the Treasury, the Bank of England, and the FSA, 'Financial Stability and Depositor Protection: Strengthening the Framework' (January 2008) Cm 7308. See also Chapter 14, paras 14.235–14.240.

[231] Bank of England, HM Treasury and FSA, 'Financial Stability and Depositor Protection: Further Consultation' (July 2008) Cm7436. See also the Bank of England, HM Treasury and the FSA, 'Financial Stability And Depositor Protection: Special Resolution Regime' (July 2008); and HM Treasury, 'Financial Stability and Depositor Protection: Cross-Border Challenges' (September 2008).

Scheme ('SLS') being extended from £100m to £200m and with guarantees being provided for money market loans for up to three years at commercial rates. The UK bail-out model was then followed by other countries within the EU and elsewhere as part of a more coordinated but still not fully integrated response to the credit crisis. These tools considerably extend the range of support options available to authorities in ensuring that money markets and inter-bank markets work effectively and in protecting the systemic stability of the financial system.

Financial stability and depositor protection

1.152 The July 2008 consultation document builds on the earlier consultation document published in January 2008 with proposed legislation to follow in autumn 2008. The report restates the five key objectives identified earlier of strengthening the stability and resilience of the financial system, reducing the likelihood of banks facing difficulties, reducing the impact of a bank in difficulties, providing effective compensation, and strengthening the Bank of England ensuring coordination between all authorities in the UK and internationally.

1.153 The Chancellor of the Exchequer, Alistair Darling, had noted that no system of regulation could or should prevent the failure of each and every institution although the authorities had to do everything possible to prevent problems that could pose a wider threat to stability. The challenge was to ensure that the authorities can act quickly and decisively when necessary to support financial institutions. The proposals were intended to give the authorities the full range of powers required. This would be achieved by entrenching the model established a decade ago with the FSA being responsible for individual institutions and the Bank of England for the stability of the financial system as a whole. Each institution would nevertheless be provided with powers and improved coordination would be facilitated.[232]

US sub-prime crisis

1.154 The conditions in the financial markets following the US sub-prime mortgage crisis during the second half of 2007 were outlined in the report. While there had been some signs of a limited recovery of financial activity in some credit markets since March 2008, central bank lending surveys had confirmed that tight credit conditions would continue for some time. Inter-bank funding markets also remained under considerable pressure although there had been some loosening of

---

[232] <http://www.hm-treasury.gov.uk/newsroombaselineandbaselinespeeches/press/2008/pressbaseline69baseline08.cfm>.

conditions following central bank intervention. The purchase of Bear Stearns by J P Morgan Chase & Co in March 2008 with financial assistance from the Federal Reserve Bank of New York was noted.

Financial Stability Forum

The Financial Stability Forum had produced an important report on *Enhancing* **1.155** *Market and Institutional Resilience* in April 2008.[233] This recommended action in five key areas of strengthening prudential oversight of capital, liquidity, and risk management, enhancing transparency and valuation, improving the role and uses of credit ratings, strengthening authorities' responsiveness to risks, and establishing effective arrangements for dealing with stress in the financial system. The recommendations had been endorsed by the G-7 Finance Ministers with a commitment to their rapid implementation with priority actions being secured within 100 days. An update on progress was provided to the G-8 Finance Ministers meeting in Osaka on 14 June 2008. The UK July 2008 report made frequent reference to the recommendations contained in the FSF report.

The Economic and Financial Affairs Council (ECOFIN) within the European **1.156** Union had endorsed a separate programme of work in autumn 2007 on the issues raised by the market disruption. A progress report was presented to the European Council in spring 2008.

UK response

The need to support Northern Rock in the UK and the enactment of the Banking **1.157** (Special Provisions) Act 2008 which received Royal Assent on 21 February 2008 (para 1.14) are referred to in the report.[234] The Building Societies (Financial Assistance) Order 2008 was approved in June 2008 under the 2008 Act (para 1.38). The Government would also allow building societies to issue floating charges in relation to the provision of liquidity support by central banks.

The report noted the main findings of the FSA audit report (para 1.16) and the **1.158** extended three-month repo open market operations ('OMOs') facility made available by the Bank of England in March and April (para 1.18). This reflected other central bank liquidity intervention activity especially by the European Central Bank and the Federal Reserve as well as the Bank of Canada and Swiss National Bank. A Special Liquidity Scheme (SLS) was also opened in April 2008

---

[233] FSF, 'Enhancing Market and Institutional Resilience' (April 2008) Report to the G-7 Finance Ministers.
[234] Chapter 14, paras 14.220–14.240.

by the Bank of England to allow banks to swap high quality mortgage-backed and other securities for UK Treasury bills for a limited period and subject to appropriate haircuts (deductions).

1.159 The report referred to the efforts undertaken by major UK banks to raise capital levels during the second half of 2007 and first half of 2008 (para 1.19). Tier 1 capital ratios had been increased by over £45bn through rights and other capital issues. Banks were also disposing of non-core assets to strengthen capital resources. The FSA and Treasury were to establish a sub-group of the High-Level Group on City Competitiveness to consider market practices with regard to equity raising and the need for more efficient and orderly practices (para 1.20). The Chancellor of the Exchequer had separately asked Sir James Crosby to examine options to improve the functioning of mortgage finance markets with an interim report published in July 2008 and specific proposals in the subsequent Pre-Budget Report and final report in November 2008.

Policy recommendations

1.160 The authorities remained committed to the five key policy objectives set out in the January consultation paper. The need for reform remained clear although the proposals set out in the July 2008 paper were considered to reflect a measured and proportionate response to mitigate risks to financial stability and to protect depositors at the same time as continuing to rely on the UK's principles-based regulatory framework (para 1.23). The authorities had considered the consultation responses received and undertaken additional research on specific points raised (Annex D).

1.161 A series of principal recommendations were made with regard to each of the five key policy objectives of strengthening the stability and resilience of the financial system (Chapter 2), reducing the likelihood of banks facing difficulties (Chapter 3), and the impact of banks in difficulty (Chapter 4), as well as providing effective compensation (Chapter 5) and strengthening the Bank of England and tripartite coordination (Chapter 6).

Stability and resilience

1.162 The FSA would ensure that the recommendations of the FSF in its April 2008 report would be implemented on the strengthening of the resilience of the global financial system. The UK had fully supported and taken a lead role in this work (para 1.24). The prudential oversight of capital, liquidity, and risk management would be strengthened through coordinated action by national and international bodies especially through the work of the Basel Committee on Banking Supervision and its Basel II proposals on structured credit and securitisation. Transparency and valuation in securitisation markets would be enhanced through additional risk disclosures by financial institutions with accounting and disclosure work being taken forward by the International Accounting Standards Board ('IASB'). The role and uses of credit ratings would be enhanced with improvements made in the quality of the rating process (including the management of conflicts of interest), expanded information on structured products provided (including differentiated ratings for corporate and structured finance products), and an enhanced assessment of underlying data quality.

The UK authorities supported the need for a strengthened and independent monitoring of credit rating agency ('CRA') performance against internationally agreed standards including the possible establishment of an EU registration system for CRAs. Regulatory authorities had also to become more responsive to risks and arrangements for dealing with stress in the financial system. UK authorities also fully supported the establishment of international supervisory 'colleges' which they had called for some time ago.[235] **1.163**

It was also proposed that supervisory colleges be created under EU law following the conclusions of the May ECOFIN Council on Colleges. The FSF had also recommended that a specific group of supervisors and central bankers be established to deal with cross-border crisis management planning issues in connection with each of the largest cross-border financial firms with parallel work being undertaken within the EU through the revised Memorandum of Understanding on Cross-Border Financial Stability. **1.164**

Bank difficulty

Effective regulation and liquidity support were necessary to prevent banks from collapsing. Individual bank failure could not and should not be prevented in all cases although the authorities had to attempt to ensure that the likelihood of collapse was reduced insofar as possible to limit consumer and stability damage. It was accepted that limited additional regulatory powers were required in this regard in light of the existing tools available to the FSA. Individual institutional supervision would nevertheless be enhanced through the adoption of a supervisory enhancement programme by the FSA following its internal audit report. **1.165**

Heightened supervision was also referred to in the January 2008 consultation document where firms faced increased risks which created a greater threat to financial stability (paras 1.28–1.30). The FSA would be given additional statutory powers to obtain and share information with the Bank of England and Treasury in connection with financial stability (para 1.31). Banks would be **1.166**

---

[235] GA Walker, *International Banking Regulation—Law, Policy and Practice* (n 226), ch 4; and GA Walker, 'International Supervisory Co-operation' (n 226).

required to provide additional information confirming how they satisfied the Threshold Conditions on a continuing basis with a consultation paper to be issued by the FSA in this regard (para 1.32). The FSA would also be given some additional enforcement powers to deal with market abuse including the ability to offer immunity from prosecution (para 1.33).

1.167　The provision of emergency liquidity assistance would be improved. The FSA would consult on changes to the Disclosure and Transparency Rules to clarify circumstances in which an issuer in receipt of liquidity support from a central bank may have a legitimate interest to delay disclosure (para 1.36). The Settlements Finality Regulations 1999 would be revised to ensure that collateral provided may be realised more effectively and charges granted to a central bank would otherwise be exempt from registration. The Bank of England was to be given a separate statutory immunity in connection with the discharge of its functions in connection with financial stability and other central bank activities (para 1.34). The Government was considering legislating to ensure that restrictions on borrowing (including negative pledges and similar provisions) were of no effect in circumstances where financial assistance is provided by the central bank (para 1.37). The report nevertheless contained no express reference to possible changes to the Market Abuse Directive implementing measures or the Takeover Code. The role of the Bank of England in the oversight of the payment system would be given a statutory basis (para 1.40).

Impact failure

1.168　A statutory 'Special Resolution Regime' ('SRR') was to be created to assist the resolution of a bank in difficulty. It was accepted that an extensive range of powers were already available including through voluntary firm and regulatory action although a new SRR may be considered necessary in specific cases. The report referred to the need to ensure that depositors were not deprived of access to their accounts and that insolvency is incompatible with the objectives of securing faster depositor payout (para 1.42) although this did not justify the need to create a new SRR as such. Wider public interests were also referred to including managing the risk to financial stability, protecting public finances, protecting depositors, and ensuring continuity of key banking and payment arrangements.

1.169　The new regime was described as consisting of a set of existing and new tools to permit the authorities to take control of a bank when it was judged to be failing and all other options had been deemed insufficient (para 1.43). Available tools would then include (a) transferring part or all of the failing bank to a private sector third party, or (b) to a publicly controlled 'bridge bank' (although undefined), (c) a new bank insolvency procedure, (d) temporary public ownership (although now available under the Banking (Special Provisions) Act 2008, and (e) financial support as currently provided. This remained one of the least clearly articulated aspects of the new reforms. The Government had clearly decided that it wished to introduce mandatory US-style 'purchase and assumption' and 'bridge bank' options within the new special insolvency procedures although the case for this was still not fully made out in light of the existing remedies already available under UK law. As the Government remains committed to these proposals, it can only be hoped that all necessary supporting amendments are made and other consequential difficulties limited.

In terms of operation of the new SRR, the Government had decided to allow the **1.170** FSA to trigger resolution (principally after a bank had failed to comply with its Threshold Conditions and alternative options were insufficient) with the Bank of England being responsible for determining which SRR option to use and its management (para 1.44). The Chancellor would remain responsible for decisions involving the temporary public ownership of an institution and for ensuring compliance with relevant international obligations. The Chancellor would sanction any option involving public finances. This may have created an unduly complicated compromise especially with the Bank's active involvement in the operational and management process. It may clearly have been preferable for this to have remained with the FSA as it has the staff, resources, and information to manage the transfer of assets and liabilities between one financial institution and another. The FSA should act in all cases where the matter can be resolved through its existing powers with the Bank being called in as necessary. The need for the Bank's involvement in the SRR decision may confuse liquidity with corporate restructuring. This is obviously closer to the FSA's function as bank supervisor and as the UK Competent Authority for Listing. There also appears to be no direct link between liquidity and asset transfer with the need for the Bank's involvement not being properly made out. The Bank has to be closely involved although operational matters could be dealt with through the FSA.

In the event of difficulties arising with a particular institution, the authorities are **1.171** to cooperate through the existing Standard Committee. An attempt is nevertheless made to clarify their roles where the SRR is triggered (para 1.45). The FSA is responsible for supervisory decisions and regulatory actions including the ongoing supervision of any firm while it continues to operate in the SRR. The Bank of England is responsible for liquidity support and the operation of the SRR with the Treasury managing public finances and the overall public interest. The Financial Services Compensation Scheme (FSCS) will be involved in the assessment of 'the readiness of a bank for payout of its depositors' (para 1.46) although this is not explained further.

The revised objectives of the Bank of England are stated to be to protect the finan- **1.172** cial stability of the UK, to protect public finances and depositors, and to ensure continuity of key banking services (para 1.47). This has to be balanced against the need to ensure sufficient protection of property rights and the rights of creditors and counterparties of failing banks. Clear criteria would be set out in the legislation to determine the operation of the special resolution tools conferred on the Bank with additional safeguards being incorporated. The decision to use the SRR would be taken by the Bank and implemented through an application to its Court (para 1.48). The Court would be assigned a formal role in overseeing the Bank's performance and financial stability with a separate Financial Stability Committee being established to support the Governor (para 1.72).

1.173 An equivalent SRR was to be established for building societies (para 1.49) with the assets of a society following closure being shared equally among creditors and societies' members under Order (para 1.50). The FSCS was separately to be required to contribute to costs arising from the use of resolution tools covered by industry levies collected under FSMA (para 1.52). Secondary legislation would be introduced in connection with financial collateral arrangements (para 1.54) with the FSA working with banks to ensure that indirect members of payment systems had contingency plans in the event that their sponsor banks fail (para 1.53).

Compensation

1.174 The FSA would consult on changes to the FSCS compensation limits in autumn 2008 (para 1.56). This would apply to payments across all sectors and not be limited to banking. The bank limit would nevertheless be increased to £50,000 on a per person per bank basis. Consultation continued on possible additional arrangements including temporary high balance cover.

1.175 It was intended that payments would be made within a seven-day period following an individual bank failure with access, at least, to a proportion of the funds being provided to minimise depositor disruption (para 1.58). The FSA and FSCS were to have power to collect all necessary information from banks before default with this information being shared with the Bank of England. New FSA rules would specify the circumstances in which consumers had to submit a formal claim to the FSCS before payment with the FSCS acquiring automatic rights of recovery (subrogation) in place of claimants (para 1.59). The FSA would also consult on requiring banks to maintain readily information on deposit balances to allow speedy FSCS payment, eligibility criteria for deposits to qualify for FSCS compensation payment, and to allow possible gross payments of FSCS compensation (para 1.60).

1.176 The FSA would consult separately on how the information held by banks in this regard was to be reviewed, including possible routine access being provided to the FSCS (para 1.61). The authorities would continue to work with the industry in connection with peer targets although no agreement had been achieved in this area (para 1.62). The Government would legislate to allow the FSCS to have access to immediate liquidity through borrowing from the public sector including the provision of loans from the National Loans Fund (para 1.66). The Government had decided not to introduce pre-funding on a mandatory basis although the matter would be reviewed and the FSCS would be given power to introduce pre-funding if considered appropriate in the future (para 1.67).

The FSA and FSCS would review how consumers can be better informed about   **1.177** the current compensation scheme arrangements (para 1.65). Work would be undertaken with banks and trade associations to ensure that depositors can open up new accounts quickly to facilitate fast compensation payments and minimise disruption (para 1.63). It had been decided that it is not necessary to legislate to give the FSCS more flexibility in the management of a wide range of claim volumes (para 1.64). Scottish and Northern Irish banks would be required to hold equivalent assets to the value of their notes which would be ring-fenced for the benefit of note holders with these assets being made up of Bank of England banknotes and UK coin or funds in interest-bearing accounts at the Bank (para 1.69).

Bank of England and coordination

It was essential to ensure that the Bank has the correct statutory and operational   **1.178** framework to deliver its new core objective of financial stability as well as its more traditional monetary policy functions. The Government has then used the monetary policy model to develop a parallel financial stability regime within the Bank (para 1.72). The Bank was specifically to be given statutory responsibility for 'contributing to the maintenance of financial stability' with improved policy instruments including the bank SRR. Hopefully, any confusion or qualification in the nature of this obligation would be clarified. Legislation would provide for the creation of a Financial Stability Committee to support the Governor and Bank using relevant external expertise (above).

The Court would have a formal role in overseeing the Bank's performance on   **1.179** financial stability with the Bank consulting with the Treasury on a periodic basis to establish detailed financial stability objectives. The size of the Bank's Court would be restricted to 12 members including a majority of non-executive members with one acting as Chair of the Court, which practice had been followed since 2003. The membership of existing non-executive members would be terminated to allow for their re-appointment on the coming into effect of the new legislation. A strengthened MOU was to be entered into between the Bank, the FSA, and the Treasury (para 1.74). All major appointments to the Bank would in future be advertised and conducted on an open competition basis (para 1.73). This would apply with regard to the Governor and Deputy Governors and external members of the Monetary Policy Committee (MPC).

1.180 Many of the key elements within the July 2008 paper are to be fully supported. Much of this nevertheless reflects ongoing work either at the international or UK FSA levels or the recapitalisation or disposals already being carried out by banks themselves. It has to be accepted that the compensation recommendations are more balanced and proportionate than originally proposed. The maintenance of the new full SRR is welcome provided that a coherent and operable set of new resolution mechanisms are adopted in practice. One of the major tasks may be ensuring that any consequential corporate, property, insolvency, liability, and human rights difficulties are avoided in practice. A meaningful and effective result may still follow provided that the Government does not insist on some of the more extreme parts of its initial post-crisis response. It is also necessary to ensure that the banking reforms are properly included within an overall revision of supervisory and regulatory practice following the recent crises in financial markets which have affected all sectors and not just the banking or deposit areas.

2

THE FINANCIAL SERVICES AND MARKETS ACT

Genesis of FSMA

It took more than four and a half years, and two parliamentary terms, to imple- **2.01**
ment on 1 December 2001 (a date known as 'N2') the statutory framework for
the incoming Labour Government's announcement on 20 May 1997 that it
would create a single regulator for financial services.[1] Each of the existing regulatory regimes was underpinned by its own statutory and in some cases non-
statutory framework. The process was a painstaking one, and care was needed to
understand and where necessary replicate existing provisions, either directly in the
Financial Services and Markets Act 2000 ('FSMA') or through secondary legislation such as statutory instruments or through Financial Services Authority ('FSA')
rules or directions, and to create a new robust framework for a modern risk-based
regulator for financial services. These aspects were considered in detail in the 1st
edition of this book.

Structure

FSMA consists of 30 separate Parts, covering topics as diverse as the chapter head- **2.02**
ings in this book: listing, prospectuses, business transfers, market abuse, passporting, controllers, collective investment schemes, ombudsmen, investment
exchanges and clearing houses, Lloyd's, professions, mutual societies, auditors
and actuaries, and insolvency.

---

[1] Statement of the Chancellor of the Exchequer to the House of Commons on the Bank of
England.

Table 2.1

Part[2]	Coverage
1. The Regulator	The FSA's general duties, statutory objectives, constitution, funding, and accountability
2. Regulated and Prohibited Activities	The Treasury's power to set the scope of regulation by order, including the regulation of financial promotions, with prohibitions for persons who are not authorised or exempt
3. Authorisation and Exemption	Setting out which persons are to be authorised, either through a permission given by the FSA or under European legislation
4. Permission to Carry on Regulated Activities	Applications for permission to carry on regulated activities, and the FSA's powers to give, vary, or revoke permissions
5. Performance of Regulated Activities	Approval of persons to perform controlled activities, specified by the FSA, and the FSA's powers to make principles and codes of conduct for approved persons, and impose censure, financial penalties and prohibitions
6. Official Listing	Powers of the FSA as UK listing authority (substantially amended to reflect the market abuse and prospectus directives)[3]
7. Control of Business Transfers	A mechanism for the transfer of banking and insurance business, with court sanction
8. Penalties for Market Abuse	The market abuse provision and the FSA's power to make a code and censure or impose penalties (also substantially amended to reflect the Market Abuse Directive)[4]
9. Hearings and Appeals	The Tribunal and its procedure; financial assistance
10. Rules and Guidance	The FSA's powers to impose rules and give guidance, procedure, and competition scrutiny for the FSA's regulating provisions and practices
11. Information Gathering and Investigations	The powers of the FSA and the BERR[5] to require the production of information and documents, require reports, and to conduct investigations
12. Control over Authorised Persons	FSA approval of persons who acquire control over authorised persons
13. Incoming Firms: Intervention by the Authority	The FSA's powers to intervene in the activities of authorised persons based in other EEA States who are exercising passporting rights
14. Disciplinary Measures	The FSA's powers to censure and impose financial penalties for breaches of requirements imposed under FSMA
15. The Financial Services Compensation Scheme	The compensation scheme and the scheme manager ('FSCS')

[2] Many users (including the FSA) still follow the Roman numbering system used at the time of Royal Assent; however, the conventional Arabic numbering system now used to draft statutory legislation is adopted here.

[3] Directives 2003/6/EC on insider dealing and market manipulation (Market Abuse Directive) and 2003/71/EC on the prospectus to be published when securities are offered to the public or admitted to trading on a regulated market (prospectus directive)—amended by SI 2005/381 and SI 2005/1433.

[4] Amended by SI 2005/381.

[5] Department for Business, Enterprise and Regulatory Reform.

16. The Ombudsman Scheme	The ombudsman scheme and the functions of the scheme operator, the Financial Ombudsman Service ('FOS')
17. Collective Investment Schemes	The regulation of collective investment schemes, including authorised unit trusts, open-ended investment companies, recognised overseas schemes, and unregulated schemes
18. Recognised Investment Exchanges and Clearing Houses	The regulatory regime for investment exchanges and clearing houses, and competition scrutiny of their regulatory provisions and practices
19. Lloyd's	Making the Society of Lloyd's an authorised person, and giving the FSA certain powers to direct its affairs and those of its members and managing and members' agents
20. Provision of Financial Services by Members of the Professions	An exemption for members of the professions providing financial services to clients under the supervision of designated professional bodies, subject to FSA oversight
21. Mutual Societies	Treasury powers to transfer certain functions under mutuals legislation to the FSA and to the Treasury and dissolve the existing statutory bodies
22. Auditors and Actuaries	The appointment of auditors and actuaries on behalf of authorised persons; their rights and duties
23. Public Record and Disclosure of Information	The FSA's public record (or Register) of regulated persons, and restrictions on disclosure of confidential information
24. Insolvency Disclosure of Information	Powers for the FSA to bring insolvency proceedings, and rights to receive information and be heard by the court
25. Injunctions and Restitution	FSA and BERR powers to seek injunctions and restitution for regulatory contraventions and offences
26. Notices	Procedures to be followed by the FSA in issuing notices
27. Offences	Offences for misleading statements and supplying false information to the FSA; prosecution of insider dealing and money laundering offences
28. Miscellaneous	Treasury powers to enforce international obligations, order past business reviews, and other miscellaneous provisions
29. Interpretation	Definitions, interpretation, and service of notices
30. Supplemental	Commencement; scope and control of statutory instruments

At Royal Assent, FSMA contained 433 sections and 22 Schedules. More than 200 **2.03** statutory instruments have since been made under or in connection with FSMA.[6] And the FSA's own Handbook of rules and guidance if printed and piled up was at one time said to be higher than its chairman and chief executive combined.[7] This is to say nothing of the various materials produced by commentators, lawyers, professional bodies, and trade associations.

---

[6] Most of these are listed on the HM Treasury website <http://www.hm-treasury.gov.uk>.
[7] <http://www.fsa.gov.uk/handbook>. See Chapter 5.

Framework

2.04 In essence the statutory framework is straightforward. FSMA creates offences for carrying on certain specified activities without authorisation. By seeking and obtaining authorisation, firms submit themselves to the jurisdiction of the FSA. FSMA sets out the FSA's functions in relation to that jurisdiction and the purposes for which they are exercised, and the associated checks and balances. FSMA says who must join the 'club' of regulated firms, and authorises the FSA to make and administer the 'club rules'.

Sources of complexity

2.05 The legislation can however seem complex because FSMA itself contains little useful information for consumers or practitioners on the substantive regulatory requirements which apply to financial services. The scope of the offences which force firms into FSA regulation is specified in secondary legislation made by the Treasury. FSMA contains roughly 100 separate powers to make statutory instruments, many of which have been exercised. The detailed procedures for most of the applications and other processes administered by the FSA are determined by it in accordance with the requirements of FSMA. Regulated persons need to look to the FSA's own Handbook for their rules.

2.06 FSMA then is primarily a rulebook for the FSA and the other bodies exercising functions under FSMA, which means that its main interest for other readers is in understanding their rights when dealing with those bodies. But to put these rights into context readers need to be familiar with the substantive regulatory framework as well.

2.07 A second reason is the diversity of the FSA's functions. Depending on how they are counted, the FSA has more than 1,000 separate statutory functions. Creating a single regulator for financial services is not as simple as giving the FSA licensing, standard-setting, and enforcement functions. Each of the previous statutory and self-regulatory regimes had its own special features, some of which could not be achieved through these simple statutory powers alone. For example, the FSA's powers to make client money rules under section 139 and impose asset requirements under section 48 on authorised persons are extended to impact on third parties through the creation of a trust or enforceable protections over assets held.

2.08 Furthermore, the creation of a single regulator with consolidated powers was an opportunity to solve some of the problems that had eluded previous regulatory systems. Thus the FSA's enforcement functions were extended to include investigation and prosecution powers for insider dealing and money laundering offences,[8] and powers to deal with market abuse through penalties, public censure, or restitution.[9] Equally, there was an accretion effect with the FSA seen as a recipient of functions without an obvious home, or in respect of firms and bodies which it already regulates. Thus when the London Stock Exchange decided to seek a listing, the role of listing authority was transferred to the new FSA in May 2000.[10]

This accretion effect has continued after implementation of FSMA, mainly **2.09** through extensions to the scope of regulation, to include funeral plans, e-money, credit unions, mortgages, insurance mediation, and home reversion and home purchase plans including certain Islamic arrangements.[11] The FSA is the supervisory authority under the Money Laundering Regulations 2007 for certain categories of authorised and other firms providing money lending services and certain other firms.[12] There are also plans to regulate other banking activities of credit rating agencies at a European level.

A third reason is the extent of the checks and balances on the FSA in discharging **2.10** its functions. One of the Government's aims was of course to create a single regulator which was more effective in protecting consumers and maintaining confidence in the financial system. But there were worries that a more powerful regulator could be over-powerful, and practitioners in particular were concerned to avoid a position in which regulatory action became too easy. Furthermore, the obligation under the Human Rights Act 1998 for Ministers to certify that FSMA was compatible with the Convention rights focused attention on the fairness of the FSA's procedures.

Finally, there is the effect of Europe. The Government was establishing a single **2.11** regulator in the UK against a background of separate single market directives for credit institutions, life and general insurance, investment services, and collective investment schemes. The Government and the FSA needed to be able to implement these directives either directly through FSMA or through secondary legislation under it. So when a directive requires duties to be imposed on the FSA as competent authority, FSMA or regulations made under it need to be capable of implementing that requirement. Equally, when a directive requires authorised

---

[8] See ss 401and 402 (proceedings for offences), which refer to Part 5 of the Criminal Justice Act 1993 (insider dealing) and prescribed regulations relating to money laundering (the Money Laundering Regulations 2007, SI 2007/2057 and the Transfer of Funds (Information on the Payer) Regulations 2007, SI 2007/3298).

[9] See s 123 (penalties and censure) and ss 383 and 384 (restitution).

[10] Official Listing of Securities (Change of Competent Authority) Regulations 2000, SI 2000/1968.

[11] Through provisions and amendments in the RAO (Regulated Activities Order) SI 2001/544 and the Exemption Order SI 2001/1201 art 6 (transitional exemption for credit unions).

[12] See Part 4 of SI 2007/2157, with reg 3(3)(a) and Sched 1.

persons to be subject to certain requirements, the FSA needs to be able to implement those requirements through its rules.

2.12 As far as possible FSMA was designed to accommodate existing and expected obligations from Europe, either through general or consolidated provisions incorporating European law such as provisions in Schedule 3 (EEA passport rights), Schedule 6 (threshold conditions), or Part 13 (incoming firms), or through powers to make secondary legislation. However, there have been concerns both to demonstrate substantive and precise implementation in new provisions and to avoid 'gold-plating'.[13] In practice, Government draftsmen have not felt satisfied with the powers in FSMA, and there has been frequent recourse to the European Communities Act 1972 both since and even before FSMA came into force.[14]

The FSA's general duties and other statutory functions

2.13 The FSA's functions are discussed in detail in other chapters. Many of these functions are conferred directly by FSMA, but FSMA also provides for functions to be conferred on it through secondary legislation. FSMA gives special significance to these functions and accordingly special consideration needs to be given to the implications of conferring new functions on the FSA through external legislation, as many provisions of FSMA will not otherwise automatically apply.

2.14 Features which apply only to functions conferred by or under FSMA include:

(i) aspects of the FSA's governance and accountability which are set out in Schedule 1—the role of the non-executive committee, delegation, monitoring and enforcement, reporting, scope of the complaints scheme and the independent investigator, records, non-Crown status of the FSA's functions, and its qualified exemption from liability in damages;

---

[13] See for example 'Implementation of EU legislation', an independent study for the Foreign and Commonwealth Office by Robin Bellis, November 2003; and 'Lost in Translation? Responding to the challenges of European law', National Audit Office, May 2005.

[14] See, for example, the Financial Services and Markets Act 2000 (Markets in Financial Instruments) Regulations 2007, SI 2007/126 and the Financial Services and Markets Act 2000 (Markets in Financial Instruments) (Modification of Powers) Regulations 2006, SI 2006/2975; the Financial Services and Markets Act 2000 (Motor Insurance) Regulations 2007, SI 2007/2403; the Reinsurance Directive Regulations 2007, SI 2007/2353; the Capital Requirements Regulations 2006, SI 2006/3221; the Prospectus Regulations 2005, SI 2005/1433; the Investment Recommendation (Media) Regulations 2005, SI 2005/382; the Financial Services and Markets Act 2000 (Market Abuse) Regulations 2005, SI 2005/381; the Financial Services (Distance Marketing) Regulations 2004, SI 2004/2095; the Financial Conglomerates and other Financial Groups Regulations 2004, SI 2004/1862; the Insurers (Reorganisation and Winding Up) Regulations 2004, SI 2004/353; the Electronic Commerce (EC Directive) Regulations 2002, SI 2002/2013; the Electronic Commerce (Financial Services and Markets) Regulations 2002, SI 2002/1775 as amended; the Financial Services (EEA Passport Rights) Regulations 2001, SI 2001/1376.

(ii) also in paragraph 17 of Schedule 1, the FSA's main fee-raising power may be exercised only to enable it to meet expenses incurred for a purpose which is incidental to carrying out its functions conferred by or under FSMA;

(iii) the FSA's information-gathering powers under section 165, which apply only to information and documents reasonably required in connection with the exercise by the FSA of functions conferred on it by or under FSMA; and

(iv) the scope of the confidentiality restriction in section 348, which protects only information received for the purposes of, or in the discharge of, any functions of the FSA (or BERR) under any provision made by or under FSMA.

Other aspects of the FSA's functions, however, are not so restricted. For example, **2.15** the FSA's general duties, the regulatory objectives, and the so-called principles of good regulation under section 2, apply to the way the FSA determines its general policy and principles for exercising any functions, not simply those conferred by or under FSMA.

The main exception to this is the FSA's functions as UK listing authority under **2.16** Part 6, which may be transferred by Treasury order to another body and are treated as separate from the FSA's other functions for many purposes. Schedule 7 disapplies the regulatory objectives when the FSA is acting as listing authority, and objectives are agreed annually with the Treasury. Fees and penalties received under Part 6 must also be accounted for separately. Similar provisions apply to the FSA's functions under mutuals legislation. See para 2.71 below.

Other bodies and their functions

FSMA confers or provides for functions to be performed by several bodies apart **2.17** from the FSA:

(i) Ministers—the Treasury, the Secretary of State, and the Lord Chancellor, generally in making statutory instruments, or making or approving appointments, although they each have additional functions to perform;

(ii) other public bodies and officials—the Office of Fair Trading, the Competition Commission, the Director of Public Prosecutions (and the Director of Public Prosecutions for Northern Ireland), and Government-appointed investigators and reviewers;

(iii) the courts and the Financial Services and Markets Tribunal, which is administered by the court service;[15]

---

[15] See Part 9 (hearings and appeals) and Sched 13, together with the Tribunal rules (SI 2001/2476) and financial assistance regulations (SI 2001/3632) and costs regulations (SI 2001/3633) made under them.

   (iv) the separate role of UK listing authority, currently performed by the FSA under Part 6, but which may be transferred to another body by order;

   (v) recognised investment exchanges and clearing houses, Lloyd's, and designated professional bodies (Parts 18 to 20);

   (vi) the scheme manager for the Financial Services Compensation Scheme ('FSCS') (Part 15);

   (vii) the scheme operator for the Financial Ombudsman Service ('FOS') and its panel of ombudsmen (Part 16); and

   (viii) various FSA officials and appointments—its Board, chairman, members, non-executives,[16] practitioner and consumer panels,[17] and independent investigator,[18] as well as persons not directly contemplated in FSMA such as members of the FSA's smaller business panel[19] and its Regulatory Decisions Committee.[20]

2.18 The functions of most of these bodies will be discussed in later chapters, as will those of the Bank of England, which operates under its own legislation. However, a number of general features are worth considering. First, although FSMA creates checks and balances on the FSA in discharging its functions, none of these is permitted to undermine the FSA's direct line of accountability to the Treasury.

2.19 Thus FSMA requires the FSA itself to create many of its own checks and balances, such as itself applying appropriate principles of corporate governance, and appointing its own practitioner and consumer panels and independent investigator, rather than have these entities imposed upon it.[21] Where this does not provide sufficient independence, so that an external body is needed as in competition scrutiny, the final say is usually reserved for the Treasury.

2.20 The role and accountability of the Treasury are worth exploring in more detail.

   (i) The FSA's constitution must provide for its Board and Chairman to be appointed and subject to removal by the Treasury, and FSMA also provides for the Treasury to approve some of the key appointments by the FSA, namely the independent investigator, and the chairmen of the statutory consultative panels, the FSCS, and the FOS.[22]

---

[16] See Sched 1, paras 2–5.

[17] Established under ss 8–11 (arrangements for consulting practitioners and consumers).

[18] Described in the FSA's complaints scheme (COAF in its Handbook) as the Complaints Commissioner.

[19] As a separate part of the FSA's arrangements for consulting practitioners established under s 8.

[20] As a decision-maker under the FSA's procedures determined under s 395—see the FSA's Decision Procedures and Penalties Manual ('DEPP') in the FSA Handbook.

[21] Obligations under ss 7–11, and Sched 1, paras 7–8 respectively.

[22] Sched 1, paras 2–5 and 7–8; ss 9(3), 10(3), and 212(4) and Sched 17, para 3(2).

(ii) The Treasury makes most of the statutory instruments under FSMA, including crucially those which determine the scope of regulation. The main statutory instruments made by other Ministers are the Tribunal rules and the Financial Assistance regulations, made by the Lord Chancellor, and provisions relating to insolvency, some of which are made by the Secretary of State.[23] Most of these require only the negative resolution procedure, and come into force unless a contrary resolution is passed in either House. However, some of the key instruments require the approval of each House, either when first made or subsequently if they extend regulation or substantively affect the FSA's powers or third parties' rights.[24]

(iii) The Treasury may under section 12 order a review of the economy, efficiency, and effectiveness with which the FSA has used its resources in discharging all or any of its statutory functions, or under section 14 order an inquiry into a serious failure in the system established by FSMA or in its operation.[25]

(iv) The Treasury has the final say in competition scrutiny of the FSA's regulating provisions and practices, as well as the recognition and scrutiny of investment exchanges and clearing houses, and their approval is required for incorporation of the Takeover Code into its code of market conduct.[26]

(v) The Treasury receives the FSA's annual report on the discharge of its functions, the extent to which the regulatory objectives have been met, and its consideration of the 'principles of good regulation' in section 2(3), and can impose additional reporting requirements.[27]

(vi) The Treasury may direct the FSA and other bodies in relation to requirements under international obligations, such as compliance with single market directive and treaty obligations, under section 410.[28]

---

[23] See Parts 9 (hearings and appeals) and 18 (insolvency) respectively.

[24] Orders under s 21 (financial promotion) and Sched 2; s 22 (regulated activities) and Sched 2—such orders come into force when made but cease to have effect after 28 days if not approved; s 144(4) (limiting the FSA's powers to make price stabilising rules); s 192(b) or (e) (amendments to controller provisions); s 236(5) (definition of an open-ended investment company); s 326 (designated professional bodies); s 327 (exemption from the general prohibition); s 404 (schemes for reviewing past business); s 419 (carrying on regulated activities by way of business); Sched 8 (transfer of listing functions); and regulations under s 90B (power to make further provision about liability for published information) and s 262 (open-ended investment companies).

[25] The first review under s 10 was undertaken by the Auditor and Comptroller General who reported on 30 April 2007: <http://www.nao.org.uk/pn/06-07/0607500.htm>.

[26] Chapter 3 of Part 10 and Chapter 2 of Part 18 (competition scrutiny)—the Competition Commission determines whether provisions or practices have a significant adverse effect on competition, but the Treasury determine whether, and if so what, action should be taken; s 120 (references to the City Code).

[27] Sched 1, para 10.

[28] See also s 405 on implementing third country decisions.

2.21 Finally, FSMA avoids direct formal accountability of the FSA to Parliament. Thus it is the Treasury which would order any inquiry or review under FSMA, a position which is preserved under the Investigations Act 2005. Similarly, the FSA's annual report is made to the Treasury, which in turn must lay it before Parliament. However, the Treasury is accountable to Parliament for its functions under FSMA and its oversight of the FSA, and in practice the Treasury Select Committee and other parliamentary committees often seek evidence and ask questions directly from the FSA and its officials, and make recommendations to it.

Scope

2.22 As we have seen, the scope of FSA regulation is determined primarily through the specification of regulated activities under Part 2 of FSMA, which in turn forces firms carrying on those activities into FSA regulation. But the scope of FSA regulation is not as simple as that. FSMA also impacts on:

(i) controllers, directors, officers, and persons who perform functions on behalf of regulated firms in respect of regulated activities (see Parts 5, 11, 12, 22, and 27);

(ii) persons who communicate financial promotions of specified activities (see Parts 2 and 27);

(iii) persons who engage in market activities covered by listing, prospectus, disclosure, takeover, market abuse, investment exchanges and clearing houses, misleading practices, and insider dealing regimes (see Parts 6, 9, 18, and 27);

(iv) persons who may be recipients or the subject of FSA guidance (under section 157);

(v) third parties who may be concerned in the activities of regulated firms (assets requirements under Part 4, business transfers under Part 7, client money and money laundering rules under Part 10, operators and participants in collective investment schemes under Part 17); and

(vi) mutual societies (in respect of registration and other functions transferred to the FSA under Part 21).

2.23 The scope of FSA regulation under FSMA is in practice specified by or as a result of secondary legislation made by the Treasury, save for the FSA's guidance functions. Even its functions as UK listing authority could be transferred to another body by statutory instrument under Schedule 8.

2.24 Yet FSMA itself also specifies the potential scope of FSA regulation, primarily through its long title ('the regulation of financial services and markets') and the matters already covered by FSMA and particularly in section 22 and Schedule 2 to FSMA.

Schedule 2 to FSMA is one of its more confusing features. It contains an indicative **2.25** list of the activities and investments in respect of such activities which may be specified for the purpose of defining regulated activities. In doing so, it also provides an indicative list of the activities and investments which may be specified for the purposes of:

(i)   the financial promotion restriction as a result of section 21(11) and consequently the FSA's financial promotion rules under section 145(3);

(ii) the jurisdiction of the FOS as a result of sections 226(4) and 227(4); and

(iii) the scope of the misleading statements offence which the FSA may prosecute as a result of section 397(11); and

(iv) the investments subject to exemption from gaming restrictions as a result of section 412(3).

The explanatory notes to FSMA suggest that Schedule 2 has a limiting effect.[29] **2.26** However, strictly the list in Schedule 2 supplements section 22 and does not limit the Treasury's powers in specifying activities, as section 22(2) and (3) and corresponding provisions in other sections make clear. Furthermore section 22 defines an investment widely as any 'asset, right or interest', and activities may in any event be specified more generally in relation to property of any kind.

In practice, several activities have already been specified by the Treasury which are **2.27** not strictly included in Schedule 2, such as those relating to funeral plan contracts and e-money.[30] However, the Government has sometimes trodden warily in departing from the activities and investments specified in Schedule 2, even where there have been obvious similarities with some of the investments already specified. Thus, the Government legislated to amend Schedule 2 to include home reversion plans and certain Islamic arrangements before specifying these in the relevant scope orders.[31]

The FSA and the FOS have gone beyond the list in Schedule 2 by specifying certain **2.28** unsecured types of lending in the FOS's compulsory and voluntary jurisdictions

---

[29] Explanatory notes for Sched 2:
'777. This Schedule does not define what activities are regulated under the Act. The regulated activities will be those activities which are prescribed using the power conferred by section 22. The Schedule sets out a list of "activities" and "investments" which, together, indicate the broad scope of activities which are potentially regulated under the Act. The scope of the Act is not strictly limited by the Schedule, but rather by the overall object and purpose of the Act. However, the general nature of the activities set out in the Schedule serves to inform and therefore indirectly limit the extent of the Treasury's power to bring further activities within the scope of the Act.
778. It is within this overall object and purpose that the power under section 22 to prescribe the regulated activities operates. Orders made under that section will be an exhaustive statement of the regulated activities'.

[30] See arts 9B, 59, 74A, and 87 of the consolidated RAO.

[31] The Regulation of Financial Services (Land Transactions) Act 2005.

respectively, even before the introduction of a specific consumer credit jurisdiction under section 226A by the Consumer Credit Act 2006, as well as specifying other ancillary activities carried on in respect of regulated activities and lending.[32]

Regulated activities

2.29   The concept of regulated activities is central to the scope of FSA regulation under FSMA. By section 19, persons carrying on or purporting to carry on regulated activities in the UK must either be authorised under FSMA, or exempt, although as we shall see below further exclusions apply. Breach of section 19 is an offence under section 23, although subsection (2) provides a defence if an accused can show he took all reasonable precautions and exercised all due diligence to avoid committing the offence. Transactions are also potentially unenforceable, and there may be a liability to pay compensation.[33]

2.30   The FSA's functions may generally be exercised to protect consumers of services provided in carrying on regulated activities, even where the FSA is exercising these functions in respect of other, non-regulated, activities of a regulated firm.[34] The FSA's consumer protection objective under section 5 applies to regulated activities even when carried on under an exemption.[35] The definition of the financial system, which specifies the scope of the market confidence and public awareness objectives in sections 3 and 4, also includes regulated activities.

2.31   A regulated activity is defined by section 22(1) as:

> an activity of a specified kind which is carried on by way of business and—
> (a)   relates to an investment of a specified kind; or
> (b)   in the case of an activity of a kind which is also specified for the purposes of this paragraph, is carried on in relation to property of any kind.

2.32   As discussed above, Schedule 2 to FSMA supplements this section by setting out an indicative list of activities and investments which may be specified, although nothing in Schedule 2 limits the Treasury's power. The range of activities which may be specified is very wide but covers in effect three broad categories:

> (i)   **dealing as principal** in investments, including through contracts or services which firms issue and perform themselves, such as deposits, insurance contracts, securities, regulated mortgages, and funeral plan contracts;

---

[32]   See the rules in DISP 2.3–2.5 of the Complaints Sourcebook in the FSA Handbook.

[33]   FSMA, ss 26–29.

[34]   For example, through general rules made under s 138, and powers to vary an authorised person's Part 4 permission to impose a requirement under ss 41, 43, 44, and 45.

[35]   See subs (3); the various definitions of 'consumer' used in FSMA have also been extended to include users of financial services which were regulated under predecessor legislation before N2—see SI 2001/1821 art 3 and SI 2002/1501 art 4 (which added customers of credit unions from 2 July 2002).

(ii) **advice and intermediation** in respect of dealing in investments, including markets themselves; and

(iii) **holding or administering** investments and other property on behalf of customers.

Because of the importance of the consolidated order made under section 22 (the **2.33** Regulated Activities Order, or 'RAO' as it is referred to here), a commitment was made by Ministers to maintain a consolidated version on the Treasury website.[36] It is outside the scope of this chapter to consider the detail of the RAO, but it is worth noting a number of features.

Firstly, the RAO specifies not regulated activities themselves but activities and **2.34** investments 'of a specified kind'.[37] In giving permissions for authorised persons to carry on a regulated activity under s 42(7), the FSA specifies its own description of the activities covered by the permission within the specified kinds of activity. The same applies to descriptions of regulated activities in other instruments, whether made by the FSA or by other bodies.

Secondly, the RAO excludes a number of activities when carried on with an **2.35** exempt or authorised person with the appropriate permission. Thus, there is scope for an element of circularity in specifying activities, and activities falling inadvertently outside regulation, which needs to be guarded against. Many of these exclusions are not therefore available to authorised persons.[38]

Thirdly, and related to this, the Treasury need to ensure that the RAO extends to **2.36** all activities required to be covered by single market directives. So, for example, the text of various directives is included as Schedules to the RAO, and article 4(4) provides for exclusions to be disregarded for an investment firm or credit institution in providing investment services and activities on a professional basis.[39]

Fourthly, paragraph 25 of Schedule 2 gives the Treasury power in specifying activ- **2.37** ities and investments to make exemptions, confer functions and jurisdiction, and make changes to other legislation including amending primary legislation. This power has been used to make supplemental or consequential changes to other legislation relating to those activities, and to FSMA itself in a number of cases.[40]

---

[36] SI 2001/544 as amended and consolidated on <http://www.hm-treasury.gov.uk>.

[37] See s 22(1) and art 4 of the RAO; also n 73 below.

[38] See for example exclusions which are not available to authorised persons under arts 16, 22, 29, 29A, 54A; and exclusions available to authorised persons under arts 33, 33A, 38 39B, 41, 42, 46, 47, 60.

[39] Any service provided to a third party listed in section A of Annex I to the markets in financial instruments directive (the text of which is set out in Sched 2 to the RAO), read with Article 52 of Commission Directive 2006/73/EC (the text of which is set out in Part 4 of Sched 2); and activity listed in Section A of Sched I to that directive.

[40] See for example the disapplication of s 49(2) for an insurance mediation activity or regulated activity involving a regulated mortgage contract in s 49(2A), inserted by SI 2001/544, art 97

2.38 Finally, the RAO is not the only determinant of whether an activity is a regulated activity. Section 22(1) also requires that the activity should be carried on by way of business, and section 419 provides for a further order specifying circumstances in which activities are and are not to be carried on by way of business.

2.39 The effect of this order is that activities in relation to deposits are not treated as carried on by way of business if they are not held out as accepted on a day-to-day basis and are accepted only on particular occasions.[41] By contrast, investment business activities are carried on by way of business only by persons who carry on the business of engaging in one or more such activities, and similar provision applies to arranging and advice on regulated mortgage contracts; insurance mediation activities are carried on by way of business only if taken up or pursued for remuneration.[42] Meanwhile trustees of occupational pension schemes may be treated as carrying on the regulated activity of managing investments unless all day-to-day decisions are delegated to a person who is authorised or exempt in relation to that activity, or involve pooled investments on the advice of an authorised or exempt person.[43]

2.40 The regulation of collective investment schemes under Part 17 also impacts on regulated activities. Units in a collective investment scheme are a specified kind of investment in the RAO, and establishing etc a collective investment scheme is a specified kind of activity.[44] However, the definition of a collective investment scheme can itself be amended; exclusions can be specified through separate orders made under section 235(5).[45]

Exemptions

2.41 FSMA provides for various types of exemption. Some of these arise directly under FSMA, although again their scope is in practice determined by secondary legislation or recognitions under FSMA:

(i) an exemption under section 285 for recognised investment exchanges and clearing houses as respects any regulated activity which is carried on as part

---

(itself inserted by SI 2003/1476, art 20(1),(2) and SI 2004/1610, art 3); and the supplemental register provisions for unauthorised persons carrying on insurance mediation activities in arts 92–96.

[41] The Financial Services and Markets Act 2000 (Carrying on Regulated Activities by Way of Business) Order 2001 SI 2001/1177, as amended, art 2.

[42] ibid, arts 3 (reflecting the test in Directive 2002/92/EC on insurance mediation) and 3A.

[43] ibid, art 4, as amended by SI 2005/922 to include inter alia insurance contracts as well as units in collective investment schemes and investment trusts.

[44] ibid, arts 51 and 81.

[45] See the Financial Services and Markets Act 2000 (Collective Investment Schemes) Order 2001, SI 2001/1062 as amended.

of its business as an investment exchange, or which is carried on for the purposes of or in connection with the provision of clearing services by it;

(ii) an exemption for appointed representatives under section 39 in respect of prescribed regulated activities for which an authorised person has taken responsibility; and

(iii) specification in an exemption order under section 38.

The exemptions for appointed representatives and persons specified in an exemption order are not available to authorised persons, who must instead have these activities covered by their permission.[46] This latter restriction applies to incoming firms which rely on a single market or Treaty passport under Schedule 3 or 4; and to so-called 'exempt investment firms' under the Financial Services and Markets Act 2000 (Markets in Financial Instruments) Regulations 2007 which are in fact authorised persons.[47] However, there is no such restriction for recognised bodies under section 285. **2.42**

Paragraph 25 of Schedule 2 provides for exemptions to be specified in the RAO. As set out above, the RAO provides for exclusions from the main types of activity specified in it. Unlike other exemptions, excluded activities are not themselves regulated activities, which means that they fall outside the FSA's scope and responsibilities for many purposes. The Collective Investment Schemes Order also provides exemptions from Part 17, and in effect creates exclusions from regulated activities.[48] **2.43**

In addition to formal exemptions certain regulated activities are not treated as carried on in breach of the general prohibition when: **2.44**

(i) they are underwriting activities carried on by a member of Lloyd's (provided the FSA has not directed that the general prohibition applies)— see section 316(1);

(ii) they are exempt regulated activities, carried on under rules made by a designated professional body and approved by the FSA under section 332;[49] or

(iii) they are not carried on in the UK (see paras 2.56–2.61 below).

There is no explicit provision for this, but it may also be assumed that the general and financial promotion prohibitions in FSMA do not apply to the Crown, or to **2.45**

---

[46] See s 38(2) and the chapeau to s 39(1).

[47] SI 2007/126 (as amended) at regs 4A–4C. The exemption relates to certain requirements of the markets in the Financial Instruments Directive and other directives. It is limited to firms which have a relevant office in the UK and do not seek to exercise passporting rights; may not hold client money; and whose permitted activities are limited to the provision of investment advice, or the reception and transmission (to certain types of firm) of orders in certain types of investment.

[48] s 235(5)—see the Financial Services and Markets Act 2000 (Collective Investment Schemes) Order 2001, SI 2001/1062 as amended.

[49] The 'exemption' is created by s 327.

the FSA and the other creatures of FSMA in performing their statutory functions under it.[50]

Financial promotions and misleading statements

2.46 As discussed above, the scope of FSA regulation is not confined to the carrying on of regulated activities, and a separate restriction and other criminal offences apply to the promotion of financial services.

2.47 The financial promotion restriction in section 21 is one of the major innovations under FSMA. Under predecessor legislation, such as the Financial Services Act 1986, the definitions of many of the activities comprising investment business included offering to carry on those activities. These were supplemented by separate prohibitions on cold-calling and investment advertising, for persons without exemption or authorisation, or approval by an authorised person.

2.48 Under FSMA, offering is no longer specified as a type of regulated activity in the RAO.[51] There is now a single prohibition in section 21(1), which applies, subject to exemptions, to any communication which is not made or approved by an authorised person:

> A person (A) must not, in the course of business, communicate an invitation or inducement to engage in investment activity.

2.49 'Engaging in investment activity' is defined by section 21(8) in terms of entering or offering to enter into an agreement the making or performance of which constitutes a controlled activity, or exercising rights conferred by a controlled investment to acquire, dispose of, underwrite, or convert a controlled investment. Controlled activities and investments are specified by the Treasury by order, and Schedule 2 is treated as providing an indicative list of activities and investments which may be specified, but which does not of course limit the powers conferred on the Treasury.

2.50 However, the main bulk of the consolidated Financial Promotion Order (often referred to as the 'FPO')[52] concerns the various exemptions which specify the circumstances in which the restriction does not apply. This is because the scope of the restriction is in effect very wide indeed:

(i) it applies to any communication of an invitation or inducement, as well as causing such a communication to be made (section 21(13));

---

[50] The FSA might otherwise need to authorise itself.

[51] 'Offering' is nevertheless still specified in much of Sched 2, and has in effect been specified as a component of 'ancillary activities' for the purposes of the FOS's jurisdiction. See DISP 2.6.4G.

[52] Remade as the Financial Services and Markets Act 2000 (Financial Promotions) Order 2005, SI 2005/1529 under s 21 and Sched 2. Like the RAO, the FPO continues to be amended frequently, as the scope of FSA regulation changes.

(ii)　most of the exclusions for regulated activities in the RAO are not replicated in the corresponding 'controlled activities' specified in the FPO—this level of detail is not always apparent in the communication so that enforcement particularly against unauthorised persons would be difficult;

(iii)　there is no automatic exemption in section 21 for exempt persons and other persons to whom the general prohibition in section 19 does not apply; and

(iv)　The business test 'in the course of business' is wider than the 'by way of business' test for regulated activities and potentially applies to any business, even one which does not involve financial services, and the Treasury have not exercised their power to specify circumstances in which this does not apply.

2.51　The exemptions generally apply to the circumstances of the communication rather than to the circumstances of the underlying controlled activity, and these circumstances often need to be widely framed in order to avoid catching legitimate communications of non-financial services inadvertently. On the other hand, the Treasury needs to be wary of making exemptions too wide,[53] and have in effect continued the distinction between different types of communication such as advertisements and cold-calling through a new classification of communications[54] as:

(i)　'real time'—in the course of a personal visit, telephone conversation, or other interactive dialogue—or 'non-real time' such as communications made by letter or e-mail or contained in a publication;

(ii)　where the communication is real time, 'solicited'—ie where the personal visit, telephone call, or other interactive dialogue is initiated by the recipient of the communication—or 'unsolicited'.

2.52　FSA rules do not permit authorised persons to approve a real time communication by an unauthorised person, because of the practical difficulties of doing so in advance and the consequences of an unapproved communication in terms of unenforceability of contracts.[55] Accordingly, particular care is required with real time communications. Exemptions for real time communications by appointed representatives for example require them to comply with financial promotion rules which means that breach of FSA rules may involve an offence.[56]

---

[53] Not least because s 145(3) restricts the FSA's powers to make financial promotion rules for authorised persons in respect of communications which would not contravene the restriction.

[54] See arts 7 and 8 of the FPO, as amended.

[55] See COB 3.12.2R in the Conduct of Business Standards Sourcebook of the FSA Handbook.

[56] See art 16(2) of the FPO.

2.53 Most of the main exemptions in the FPO involve one or more of the following features:[57]

   (i) communications to specific types of recipient—suppliers, existing customers, shareholders, employees, creditors, trustees and beneficiaries, sophisticated investors, high net worth individuals, investment professionals, overseas persons;

  (ii) communications by specific types of person—advice centres, employers, exempt persons, appointed representatives, issuers, journalists, directors, members of a profession, trustees, persons acting as a mere conduit, clients of an authorised person;

 (iii) communications in particular circumstances or through a particular medium—one-off, follow-up and solicited communications, introductions and generic promotions, electronic commerce communications, interviews and broadcasts, communications relating to a takeover or subject to other safeguards or rules, communications which contain a specified message or warning; and

 (iv) communications relating to particular types of investment activity or investment—deposits, insurance, dealing, securities.

2.54 These differences mean that it is usually quite difficult to reconcile the regulated activities and the financial promotion regimes, and it is often the financial promotion restriction which has the wider scope. Consequently, the FPO has been amended several times, including before N2, and was one of the main aspects of FSMA considered as part of the two-year review of FSMA. The Treasury maintains a consolidated version of the Order on its website.[58]

2.55 A further determinant of the scope of FSA regulation is the misleading statements offence in section 397, the scope of which is specified in terms of types of activities and types of investments by the Treasury. The effect of the section is to give the FSA jurisdiction to prosecute misleading statements, so that exclusions are generally inappropriate. The existence of the offence also gives the FSA jurisdiction to seek an injunction, including a remedial injunction, or restitution under Part 25.

Territorial scope

2.56 The territorial scope of regulation is determined partly in FSMA and partly in secondary legislation. Again territorial scope can differ according to the aspect

---

[57] See the consolidated FPO generally.

[58] A similar order is made under s 238 for communications by authorised persons in relation to unregulated collective investment schemes.

being considered. It is worth bearing in mind, however, that there is a practical limit on the territorial application of any national law, since in general only national courts can be expected to uphold it. It is of course possible that in some cases foreign courts will be authorised or required by their own national law to take account of whether a person is acting in breach of UK law, for example where an international treaty applies. This applies to some extent with the single market directives. However, such questions are outside the scope of this chapter.

The definition of regulated activity in section 22 contains no territorial restriction, although the RAO itself contains a number of exclusions for activities carried on by, through, or to overseas persons.[59] The definition of regulated mortgage contract for example applies only if the loan is secured on property in the UK.[60]   **2.57**

However, the main territorial restriction lies in the general prohibition in section 19, which applies the prohibition to regulated activities carried on in the UK. This is supplemented by section 418, which provides that any regulated activity is treated as carried on in the UK if it is carried on from an establishment maintained in the UK, or by a firm with its registered office in the UK if day-to-day management is in the UK or it is exercising passporting rights as a UK firm.   **2.58**

There is no such territorial limit, however, on the restriction in section 20 which applies to authorised persons, so that their permissions in theory need to extend to regulated activities carried on by them worldwide. Similarly, there is no restriction on the scope of most of the FSA's rule-making powers, although in practice the FSA often imposes a restriction through the application provisions in its rules.   **2.59**

There is equally no territorial limit on references to regulated activities in the regulatory objectives, although the financial system is defined for the purposes of the market confidence and public awareness objectives in terms of 'the financial system operating in the United Kingdom'.[61] Section 2(3)(e) requires the FSA in discharging its general policy or rule-making functions to have regard to the international character of financial services and UK competitiveness; the FSA may decide that a different approach is appropriate, for example where a firm is supervised by another regulator.   **2.60**

Finally, the FPO includes a number of exemptions, for both incoming and outward communications, whereas the misleading statements offences in section 397 require the statement, the intended person to be induced, or the agreement, to take place in the UK. The move to home State supervision means that exemptions will increasingly apply to incoming communications, as they already do for   **2.61**

---

[59] See art 72 of the RAO.
[60] See art 61(3)(a)(ii).
[61] See s 3(2).

electronic commerce communications, while the FSA will be responsible for policing outward communications by UK firms.[62]

Markets

2.62 FSMA provides for regulation of markets both through the specification of dealing and of markets themselves as regulated activities,[63] and through Part 6 provisions relating to listing and prospectuses, as well as market abuse and powers to prosecute for insider dealing. Thus the scope of the market abuse regime is specified in terms of an order under section 118. These provisions have been substantially amended following implementation of the Market Abuse Directive and the Prospectus Directive.[64]

Miscellaneous

Confidentiality and disclosure

2.63 Section 348 protects the confidentiality of information obtained by the FSA in the discharge of its functions, as well as information obtained by other 'primary recipients', namely investigators, the BERR, their employees, and other persons appointed as skilled persons, auditors, and experts on their behalf.

2.64 Section 349 gives the Treasury power to prescribe exemptions or 'gateways' from the restriction on disclosing confidential information without permission, subject to restrictions on its use. These regulations,[65] which are one of the most amended instruments under FSMA, aim to provide the FSA and other recipients of confidential information with sufficiently wide gateways either to enable or assist them to perform any of their public functions, or to enable or assist other public bodies to perform their functions.

2.65 In practice, the main restriction here is the duty of professional secrecy imposed under the various single market directives, and the regulations distinguish between directive information (which has narrower gateways) and non-directive information (which enjoys wider gateways).

---

[62] See Chapter 3.

[63] RAO, arts 14 and 25.

[64] The Financial Services and Markets Act 2000 (Market Abuse) Regulations 2005, SI 2005/381, which also specify the markets covered by s 118, and the Prospectus Regulations 2005, SI 2005/1433.

[65] SI 2001/2188 as amended; s 352 makes breach of these regulations, and of ss 348 and 350 (Revenue information) an offence, subject to defences.

The section 348 restriction provides an absolute exemption under section 44 **2.66** of the Freedom of Information Act 2000, but the self-help gateways might in theory permit the FSA to disclose information to enable or assist it to give guidance under section 157 or as part of the public record it must maintain under section 347. The function of giving guidance applies to such information and advice as it 'considers appropriate', and the contents of the register are similarly governed. The FSA would take into account the restriction, and any single market provisions, in deciding whether this was appropriate or not.

Section 348 is not the only restriction on disclosure. The procedural provisions **2.67** of FSMA require the FSA to issue warning and decision notices before publishing:

(i) statements of an approved person's misconduct under section 66;
(ii) statements censuring an issuer or applicant under section 91;
(iii) statements that a person has engaged in market abuse under section 123; and
(iv) statements to the effect that an authorised person has contravened a requirement imposed on him by or under FSMA under section 205.

Furthermore section 391 prohibits either the FSA or any recipient of a notice **2.68** (including a third party) from publishing details of any warning or decision notice until the FSA has issued a final notice, or the FSA has withdrawn it. As a matter of policy, the FSA does not usually publish details of supervisory or enforcement action until it takes effect.[66] Section 413 also protects communications with legal advisers in connection with legal advice or legal proceedings from any requirement of production, disclosure, or inspection under FSMA. This applies both to regulated firms and to the FSA itself.

Finally, section 353 provides for the Treasury to make regulations permitting the **2.69** disclosure of information to the FSA to enable or assist it to discharge its functions or to any person to enable or assist the discloser without contravening any duty to which the discloser may be subject. The regulations made under this section permit disclosures by the FOS and the FSCS, as well as by skilled persons and other experts appointed in respect of regulated firms.[67] This and the duty for the FSA to cooperate with other regulators under section 354 are subject to the confidentiality restriction in section 348.

---

[66] See Chapter 6 of the FSA's Enforcement Guide; by contrast the Tribunal Rules 2001, SI 2001/2476 contain a presumption of publicity—see rule 17.

[67] The Financial Services and Markets Act 2000 (Disclosure of Information by Prescribed Persons) Regulations 2001, SI 2001/1857 as amended.

Relationship to external legislation

2.70 The implementation of FSMA impacted a large volume of legislation which referred to predecessor legislation,[68] and FSMA is referred to in much other legislation.

2.71 Some of this legislation confers functions directly on the FSA, in which case there is usually provision for some or all of those functions to be treated as conferred by or under FSMA. For example:

    (i) functions in relation to mutual societies, which are treated as conferred by or under FSMA for most purposes of Schedule 1, but not for other purposes, since mutuals legislation makes specific provision for these;[69]

   (ii) functions as investigating authority under the Proceeds of Crime Act 2002, which are treated as conferred under FSMA by virtue of paragraph 19A of Schedule 1 to FSMA;

  (iii) functions as a qualifying body under the Unfair Terms in Consumer Contracts Regulations 1999, and as a designated enforcer under Part 8 of the Enterprise Act 2002, which are treated as conferred by or under FSMA;[70]

  (iv) functions in relation to insolvency legislation, which are treated as conferred by or under FSMA.[71]

2.72 However, certain functions conferred on the FSA, for example the Treasury's functions delegated to the FSA under the Uncertificated Securities Regulations 2001, are not treated as conferred by or under FSMA. In this case the legislation itself provides for the appropriate governance, accountability, and fee-raising powers.[72]

2.73 Most of the other references to FSMA in external legislation are to:

    (i) definitions of bank, insurer, and other authorised persons—care may be needed here to ensure that authorisation by the FSA is not taken to imply FSA approval or supervision of the firm in respect of the right, activity, or other privilege referred to in the legislation;[73]

---

[68] See eg the Financial Services and Markets Act 2000 (Consequential Amendments and Repeals) Order 2001, SI 2001/3649, as well as further orders SI 2001/3629, SI 2001/3801, SI 2001/3647.

[69] See Sched 2 to the Financial Services and Markets Act 2000 (Mutual Societies) Order 2001, SI 2001/2617; the FSA's monitoring and enforcement duties and the general duties in s 2 (see paras 2.13–2.16) are expressly disapplied.

[70] See reg 16 of SI 1999/2083 as amended, and art 3 of the Designation Order SI 2004/935.

[71] See the Insolvency Act 2000 Scheds 1, 2.

[72] SI 2001/3755—see regs 6 and 11.

[73] Because the activities that such entities have permission or exemption to carry on are defined in secondary legislation and generally need to be kept up-to-date or 'ambulatory' (ie reflecting the latest version of the RAO as amended from time to time), provision is generally made for the definition to be 'read' with reference to s 22, Sched 2, and any relevant order made under s 22.

(ii) the FSA and its functions conferred by or under FSMA, usually for the purpose of conferring gateways from confidentiality provisions applying to other regulators.

2.74

Increasingly, new functions have been conferred on the FSA through regulations implementing single market directives under the European Communities Act 1972. Usually, the regulations themselves provide for the FSA's functions—including functions as a competent authority—to be treated as conferred under FSMA.[74] However, the functions conferred or required may sometimes fall already within an existing FSA function under FSMA, for example the function of giving guidance under section 157; or by virtue of requirements on regulated persons being treated as conferred under FSMA, which activates the FSA's monitoring and enforcement functions.

Evolution

As discussed above, FSMA built a substantial degree of flexibility into the regulatory regime so that it could evolve without the need for further primary legislation. So far FSMA has been able to accommodate major domestic changes such as depolarisation and its extension to mortgage and general insurance intermediaries successfully, although it has not fully been able to anticipate all changes from Europe.

2.75

Two-year review

The first major test for FSMA after N2 was the Government's two-year review. This arose from a commitment to review the impact of FSMA on competition after two years promised by the Government in response to the Cruickshank report into competition in UK banking.[75] However, the Government quickly extended this to other aspects of its operation.

2.76

The Government announced the scope of the review on 4 November 2003.[76] It covered:

2.77

(i) a review of the impact of FSMA on competition, which was undertaken by the Office of Fair Trading;

(ii) a review of the scope of regulation, to be performed by the Treasury;

---

[74] For example, reg 23 of the Financial Services (Distance Marketing) Regulations 2004, SI 2004/2095; reg 27 of the Capital Requirements Regulations 2006, SI 2006/3221; and reg 5 of the Transfer of Funds (Information on the Payer) Regulations 2007, SI 2007/3298 and reg 24 of the Money Laundering Regulations 2007, SI 2007/2157.

[75] 'Banking Review Competition and Regulation in Financial Services: Striking the Right Balance' (July 1999); Final Report (March 2000); Government response: HM Treasury (August 2000).

[76] Statement by the then Financial Secretary, the Rt Hon Ruth Kelly MP. See the Treasury website: <http://www.hm-treasury.gov.uk>.

    (iii) a review by the FSA of the way it had exercised its functions, including the simplicity of its Handbook, the burden of consultation, and the way it gave guidance;

    (iv) a joint review by the FSA and the FOS of the way they worked together and whether there was a need for an appeal from an ombudsman's decisions.

2.78 Progress and outcomes of the review were announced on 2 December 2004.[77] Broadly, the review concluded that FSMA was working well and recommendations could be incorporated either in changes to secondary legislation or in changes to the FSA's (and where appropriate the FOS's) procedures. However, the Treasury identified a number of deregulatory amendments to FSMA itself through an order under the Regulatory Reform Act 2006.[78]

Further developments

2.79 Following the review, FSMA has seemed relatively secure and has continued to act as a model for other regulatory regimes introduced in the UK since 1997.[79] There has been general acceptance of the single regulator model, and FSMA itself was able to accommodate almost all the conclusions of the Treasury's review through secondary legislation. At the same time, FSMA still does not cover all financial services for all purposes and in that sense the FSA cannot be said to be a single regulator. Occupational pension schemes continue to have their own regulator, the Pensions Regulator, and consumer credit continues to be regulated by the Office of Fair Trading. Both areas have recently been the subject of substantial legislative reform, and there appears to be no appetite for further extension of FSA responsibility.[80] Nevertheless, the extension of the FSA's jurisdiction to include mortgage and general insurance intermediaries has underlined the difference between the FSA's regulatory approach to product providers on the one hand and to intermediaries on the other.[81]

2.80 Domestic scrutiny of the legislation including the two-year review initially focused on industry concerns about fairness of procedures and the burden of regulation under FSMA. Many of these concerns were not specific to financial services, and

---

[77] Statement by the then Financial Secretary, Hon Stephen Timms MP. See the Treasury website: <http://www.hm-treasury.gov.uk>—FSMA Bulletin 43 sets out the main changes to statutory instruments.

[78] The Regulatory Reform (Financial Services and Markets Act 2000) Order 2007.

[79] For example, the Communications Act 2003; the Pensions Act 2004; the Gambling Act 2004; the Consumer Credit Act 2006.

[80] The Pensions Act 2004 and the Consumer Credit Act 2006. See also the Thornton Review of Pensions Institutions, 5 June 2007.

[81] Hampton Review of Regulatory Inspection and Enforcement, 16 March 2005.

as discussed above have been matched to some extent by the Government and regulators themselves under the existing framework.[82]

Recently, however, there have been more serious concerns about the adequacy of **2.81** the arrangements to protect consumers, for example in criticism of the role of the FSA and other bodies in supervising Northern Rock plc and providing adequate protections for bank depositors and insurance policyholders.[83] Many of these concerns arguably relate to alleged operational failings by the FSA and other bodies in the pursuit of the regulatory objectives through their statutory functions, rather than a failing in the legislation itself. However, the Government now appears readier to introduce legislation to protect consumers directly rather than simply leave this to the FSA in exercising its functions under FSMA.[84] There have also been renewed calls for the Bank of England to resume some or all of its previous functions in the supervision of banks, which would if implemented lead to some unpicking of the single legislative framework.

Further stand-alone materials from Europe could also undermine the coherence **2.82** of FSMA as the single Act, as could further expansion of the separate comitology arrangements established under the Lamfalussy process.[85] However, the implementation of a single statutory framework for regulation continues to stand the UK in good stead, both as a model for influencing future European legislation and in accommodating it.

---

[82] For example, the Government's 2005 Pre-Budget Report set out a 10-point plan of reforms to deliver better regulation in financial services. The plan included a review of the RAO and the FPO, the controllers' regime, and exemptions for employers, a Regulatory Reform Order allowing the FSA to reduce the burden of consultation, and a value for money review of the FSA: HM Treasury, December 2005. This process led to changes in secondary legislation and to FSMA itself by virtue of the Regulatory Reform (Financial Services and Markets Act 2000) Order 2007, SI 2007/1973.

[83] 'The run on the Rock', Treasury Select Committee, 26 January 2008 and 10 July 2008; 'Inherited estates', Treasury Select Committee, 19 June 2008.

[84] See for example the Banking (Special Provisions) Act 2008 which enabled the transfer of Northern Rock plc into public ownership, and the public consultations undertaken in respect of the scope and application of the FSCS.

[85] Including UK regulations and secondary European materials. The largest of these so far, the Directive on markets in financial instruments (MiFID) (EC) 2004/39 has now been accommodated.

3

EUROPEAN FINANCIAL SERVICES

Introduction

The purpose of this chapter is to assess the impact of European law on the devel- **3.01** opment of financial services law in the United Kingdom—in short, to answer the question 'why does European financial services law matter?' To understand the significance of European financial services law, we need to understand its origins and the way in which it has developed.

Since the establishment of the European Economic Community in 1957, Member **3.02** States have been committed to the creation of a single integrated market, free of restrictions on the movement of services, capital, goods, and persons. Initially it was assumed that this could only be achieved through the harmonisation of national laws, but when the legislative process was becalmed, the European Court of Justice proved to be a major force for integration, through its case law interpreting the provisions of the Treaty establishing the four freedoms. The Treaty of Rome set out the basis for ensuring fair competition and envisaged a system of harmonisation of laws to the extent necessary for the proper functioning of the Common Market.

The original Community of six Member States has now become a European **3.03** Union of 27 Member States, and the Agreement on the European Economic Area of 1992 has the effect of extending the application of European financial services law to Norway, Iceland, and Liechtenstein. In this chapter the terms 'EC law' and 'EU law' will be used interchangeably. References to the 'Treaty' are to the Treaty of Rome as amended by the Treaty of Amsterdam. The 'United Kingdom' comprises Great Britain and Northern Ireland, thus excluding the Channel Islands and the Isle of Man. But the 'UK' includes Gibraltar in relation to financial services law. The UK Government is thus in the awkward position of being responsible under Community law for ensuring that the Government of Gibraltar implements all EU financial services legislation, despite having no powers to enforce compliance.

3.04   The basic goal of a single integrated market has remained unaltered through a number of Treaty changes, though the timetable for completion of the single market has inevitably slipped. Successive deadlines for the realisation of a single market in financial services were set by political leaders from 1992 up to 2005.

3.05   There are several reasons why it is important for the financial services practitioner to understand the basic principles of European Community law. First, an ever-growing proportion of UK financial services law is directly derived from EC law in that it has been enacted in order to implement European Community directives. Implementing legislation must be interpreted and applied in the UK in accordance with the provisions of the relevant directive and with the general principles of Community law.[1] Community law is unique in that it takes precedence over any conflicting provision in UK law.[2]

Breach of Community obligations

3.06   It would be wrong, however, to assume that Community law can be ignored by the practitioner until it has been implemented in UK law. Even where a directive has not yet been implemented by a Member State, the European Court of Justice has held that a State may be liable in damages for failure to implement by the directive deadline.[3] In some cases, an individual may be able to rely on the provisions of a directive against a government which has not implemented by the due implementation date.[4]

Direct effect

3.07   A knowledge of the general principles of Community law is also necessary since a claim may lie against a Member State or public authority for failure to comply with Treaty obligations. In a series of landmark rulings, the European Court of Justice ruled that Articles 43[5] and 49[6] of the Treaty were directly effective without the need for implementing EU directives. In the *Brasserie du Pêcheur* case,[7] an action was brought against Germany for breach of Community law, in that it had failed to adapt German law to the requirements of Article 28 of the Treaty.

---

   [1] s 3(1) of the European Communities Act 1972; Case C 106/89 *Marleasing v La Comercial Internacional de Alimentacion* [1990] ECR I-4135.
   [2] Case 6/64 *Costa v ENEL* [1964] ECR 585.
   [3] Cases C-6 and 9/90 *Frankovich and Bonafaci v Italy* [1991] ECR 1–5357.
   [4] Case 8/81 *Becker* [1982] ECR 53.
   [5] Case 2/74 *Reyners v Belgium* [1974] ECR 631.
   [6] Case 33/74 *Van Binsbergen v Bestuur van de Bedrijfsvereniging voor de Metaalnijverheid* [1974] ECR 1299.
   [7] Cases C-46/93 and 48/93 [1996] ECR I-1029.

The principle of 'vertical direct effect' has been extended by the Court to cover **3.08**
'horizontal direct effect'. The Court has ruled that some articles of the Treaty are
capable of conferring rights on private individuals or undertakings which may be
relied on against other private undertakings. In the *Viking*[8] and *Laval*[9] cases, the
Court firmly rejected the argument that the horizontal direct effect of the Treaty
fundamental freedoms could only apply as against public and quasi-public
authorities. The significance of these cases for financial services practitioners is
that discriminatory conduct by private market operators may be open to challenge on the grounds that it restricts fundamental Treaty freedoms. The Court had
indicated in an earlier case that Article 49 which prohibits discrimination on
grounds of nationality could apply to premiums charged by an insurance company if they were found to be discriminatory.[10]

Sources of Community law

The primary sources of EC law are found in the EC Treaty as amended, other **3.09**
international agreements to which the EU is party, such as the GATT, and the
general principles of law developed by the European Court of Justice in its case
law (Article 220 of the EC Treaty). These are derived inter alia from the European
Convention on Human Rights.

A secondary source of EC law is the legislation made under the Treaty, in the form **3.10**
of regulations, directives, and decisions.[11] Primary sources of EC law take precedence over secondary sources. Thus the validity of an EU directive may be challenged before a national court or before the European Court of Justice on the
grounds that it does not comply with the general principles of EC law or that the
Treaty base chosen for the directive is incorrect.[12]

It is rarely a straightforward process to identify a provision of UK law as having an **3.11**
EU derivation, and the EU origins of much of UK law are becoming increasingly
invisible. Because the EU tends to legislate in the financial services area by way of
directives, which have to be implemented in national law through domestic legislation, the EU derivation of a particular provision of UK law tends to get overlooked in time, as it is absorbed into the general body of law. But it remains vitally
important to be able to trace the origins of such a provision, since its EU derivation will affect its continuing interpretation and application and constrain the

---

[8] Case C-438/05, 11 December 2007.

[9] Case C-341/05. The judgment of the ECJ was handed down on 18 December 2007.

[10] Case 251/83 *Eberhard Haug-Adrion* v *Frankfurter Versicherungs AG* [1984] ECR 4277.

[11] Art 249 of the EC Treaty.

[12] Case 233/94 *Germany* v *European Parliament and Council* (Deposit Guarantee Directive)
[1997] ECR I-2045.

ability of the UK Government or the Financial Services Authority ('FSA') to change it. Both the Treasury and the FSA now refer explicitly to the EU source when implementing major pieces of legislation such as the Directive on Markets in Financial Instruments ('MiFID').

Impact on UK law

3.12 It is easy to lose sight of the many ways in which UK law has had to adjust to meet the demands of EU law. Some effects are more visible than others, for example, the major legislative changes required to accommodate the Single Market Directives conferring the so-called 'passport' on banks, investment firms, and insurance companies.[13]

3.13 Other changes have been more subtle. The increasing constraints on the UK's legislative discretion prevent it, for example, from pursuing a policy of deregulation in areas where this would conflict with Community obligations to regulate in accordance with agreed EU minimum standards. Conversely, it is more difficult for the UK to raise standards unilaterally if those standards can only apply to UK firms who have to compete in EU markets with firms from other Member States operating under the minimum Community standards. More recently, efforts by the FSA to introduce more principle-based regulation have come up against the obstacle of extremely detailed prescriptive EU legislation.[14]

3.14 The relationship between EU law and UK law, particularly in the area of securities law, is very much one of cross-fertilisation. The UK was one of the few Member States to have established a sophisticated system of securities regulation and had a thriving international financial market by the time the Community launched its programme on investment services. Consequently the UK was in a position to inject ideas based on practical experience into the Community process. But whatever the inspiration for a particular directive, the final product is never going to replicate the regime in one Member State. The result will be a compromise between Member States with widely differing traditions, markets, and ambitions. The directive will inevitably require a number of changes to existing law. It will often, however, only cover a small proportion of the matters already covered by domestic law. Thus, the 1992 Investment Services Directive stopped short of imposing licensing requirements on investment advisers and commodity futures traders, although they had been required to be licensed in the UK since the Financial Services Act 1986 ('FSA 1986'). It was not until November 2007 with the

---

[13] See FSMA, Sched 3.
[14] See FSA, 'Principles-Based Regulation: Focusing on the Outcomes that Matter' (April 2007). See below Chapter 5.

implementation of MiFID[15] that all Member States were required to license investment advisers and commodity derivatives firms, who were then able to benefit from the single passport.

Implementation: Copy-out v gold-plating

When implementing any directive which applies only to a subset of FSA regulated **3.15** firms, such as MiFID, the UK is almost invariably faced with the dilemma of whether to extend the directive requirements to all UK regulated firms, where relevant, or whether to leave the rules for non-MiFID firms unaltered. The latter option can rapidly result in a confusing and incoherent rulebook. But the former can equally be unattractive in policy terms, given the widespread resistance to gold-plating implementation measures. To avoid accusations of gold-plating, the Treasury and the FSA have increasingly resorted to 'copying out' the relevant directive provisions in statutory instruments and FSA rules.

On the other hand, where it is a question of tidying up the statute book following **3.16** EU legislation, it may not be possible to make the desired changes by means of secondary legislation under the European Communities Act 1972. Although this has the great advantage of speed and convenience, there are severe constraints on the amendments to primary legislation that can be made under the European Communities Act. Under section 2(2) of the Act regulations may be made:

(a) for the purpose of implementing any Community obligation of the United Kingdom, or enabling any such obligation to be implemented, or of enabling any rights enjoyed or to be enjoyed by the United Kingdom under or by virtue of the Treaties to be exercised; or

(b) for the purpose of dealing with matters arising out of or related to any such obligation or rights . . .

It will be apparent that section 2(2) cannot be used, therefore, to tidy up UK pri- **3.17** mary legislation, if this is not required by the provisions of the directive itself,[16] even where this would be highly desirable in the interests of a more coherent statute or rule book. But all too often this is simply the price to be paid for pioneering a system of financial services regulation, rather than starting from scratch with the directive.

---

[15] Directive 2004/39/EC [2004] OJ L145/1.
[16] See n 37 below.

Establishing the Single Market in Financial Services

3.18 Early efforts to establish a single market in financial services through harmonisation of national laws were largely unsuccessful. Harmonisation directives required unanimity in the Council to be adopted but since they tended to contain an excessive amount of detail, it often took years to reach agreement, by which time the directive might already be out of date. Because Member States were only prepared to agree on minimum standards, they remained free to impose stricter standards domestically which they imposed on their own firms and incoming firms alike.

Commission White Paper on Completing the Internal Market

3.19 The Commission White Paper of 1985 on 'Completing the Internal Market' called for a new approach to financial services legislation, arguing that the principle of mutual recognition established by the Court of Justice in the *Cassis de Dijon* case could be adapted to allow the free movement of financial services within the EU. The Commission proposed that banks and other financial institutions should be able to provide financial services in any EU Member State, provided that they were authorised by their home State, in accordance with harmonised prudential standards. Other Member States would be required to recognise their home State authorisation and would be unable to impose additional licensing requirements. Thus the foundations of the passporting system for banks, insurance companies, and investment firms were laid.

3.20 The Commission White Paper was followed by the Single European Act of 1986, which introduced qualified majority voting for almost all internal market measures. The momentum generated by these initiatives continued until the Maastricht Treaty in 1993, which set a new objective of economic and monetary union, including the creation of a single currency. In terms of legislative process, the most important change brought in by the Maastricht Treaty was the increase in the powers of the European Parliament through the introduction of the so-called 'co-decision' procedure.[17] From then on, the European Parliament had the power to veto Community legislation and both the Commission and the Council had to take its views much more seriously than hitherto.

3.21 The enlargement of the Community from 12 to 15 Member States in 1995 and renewed concentration on the preparations for the introduction of the single currency deflected attention from the goal of the single market in financial services. However, the European Commission seized the initiative in 1998 with the launch

---

[17] Set out in Art 251 of the Treaty.

of the Financial Services Action Plan (FSAP),[18] designed to capitalise on the future introduction of the euro.

Financial Services Action Plan

The FSAP was an extremely ambitious programme of legislative activity designed **3.22** to achieve a 'single deep and liquid capital market' in Europe. A target date of 2005 was eventually set, by which time some 42 separate regulatory measures were due to be adopted, covering the wholesale and retail markets, 'state of the art' prudential rules, and supervision and tax harmonisation. The Commission recognised that, some 40 years after the Treaty of Rome, markets remained fragmented, while the costs of capital and intermediation stayed high. In the view of the Commission, economic growth depended on the integration of the EU financial markets and that integration could not be achieved without EU regulatory intervention.

The Commission saw an urgent need for reform, following the coming into force **3.23** of the Investment Services Directive in 1996 and the consequent shift of emphasis from regulation of banking to regulation of securities business, coupled with growing interest in market regulation.

In the Commission's view, this necessitated action on two fronts—to enable EU **3.24** legislation to be amended more quickly to adapt to fast moving securities markets, and to introduce a streamlined approach to drafting legislation. The Commission pressed for framework legislation in place of detailed directives, which could be supplemented by guidance, a plea which was to be later endorsed by the Lamfalussy Report in 2001.

Lamfalussy Report

In July 2000, the so-called Committee of Wise Men, chaired by Baron Lamfalussy, **3.25** was appointed by the Council to assess progress in the long-running struggle to establish an integrated securities market. The Lamfalussy Report[19] was delivered to the Council in February 2001 and was fiercely critical of the structures then in place for agreeing, implementing, and enforcing EU securities legislation.

The Report concluded that the chances of delivering the FSAP commitments on **3.26** time were 'close to zero'. Legislative procedures were too slow, the average time for agreeing a directive under co-decision was about two years, and the Council continued to introduce what was seen as unnecessary complexity into draft legislation

---

[18] COM (1998) 625.
[19] Final Report of the Committee of Wise Men on the Regulation of European Securities Markets, February 2001.

during negotiations. Member States were criticised for incorrect and uneven implementation of directives. The legislative process was unable to respond quickly to changing market conditions, it produced badly drafted and ambiguous texts, and no clear distinction was drawn between essential framework principles and detailed implementing rules—essentially the same criticisms that had been voiced by the Commission in the 1985 White Paper and again when drawing up the FSAP.

3.27 The Lamfalussy Report, endorsed by the Stockholm Council in March 2001 and by the European Parliament, recommended a new four-level structure of regulation for the securities markets in the first instance:[20]

- Level 1: principle-based legislation, adopted as before in accordance with the co-decision procedure by the Council and the European Parliament. Level 1 legislation should define the implementing powers for the Commission under Level 2.

- Level 2: detailed implementing measures, consisting either of Commission directives or regulations, made under powers conferred by the Level 1 directive, under a new streamlined accelerated legislative procedure, in which the Commission is assisted by two institutional committees. Technical advice is prepared by the Committee of European Securities Regulators ('CESR'),[21] following a request from the Commission and after consultation with market users. A vote is taken by qualified majority of the Member States represented in the European Securities Committee ('ESC').[22] The European Parliament has power to pass a resolution within three months on the draft implementing measures, and within one month of the vote by the ESC if the Level 2 measures go beyond implementing powers.

- Level 3: enhanced cooperation between the members of CESR to ensure proper implementation of Level 1 and Level 2 measures. CESR may issue guidance and common, non-binding standards. It also reviews national regulatory practice.

- Level 4: The Commission, which is responsible for policing the implementation of EU legislation, concentrates on more effective enforcement of compliance, if necessary bringing infringement proceedings under Article 226 of the Treaty against a Member State in the European Court of Justice for non-implementation or incorrect implementation of EU legislation.

3.28 A key theme of the Lamfalussy Report was its emphasis on consultation—consultation of all the parties likely to be affected by a particular measure, so that

---

[20] The system was extended to the banking and insurance sectors in 2003; see para 3.29 below.
[21] CESR replaced the former FESCO (the Federation of European Securities Commissions); see Commission Decision 2001/527 [2001] OJ L191/43.
[22] Set up by Commission Decision of 6 June 2001.

problems could be identified and an agreed solution found before either Level 1 measures were published in draft form or Level 2 measures were adopted by the Commission. While CESR has consulted widely on proposed advice to the Commission and before issuing recommendations or guidelines, the Commission itself was criticised for failing to consult properly before publishing the draft directives on market abuse and prospectuses.

Lamfalussy: banking and insurance

Although the Lamfalussy Report was concerned only with the securities markets, **3.29** its recommendations were subsequently adopted in relation to banking and insurance. The Level 3 Committee of European Banking Supervisors ('CEBS') was set up by Commission Decision on 5 November 2003,[23] as was the Committee of European Insurance and Occupational Pension Supervisors ('CEIOPS'). The former Banking Advisory Committee ('BAC') created under the First Banking Directive, which had acted both as an advisory and as a comitology committee, divided into two, becoming at Level 2 the European Banking Committee ('EBC') and CEBS at Level 3, while the European Insurance and Occupational Pensions Committee ('EIOPC') replaced the former Insurance Committee under a 2005 Directive establishing a new organisational structure for the financial services committees.[24]

After the FSAP

The Lamfalussy recommendations came too late to have a major influence on the **3.30** shape of the legislation coming out of the FSAP. Four directives have been adopted under the Lamfalussy procedures—the Market Abuse and Prospectus Directives, MiFID, and the Transparency Directive. While all four made use of the Level 2 facility, the Level 1 directives hardly measured up to the Lamfalussy model of framework principles. MiFID in particular contained an excessive amount of detail and prescription at Level 1, which was supplemented by further detail at Level 2.[25] With the adoption of virtually all the measures envisaged in the FSAP, the Commission has now turned its attention away from new legislation and is focusing on other priorities—making the Lamfalussy process work, implementing 'Better Regulation' through consultation, impact assessments, simplification and codification of existing legislation, and strengthening the enforcement of

---

[23] Commission Decision 2004/5/EC.
[24] Directive 2005/1/EC [2005] OJ L79/9.
[25] See Commission Decision 2006/73/EC [2006] OJ L241/26; Commission Regulation 1287/2006 [2006] OJ L241/1.

Member State implementation.[26] However the Commission has not ruled out bringing forward new legislative measures where circumstances have changed or non-legislative measures are judged to have been ineffective.[27] Harmonising the rules relating to company law and corporate governance,[28] as well as to accounting and auditing, are seen as essential for creating a single market in financial services, though they do not form part of mainstream financial services policy.

Dominant themes

3.31 Certain trends can be observed in EU financial services legislation. The initial focus was on authorisation and prudential supervision of financial institutions such as credit institutions (banks and building societies in the UK) and insurance companies. Subsequently there was a move away from institutional supervision to functional supervision, with the development of policies designed to impose similar requirements on institutions carrying on the same type of business. This coincided with the emergence of a system of securities and market regulation in the EU, which also heralded the development of more sophisticated risk-based capital requirements.

Home/host jurisdiction

3.32 The introduction of securities regulation necessitated a formal distinction being drawn between prudential supervision, which was the responsibility of the home State competent authority under the single market directives, and conduct of business rules, which remained within the competence of the 'host' State (although, as will be seen below,[29] it was far from clear in many cases which State was the host State).

Minimum/maximum harmonisation

3.33 Failure to agree on allocation of regulatory responsibility for conduct of business rules frustrated the efforts of those European firms seeking to take advantage of the pan-European market, who could find themselves subject to dual and possibly conflicting regulation in respect of the same business. This would have mattered less if the rules applied by each regulator were the same. In practice, however, they

---

[26] Commission White Paper on Financial Services Policy 2005–2010.

[27] Thus the Commission is still prepared to take legislative action, should the market fail to come up with satisfactory solutions to the problems besetting clearing and settlement. See too the draft proposals for regulation of credit rating agencies published by the Commission on 31 July 2008, and the draft Regulation published in November 2008, COM (2008) 704.

[28] See paras 3.107–3.111 below.

[29] See para 3.63 below.

varied considerably, which led to increasing pressure for greater harmonisation and, in particular, for the introduction of maximum harmonisation rules at EU level. This has proved to be a highly contentious issue, with Member States clinging to their power to protect their domestic, particularly their retail, investors as they see fit. Attempts to introduce maximum harmonisation have had mixed success[30] and it could be argued that only the Prospectus Directive[31] contains a clear and unambiguous statement that Member States cannot introduce additional requirements in the field covered by the directive.

Differences of opinion between Member States on jurisdiction and the interpreta- **3.34** tion of directives will feed through to implementation and firms relying on the UK implementation of a particular directive may find that other Member States have interpreted the directive very differently. This is where CESR can play a valuable role in seeking consensus and issuing guidance on interpretation and implementation, supported by the Commission, which is ultimately responsible for monitoring compliance with Community obligations.

Single Market Legislation—Banking

Much of the UK law on the regulation of banks, securities business, and insurance **3.35** companies is derived from EU law. A UK statutory system[32] for licensing banks or deposit-taking institutions was introduced in 1979 following the adoption of the First Banking Directive in 1977. That Directive laid down the basic requirements for obtaining a banking licence—separate and adequate own funds, effective management by at least two persons of sufficiently good repute, and experience— requirements which continue to apply, as supplemented by the later Banking Directives.

Second Banking Directive

The Second Banking Directive, adopted in 1989,[33] introduced the principle of **3.36** home State authorisation and prudential supervision for EC credit institutions (ie, banks and building societies). This meant that a bank, once authorised as a credit institution in its home State, could provide a wide range of banking and

---

[30] See below paras 3.75–3.78; 3.91–3.92.
[31] See below, para 3.103.
[32] Banking Act 1979.
[33] Directive 89/646/EEC [1989] OJ L386/1. The Second Banking Directive was consolidated in 2000 with the Banking Consolidation Directive 2000/12/EEC of 20 March 2000 and then amended and reissued as the recast Capital Requirements Directive 2006/48/EC at para 3.43 and n 43 below.

investment services throughout the EC by opening branches or by supplying services in other Member States, without being subjected to any local licensing requirements. The Second Banking Directive retained the definition of 'credit institution' which had been adopted in the First Banking Directive, ie an institution 'whose business is to receive deposits or other repayable funds from the public and to grant credits for its own account'.[34] Banks and other financial institutions already benefited from the right under the Treaty to set up branches or provide services in other Member States, but until the Second Banking Directive, the host State of the branch would insist on the bank applying for local authorisation.

3.37 The licensing conditions were expanded under the Second Banking Directive to include minimum initial capital and own funds requirements, together with provisions allowing home State regulators to vet the suitability of controlling shareholders of banks.[35] Some, but not all, of the directive licensing requirements can be found in the Threshold Conditions for authorisation set out in Schedule 6 to FSMA.

3.38 The provisions dealing with qualifying or controlling shareholders are now found in Part XII of FSMA. They are a good illustration of the difficulties involved in disentangling provisions designed to implement an EU obligation from other cases where the UK has decided to extend their application.

3.39 In line with EC law, Part XII applies only in respect of UK incorporated entities and not to branches of firms incorporated in other Member States. Nor does it apply to branches of firms incorporated in third countries. The FSMA provisions do, however, apply to UK authorised firms other than those operating under a passport, so go beyond the minimum requirements of the banking and other financial services directives. The significance of this is that the UK could decide at any time to cut back regulation in this area to the minimum directive requirements. The super-equivalent provisions do not have to be interpreted in line with the directives, but they would have to be compatible with EC law generally where relevant.

Post-BCCI Directive

3.40 Following the collapse of the Bank of Credit and Commerce International, the prudential requirements in the banking and other financial services directives were tightened up in Directive 95/26/EC[36] to deal with the type of abuse which

---

[34] Art 4, Directive 2006/48EC.

[35] See the Communication from the Commission on Intra-EU Investment in the Financial Services Sector, C/2005/4080, 21 October 2005, reminding Member States of the relevant Treaty freedoms and their application to supervisory decisions in relation to cross-border consolidation.

[36] Directive 95/26/EC on reinforcing prudential supervision, now consolidated in Directive 2006/48/EC.

had emerged in that case. In particular, where a bank or financial institution formed part of a group, the group structure had to be sufficiently transparent to enable effective prudential supervision of the authorised firm. Banks and insurance companies were required to locate their head office in the same Member State as their registered office—a requirement which already applied to investment firms under the 1993 Investment Services Directive.[37] More controversially, external auditors of banks and other financial institutions were required henceforth to report to the 'competent' or supervisory authorities on any irregularities which might suggest a material breach of the law applying to financial institutions or which might affect the continuation of the business.

The first two requirements are now implemented in the threshold conditions in **3.41** Schedule 6 to FSMA, but again extend beyond the requirements of Directive 95/26/EC to apply to authorised firms which do not benefit from a passport. Moreover, the group structure or 'close links' provisions apply in the case of a non-EU firm seeking to carry on regulated activities in the UK though a branch. Similarly the auditors' reporting obligations, found in Part XXII of FSMA and the Communication by Auditors Regulations 2001, extend beyond UK and passporting firms.

Capital Directives

Considerable efforts were devoted to harmonising capital requirements as a key **3.42** part of the licensing and prudential supervision requirements for banks. The Own Funds Directive[38] was the first attempt in EC law to harmonise definitions and standards relating to bank capital ('own funds'). This was followed by the Solvency Ratio Directive[39] and the Large Exposures Directive[40] on the monitoring and control of large exposures. The Capital Adequacy Directive, adopted in 1993,[41] set out for the first time ongoing capital requirements to cover risks inherent in the trading book business of banks, such as position risk, settlement and counterparty risk, and large exposures. CAD II, the amending Directive adopted in 1998 on the capital adequacy of investment firms and credit institutions[42] allowed the use of internal risk management models for calculating capital requirements in relation to market risk.

---

[37] The Second Banking Directive did not impose a substantive obligation to this effect, but contained only a recital reference. This was not sufficient to allow the European Communities Act 1972 to be used to introduce an amendment to primary legislation.

[38] Directive 89/299/EEC, now consolidated, as amended, in Directive 2006/49/EC.

[39] Directive 89/647/EEC, now consolidated, as amended, in Directive 2006/49/EC.

[40] Directive 92/121/EEC, now consolidated, as amended, in Directive 2006/49/EC.

[41] Directive 93/6/EEC, now consolidated, as amended, in Directive 2006/49/EC.

[42] Directive 98/31/EC [1998] OJ L204/13, now consolidated, as amended, in Directive 2006/49/EC.

Capital Requirements Directive

3.43 The Capital Requirements Directive ('CRD')[43] is designed to bring EU legislation into line with the Basel 2 Accord—the Agreement on Capital Requirements drawn up by the Basel Committee on Banking Supervision, whose members are drawn from the 13 'G10' countries. Although the Basel Accords are applied to banks in more than 100 countries, they are not legally binding, unlike EU capital requirements. The EU has traditionally followed Basel in setting capital requirements, but this is not necessarily a straightforward process. First there is inevitably a delay in translating Basel requirements into EU law, since adjustments have to be made to provisions originally designed for large international banks to cater for the wide range of banks and investment firms in the EU. There is also a natural reluctance on the part of those EU Member States who are not members of the Basel Committee to adopt without question requirements which they have had no hand in shaping. This awkward interface between the two regimes has caused difficulties in the past, when EU banks have been unable to take advantage of a relaxation of the Basel requirements, because they were still bound by tighter EU requirements, until the necessary changes were made.

3.44 The CRD consists of three pillars:

- Pillar 1 sets out the minimum capital requirements for credit, market, and operational risk.
- Pillar 2 requires banks and supervisors to take a view on whether additional capital should be held against risks not covered in Pillar 1 and to take action where necessary.
- Pillar 3 requires banks to publish details of their risks, capital and risk management.

The CRD is more sensitive to the risks that banks face—the new framework includes an explicit measure for operational risk and includes more sensitive risk weightings against credit risk. The internal ratings-based approach allows banks to rely to some extent on their own estimate of credit risk. The CRD also provides incentives for banks to improve their risk management, with more sensitive risk weights as firms adopt more sophisticated approaches to risk management. Overall the level of capital held by banks collectively has remained broadly unchanged as a result of the CRD.

---

[43] The CRD comprises 2 directives: Directive 2006/48/EC relating to the taking up and pursuit of the business of credit institutions (recast) [2006] OJ L177/1 and Directive 2006/49/EC relating to the capital adequacy of investment firms and credit institutions (recast) [2006] OJ L177/201.

Consolidated supervision

The principle of consolidated supervision was accepted early on in relation to   **3.45**
banking groups. The First Consolidated Supervision Directive in 1983 required
Member States to take into account the risks to the solvency of an authorised bank
posed by other group companies. The 1983 Directive was replaced by the Second
Consolidated Supervision Directive[44] which expanded the reach of consolidated
supervision to cover a wider range of banking groups, but the focus remained on
the risks posed by other group companies to the bank. In particular the responsibilities of any 'solo' supervisor of other companies in the group remained unaffected, though the directive introduced the requirement that the various banking,
insurance, and securities supervisors must cooperate closely and exchange relevant
information in respect of group companies covered by the directive. CAD I
extended the provisions of the Second Consolidated Supervision Directive to
those non-banking groups which contained an investment firm covered by the
Investment Services Directive. The drafting of these provisions was very unsatisfactory, but the FSA has now put in place a single set of rules for the consolidated
supervision of investment groups.

Financial Conglomerates Directive

The Financial Conglomerates Directive,[45] adopted in 2002 and implemented in   **3.46**
the UK in January 2005,[46] made significant changes to the former regimes for the
supervision of banking/investment groups and insurance groups. The Directive is
aimed at the supervision of those conglomerates with group companies in both
the banking or investment sectors and in the insurance sector, with a significant
volume of business in each. The banking/investment sector is widely defined and
has been expanded by MiFID to include activities such as investment research and
financial analysis, as well as including activities which are not regulated by the
FSA, such as finance leasing and the financing of commercial transactions. Such
conglomerates pose significant regulatory challenges to ensure that there are no
regulatory gaps in the assessment of business risks, controls, and financial resources
in groups, whose business spans different financial sectors and is likely to be
located in different jurisdictions, both inside and outside the EU. This makes
cooperation between home and host States essential. The Directive builds on the
concept of the Co-ordinating Supervisor in the CRD instead of attempting to

---

[44] Directive 92/30/EEC on the supervision of credit institutions on a consolidated basis [1992]
OJ L110/52.
[45] Directive 2002/87/EC [2002] OJ L35/1.
[46] See Chapters 14 and 16 below.

introduce a single European regulator for the group. CEBS has produced guide-lines on how the home/host supervisory arrangements should work.

3.47   The directive must also be applied to financial conglomerates which are only sub-groups within a wider financial group. There are special provisions for non-EEA conglomerates. Different arrangements apply depending on whether supervision of the conglomerate in the third country is considered to be equivalent to the EU regime. The FSA rules implementing the directive apply only to those conglomer-ates for which the FSA is the coordinating supervisor. Either the FSA's insurance or its banking/investment capital rules apply, depending on the dominant busi-ness of the group. But until the insurance solvency requirements are updated by Solvency II, this is likely to produce very different results.[47]

Single Market Legislation—Insurance

3.48   The pattern of EC legislation in the last 15 years has been to legislate for banks in the first instance and then to apply the same rules with minor modifications to investment firms. Insurance regulation has followed a slightly different path and there have been very few attempts to integrate insurance regulation with regula-tion of banking and investment business at European level. Indeed, EU law pro-hibits an insurance company from carrying on any business other than insurance business.[48] Consequently the FSA is limited in what it can do to achieve a more integrated Prudential Sourcebook, given the constraints imposed by the relevant directives.[49]

3.49   EC insurance regulation did, however, follow the same system of home State authorisation and prudential supervision, but with separate regimes applying to life and non-life business. It is fair to say that the concept of a single market for insurance took rather longer to gather support and some of the early insurance directives seemed to be drafted with little respect for the principles of the Treaty, as interpreted by the European Court of Justice. Some insurance regulators found it difficult, for example, to accept the right of insurance companies to provide insurance for a policyholder in another Member State if they had not established a branch in that Member State.

---

[47]   ibid.
[48]   See FSMA, s 141(1), implementing the EU prohibition found eg, in Art 6(1)(b) of Directive 2002/83/EC, n 50 below.
[49]   See Chapter 11 below.

Life assurance

Although the Second Life Assurance Directive of 1990[50] was ostensibly designed **3.50** to facilitate cross-border services business, it nevertheless allowed the Member State where the policyholder was based to impose a highly restrictive regime on the insurance company, regulating matters such as premium scales, policy terms, and conditions, and imposing requirements such as the localisation of assets. Fortunately the Third Life Directive, adopted in 1992,[51] cut back on the powers of host States to restrict services business. The Third Directive laid down a system of home State authorisation and prudential supervision for life assurance companies, replicating to a large extent the banking regime.

Non-life assurance

The same pattern was followed in relation to non-life assurance. A licensing sys- **3.51** tem was established under the First Non-Life Directive in 1973,[52] followed by a Directive on Services[53] and the Third Non-Life Directive in 1992.[54]

The insurance directives were initially implemented in the Insurance Companies **3.52** Act 1982. They are now implemented in FSMA and rules made under that Act. Although a valiant attempt was made to harmonise the provisions covering the exercise of passporting rights by UK and EEA firms in Schedule 3 to the Act, the variations in the relevant sectoral directives made this impossible. The different notification procedures where an institution is passporting into or out of the UK, must therefore be retained until the directives themselves are changed.

Consolidated supervision of insurance groups

The EU provisions on consolidated supervision of insurance companies followed **3.53** the same model adopted for banks and investment firms. The 1998 Directive on Supervision of Insurance Undertakings in a Group[55] focused on the solo supervision of the insurance company in the group and the risks posed by other group companies to policyholder security. There was no attempt to supervise non-insurance companies within the group. The Financial Conglomerates Directive

---

[50] Directive 90/619/EEC, now consolidated in Directive 2002/83/EC on Life Assurance [2002] OJ L345/1.

[51] Directive 92/96/EEC, now consolidated in Directive 2002/83/EC on Life Assurance.

[52] Directive 73/239/EEC [1973] OJ L228/19.

[53] Directive 88/357/EEC [1988] OJ L172/1.

[54] Directive 92/49/EEC [1992] OJ L228/1.

[55] Directive 98/78/EC [1998] OJ L330/1.

now remedies this omission, at least in relation to those financial conglomerates with a significant amount of banking or investment business.[56]

Reinsurance

3.54 Although most Member States already regulated reinsurance, it was not until 2005 that an EU Directive setting up a home State licensing system for EU reinsurers was agreed. The Directive [57] was implemented in the UK by FSA rules in 2007.

Solvency II

3.55 The capital requirements for insurers date back in some cases to the 1970s. The draft Solvency II directive[58] represents an ambitious attempt to introduce an EU risk-based approach to the solvency requirements of life and non-life insurers and reinsurers, replacing the existing Solvency I directives. The draft directive, like the CRD, consists of three pillars:

- Pillar 1 sets out a valuation standard for liabilities to policyholders and the capital requirements for insurers in relation to insurance, credit, market, and operational risk. Firms may use their own capital models if they obtain the approval of their supervisor.

- Pillar 2 establishes the supervisory review process, which focuses on evaluating the adequacy of capital and risk management systems and processes. Supervisors may require a firm to hold additional capital against risks not adequately covered in Pillar 1.

- Pillar 3 requires firms to publish details of their risks, capital, and risk management processes.

3.56 Solvency II, as drafted, also gives supervisors considerable discretion and flexibility in the application of group supervision to sub-groups within a larger insurance group, a discretion which is not available to supervisors under the FCD. It also proposes a new group capital regime which could allow insurance groups meeting the criteria to maintain their solvency capital requirement at group level rather than at solo level, in return for guarantees of group support. An amended proposal was published in February 2008[59] and could be agreed in principle by the end

---

[56] See paras 3.46–3.47 above.
[57] Directive 2005/68/EC on Reinsurance and amending Council Directives 73/239/EEC, 98/78/EC, and 2002/83/EC [2005] OJ L323/1.
[58] An amended Commission proposal was published in February 2008, COM (2008) 119.
[59] See n 58 above.

of 2008. Solvency II will be a Lamfalussy directive and CEIOPS is already preparing advice on the future Level 2 implementing measures.

Single Market Legislation—Collective Investment Schemes

UCITS

The first example of a home State licensing system for financial services arose as **3.57** early as 1985 with the first UCITS Directive,[60] which provided a passport for certain types of securities collective investment schemes which could be marketed to the public in any Member State once they had been authorised by their home State. The 1985 UCITS Directive is also notable in that it introduced the division of responsibilities between the home State, responsible for licensing and prudential supervision of the UCITS, and the host State, responsible for regulation of marketing of the product and other conduct of business rules. This was a distinction which was to be endorsed in later directives, such as the Banking Directive, the Insurance Directives, and MiFID. The precise dividing lines are, however, unclear in practice and continue to generate considerable controversy and debate between financial institutions and Member States.[61] The UCITS Directive, as amended by two later directives in 2002,[62] is unique in that it is the only example of product regulation found in EU financial services law. As such it has proved difficult to reconcile and develop in line with mainstream EU financial services regulation, which focuses on regulation of the product provider.

UCITS amending directive

In July 2008 the Commission published a draft directive[63] amending the UCITS **3.58** directives which was intended to overcome some of the barriers to the cross-border management and distribution of funds. The amendments will:

- Remove administrative barriers to the cross-border marketing of UCITS. Marketing the fund in another Member State will be able to start immediately the regulator of the fund has notified the host State regulator.

---

[60] Directive 85/611/EEC on undertakings for collective investment in transferable securities [1987] OJ L375/10.

[61] See below, paras 3.62–3.63.

[62] Directive 2001/107/EC on management companies and simplified prospectuses [2002] OJ L41/20; Directive 2001/108/EC on investments of UCITS [2002] OJ L41/35.

[63] COM (2008) 458.

- Replace the simplified prospectus with a Key Investor Information (KII) document, providing investors with key facts to enable them to make an informed investment decision.
- Facilitate national and cross-border mergers between UCITS funds and allow the use of master feeder structures.
- Improve cooperation between national supervisors.

3.59 One issue which the draft directive does not address is that of the UCITS management company passport (ie the possibility for UCITS authorised in one Member State to be managed remotely by a management company established in another Member State). Following a request from the Commission, CESR published its advice[64] at the end of October 2008 on the supervisory issues arising if a UCITS were managed by a management company situated in another Member State. The advice is designed to help the Commission to devise a regime which would meet the concerns of supervisors and investors. A full passport for UCITS depositaries is currently ruled out by the UCITS Directive which requires the depositary to be established in the same Member State as the management company. This would allow a branch of a credit institution authorised in another Member State to act as depositary, though this is currently prohibited by some Member States, but it would not allow depositaries to offer their services remotely from another Member State. The Commission has decided not to take further action in respect of depositaries because it believes that a condition precedent for a full passport would be the harmonisation of the role and responsibilities of the depositary. Moreover, since it is possible in practice to delegate to sub-custodians in other Member States, it is thought that the potential benefits of further legislation are outweighed by the cost.

Single Market Legislation—Investment Services

Investment Services Directive

3.60 The regulation of investment services was closely modelled on the regime which had already been established for banks, but it departed from the banking model with the introduction of conduct of business rules and market rules, both of which proved controversial. The Investment Services Directive[65] introduced a licensing system for a range of investment services, together with the introduction of home State authorisation and prudential supervision, thus achieving in one directive what had taken two or three attempts for banking and insurance. The ISD adopted a functional approach to securities regulation by requiring Member States to set up a prior licensing system for any firm whose business was to provide one or more

---

[64] CESR/08-867.
[65] Directive 93/22/EEC [1993] OJ L194/27, now replaced by MiFID.

of the investment services listed in Section A of the Annex to the directive. This approach can be contrasted with the previous institutional approach of the Second Banking Directive under which a bank, once authorised as a credit institution, could provide any of the services listed in the Annex to the directive, provided that such services were covered by its authorisation as a credit institution.

The Annexes to the two Directives served very different purposes. In the case of **3.61** the Second Banking Directive, the Annex listed a range of activities which could be carried on by a bank throughout the EU without being subjected to any local licensing requirements. In the case of the ISD, Section A of the Annex contained a list of investment services, each of which was subject to a prior licensing requirement. The early enthusiasm for an ISD passport and consequent pressure from some trade associations in the UK to have identical provisions in the two Annexes soon evaporated when it was realised that this would mean setting up a licensing system for activities such as 'advice to undertakings on capital structure, industrial strategy and related matters and advice and services relating to mergers and the purchase of undertakings'. The awkward interplay between the two Annexes is carried over in MiFID where Annex 1 serves the same purpose as the ISD Annex. MiFID has however, resolved many of the problems which emerged after implementation of the ISD.

Home/host conflict

The conduct of business regime and the division of responsibilities between home **3.62** and host state proved to be one of the more intractable issues needing a solution. The ISD required Member States to establish rules of conduct to be observed by authorised ISD firms. These were to be applied and enforced by the Member State 'in which a service was provided'. Unfortunately Member States could take diametrically opposite views about where services were provided and hence whose rules should apply to services business.

Both banks and investment firms suffered as a result of this difference of views, **3.63** because banks providing investment services were subject to the same conduct of business rules as investment firms under the ISD and both were required to notify the relevant competent authority of their intention to provide services 'within the territory of another Member State' for the first time. Firms could find themselves subject not only to home State rules but also to rules in another Member State, if they happened to have a client in that State. Efforts by the Commission to resolve the impasse proved unsuccessful. The Commission attempted to provide guidance in its Interpretative Communication on 'Freedom to Provide Services and the Interest of the General Good in the Second Banking Directive'[66] on the vexed

---

[66] [1997] OJ C209/6.

question of where services were provided. Although the Communication was expressly restricted to 'problems specifically related to the Second Directive', it was equally relevant to the ISD, because of the similar provisions in both directives and because of the application of the ISD to bank investment firms. But the 'characteristic performance' test advocated in the Communication was rejected by many Member States, though supported by the UK and the battle over jurisdiction continued to generate tension between Member States. It was left to MiFID to resolve the issue.[67]

Professional/retail business

3.64 Another obstacle facing investment firms seeking to carry on business in another Member State under the ISD was the failure of many Member States to observe the requirement in Article 11(1) of the ISD that conduct of business rules should be 'applied in such a way as to take account of the professional nature of the person for whom the service is provided'. Not only did the conduct of business regime vary widely from one Member State to another, but many States did not distinguish between wholesale institutional clients and retail clients of an investment firm. The ISD did not contain any agreed definition of professional investor. Nor did it attempt any meaningful harmonisation of conduct of business rules; such harmonisation as there was took the form of minimum harmonisation, allowing Member States to impose more rigorous requirements on domestic and incoming firms alike, subject only to the constraints of Community law and the general good test developed by the European Court of Justice in particular.

General good test

3.65 The European Court has developed the 'general good' test as a measure of whether a Member State is allowed to impose its own rules (mainly but not necessarily conduct of business rules) on EEA firms where those rules have the effect of restricting the firm's exercise of its freedoms under the Treaty.

3.66 The test is not defined in EU legislation but originates in the case law of the European Court of Justice. It is essentially a negative test in that Member States are only allowed to impose their domestic rules on firms if those rules meet certain conditions. Those conditions are that the rule in question:

(i)   must be non-discriminatory;
(ii) must not duplicate equivalent home State rules to which the firm is already subject;
(iii) must be objectively necessary to achieve a general good objective (such as consumer protection);

---

[67] Even now, the problem awaits full resolution, see para 3.74 below.

    (iv) must be proportionate, that is, it must be the least restrictive method of attaining a general good objective; and

    (v) must not cover a matter which has already been harmonised at Community level.[68]

The *Alpine Investments* case[69] provides an example of a challenge to a financial **3.67** services rule on the grounds that it interfered with a firm's right to provide investment services from its home State into other Member States. The case concerned a Dutch law effectively banning cold calls made from the Netherlands to other Member States to persuade potential investors to buy commodity futures. The European Court upheld the Dutch restrictions on the basis that, although they amounted to a restriction on the right to provide services, they nevertheless met the conditions necessary to satisfy the general good test and consequently could be applied.

Another example of a firm challenging a domestic restriction which applied equally **3.68** to national and incoming EEA firms can be found in the *Caixa Bank* case.[70] Here the French banking subsidiary of a Spanish bank challenged the prohibition under the French Monetary and Financial Code on the provision of interest-bearing current accounts. The case was referred by the Conseil d'Etat to the European Court of Justice for a preliminary ruling on the question whether the prohibition constituted an obstacle to freedom of establishment under the Treaty.

The European Court upheld the challenge in a preliminary ruling in October **3.69** 2004, concluding that the prohibition did constitute a restriction on freedom of establishment, in that it was a serious obstacle for companies from other Member States carrying on business in France via a subsidiary and seeking to raise funds from the public. Although the prohibition was alleged to be justified on consumer protection grounds and as a means of encouraging long-term savings, the court found that the prohibition was disproportionate, in that there were other less restrictive means of securing those objectives.

These cases illustrate the fact that EC law can be used successfully to challenge **3.70** national laws which may have been accepted without question by financial institutions. They demonstrate that the general good test is available not only to firms passporting into a Member State under a Single Market Directive, but also to other EEA firms engaged in cross-border services or branch business, and to nationals of that Member State, if they are in a position to invoke any of the Treaty freedoms.

---

[68] See *Gebhard v Consiglio dell'Ordine degli Avvocati e Procuratori di Milano* [1995] ECR 4165; Case 205/84 *Commission v Germany (the German Insurance case)* [1986] ECR 3755.

[69] Case 384/93 *Alpine Investments v Minister van Financien* [1995] ECR I–1141.

[70] Case C-442/02 *Caixa Bank France v Ministry for Economy, Finance and Industry* (2005) 1 CMLR 39.

Markets in Financial Instruments Directive ('MiFID')

3.71 MiFID is a major piece of legislation, the most ambitious directive to have come out of the FSAP. It was adopted under the Lamfalussy procedures. Like its predecessor, the ISD, it applies to bank and non-bank investment firms providing investment services. MiFID introduces significant changes to the ISD in relation to scope, organisation and internal controls, harmonisation of conduct of business rules, and regulatory responsibilities. A large part of the directive deals with the regulation of markets and alternative trading systems, henceforth known as 'Multilateral trading facilities' or 'MTFs'.[71]

3.72 The main changes introduced by MiFID were the following:

- Scope: MiFID enlarged the definition of investment services to include investment advice and commodity derivatives business.
- MiFID provided for detailed harmonisation of conduct of business.
- MiFID introduced a definition of professional client.
- MiFID largely clarified the responsibilities of home and host regulators.

Agreed definition of professional client

3.73 By introducing a definition of 'professional client' in Annex II and by requiring Member States to distinguish between professional investors and retail investors when applying their conduct of business rules, MiFID paved the way for more proportionate regulation of conduct of business in all Member States.

Resolving the home/host conflict

3.74 MiFID dealt with the conflict of regulatory jurisdiction over services business which had emerged under the ISD by allocating sole jurisdiction over the application of MiFID conduct of business rules in relation to services business carried on by a MiFID firm to the home State of that firm.[72] Services provided by a branch 'within its territory' would be the responsibility of the State of the branch. But this did not answer the question of when services were provided within the territory of a Member State—the same question which had bedevilled regulatory relations since the implementation of the Second Banking Directive and the ISD.[73] The Electronic Commerce Directive ('ECD') had earlier sidestepped the issue by allocating jurisdiction over services provided via the Internet etc ('information society services') to the country of origin, ie the country from which they were provided, irrespective of the country of destination and irrespective of

---

[71] For a detailed account of the market aspects of MiFID, see *Financial Markets and Exchanges Law* (OUP, 2007), ch 11.

[72] Art 31(1).

[73] See paras 3.62–3.63 above.

whether they were provided from the home State or from a branch in another Member State.[74] CESR issued a consultation paper in December 2006 dealing with services jurisdiction and other MiFID issues. But it was clear that it felt unable to impose a common interpretation on CESR members. In guidance issued in May 2007[75] CESR summarised the views of consultees and indicated that it was seeking a definitive interpretation from the Commission of Article 32(7).

MiFID and maximum harmonisation

The changes introduced by MiFID purporting to provide for maximum harmo-   **3.75**
nisation of conduct of business rules are also open to differing interpretations. It is debatable whether MiFID clearly provides for maximum harmonisation. Article 19(10) of MiFID authorises the Commission to adopt Level 2 measures in 'order to ensure the necessary protection of investors and the uniform application of paragraphs 1 to 8 . . .'. Is the reference to 'uniform application' sufficient to convert the harmonisation provisions into maximum harmonisation?

The wording of the Level 2 Directive, Directive 2006/73, is much clearer;   **3.76**
Article 4(2) states that:

> Member States may retain or impose requirements additional to those in this direc-
> tive only in those exceptional cases where such requirements are objectively justified
> and proportionate so as to address specific risks to investor protection or to market
> integrity that are not adequately addressed by this Directive and provided that one of
> the following conditions is met . . .'

But although the Level 2 Directive spells out that Member States cannot go fur-   **3.77**
ther than the directive, except in certain circumstances, this is wording that one would expect to find in MiFID itself if Member States genuinely intended it to be a maximum harmonisation directive. Moreover the proposition that MiFID is a maximum harmonisation measure is based on the premise that it and the Level 2 implementing measures deal adequately at EU level with investor protection. It seems odd, to say the least, to allow the Level 2 Directive, rather than MiFID, to provide for exceptions on the grounds that it does not address specific risks. If the MiFID Level 1 provisions constitute maximum harmonisation, they ought also to authorise any exceptions. A Level 2 measure should not be able to provide for exceptions to a Level 1 measure except where expressly authorised by the Level 1 measure, nor can a Level 2 measure convert Level 1 provisions into maximum harmonisation provisions, if the wording of the Level 1 measure does not clearly and unambiguously support that interpretation.

---

[74] See para 3.93 below.
[75] CESR, 'The Passport under MiFID: Recommendations for the Implementation of the Directive 2004/39/EC' (May 2007). The Commission response of 18 June 2007 was disappoint-ing: it did not come up with a definitive view.

3.78 As against this, it can be argued that MiFID is a Lamfalussy directive and maximum harmonisation was one of the main recommendations in the Lamfalussy Report.[76] Moreover, Member States appear to have accepted the provisions of the Level 2 Directive at face value, at least for the time being. The UK has sought Commission approval for a few additional provisions[77] and has concluded that other domestic provisions which might be judged inconsistent with Article 4(2) fall outside the scope of MiFID.

Single Market Legislation—Compensation

Deposit insurance and investor compensation

3.79 The impact of EU law extends to investor compensation and depositor protection but not as yet to the protection of policyholders, though a proposal on insurance guarantee schemes is now in the pipeline. Broadly speaking, the Deposit Guarantee Directive[78] and the Investor Compensation Directive[79] provide for small depositors and investors to be compensated by the protection scheme established under the relevant directives in the home State of the authorised bank or investment firm, even where the claim arises in respect of business done with a branch in another Member State.

3.80 It is therefore important to be aware of the requirements of the Investor Compensation Directive and the Deposit Guarantee Directive and the way in which they have been implemented, not only in the UK but also in other Member States. UCITS Management Companies which benefit from a passport under the UCITS Management Companies Directive[80] are now also covered by the Investor Compensation Directive.

3.81 It proved easier to integrate the Deposit Guarantee Directive with UK law than the later Investor Compensation Directive. The difficulty in implementing the Investor Compensation Directive was mainly due to the fact that the UK had already established a comprehensive system of investor compensation under the Financial Services Act, applying to a far wider range of investment firms and investment business than those covered by the directive and providing a higher

---

[76] Though neither the Market Abuse Directive nor the Transparency Directive purports to be a maximum harmonisation measure.

[77] See the Article 4 Notification made by HM Treasury on 18 September 2007 covering inter alia dealing commissions and packaged products. Available at <http://www.hm-treasury.gov.uk>.

[78] Directive 94/19/EEC on deposit guarantee schemes [1994] OJ L135/5.

[79] Directive 97/9/EC on investor compensation schemes [1997] OJ L22.

[80] Directive 2001/107/EC on management companies and simplified prospectuses [2002] OJ L41/20.

level of compensation. Compensation was, however, restricted under the previous UK scheme to claims in respect of investment business carried on in the UK.

Reconciling the two regimes has resulted in a complicated set of provisions in the **3.82** Compensation Sourcebook in the FSA Handbook. Any claim for compensation needs to be analysed in terms of whether it falls within the scope of either of the two Directives in the first instance. The level of compensation available will depend on which scheme is responsible for compensating investors, whether the claim arose in respect of branch business outside the home State, the level of compensation provided by the branch State (the 'host State'), and the level of compensation provided by the home State.

The reason why both home and host State compensation schemes may need to be **3.83** considered in relation to a directive claim is because under the Deposit Guarantee Directive and the Investor Compensation Directive, investment firms are entitled, but not required, to seek 'top-up' cover for their branch business in other Member States, where the host State's scheme is more generous than their home State scheme.[81]

Member States must ensure that, if they raise the level of compensation under **3.84** their domestic scheme, the same amount of compensation is available to depositors or investors who have done business with domestic firms through branches established in other Member States. Any discrimination against EEA depositors, investors, or policyholders will be in breach of the Treaty provisions on non-discrimination, whether or not the matter is covered by a directive. The FSA has announced[82] that it is changing the rules of the Financial Services Compensation Scheme to cover contracts of insurance issued by UK insurance undertakings through establishments in other Member States in relation to EEA risks. Previously, only contracts of insurance issued by UK insurers through an establishment in another Member State in relation to UK risks were covered.

Insurance

Plans are now underway to fill the gap at Community level for compensation to **3.85** be made available in the event of the insolvency of an insurance company. The European Commission set up a working group in February 2002 to examine the need for insurance guarantee schemes. Progress has been slower than expected, but a Commission Consultation Paper on Insurance Guarantee Schemes appeared

---

[81]   The export ban in the Deposit Guarantee Directive and the Investor Compensation Directive lapsed in 1999.

[82]   Policy Statement 08/8, Financial Services Compensation Scheme: EEA branches of UK insurers.

in May 2008,[83] analysing the problems and evaluating the options. A statement on how the Commission proposes to proceed should appear by the end of the year.

Compensation and group supervision

3.86 Home State compensation based on the default of a single entity, whether a bank, investment firm, or insurance company, may prove increasingly difficult to recon-cile with the principle of group or consolidated supervision under the Financial Conglomerates Directive and Solvency II and with any move to introduce the concept of group insolvency in EU legislation.[84]

Consumer Protection

3.87 EU harmonisation of conduct of business rules is principally designed to harmo-nise those rules aimed at protecting the retail investor or retail policyholder, on the basis that differences in national law in this area constitute a barrier to free move-ment of services and Community measures can facilitate the further integration of the internal market. In the financial services area, most EU harmonisation legislation is devised on a sectoral basis and aimed at specific types of financial institution such as banks, insurance companies, and investment firms. In general, however, the attempts to harmonise conduct of business rules apply only to invest-ment business and the marketing of insurance.[85]

Consumer protection directives

3.88 UK financial institutions have to contend not only with the specific 'vertical' sec-toral directives such as MiFID and the Life Assurance Directive, but also with the 'horizontal' consumer protection directives, so-called because they apply across the board to all businesses dealing with consumers. Directives such as the Unfair Contract Terms Directive,[86] and the Distance Marketing Directive ('DMD')[87] have had a significant impact on the domestic law governing the marketing of

---

[83] Markt 2008/08.

[84] See for example the Commission Report on Responses to the Public Consultation on Reorganisation and Winding up of Credit Institutions.

[85] Insurance Mediation Directive (Directive 2002/92/EC [2002] OJ L9/3).

[86] Directive 93/13/ EEC on unfair terms in consumer contracts [1995] OJ L95/29. See below para 3.95.

[87] Directive 2002/65/EC on the distance marketing of consumer financial services [2002] OJ L271/16.

financial services, together with the Electronic Commerce Directive,[88] which is not, however, limited to consumer business.

Definition of consumer

EU consumer protection law protects all consumers, usually defined as 'any natural person who is acting for purposes which are outside his trade, business or profession',[89] regardless of the consumer's level of sophistication. EU sectoral directives on the other hand, such as MiFID, aim to tailor regulation more appropriately to the needs of the end user by requiring conduct of business rules to take into account the retail or professional client or potential clients. The result at the UK level may be that the FSA is obliged to require firms to provide unnecessary and unwanted protections for sophisticated individual customers, because of the obligation to implement a particular consumer protection directive. Conversely, small and medium-sized companies are unprotected under EU consumer laws, though they are treated in the same way as consumers under financial services directives such as the Investor Compensation Directive and the Deposit Guarantee Directive.

3.89

Distance Marketing Directive

The DMD requires Member States to distinguish between the information to be given to investors, policyholders, and other consumers before they enter into a distance contract for the provision of financial services and non-distance contracts. The Directive is based on the premise that distance selling creates additional risks for investors, though some Member States, including the UK take the view that high pressure sales techniques carried out face to face could be equally, if not more, damaging. The DMD requires information to be given to the consumer about the firm, the service being provided, including any risks attached, the contract and the applicable law, the price payable, cancellation rights, and redress mechanisms. The effect of the DMD provisions on cancellation rights has been to add substantially to the complexity of the cancellation provisions in the FSA Handbook. The DMD presented the FSA with the classic dilemma of whether to apply the new requirements to all products and services or whether to create a new distinction in the rulebook between distance and non-distance selling. In the end, the FSA decided to create two regimes, ostensibly to avoid imposing additional costs on firms, and while the resulting complexity has avoided accusations of goldplating, it does little to improve the coherence of the Rulebook.

3.90

---

[88] See below para 3.93.
[89] Art 2 of the Distance Marketing Directive.

3.91 The DMD also raises questions about regulatory jurisdiction in relation to cross-border distance selling. The Directive started off as an attempt to impose 'maximum harmonisation' rules to be applied by the 'country of origin'. Had it been successful, this would have meant that a Member State would no longer be able to impose higher standards than the Community norm, even on its own nationals. This would have allowed financial institutions to market their products and services throughout the EU on the basis of a single set of Community standards. It would also have had the advantage of defusing the arguments over jurisdiction since, if all Member State rules are the same, the question of whose rules apply becomes much less important.

3.92 Unfortunately, the agreed text of the Distance Marketing Directive did not adopt the maximum harmonisation approach throughout. Nor did it opt unambiguously for country of origin control. The final version contains some maximum harmonisation provisions but also allows Member States for example to continue to apply the additional information requirements of the Life Assurance Directive, requirements which are based on minimum harmonisation and which are the responsibility of the host State. The result is uncertainty not only about whose rules apply in relation to a particular issue, but also whether those rules are maximum or minimum requirements. The UK has, however, taken the view that it is implicit on the basis of the transitional provisions in Article 16 of the DMD that it should be implemented on a country of origin basis. Whether this has succeeded in defusing any potential regulatory conflict depends on whether other Member States have taken the same approach.

Electronic Commerce Directive

3.93 The 'country of origin' test for jurisdiction had first appeared in the ECD[90] and should be distinguished from both the home and host State approaches. The Directive was designed to liberalise the provision of 'information society services', essentially services provided via the web, email, or mobile phones. The Member State where the service provider is established is responsible for ensuring compliance with the directive in respect of services provided from that State. The State of establishment, or the country of origin as it has come to be known, is the State where the service provider pursues an economic activity through a fixed establishment for an indefinite period. Thus where internet services are provided from a branch of a financial institution in another Member State, the branch State, as opposed to the home State, will be responsible for ensuring compliance with the ECD. The State into which the services are provided—the country of destination—is

---

[90] Directive 2000/31/EC [2000] OJ L178/1. For a detailed analysis of the ECD, see *Financial Markets and Exchanges Law* (OUP, 2007), ch 12.

not allowed to impose restrictions on the inward provision of information society services.

The ECD applies to all undertakings providing information society services, **3.94** including financial institutions, but its provisions have posed particular problems in implementation, because of its territorial scope which differs from that of the DMD and many of the sectoral directives.[91]

Unfair Contract Terms Directive

The Unfair Contract Terms Directive aims to protect consumers against unfair **3.95** contract terms by requiring terms in consumer contracts to be drafted in plain and intelligible language, with any ambiguities being interpreted in the consumer's favour. The FSA is one of the authorities in the UK designated to enforce the provisions of the UCTD in the UK. Its powers under the Unfair Terms in Consumer Contracts Regulations enable it to challenge unfair contract terms used by regulated firms in standard form contracts. Ultimately it can force firms to stop using such terms.

Single Market Legislation—Issuer Disclosure

EU law has had a significant impact on issuer disclosure requirements. The first **3.96** step was taken in 1979 with the Admissions Directive[92] which harmonised the conditions applicable to official listing. This was followed by the Listing Particulars Directive,[93] the Regular Information Directive,[94] the Directive on Acquisition of Major Shareholdings,[95] and the Directive on Mutual Recognition of Listing Particulars.[96] Together these resulted in a comprehensive disclosure regime for securities admitted to official listing.

It was not until 1989 that disclosure requirements for unlisted securities were **3.97** addressed. The Public Offers Directive[97] laid down a similar disclosure regime to apply to unlisted securities offered to the public for the first time in a Member State.

---

[91] See Chapter 13 below.
[92] Directive 79/279/EEC on admission of securities to Official Stock Exchange Listing [1979] OJ L66/21, now consolidated in Directive 2001/34/EC [2001] OJ L184/1.
[93] Directive 80/390/EEC [1980] OJ L100/1 now consolidated in Directive 2001/34/EC.
[94] Directive 82/121/EEC [1982] OJ L48/26. The directive has been replaced by the Transparency Directive whose provisions are now consolidated in Directive 2001/34/EC.
[95] Directive 88/627/EEC, now consolidated in Directive 2001/34/EC.
[96] Directive 90/211/EEC [1990] OJ L112/24.
[97] Directive 89/298/EEC [1989] OJ L124/8, replaced by the Prospectus Directive (Directive 2003/71/EC).

3.98   The harmonisation of disclosure requirements was seen as an essential step in the integration of capital markets in the EU, by providing equivalent protection for investors throughout the EU. This, it was hoped, would encourage issuers to seek official listing on a number of stock exchanges or to engage in multiple issues by reducing the costs involved in complying with widely differing requirements. Common disclosure standards were also designed to foster investor confidence, thereby leading to greater interpenetration of the national securities markets.

3.99   Unfortunately these ambitions were not realised. During the 1990s it became clear that the EU was still a long way from achieving the benefits of a single capital market. One of the more visible failures was the lack of any significant number of cross-border issues, due largely to the ability of host Member States to impose additional requirements on the issuer and to require the translation of the prospectus into the local language. Another defect of the former EU regime was its concentration on officially listed securities while ignoring the requirements applying to admission to trading on a regulated market.

Prospectus Directive

3.100   The result was the adoption of two major directives under the Lamfalusssy procedures—the Prospectus Directive ('PD')[98] and the Transparency Directive.[99] The PD has been implemented in the UK in the Prospectus Regulations 2005 and the FSA's Prospectus Rules.

3.101   The main significance of the PD is that it introduces a passporting system for issuers so that a prospectus approved by the competent authorities of one Member State must be accepted by any other Member State as valid for an offer of securities to the public in that Member State or for admission of securities to trading on a regulated market operating in the Member State. The PD also contains a definition of 'offer to the public' which was conspicuously lacking in the old Prospectus Directive. The definition is, however, very wide and may be interpreted differently by Member States.[100]

3.102   The host Member State has no power to approve the prospectus or to impose additional requirements. Nor can a host Member State require a translation of the whole listing particulars, if the original is drawn up in English. Only a translation of the summary note prepared by the issuer can be required in this case. If the issuer seeks admission to trading on a regulated market in the host State, it may be

---

[98]   Directive 2003/71/EC [2003] OJ L345/64.
[99]   Directive 2004/109/EC [2004] OJ L390/38.
[100]   See Chapter 18 below.

required to comply with additional admission requirements, provided that these meet the general good test laid down by the European Court.[101]

The PD is also significant in that it is a 'maximum harmonisation' Directive. **3.103** Member States are not permitted therefore to impose requirements on issuers, even domestic issuers, beyond those laid down in the directive in respect of matters covered by the directive. This raises questions about the continuing ability of the FSA as the UK competent authority to impose rules on issuers which go beyond the requirements of the directive. The validity of FSA requirements going beyond those of the PD will depend on analysis of the scope of the directive, as determined by the provisions of the directive itself, the legal base for the directive, and any clarification provided by the recitals to the directive.

Finally the PD is significant in that non-EU issuers can take advantage of rights **3.104** under the directive—rights which were previously only available to EU issuers, ie EU nationals—by selecting the EU home State of their choice. The new open market policy was dictated largely by economic and political considerations, the EU seeking to encourage the increasing numbers of third country issuers seeking access to EU capital markets,[102] in line with the FSAP aspiration of creating a 'single deep liquid EU market'.

Transparency Directive

The Transparency Directive ('TD')[103] was adopted in 2004 under the Lamfalussy **3.105** procedures. Implementation should have been completed by all Member States by January 2007. Although the TD is a Lamfalussy directive, unlike the PD it is not a maximum harmonisation directive. It was designed to improve the quality, quantity, and timeliness of periodic information for investors in securities admitted to trading on a regulated market and is a key measure in improving corporate governance.[104] Responsibility for ensuring compliance by issuers rests with the regulator in the home State of the issuer, ie the state of incorporation for EU issuers. Third country issuers can choose a 'home State' within the EU, as under the PD. The home State of the issuer can impose more stringent requirements than those in the TD, whereas the host State of the regulated market is prohibited from going further than the directive.

The TD requirements build on the provisions of Regulation 1606/2002 on the **3.106** application of international accounting standards and introduce requirements on

---

[101] See paras 3.65–3.70 above.
[102] Contrast the approach taken in the E-Commerce Directive whose benefits are available only to EU nationals.
[103] Directive 2004/109/EC [2004] OJ L390/38.
[104] See paras 3.107–3.111 below.

the content and timing of annual and half-yearly financial reports, together with interim management statements for issuers of shares who did not already produce quarterly reports. The provisions on disclosure of major shareholdings, which originally applied only to officially listed companies under the Major Shareholdings Directive, are amended and now extend to companies admitted to trading on a regulated market.

Corporate Governance

3.107 There is no generally accepted definition of 'corporate governance'. Within the EU it is used to describe the way in which companies are directed and controlled and the law and practice in Member States varies widely. Before September 2001, when the Commission set up the High-Level Group of Company Law Experts, it was looked on as a matter for national company law. The High-Level Group soon turned its attention to corporate governance issues, producing recommendations in November 2002. The Commission response was that there was no need for a European Corporate Governance Code. However, the collapse of Enron in the USA and of Parmalat in the EU focused attention on the damage caused to investor confidence by large corporate failures. The Commission in its 2003 proposals for 'Modernising Company Law and Enhancing Corporate Governance in the European Union—a Plan to Move Forward' concentrated on strengthening shareholder rights and on improving transparency in the way companies are run.

Takeover Directive

3.108 The Takeover Directive proved to be a lamentable failure in improving shareholder rights in relation to takeover bids. The Directive has entrenched rather than removed many of the barriers to cross-border takeovers and several Member States seem to have taken full advantage of the options and exemptions available to exclude shareholders from exercising control.[105]

Accounting Directives

3.109 Directive 2006/46[106] amended the earlier accounting directives. Significantly this required EU incorporated companies which are admitted to trading on an EU regulated market to produce an annual corporate governance statement as a separate part of the annual report. The statement should provide shareholders with

---

[105] See Report on Implementation of the Takeover Directive, February 2007.
[106] Directive 2006/46/EC [2006] OJ L224/1.

key information about the corporate governance practices of the company, including a description of the risk management systems and internal controls in relation to the financial reporting process. In particular, the statement should make clear whether the company applies any corporate governance practices other than those stipulated by national law.

Directive on Shareholders' Rights

In June 2007, the Directive on Shareholders' Rights[107] was adopted. This again **3.110** applies to EU companies admitted to trading on an EU regulated market and imposed minimum standards in respect of information to be provided to shareholders before the general meeting. It also requires shareholders to be given simple means to vote at a distance and abolishes share blocking.

One share, one vote

As a result of the 2006 consultation on future priorities for the Company Law **3.111** Action Plan, the Commission decided to rethink its strategy in this area. In line with its capital markets policy following completion of the FSAP, the Commission concluded that the case for EU legislative intervention needed to be supported by clear evidence of market need. It took the opportunity in October 2007 to abandon its 'one share, one vote' plans after publication of a study which demonstrated no economic evidence of a causal link between deviations from the so-called 'proportionality principle' and the economic performance of companies. The Commission's view was that shareholders should use their existing voting rights to press for enhanced transparency and better dialogue between companies and their shareholders and that EU legislation now provided ample provisions on transparency.

Insider Dealing and Market Abuse

The other aspect of market regulation that received attention at EU level was that **3.112** of insider dealing. The 1989 Insider Dealing Directive ('IDD')[108] was the first attempt to outlaw insider dealing in all EC Member States.

The IDD emphasised the importance of equality of access to information. The **3.113** obligation imposed on issuers in the Admissions Directive to inform the public as soon as possible of any major developments which were likely to affect the price

---

[107] Directive 2007/36/EC [2007] OJ L184/17.
[108] Directive 89/592/EEC [1989] OJ L334/30.

of the issuers' shares was extended by the IDD to all companies whose securities were admitted to trading on an official market.

Market Abuse Directive

3.114 The EU provisions on insider dealing were to remain unchanged until the adoption of the Market Abuse Directive ('MAD')[109] in 2003. The Directive was intended to enhance the integrity of EU financial markets by establishing a common EU-wide framework for preventing and detecting market abuse and for ensuring a proper flow of information to the market. MAD not only updated the insider dealing provisions in the IDD but also introduced the concept of market manipulation, the opportunities for which had grown considerably due to the increase in cross-border trading, the development of common trading platforms by investment exchanges, the variety of new investment products and trading venues, and the growing number of market participants. 'Market manipulation' was designed to cover the case where a person seeks to distort the price of financial instruments, or effect transactions or orders to trade, or disseminates information in a manner which gives or is likely to give false or misleading signals about financial instruments.

3.115 On insider dealing, MAD prohibits anyone in possession of inside information from dealing (or attempting to deal) in relevant 'securities', a term which, for the purposes of the directive, includes financial and commodity derivatives. MAD sets out three categories of inside information to cater for:

- financial instruments which are not commodity derivatives
- commodity derivatives
- intermediaries executing client orders.

3.116 MAD also defines three ways in which financial markets can be manipulated, for example through the dissemination of false or misleading rumours, using some form of deception when trading, or where transactions or orders to trade could give false or misleading signals as to the demand or supply of a price, or where the price was deliberately fixed at an abnormal or artificial level, unless this was for a legitimate reason and it conformed to accepted market practice.

3.117 As well as prohibiting market abuse, MAD aims to improve the flow of information to the market by requiring prompt disclosure of inside information by all issuers whose securities were admitted to trading on a regulated market. Share dealings by insiders, as defined under the directive, now have to be disclosed, and anyone producing investment research has to ensure that the information is

---

[109] Directive 2003/6/EC [2003] OJ L96/16. See below Chapters 8 and 9.

presented fairly and any interests or conflicts of interest are disclosed. MAD also requires those arranging financial transactions to notify the competent authority of any suspicious transactions which might constitute market abuse.

The trigger for application of the directive is the admission to trading (or an application for admission to trading) of any financial instrument on any EU regulated market. The directive then applies to all transactions in the EU in that instrument, whether the transaction is undertaken on or off a regulated market. MAD is the first directive to stipulate that each Member State should designate a single competent authority with ultimate responsibility for ensuring compliance with the directive. The directive also goes further than other directives in requiring competent authorities to be given a range of powers to enforce the provisions of the directive. Although MAD requires Member State competent authorities to cooperate in dealing with market abuse, in recognition of the fact that securities trading was increasingly international in nature, the provisions on jurisdiction in the directive are not always clear. For example Article 10 of MAD envisages the authorities in the Member State where the conduct took place having jurisidiction to take action, as well as the authorities in the Member State on whose market the securities were admitted to trading. **3.118**

Money Laundering

The origins of EU money laundering legislation can be found in the Recommendations issued by the Financial Action Task Force on Money Laundering (FATF)—a body set up by the G-7 in 1989. The First EU Directive (1MLD), which was adopted in 1991[110] implemented in EU law the 40 FATF recommendations which had been adopted at that stage. 1MLD concentrated on the laundering of drugs money through banks (or credit institutions) and other financial institutions. **3.119**

The Second Money Laundering Directive ('2MLD')[111] extended the definition of money laundering to cover the laundering of the proceeds of 'serious crime' while a range of non-financial institutions were brought within the net for the first time, such as lawyers, notaries, accountants, estate agents, art dealers, jewellers, auctioneers, and casinos. The customer identification requirements were tightened up and a prohibition on 'tipping off' was introduced. **3.120**

---

[110] Directive 91/308/EEC [1991] OJ L166/77, now replaced by the Third Money Laundering Directive.
[111] Directive 2001/97/EC [2001] OJ L344/76, now replaced by the Third Money Laundering Directive.

Third Money Laundering Directive

3.121   The Third Money Laundering Directive[112] ('3MLD') was adopted in 2005, and should have been implemented by all Member States by December 2007.[113] 3MLD implements the June 2003 FATF recommendations and replaces 1 and 2MLD; it extends the definition of money laundering still further to cover not only concealing or disguising the proceeds of serious crime, but also the financing of terrorism. This is caught irrespective of whether the funds involved have been lawfully or criminally acquired.

3.122   The other major changes introduced by 3MLD involve new definitions of 'politically exposed person', 'beneficial owner', and 'trust or company service provider'. The provisions dealing with beneficial owners and trusts have presented problems for the UK in implementation.[114] The Directive also incorporates the FATF recommendations on the adoption of a risk-based approach to identification and verification of customer identity, introducing a simplified due diligence procedure for some cases and enhanced due diligence in others. 3MLD widens the possibility of relying on third parties for identification and verification purposes but leaves ultimate responsibility with the firm itself. Reliance can also be placed on third parties in other jurisdictions where those jurisdictions are deemed to have regimes equivalent to the EU. The Commission is authorised to draw up a list of non-equivalent jurisdictions, which is binding on Member States.

---

[112]   Directive 2005/60/EC of 26 October 2005 on the prevention of the use of the financial system for the purpose of money laundering and terrorist financing [2005] OJ L309/15.

[113]   The Commission announced in June 2008 that it was opening infringement proceedings against 15 Member States for failure to implement 3MLD by the deadline of December 2007—see Chapter 10 below.

[114]   See Chapter 10 below.

4

INTERNATIONAL AGREEMENTS AND SUPRANATIONAL BODIES

Issues of extra-territoriality or disputes of jurisdictional authority inevitably come to the fore as spaces and the rules which govern them are contested. Spaces and rule-making authority may come to be shared, but the ways in which they are shared and the outcomes of such sharing depend upon the institutional mechanisms which are established to deal with jurisdictional disputes.[1]

Global Markets, Local Regulation

Much has been written and said about globalisation and whether it is, in fact, now an irresistible force, particularly in the global economy.[2] The financial markets have shown themselves increasingly to be a global process 'not hindered or prevented by territorial or jurisdictional boundaries'[3] but they are, nonetheless, markets which continue to operate within the bounds of both economic activity and national political and legal regulation[4] or a system of 'international cooperation based on home country control'.[5]   **4.01**

'All legislation is prima facie territorial'[6] but in the past 60 years, national legal and regulatory systems have had to deal increasingly with the impact of trans-national   **4.02**

---

[1] A Hudson, 'Beyond the Borders: Globalisation, Sovereignty and Extra-territoriality' (1998) *Geopolitics* 3(1), 89–105.

[2] 'With global flows of capital and the internationalisation of production, we live in a world in which the complexity of spatial relations is more obvious than the simple legalistic maps of state sovereignty' RBJ Walker, *Inside/Outside: International Relations as Political Theory* (1993).

[3] Rosenau, 'The dynamics of globalisation: toward an operational framework', (1996) *International Studies Association.*

[4] AC Hudson, 'Reshaping the regulatory landscape: border skirmishes around the Bahamas and Cayman offshore centres', (1998) *Review of International Political Economy*, 5:3.

[5] EB Kapstein, 'Shockproof, the end of the Financial Crisis', (1996) *Foreign Affairs*, Jan/Feb.

[6] *American Banana Co v United Fruit Co* 213 US 347, 357 (1909) ('The foregoing considerations would lead, in case of doubt, to a construction of any statute as intended to be confined in

effects in relation to competition and anti-trust issues (the US Uranium anti-trust cases of the 1970s and more recently the Hartford Fire and Boeing/McDonnell Douglas investigations), environmental issues (Chernobyl and other environmental and pollution cases), human rights issues, the 'war on terrorism' (intelligence sharing and stopping terrorist financing), and economic turmoil created by the 'credit crunch' and its consequences.[7] Numerous agreements have been negotiated and international or supranational bodies have been established in order to foster cooperation between governments, between regulators, and between industry participants to overcome the obstacles to the continued development of the financial markets and to maximise the benefits of a global financial market.[8]

4.03 However, the growth of globalisation can also lead to political problems resulting from the loss of national sovereignty and the diminution of governmental autonomy; and the economic and social problems resulting from the impact of trade internationalisation.[9] Supranational bodies have tended to be comprised of the powerful, eg the Group of 10 ('G-10'),[10] who have the greatest interest and the most to gain by a global, collaborative approach. This does not mean that regional multilateral bodies and cooperation are ineffective, only that their impact is generally less than those comprised of and representing the interests of the more developed countries. Nor does it mean that the developed countries will always take a cooperative approach especially if they perceive their national or economic interests would be damaged thereby. However, all of these bodies depend upon the give and take of discussion, negotiation, and collaboration to reach their objectives, and some have been more successful than others in achieving those goals.

4.04 This chapter sets out some of the international agreements and supranational bodies in the banking and financial services sector that carry out a wide range of functions including collating collective research and the compilation of statistics, acting as a forum for discussion and debate, providing a framework for standard setting, establishing compliance and monitoring standards or rules, and mediating disputes between national interests.

---

its operation and effect to the territorial limits over which the lawmaker has general and legitimate power. "All legislation is prima facie territorial"' quoting *Ex parte Blain*, LR 12 Ch Div 522, 528).

[7] See Joacquin Almunia, 'Building and Sustaining Solid Financial Markets: challenges for international cooperation', Economic and Social Council of the United Nations (Speech 08/192) 14 April 2008.

[8] For a useful overview, see Ethan B Kapstein, BIS Working Papers, No 199, *Architects of stability? International cooperation among financial supervisors*, BIS Monetary and Economic Department, February 2006 <http://www.bis.org/publ/work199.pdf>.

[9] VA Schmidt, 'The New World Order, Incorporated: The Rise of Business and the Decline of the Nation State', (1995) *Daedalus*, Vol 124, no 2 spring.

[10] See n 86 below.

International Bodies and International Agreements

International bodies and international agreements in the banking and financial **4.05**
services sector have tended to follow the trend in capital flows and generally have
served to expand cross-border competition or to promote financial stability or to
facilitate cross-border financial transactions.[11]

Broadly speaking, international bodies and agreements can be broken down into **4.06**
several broad categories: inter-governmental trade and services agreements, inter-
regulator agreements, international technical agreements and trade and professional body agreements, and industry codes of conduct.[12]

There are a number of inter-governmental trade and services agreements that have **4.07**
an impact on the financial sector. The World Trade Organisation ('WTO') is
probably the most notable and its role and structure will be dealt with later in this
chapter. However, there are other organisations such as the United Nations
Conference on Trade and Development ('UNCTAD') that have had a significant
impact on the development of banking and capital markets around the world.

UNCTAD, established in 1964 to promote the development-friendly integration **4.08**
of developing countries into the world economy, provides a forum for inter-
governmental deliberations supported by discussions with experts and exchanges
of experience. It also undertakes research, policy analysis, and data collection for
the debates of government representatives and experts. It also provides technical
assistance to developing countries with special attention to the needs of the
least developed countries and of economies in transition. UNCTAD also jointly
sponsors with the WTO the International Trade Centre ('ITC') that deals with
the operational aspects of trade development with an emphasis on trade promotion. The ITC is industry facing in contrast to UNCTAD's primarily government
facing role and ITC's technical assistance focuses on assisting businesses in developing countries. UNCTAD also cooperates with UN regional commissions to
support international projects in various developing countries.[13]

The second category of international agreement is that of inter-regulator agree- **4.09**
ments and memoranda of understanding ('MOU') particularly in the areas of
international cooperation and information sharing. Bodies such as the International

---

[11] WR White, 'International agreements in the area of banking and finance: accomplishments
and outstanding issues', BIS Working Paper No 38, October 1996. See also GA Walker, *International
Banking Regulation Law, Policy and Practice* (2001) ch 5.

[12] White, n 11 above, 4.

[13] <http://www.unctad.org>. See also Report of the Panel of Eminent Persons: *Enhancing
the Development Role and Impact of UNCTAD* (June 2006). (<http://www.unctad.org/sections/
edm_dir/docs/osg20061_en.pdf>)

Organisation of Securities Commissions ('IOSCO') have led the way in promoting the use of MOUs as an effective regulatory device. In 1991, the Technical Committee of IOSCO released its 'Principles for Memoranda of Understanding'[14] which provided a blueprint for securities and futures regulators to use when developing MOUs with their counterparts. These Principles covered the subject matter of the MOU, confidentiality, implementation procedures, the rights of persons subject to an MOU request, consultation, public policy exception, types of assistance, permitted uses, participation by the requesting authority, and cost-sharing.

4.10 In many cases, MOUs have enabled regulators to agree the basis on which they will be able to share information on a bilateral basis between the relevant requesting and requested market authorities. Although not legally enforceable, these MOUs are usually trigger-based agreements where information is shared once certain triggering events have occurred. Pre-agreed exposure levels are part of this triggering mechanism because they permit an integrated multilateral assessment of market risks. So a significant decrease in a member's capital position, or large cash flows in proprietary or customer accounts, or a concentration of positions in any futures or options contract may all trigger the need for information sharing between regulatory authorities. All information shared is generally kept confidential, even if the MOU is terminated.

4.11 Whilst home supervisors have organisation-wide supervisory oversight responsibility, cooperation with host supervisors on issues related to the operation of firms in host markets is essential. In May 1996, the Basel Committee[15] and IOSCO agreed to promote additional cooperative and collaborative arrangements to improve their supervision of diversified financial groups.[16] The principal focus of their initiative is the types of groups or institutions for which such arrangements would be useful and appropriate, the types of information that may need to be exchanged, ways to facilitate the resolution of possible legal, confidentiality, policy, or practical issues that may arise, and any additional arrangements that may be appropriate to coordinate the activities of the relevant supervisors. Other initiatives as between regulatory bodies have included 'A Report from the Regulators Participating in the Windsor Meeting'[17] that detailed the progress domestic

---

[14] <http://www.iosco.org/library/pubdocs/pdf/IOSCOPD17.pdf>. For comment, see GA Walker, 'International Supervisory Co-operation', in W Blair, A Allison, G Morton, P Richards-Carpenter, GA Walker, and N Walmsley, *Banking and Financial Services Regulation*, (3rd edn, 2002) ch 1.

[15] See para 4.117.

[16] IOSCO, 'A Resolution Concerning Cross-Border Transactions' <http://www.iosco.org/library/resolutions/pdf/IOSCORES12.pdf.>

[17] The Windsor Declaration arose out of a meeting in May 1995 of representatives of the regulatory authorities of 16 countries responsible for supervising the activities of the world's major futures and options markets. The Windsor declaration sought to address the areas of cooperation between market authorities, protection of customer positions, funds and assets, default procedures, and regulatory cooperation in emergencies. The President's Committee of IOSCO adopted a resolution supporting further work by the IOSCO Technical Committee as discussed in the Windsor Declaration.

regulators[18] had made towards sharing information with their peers from other countries.

However, instances have arisen where regulatory cooperation may not always be **4.12** the case. The Technical Committee of IOSCO addressed the issue in its 'Report on Issues Raised for Securities and Futures Regulators by Under-Regulated and Uncooperative Jurisdictions'[19] and the consequent resolution committing IOSCO members to provide cooperation and assistance in regulatory matters.[20] Similarly, following the *Sumitomo* case, supervisors of commodity futures markets from 17 countries met in London to discuss the oversight of commodity futures markets. The 'London Communiqué on the Supervision of Commodity Futures Markets'[21] was subsequently released by the Japanese Ministry of International Trade and Industry in conjunction with the Japanese Ministry of Agriculture, Forestry and Fisheries, the US Commodity Futures Trading Commission, and the UK Securities and Investments Board. Such communiqués are, however, statements of intent rather than enforceable agreements but they form an important part of the regulator's armoury.

Similar agreements have arisen in the funds industry[22] where the insolvency or **4.13** threatened insolvency of a fund manager, trustee, custodian, or affiliated companies of any of these entities can often trigger a crisis of confidence. The IOSCO Discussion paper, 'Regulatory Cooperation in Emergencies'[23] identified the main scenarios of emergencies in the funds industry and considered the relevant regulatory cooperation policies and, in particular, the policies for determining suspension of redemption of units in collective investment schemes.

Cooperation between home and host country supervisors also needed addressing **4.14** in relation to Year 2000 cross-border issues. In a paper titled, 'Supervisory Cooperation on Year 2000 Cross-Border Issues',[24] the Basel Committee put forward five recommendations to ensure that banking supervisors were prepared. Finally, the issue of global financial conglomerates has given rise to a number of other regulatory responses and the Principles for the Supervision of Financial

---

[18] The following countries participated in the Windsor meeting: Australia, Brazil, Canada, France, Germany, Hong Kong, Italy, Japan, the Netherlands, Singapore, South Africa, Spain, Sweden, Switzerland, United Kingdom, and the United States of America.

[19] <http://riskinstitute.ch/140190.htm>.

[20] <http://www.iosco.org/library/resolutions/pdf/IOSCORES11.pdf>.

[21] <http://www.cftc.gov/opa/press96/opaderiv2.htm>.

[22] See 'Discussion Paper on International Cooperation in Relation to Cross-Border Activity of Collective Investment Schemes' (1996) that included a template of a mutual recognition agreement and a declaration on Co-operation and Supervision of Cross-Border Investment Management Activity that provides a framework for providing regular information about relevant cross-border activity.

[23] IOSCO, Technical Committee, Working Group 5.

[24] Basel Committee on Banking Supervision, Publication 38.

Conglomerates[25] prepared by the tripartite group of bank, securities, and insurance regulators, and the Joint Forum's Framework for Supervisory Information Sharing[26] built upon the Tripartite Committee's recommendations that supervisory cooperation should be one of the eight major principles of financial supervision.[27]

4.15 In banking, regulatory cooperation began with the bank supervisors' Concordat of 1975.[28] A revised version of the Concordat was issued in 1983, a supplement in 1990, and a normative version in 1992 ('Minimum Standards for the Supervision of International Banking Groups and Their Cross-Border Establishments')[29] that addressed the respective roles of the home and host supervisor, the need for effective consolidated supervision by the home supervisor, and the mechanics of supervisory information exchanges. Other regulatory responses have been directed to improving the global supervision of banks' international activities and BIS's 'The Supervision of Cross-Border Banking',[30] making it clear that the financial activities of international banks must be subject to effective home and host supervision. Regulators are keen to ensure that all cross-border banking operations are subject to effective home and host supervision and the BIS's 'Minimum Standards for the Supervision of International Banking Groups and their Cross-Border Establishment'[31] provided a detailed summary of the requirements and the principles for supervision.

4.16 These principles were further elaborated on in 10 key principles of information sharing issued by the G-7 finance ministers in May 1998.[32] Given the goal of improving cooperation through information-sharing, the objective of this agreement was to provide supervisors with guidance for the possible identification of a coordinator or coordinators, and identify the mechanisms from which supervisors can select in emergency and non-emergency situations. The need for regulatory cooperation across banking and financial services industry groups is also taken up by the Group of Thirty ('G-30')[33] in their report on reducing systemic risk.

---

[25] Basel Committee on Banking Supervision, Publication 47.

[26] Basel Committee on Banking Supervision, Publication 45.

[27] Basel Committee on Banking Supervision, Paper 20.

[28] Committee on Banking Regulations and Supervisory Practices, Report to the Governors on the supervision of banks' foreign establishments, BS/75/44e.

[29] Basel Committee on Banking Supervision, Publication 314.

[30] Basel Committee on Banking Supervision, Publication 27.

[31] See n 29 above.

[32] The Coordinator Paper, Bank for International Settlement, 1999.

[33] The Group of Thirty was established in 1978 as a private, non-profit, international body composed of senior representatives of the private and public sectors and academia. Its objectives are to deepen understanding of international economic and financial issues, to explore the international repercussions of decisions taken in the public and private sectors, and to examine the choices available to market practitioners and policymakers.

'Global Institutions, National Supervision and Systemic Risk'[34] examined the potential for systemic risk arising from the gap between the global operations of financial institutions and markets and nationally based systems of accounting, reporting, law, and supervision. This G-30 report concluded that regulatory cooperation across borders and functions will come about only 'if supervisors recognise their mutual interdependence and adopt common supervisory techniques'.[35,36]

Another area of development in international agreements has been in what White **4.17** calls the 'plumbing' of global banking and finance,[37] which are those technical agreements between countries, regulators, or industry participants which simply allow the system to work on a global basis. Examples of this type of agreement are the International Standards Organisation's SWIFT (Society for Worldwide Interbank Financial Telecommunication)[38] agreements. SWIFT's primary function is to establish standards and agreements between industry members and to lay down the standards for inter-bank communications and messaging. The ISO has also developed other new standards such as UNIFI to achieve standards of convergence among all organisations that develop messages to support financial business transactions.[39] Other such architectural agreements include those global standards in private law promulgated by UNIDROIT (the International Institute for the Unification of Private Law) whose basic statutory objective is to modernise and, where appropriate, harmonise uniform rules of private law. The uniform rules prepared by UNIDROIT are concerned with substantive law rules but they address legal issues arising from new technologies and changing commercial practices where transactions are trans-national by their nature.

---

[34] The Group of Thirty, A Study Group Report, 1997.

[35] Quoted in 'Risk Mitigation, Overview: Regulatory Co-operation', International Financial Risk Institute, (1999) <http://riskinstitute.ch/00013408.htm>.

[36] The G-30 has also recently established a working group on Financial Regulatory Systems. The purpose of this Financial Regulatory Systems Working Group is to assess the strengths and weaknesses of different types of regulatory systems, including looking at the three main regulatory structures adopted: integrated single financial regulator, the functional approach, and the institutional or sector-by-sector approach in the key markets including: Australia, Brazil, Canada, China, France, Germany, Hong Kong, India, Italy, Japan, Mexico, the Netherlands, Singapore, Spain, South Africa, Switzerland, the United Kingdom, and the United States. The Working Group will report in 2008.

[37] White, n 11 above, 8.

[38] SWIFT is a cooperative society under Belgian law, which its member-shareholders own and control. With 7,600 members and participants in 200 countries whose daily messaging through the system regularly exceed 9 million, SWIFT has a Board of 25 independent directors, appointed by the shareholders which is responsible for overseeing and governing the company.

[39] ISO 20022-UNIversal Financial Industry Message scheme ('UNIFI') is the international standard that defines the ISO platform for the development of financial message standards.

4.18   The final category of international cooperation is the multitude of trade body and professional organisations that establish standards, agree protocols, and adopt standard forms in the interests of their sector of the banking and financial services industry. Organisations such as International Swaps and Derivatives Inc,[40] the International Capital Markets Association,[41] and G-30 have all been instrumental in obtaining industry cooperation in a wide range of areas and developing standardised documentation and articulating industry best practice.

The World Trade Organisation and Financial Services

4.19   The World Trade Organisation ('WTO') was established in 1995 as the successor body to the General Agreement on Tariffs and Trade ('GATT') whose origins as a forum for global trade date back to the post-World War II period. Originally a system developed through a series of trade negotiations, or rounds, held under GATT, the first GATT rounds dealt mainly with tariff reductions as between member countries, but later negotiations included other areas such as antidumping and non-tariff measures and the 1986–94 Uruguay Round led to the WTO's creation.

4.20   Still fundamentally a negotiating forum, the WTO has 153 member countries accounting for over 97 per cent of world trade and another 30 countries are currently negotiating membership.

4.21   Decisions are made by the entire membership of the WTO. This is typically by consensus, and although a majority vote is also possible, it has never been used in the WTO. The WTO's agreements must be ratified by all members in accordance with their local requirements in order to be effective.

---

[40] The International Swaps and Derivatives Association Inc was founded in 1985 and is the global trade association representing participants in the privately negotiated derivatives markets such as swaps and options in all asset classes (including interest rate, currency, commodity and energy, credit and equity derivatives). ISDA has over 650 member institutions from 47 countries and has developed standard master agreements (the ISDA Master Agreement) as well as publishing a wide range of other related market documentation materials and instruments covering a variety of transaction types. It has also produced legal opinions on the enforceability of netting and collateral arrangements and acts to secure recognition of the risk-reducing effects of netting in determining capital requirements.

[41] The International Capital Market Association, which came into being on 1 July 2005 as a result of a merger between the International Securities Market Association ('ISMA') and the International Primary Market Association ('IPMA'), is the self-regulatory organisation and trade association representing the investment banks and securities firms issuing, trading, and dealing in the international capital markets worldwide. ICMA's 430 members represent all of the major participants in the global capital markets and are located in some 50 countries across the world.

The WTO's decision-making body is the Ministerial Conference that meets at   **4.22**
least once every two years. The WTO General Council is comprised of ambassadors to the WTO and heads of delegation who meet at the WTO's headquarters
in Geneva several times a year. The General Council also meets as the Trade Policy
Review Body and the Dispute Settlement Body. More specialised councils such as
the Goods Council, Services Council, and Intellectual Property (TRIPS) Council
report to the General Council as well as a number of other specialised committees,
working groups and working parties deal with the individual agreements and
other areas such as the environment, development, membership applications, and
regional trade agreements.

WTO Agreements

The WTO agreements, negotiated and signed by the member nations, provide   **4.23**
the legal ground-rules for international commerce. The WTO system's overriding
purpose is to help trade flow as freely as possible and to remove obstacles by ensuring
that individuals, companies, and governments comply with the both transparent
and predictable trade rules. There are three major areas of trade which are covered
by the WTO: the General Agreement on Tariffs and Trade ('GATT'), which
governs trade in goods, the General Agreement on Trade in Services ('GATS'),
and the Agreement on Trade-Related Aspects of Intellectual Property Rights
('TRIPS'). GATS provides for four methods of supply of services: cross-border
supply, consumption abroad, commercial presence, and presence/movement of
natural persons.

Under the WTO agreements, countries cannot normally discriminate between   **4.24**
their trading partners. Obligations contained in GATS can be categorised into
two categories: general obligations which apply directly and automatically to all
member countries of the WTO, regardless of the existence of commitments made
for each sector; and conditional obligations which apply to sectors where the
WTO member country has assumed market access and national treatment
obligations.

Granting more favourable access to one member (for example, a lower customs   **4.25**
duty rate for one of their products) requires that State to extend the same treatment to all other WTO members. This principle is known as most-favoured-
nation treatment. This 'most-favoured-nation' principle is the backbone of the
three major areas of trade: GATT, GATS, and TRIPS. Other general obligations
include transparency by which WTO member countries are required to publish
all measures of general application relevant to the WTO's functions and to
establish national enquiry points to respond to other members' information
requests.

4.26 The granting of market access is another commitment undertaken by individual WTO members in specified sectors after negotiations that may be made subject to one or more limitations. The other general obligation of WTO members is that of 'national treatment' which means treating one's own nationals and foreigners equally. In services, it means that once a foreign company has been allowed to supply a service in one's country there should be no discrimination between the foreign and local companies. Under GATS, a country only has to apply this principle when it has made a specific commitment to provide foreigners access to its services market. It does not have to apply national treatment in sectors where it has not made any commitment even though the service is permitted under a liberalised regime. Even in the sectors where it has made commitment for market access, GATS does allow limitations on national treatment to be taken fully or partially.

Dispute Resolution under WTO Proceedings

4.27 The WTO also provides a dispute resolution role in interpreting agreements and resolving conflicts between member countries. Disputes in the WTO may arise where one country adopts a trade policy measure or takes some action that one or more fellow WTO members considers to be breaking the WTO agreements or to be a failure to comply with its obligations under the agreements.

4.28 The Uruguay Round agreement introduced a more structured process with more clearly defined stages in the procedure, and imposed greater discipline for the length of time a case should take to be settled. The Uruguay Round agreement emphasised that prompt settlement is essential if the WTO is to function effectively, and it set out in considerable detail the procedures and the timetable to be followed in resolving disputes. Cases referred under the WTO's dispute resolution procedures usually take about one year to reach resolution, or up to 15 months if the case is appealed. The Uruguay Round agreement also strengthened the enforcement mechanisms, and rulings are automatically adopted unless there is a consensus to reject a ruling. Although WTO procedures do resemble a court or tribunal, the preferred solution is for the WTO member countries to negotiate and settle the dispute between them. The first stage is therefore consultations between the governments concerned, and even when the case has progressed to other stages, consultation and mediation are still the objective of the enforcement process.

4.29 Such a dispute was the request made on 13 March 2003 by Antigua and Barbuda pursuant to Article 4 of the Understanding on Rules and Procedures Governing the Settlement of Disputes ('DSU')[42] and Article XXIII of GATS regarding

---

[42] WTO, Dispute Resolution Panel, DS285.

certain legal and regulatory measures applied by authorities in the USA that affected the cross-border supply of gambling and betting services whose cumulative impact resulted, according to Antigua, in making unlawful the supply of gambling and betting services on a cross-border basis. Antigua and the USA held consultations in April 2003, but these consultations did not resolve the dispute. Antigua therefore requested the WTO Disputes Settlement Board ('DSB') to establish a Panel to examine, in the light of the relevant provisions of the covered agreements and to make such findings as will assist the DSB in making the recommendations or in giving the rulings provided for in those agreements. Antigua and Barbuda requested the Panel to find that the USA's prohibition on the cross-border supply of gambling and betting services and its measures restricting international money transfers and payments relating to gambling and betting services are inconsistent with the USA's Schedule of specific commitments under the GATS and Articles XVI:1, XVI:2, XVII:1, XVII:2, XVII:3, VI:1, VI:3, and XI:1 of the GATS.

Antigua argued that a vast array of gambling and betting games and services were **4.30** being offered on a commercial basis in the USA and elsewhere, and since the mid-1990s Antigua had built up a primarily Internet-based, 'remote-access' gaming industry as part of its economic development strategy. Antigua submitted that US federal and state laws were preventing Antigua's on-line gaming industry from competing with US-based gambling firms.

The initial WTO panel decision had found that these services were outside the **4.31** WTO rules for trade in services on the basis that the USA could use federal gaming laws to protect public morals or maintain public order. However, on appeal it was held that the USA had to clarify its laws that were deemed to be overbroad in certain areas and therefore limited the cross-border trade in these services. The parties, both of whom claimed victory, referred the implementation of this ruling to arbitration.

Since this decision, Antigua referred the matter to a WTO Compliance Panel **4.32** which found that the US had not taken measures to bring its federal gambling laws into line with its commitments and in June 2007, Antigua filed a request to suspend its trade concessions and the matter has been referred to a WTO arbitrator. The US has also taken steps to remove gambling and betting from its schedule of Article XXI WTO commitments in an effort to frustrate the outcome of the dispute resolution process in this case.[43]

---

[43] See <http://www.ustr.gov/Document_Library/Press_Releases/2007/May/Statement_of_ Deputy_United_States_Trade_Representative_John_K_Veroneau_Regarding_US_Actions_ under_GATS_Article_XXI.html>.

Financial Services under the WTO

4.33 In 1997, 70 WTO members concluded a financial services agreement (the Financial Services Annex)[44] covering more than 95 per cent of trade in banking, insurance, securities, and financial information. The WTO's current work programme, the Doha Development Agenda ('DDA'), adds negotiations and other work on non-agricultural tariffs, trade, and environment, WTO rules such as anti-dumping and subsidies, investment, competition policy, trade facilitation, transparency in government procurement, intellectual property, and a range of issues raised by developing countries as difficulties they face in implementing the present WTO agreements.[45]

4.34 The Financial Services Annex to the GATS Agreement applies to measures affecting the supply of financial services in WTO member States. A financial service is defined as any service of a financial nature offered by a financial service supplier of a member country. Financial services includes all insurance and insurance-related services, and all banking and other financial services (excluding insurance) and includes the following activities:

Insurance and insurance-related services including:

   (i) direct insurance (including co-insurance):
      (A) life,
      (B) non-life;
  (ii) reinsurance and retrocession;
 (iii) insurance intermediation, such as brokerage and agency;
 (iv) services auxiliary to insurance, such as consultancy, actuarial, risk assessment and claim settlement services.

Banking and other financial services (excluding insurance) including:
  (v) acceptance of deposits and other repayable funds from the public;
 (vi) lending of all types, including consumer credit, mortgage credit, factoring and financing of commercial transaction;
 (vii) financial leasing;
(viii) all payment and money transmission services, including credit, charge and debit cards, travellers cheques, and bankers drafts;
 (ix) guarantees and commitments;

---

[44] Fifth Protocol to the General Agreement on Trade in Services, S/L/45, <http://www.wto.org/english/tratop_e/serv_e/10-anfin_e.htm>.

[45] The Doha Round of negotiations broke down in July 2008 as a result of a failure to agree various agricultural reforms and protections for agriculture in developing and emerging member countries. The status of the remainder of the commitments, including those relating to access to financial services (see Testimony of Dr Sydney J Key to the US House of Representatives, 15 November 2005 <http://financialservices.house.gov/media/pdf/111505sk.pdf>) remains unclear.

   (x) trading for own account or for account of customers, whether on an exchange, in an over-the-counter market or otherwise, the following:

     (A) money market instruments (including cheques, bills, certificates of deposit);

     (B) foreign exchange;

     (C) derivative products including, but not limited to, futures and options;

     (D) exchange rate and interest rate instruments, including products such as swaps, forward rate agreements;

     (E) transferable securities;

     (F) other negotiable instruments and financial assets, including bullion.

  (xi) participation in issues of all kinds of securities, including underwriting and placement as agent (whether publicly or privately) and provision of services related to such issues;

 (xii) money broking;

(xiii) asset management, such as cash or portfolio management, all forms of collective investment management, pension fund management, custodial, depository, and trust services;

 (xiv) settlement and clearing services for financial assets, including securities, derivative products, and other negotiable instruments;

  (xv) provision and transfer of financial information, and financial data processing and related software by suppliers of other financial services;

 (xvi) advisory, intermediation, and other auxiliary financial services on all these activities listed, including credit reference and analysis, investment and portfolio research and advice, advice on acquisitions and on corporate restructuring, and strategy.

4.35 For the purposes of Article I of the GATS Agreement, 'services supplied in the exercise of governmental authority' means activities conducted by a central bank or monetary authority or by any other public entity in pursuit of monetary or exchange rate policies, activities forming part of a statutory system of social security or public retirement plans, and other activities conducted by a public entity for the account or with the guarantee or using the financial resources of the Government.

4.36 WTO members have agreed, however, that they will not be prevented from taking measures for prudential reasons, including for the protection of investors, depositors, policyholders, or persons to whom a fiduciary duty is owed by a financial service supplier, or to ensure the integrity and stability of the financial system. Where such measures do not conform to the provisions of the Agreement, they will not be used as a means of avoiding the member's commitments or obligations under the Agreement. Furthermore, nothing in the Agreement requires a member to disclose information relating to the affairs and accounts of individual customers or any confidential or proprietary information in the possession of public entities.

A WTO member may also recognise prudential measures of any other country in determining how the member's measures relating to financial services are to be applied. Such recognition, which may be achieved through harmonisation or otherwise, may be based upon an agreement or arrangement with the country concerned or may be accorded autonomously.

4.37   A WTO member that is a party to such an agreement or arrangement is required to afford adequate opportunity for other interested WTO members to negotiate their accession to such agreements or arrangements, or to negotiate comparable ones with it, under circumstances in which there would be equivalent regulation, oversight, implementation of such regulation, and, if appropriate, procedures concerning the sharing of information between the parties to the agreement or arrangement. Where a WTO member accords recognition autonomously, it must afford adequate opportunity for any other WTO member to demonstrate that such circumstances exist.

4.38   Participants in the Uruguay Round, which came into force on 1 January 1995, have also taken on specific commitments with respect to financial services under GATS on the basis of an alternative approach to that covered by the provisions of Part III of that Agreement.[46] It was agreed that this approach could be applied subject to the understanding that it does not conflict with the provisions of the Agreement, it does not prejudice the right of any member to schedule its specific commitments in accordance with the approach under Part III of the Agreement, the resulting specific commitments apply on a most-favoured-nation basis, and no presumption has been created as to the degree of liberalisation to which a member is committing itself under the Agreement.

4.39   Interested WTO members have also subscribed to the following specific commitments in relation to financial services.[47]

4.40   In addition to Article VIII of the Agreement, each member has agreed to provide a list of provisions in its schedule pertaining to financial services that contain existing monopoly rights and will endeavour to eliminate them or reduce their scope.

4.41   Notwithstanding Article XIII of the Agreement, each member will ensure that financial service suppliers of any other member established in its territory are accorded most-favoured-nation treatment and national treatment as regards the purchase or acquisition of financial services by public entities of the member in its territory.

---

[46]   Uruguay Round Agreement, Decision on Financial Services.
[47]   WTO, Understanding on Commitments in Financial Services <http://www.wto.org/english/tratop_e/serv_e/21-fin_e.htm>.

Each member will permit non-resident suppliers of financial services to supply, as **4.42** a principal, through an intermediary, or as an intermediary, and under terms and conditions that accord national treatment, the following services:

- insurance of risks relating to maritime shipping and commercial aviation and space launching and freight (including satellites), with such insurance to cover any or all of the following: the goods being transported, the vehicle transporting the goods and any liability arising as a result and goods in international transit, as well as reinsurance and retrocession, and the services auxiliary to insurance as referred to in sub-paragraph 5(a)(iv) of the Annex;

- the provision and transfer of financial information and financial data processing as referred to in sub-paragraph 5(a)(xv) of the Annex and advisory and other auxiliary services, excluding intermediation, relating to banking and other financial services as referred to in sub-paragraph 5(a)(xvi) of the Annex.

Each member will also permit its residents to purchase in the territory of any other **4.43** member the financial services indicated in sub-paragraph 3(a), sub-paragraph 3(b), and sub-paragraphs 5(a)(v) to (xvi) of the Annex.

Each member will grant financial service suppliers of any other member the right **4.44** to establish or expand within its territory, including through the acquisition of existing enterprises, a commercial presence.

A WTO member may, however, impose terms, conditions, and procedures for **4.45** authorisation of the establishment and expansion of a commercial presence in so far as they do not circumvent the member's obligation and they are consistent with the other obligations of the Agreement.

A member will permit financial service suppliers of any other member established **4.46** in its territory to offer in its territory any new financial service. A new financial service is a service of a financial nature, including services related to existing and new products, or the manner in which a product is delivered, that is not supplied by any financial service supplier in the territory of a particular member but which is supplied in the territory of another member.

No WTO member will take measures that prevent transfers of information or the **4.47** processing of financial information, including transfers of data by electronic means, or that, subject to importation rules consistent with international agreements, prevent transfers of equipment, where such transfers of information, processing of financial information, or transfers of equipment are necessary for the conduct of the ordinary business of a financial service supplier. Nothing in this paragraph, however, restricts the right of a WTO member to protect personal data, personal privacy, and the confidentiality of individual records and accounts so long as such right is not used to circumvent the provisions of the Agreement.

4.48 Each WTO member will permit temporary entry into its territory of the following personnel of a financial service supplier of any other member that is establishing or has established a commercial presence in the territory of the member:

(a) senior managerial personnel possessing proprietary information essential to the establishment, control, and operation of the services of the financial service supplier; and

(b) specialists in the operation of the financial service supplier.

4.49 Each WTO member will also permit, subject to the availability of qualified personnel in its territory, temporary entry into its territory of the following personnel associated with a commercial presence of a financial service supplier of any other member:

(a) specialists in computer services, telecommunication services, and accounts of the financial service supplier; and

(b) actuarial and legal specialists.

4.50 Each member will endeavour to remove or to limit any significant adverse effects on financial service suppliers of any other member of:

(a) non-discriminatory measures that prevent financial service suppliers from offering in the member's territory, in the form determined by the member, all the financial services permitted by the member;

(b) non-discriminatory measures that limit the expansion of the activities of financial service suppliers into the entire territory of the member;

(c) measures of a member, when such a member applies the same measures to the supply of both banking and securities services, and a financial service supplier of any other member concentrates its activities in the provision of securities services; and

(d) other measures that, although respecting the provisions of the Agreement, affect adversely the ability of financial service suppliers of any other member to operate, compete, or enter the member's market, provided that any action taken under this paragraph would not unfairly discriminate against financial service suppliers of the member taking such action.

4.51 WTO members are also required to endeavour not to limit or restrict the present degree of market opportunities nor the benefits already enjoyed by financial service suppliers of all other members as a class in the territory of the member, provided that this commitment does not result in unfair discrimination against financial service suppliers of the member applying such measures.

4.52 Under terms and conditions that accord national treatment, each WTO member also commits to grant to financial service suppliers of any other member established in its territory access to payment and clearing systems operated by public entities, and to official funding and refinancing facilities available in the normal course of ordinary business.

In addition to the existing WTO agreements, the WTO Financial Leaders Group   **4.53**
that is comprised of private sector representatives from Canada, the European
Union, Hong Kong, Japan, Switzerland, and the USA have also commented on
the various negotiating proposals relating to financial services that have been
tabled in the WTO Council for Trade in Services ('CTS').[48] In particular, this
group found that in the future the WTO financial services negotiations should
reflect the following goals.

- Foreign investors should have the right to establish through a wholly-owned presence or other form of business ownership, and to operate competitively through
  established vehicles available to national businesses. Thus, limits to investment in
  joint ventures and domestic financial institutions should be lifted and fully-owned
  subsidiaries, branches, and representative offices should be allowed for foreign
  financial services providers. In addition, arbitrary 'economic needs tests' and
  restrictions on regional and product-specific activity should be abolished.

- Foreign direct investors should have the same access to domestic and international markets as domestic companies. They should be treated for regulatory
  and other purposes on the same basis as domestic companies.

- Unnecessary restrictions on cross-border financial services business and consumption of services abroad should be removed, to encourage trade without
  requiring establishment, particularly taking account of technological advance-
  ment, including electronic commerce.

- The temporary posting of key business personnel should be facilitated by the
  creation of a system of easily obtained and renewable permits.

- Existing investments should be grandfathered by WTO member countries that
  did not commit to do so in the 1997 Agreement.

- Countries wishing to accede to membership in the WTO should do so on the
  basis of commitments to substantial financial liberalisation consistent with the
  1997 Financial Services Agreement and the goals set forth above, resulting in
  commercially meaningful access.

- In order to ensure that market access and national treatment commitments
  achieve their promised objectives, there is a pressing need to supplement them
  with new commitments on improved transparency and, in addition, domestic
  regulatory reform as necessary and appropriate for each specific sector.

- Transparent domestic rules and administrative procedures are an essential part of
  liberalising financial services. Clear and reliable information about a country's financial services laws and practices promotes equitable trade and competition. Regulatory
  regimes, even restrictive ones, should be made more transparent. This is an obligation on all WTO members, whether they make specific commitments or not.

---

[48] Financial Leaders Group, Commentary on Proposals for Liberalisation in Financial Services,
21 September 2001.

- To encourage private savings for retirement, in recognition of worldwide ageing populations, WTO members should commit to lock in and improve market access in the provision of pension and asset management products and services.

- The dissemination and processing of financial information to provide clients with competitive services necessary for the conduct of ordinary business should be permitted.

4.54 The WTO does and will continue to fulfil an important role in the international arena of financial services but it depends heavily upon the goodwill and good faith of all of its members to negotiate, adopt, and fulfil the commitments to create a global financial services market.[49]

Regional Trade Agreements

4.55 Trade liberalisation is also increasingly important in other areas of financial services and there are a number of regional trade agreements that affect financial services.

4.56 The largest of the regional trade organisations is that established under the North American Free Trade Agreement ('NAFTA'),[50] a regional agreement between the Government of Canada, the Government of the United Mexican States, and the Government of the United States of America to implement a free trade area.

4.57 The objectives of this agreement, which includes national treatment, most-favoured-nation treatment, and transparency, are to eliminate barriers to trade in, and facilitate the cross-border movement of, goods and services between the territories of the parties, promote conditions of fair competition in the free trade area, increase substantially investment opportunities in the territories of the parties, provide adequate and effective protection and enforcement of intellectual property rights in each party's territory, create effective procedures for the implementation and application of this agreement, for its joint administration, and for the resolution of disputes, and establish a framework for further trilateral, regional, and multilateral cooperation to expand and enhance the benefits of NAFTA.

4.58 NAFTA is operated through the NAFTA Secretariat, a unique organisation established pursuant to Article 2002 of the Agreement to administer the mechanisms specified under NAFTA to resolve trade disputes between national industries and/or governments in a timely and impartial manner. Under NAFTA each of the

---

[49] See n 45 above.
[50] North American Free Trade Agreement, <http://www.nafta-sec-alena.org>. The enlarged European Union (see Chapter 3) represents a market which is about 10% larger than the USA.

participating governments have established permanent, national section offices in each country.

The financial sector provisions of NAFTA (Chapter Fourteen) set out a declara- **4.59** tion of principles with respect to openness of the financial sector, together with safeguards to permit participating parties to maintain distinct approaches to the regulation of their financial sectors, including safeguards that protect each party's approach to regulation,[51] the supply of financial services from outside a country,[52] the terms and conditions under which financial institutions from one country can operate in another country,[53] and the settlement of disputes in the financial sector.[54]

NAFTA was intended to open the participants' financial sectors to the supply of **4.60** services through cross-border trade or establishment by financial suppliers from the other countries without interfering with national approaches to financial sector regulation.[55] The Agreement declares the general principle that freedom of cross-border trade requires each party to permit its residents and nationals to pur- chase financial services from suppliers of other parties located anywhere in the free trade area. On the other hand, the cross-border provision states explicitly that it does not entail any obligation on the parties to permit providers either to do business or to solicit in their territory.

Another key provision of the Agreement was in relation to the right of establish- **4.61** ment in other participant countries. While Article 1404 states that 'financial serv- ices providers of a Party should be permitted to establish financial institutions in the territory of another Party in the juridical form determined by the provider', it continues to specify that the participation of the external providers be 'through separate financial institutions as may be required by that Party'.[56] Establishment alone does not ensure that foreign firms are able to serve another country's needs for financial services. They must also be free to supply their services once they become established. The 'National Treatment' provisions[57] determine the operat- ing conditions for those institutions that have been permitted to operate under the Establishment Article. NAFTA clearly takes the broader concept of competi- tive national treatment and while defining national treatment as 'treatment no less favourable than that accorded by a party'[58] to its own nationals; the Agreement

---

[51] NAFTA Agreement, Art 1403, Regulatory Measures.
[52] ibid, Art 1405, Cross-border Trade.
[53] ibid, Art 1404, Establishment and Art 1407, National Treatment.
[54] ibid, Art 1413, Consultations; Art 1414, Financial Services Committee; Art 1415, Dispute Settlement and Art 1416, Investment Disputes in Financial Services.
[55] NAFTA Agreement, Art 1403.
[56] ibid, Art 1403(2).
[57] ibid, Chapter Three.
[58] ibid, Art 1405(2).

nonetheless requires that policies, whether providing different or identical treatment, must offer 'equal competitive opportunities',[59] the condition that foreign providers not be disadvantaged relative to domestic suppliers.

4.62 The application of many of the principles of the financial sector portion of NAFTA must rely on interpretation and enforcement, and even the results of most careful negotiations may fail to meet their expectations in practice. On the whole, the dispute settlement provisions follow the general provisions in Chapter Eleven of the Agreement with allowance for the needs of the financial sector. The Agreement also provides for a Financial Services Committee[60] to supervise implementation, to consider issues referred to it, and to participate in dispute settlement. Under the procedure laid down by NAFTA, disputes will be referred to a Tribunal consisting of panelists drawn from a roster of individuals with expertise in the financial sector. If the complaint is upheld by the Tribunal, the complaining party may suspend benefits in the financial services sector.

4.63 In addition, the Agreement contains a number of reservations in the area of financial services. As NAFTA is a multilateral agreement, the participants, rather than making specific commitments, have agreed on a set of general principles. Schedule A of the Agreement sets out the reservations to the Agreement of both federal and provincial or State governments, and Schedule B contains the areas where the parties reserve the right to derogate (or reverse) provisions of the agreement in the future. Canada, at one extreme, presented a single reservation of the national government, whereas the USA presented 18, and Mexico, 26.

4.64 Of the three parties, Canada appears to have fared the best in the short run as a result of NAFTA but the USA would probably gain the most benefits in the long run with the opening up of two major markets to its financial institutions under the Agreement. Access to Mexican financial markets will be more valuable to US banks than to Canadian ones, but Mexico has undoubtedly benefited from the opening up of its financial sector while being able to shelter its financial system from substantial foreign competition during the period of its transition from State to private ownership.

The Security and Prosperity Partnership of North America

4.65 In addition to NAFTA, the US, Canada, and Mexico launched their joint Security and Prosperity Partnership of North America ('SPP') in March of 2005 as part of a trilateral effort to increase security and enhance prosperity among the participat-

---

[59] ibid, Art 1405(5).
[60] ibid, Art 1412, Annex 2001(2).

ing countries through greater cooperation and information sharing. SPP is neither an agreement nor a treaty but is intended to complement, rather than replace, existing bilateral and trilateral fora and working groups and it is intended to establish agreed priorities for ongoing and new trilateral and bilateral initiatives, give existing efforts additional momentum, and create new programmes and initiatives where necessary and appropriate.

The SPP was designed to establish a cooperative approach to advance common **4.66** security and prosperity and identified five priorities for cooperative approaches to common challenges and opportunities including:

- Competitiveness
- Safe food and products
- Energy and environment
- Smart and secure borders
- Emergency management and preparedness

SPP Prosperity working groups include a financial services group that is intended **4.67** to work towards the freer flow of capital and the efficient provision of financial services throughout North America including facilitating cross-border electronic access to stock exchanges without compromising investor protection, promoting further collaboration on training programmes for bank, insurance, and securities regulators and supervisors, and seeking ways to improve convenience and cost of insurance coverage for carriers engaged in cross-border commerce.

Latin America has a number of other regional trade agreements in place including **4.68** the Dominican Republic–Central America Free Trade Agreement ('DR–CAFTA')[61] whose objective is to open new opportunities and to help those regional economies to expand their opportunities for growth in the USA.

In particular, DR–CAFTA seeks to level the playing field for US financial services. **4.69** While the US finance and insurance markets are largely open to imports from all countries, including Costa Rica, El Salvador, Guatemala, Honduras, Nicaragua, and the Dominican Republic, the same is not true for current US access to those countries' finance and insurance markets. DR–CAFTA gives US companies the opportunity to export financial services and products to the region. Costa Rica, which has the most developed insurance sector in the region, committed for the first time to liberalise its insurance market. In addition, DR–CAFTA contains provisions allowing the establishment of foreign insurance providers through

---

[61] The US Congress approved the Central American–Dominican Republic Free Trade Agreement (CAFTA–DR) in July 2005 and the President signed it into law on 2 August 2005. As at the date of publication, El Salvador, Honduras, Nicaragua, Guatamala, the Dominican Republic, and Costa Rica have taken the legislative steps required to ratify the DR-CAFTA Agreement.

branches or subsidiaries and new rules permitting cross-border provision of marine, aviation, and transportation insurance.

4.70 DR–CAFTA also liberalises the region's banking and securities sectors. Parties must provide market access for financial institutions without limits on the value of transactions, number of operations, or number of persons employed. Central American parties must permit cross-border trade in financial services and allow other parties' financial institutions to provide any new financial services that it would permit its own institutions to provide. DR–CAFTA contains specific binding commitments affecting asset management services and El Salvador, Guatemala, Honduras, and Nicaragua have committed to allow branch banking and generally opened up other areas of financial services to US financial product providers.

4.71 Other regional trade agreements that include provisions on banking and financial services include the Free Trade Area of the Americas ('FTAA'), the Caribbean Community ('CARICOM'), the Asia Pacific Economic Cooperation ('APEC'), the Gulf Co-operation Council ('GCC'), the Association of Southeast Asian Nations ('ASEAN'), the African Union, the East African Community, the Japan/Singapore Economic Partnership Agreement, the South Asian Association for Regional Cooperation, and the Southern Africa Development Community.[62]

---

[62] The regional trade associations are:

AFTA	ASEAN Free Trade Area	Brunei Darussalam Cambodia Indonesia Laos Malaysia Myanmar Philippines Singapore Thailand Vietnam
ASEAN	Association of South East Asian Nations	Brunei Darussalam Cambodia Indonesia Laos Malaysia Myanmar Philippines Singapore Thailand Vietnam
BAFTA	Baltic Free-Trade Area	Estonia Latvia Lithuania
BANGKOK	Bangkok Agreement	Bangladesh China India Republic of Korea Laos Sri Lanka
CAN	Andean Community	Bolivia Colombia Ecuador Peru Venezuela
CARICOM	Caribbean Community and Common Market	Antigua & Barbuda Bahamas Barbados Belize Dominica Grenada Guyana Haiti Jamaica Monserrat Trinidad & Tobago St. Kitts & Nevis St. Lucia St. Vincent & the Grenadines Surinam
CACM	Central American Common Market	Costa Rica El Salvador Guatemala Honduras Nicaragua
CEFTA	Central European Free Trade Agreement	Bulgaria Croatia Romania
CEMAC	Economic and Monetary Community of Central Africa	Cameroon Central African Republic Chad Congo Equatorial Guinea Gabon

CER	Closer Trade Relations Trade Agreement	Australia New Zealand
CIS	Commonwealth of Independent States	Azerbaijan Armenia Belarus Georgia Moldova Kazakhstan Russian Federation Ukraine Uzbekistan Tajikistan Kyrgyz Republic
COMESA	Common Market for Eastern and Southern Africa	Angola Burundi Comoros Democratic Republic of Congo Djibouti Egypt Eritrea Ethiopia Kenya Madagascar Malawi Mauritius Namibia Rwanda Seychelles Sudan Swaziland Uganda Zambia Zimbabwe
EAC	East African Cooperation	Kenya Tanzania Uganda
EAEC	Eurasian Economic Community	Belarus Kazakhstan Kyrgyz Republic Russian Federation Tajikistan
EC	European Communities	Austria Belgium Bulgaria Cyprus Czech Republic Denmark Estonia Finland France Germany Greece Hungary Ireland Italy Latvia Lithuania Luxembourg Malta Netherlands Poland Portugal Romania Slovak Republic Slovenia Spain Sweden United Kingdom
ECO	Economic Cooperation Organization	Afghanistan Azerbaijan Iran Kazakhstan Kyrgyz Republic Pakistan Tajikistan Turkey Turkmenistan Uzbekistan
EEA	European Economic Area	EC Iceland Liechtenstein Norway
EFTA	European Free Trade Association	Iceland Liechtenstein Norway Switzerland
GCC	Gulf Cooperation Council	Bahrain Kuwait Oman Qatar Saudi Arabia United Arab Emirates
GSTP	General System of Trade Preferences among Developing Countries	Algeria Argentina Bangladesh Benin Bolivia Brazil Cameroon Chile Colombia Cuba Democratic People's Republic of Korea Ecuador Egypt Ghana Guinea Guyana India Indonesia Islamic Republic of Iran Iraq Libya Malaysia Mexico Morocco Mozambique Myanmar Nicaragua Nigeria Pakistan Peru Philippines Republic of Korea Romania Singapore Sri Lanka Sudan Thailand Trinidad and Tobago Tunisia United Republic of Tanzania Venezuela Vietnam Yugoslavia Zimbabwe
LAIA	Latin American Integration Association	Argentina Bolivia Brazil Chile Colombia Cuba Ecuador Mexico Paraguay Peru Uruguay Venezuela
MERCOSUR	Southern Common Market	Argentina Brazil Paraguay Uruguay
MSG	Melanesian Spearhead Group	Fiji Papua New Guinea Solomon Islands Vanuatu
NAFTA	North American Free Trade Agreement	Canada Mexico United States
OCT	Overseas Countries and Territories	Greenland New Caledonia French Polynesia French Southern and Antarctic Territories Wallis and Futuna Islands Mayotte Saint Pierre and Miquelon Aruba Netherlands Antilles Anguilla Cayman Islands Falkland Islands South Georgia and South Sandwich Islands Montserrat Pitcairn Saint Helena Ascension Island Tristan da Cunha Turks and Caicos Islands British Antarctic Territory British Indian Ocean Territory British Virgin Islands

PAN-ARAB	Pan-Arab Free Trade Area	Bahrain Egypt Iraq Jordan Kuwait Lebanon Libya Morocco Oman Qatar Saudi Arabia Sudan Syria Tunisia United Arab Emirates Yemen
PATCRA	Agreement on Trade and Commercial Relations between the Government of Australia and the Government of Papua New Guinea	Australia, Papua New Guinea
PTN	Protocol relating to Trade Negotiations among Developing Countries	Bangladesh Brazil Chile Egypt Israel Mexico Pakistan Paraguay Peru Philippines Republic of Korea Romania Tunisia Turkey Uruguay Yugoslavia
SACU	Southern African Customs Union	Botswana, Lesotho, Namibia, South Africa, Swaziland
SADC	Southern African Development Community	Angola Botswana Lesotho Malawi Mauritius Mozambique Namibia South Africa Swaziland Tanzania Zambia Zimbabwe
SAPTA	South Asian Preferential Trade Arrangement	Bangladesh Bhutan India Maldives Nepal Pakistan Sri Lanka
SPARTECA	South Pacific Regional Trade and Economic Cooperation Agreement	Australia New Zealand Cook Islands Fiji Kiribati Marshall Islands Micronesia Nauru Niue Papua New Guinea Solomon Islands Tonga Tuvalu Vanuatu Western Samoa
Trans-Pacific	Tripartite	Egypt India Yugoslavia
SEP	Agreement Trans-Pacific Strategic Economic Partnership	Brunei Darussalam Chile New Zealand Singapore
UEMOA WAEMU	West African Economic and Monetary Union	Benin Burkina Faso Côte d'Ivoire Guinea Bissau Mali Niger Senegal Togo

Reproduced with the kind permission of the World Trade Organization, Regional Trade Agreement gateway,<http://www.wto.org/english/tratop_e/region_e/region_e.htm>.

PAN-ARAB currently only covers goods and commodities but in 2007 the Union of Arab Banks held a conference to consider the social legal and practical issues underpinning cooperation between Arab banks and financial institutions with a view to strengthening regional economic cooperation on both trade and investment levels between the Arab countries in line with the establishment of the Arab Customs Union following on from PAN-ARAB.

Global Bankers—the World Bank and the International Monetary Fund

The International Monetary Fund ('IMF') and the World Bank Group[63] are the world's bankers and yet they carry out a unique joint role as a flywheel to the global economy. They play an important, if sometimes controversial, role in global banking and financial services although recent years have seen the increasing politicisation of these economic institutions—from all sides of the political spectrum. As a result, the IMF and the World Bank have become at once more critical to global economic stability but also have generated considerable political resistance to their global economic policies.

4.72

The two organisations are intended to complement each other's work. While the IMF's focus is chiefly on macroeconomic performance and on macroeconomic and financial sector policies, the World Bank is concerned mainly with funding project-based economic measures and longer term development and poverty reduction issues. The World Bank's activities include lending to developing countries and countries in transition to finance infrastructure projects, the reform of particular sectors of the economy, and broader structural reforms. The IMF provides financing not for particular sectors or projects but for general support of a country's balance of payments and international reserves while the country takes policy action to address its difficulties.

4.73

Established in 1945[64] both the World Bank and the IMF were founded to help promote the health of the world economy and they are still the central institutions of the international monetary system. The IMF and the International Bank for Reconstruction and Development ('IBRD'), now more commonly known as the World Bank, were set up to promote long-term economic development, including through the financing of infrastructure projects, such as road-building and improving water supply. Together these institutions provide a wide variety of low-interest loans, interest-free credit, and grants to developing countries. The World Bank also works with countries in their anti-corruption efforts and has as well a

4.74

---

[63] The World Bank is not a bank but a specialised agency which has become a group of five closely associated development institutions: the International Bank for Reconstruction and Development ('IBRD'), the International Development Association ('IDA'), the International Finance Corporation ('IFC'), the Multilateral Investment Guarantee Agency ('MIGA'), and the International Centre for Settlement of Investment Disputes ('ICSID').

[64] The IMF was conceived in July 1944 at the Bretton Woods Conference (see n 79) where a charter (or Articles of Agreement) of an international institution to oversee the international monetary system and to promote both the elimination of exchange restrictions relating to trade in goods and services, and the stability of exchange rates was drawn up. The IMF came into existence in December 1945, when the first 29 countries signed its Articles of Agreement <http:// www.imf. org/external/pubs/ft/aa/index.htm>.

number of mechanisms[65] in place to prevent corruption and fraud in bank-financed projects.

4.75 The World Bank is operated as a cooperative, with its member countries as shareholders.[66] A Board of Governors that is composed of the finance ministers or development ministers of their respective countries represents the World Bank's shareholders. The governors, who meet once a year at the Bank's annual meetings, are the ultimate policymakers. The Board of Governors to the President and the Executive Directors delegates day-to-day decision-making at the Bank. The Bank's President is, by tradition, a national of the largest shareholder, the USA.[67] Elected for a five-year renewable term, the President of the World Bank chairs meetings of the Board of Directors and is responsible for overall management of the Bank. Every member government of the World Bank Group is represented by an Executive Director. The five largest shareholders—France, Germany, Japan, the UK, and the USA—each appoint an Executive Director, while other member countries are represented by 19 Executive Directors. Approximately 9,000 economists, educators, environmental scientists, financial analysts, anthropologists, engineers, and many others who come from over 160 different countries and many of whom work in local country offices carry out the work of the Bank.

4.76 The IMF is also accountable to its member countries and operates through its Board of Governors. Key policy issues relating to the international monetary system are considered twice-yearly in a committee of the governors called the International Monetary and Financial Committee ('IMFC'). A joint committee of the Boards of Governors of the IMF and World Bank called the Development Committee also advises and reports to the governors on development policy and other matters of concern to developing countries.

4.77 However, the day-to-day work of the IMF is carried out by an Executive Board whose powers to conduct the business of the IMF are delegated to it by the Board of Governors. The Executive Board has 24 Executive Directors, with the Managing Director as chairman. In addition, a First Deputy Managing Director and two other Deputy Managing Directors assist the Managing Director.

4.78 The Executive Board of the IMF usually meets three times a week, in full-day sessions at the IMF's headquarters in Washington, DC. The IMF's five largest

---

[65] The World Bank has established a Department of Institutional Integrity for whistleblowing and reporting in relation to projects funded by it.

[66] The number of shares a country has in the World Bank is based roughly on the size of its economy. The USA is the largest single shareholder, with 16.41% of votes, followed by Japan (7.87%), Germany (4.49%), the UK (4.31%), and France (4.31%). The rest of the shares are divided among the other member countries.

[67] American Robert Zoellick was elected as president of the World Bank in July 2007.

shareholders[68]—the USA, Japan, Germany, France, and the UK—along with China, Russia, and Saudi Arabia, have their own seats on the Board. The other 16 Executive Directors are elected for two-year terms by groups of countries, known as constituencies.

The IMF's aims include promoting the balanced expansion of world trade, the **4.79** stability of exchange rates, the avoidance of competitive devaluations of currencies, and the orderly correction of balance of payment problems. It serves to prevent economic crises in the system by providing technical assistance and training to member states and encouraging countries to adopt sound economic policies, and it provides a global funding system that allows members needing temporary financing to address balance of payments problems to borrow but also to implement adjustment and reform economic policies. The IMF has, therefore, become the principal forum for discussion of the stability of the international monetary and financial system, but also of national economic policies in a global context.

In September 2000 at the annual meetings of the IMF and World Bank, the IMF **4.80** set out some new major priorities including striving to promote sustained non-inflationary economic growth that benefits all people of the world and to be the centre of competence for the stability of the international financial system.[69] It also made commitments that it would focus more clearly on its core macroeconomic and financial areas of responsibility and work with other institutions established to safeguard global public goods and be an open institution, learning from experience and dialogue, and adapting continuously to changing circumstances.

The IMF's financing comes from quotas that are intended broadly to reflect the **4.81** individual members' relative size in the world economy: the larger a country's

---

[68] Unlike some international organisations that operate under a one-country-one-vote principle, the IMF has a weighted voting system such that the larger a country's quota in the IMF—determined broadly by its economic size—the more votes it has. The IMF's resources come mainly from the quota (or capital) subscriptions that countries pay when they join the IMF, or following periodic reviews in which quotas are increased. Countries pay 25% of their quota subscriptions in Special Drawing Rights (SDRs) or the major currencies; the IMF can call on the remainder, payable in the member's own currency, to be made available for lending as needed. Quotas determine not only a country's subscription payments, but also the amount of financing that it can receive from the IMF, and its share in SDR allocations. Quotas also are the main determinant of countries' voting power in the IMF. See <http://www.imf.org/external/np/sec/ memdir/members.htm>.

[69] The Heavily Indebted Poor Countries ('HIPC') Initiative grew out of the United Nation's Millennium Declaration and the World Bank has adopted its 'Millennium Development Goals' as part of its commitment to 'an expanded vision of development, one that vigorously promotes human development as the key to sustaining social and economic progress in all countries, and recognises the importance of creating a global partnership for development'. In the spring of 2005, the World Bank and IMF implemented a new Debt Sustainability Framework in Low-Income Countries, which is seeking to reduce the challenge to low income countries by providing guidance on new lending to those countries whose main source of financing is official loans. The framework has been developed with the intention to provide better monitoring and prevent the accumulation of unsustainable debt—see <http://www.worldbank.org>.

economy in terms of output, and the larger and more variable its trade, the higher its quota tends to be. The USA therefore contributes the most to the IMF,[70] whereas Palau, the world's smallest, only contributes 0.001 per cent. The most recent (eleventh) quota review came into effect in January 1999 and raised IMF quotas about $300 billion. In addition, the IMF may borrow to supplement the resources available from its quotas. The IMF has two sets of standing arrangements to borrow if needed to cope with any threat to the international monetary system. These are the General Arrangements to Borrow ('GAB') established in 1962 between the G-10 governments and Switzerland, and the New Arrangements to Borrow ('NAB') introduced in 1997 with 25 participating lender countries and institutions. Under the two arrangements, the IMF currently has up to SDR 34 billion (about $50 billion) available to lend.

4.82 The IMF's Articles of Agreement call for it to oversee the international monetary system, including by exercising firm 'surveillance'—that is, oversight—over its member countries' exchange rate policies. Under the Articles, each member country undertakes to collaborate with the IMF in its efforts to ensure orderly exchange arrangements and to promote a stable system of exchange rates. More specifically, member countries agree to direct policies toward the goals of orderly economic growth with reasonable price stability, together with orderly underlying economic and financial conditions, and to avoid manipulating exchange rates for unfair competitive advantage. In addition, each country undertakes to provide the IMF with the information necessary for its effective surveillance. The membership has agreed that the IMF's surveillance of each member's exchange rate policies has to be carried out within the framework of a comprehensive analysis of the general economic situation and economic policy strategy of the member.

4.83 The regular monitoring of economies, and associated provision of policy advice, that IMF surveillance involves can help signal dangers ahead and enable members to act in a timely way to avoid trouble.

4.84 The IMF conducts its oversight in three ways: country surveillance, which takes the form of regular (usually yearly) comprehensive consultations with individual member countries about their economic policies, with interim discussions as needed; global surveillance, which entails reviews by the IMF's Executive Board of global economic trends and developments; and regional surveillance, under which the IMF examines policies pursued under regional arrangements. This includes IMF Board discussions of developments in the European Union, the euro area, the West African Economic and Monetary Union, the Central African Economic and Monetary Community, and the Eastern Caribbean Currency Union. IMF also

---

[70] US contributions are 17.5% of total quotas.

participates in surveillance discussions of such groups of countries as the G-7 and Asia Pacific Economic Community.

Any IMF member country can request IMF support if it has a balance of pay-   **4.85**
ments need. The IMF is not, however, an aid agency or a development bank.
It lends to help its members tackle balance of payments problems and restore
sustainable economic growth. Once IMF assistance has been agreed, limits on
which are set in relation to a member's quota in the IMF, foreign exchange funds
are deposited with the country's central bank to supplement its international
reserves and thus to give general balance of payments support.

When a country approaches the IMF for financing, either in the form of standby   **4.86**
arrangements or by extended fund facilities,[71] it may be in a state of economic
crisis or near-crisis and the IMF provides the country's authorities with advice on
the economic policies that may be expected to address the problems most effectively. For the IMF also to provide financing, it must agree with the country's
authorities on a programme of policies aimed at meeting specific, quantified goals
regarding external viability, monetary and financial stability, and sustainable
growth. Details of the programme are spelled out in a 'letter of intent' from the
government concerned to the Managing Director of the IMF. IMF lending is
conditional upon the acceptance of this IMF programme of policies to correct the
borrower country's balance of payments problem and both the borrower country
and the IMF must agree on specific economic policies that are required; the IMF
disburses funds in phases linked to the borrowing country's actually meeting its
scheduled policy commitments.

IMF funding is also intended to be temporary and repayment periods are rela-   **4.87**
tively short[72] and the IMF expects borrower countries to give priority to the repayment of their loans. IMF borrowers are generally developing countries, countries
in transition from central planning to market-based systems, or emerging market
countries recovering from financial crises whose access to the international capital
markets is limited.

The IMF is also known for its policy advice and its policy-based lending to   **4.88**
countries in times of economic crisis. The objective of this advice is to help

---

[71] As the credit crunch began to affect developing country economies in October 2008, the IMF
announced that it had received requests from Belarus, Pakistan, and Hungary to provide financial
assistance. The IMF also operates a Poverty Reduction and Growth Facility for certain countries and
a supplemental reserve facility to provide short-term financing.

[72] The repayment period is 3¼–5 years for short-term loans under IMF Stand-By Arrangements
or 4½–10 years for medium-term financing under Extended Arrangements. However, in November
2000, the Executive Board agreed to introduce the expectation of earlier repayment (2¼–4 years
for stand-by arrangements and 4½–7 years for extended arrangements). The repayment period for
loans to low-income countries under the IMF's Poverty Reduction and Growth Facility is 10 years,
with a 5½-year grace period on principal payments.

strengthen the design and implementation of members' economic policies, including by strengthening skills in the institutions responsible, such as finance ministries and central banks. The IMF began providing technical assistance in the mid-1960s when many newly independent countries sought help in setting up their central banks and finance ministries. The IMF also provided technical assistance in the early 1990s, when countries in central and eastern Europe and the former Soviet Union began their shift from centrally-planned to market-based economic systems. The IMF offers training courses for government and central bank officials of member countries at its headquarters in Washington and at regional training centres, and through visits by IMF staff, supplemented by hired consultants and experts.

4.89 The IMF also works with national governments and other international institutions to:
- strengthen the legal, regulatory, and supervisory frameworks for banks;
- review minimum capital requirements for banks and financial institutions;
- develop a core set of international accounting standards;
- finalise a set of core principles for good corporate governance;
- avoid exchange rate regimes that are vulnerable to attack; and
- ensure a freer flow of timely financial data to markets.[73]

4.90 The IMF has also been working with the Basel Committee on Banking Supervision to improve regulatory standards.

4.91 Although the financing capacity of the IMF itself is considerable, the greater part of international financial flows are private flows. The IMF therefore works with the private sector to manage and resolve financial crises and to reduce the impact of economic turmoil by improving risk assessment and encouraging closer and more frequent discussion between countries and private investors. In September 2000, the IMF has established a Capital Markets Consultative Group to provide a basis for regular communication between international capital market participants and the IMF on matters including global economic and market developments and the development of measures to strengthen the global financial system.

4.92 When economic or financial crises do occur, IMF-supported programmes are expected to be able to restore stability through their mix of official financing, policy adjustments, and associated gains in confidence among private investors. In certain cases, however, such actions as coordinated debt restructuring by private creditors may be needed. IMF members have agreed on some principles to guide the involvement of the private sector in crisis resolution.

---

[73] See para 4.213.

The IMF collaborates actively with the World Bank, the regional development **4.93** banks, the World Trade Organization, the United Nations agencies, and other international bodies. The IMF is also a member of the Financial Stability Forum, which brings together the national authorities responsible for financial stability in significant international financial centres, international regulatory and supervisory bodies, committees of central bank experts, and international financial institutions.

The World Bank Group, on the other hand, provides funding to many of the **4.94** world's low-income countries who are generally excluded from the international money markets or who cannot afford to do so at high interest rates. Direct contributions and loans from developed countries are made by the World Bank Group to these countries who receive grants, interest-free loans, and technical assistance from the World Bank to enable them to provide basic services including education and medical programmes (including HIV/AIDS). In the case of the World Bank loans, countries have 35 to 40 years to repay, with a 10-year grace period.

Interest-free credit and grant financing from the IDA is funded by 40 of the devel- **4.95** oped countries that provide the money for this funding by making contributions every four years. IDA credits make up about one quarter of the Bank's financial assistance but aside from IDA funds, very little of the Bank's income is provided by its member countries.

In 1996, with the IMF, the World Bank launched the Heavily Indebted Poor **4.96** Countries ('HIPC') Initiative in an effort to cut the debts of the world's poorest, most indebted countries. The HIPC Initiative, combined with other types of debt relief, will cut by two-thirds the external debt in these countries, lowering their debt levels to below the overall average for developing countries.

Higher-income developing countries can receive loans from the IBRD. Countries **4.97** that borrow from the IBRD can repay over longer time periods than if they had borrowed from a commercial bank.[74] Developing country governments borrow money for specific programmes, including poverty reduction efforts, delivery of social services, protection of the environment, and promotion of economic growth that will improve living standards.[75] The IBRD raises almost all its money in the world's financial markets—$13 billion in fiscal 2004. With an AAA credit rating, the IBRD issues bonds to raise money and then passes on the low interest rates to its borrowers.

---

[74] IBRD loans are repaid by borrowers in periods between 5–20 years with a 3–5-year grace period before the repayment of principal begins.
[75] In fiscal 2007 IBRD provided loans totalling $12.8 billion in support of 112 projects.

4.98   The World Bank Group also acts in collaboration with other institutions in fighting international poverty. For example, it has worked with governments and the private sector to launch the new BioCarbon Fund and with the International Emissions Trading Association ('IETA') to launch the Community Development Carbon Fund ('CDCF'). It has also joined with the Food and Agriculture Organisation ('FAO') and the United Nations Development Programme ('UNDP') to sponsor the Consultative Group on International Agricultural Research ('CGIAR') to reduce hunger and poverty, improve human nutrition and health, and protect the environment. Through the Consultative Group to Assist the Poor ('CGAP'), the World Bank has worked with the donor organisations to provide access to financial services (such as loans and savings) for the poor, including microfinance.

The Bank for International Settlements

4.99   The Bank for International Settlements ('BIS') was established in 1930,[76] making it the oldest international financial institution and the principal centre for international central bank cooperation.

4.100   In the aftermath of World War I, the BIS was established as part of the Young Plan (1930)[77] to deal with the issue of the reparation payments imposed on Germany by the Treaty of Versailles. The BIS quickly outgrew this role and the Bank's activities focused on cooperation among central banks and other agencies with a special function in promoting monetary and financial stability.

4.101   Central bank cooperation through the BIS has taken place through the regular meetings in Basel, the Bank's headquarters,[78] of central bank governors and

---

[76] Hague Convention respecting the Bank for International Settlements of 20 January 1930, 104 League of Nations Treaty Series 441.

[77] The Young Plan was adopted by the Allied Powers in 1930 and set the total war reparations at $26,350,000,000 to be paid by Germany to the Allies over a period of 58½ years. Global economic depression of the 1930s was already deepening and a payment moratorium was called for the fiscal year 1931–32. When the Nazi party took over Germany, Germany defaulted on the unpaid reparations debt. After Germany's defeat in World War II, an international conference decided in 1953 that Germany would pay the remaining debt only after the country was reunified. Nonetheless, West Germany paid off the principal by 1980; then in 1995, after reunification, the new German government announced it would resume payments of the remaining interest.

[78] BIS has recognised international status through the Agreement between the Swiss Federal Council and the Bank for International Settlements to determine the Bank's legal status in Switzerland of 1 February 1987 as amended, Compendium of Swiss Laws (0.192.122.971.3) such that the property and assets of the BIS—along with assets of third parties entrusted to the BIS—have immunity in Switzerland and certain other jurisdictions from such measures as expropriation, seizure, or confiscation. The BIS has also been granted various immunities in the People's Republic of China, where the BIS has a representative office in Hong Kong SAR, and in Mexico.

other experts. The Bank has its own secretariat and has developed its own research facilities in financial and monetary economics. It also performs an international function in collating and disseminating global economic and financial statistics.

International cooperation came to the fore again in the aftermath of World War II, **4.102** and until the early 1970s BIS focused on implementing and defending the Bretton Woods system.[79] In the 1970s and 1980s, the BIS's focus was on managing cross-border capital flows during the oil crises and the international debt crisis. The 1970's banking crisis also brought the issue of regulatory supervision of internationally active banks to the fore, resulting in the 1988 Basel Capital Accord and its 'Basel II' revision of 2001 to 2006. More recently, as a result of the 1997 Asian economic crisis, the issue of financial stability in the wake of economic integration and globalisation has been at the BIS's centre of attention.

The Bank operates within the terms of its Statutes[80] and its three most important **4.103** decision-making bodies are:

- the General Meeting of member central banks;
- its Board of Directors; and
- the Management of the Bank.

The BIS has 55 member central banks,[81] all of which are entitled to be represented **4.104** and vote in the General Meetings. Voting power is determined by the number of BIS shares issued in the country of each member represented at the meeting.

The BIS Board of Directors has six ex officio directors, comprising the governors **4.105** of the central banks of Belgium, France, Germany, Italy, and the UK, and the

---

[79] The Bretton Woods system of international economic management was established in 1944 to set out the rules for commercial and financial relations among the world's major industrial states. In July 1944 delegates from all 44 Allied nations gathered at the Mount Washington Hotel, situated in the New Hampshire resort town of Bretton Woods, for the United Nations Monetary and Financial Conference and the resulting Bretton Woods Agreement set up a system of rules, institutions, and procedures to regulate the international political economy. The Agreement established the framework for the International Bank for Reconstruction and Development (later the World Bank) and the International Monetary Fund. The chief features of the Bretton Woods system were an obligation for each country to adopt a monetary policy that maintained the exchange rate of its currency within a fixed value—plus or minus one %—in terms of gold; and the provision by the International Monetary Fund of finance to bridge temporary payments imbalances. The system eventually collapsed in 1971 following the United States' suspension of convertibility from dollars to gold.

[80] <http://www.bis.org/about/statutes-en.pdf>.

[81] Members are the central banks or monetary authorities of: Algeria, Argentina, Australia, Austria, Belgium, Bosnia and Herzegovina, Brazil, Bulgaria, Canada, Chile, China, Croatia, the Czech Republic, Denmark, Estonia, Finland, France, Germany, Greece, Hong Kong SAR, Hungary, Iceland, India, Indonesia, Ireland, Israel, Italy, Japan, Korea, Latvia, Lithuania, the Republic of Macedonia, Malaysia, Mexico, the Netherlands, New Zealand, Norway, the Philippines, Poland, Portugal, Romania, Russia, Saudi Arabia, Singapore, Slovakia, Slovenia, South Africa, Spain, Sweden, Switzerland, Thailand, Turkey, the UK, and the USA, plus the European Central Bank. The legal status of the central bank of Yugoslavia for BIS purposes is currently under review.

Chairman of the Board of Governors of the US Federal Reserve System. Each ex officio member appoints another member of the same nationality. The BIS Statutes also provide for the election to the Board of not more than nine governors of other member central banks.[82] The Board of Directors elects a chairman and vice-chairman from among its members for a three-year term.

4.106   The Board, which meets at least six times per year, is responsible for determining the strategic and policy direction of the BIS, supervising the management, and fulfilling the specific tasks given to it by the Bank's Statutes. The Consultative Committee and the Audit Committee, made up of selected Board members, also assist the Board in its work.

4.107   Apart from providing the forum for monetary policy cooperation, the BIS also carries out certain banking functions for the central bank community (eg gold and foreign exchange transactions), as well as trustee and agency functions. The BIS's statutes require it 'to serve as a prime counterparty for central banks in their financial transactions, by providing an appropriate range of banking services and maintaining its reputation for absolute confidentiality and security'.

4.108   The BIS has, therefore, developed a range of banking services specifically designed to assist central banks and monetary authorities in the management of their foreign exchange and gold reserves. It also acts as a banker to, and manages funds for, international financial institutions. The BIS does not accept deposits from, or generally provide financial services to, private individuals or corporate entities, nor is it permitted to make advances to governments or open current accounts in their name. The BIS was the agent for the European Payments Union,[83] helping the European currencies restore convertibility after World War II. Similarly, the BIS has acted as the agent for various European exchange rate arrangements, including the European Monetary System[84] which preceded the move to a single currency.

---

[82] The governors of the central banks of Canada, Japan, the Netherlands, Sweden, and Switzerland are currently the elected members of the Board.

[83] The European Payments Union ('EPU') was established on 1 July 1950 by the country members of the Organization for European Economic Cooperation ('OEEC') as an organisation of European recipients of US economic assistance. The EPU was intended to be a temporary system, designed to assist European countries 'until they are fully able to take their place in a world-wide system'. The EPU was a multilateral settlement scheme set up to achieve the ideal of trade equilibrium among members and removal of trade discriminations.

[84] The European Monetary System was organised in 1979 to stabilise foreign exchange and counter inflation among its members. After 1986, changes in national interest rates were used to keep the currencies within a narrow range (the Exchange Rate Mechanism) but in the early 1990s the EMS was strained by the differing economic policies and conditions between its members, and in September 1992 Britain permanently withdrew from the system.

The BIS has also provided or organised emergency financing to support the inter-   **4.109**
national monetary system when required. During the Great Depression, the BIS
organised support credits for both the Austrian and German central banks and, in
the 1960s, the BIS arranged special support credits for the Italian lira and the
French franc and the Group Arrangements to support sterling.[85] More recently,
the BIS has provided finance for Mexico in 1982 and Brazil in 1998 in the context
of IMF-led stabilisation programmes.

In addition to the BIS's secretariat, a number of other international committees   **4.110**
and organisations focusing on financial stability and the international financial
system have their headquarters at the BIS. These include the Group of Ten[86]
which is comprised of the governors of the central banks of Belgium, Canada,
France, Germany, Italy, Japan, the Netherlands, Sweden, Switzerland, the UK,
and the USA which has established a number of standing committees to study the
functioning and architecture of international financial markets. The most important of these standing committees are the Markets Committee,[87] the Committee
on the Global Financial System,[88] the Basel Committee on Banking Supervision,
and the Committee on Payment and Settlement Systems.[89]

---

[85] See FJ Garvin, *Gold, Dollars and Power: the politics of monetary relations 1958–1971* (2003).

[86] The Group of Ten (G-10) refers to the group of countries (Belgium, Canada, France, Germany,
Italy, Japan, the Netherlands, Sweden, Switzerland, the UK, and the USA) that have agreed to
participate in the General Agreements to Borrow, a supplementary borrowing arrangement that
can be invoked if the IMF's resources are estimated to be below its members' needs. The General
Agreements to Borrow was established in 1962 when the governments of eight IMF members—
Belgium, Canada, France, Italy, Japan, the Netherlands, the UK, and the USA—and the central
banks of two others, Germany and Sweden, agreed to make resources available to the IMF for
drawings by participants, and, under certain circumstances, for drawings by non-participants. The
Group was strengthened in 1964 by the association of Switzerland, then a non-member of the IMF,
but the name of the G-10 remained the same, hence there are actually 11 members. The Bank for
International Settlements (BIS), European Commission, IMF, and OECD are also official observers
of the activities of the G-10. Source: IMF, Factsheet: a Guide to Committees, Groups and Clubs,
September 2005.

[87] The Markets Committee (formerly known as the Committee on Gold and Foreign Exchange)
was established in 1962 and when the Gold Pool arrangements collapsed in 1968, members continued
to meet at the BIS for open and informal exchanges of views focusing on recent developments in foreign
exchange and related financial markets, an exchange of views on possible future trends, and consideration of the short-run implications of particular current events for the functioning of these markets.

[88] The Committee on the Global Financial System monitors and exams broad issues relating to
the financial markets and systems with a view to elaborating appropriate policy recommendations
and assisting the governors of the G-10 central banks in recognising, analysing, and responding to
threats to the stability of financial markets and the global financial system.

[89] See para 4.141; The Committee on Payment and Settlement Systems ('CPSS') was originally established in 1980 to address issues concerning the development of electronic funds transfer
systems and the question of competition and cooperation in payment systems. In 1989 the G-10
Governors set up an ad hoc Committee on Interbank Netting Schemes to study in more detail the
policy issues relating to cross-border and multicurrency inter-bank netting schemes, including a set
of minimum standards for the operation of bilateral and multilateral netting schemes and an agreed
approach for the joint oversight of such systems.

4.111 These standing committees promote cooperation through the exchange of information and expertise. Committees are usually chaired by senior officials of member central banks and are composed of experts from the central banks. In the case of the Basel Committee, members also include non-central bank supervisory authorities. Committee members are mainly (but not exclusively) from G-10 countries. Some committees also develop and propose common international standards that are implemented through national legislation.

4.112 The BIS headquarters also hosts the secretariats of a number of independent organisations that do not have any direct reporting links to the BIS or its member central banks. These are the Financial Stability Forum (FSF), the International Association of Insurance Supervisors (IAIS), and the International Association of Deposit Insurers ('IADI').[90]

4.113 Established in 1994, the IAIS represents insurance supervisory authorities of some 180 jurisdictions. The IAIS was formed to promote cooperation among insurance supervisory authorities, to set international standards for insurance supervision and regulation, to provide training to members, and to coordinate work with regulators in the other financial sectors and international financial institutions, and its secretariat is hosted by the BIS.

4.114 The IAIS issues global insurance principles, standards, and guidance papers for the industry and provides its members with training and support on issues related to insurance supervision. It also organises meetings and seminars for insurance supervisors and holds an annual conference for supervisory and industry representatives. The IAIS works closely with other standard setting bodies such as the International Insurance Foundation and the International Insurance Society. The day-to-day operations of the IAIS are carried out by its Executive Committee, whose members represent different geographical regions. It is supported by three main committees—the Technical Committee which oversees global insurance regulatory and supervisory standards; the Emerging Markets Committee which assists emerging insurance markets to establish sound insurance supervisory systems; and the Budget Committee which controls the finances of the IAIS. These committees organise a number of working groups to accomplish their objectives including the Financial Conglomerates Subcommittee which coordinates the

---

[90] The IADI's objectives are to contribute to the stability of financial systems by promoting international cooperation in the field of deposit insurance and to encourage wide international contact among deposit insurers and other interested parties. The Association seeks to enhance the understanding of common interests and issues related to deposit insurance, set out guidance to enhance the effectiveness of deposit insurance systems, with such guidance taking into account different circumstances, settings, and structures, and facilitate the sharing and exchange of expertise on deposit insurance issues through training, development, and educational programmes as well as providing advice on the establishment or enhancement of effective deposit insurance systems.

work of IAIS members for the Joint Forum, the Insurance Fraud Subcommittee which analyses fraudulent activities by or on insurance companies and seeks to help prevent and detect insurance fraud in the industry, and the Insurance Laws, Regulations, Practices and Standards Subcommittee which collects and analyses information through a global insurance laws database.

The IAIS has issued a number of documents relating to the regulation and super-   **4.115**
vision of insurance including its insurance core principles and methodology,[91] the Insurance Concordat regarding the supervision of cross-border insurance activities,[92] principles for the conduct of insurance business,[93] and principles for carrying on insurance business over the Internet.[94] IAIS has also been active in establishing detailed standards relating to capital adequacy and solvency for insurers and reinsurers.[95]

IAIS has also been very involved in the establishment of certain standards for the   **4.116**
industry and the development of best or most prudent practices. In some cases, these standards set out best practices for a supervisory authority; in others, they describe the practices a well managed insurer would be expected to follow and thereby assist supervisors in assessing the practices that companies in their jurisdictions should have in place.

The Basel Committee

The Committee on Banking Regulations and Supervisory Practices or the Basel   **4.117**
Committee was established at the end of 1974 and is comprised of members from Belgium, Canada, France, Germany, Italy, Japan, Luxembourg, the Netherlands, Spain, Sweden, Switzerland, the UK, and the USA. These countries are represented by their respective central banks and also by the authority with formal responsibility for the prudential supervision of banking business where this is not the central bank, such as the UK Financial Services Authority. The Basel Committee meets regularly four times a year and it has 25 technical working groups[96] and task forces on specific topics that also meet regularly.

---

[91] Insurance core principles and methodology, October 2003.

[92] Principles applicable to the supervision of international insurers and insurance groups and their cross-border business operations, December 1999.

[93] Principles for conduct of insurance business, December 1999.

[94] Principles for the supervision of insurance activities on the Internet, October 2004.

[95] Principles on capital adequacy and solvency, January 2002.

[96] These working groups include the Accord Implementation Group, Accounting Task Force, the Capital Task Force, International Liaison Group (with 16 non-G-10 countries), Working Group on Corporate Governance, Cross-Border Banking Group, Electronic Banking Group, Joint Forum (with IAIS and IOSCO), Joint IOSCO–BCBS Working Group on Trading Book and the Research Task Force.

4.118 The Basel Committee's role is to provide a forum for banking supervisors and to formulate broad supervisory standards and guidelines and to recommend statements of best practice for the banking industry. It has no power to make or enforce those standards and individual national authorities must take the necessary steps—statutory or otherwise—to implement them. The Committee does not, therefore, have any formal supranational supervisory authority, and its conclusions do not, and were never intended to, have legal force. The role of the Committee is therefore to encourage convergence among its members and other countries to adopt common approaches and common standards without harmonisation of the detail of member countries' supervisory techniques.

4.119 The Basel Committee reports to the central bank governors of the G-10 countries and seeks the G-10 governors' endorsement for its major initiatives. The Committee's Secretariat is provided by the BIS. The Secretariat is staffed mainly by professional supervisors on temporary secondment from member institutions and in addition to its secretarial work for the Committee and its many expert subcommittees, the Secretariat also provides advice to supervisory authorities in both member and non-member countries.

4.120 In 1983 the Committee finalised an agreement (the Concordat) that set out the principles for sharing supervisory responsibility for foreign banks and their branches (Principles for the Supervision of Bank's Foreign Establishments) on the basis that no foreign banking establishment should be able to avoid supervision and that supervision should be adequate. Further amendments of this Concordat have added to it further minimum standards for the supervision of banks and mechanisms for the sharing of information, the consolidated supervision of banking groups, and the exchange of prudential information between banking supervisors in different countries.

The Basel Accord

4.121 In 1988, the Committee introduced a capital measurement system commonly referred to as the Basel Capital Accord which sought to introduce a credit risk measurement framework with a minimum capital standard of 8 per cent by 1992 for all banking institutions in the member States. This framework has been progressively introduced not only in member countries but also in virtually all other countries with active international banks. This document set out the agreement among the G-10 central banks to apply common minimum capital standards to their banking industries, to be achieved by end-year 1992. The standards adopted are almost entirely addressed to credit risk, the main risk incurred by banks and the agreement contains two main sections, (a) the definition of capital, and (b) the structure of risk weights.

The agreement also defines the target standard ratio and the transitional and **4.122**
implementing arrangements and four technical annexes covering the definition of
capital, the counterparty risk weights, the credit conversion factors for off-
balance-sheet items and the transitional arrangements as also included. Since
1988, five amendments to the Accord have been made to the agreement.

Basel II

In June 1999, the Committee issued a new proposal for a New Capital Adequacy **4.123**
Framework (Basel II)[97] to replace the 1988 Accord that was finally adopted in
June 2004 and implemented from 1 January 2007, although certain provisions
were deferred to year-end 2007. This text is intended to serve as the basis for
national rule-making and approval processes to continue, and for banking organisations to complete their preparations for Basel II's implementation.

Basel II represents a major revision of the international standard on bank capital **4.124**
adequacy that was introduced in 1988. It aligns the capital measurement framework with sound contemporary practices in banking, promotes improvements in
risk management, and is intended to enhance financial stability.

The Basel II capital framework consists of three pillars: minimum capital require- **4.125**
ments, which seek to refine the standardised rules set forth in the 1988 Accord;
supervisory review of an institution's internal assessment process and capital
adequacy; and effective use of disclosure to strengthen market discipline as a
complement to supervisory efforts.

The Basel II framework represents the work of the Committee to secure interna- **4.126**
tional convergence on supervisory regulations governing the capital adequacy of
internationally active banks.

Following the publication of the first round of proposals for revising the capital **4.127**
adequacy framework in June 1999,[98] a consultation process was carried out by all
of the Committee's member countries as well as quantitative impact studies, and
the proposals were circulated to supervisory authorities worldwide.

The result of that process, which was endorsed by the Central Bank Governors **4.128**
and Heads of Banking Supervision of the G-10 countries, is an agreed framework
for measuring capital adequacy and the minimum standards to be achieved which

---

[97] Basel Committee on Banking Supervision: 'Basel II, International Convergence of Capital
Measurement and Capital Standards: a Revised Framework', Publication 107 (June 2004).
[98] Basel Committee on Banking Supervision: 'A New Capital Adequacy Framework', Publication
50 (June 1999).

the national supervisory authorities represented on the Committee proposed for adoption in their respective countries.

4.129 The Basel II framework is designed to establish minimum levels of capital for internationally active banks. As under the 1988 Accord, national authorities are free to adopt arrangements that set higher levels of minimum capital and may put in place supplementary measures of capital adequacy for the banking organisations they authorise or license. More generally, under the second pillar, supervisors should expect banks to operate above minimum regulatory capital levels.

4.130 National authorities may use a supplementary capital measure as a way to address, for example, the potential uncertainties in the accuracy of the measure of risk exposures inherent in any capital rule or to constrain the extent to which an organisation may fund itself with debt. Where a national authority uses a supplementary capital measure (such as a leverage ratio or a large exposure limit) in conjunction with the measure set forth in this framework, in some instances the capital required under the supplementary measure may be more binding. This framework is intended to promote stronger risk management practices within the banking industry based on the three pillars of minimum capital requirements, supervisory review, and disclosure for market discipline. The Committee specifically sought to establish more risk-sensitive capital requirements that are conceptually sound, and paid due regard to particular features of the present supervisory and accounting systems in individual member countries.

4.131 One significant innovation of the Basel II framework is the greater use of risk assessments provided by banks' internal systems as inputs to regulatory capital calculations. Basel II also sets out a detailed set of minimum requirements designed to ensure the integrity of these internal risk assessments, and each supervisor must develop their own set of review procedures for ensuring that banks' systems and controls are adequate to serve as the basis for the capital calculations.

4.132 The Basel II framework provides a range of options for determining the capital requirements for credit risk and operational risk in order to allow banks and supervisors to select approaches that are most appropriate for their operations and their financial market infrastructure, and it allows for a limited degree of national discretion in the way in which each of these options may be applied, to adapt the standards to different conditions of national markets. Monitoring and review of the Basel II framework will be carried out by the Accord Implementation Group ('AIG') to promote consistency in the framework's application by encouraging supervisors to exchange information with each other on their implementation approaches. Based on the work of the AIG, the Committee has issued general principles for the cross-border implementation of the Basel II framework, and more focused principles for the recognition of operational risk capital charges under advanced measurement approaches for home and host supervisors.[99]

The Basel II framework also highlights the need for banks and supervisors to give **4.133** attention to the second (supervisory review) and third (market discipline) pillars. The Basel Committee has also stated its awareness of the need for interaction between regulatory and accounting approaches at both the national and international level and the impact that the comparability of the resulting measures of capital adequacy and for the costs associated with the implementation of these approaches has on the industry.[100]

The Basel Committee is continuing to look at evolving issues for the industry **4.134** such as combating terrorist financing, supervisory practices for dealing with weak banks, risk management in electronic banking, the management and supervision of operational risk, transparency and disclosure by banks, accounting and auditing issues, and the cooperation between banking supervisors including discussion and information sharing.

More recently, the Committee has moved more aggressively to promote other **4.135** supervisory standards worldwide. In collaboration with many non-G-10 supervisory authorities, the Committee in 1997 developed 'Core Principles for Effective Banking Supervision',[101] that provides a comprehensive blueprint for an effective supervisory system and to facilitate implementation and assessment for supervisory purposes, the Committee developed the 'Core Principles Methodology'[102] in 1999.

The Committee has encouraged contacts and cooperation between its members **4.136** and other banking supervisory authorities and other supervisors in financial services, in particular the International Organisation of Securities Commissions ('IOSCO') in areas of mutual concern such as the management of derivatives activities in banks and securities houses, and it has worked closely with IOSCO and the IAIS to consider the risk and prudential requirements for diversified financial conglomerates.

---

[99] Basel Committee on Banking Supervision: 'Implementation of Basel II: Practical Considerations', Publication 109 (July 2004).

[100] Basel II: International Convergence of Capital Measurement and Capital Standards: A Revised Framework, June 2004; <http://www.bis.org/publ/bcbs107.htm>.

[101] Basel Committee on Banking Supervision: 'Core Principles for Effective Banking Supervision', Publication 30 (September 1997).

[102] Basel Committee on Banking Supervision: 'Core Principles Methodology', Publication 61 (October 1999).

4.137 The Basel Committee also circulates to supervisors throughout the world research papers and statistical information, and it holds an International Conference of Banking Supervisors that takes place every two years.

Financial Stability Institute

4.138 In 1999, the BIS and the Basel Committee created the Financial Stability Institute (FSI) to assist supervisors around the world in improving and strengthening their financial systems. The objectives of the FSI are to promote sound supervisory standards and practices globally, and to support full implementation of these standards in all countries, to provide supervisors with the latest information on market products, practices, and techniques to help them adapt to rapid innovations in the financial sector, to help supervisors develop solutions to their multiple challenges by sharing experiences in focused seminars and regional workshops, and to assist supervisors in employing the practices and tools that will allow them to meet everyday demands and tackle more ambitious goals.

4.139 The aim of FSI is to produce skilled supervisors who are key to the effective supervision of the financial sector. Supervisors need to understand the risks inherent in financial activities and establish an adequate framework of supervision and regulation. The FSI therefore provides banking supervisors with information and technical support including organising topical seminars and special meetings for banking supervisors, holding regional workshops and seminars for banking supervisors, and providing both document and Internet-based information through its FSI Connect and FSI Information programme.

The Committee on Payment and Settlement Systems

4.140 In 1980 the governors of the central banks of the G-10 countries established a Group of Experts on Payment Systems whose purpose was to take forward work on payment system issues including addressing concerns about the development of electronic funds transfer systems. The Group of Experts on Payment Systems also studied the characteristics of new types of inter-bank netting schemes, on which the Bank for International Settlements published a report in 1989.[103] In 1989 the G-10 Governors set up an ad hoc Committee on Interbank Netting Schemes to study the policy issues relating to cross-border and multicurrency inter-bank netting schemes.

---

[103] Bank for International Settlements: 'Report on Netting Schemes' (February 1989).

As a follow-up to the work of the Committee on Interbank Netting Schemes, and **4.141** more generally to take over and extend the activities of the Group of Experts on Payment Systems, the G-10 Governors established in 1990 the Committee on Payment and Settlement Systems ('CPSS'). The CPSS is one of the permanent G-10 central bank committees reporting to the G-10 Governors whose secretariat is provided by the BIS in Switzerland.

The principal purpose of the CPSS is to analyse and promote awareness of risks **4.142** and to develop minimum standards or best practices, and the CPSS and its member central banks have played a leading role in promoting efficient and robust payment and settlement arrangements. The CPSS therefore serves as a forum to monitor and analyse developments in domestic payment, settlement, and clearing systems as well as in cross-border and multicurrency settlement schemes, and also developments in domestic payment, settlement, and clearing systems and in cross-border and multicurrency settlement schemes.

The CPSS also provides a means of coordinating the oversight functions exercised **4.143** by the central banks with respect to payment systems. In addition to addressing general concerns regarding the efficiency and stability of payment, clearing, settlement, and related arrangements, the CPSS also considers the relationships between payment and settlement arrangements, central bank payment and settlement services, and the major financial markets that are relevant for the conduct of monetary policy.

Since its creation, the CPSS has published various reports covering large-value **4.144** funds transfer systems, securities settlement systems, settlement mechanisms for foreign exchange transactions, clearing arrangements for exchange-traded derivatives and retail payment instruments, including electronic money. The CPSS's 'Red Book' on payment systems also provides extensive information on the most important payment and settlement systems in the CPSS countries.

CPSS also has a role as a standard setter and through the publication of the Core **4.145** principles for systemically important payment systems, the CPSS/IOSCO Recommendations for Securities Settlement Systems,[104] and the CPSS/IOSCO Recommendations for Central Counterparties,[105] the CPSS has contributed to the establishment of best practice. The CPSS has cooperated with other bodies, including the IOSCO, the Basel Committee, and the G-10 Deputies, to address issues of common concern as well as maintaining contact with many global payment system providers, industry associations, and other regulatory authorities. The Committee

---

[104] Bank for International Settlements: 'Committee on Payment and Settlement Systems, Recommendations for Securities Settlement Systems', Publication 46 (November 2001).
[105] Bank for International Settlements: 'Committee on Payment and Settlement Systems, Recommendations for Central Counterparties', Publication 64 (November 2004).

has undertaken an active work programme concerning the arrangements for the settlement of securities transactions, and has worked jointly with the Technical Committee of IOSCO to improve the efficiency and security of securities settlement systems worldwide, including cross-border securities settlement arrangements.[106] CPSS also works with other regional payment and settlement bodies in emerging regional central bank groups focusing on payment systems, for instance in eastern and central Europe, in Asian EMEAP countries, and in Latin America.

4.146 The CPSS has also contributed to the discussions surrounding the need for sound risk management in large-value funds transfer systems.[107] Recent work of the CPSS, such as the Core Principles, has emphasised the importance of payment systems that are 'systemically important', rather than drawing a line exclusively between 'large-value' and 'retail', and looked at the introduction of real-time gross settlement systems.[108] The CPSS has recently started new work in the area of large-value payment systems.[109]

4.147 Another key aspect of the Committee's work remains the implementation of a strategy to mitigate foreign exchange settlement risk. In 1996 the G-10 Governors endorsed a report prepared by the CPSS entitled 'Settlement risk in foreign exchange transactions'[110] which provided a clear definition of settlement risk in foreign exchange transactions and a corresponding method to measure it properly. The G-10 central banks decided to reaffirm and strengthen the strategy as set out in the July 1998 follow-up report 'Reducing foreign exchange settlement risk: a progress report'.

4.148 In August 2003 the CPSS published a report on 'The role of central bank money in payment systems'[111] which looked at the issue of competition and cooperation between central banks, and commercial banks and practical issues such as which institutions may have accounts at the central bank, the range of services provided by central banks to meet the needs of account holders, and ways to mitigate credit and liquidity risks.

4.149 The CPSS has also undertaken substantial work in the area of retail payment instruments and systems, to identify current market trends, and to explore policy issues that may arise for central banks in this context, and it has published three

---

[106] Both Committees published the final report on the Recommendations for Securities Settlement Systems, see n 103 above.

[107] Estimates compiled by the CPSS indicate that these systems transfer the equivalent of several trillion dollars per day in CPSS countries, a large portion of which is related to the settlement of financial market transactions.

[108] See CPSS report: 'Real-time gross settlement systems', Publication 22 (March 1997).

[109] Bank for International Settlements: 'Committee on Payment and Settlement Systems, New Developments in Large Value Payment Systems', Publication 67 (May 2005).

[110] CPSS report: 'Settlement risk in foreign exchange transactions', Publication 17 (March 1996).

[111] Bank of International Settlements: 'Committee on Payment and Settlement Systems, The role of central bank money in payment systems', Publication 55 (August 2003).

reports[112] analysing the characteristics of systems used in these countries to effect, clear, and settle payments initiated with particular retail payment instruments. The CPSS has also been involved in developing the legal and regulatory framework for 'electronic money'[113] and the G-10 Governors have asked the BIS, in cooperation with the CPSS, to closely monitor global developments of electronic money products and their potential impact on policy issues.

Following the failure of Barings in the early 1990s, the CPSS undertook a systematic **4.150** review and analysis of risks in clearing arrangements for derivatives in the G-10 countries. It published a report in March 1997[114] which describes the structure of the clearing arrangements for exchange-traded derivatives, and which identifies possible weaknesses in such arrangements. The CPSS has also been involved in the development of new payment system services by various providers, both domestic and international, and in this connection, the CPSS, together with the Group of Computer Experts, has undertaken various surveys on the development of e-money[115] and an internal survey on certification authorities and public key infrastructure.

Finally, in 2005 the CPSS set up a new working group on oversight, whose task is **4.151** to map and compare the objectives that central banks have for their oversight of payment and securities settlement systems[116] and the methods they use to achieve these objectives, and other recent projects include work on international remittance systems in considering and comparing the remittance markets in different countries to identify general principles for international money transfers.

Securities and the International Organisation of Securities Commissions

The International Organisation of Securities Commissions ('IOSCO') is an inter- **4.152** national organisation of securities exchange regulators who cooperate in setting guiding principles for the world's capital markets. IOSCO was formed in 1983, when an inter-American regional association was transformed into an international

---

[112] See 'Retail payments in selected countries: a comparative study', published in September 1999, describing and comparing the retail payment instruments in use in G-10 countries and Australia; 'Clearing and settlement arrangements for retail payments in selected countries', September 2000; and 'Policy issues for central banks in retail payments', March 2003.

[113] Bank of International Settlements: 'Committee on Payment and Settlement Systems, Survey of developments in electronic money and internet and mobile phone payments', Publication 62 (March 2004).

[114] Bank of International Settlements: 'Committee on Payment and Settlement Systems, Clearing arrangements for exchange-traded derivatives', Publication 23 (March 1997).

[115] Bank of International Settlements: 'Committee on Payment and Settlement Systems, Survey of electronic money developments', Publication 48 (November 2001).

[116] Bank of International Settlements: 'Committee on Payment and Settlement Systems, Central Bank Oversight of payment and settlement systems', Publication 68 (May 2005).

cooperative body. IOSCO is the most important cooperative forum for securities regulatory agencies and is now one of the key global standard setting bodies whose members regulate over 90 per cent of the world's security markets.[117] The decision to form the IOSCO was taken by 11 regulatory agencies from North and South America at a gathering in Ecuador in April 1983. In 1984 securities regulators from France, Indonesia, Korea, and the UK joined the organisation. There are currently 181 members of IOSCO.

4.153 The member bodies of the IOSCO have resolved:
- to cooperate together to promote high standards of regulation in order to maintain just, efficient, and sound markets;
- to exchange information on their respective experiences in order to promote the development of domestic markets;
- to unite their efforts to establish standards and an effective surveillance of international securities transactions; and
- to provide mutual assistance to promote the integrity of the markets by a rigorous application of the standards and by effective enforcement against offences.

4.154 IOSCO has three categories of members, Ordinary, Associate, and Affiliate. Ordinary members include government bodies such as a securities commission or a self-regulatory body such as a stock exchange, where there are no governmental regulatory bodies in a particular country. Associate members are national regulatory bodies of a country which is already an ordinary member or any other eligible body with an appropriate responsibility for securities regulation.[118] Affiliate members are other regulatory bodies where the national regulatory body is already an ordinary member of IOSCO[119] and are therefore members of the SRO Consultative Committee. An SRO or international body is eligible for affiliate membership provided it has an appropriate interest in securities regulation.

4.155 IOSCO and its General Secretariat are based in Madrid, Spain but most of its work is carried out by its members through a number of committees. The Presidents' Committee meets once a year during the IOSCO's annual conference and is comprised of all the Presidents of member agencies. The Presidents' Committee has wide powers to take such decisions as are necessary to provide the overall policy for the organisation. The Executive Committee is composed of

---

[117] <http://www.iosco.org>.

[118] ibid.

[119] Affiliate members include the Alberta Securities Commission, the British Columbia Securities Commission, the Dubai Financial Services Authority, the Indian Forward Markets Commission, the Japanese Ministries of Agriculture, Forestries, and Fisheries and International Trade and Industry, the Japanese Securities and Exchange Surveillance Commission, the Korea Insurance Deposit Corporation, the Lubuan Offshore Financial Services Authority, the North American Securities Administrators Association, and the US Commodities and Futures Commission.

19 members including the Chairmen of the Technical and Emerging Markets Committees, the Chairmen of the Regional Committee, a single ordinary member elected by each Regional Committee, and nine ordinary members elected by the Presidents' Committee. This committee meets periodically throughout the year and is subject to the by-laws of the organisation. The Executive Committee, which is chaired by a Chairperson who is elected from among the members of the Committee, takes all of the decisions and actions that are necessary to achieve the objectives of the organisation.

The Regional Standing Committees, of which there are four, meet to discuss specific regional problems and issues of the members of the organisation that constitute them. The four Regional Standing Committees include the Africa/Middle East Regional Committee, the Asia-Pacific Regional Committee, the European Regional Committee, and the Inter-American Regional Committee. **4.156**

The Executive Committee has established two specialised Working Committees: the Technical Committee and the Emerging Markets Committee. The Technical Committee is comprised of 15 national securities regulators that regulate the world's larger and more developed internationalised markets. The Committee reviews major regulatory issues and coordinates IOSCO's practical responses to these issues. The work of this particular committee is divided into five functional subject areas: Multinational Disclosure and Accounting, Regulation of Secondary Markets, Regulation of Market Intermediaries, Enforcement and Exchange of Information, and Investment Management. These subject areas are addressed by specialised Working Groups that meet regularly throughout the year to tackle the issues they are given by the Technical Committee. **4.157**

The Emerging Markets Committee promotes the development and improvement of efficiency of emerging securities and future markets by establishing principles and minimum standards, preparing training programmes for members, and the transfer of technology and expertise. This Committee has also established Working Groups, which address the same functional subject areas as the Working Groups of the Technical Committee. **4.158**

SROs, which are affiliate members of IOSCO, are members of the Self Regulatory Committee. This Committee is designed to implement IOSCO's recognition of the importance of maintaining a close relationship with its affiliate members, including SROs, thus allowing them to make a constructive input into the work of IOSCO as a whole. **4.159**

The IOSCO meets on an annual basis in order to discuss any important issues that relate to world securities and future markets. The Annual Conference is staged in a different city every year in a member country. The various Committees and members of the IOSCO also meet, but according to their own agendas and requirements. **4.160**

4.161   IOSCO does not have the power to make any rules or legally enforceable standards, but its members (the national securities authorities) resolve to cooperate with each other to ensure better regulation of the markets, on a domestic and international level, in order to maintain just, efficient, and sound markets.

4.162   These authorities agree to implement certain principles of securities regulation that are based upon the organisation's three principal objectives:

- the protection of investors;
- ensuring that markets are fair, efficient, and transparent; and
- the reduction of systematic risk in the markets.[120]

4.163   Implementation may therefore require implementation through a variety of methods depending upon the jurisdiction in question. It may be necessary to implement a change in legislation or regulation, a change in policy or practice by the regulatory body, or a bilateral or multilateral agreement.

4.164   To achieve these objectives, the principles need to be implemented under the relevant national legal framework. The principles are grouped into eight categories including Principles relating to the Regulator, Principles for Self Regulation, Principles for the Enforcement of Securities Regulation, Principles for Cooperation in Regulation, Principles for Issuers, Principles for Collective Investment Schemes, Principles for Market Intermediaries, and Principles for the Secondary Market.

4.165   The Technical Committee, the Working Groups, and the Emerging Markets Committee all carry out and produce various reports published by IOSCO that are a valuable source of information on the principles that underlie effective securities regulation and the tools and techniques necessary to give effect to those principles.

4.166   Part of IOSCO's role is to allow national securities regulators to share information on a domestic and international level, and to remove impediments to international cooperation.

4.167   In recent years, IOSCO has been putting greater emphasis on the Multilateral Memorandum Concerning Consultation and Cooperation and the Exchange of Information ('IOSCO MOU'). To date, 47 members have signed the IOSCO MOU and a further 15 have expressed their commitment to doing so in accordance with the document's Appendix B.[121] The IOSCO MOU is now proving to be an effective tool, particularly in combating cross-border financial crime.

4.168   In broad terms, IOSCO's priorities are to maintain and enhance its programmes for setting new standards and principles in specific areas, to continue with

---

[120] IOSCO, 'Objectives and Principles of Securities Regulation', p 5.
[121] IOSCO, Annual Report 2007, Statement of the Secretary General.

implementation of the IOSCO Principles, and to strengthen and extend cross-border cooperation between regulators, especially for enforcement purposes. IOSCO's achievements over the past year are many and varied. They include promulgation of the Code of Conduct Fundamentals for Credit Rating Agencies;[122] new Principles on Client Identification and Beneficial Ownership for the Securities Industry;[123] key reports on Strengthening Capital Markets Against Financial Fraud[124] and on Islamic Capital Markets; a survey on the implementation of the IOSCO Principles as they relate to auditor oversight and productive cooperation with global banking and insurance regulators through the Joint Forum.[125]

It is undoubtedly the world's leading standards setter for securities regulation. Its **4.169** high profile is now widely acknowledged by members and by other bodies in the international financial community who recognise IOSCO's achievements over recent years. The IOSCO Objectives and Principles of Securities Regulation have become the fundamental reference for benchmarking and assessing securities regulation in any jurisdiction worldwide, and a powerful basis for setting standards in specific areas of regulation and for addressing new issues as they emerge.[126]

Joint Forum

The IOSCO shares a relationship with the Basel Committee and the IAIS through **4.170** the Joint Forum.[127] The Joint Forum traces its origins from the Tripartite Group, which was formed in early 1993 to address a range of issues relating to the supervision of financial conglomerates. The Tripartite Group was created at the initiative of the Basel Committee and composed of bank, securities, and insurance supervisors, acting in a personal capacity but drawing on their experience of supervising different types of financial institutions. The Tripartite Group recognised the trend towards cross-sector financial conglomerates and issued a report in July 1995 raising issues of concern in the prudential supervision of financial conglomerates.[128] The purpose of this report, published as a discussion document, was to identify

---

[122] IOSCO, 'Code of Conduct Fundamentals for Credit Rating Agencies' (December 2004).

[123] IOSCO, 'Principles on Client Identification and Beneficial Ownership for the Securities Industry' (May 2004).

[124] IOSCO, 'Strengthening Capital Markets Against Financial Fraud' (February 2005).

[125] 30th IOSCO Annual Conference Opening Ceremony—speech by Jane Diplock AO Chairman of the IOSCO Executive Committee and New Zealand Securities Commission: <http://www.iosco.org>, p 2.

[126] ibid, p 3.

[127] The Joint Forum was original referred to as the 'Joint Forum on Financial Conglomerates'.

[128] Basel Committee: 'The supervision of financial conglomerates' (A report by the tripartite group of bank, securities and insurance regulators) (July 1995).

challenges that financial conglomerates pose for supervisors and to consider ways in which these problems may be overcome. To carry this work forward, the Joint Forum was established in 1996 as a cooperative cross-sectoral forum whose parent bodies are IOSCO, the Basel Committee, and the IAIS. Thirteen countries are currently represented in the Joint Forum: Australia, Belgium, Canada, Denmark, France, Germany, Italy, Japan, Netherlands, Spain, Switzerland, the UK, and the USA. The EU Commission attends in an observer capacity. The chairmanship of the Joint Forum rotates between the three sector committees and is named for a two-year term.

4.171 These three parent bodies, IOSCO, Basel Committee, and IAIS, approve the Joint Forum's mandates and reports. The Joint Forum has a specific mandate to undertake work on risk assessments and capital and, if appropriate, to develop further guidance and principles and/or identify best practices, with special focus on risk aggregation, operational risk management, credit risk management and transfer, business continuity, outsourcing and the disclosure of financial risks.[129]

4.172 Comprised of an equal number of senior bank, insurance, and securities supervisors representing each supervisory constituency, the Joint Forum usually meets three times per year, and has three main subgroups, which are the risk assessment and capital, the business continuity, and the regulatory and market differences subgroups. The growing emergence of financial conglomerates and the blurring of distinctions between the activities of firms in each financial sector have heightened the need for cooperative efforts to improve the effectiveness of supervisory methods and approaches. The Joint Forum has studied issues of common interest to the three financial sectors and developed guidance and principles so as to identify best practices, as appropriate, in particular for:

- risk assessments and management, internal controls, and capital;
- the use of the audit and actuarial functions in the supervision of regulated entities and corporate groups containing regulated entities;
- corporate governance, including fit and proper tests;
- outsourcing by regulated firms of functions and activities; and
- different definitions of banking, insurance, and securities activities, and the potential that they may lead to regulatory arbitrage.

The Joint Forum provides the framework to permit different sectoral regulators to address these issues.[130]

---

[129] <http://www.bis.org>.
[130] Basel Committee on Banking Supervision: 'The Joint Forum, Core Principles: Cross sectoral comparison' (November 2001).

The Organisation for Economic Co-operation and Development

The Organisation for Economic Co-operation and Development ('the OECD') **4.173** developed out of the Organisation for European Economic Co-operation ('OEEC') that was established in 1947 to coordinate the Marshall Plan[131] for the reconstruction of Europe following World War II.

An economic counterpart to the North Atlantic Treaty Organisation ('NATO'), **4.174** the OECD took over from the OEEC in 1961 with a mandate to be an effective means of international coordination and to assist sound economic expansion in member countries and other countries in the process of economic development, and to contribute to growth in world trade on a multilateral, non-discriminatory basis.

There are 30 member countries of the OECD whose members produce 60 per **4.175** cent of the world's goods and services, but increasingly the OECD has been expanding its remit to include work on issues such as sustainable development, bringing together environmental, economic, and social concerns across national frontiers for a better understanding of the problems, and the means to tackle them together.

Decision-making power is vested in the OECD's Council. The Council is com- **4.176** prised of one representative per member country and the European Commission. The Council meets regularly at the level of ambassadors to the OECD, and decisions are taken by consensus. The Council meets at ministerial level once a year to discuss key issues and set priorities for OECD work. The OECD Secretariat's various directorates carry out the work mandated by the Council.

The OECD Secretariat is based in Paris and has a staff of 2,500 to support the **4.177** activities of its committees.[132] A Secretary-General, assisted by four Deputy Secretaries-General, heads the OECD Secretariat. The Secretary-General also chairs the Council. As well as running the day-to-day operations of the OECD, the

---

[131] The Marshall Plan grew out of a speech by then US Secretary of State George C Marshall on 5 June 1947 that outlined a proposal for the economic regeneration of Europe post-World War II. The USA offered up to $20 billion for relief provided the European nations could agree a plan on how they would use the aid, thus cooperating and acting as a single economic unit for the first time.

[132] The OECD Secretariat is organised in departments or directorates and these include the Executive Directorate, the Economics Department, the Development Co-operation Directorate, the Directorate for Financial and Enterprise Affairs, the Directorate for Employment, Labour and Social Affairs, Public Affairs and Communications Directorate, Statistics Directorate, Public Governance and Territorial Development Directorate, Centre for Tax Policy and Administration, Directorate for Education, the Environment Directorate, the Trade Directorate, the Directorate for Science, Technology and Industry, the Directorate for Food, Agriculture and Fisheries, and the Centre for Co-operation with Non-members.

OECD Secretariat collects data, monitors trends, and analyses and forecasts economic developments, and carries out and publishes research on social changes or evolving patterns in trade, environment, agriculture, technology, taxation, and more.

4.178   Representatives of the OECD member countries meet in specialised committees to discuss ideas and to review progress in specific policy areas, such as economics, trade, science, employment, education, or financial markets. There are approximately 200 OECD committees, working groups, and expert groups.

4.179   The OECD, unlike the World Bank or the International Monetary Fund, is not a financial institution and it does not act as a bank or financial institution. The OECD's focus is on the determination of key issues through the collection of data and its analysis, and then moving on to collective discussion of policy and decision-making, and finally implementation. Discussions at the OECD sometimes evolve into negotiations where OECD countries agree on the 'rules of the game' for international cooperation, and they may culminate in formal agreements, for example agreements on combating bribery, on export credits, or on capital movements; or they may produce standards and models for international taxation, or recommendations and guidelines covering corporate governance or environmental practices.

The Financial Action Task Force

4.180   In 1989 in response to mounting concern over money laundering, the Financial Action Task Force on Money Laundering ('FATF') was established by the G-7 Summit that was held that year in Paris. The G-7 Heads of State or Government and the President of the European Commission, recognising the threat posed to the banking system and to financial institutions, convened the Task Force from the G-7 Member States, the European Commission, and eight other countries.[133]

4.181   FATF was given the responsibility of examining money laundering techniques and trends and reviewing the action that had already been taken at a national or international level. In April 1990, FATF issued a report containing a set of Forty Recommendations, which provide a comprehensive plan of action needed to fight

---

[133] During 1991 and 1992, the FATF expanded its membership from the original 16 to 28 members which are Argentina, Australia, Austria, Belgium, Brazil, Canada, Denmark, the European Commission, Finland, France, Germany, Greece, Gulf Co-operation Council—whose members include Bahrain, Kuwait, Oman, Qatar, Saudi Arabia, and the United Arab Emirates—Hong Kong (China SAR), Iceland, Ireland, Italy, Japan, Luxembourg, Mexico, Kingdom of the Netherlands, New Zealand, Norway, Portugal, Russian Federation, Singapore, South Africa, Spain, Sweden, Switzerland, Turkey, the UK, and the USA.

against money laundering. Since then FATF has continued to examine the methods used to launder criminal proceeds and has completed two rounds of mutual evaluations of its member countries and jurisdictions. It has also updated the Forty Recommendations to reflect the changes that have occurred in the fight against money laundering, and has sought to encourage other countries around the world to adopt anti-money laundering measures. FATF also conducts research into anti-money laundering measures and the typologies employed by money launderers and FATF publishes reports and other information on the schemes being employed by both money launderers and terrorists to infiltrate the global banking and financial system.

In 2001, the development of standards in the fight against terrorist financing was **4.182** added to the mission of the FATF and FATF has promulgated nine special recommendations regarding terrorist financing including putting in place agreements to ratify and implement UN instruments on terrorist financing, criminalising the financing of terrorism and money laundering associated with it, freezing and confiscating terrorist assets, requiring reporting of suspicious transactions relating to terrorist financing, providing international cooperation in relation to stopping terrorist financing, the licensing and registration of money transmission activities to prevent informal or 'hawala' networks from being used to finance terrorism, recording basic information regarding wire transfers of money to prevent its use for money laundering, and reviewing the adequacy of national laws to prevent non-profit and charitable organisations from being exploited for terrorist financing.

FATF member countries are committed to the discipline of multilateral monitor- **4.183** ing and peer review and regularly carry out monitoring programmes in relation to their implementation of the FATF Recommendations. In the self-assessment programme, each member country provides information on the status of its implementation of the Forty Recommendations and Eight Special Recommendations by responding each year to a standard questionnaire. This information is then compiled and analysed, and provides the basis for assessing the extent to which both individual countries and the group as a whole have implemented the Recommendations. The second element for monitoring the implementation of the Forty Recommendations is the mutual evaluation process whereby each member country receives an on-site visit conducted by a team of three or four selected experts in the legal, financial, and law enforcement fields from other member governments. Following the monitoring visit the team draws up a report assessing the extent to which the evaluated country has moved forward in implementing an effective system to counter money laundering and to highlight areas in which further progress may still be required. Countries that are found to be non-complying with the Forty Recommendations may have other members tighten their anti-money policies in relation to those countries, and FATF may apply various types of moral pressure to secure compliance. Ultimately FATF can also apply Recommendation 21 to that non-cooperative country which would result in FATF issuing a statement to its members and their financial institutions to give 'special attention' to business relations and transactions with persons, companies, and financial institutions domiciled in the non-cooperative country. Such measures can have a very substantial effect on the financial and banking systems of a country that has failed to comply with FATF standards and, as a final measure, the FATF membership of the non-cooperative country can be suspended.[134]

4.184 FATF also has a number of associate regional bodies including the Asia/Pacific Group on Money Laundering ('APG'), the Caribbean Financial Action Task Force ('CFATF'), the Council of Europe Select Committee of Experts on the Evaluation of Anti-Money Laundering Measures ('MONEYVAL'), the Eurasian Group ('EAG'), the Eastern and Southern Africa Anti-Money Laundering Group ('ESAAMLG'), the Financial Action Task Force on Money Laundering in South America ('GAFISUD'), the Middle East and North Africa Financial Action Task Force ('MENAFATF'), and the Egmont Group of Financial Intelligence Units ('EGMONT') that cooperate on the exchange of information relating to money laundering activities.

4.185 The private sector also has an interest in preventing the use of financial institutions for money laundering activities and the Wolfsberg Group of international private banks[135] has adopted the Wolfsberg AML Principles that include guidelines for client acceptance and client identification as a means of establishing best practice in anti-money laundering procedures.[136]

IASB and International Accounting Standards

4.186 The history of international accounting standards which began in 1966 with the proposal to establish an International Study Group whose members included the Institute of Chartered Accountants in England and Wales ('ICAEW'), the American Institute of Certified Public Accountants ('AICPA'), and the Canadian Institute of Chartered Accountants ('CICA') has been fundamental to the development of the global capital markets. The working group that was formed (the Accountants International Study Group ('AISG')) published a number of papers and in June 1973 the International Accounting Standards Committee ('IASC')

---

[134] As at the date of publication, no countries were on the list of non-cooperative countries: <http://www.fatf-gafi.org/document/4/0,3343,en_32250379_32236992_33916420_1_1_1_1,00.html>.

[135] Banco Santander, Bank of Tokyo-Mitsubishi UFJ, Barclays Bank PLC, Citigroup, Credit Suisse, Deutsche Bank, Goldman Sachs, HSBC, JP Morgan Chase, Société Générale, UBS.

[136] <http://www.wolfsberg-principles.com/standards.html>.

was established[137] to agree and set out international standards. However, agreement on these fundamental issues has been neither easy nor straightforward and there are still substantive differences that the successors of these bodies are still trying to reconcile.

The IASC was disbanded in 2001 and its successor, the International Accounting **4.187** Standards Board ('IASB'), is an independent, privately funded accounting standard setter located in London. The IASB has 14 members who report to an oversight body (the Trustees of the International Accounting Standards Committee Foundation) that was formed as a Delaware not-for-profit corporation in 2000/2001. The objectives of the IASC Foundation are to develop, in the public interest, a single set of high quality, understandable, and enforceable global accounting standards that require high quality, transparent, and comparable information in financial statements and other financial reporting to help participants in the world's capital markets and other users make economic decisions, to promote the use and rigorous application of those standards, to take account of, as appropriate, the special needs of small and medium-sized entities and emerging economies, and to bring about convergence of national accounting standards and International Accounting Standards ('IAS')[138] and International Financial Reporting Standards ('IFRS').

The IASB also has a Standards Advisory Council that acts as a standards advisory **4.188** body and it provides a forum for organisations and individuals with an interest in international financial reporting to take part in standard setting. The Council has approximately 50 members and individual members are appointed for a renewable term of three years and have diverse geographical and professional backgrounds. The Council is responsible for giving advice to the IASB on agenda decisions and priorities in the IASB's work, and for informing the IASB of the views of the organisations and individuals on the Council on major standard setting projects, and giving other advice to the IASB or the Trustees.

---

[137] The IASC was founded in June 1973 as a result of an agreement between the accountancy bodies in Australia, Canada, France, Germany, Japan, Mexico, the Netherlands, the UK and Ireland, and the USA, and these countries constituted the Board of IASC at that time. The international professional activities of the accountancy bodies were organised under the auspices of the International Federation of Accountants (IFAC) in 1977 but in 1981, IASC and IFAC agreed that IASC would have full and complete autonomy in setting international accounting standards and in publishing discussion documents on international accounting issues. At the same time, all members of IFAC became members of IASC but this membership link was discontinued in May 2000 when IASC's constitution was changed as part of the reorganisation of IASC.

[138] Statements of International Accounting Standards issued by the Board of the International Accounting Standards Committee ('IASC') between 1973 and 2001 are designated 'International Accounting Standards' ('IAS').

4.189 The IASB has a separate interpretative body (the International Financial Reporting Interpretations Committee—formerly the Standing Interpretations Committee) which is comprised of 12 members representing the wider accounting and financial community. The Committee reviews various accounting issues that are likely to receive divergent or unacceptable treatment in the absence of authoritative guidance, with a view to reaching consensus on the appropriate accounting treatment. In developing interpretations, the Committee meets approximately every six weeks to address issues including newly identified financial reporting issues not specifically dealt with in International Financial Reporting Standards, or issues where unsatisfactory or conflicting interpretations have developed, or seem likely to develop in the absence of authoritative guidance, with a view to reaching a consensus on the appropriate treatment.

4.190 The IASB announced in April 2001 that its accounting standards would be designated 'International Financial Reporting Standards' ('IFRS') and that it would adopt all of the International Accounting Standards issued by the IASC. The Interpretations of International Accounting Standards issued by the International Financial Reporting Interpretations Committee do not have the same status as IASs, although financial statements should not be described as complying with International Accounting Standards unless they comply with all the requirements of each applicable Standard and each applicable interpretation of the Standing Interpretations Committee. The IASB has adopted a conceptual framework underlying its financial reporting standards and interpretations, the Framework for the Preparation and Presentation of Financial Statements (the Framework)[139] that sets out the concepts that underlie the preparation and presentation of financial statements for external users as well as publishing the IFRSs, and the interpretations of International Accounting Standards developed by the International Financial Reporting Interpretations Committee. These standards have been adopted by various countries, including the European Commission, to require the use of IASC Standards for all listed companies no later than 2005.

The Financial Accounting Standards Board

4.191 The US-backed Financial Accounting Standards Board ('FASB') was established in 1973[140] as the designated organisation in the private sector for establishing standards of financial accounting and reporting. Those standards govern the

---

[139] Available from the IASB.

[140] Prior to the current structure being put in place, financial accounting and reporting standards in the US were established by the Committee on Accounting Procedure of the American Institute of

preparation of financial reports and have been officially recognised as authoritative by the Securities and Exchange Commission (Financial Reporting Release No 1, Section 101 and reaffirmed in its April 2003 Policy Statement) and the American Institute of Certified Public Accountants (Rule 203, Rules of Professional Conduct, as amended May 1973 and May 1979).

The FASB was established to improve standards of financial accounting and **4.192** reporting for the guidance and education of the public, including issuers, auditors, and users of financial information, and the FASB seeks to improve the usefulness of financial reporting by focusing on the primary characteristics of relevance and reliability and on the qualities of comparability and consistency, to keep standards current to reflect changes in methods of doing business and changes in the economic environment, to consider promptly any significant areas of deficiency in financial reporting that might be improved through the standard-setting process, to promote the international convergence of accounting standards concurrent with improving the quality of financial reporting, and to improve the common understanding of the nature and purposes of information contained in financial reports. The FASB also develops broad accounting concepts as well as standards for financial reporting and provides guidance on implementation of standards. Research is conducted by the FASB staff and others, including foreign national and international accounting standard setting bodies, on various accounting matters.

Like the IASB, the FSAB reports to an independent Financial Accounting **4.193** Foundation ('FAF') that is separate from all other constituent organisations. However, its Board of Trustees is made up of members from these constituent organisations[141] having interest in financial reporting and approved by the FAF Trustees. There also are a number of Trustees-at-large who are not nominated by those organisations, but are chosen by the sitting Trustees and who are responsible for selecting the members of the FASB and its advisory council as well as ensuring adequate funding of their activities and for exercising general oversight with the exception of the FASB's resolution of technical issues.

Financial Accounting Standards Advisory Council ('FASAC') has responsi- **4.194** bility for consulting with the FASB on technical issues on the Board's agenda

---

Certified Public Accountants (1936–59) and then by the Accounting Principles Board, also a part of the AICPA (1959–73). The pronouncements of those predecessor bodies remain in force unless amended or superseded by the FASB.

[141] FAF Constituent Organisations are: the American Accounting Association, American Institute of Certified Public Accountants, the CFA Institute, the Financial Executives International, the Government Finance Officers Association, the Institute of Management Accountants, the National Association of State Auditors, Comptrollers, and Treasurers, and the Securities Industry Association.

including project priorities, matters likely to require the attention of the FASB, selection and organisation of task forces, and such other matters as may be requested by the FASB or its chairman. The Council has more than 30 members who are broadly representative of preparers, auditors, and users of financial information.

4.195 Finally, in 1984, the FAF established the Governmental Accounting Standards Board ('GASB') to set standards of financial accounting and reporting for State and local governmental authorities such as State bodies and municipal or city governments. As with the FASB, the FAF is responsible for selecting its members, ensuring adequate funding, and exercising general oversight.

Sarbanes-Oxley and its Impact on Non-US Entities

4.196 Although not a supranational body, one of the most far-reaching pieces of legislation in the global financial services and particularly the capital markets and banking sector in recent years is the US's Sarbanes-Oxley Act of 2002.[142] This law, passed in the wake of the Enron and WorldCom financial scandals, was designed to strengthen corporate governance and to restore investor confidence in the US markets. However, the legislation is extremely wide ranging and establishes new or enhanced standards for all US public company[143] boards, management, and public accounting firms, and its impact both within and outside the US has been seismic in terms of corporate reporting.

4.197 The impact of Sarbanes-Oxley has been far wider—wider even than the extraterritorial reach of the US legislation—in that it has driven many of the major developed markets to consider and implement similar corporate governance legislation and has resulted in a step change in the approach of regulators to many issues including public company reporting, senior management responsibility, and auditor independence.

4.198 The Act was intended 'to protect investors by improving the accuracy and reliability of corporate disclosures made pursuant to the securities laws, and for other purposes'. One of these 'other purposes' has been to extend the reach of US law and the regulatory authority of the US Securities and Exchange Commission

---

[142] Pub L No 107–204, 116 Stat 745 (2002).

[143] Public companies include all companies required to file reports under the Securities and Exchange Act of 1934 or to file registration statements under the Securities Act of 1933. Certain other 'listed companies'—ie those having listings on one or more US exchanges—and small business issuers are also required to comply with some of its provisions.

('SEC') to foreign corporations registered on US stock exchanges. European companies, their directors and officers, as well as their independent auditors and legal advisors have therefore had to address the many issues arising from this legislation.

The key feature of the law was to expand greatly the responsibilities of audit **4.199** committees and to impose stringent independence requirements, effectively prohibiting international accounting firms from providing certain non-audit services including legal services, management consultancy services, and other professional services to any of their audit clients listed or registered on US exchanges. The law also required sweeping new certification requirements for directors and officers of US registrant corporations that financial reports contain 'no untrue statement or omissions of material facts' and required accountants to attest to some new representations as to a company's compliance with financial reporting requirements.

The Sarbanes-Oxley Act requires companies to establish mandates for directors **4.200** and officers, regarding 'corporate responsibility' certifications and assessments, in connection with each and every quarterly or annual financial report, including representations by the company's chief executive officer and chief financial officer that they have reviewed the quarterly and annual reports, assertions by these officers that they are responsible for the company's system of internal control, certification, based on evaluations made within 90 days of the respective financial reports, that such internal controls are adequate and effective, and certification that these officers have disclosed, both to the company's audit committee of the board of directors and to the company's independent auditors any significant deficiencies in controls, and all instances of possible fraud (whether or not material) involving management or any employees with significant control responsibilities. The law also contains provisions for the protection of corporate whistleblowers in some circumstances.[144] Finally, the law imposes very wide criminal and civil penalties and sanctions for companies and their officers that violate US securities laws and regulations with criminal penalties of up to 20 years' imprisonment for the destruction, alteration, or falsification of any documents, corporate records, or audit records subject to any investigation of any agency or department of the US Government.

---

[144] The US First Circuit Court held in *Carnero v Boston Scientific Corp*, 433 F.3d 1 (1st Cir. 2006) that Congress did not intend the whistleblowing provisions of Sarbanes-Oxley to apply extraterritorially. However the US Federal Courts for the Southern District of New York have recently held that these provisions may still apply to US company's conduct overseas. See *O'Mahony v Accenture*, 07 Civ. 7916, 2008 U.S. Dist. LEXIS 10600 (S.D.N.Y. Feb. 5, 2008).

4.201   The Sarbanes-Oxley Act also established a new Public Companies Accounting Oversight Board ('PCAOB'), under ultimate oversight of the SEC, with authority over registered public accounting firms (whether domestic or foreign) regarding auditing and audit standards, audit quality control, and auditor independence standards and rules, inspections of accounting firms registered with the Board, and the ability to carry out investigations and disciplinary proceedings against auditors of US registered public companies. The board is not a US government agency but is made up of five individuals who are selected by the chairman of the Board of Governors of the Federal Reserve System and the Secretary of State of the Department of the Treasury, and who report to the Securities and Exchange Commission. The law also proposed mandatory rotation of registered public accounting firms.

4.202   The Act also acknowledged the role of the Financial Accounting Standards Board ('FASB'), under the oversight of the SEC, to promulgate and define US generally accepted accounting principles ('GAAP').

4.203   The company's auditors are required to attest to management's assessment of the adequacy and effectiveness of internal controls, and new financial reporting disclosure requirements have been adopted including a mandatory financial reports feature whereby all material correcting adjustments required by the company's independent auditors are disclosed, that all material off-balance sheet transactions, arrangements, obligations (including contingent obligations) have been disclosed, the requirement of pro forma financial information, provided in any public filings or press releases or other public disclosures, and the confirmation that these contain no untrue statements, or any omissions, of material facts. The law has also established new conflicts of interest standards and rules of conduct for securities analysts.

4.204   Non-US companies whose securities are not registered on US stock exchanges will not be directly affected by Sarbanes-Oxley, but for those companies that are registrants with the SEC and on US stock exchanges, the effects are far-reaching. The Act expressly applies to any non-US company registered on US exchanges under either the Securities Act or the Exchange Act, regardless of such company's country of incorporation or corporate domicile. The Act requires that auditors of such registrants, regardless of their nationality or place of business, be subject to the oversight of the PCAOB and to the statutory requirements of Sarbanes-Oxley. Directors and officers of registrants, namely chief executive officers and chief financial officers (or finance directors) and regardless of nationality, are required by Sarbanes-Oxley to provide the enumerated certifications and to conduct the internal controls assessments set forth in the Act.[145] Penalties and sanctions—both

---

[145] See PricewaterhouseCoopers Securities Litigation Review 2007, <http://10b5.pwc.com/PDF/2007%20SECURITY%20LIT%20STUDY%20W-LT.PDF>.

criminal and civil—under Sarbanes-Oxley apply equally to US and non-US corporate registrants,[146] and their directors and officers, and their independent auditors and legal advisors.

The application of Sarbanes-Oxley to US registered companies and its wider **4.205** impact abroad had not, however, been without criticism or comment.[147] However, several European countries have also adopted legislation comparable in scope to the Sarbanes-Oxley Act. The French Financial Security Act (Loi de Sécurité Financière—LSF) of August 2003 introduced new requirements on disclosures to shareholders and the market for the purposes of corporate governance and internal control. The Autorité des Marchés Financiers ('AMF') has also indicated that it will be requiring non-EU issuers listed or offering their securities in France to comply with their requirements that are, in some respects, more stringent than the Sarbanes-Oxley requirements.

The UK has similar provisions in that in July 2003, the revised non-statutory **4.206** Combined Code on Corporate Governance promulgated by the Financial Reporting Council was issued which supersedes the Combined Code issued by the Hampel Committee in 1998 and includes the Turnbull guidance on internal control, the Smith guidance on audit committees, and various items of good practice guidance from the Higgs Report. The Code, although non-statutory, is referred to in the UK Listing Rules, which are published by the Financial Services Authority as the UK Listing Authority ('UKLA'), and all UK listed companies subject to the Listing Rules must include in their annual report a statement of their compliance with their Combined Code or explain matters of non-compliance. The Financial Reporting Council has instigated a review of the Turnbull guidance, and the Companies Act 2006 now provides a statutory statement of

---

[146] These new powers have already been exercised by the SEC Department of Enforcement and other US enforcement agencies including the Department of Justice against a number of non-US firms including: A.C.L.N. (Belgium); Adelphia; Allied Irish Bank (Ireland); AOL Time Warner; Cendant; Elan (Ireland); Enron; Global Crossings; ImClone; Learnout & Hauspie (Belgium); Livent (Canada); McKesson HBOC; Microsoft; Microstrategies; Montedison (Italy); National Steel; Paracelsus (Germany); Rite-Aid; Sensormatic; Sunbeam; Tyco (Bermuda); UBS PaineWebber (Switzerland); Waste Management; WorldCom; and Xerox. See D Dooley, *Sarbanes-Oxley: A Guide for Europeans, Part I*, European Business Forum.

[147] 'Political blindness to the international relations viewpoint was evident from the US failure to consult regulatory counterparts abroad and from the heated political rhetoric accompanying SOX, advertised as the most sweeping reform of American business practices since the 1930s. By US standards, SOX is a codification, fitting easily if clumsily into the US corporate template, more nearly incremental tinkering than substantive reform. This rhetoric-reality gap reflects uncertainty about how bad things were on the one hand and public perceptions that they are certainly awful on the other. Sweeping rhetoric lets the public think Congress is doing something; limited substance enables regulators to hold back in case less is wrong than many think.' Lawrence A Cunningham (Professor of Law and Business, Boston College), speech to the FESE Convention at the Guildhall, London on Thursday, 12 June 2003.

directors' duties and the extension of criminal sanctions for breaches of directors' duties. The Companies Act 2006 also allows auditors to limit their liability subject to shareholder approval and the UK has implemented the various provisions of the EU Transparency Directive[148] on shareholder reporting.[149]

Global Regulatory Convergence—The Credit Crunch and the Role of Supranational Bodies in Creating Financial Stability in the Global Market

4.207 In the second half of 2007 and 2008, the increasingly difficult economic and market conditions arising (in part but not wholly) from the collapse of the US sub-prime mortgage market and the accompanying reluctance of global banks to lend to one another at inter-bank rates approximating central bank policy rates (the 'credit crunch') triggered a number of international reactions to try to bring financial stability back into the markets.

4.208 The traditional role of the national central banks in dealing with the effects of global financial instability was called into question by the credit crunch. Foreshadowing the coming storm, former US Treasury Secretary Robert Rubin put the sentiments bluntly when he wrote in 2003: 'Our politics may not be well suited to coping with the new risks of the global economy'.[150]

Financial Stability Forum and the Credit Crunch

4.209 In October 2007, the G-7 Ministers and Central Bank Governors asked the Financial Stability Forum ('FSF') to undertake an analysis of the causes and weaknesses that produced the credit crunch and to set out recommendations for increasing the resilience of markets and institutions. The FSF, whose work drew on a number of supranational bodies including the Basel Committee on Banking Supervision ('BCBS'), the International Organization of Securities Commissions ('IOSCO'), the International Association of Insurance Supervisors ('IAIS'), the Joint Forum, the International Accounting Standards Board ('IASB'), the Committee on Payment and Settlement Systems ('CPSS'), the Committee on the Global Financial System ('CGFS'), the International Monetary Fund ('IMF'), the Bank for International Settlements ('BIS'),

---

[148] Directive 2004/109/EC.
[149] FSA: Transparency Obligations Directive (Disclosure and Transparency Rules) Instrument 2006 amending the Disclosure and Transparency Rules.
[150] RE Rubin, *In an Uncertain World* (Random House, 2003).

reported to the G-7 Ministers and Governors at their meeting in Washington in April 2008.[151]

In order to re-establish confidence in the soundness of markets and financial insti-   **4.210**
tutions, national authorities including central banks took exceptional steps including monetary and fiscal stimulus, central bank liquidity operations, policies to promote asset market liquidity, and actions to resolve problems at specific institutions with a view to facilitating adjustment and dampening the impact on the real economy. The financial system has, however, remained under stress and the FSF proposed concrete actions in the five specific areas:

- Strengthened prudential oversight of capital, liquidity, and risk management;
- Enhancing transparency and valuation;
- Changes in the role and uses of credit ratings;
- Strengthening the authorities' responsiveness to risks;
- Robust arrangements for dealing with stress in the financial system,

the goal being to strengthen the efficiency and resilience of the system without hindering the processes of market discipline and innovation that are essential to the financial system's contribution to economic growth.

The report set out a number of specific recommendations including: **4.211**

- The Basel II capital framework should be implemented on a timely basis.

- National supervisors would strengthen the Basel II capital treatment of structured credit and securitisation activities.

- Capital requirements for certain complex structured credit products such as collateralised debt obligations of asset-backed securities would be studied and raised.

- Proposals would be put forward to strengthen the capital treatment for banks' liquidity facilities to off-balance sheet asset-backed commercial paper conduits.

- Authorities should ensure that the capital buffers for monoline insurers and financial guarantors are commensurate with their role in the financial system.

- Banking supervisors would issue for consultation sound practice guidance on the management and supervision of liquidity.

- Banking supervisors would use Basel Pillar 2 to strengthen banks' risk management practices, to sharpen banks' control of tail risks and mitigate the build-up of excessive exposures and risk concentrations.

---

[151] Report of the Financial Stability Forum on Enhancing Market and Institutional Resilience, <http://www.fsforum.org/publications/r_0804.pdf> and its October 2008 follow up report on implementation, <http://www.fsforum.org/press/pr_081009f.pdf>.

- Banking supervisors would strengthen guidance relating to the management of firm-wide risks, including concentration risks.

- The IASB would improve the accounting and disclosure standards for off-balance-sheet vehicles on an accelerated basis and work with other standard setters toward international convergence.

- The International Auditing and Assurance Standards Board, as well as the major national audit standard setters and relevant regulators should consider the lessons learned during the market turmoil and, where necessary, enhance the guidance for audits of valuations of complex or illiquid financial products and related disclosures.

- Credit rating agencies should improve the quality of the rating process and manage conflicts of interest in rating structured products and IOSCO has reissued its Code of Conduct Fundamentals for Credit Rating Agencies.

- Supervisors, regulators, and central banks—individually and collectively—would take additional steps to more effectively translate their risk analysis into actions that mitigate those risks.

- At the international level, the FSF would give more force to its own risk analysis and recommendations, both directly and through the actions of its members, by initiating and following up action to investigate and mitigate risk.

- Authorities' exchange of information and cooperation in the development of good practices will be improved at national and international levels so that, by end-2008, a college exists for each of the largest global financial institutions.

- Banking supervisors and central banks should improve cooperation and the exchange of information including in the assessment of financial stability risks. The exchange of information should be rapid during periods of market strain.

- International bodies should enhance the speed, prioritisation, and coordination of their policy development work including encouraging joint strategic reviews by standard setting committees to better ensure policy development is coordinated and focused on priorities.

- Central bank operational frameworks should be sufficiently flexible in terms of potential frequency and maturity of operations, available instruments, and the range of counterparties and collateral, to deal with extraordinary situations.

- Banking authorities should clarify and strengthen national and cross-border arrangements for dealing with weak banks and review, and where necessary, strengthen deposit insurance arrangements.

- For the largest cross-border financial firms, the most directly involved supervisors and central banks should establish a small group to address specific cross-border crisis management planning issues and this group should hold its first meeting before the end of 2008.

However, both the US Federal Reserve[152] and the UK Bank of England[153] found **4.212** that although there was general agreement as to the broad principles of regulation, the regulatory tools at their command were limited in the face of a serious and widening crisis in the financial markets. Initially they responded with the tools of monetary policy such as raising interest rates but these seemed to have little effect on the spiral of inter-connected economic and regulatory failures that were not limited to one country's markets or economy.

The IMF as the Lender of Last Resort

In the first half of 2008 as the impact of the credit crunch deepened, several bank- **4.213** ing institutions found themselves in financial difficulties which required national central banks to step in to maintain financial stability and avoid contagion in the

---

[152] See statements by US Treasury Secretary Paulson and Federal Reserve Chairman Bernanke at <http://www.house.gov/apps/list/hearing/financialsvcs_dem/hr071008.shtml>. In April 2008, US Treasury Secretary Henry Paulson announced proposals for wide-ranging changes to the whole regulatory structure of the financial services industry in the US. As a result the Federal Reserve would have the power to regulate virtually the entire US financial services industry. These proposals are part of a sweeping overhaul of the US Government's regulatory foreshadowed by the President's Working Group on Financial Markets which recently released a series of recommendations addressing issues including ratings agencies, securitisation, mortgage origination, and OTC derivatives. A new style Federal Reserve would replace the Federal Reserve's more limited role of bank holding company supervision because the US Treasury says that it recognises the need for enhanced regulatory authority to complement market discipline to deal with systemic risk. Other proposals included:
- modernising the President's Working Group on Financial Markets;
- creating a new Federal Commission for Mortgage Origination to evaluate, rate, and report on the adequacy of each state's system for licensing and regulation of participants in the mortgage origination process;
- creating a Federal Charter for Insurance to encourage a more competitive US industry and taking away some of the powers of the states to regulate insurance;
- merging the Securities and Exchange Commission and the Commodities and Futures Trading Commission and their regulatory philosophies;
- developing an objectives-based regulatory approach for the future which will consist of a market stability regulator, a prudential regulator and a business conduct regulator with a focus on consumer protection giving the Federal Reserve authority to look at the financial status of any institution that could affect market stability;
- giving stock exchanges more room for self-regulation.

[153] The UK 'Tripartite Authorities' of the UK Treasury, the Bank of England and the UK Financial Services Authority published a joint consultation paper in January 2008, 'Financial stability and depositor protection: strengthening the framework' (CM 7308) on issues arising from the regulatory failures which the Northern Rock plc situation and the ongoing credit crunch had given rise to. This was followed up in July 2008 by a further consultation (CM 7436) setting out the UK Government's proposals to:
- strengthen the stability and resilience of the financial system—in the UK and internationally;
- reduce the likelihood of individual banks facing difficulties—including regulatory interventions and liquidity assistance;
- reduce the impact if, nevertheless, a bank does get into difficulties;
- provide effective compensation arrangements in which consumers have confidence; and
- strengthen the Bank of England, and ensuring effective coordinated actions by authorities, both in the UK and internationally.

banking sector. In the UK, Northern Rock plc, was finally taken into public ownership by the UK Government in February 2008[154] and US investment bank, Bear Stearns, was 'rescued' by JP Morgan Chase at the behest of the US Federal Reserve. The Danish Central Bank (Danmarks Nationalbank) was also called upon to take over the assets of Roskilde Bank A/S[155] and questions began to arise regarding the role of the IMF as the lender of last resort.

4.214 From Bretton Woods onwards, the IMF had stepped in to help resolve currency crises such as those that afflicted developing economies such as Mexico, Asian countries, and Argentina in the 1990s.[156] The situation in 2008 is, however, arguably different because the IMF was now being asked to help the central banks of the major developed economies, in particular the US and the UK. Previously, there had always been an assumption that the US would bail out whoever needed to be bailed out because it is the main contributor of funds to the IMF;[157] however, when the US economy was experiencing major economic problems leading to global contagion in the markets then the supranational regulatory authorities were in largely uncharted territory.[158]

4.215 The question then arose of whether the IMF should become the international lender of last resort to the national lenders of last resort or even whether the IMF should become a global supervisor with an 'early warning system' for bank failures.[159] The IMF lacks the fundamental requirement for such a role, however, in that it has no power to print money in order to create liquidity in the system.[160] In addition, the IMF acts by consensus and as we have seen national regulators have needed to take decisive action to shore up the markets and do not have the luxury of time to consider, debate, and consult a wide range of interests.

4.216 It has also been suggested that the IMF might become a super-regulator for banks given the global reach of the major investment banking institutions but it would

---

[154] See The Northern Rock PLC Transfer Order 2008, SI 2008/432.

[155] See Press release dated 24 August 2008, Danish Central Bank: <http://www.nationalbanken. dk/DNUK/PressRoom.nsf/side/PressDNN20087204/$file/DNN20087204.pdf>.

[156] There was, of course, the sterling crisis in the mid 70's but that was a UK-specific problem rather than a global one. For a historical analysis of the history of the lender of last resort theory see: WR Cline, 'The Case for a Lender-of-Last-Resort Role for the IMF', Center for Global Development and Institute for International Economics, 23 September 2005. (<http://www. petersoninstitute.org/publications/papers/cline0905imf.pdf>).

[157] See 'An International Lender of Last Resort, the IMF and the Federal Reserve', Representative Jim Saxton, Vice Chairman, US House of Representatives, Joint Economic Committee, February 1999. (<http://www.house.gov/jec/imf/lolr.pdf>).

[158] See EB Kapstein, BIS Working Papers No 199, *Architects of stability? International cooperation among financial supervisors, BIS Monetary and Economic Department*, February 2006, p 15.

[159] See JD Sachs, *The International Lender of Last Report: What are the Alternatives?* (<http:// www.bos.frb.org/economic/conf/conf43/181p.pdf>)

[160] S Fischer, *On the Need for an International Lender of Last Resort*, New York, 3 January 1999 (<http://www.imf.org/external/np/speeches/1999/010399.htm>)

appear that the IMF is too far away from the day-to-day supervision of institutions to do so effectively. However, the IMF continues to play an important role in ensuring multilateralism because the challenges facing the world economy are of a global nature, requiring strong action and close cooperation.[161]

The Global Economy and the Future of Supranational Bodies

In a response to a 2006 BIS Working paper on financial stability, Peter Praet of the National Bank of Belgium had said: 'Contrary to monetary policy, the responsibility for financial stability is shared with other authorities; in particular, supervisors and treasuries. The governance of the process is—unavoidably—complex, and the potential for frictions, both domestic and international, is high, especially given that public money is at stake'.[162] This was now being borne out by the credit crunch and governments have increasingly turned to the supranational bodies for a solution. **4.217**

In considering the role of the IMF, Alistair Darling, the UK Chancellor of the Exchequer, has called for reform of both the IMF and World Bank, institutions he says that were set up over 60 years ago and designed for another age.[163] These bodies, the Chancellor argued, needed to be reformed and refocused to deal with the challenges of which financial stability was perhaps the most pressing but not the only example of where the various member nations need to act together. **4.218**

In a speech at the Washington think tank, the Brookings Institute, Darling urged that urgent action was required on the big challenges facing the global economy—financial stability and how to deal with rising food and commodity prices that are already impacting developing and developed countries alike. **4.219**

Although both governments and central banks around the world have already taken action in response to these developments and made coordinated efforts to improve liquidity in money markets, the issue remains as to how to inject and maintain confidence in the financial markets in the face of the ongoing uncertainty in the financial markets. Darling did recognise that some of the instability has arisen through investors and institutions chasing 'the search for yield' during **4.220**

---

[161] IMF, Communiqué of the International Monetary and Financial Committee of the Board of Governors of the International Monetary Fund, Press Release No 08/78, 12 April 2008.

[162] BIS Working Paper 199, 'Observations on the paper by E Kapstein' (P Praet, National Bank of Belgium), p 22 (<http://www.bis.org/publ/work199.pdf>).

[163] Alistair Darling, MP, 'The Response to Global Economy Issues', Brookings Institution, 11 April 2008 (<http://www.brookings.edu/~/media/Files/events/2008/0411_global_economics/0411_global_economics_darling.pdf>).

a period where the markets have experienced historically low interest rates. He said:

> Financial innovation has brought considerable benefits. It has allowed increased access to finance, with the easier and more efficient allocation of capital with, and between, economies. It has also increased the scope for risk to be diversified. That is all to the good. But recent events have also highlighted that the increased complexity and sophistication of markets carry risks that need to be better managed and understood. Innovation brings huge benefits provided institutions and regulators can understand what they are doing. The problem is that too many institutions, too many boards who have primary responsibility for what their firms are doing, failed to understand the risks to which they became exposed. There must therefore be greater transparency in the financial markets, providing greater certainty and confidence. That is why today, in the present context, the sooner institutions disclose their positions the better. This is not just a matter for individual banks. It matters to us all. I see that in the past few days some banks have pleaded mea culpa. Indeed, but we are all feeling the consequences.

4.221 The Chancellor indicated that international coordination is necessary and cooperation between supervisors is important—so that problems can be identified before they take hold and spread. However, he warned that:

> [o]ur response needs to be measured and proportionate—we must not repeat what I might call the 'Enron mistake', where in an attempt to deal with an undoubted problem, there were unintended and undesirable consequences. It is not a question of more regulation—often it is a question of regulators and management doing their job effectively.

Darling said that there were two key lessons that can be drawn from the current crisis: first, that national economies are inextricably linked and that events in one country can impact on others around the world and second that there is a need for governments and regulators to take action in response to the risks that have been identified. He called for the IMF to work with the Financial Stability Forum to develop an early warning system, focusing its surveillance more closely on financial sector issues and on the links between developments in the financial sector and the wider economy and to strengthen its analysis of 'spillovers' between national economies.[164] However, this new role would require reform of these institutions in order to make the IMF more representative of its members' roles in the global economy and that these long-standing and established organisations needed to be ready to change otherwise they risk becoming marginalised and

---

[164] The Financial Stability Forum published its paper on *Credit Risk Transfer: developments from 2005–2007* in July 2008 but its recommendations to regulators and supervisors including that 'Supervisory authorities need to ensure that they have the requisite resources and expertise to oversee CRT activities at the firms they supervise, and should ensure that these firms in turn have the capacity to understand and manage all of the risks in their CRT positions' is, in the case of the credit crunch, definitely a case of shutting the stable door after the horse has bolted.

ineffective in supporting the cooperation needed to deal with global events and issues.

However, the debate continues and a global regulatory solution remains at some distance; the supranational bodies must, therefore, continue to fulfil their role in providing fori for cooperation and discussion and in keeping the lines of communication between the regulators and between the regulators and market participants open.[165]

4.222

---

[165] As Benjamin Franklin told the US Continental Congress, 'We must all hang together or assuredly we shall all hang separately.' An admonition that has resonances for the global markets today just as it did in 1776.

Part II

FINANCIAL SERVICES REGULATION

5

FSA HANDBOOK AND HIGH-LEVEL STANDARDS

Introduction

What is the Handbook?

The FSA exists to perform functions connected with the regulation of financial **5.01**
services. FSMA distinguishes the FSA's particular functions from its general functions.[1] Its particular functions are not defined as such. They include all the myriad
tasks that the FSA is required to perform under FSMA, other primary legislation,
subordinate legislation, and European legislation. These include the enforcement
of the regulatory perimeter; the authorisation, supervision, and discipline of
financial services firms and their employees; cooperation with other regulators at
local, European, and international level; the prevention of financial crime; providing public information about financial services; and reporting to Parliament and
the public.

The FSA's general functions are defined[2] as: **5.02**

(a) Its function of making rules under FSMA (considered as a whole);
(b) Its function of preparing and issuing codes under FSMA (considered as a
    whole);
(c) Its functions in relation to the giving of general guidance (considered as a
    whole); and
(d) Its function of determining the general policy and principles by reference to
    which it discharges its particular functions.

The general functions are, therefore, the instrumentality by which the FSA dis- **5.03**
charges its particular functions. It is no surprise that the FSA's obligation to pursue

---

[1] FSMA, s 2(4).
[2] ibid.

statutory objectives[3] and to have regard to seven 'principles of good regulation'[4] attach to its performance of general functions.[5] The FSA's Handbook of Rules and Guidance ('the Handbook') is one of the most important products or physical expressions of the FSA's general functions: it is the primary re-statement of the rules, codes, and general guidance through which the FSA performs its particular functions. It is therefore also the most obvious physical expression of the FSA's policy.

Current pressures on the Handbook

5.04 Because it is such an important expression of how the FSA performs its general functions, the Handbook is a focal point for debate about how well the FSA regulates and how well it meets the objectives of 'better regulation' as originally enunciated in the Hampton and Arculus Reports of 2005 (and which can be traced through the Better Regulation Task Force to the Legislative and Regulatory Reform Act 2006 and to the present Better Regulation Executive, part of HM Government's Department for Business, Enterprise and Regulatory Reform).

5.05 A key early strategy for better regulation enunciated by the Better Regulation Task Force, and accepted (in principle at least) by Government, was 'one in, one out'. In a speech to the FSA in June 2005, Sir David Arculus (then head of the Better Regulation Task Force) explained that strategy as follows:

> its much too easy for . . . regulators to react to events . . . by producing yet another equivalent of the Dangerous Dogs Act. Most times there is already a law in place which is perfectly adequate but which is not being followed properly. Sometimes of course there does need to be a change in the law, and when that is the case, [the BRTF proposes] . . . that a compensatory simplification measure be brought in.

Simplification might mean deregulation or it might mean consolidation of an existing regulation or it might mean rationalisation—using horizontal regulation (such as a general duty not to trade unfairly) to replace a variety of sector specific regulations. Alternatively, it might mean a targeted sectoral guide.[6]

---

[3] FSMA, s 2(1).

[4] ibid, s 2(3).

[5] The FSA's designation as a body whose regulatory functions are subject to the Legislative and Regulatory Reform Act 2006, ss 21 and 22 (see the Legislative and Regulatory Reform (Regulatory Functions) Order 2007, SI 2007/3544, art 2 and Sched 1) means that in addition to the principles of good regulation in FSMA the FSA must also have regard to the principles contained in the *Statutory Code of Compliance for Regulators* (Department for Business, Enterprise and Regulatory Reform, 17 December 2007) when exercising its general functions of determining its policy and issuing guidance.

[6] The speech can be found at <http://www.fsa.gov.uk/Pages/Library/Communication/Speeches/2005/0705_sda.shtm>l.

Better regulation is an idea whose time has come in Europe as well as in the UK: **5.06**

> To my mind better regulation should mean not only fewer, and where they do exist, better targeted rules, but also that the design of these rules is based on open consultation and detailed economic impact analysis. This is vital. We must change our mindset in the EU from a presumption of rule making to deal with problems to a presumption of no rule making unless a vigorous set of tests are passed. Starting with: is there a market failure? Indeed the success, or failure, of any measure—be it legislative or non-legislative—largely depends on the input received from regulators, supervisors and market participants.[7]

It is that rationalisation, making the most of existing general duties, as a deliberate **5.07** substitute for making additional specific rules, driven by the political, commercial, and common-sense desire for better regulation, that underlies the FSA's current focus on 'principle-based regulation'.

That focus has had (and will continue to have) important consequences for the **5.08** Handbook. In summary:

(a) Increased reliance on the FSA Principles for Businesses and other high-level rules as a substitute for detailed rule-making should gradually make the Handbook leaner, though it also poses risks for firms and for the FSA in terms of the predictability and enforceability of FSA rules (see para 5.19 *et seq.* below). Recent examples of the FSA's new approach can be seen in the simplified Conduct of Business Sourcebook ('COBS') and in the individual capital adequacy regimes for insurers, which rely overtly on high-level 'principle-based' requirements.[8]

(b) The FSA has articulated its approach to the mass of general public material that it publishes, but which sits outside the Handbook. Importantly, that approach puts general guidance (including guidance re-stated in the Handbook) and individual guidance on the same footing as other FSA public material relevant to compliance with rules (see para 5.77 *et seq.* below).

(c) The FSA is likely to rely more on FSA-confirmed industry guidance as a substitute for its own guidance (see para 5.77 *et seq.* below).

What material goes into the Handbook?

Although it is accurate to describe the Handbook as the primary re-statement of **5.09** the rules, codes, and general guidance, through which the FSA performs its

---

[7] C McCreevy, *The Blueprint for the Development of European Financial Services—The Legislative and Regulatory Programme,* Speech to the Association of Compliance Officers in Ireland Conference, Dublin, 26 November 2007:

[8] FSA, 'Policy Statement 06/14: Prudential Changes for Insurers' (December 2006) and INSPRU 7.

particular functions (see para 5.03 above), that description needs explanation and elaboration:[9]

(a) The FSA is under statutory obligation to make some of its written output public. For example, FSMA, s 153 requires the FSA to exercise its rule-making powers in writing, in a document that FSMA identifies as a 'rule-making instrument'.[10] FSMA also requires the FSA to publish all its rule-making instruments.[11] Most other legislative provisions made by the FSA (such as general guidance and codes) are also in practice made by instrument. The FSA publishes the instruments it makes on its website. That fulfils the FSA's obligations to publish its rules. The definitive version of the FSA's rules at any time is the version contained in the legal instruments.[12] (See generally, para 5.104 below.) What appears in the Handbook is not the instruments themselves, but a consolidated re-statement of the instruments in force at a given time.

(b) In fact, there are several versions of the Handbook. At the time of writing, the online consolidated Handbook is updated daily and the CD-Rom and printed versions are updated monthly. The consolidated Handbook may contain typographical improvements, with no legal effect (such as cross-referencing and spelling corrections), which do not appear in the underlying legal instruments. The FSA has made increasingly sophisticated use of its website to make the consolidated online version of the Handbook a useful tool for itself and for firms. For example, the website offers the functionality for users to 'time travel' (that is, to view versions of the Handbook that were in force on a specified date in the past) and create 'tailored handbooks' containing only the provisions of the Handbook that are relevant to their business. At the time of writing there are 14 sector-specific handbooks of this kind that are each some 90 per cent shorter than the full Handbook. Tailored handbooks are accessed through a web-based process in which firms answer questions designed to identify the scope of their regulated activities. A truncated version of the Handbook is then compiled by matching meta-data[13] attached to each electronic Handbook provision with the information provided. The FSA has indicated that, provided a firm follows the published instructions relating to tailored handbooks, it will not take disciplinary action against a firm that

---

[9] The FSA has published a Reader's Guide to the Handbook, from which some of what follows is extracted and which readers are recommended to review.

[10] FSMA, s 153(2).

[11] ibid, s 153(4).

[12] ibid, s 154.

[13] When the electronic version of the Handbook is compiled, an electronic tag (the 'meta-data') is attached to each provision indicating the firms and activities to which it is relevant.

breaches a requirement in the Handbook because it reasonably relied on the fact that it was not included in a tailored handbook.[14]

(c) What goes into the Handbook is essentially a matter of choice by the FSA. That has several consequences. First, not all the rules made by the FSA appear in the Handbook, though the class of rules that does not appear in the Handbook is relatively small and deals mainly with specific types of fees.[15] Second, the FSA publishes a great deal of general guidance that is closely connected with the Handbook, but which does not form part of it.[16] 'Handbook guides' are guides to the Handbook as a whole. They indicate which material in the Handbook is likely to be relevant to firms of a particular type. 'Regulatory guides' address particular topics in the Handbook. They include the Perimeter Guidance Manual ('PERG') which address the perennial issue of which activities are regulated and which are not, and the Enforcement Guide ('EG'). Although the Regulatory Guides contain general guidance (on which see para 5.74, below), they are not part of the Handbook as such.[17] Third, the FSA operates (increasingly web-based) systems to deal with applications for authorisation and regulatory reporting. Each of those systems reflects policy choices and imposes requirements (for example as to the form of application or reporting) that are the product of the performance of the FSA's functions and the exercise of FSA powers,[18] but they do not form part of the Handbook. Fourth, and finally, the Handbook includes some requirements not made by the FSA. The powers to make rules relating to the Ombudsman scheme are shared between the FSA and the Financial Ombudsman Service ('FOS'). FOS rules are subject to FSA consent or approval and appear in the Handbook. The rules made exclusively by FOS are indicated in the schedules to the Dispute Resolution: Complaints Sourcebook ('DISP').

(d) The Handbook does not generally include statutory instruments such as orders, regulations, and the rules of the Financial Services and Markets Tribunal; or insolvency or winding-up rules; or rules made by self-regulatory bodies such as designated investment exchanges or recognised professional bodies. However, Handbook provisions may include extracts from or cross-references to directly applicable non-FSA legislative materials. These are

---

[14] Readers' Guide, p 17.

[15] ibid, p 20.

[16] The distinction is important to the FSA, because it reduces the nominal size of the Handbook, a measure that is sometimes used as an indicator of how effective the FSA has been in achieving 'better regulation' (see para 5.03 above). But it is invisible to the ordinary user of the online Handbook, where this guidance appears alongside the Handbook. It is also irrelevant, because the general guidance in the Regulatory Guides and Handbook Guides has the same status as general guidance in the Handbook proper (see para 5.79, below).

[17] See, for example, EG 1.8.

[18] For example, the power to give directions as to the form of applications for the variation of a firm's permission, in FSMA, s 51(3).

labelled 'UK' or indicated with a Union Jack icon alongside the text. European legislation affecting financial services is ever more voluminous, detailed, and prescriptive. In response, the FSA has where possible adopted a policy of implementing European requirements by 'intelligent copy-out'. The provisions of COBS that implement MiFID are a good example. Allied to that, Handbook provisions increasingly include a note indicating precisely which European requirement they are intended to implement. In addition, the Handbook may include extracts from and cross-references to non-FSA, European legislative material, such as directives and directly applicable regulations. This material is labelled 'EU' in the Handbook, or indicated with an EU flag icon alongside the text.

An overview of the structure and content of the Handbook

5.10 The structure of the Handbook was consulted on in April 1998,[19] and the current structure broadly reflects the original proposals, with the content of the Handbook reflecting the choices outlined in the preceding paragraphs. The following table sets out the structure of a summary of the content of the Handbook as it stands at the time of writing, both to provide an overview of the Handbook at large and to introduce FSA abbreviations for each sourcebook or module of the Handbook, which are used throughout the rest of this chapter:

Table 5.1

High-Level Standards (Block 1)	PRIN	Principles for Businesses (the fundamental obligations of all firms under the regulatory system)
	SYSC	Senior management arrangements, systems, and controls (the responsibilities of directors and senior management)
	COND	Threshold conditions (the minimum standards for becoming and remaining authorised)
	APER	Statements of principle and code of practice for approved persons (the fundamental obligations of approved persons)
	FIT	The fit and proper test for approved persons (the minimum standards for becoming and remaining an approved person)
	GEN	General provisions (interpreting the Handbook, fees, approval by the FSA, emergencies, status disclosure, the FSA logo, and insurance against fines)
	FEES	Fees manual (the fees provisions for funding the FSA, FOS, and FSCS).

[19] FSA, 'Consultation Paper 8: Designing the FSA Handbook of Rules and Guidance' (April 1998).

Prudential Standards (Block 2)	GENPRU	General Prudential Sourcebook (General Prudential Sourcebook for Banks, Building Societies, Insurers, and Investment Firms)
	BIPRU	Prudential Sourcebook for Banks, Building Societies and Investment Firms
	INSPRU	Prudential Sourcebook for Insurers
	MIPRU	Prudential Sourcebook for Mortgage and Home Finance Firms and Insurance Intermediaries
	UPRU	Prudential Sourcebook for UCITS firms
	IPRU(BANK)	Interim Prudential Sourcebook for Banks (residual prudential and notification requirements)
	IPRU(BSOC)	Interim Prudential Sourcebook for Building Societies (residual prudential and notification requirements)
	IPRU(FSOC)	Interim Prudential Sourcebook for Friendly Societies (residual prudential and notification requirements)
	IPRU(INS)	Interim Prudential Sourcebook for Insurers (residual prudential and notification requirements)
	IPRU(INV)	Interim Prudential Sourcebook for Investment Business (residual prudential and notification requirements)
Business Standards (Block 3)	COBS	New Conduct of Business Sourcebook (the conduct of business requirements applying to firms with effect from 1 November 2007)
	ICOBS	Insurance: New Conduct of Business Sourcebook (the non-investment insurance conduct of business requirements)
	MCOB	Mortgages and Home Finance: Conduct of Business Sourcebook (the requirements applying to firms with mortgage business and other home finance business customers)
	CASS	Client assets (the requirements relating to holding client assets and client money)
	MAR	Market conduct (Code of Market Conduct, Price stabilising rules, Inter-professional conduct, Endorsement of the Takeover Code, Alternative Trading Systems, what is acceptable market conduct, and what is market abuse)
	TC	Training and Competence (the commitments and requirements concerning staff competence)
Regulatory Processes (Block 4)	SUP	Supervision (supervisory provisions including those relating to auditors, waivers, individual guidance, notifications, and reporting)
	DEPP	Decision Procedures and Penalties manual (a description of the FSA's procedures for taking statutory notice decisions, the FSA's policy on the imposition and amount of penalties, and the conduct of interviews to which a direction under section 169(7) of the Act has been given or the FSA is considering giving with effect from 28 August 2007)
Redress (Block 5)	DISP	Dispute resolution: Complaints (the detailed requirements for handling complaints and the Financial Ombudsman Service arrangements)
	COMP	Compensation (the rules governing eligibility under, and levies for, the Financial Services Compensation Scheme)
	COAF	Complaints against the FSA (details of the scheme for handling complaints against the FSA)

Table 5.1 *Cont.*

Specialist Sourcebooks (Block 6)	COLL	Collective Investment Schemes
	CRED	Credit unions
	ELM	Electronic money (requirements for firms issuing electronic money)
	PROF	Professional firms (requirements applying to professional firms whether exempt or authorised)
	RCB	Regulated Covered Bonds
	REC	Recognised investment exchanges and Recognised Clearing Houses
Listing, Prospectus and Disclosure (Block 7)	LR	Listing Rules
	PR	Prospectus Rules
	DTR	Disclosure Rules and Transparency Rules

High-Level Standards and Principle-based Regulation

A brief history of regulation by reference to high-level standards

5.11 The Financial Services Act 1986 ('FSA 1986') created the Securities and Investments Board ('SIB') as the regulator of the various self-regulating organisations ('SROs') operating in the financial services industry. The SIB rulebook grew rapidly in its complexity and density.

5.12 As a reaction to this complexity, the then chairman of the SIB, Sir David Walker, secured the passage of a series of amendments to FSA 1986, by way of the Companies Act 1989. In particular, the 1989 Act inserted FSA 1986, s 47A, which conferred the power to:

> issue statements of principle with respect to the conduct and financial standing expected of persons authorised to carry on investment business.

5.13 FSA 1986, s 47A(2), provided that failure to comply with a statement of principle was a ground for taking disciplinary action or exercising powers of intervention, but did not of itself give rise to any right of action by investors, or affect the validity of any transaction.

5.14 SIB then promulgated 10 Principles for Businesses and 40 'designated rules', which were directly applicable to members of the SROs and formed the backbone of SIB's regulatory rulebook.

High-level standards in the Handbook

5.15 Following the SIB model, the Handbook includes high-level standards that apply generally (GEN, FEES); to authorised persons (PRIN and COND); to approved persons (APER and FIT); and to senior management (SYSC and to an extent APER and FIT). Apart from GEN, FEES, and parts of SYSC (for example, guidance on the Public Interest Disclosure Act 1998 and whistleblowing in SYSC 18), these high-level standards are essentially principles-based:

(a) principles for authorised persons (rules and guidance in PRIN);
(b) principles by reference to which the FSA will determine whether a firm meets the threshold conditions in order to be given and retain authorisation (the threshold conditions in Schedule 6 and guidance in COND);
(c) principles for senior management (rules and guidance in SYSC);
(d) principles for approved persons (statements of principle breach of which constitutes misconduct, and the code and guidance in APER);
(e) principles by reference to which the FSA will assess whether a person is fit and proper to perform a controlled function (guidance in FIT).

Central to all of these are the Principles for Businesses ('PRIN'). The FSA's **5.16** approach to the suitability and other threshold conditions in Schedule 6 ('COND'), for example, will depend on whether the firm is ready, willing, and organised to abide by the Principles. Senior management are responsible for ensuring that they have appropriate arrangements ('SYSC') to assure compliance with the Principles. Whether a person is fit and proper to perform a controlled function for an authorised person ('FIT'), and the standards which will be expected of him or her in performing those functions ('APER'), will be assessed ultimately by reference to whether their employer will be able to comply with the Principles.

Like the SIB, the FSA has exercised its legislative powers to ensure that its high- **5.17** level rules are enforceable by the regulator, but breach of them is not actionable by consumers or other persons affected by that breach (see para 5.63 below).

High-level rules in European financial services legislation

In keeping with the political and rhetorical emphasis in Europe on the impor- **5.18** tance of high-level rules (see para 5.06 above for an example), some recent European financial services legislation, for example MiFID,[20] has included high-level principles in its architecture. There is, however, a tension between the policy aim of better regulation and the policy aim of the deeper integration of European financial markets. The latter aim tends to have priority in Europe and to compel the production of ever more detailed, prescriptive legislation.

---

[20] See in particular MiFID, Art 19.

Principle-based regulation

5.19 That is the background against which the FSA framed its response to the wider 'better regulation' initiative described in para 5.04 *et seq.* above. In March 2005, the FSA (in partnership with the Financial Services Practitioner Panel) launched a study of the costs of FSA regulation, in parallel with a government review of the costs of regulation generally. The results of the FSA study were published in 2006.[21] In Consultation Paper 05/10 published in July 2005, the FSA outlined its strategy for reviewing its Handbook of rules and guidance. The FSA commented that a key reason for undertaking a review of the Handbook was that it wanted the Handbook to reflect its vision and values, which include:

> an approach to rule-making based as far as possible on principles rather than prescription; a focus on senior management responsibility; and acting in a proportionate and risk-based way.[22]

5.20 But it is clear that the FSA has expanded the notion of principle-based regulation beyond its role as a device to guide and reduce the content of the Handbook and towards a new relationship with the firms it regulates. The following is an extract from the FSA's flagship statement on principle-based regulation in 2007:

> Principles-based regulation ... means a different approach to how we deal with regulated entities whether in the context of day to day supervisory contact, the information we request, or when necessary, the way we use our enforcement powers. It also means different expectations of firms and how they engage with the regulatory issues they face. Our aim is to focus more clearly on the outcomes we as regulators want to achieve, leaving more of the judgement calls on how to achieve those outcomes to the senior management of firms.[23]

5.21 Other chapters of this book contain commentary on how the Principles for Businesses and other high-level rules impact on particular aspects of the FSA regulation of financial services. The following paragraphs tackle a set of rather broader issues, raised by principle-based regulation in general: what principle-based regulation might mean in practice and the kinds of issues that it might raise for both the regulated and the regulator.

What are 'principles'?

5.22 Principles are rules (made using the FSA's legislative powers) that are expressed at a high level of generality. The most obvious examples are are the FSA Principles for Businesses in PRIN, but it is important to be clear that when the FSA speaks

---

[21] Deloitte, 'The Cost of Regulation Study' (June 2006).
[22] FSA, 'Consultation Paper 05/10: Reviewing the FSA Handbook' (July 2005).
[23] FSA, 'Principles-based Regulation: Focusing on the outcomes that matter' (April 2007), p 6.

about 'principle-based regulation' it means regulation on the basis of high-level rules in general. In practice, this means:

(a) principles cannot be invented 'on the hoof'. They are the product of the FSA's formal legislative processes (including where necessary, consultation, CBA, feedback, making by the FSA Board—see paras 5.84 *et seq.* below);

(b) principles are aimed at outcomes or behaviours that are required from a number of (or indeed, all) regulated firms, no matter how diverse their business, structure, or governance. For example, under PRIN firms must 'act with integrity', 'treat their customers fairly', 'maintain adequate financial resources';

(c) principles are specific as to outcome, but not as to the method by which each firm is to achieve that outcome;

(d) deciding whether (or not) a firm has achieved the outcome required by a principle almost always requires judgement by the regulator. The central role of that judgement is reflected in the language in which principles (including those in PRIN) are drafted: for example, capital must be *adequate*, behaviour must be *reasonable* or *fair*;

(e) because principles are rules, they are capable of being breached. Breach can be the basis for the exercise of supervisory or enforcement powers by the FSA, as a public body (see para 5.59 below);

(f) there is a well established body of public law that sets out the standards against which the courts will test the adequacy of the exercise of powers by a public body on the basis of judgements by its officials.

Practical limitations on principle-based regulation

Principle-based regulation is not a one size fits all solution. There are areas of **5.23** financial services regulation where detailed prescriptive rules are necessary and desirable and are likely to remain in place. Areas in which detailed rules are likely to predominate include prudential regulation (for example detailed rules specifying the basis for the valuation of assets and liabilities, the quality of capital firms are required to hold and the level or amount of capital that firms must hold). It is likely that the international banking crisis that emerged during 2008 will result in renewed scrutiny of both detailed prudential rules and of the role of principles as the basis for regulation. But at the time of writing, the indications are that the FSA remains committed to principle-based regulation, not least because high-level rules offer the means by which firms and the regulator can respond quickly and flexibly to unexpected changes in circumstances.

The FSA operates in a wider arena than just the United Kingdom. The impetus **5.24** for financial services regulation comes from a variety of sources, for example from international bodies such as the BIS, the IAIS, and international initiatives on accounting standards.

5.25 More locally, the European Community has significant legislative competence in the financial services field. Notwithstanding its rhetoric in favour of principle-based regulation, its legislation, which the UK is required to implement, is often prescriptive (see para 5.18 above) or maximum-harmonising. That drives the kind of 'copy-out' implementation strategies outlined in para 5.09(d) above. The result may be principle-based, if that is the character of the underlying rules, but that is often not the case.

The relationship between principles and other FSA rules

5.26 Because principles are rules of general application, they will apply in areas where the FSA has made other, more detailed rules and guidance.

5.27 Sometimes the more detailed rules will be expressed as an expansion or explanation of what a particular principle means. An example is COBS 20 (With profits) which expands on Principle for Businesses 6 as it applies to with-profits policyholders. But this will not always be the case. Often, detailed rules will simply occupy space that is also occupied by a principle. Detailed prudential rules, for example, occupy the same space as Principle for Businesses 4 (adequate resources).

5.28 If both a principle and a detailed rule apply to the same situation, a court will construe the detailed rule and the principle together, based on the ordinary meaning of the words in which both are expressed (if there is no defined meaning—on which see para 5.112 *et seq.* below). If the defined or ordinary meaning of the words is unclear or ambiguous, the court will look to the purpose of both the rule and the principle. In practice it is likely that the outcome of this process will be that the more detailed rule will control the outcome required. So, there may be little scope for the application of a general rule if a detailed rule clearly applies and is unambiguous as to what the firm must do.

5.29 The FSA may dispense with the application of its detailed rules in favour of the more general principles only:

(a) on application by a firm for a waiver or modification of the detailed rule, where the FSA is satisfied that the rule may be waived or modified and that the criteria in FSMA 2000, s 148 are met (see para 5.65 below); or

(b) by consulting on and then making rules that substitute principles for more detailed rules.

5.30 Other than by these means, the FSA has no power to dispense with the application of the detailed rules it has made. The approach to principle-based regulation will, therefore, be iterative, as the FSA identifies areas in which principles can substitute for detailed rules and legislates accordingly.

As a corollary, principles will be directly relevant when detailed rules do not apply, **5.31** do not cover the situation under consideration, or are ambiguous as to the outcome that is required in the particular circumstances. One of the reasons for relying more on principles is that detailed rules often become obsolete as circumstances change.

Principles and statutory obligations

The FSA must act lawfully. That includes complying with any statutory or other **5.32** legislative requirements that apply to it. Only Parliament can dispense with statutory obligations in favour of principles. For example, FSMA specifies the grounds on which the FSA can approve a change of the controllers of an authorised person. The FSA has no power to approve a change of control on a different basis, principle-based or not.

Where the FSA's statutory obligations give it a discretion, or leave an issue to the **5.33** FSA's judgement, the FSA may exercise that discretion or judgement having regard to any relevant policy that it has expressed and in a way that is consistent with its existing rules and guidance.[24]

Principles and consistency of outcome

Principles are (by definition) not specific as to the method by which a firm must **5.34** achieve the outcome at which the principle is aimed. So different firms may do different things to comply with a principle. The range of different things that different firms do will be affected by, amongst other things:

(a) the actual circumstances in which the firm finds itself;
(b) the firm's commercial strategy;
(c) the quality of the firm's advisers and the firm's judgement; and
(d) the firm's appetite for risk.

It follows that, across any population of firms to which a principle applies, there **5.35** will be a range of actions that firms take to comply with the principle, and a range of acceptable outcomes.

Consistent application of a principle, or consistent intervention to secure the **5.36** application of a principle, cannot mean compelling all firms to do the same thing.

---

[24] The FSA is 'required to discharge its statutory responsibilities in accordance with the provisions of [FSMA] and its Handbook of Rules and Guidance': *R v FSA, ex parte Davis* [2004] 1 WLR 185 (CA), per Mummery LJ at [3], upholding the earlier decision of Lightman J (*R v FSA, ex parte Davies* [2003] 1 WLR 1284) that the FSA had not, in deciding to pursue proceedings to prohibit a person from carrying on a controlled function under FSMA, acted inconsistently with the guidance in its enforcement manual setting out its policy as to the exercise of the prohibition power.

Consistent application of a principle means that firms and the regulator take the actions necessary to secure that each firm achieves the outcome that the principle requires. The actions taken by each firm (and the actions taken by the FSA) may be different in each case and the customers, market counterparties, and other firms that benefit from the protection offered by the principle may experience different results.

5.37 Principle-based regulation requires a shift in regulatory approach. Detailed rules constrain firms to a particular action (which the rule-maker has determined will produce the required regulatory outcome). Principle-based regulation is permissive of a range of actions. It is the regulator's function to identify, on a reasonable and rational basis, the range of actions that are likely to produce the outcome required by the principle. It is the regulator's function to object (and if necessary to intervene) if the actions that a particular firm proposes to take do not fall within the range of actions likely to produce the required outcome.

5.38 Put another way, the regulator's function is to determine whether the action proposed by a firm falls inside or outside the range of acceptable actions. The key, therefore, is to be able to identify those actions that, in the particular circumstances of a firm, define the end point of the acceptable range of actions. It is not the regulator's function to necessarily approve particular actions, or to compel the firm to choose a particular action from the range of acceptable actions. In this way, consistent regulatory outcomes are achieved through the exercise of choice and judgement by well informed firms. That is the essence of genuinely principle-based regulation.

Principle-based regulation and legal challenge

5.39 There are two main mechanisms by which firms may mount a legal challenge to principle-based regulation. First, firms may challenge enforcement action for breach of a principle on the grounds that the FSA has failed to establish, on the evidence presented, that the relevant rule has been breached. Second, firms may seek judicial review of supervisory decisions taken on the basis of principles.

5.40 There are three main questions that a court or tribunal is likely to ask:[25]

(a) what did the totality of the rules on which the FSA relies to act or to enforce (construed together) require the firm to do in this particular case? What are the controlling rules?[26]

---

[25] Though there is at present little direct authority on the point.

[26] See *R v Financial Services Authority, ex parte Davis and others* [2004] 1 WLR 185 (CA), for the relationship between judicial review and the statutory scheme for challenge of FSA decisions, established under FSMA. The FSA has not yet been subject to judicial review.

(b) if the controlling rule is a principle (a high-level rule):
   (i) in taking supervisory action, did the FSA act reasonably in deciding that the action taken by the firm was outside the range of actions likely to achieve the outcome required by the principle; or
   (ii) in taking an enforcement case, has the FSA established to the required standard of proof that the firm knowingly or recklessly did something prohibited by the relevant principle, or failed to do something required by it?
(c) in evaluating (b) the court or tribunal will ask itself:
   (i) was the outcome required by the principle, or the conduct prohibited by it, sufficiently clear that the firm knew, or ought to have known, what the principle required, or that its action was prohibited?
   (ii) was there a course of communication between the firm and the FSA relevant to the outcome required by the principle, or the action prohibited and what was the effect of that?[27]
   (iii) in deciding whether the action taken by the firm was outside the range of acceptable actions, or prohibited, did the FSA follow any relevant procedures if has established, have regard to all relevant information, disregard irrelevant information and act logically and rationally?

Consistency in decision-making by the regulator

The risk (to the FSA) of a successful challenge to a principle-based decision will be minimised if the FSA acts logically and rationally, sensibly following its own procedures and relying only on relevant information. The most general proposition is that rational (and so legally defensible) decision-making requires the FSA to treat like cases alike, unless there are good reasons to treat them differently. **5.41**

Rational (and from the FSA perspective, defensible) decision-making therefore requires: **5.42**

(a) a clear understanding of the regulatory issue raised by the firm or individual under consideration;
(b) a clear understanding of the circumstances of the firm or individual which identify it as similar to or different from other firms or individuals that raise the same regulatory issue;
(c) a clear understanding of the applicable rules (whether high-level or detailed) and the FSA's expressed policy and other material on that regulatory issue;
(d) proper application of any relevant process that the FSA has put around decision-making.

---

[27] See, for example, *Fox Hayes v FSA*, FSMT Case 047, 24 September 2007, where the Financial Services and Markets Tribunal took account of the inadequacy of FSA guidance in deciding that there had been no breach of Principle for Businesses 2.

5.43 The courts are likely to support differential treatment when it is reasoned and objectively justifiable, taking all this information into account. Whether in any particular case differential treatment is sufficiently reasoned and sufficiently justifiable to survive challenge is a question of judgement on a case-by-case basis.

5.44 Rationality (and legal defensibility) are not the same as consistency. For example:

(a) It is rational (and legally acceptable) for a public body with enforcement powers *not* to pursue every instance in which its rules are breached. A rational choice of which breaches to pursue may be made taking into consideration the availability of resources, degree of risk to objectives, quality of evidence, and other relevant factors. The courts are likely to uphold a rational choice of this kind, even though it produces inconsistency—some firms face enforcement, others do not.

(b) It is rational (and legally acceptable) to take action aimed at consistency of high-level outcomes or behaviour across a population of firms, even though doing so sacrifices consistency of action by all firms and so may produce an inconsistency of result for different customers. A rational choice to pursue high-level outcomes or behaviour may, for example, be based on a judgement that this strategy is likely to lead to better overall outcomes for consumers, even though some individual outcomes may be worse. For example, Principle for Businesses 6 requires a firm to treat its 'customers' fairly. The FSA interprets that as relating to a firm's customers overall, not to customers individually.

5.45 Each of the preceding paragraphs exemplifies a case in which rational, legally defensible decisions do not require consistency of result for firms and consumers. In each case, the decision is defensible because there are good reasons for not treating like cases alike.

5.46 There is no requirement for (and probably no such thing as) absolute consistency. But a firm is more likely to be able to show that a decision by the FSA is irrational, and unenforceable, if the FSA acts inconsistently, without good, objectively justifiable reasons for doing so.

5.47 To use a supervisory example, say the FSA is approached by two substantially similar firms that wish to market a substantially similar product to the public. In one case the FSA decides that the applicable principle requires the firm to do minimal due diligence to determine whether the product is suitable for its customers. In the other case the FSA decides that the applicable principle requires extensive, and substantially more expensive, due diligence. The FSA imposes requirements on the firms accordingly. Both requirements achieve the outcome that customers are treated fairly. But the firm forced to undertake the more expensive process may have good grounds for challenging the FSA's action. Its challenge is more likely to succeed if the FSA cannot show any objectively justifiable reasons for the differential treatment it has applied. So, consistency of outcome can lead to challenge if the FSA does not conduct itself in a rational way.

But, say the same two firms approach the FSA and each sets out the approach it **5.48** proposes to take to ensure that it treats its customers fairly. One firm proposes an extensive, expensive approach. The other proposes a shorter and cheaper approach. In each case the FSA considers, on the basis of the available relevant information and in a consistent way, whether the approach is within the range of approaches that are likely to produce compliance with Principle for Businesses 6. It decides that both approaches are acceptable and tells each firm that it does not object to the approach that the firm proposes to take.

The essential difference between the two cases is not that in the first the FSA has **5.49** exercised its power to require the firms to act in a particular way and in the second it has simply not objected to what the firms wanted to do. Both of those are decisions by the FSA that can be challenged by the courts. The difference is that in the first case the exercise of power has been inconsistent, because it imposed a differential burden on the firms, for no good reason. In the second case, the FSA has acted in an internally consistent way to decide, for good reason, that the actions the firms proposed produced an equivalent outcome and should be treated in the same way (non-objection) for that reason.

The second case raises interesting issues about the extent to which (and how) the **5.50** FSA should publicise the range of acceptable actions that firms can take to comply with a principle. The FSA has made important commitments to be transparent in its regulation, which firms are entitled to expect it to meet. Those commitments and the range of legal issues raised by principle-based regulation are the main reasons why the FSA has put so much recent effort into articulating the status and effect of the material it includes in its Handbook and the other material that it makes public outside the Handbook. They are also the reason why the FSA has recently articulated its willingness to endorse industry guidance in certain cases. But before turning to look at what the FSA has said in that regard (in para 5.79 *et seq.* below) it is useful first to survey the range of different Handbook provisions and public material that the FSA produces.

Handbook Components

The powers exercised to make the material re-stated in the Handbook

By far the largest component of the material that is re-stated in the Handbook is **5.51** the product of the FSA's legislative functions (see para. 5.84 below). But by no means all the material in the Handbook is the product of those functions. An FSA rule-making instrument (see para 5.102 below) must specify the statutory or other provision under which it is made.[28] When an instrument is consolidated into the Handbook that information is included in a Schedule to the relevant module of the Handbook in which the material in that instrument belongs. For reasons of consistency and clarity, the FSA has adopted the practice of including that schedule in each module of the Handbook. The full range of the powers exercised to make the material in the Handbook as a whole can, therefore, be seen in GEN Schedule 4 to the General Provisions Sourcebook.

Rules

5.52 The FSA's most obvious legislative function (see para 5.84 below) is its function of making rules. For example, the FSA's main high-level standards, its Principles for Businesses ('PRIN'), are rules. Through rules, the FSA may impose binding and enforceable requirements on the persons it regulates, and these may impact on third parties.[29] Most rules (other than evidential provisions, on which see para 5.60 below) are labelled 'R' in the Handbook.

5.53 Although the FSA has many rule-making powers, foremost is the general rule-making power in FSMA, section 138. The FSA has the power to make general rules applying to both regulated and unregulated activities of authorised persons.[30] Moreover, since the advent of MiFID, the FSA may make general rules applying to investment firms and credit institutions with respect to the provision by them of ancillary services,[31] the provision of which does not involve carrying on a regulated activity.[32]

5.54 Nevertheless, there is a clear link between rules and regulated activities: first, because authorised persons have, and generally need, a permission to carry on regulated activities; second, because the main feature of general rules is that they must be made for the purpose of protecting the interests of consumers.[33]

5.55 Consumers are defined in FSMA, section 138(7) as persons who use, have used, or are or may be contemplating using any of the services provided by authorised persons or their appointed representatives in carrying on regulated activities or providing ancillary services under MiFID. The definition is not limited to private individuals and can include other authorised persons. The definition includes

---

[28] FSMA, s 153(2).

[29] For example, breach of rules may confer rights of action under s 150; rules under s 139 may provide for client money to be held on trust.

[30] However, GEN 2.2.17R makes clear that general rules are to be interpreted in the Handbook as applying only to regulated activities, unless the contrary intention appears.

[31] Defined in MiFID Annex 1, Section B.

[32] FSMA, s 138(1A) to (1C).

[33] See tailpiece of FSMA, s 138(1).

those with rights or interests which are derived from or attributable to such services, or which may be adversely affected by the use of such services by others on their behalf. The FSA's consumer protection objective in FSMA, section 5 uses the definition of consumers in FSMA, section 138, but extends it to users of services provided by other persons such as those enjoying an exemption or otherwise carrying on regulated activities without permission.

The link to consumers in the general rule-making power appears to give primacy **5.56** to the consumer protection objective, at least in respect of the regulation of authorised persons. The primacy of this objective is mirrored by specific references to protecting consumers, for example in FSMA, sections 41(3) and 45(1)(c) in relation to Part 4 permissions, and to threats to the interests of consumers in the FSA's consideration of controllers in FSMA, section 186(2)(b). Although the FSA is not required by FSMA, section 138 to make general rules, the FSA's responsibility through its general duties to secure the appropriate degree of protection for consumers drives it to do so, and in doing so to consider the matters set out in FSMA, section 5, including the degree of risk involved, the experience and expertise of different consumers, and their need for accurate information and advice, but also the principle that consumers should take responsibility for their decisions.

The regulatory objectives are not mutually exclusive. By promoting public aware- **5.57** ness and reducing financial crime, the FSA protects consumers. By securing the appropriate degree of protection for consumers, the FSA maintains confidence in the financial system. General rules may be used directly to maintain market confidence by protecting the interests of consumers who are not customers of the authorised persons concerned, and by protecting the interests of indirect clients such as beneficiaries and of market counterparties (see Principle for Businesses 5 and Principle for Businesses 10). In discharging its rule-making functions, the FSA must have regard to all the regulatory objectives and the seven principles of good regulation set out in FSMA, section 2(3), including economy and efficiency, management responsibility, proportionality, innovation, competition, and competitiveness.

Certain rules may apply to other persons who are not authorised, but are never- **5.58** theless within the FSA's regulatory scope, or impact on third parties:[34]

(a) rules under Part 6 (listing, disclosure, prospectus, transparency, and corporate governance rules) apply to issuers, offerors, and applicants (many of which are authorised), and in effect to directors, sponsors, employees, and the FSA as listing authority itself;

(b) client money rules under Part 10, to the extent that they impact on the rights of third parties;

---

[34] Most of these are considered in more detail in other chapters.

(c) the scheme manager under the Financial Services Compensation Scheme ('FSCS') and the FOS, as well as individual Ombudsmen, under rules made by the FSA and the FOS for the compensation and Ombudsman schemes, under Parts 15 and 16—having effect on claimants, former authorised persons, voluntary jurisdiction participants, and parties to a complaint generally;

(d) trustees, depositaries, auditors, and other operators of regulated and unregulated collective investment schemes, under Part 17—some but not all of which are required to be authorised;

(e) recognised investment exchanges and clearing houses, under Part 18—in respect of notification rules;

(f) former underwriting members of Lloyd's, and current members to the extent that the FSA has made a direction applying Part 10 as a core provision to the Lloyd's market, under Part 19;

(g) exempt professional firms in respect of rules for the purpose of ensuring that their clients are aware they are not authorised, under Part 20;

(h) auditors and actuaries on whom duties are imposed under Part 22;

(i) persons qualifying for authorisation under Schedule 3 (EEA passport rights) and Schedule 4 (Treaty rights);

(j) exempt persons such as appointed representatives in respect of their exemptions under the financial promotion order,[35] and certified e-money issuers under the RAO,[36] who are effectively subject to FSA rules under or by virtue of secondary or external legislation; and

(k) persons liable to pay fees in connection with the discharge of FSA functions, pursuant to fees rules made under FSMA, Schedule 1, para 17.[37]

Breach of rules

5.59 Breach of rules does not itself constitute an offence,[38] although breach may result in an offence, for instance if compliance with rules is a condition for an exemption under the financial promotion order (as for appointed representatives)[39] or the misleading practices offence under FSMA, section 397(4).[40] False or misleading statements given to the FSA in purported compliance with a rule may involve an offence under FSMA, section 398. However, the primary significance of rules for

---

[35] See art 16(2)(b) of the Financial Services and Markets Act 2000 (Financial Promotions) Financial Promotion Order 2005, SI 2005/1529.

[36] See ELM 8.7, using powers under RAO, art 9G.

[37] Such as persons making applications or seeking FSA approvals.

[38] FSMA, s 151(1).

[39] See art 16(2)(b) of the Financial Promotion Order 2005, 2005/1529.

[40] As with price stabilising rules made under FSMA, s 144 and control of information rules under FSMA, s 147.

authorised persons is that breach triggers the FSA's investigation, disciplinary, and other enforcement powers, including public censure, financial penalties, injunctions, and restitution.[41]

Evidential provisions

Rules made under FSMA, section 149 may provide for breaches to give rise to no **5.60** consequences under FSMA except that breach may be relied on as tending to establish breach of another specified rule, and conversely that compliance may be relied on as tending to establish compliance with the other specified rule. Such 'evidential provisions' are labelled 'E' in the Handbook.

Effect of breach on non-authorised persons and transactions

Most rules and other requirements apply only while firms remain authorised, so **5.61** that the FSA may in some instances keep a firm's Part 4 permission in place even if there are no activities that it is able to carry on.[42] Breaches of requirements imposed through rules generally only expose other non-authorised persons to the risk of injunctions or restitution orders imposed by the courts under FSMA, sections 380 and 382. The FSA may, however, take action to remove or restrict the status or rights of non-authorised persons who are concerned in a breach of rules. For example, approved persons may be found unfit to perform controlled functions, or indeed any functions, on behalf of an authorised person, or disciplined for misconduct if they are knowingly concerned in a breach by the authorised person for whom they perform a controlled function.[43]

Breach of rules does not make a transaction void or unenforceable.[44] However, **5.62** private contractual terms between parties may have that effect.

Private rights of action for contravention of a rule

The general position is that contravention of a rule by an authorised person **5.63** is actionable at the suit of a private person who suffers loss as a result of the

---

[41] Breaches of rules including the Principles for Businesses are relevant to the FSA's consideration of whether an authorised person continues to meet the threshold conditions ('COND') and its protection of consumers objective, so that breaches may trigger variation, including imposition of limitations or requirements, or cancellation of the firm's permission. However, FSMA s 206(2) provides that the FSA may not fine a firm and withdraw its authorisation.

[42] As envisaged under FSMA, ss 44(4) and 45(3).

[43] See FSMA, ss 56 (prohibition orders), 63 (withdrawal of approval) and 66 (disciplinary powers).

[44] See ibid, s 151(2).

contravention, subject to defences and other incidents applying to actions for breach of statutory duty.[45] The Treasury may make (and has made) regulations providing that in specified cases, breach of a rule is actionable not only at the suit of a private person, but also at the suit of other persons).[46] The FSA has the power to prevent private actions by making rules specifying that particular provisions do not give rise to private rights of action if breached.[47] The FSA has exercised that power to remove private rights of action for certain high-level rules such as PRIN, SYSC, and listing and financial resources rules.[48]

Incidental and supplementary powers

5.64   FSMA, section 156 provides that FSA rules may contain incidental, supplemental, consequential, and transitional provisions, and make different provision for different cases. The general rule-making power and powers to make most other rules do not normally authorise the FSA to vary or otherwise sub-delegate the contents of those rules for individual firms. However, there are exceptions such as FSMA, section 214 which permits the FSA to authorise the FSCS to determine certain matters for the purposes of the compensation scheme, and FSMA, Schedule 17 para 13, which provides for individual ombudsmen to be able to waive time limits for referral of complaints.

Waiver and modification of rules

5.65   The FSA has a general power to waive or modify the majority of its rules,[49] with the consent of, or on the application of, the person who is subject to the relevant rules.[50] A waiver and modification power in this wide form is very recent and is the product of a Regulatory Reform Order[51] that came into effect on 12 July 2007, made under the Legislative and Regulatory Reform Act 2006. The previous position was that the general waiver or modification power was exercisable only in respect of a specified subset of FSA rules, and only exercisable on the application of or with the consent of an authorised person to whom the rules applied.

---

[45]   ibid, s 150(1).

[46]   ibid, s 150(3). See the Financial Services and Markets Act 2000 (Private Rights of Action) Regulations 2001, SI 2001/2256 and the Financial Services and Markets Act 2000 (Fourth Motor Insurance Directive) Regulations 2002, SI 2002/2706.

[47]   FSMA, s 150(4).

[48]   ibid, s 150 is not disapplied for the rules in GEN or FEES.

[49]   Trust scheme rules and Scheme particulars rules, under FSMA, ss 247 and 248 are excluded, but there is a parallel waiver power for those rules in FSMA, s 250.

[50]   FSMA, s 148(2). There are other waiver powers associated with particular rule-making powers, elsewhere in FSMA.

[51]   The Regulatory Reform (Financial Services and Markets Act 2000) Order 2007, SI 2007/1973.

That had a number of restrictive consequences. For example, it prevented auditors and actuaries (who are subject to FSA rules but not authorised persons) from applying for a waiver or modification.

If the FSA is satisfied that: **5.66**

(a) compliance with the unmodified rule would be unduly burdensome or would not achieve the purpose for which the rule was made; and

(b) there is no undue risk to persons whose interests the rules are intended to protect,[52]

it may direct that a rule does not apply to the applicant (a waiver) or that the rule applies subject to the modifications specified in the direction (a modification). The direction may be subject to conditions,[53] which generally take effect as limits on the scope of extent of the direction (for example a time limit) or conditions precedent to the continued validity of the direction (for example, a requirement that a firm should hold additional capital or take some other step while the direction is in force). The FSA may revoke a direction of its own accord or vary it with the consent of or on the application of the firm concerned.[54]

The FSA will generally publish directions waiving or modifying rules in the FSA **5.67** register; indeed it is required to publish unless it is satisfied that it is unnecessary or inappropriate to do so, and if necessary to consider publishing in an anonymised form.[55] Publication serves a number of interests, including maintaining consistency of decision-making ensuring that all firms of a similar kind are aware of what concessions might be available and ensuring that private rights of action are not unnecessarily undermined.

The FSA has made increasingly sophisticated use of the waiver power. For exam- **5.68** ple, if it is necessary temporarily to adjust the impact of a rule on a class of firms, say in response to a fall in stock market values, the FSA may publicise a standard-form direction and indicate that firms that meet a specified set of criteria may have the benefit of the direction simply by indicating to the FSA that they consent to the variation or modification embodied in the direction. In extremis, the FSA may also use this 'waiver by consent' strategy quickly to effect critical changes to its rules while the formal processes of a permanent amendment to rules and guidance (on which see para 5.84 below) are underway.

---

[52] FSMA, s 148(2) and (4).
[53] ibid, s 148(5).
[54] ibid, s 148(9).
[55] ibid, s 148(6) and (7).

Statements of principle, codes, directions, and requirements

5.69 For approved persons,[56] FSMA, section 64 provides for both statements of principle and a code describing the conduct expected of them.[57] The classification of the statements of principle in FSMA, section 64 is difficult.[58] FSMA, section 64(11) provides that the power to issue statements of practice is to be treated as part of the FSA's rule-making function and in many respects statements of principle are treated as rules. Chapter 6 of the Reader's Guide says that the principles are binding on approved persons. However, many of the statutory provisions that apply to rules do not apply to statements of principle, or have to be replicated.[59] There is no power to waive or modify statements of principle, and misconduct does not itself give rise to private rights of action. Statements of principle are labelled with the letter 'P' in the Handbook.

5.70 FSMA, section 119 provides for a code (known as the Code of Market Conduct[60]) giving guidance to those determining whether or not behaviour amounts to market abuse. The Code is supplemented by guidance. Making codes is a general function subject to the FSA's general duties in FSMA, section 2 (see para 5.02 above) and one of the FSA's legislative functions (see para 5.86 below). Although similar in many ways to general guidance (on which see para 5.74 below), the Code of Market Conduct is distinct in that breach of its provisions may be indicative of misconduct or market abuse. In this respect the provisions of the Code are similar to evidential provisions and are labelled 'E' in the Handbook.

5.71 The Code of Market Conduct also has another distinctive feature. Because of concerns about the breadth of the definition of market abuse, FSMA, section 122(1) provides a formal safe harbour for those who behave in a way that is described in the code applicable at the time as behaviour that, in the opinion of the FSA, does not amount to market abuse. These conclusive provisions are labelled 'C' in the Handbook.

5.72 There is no such formal safe harbour for conduct that conforms with individual or general guidance given by the FSA, but the FSA has recently articulated the policy that if a firm takes a reasonable course of action that the FSA has indicated, in general public material or in a specific individual exchange (such as

---

[56] Persons approved by the FSA under FSMA, s 59 to perform controlled functions on behalf of an authorised person in respect of regulated activities.

[57] Set out in APER.

[58] They are not to be confused with the Principles for Businesses in PRIN, which apply to authorised persons. However, several of the principles for approved persons in APER are the same as or derived from those in PRIN.

[59] See for example FSMA, s.64(11) which replicates for statements of principle the power in FSMA, s 156 to make different provision for different circumstances or cases.

[60] Set out in MAR.

a supervisory letter), as being in compliance with a rule, then the FSA will not take action against the firm for not having complied with the rule. In relation to guidance, that policy is not new. But the policy is new in relation to the FSA's general public material. This is considered further in para 5.79 below.

Directions

Certain directions and requirements imposed by the FSA under FSMA are treated **5.73** as made in the exercise of legislative functions.[61] All such provisions are labelled 'D' in the Handbook.

General guidance and individual guidance

The FSA's guidance function described in FSMA, section 157(1) is very wide, and **5.74** includes the giving of guidance consisting of such information and advice as the FSA considers appropriate:

(a) with respect to the operation of FSMA and of any rules made under it;
(b) with respect to any matters relating to functions of the FSA;
(c) for the purpose of meeting the regulatory objectives; and
(d) with respect to any other matters about which it appears to the FSA to be desirable to give information or advice.

FSMA, section 157(5) provides that (with one exception[62]) references to guidance **5.75** given by the FSA include references to any recommendation made by the FSA to persons generally, to regulated persons generally, or to any class of regulated person.[63] By far the largest component of the Handbook is 'general' guidance in that sense, labelled 'G' in the Handbook. The majority of the guidance re-stated in the Handbook, or associated with the Handbook (for example in the Handbook Guides and Regulatory Guides—on which see para 5.09 above) is also 'general guidance' within the formal definition in FSMA, section 158(5): guidance which is 'general' in the sense outlined above, but also 'intended to have continuing effect and given in writing or other legible form'.

---

[61] Directions under FSMA ss 316, 318, and 328.
[62] Guidance on outsourcing, which the FSA must give in order to comply with the UK's obligation under MiFID to set out policy on outsourcing by banks and investment firms.
[63] 'Regulated person' is defined in FSMA, s 157(6) as any (a) authorised person; (b) person who is otherwise subject to FSA rules, so arguably does not apply to approved persons, even though the need for approval is triggered by the FSA's controlled functions rules made under FSMA, s 59. Advice to consumers is not regarded as given to 'persons generally', and is not included in the Handbook, except in relation to the [Block 5] of the Handbook covering dispute resolution: complaints ('DISP'), compensation ('COMP'), and complaints against the FSA ('COAF').

5.76   But other forms of guidance, which are not 'general guidance', are equally significant to the performance of the FSA's regulatory functions. In particular there is
'individual guidance', given to authorised firms at their request or at the FSA's
own initiative, addressing issues of individual relevance or concern to the firm.
The distinction between general guidance and individual guidance has procedural consequences because specific requirements attach to the issue of general
guidance on rules (considered in para 5.103 below), although these consequences
have become less significant since secondary legislation made under the Legislative
and Regulatory Reform Act 2006 has begun to have an impact on FSMA.

Other public material published by the FSA and industry guidance

5.77   The FSA publishes a mass of general public material, which sits outside the
Handbook. This includes everything from market bulletins, through regulatory
updates to speeches, case studies, 'Dear CEO letters', and FAQs. The FSA's
usual approach has been to append a statement to that material indicating that it
is not general guidance. That statement encapsulated the FSA's conclusion that
(for one or other technical reason, including, for example, that the material
did not relate to FSA rules, or that it was not intended to have continuing effect)
the FSA was not required to consult or to undertake any other statutory processes
(on which see para 5.84 *et seq*. below) before publishing the material, and had
not done so. But that made it difficult for firms to decide exactly what weight to
give to such material when deciding what was required to comply with FSA
rules.

5.78   In November 2006 the FSA published a Discussion Paper[64] opening debate on
whether and in what circumstances the FSA should rely on industry guidance
instead of publishing public material of its own, whether included in the Handbook
or not. From the FSA's perspective, industry guidance has the dual benefit of
directly engaging industry associations and practitioners in constructive debate
about what is required to comply with particular rules and of distributing responsibility for the volume and complexity of regulatory guidance. But, as with the
FSA's general public material, a critical question for firms was whether, and to
what extent, the FSA would have regard to industry guidance and a firm's compliance with it, in deciding whether the firm had complied with or breached a relevant FSA rule. That, and other issues relating to the effect of guidance generally,
are considered in the following paragraphs.

---

[64]   FSA, 'Discussion Paper 06/5: FSA Confirmation of Industry Guidance' (November 2006).

The effect of guidance, other FSA public material, and confirmed industry guidance

SUP 9.4 sets out the effect of individual guidance. The previous edition of this **5.79** work noted that Chapter 6 of the Reader's Guide indicated that if a person acted in accordance with general guidance, or current individual written guidance given to him by the FSA, in the circumstances contemplated by that guidance, the FSA would proceed on the footing that the person had complied with the aspects of the rule or other requirement to which the guidance related.

As far as individual and general guidance is concerned, that position is essentially **5.80** unchanged. But the FSA's approach has developed, so that it now puts other public material relevant to compliance with rules explicitly on the same footing as general guidance in the Handbook and individual guidance:

> If a firm has complied with the Principles, high-level rules and other rules then it is irrelevant whether they have complied with any other material we have issued. But firms can rely on all the material we publish. This is fundamental to our approach. So if a firm takes a reasonable course of action which we have indicated, in general public material or in a specific individual exchange (such as a supervisory letter), as being in compliance with a rule, then we will not take action against the firm for not having complied with the rule. The status of the general public material—the process it has been through, the format in which it has been published—does not affect that. For example it does not matter whether it is a specific rule or formal guidance in the Handbook, or a case study or 'Dear CEO' letter on our website.[65]

The FSA approach to confirmed industry guidance follows its approach to guid- **5.81** ance generally:

> Firms are not required to adhere to any guidance, whether given directly by us or confirmed by us. However, case studies and other useful examples of how to meet our principles and rules, particularly when tailored to specific groups of firms, can clearly be helpful. . . . If a firm takes a reasonable course of action that is indicated by FSA-confirmed industry guidance to be in compliance with a specific rule or principle (or part of it), we will treat them as having complied with that rule or principle providing that guidance was appropriate to them.[66]

The FSA's conclusions following feedback on its discussion paper on industry **5.82** guidance are set out in its Policy Statement of September 2007.[67] As might be expected, they follow the same general approach. The FSA has confirmed that, subject to the conditions and processes set out in the Policy Statement, it will confirm appropriate industry guidance. Perhaps the most significant conditions are that the wording of the FSA's confirmation does not offer firms a safe harbour

---

[65] FSA, 'Principles-based regulation: focusing on the outcomes that matter' (April 2007), p 10.
[66] ibid, p 11.
[67] FSA, 'Policy Statement 07/16: FSA Confirmation of Industry Guidance' (September 2007).

for compliance with industry guidance,[68] that the obligation is on the producer of the guidance to keep it up to date and to notify the FSA of material changes, and that FSA confirmation will last for three years, after which it will lapse, unless there has been a review in the interim.

5.83 The general position, therefore, is as follows:

(a) DEPP 6.2.1G(4) indicates that:

the FSA will not take action against a person for behaviour that it considers to be in line with guidance, other materials published by the FSA in support of the Handbook, or FSA-confirmed industry guidance which were current at the time of the behaviour in question.

(b) Guidance is not binding on those to whom the FSA's rules apply. Nor are the variety of other public materials that the FSA publishes to support the rules and guidance in the Handbook. Such materials are intended to illustrate the ways, but not the only ways in which a person can comply with the relevant rules.[69]

(c) Guidance does not set the minimum standard required to comply with a rule, nor is there any presumption that a failure to comply with guidance is indicative of a failure to comply with the rule to which it relates: there may be a number of different ways of complying with a rule. An important facet of principle-based regulation (on which see para 5.19 *et seq.* above) is that firms should be able to choose how best to comply with particular rules in the specific circumstances that apply to them. The Enforcement Guide indicates that the FSA will take care to ensure that this is recognised in relation to industry guidance, so that industry guidance does not become 'a prescriptive regime in place of FSA rules'.[70]

(d) The absence of guidance or other public material on a particular issue does not prevent the FSA from taking supervisory or enforcement action.[71]

(e) Guidance and supporting materials are, however, potentially relevant to an enforcement case[72] (and so also to the exercise of the FSA's supervisory and other powers short of enforcement). A decision-taker may take guidance and supporting materials into account:

(i) To help assess whether it could reasonably have been understood or predicted at the time that the conduct in question fell below the

---

[68] The wording of the confirmation is that 'the FSA has reviewed this [industry guidance] and has confirmed that it will take account of it when exercising its regulatory functions. This [industry guidance] is not mandatory and is not FSA guidance. This FSA view cannot affect the rights of third parties.' See PS 07/16, para 2.32.

[69] EG 2.23.

[70] EG 2.30.

[71] EG 2.27.

[72] EG 2.25.

    standards required by PRIN.[73] Supporting material will have the same function in relation to other high-level rules that the FSA may make in pursuit of principle-based regulation;

  (ii) To explain the regulatory context;

 (iii) To inform a view of the overall seriousness of the breaches;

 (iv) To inform consideration of a firm's defence that the FSA was judging the firm on the basis of retrospective standards;

  (v) To be considered as part of expert or supervisory evidence about the standards that applied at the time of the breach.[74]

(g) It will be for the FSA (or the relevant decision-taker in an enforcement context) to determine whether and to what extent the supporting material is relevant to compliance with the particular rule. That will depend, for example, on the type and accessibility of the supporting material and (in an enforcement context) on the nature of the firm's defence.[75]

(h) Guidance on rules, FSMA, or any other matter represents the FSA's view, and does not bind the courts, for example in relation to action by or on behalf of a third party. Nevertheless, FSA guidance may be persuasive, and its existence may in some circumstances affect the factual matrix within which a claim is determined. FSA guidance will also be taken into account by the Ombudsman in considering what is fair and reasonable in all the circumstances.[76]

Handbook Processes

The FSA's legislative functions

The Delegated Powers and Deregulation Committee of the House of Lords **5.84** reviewed the powers of the FSA to make secondary legislation under FSMA and accepted in principle that the delegation of powers to the FSA was appropriate, subject to safeguards, for example that the Treasury rather than the FSA should prescribe the definition of 'private person' eligible to seek damages for breaches of FSA rules, on which see para 5.63 above.

The Committee also recommended that, in the light of its obligations under the **5.85** Human Rights Act 1998, the FSA should include a statement in its annual report that, in its view, the provisions of the delegated legislation it has made in the reporting period are compatible with the Convention rights as defined in Human Rights Act 1998, section 1. This recommendation was accepted by the FSA.

---

[73] EG 2.25(1).
[74] EG 2.25(2) to (5).
[75] EG 2.26.
[76] See DISP 3.6.4R(1).

5.86 The FSA's legislative functions are a subset of its general functions (see para 5.03 above). The legislative functions are defined in FSMA, Schedule 1 para 1 as:

(a) making rules;
(b) issuing codes;
(c) issuing statements;
(d) giving directions;
(e) issuing general guidance as defined by FSMA, section 158(5); and
(f) giving guidance under FSMA, section 158A to meet the requirement under MiFID to set out a statement of policy on outsourcing.

5.87 The general position is that the FSA may make arrangements for any of its functions to be discharged by a committee, sub-committee, officer, or member of staff. That was originally subject to the limitation that the FSA could only exercise its legislative functions through its governing body, the FSA Board. Following consultation by HM Treasury during 2005 and the passage of the Regulatory Reform Act 2006, FSMA was amended to provide greater flexibility. As a result:

(a) The legislative functions in para 5.86(a) to (d) above must still be exercised by the FSA Board; but
(b) Although an FSA officer or member of staff may not give general guidance, it is no longer a requirement that general guidance must be given by the FSA Board. The result is that general guidance may now be given by an appropriate committee or sub-committee of the FSA Board.

5.88 The FSA has indicated that in future, the function of giving general guidance will be exercised by a sub-committee of the FSA Board with the same composition as the Regulatory Policy Committee (see para 5.90 below) unless the guidance is included in a rule-making instrument, in which case the function of making the instrument as a whole will be exercised by the FSA Board.[77]

5.89 FSMA, Schedule 1 para 7 provides that the arrangements that the FSA must make for the investigation of complaints arising in connection with the exercise of (or failure to exercise) its functions need not extend to complaints arising in connection with the FSA's legislative functions. Instead, most of the FSA's legislative functions as well as other functions which are exercised to make the materials re-stated in the FSA Handbook are subject to other provisions in FSMA such as requirements for consultation, notification, publication, and competition scrutiny. These are considered in paras 5.91 *et seq.* below. The FSA's 'Handbook processes' are the internal mechanisms and procedures by which it complies with these requirements.

---

[77] FSA, 'Policy Statement 07/10: Implementing the Regulatory Reform Order in relation to guidance' (July 2007).

The FSA's Handbook processes also include the internal procedures by which it **5.90** pursues its policy objectives in relation to the Handbook. Foremost amongst these (for the present at least) is principle-based regulation (on which see para 5.19 above). Other than the FSA Board, the most significant decision-making body in this context is the FSA's Regulatory Policy Committee ('RPC'). At the time of writing the RPC consists of the Chief Executive, the three Managing Directors, the General Counsel to the Board, the Director of Enforcement, the Director of Regulatory Strategy and Risk, and the Director of Communications. Its functions include reviewing proposals for the exercise of the FSA's legislative powers at an early stage, before they are put to the FSA Board, in particular before significant resources are committed to a legislative drafting project.

Consultation

There are many different but similar consultation provisions in FSMA, and paral- **5.91** lel changes to these provisions accounted for many of the amendments made to FSMA during its passage through Parliament. A statutory requirement for consultation is something of an innovation in financial services legislation. The Financial Services Act 1986 required the Securities and Investments Board to have regard to the costs of compliance.[78] Consultation was simply a good way of informing and improving its decision-making by offering firms and consumer bodies the opportunity to make observations on its proposals and on the associated costs and benefits. The practice of consulting has developed across the public sector, driven by work and guidance by the Cabinet Office. However, the requirements under FSMA are more prescriptive and, because they are binding on the FSA there is little flexibility to dispense with the requirements.

The main consultation requirement in relation to the Handbook, namely that for **5.92** rules, is set out in FSMA, section 155. The FSA must publish its draft rules in the way appearing to it to be best calculated to bring them to the attention of the public.[79] The draft rules must be accompanied by:

(a) a cost benefit analysis;
(b) an explanation of the purpose of the proposed rules;
(c) an explanation of the FSA's reasons for believing that making the proposed rules is compatible with its general duties under FSMA, section 2 (commonly known as a 'compatibility statement'); and
(d) notice that representations about the proposals may be made to the FSA within a specified time.

---

[78] Under Financial Services Act 1986, Sched 7 para 2A.
[79] See s 155(1) for rules.

5.93   FSMA, section 155(7) allows the FSA to dispense with consultation on proposed rules if it considers that the delay in consultation would be prejudicial to the interests of consumers. But the FSA has no discretion to dispense with consultation requirements if, for example, it considers that delay would prejudice someone other than a consumer, or that no useful purpose would be served by consultation, for example because the proposed amendments are minor in nature. That is difficult enough, but in fact the majority of the FSA's legislative functions require consultation in all cases, with no discretion not to consult.[80] That drives the FSA to adopt other strategies to minimise the prejudicial impact on firms and individuals other than consumers of the delay entailed in complying with consultation requirements. One such strategy is the 'waiver by consent' considered in para 5.68 above.

5.94   The Treasury consulted in December 2005 and May 2006 on a Regulatory Reform Order to relax the requirements to consult.[81] The result was that although the consultation requirements in relation to general guidance were reduced (on which see para 5.103 below) the consultation requirements in relation to rules and the product of other legislative functions (codes, directions, and the like) were left unchanged.

Cost-benefit analysis

5.95   The requirement for a cost–benefit analysis does not apply to rules which raise fees or levies, for the financial assistance scheme, for the FOS or establishment of the FSCS, for the FSA's functions under Part 6, or for other functions.[82] Instead the proposed rules must be accompanied by details of the expected expenditure by reference to which the proposal is made. The fees rules for the FSA, listing, and the FOS general levy are consulted on each financial year, generally at the same time as the FSA's budget or business plan. The draft Financial Services and Markets Bill defined cost–benefit analysis as an estimate of the costs of complying with the rules[83] together with an analysis of the benefits. However, this was amended

---

[80] For example, issuing statements of policy under FSMA, s 121 as to what behaviour constitutes market abuse; and issuing statements of policy on the imposition of disciplinary measures on authorised firms under FSMA, s 211. A full list of consultation requirements is set out in HM Treasury's second consultation on the Regulatory Reform Order, in May 2006, p 18. By contrast, the FSA may dispense with consultation in respect of the code of market conduct if it considers that there is an 'urgent need' to publish the code. See FSMA, s 121(6) and (9) in relation to alterations or replacements of the code.

[81] See HM Treasury, 'Regulatory Reform Order: A consultation on proposed changes to the Financial Services and Markets Act 2000' (December 2005), chs 2 to 4. A second consultation followed: HM Treasury, 'Regulatory Reform Order: A second consultation on proposed changes to the Financial Services and Markets Act 2000' (December 2005).

[82] See FSMA, s 155(3); subs (9) sets out the above excluded provisions.

[83] Along the lines of the provision in the Financial Services Act 1986, Sched 7 para 2A.

following the interim Cruickshank Report on competition in UK banking[84] to make clear that costs should include all economic costs, and not just compliance costs. The obligation to publish a cost–benefit analysis need not deter the FSA from making deregulatory changes. The FSA is not required to publish a cost–benefit analysis if it considers that its proposals, if complied with, will result in no increase in costs or that any increase will be of minimal significance.[85]

Purpose

The explanation of the purpose of the proposed rules is given in the FSA's consul- **5.96** tation paper on the proposed rules. The FSA also includes a high-level 'purpose' statement at the beginning of each section of the Handbook, to facilitate a purposive interpretation of the chapter.[86] Many legislative functions have a purpose test: for example, general rules under FSMA, section 138 are made for the purpose of protecting the interests of consumers, and the explanation provided clearly needs to reflect that test. Finally, the tests for giving a waiver or modification of rules under FSMA, section 148 (see para 5.65 above) may be informed by the explanations given in the Handbook and the consultation paper.

Compatibility with the general duties

The so-called compatibility statement[87] in respect of the general duties in FSMA, **5.97** section 2 (or the general duty in FSMA, section 73 for listing rules) applies only to consultation on rules. The statement is not required for other general functions such as the making of codes or the making of principles for approved persons, even though, like rules, they too are expressly subject to the general duties.

Compatibility with the general duties implies not just compatibility with the reg- **5.98** ulatory objectives as required by FSMA, section 2(1)(a), but also compatibility with 'acting in a way which the FSA considers most appropriate for the purpose of meeting those objectives' under FSMA, section 2(1)(b), and 'having regard' to the principles of good regulation in FSMA, section 2(3). In one sense, having to give its reasons should be no hardship, and consultation on those reasons should help the FSA improve its decision-making, since the FSA must already comply with the general duties in making the rules and giving general guidance. Nevertheless, a full

---

[84] Banking Review Competition and Regulation in Financial Services: Striking the Right Balance (July 1999); Final Report (March 2000); Government response (August 2000).
[85] FSMA, s 155(8) and (11), and equivalent provisions in other consultation requirements.
[86] Every provision in the Handbook must be interpreted in the light of its purpose: GEN 2.2.1R.
[87] Required by FSMA, s 155(2)(c) and s 157(4).

statement of compatibility with the general duties, on top of a cost–benefit analysis, can add considerably to the length of a consultation paper.

5.99 Furthermore, the obligation overlaps substantially with the FSA's general duty to consult practitioners and consumers, including two statutory panels and an additional panel for smaller businesses, on the extent to which its policies and practices are consistent with its general duties.[88] The FSA tends to consult the panels at an early stage in its policy-making process, although they are of course free, in addition, to respond to the FSA's consultation papers.

Consultation periods and implementation

5.100 Finally, the FSA must include in its consultation a statement that representations about the proposals may be made to the FSA within a specified period, and must pay regard to these representations before taking the proposed action.[89] Following consultation, the FSA must publish a feedback statement, and if the proposals have changed significantly (which implies that the FSA may change its proposals), a revised cost–benefit analysis.[90] The FSA will generally follow the public sector standard of 12 weeks, although a longer period may be specified where appropriate or a shorter period where necessary.

5.101 Nevertheless, FSMA does not expressly provide that an inappropriate failure to consult would automatically invalidate the rules made; nor does it expressly require the FSA to consult when it amends or revokes rules,[91] although an amendment would arguably involve the insertion of new rules. Nor would a failure to publish a feedback statement with a revised cost–benefit analysis or notify the Treasury as required[92] necessarily invalidate the making, amendment, or revocation of an instrument.

Publication

5.102 FSMA requires that the function of making rules is executed in writing[93] and that a rule-making instrument must be published. A failure to publish a rule-making instrument will invalidate that instrument at least in the case of the rules that it contains. The definitive version of a rule is that contained in the rule-making instrument and there are provisions for a copy of the instrument to be verified by

---

88 FSMA, ss 8 to11.
89 ibid, s 155(2)(d) and (4), in the case of consultation on proposed rules.
90 ibid, s 155(5) and (6), in the case of consultation on proposed rules.
91 Compare the reference to altering or revoking rules in FSMA, s 152.
92 FSMA, ss 152 and 158.
93 ibid, s 153(1)

the FSA for the purposes of legal proceedings.[94] There can be no breach of a rule if the relevant rule-making instrument has not been published in accordance with FSMA, section 153, and a rule-making instrument will be void to the extent that it does not specify the provisions of FSMA under which the rules are made.[95]

Reduced consultation on guidance

When FSMA came into force, the consultation provisions applicable to general **5.103** guidance (on which see para 5.74 above) were a close match of the consultation provisions for rules, outlined above. Following consultation in 2005 and 2006, the Treasury laid a Regulatory Reform Order before Parliament, which came in to force on 12 July 2007. One effect of that Order was to reduce the consultation requirements applicable to general guidance on rules,[96] so that the position is now as follows:[97]

(a) The FSA is required to publish a draft of the proposed general guidance in the way best calculated to bring it to the attention of the public;

(b) That publication must indicate that the FSA is open to representations about the proposed general guidance;

(c) The FSA must have regard to any representations received before making the proposed general guidance;

(d) The FSA may dispense with these consultation requirements if it considers that the delay in complying with them would be prejudicial to the interests of consumers; and

(e) If the FSA gives general guidance that it intends to have continuing effect and that is in written or other legible form, it must give the Treasury a copy of that guidance without delay. It must also notify the Treasury if that guidance is later altered or revoked.[98]

Competition scrutiny

To match the exemptions[99] from the Competition Act 1988 for behaviour which **5.104** is encouraged by the FSA's regulating provisions,[100] those regulating provisions

---

[94] ibid, s 154.
[95] ibid, ss 153(3) and (6).
[96] ibid, s 157(1).
[97] ibid, s 157(3).
[98] ibid, s 158.
[99] Set out in FSMA, s 164.
[100] 'Regulating provisions' are defined in FSMA, s 159(1) to mean any (a) rules; (b) general guidance (as defined by FSMA, s 158(5)); (c) statement issued by the Authority under FSMA, s 64; or (d) code issued by the Authority under FSMA, ss 64 or 119.

and the FSA's practices[101] are themselves subject to competition scrutiny under Part 10 of FSMA,[102] as are the recognition and regulatory provisions and practices of investment exchanges and clearing houses under Part 18. The FSA is not itself a competition regulator,[103] so that a full competition objective would be inappropriate. However, following the Cruickshank Report on competition in UK banking,[104] competition is an important part of the FSA's decision-making:

(a) In discharging its general functions (which include making rules and codes and giving general guidance as well as general policy-making), the FSA must have regard inter alia to:[105]

    (i) the need to minimise the adverse effects on competition that may arise from anything done in the discharge of those (general) functions; and

    (ii) the desirability of facilitating competition between those who are subject to any form of regulation by the FSA; this is primarily an objective of the OFT and the Competition Commission and the FSA must have regard to it only to the extent that it concerns regulated firms.

(c) The FSA's compatibility statement (see para 5.97 above) must include its reasons for believing that making the relevant regulating provision is compatible with having regard to these matters.[106]

(d) The cost–benefit analysis provisions include all economic costs, rather than simply costs of compliance, and the Competition Commission must have regard to any cost–benefit analysis produced by the FSA.[107]

5.105 Under the competition scrutiny provisions in FSMA Part 10, the Office of Fair Trading ('OFT') must keep under review the FSA's regulating provisions and practices, and must make a report if it considers that they or any combination of them are having an adverse effect on competition, in which case the Competition Commission must investigate.[108] The OFT may also make a report if it does not consider they are having an adverse effect on competition, but wishes to refer the matter for review by the Commission.

---

[101] Defined in FSMA, s 159(1) to mean 'practices adopted by the FSA in the exercise of functions under FSMA'.

[102] See also the parallel provisions in FSMA, s 59. Competition scrutiny is not the only form of scrutiny: the Financial Services and Markets Tribunal may, in determining a case before it, make recommendations as to the FSA's regulating provisions or its procedures, under FSMA, s 133(8).

[103] Enterprise Act 2002, s 209 permits the Secretary of State to add new domestic competition authorities in conjunction with powers to enforce European competition provisions.

[104] HM Treasury, Banking Review Competition and Regulation in Financial Services: Striking the Right Balance (July 1999); Final Report (March 2000); Government response (August 2000).

[105] ibid, s 2(3).

[106] ibid, s 155(2)(c).

[107] ibid, Sched 14 para 2(b).

[108] ibid, s 160.

The Competition Commission must investigate the matter and make a report **5.106** unless it considers that, as a result of a change of circumstances, for example if the FSA were to change its regulating provisions or practices in response, no useful purpose would be served by a report.[109] A report must include a conclusion as to whether the regulating provisions or practices have a significantly adverse effect on competition, and if so, state whether it considers that effect is justified and specify what action if any it considers the FSA ought to take in accordance with the restrictions in FSMA.

The Treasury must, having regard to any representations made by the FSA or by **5.107** other persons affected, then direct the FSA to take specified action, unless it considers that FSA action has already made this unnecessary or that, in the exceptional circumstances of the case, a direction would be inappropriate or unnecessary.[110] In exceptional circumstances the Treasury may direct the FSA to take action even if the Commission concludes the adverse effect on competition is justified.

Although the competition provisions are set up with an ongoing review obligation **5.108** and formal escalation procedures, in practice most competition scrutiny takes place at an informal level, with the FSA seeking the OFT's views at an early stage and taking these into account in formulating its Handbook provisions. There is scope for compromise at each stage.[111] The FSA and the OFT have formalised working arrangements to facilitate dialogue and effective cooperation on matters of mutual interest or where functions overlap.[112]

Interpretation of the Handbook

It is important to remember that the Handbook is for the most part a re-statement **5.109** of separate FSA rule-making instruments, each containing legislative provisions. The definitive version of the Handbook is contained in these instruments, and Handbook provisions are verified for court proceedings by reference to these[113] (see para 5.102 above).

As secondary legislation, rules are already subject to the provisions of the **5.110** Interpretation Act 1978, although most of these do not apply if the contrary

---

[109] ibid, s 162.

[110] ibid, s 163. These provisions reflect a more general retreat from ministerial interference in competition matters, as reflected in the Enterprise Act 2002, compared say with the position under the Financial Services Act 1986, although the Treasury retains a final say in exceptional circumstances under FSMA.

[111] See FSMA, ss 162(2) and 163(3)(a).

[112] Office of Fair Trading, FSA, 'The roles and responsibilities of the Financial Services Authority and the Office of Fair Trading' (July 2007).

[113] FSMA, s 154.

intention appears. Indeed GEN 2 establishes its own rules of interpretation for the Handbook:

(a) Every provision in the Handbook must be interpreted in the light of its purpose[114] (on which see para 5.96 above). GEN 2.2.2G goes on to explain:

> The purpose of any provision in the Handbook is to be gathered first and foremost from the text of the provision in question and its context among other relevant provisions. The guidance given on the purpose of a provision is intended as an explanation to assist readers of the Handbook. As such, guidance may assist the reader in assessing the purpose of the provision, but it should not be taken as a complete or definitive explanation of a provision's purpose.

(b) Evidential provisions indicated by the use of the letter 'E' (see para 5.60 above) are to be taken to provide that contravention of the rule does not give rise to any of the consequences provided for by provisions of the Act other than FSMA, section 149.[115]

(c) In the Handbook (except IPRU, unless otherwise indicated) an expression in italics which is defined in the Glossary has the meaning given there. An expression in italics which relates to an expression defined in the Glossary must be interpreted accordingly.[116] When italics have not been used, then (unless the context otherwise requires) an expression bears its natural meaning subject to the provisions of the Interpretation Act 1978.[117]

(d) GEN 2.2.11R nevertheless applies the Interpretation Act to the entire Handbook, and in particular, unless the contrary intention appears:
   (i) expressions in the Handbook have the same meanings as in FSMA;
   (ii) references to an enactment are references to that enactment as amended;
   (iii) words importing the masculine gender include the feminine gender, and words importing the singular include the plural, and vice versa;
   (iv) GEN 2.2.13R goes further and provides that references to other provisions in the Handbook are references to those provisions as amended *from time to time* (rather than at the time they were made)—in other words references to other provisions in the Handbook are ambulatory and do not have to be updated when those provisions are amended;

---

[114] GEN 2.2.1R.
[115] GEN 2.2.3R. But see GEN 2.2.4G(2): Other provisions in the Handbook, although also identified by the status letter 'E' in the margin or heading, are actually not rules but provisions in codes and GEN 2.2.3R does not apply to them. These code provisions are GEN 2.1.4 E, and those provisions in the Code of Practice for Approved Persons (APER 3 and APER 4) and the Code of Market Conduct (MAR 1) with the status letter 'E'.
[116] GEN 2.2.7R.
[117] GEN 2.2.9G.

(v) References to step-children and step-siblings (for example in control-lers and close links provisions) include (from 5 December 2005) chil-dren and siblings whose parents are in a civil partnership under the Civil Partnership Act 2004;[118]

(vi) A requirement for a communication or notice or similar to be 'in writ-ing' means that (unless the contrary intention appears) the communi-cation etc must be in legible form and capable of being reproduced on paper, irrespective of the medium used. References to 'writing' are interpreted accordingly;[119]

(vii) A document includes information recorded in any form, including electronic form;[120]

(viii) General rules (made under FSMA, section 138, see para 5.53 above) are to be treated as applying to a firm with respect to the carrying on of all regulated activities, and not the carrying on of other activities, unless and to the extent that a contrary intention appears.[121]

(ix) If a partnership or unincorporated association is dissolved, but its authorisation is preserved under FSMA, section 32, any partnership or unincorporated association which succeeds to the business is to be regarded as the same firm for the purposes of the Handbook.[122]

---

[118] GEN 2.2.12A.
[119] GEN 2.2.14R.
[120] GEN 2.2.16G.
[121] GEN 2.2.17R.
[122] GEN 2.2.18R.

6

REGULATORY PROCESSES— AUTHORISATION, SUPERVISION, ENFORCEMENT

Authorisation

Authorised and exempt persons

Authorised persons

This Part describes the process by which a person obtains a permission under **6.01** Part IV of the Financial Services and Markets Act 2000 ('FSMA') and thereby becomes an 'authorised person', this being the basis on which the majority of persons attain that status. It is important to understand that authorised persons must be distinguished from approved persons and from exempt persons—the terminology often causes confusion, but the different categories operate under very different regimes. Under section 31 the following persons are authorised persons:

 (i) A person who has a Part IV permission to carry on one or more regulated activities.

 (ii) An EEA firm qualifying for authorisation under Schedule 3 to FSMA. This is a reference to provisions which implement the Banking Consolidation Directive,[1] the Life and Non-life Insurance Directives,[2] the Markets in

---

[1] Directive 2006/48/EC of the European Parliament and of the Council of 14 June 2006 relating to the taking up and pursuit of the business of credit institutions (recast).

[2] Council Directive of 24 July 1973 on the coordination of laws, regulations, and administrative provisions relating to the taking up and pursuit of the business of direct insurance other than life assurance (No 73/239/EEC) (First Non-life Insurance Directive); Council Directive of 22 June 1988 on the coordination of laws, etc and laying down provisions to facilitate the effective exercise of freedom to provide services and amending Directive 73/239/EEC (No 88/357/EEC) (Second Non-life Insurance Directive); and Council Directive of 18 June 1992 on the coordination of laws, etc and amending Directives 73/239/EEC and 88/357/ (92/49/EEC) (Third Non-life Insurance

Financial Instruments Directive ('MiFID'),[3] the Insurance Mediation Directive,[4] and the UCITS Directives.[5] Under these directives firms incorporated in other Member States may have rights to provide services into or establish branches in the UK. To the extent that such firms are able to do so under these directives and provided they satisfy the conditions in FSMA, they are treated as qualifying for authorisation and are also 'authorised persons'. They do not have to go through the process described in this chapter; instead they have to follow the procedures for exercising the relevant passport rights. However if their 'passport' does not cover all the activities for which authorisation is required they have to 'top up' their permission by application for the relevant Part IV permission(s).

(iii) A Treaty firm qualifying for authorisation under Schedule 4 to FSMA. These are firms which are nationals of other EEA States, which are not entitled to passporting rights under the directives referred to above, but which may be eligible, on the basis of their home State authorisation, to be treated as authorised firms. They must satisfy the conditions in Schedule 4, and again do not have to apply for permission in the manner described in this chapter.

(iv) A person who is otherwise authorised by a provision of, or made under, FSMA. This is a relatively limited class—for example, under section 315 of FSMA, the Society of Lloyd's is an authorised person for the activities specified in that section.

All references to 'authorised person' in FSMA and the regulations made under it are to persons who are authorised as described above.

Exempt persons

6.02 It is essential to understand that an exempt person is not an authorised person and references in FSMA to 'authorised persons', for example in section 21 (financial

---

Directive); and Directive 2002/83/EC of the European Parliament and of the Council of 5 November 2002 concerning life assurance (Life Assurance Consolidation Directive).

[3] Directive of the European Parliament and of the Council of 21 April 2004 on markets in financial instruments amending Council Directive 85/611/EEC and 93/6/EEC and Directive 2000/12/EC of the European Parliament and of the Council and repealing Council Directive 93/22/EEC (2004/39/EC).

[4] European Parliament and Council Directive of 9 December 2002 on insurance mediation (2002/92/EC).

[5] Council Directive of 20 December 1985 on the coordination of laws, regulations, and administrative provisions relating to undertakings for collective investment in transferable securities (85/611/EEC) (the UCITS I Directive), as amended by: European Parliament and Council Directive 95/26/EC, European Parliament and Council Directive 2000/64/EC, European Parliament and Council Directive 2001/107/EC (the 'Management Directive'), European Parliament and Council Directive 2001/108/EC (the 'Product Directive'), European Parliament and Council Directive 2004/39/EC ('MiFID'), European Parliament and Council Directive 2005/1/EC and European Parliament and Council Directive 2008/18/EC.

promotion), do not include exempt persons. A person is not an 'exempt person' because his activities do not require authorisation as a result of an exclusion under the Regulated Activities Order.[6] Exempt persons can be exempt because FSMA provides that they are to be exempt—for example, recognised investment exchanges and recognised clearing houses are exempt persons under section 285 of FSMA. Their exemption applies to the regulated activities specified in that section. Appointed representatives are exempt persons by virtue of section 39 of FSMA. Persons can also become exempt under an order made by the Treasury: under the Financial Services and Markets Act 2000 (Exemption) Order 2001 (SI 2001/1201) a number of named entities (and types of entity) are exempt in relation to certain types of specified regulated activity. So, for instance, the Bank of England is exempt in respect of any regulated activity (with the exception of effecting or carrying out insurance business). By contrast, a local authority is exempt in respect of deposit-taking, but not otherwise.

By virtue of section 38 of FSMA a person cannot be an exempt person as a result of the Order if he is authorised under Part IV of FSMA. The effect of this is that as soon as a person is authorised, the Order becomes irrelevant. So, even if, in relation to a particular activity, that person is explicitly named in the Order or is of a type covered by the Order, if he intends to carry on that activity he will need to obtain specific Part IV permission for that activity as part of his authorisation. In a similar vein, under section 39 of FSMA an authorised person can also never be exempt from the general prohibition as an appointed representative—again his authorisation has to cover all his activities. However, if a person is exempt because of activities as a recognised investment exchange or recognised clearing house, then he may be authorised for another regulated activity. **6.03**

Is authorisation required?

The question of whether a person requires authorisation is a matter of law and the answer depends on the facts when construed in the light of sections 22 and 418 of FSMA and the Regulated Activities Order.[7] **6.04**

The interpretation of the Regulated Activities Order is not always straightforward, and certain categories of activity can give rise to a number of complexities (particularly the 'making arrangements with a view to' activity under article 25(2)). There is a facility for contacting the FSA by telephone or email to ask particular **6.05**

---

[6] The Financial Services and Markets Act (Regulated Activities) Order 2001, SI 2001/544.
[7] ibid.

queries about whether proposed activities will require authorisation—contact details of the Perimeter Guidance Team (for queries about whether proposed activities will require authorisation) are on the FSA website. In addition, Chapter 9 of the SUP section of the Handbook provides a process for obtaining individual guidance from the FSA. This process may be used where it is not clear if, in the particular circumstances, a person's activities fall within the authorisation requirement (for instance, where submitting a query to the Perimeter Guidance Team). SUP Chapter 9 is therefore unusual in that it applies both to authorised firms and to all other persons. The guidance is given by the FSA using its powers under section 157 of FSMA. Therefore, a person may request individual guidance from the FSA where it is not clear in the circumstances as to whether authorisation is required. The FSA does not enter into discussions on a 'no names' basis in connection with such requests. It has also made it very clear that it is not the first point of call for guidance on authorisation issues and expects the person to have taken proper steps to ascertain his own position. This will usually involve taking professional legal advice. This advice may however identify an uncertainty in the scope, say, of an exemption, when applied to particular activities. In such a case, the FSA needs to be given a full written description of the activities accompanied by the legal analysis of the position. Where a reasonable request is made to the FSA it will give the person guidance. If a person acts in accordance with current individual written guidance given to him by the FSA on the basis contemplated by that guidance, then the FSA will deal with him on the basis that he is in compliance with FSMA. Obtaining such guidance under the procedure in SUP 9 may therefore be extremely helpful in establishing the defence under section 23(3) of FSMA—namely, that the person took all reasonable precautions and exercised all due diligence to avoid contravening the general prohibition against carrying on a regulated activity without permission. Guidance, however, cannot affect the rights of third parties.

Who can be authorised?

6.06 Individuals, bodies corporate, partnerships, and unincorporated associations are eligible to apply for authorisation (although certain activities may only be carried on by persons with a particular legal status—see para 6.10(i)). Particular provision is made in FSMA for partnerships and unincorporated associations—under section 32 their authorisation is not affected by any change in membership. Firms which are incorporated overseas may also apply for authorisation if their activities are such that authorisation is required. This is particularly likely to be the case if they establish a branch in the UK. In such cases, it is the entity which is authorised, albeit in respect of the activities of its UK branch. As a result, some (but not all) of the FSA requirements apply to the entity and not just to the UK branch.

Consequences of authorisation

Position under FSMA

Once a firm is authorised it cannot breach the prohibition in FSMA against **6.07** carrying on regulated activities without permission. However, under section 20 of FSMA, if an authorised person carries on a regulated activity in the UK or purports to do so otherwise than in accordance with his permission, he will be taken to have contravened a requirement imposed on him by the FSA under FSMA. This can give rise to FSA disciplinary action as well as actions for breach of statutory duty by private persons (or fiduciaries or representatives acting on their behalf).[8] However, a contravention of section 20 of FSMA by an authorised person does not make him guilty of an offence or make any transaction void or unenforceable (in contrast to a breach of section 19 of FSMA by an unauthorised person).

FSA rules

The other obvious consequence of authorisation is that the authorised person is **6.08** subject to the rules contained in the FSA Handbook. It will also be an authorised person for the purposes of the financial promotion regime. As a result (and subject to any conditions on the scope of its authorisation), it will be able to both communicate and approve financial promotions (subject to specific FSA financial promotion rules and a statutory regime which restricts promotion of unregulated collective investment schemes by authorised firms). The authorised person will also be subject to the FSA disciplinary regime, and certain individuals employed in it will be separately registered with the FSA under the Approved Persons regime, also leading them into the disciplinary jurisdiction of the FSA.

The authorisation process

The threshold conditions

Section 41 of FSMA requires that in giving or varying permission, or imposing or **6.09** varying any requirement, the FSA must ensure that the applicant will satisfy and continue to satisfy the threshold conditions in relation to all of the regulated activities for which he has or will have permission. The threshold conditions therefore form the basis for many of the information requirements that have to be satisfied in connection with the application for authorisation. When preparing the information, it is helpful to bear in mind that the purpose is to enable the FSA

---

[8] Under the Financial Services and Markets Act 2000 (Rights of Action) Regulations 2001, SI 2001/2256.

to be satisfied that these conditions are met, and that it can reasonably expect that they will continue to be met following authorisation.

6.10 Schedule 6 to FSMA sets out the threshold conditions. The key aspects are as follows:

(i) There are some limitations on legal status, depending on the regulated activity concerned. Thus, the effecting and carrying out of contracts of insurance can only be effected by a body corporate (other than a limited liability partnership), a registered friendly society, or a member of Lloyd's. If a person wants to carry on the activity of accepting deposits or issuing electronic money, then it must be a body corporate or a partnership. However, these are the only activities for which there is a legal status requirement.

(ii) There are some restrictions in relation to the location of offices. If the person is a body corporate constituted under the law of any part of the UK, then both its head office and any registered office must be in the UK. This does not apply if the only regulated activity concerned is insurance mediation, in which case there are specific rules. If the person concerned has his head office in the UK but is not a body corporate, then it must carry on business in the UK. There are no other requirements as to the location of offices.

(iii) Where the activity concerns effecting and carrying out contracts of insurance against damage arising out of the use of motor vehicles on land there must be a claims representative in each EEA State other than the UK—that is a person with responsibility for handling and settling claims arising from certain motor accidents.

(iv) The FSA must be satisfied that the applicant's 'close links'[9] do not prevent the FSA's effective supervision. Where the person who is a close link is subject to laws or other provisions of a territory which is not an EEA State, the FSA must also be satisfied that this would not prevent it being able to supervise the applicant effectively. The essential purpose of the arrangements for close links is to give the FSA an overview of those persons who own or control the applicant, and/or of those whom it owns or controls. In many cases, this can be a very complex disclosure, and the need to provide close links information is a matter that should be identified and dealt with at an early stage in the preparation of an application, as it may involve the gathering of information from a wide range of persons. Once authorised, the applicant will have ongoing obligations in relation to notification of changes in its close links.

(v) The applicant must have resources which are adequate in relation to the activities that he seeks to carry on, or carries on. The FSA may, in judging

---

[9] See definition in FSMA, Sched 6, para 3(2).

whether or not this condition is met, take into account the fact that that entity is a member of a group, and the provisions which he makes or which the group makes in respect of liabilities and the means by which both the applicant and the group manages risk in connection with the applicant's business. This is a very important and potentially wide-ranging threshold condition. It requires the FSA, in effect, to form a view as to the resources available to the applicant and to have regard to the impact (whether positive or negative) that membership of a group may have on the applicant's individual position.

(vi) Suitability—the FSA has to be satisfied that the applicant is a fit and proper person having regard to all the circumstances, including:
   (a) his connection with any person;
   (b) the nature of the regulated activities he wishes to carry on;
   (c) the need to ensure that his affairs are conducted soundly and prudently.

The permission concept

6.11 As explained above, most authorised persons attain their authorised status by being granted a permission under Part IV of FSMA.

6.12 Permissions are given in respect of regulated activities—that is, the final FSA permission granted will relate to one or more activities which are regulated activities by virtue of the Regulated Activities Order.

6.13 The FSA has powers[10] to:

(i) impose limits on the carrying on of any particular regulated activity, for example, as to circumstances in which the activity may or may not be carried on. This power is frequently used;
(ii) grant a narrower or wider scope of permission for a particular regulated activity than that for which application is made;
(iii) give permission for an activity which has not been included in the application itself.

6.14 The FSA also has power[11] to impose requirements on any permission which it grants. Requirements may be very wide-ranging—they may in particular be imposed:

(i) so as to require the person concerned to take specified action; or
(ii) to require him to refrain from doing so.

---

[10] FSMA, s 42(7).
[11] ibid, s 43.

6.15 Requirements may cover activities which are not regulated activities and can be imposed by reference to membership of a group. They may also be time limited.

6.16 Requirements and limitations are published on the FSA register as they are an essential part of a firm's permission.

6.17 Some firms have extremely complicated permissions. In many cases this is not a reflection of their business but is a result of the complex transition process by which firms which were authorised under the pre-FSMA legislation (mainly the Financial Services Act 1986) were automatically granted authorisation and Part IV permissions under FSMA when it came into force on 1 December 2001. In some cases this resulted in firms with substantially similar businesses having different permissions—particularly in relation to limitations and requirements imposed. Indeed the FSA's approach to limitations and requirements has developed over time. This needs to be borne in mind when looking at any existing permission for purposes of information or comparison where the firm was authorised before 1 December 2001 under the Financial Services Act 1986.

Variations and cancellations

6.18 Once a person is authorised, he may apply to have his permission varied by adding or removing regulated activities, varying descriptions, and varying or cancelling requirements and limitations.[12] The FSA also has certain powers to vary and cancel permissions on its own initiative.[13]

Application procedure

General

6.19 The basis for the FSA application procedure is provided for in FSMA.[14] This requires the application to contain a statement of the regulated activities proposed, to provide an address in the UK for service. The FSA is empowered to make provision as to the manner in which applications may be made and to make different provision for different cases. The FSA has made such provision through its website: see the page headed 'How do I get authorised?' at <http://www.fsa.gov.uk/Pages/Doing/how/index.shtml> through which, by following a 'build your own application pack' process appropriate to the type of proposed business, the prescribed application forms, together with guidance notes, are available. There is also some perimeter guidance in PERG 2 in relation to authorisation and

---

[12] ibid, s 44.
[13] ibid, s 45.
[14] ibid, ss 51–55.

regulated activities. The question often arises as to whether the FSA needs to be contacted before an application is submitted. There is no requirement to contact the FSA in advance of submission of an application. It often happens that, during the preparation of the application, it is necessary to contact the authorisation team (by telephone or email) to discuss a particular aspect of completion of the forms, but it is not usual to meet with the FSA authorisation team before the application is submitted. There can be cases, however, where this is either necessary or desirable. This is likely to be the case where the application is complex or unusual, or involves particular time pressures. In such circumstances it is sensible to write or telephone to the authorisations team to explain why it is thought a meeting would be helpful. See also para 6.05 above in relation to contacting the Perimeter Guidance Team and the seeking of individual guidance.

It is common for firms to wish to submit the application to the FSA as quickly as **6.20** possible—often the FSA authorisation is seen merely as a step in a chain to starting a particular business. It is important to appreciate that the issues associated with the application process will continue to be core to the firm's business. If time is taken at this initial stage by senior management to understand the applicable rules and consider how best to comply with them in the context of their business on an ongoing basis, they will be on their way to integrating compliance into the business, instead of seeing it as an unnecessary and expensive 'add on'.

Time limits

Section 52 of FSMA requires the FSA to determine an application before the end **6.21** of the period of six months beginning with the date on which it received the completed application. There can, however, be some scope for debate as to whether the FSA has in fact received a 'completed application'. An applicant may often feel that it has delivered a complete application, but the first response from the FSA following receipt may well indicate the FSA does not regard the application as complete. It is therefore essential for any applicant who wishes his application to be considered expeditiously to ensure that it is complete when delivered.[15] FSMA sets the maximum time scales for the determination of applications—under the FSA's service standards the Regulator states that it aims to determine 75 per cent of applications within three months of receipt. In practice, whether or not the FSA's objective is reached at any time depends on both the volume of applications received, available staff resources, and the complexity of any particular application.

---

[15] FSMA enables the FSA to determine incomplete applications if it considers it appropriate to do so, and it must in any event determine incomplete applications within 12 months of receipt.

Application pack

6.22 There is a wide range of businesses which now need to be authorised—ranging from motor vehicle dealers who introduce certain types of insurance, through to international investment banks. The FSA authorisation process is commenced by the submission of a completed application pack to the FSA.

6.23 The FSA now provides a facility on its website allowing an applicant to build its own application pack. The applicant enters the 'build your own' application pack section of the website by selecting one of six different 'portals' depending upon the type of firm it will be and then answering a series of initial questions. The types of firm are:

(a) retail intermediaries (financial advisers, home finance intermediaries, insurance intermediaries, connected travel insurance intermediaries);

(b) wholesale investment firms (simple and complex securities and futures firms, advisers and arrangers of wholesale funds and investment managers);

(c) insurance firms (which will not be insurance intermediaries);

(d) other provider firms and deposit-takers (banks, home finance providers, personal pension providers, and e-money issuers);

(e) small e-money issuers;

(f) credit unions.

6.24 A glossary is also available on the application section of the website which is intended to assist the applicant in determining what type of firm it will be based on its proposed activities (which in turn will have a bearing on the shape and content of the application pack). Although the glossary may be helpful to a degree, it is likely that the applicant will require further assistance from its professional adviser as to the precise scope of the definitions.

The application forms

Core details form

6.25 All application packs will have a core details form. The purpose of the form, as the name suggests, is to provide basic information about the identity and legal status of the applicant and some initial information about personnel. Completion of the core details form is straightforward, particularly when compared with the business-specific supplement. However, it is nevertheless important to have regard to the accompanying guidance notes which explain the purpose of some of the questions and will assist in completing the application. In the core details form the applicant must record, amongst other things:

(a) its contact details;

(b) details of any professional advisers acting for it;

(c) whether or not there are any specific timing issues. The firm may wish to be authorised by a specific date—for example, where the applicant is currently an appointed representative (which means that it is exempt from FSMA) but that status is due to expire by a certain date. The FSA will try to meet the applicant's desired date, but does not make any guarantees in this regard. See para 6.21 above in relation to the FSA's statutory obligations and its performance standards for dealing with applications;

(d) its legal status (eg whether it is a private or public limited company, partnership, limited partnership, limited liability partnership, etc). Note that if the applicant is a partnership or limited liability partnership it will be required to attach copies of the relevant deeds;

(e) details of its auditor or reporting accountant (if any);

(f) details of the directors or partners who have shareholding or voting rights in the firm—note that separate forms will need to be completed in relation to external controllers of the firm;

(g) details of personnel—a staff organisational chart must be included on a separate sheet of paper. The FSA may decide to take up references for any individuals that will perform controlled functions—it will most likely do this in the case of individuals who will perform significant influence functions (ie anyone who will be performing any one of the controlled functions other than the customer function). The form therefore asks whether any of the proposed approved persons would want the FSA to wait until a certain date before writing to their employer. If this is the case, this may obviously delay the processing of the application by the FSA. The information as regards personnel in the core details form is quite basic: further information will be required in the relevant supplement that the firm will be required to submit;

(h) details of its IT systems and its arrangements for business continuity and disaster recovery.

The guidance notes to the core details form also provide an overview of the FSA Handbook and an introduction to the threshold conditions which applicant firms must satisfy to be and remain authorised.

Business-specific supplement

In addition to the core details form, there will be a specific supplement depending **6.26** upon the proposed business of the applicant—so there are different supplements for firms selling non-investment insurance contracts, for non-complex securities and futures firms, for investment managers, etc. Each of these specific supplements is accompanied by guidance notes. The following paragraphs summarise the component sections of a supplement by using the specific supplement for an application pack built for a complex securities and futures firm as an example.

The specific provisions of supplements for other types of firms are likely to have different requirements of detail (for instance as regards financial resources).

Business-specific supplement form—Section 1: Regulatory Business Plan

6.27 In many ways the first section of the supplement, the 'regulatory business plan', is the most important part of the entire application because its purpose is to describe to the FSA the applicant's proposed business and how it will be carried on. Section 1.1 sets out a series of matters which the applicant must explain or describe in relation to its proposed business: but those explanations and descriptions must be set out on separate sheets of paper. The notes to the supplement provide more information as to the style and nature of detail required. It is important for the applicant to read the notes carefully before it writes its business plan document. The FSA will find it easier to process an application where this part of the business plan follows the structure of the explanations and descriptions required in Section 1.1 of the supplement.

6.28 It is not necessary in most cases for the written description of the proposed business to run to hundreds of pages. What is appropriate depends on the scale and complexity of the business concerned. The written plan must convey the nature of the business and how it will be carried on. This does not always mean that it has to be particularly lengthy. Its purpose is to ensure that the FSA understands the proposed business, can feel comfortable that there is a coherent business plan for managing and developing the business, and that the necessary expertise will be available.

6.29 The threshold conditions concerning adequate resources and suitability are, in the FSA's general view, only likely to be satisfied if the applicant can demonstrate previous experience in the type of business for which the application is made. Thus at least some of the senior management would be expected to have proper experience in the financial services industry with relevant experience in the sector for which authorisation is sought. These issues can all be conveyed to the FSA through a carefully written business plan.

6.30 In addition to the separately written document which the applicant must provide, other regulatory business plan details must be completed on the form itself, including:

(a) whether it will be carrying on MiFID or non-MiFID business—this will have an impact upon the precise application of the FSA rules to the firm once authorised and its financial resources requirements. Guidance on the scope of MiFID and the recast Capital Adequacy Directive is set out in Chapter 13 of the FSA's Perimeter Guidance Manual ('PERG'). The applicant is also required to indicate whether or not it will be intending to passport any of its activities into other EEA States (whether on a cross-border basis or by establishing a branch);

(b) details in relation to its prospective clients—ie how the firm will source its clients, the number of clients it expects to have on authorisation and 12 months after authorisation;

(c) how the applicant expects to derive its income, what external and internal business risks its perceives, and how it intends to manage those risks;

(d) whether the applicant will be outsourcing any of its functions to third parties and, if so, how it will monitor and control those functions;

(e) a summary assessment of the competence and capability of those persons who will perform significant influence functions;

(f) whether the firm's IT systems are complex, whether the firm will be heavily dependant on those systems, and/or whether the systems will automatically interface with customers (which will be relevant to firms that deal with customers through the Internet, for example in relation to the provision of services such as broking and banking). The notes provide some guidance as to how to determine these issues. Where there is such complexity, dependency, or automatic interface the firm is required to complete a separate Detailed IT Controls Form (Annex 1) which must also be signed off both by the firm's auditor or reporting accountant (no sign-off from the auditor/reporting accountant is required where the firm does not have complex IT systems). Therefore, it is important at an early stage in considering the application to determine whether the Detailed IT Controls Form will be required. If so it will be necessary to notify the auditors so that they can advise as to what they will require before being able to complete and sign their section of the form. In addition, various supporting documents must be attached to the Detailed IT Controls Form, including systems and network diagrams and information security policies. Some significant preparatory work may therefore need to be done by the firm's IT department or IT consultants and, as stated above, the firm's auditors.

Business-specific supplement form—Section 2: Scope of Permission

6.31 Many applicants (including complex securities and futures firms) have to complete a permission profile table.[16] This sets out all the possible types of regulated activity for which permission may be sought, the types of investments in respect of which those activities may be performed, and the types of customer for which the service or activity may be performed. Such an applicant must also specify any applicable limitations or requirements.

6.32 Where an applicant decides to apply for a requirement or limitation that reduces the scope of its permission it will only be required to demonstrate that it can satisfy the threshold conditions in respect of that reduced scope. The use of limitations

---

[16] Exceptions include insurance intermediaries and sole traders, who have to select a particular 'permission profile' instead.

and requirements can therefore help the FSA to be satisfied that firms will meet the threshold conditions.

6.33 Requirements are imposed on an applicant in order to require it to take or refrain from taking a particular action and can extend to activities which are not regulated activities. Requirements generally relate to all or a number of activities which are carried on, in contrast to limitations which are specific to one particular activity. Having said this, the FSA's practice is not entirely consistent and has changed over time, and there are firms which have multiple limitations on their permissions which are also replicated as requirements. The use of limitations can also sometimes seem rather excessive or indeed unnecessary and the phrasing can be difficult to understand.

6.34 The supplement form sets out certain standard requirements which may be imposed. These include requirements that the firm does not hold client money or that it does not control client money or that the firm is exempt from MiFID by virtue of one or more exemptions in Article 2 of the directive. The FSA or the firm may also seek to impose other specific requirements. For example, requirements often limit the scope of a firm's activities so as to bring it within a particular differentiated regulatory regime. Such regimes include those for oil and energy market participants, venture capital firms, corporate finance advisory firms, and service companies. If the firm is applying to be a service company it will be subject to requirements that it must not guarantee or accept responsibility for the performance of participants in arrangements which it makes, that it must not approve financial promotions for other persons, or provide its services otherwise than in accordance with documents provided by the firm to the FSA.

6.35 Other types of requirement might relate to the way in which the firm carries on other activities or to the type of reporting that it does. There may be a requirement to submit financial returns more often than normal—this might be for a limited period of time in order for the FSA to remain satisfied that the firm has adequate financial resources. Similarly a firm might sometimes be required to have independent periodic compliance reviews—particularly during its initial period of operations.

6.36 Unlike requirements, each limitation is specific to a particular regulated activity or specified investments in order to restrict the basis on which any particular activity is carried on—for example firms who wish to accept deposits can apply for a limitation so that the activity is limited to wholesale deposits. Applicants may wish to apply for certain limitations or the FSA may itself impose them where it considers it appropriate to do so after reviewing the application. Common limitations include:

(a) limits on the types of client that a firm may deal with;

(b) limits on the number of clients with whom a firm may carry on particular activities—this might be a limitation imposed at the outset, which the

FSA would be prepared to review once the firm has further developed its systems;

(c) limits on the types of investments—for example a limitation to venture capital investments for venture capital firms. The use of limitations can assist firms as it may enable them to fall within a lighter capital or reporting requirements regime.

Following authorisation, requirements and limitations may be varied as part of the procedure for varying an authorisation.

Business-specific supplement form—Section 3: Financial Resources

The purpose of this section of the supplement form is to enable the FSA to under-   **6.37**
stand the financial position of the applicant, to identify its capital requirements, and to be satisfied that on authorisation it will meet and thereafter will continue to meet its capital requirements. For new businesses this calculation is prepared on the basis of forecasts and pro forma figures. It is important for an applicant to understand its likely capital requirements and how it will meet them—it is unde- sirable to get too far down the process of completing an application pack before discovering that the capital requirements are far greater than originally envisaged.

Although there is no FSA requirement for professional advisers (such as auditors/   **6.38**
reporting accountants) to review the information given in the Financial Resources section of the supplement form or to provide a 'sign off' it is advisable for the applicant to seek appropriate professional advice in preparing this section. This can prove to be a complex area with many pitfalls.

The precise prudential rules which will apply to a firm once authorised will depend   **6.39**
on the nature of its activities and in particular whether it is subject to one or both of MiFID and the recast Capital Adequacy Directive. A firm which is subject to both directives will be subject to the FSA's prudential rules set out in the Prudential Sourcebook for Banks, Building Societies and Investment Firms ('BIPRU') and the General Prudential Sourcebook ('GENPRU'). A firm which falls outside the recast Capital Adequacy Directive will be subject to the prudential rules in the Interim Prudential Sourcebook for Investment Businesses ('IPRU(INV)'). Which of the rules within IPRU(INV) apply to such a firm is determined in part by whether it falls within MiFID.

Having determined whether it will be subject to the prudential rules in GENPRU   **6.40**
and BIPRU or to the rules in IPRU(INV), an applicant firm must determine and state the sub-category into which it will fall. The sub-categorisations will deter- mine which of the regulatory capital rules will apply once the firm is authorised. For instance, if the firm is a BIPRU investment firm it must determine whether it is a BIPRU limited licence firm, a BIPRU limited activity firm, or a full scope BIPRU investment firm. The Q&As in PERG 13 provide guidance as to what

these sub-categories mean, but it may be prudent to seek professional advice. At the same time, such an applicant must specify whether it is a BIPRU 50K firm, a BIPRU 125K firm, or a BIPRU 730K firm. There are also different prudential sub-categories for firms which fall outside the recast Capital Adequacy Directive (such as 'Broad Scope', 'directive fund manager', and 'exempt CAD firm'). Certain firms will fall within more than one sub-category. The relevant sub-categorisation(s) will determine the scope of the IPRU(INV) rules that will apply.

6.41 An applicant is not required to have the necessary capital in place at the time that the authorisation application is submitted to the FSA—but it will need to satisfy the FSA that the relevant funds have been contributed before the FSA will finally issue its authorisation.

Business-specific supplement form—Section 4: Personnel

6.42 This section of the business-specific supplement requires the applicant to list the names of individuals in respect of whom the firm is applying for approval to perform controlled functions. A person who is approved by the FSA to perform a controlled function is called an 'approved person'. Approved persons are not the same as 'authorised persons'. The status of approved person is given to certain persons who carry out certain functions in relation to an authorised person. Their status is dependent on their position with the authorised firm—it is not transferable, they are not authorised in their own right. This is an important point which is often misunderstood, particularly by the individuals concerned. Section 59 of FSMA provides for certain categories of person to have the status of approved persons. The principal effect of being an approved person is that one is subject to the FSA's disciplinary regime—in particular its powers to impose unlimited fines and make public statements about the approved person.

6.43 The Handbook provisions relating to the approved persons regime are not all to be found in the same place, which can cause confusion. The Senior Management Arrangements, Systems and Controls Sourcebook ('SYSC') contains the rule as to who must be registered for the required function known as the 'apportionment and oversight function' (normally the chief executive). SYSC also requires firms that carry on designated investment business to allocate the compliance oversight function to a director or senior manager. However for further detail on what each of the controlled functions comprises one has to look at the Supervision Manual ('SUP') Chapter 10, and the Statements of Principle and Code of Practice for Approved Persons ('APER') contains the Principles applicable to approved persons and the Code of Practice that applies to those Principles. There are special rules as to the functions which apply for overseas firms and incoming firms. However, for most firms the position is that they must:

(a) register each director or partner and non-executive director in respect of the relevant 'Governing Function' (ie one of CF1 to CF6 as appropriate);

(b) appoint someone to each of the 'Required Functions' (ie CF8 to CF12B)—the Required Functions include the apportionment and oversight function (CF8), the compliance oversight function (CF10), and the money laundering reporting function (CF11) and these will be relevant in all cases. Other Required Functions (such as the EEA investment business oversight function (CF9) or the actuarial function (CF12) are applicable only to certain types of business;

(c) consider if they need to register one or more individuals for each of the systems and controls function (CF28), the significant management function (CF29), and/or the customer function (CF30).

As a practical matter therefore at an early stage in the application a firm needs **6.44** to decide which controlled functions are relevant to it and who will fulfil them. It is likely that most firms carrying on designated investment business will need to register one or more persons with a customer function (CF30). This is because these persons will be involved in advising, managing, or trading on behalf of customers. In many cases, where a firm has retail clients or deals with consumers, there is an associated examination requirement for the customer functions. It is important to identify if there are any qualification requirements which need to be satisfied and whether or not the persons who will be registered already meet the necessary requirement. If not, arrangements need to be made for them to take the appropriate examinations—they will not be registered for the customer functions until they can satisfy the FSA that they meet the necessary criteria. This can in turn delay the granting of an authorisation. In some cases it is possible to apply for a waiver of particular training requirements—such an application is made at the same time as the authorisation application. In any event the applicant needs to be satisfied that all of the persons who will be registered as approved persons are competent for the roles which they are to carry on and that it can substantiate its belief in that competence.

It should be noted that specifying the names of potential approved persons in **6.45** section 4 of the supplement does not amount to an application for approval of that person: separate application forms[17] must be completed in relation to each of those individuals who will perform controlled functions under the approved persons regime.

Business-specific supplement form—Section 5: Compliance Arrangements

The completion of this section of the form is relevant to the FSA's assessment of **6.46** the applicant's systems and controls for compliance. The section requires the

---

[17] Form A—Application to perform controlled functions under the approved persons regime.

applicant firm to have established and documented compliance procedures, including a compliance manual. The applicant is not required to send a copy of the compliance manual or other documented procedures to the FSA but these documents must be ready for inspection at any time should the FSA request sight of them—on the application form the firm must tick a box confirming that it has such documented compliance procedures in place. The FSA warns that the manual should be designed so that it is specifically tailored to the business of the applicant and is easy to use as well as easy to amend and keep up to date. The FSA has had concerns in the past that some firms simply use 'off the shelf' compliance manuals, procedures, and programmes which have not been tailored to their businesses and which do not properly reflect the sort of steps which that particular kind of firm should be considering. The guidance notes indicate that if a firm has any doubts as to what should be included within the compliance manual it should seek professional advice.

6.47   The applicant must establish and maintain a compliance monitoring programme, a copy of which (unlike the compliance manual) must be attached to the application. The guidance notes include an example of a compliance monitoring programme (at least as regards the headings of the contents that should be included) but the FSA stresses that an applicant firm will need to devise its own compliance monitoring programme based on its own proposed business.

6.48   The compliance arrangements section of the supplement does not require the firm to provide details of the compliance officer as such. Note that a director or senior manager of the applicant firm must be allocated to the compliance oversight function (CF10) and this person must be named in Section 4 on personnel (see para 6.42 on approved persons). However, this approved person—who must occupy a senior position—will not necessarily be the compliance officer himself. For very small firms the person nominated as compliance officer might also be an executive working in the business. Where the proposed compliance officer does not have historical experience of compliance matters it is desirable to show that he has or will receive training (from a combination, perhaps, of professional advisers, attendance at courses, and the taking of the regulatory section of one of the approved exams). It may well be possible in some cases to demonstrate that through such training and through the understanding that the person has of the business, he will be suitable to carry out the function. The FSA is keen for firms not to become over-dependent on third parties, partly because it is concerned that this leads a firm's senior management to feel more distant from its own responsibility for understanding and controlling the compliance issues that affect the firm.

6.49   The fight against financial crime is a key issue for the FSA. The compliance arrangements section of the supplement requires the applicant to provide a brief description of the steps it has put into place to counter the risks that the firm might be used to further financial crime. Financial crime in this context includes fraud or dishonesty and money laundering. The description should include the steps that the firm will take to ensure that its money laundering reporting officer (MLRO) understands his duties and how to perform them, the firm's client identification procedures and other anti-money laundering procedures (including 'know your business' information gathering and staff training). In addition, the firm should describe the controls and procedures it has instituted to mitigate the risk of market abuse and to monitor those controls and procedures. It should also provide details of the anti-market abuse training that will be provided to its relevant staff.

Another key issue for the FSA is that of treating customers fairly ('TCF'). The **6.50** supplement requires the applicant firm to outline the measures that it has put in place to deliver and demonstrate the TCF outcomes.

Business-specific supplement form—Section 6: Fees and Levies

This section of the supplement form relates to the periodical fees and levies to **6.51** which the firm will be subject on an ongoing basis once authorised (to be contrasted with the application fee that the firm must pay when seeking authorisation— see para 6.57 below). The relevant periodical fees are calculated on the basis of the relevant fee block applicable to the applicant depending upon what type of business it will undertake and its consequent scope of permission. It should be noted that levies are also raised for the Financial Ombudsman Service ('FOS') and the Financial Services Compensation Scheme ('FSCS') unless the firm can show that it will not have any eligible claimants or eligible complainants as clients.

Individual forms

As stated above (see para 6.48) an applicant firm must submit a separate Form A **6.52** (Application to perform controlled functions under the approved persons regime) in relation to each of those individuals who will perform controlled functions under the approved persons regime.

Owners and influencers appendix

This document must be filled in whenever a firm will not be solely owned by its **6.53** directors or partners. It is designed to elicit information in relation to controllers and close links. If relevant, information must also be provided if the firm is part of a financial conglomerate or a third country banking or investment group. Again, guidance notes accompany the form.

Supporting documents

In addition to the application pack components outlined above, certain specified **6.54** supporting documents will need to be submitted. Depending upon the nature of the firm, this may include a staff organisation chart, business plan information, compliance procedures, and monthly forecasts for profit and loss, balance sheet, and cash flow. Applicants must ensure that the relevant supporting documents are attached to the application. It is often a failure to deal with easily missed details of this kind that leads to delays in the handling of the application.

Change of legal status application pack

6.55 An existing authorised firm wishing to change its legal status only may qualify to use this pack which enables an existing authorised firm to cancel its permission at the same time as the applicant applies for authorisation. This type of pack might be most suitable where an existing authorised firm which is a limited company is transferring its business into a limited liability partnership.

Credit union application pack

6.56 Applicants wishing to be authorised as a credit union should apply using the separate credit union application pack. This includes the registration element of the process.

Application fees

6.57 All applicants have to pay a one-off authorisation fee to the FSA and until the fee is paid the application will be treated as incomplete and is unlikely to be considered. The amount of the fee varies—applications which are considered 'straightforward' cost £1,500, applications which are 'moderately complex' cost £5,000, and applications which are complex cost £25,000. (The application fee for change of legal status applications is charged at 50 per cent of the full authorisation fee—ie £750 for a straightforward application and £2,500 for a moderately complex application.) Fund management is regarded as 'moderately complex' whereas the businesses of financial advisers, mortgage brokers, and general insurance intermediaries are considered to be 'straightforward'. It is important to be aware that the application fee is non-refundable—the applicant will not get its money back if, having submitted an application, it decides not to proceed to authorisation or if the FSA refuses to grant authorisation for some reason.

Determining applications

6.58 In the normal course the application is handled by staff within the Authorisations Department who have the power to grant applications on the terms applied for. During discussions on the application that the FSA may have with the applicant it may become apparent that the firm should apply for a further or different limitation or requirement or permission, and in such circumstances may revise its application. The internal staff then have the power to grant the application. The internal staff procedures at the FSA are relatively flexible and have been designed to ensure that the majority of applications can be processed using a degree of necessary, but not excessive, formal committee procedures. Where a decision concerns the refusal or proposed refusal of an application or the grant of an application subject to a limitation or requirement not applied for by the applicant, the decision will be made under executive procedures (as specified in the Decision Procedure and Penalties manual ('DEPP')) unless the applicant makes representations to the FSA, in which case the decision will be made by the Regulatory Decisions Committee ('RDC').

During the authorisation process there may, in very limited cases, be a warning **6.59** notice issued. Where FSA staff members consider that an application should be refused or should be granted subject to a limit or requirement which was not applied for, or for a narrower description of regulated activity than that to which the application relates, they will recommend to the RDC that a warning notice be given. The warning notice procedure is a matter for decision by the RDC and enables the person concerned to make representations to the RDC before any decision notice is issued. After considering representations the RDC may decide to grant the application and, if appropriate, issue a decision notice. The concept of warning notices and decision notices is described in more detail in paras 6.86 to 6.89 of this chapter.

Supervision Process

A risk-based approach

FSMA requires the FSA to 'maintain arrangements designed to enable it to deter- **6.60** mine whether persons on whom requirements are imposed by or under this Act, or by any directly applicable community regulation made under the markets in financial instruments directive, are complying with them'.[18]

The FSA has therefore had to develop an approach to enable it to supervise the **6.61** firms and individuals who fall within its jurisdiction, and in doing so has had to have regard to the regulatory objectives specified in FSMA and to section 2(3) of FSMA—described as the principles of 'good regulation'. SUP is the principal part of the Handbook that applies to the continuing relationship between the FSA and an authorised person. While the Conduct of Business rules apply to the conduct of the firm's regulated business, it is the rules in SUP that are more directly relevant to the firm/regulator relationship.

The FSA has long since decided on a risk-based approach to supervision. The **6.62** breadth of firms and activities authorised by the FSA, when seen in the context of

---

[18] FSMA, Sched 1, para 6(1).

the FSA's resources, leads to the conclusion that a risk-based approach is the only proper use of the FSA's supervisory procedures.

6.63 The FSA's risk-based approach to regulation in the context of supervision is realised by way of 'ARROW'—the Advanced Risk-Responsive Operating Framework.[19] In broad terms, the FSA uses ARROW to carry out impact and probability assessments against firms to decide how to regulate them. The risk that is assessed is the risk that the firm presents to the FSA's ability to meet its regulatory objectives. Under ARROW the FSA assesses the impact of the firm (ie broadly, how significant would it be to the FSA if the firm were to fail in some way) and the probability that a particular perceived risk will materialise. The FSA uses its impact assessment on a firm to classify it into one of four bands—high (A), medium high (B), medium low (C), and low (D). Depending upon the impact scoring for the firm, the FSA will use one of the following approaches: the 'ARROW Small Firms' approach (for low risk firms—eg advisory firms and credit unions), the 'ARROW Light' approach (for medium high or medium low risk firms) and the 'full ARROW' approach (for high risk firms—eg medium-sized businesses assessed as high risk and large businesses and groups).

6.64 In assessing the impact that a firm might have the FSA has regard to such factors as:

   (i) the extent to which consumers may be affected by failures of the firm;
  (ii) the degree to which risks related to the firm could, if they were to materialise, damage market confidence;
 (iii) the incidents and materiality of any financial crime which could be perpetrated through or by the firm.

6.65 In practice an impact assessment of this kind is likely to produce the result that a firm which does not deal with retail customers, which does not take deposits, and whose regulated activities are limited, say, to arranging corporate finance deals, is likely to be assessed as being a relatively low impact firm.

6.66 The probability part of the process focuses on issues such as:

  (a) the firm's strategy;
  (b) its financial soundness;
  (c) its customers and products and services;
  (d) its internal systems and controls;
  (e) the business risks that it faces—for example the types of credit, market, and operational risks which are inherent in its kind of business.

---

[19] In 2006 the FSA introduced an improved version of the framework—ARROW II. Improvements include enhancements to the FSA's internal processes, better communication to firms of the FSA's risk assessment, and integration of the FSA's capital assessments (eg under Pillar 2 of the Capital Requirements Directive).

The nature and scope of the probability assessment will differ depending upon which approach (ie impact risk assessment) applies. Low-impact firms subject to the ARROW small firms approach are unlikely to receive site visits and instead the assessment will be carried out by the FSA on a 'desk-based' basis, with FSA staff looking at returns and other sources. However, for those firms subject to full ARROW (and also to a lesser extent for those subject to ARROW Light) the process is likely to involve significant interaction between the firm and the supervisory team, including visits to facilities, provision of information, and detailed discussion.

At the pre-assessment stage at the outset of the ARROW process the FSA will **6.67** usually send the firm a list of documents that it would like to see before the ARROW visit (the FSA sometimes refers to these as 'Deliverables'). Depending upon the nature of the firm this can include (amongst many other documents) structure charts, staffing details, financial statements, board minutes, an up-to-date copy of the Compliance Manual, the Compliance Monitoring plan, the firm's ICAAP, TCF information, transactional information and client categorisation information. Even for a medium risk firm delivering this requested information can involve considerable work, particularly for MiFID firms—more than 100 separate and detailed documents may be requested, some of which may involve having to draft explanations of certain matters in response to questions raised.

The ARROW visit itself will also be an intensive experience for the firm and its **6.68** senior staff. The FSA will want to interview certain key individuals (including senior managers, non-executive directors, and approved persons). Interviewees are likely to be asked to bring certain documents with them, such as management information, structure charts, and strategy documents.

Following the visit the FSA will complete its risk assessment. The risks identified **6.69** are assessed against the FSA's statutory objectives, and result in the production of a risk mitigation plan which is a tool for the prudential supervision of medium and high risk firms. The risk mitigation plan will highlight the risks that the FSA has identified as a result of its review, and prescribe actions that must be taken by the firm to counter, mitigate, or deal with the risks that have been identified. The FSA sends a copy of the risk mitigation plan with its ARROW letter, first in draft form to enable the firm to correct any factual errors, and then in final form addressed to the firm's board or governing body. Firms are given a timetable against which the range of risk mitigation actions must be taken, and failure to take the ARROW process and the resultant ARROW letter seriously and to deal with its requirements could well lead a firm into enforcement.

As stated above, these assessments enable the FSA to determine how it will deal with **6.70** a firm. A very large number of firms have been almost automatically classified as 'low risk' and in consequence do not have a relationship with a particular supervisor, but rather are dealt with through the FSA Contact Centre. This has advantages and disadvantages, a principal disadvantage being that there is no person or team at the FSA dedicated to having an understanding of a particular firm's business. Being assessed as a low risk firm does not, however, mean that the firm will not hear from the FSA—see the description of supervisory tools below.

Supervisory tools

6.71 The FSA classifies the procedures which it uses to supervise firms under the following headings:

(a) diagnostic—processes which are designed to identify, assess, and measure risk;
(b) monitoring—processes for the tracking of identified risks;
(c) preventative—processes for limiting and reducing identified risks;
(d) remedial—processes for responding to crystallised risks.

6.72 These processes include:

(a) desk-based reviews—which may for example require firms to supply the FSA with certain information—for example as to the procedures it uses in a particular area such as its client classification and anti-money laundering procedures. Firms that fail to take desk-based reviews seriously are likely to receive a follow-up visit;

(b) reviews and analysis of periodic returns. For many firms their principal contact with the FSA is through the completion of the various reports which are required by SUP. Again failures to supply such reports on time or the supply of incomplete reports may provoke action from the FSA. There are numerous reports and notifications that a firm may need to make to the FSA. These include the annual controllers and annual close links reports, both of which must be submitted within four months of the firm's accounting reference date. Certain types of firm have to make annual compliance reports. All firms have to make financial reports—the timing and content of these reports is specific to the type of firm concerned. The FSA imposes automatic penalties for late filing of returns. The preparation of all these reports (but particularly the financial report) is a serious matter and incomplete, incorrect, or late reports are taken seriously by the FSA.

(c) Review and analysis of notifications. There are a wide range of matters that must be notified to the FSA by a firm. Again these are detailed in SUP and they include:
(i) any matters which could have a significant adverse impact on the firm's reputation;

    (ii) any matter which could affect the firm's ability to continue to provide adequate services to its customers;

    (iii) civil proceedings where the amount of the claim is significant in relation to the firm's financial resources or its reputation;

    (iv) the fact that the firm is prosecuted for or convicted of any offence involving fraud or dishonesty or that penalties are imposed on it for tax evasion;

    (v) the fact that it becomes aware that an employee may have committed a fraud against one of its customers;

    (vi) the fact that it becomes aware of a significant breach of a FSA rule or principle.

The above sets out only a few examples from the list of notification requirements—all authorised firms need to make sure that they are aware (see SUP 15) of the notification requirements applicable to them. Firms should also be aware of the need to give the FSA advance notice of changes in name, business name, principal place of address, or if they become subject to or cease to be subject to the supervision of an overseas regulator. SUP sets out the basis on which notifications may be made to the FSA.

(d) Review and analysis of transaction reports. Many firms which enter into reportable transactions must also comply with the transaction reporting requirements of SUP 17. These reports enable the FSA to monitor both the activities of firms and oversee the markets in transferable securities.

(e) The use of auditors. Auditors have a key role to play in assisting the FSA in its supervisory function. All authorised firms are required to appoint an auditor (regardless of whether they would otherwise be obliged to do so) and an auditor must be qualified in a way which satisfies the requirements of SUP. Firms are required by FSA rules to cooperate with their auditors and auditors are required to cooperate with the FSA in the discharge of its statutory functions. Auditors are obliged by regulations made under FSMA to report certain matters to the FSA and the auditors of certain types of business are required to make annual reports to the FSA on specific matters. In particular the auditors' report to the FSA covers the firm's financial statements and regulatory reporting—and the auditor must submit a letter annually commenting on the firm's internal controls—however this letter need only cover matters which have come to the auditor's attention while undertaking the work required to produce the reports on the financial statements and accounting records. Auditors of firms are also required to provide client assets reports to the FSA which contain an opinion on the firm's systems for the custody, identification, and control of custody assets and compliance with client money rules. Auditors are independent and have no privilege against disclosure of this information to the FSA.

(f) Meetings with management and other representatives and on-site inspections.

(g) Sectoral reviews and thematic work. The FSA identifies themes which it considers may raise particular regulatory concerns—for example the adequacy of financial promotions to retail customers—and may then conduct theme visits or desk-based theme reviews designed to enable it to gather information on a particular industry sector (eg hedge funds) or on a particular type of matter (eg financial crime). Thematic work can help the FSA to form a view as to whether its risk assessments of sectors or activities is likely to be sound. The FSA has stated that the selection of a firm for participation in the FSA's thematic work does not imply that the FSA has already decided that there is a problem in that firm. Rather it reflects a number of factors including the desire to create a representative sample of firms reviewed. Nevertheless there is still likely to be a view in many firms that if a firm is included in a sample for thematic work it is, by definition, more likely to be considered for enforcement action. The FSA regularly publicises its key themes—authorised firms should ensure that they are aware of these themes and the extent to which they are relevant to the firm's business—and make sure that if asked questions relating to such themes, they would be in a position to do so without embarrassment.

(h) Own initiative information gathering. The use of this tool relies on Principle 11 which requires a firm to cooperate with its regulator. From time to time the FSA will, through visits or desk-based reviews, ask firms to provide information, documentation, or to attend meetings in order to enable the FSA to gather information for supervisory purposes. In addition the FSA carries out mystery shopping where the FSA or persons appointed by it may pose as potential retail customers to enable them to assess the selling of financial products to consumers.

(i) Other tools. As considered further below other supervisory tools include the ability to require a report by a skilled person, the ability to vary and cancel permissions, and to set individual requirements on a firm of the FSA's own volition.

Enforcement Processes

Relevant statutory provisions

Information gathering and investigations

6.73 The remaining paragraphs of this chapter consider the FSA's processes in relation to enforcement, and in particular in relation to the imposition of disciplinary measures. Sections 165 to 169 and section 284 of FSMA confer wide-ranging information gathering and investigation powers on the FSA. These powers are summarised in the Enforcement Guide ('EG'). Failure to comply with requirements imposed in the exercise of these powers can give rise to the commission of criminal offences punishable by imprisonment and/or a fine. In any event, it is an extremely serious matter not to take care in the provision of information to an investigator or in response to an information request, and any firm in receipt of such must ensure that it devotes the necessary resources to dealing properly with the matter.

Through the use of these information gathering and investigation powers the FSA   **6.74**
is able to acquire information from authorised firms, persons who work in such firms, and, in certain circumstances, third parties. This enables it to investigate the wide range of matters for which it is the enforcement authority, including contraventions of FSA rules, the commission of insider dealing offences, and of market abuse and breaches of anti-money laundering requirements.

Skilled person reports

Section 166 of FSMA confers power on the FSA to require a firm to appoint   **6.75**
a third party (usually a firm of solicitors or accountants) to provide the FSA with a report on any matter about which the FSA could require the provision of information or production of documents under section 165 of FSMA. The imposition of this requirement (known as a 'skilled persons report') can be applied both to an authorised person and any other member of the authorised person's group. The preparation of such reports is a matter of some controversy and there have been concerns expressed that the FSA has used the power to require a skilled persons report instead of devoting its own resources to investigating a particular matter. A skilled person acts independently of the authorised firm, but the authorised firm is required to pay its fees. The skilled person report exercise can be a source of considerable disruption to a firm—requiring it to commit significant resources to providing information and assistance to the skilled person—and also involves significant expense.

SUP 5 sets out guidance on the FSA's approach to the use of skilled person reports   **6.76**
which makes it clear that the reports may be required in connection with monitoring, remedial, and preventative purposes. There is a perception that skilled person reports lead to enforcement action: in practice, only a tiny proportion of the skilled reports that are commissioned actually result in enforcement action in the form of a Final Notice. However it is difficult to predict if this will continue. Following the events in relation to Northern Rock and the increased emphasis on certain areas such as market conduct, it could be anticipated that the FSA will seek to be more vigorous in the use of the enforcement process in order to send firm messages to the market.

6.77 If a skilled person is appointed, SUP 5 imposes particular duties on the firm. It sets out the terms which must be included in a contract between the firm and the skilled person. In particular the firm is required to waive any duty of confidentiality owed by the skilled person to the firm which might limit the provision of information or opinion by the skilled person to the FSA. The contract must be governed by the laws of a part of the UK and provide that the FSA will have a right to enforce the provisions which are included in the contract in order to comply with the SUP requirements. The FSA rules require the firm to provide all reasonable assistance to any skilled person. This includes providing access at all reasonable business hours to the firm's accounting and other records in whatever form, providing such information and explanations as the skilled person reasonably considers necessary or desirable, and permitting the skilled person to obtain information directly from the firm's auditor to the extent the skilled person reasonably considers he needs such information or it is desirable for the proper performance of his duties.

Disciplinary measures

6.78 Part XIV of FSMA specifies the main disciplinary measures in relation to firms available to the FSA. However there are additional powers elsewhere within FSMA and, as regards private censures, the FSA operates its own, non-statutory procedure.

Public censure

6.79 If the FSA considers that an authorised person has contravened a requirement of FSMA, the FSA may publish a statement to that effect.[20] Requirements imposed under FSMA include FSA rules.

Private warnings

6.80 The FSA operates a private warning procedure as described in EG 7. FSMA makes no specific reference to any such procedure, and its scope and its use therefore falls to be governed only by the EG provisions. According to EG 7, the private warning procedure may be used in a wide range of circumstances—and indeed private warnings may be given not only to approved persons and authorised persons but also to unauthorised persons—for example, in the context of potential market abuse. Private warnings may be given in a wide range of cases—both where the FSA has power to bring formal disciplinary action but, for whatever reason, has determined that it is not appropriate to do so, and more generally.

6.81 Private warnings do not constitute formal disciplinary action, nor do they amount to a determination that there has been a contravention of a requirement or that there has been misconduct. Nevertheless the private warning forms part of an

---

[20] FSMA, s 205.

authorised firm's or approved person's compliance history. They may therefore be relevant in the future if the FSA is deciding whether to commence disciplinary action in relation to a future breach—but they cannot be relied on to determine whether or not that future breach has taken place or in determining the level of the sanction for it.

Whilst private warnings are a useful tool, and may be welcomed by firms and **6.82** approved persons for the reason that they avoid the publicity of a public censure or fine, there are nevertheless some concerns associated with the private warning process. For example, a person who receives a private warning is not able to raise the matter with the RDC. A private warning may be given in circumstances where no action could be brought against that individual in respect of a rule breach; nevertheless the private warning will be on his regulatory record. The fact that the warning is private does not affect the fact that it is a fairly serious matter for anyone who receives it. Recipients of such a warning should ensure that any comments they have on the matter are recorded by them in writing to the FSA for placing on their file.

Financial penalties

If the FSA considers that an authorised person has contravened a requirement **6.83** imposed by or under FSMA, it may impose on him a penalty of such amount as it considers appropriate.[21] The penalty is potentially unlimited and is payable to the FSA. A person cannot be required both to pay a penalty and have his authorisation withdrawn. FSMA requires the FSA to issue a statement of policy with respect to the imposition of penalties and in particular for determining what the amount of a penalty may be. In practice this policy statement is fulfilled through the provisions of EG and the Decision Procedures and Penalties Manual ('DEPP'). As explained below, a financial penalty is accompanied by the publication of a public notice which contains a fair amount of detail—a financial penalty might therefore be distinguished from a public censure/statement in a legal sense, but in practice the imposition of a financial penalty also results in a public statement which can be written in a censorious manner.

Other disciplinary measures

In addition to the disciplinary measures of public statements and financial penal- **6.84** ties the FSA has other measures available to it where it considers it necessary to take protective or remedial action. These include varying and cancelling permissions and withdrawing a firm's authorisation or an individual's status as an approved person, or prohibiting an individual from performing specified functions.[22]

---

[21] ibid, s 206.
[22] ibid, ss 45, 46, and 54.

The FSA also has powers to intervene against a firm which is exercising passport rights and EG Chapter 8 sets out the grounds for exercising these powers.[23]

6.85 The FSA also has powers to apply to court for injunctions[24] and EG Chapter 10 provides guidance on the use of the FSA's powers to apply for such orders. The FSA has used these powers, but in practice they tend to be used in situations where firms are not authorised but should be, or in other very serious cases. If the average authorised firm encounters the FSA's enforcement powers, it is most likely to be in the context of an action for breach of FSA rules resulting in the imposition of a financial penalty or the issuing of a public censure. Thus, whilst the other powers available to the FSA are noted, the following paragraphs deal principally with the disciplinary powers and processes available to the FSA for breach of the FSA's requirements by authorised firms and approved persons.

Warning notice

6.86 If the FSA proposes to publish a statement or impose a penalty it must give the authorised person a warning notice which sets out the terms of the statement or the amount of the penalty. Section 387 of FSMA provides that a warning notice must both state the action which the FSA proposes to take and give reasons for it. When the FSA proposes to impose a financial penalty or issue a public censure (and in most other cases where a warning notice or decision notice is given[25]), the FSA will be subject to section 394 of FSMA. This means that it must allow the authorised person access to the material on which it relied in taking the decision which gave rise to the notice and allow him access to any secondary material which, in the opinion of the FSA, might undermine that decision. Secondary material is material on which the FSA did not rely but which it considered in reaching its decision, or which was obtained by it in connection with the matter to which the notice relates. There has been and still is considerable controversy over the scope of section 394 since it does not require the FSA to give a person access to all the material which it has. It remains for the FSA to decide whether it has 'secondary material' which might undermine its decision. Section 394 limits the material that may need to be provided, such that certain excluded material, including material which is subject to legal advice privilege, does not have to be disclosed.

6.87 The warning notice must give at least a 28-day period during which representations may be made. After the expiry of that period the FSA must then decide 'within a reasonable period' whether to issue a decision notice.

---

[23] ibid, ss 194 to 201.
[24] ibid, s 380; market abuse: s 381; incoming firms: s 198.
[25] See s 392 of FSMA.

Decision notice

If the FSA decides to publish a statement or impose a penalty, it must give the **6.88** authorised person concerned a decision notice which sets out the terms of the statement or the amount of the penalty. If the FSA publishes a statement or imposes a penalty then the authorised person has the right to refer the matter to the Financial Services and Markets Tribunal ('the Tribunal') within 28 days of the decision notice (see s 133(1) of FSMA).

A decision notice must state the FSA's reasons and other matters, as required for **6.89** the warning notice. It must also indicate the recipient's right to have the matter referred to the Tribunal.

Final Notices

Once a decision notice has been issued, if the authorised person does not refer the **6.90** matter to the Tribunal within the appointed period of 28 days (see para 6.88 above) the FSA must, on taking the action to which the decision notice relates, give the person concerned a Final Notice. The Final Notice sets out the terms of the statement/the amount of the penalty and, unlike the warning notice and decision notice, it is made public. Copies of all the Final Notices which have been issued in enforcement proceedings are available on the FSA website. It can be extremely valuable to review these notices, as the FSA uses them to report more than just the very basic details of the matter concerned. Final Notices can be quite lengthy. They set out the facts on which the FSA relies, the opinions of the FSA on the issues raised, and details of its reasoning for the action taken. In practice the FSA uses the Final Notice (and the accompanying press release) to send messages to the industry generally as part of its 'credible deterrence' strategy.

FSA procedures

Section 395 of FSMA requires the FSA to determine the procedures which it will **6.91** follow for the giving of supervisory, warning, and decision notices. The section provides a considerable degree of flexibility for the FSA in determining these procedures. Once the FSA has stated its procedure FSMA requires it to follow that procedure and, if it changes it in a material way, to publish a revised statement. A failure in a particular case to follow a procedure does not affect the validity of a notice given, but may affect any consideration of the matter by the Tribunal.

The Financial Services and Markets Tribunal

During the course of development of FSMA there was considerable concern **6.92** expressed about the breadth of the FSA powers to impose penalties on authorised firms and the fact that, under FSMA, the FSA will in many cases be investigator, jury, and judge. As a result, FSMA provided for the establishment of the Tribunal, to which references may be made within a relatively short period beginning on the date on which decision notices or supervisory notices have been issued.[26] Of the 60 or so hearings that have been held before the Tribunal, it is clear that it acts wholly independently of the FSA and is not shy of criticising the regulator where it thinks it appropriate. The most publicity has probably been given to the Tribunal decision in a reference made by Legal & General. The Tribunal's comments on the FSA's conduct of the enforcement proceedings against Legal & General were a significant trigger for a review and restructuring of the FSA enforcement process. In another case (*Hoodless and Blackwell*) the Tribunal overturned the decision of the FSA in relation to Mr Hoodless and, whilst it upheld the conclusion of a decision notice in relation to Blackwell, it specifically directed that the Final Notice be read in the light of the Tribunal finding which upheld only certain of the matters relied on by the FSA. Indeed the Tribunal commented 'it did seem to us that the allegations made in the decision notices went substantially beyond what was justified by the evidence that we had heard'.

6.93 Nevertheless, proceedings before the Tribunal are not lightly taken, not least because its hearings are held in public. In the *Legal & General* case the Tribunal expressed concern that simply because that case had been complex and expensive, it would not want potential applicants to feel daunted by the exceptional features of that case when considering the exercise of their own legal rights. The relatively limited number of cases which have gone to the Tribunal may therefore be attributed to a number of features—cost and continuing publicity being probably the most significant.

6.94 A hearing before the Tribunal is not an appeal but a review from the beginning of the facts and matters concerned. The Tribunal may consider any evidence relating to the subject matter of the reference whether or not it was available to the FSA at the material time. The parties are permitted to raise matters not directly brought before the Regulatory Decisions Committee of the FSA—but save in exceptional cases the Tribunal will expect the FSA to confine its position to the charges already set out in its statement of case.

The FSA Handbook and enforcement matters

The Enforcement Guide and the Decision Procedures and Penalties Manual

6.95 Both EG (which is technically not part of the FSA Handbook) and DEPP (which is) contain significant provisions which expand on the FSA's enforcement policy and set out applicable rules and guidance which apply when the FSA exercises its statutory powers. EG 2 sets out the FSA's approach to enforcement generally

---

[26] FSMA, ss 132 to 137 and Sched 13.

when considering whether to exercise its enforcement powers: it includes descriptions of the case selection criteria it uses in different types of cases. EG Chapter 3 sets out the FSA's policy on using its powers to require information and reports, and on carrying out investigations. Annex 2 to EG sets out guidelines on investigation where a case may concern both the FSA and other prosecuting and investigating agencies. The guidelines set out some broad principles which the various agencies have agreed should be applied in order to assist in determining which of them should investigate cases to avoid duplication and similar matters. Any firm which is facing a serious enforcement matter may find that other agencies are or could be involved, in which case these guidelines may be relevant.

When is disciplinary action involving a penalty or censure likely?

DEPP 6.2 sets out a non-exhaustive list of factors that will be considered by the FSA in determining whether to take disciplinary action involving a financial penalty or censure. These include: **6.96**

 (i) the nature and seriousness of the suspected breach. This can include consideration of whether the breach was deliberate or reckless, its duration and frequency, whether it reveals serious or systemic weaknesses in the firm, and whether it caused a loss or risk of loss to consumers or other market users. It is also expressly noted that in judging nature and seriousness the FSA may also consider whether there are a number of smaller issues, which individually may not justify disciplinary action, but which do so when taken collectively. This could arise for example where the FSA identifies a number of relatively small rule breaches, which taken together indicate a general concern with the firm's approach to systems and controls on compliance matters;

 (ii) the conduct after the breach. This particularly takes into account whether the breach was brought to the attention of the FSA by the firm or approved person concerned and the degree of cooperation shown during investigation of the breach. It will also be relevant to have regard to remedial steps that have been taken—in particular whether consumers have suffered loss and been compensated and whether disciplinary action has been taken against staff involved (where appropriate);

 (iii) the previous regulatory record of the firm or approved person (and this might take into account previous private warnings);

 (iv) whether the behaviour contravenes guidance published by the FSA;

 (v) action taken by the FSA in previous similar cases and action taken by other regulatory authorities. In particular, where action may be taken by another regulatory authority, the FSA will consider whether that action would be adequate to address the FSA's concerns. Nevertheless the involvement of an overseas regulator will not necessarily prevent the FSA from taking its own action. In the case of Credit Suisse First Boston International (and certain of its employees)[27] the FSA imposed penalties and other disciplinary measures as a result of conduct that took place in Japan in relation to Japanese business activities, which included attempts to mislead the Japanese authorities.

6.97 DEPP 6.4 sets out the criteria that the FSA will use in deciding whether it is appropriate to issue a public censure rather than impose a financial penalty, while DEPP 6.3 sets out the specific factors that the FSA will take into account when deciding whether to impose a penalty for market abuse.

Action against approved persons

6.98 DEPP 6.2.4G to DEPP 6.2.9G set out further particular guidance on the circumstances in which an approved person might face disciplinary action. The FSA has made it clear that it will only take disciplinary action where there is evidence of personal culpability on the part of the approved person. In practice this means that his behaviour must either have been deliberate or below the standard which would be reasonable in all the circumstances. The FSA has issued Statements of Principle which apply to approved persons and a Code of Practice for Approved Persons which is relevant in helping to determine whether conduct amounts to a breach of a Principle.[28] The issues referred to in paras 6.96, 6.97, and 6.101 are relevant in determining the type of action taken.

6.99 The FSA's statutory powers to take disciplinary action against approved persons are based on section 66 of FSMA. This provides that action may be taken against an approved person where it appears to the FSA that he is guilty of misconduct. He will be guilty of misconduct if, while an approved person:

(i) he has failed to comply with a Statement of Principle (being the principles applicable to approved persons); or

(ii) he has been knowingly concerned in a contravention by the firm of a requirement imposed on it by or under FSMA.

Thus there are two separate bases on which action may be brought against an approved person. The concept of 'being knowingly concerned' in a contravention is potentially quite wide—a person may be knowingly concerned by knowing the facts involved, he does not necessarily need to know that that amounts to a contravention by the firm of a requirement.

---

[27] Final Notice against Credit Suisse First Boston International dated 11 December 2002, <http://www.fsa.gov.uk/pubs/final/creditsuisse-fb_11dec02.pdf>; Final Notice against Christopher Allan Goekjian dated 22 September 2003, <http://www.fsa.gov.uk/pubs/final/goekjian_22sept03.pdf>; Final Notice against Anthony Blunden dated 10 November 2003, <http://www.fsa.gov.uk/pubs/final/blunden_10nov03.pdf>.

[28] See FSMA, s 64.

Discipline for breaches of the Principles for Businesses

The FSA Principles are, as a matter of law, FSA rules. They are rules which are   **6.100**
drafted in general rather than specific terms. Nevertheless it is possible for the FSA
to discipline a firm for breach of a Principle alone—the FSA has done so in the
past and intends to do so in the future. In fact, the FSA has made it clear that, as
part of the move towards more principles-based regulation generally, it will where
appropriate take enforcement action based on a breach of the Principles alone—
and FSA enforcement practice is bearing this out.[29] The Citigroup decision
attracted some comment because Citigroup was penalised £14 million for breach
of FSA Principles (Principle 2, requiring the firm to exercise due skill, care, and
diligence, and Principle 3, requiring the firm to have adequate systems and controls), despite the fact that the conduct concerned did not give rise to any breach
of any particular rule or breach of any law.[30] In December 2007 five Norwich
Union life companies were fined a total of £1.26 million in aggregate for breaches
of Principle 3 in disclosing confidential customer information to fraudsters—
other than Principle 3 there were no specific rule breaches specified. This move
towards enforcement for breach of FSA Principles alone naturally raises concerns
because of the lack of particularity in the Principles themselves and the fear that
the FSA might apply its current enforcement standards retrospectively to conduct
which occurred in the past. The FSA acknowledges that there is an issue here and
that firms must be able reasonably to predict, at the time a particular course of
conduct occurred, whether that conduct would breach the Principles—this is
referred to in para 2.20 of EG as the 'reasonable predictability test' or 'condition
of predictability'. The FSA says that the standards which will apply to an enforcement action in relation to a breach of Principle will be those standards which
applied at the time the conduct took place—it says it will not apply later, higher
standards to behaviour. This perhaps provides a degree of comfort, but the fact
remains that the Principles are drafted in the highest terms and are open to interpretation (perhaps with the FSA having the 'benefit of hindsight' as is sometimes
claimed)—this makes day-to-day compliance with FSA rules in the context of
principles-based regulation difficult.

When might there be a public censure or public statements?

Public censures may be issued under section 205, public statements may be made   **6.101**
about approved persons under section 66, and public statements may be made

---

[29] In fact, in its 2007/2008 financial year, most of the FSA's enforcement actions were based on
Principles only or on a combination of Principles and rules. Of 48 disciplinary cases, 21 (44%) were
based on Principles alone and almost all of the remaining cases were a combination of Principles and
rules. (FSA 'Enforcement annual performance account 2007/08'.)

[30] Final Notice against Citigroup Global Markets Limited dated 28 June 2005 <http://www.fsa.
gov.uk/pubs/final/cgml_28jun05.pdf>.

under section 123 and section 91 respectively in cases of market abuse and contravention of listing rules. As already noted the warning notice procedure applies to any decision to issue such a public censure or statement. In determining whether it is appropriate to issue a public statement rather than impose a financial penalty the FSA states (in DEPP 6.4) that it considers all relevant circumstances including the following:

(i) where a profit has been made or loss avoided as a result of the breach or misconduct this may be a factor in favour of a financial penalty;

(ii) the more serious the breach or misconduct whether in nature or degree, the more likely it is that a financial penalty will be considered appropriate;

(iii) a poor disciplinary record or compliance history may be a factor in favour of a financial penalty as it may act as a deterrent to future cases;

(iv) whether the person has inadequate means to pay an appropriate financial penalty.

What factors influence the level of financial penalties?

6.102 DEPP 6.2 sets out some of the factors involved in a decision as to whether to impose a financial penalty on a firm or an approved person (see para 6.96 above). Where the FSA has decided to impose a financial penalty, some of the factors it will have regard to in determining the level of that penalty are set out in DEPP 6.5 and include:

(i) the seriousness of the misconduct or contravention (which can include its duration and frequency and the loss or risk of loss caused to consumers and market users);

(ii) the extent to which the contravention or misconduct was deliberate or reckless. This can include having regard to whether there has been a failure to comply with the firm's procedures and whether there has been no apparent consideration given to the consequences of the behaviour that constitutes the contravention. Deliberate or reckless behaviour is likely to result in a higher penalty than would otherwise be the case;

(iii) regard will be had as to whether the penalty is to be imposed on an individual and as to the size, financial resources, and other circumstances of the firm or individual. The FSA will not impose a financial penalty that could cause serious financial hardship or financial difficulties. However, this has not prevented it from imposing significant penalties on individuals where it has thought it appropriate to do so—for example, a CSFB employee was subject to a penalty of £150,000 for his involvement in the matter referred to above[31] and the Head of Trading at Evolution Beeson Gregory was ordered

---

[31] Final Notice against Christopher Allan Goekjian dated 22 September 2003 <http://www.fsa.gov.uk/pubs/final/goekjian_22sept03.pdf>.

to pay £75,000 for his part in a matter which led to a breach of market conduct rules by his firm;[32]

(iv)   the amount of profits accrued or loss avoided;

(v)   conduct following the contravention;

(vi)   disciplinary record and compliance history;

(vii) previous action taken by the FSA;

(viii) action taken by other regulators.

The FSA has always operated a practice of taking into account a firm's cooperation   **6.103**
in determining the level of any financial penalty. The FSA will continue to take account of a firm's overall cooperation in setting the level of a penalty.[33] However, in addition the FSA operates a formal discount scheme specifically for early settlement. This scheme is clearly designed to do two things: to encourage the earliest possible settlement—there is a sliding scale of discount percentages depending upon how early in the enforcement process settlement is reached—and to distinguish early settlement from other types of cooperation with the Regulator. The purpose is to give a clear encouragement to early settlement. See para 6.114 below for further details.

FSA procedures

The decision-making process

A referral to the Enforcement Division can be made by a number of different FSA   **6.104**
divisions, including the Markets Division which covers market abuse and Listing Rule cases, and the Retail Themes Division which covers both financial promotions and visits to certain firms as part of the ARROW reviews. Consequently, the question of whether a firm may be referred to enforcement may not always be because of a matter that has arisen in the course of its normal supervisory relationship. A document called the Enforcement Referral Document is prepared to justify why use of the enforcement procedure is correct for a particular case. Where a referral is generated other than by the division responsible for supervision, the supervisor should be informed promptly and should sign the Enforcement Referral Document.

---

[32] Final Notice against Evolution Beeson Gregory Limited and Christopher Potts dated 12 November 2004 <http://www.fsa.gov.uk/pubs/final/evolution_12nov04.pdf>.

[33] In the context of market abuse cases, the FSA will also be introducing a specific 'leniency factor' whereby it will take into account the cooperation shown by an individual suspected of having been involved with other individuals in determining whether to pursue a criminal or civil case against him. This was consulted on over the summer of 2008. The indicative date on the draft instrument in the consultation paper suggested that the 'leniency factor' concept would come into force in December 2008.

6.105 Once a case has been accepted by the Enforcement Division a case team is established which will usually hold an initial scope meeting with the person/firm concerned as part of the planning process. The purpose of these meetings is to give an indication of the scope of the investigation, the type of documents to which access will be required, and similar matters. These discussions should be a matter of course and should include the supervisor of relationship managed firms. As a minimum the FSA case team should set out the nature of and reasons for its concerns and a clear explanation of why the matter has been referred to enforcement. If, as the investigation progresses, the nature of the FSA's concerns change significantly then it should reassess them so as to satisfy itself that the investigation remains appropriate.

6.106 As the case progresses the FSA prepares a draft preliminary investigation report. The draft investigation report should clearly set out the facts found by the investigation and the rule breaches alleged so that those who are the subject of the investigation can comment properly, with a full understanding of the rule breaches which form the basis of the proposed action.

6.107 EG 4.30 to 4.33 provide that the FSA will usually send a preliminary findings letter to any person under investigation before considering whether to recommend to the RDC that enforcement action be initiated. That letter will set out the facts which the FSA considers relevant, will usually annex the investigator's preliminary investigation report (referred to above), and will invite the person concerned to comment on whether those facts are complete and accurate. It is important for a firm to deal with the preliminary findings letter and preliminary investigation report seriously and devote sufficient resources to dealing with them fully, since they will form the basis of subsequent decisions and actions taken by the FSA. The firm should use its response to correct any errors of fact, explaining why it believes the FSA's assertions of fact are deficient, and/or to provide further information where it feels that the FSA has not obtained a complete picture. It should ensure that the response includes any mitigating factors or other comments which it wishes to advance. A reasonable period (normally 28 days) is allowed for a response—responses received outside any deadline set by the FSA are not likely to be taken into account.

The decision-maker—the Regulatory Decisions Committee

6.108 FSMA's requirements for decision-making procedures in relation to the issue of warning and decision notices are broadly expressed:

> the procedure must be designed to secure, among other things, that the decision which gives rise to the obligation to give any such notice is taken by a person not directly involved in establishing the evidence on which that decision is based.[34]

---

[34] FSMA, s 395.

It must be noted therefore that this is deliberately constituted as an administrative **6.109** and not a judicial procedure. The warning notice procedure must set out not only the proposed action but the reasons for it—it is not the same as a charge sheet in criminal proceedings. The decision must be taken by the FSA, not by an independent body—in the FSA's view FSMA requires any decision-making body to be part of the FSA and not entirely independent of it.

Thus the system for decision-making established by the FSA is an internal proc- **6.110** ess. In practice the function is generally carried out by the Regulatory Decisions Committee ('RDC') which is a committee of the FSA's Board whose members are appointed by the Board. However, apart from the chairman, none of the members of the RDC is an FSA employee. In addition, the RDC has its own dedicated legal advisers and support staff—all RDC staff are separate from the FSA staff involved in conducting investigations and making recommendations to the RDC. So while the RDC is determinedly part of the FSA as regards its decision-making, there is independence between it and between the Enforcement team prosecuting the relevant case. This is designed to ensure that there is a degree of objectivity on the part of the RDC when it comes to hearing the Enforcement team's submissions.

Where FSA enforcement staff consider that there is a case, they will make a recom- **6.111** mendation to the RDC that a warning notice or supervisory notice be given. The RDC considers whether the material on which the case is founded is sufficient to support the action. Where it decides to issue the warning notice or first supervisory notice the notice will specify that the recipient has at least 28 days to make representations—and will also stipulate a timeframe within which the recipient is allowed to indicate that he wishes to make oral representations.

As an additional measure of independence and objectivity, when the FSA has **6.112** given the relevant notice, the RDC will not meet with or discuss the matter with FSA enforcement staff without the recipient being present or otherwise able to respond. Where the recipient so indicates, a meeting will be convened to allow the recipient of the notice the opportunity to make oral representations and to allow relevant FSA staff to respond to those representations. The recipient may be legally represented if he wishes.

The FSA has published some useful Q&As on how the Regulatory Decisions **6.113** Committee works in practice: <http://www.fsa.gov.uk/Pages/About/Who/board/ committees/RDC/faqs/index.shtml>

Settlement of enforcement cases

The FSA is keen that, wherever possible, enforcement cases settle early. This is **6.114** largely because enforcement investigations are resource-intensive and time consuming and settlement can result in consumers obtaining compensation earlier than would otherwise be the case. As noted above, the FSA has now introduced a formal discount scheme for early settlement of cases, with discounts of 30 per cent, 20 per cent, or 10 per cent depending on how early in the enforcement process settlement is reached, from the initial stages up until the issuance of the decision notice.

6.115 Settlements of enforcement cases are not the same as settlements of commercial litigation—in particular they are not confidential. They result in the publication of a Final Notice which sets out the terms of the agreed settlement (usually a financial penalty and, where it has been considered appropriate, the payment of compensation to consumers).

6.116 Settlement of a case can take place at any time. Settlement decisions are taken by the FSA Executive (ie by two FSA directors, one of whom will usually be the Director of Enforcement). The RDC is not involved in taking any decisions on statutory notices that result from settlement leaving it as an FSA body with the responsibility of taking enforcement decisions in the absence of agreed settlement—this ensures that there is a proper separation and transparency between the Enforcement Division and the RDC. However, despite this separation and as already noted, it is not until disputes reach the Tribunal that there is a process which can be said to be entirely independent of the FSA.

6.117 Where a settlement is agreed this will not obviate the need for a decision notice, which will be in agreed form. The vast majority of disciplinary cases that result in a financial penalty have, in the past, been 'settled' and this is likely to continue in the future.[35] The effect of this is that the Final Notice is likely to have been negotiated with the FSA—both as to its content and indeed as to the final decision, for example on the rules or Principles which are held to have been breached. Therefore, whilst Final Notices can be extremely educational to read, it must be borne in mind that they are often the result of a negotiation and may well therefore not give as complete a picture as if the matter had proceeded to a full and unnegotiated decision.

The role of mediation in the settlement process

6.118 The FSA Handbook only briefly mentions settlement by mediation: under DEPP 5.1.9G the FSA states that it and other parties 'may agree to mediation as a way of facilitating settlement in appropriate cases'. More detail is provided in a specific note on mediation in the 'Enforcement in focus' section of the FSA

---

[35] In the FSA's financial year between 1 April 2007 and 31 March 2008, '36 cases were concluded by executive settlement. Approximately three-quarters of cases with a disciplinary outcome settled before reaching the RDC and almost all cases involving a financial penalty settled during the first settlement stage, receiving the full 30% discount on the financial penalty' (FSA, 'Enforcement annual performance account 2007/08').

website: <http://www.fsa.gov.uk/pages/doing/regulated/law/focus/mediation. shtml>. The FSA sees mediation working within regulation 'to supplement the informal settlement discussions which can be part of the regulatory process and to provide a way of progressing a case where settlement discussions are unlikely to lead to an agreed settlement'.

Mediation is not appropriate in all enforcement actions: in particular, the FSA **6.119** says that mediation is 'unlikely' to be appropriate in cases involving allegations of criminal conduct: in fact it is difficult to see how mediation would ever be appropriate in any criminal enforcement action. The FSA is also unlikely to agree to mediation where it feels that urgent enforcement action is necessary. Otherwise, the use of mediation is possible in a wide array of enforcement cases.

Mediation involves an alternative form of dispute resolution between the FSA and **6.120** the subject of the enforcement action. An independent and neutral mediator is appointed with the consent of both parties: his role is to act purely as a facilitator of negotiations and settlement discussions between the two parties. He does not make any judgment on the relative merits of each side's arguments. There are no prescribed statutory or FSA rules with regards to how a mediation progresses. However, at the outset of the process the parties will sign a mediation agreement setting out the terms which will apply. A mediation will either terminate without a settlement on the withdrawal of one or both of the parties, or it will result in an agreed settlement.

Mediation can, in theory, take place at any stage along the enforcement process **6.121** (provided both the parties agree); however, the FSA says that mediation is generally available to firms or individuals only once during the enforcement process.

7

FINANCIAL REDRESS—COMPLAINTS, DISPUTES, AND COMPENSATION

Introduction: Regulatory Objectives

The Financial Services and Markets Act 2000 ('FSMA') identified four regulatory **7.01** objectives,[1] of which 'the protection of consumers' (or 'securing the appropriate degree of protection for consumers')[2] and 'market confidence' (or 'maintaining confidence in the financial system')[3] are relevant to the topic of complaints, disputes, and compensation. Effective complaints, dispute resolution, and compensation arrangements both protect consumers and assist stability adding to market confidence. These two objectives are regularly identified in the regulator's work, for example in the recent publications of the Tripartite Authorities on the deposit protection reforms proposed in the aftermath of Northern Rock.

In addition to the Financial Services Authority ('FSA'), FSMA created three bod- **7.02** ies of particular relevance to the protection of consumers: the Consumer Panel, the Financial Ombudsman Service ('FOS'), and the Financial Services Compensation Scheme ('FSCS'). The first, the panel set up to 'represent the interests of consumers',[4] is not considered further in this chapter. FOS and the FSCS are described below. Both FOS and the FSCS are going through periods of potentially significant change, in response to the Hunt Report and the reforms to the framework for financial stability and depositor protection respectively. Since going into production, further implications of the credit crisis have arisen and the impact on FSCS has been taken into account in this chapter.

The 'single complaints and compensation schemes' were identified at Chapter 10 **7.03** of HM Treasury's consultation document on the Financial Services and Markets

---

[1] FSMA, s.2(2).
[2] ibid, s.5.
[3] ibid, s.3.
[4] ibid, s.10.

Bill.[5] The purpose and need for single complaints and compensation schemes was set out:

> No regulatory system can guarantee that regulated firms will always comply with the rules or generally accepted standards of conduct. It is important that consumers should have access to cheap, quick, informal and effective dispute resolution arrangements. Nor can regulation guarantee that firms will always be able to meet their liabilities to consumers, so it is also important to put in place effective compensation arrangements. The Government intends to rationalise the existing arrangements through the creation of a single ombudsman scheme and a single compensation scheme. This will reduce the scope for confusion about the roles and responsibilities of different schemes. It will also ensure improved access for consumers by providing single points of entry.[6]

7.04 The creation of the 'one-stop shops' for complaints and dispute resolution and for compensation recognised the range of pre-existing arrangements developed under an array of predecessor legislation. The development of the complaints and compensation schemes under FSMA built on pre-existing arrangements rather than started from scratch. However, it is beyond the scope of this chapter to provide a history of the predecessor arrangements and schemes or the transitional arrangements under FSMA.

7.05 In addition to the single complaints and compensation schemes, FSMA also equipped the FSA itself with responsibilities and powers to act on behalf of consumers, for example to direct financial redress for the benefit of consumers.

Routes to Financial Redress

Claims for financial redress outside FSMA

7.06 Although consumers have enhanced protection and alternative routes to financial redress under FSMA, it is worth noting some of the remedies existing outside the scope of this legislation. In the investment sector, this has developed alongside conduct of business regulation, as discussed below. In other sectors, for example insurance broking, there is a long and substantial body of case law (not considered in this chapter).

7.07 Investors seeking redress may have received advice from an individual or firm acting in a professional capacity or bought an investment (or other regulated) product directly from a provider. The advisory relationship is likely to give rise to a

---

[5] HM Treasury, 'Financial Services and Markets Bill: a consultation document—Part 1: Overview of Financial Regulatory Reform' (July 1998).

[6] ibid, para 10.1.

duty of care, concurrent in contract and tort.[7] The consumer would be owed a duty of skill and care to the standard expected from the reasonably competent professional adviser at the time.

The duty of care in the investment context was considered in *Seymour and others*   **7.08**
v Christine Ockwell & Co and others.[8] *Seymour* confirmed that the advisory duty was not delegated by the firm, so that insofar as the adviser lacked the necessary expertise, the customers should have been referred to an expert. When determining the duty of care, the court will have regard to the level of advice which might have been expected by a consumer. Where the investor is highly experienced and sophisticated, and so more likely to have been prepared to accept the risk of trading losses, in the absence of an express contractual duty, an advisory duty, in contract or in tort, is unlikely.[9]

The consumer might also have a claim against the product provider for misrepre-   **7.09**
sentation (giving rise to a claim for damages under the Misrepresentation Act 1967) or for negligent misstatement. The circumstances of the investor will again be relevant to determining whether he is owed any liability by a firm. In the financial services sector, (overturning the judgment at first instance) the Court of Appeal, in the case of *Peekay Intermark Ltd and another v Australia and New Zealand Banking Group Ltd*,[10] found that the experienced and sophisticated investor did not rely on pre-contractual representations, which were displaced by subsequent documentation making clear the nature and risks of the investment, but on 'his own assumption that the investment product . . . corresponded to the description he had previously been given'. Following the principles in *Hedley Byrne v Heller*,[11] if a product provider has disseminated information to an identified category of person such as the consumer for an identified purpose and on which the consumer relied, a duty of care may also arise on which the claim for negligent misstatement (although not for suitability) would be based.

Whether for negligence or negligent misstatement, in common with claims for   **7.10**
professional negligence generally, the consumer would be entitled to expect to recover his economic loss in accordance with usual principles. The Court of Appeal confirmed that in claims for negligent financial advice, the conventional, negligence, approach to causation should apply (*Beary v Pall Mall Investments*),[12]

---

[7] *Henderson v Merrit Syndicates Limited* [1993] 2 AC 145.
[8] [2005] PNLR 39.
[9] These factors were material in *Springwell Navigation Corp v J P Morgan Chase* [2008] EWHC 1186 (Comm).
[10] [2006] EWCA Civ 386.
[11] [1964] AC 465.
[12] [2005] EWCA Civ 415.

so that there was no scope for following 'exceptional departures' from the established principles.[13]

7.11 Although claims in negligence or misrepresentation are likely to provide the most obvious causes of action for consumers seeking financial redress in this sector, deceit would also be available as the basis for a claim, not just for fraud or theft but in the event of deliberate misrepresentations of facts or opinions. Further, a relationship of trust and confidence is likely to exist or be built up between a client and his financial adviser, giving rise to fiduciary duties on the firm.

7.12 Under the FSMA structure, *Seymour* confirmed that, generally, a product provider, rather than an adviser, does not owe an advisory duty of care to investors, absent negligent misstatement. In that case, the individual adviser remained the party solely liable to the customers, but was entitled to a contribution from the provider. The court was influenced in part by the view that any duty of care on the provider would be a duty 'which by-passed the regulatory regime and sidestepped the contractual remedy'[14] ie that the FSMA structure does not impose a general advisory duty on the provider, although there may be exceptions. A provider may assume a responsibility to the investor by its conduct, for example in meetings with the investor, and be found to have provided investment advice to which conduct of business rules apply.[15] Previously a duty of care owed to investors has been extended to lenders found to have operated in close collaboration with offices of authorised intermediaries.[16] Although generally not responsible for investment advice given by firms of authorised independent financial advisers, or the risks of borrowing, a lending building society was held to be responsible for torts committed by the advisers on the basis of a 'joint enterprise'. The judge was satisfied that there had been a sufficient degree of cooperation between the advisers and the lender to develop and market the lender's product (in this case, equity release mortgages) to consumers such that the lender owed a liability to investors arising from the conduct of the advisers.

7.13 In the context of the ongoing 'Treating Customers Fairly' ('TCF') work, the FSA has published guidance on the rules and responsibilities of distributors and providers, under section 157 of FSMA, for example, the Providers and Distributors Regulatory Guide Instrument 2007.[17] The FSA described this guidance as articulating 'the existing responsibilities in the Principles, detailed rules and guidance in

---

[13] Such as developed by the House of Lords in *Chester v Afshar* [2005] 1 AC 134.
[14] His Honour Judge Havelock-Allan QC, p 59.
[15] *Walker v Inter-Alliance Group plc and Scottish Equitable plc* [2007] EWHC 1858.
[16] *Investors Compensation Scheme v West Bromwich Building Society* [1999] Lloyd's Rep PN 496.
[17] FSA Instrument 2007/41.

FSMA and subordinate legislation, and case law'.[18] The industry has also published guidelines, for example by the Association of British Insurers together with the Association of IFAs,[19] and by the Joint Associations Committee in respect of structured products.[20]

Claims for financial redress under FSMA

Unauthorised persons

FSMA provides for consumers to make claims for losses sustained as a result of parting with money or property pursuant to agreements made by or through unauthorised persons carrying on regulated activities. Such agreements are both unenforceable and give rise to rights to recover both money paid and compensation for any loss sustained as a result.[21] This enforces the 'perimeter' of regulation and protects the consumer. The amount of compensation may be agreed by the parties or awarded by the court. The court has the power, if it 'is satisfied that it is just and equitable in the circumstances of the case', to allow the agreement to be enforced and money or property to be retained.[22] In exercising this discretion the court is directed to 'whether the person carrying on the regulated activity concerned reasonably believed that he was not contravening the general prohibition by making the agreement'[23] or whether (if applicable) 'the provider knew that the third party was (in carrying on the regulated activity) contravening the general prohibition'.[24] If deposits have been taken, in breach of the general prohibition, the 'depositor' has the statutory right to apply for an order returning the money, if he is not entitled under the agreement with the deposit taker to recover his money without delay.[25]

7.14

---

[18] FSA Policy Statement 07/11: 'Responsibilities of providers and distributors for the fair treatment of customers—Feedback on DP 06/4' (July 2007).

[19] 'Working Together to Deliver Good Customer Experiences—Responsibilities of Providers and Advisers: a joint paper by the Association of IFAs and ABI' (October 2006).

[20] The Joint Associations Committee ('JAC') comprises the following trade associations: European Securitisation Forum ('ESF'), International Capital Market Association ('ICMA'), London Investment Banking Association ('LIBA'), the International Swaps and Derivatives Association ('ISDA') and Securities Industry and Financial Markets Association ('SIFMA'). In July 2007, the JAC released 'Principles for Managing the Provider—Distributor Relationship', followed in July 2008 by 'Structured Products: Principles for Managing the Distributor—Individual Investor Relationship'.

[21] FSMA, ss 26 and 27. See also, *Brodenik and others v Centaur Tipping Services Ltd* (27 July 2006).

[22] ibid, s 28(3).

[23] ibid, s 28(5).

[24] ibid, s 28(6).

[25] ibid.

7.15 In addition, if a consumer deals with an authorised person who carries out a regulated activity otherwise than in accordance with a permission under FSMA, the contravention is actionable at the suit of a person who suffers loss as a result.[26]

7.16 These statutory remedies were recently considered on a liquidators' application for directions *(Re Whiteley Insurance Consultants (also known as Kingfisher Travel Insurance Services) (a firm))*.[27] As the firm traded first as unauthorised and then as authorised, both sections 26 and 28 and section 20 applied. On the facts, the court declined to exercise the discretion under section 28, so that agreements were unenforceable, but in respect of (what the court described as) the 'later period', the court considered whether policyholders had suffered any loss and could make a claim under section 20(3) for damages or otherwise.

Breach of statutory duty—Conduct of Business Rules

7.17 Consumers have the right to bring actions for breach of statutory duty. Section 150 provides that 'a contravention by an authorised person of a rule is actionable at the suit of a private person who suffers loss as a result of the contravention, subject to the defences and other incidents applying to actions for breach of the statutory duty'. Breach of statutory duty as a cause of action is available in respect of Conduct of Business Rules made by the FSA, but before considering the claims of consumers under section 150, it is worth noting the framework (and spirit) of the general principles established by the FSA.

7.18 The PRIN Sourcebook contains the following 11 Principles, most of which although not actionable themselves, are directly relevant to consumers:

1. Integrity—a firm must conduct its business with integrity;
2. Skill, care and diligence—a firm must conduct its business with due skill, care, and diligence;
3. Management and control—a firm must take reasonable care to organise its affairs responsibly and effectively, with adequate risk management systems;
4. Financial prudence—a firm must maintain adequate financial resources;
5. Market conduct—a firm must observe proper standards of market conduct;
6. Customers' interests—a firm must pay due regard to the interests of its customers and treat them fairly;
7. Communications with clients—a firm must pay due regard to the information needs of its clients and communicate information to them in a way which is clear, fair, and not misleading;
8. Conflicts of interest—a firm must manage conflicts of interest fairly, both between itself and its customers and between a customer and another client;

---

[26] FSMA, s 20.
[27] [2008] EWHC 1782.

9. Customers: relationships of trust—a firm must take reasonable care to ensure the suitability of its advice and discretionary decisions for any customer who is entitled to rely upon its judgement;

10. Clients' assets—a firm must arrange adequate protection for clients' assets when it is responsible for them; and

11. Relations with regulators—a firm must deal with its regulators in an open and cooperative way, and must disclose to the FSA appropriately anything relating to the firm of which the FSA would reasonably expect notice.[28]

Principle 6 was highlighted by the FSA as part of the 'TCF' work,[29] which will   **7.19** have drawn to the attention of firms the FSA's attitude towards (amongst other issues) the identification of complaints, causes of complaints, and remedial action taken by firms to avoid complaints.[30] This will be particularly relevant to a firm's practices, or any finding by an Ombudsman, which might affect a large number of customers. Firms must now have systems in place for recording complaints and being able to carry out follow up or remedial work.

Rules, enforceable under section 150, are developed from the Principles, but the   **7.20** FSA regards the Principles as a 'general statement of the fundamental obligations of firms under the regulatory system'.[31] A breach of a Principle makes a firm liable to disciplinary sanction,[32] although a contravention of the Principles does not give rise to a right of action by a private individual under section 150.[33]

For consumers who have received investment advice and are able to bring a claim   **7.21** in common law, the claim for breach of statutory duty under section 150 strengthens the position. Further, when determining the standard and duty of skill and care of the reasonably competent professional adviser, courts are likely to have regard to the Conduct of Business Rules a firm would have been expected to follow. For example, in *Loosemore v Financial Concepts*[34] the investor's claim raised the obligation to ascertain sufficient information regarding the investor's personal and financial circumstances, and give suitable advice on the clients' investments, on the basis such advice would reflect the risks inherent in the recommended financial products. The court was satisfied that the relevant test applied to a firm would 'ordinarily include compliance with the rules'.[35] Similarly, in *Seymour*, the

---

[28] PRIN 2.1.1R.
[29] FSA, 'Treating customers fairly—progress and next steps' (July 2004).
[30] At Annex 1, as part of the 'retail reform agenda', FSA stated it would 'continue to focus on the quality of firms' complaint handling processes as, despite some improvement after previous mis-selling, standards are generally too low' (para 3).
[31] PRIN 1.1.2G.
[32] PRIN 1.1.7G.
[33] PRIN 4.4.4R.
[34] [2001] 1 Lloyd's Rep 235.
[35] HHJ Raymond Jack QC, at 241.

court found that 'the regulations afford strong evidence as to what is expected of a competent adviser in most situations'.[36]

7.22 Although the application of conduct of business rules may bolster the duty of care owed by a firm, it does not delineate the scope of such duty. In *Seymour*, the judge accepted that they were not 'necessarily co-extensive'.[37] In *Gorham and others v British Telecommunications plc and others*[38] it was seen as part of the giving and receiving of advice on pension provision and life assurance that the interests of the policyholder customer's dependant family should have been considered. Accordingly, the adviser owed a duty to the family dependants not to give negligent advice to the policyholder which adversely affected their interests. In this case, the investor had been advised not to be a member of his employer's pension scheme but to contribute to a personal pension plan. The investor did not join the occupational pension scheme and, following his death, the family dependants did not qualify for the lump sum death benefit payable. Operating under the Conduct of Business Rules by its then regulator, LAUTRO, the pension provider suggested those rules defined the scope of any duty of care, and the omission of any obligation under the rules to take into account interests of third parties, such as family members, indicated there was no duty owed to family members in those circumstances. This view was rejected by the Court of Appeal.[39] Accordingly, although generally firms might expect the duty of care not to exceed widely the scope of conduct of business rules, it is clear from the *Gorham* case that a duty of care may exist at common law which is broader than the duty under conduct of business rules and that statutory remedies do not exclude common law remedies.[40] In its work to simplify the Conduct of Business Rules for insurance intermediation, the FSA has made it clear that this does not affect the standard previously expected.

7.23 A claim for breach of statutory duty is usually quantified as for 'negligence' claims, and may be subject to contributory liability.[41]

7.24 In the investment and insurance sectors, the FSA has implemented conduct of business standards (now in part required by European Directives). The Conduct

---

[36] At 34.

[37] ibid. See also *Shore v Sedgwick Financial Services Ltd and others* [2007] EWHC 2509.

[38] [2000] 1 WLR 2129.

[39] It is summarised in *Seymour*: 'the Court was not impressed by an argument that because of the statutory and regulatory duties superimposed by the Financial Services Act on the common law duty of care owed . . . it was unnecessary and inappropriate to widen that common law duty so as to include a duty to Mrs Gorham as well'.

[40] In *Seymour*: 'the existence of a regulatory regime is not preclusive of a common law liability not duplicated by that regime'; see also *Re Whiteley Insurance Consultants (also known as Kingfisher Travel Insurance Services) (a firm)* [2008] EWHC 1782,

[41] Illustrated by the circumstances of an 'intermediate customer' in *Spreadex Ltd v Sanjit Sekhon* [2008] EWHC 1136 (Ch).

of Business Rules for investment business are now contained in the COBS
Sourcebook of the FSA Handbook. A firm must act 'honestly, fairly and professionally' in accordance with the best interests of the client.[42] A firm must take
reasonable steps to ensure that a 'personal recommendation is suitable'[43] and has
an obligation to obtain necessary information[44] without which a firm must not
make a 'personal recommendation'.[45] There are detailed rules for specific areas of
business, and separate rules for general insurance mediation ('ICOBS') and home
finance advice and arranging ('MCOB').[46] In addition to general standards, conduct of business rules may include particular requirements for certain products,
generally those with higher risks for consumers.[47]

Although an enforcement case, the first decision of the Financial Services and   **7.25**
Markets Tribunal in the proceedings between Legal & General Assurance Society
Limited and the FSA[48] considered comparable LAUTRO Rules. An advising firm
was obliged 'to use best endeavours to enable the investor to understand the nature
of any risk involved';[49] and to have regard to the investor's financial position generally and to all other relevant circumstances and to use best endeavours to ensure that
it recommended only that contract suited to the investor.[50] In the attachment to the
judgment, the Tribunal noted its conclusions 'about 13 alleged mis-sales about
which we heard evidence from customers'.[51] In doing so, the Tribunal considered in
particular Rule L8(1) to determine whether the adviser 'did not have regard to all
the relevant circumstances and/or did not do his best endeavours to ensure that he
recommended only a contract which was suitable to that customer'.[52]

Agents and appointed representatives

A provider may be liable to an investor if the investor dealt via its agent, such as an   **7.26**
appointed representative. FSMA provides that 'the principal of an appointed representative is responsible, to the same extent as if he had expressly permitted it, for
anything done or omitted by the representative in the carrying on of business
for which he has accepted responsibility'.[53] In *Martin v Britannia Life Ltd*,[54] the

---

[42] COBS 2.1.1R.
[43] COBS 9.2.1R.
[44] COBS 9.2.2R.
[45] COBS 9.2.6R.
[46] For example, at ICOBS 5.3 and MCOB 4.7.4.
[47] For example payment protection insurance (ICOBS 5.3.2R) or pensions (COBS 19).
[48] 13 January 2005.
[49] Rule L6 (aa).
[50] Rule L8(1), Sched L2.
[51] Para 6.
[52] Attachment 1, para 2.
[53] s 39(3).
[54] [2000] Lloyd's Law Reports PN 412.

court looked at both ostensible and apparent authority of the agent to determine whether the principal was liable. Where the appointed representative acts with ostensible authority to advise beyond the terms of the written appointment, the principal may be liable for the financial advice given by its appointed representative, even if it is outside the terms of appointment.

7.27 However, it would be wrong to expect that the appointed representative's conduct will always fix the principal with liability. Albeit considered under section 44 of the Financial Services Act 1986, in *Emmanuel & Emmanuel v DBS Financial Management plc*,[55] the court identified the relevant transactions as completed directly between the appointed representative and the investors outside the scope of the appointed representative's agreement to act as agent for the principal, and so could not be seen to have been as agent for the principal. The mere fact that dealings with the investor were in the course of the appointed representative's business did not establish that the principal was responsible or had accepted responsibility.

Clients' assets

7.28 Consumers are also protected by the detailed rules contained in the CASS Sourcebook of the FSA Handbook, developing Principle 10 (Clients' assets), for the holding and segregation of client money and assets.[56] The rules provide for the segregation of investors' assets and funds, imposing obligations on firms to ensure funds are properly held and to report any breaches of client money requirements.

7.29 There are obligations of 'safe custody' on firms for the 'safeguarding and administration of assets' (as a regulated activity). The rules 'are designed primarily to restrict the commingling of client and firm's assets and minimise the risk of the client's safe custody investments being used by the firm without the client's agreement or contrary to the client's wishes, or being treated as the firm's assets in the event of its insolvency'.[57] The segregation of clients' money and assets should therefore put the investor in a better position to recover his property in the event of a dispute or the failure of a firm.

Promotions and public statements

7.30 In addition to conduct of business rules, there are the restrictions imposed on financial promotions, breach of which gives rise to actions by consumers. Under FSMA,[58] in order to communicate an invitation or inducement to engage in

---

[55] Unreported, 16 March 1994.
[56] A firm must 'arrange adequate protection for clients' assets where it is responsible for these'.
[57] CASS 2.1.12G.
[58] s 21.

investment activity a person must be authorised or the content of the communication approved by an authorised firm. An agreement entered into in consequence of an unlawful communication is unenforceable.[59] The investor is entitled to recover money or property paid and compensation for 'any loss sustained by him as a result of having parted with [any money or other property]'.[60] The detailed implementation of the financial promotions regime is to be found in regulations[61] and the COBS rules:

> a firm must ensure that a communication or financial promotion is fair, clear, and not misleading',[62] although it is a defence to an action for damages under s.150 if a firm took 'reasonable steps'.[63] The 'general rule' when communicating with retail clients is that 'a firm must ensure that information: (1) includes the name of the firm; (2) is accurate and in particular does not emphasise the potential benefits of relevant business or relevant investment without also giving a fair and prominent indication of any relevant risks; (3) is sufficient for, and presented in a way that is likely to be understood by, the average member of the group to whom it is directed, or by whom it is likely to be received; and (4) does not disguise, diminish or obscure important items, statements or warnings'.[64]

Additional requirements apply to different products, or to 'direct offers' promotions that include a form by which any response may be made (eg letters with tear-off application forms attached)[65] so that the potential investor is able to make an 'informed assessment'.[66]

It is also a specific offence under FSMA to make misleading, false, or deceptive **7.31** statements.[67] This is not expressed to give rise to a claim for breach of statutory duty but the investor would be protected in such circumstances by common law remedies and rules in COBS.

There is a further right of redress for investors in collective investment schemes. **7.32** Part XVII of FSMA includes an action for damages. In the event of a contravention by an authorised firm of section 238 or section 240, which apply where an authorised firm communicates invitations or inducements to participate in a collective investment scheme, an investor has the right to claim damages.[68]

---

[59] s 30.
[60] s 30(2).
[61] SI 2001/1335 (as amended).
[62] COBS 4.2.1R.
[63] COBS 4.2.6R.
[64] COBS 4.5.2R.
[65] COBS 4.7.
[66] COBS 4.7.4G.
[67] FSMA, s 397.
[68] ibid, s 241.

Redress by the FSA

7.33 A consumer's complaint may also be pursued by action taken by the FSA under Part XXV of FSMA (Injunctions and Restitution). Restitution orders may be made[69] in circumstances where 'a person has contravened a relevant requirement', and that person has derived profits as a result or others have suffered loss. Payment may be made to those affected of the profits and/or to the extent of the loss.[70] The FSA is under an obligation to distribute any such receipts to those affected persons.[71]

7.34 Restitution orders may be sought by the FSA in circumstances where a firm has failed to comply with orders for the payment of redress to investors, eg by FOS. Firms are obliged to meet FOS awards (under the DISP Rules) and if they fail to do so, the FSA may take action against the firm for the benefit of investors. As in the *FSA v Matthews and others*,[72] orders made by a court may reflect the resources of defendants and accordingly may not provide for payment to the same extent as an award of damages by a court (or even an FOS award).

7.35 The FSA may also secure the payment of redress for investors as part of its enforcement function. For example, in 2003, the FSA imposed a penalty on Lloyds TSB of £1.9 million for the mis-selling of precipice bonds but the firm also agreed to provide compensation of around £98 million in respect of 22,500 sales.[73] In connection with the FSA's investigations into split capital investment trusts, the settlement agreed with over 20 firms led to the creation of Fund Distribution Limited, a company set up to receive and distribute settlement payments from firms to individual investors who lost funds as a result of investing in 'zeros'.[74]

7.36 Other action to secure financial redress for consumers may include an industry-wide review into mis-selling. Under the previous regime of the Financial Services Act 1986, The Securities and Investments Board ('SIB') established the 'Pension Review', followed by the 'FSAVC [Free Standing Additional Voluntary Contributions] Review'. The Pension Review imposed a large, wide scale proactive obligation on firms to identify investors who may have been mis-sold personal pension plans between 1988 and 1994; and where such sales were not compliant, and caused the investor loss, to calculate, offer, and pay redress. The SIB issued detailed guidance (supplemented by the Personal Investment Authority) on determining both the eligibility of claims (ie the 'liability' of firms to investors) and

---

[69] ibid, s 382.
[70] ibid, s 382(2).
[71] ibid, s 382(3).
[72] [2004] EWHC 2966 (Ch).
[73] Final Notice dated 24 September 2003.
[74] FSA Press Release dated 24 December 2004.

quantifying investors' losses. Over the course of the Pension Review, it is estimated that £13–£14 billion has been paid by way of redress to investors. Under FSMA, industry-wide reviews may now be ordered by HM Treasury.[75] Such authorisation from HM Treasury can fix both the scope of the review and the amounts payable by way of compensation. To date, no review has been so ordered by HM Treasury.

Claims against the FSA

In addition to making claims or complaints on its own behalf or for the benefit of   **7.37** investors, the FSA might also be on the receiving end of claims from consumers or authorised firms. Part IV of Schedule 1 to FSMA provides the FSA with an exemption from liability to damages for 'anything done or omitted in the discharge or purported discharge of the Authority's functions',[76] although this is not available in the event of bad faith or an unlawful act or omission under section 6(1) of the Human Rights Act 1998. In the case of *Tee v Lautro Ltd*,[77] the claimant proceeded against LAUTRO for negligence and misfeasance in public office following enforcement action taken against the individual's company. While the claim was struck out following the defendant's reliance upon a similar immunity from damages provided by the Financial Services Act 1986,[78] the court was also satisfied that there was no duty of care owed by LAUTRO in negligence, and misfeasance required proof of malice, not mere recklessness.

Under FSMA, the FSA is obliged to make arrangements for the investigations   **7.38** of complaints against it.[79] This includes the appointment of an independent person[80] who, following completion of any investigation, may make remedial recommendations including that the FSA make a 'compensatory payment'.[81] The FSA has established its procedure in its COAF Sourcebook as 'guidance' (as the FSA is unable to make rules against itself). This covers complaints against both the FSA and certain predecessors.[82] A complaint is defined as 'any expression of dissatisfaction about the manner in which the FSA has carried out or failed to carry out its functions . . . other than its legislative functions' and is to cover

---

[75] FSMA, s 404.
[76] Para 19(1).
[77] Unreported 16 July 1996.
[78] FSA 1986, s 187.
[79] FSMA, Sched 1, para 7.
[80] COAF 1.3; Sir Anthony Holland is the present Complaints Commissioner appointed by the FSA with the benefit of input from both the Consumer Panel and the Practitioner Panel and one independent person; COAF 1.5.10.AG.
[81] Para 8(5).
[82] COAF 1 and COAF 2.

'allegations of misconduct'; it does not cover complaints about FOS, the FSCS, or the FSA's relationship with its employees.[83]

7.39 The complaints scheme operated by the FSA reflects changes made following further consultation.[84] There are two stages—firstly an investigation by the FSA and secondly an investigation by the Commissioner. The FSA has developed a 'fast track' process for dealing with 'low impact' complaints which can be resolved within five days.[85] Claims not suitable for such 'fast track' are dealt with by the FSA's 'Stage one' internal investigation or (normally if the complainant is dissatisfied with the FSA's determination or handling) a 'Stage two' investigation by the Complaints Commissioner.[86] The FSA is no longer obliged to complete its investigations within eight weeks (which its experience indicated was not feasible) but is required to complete investigations as soon as possible, within four weeks if possible, but if not to write with an indication of the reasonable timescale.[87] The Commissioner may conduct his investigation 'in whatever manner he thinks appropriate . . . at the FSA's expense'.[88] The Commissioner must have 'sufficient financial and other resources to allow him to fulfil his role under the complaints scheme properly'.[89] A final report is issued to the FSA and the complainant.[90] Beforehand, the FSA and complainant will receive a 'preliminary report' on which to comment.[91] The Commissioner may publish his final report.[92] The FSA must respond if the complaint is upheld or it is criticised.[93] Instead of, or in addition to, a 'compensatory payment', following complaints the FSA might make an apology and implement steps to rectify any errors.

7.40 Generally, as well as those relating to its legislative function, the FSA will not investigate complaints merely expressing dissatisfaction with its general policies or the alleged unreasonable exercise of its discretion where no unreasonable, unprofessional, or other misconduct is alleged.[94] Complaints should be made within 12 months.[95] The FSA does not make any charge.[96] Each year, the Commissioner

---

[83] COAF 1.1.5G; COAF 1.4.2G.
[84] Consultation Paper 04/6: 'Changing the FSA's Complaint Scheme' (March 2004).
[85] COAF 1.5.1AG.
[86] COAF 1.5.6G.
[87] COAF 1.5.3G.
[88] COAF 1.5.10G.
[89] COAF 1.3.3G.
[90] COAF 1.5.19G.
[91] COAF 1.5.19.AG.
[92] COAF 1.5.21G.
[93] COAF 1.5.22G.
[94] COAF 1.4.2A.
[95] COAF 1.4.6.G.
[96] COAF 1.4.7G.

must submit a report to the FSA for publication.[97] As at 17 March 2004,[98] in the period from 3 September 2001, the FSA had dealt with 259 complaints at Stage one, 38 had been dealt with by the Complaints Commissioner, of which 12 had given rise to recommendations by the Commissioner for action by the FSA. The FSA's Annual Report for 2007/08 noted that 212 complaints were concluded in the year at Stage one, and the Commissioner concluded 17 full Stage two complaints.

Complaint Handling by Firms

DISP

For an authorised firm (and certain others), the FSA Handbook prescribes a complaints handling process. Generally, this is applicable to all authorised firms, with some exceptions, such as credit unions or authorised professional firms for non mainstream regulated entities[99] or with a professional body to handle complaints;[100] for members of Lloyd's, complaint procedures at Lloyd's must first be completed.[101] Although complaint handling may be outsourced,[102] firms are responsible for the acts and omissions of an outsourcer. **7.41**

The complaint handling requirements for firms are contained in the DISP Rules.[103] These Rules are to ensure that complaints are dealt with promptly, fairly, and that firms take action to rectify the cause of complaints. An action may arise under section 150 for breach of these Rules.[104] Chapter 1 deals with complaint handling procedures for firms ('Treating Complainants Fairly'); Chapters 2 to 5 deal with FOS. The key issues were subject to consultation before N2.[105] Draft DISP Rules were then consulted on.[106] The framework for a firm's own complaints procedures was recently reviewed and revised as part of the FSA's work on principles-based regulation (and TCF) and the implementation of the Markets in Financial Investment Directive ('MiFID')[107] in November 2007.[108] **7.42**

---

[97] COAF 1.6.2G.

[98] Reported in CP 04/6.

[99] DISP 1.1.5R.

[100] DISP 2.3.4R.

[101] DISP 1.11.

[102] DISP 1.1.19G.

[103] Or in CRED for credit unions.

[104] DISP Sched 5.

[105] FSA Consultation Paper 4: 'Consumer Complaints' (December 1997); FSA Consultation Paper 33: 'Consumer complaints and the new single ombudsman scheme' (November 1999).

[106] Consultation Paper 49: 'Complaints Handling Arrangements: Feedback Statement on CP33 and Draft Rules' (May 2000).

[107] 2004/39/EC.

[108] FSA Consultation Paper 06/19: 'Reforming Conduct of Business Regulation'; FSA Policy Statement 07/9: 'Treating Complainants Fairly' (July 2007).

7.43 DISP 1 sets out the general requirements for firms to have internal complaint handling procedures. The procedures must be effective and transparent for the 'reasonable and prompt handling of complaints', and deal with 'any expression of dissatisfaction whether oral or written, and whether justified or not', relating (if not MiFID business) to the provision of financial services or products, which alleges financial loss, material distress, or material inconvenience.[109] Complaints should be used by firms to identify any 'root causes' affecting other processes or products which should be remedied.[110] For MiFID business the information from complaints should be used to assess compliance procedures.[111] The complaints procedures should provide for receiving complaints, responding to complaints, referring complaints to other firms, the appropriate investigation of complaints, and notifying complainants of their right to go to FOS where relevant.

7.44 Firms must publicise summary details (in writing) of their internal complaints process, refer customers to the availability of these details 'at, or immediately after, the point of sale', on request or on receipt of a complaint.[112] Firms may display in branches and offices a notice indicating that the firm is covered by FOS.[113]

7.45 A complaint must be investigated 'competently, diligently and impartially'; the subject matter, outcome, and any remedial action or redress must be assessed 'fairly, consistently and promptly'.[114] If upheld, redress or remedial action must be offered, and promptly complied with if accepted, and the review and decision explained in a way that is 'fair, clear and not misleading'.[115] Relevant factors in the assessment of a complaint by a firm include any FSA guidance and FOS decisions concerning similar complaints against that firm.[116] Time barred complaints may be rejected without considering the merits.[117]

7.46 With some exceptions, complaints must be dealt with within prescribed time limits at DISP 1.6. The time limits require firms to send a prompt acknowledgement of a complaint and to keep the complainant informed of progress.[118]

7.47 A 'final response' must be sent by the end of eight weeks.[119] The FSA expects firms to have dealt with 'almost all' complaints within eight weeks.[120] If unhappy with

---

[109] DISP 1.3.1R.
[110] DISP 1.3.3R.
[111] DISP 1.3.4G; SYSC 6.1.
[112] DISP 1.2.1R.
[113] DISP 1.2.5G.
[114] DISP 1.4.1R.
[115] DISP 1.4.1R.
[116] DISP 1.4.2G.
[117] DISP 1.8.1R.
[118] DISP 1.6.1R.
[119] DISP 1.6.2R.
[120] DISP 1.6.7G.

the outcome, or if a firm is not in a position to give a final response within eight weeks, the complainant is entitled to refer the matter to FOS (and must be advised of this).[121] The FSA expects firms to set out 'prominently' the information regarding FOS.[122]

DISP does acknowledge some firms may have a 'two-stage' complaints procedure, **7.48** for example, allowing for a complaint to be returned to an office of the firm and then referred to head office after an initial response has been given.[123] If a full initial response is sent within eight weeks, the complaint can then be regarded as closed if there is no reply within eight weeks. If the complainant takes more than one week to reply, the time limits are extended accordingly.[124] The FSA has observed that a two-stage process 'should mean just that. Iterations are likely to be justifiable only in a minority of cases.'[125]

DISP also deals with the possibility that the recipient of the complaint may not be **7.49** solely responsible for the matter complained of, in which case it may refer the complaint to the other firm provided that it does so promptly, confirms the complaint by 'final response' and complies with its own obligations if jointly responsible for the complaint.[126]

In addition to the handling of a complaint, DISP requires record keeping and **7.50** reporting (with some exceptions for complaints resolved by close of business on the business day following receipt).[127] Complaint records must be retained for at least three years from the date of receipt of the complaint,[128] and five years for MiFID business and complaints must be reported to the FSA twice a year in the prescribed format (at Annex 1R to DISP 1).[129] Reporting includes not only the total number of complaints, to be broken down by categories and generic product types, but also the time taken for dealing with complaints and total redress paid.[130] A complaint is 'closed' when the final response has been sent, or where an earlier response has been accepted in writing by the complainant, or, if a two-stage process applies, where the complainant has not indicated dissatisfaction with the first response.[131] The report to the FSA is to confirm the details of a single contact at

---

121 DISP 1.6.2.R; see also DISP 1.6.4R.
122 DISP 1.6.6AG.
123 DISP 1.6.5R.
124 DISP 1.6.6R.
125 The FSA's 'Dear CEO letter' dated 27 October 2007.
126 DISP 1.7.1R.
127 DISP 1.5.1R.
128 DISP 1.9.1R.
129 DISP 1.10.1R.
130 DISP 1.10.2.R.
131 DISP 1.10.7.R

the firm for complainants.[132] In any event, adequate management information about complaints is important as part of a firm's TCF obligations.

7.51 Following Principle 6, customers must be treated fairly in the complaints process. This is reflected in industry guidance.[133] A firm is expected to adopt a helpful attitude towards a customer making a legitimate complaint and make reasonable enquiry, rather than adjudicating a complaint purely on the words and evidence of the customer alone. The FSA's interpretation of the DISP obligations is apparent from various publications such as the 'Dear CEO letters'. Firms are under an express obligation to cooperate with FOS and meet any awards made against them by FOS—prompt compliance is required.[134] The FSA has taken enforcement action where firms have failed to comply with FOS awards. In the case of *Heather Moor & Edgecomb Ltd*, the Financial Services and Markets Tribunal[135] ordered the firm's permission be cancelled unless an award was paid (and leave to appeal has been refused).[136] The FSA has also acted where firms have failed to ensure effective complaints handling procedures and adequate resources for handling complaints or personnel trained to carry out fair investigations.[137]

7.52 The DISP Sourcebook identifies two particular categories of complaint to which prescriptive or different treatment applies. Firstly, complaints which are subject to the FSAVC Review are not subject to the time limit requirements for dealing with complaints, or the reporting requirements to the FSA. The FSAVC Review commenced before the implementation of the FSMA regime and the time limits might not be achievable due to the complicated nature of dealing with such complaints, in particular assessing and quantifying any loss and redress. The second particular area is mortgage endowment complaints.

Mortgage endowment complaints

7.53 To date, the largest single source of complaints to FOS has been mortgage endowments, ie the sales of endowment policies as repayment vehicles for mortgages taken out to buy the investor's home.[138] The DISP Rules set out both the approach and standards firms should use when investigating such complaints, and how any financial loss should be assessed and what redress should be offered as 'fair and appropriate compensation'.[139] The complaint handling process requires the

---

[132] DISP 1.10.9.R.

[133] Joint paper by the Association of IFAs and ABI: 'Working Together to Deliver Good Customer Experiences—Responsibilities of Providers and Advisers' (October 2006).

[134] DISP 1.4.4R; 3.7.12(1)R.

[135] 19 May 2008.

[136] 1 July 2008.

[137] For example, the FSA's final notice to Mandrake Associates Limited dated 17 July 2008.

[138] The history of these complaints was examined for FOS by David Severn (see para 7.120 below).

[139] Appendix 1.

gathering of all relevant facts and information, making a fair and objective assessment of whether the firm has failed to comply with the relevant duty owed to the complainant, and assessing whether any failure of duty by it was in the circumstances a material failure, in the sense that if it had not occurred the complainant would have been likely to have acted differently.[140] It also directs that certain assumptions should be made in favour of the complainant 'unless the contrary is demonstrated' (for example, that the complainant could have afforded a repayment mortgage).[141]

The FSA took action to enforce the proper handling of endowment mis-selling **7.54** complaints, which illustrates its view of firms' complaint handling obligations. On 4 April 2002, the FSA wrote to large firms dealing with mortgage endowment claims raising concerns about, and providing 'urgent guidance' for, the handling of those complaints.[142] The FSA sent a follow-up letter in December 2004[143] to remind firms 'of the importance of handling complaints in a way that is consistent with the principle of treating customers fairly and to warn of enforcement action.[144] The action taken by the FSA against firms and its further publications[145] further illustrated the FSA's attitude to complaint handling.

---

[140] DISP App 1.1.6G.
[141] DISP App 1.2.2G.
[142] The Tiner letter.
[143] Published on 4 January 2005 (The 'follow up letter').
[144] The Annex to the Tiner letter listed nine specific action points to assist firms to deal with complaints fairly:

(1) recognise in the assessment of the complaint that the key risk for the consumer is that the endowment may not repay the mortgage loan;
(2) avoid too narrow a view of the scope of the advisory duty in the context of mortgage advice;
(3) recognise that oral evidence can be good and sufficient evidence, avoiding too ready a dismissal of evidence from the consumer which is not supported by documentary proof;
(4) investigate the issue diligently in particular so as to take into account the selling practices at the time, the training, instruction, sales scripts, and incentives given to advisers at the time, and the track record of the particular adviser;
(5) go the extra mile to clarify ambiguous issues or conflicts of evidence before finding against the consumer;
(6) avoid making a conclusive assumption that a pre-existing endowment held at time of sale, whether for purposes of savings or mortgage repayment, is sufficient evidence of understanding and acceptance of the key risk;
(7) avoid making too literal and narrow an interpretation of the issue of the complaint as expressed by the consumer;
(8) avoid rejecting complaints solely on the basis that the consumer signed a proposal form or failed to exercise the cancellation right and so must be presumed to have been satisfied with the advice and the product at time of sale; and
(9) avoid claiming as evidence of risk warning at time of sale (so as to justify rejection of the complaint) either:
  (a) the absence of a statement in product literature that repayment of the mortgage was guaranteed; or
  (b) a statement in product particulars that the firm will monitor the plan and advise the consumer if the level of contribution is insufficient for the target amount to be repaid.
[145] For example, 'Mortgage endowments: Progress report and next steps' (July 2005).

7.55 In December 2003, the FSA imposed a penalty on Friends Provident Life and Pensions Limited for the mishandling of endowment mortgage complaints.[146] The FSA found that the complaints handling procedures were unfair towards the customers. In particular, the FSA concluded that the firm's complaints handling procedures meant that the firm dismissed a consumer's case where the complainant's evidence was not supported by contemporaneous documentation, the firm had made assumptions that customers understood risks associated with the endowment policy if the customer had had a pre-existing endowment policy, and the firm had assumed that the customers were satisfied with the advice if they did not exercise cancellation rights. The FSA did not consider that the firm had put in place effective and appropriate complaints procedures.[147]

7.56 In March 2004, the FSA imposed a penalty on Allied Dunbar Assurance plc of £725,000 for flaws in its procedures for handling mortgage endowment complaints.[148] The FSA identified that its complaint handlers had conducted poor quality investigations and there was a failure to collect sufficient evidence to make a fair assessment to both the consumer's attitude to risk and the suitability of sale. In particular, the firm did not give clear instructions to its complaints handling staff about the types of evidence it should consider (including the customer's version of events), did not give clear instructions about the weight to be attached to the different types of evidence when coming to a decision, unfairly restricted (by the written procedures) the ability of a complaint handler to uphold a complaint where a sale was plainly unsuitable if, for example, the customer did not complain specifically that the sales advice failed to explain the risks of an endowment policy, and tended to give disproportionate weight to the views of the sale adviser when assessing the facts. Unfair assumptions were made that customers had accepted the risks associated with an endowment mortgage, for example if the customer had held a pre-existing endowment. The FSA concluded investigations were of poor quality, did not gather sufficient evidence, or make a fair assessment, so that unsound decisions were made to reject complaints.[149]

7.57 In May 2005, the FSA imposed a penalty on Abbey National plc of £800,000 for mishandling mortgage endowment complaints.[150] The FSA found that '[b]y putting its own interests ahead of those of its customers with a mortgage endowment complaint, Abbey had singularly failed to treat its customers fairly'.[151] In particular, the FSA found that insufficient steps had been taken to establish the

---

[146] Final Notice dated 15 December 2003.
[147] FSA Press Release dated 17 December 2005.
[148] Final Notice dated 18 March 2004.
[149] FSA Press Release dated 19 March 2004.
[150] Final Notice dated 25 May 2005.
[151] FSA Press Release dated 25 May 2005.

customer's attitude to risk at the point of sale, and the subject matter of the complaint had not been fully investigated. The firm had an obligation to carry out an objective investigation to make a genuine enquiry and assessment, and in the FSA's view the firm had breached Principle 2 in failing to conduct its business with due skill, care, and diligence in relation to its handling of mortgage endowment complaints, and Principle 6 in failing to pay due regard to the interests of its customers or to treat them fairly.

Unauthorised bank charges

In some circumstances, the FSA may grant firms a waiver from the DISP Rules.[152] **7.58**
The recent complaints about bank charges, which is the subject of test case litigation brought by the Office of Fair Trading, are on hold. A waiver granted by the FSA on that basis has been extended pending a decision from the Court of Appeal.[153] The FSA also wrote to firms about the handling of complaints about overdraft charges, as its thematic work had 'identified that some firms' processes were so protracted, incremental and iterative that they do not appear to comply with our rules'.

Complaint history

The making and outcome of a complaint might also be relevant to an individual's **7.59**
employment and status. Although the DISP reporting requirements are limited to complaints against a firm, a firm must have regard to a person's complaints history if considering appointing that person to a customer function, and former employers are to include within a job reference, for anyone who applies for a customer function role, all relevant information of which they are aware, and in doing so must 'have regard to the purpose of the request and in particular to: . . . (b) any relevant outstanding or upheld complaint from an eligible complainant against that person'.[154]

The FSA, when considering the fitness and propriety of an individual, will also **7.60**
have regard to that individual's complaint history.[155] For these reasons, as well as general principles, in the event a complaint is made against an individual, the firm should, if possible, seek to obtain that individual's response to the substance of the complaint. The compliance record of an individual may be taken into account by the FSA when considering the fitness and propriety of a person to carry out

---

[152] The FSA granted a waiver for mortgage endowment complaints whilst firms 'put additional resource and systems in place to eliminate backlogs'.

[153] Press notice dated 21 July 2008.

[154] SUP 10.13.12R.

[155] FIT 2.1.3(6)R.

a controlled function and a history of complaints could lead the FSA to exercise its powers to withdraw its approval from an individual.

7.61 Recently, the FSA has issued proposals for publishing complaints data about firms.[156] As part of its approach to increased transparency, league tables of the numbers of complaints and how they are handled may be compiled. The proposal is to publish data for 'those firms handling the largest number of complaints'. The FSA reported that 400 firms account for 99 per cent of reported complaints. This work may be alongside FOS—the recent Hunt Report (discussed at para 7.134 below) recommended that FOS 'should work with the FSA, industry and consumer stakeholders to define a common complaints dataset to enable joint publication of performance data on a firm-specific basis in the medium term'.

Financial Ombudsman Service

Introduction

7.62 Part XVI of FSMA provides for the Financial Ombudsman Service ('FOS'), described as 'a scheme under which certain disputes may be resolved quickly and with minimum formality by an independent person'.[157] FOS describes itself as 'settling financial disputes, not taking sides'. In July 1998, as part of the consultation on the Financial Services and Markets Bill, HM Treasury had identified that 'it is important that consumers should have access to cheap, quick, informal and effective dispute resolution arrangements'.[158] For this purpose, a single ombudsman scheme was proposed. This single scheme was to replace the 'patchwork quilt'[159] of eight pre-existing dispute resolution schemes: the Banking Ombudsman; the Building Societies Ombudsman; the FSA Complaints Services; the Insurance Ombudsman; the Investment Ombudsman; the Personal Insurance Arbitration Services; the PIA Ombudsman; and the SFA Complaints and Arbitration Services.

7.63 According to HM Treasury's consultation, the new scheme was intended to operate 'if a consumer fails to obtain satisfaction from a firm's internal complaints handling arrangements', and firms were to be required 'to cooperate with the Scheme's investigation of a case'. It was not to be for or against firms or customers. A decision in favour of the consumer was to be binding on the firm, but not consumers.

---

[156] FSA Discussion Paper 08/3: 'Transparency as a Regulatory Tool' (May 2008).
[157] FSMA, s 225(1).
[158] Financial Services and Markets Bill: A Consultation Document, Part 1, Overview of Financial Regulatory Reform.
[159] As described in the FSA's Consultation Paper 4: 'Consumer Complaints' (December 1997).

FOS has since been subject to review by the FSA, at the request of HM Treasury, **7.64** as part of the review of implementation of the Act with the benefit of two years' experience (the 'N2 plus 2' review) but HM Treasury limited the scope of the review. HM Treasury noted key, non-negotiable safeguards for FOS, in particular that it remained independent, decisions are dealt with on the merits, and the service remained free to consumers (even those with unsuccessful complaints).[160] The informality of procedure and protection for consumers from adverse costs consequences are important features of FOS and have been approved by Lord Hunt in his recent report 'Opening up, reaching out, and aiming high—an agenda for accessibility and excellence in the Financial Ombudsman Scheme' ('the Hunt Report') published in April 2008 (and discussed at para 7.134).

The scheme operator

The Financial Ombudsman Service Limited is the 'scheme operator' (as defined **7.65** by FSMA) of the Financial Ombudsman Service. The company was established by the FSA to carry out the statutory functions of the scheme operator under Part XVI of FSMA. The 'body corporate' is a company limited by guarantee, set up under Part II of Schedule 17 to FSMA.

As required by Schedule 17, the scheme operator has a chairman and a Board who **7.66** are responsible for the operation of the scheme but who have no involvement in considering individual complaints. The chairman and Board members are subject to appointment, and removal, by the FSA. The chairman's appointment must be approved by HM Treasury. Although Board members are appointed by the FSA, 'the terms of their appointment (and in particular those governing removal from office) must be such as to secure their independence from the [FSA] in the operation of the scheme'.[161] The Board are public interest appointments. Issues decided by the Board include the appointment of the Ombudsmen, the making of rules in respect of the scheme's voluntary jurisdiction (subject to the approval of the FSA), the making of rules relating to the levying of case fees (subject to the approval of the FSA), and the approval and recommendation to the FSA of the annual budget.[162] A Memorandum of Understanding ('MOU') is in place between the FSA and FOS. In addition to describing the FSA's and FOS's responsibilities (for example, the FSA appoints the directors, but the FSCS is responsible for the operation of the scheme and appointing the Ombudsmen), the MOU provides for general cooperation, information sharing, and consultation. As long as he has

---

[160] The Financial Secretary to the Treasury's Statement on the Two Year Review of the Financial Services and Markets Act (dated 4 November 2003).

[161] FSMA, Sched 17, Part II, Clause 3(3).

[162] Lastly, the Corporate Plan & 2008/09 Budget (January 2008).

regard to the parties' rights of privacy, the Ombudsman may disclose information to the FSA and other regulatory or statutory bodies to assist those bodies (or FOS) to discharge those functions.[163] FOS and the FSA may also share information for the discharge of their respective statutory functions under FSMA regulations,[164] and FOS may make similar disclosure to the OFT. FOS also has an MOU with the OFT.

7.67 Part II of Schedule 17 requires an annual report from FOS and the Chief Ombudsman,[165] and an annual budget to be approved by the FSA.[166] The budget must be approved before each financial year and must 'include an indication of (a) a distribution of resources deployed in the operation of the scheme, and (b) the amounts of income of the scheme operator arising or expected to arise from the operation of the scheme'.

7.68 Part II of Schedule 17 provides for 'a panel of persons, appearing to [the scheme operator] to have appropriate qualifications and experience, to act as Ombudsmen for the purposes of the scheme'[167] and for one member of the panel to act as Chief Ombudsman.[168] All Ombudsman appointments, by the scheme operator, are to ensure the independence of the individuals. In addition to dealing with complaints, the Chief Ombudsman is responsible for the day-to-day functioning of the organisation (akin to a chief executive role). As at the end of 2007/08, there were 37 FOS ombudsmen but the bulk of cases are dealt with by teams of case workers and adjudicators.[169] In practice, although the determination of complaints is reserved to an Ombudsman,[170] investigations may be delegated to staff and cases may only be seen by an Ombudsman if they are unusual, difficult, or contentious. The Court of Appeal has upheld the delegation by the Ombudsman under DISP 3.3, in particular for summary dismissal.[171]

7.69 Part XVI of FSMA and Schedule 17 also provide some particular powers, and protection, to FOS. The Ombudsman has the power to compel production of documents or information from 'a party to a complaint'.[172] This is limited to 'information and documents, the production of which the Ombudsman considers necessary for the determination of the complaint'.[173] Failure to comply may lead the 'defaulter'

---

[163] DISP 3.8.3.R.
[164] The Financial Services and Markets Act 2000 (Disclosure of Information and Prescribed Pensions) Regulations 2001, SI 2001/1857; The Financial Services and Markets Act 2000 (Disclosure of Confidential Information) Regulations 2001, SI 2001/2188.
[165] Para 7.
[166] Para 9.
[167] Para 4.
[168] Para 5.
[169] DISP 3.9.1A.R.
[170] Sched 17, para 14(2)(f).
[171] *FOS v Heather, Moor & Edgecomb Ltd* [2008] EWCA 643.
[172] FSMA, s 231(1).
[173] ibid, s 231(3).

to be treated as if in contempt of court.[174] However, FOS has no such powers to obtain information from third parties who might hold relevant material. It is for the parties to the complaint to seek to obtain and present such evidence.

FOS has immunity from liability for damages for acts or omissions 'in the **7.70** discharge, or purported discharge, of any functions under this Act in relation to the compulsory jurisdiction'.[175] This does not apply in the event of bad faith or in respect of an award of damages under section 6(1) of the Human Rights Act 1998.[176]

The operation of FOS

Part XVI of FSMA, and Schedule 17, set out the keystones for the operation of **7.71** FOS: compulsory jurisdiction (including determination under the compulsory jurisdiction and awards), voluntary jurisdiction, costs, and funding. This framework is built upon by the DISP Rules contained in the FSA Handbook (in the Redress Module).

Compulsory jurisdiction—framework

Under section 226, compulsory jurisdiction applies to any firm, against which a **7.72** complaint is made, being authorised at the time of the act or omission to which the complaint relates, and the complaint relates to an activity regulated under the Act and subject to the compulsory jurisdiction rules.[177] The Ombudsman can consider all disputes arising from the carrying on of such regulated activity. FOS's compulsory scope has extended since N2, adding credit unions, mortgage and general insurance brokers (like the FSA and the FSCS), and also (from 6 April 2007) consumer credit.[178] From 1 November 2009, it is proposed that FOS provide the 'out of court' redress mechanism under the Payment Services Directive.[179] The 'Thornton Review' also recommended combining the functions of FOS and the Pensions Ombudsman.[180] The FSA is responsible for making the DISP Rules dealing with the compulsory jurisdiction. These rules determine the scope of compulsory jurisdiction, those eligible to claim, and in what circumstances a claim may be made. FSMA also identifies, in particular, the application of relevant

---

[174] ibid, s 232(4).
[175] ibid, Sched 17, para 10.
[176] ibid, para 10(2).
[177] ibid, s 226(2) and (4).
[178] ibid, s 226A (added by the Consumer Credit Act 2006).
[179] Consultation Paper 08/14: 'Implementation of the Payment Services Directive' (August 2008).
[180] Paul Thornton: *A Review of Pensions Institutions* (June 2007).

time limits and a requirement on consumers to communicate first the 'substance' of a complaint to the firm giving it a 'reasonable opportunity to deal with it'.[181]

7.73 FSMA provides for the determination of complaints under the compulsory juris-diction to be 'by reference to what is, in the opinion of the Ombudsman, fair and reasonable in all the circumstances of the case'[182] for which relevant factors may be specified.[183]

7.74 FSMA also requires a written statement of a decision, with reasons, signed by the Ombudsman, which 'determination' the complainant must accept or reject.[184] If accepted by the consumer, the Ombudsman's decision is binding on the con-sumer and the firm, and is 'final'.[185] Such decision may include an award against the firm for the payment of 'fair compensation for loss or damage', not to exceed a monetary limit (fixed by the FSA), although recommendation of a higher amount may be made, or a direction to take 'just and appropriate' steps, and is enforceable by the consumer.[186] It is possible to make both a money award and a direction to take steps.[187] Although 'prompt compliance' is required, Schedule 17 identifies that money awards 'registered in accordance with scheme rules' may be enforced by the County Court in England and Wales, and by similar procedures in Scotland and Northern Ireland.[188] FOS is required to maintain 'a register of each money award'.[189] This is satisfied by an internal database at FOS,[190] although the Court of Appeal has suggested that the register, as an official list or record, needs to open to public inspection.[191]

7.75 FOS does make some of the DISP Rules,[192] such as the procedures for reference of complaints and for their investigation, consideration, and determination by an Ombudsman.[193] FOS must publish such rules in draft for consultation, inviting

---

[181] FSMA, Sched 17, para 13.
[182] ibid, s 228(2).
[183] ibid, Sched 17, para 14.
[184] ibid, s 228(3) and (4).
[185] ibid, s 228(5).
[186] ibid, s 229(2)(b), and (9).
[187] *Bunney v Burns Anderson plc* [2007] EWHC 1740 (Ch).
[188] Para 16.
[189] DISP 3.7.7.R.
[190] See the judgment of the Financial Services and Markets Tribunal in *Heather, Moor & Edgecomb Ltd v FSA* (sitting on 19 May 2008).
[191] *R (Heather, Moor & Edgecomb Ltd) v FOS* [2008] ECWA Civ 642.
[192] Sched 17, para 14.
[193] Sched 17, para 14(2) contains a non-exhaustive list of issues which may be dealt with by these rules, which may: '(a) specify matters which are to be taken into account when determining whether an act or omission was fair and reasonable; (b) provide that a complaint may in specified circum-stances be dismissed without consideration of its merits; (c) provide for the reference of a complaint, in specified circumstances and with the consent of a complainant, to another body with a view to its being determined by that body instead of by an ombudsman; (d) make provision as to the evi-dence which may be required or admitted, the extent to which it should be oral or written and the consequences of a person's failure to produce any information or document which he has been

representations, which rules then may only be made with the consent of the FSA.[194]

Voluntary jurisdiction—framework

Section 227 adds the 'voluntary jurisdiction'. This relates to activities which are or **7.76** would be made subject to the compulsory jurisdiction. With the approval of the FSA, FOS makes rules for the operation of its voluntary jurisdiction. Such rules may determine who is an eligible claimant, and make different provisions for complaints arising from different activities.[195] These FOS rules are described as 'standard terms'.[196] The standard terms may require funding to FOS 'by participants' of the voluntary jurisdiction scheme, and make 'provision as to the ordering of costs'.[197] FSMA also provides for the 'standard terms' to include an immunity from damages for FOS, on the same basis as for the compulsory jurisdiction.[198]

Any part of the voluntary jurisdiction may also be delegated by FOS to a body **7.77** responsible 'for the operation of broadly comparable scheme . . . for the resolution of disputes'.[199]

The FSA is to receive from FOS a copy of the voluntary jurisdiction rules once **7.78** made 'without delay' and written notice of the revocation of any such rules.[200] These rules must be printed and available to the public immediately after being made. As with the compulsory jurisdiction, any proposed voluntary jurisdiction rules must be published in draft for consultation and representations invited within a specified time; a 'statement of the difference' must be published if significant changes follow the consultation period.[201]

Costs

As already noted, costs awards may not be made by FOS against a complainant in **7.79** respect of the firm's costs.[202] However, FOS may make costs orders, including

---

required (under Section 231 or otherwise) to produce; (e) allow an Ombudsman to fix time limits for any aspect of the proceedings and to extend a time limit; (f) provide for certain things in relation to the reference, investigation, or consideration (but not determination) of a complaint to be done by the member of the scheme operator staff instead of by an ombudsman; (g) make different provision in relation to different kinds of complaint'. Para 14(3) allows for the dismissal of complaints 'without consideration of its merits' to include complaints which are frivolous or vexatious, complaints best dealt with in legal proceedings, or if there are 'other compelling reasons'.

[194] Sched 17, para 14(4)–(7).
[195] Sched 17, Part IV.
[196] Sched 17, para 18.
[197] Para 18(3).
[198] Para 18(5).
[199] Para 19.
[200] ibid.
[201] Para 22.
[202] FSMA, s 230(3).

an award against a complainant 'for the purpose of providing a contribution to resources deployed in dealing with the complaint' under the compulsory jurisdiction if the consumer's conduct was improper or unreasonable or responsible for an unreasonable delay.[203] Costs awards due to FOS are recoverable as a debt,[204] and costs awards against the respondent firm are to be treated as a money award for the purposes of enforcement.[205]

Funding

7.80　FOS is funded by the financial services industry under rules made by the FSA (see below).[206] Complainants are not to be charged. Fees are to be paid to FOS by firms (or via the OFT for consumer credit jurisdiction) but FSMA allows for the rules to include a reduction or waiver of fees, different fees for different stages of a complaint, a refund of fees, and different arrangements for different complaints.[207]

DISP—jurisdiction of FOS

7.81　The essential requirements for a complaint to FOS are that the complainant is an 'eligible complainant'; the complaint is subject to the compulsory or voluntary jurisdiction, both in terms of the firm and the activity giving rise to the complaint; for compulsory jurisdiction, the act or omission complained of occurred after N2 (otherwise the complaint has to be dealt with on the terms of the relevant predecessor scheme, if any); and the firm must have failed to resolve the complaint (to the complainant's satisfaction) within eight weeks.

7.82　There are transitional arrangements dealing with complaints which were, or would otherwise have been, made to one of the pre-existing dispute resolution services (which are part of the compulsory jurisdiction for former members).[208] The procedures for such claims may be modified by DISP to follow the rules of the relevant predecessor scheme, which are not considered here.

7.83　DISP Chapter 2 deals with FOS's jurisdiction.

Time limits

7.84　There are time limits for making complaints to FOS.[209] A complaint cannot be made to FOS less than eight weeks after receipt of the complaint by the firm,

---

[203] ibid, s 230(4).
[204] ibid, s 230(6).
[205] ibid, s 230(7).
[206] ibid, ss 234, 234A.
[207] ibid, Sched 17, para 15.
[208] Financial Services and Markets Act 2000 (Transitional Provisions) (Ombudsman Scheme and Complaints Scheme) Order 2001.
[209] DISP 2.8.1R.

unless the firm has already sent its 'final response'. After the final response has been sent, properly advising the complainant of the possibility of referring the matter to FOS (including contact details), a complaint cannot be made to FOS more than six months later. Complaints cannot be first made (to the firm or FOS) more than six years from the event complained of or, if later, more than three years from the date on which the complainant became aware or ought reasonably to have become aware of the cause for complaint, in the absence of any prior (and acknowledged or recorded) referral within that period of the complaint to the firm or FOS.[210] This reflects the law on limitation in England and Wales, ie the standard six-year limitation period for claims in contract and tort, subject to the three-year extension applicable in negligence claims, save that a 15-year 'long stop' is not applied under DISP. The time limits do not apply in exceptional circumstances or where the firm does not object, but otherwise the firm can reject such complaints without considering the merits.[211]

7.85 The position on limitation is modified for mortgage endowment 'risk' complaints.[212] For these complaints, the firm must have written to the complainant warning of a high risk that the endowment policy will not produce a sum large enough to repay the target amount (known as a 'red letter') which triggers the three-year period of knowledge for the complaint, together with a warning (of at least six months) of the expiry of the time limit. Failure to give such warning will mean that time for making the complaint will not start to run for the purpose of a complaint to the FOS. These time limits do not apply to claims in respect of past business reviews, in particular the Pension Review and the FSAVC Review, and also for any future review of past business approved by HM Treasury.[213]

Eligible complainant

7.86 FOS is to serve consumers, ie private individuals and small businesses and organisations. The protection is made available to those consumers who need it most. A business, charity, or trust, is 'eligible' subject to group annual turnover, annual income, or net asset value respectively being less than £1 million. [214] This test for eligible complainant was unchanged after consultation as part of the FSA and FOS Consultation Paper 05/15 (Review of Compensation Scheme and Ombudsman Scheme limits and miscellaneous amendments to the Compensation Sourcebook; dated 15 December 2005) but the 'small business' test is proposed to change to 'micro-enterprise' once FOS's jurisdiction is extended to cover payment service providers. Following implementation of MiFID, a 'professional client' or

---

[210] DISP 2.8.2.R.
[211] DISP 1.8.1.R.
[212] DISP 2.8.7.R.
[213] DISP 2.8.5R.
[214] DISP 2.7.3R.

an 'eligible counterparty' is excluded,[215] as well as firms complaining in respect of an activity for which they hold a permission.[216] For consumer credit business, further exclusions apply, eg a body corporate or a partnership of more than three persons,[217] A complainant must have had one of the specified relationships with the firm: a complaint is generally only accepted by FOS if it arises out of a customer or potential customer relationship.[218] There are specific categories of eligible 'indirect complaints' which allow complaints where the complainant may have a legitimate ground for dispute with the regulated firm but is not the identified customer.[219]

7.87   Complaints may be made by a representative of a complainant, where authorised by the complainant or by law.[220] The complainant does not need to live or be based in the UK.

Firms and activities—the compulsory jurisdiction

7.88   With some limited exceptions, all authorised firms are subject to the compulsory jurisdiction.[221] Compulsory jurisdiction applies to acts or omissions by an authorised firm carrying out a regulated activity, and firms are responsible for complaints against their appointed representatives.[222] Compulsory jurisdiction was extended to credit unions from 2 July 2002, to mortgage business on 31 October 2004 and to general insurance broking from 14 January 2005—the Insurance Mediation Directive ('IMD')[223] requires adequate complaints handling processes. MiFID also refers to an 'extra-judicial mechanism for investors' complaints'.[224] A list of regulated activities is at DISP 2 Annex 1. In addition to the FSA regulated firms, covering about 21,000 firms, consumer credit (regulated by the Office of Fair

---

[215] DISP 2.7.9(2)R.
[216] DISP 2.7.9(1)R.
[217] DISP 2.7.9(3)R.
[218] DISP 2.7.6.R.
[219] The examples are beneficiaries of personal or shareholder pension schemes, beneficiaries or intended beneficiaries of insurance contracts (eg employees covered by a group permanent health policy taken out and arranged by the employer but which provides benefits for the employee); those who have given a firm a guarantee or security for a mortgage or loan; those who have relied upon a cheque guarantee card issued by a firm; the true owner of a cheque or bill of exchange collected by a firm for someone else's account; the recipient of a banker's reference given by a firm; or the holder of units in a collective investment firm or a holder of units in a collective investment scheme where the firm is the 'operator' or 'depository', as defined by the FSA Handbook Glossary, providers of guarantees or securities for mortgages or loans, various complaints under the Consumer Credit Act, as well as complaints by a beneficiary against a trust or estate of which the respondent firm is trustee or personal representative.
[220] DISP 2.7.1–2R.
[221] DISP 2.3.
[222] DISP 2.3.3G.
[223] 2002/92/EC, Art 10.
[224] Art 53.

Trading) was added from April 2007 and includes 'licensees' under the Consumer Credit Act 1974, not just FSMA authorised firms.[225] Compulsory jurisdiction also includes some banking services—lending money secured by a charge on land (ie mortgages), lending money other than 'restricted credit', paying money by a 'plastic card' (ie credit cards), and 'ancillary banking services',[226] which services'[227] include the operation of cash machines and of safe deposit boxes. Compulsory jurisdiction also catches any connected ancillary activities.[228] With effect from 1 January 2009, 'connected travel insurance' is due to become a regulated activity and part of FOS's compulsory jurisdiction.[229]

The scope of voluntary jurisdiction is offered for activities which were not, but are **7.89** now, regulated or would be regulated activities (or consumer credit activities) if carried on from an establishment in the UK, the banking activities noted above, general and long-term insurance mediation and National Savings & Investments.[230] The Post Office also joined with effect from February 2008. It allows participation for activities before they become regulated. Voluntary jurisdiction also includes 'ancillary activities' provided in connection with these identified activities.

The territorial scope of FOS jurisdiction is limited to activities carried on from an **7.90** establishment in the UK.[231] There is some extension under voluntary jurisdiction for insurance and banking, if the activity is elsewhere in the EEA and directed wholly or partly at the UK, is governed by contracts made under the law of England and Wales, Scotland, or Northern Ireland, and the home State EEA Regulator has been notified by the firm that it intends to participate in the FOS voluntary jurisdiction.[232]

FOS procedures

DISP 3 sets out the procedures for assessing complaints and grounds for rejection, **7.91** including evidence and time limits, how FOS will determine what is 'fair and reasonable', the types of loss and damage for which awards may be made, the limits on awards, and what awards may be made for costs.

---

[225] DISP 2.4.1R.
[226] DISP 2.3.1R.
[227] Previously at DISP 2.6.6G.
[228] DISP 2.3.1R.
[229] FSA Consultation Paper 07/22: 'Regulating Connected Travel Insurance' (December 2007).
[230] DISP 2.5.1R.
[231] DISP 2.6.1.R, 2.6.3R.
[232] DISP 2.6.4R.

Dismissal of a complaint

7.92 Before assessing the merits of a complaint, the Ombudsman may make a decision that the complaint (or complainant) is ineligible, or that the complaint should otherwise be dismissed without consideration of its merits.[233] Before a complaint is dismissed as 'out of jurisdiction', the parties must have the opportunity to comment and, when making the decision, FOS must give reasons to the complainant.[234]

7.93 Before complaints are dismissed 'without consideration of the merits',[235] the complainant will be given an opportunity to make representations and receive a reasoned decision. Dismissal might arise where the Ombudsman is satisfied the complainant has not suffered real loss or harm, the complaint is 'frivolous or vexatious', or has no 'reasonable prospect of success'. Firms may be reassured that a complaint may be dismissed if it is about 'the legitimate exercise of a firm's commercial judgement'. Complaints about investment performance (not involving negligence or maladministration) or the exercise of discretion under a rule, or the failure to consult beneficiaries before exercising such discretion where there is no legal obligation to do so, or where not all potential complainants have consented to the referral of the complaint, may also be dismissed. Other grounds to reject a complaint at this stage include if the matter has been subject to scrutiny either under and in accordance with standards of a past business review, or by FOS (unless new evidence is available) or a former scheme or a comparable dispute resolution process or by the court, or is more suitable for such scrutiny. Employee disputes can also be dismissed. DISP includes, as a catch all, 'other compelling reasons'.[236] If the complainant consents, complaints may also be referred to another more suitable complaints scheme.[237]

7.94 In addition, a complaint may be dismissed where a firm has made an offer which is 'fair and reasonable in relation to the circumstances alleged by the complainant and which is still open for acceptance'.[238] FOS might seek to negotiate a settlement between the parties, and it is expressly contemplated FOS will seek to resolve complaints between the parties by mediation or other means, such as an investigation and provisional assessment.[239]

Test cases

7.95 A test case procedure was introduced after the 'N2 plus 2' review of FOS. If satisfied that a complaint raises an 'important or novel point of law, which has

---

[233] FSMA, Sched 17, para 14(2)(b).
[234] DISP 3.2R.
[235] DISP 3.3.1R.
[236] DISP 3.3.4(17)R.
[237] DISP 3.4.1R.
[238] DISP 3.3.4(4)R.
[239] DISP 3.5.1R.

important consequences', the complaint may be dismissed, to be considered by a court as a test case.[240] If at the request of the firm, the firm must undertake to meet the complaint's costs.

Complaint investigation procedures

FOS's processes are designed to comply with requirements of the Human Rights **7.96** Act 1998, and in particular Article 6 of the European Convention on Human Rights ('ECHR'). Under Article 6, parties are entitled to 'a fair and public hearing within a reasonable time by an independent and impartial tribunal established by law' in the determination of any civil rights and obligations. FOS makes awards binding on firms. Accordingly, complainants and firms have the opportunity of making representations to FOS, and commenting on a 'provisional assessment' (sometimes referred to as a 'view').[241] This provisional determination should summarise the complaint and relevant facts and indicate a proposed decision, on which the 'losing' party (or sometimes both sides) can comment. If disputed, the matter is reconsidered. Alternatively an 'adjudication' may be issued to both parties, which is referred to an Ombudsman if disputed by any party (in effect, an 'appeal'). In 2007/08, nine out of every 10 cases were resolved by adjudicators (by adjudication, settlement, or mediation).[242] Generally complaints are decided on the basis of paperwork but parties may seek to make oral representations at a hearing, before the complaint is finally determined, subject to satisfying the Ombudsman that the issues are material and that a hearing will help.[243] The Ombudsman will decide whether a hearing should be held (usually after an adjudication and before any final decision) and, if so, whether by telephone, in public or in private,[244] having regard to the ECHR.[245] In practice, hearings are rare and if a firm requests a hearing, the complainant must also have the opportunity of attending, if necessary with representation. The hearing is not a 'trial' on an adversarial basis at which there is a cross-examination of the complainant or witnesses at the end of which 'judgment' is delivered, but part of FOS's investigation into the issues which allows the parties to address the Ombudsman directly. The Ombudsman is likely to reserve the matter for further consideration.

The flexibility and informality of the complaint process allows the Ombudsman **7.97** to consider what evidence is required and how that should be presented.[246] Firms are to cooperate fully with FOS in the handling of complaints.[247] Normally a

---

[240] DISP 3.3.5R.
[241] DISP 3.5.4R.
[242] FOS Annual Review 2007/08.
[243] DISP 3.5.5R.
[244] DISP 3.5.6.R.
[245] DISP 3.5.7G.
[246] DISP 3.5.8R.
[247] DISP 1.4.4R.

written complaint form is submitted, and further issues are dealt with in correspondence or by telephone, not usually by face-to-face meetings. A firm may be
asked to submit witness statements. A respondent firm would be expected to be
able to produce contemporaneous letters and notes from its file. Complaints may
be decided on the basis of evidence available or dismissed in the absence of information.[248] Evidence of third parties, including the FSA and experts, may be taken
into account.[249] Evidence may be excluded if it would be inadmissible before a
court, but the Ombudsman is not bound by rules of admissibility. Evidence may
also be received by FOS in confidence[250] so that the other party only sees an edited
version. Facts are determined on the balance of probabilities.

7.98 When considering or investigating a complaint, FOS is entitled to disclose information to parties to the complaint or as part of his determination process. For
compulsory jurisdiction, a party's dealings with the Ombudsman attract the privilege from defamation allowed for court proceedings.[251] The Ombudsman must
have regard to the parties' rights to privacy,[252] and does not have to disclose information under the Data Protection Act 1998 if that would prejudice performance
of its function.[253] As noted above, the Ombudsman has the power to require parties to the complaint to provide specified information which it considers necessary
for the fair determination of the complaint.[254] Failure to comply with a requirement allows the court to deal with the person as if they were in contempt.[255]

7.99 The Ombudsman has the discretion to fix, and extend, any time limits during the
determination process.[256] A failure by a firm to comply with time limits might
lead to an award for any material distress or material inconvenience caused to the
complainant.[257] If a time limit is not met by either party, the Ombudsman may
proceed regardless or dismiss the complaint.[258]

The decision

7.100 An important feature of the FOS process is that complaints are determined by
what is 'fair and reasonable in all the circumstances of the case'.[259] This includes,
but is not limited to, legal liability. The Ombudsman is to 'take into account the

---

[248] DISP 3.5.9R.
[249] DISP 3.5.12G.
[250] DISP 3.5.10G.
[251] FSMA, Sched 17, para 11.
[252] DISP 3.8.1R.
[253] FSMA, s 233.
[254] ibid, s 231.
[255] ibid, s 232.
[256] DISP 3.5.13R.
[257] DISP 3.5.14R.
[258] DISP 3.5.14(1)R, 3.5.15R.
[259] FSMA, s 228(2).

relevant law, and regulations, Regulator's rules, guidance and standards, codes of practice and, where appropriate, what he considers to have been good industry practice at the relevant time'.[260] For example, FOS welcomed the ABI guidance on handling health insurance complaints, which set standards for the industry.[261] The FSA may also approve Industry Guidance—although that cannot affect the rights of third parties, such as consumers, it may help FOS to establish what was thought a good practice at the time or explain that a firm's approach was not unique.[262] FOS seeks to be consistent in its interpretation of the law, and its approach to complaints of a similar type. In practice this may be done by identifying 'lead cases'. The outcome of a lead case is then applied to 'follow on' cases, ie those which turn on the same findings required to determine the lead case. The Court of Appeal, in *R (Heather Moor & Edgecomb Ltd) v FOS*, approved FOS's approach to a complaint based on legal analysis of the relevant standard of care, and noted the need for FOS to be consistent in its decisions.

7.101 The determination of an Ombudsman must be made in writing, signed with reasons.[263] If accepted by the complainant, it is binding on the complainant and the firm—if rejected by the complainant it is not binding on either the complainant or the firm. Following the 'N2 plus 2' review, the FSA confirmed there was not to be any right of appeal from an Ombudsman decision, which the Hunt Report supports.

7.102 A decision may include a money award of 'fair compensation', an interest award, a costs award, or a direction to take 'just and appropriate' steps.[264] The money award may include both financial loss and pain and suffering or damage to reputation or distress and inconvenience (including distress and inconvenience suffered during the course of the complaint).[265] The maximum money award is £100,000[266] plus any interest and costs, although more may be recommended.[267] The FSA consulted on a proposal to increase the limit to £200,000 but did not do so.[268] Where the complaint involves more than one firm, the Ombudsman may direct how the award is allocated[269] after investigating such connected complaints together.[270]

---

[260] DISP 3.6.4R.

[261] FOS Corporate Plan & 2008/09 Budget (January 2008).

[262] FSA: 'Policy Statement 07/16 on Industry Guidance' (September 2007).

[263] DISP 3.6.6.R.

[264] DISP 3.7.1R.

[265] DISP 3.7.2R.

[266] DISP 3.7.4R.

[267] DISP 3.7.6G.

[268] FSA Consultation Paper 05/15: 'Review of Compensation Scheme and Ombudsman Services limits and miscellaneous amendments to the Compensation Sourcebook' (December 2005).

[269] DISP 3.6.3G.

[270] DISP 3.5.3G.

7.103 After consultation, the FSA withdrew the original proposal to cap amounts awarded for distress and inconvenience, but the usual amount is £100–£500. Awards of £1,000 or more are exceptional. FOS has published details of how such awards are usually approached.[271] Any award for interest[272] or costs 'reasonably incurred by the complainant' is not subject to the £100,000 cap,[273] but FOS tells complainants that usually they do not require professional advice, and costs awards are uncommon.[274] A firm must comply with an award accepted by the complainant[275] which is binding (or any earlier agreed settlement) and FOS must maintain a register of money awards and directions made[276]—as noted, a money award can be recovered or enforced with the courts,[277] and a direction can be enforced by injunction.[278]

7.104 FOS is not able to direct a firm to pay redress, the cost of which exceeds the monetary limit (currently £100,000). Any such direction is subject to an 'implicit limitation that it will not be enforced' against the firm.[279]

7.105 In December 2003, the Board of FOS commissioned the Personal Finance Research Centre at the University of Bristol 'to carry out an independent assessment of the work of FOS'. The report, dated July 2004,[280] concluded that the 'case handling process' was 'both robust and fit for purpose. It complies with principles of due and fair process, and ensures that cases are considered on their merits'.

Voluntary jurisdiction

7.106 Unlike the DISP Rules made by the FSA prescribing the scope of compulsory jurisdiction, voluntary jurisdiction is subject to the 'standard terms' made by FOS, with the approval of the FSA, and set out at DISP Chapter 4, to which firms commit on a contractual basis. In short, the DISP Rules otherwise applicable are generally extended for voluntary jurisdiction participants, including the complaint handling procedures of the firms themselves (at DISP 1), the rules and guidance (at DISP 2), and the complaints handling procedures (at DISP 3).

---

[271] Technical Note: 'Compensation for distress, inconvenience or other non-financial loss' (July 2008).
[272] DISP 3.7.8R.
[273] DISP 3.7.9R.
[274] DISP 3.7.10G.
[275] DISP 3.7.12R.
[276] DISP 3.7.7R.
[277] FSMA, Sched 17, para 16.
[278] ibid, s 229(9).
[279] *Bunney v Burns Anderson plc* [2007] EWHC 1240 (Ch).
[280] 'Fair and reasonable. An assessment of the Financial Ombudsman Service'.

The exemption from liability in damages in Schedule 17 to the Act is included in   **7.107**
DISP for the voluntary jurisdiction function,[281] and the provisions for the making
of awards and their enforcement are similarly extended by the Rules.[282]

Firms may withdraw from voluntary jurisdiction, subject to satisfying FOS's con-   **7.108**
ditions.[283] In particular, a firm must provide to FOS a written plan explaining how
customers will be notified to offer withdrawal from voluntary jurisdiction and the
continuing of handling complaints prior to this withdrawal, which plan must be
approved by FOS. The firm must also be up to date in meeting levies and fees.

Funding

With effect from 1 January 2006, the funding regime is now in Chapter 5 of the   **7.109**
FEES Module of the Handbook. Firms (including those under the consumer
credit and voluntary jurisdictions) are to pay annual fees of a general levy and case
fees, unless a firm is exempt (ie has no reasonable likelihood of conducting business with eligible claimants).[284] As such, large institutional firms, market counterparties, and the like do not contribute to the funding of FOS.

The raising of levies follows the approval by the FSA of FOS's annual budget.[285]   **7.110**
Generally, firms pay both a general levy and case fees (but for consumer credit,
different rules apply). A 'supplementary levy' was previously raised for the costs
of establishing FOS.[286] In 2007/08, £19.5 million was to be raised by levy and
£35 million received in case fees. The budget for 2008/09 provides a levy/case
fee split of about 30/70 (in line with previous years). Firms must contribute to the
general levy.[287] The general levy is apportioned between firms according to the
relevant 'tariff basis' and the extent of 'relevant business' of the firm, detailed for
15 (of the 17) industry blocks.[288] Firms with higher levels of relevant business
generally pay a higher levy, although the methodology varies between industry
blocks—some firms pay a flat fee, others pay a variable fee calculated by reference
to size and levels of business. The calculation of the general levy is based on information submitted by firms each year to the FSA (and is collected for FOS by the
FSA).[289] In addition there is a 'standard case fee' which is payable in respect of

---

[281] DISP 4.2.8R.
[282] DISP 4.2.4–5R.
[283] DISP 4.2.7R.
[284] FEES 5.1.4R.
[285] FSMA, Sched 17, para 9.
[286] FEES 5.6.
[287] FEES 5.3.6R.
[288] FEES 5 Annex 1R.
[289] FEES 5.4.1R.

complaints closed by FOS.[290] This is to ensure that firms which generate complaints contribute proportionately higher amounts to FOS's costs, although small credit unions, cash plan heath providers, and small friendly societies are exempt.[291] The standard case fee is consulted on each year, and is presently £450,[292] but firms are not now charged for the first three complaints each year.[293] A 'special case fee' is payable in respect of complaints from small businesses, complaints against firms which ceased to be authorised, and complaints against persons who are subject to a former scheme (where complaints are dealt with under the transitional provisions) and who do not pay the general levy. The special case fee is also £450.

7.111 The voluntary jurisdiction firms pay under the 'standard terms'.[294] There are seven voluntary jurisdiction 'blocks' applying a range of general tariff measures (eg for National Savings & Investments a £10,000 flat fee applies). For the consumer credit jurisdiction, the contribution under section 234A may comprise the costs of establishing FOS for this purpose, FOS's operation of this jurisdiction, and 'collection costs'. The OFT imposes and collects the contributions from each relevant firm.

7.112 Whether the general levy, or a case fee, payment is to be made by a firm within 30 calendar days of the date of the invoice[295]—issued by the FSA for the general levy or by FOS for case fees.[296]

7.113 Unpaid levies or case fees attract an administrative fee of £250 and interest at a rate of 5 per cent over the Bank of England's repo rate on the outstanding portion.[297] FOS may take steps to recover payment and refer non-paying firms to the FSA.[298] Both the FSA and FOS have the discretion to reduce or refund a fee if it is inequitable due to exceptional circumstances of a particular case but firms may not seek to recover any overpayment due to mistake after two years.[299]

7.114 New joiners to FOS receive a discounted general fee depending on which quarter of the financial year the firm joins. The fee is reduced by 25 per cent per quarter.[300] Departing firms remain liable to pay both standard and special case fees, and do not receive a refund of any general levy, except in exceptional circumstances.[301]

---

[290] FSMA, Sched 17, para 15; FEES 5.5.1R.
[291] FEES 5.5.3–4R.
[292] FEES 5 Annex 1.
[293] FEES 5.5.15R.
[294] FSMA, Sched 17, para 18.
[295] FEES 5.7.
[296] FEES 5.7.2R.
[297] FEES 2.2.1R.
[298] FEES 2.2.3–4G.
[299] FEES 2.3.
[300] FEES 5.8.1R.
[301] FEES 5.9.

In its report, the Personal Finance Research Centre identified alternative methods **7.115** of raising fees, including a tiered structure by reference to 'detriment' or charges linked to time spent on a case, but preferred the current system.

The Court of Appeal considered FOS's funding in the recent case of *FOS v Heather,* **7.116** *Moor & Edgecomb Ltd*.[302] The Trowbridge County Court had found FOS's case fees to be 'unreasonable' and dismissed FOS's claim to enforce payment against a firm. On appeal, it was found that the rule requiring payment of the standard case fee was not unreasonable and not unlawful, so that if a complaint is investigated the case fee is properly payable. Stanley Burnton LJ commented that 'a system under which firms make a payment of a fee in respect of the services of the Ombudsman in investigating and deciding complaints against them is, in my judgement, a perfectly rational response to the need to fund the scheme'.[303]

FOS's experience

FOS's Annual Review for 2007/08 confirmed the huge growth in the number of **7.117** complaints to FOS. From 28,400 complaints, 340 staff, and a budget of £21 million reported for 2000/02, FOS received 123,089 new cases, had 825 staff, and a budget of £55 million in 2007/08.

FOS—cases arising

FOS has been faced with significant and difficult cases to resolve. Of the early **7.118** caseload, the decisions regarding dual rate mortgages received much attention. FOS received complaints from borrowers whose lender was operating two 'stand-ard' variable borrowing rates, and pre-existing borrowers were being placed on the higher of the two rates upon the expiry of fixed term mortgage deals. The lower standard rate was not being made available to such pre-existing customers. FOS dealt with these complaints by using the 'lead case' procedure. The decision against the use of dual standard variable rates led to mortgage lenders changing their practice. FOS determined the complaint by reference to what was 'fair in the circumstances of the case taking into account the law, the principles of the mort-gage code, and good industry practice'.[304]

The uncertainties surrounding the Equitable Life Assurance Society Limited **7.119** ('ELAS') have also included a large number of complaints against that firm. By its

---

[302] [2008] EWCA Civ 643.
[303] Stanley Burnton LJ also noted that the 'FSA rules require firms to deal with complaints fairly and effectively and a complaint to FOS is likely to be made only when a firm's response to a complaint is regarded by the complainant as unsatisfactory'.
[304] FOS briefing note dated 12 September 2002.

'lead' case procedure, FOS upheld a complaint from a guaranteed annuity rate policyholder (decision dated March 2005), clearing the way for 'follow-on' cases. In contrast, by a decision dated 22 March 2005, the Chief Ombudsman dismissed a batch of complaints regarding alleged 'over bonusing' by ELAS, as referred to by Lord Penrose.[305] Because of the number of complaints, and level of both policyholders' and public interest, FOS published the reasons for its decision to dismiss the complaints in this case. FOS noted that the issue had already been considered in detail by the FSA, that the complaints by policyholders would be better dealt with by the court, and that if successful, the outcome of complaints could have wider implications in terms of the company's policyholders and would have added to the 'turbulence affecting this aspect of the affairs of [ELAS] and its members'. The Chief Ombudsman exercised the discretion to dismiss the complaints without consideration of their merits.

7.120 Mortgage endowment cases have been the largest single source of complaints for FOS, totalling over 265,000 complaints. FOS has published David Severn's report on the history of these complaints.[306]

7.121 In the light of the waiver from DISP granted to banks for complaints about unauthorised overdraft charges, in July 2007, FOS decided to put individual complaints on hold until the outcome of the OFT test case is known (except for hardship cases) as 'the law is one of the things that the ombudsman has to take into account when [FOS] decide cases. So [FOS has] decided not to continue our work on unauthorised overdraft charges until the legal position has been clarified'.[307]

Challenges to FOS

7.122 As the FOS exercises a public function, and may make decisions based on 'fair and reasonable', a firm wishing to challenge a decision needs to overcome the threshold and test of judicial review proceedings. The applicant is to show that the decision was illegal, procedurally improper, or irrational, and may fail to do so even if the court accepts it does not owe any legal liability or that the Ombudsman had misinterpreted the relevant contracts and applicable code of practice.[308] Although in the *Norwich and Peterborough Building Society* case the court found that the decision had failed to take a material consideration into account, the Ombudsman

---

[305] Report of the Equitable Life Inquiry by Lord Penrose printed on 8 March 2004.

[306] The Financial Ombudsman Service and mortgage endowment complaints, published by FOS on 29 May 2008.

[307] FOS FAQ on complaints about bank charges (updated 23 May 2008).

[308] *R v Financial Ombudsman Service Ltd, ex parte Norwich & Peterborough Building Society & others* [2002] EWHC 2379.

was entitled to exercise his own judgement as to fairness and in doing so had not acted irrationally. Accordingly, the court did not impose its own view of fairness, and the decision was upheld. In a later case,[309] the court upheld the decision of the Ombudsman as to 'fair' compensation, even though damages would not have been awarded by a court for the loss. Under section 228(2) and DISP 3.8.1R, provided the position at law had been taken into account, the court held that the Ombudsman was free to make an award above the damages a court would find: 'the Ombudsman is free to make an award which differs from that which a court applying the law would make, provided he concludes that the award he wishes to make is one which is fair and reasonable in all the circumstances of the case and provided he has taken into account matters identified in Rule 3.8.1, paragraph (2)'.[310] Most recently, the Ombudsman's determination was upheld in *R (on the application of Williams) v FOS*[311] where the court was satisfied that the Ombudsman had been entitled to rely on his own expertise in considering the risks of an investment. The court noted that this would not be appropriate where the financial products were rare or complex, or their practical application was unknown, in which circumstances the Ombudsman would be expected to call on additional expertise.

7.123 FOS's approach to dealings with partners of a dissolved partnership was also upheld by the court, where despite writing to all former partners, FOS had only received, and taken into account, comments from one partner.[312] Hodge J found that the partner was 'clearly on notice and clearly had plenty of opportunity to put its submissions'. This approach of dealing with the one partner who can communicate with the others is now included in DISP.[313]

7.124 Although the upholding of a complaint was not overturned, in the *Garrison* case the court[314] did quash a decision as to the money award, which was returned to FOS for reconsideration. The court found that there was 'no logical connection between the redress ordered and the error found. In short, the redress does not fulfil the aim set by the Ombudsman himself and is, therefore, on its face, irrational'. FOS had applied a standard benchmark for the calculation of the award, not suited to the particular facts of the case.

---

[309] *R (IFG Financial Services Ltd) v Financial Ombudsman Service Ltd & others* [2005] EWHC 1153.

[310] Stanley Burnton J, para 76.

[311] [2008] All ER(D) 35 (Jul)

[312] *R v FOS, ex parte Bruce* [2007] EWHC 1646 (Admin).

[313] DISP 3.1.3.R.

[314] *R v FOS, ex parte Garrison* [2006] EWHC 2466 (Admin).

7.125 The Court of Appeal has recently examined FOS's statutory footing and responsibilities.[315] The firm challenged the decision of FOS on the following grounds:

    a) on its true construction Section 228(1) of [FSMA] requires FOS to determine complaints in accordance with the rules of English law;[316]

    b) that construction of [FSMA] is required in order to avoid an infringement of the [firm's] Convention rights under Article 6 and Article 1 of the First Protocol;

    c) in the present case, the Ombudsman failed to apply the rules of English law, or to take them into account, but instead made a decision by reference to what he considered to be fair and reasonable. It follows that his decision falls to be quashed for error of law. For this reason, his decision was one that no reasonable Ombudsman could have made;

    d) in any event, the Ombudsman should have held an oral hearing in public and he should have given his decision in public, but he wrongfully refused to do so.

7.126 The Court of Appeal dismissed the challenge; the reasons may be summarised as follows:

    (a) 'by the use of the formula in Section 228, Parliament excluded that possibility';

    (b) 'the rules applied by the Ombudsman are sufficiently predictable . . . Arbitrariness on the part of the Ombudsman including an unreasoned and unjustified failure to treat like cases alike, would be a ground for judicial review';

    (c) 'the Ombudsman was entitled to reach this conclusion on the evidence before him' and had applied the appropriate test; and

    (d) 'in the present case, the court is concerned with a scheme under which disputes may be resolved quickly and with minimum formality, a consideration that justifies holding a public oral hearing only when that is necessary fairly to determine the dispute in question . . . So far as the requirement under Article 6 of a public hearing is concerned, there has been a public hearing before this court, and a public hearing in judicial review proceedings is available to any complainant or respondent who considers that the Ombudsman has made an unlawful decision. More generally, where, as in the present case, a complaint can fairly be determined on written evidence and without oral submissions . . . given the nature of the jurisdiction and the desirability of speedy decision and minimum cost and with minimum formality, it is normally not necessary for the Ombudsman to hold a public hearing . . . the purpose of ensuring public scrutiny of the decisions of FOS is satisfied by the availability of judicial review proceedings in which any decision alleged to have been unfair or arbitrary or otherwise unlawful will be published. It follows that no breach of Article 6 has been established.'

---

[315] *R (Heather, Moor & Edgecomb Ltd) v FOS* [2008] EWCA Civ 642.
[316] Not on a 'fair and reasonable' basis.

FOS—the two-year review, DISP simplification, and the Hunt Report

Two issues were raised by the two-year review of FSMA in a joint consultation **7.127**
paper issued by the FSA and FOS.[317] This work was part of the FSA's TCF work.

The first issue was whether the decisions of FOS should be subject to an appeal, **7.128**
and the second was whether regulatory action by the FSA should replace decisions
on individual cases by FOS. FOS already referred to the FSA issues with regulatory implications under the existing MOU, but this was considered further. The
outcome of the consultation, reported in a joint FSA and FOS policy statement,[318]
rejected the prospect of appeals but agreed there would be benefit in greater
involvement of the FSA in cases with 'wider implications' and an improved
process for test cases.

This 'N2 plus 2' review took into account industry concerns that firms had no **7.129**
effective method of challenging decisions of FOS.[319] Firms expressed concern as
to the binding nature of FOS's decisions and the use of decisions as precedents
which impacted on firms' future conduct. Further, challenge was accepted as
being more difficult due to FOS's 'fair and reasonable' scope. The FSA concluded
that not only would amendment to primary legislation be required to provide
for an external appeals procedure but the current decision-making process of
an adjudicator and Ombudsman, and the availability of judicial review, was
adequate. Further, an appeal mechanism would increase FOS's costs and impede
speed and informality.

Notwithstanding the MOU between FOS and the FSA, and FOS's ability to **7.130**
disclose information to the FSA, the FSA acknowledged that communications
could be improved for cases with 'wider implications'. FOS and the FSA agreed to
liaise to identify and understand such cases. A test case procedure is now available
to firms to determine a novel point of law with significant consequences, providing the firm funds the complainant's case as well as its own, including in respect of
any appeal by the firm. When considering 'wider implications', FOS and the FSA
will have regard to factors such as a large number of customers, a large number of
firms, the financial integrity of a firm, interpretation of the FSA's rules or guidance, or common industry practice. The FSA will consider whether it needs to
comment on the interpretation or application of its rules, whether the case raises

---

[317] Consultation Paper 04/12: 'FSMA 2 Year Review: Financial Ombudsman Service' (July 2004).

[318] FSMA 2 Year Review: 'Financial Ombudsman Service, Feedback on CP 04/12 and supplementary FOS consultation on procedural rules' (March 2005).

[319] In HM Treasury's statement dated 4 November 2003, it was considered 'appropriate to examine
whether Ombudsman decisions should be subject to some form of appeal in specific circumstances.
It is vital that firms and consumers alike have confidence in the Ombudsman's decisions even when
they do not like them' (para 36).

material issues about existing FSA policy that require new rules or guidance, whether the FSA intends to take action either to obtain (more advantageous) redress for consumers or for enforcement, whether the FSA's investigation is likely to be more effective and timely than FOS's process, and whether HM Treasury should be asked to authorise an industry-wide review (under section 404 of FSMA). If the FSA does become involved, it may clarify the interpretation or application of a rule before FOS decides a case, or submit material to FOS for it to take into account in its decision.

7.131 The FSA has stated that FOS's decisions are not about enforcing FSA Rules; they are 'about protecting the rights of consumers'.[320] For a wider implications issue in which the FSA does not become involved, FOS may seek industry and consumer input. This might cover the wider context such as how widespread and longstanding the commercial practice in the market has been, why it was adopted, those affected (both firms and consumers), and their legitimate expectations, the relevant rules and codes of practice and generally accepted industry practice at the material time, consequences for the industry and consumers if the Ombudsman upholds or rejects a practice in an individual case, and the potential effect and practicability of different redress options.

7.132 In addition, the FSA confirmed the procedure which the Ombudsman would follow to obtain industry, consumer and expert input. Where and to the extent possible without breach of confidentiality, the FSA and FOS will publish information about wider implications, cases, and processes. The policy statement included details of cases where this had already been considered.

7.133 Since the 'N2 plus 2' review, DISP has undergone substantial amendment. Amended rules (at DISP 1) for handling complaints by firms generally came into force on 1 November 2007 and the revised ('clearer, shorter and easier to use') rules on the Ombudsman's jurisdiction and procedures came into force on 6 April 2008, so that DISP 2–4 is about a third shorter as a result.[321]

7.134 More recently, Lord Hunt carried out, at the invitation of the FOS, a review of FOS's relationship with consumers, the financial services industry, and other stakeholders. The Hunt Report made 73 recommendations. The core foundation of a 'fair and reasonable' decision, file-based reviews, no appeals, and no charge for complainants, were all approved by Lord Hunt. Lord Hunt called on FOS to

---

[320] FSA Policy Statement 07/16 (September 2007).

[321] FSA Consultation Paper 06/19: 'Reforming Conduct of Business Regulation' (October 2006) and FSA Policy Statement 07/09: 'Treating Customers Fairly—feedback on CP 06/19 (part) and made rules' (July 2007). Policy Statement 07/2: 'Implementing the Markets in Financial Instruments Directive' (January 2007). FSA and FOS Consultation Paper 07/14: 'Dispute Resolution; The Complaints Sourcebook—Further Simplification and Minor Changes' (July 2007); Policy Statement 08/3 (March 2008).

refocus on its founding principles of speed, informality, and independence, and noted 'if my conclusions are accepted and my recommendations implemented, I believe that the demographic profile of those using the FOS should, must, and will broaden . . .'. The Court of Appeal in *Edgecomb* acknowledged that FOS should not be stifled by the imposition of legal doctrine, and that the recommendations of the Hunt Report 'can do much to allay any concerns, in any important area of consumer dispute resolution, about the values and principles of what we know by the expression "the rule of law"'.

FOS welcomed the 'detailed and thought provoking report' noting that some of **7.135** the recommendations 'involved innovative—and sometimes radical—departures from current practice'.[322] FOS has since published two policy statements on accessibility and transparency setting out its 'decisions of principle' on these issues.[323] Responding to recommendations of the Hunt Report on accessibility, the policy statement reports, for example, that the FOS do not plan a name change, will

---

[322] FOS press release dated 9 April 2008. The press release summarised the report as follows:

In his review, Lord Hunt concludes that:
- the ombudsman's approach to settling disputes on the basis of 'what is fair and reasonable' is essential—to underpin the ombudsman's credibility as an informal non-legalistic alternative to the courts;
- charging consumers to access the ombudsman—as some have proposed—would comprehensively damage accessibility;
- there is no convincing case for an external appeals mechanism—on top of the ombudsman service's current internal appeals procedure;
- there should be no change to the ombudsman's current approach to formal hearings (holding them only where absolutely necessary—as most disputes can be decided on the basis of paper evidence);
- there is no requirement for a small firms' division—as long as the ombudsman's Small Businesses Taskforce continues to focus on the particular needs of small firms;
- there should be closer monitoring and regulation of the activities of claims management companies;
- there should be greater openness—in relation to the ombudsman's approach, the relationship between the ombudsman and the regulatory system, and the performance of individual financial services businesses in handling customer complaints.

Lord Hunt's review includes 73 specific recommendations for the ombudsman service, including:

- significantly increasing investment in pro-active communications—including TV advertising, consumer campaigns and strategic partnerships with government and others;
- commissioning a new consumer–friendly brand name instead of 'Ombudsman';
- offering a freephone service (instead of the current subsidised 0845 number) and extended opening hours;
- appointing 'case advisers'—working alongside adjudicators and ombudsmen —to guide the most vulnerable consumers through the complaints-handing process;
- launching an awards scheme to identify and reward businesses who handle complaints well—matched by a 'wooden spoon' for the worst performers;
- publishing comprehensive information on all aspects of ombudsman policy and methodology (but not decisions on all cases)—as well as benchmarked data on how individual financial services businesses handle complaints;
- placing all the ombudsman service's formal communication with the regulators on the public record.

[323] Policy statement: 'Improving service to our users: Our strategic approach to accessibility' (July 2008); Policy Statement: 'Our strategic approach to transparency' (July 2008).

consider the 'overall budgetary impact of providing calculations in compensation awards that involve a formula', and do not 'propose any changes to the status of ombudsman decisions—or to the current system involved in delivering ombudsman decisions'. The Policy Statement also considers numerous awareness and consumer proposals. FOS explain that the 'next corporate plan and budget (to be published in January 2009) will cover the impact on resources and cost—and therefore the timing of implementation'. On transparency, FOS have decided that its 'published material will continue to focus on how we approached the kinds of complaints that we have actually received . . .' and 'so do not propose to publish what our approach might be to hypothetical future cases'; 'case reports that focus on key principles' will also be published, to be integrated with an 'evolving online digest of [FOS] processes and approach'. Alongside the FSA's proposal to publish firms' complaints data, the FOS plan to publish 'information about individual businesses—both the numbers of cases and the proportion upheld', in 2009. A discussion paper will be published to explain what and how data could be published.

Financial Services Compensation Scheme

Introduction

7.136   One of the aims of FSMA was to 'rationalise the existing arrangements through the creation of a single ombudsman scheme and a single compensation scheme'.[324] Part XV provides for the Financial Services Compensation Scheme ('FSCS'). The FSCS replaced eight pre-existing compensation schemes or arrangements: the Deposit Protection Scheme;[325] the Building Societies Investor Protection Scheme;[326] the Policyholders Protection Scheme;[327] the Friendly Societies Protection Scheme;[328] the Investors Compensation Scheme ('ICS');[329] the PIA Indemnity Scheme;[330] the FSA's scheme covering 'Section 43 firms';[331] and the ABI Spouses and Dependants Scheme.[332] From 1 December 2001 to 2008, the FSCS paid total compensation of over £1 billion, of which about £500 million is in the insurance sector, and £400 million for investment claims (including Pension Review).[333]

---

[324]   HM Treasury: 'Financial Services and Markets Bill: a consultation document—Part 1, overview of financial regulatory reform' (July 1998).
[325]   Banking Act 1987.
[326]   Building Societies Acts 1986 and 1997.
[327]   Policyholders Protection Act 1975.
[328]   Friendly Societies Act 1992.
[329]   Financial Services Act 1986.
[330]   ibid.
[331]   ibid.
[332]   A voluntary industry scheme.
[333]   FSCS Annual Report 2007/08.

Following the banking crisis, in the autumn of 2008, FSCS paid billions of pounds to fund the transfers of deposit accounts. After events at Northern Rock in 2007, the nature and purpose of the FSCS had come under close scrutiny, which has continued with the Banking Bill.

As noted in HM Treasury's 1998 consultation, the regulatory system does not **7.137** guarantee the solvency or survival of authorised firms, as repeated recently by the Tripartite Authorities.[334] In its early consultation,[335] the FSA noted that 'effective compensation arrangements for customers where individual firms authorised by the FSA are no longer able to meet their liabilities to [consumers of financial services] will have a key role to play in achieving [the protection of consumers]'.[336] In addition to the consumer protection objective, the existence of a compensation scheme also supports the FSA's 'market confidence' objective. The CP noted that 'as well as providing protection in the last resort for consumers, the existence of compensation also helps to reduce the systemic risk that a single failure of a financial firm may trigger a wider loss of confidence in the rest of the financial sector concerned (eg through a run on deposit-taking institutions)'.[337] In the light of Northern Rock, significant reforms are proposed to improve the scheme from both consumer protection and market confidence perspectives, which are addressed below.

Firms are obliged to disclose the existence of the FSCS, and the availability of **7.138** compensation, to consumers, although firms are not to advertise prominently membership of a compensation scheme.[338] References in advertising are to be limited to a 'factual reference'. The reason for this is that it might otherwise affect 'stability of the financial system or investors confidence'.[339]

The Scheme Manager

The structure of compensation arrangements under the Act is similar to that **7.139** put in place for the scheme operator of FOS. The FSA 'must establish a body corporate' to act as the 'Scheme Manager' of the Financial Services Compensation Scheme.[340] Financial Services Compensation Scheme Limited, a company limited by guarantee, was established by the FSA as the Scheme Manager. The Scheme

---

[334] 'Financial stability and depositor protection: strengthening the framework' (January 2008).
[335] FSA Consultation Paper 5: 'Consumer Compensation' (December 1997) (CP5).
[336] Para 1.
[337] Para 11.
[338] COBS 4.4.1.R; COBS 5 Annex 1R; the Credit Institutions (Protection of Deposits) Regulations 1995 also apply to banks and building societies.
[339] Article 10(3) of the Investors Compensation Directive (1997/9/EC); see also Article 9(3) of the Deposit Guarantee Schemes Directive (1994/19/EC).
[340] FSMA, s 212(1).

Manager is to have a chairman and a Board, and its members are the Scheme Manager's directors.[341] The chairman and other members of the Board are appointed and removed by the FSA, with the approval of HM Treasury in the case of the chairman.[342] As explained by the FSA,[343] directors are recruited 'using Nolan-type procedures' and sit as 'public interest members, not as representatives of a particular group or industry sector'.[344]

7.140 The FSCS is to be accountable to, but operationally independent from, the FSA. The FSA must ensure that the FSCS is 'at all times capable of exercising' its functions under FSMA,[345] but the appointment of directors is to be on terms 'such as to secure their independence from [the FSA] in the operation of the compensation scheme'.[346] In CP5, the FSA explained: 'where the compensation arrangements are separate but still closely related to the regulator . . . this has the advantage of separating policy-making for the compensation arrangements, allowing the Board of the Scheme to concentrate on management of the claims process.'[347] The FSA/FSCS relationship was modelled on the pre-existing arrangements between SIB and the ICS. An MOU has been agreed (and published) between the FSA and the FSCS which recognises the FSCS's independence but addresses the 'need to cooperate and communicate constructively'.[348] The FSCS is required to provide an annual report to the FSA.[349] The FSA exercises further oversight by fixing the amount of 'management expenses' which may be levied by the FSCS.[350]

The Scheme

7.141 The FSA is to 'by Rules establish a scheme for compensating persons in cases where relevant persons are unable, or are likely to be unable, to satisfy claims against them'.[351] This set of rules, the Compensation ('COMP') Sourcebook in the FSA's Handbook, is the 'Financial Services Compensation Scheme'.[352] This framework followed the approach of section 54 of the Financial Services Act 1986.

---

[341] ibid, s 212(3).

[342] ibid, s 212(4).

[343] FSA Consultation Paper 24: 'FSA—Consumer Compensation: Further Consultation' (June 1999).

[344] Para 7.3.

[345] FSMA, s 212(2).

[346] ibid, s 212(5).

[347] Para 64.

[348] Para 1.

[349] ibid, s 218.

[350] ibid, s 223; 'management expenses' are defined at s 223(3) as 'expenses incurred, or expected to be incurred, by the Scheme Manager in connection with its functions under this Act other than those incurred (a) in paying compensation; (b) as a result of any provision of the scheme made by virtue of Section 216(3) or (4) or 217(1) or (6)' (which sections provide for alternative forms of protection).

[351] FSMA, s 213(1).

[352] ibid, s 213(2).

'Relevant person' includes 'an authorised person at the time the act or omission **7.142** giving rise to the claim against him took place' and 'an appointed representative at that time'.[353] Business carried on by interim authorised firms is not protected.[354] 'Claims' is not defined by FSMA, but in the FSA's Glossary (as 'a valid claim made in respect of a civil liability'). The Scheme is to deal both with the assessment and payment of compensation 'in respect of claims made in connection with regulated activities', and its funding with 'power to impose levies on authorised persons, or any class of authorised person'.[355] The further provisions in Part XV are not to limit FSA general power to establish the Scheme.[356]

FSMA provides the FSCS with certain powers to obtain information for the **7.143** 'efficient settlement of claims'.[357] The FSCS may seek from a 'relevant person', in respect of whom a claim is made under the Scheme, 'specified information' or 'specified documents' where these are considered to be 'necessary for the fair determination of the claim' or alternatively 'to be necessary (or likely to be necessary) for the fair determination of other claims made (or which the FSCS expects may be made) in respect of the relevant person concerned'.[358] These powers may be enforced by contempt proceedings.[359] In addition, information may also be obtained from a person 'knowingly involved in the act or omission giving rise to the claim' (but not generally from third parties holding information). The FSCS has the right to inspect relevant documents held by insolvency practitioners[360] and by the Official Receiver.[361] The FSA and the FSCS may also disclose information to each other for the discharge of their respective functions.[362]

As with the FSA and FOS, the FSCS has statutory immunity under FSMA.[363] **7.144** Subject to the same exceptions for acts or omissions in bad faith or unlawful as a result of section 6(1) of the Human Rights Act 1998, statutory immunity is provided for damages 'for anything done or omitted in the discharge, or purported discharge, of the Scheme Manager's functions'. The FSA must, however, establish ECHR compliant procedures 'for the handling of any complaints of

---

[353] ibid, s 213(9).
[354] See the treatment of mortgage and insurance brokers with interim authorised status after 31 October 2004 and 14 January 2005 respectively.
[355] FSMA, s 213(3)(b).
[356] ibid, s 213(7).
[357] FSMA Explanatory Notes.
[358] FSMA, s 219.
[359] ibid, s 221.
[360] ibid, s 220.
[361] ibid, s 224.
[362] Financial Services and Markets Act 2000 (Disclosure of Information by Prescribed Persons) Regulations 2001, SI 2001/1857; Financial Services and Markets Act 2000 (Disclosure of Confidential Information) Regulations 2001, SI 2001/2188.
[363] FSMA, s 222.

maladministration relating to any aspect of the operation of the compensation scheme'.[364]

Provisions of the Scheme

7.145 FSMA allows for the COMP Rules to provide for the circumstances in which a relevant person may trigger the scheme; the type of eligible claimant and eligible claim; the procedure to be followed in making a claim; the making of interim payments; limits on the compensation amounts; and for payment to be made to persons other than the claimant, as well as for its funding by levy on authorised firms.[365] This is a non-exhaustive list. FSMA notes that 'different provision may be made with respect to different kinds of claim'.[366]

7.146 In contrast to FOS's regime under the DISP Rules, the FSCS operates five different 'sub-schemes', some of which are markedly different to the others. This reflects the different policy approaches towards different sectors of the financial services market. It is also a legacy of the pre-existing compensation arrangements; there are transitional arrangements for claims against firms which failed, or claims which arise in respect of acts or omissions which occurred, before FSMA took effect.[367]

7.147 At 1 December 2001, the Scheme comprised three sub-schemes—accepting deposits, insurance business, and designated investment business. In these three sectors, the most active, pre-existing, compensation bodies were the Deposit Protection Board, the Policyholders Protection Board ('PPB'), and the ICS respectively. Each was set up independently from the other, in response to particular events or policy needs, and reflected the types of business protected by each, with differences in scope, the approach to claims, and levels of protection. Many of those differences are preserved within the FSCS. A further two sub-schemes have since been added, reflecting the increased regulatory responsibilities of the FSA— the home finance mediation sub-scheme, with effect from 31 October 2004 (and now including Islamic home finance) and the general insurance mediation sub-scheme, with effect from 14 January 2005. For the same reason, the scope of the accepting deposit sub-scheme was also extended to include credit unions, with effect from 2 July 2002, and the general insurance mediation sub-scheme will extend to cover 'combined travel insurance' from 1 January 2009.[368]

---

[364] COMP 2.2.8R.

[365] FSMA, s 214(1).

[366] ibid, s 214(2).

[367] Financial Services and Markets Act 2000 (Transitional Provisions, Repeals and Savings) (Financial Services Compensation Scheme) Order 2001, SI 2001/2967 as amended.

[368] FSA Policy Statement 08/4: 'Regulating connected travel insurance—feedback on CP07/22 and final rules' (May 2008).

When considering the application of the Scheme's rules, it is important to identify **7.148** the relevant sub-scheme.

The accepting deposits and designated investment business sub-schemes also **7.149** serve to implement two European Directives—the Deposit Guarantee Schemes Directive[369] ('DGD'), and the Investor Compensation Directive[370] ('ICD'). The ICD notes that 'whereas the protection of investors and maintenance of confidence in the financial system are an important aspect of the completion and proper functioning of the internal market in this area; whereas to that end it is therefore essential that each Member State should have an investor compensation scheme'.[371] The Directives were initially implemented by the amendment to the Deposit Protection Scheme and the ICS. Each Directive stipulates minimum requirements for compensation schemes in Member States (including compensation to €20,000 but expected to rise to €50,000). As such, when exercising its policy-making responsibility, the FSA cannot put in place arrangements which do not satisfy the requirements of the directives, although in fact the FSCS offers greater levels of protection. The European Commission is presently considering amendment to the DGD (in particular, on time for payment, 'co-insurance' and further convergence to a uniform coverage level)[372] which might mean changes to the FSCS. The Commission has also issued a consultation paper on the introduction of a directive for insurance guarantee schemes in Member States.[373] Subject to the terms of any such directive, if implemented, the FSCS insurance business sub-scheme may require amendment in order to comply.

The COMP Rules

There are 13 Chapters to the COMP Rules. The following paragraphs consider, **7.150** in particular, the implementation in COMP of those possible provisions identified at section 214 of FSMA.

'The circumstances in which a relevant person is taken (for the purposes of the Scheme) to be unable, or likely to be unable, to satisfy claims made against him' (section 214(1)(a))

The purpose of the scheme is to be effective on the insolvency, or other inability **7.151** (but not unwillingness) of an authorised firm to meet claims against it.

---

[369] 1994/19/EC.
[370] 1997/9/EC.
[371] Recital 4.
[372] European Banking Committee EU Newsletter dated 4 July 2008.
[373] Consultation Paper on Insurance Guarantee Schemes: MARKT 2508/08 (7 May 2008).

Compensation may only be paid in respect of a claim against 'a relevant person who is in default'.[374] The 'default' process is set out at COMP Chapter 6.

7.152 Only a 'relevant person' may be declared in default. 'Relevant person' as defined by FSMA[375] is modified for the FSCS to 'a participant firm' (or an appointed representative),[376] which excludes incoming EEA firms which are credit institutions, ISD investment firms, or UCITS management companies, although the first two may 'top up' into the FSCS (discussed further below). 'Participant firm' also excludes firms subject to the rules of the Law Society (England and Wales) or the Law Society of Scotland, which operate their own compensation arrangements, but other 'professional' firms (such as accountants and actuaries), authorised to carry on regulated activities under FSMA, are participants in the Scheme.

7.153 The COMP Rules transpose the 'unable or likely to be unable' test from FSMA, enabling the FSCS to declare firms 'in default' if so satisfied.[377] Further, if a 'protected claim' exists, the FSCS may determine a default following an insolvency event (eg a winding up, a court order appointing a liquidator, administrator, or provisional liquidator, or a company voluntary arrangement), or a determination by a 'home State regulator' of an inability of the firm to pay claims with no early prospect of being able to do so.[378]

7.154 For the designated investment business, home finance mediation and general insurance mediation sub-schemes, where the FSCS may receive claims against smaller 'high street firms', the FSCS has power to declare the firm in default if it is satisfied that the firm 'cannot be contacted at its last place of business and that reasonable steps have been taken to establish a forwarding or current address, but without success; and there appears to the FSCS to be no evidence that the relevant person will be able to meet claims against it'.[379] For example, where a sole trader has disappeared, and no evidence is available on which to be satisfied that the individual is unable, or likely to be unable, to meet claims, the FSCS may still declare the firm in default.

7.155 The COMP Rules also reflect the requirement of the DGD and ICD that, for claims covered by these Directives, the default decision is by the competent authority (ie the FSA) or follows a judicial ruling that has the 'effect of suspending the ability of eligible claimants to bring claims against the participant firm'.[380] In practice, for larger firms, such as banks and insurers, the FSCS is likely to be

---

[374] COMP 3.2.1R(2).
[375] FSMA, s 213(9)(a).
[376] COMP 6.2.1R.
[377] COMP 6.3.2R.
[378] COMP 6.3.3R.
[379] COMP 6.3.4R.
[380] COMP 6.3.1R(2).

triggered by a judicial ruling or other appointment of an insolvency practitioner. However, for smaller firms, such as credit unions and many IFAs, the FSCS carries out its own 'solvency' investigation before being able to declare a firm in default.

If necessary, the FSCS has the power to fund insolvency proceedings by a claimant **7.156** against a firm where it would help the FSCS 'to discharge its functions'.[381]

Following a declaration of default of a firm, the FSCS 'must take appropriate steps **7.157** to ensure that potential claimants are informed of how they can make a claim for compensation as soon as possible',[382] although there is no time limit on making applications to the FSCS. The FSCS is to publish information generally on the operation of the scheme.[383]

'For a claim to be entertained only if it is made by a specified kind of claimant' (section 214(1)(f))

The FSA's view was that 'in general cover should focus primarily on private **7.158** individuals and smaller commercial entities' to be available to those least able to sustain loss.[384] COMP Chapter 4 defines 'eligible claimant' by listing a table of exclusions.[385] These exclusions are directed to professional and governmental parties and reflect those permitted under the DGD and ICD[386] including a size test for companies with a higher threshold than under DISP (in particular, a turn-over limit of £6.5 million).[387] Individuals and small businesses are generally protected, although there are exclusions for those deemed to be connected to a firm which has failed, eg directors and 'managers', and their 'close relatives' (as defined in the Glossary), or those 'who in the opinion of the FSCS are responsible for, or who have contributed to, the relevant person's default'. Those with claims connected to money laundering transactions are also excluded. Claimants need not be UK residents. There are no exceptions to the list of exclusions for claims under the designated investment sub-scheme or the home finance media-tion sub-scheme. There are limited exceptions to the exclusions in the accepting deposits sub-scheme,[388] in particular 'large partnerships'.[389]

Although there are no exceptions to the exclusions for the designated investment **7.159** sub-scheme, the COMP rules do permit in some circumstances a claim of this

---

[381] COMP 2.2.4R.
[382] COMP 2.2.7R.
[383] COMP 2.2.3.R.
[384] CP5, para 83.
[385] COMP 4.2.2R.
[386] Annex 1.
[387] Adopted from the Companies Act 2006 (Amendment) (Accounts and Reports) Regulations 2008, SI 2008/395.
[388] Net assets over £1.4 million.
[389] COMP 4.3.1R(1).

type to be made on behalf of an individual by an individual's pension fund, or by small employers' pension schemes.[390] Where a claimant may be a bare trustee or 'nominee company', the FSCS is to treat the underlying beneficiaries as having the claim.[391]

Insurance

7.160 The position for the insurance business and general insurance mediation sub-schemes is more complicated. First, a 'small business' test[392] applies, as opposed to the 'large companies'[393] or 'large partnerships' exclusions. Further, to preserve protected status available under the Policyholders Protection Act 1975 ('PPA') for insurance contracts, all partnerships are eligible in respect of contracts entered into before 1 December 2001.[394]

7.161 All types (and sizes) of policyholder may be an 'eligible claimant' in the insurance business and general insurance mediation sub-schemes for claims 'in respect of a liability subject to compulsory insurance'. The defined compulsory insurances are under the Road Traffic Act 1988, the Employer's Liability (Compulsory Insurance) Act 1969, the Nuclear Installations Act 1965, and the Riding Establishments Act 1964, and their Northern Ireland equivalents. Accordingly, a company of any size with compulsory employer's liability insurance from a failed insurer may be eligible for protection from the FSCS. Albeit under the terms of the Policyholders Protection Act 1975 ('PPA'), the Court of Appeal considered the scope of 'in respect of' compulsory insurance in the context of a claim for defence costs under employers' liability insurance.[395]

7.162 The 'eligible claimant' exclusions generally apply to persons whose claims arise under the Third Parties (Rights Against Insurers) Act 1930[396] but this is modified for claims under general insurance contracts: if the policyholder himself would otherwise be eligible, so the third party will be;[397] the exclusion does not apply to claims under contracts of employer's liability insurance where the liability is or would have been the subject of compulsory employer's liability cover;[398] finally, if the liability to the third party had been agreed or established before the insurer's default, the third party will be eligible.[399] The adjustment for third

---

[390] COMP 12.6.2AR.
[391] COMP 12.6.2R.
[392] Turnover of less than £1 million.
[393] Defined by reference to s 382 of the Companies Act 2006.
[394] COMP 4.3.4R.
[395] *R v FSCS, ex parte Geologistics Ltd* [2005] EWCA Civ 1905.
[396] COMP 4.2.2R(16).
[397] COMP 4.3.5R(1).
[398] COMP 4.3.5R(2).
[399] COMP 4.3.5R(3).

parties' employer's liability claims provides a significant extension for these type of claims which are often for latent disease and therefore predate compulsory employer's liability insurance. The particular role of the FSCS in the handling of mesothelioma claims was addressed by HM Treasury and the FSA following the House of Lords decision in *Barker v Corus*.[400] Following consultation[401] the Transitional Order and COMP rules[402] were amended to allow the FSCS to contribute to employers' and 'live' insurers' settlements of such claims.

The insurance business sub-scheme is also divided between general insurance **7.163** contracts and long-term insurance business. For long-term insurance business, the exclusions to eligible claimant are disapplied save for those connected to the firm in default, or its failure, or those whose claim arises from a money laundering transaction.[403]

'A claim to be entertained only if it falls within a specified kind of claim' (section 214(1)(g))

The scope of 'protected claims',[404] reflects the five different sub-schemes. Generally **7.164** a 'claim' requires the firm to owe the claimant a 'civil liability' (unlike FOS's 'fair and reasonable' approach). Although the Scheme is limited to certain activities under the scope of FSMA, compensation is not restricted to claims against firms for activities for which a firm had a permission.

A claim may be 'for' a deposit,[405] or 'in connection with' investment business, **7.165** mortgage business, or non-investment insurance mediation,[406] and the insurance business sub-scheme protects claims 'under a protected contract of insurance'.[407]

A 'protected deposit' is a 'deposit', as defined under the Financial Services and **7.166** Markets Act 2000 (Regulated Activities Order) 2001 ('RAO'),[408] but extended for credit unions, made with the relevant person in the UK and, in certain circumstances, with an EEA branch of a UK firm.[409] Deposits in all currencies are protected. A bond issued by a credit institution as part of its capital, a secured

---

[400] [2006] UK HL 20.
[401] 'Mesothelioma compensation: amending the Financial Services Compensation Scheme' (September 2006).
[402] COMP 4.4.
[403] COMP 4.3.2R.
[404] COMP Chapter 5.
[405] COMP 5.2.1(R)1.
[406] COMP 5.2.1R(3)–(5).
[407] COMP 5.2.1R(2).
[408] SI 2001/544, as amended.
[409] COMP 5.3.1R.

deposit, a deferred share issued by a building society, and a non-nominative deposit are all excluded from protection.[410]

7.167 For protected deposits, the FSCS was set up as a 'pay box' facility. It protects the balances of transactional and savings accounts. It does not protect claims concerning advice on deposit accounts or the arranging of deposit accounts. Nor does the FSCS have any role to intervene in the case of a failing deposit taker. However, as discussed below, the nature of depositor protection and the FSCS's role is under review.

7.168 The designated investment business sub-scheme, the home finance mediation sub-scheme, and the general insurance mediation sub-scheme all protect claims for bad advice, including breach of Conduct of Business Rules (giving rise to a liability under section 150), as well as loss of funds.

7.169 'Protected investment business' comprises 'designated investment business'[411] which includes a range of regulated activities, such as advising, managing, arranging, agreeing to arrange (contained in the RAO), and investments (also defined in the RAO). 'Protected investment business' includes, for example, claims by investors against advisers for misappropriation of investments or funds, bad advice on the buying or selling of investments, or mismanagement of investments. The FSCS's scope exceeds the requirements of the ICD, which states only that 'each scheme must cover money and investments held by an investment firm in connection with an investor's investment operations which, where an investment firm is unable to meet its obligations to its investor clients, cannot be returned to the investor'[412] and applies to a limited list of 'investments'[413], and does not include, for example, long-term insurance products such as personal pension plans or endowment policies.

7.170 'Protected investment business' also covers the activity of a manager or trustee of an authorised unit trust and of an authorised corporate director or depositary of an open ended investment company, providing the claim is made by the holder of underlying units.[414]

7.171 'Protected home finance mediation' follows the scope of the RAO and includes 'home finance transactions' such as advising, arranging, or making arrangements with a view to 'regulated mortgage contracts'.[415] In so far as 'arranging' is conducted

---

[410] COMP 5.3.1(2).
[411] COMP 5.5.1R(1).
[412] Recital 8.
[413] Previously defined at Article 1 by reference to the Investment Services Directive (93/22/EC) and now by the Markets in Financial Instruments Directive (2004/39/EC).
[414] COMP 5.5.1R(2) and (3).
[415] COMP 5.6.1R.

by a 'mortgage lender', that is also protected. However, mortgage lending and mortgage administration are not protected, despite being regulated activities. After consultation, the FSA concluded it would 'not be proportionate or cost effective to include mortgage lending or administration within the scope of the Scheme'.[416]

Insurance

The scope of 'protected non-investment [ie general] insurance mediation' refers to 'insurance mediation activities', defined by the RAO, in connection with 'relevant general insurance contracts' or 'pure protection contracts'.[417] These defined terms exclude reinsurance and aviation, marine, and credit insurance, for which individuals and small businesses are unlikely to need protection. Mediation of long-term care insurance contracts is dealt with as an 'investment' under the designated investment sub-scheme.
7.172

For insurance business, different rules apply depending on whether the contract of insurance under which a claim is made was issued before or after 1 December 2001. This is to preserve protection for claimants under contracts issued before FSMA came into force, who would have had an expectation of protection. There are also the particular arrangements in place for third party claims under employers' liability policies written before this insurance became compulsory.
7.173

The definition of 'relevant general insurance contract'[418] excludes certain classes such as aviation, marine, goods in transit, and credit insurance (although credit insurance was a protected class under the PPA). Reinsurance contracts are not protected.[419] With effect from 1 January 2004, insurance contracts issued after that date at the Society of Lloyd's are protected, although only in the event that the Lloyd's Central Fund is unable to meet claims to the FSCS level of protection.[420] Long-term insurance contracts are protected[421] whether issued before or after commencement.
7.174

For contracts of insurance issued before commencement, a claim is protected if made under a 'United Kingdom policy', as defined for the purposes of the PPA,[422] or certain employer's liability contracts. A policy is a 'United Kingdom policy' 'if, had any of the obligations under the contract evidenced by the policy been performed at the relevant time, such performance would have formed part of
7.175

---

[416] FSA Consultation Paper 146: 'The FSA's approach to regulating mortgage sales' (August 2002).
[417] COMP 5.7.1R.
[418] COMP 5.4.2R(3).
[419] COMP 5.4.2R(4).
[420] COMP 5.4.2R(5), COMP 6.3.6R.
[421] COMP 5.4.2R(3).
[422] COMP 5.4.5R(1)(a).

an insurance business which the insurer was authorised to carry on in the United Kingdom, whether or not such obligation(s) would have been performed in the United Kingdom'.[423]

7.176 The COMP Rules also require certain claims to be treated as liabilities 'under a protected contract of insurance', in particular claims for premiums paid to insurers for policies which have not commenced or the unexpired portion, third party claims under section 151 of the Road Traffic Act 1988 (where the insurer would otherwise be entitled not to meet a claim from the policyholder), and claims for the proceeds of long-term insurance contracts which have matured or been surrendered but which proceeds have not been paid to the claimant.[424]

'The procedure to be followed in making a claim' (section 214(1)(h))

7.177 The COMP Rules are largely silent as to the procedure to be followed by the FSCS when determining claims for compensation. The FSCS's process must be 'procedurally fair and in accordance with the ECHR'.[425] However, other than for claims under a contract of insurance, claimants are to make an application for compensation.[426] Claims may be made on behalf of eligible claimants.[427]

7.178 Usually, the FSCS requires completion of a written application form from claimants, for example in the designated investment business sub-scheme setting out the details of their personal and financial circumstances, the history of dealings with the firm and the basis of the claim for compensation. Where, for example, the claim is for breach of conduct of business rules, the facts of the advice given by the firm to the claimant require more detailed description than, say, a claim 'for' a deposit balance. In the event of an application containing 'any material inaccuracy or omission, the FSCS may reject the application unless this is considered by the FSCS to be wholly unintentional'.[428]

7.179 Payments of compensation may be conditional upon an assignment to the FSCS of a claimant's rights against the relevant person or third parties.[429] The FSCS's usual practice is to take a written assignment of rights. An offer of compensation may be withdrawn if it 'is not accepted or if it is not disputed within 90 days of the date on which the offer is made',[430] although any such offers may be repeated.[431]

---

[423] *Ackman and Scher v Policyholders Protection Board* [1994] 2 AC 57, Lord Goff of Chieveley at 103–4.
[424] COMP 5.4.7R.
[425] COMP 2.2.1.R.
[426] COMP 3.2.1R(1).
[427] COMP 3.2.3G.
[428] COMP 8.2.1R.
[429] COMP 7.2.1R.
[430] COMP 8.3.1R.
[431] COMP 8.3.3R.

In the event that offers were made when they should not have been, the FSCS 'must withdraw any offer'.[432]

For the designated investment, home finance mediation, and general insurance **7.180** mediation sub-schemes, there are modifications to the 'civil liability' test. Where it is reasonable to do so, the FSCS may disregard a defence of limitation[433] and (save for protected home finance mediation) the FSCS is also to ignore the fact a claim is extinguished by operation of law if solely as a result of the dissolution of the company against which the claim is made.[434] Claims which have already been dealt with by a firm under an industry review (eg the Pension Review or the FSAVC review) may also not be reopened.[435]

'The making of interim payments before a claim is finally determined' (section 214(1)(i))

Payment of a claim is generally to be made 'as soon as reasonably possible' after the **7.181** FSCS has calculated the amount of compensation due, which would follow the FSCS's determination of eligibility, and in any event 'within three months', although the FSA may grant a three-month extension.[436] This reflects the time for payment of compensation under the DGD[437] and ICD,[438] although the rule applies to all the sub-schemes. The rule does not require payments within a certain period of a firm's failure—the time period commences from the FSCS's calculation of the compensation amount. Other than for claims covered by the DGD and ICD, the FSCS may pay a lesser sum in final settlement, if the amount of the claim is uncertain and it would be prudent to do so.[439] For all types of claims, a payment may be made 'on account' in similar circumstances.[440]

In the event that the claimant may have 'any reasonable prospect of recovery in **7.182** respect of the claim from any third party or by applying for compensation to any other party', the FSCS may make a payment on account or pay a lesser sum in final settlement,[441] save for DGD and ICD claims. Alternatively, for protected investment business or home finance mediation, instead of a payment on account or payment of a lesser sum, as the FSCS is the fund of 'last resort', payment may be postponed by the FSCS in these circumstances (again, with the exception of

---

[432] COMP 8.3.4R.
[433] COMP 8.2.4R.
[434] COMP 8.2.5R.
[435] COMP 8.2.7R.
[436] COMP 9.2.1R.
[437] Art 10.
[438] Art 9.
[439] COMP 11.2.4R, and 11.2.6R.
[440] COMP 11.2.4R.
[441] COMP 11.2.5R.

an ICD claim)[442] or where recovery may be made from the principal of an appointed representative.[443]

7.183 The FSCS may postpone payment of insurance business compensation where the liability is covered 'by another contract of insurance with a solvent insurance undertaking or where it appears that a person other than the liquidator may make payments or take such action to secure the continuity of cover as the FSCS would undertake'.[444] The payment of compensation in respect of certain bonuses under long-term insurance contracts may also be postponed where uncertain but otherwise this compensation, and compensation in respect of liabilities subject to compulsory insurance, is to be paid as 'soon as reasonably practicable' (after the benefit has fallen due or the insurer was declared in default).[445]

7.184 Time for payment of compensation is also extended for claims subject to the Pension Review (ie subject to the Specification of Standards and Procedures issued by the FSA in October 1994, as supplemented and modified by subsequent guidance issued by the FSA), or subject to the FSAVC Review Model Guidance (issued by the FSA in May 2000).[446] This reflects the particular redress processes applicable to these two classes of claim for which the regulator has prescribed particular methods of quantification and payment of redress, which might not be achievable within a three-month timescale.

7.185 Reflecting the exclusion to 'eligible claimant',[447] claimants subject to pending money laundering proceedings may have payment of compensation postponed.[448]

'Limiting the amount payable on a claim to a specified maximum amount or a maximum amount calculated in a specified manner' (section 214(1)(j))

7.186 Compensation for protected deposits, protected investment business, and protected home finance mediation is subject to a maximum sum, per claimant, per firm.[449] For protected deposits the limit is now £50,000; before 7 October 2008 it was £35,000, and before 1 October 2007 it was £31,700 (comprising 100 per cent of the first £2,000 and 90 per cent of the next £33,000). A maximum payment of £48,000 is provided for the other two sub-schemes, comprising 100 per cent of the first £30,000 and 90 per cent of the next £20,000. The shared portion of loss is known as 'coinsurance'. Interest may be paid, which is not taken into account when applying these limits.[450]

---

[442] COMP 9.2.2R(2).
[443] COMP 9.2.2R(1).
[444] COMP 9.2.2.R(3).
[445] COMP 9.2.2R(6), COMP 12.4.11AR, and COMP 12.4.9R.
[446] COMP 9.2.2R(4).
[447] COMP 4.2.2R.
[448] COMP 9.2.2R(5).
[449] COMP 10.2.3R.
[450] COMP 11.2.7R and 11.2.8R.

For insurance business and general insurance mediation claims, compensation is **7.187** generally payable to 100 per cent of the first £2,000 and 90 per cent of the remainder, without limit, but compensation in respect of a liability subject to the compulsory insurances is in full (although third party claims for pre-compulsory employer's liability are protected to 90 per cent).[451] The absence of a limit reflects the exposure of an individual or small business to the type of loss for which insurance might have been purchased. The amount of a claim under an insurance policy may be disproportionate to the premiums paid and exceed the means of the policyholder, for example the cost of rebuild and repair to a house. The unlimited level of compensation is available for claims against both insurers and brokers, as the failure of a broker to arrange suitable (or any), say, home insurance, can have consequences for the client equally drastic as the failure of the insurer to meet the claim. Further, 'enhanced' protection to 100 per cent is provided by the FSCS for an insurer's periodical payments, under section 101 of the Courts Act 2003.

The absence of a cap for insurance claims means that compensation from the **7.188** FSCS may exceed the award which FOS might make (which is limited to £100,000).

Each claimant is entitled to his own limit. Unless a bare trust, a trust is a single **7.189** claimant irrespective of the number of beneficiaries and the compensation payable to a trust may be adjusted if not all the beneficiaries would be 'eligible claimants'.[452] Clients with funds in a client account are entitled to make claims for their own share.[453] Each person sharing a joint claim is entitled to his or her own maximum limit, and joint claims are presumed to be equal in the absence of evidence to the contrary,[454] although claims by a business trading in partnership are treated as one claim and therefore only one limit is available.

After consultation in 2005, the FSA decided not to adjust the compensation limits **7.190** at that time.[455] However, following the events at Northern Rock, coinsurance was removed from the protected deposits limit and the FSA is expected to consult again on all the FSCS compensation limits in the autumn of 2008.

Quantification

The quantification of claims for compensation is dealt with at COMP Chapter 12. **7.191** Compensation is paid in respect of an 'overall net claim', ie after taking account of any other payments the claimant might have received from the firm, the FSCS, or

---

[451] COMP 10.2.3R.
[452] COMP 12.6.5R.
[453] COMP 12.6.7R.
[454] COMP 12.6.10R.
[455] FSA Consultation Paper 05/15: 'Review of Compensation Scheme and Ombudsman Service limits and miscellaneous amendments to the Compensation sourcebook' (December 2005).

any third party, and after application of 'set off'.[456] Such amounts are deducted from the total claim, not the amount of compensation. Once satisfied the conditions for a claim have been met, the FSCS is to calculate the amount of compensation 'as soon as reasonably possible'.[457]

7.192 Claims for protected deposits are quantified at the date of default or date the protected deposit is 'due and payable if later' (eg fixed term accounts).[458] As a 'pay box', the quantification for deposit claims will verify account balances with the failed bank (or the appointed insolvency practitioner) as at the relevant date.

7.193 For protected investment business, home finance mediation, and general insurance mediation, the FSCS has discretion as to the date at which claims are quantified[459] (save that the category of an 'ICD claim' must be quantified as at the date of the firm's default).[460]

7.194 Claims for return of property or in respect of uncompleted transactions are compensated to the extent of the investor's loss. For other claims in these three sub-schemes (eg claims for bad advice), the FSCS 'may pay compensation for any claim . . . only to the extent that the FSCS considers that the payment of compensation is essential in order to provide the claimant with fair compensation'.[461] This rule gives the FSCS discretion to develop and apply its own methods or bases of quantification. The FSCS is not obliged to follow the assessment of damages which a court would undertake.

7.195 The wording of this rule reflects a previous rule applicable to claims to ICS.[462] In *R v Investors Compensation Scheme, ex parte Bowden*,[463] the House of Lords considered the interpretation of that ICS Rule. In short, when quantifying the relevant investors' claims, ICS had deducted the amount of the 'benefit' (or income) investors had received as a result of the authorised firm's advice and limited the recovery of professional fees. Whether or not such deductions would have been followed by a court when assessing damages for those claims, the House of Lords was satisfied that ICS had the discretion to determine its own basis of compensation which did not need to match the damages a court would award. Lord Lloyd of Berwick found 'a broad discretion to include within the definition of a compensatable claim either the claim as a whole, or those elements of the claim which the

---

[456] COMP 12.2.7R and 12.2.4R.
[457] COMP 12.2.8R.
[458] COMP 12.3.1R.
[459] COMP 12.3.5R, 12.3.7R, and 12.3.8R.
[460] COMP 12.3.6R.
[461] COMP 12.4.2R, 12.4.17R, 12.4.20R.
[462] Securities and Investments Board: The Financial Services (Compensation of Investors) Rules 1994, Rule 2.04.1.
[463] [1995] 3 All ER 605.

management company considers essential in order to provide fair compensation and to exclude those elements which do not meet that requirement'.[464] Accordingly, for 'advice' claims, the FSCS's approach is to determine what it considers to be a reasonable basis to provide 'fair compensation'. The House of Lords also confirmed that it was legitimate to develop policies for the quantification of classes of claim of a similar type.

Certain losses are excluded from compensation in the investment sub-scheme if **7.196** they relate to or depend on: [1] a failure of investment performance to match a guarantee given or representation made; or [2] a contractual obligation to pay or promise to pay which the FSCS considers to have been undertaken without full consideration passing to the relevant person or in anticipation of possible insolvency; or [3] the mere fluctuation in the value of an investment.[465] Similar (appropriately adjusted) exclusions apply to claims for protected home finance mediation.[466]

Compensation for investment business claims may also be reduced if the FSCS is **7.197** satisfied of contributory negligence on the part of the claimant or where 'payment of the full amount would provide a greater benefit than the claimant might reasonably have expected or than the benefit available on similar investments with other relevant persons', which it would be inequitable for the FSCS to ignore.[467] Because these provisos are not in the ICD, they cannot be applied to that class of claim. Further, neither this nor the general discretion on the method of quantification is available to claims covered by either the Pension Review or FSAVC Review, for which redress is to be calculated in accordance with the regulatory guidance.[468] In contrast to DISP, which appends the methodology for the quantification of claims for endowment mis-selling, the FSA guidance for the quantification of those claims is not referred to in the COMP Rules.

As well as the 'essential in order to provide the claimant with fair compensation' **7.198** discretion, compensation for mortgage advice and arranging or general insurance mediation may also be reduced for contributory negligence[469] and in general insurance mediation for 'excessive benefits'.

Insurance business sub-scheme

Reflecting the predecessor scheme, the nature of payments by the FSCS in the **7.199** insurance business sub-scheme is as much about 'protection' as 'compensation'.

---

[464] At 611.
[465] COMP 12.4.3R.
[466] COMP 12.4.18R.
[467] COMP 12.4.8R.
[468] COMP 12.4.6 and 7R.
[469] COMP 12.4.19R and COMP 12.4.21R.

In addition to the compensation function, there is the objective of continuity of insurance, both for long-term and general insurers. Compensation 'may not necessarily be enough to enable [long term] policyholders to find alternative cover' and general insurance claims can have a long tail resulting in costs and delays for policyholders.[470] Compensation is payable if continuity is not achieved.[471]

7.200   The provisions for continuity are derived from sections 216 and 217.[472] For long-term insurance, the FSCS 'must make arrangements to secure continuity of insurance',[473] which may comprise the transfer of business or the issue of substitute policies.[474] Continuity for long-term insurance policyholders is only to be provided where it is 'reasonably practicable' and if, in the opinion of the FSCS at the time it proposes to make the arrangements, the cost is justified by the benefits.[475] The obligation to consider continuity for a long-term insurer is triggered by insolvency proceedings,[476] not by the FSCS exercising any discretion or making any assessment of 'unable or likely to be unable' to pay claims. The level of protection is limited to 90 per cent of benefits under the contracts, with future premiums to be adjusted accordingly.[477]

7.201   Whether the FSCS can arrange continuity will depend on a number of factors including the state of the insurer itself and identifying a willing transferee for the business. Whilst investigating or pursuing continuity, the FSCS is to meet 90 per cent of the benefits falling due under the insurer's long term contracts.[478] Recognising the involvement of an insolvency practitioner, and the possibility that continuity may be required to meet short-term cash flow needs, claims falling due may in fact be funded by the insolvency practitioner with the benefit of an indemnity from the FSCS (which option is also available for a compensation payout).[479] Benefits falling due do not include bonuses unless 'declared and vested' before the date of trigger for the FSCS.[480] Further, benefits which the FSCS considers are 'excessive' are also not protected.[481] However, continuity must be provided for benefits not yet determined to be excessive, even if under investigation

---

[470] FSMA Explanatory Notes.
[471] COMP 3.2.1R.
[472] COMP 3.3.
[473] COMP 3.3.1R.
[474] COMP 3.3.2R.
[475] COMP 3.3.1R.
[476] COMP 3.3.1R, incorporating COMP 3.3.3R.
[477] COMP 3.3.2AR and COMP 3.3.2BR.
[478] COMP 3.3.2CR.
[479] COMP 3.3.2CR(4) (and COMP 11.2.3R).
[480] COMP 3.3.2DR(1).
[481] COMP 3.3.2DR(2).

by the FSCS, unless the claim for protection (ie the benefit falling due) 'arises out of the exercise of any option under the policy'.[482]

Although expressed as a power ('may') rather than an obligation ('must'), for an **7.202** insurance undertaking 'in financial difficulties', the COMP Rules make similar provision for continuity, for both general and long-term insurance.[483] In addition to transfers of the business, or the issue of substitute policies, the additional measure of 'assistance to the relevant person to enable it to continue to effect contracts of insurance or carrying out contracts of insurance' is included.[484] The FSCS may therefore fund payments by the insurer. This might be implemented under the terms of a scheme of arrangement. Again, a 'costs test' applies.[485]

This continuity regime reflects section 216 of FSMA, which provides for continu- **7.203** ity of long-term insurance policies, and section 217, which deals with insurers in financial difficulties. These two sections, in turn, followed the approach of the PPA.[486]

In the event that continuity of insurance cannot be achieved, the FSCS may pay **7.204** compensation. As for all sub-schemes, compensation is payable on the 'overall net claim',[487] allowing deduction of liabilities owed by policyholders to the insurer. The FSCS must determine a specific quantification date for a claim.[488]

Compensation for claims under general insurance contracts are to be calculated in **7.205** respect of a liability subject to compulsory insurance or 'in accordance with the terms of the contract',[489] and for long-term insurance contracts 'in accordance with the terms of the contract as valued in the liquidation' (to which the Insurers (Winding Up) Rules 2001 currently apply), or in the absence of a liquidation valuation, 'in accordance with such reasonable valuation techniques as the FSCS considers appropriate' to include benefits fallen due and bonuses to which a value has been or is likely to be attributed.[490] Long-term insurance contract compensation may be adjusted by the FSCS for any 'excessive benefit', defined as a benefit 'no reasonable and prudent insurer in the position of the relevant person would have so decided given the premiums payable and other contractual terms'.[491]

---

[482] COMP 3.3.2ER.
[483] COMP 3.3.3R and COMP 3.3.6R.
[484] COMP 3.3.4R(2).
[485] COMP 3.3.3R(1) and COMP 3.3.7R.
[486] PPA, ss 11 and 16.
[487] COMP 12.2.4R.
[488] COMP 12.3.2R.
[489] COMP 12.4.9R and 12.4.10R.
[490] COMP 12.4.11R, 12.4.11AR, and 12.4.12R.
[491] COMP 12.4.13R(2).

Such reduction to or disregard of a claim may only be made following an actuary's written recommendation.[492]

'For payment to be made, in specified circumstances, to a person other than the claimant' (section 214(1)(k))

7.206 Generally, payment is to be made to the claimant 'or as directed by the claimant'.[493] Pension Review compensation must usually be paid to the trustee of an occupational pension scheme or to a personal pension scheme or other product provider (or both).[494] The COMP Rules expressly allow for payments to be made other than to the eligible claimant, for example to personal representatives or beneficiaries of a trust.[495] Similarly, those entitled to funds held on client account are regarded as the claimant, rather than the firm in whose name the account is held.[496] The COMP Rules make clear that claims by personal representatives, agents, or trustees, are distinct from the individual acting in that capacity.[497]

'The scheme may provide for the determination and regulation of matters relating to the scheme by the scheme manager' (section 214(3))

7.207 Save for claims under a protected contract of insurance, an application for compensation is required.[498]

7.208 Claimants are not required to be legally represented and the FSCS does not meet the costs of representation. In assessing claims, the FSCS will have regard to all available evidence, such as contemporaneous client files and information provided by the firm in default, as well as the claimant's evidence. The FSCS has specific power to deal with claims under an insurance policy where it is not 'evidenced by a policy'.[499]

7.209 The FSCS is to be procedurally fair and act in accordance with the ECHR. The recourse for discontented claimants, once the FSCS's internal review procedure has been exhausted, is by judicial review. This meets the requirement of the ICD that 'Member States shall ensure that an investor's right to compensation may be the subject of an action by the investor against the compensation scheme' (Article 13). There is no external 'appeal' procedure.

---

492 COMP 12.4.14R.
493 COMP 11.2.1R.
494 COMP 11.2.2R.
495 COMP 3.2.2R.
496 COMP 12.6.7R.
497 COMP 12.6.
498 COMP 3.2.1R.
499 COMP 5.4.6R.

Recent cases have confirmed that judicial review is the appropriate method of **7.210** challenge.[500]

'Specified territories, areas, or localities' (section 214(4))

Dealings in the UK with an authorised firm are generally protected. Deposit, **7.211** investment, and general insurance mediation protection is extended to 'passport-ing' firms under the home State principle, ie claims against a UK authorised firm, exercising an EEA right to trade in another EEA State, will be protected by the FSCS to the extent that the claim is covered by the scope of the DGD or ICD or IMD respectively.[501] Protected home finance mediation depends on the customer being a UK resident, or the firm's establishment being in the UK,[502] as well as the relevant property being in the UK (under the Glossary definition of 'regulated mortgage contract').

The DGD and ICD also provide for incoming EEA firms to be able to 'top up' the **7.212** level of compensation offered by their home States by joining the FSCS. The minimum level of compensation under the DGD and ICD is €20,000. As a result, for example, banks from those Member States opening branches in the UK may elect to top up the level of protection available to depositors with the UK branches by joining the FSCS, so that their customers will receive the same limit of protection as customers of UK banks, albeit the first €20,000 would be met by the home State scheme, and the remainder by the FSCS. Incoming EEA firms may elect to participate in the FSCS,[503] and under the Electing Participants Regulations,[504] topping up is available to EEA credit institutions, MiFID invest-ment firms, UCITS management companies, or IMD insurance intermediaries who establish UK branches in the exercise of an EEA right.[505] When subsequently quantifying compensation, the FSCS must 'take account of the liability of' the home State scheme.[506] If preferred, for reasons of expediency or otherwise, FSMA allows for rules to enable the FSCS to make the full payment of compensation, including that portion due from an overseas scheme, facilitating a single payment to claimants, and then recover that cost from the overseas scheme (although this section could apply to other governmental schemes).[507]

---

[500] *R v FSCS, ex parte Geologistics Ltd* [2003] EWCA Civ 1905, *Murphy v FSCS*, unreported, 2 September 2004.

[501] COMP 5.3, 5.5, and 5.7.

[502] COMP 5.6.2.R.

[503] FSMA, s 213(10).

[504] Financial Services and Markets Act 2000 (Compensation Scheme: Electing Participants) Regulations 2001, SI 2001/1783.

[505] COMP 14.2.

[506] COMP 12.4.1R and 12.4.4R.

[507] FSMA, s 214(6).

7.213 For the insurance business sub-scheme, the geographical location of risk is relevant to whether a claim is protected. The COMP Rules implemented the changes in the Policyholders Protection Act 1997, so that if the contract was issued (i) in the UK, risks in the UK, the EEA, and the Channel Islands and the Isle of Man are protected; (ii) in another EEA State, only risks in the UK are protected; and (iii) in the Channel Islands or Isle of Man, risks in the UK, the Channel Islands, or the Isle of Man are protected.[508] How to determine the situation of a risk is addressed by the COMP Rules.[509] In May 2008, for policies issued by EEA branches of UK insurers, the FSA consulted on extending the scope of protection to risks in the EEA, which rule change has now been made.[510]

Recovery of cost of compensation

7.214 The FSCS is funded by a levy on regulated firms. To mitigate the cost of compensation, the FSCS seeks to recover from firms in default and third parties in respect of claims paid.[511]

7.215 Many firms declared in default are subject to formal insolvency proceedings. The FSCS has certain rights to participate in insolvency proceedings of authorised firms.[512] This recognises the FSCS's position as a likely creditor of such firms, often becoming the largest single creditor once compensatable claims have been paid.

7.216 The rights to participate in insolvency proceedings no longer include those provided to the Deposit Protection Board,[513] which was entitled to sit on creditors committees and had preferred rights to receive dividends on all the claims of compensated depositors, not just the compensated claim. However, the FSCS does have the benefit of the priority afforded to policyholders or direct insurance creditors of insolvent insurers.[514]

7.217 As part of the claim process, the FSCS seeks an assignment of the claimant's rights against the firm in default, but also third parties.

7.218 Where the FSCS takes an assignment of rights from a claimant 'it must pursue all and only such recoveries as it considers are likely to be both reasonably possible

---

[508] COMP 5.4.3R.

[509] COMP 5.4.4R.

[510] FSA Consultation Paper 08/9: 'Financial Services Compensation Scheme: EEA branches of UK insurers' (May 2008); FSA Policy Statement 08/8 (July 2008).

[511] FSMA, s 215, DGD Art 11, ICD Art 12.

[512] FSMA, s 215(3)–(5).

[513] Banking Act 1987, s 58.

[514] Under reg 32 of the Insurers (Reorganisation and Winding Up) Regulations 2004, SI 2004/353, implementing the EC Directive on the reorganisation and winding up of insurance undertakings (2001/17/EC).

and cost effective to pursue'.[515] The FSCS retains amounts recovered to set against future levy needs, but where an amount exceeds the compensation paid to the claimant (whose assigned rights have given rise to the recovery) the surplus (less reasonable costs) are forwarded to the claimant.[516]

In addition, to avoid claimants with large losses awaiting a dividend distribution **7.219** from an insolvency practitioner before accepting any offer of compensation (and assigning their rights to dividends to the FSCS), the FSCS is to 'ensure that the claimant will not suffer disadvantage' in such circumstances by, after the event, reconciling the position had the investor awaited receipt of the dividend before applying for compensation.[517]

The construction and effect of a form of assignment of rights previously relied on **7.220** by ICS under a similar regime was considered by the courts[518] and in *FSCS v Abbey National Treasury Services plc*,[519] the power of the FSCS to take assignments of investors' claims was disputed. This challenge was rejected on the basis that the FSA had power under FSMA to include provision in the COMP Rules for assignment to the FSCS of investors' claims against third parties. The court found such provision to be 'obvious' and an 'integral' component of a compensation scheme, such that the power falls within section 213(1), or as an incidental or supplemental matter within section 156(2). Further, the court rejected the defence that compensation paid by the FSCS to investors is to be taken into account in the calculation of loss recoverable by the FSCS as assignee of the investors' claims, finding 'no reason in principle . . . why assigned claims should be restricted to the net loss'. Accordingly, FSCS may pursue recoveries where a claimant's losses do not exceed the compensation paid.

Funding: Section 214(1):(b) 'the establishment of different funds for meeting different kinds of claim'; (c) 'the imposition of different levies in different cases'; (d) limiting the 'levy payable by a person in respect of a specified period'

The principle is that the 'good' subsidise the 'bad', ie those firms still trading fund **7.221** the costs of the FSCS for those firms which have failed.[520] With effect from 1 January 2006, the funding rules are in the FEES Module of the Handbook. The FSCS has two types of cost—compensation costs and management expenses[521] and may levy for what it has incurred or for what it expects to incur. Compensation costs

---

[515] COMP 7.2.3R.
[516] COMP 7.2.4R.
[517] COMP 7.2.5R, 7.2.6G.
[518] *ICS v West Bromwich Building Society* [1998] 1 All ER 98.
[519] [2008] EWHC 1897.
[520] FSMA, s 213(3)(b).
[521] FEES 6.1.5G.

are costs incurred in paying compensation ie. the amounts paid to claimants (or for their benefit). Management expenses are the costs of establishing, maintaining, and operating the FSCS. Management expenses are split between 'base costs' and 'specific costs'. 'Base costs' are those costs which are incurred irrespective of the level of activity of the scheme (eg the salary of board members), and are charged to all firms liable for the FSCS levy (by reference to regulatory fees).[522] Compensation costs and specific costs reflect the level of claims activity and are charged to a class or sub-class by reference to the activity giving rise to the claim (and not a firm's permissions).[523] 'Establishment costs', recoverable for the first three years of the FSCS, have now been collected.

7.222 After detailed consultation,[524] the FSA adopted an ICS style funding model and a 'pay as you go' model for the FSCS. The approach is that the costs of claims are allocated to sectors or sub-sectors with responsibility for the business giving rise to claims reflecting the obligation 'to take account of [this] desirability'.[525]

7.223 With effect from 1 April 2008, a revised funding system was put in place, following a detailed review.[526] There are now five funding classes: deposit, life and pensions, investment, home finance, and general insurance. Save for deposit, each class is split into two sub-classes: providers and intermediaries. Costs are borne by the relevant sub-class, to an annual limit, then by the connected sub-class to its limit, and if further funds are required, the remaining classes may be levied as part of this 'general retail pool' (with the exception of the home finance provider sub-class which does not contribute to the general retail pool). A 'clean break' was implemented from the previous system, with firms receiving debits or credits for amounts owed to or by the previous contribution groups. Firms who do not carry out business which could give rise to potential claims (and have no reasonable likelihood of doing so) are exempt from the levy (except for base costs).[527]

7.224 There is no limit on the compensation which the FSCS may pay in each year, but there are limits on the levies which may be raised on each class or sub-class.[528] Those limits are set by reference to affordability (and will be kept under review by the FSA). The total levy capacity is £4.03bn (or £4.73bn including home finance providers). The FSCS allocates its compensation costs levy to the classes and

---

[522] FEES 6.4.5R.
[523] FEES 6.5.2–3R.
[524] Concluding with FSA Consultation Paper 86: 'Financial Services Compensation Scheme Draft Funding Rules' (March 2001).
[525] FSMA, s 213(5).
[526] FSA Consultation Paper 07/5: 'FSCS Funding Review and FSA Policy Statement 07/19' (November 2007).
[527] FEES 6.2.1R.
[528] FEES 6 Annex 2R.

sub-classes and each has its own tariff base.[529] Certain tariff bases are still under review.[530]

The FSCS raises a levy for costs expected for each financial year (for management **7.225** expenses) or the following 12 months (for compensation costs).[531] Further levies may be raised during a year. There is no 'joining fee' but firms leaving regulation may be subject to an exit levy.[532] Topped up EEA firms receive a discount for the level of their home State cover.[533]

Since 1 December 2001, the FSCS has raised total levies of over £800 million, **7.226** mainly paid by the general insurers, and for investment claims.

Funds are raised against and held for the benefit of individual classes and sub- **7.227** classes. The FSCS is to use its resources 'in the most efficient and economic way' and in managing funds the FSCS is to act 'prudently'.[534] Although the FSCS may levy for the cost of claims paid in error but in good faith,[535] it must also try to recover those amounts unless unreasonable or uneconomic to do so.[536]

In the event of a short-term lack of funds for claims, the FSCS may raise a further **7.228** levy or arrange borrowing between classes, the cost of which (at the Bank of England's repo rate) will be added to a future levy raised on the borrowing class.[537] The FSCS has also arranged external borrowing facilities in the event of short-term cash flow need. If the FSCS has more funds than required, it may pay a refund to the relevant class or sub-class 'on any reasonable basis'.[538]

Recoveries are allocated to the relevant sub-class, but if the general retail pool or **7.229** other sub-class contributed to the relevant compensation costs, recoveries are paid first in that order.[539]

Current practice is for the FSA to raise its fees, FOS's fees, and the FSCS's levy at **7.230** the same time, on a single invoice. Firms must notify the FSCS of relevant sub-classes and tariff data, but the FSCS may rely on the information supplied to the FSA.[540] Failure to submit information leads to an administrative fee of £250 and

---

[529] FEES 6, Annex 3R.
[530] FSA Consultation Paper 08/8: 'FSCS Funding: tariff changes' (April 2008).
[531] FSMA, s 213(5).
[532] FEES 6.4.8R and 6.7.6R.
[533] FEES 6.6.1R.
[534] FEES 6.3.12R.
[535] FEES 6.3.10R.
[536] COMP 8.3.5R.
[537] FEES 6.3.3G, 6.3.15R, and 6.3.17R.
[538] FEES 6.3.21R.
[539] FEES 6.3.19–20R.
[540] FEES 6.5.13–14R.

the default option for calculating the tariff.[541] As for the FSA and FOS, if the FSCS levy is calculated on mistaken data, a firm is to have two years in which to seek an adjustment.[542] Adjustments may be made to a levy on a number of grounds, including 'on any reasonable basis'.[543] The levy raised on behalf of the FSCS is enforceable as a debt.[544] Levies are to be paid within 30 days[545] (or quarterly by direct debit with the FSCS's agreement) failing which 'additional administrative fees' of £250 are payable to the FSCS, together with interest at a rate of 5 per cent over the Bank of England repo rate.[546]

7.231 Each year, the FSA consults on the FSCS's proposed expenditure for the following year. Under section 223, the FSCS cannot levy for 'management expenses' an amount in excess of a limit fixed by the Rules as applicable to that period. The FSA consults on that limit each year based on the FSCS's budget.[547] The limit is then incorporated in the FEES Rules.[548]

Financial Stability and Depositor Protection

7.232 On 31 January 2008, the Bank of England, HM Treasury, and the Financial Services Authority ('the Authorities') published a consultation paper which addressed five key objectives: strengthening the financial system, reducing the likelihood of banks failing, reducing the impact of failing banks, effective compensation arrangements in which consumers have confidence, and strengthening the Bank of England and improving coordination between authorities. The Consultation Paper followed a discussion paper issued by the Authorities in October 2007 (Banking Reform—Protecting Depositors: Discussion Paper). Following the responses to consultation, the Authorities have now published two further papers: a 'Further Consultation', on 1 July 2008, and the 'Financial stability and depositor protection: Special Resolution Regime', on 22 July 2008. It is intended to introduce legislation to Parliament later in 2008.

7.233 The initial Discussion Paper, and later work, was prompted by the 'credit crunch' in the summer of 2007, and the consequent market turmoil, in particular the events of Northern Rock. In addition the House of Commons Treasury Select

---

[541] FEES 6.5.16R.
[542] FSA Consultation Paper 08/8: 'FSCS funding—tariff charges' (April 2008); draft rules FEES 2.3, 6.3.22AR, BG.
[543] FEES 6.3.22R.
[544] FSMA, s 213(6) and FEES 2.2.3G.
[545] FEES 6.7.3R.
[546] FEES 2.2.1R.
[547] Lastly, FSA Consultation Paper 08/2: 'Regulatory fees and levies 2008/09' (January 2008).
[548] FEES 6. Annex 1R.

Committee has carried out its own investigations and its report, 'The Run on the Rock' published on 26 January 2008, also contained proposals for depositor protection.

In the Consultation Papers, of direct relevance to deposit insurance, are the **7.234** proposals for 'effective compensation arrangements in which consumers have confidence'. These proposals consider issues such as possible increases to compensation limits, including whether (and how) to deal with temporary high balances (caused by, say, the proceeds of a house sale), changes to the FSCS to be able to make payments to depositors 'within one week', and increased consumer awareness.

The FSA will review the compensation limits for other sectors, such as investments, **7.235** as well as for deposits. The Further Consultation identifies that one proposal will be an increase in the deposit guarantee limit to £50,000 (per person, per bank); it also notes the limit could apply by 'brand', not by individual bank entity. The key measures for a faster compensation payment have been identified: the FSCS must have early access to information in respect of the depositors of a failing or failed bank; such information would usually be obtained via the FSA, as the supervisor, on the request of the FSCS. For the purposes of identifying the depositors entitled to receive compensation, banks should have readily available information on account balances—this might include a 'single view of each customer' so that the FSCS would immediately be able to ascertain the amounts to which individual depositors would be entitled. The Further Consultation maintained this target payout, for at least part of depositors' funds, with the balance soon after.

The complicated eligibility exclusions, fully adopted from the DGD, are seen to **7.236** restrict speedy payout, as ineligible claimants needed to be identified and excluded. Although corporate bodies may remain ineligible, it is important for the FSCS objectives that payout to individuals is speedy. Insofar as exclusions are retained, the Further Consultation suggested any ineligible accounts (and dormant accounts) be flagged by banks so that the FSCS could identify those accounts straightaway. Applying 'set off' under the current arrangements also requires bank records to provide an overall 'net' balance. Further, set-off affects short-term consumer liquidity as although a debt, such as a mortgage, may be reduced in value, the depositor loses access to cash for daily living costs. To the extent set off is disapplied under these reforms, it is to be fair to other depositors and levy payers, and the depositor will still be indebted in full to the bank. Other measures proposed include the removal of claim forms and the automatic conferral of rights of recovery. The Authorities acknowledge the logistical demands of a large scale payout, including payment channels which may be vulnerable to fraud, and the burden on banks opening a large number of new accounts. Further work with the industry is proposed on both this and consumer awareness.

7.237 The funding arrangements for the FSCS were also reviewed. The FSCS needs access to immediate liquidity in order to fund a large scale payout, which is now proposed to be provided by Government (in the National Loans Fund). The Further Consultation raises the possibility of a pre-fund at some time in the future, which may or may not levy risk-based premiums.

7.238 The measures described above would be designed to improve the speed of the payout of compensation following failure. However, the Authorities also propose a number of pre-insolvency interventions under a 'special resolution regime' ('SRR'). The 'tools' of such a regime are identified as directed transfers, ie the ability of the Authorities to direct (and accelerate) the transfer of business; the establishment and operation of a 'bridge bank', and 'temporary public owner-ship'. The SRR may apply when in the public interest and for financial stability reasons and be operated by the Bank of England. In addition, as part of the SRR, a new 'bank insolvency procedure' would apply to banks. This would include, as an express obligation of the bank liquidator, the facilitating of an account transfer or the FSCS compensation payout (which would be triggered by the liquidation).

7.239 As the regulator, the FSA will trigger the SRR, and the Bank of England will be the 'Special Resolution Agency' ie the body to decide upon and operate the tools of the SRR. The FSA will continue to supervise the bank in the SRR. HM Treasury will have to approve the use of public funds and any decision with implications for public finances; the Chancellor of the Exchequer will decide upon temporary public ownership, and remains responsible for ensuring compliance with the UK's international obligations. At the conclusion of any SRR, other than the FSCS payout, it is proposed that the FSCS may contribute to any shortfall in the costs of the SRR.

7.240 The Banking Bill was introduced to Parliament on 7 October 2008, and received its second reading on 14 October 2008. The Bill has received cross party support and the Government hopes to complete its passage through Parliament by 20 February 2009, when sunset provisions in the Banking (Special Provisions) Act 2008 ('BSPA') take effect.

7.241 As part of the progress of the Bill, the House of Commons has set up a Bill Committee to scrutinise the draft clauses. HM Treasury published a fourth consul-tation paper, in November 2008, entitled 'Special Resolution Regime: Safeguards For Partial Property Transfers'. This Consultation Paper acknowledged the impor-tance of property transfer powers to be provided to the Authorities by the Bill, but also the concerns of stakeholders, in particular relating to partial transfers. In response to those concerns, the Government has established an 'expert liaison group' and published for consultation draft secondary legislation dealing with the proposed 'safeguards' and a draft code of practice. The Treasury Select Committee also published its own report on 16 September 2008.[549]

The Consultation Paper referred to the 'decisive action' taken by the Authorities **7.242** and the FSCS in respect of the banking crisis, including 'steps to resolve difficulties with specific failing banks'. In September and October 2008, the first banks were declared in default by the FSA under the COMP Rules. The FSA made declarations of default for Bradford & Bingley Plc, Heritable Bank Plc, Kaupthing Singer & Friedlander Limited, and the UK branch of Landsbanki Islands hf.

In respect of the first three, exercising its powers under the BSPA, HM Treasury **7.243** made Orders for the transfer of deposit business to a third party.[550] These Orders provided for the transferee bank (rather than individual depositors) to receive payment from FSCS in the amount which FSCS would otherwise have paid in respect of claims for protected deposits following the default of the banks. If and to the extent that those deposits were not FSCS protected, HM Treasury meets the cost. Any protected deposits not so transferred, and remaining with the banks in default, are dealt with by the FSCS under the COMP Sourcebook.

In order to fund its contribution to the cost of transfer of the protected deposits, **7.244** which exceeded the maximum amount FSCS is able to raise by levy, FSCS borrowed from the Bank of England, on a short-term basis, to be refinanced with HM Treasury. To protect the levy payers, for reasons of financial stability, FSCS is not to make repayments of the borrowing other than from recoveries (received from the banks in default) or in respect of interest accrued on the borrowing, together with other management costs, subject to an annual (aggregate) cap of £1 billion.

In addition to the Orders, the FSA has made rule changes to COMP. As noted, **7.245** the maximum compensation limit for protected deposits was increased to £50,000 (from £35,000).[551] The FSA also issued its consultation on limits for all sub-schemes.[552] The deposit compensation limit has also been increased by many EU Member States and the European Commission is considering amendments to the DGD, both to increase the minimum level of compensation and to shorten timescales for payment. The FSA has also amended the 'exit levy'

---

[549] Banking Report.

[550] The Bradford & Bingley Plc Transfers of Securities and Properties etc Order 2008 (SI 2008/2546), the Kaupthing Singer & Friedlander Limited Transfer of Certain Rights and Liabilities Order 2008 (SI 2008/2674), the Heritable Bank Plc Transfer of Certain Rights and Liabilities Order 2008 (SI 2008/2644), and the Transfer of Rights and Liabilities to ING Order 2008 (SI 2008/2666).

[551] COMP 10.2.3R.

[552] CP08/15: Financial Services Compensation Scheme: Review of limits (October 2008).

rules[553] to enable the FSCS to raise exit levies, on firms which cease to be 'participant firms', in respect of prospective compensation costs for past defaults.

7.246   In respect of Landsbanki Islands hf, the UK branch had elected to 'top up' (under COMP 14) so that depositors entitled to the first tranche of compensation from the home State compensation scheme were protected for the 'top up' payment by the FSCS. In advance of the reforms under the Banking Bill, and in the absence of powers under the BSPA, it was recognised that the provisions in the COMP Sourcebook did not adequately address the handling of claims in respect of over 300,000 accounts with the UK branch. By the Compensation Sourcebook (Accelerated Compensation for Depositors) Instrument 2008, made on 29 October 2008, the FSA added COMP 15 to the Compensation Sourcebook 'to facilitate an accelerated payment of compensation' for depositors under which FSCS may modify the general claims handling and payment process (as described above).[554] In order to use powers under COMP 15, the FSCS must make a determination that the power '(1) would be beneficial to the generality of eligible claimants with protected deposits made with the relevant person in default in respect of whom the power is to be used; and (2) is unlikely to result in any additional cost to the FSCS which would require the imposition of increased levies on participant firms, over and above those required if the power was not exercised, or any additional cost is likely to be justified by the benefits'.[555] Such determination is to be published.[556] COMP 15 provides the FSCS with a variety of powers in respect of the payment of compensation without an application, early compensation for term or notice accounts, the form and method of paying compensation, the payment of compensation to which a claimant is entitled from another scheme, and the rights and obligations of the relevant person and third parties. Relying on such powers, on 4 November 2008, the FSCS made a determination in respect of Landsbanki.

7.247   Recent events have confirmed the FSCS's role as a participant in the 'safety net' for authorised firms. For deposit takers in particular, this experience supports the reform programme 'to provide for a new, permanent framework for dealing with banks before and after they experience financial stress'[557] and the resolution measures taken confirm that 'in the light of recent events in the financial markets, it has become apparent that preserving the flexibility of the Authorities is crucial'.[558]

---

[553]   FEES 6.7.6R.
[554]   15.1.2G.
[555]   COMP 15.1.4R.
[556]   COMP 15.1.7(3)R.
[557]   Consultation Paper (November 2008), paragraph 1.8.
[558]   ibid, para 1.46.

8

MARKET ABUSE

Background to the Introduction of the Market Abuse Regime

Introduction

Part VIII of the Financial Services and Markets Act 2000 ('FSMA') introduced a **8.01**
broad new power to tackle suspected wrongful behaviour on financial markets,
namely the 'civil offence' of market abuse under section 118 of FSMA. These
market abuse provisions sit alongside those powers that pre-date FSMA, most
importantly, the criminal offences of misleading statements and practices[1] and
insider dealing,[2] as well as the regulatory regime applying to regulated firms and
individuals, members of exchanges, and listed companies. The details of the new
market abuse regime are considered further in para 8.54 *et seq.*, but firstly this section will consider the background to the introduction of the market abuse provisions and, in particular, will focus on the practitioner and academic criticisms
levelled against the pre-FSMA criminal law powers and the failure of certain high-
profile prosecutions relating to wrongdoing on financial markets. This section
also considers the impact of the EU directive on insider dealing and market
manipulation (market abuse) ('MAD') which now forms part of the market abuse
regime,[3] and ongoing reviews and work undertaken at the European level.

Market abuse provisions in FSMA intended to fill a legislative 'gap'

The intended role of the FSMA market abuse regime was made clear in a state- **8.02**
ment made by the Economic Secretary to the Treasury during parliamentary
consideration of FSMA:

> We protect the financial markets in two ways. First, there are the criminal regimes for
> market manipulation and insider dealing. Those are both serious criminal offences,

---

[1] s 47 of the Financial Services Act 1986, now largely replicated as s 397 of FSMA.
[2] Part V of the Criminal Justice Act 1993.
[3] Directive 2003/6/EC on insider dealing and market manipulation (market abuse) and related
directives.

which carry a maximum sentence of seven years in jail and an unlimited fine. Secondly, there is the regulatory regime under which various regulatory bodies can take action against regulated persons for market abuse. However, there is a gap in the protections.[4]

The market abuse offences were intended by the government of the time to fill this 'gap'.[5] This is seen as supporting the FSA's regulatory objectives, namely market confidence, the protection of consumers, and the reduction of financial crime.[6] As the Economic Secretary stated, 'We are perceived to have fair and clean markets. We need to ensure that we keep it that way.'[7]

The failure of legislation adequately to protect against market misconduct

8.03 Before the introduction of the civil offence of market abuse in Part VIII FSMA, the main provisions to combat market misconduct were the statutory criminal offences of insider dealing,[8] and misleading statements and practices[9] and common law criminal offence of conspiracy to defraud. The first of the pre-FSMA legislative weapons against market misconduct, the criminal insider dealing offence, was considered by commentators and practitioners to be unsatisfactory at targeting market abuse not least as a result of the perception that a criminal offence was not a suitable means of regulating complicated market behaviour, due to the structural restrictions of prosecuting a criminal offence (for example, the need to comply with criminal procedure, ie a trial by a lay jury, with the presumption of innocence, the required standard of proof that the offence has to be proved beyond reasonable doubt, and the fact that the legislation should always be construed in the defendant's favour where there is ambiguity). In practice, very few

---

[4] Melanie Johnson, Economic Secretary to the Treasury, Standing Committee A, 2 November 1999, HMSO.

[5] See also the First Report (29 April 1999) and Second Report (2 June 1999) of the House of Lords and House of Commons Joint Committee on Financial Services and Markets (the 'Burns Reports'). The First Report commented that: 'The market abuse regime is intended to supplement, but not replace, the existing criminal sanctions for insider dealing, misleading the market and market manipulation. It is designed to allow the FSA to deal with any conduct that is damaging to the markets and in particular it is intended to enable the FSA to deal with market-abusive behaviour by non-authorised persons which is not caught by the existing criminal offences.' The two Burns Reports and the governmental responses provide illuminating background on the drafting history of the pre-MAD version of FSMA.

[6] FSMA, s 2(2).

[7] Melanie Johnson, n 4 above. See for further practitioner commentary on this point, Freshfields Bruckhaus Deringer, *Financial Services: Investigation & Enforcement* (2001) at para 13.9 (2nd edn, 2005), and Bagge, Evans, Wade and Lewis, 'Market Abuse: Proposals for the new regime', (2000) PLC 11(9), 35–42, at 36.

[8] CAJ, Part V.

[9] Financial Services Act 1986, s 47, now largely replicated as FSMA, s 397.

successful prosecutions were brought under the offence[10]—in a 12-year period up to 1997 just 30 prosecutions resulted in only 13 successful convictions. As Howard Davies, then Chairman of the FSA, commented on these statistics: 'Perhaps London's markets have been perfectly clean throughout this period. I beg leave to doubt it.'[11] Much as with insider dealing, the lack of prosecutions resulting in successful convictions was also perceived as a flaw in the 'misleading statements and practices' regime, with one practitioner citing 'a widespread perception that the current legislation has failed to deter or punish abuses effectively'.[12]

How the new regime has fared, seven years on and the ongoing role of the criminal **8.04** offences, is discussed further in para 8.187 *et seq*.

The failure of high-profile prosecutions to bring to justice those suspected of market misconduct offences

The debate leading up to the eventual introduction of the market abuse regime **8.05** was fuelled by the failure of a number of landmark prosecutions during the 1980s and 1990s, which attracted considerable media and public attention, and were perceived as having failed in their attempts to bring to justice those suspected of market misconduct. These failures were often attributed to procedural technicalities or inadequacies in the structure of the regime, most notably, in the *Blue Arrow* and *Guinness/Saunders* cases, discussed below.

The *Blue Arrow* case and the failure of the 'conspiracy to defraud' offence to catch market misconduct

The *Blue Arrow* case[13] concerned behaviour during a rights issue in Blue Arrow plc **8.06** which was intended to raise capital for the takeover by Blue Arrow of Manpower Inc. It was alleged that the market was misled by Blue Arrow's directors and financial advisers overstating how many of the shares in the Blue Arrow rights issue had been taken up at the close of the issue. This resulted in the prosecution of 14 parties involved with the rights issue for conspiracy to defraud, including the directors of Blue Arrow, and its financial advisers County NatWest. Ultimately, just four of the initial defendants were convicted by the jury, with these convictions being overturned by the Court of Appeal due to procedural difficulties

---

[10] Statistics cited by Mr Paul Boateng, MP, in Hansard written answers, 1 February 1999, Column 430.

[11] Mr Howard Davies, Chairman, FSA, Chancery Bar Association and Combar Spring Lecture (3 March 1999).

[12] Sykes, 'Market Abuse: A Civil Revolution?' (1999) *JIFM* 1(2) 59–67, at 67.

[13] *R v Cohen* [1992] 142 NLJ 1267.

experienced by the defendants. In the opinion of Mann LJ, giving the judgment of the court, their conviction was flawed for the following reasons.

• The trial judge had directed the jury to consider only a limited number of the offences alleged by the indictment, in an attempt to make the trial more manageable. However, this meant that the judge summed up on different matters than that on which counsel had addressed the jury, which was a material irregularity in the course of the trial. The judge should instead have used his severance powers at the start of the trial to cut down the unmanageably large indictment.

• The trial lasted for 184 days, of which the jury was absent from court on a total of 126 days. Mann LJ held that there was a basic assumption that juries should determine guilt or innocence on evidence it could comprehend, remember, and that had been given at such a time as to make an impression on the jury's deliberation. This was not the case on these facts, and so the conviction could not stand.

Criticisms of the failure of the prosecution in the *Blue Arrow* case

8.07 The failure of the prosecution of the *Blue Arrow* case to provide a (lasting) conviction for market misconduct generated considerable criticism, with commentators again questioning the role of criminal prosecutions in essentially regulatory domains, particularly where there is no element of direct personal gain.[14] The difficulties faced by a criminal prosecution were primarily in finding a manageable indictment, and presenting the case in an understandable manner to a lay jury.

The *Saunders* saga and the involvement of human rights to frustrate successful prosecutions for market misconduct

8.08 In the *Saunders* case,[15] Ernest Saunders, a former director of Guinness plc, was compelled by Department of Trade and Industry Inspectors to provide evidence relating to their investigation of suspected wrongdoing connected with Guinness plc's takeover of Distillers Company plc. Evidence obtained in these investigations was subsequently used in criminal proceedings against Saunders, in which he was found guilty of a number of fraud offences. The European Court of Human Rights ('ECtHR') held that the use in a criminal trial of evidence obtained under compulsory powers, 'was oppressive and substantially impaired his ability to defend himself against the criminal charges facing him'. The ECtHR concluded that Saunders was therefore: 'deprived of a fair hearing within the meaning of

---

[14] See for example Kirk, 'Blue Arrow: The SFO on trial', (1992) *ICCLR*, 3(1)), 331–3.

[15] *Saunders v United Kingdom* [1996] 23 EHRR 313.

article 6(1) . . .'.[16] This judgment, the basic effect of which was to limit greatly the authorities' powers to use self-incriminating evidence in proceedings for market misconduct, was again greeted with considerable criticism. One commentator highlighted a lack of proportionality in the decision, criticising the ECtHR's unwillingness to accept 'that the complexity of corporate fraud and the vital public interest in the investigation of such fraud and the punishment of those responsible should be taken into account in assessing whether statements made before the inspector . . . properly violated the right to a fair hearing'.[17]

The Market Abuse Directive

The detail of the current market abuse regime under section 118 has also been underpinned by the intervention of the European Commission to introduce under MAD EU-wide harmonised requirements relating to insider dealing and market manipulation,[18] implemented in the UK on 1 July 2005. This philosophical approach of MAD, embedded in its recitals, is derived from the premise that the smooth functioning of securities markets and public confidence in markets are considered by the EU to be prerequisites for economic growth and wealth, and that market abuse harms the integrity of markets. This in turn risks diminishing public confidence or stifling economic growth.[19] At the same time, it was noted that the effectiveness of legislation against market abuse varied considerably throughout the EU, as did the consistency in national enforcement of such legislation. Therefore, MAD may be understood as an attempt both to tackle the problem of market abuse and to harmonise across the EU national governments' approach to market abuse through effective laws consistently applied in all EU Member States.[20] **8.09**

---

[16] ibid, para 76 of the Judgment. Article 6(1) of the European Convention on Human Rights grants the right to a fair trial: 'a fair and public hearing within a reasonable time by an independent and impartial tribunal established by law'.

[17] Andrews, 'Hiding behind the veil: financial delinquency and the law', (1997) *EL Rev*, 22(4), 369–73. See also Stallworthy, 'Company investigations and the prosecution of fraud in the United Kingdom: conflicting public interests', (1997) *ICCLR*, 8(4), 115–19, for a similar discussion.

[18] MAD was the first directive introduced under the so-called Lamfalussy process—for a further discussion see Chapter 3. MAD was followed by Regulation 2273/2003 on buy-backs and stabilisation, Directive 2003/125/EC on investment research, 2003/124/EC on public disclosure of inside information, and 2004/72/EC which considered insider lists and suspicious transaction reporting.

[19] MAD, Recital 2.

[20] MAD, Recitals 11–13.

Access to and fairness of information

8.10   The focus of European initiatives has not merely related to detection and punishment—it has also addressed the need to enhance the timely and equal distribution of information and the fairness of that information.[21]

8.11   For example, MAD[22] has introduced across the EEA requirements that investment research be fairly presented and conflicts properly disclosed. The obligations on listed companies to announce price-sensitive information previously contained in Chapter 9 of the United Kingdom Listing Authority (UKLA) Listing Rules have also been modified as a result of MAD.[23] The Disclosure Rules (which comprise three chapters of the Disclosure Rules and Transparency Rules ('DTR')) issued by the FSA contain an obligation[24] on issuers to announce inside information as soon as possible (subject to a right in certain circumstances to delay announcement so as not to prejudice the issuer's 'legitimate interests'), as well as clarifying the circumstances and manner in which announcements should be made. This replaced the obligation under the former listing rules regime to make an announcement of 'major new developments', or changes in its 'financial condition', the 'performance of its business', or its 'expectation as to its performance', where such information was price-sensitive.[25] The impact and operation of a common threshold (inside information) applying to both the disclosure requirement and the MAD market abuse offences concerning inside information have been the subject of recent debate at European level and this is discussed further at para 8.193 *et seq*.[26] At the same time, issuers are subject to an obligation in the

---

[21]   Although in the UK the importance of this issue from the regulatory perspective can be seen from the number of enforcement actions under the Listing Rules for late or misleading announcements by listed companies. See, for example, FSA Final Notices to Marconi plc dated 11 April 2003; SFI Group plc dated 11 December 2003; Universal Salvage plc and Martin Christopher Hynes dated 19 May 2004; Sportsworld Media Group plc and Geoffrey John Brown dated 29 March 2004; the 'Shell' Transport and Trading Company plc and the Royal Dutch Petroleum company NV dated 24 August 2004 (also a market abuse decision); Pace Micro Technology plc dated 26 January 2005 and most recently Woolworths Group plc dated 11 June 2008.

[22]   Art 6(5), MAD, implemented further by the Commission Directive 2003/125/EC of the European Parliament and of the Council as regards the fair presentation of investment recommendations and the disclosure of conflicts of interest and implemented in the UK by amending the then FSA Conduct of Business Rules.

[23]   For a discussion of the Listing Rules, Prospectus Rules, and the Disclosure and Transparency Rules, see Chapter 9 at para 9.73 *et seq*.

[24]   Note that under FSMA, s 91, the FSA in its capacity as competent authority for the purposes of official listing (per FSMA, s 72) can impose sanctions for breaches of the Listing Rules, Prospectus Rules, and Disclosure and Transparency Rules.

[25]   UKLA Listing Rules 9.1–9.2 (no longer in force).

[26]   'As we explained in the joint Consultation Paper, we believe that the Directive regime is conceptually and operationally similar to the existing Listing Rules regime. We believe that in most cases determining what information should be disclosed and in what format should not lead to a different conclusion than under the current regime.' See FSA PS 05/03 para 3.6.

Listing Rules ('LR') to comply with 'listing principles'. Principle 2 (at LR 7.2.1R) requires that listed companies take reasonable steps to establish and maintain adequate procedures, systems, and controls to enable them to comply with their obligations. The concern is not so much the substance of the disclosures that issues will have to make regarding inside information, but rather the adequacy of the systems in place for identifying and disclosing such information.

In addition to the basic disclosure rule and exceptions from that rule and the list- **8.12** ing principles, the Disclosure Rules also impose rules on issuers relating to the control of insiders and inside information. For example, issuers are required to establish effective arrangements to deny access to inside information to persons other than those who require it for the exercise of their functions within the issuer,[27] and to have in place measures which enable public disclosure to be made via a regulatory information service (RIS) as soon as possible in case the issuer is not able to ensure the confidentiality of the relevant inside information.[28]

Further, in a move criticised for its lack of clarity and the administrative burden it **8.13** imposes, issuers are required to draw up and maintain lists of persons who have access to inside information.[29]

Finally, in a broadening of the previous obligations, persons discharging manage- **8.14** rial responsibilities and 'their connected persons' must notify the issuer in writing of the occurrence of all transactions conducted on their own account in the shares of the issuer, or derivatives or any other financial instruments relating to those shares within four business days of the day on which the transaction occurred. The issuer must in turn inform the RIS of any disclosure by such a person.[30] This is in addition to the Model Code which has been carried through into the Listing Rules in substantially similar form.

The Nature of the Market Abuse Regime and Underlying Processes

Introduction

As discussed at para 8.02, the FSMA market abuse regime was introduced as a civil **8.15** offence to fill the 'gap in the protections' between existing criminal offences on the

---

[27] DTR 2.6.1R.

[28] DTR 2.6.2R.

[29] DTR 2.8.1R, implementing Art 6(3) of MAD. Discussion relating to insider lists is also continuing as part of the EU-led review of the implementation and effectiveness of the MAD regime—see para 8.193 *et seq*.

[30] The Rules are set out in full at DTR 3.1 and implement Art 6(4) of MAD.

one hand and the regulatory enforcement powers on the other.[31] This section will outline the significance of the distinction between civil and criminal offences with particular emphasis placed on procedural rules. It will also look at human rights issues and how these affect the market abuse regime.

European Court of Human Rights—clarification of criminal offences

8.16 In the *Saunders* case,[32] as noted at para 8.08 above, the ECtHR passed judgment on the use of statements that a person has been compelled to make in a civil investigation for market misconduct being used in a subsequent criminal trial. Under the European Convention on Human Rights ('ECHR'),[33] it is a breach of the right to a fair trial where evidence that has been obtained by compulsion in the course of an investigation into market misconduct is used in a subsequent criminal trial. One might ask, then, why this impacts on the market abuse regime under Part VIII of FSMA, which is stated to be a civil regime.[34] Although the UK Government has classified the market abuse regime as civil in nature, the ECtHR has indicated that it is prepared to look beyond the classification of an offence by a national government, and re-classify it as a criminal offence for the purposes of the ECHR, if appropriate.[35]

The significance of the distinction between criminal and civil offences

8.17 The question as to whether or not the market abuse regime is in reality a criminal regime rather than a civil regime has sparked a considerable amount of debate and indeed was discussed at the time the regime as introduced.[36] The discussion is clearly one of significance for a number of reasons: the standard of proof in a criminal matter is such that the tribunal of fact must consider 'beyond all reasonable doubt' that the accused is guilty of the offence; by contrast, in a civil matter, the standard of proof is a belief that 'on the balance of probabilities' a matter has been proved; in serious criminal matters, the prosecution ordinarily needs to prove that the defendant had the requisite *mens rea* (mental element) to commit the offence (eg, intention to commit the crime, subjective recklessness as to its

---

[31] Melanie Johnson, n 4 above, and see generally para 8.01 *et seq.* of this chapter.

[32] *Saunders v United Kingdom*, n 15 above.

[33] Art 6(1) of the ECHR.

[34] See para 8.17 *et seq.*

[35] See for example *Bendenoun v France* [1994] 18 EHRR 54.

[36] Note also that the classification of the offence for the purposes of the ECHR was discussed in the First Burns Report (see the notes at para 8.02 for further discussion of the Burns Reports). In the section of the Report considering the proposed market abuse regime, it was observed that, 'although the draft Bill classifies the market abuse regime as civil, such classification under the domestic law is not conclusive for the ECHR and that, for that purpose, is likely to be regarded as criminal' (para 278).

commission, dishonesty or a specific level of knowledge); there is no *mens rea* for a civil matter; certain privileges are granted to the defendant in a criminal matter, for example, the privilege against self-incrimination;[37] such rights are not available in a civil matter; and as a general principle, in criminal matters, legislation is construed in the defendant's favour where there is any ambiguity. Finally, the ECHR[38] grants defendants in a criminal trial the right to a fair trial; these rights are not guaranteed to the same extent for civil matters.

In order to address this concern, a number of procedures were factored into the **8.18** FSMA regime, which in effect seek to preserve the right against self-incrimination in respect of statements made under compulsion.[39] These are described at para 8.37 *et seq.*[40]

The question of whether the market abuse regime offences are criminal for the **8.19** purposes of Article 6 of the ECHR has now been considered in a number of cases.

In the *Davidson and Tatham* case[41] the FSMT considered as a preliminary matter[42] **8.20** whether market abuse was a criminal or civil charge, and concluded that, whilst not being criminal charges for the purposes of domestic law, the penalties for

---

[37] It is a central principle of English criminal procedure that a defendant may not be compelled to testify against himself when he is charged with a criminal matter, a procedure known as the 'privilege against self-incrimination'. Criminal Evidence Act 1898 (as amended), s 1(1) provides as follows: 'A person charged in criminal proceedings shall not be called as a witness in pursuance of this Act in the proceedings except upon his own application.' In practice, this means that during the course of an investigation, a person should not be compelled (through the use of sanctions for non cooperation) to give evidence that would incriminate him as having committed the suspected offence.

[38] Convention for the Protection of Human Rights and Fundamental Freedoms, agreed by the Council of Europe at Rome on 4 November 1950, as it has effect for the time being in relation to the UK through the Human Rights Act 1998 ('HRA'), s 1(2): 'Those Articles (i.e., the Articles of the ECHR) are to have effect for the purposes of this Act . . .'

[39] Melanie Johnson, n 4 above, discussing the criticism that an early draft of the Financial Services and Markets Bill was not compatible with the ECHR: 'We recognised that there was a possibility that it would be classified as criminal for convention purposes and to avoid any risk of a finding that the Bill does not fully comply with the convention requirements, we decided to introduce the relevant protections. The first protection is against the use of compelled statements in proceedings to impose a market abuse penalty on the person who gave those statements.' It has been pointed out that the privilege against self-incrimination, in the context of the market abuse regime, only applies to *statements* made under *compulsion*. The privilege does not extend to documents (whether given under compulsion or not), or statements voluntarily made to FSA investigators. See Freshfields Bruckhaus Deringer, *Financial Services: Investigation & Enforcement*, n 7 above, at para 4.224.

[40] In response to the concerns of and the recommendation in the First Burns Report that the Government 'could incorporate criminal justice safeguards . . . into the enforcement regimes' (para 281), the Government introduced the procedural safeguards into FSMA discussed at para 8.37. In response to these changes, the Second Burns Report acknowledged that the changes would 'increase certainty and reduce the chance of successful legal challenge on ECHR grounds' (para 19).

[41] *Paul Davidson and Ashley Tatham v FSA*, FSMT Case 031, 16 May 2006.

[42] The FSMT had previously decided that this issue could be considered as a preliminary matter in the main hearing but did not need to be considered separately in a pre-hearing: *Paul Davidson v FSA*, FSMT Case 010, 9 August 2004 – Reasons for Directions.

market abuse were criminal charges for the purposes of the ECHR. In reaching a decision in the *Davidson and Tatham* case the FSMT referred to the judgment of the Court of Appeal in *Han v Customs and Excise Commissioners* [2001] EWCA Civ 1048 which concerned a civil penalty for dishonest evasion of tax. The issue was whether such a civil penalty was a criminal charge for the purposes of Article 6 of the ECHR. In that case the court summarised the relevant jurisprudence of the ECtHR and identified three criteria routinely applied by that court for the purpose of determining whether an applicant was the subject of a criminal charge.

8.21 The first criterion is the categorisation of the allegation in domestic law. In the case of the market abuse regime, the FSMT concluded that the market abuse offences were not categorised as criminal offences in domestic law. However, as was stated in the *Han* case, that was no more than a starting point and was not decisive of the nature of the allegation and it would therefore be necessary to look at the second and third criteria, namely the nature of the offence and the severity of the penalty.

8.22 It was concluded in the *Han* case that, under the second criterion, the court considers whether or not, under the law concerned, the 'offence' is one which applies generally to the public at large or is restricted to a specific group. In the case of market abuse, the FSMT in the *Davidson and Tatham* case noted that sections 118 and 123 of FSMA apply generally to the public at large and the penalty was not imposed as a disciplinary matter. As to the third criterion (the severity of the penalty), the sizes of the penalties imposed were clearly of a substantial, punitive, and deterrent nature rather than of a compensatory nature. As discussed above, the first criterion was considered to be no more than a starting point and was not in itself decisive, and accordingly in the decision, consideration of the second and third criteria prevailed.

8.23 The issue was again considered in the *Parker* case.[43] In that case, the FSA contested the proposition that an allegation of market abuse would give rise to a criminal charge within the meaning of Article 6, ECHR, the significance being relevant to a potential argument which would have been unfavourable to the FSA, on the standard of proof (as to which, see para 8.27).

8.24 The FSMT then analysed a number of the underlying cases (which did not appear to have been cited to the FSMT in the *Davidson and Tatham* decision) including the *Fleurose* Court of Appeal case.[44] That case related to a 'registered person' subject to the jurisdiction of the Disciplinary Tribunal and Disciplinary Appeals Tribunal of the Securities and Futures Authority ('SFA'), a self-regulatory

---

[43] *James Parker v FSA*, FSMT,Case 037, 18 August 2006.
[44] *Fleurose v Disciplinary Appeal Tribunal of the Securities and Futures Authority Limited* [2001] EWCA Civ 2015.

organisation under the pre-FSMA regime. The function of those bodies found their broad equivalence in the FSA's Regulatory Decisions Committee ('RDC') and the FSMT, although the analogy was not exact. Fleurose had been suspended from acting as a registered person for two years and ordered to contribute £175,000 towards the FSA's cost because of his improper conduct as a trader in manipulating the FTSE 100 Index. In *Fleurose*, Schiemann LJ, giving the judgment of the court, quoted extensively from the judgment of Potter LJ in *Han and others*, mentioning in particular the three criteria referred to above and it would seem concluded that the fact that only a registered person was subject to the disciplinary authority of the tribunals, and that no punitive or deterrent penalty was imposed, meant that the offence in *Fleurose's* was not criminal in character. A similar view had prevailed in other cases relating to disciplinary tribunals, (see *Pine v Law Society* [2001] EWCA Civ 1574, (where it was accepted without argument that the solicitors' disciplinary tribunal exercised a civil jurisdiction), and for example, *Rayner* and *Townsend v FSA*, FSMT Case 009, 6 August 2004).

The FSMT in the *Parker* case came to the conclusion that in its view the analogy **8.25** with the disciplinary tribunal cases was weak, and that Parker's position was much closer to that of the appellants in *Han* and therefore agreed with the FSMT in the *Davidson and Tatham* decision that an allegation of market abuse, even when punished in accordance with section 123 of FSMA, and therefore by a route which is classed as civil for domestic law purposes, has to be treated for ECHR purposes as a criminal charge. In reaching this view, the FSMT considered that the conduct in the *Parker* case, if proved, could lead to the imposition not only of the civil penalty but could also expose the person to criminal prosecution (in the instant case, by reason of FSMA section 402(1)(a) under the Criminal Justice Act 1993, section 52) and it was not necessary to be a member of a close group (for example, an 'approved person' for FSA purposes) to be subject to a penalty. The FSMT also concluded that the penalty imposed on Parker was both punitive and deterrent in character and was intended so to be.

Burden of proof and the standard of proof applicable to the market abuse offence

Burden of proof

The FSMT in the *Davidson and Tatham* case addressed the question of what **8.26** consequences would follow from its finding as to the categorisation of the market abuse offences.[45] As an initial point, the FSMT found that it was clear from

---

[45] Article 6 of the ECHR gives the right to a fair trial. Article 6(1) relates to civil rights and obligations and provides that everyone is entitled to a fair and public hearing within a reasonable time

Article 6(2) of the ECHR that the first consequence would be that the burden of proof would indeed lie on the FSA to prove their case.[46] Of the other five minimum rights mentioned in Article 6(3) the most relevant, according to the FSMT, was the right to legal assistance and they were addressed in statutory provisions in FSMA (sections 134 to 136).[47]

Standard of proof

8.27 The standard of proof in a criminal matter is that the tribunal of fact must consider 'beyond all reasonable doubt' that the accused is guilty of the offence; by contrast, in a civil matter, the standard of proof is a belief that 'on the balance of probabilities' a disputed matter has been proved, a less arduous standard. Under the market abuse provisions in section 123(1), the required standard of proof for market abuse is not specifically stated as either civil or criminal. Rather, it is stated that the FSA only needs to be 'satisfied' (subject to the defences that may apply under section 123(2)) that market abuse took place to impose a penalty on the guilty party.[48] The question is therefore: on what basis will the FSA be 'satisfied' that market abuse has taken place? Clear guidance on this question was provided by the FSA at the introduction of the FSMA regime: 'In such proceedings, the burden will be on the FSA and the FSA will plainly have to prove its case on a balance of probabilities.'[49]

---

by an independent and impartial tribunal. Article 6(2) relates to criminal offences and provides that everyone charged with a criminal offence shall be presumed innocent until proved guilty according to law. Article 6(3) defines five minimum rights which apply to everyone charged with a criminal offence. These five minimum rights are: the right to be informed promptly of the nature and cause of the accusation; the right to have adequate time and facilities for the preparation of the defence; the right to defend himself in person or through legal assistance of his own choosing, or, if he has not sufficient means to pay for legal assistance, to be given it free when the interests of justice so require; the right to examine witnesses against him and to obtain the attendance and examination of witnesses on his behalf; and the right to an interpreter.

[46] The point was also discussed by the FSMT in *Parker*, where the FSMT, commenting on the fact that the FSA accepted that the burden of proof would lay on it, expressed the view that this would be the case in any case in which a penalty has been imposed, apart perhaps from a minor penalty occasioned by a technical regulatory breach and with no suggestion of moral turpitude, regardless of Article 6(2) of the ECHR (which provides that anyone charged with a criminal offence is to be presumed innocent until proved guilty).

[47] In *Davidson v FSA*, FSMT Case 010, 9 August 2004, Davidson was indeed granted the right to apply for legal assistance (although in the event it was refused).

[48] Although note that the FSA may not impose a sanction if there are reasonable grounds for it to be satisfied that the person in question believed his behaviour did not constitute market abuse or 'requiring and encouraging'. Also note that under the COMC in certain circumstances the intention, purpose, or knowledge of the person in question may be taken into account in determining whether or not market abuse has been committed—see discussion at para 8.73.

[49] FSA Policy Statement 59 (April 2001)—Code of Market Conduct Feedback on CP59 and CP76, para 4.11.

Application of the balance of probabilities test

What the standard of proof should be, and how this should be applied, has been **8.28** considered in a number of FSMT cases. In *Arif Mohammed*,[50] the applicant, Arif Mohammed, submitted that a market abuse case is akin to a criminal offence, and that the burden of proof would therefore be on the FSA to prove its case beyond reasonable doubt. The FSA, conversely, submitted that the burden should be a 'balance of probabilities', albeit subject to the principle adopted by the FSMT in previous decisions[51] that the more serious the allegation, the more cogent the evidence needs to be to prove it (the so-called 'sliding scale principle'). Whilst recognising that the previous decisions referred to were not market abuse cases, and that specific considerations arise in such cases (including the fact that enforcement action may be taken against persons who are not regulated by the FSA) the FSMT agreed with the FSA that the sliding scale principle would apply.

The point was also considered in subsequent FSMT cases. In the *Davidson and* **8.29** *Tatham* case where the FSMT considered at length the various authorities cited to it. As part of this, the FSMT referred to the Court of Appeal judgment in *R v Mental Health Review Tribunal*[52] and in particular the comments in the judgment that: 'the essential point that runs through the authorities is that the civil standard of proof is flexible in its application and enables proper account to be taken of the seriousness of the allegations to be proved and of the consequences of proving them'. According to the judgment, the more serious the allegation, or the more serious the consequences if the allegation is proved, the stronger the evidence would have to be for the allegation to be proved on the balance of probabilities. Although there remained a distinction in principle between the civil standard and the criminal standard, the practical application of the flexible approach, according to the judgment, was that they were likely in certain contexts to produce the same or similar results.[53]

In the light of the authorities reviewed, the FSMT formed the view that,[54] although **8.30** the market abuse offences were criminal charges for the purposes of Article 6 of the ECHR, there was no provision in Article 6 that the appropriate standard of proof is the criminal standard. The FSMT concluded that the civil standard of proof was sufficiently strong to establish what has to be established.

---

[50] *Arif Mohammed v FSA*, FSMT, Case 012, 29 March 2005. See also the discussion at para 8.117.

[51] *Geoffrey Alan Hoodless and Sean Michael Blackwell v FSA*, FSMT Case 007, 3 October 2003, at 21, *Legal & General Assurance Soc Ltd v FSA*, FSMT Case 011, 18 January 2005, at 19.

[52] *R (On the Application of An) (Appellant) v Mental Health Review Tribunal* [2005] EWCA Civ 1605.

[53] In the *Davidson and Tatham* case, the FSMT concluded that the allegations of market abuse in question were very serious allegations, and although there remained a distinction in principle between the civil standard and the criminal standard, the practical application of the flexible approach meant that they were likely, in the context of Davidson and Tatham, to produce the same or similar results.

[54] Following *B v Chief Constable of Avon and Somerset Constabulary* [2001] 1 WLR 340.

8.31 The position was also considered in the *Parker* case and the FSMT agreed with the FSMT in *Davidson and Tatham*, for the same reason. In the *Parker* case, the FSMT referred in particular to the judgment of Lord Nicholls in *Re H* [1996] 1 All ER 1 at pages 16–17:

> The balance of probability standard means that a court is satisfied an event occurred if the court considers that, on the evidence, the occurrence of the event was more likely than not. When assessing the probabilities the court will have in mind as a factor, to whatever extent is appropriate in the particular case, that the more serious the allegation the less likely it is that the event occurred and, hence the stronger should be the evidence before the court concludes that the allegation is established on the balance of probability. Fraud is usually less likely than negligence . . . Built into the preponderance of probability standard is a general degree of flexibility in respect of the seriousness of the allegation.
>
> Although the result is much the same, this does not mean that where a serious allegation is in issue the standard of proof required is higher. It means only that the inherent probability or improbability of an event is itself a matter to be taken into account when weighing the probabilities and deciding whether, on balance, the event occurred. The more improbable the event, the stronger must be the evidence that it did occur before, on the balance of probability, its occurrence will be established.

Lord Nicholls also referred to the comments of Ungoed-Thomas J in *Re Dellow's Will Trusts*:[55]

> The more serious the allegation, the more cogent is the evidence required to overcome the unlikelihood of what is alleged and thus to approve it.

8.32 In the *Parker* case, the FSMT concluded there could be no doubt that an allegation that a person had been guilty of conduct for which he should be punished by a penalty of £300,000 was a very grave charge and compelling evidence had to be adduced if it was to be established. In other words, if one applies the 'sliding scale', the slide must be very close to the upper end of the scale. Importantly, the FSMT found that in a practical sense, even if not semantically, it was difficult to draw a meaningful distinction between the standard it had to apply and the criminal standard.

How the test has been applied in practice

8.33 As can be seen from the above, the FSMT has come to the view over a number of cases that a high standard would need to be satisfied and this led to a number of perceived setbacks for the FSA, notably in the *Davidson and Tatham* case.

---

[55] *Re Dellow's Will Trusts, Lloyds Bank Ltd v Institute of Cancer Research* [1964] 1 All ER 771 at 773, [1964] 1 WLR 451 at 455.

Again, in the *Baldwin* case[56] (a case of alleged market abuse: misuse of informa- **8.34** tion) the FSMT concluded in favour of Baldwin and WRT that there was no evidence that a disputed telephone call had taken place. The FSMT also rejected the FSA submission of the expert evidence provided. It did not establish that an expert investor would not have acted in the way that Baldwin did in the absence of inside information.

Notwithstanding the requirements as to cogency of evidence, circumstantial evi- **8.35** dence can be sufficient.[57] In the *Shevlin* case (an RDC decision),[58] Shevlin argued that the FSA, in the absence of clear evidence that Shevlin had access to inside information, did in fact access that information and based his decision to trade upon it, had failed to prove their case. He argued they were relying exclusively on circumstantial evidence. Those circumstances included the FSA's admission that they were unable to confirm with any precision when Shevlin was alleged to have logged into the email accounts of senior executives and accessed the relevant information. Whilst acknowledging that it was unable to demonstrate conclusively Shevlin's access to inside information, the FSA stated it was able to draw inferences from the weight of the circumstantial evidence in the case when it was considered as a whole and draw conclusions from the material.

In the recent *Harrison* decision (an FSA decision settled at stage 1)[59] the FSA **8.36** found that inside information had passed to Harrison, even though it had not been possible to determine the precise circumstances and terms in which the information had passed to Harrison as the relevant telephone calls had not been taped.[60]

The privilege against self-incrimination as it relates to the market abuse offence

As mentioned above, a number of procedures have been factored into the FSMA **8.37** regime which in effect seek to preserve the right against self-incrimination in respect of statements made under compulsion.[61] An FSA investigator may require

---

[56] *Timothy Edward Baldwin and WRT Investments Ltd v FSA*, FSMT, Case 026, 24 January 2006.

[57] In her speech on 22 May 2007 (*Market Abuse Policy & Enforcement in the UK*), Sally Dewar, Market Abuse Policy & Enforcement in the UK, commented that 'it is rare to find a "smoking gun"; and often cases hinge on circumstantial evidence. It is quite common for insider traders to come up with alternative rationales for their trading strategies that can be difficult to disprove.'

[58] FSA Final Notice to John Shevlin dated 1 July 2008.

[59] FSA Final Notice to Steven Harrison dated 8 September 2008 SDM.

[60] The finding also concluded that the conduct in question had not been deliberate.

[61] Melanie Johnson, n 4 above, discussing the criticism that an early draft of the Financial Services and Markets Bill was not compatible with the ECHR: 'We recognised that there was a possibility that it would be classified as criminal for convention purposes and to avoid any risk of a finding

the person who is the subject of an FSA investigation, or persons connected to such a person, to attend an interview with the investigator and answer specific questions, and otherwise provide such information as the investigator may require.[62] However, there is a specific limitation on the use to which this information can be put in the context of market abuse. According to section 174(2) of FSMA, no evidence relating to such statements may be adduced and no question relating to it may be asked by the prosecution or the FSA unless the statement is first raised by or on behalf of the person who made the statement.

European Convention on Human Rights—obligations on public authorities

The FSA's obligation to act compatibly with the ECHR, which underlies the market abuse offence

8.38 In addition to the issue of the privilege against self incrimination, there is a broader obligation on the FSA for its acts to be compatible with human rights. The Human Rights Act ('HRA') states that it is unlawful for a 'public authority' to act in a way which is 'incompatible' with an ECHR right.[63] For these purposes, a 'public authority' is defined as any person who exercises functions of a public nature, which would seemingly include the FSA in its role as the regulator of the financial services industry in the UK.[64] On this basis, the FSA must comply with the ECHR rights and, in particular, must not act in a way that is incompatible with a person's right to a fair trial. The view expressed by HM Treasury is that the structural safeguards built into the system in terms of the structure and process of the FSMT, as well as the rules relating to the use of statements obtained under compulsion, are such as to be compatible with the FSA's human rights obligations when policing

---

that the Bill does not fully comply with the convention requirements, we decided to introduce the relevant protections. The first protection is against the use of compelled statements in proceedings to impose a market abuse penalty on the person who gave those statements.' It has been pointed out that the privilege against self-incrimination, in the context of the market abuse regime, only applies to *statements* made under *compulsion*. The privilege does not extend to documents (whether given under compulsion or not), or statements voluntarily made to FSA investigators. See *Freshfields Bruckhaus Deringer on Financial Services: Investigation & Enforcement*, n 7 above, at para 4.224. In response to the concerns of and the recommendation in the First Burns Report that the government 'could incorporate criminal justice safeguards . . . into the enforcement regimes' (para 281), the Government introduced the procedural safeguards into FSMA discussed at para 8.37. In response to these changes, the Second Burns Report acknowledged that the changes would 'increase certainty and reduce the chance of successful legal challenge on ECHR grounds' (para 19).

  [62] FSMA, s 171(1) and (4).
  [63] HRA, s 6(1).
  [64] ibid, s 6(3)(b) and FSMA, s 2 (the Authority's general duties). In addition, Lomnicka argues that the FSA is impliedly considered to be a public authority by FSMA, on the basis that the exemption of liability in Sched 1, para 19 of FSMA does not extend to acts which are unlawful as a result of s 6(1) of the HRA. Eva Lomnicka, *The Financial Services and Markets Act: An Annotated Guide* (2002).

the market abuse provisions (as well as when carrying out its public functions generally).[65]

Fair process

A couple of FSMT decisions illustrate the significance of fair process considera- **8.39**
tions. The first of these involves the *Davidson and Tatham* case[66] discussed at para
8.20 above, where the first FSMT hearing was aborted on the application of the
FSA, after it emerged that the chairman of the FSA's RDC had discussed the proceedings privately with one of the members of the FSMT panel.[67] A subsequent
hearing took place with a reconstituted panel.

The FSMT has also considered on a couple of occasions the position of parties **8.40**
'identified' in Decision Notices.

The first relates to Sir Phillip Watts, the former chairman of Shell, who took **8.41**
action against the FSA before the FSMT in relation to the FSA's Final Notice
against Shell[68] for market abuse. Watts alleged that the Final Notice improperly
and unfairly implicated him in Shell's wrongdoing (although he was not mentioned by name, he argued that there are implicit references to him). Watts argued
that the unfairness stemmed from the fact that ordinarily where an FSA notice
would be prejudicial to an identified third party, that third party should be given
a copy of the notice before a final decision is made, with the right to refer the decision to the FSMT.[69] The FSMT held[70] that the purpose of the warning procedure
is to provide rights to third parties, but it limited the availability of such rights to
persons who are 'identified in the decision notice' and not, as Watts argued, to a
person who is identified only through the matter to which the reasons in the decision notice relates.[71] The FSMT further decided that where a market abuse allegation is directed against a company, this does not necessarily impute criticism to
individuals associated with the running or management of the company, although
it tempered this by adding that whether it is fair to take separate action against

---

[65] In *Rayner & Townsend v FSA*, FSMT Case 009, 6 August 2004, it was noted that the FSMT
had been set up to ensure that the regulatory decision making process as a whole was compatible
with the ECHR by providing an independent, impartial FSMT. The FSMT also has 'original jurisdiction' ie hearing before it are full rehearings—see for example the discussion in *Davidson and
Tatham*. However, see para 8.44 as to criticisms of the FSA processes in the *Legal & General* case and
the subsequent Strachan Report.
[66] *Paul Davidson and Ashley Tatham v FSA*, FSMT Case 031, 16 May 2006.
[67] The original market abuse Final Notice from the FSA to Davidson is not available to the
public.
[68] FSA Final Notice to Shell Transport and Trading Company, plc and The Royal Dutch
Petroleum Company NV dated 24 August 2004.
[69] FSMA, s 393.
[70] *Sir Philip Watts v FSA*, FSMT Case 020, 7 September 2005.
[71] ibid, para 49.

companies and the individuals running that company would depend on the facts of the case.[72]

8.42 A similar point arose in the FSMT decision relating to *Jan Laury*.[73] Laury was the compliance officer at an FSA regulated firm. Laury took objection to the fact that the Final Notice relating to the firm on the basis that it contained implied criticism of him, which was unjustified, and which he had no opportunity to contest or correct.

8.43 The FSMT considered the two potentially conflicting propositions that, on the one hand (as argued by Laury) identification need not be expressed and may be implicit, and on the other (as argued by the FSA) that reference to external sources is not permissible, and concluded that there was in reality no true inconsistency, citing as an example that if a managing director was the subject of criticism in the notice, the description 'managing director' was itself a sufficient identification and there was no need to go to outside sources to discover his or her name. According to the FSMT, what one was not allowed to do was to add material from external sources to the material in the notice in order to identify an individual as impliedly the subject of the criticism. On the facts of the *Jan Laury* case, the FSMT did not consider that the argument that a reader might possibly take loosely expressed criticisms as referring to Laury was sufficient—only a positive identification could satisfy the terms of section 393 of FSMA ('identifies a person'). Accordingly to the FSMT, where a particular function or particular department of a firm was referred to as having failings, it did not necessarily follow that a particular individual could be inferred to have been at fault, even if that individual was held by the head of department or the person responsible for that function.

8.44 Finally, it is also relevant to consider the procedural changes introduced by the FSA to its processes following criticism relating to the fairness and transparency of the FSA's enforcement approach raised in the *Legal & General* case[74] and addressed in the so-called Strachan report.[75]

---

[72] ibid, paras 50 and 54. Note also that the FSMT stated that where an individual is identified by sources external to the Final Notice (as Watts was identified by the media), s 393 would not require that individual to be given a right of response (para 52). As it transpired, on 9 November 2005, the FSA announced that they had decided to close their investigation against Watts. FSA: 'FSA closes enquiries into Shell individuals', FSA/PN/118/2005, 9 November 2005 (<http://www.fsa.gov.uk/Pages/Library/Communication/PR/2005/118.shtml>).

[73] *Jan Laury v FSA*, FSMT Case 046, 2007.

[74] In *Legal & General Assurance Society v FSA* the FSMT commented (at para 191) that: 'it was for FSA not L&G to control the process so that it was fair, effective and reasonably prompt. If L&G was not cooperating in securing a review which could be used effectively for enforcement, it was for FSA to impose a suitable exercise.'

[75] FSA, 'Enforcement process review—Report and recommendations' (July 2005), available at <http://www.fsa.gov.uk/pubs/other/enf_process_review_report.pdf>. See in particular paras 3.2–3.8

Unreasonable behaviour and costs

A number of cases have addressed the question of whether the FSA's conduct has **8.45** been unreasonable. This has occurred in the context of applications to recover costs.

The legislation which governs the awards of cost by the FSMT is found in para- **8.46** graph 13 of Schedule 13 to FSMA and in Rule 21 of the Financial Services and Markets Tribunal Rules 2001 (SI 2001/2476). Paragraph 13 of Schedule 13 to FSMA provides:

> (1) If the FSMT considers that a party to any proceedings on a reference has acted vexatiously, frivolously, or unreasonably it may order that party to pay another party to proceedings the whole or part of the costs or expenses incurred by the other party in connection with the proceedings.
>
> (2) If, in any proceedings on a reference, the FSMT considers that a decision of the FSA which is the subject of the reference was unreasonable, it may order the FSA to pay to another party to the proceedings the whole or part of the costs or expenses incurred by the other party in connection with the proceedings.

Rule 21(3) provides that where the FSMT makes a costs order it may either (a) fix the amount or (b) direct that the costs should be assessed on such basis as it should specify by a costs official (of the court).

In the Cost Decision of *Davidson and Tatham*[76] an application made to the FSMT **8.47** following the *Davidson and Tatham* decision, the FSMT sought to address whether the FSA's decision had been unreasonable. The approach adopted by the FSMT was to look at this, given the facts and circumstances which were known or ought to have been known to the FSA at the time when the decision was made. In taking this approach, the FSMT took note of the fact that the process leading to the FSA's decision was not a full judicial hearing of the kind conducted by the FSMT.[77]

In terms of paragraph 13(2), from the arguments of the parties, the FSMT identi- **8.48** fied three elements of the disputed decision which they claimed to be unreasona- ble, and which the FSMT considered relevant, namely the approach to the evidence and the facts; the approach to the law; and the approach to the penalties. As to the first, the FSMT found on the facts that it was unreasonable that the evidence of one particular party had been preferred to the evidence of another (Davidson). The FSMT also noted that the decision-making process at the time of the disputed decision had the defects identified in the enforcement process review which

---

which explain the criticisms of the lack of fairness and transparency in the enforcement process. See discussion in Chapter 1 at paras 1.77 *et seq.*

[76] *Paul Davidson and Ashley Tatham v FSA*, FSMT Case 040, 16 May 2006.

[77] See also *Legal and General Assurance Society Ltd v FSA*, Case 015, 18 January 2005: 'when deal- ing with a large volume of regulatory matters informally and speedily, FSA should not be expected to follow procedures, or express its conclusions, as required of a court'.

had taken place in the light of the *Legal & General* decision. Finally, the FSMT concluded that in its view it was not reasonable to decide against criminal proceedings on the ground that a higher penalty could be imposed by a civil penalty. It was also unreasonable to proceed to ignore the same mitigating factors as would have applied in criminal proceedings to reduce the level of the penalties. The FSMT found that in its view the amount of the final differential between the penalties imposed on two of the parties was not reasonable. It also found that after hearing Tatham's representations, it was unreasonable for the RDC not to form the view that Tatham reasonably believed that his behaviour did not amount to market abuse and that consequently they did not have the legal power to impose the penalty. In terms of the level of the penalty on Davidson, appearing in the Decision Notice, the FSMT found that although the notice took account of some mitigating factors it did not take account of all the factors that should have been borne in mind and was of the view that it was unreasonable of the RDC not to mitigate the levels of the penalties more than they did.[78] As to paragraph 13(1), the FSMT considered it unfortunate that the FSA allowed the proceedings to continue after all the evidence and expert evidence had been adduced, but could not say that it was unreasonable not to withdraw the disputed decision during the course of the hearing.

8.49 The question of costs on the basis of Schedule 13 had also been considered in an earlier FSMT decision relating to *Davidson*, (*Davidson v FSA* FSMT Case 10, 9 August 2004 – Reasons for Directions) where an application was made relating to costs thrown away in a previous hearing. This resulted from the FSA announcing that it had become aware that a conversation had taken place between the chairman of the RDC and a member of the FSMT selected from the panel of chairmen hearing the reference. As a result of this the chairman of the RDC tendered his resignation and the FSA issued a statement that it regarded his actions in connection with the conversation as inappropriate. The relevant member of the FSMT, and subsequently the other members, recused themselves. The FSMT concluded that in the circumstances, the FSA (via the RDC) had acted unreasonably. A later FSMT direction[79] that followed the main FSMT decision directed that Davidson's application for a costs order be allowed to the extent of 50% of the costs thrown away.[80]

---

[78] The FSMT added that matters identified as being unreasonable were unlikely to recur in the future as the decision notice in these references was issued before the many changes in the decision-making process recommended by the enforcement process review of 2005, were implemented.

[79] *Paul Davidson and Ashley Tatham v FSA*, FSMT Case 040, 11 October 2006.

[80] The reason for the limitation as to the quantum (to 50%) was that the FSMT should also be considered partly responsible, and the FSMT was not a party to the reference and therefore the legislative provisions relating to costs would not apply.

A costs application was also made in the *Baldwin* case[81]—(Costs Decision). The **8.50** applicants had been accused of market abuse but the FSMT had found that they were not guilty and that no penalty should be imposed. In the case of paragraph 13(2), the FSMT found it was required to look at the decision itself. Arguments were raised in the proceedings that the 'Wednesbury' test should be applied (a decision is 'Wednesbury unreasonable' if it is 'so unreasonable that no reasonable authority could ever have come to it') but the FSMT did not consider this test would be appropriate, helpful, or conducive and the FSMT considered paragraph 13 required it to make its own judgement as to what was reasonable. On the facts, the FSMT did not find itself able to conclude that the FSA's decision was unreasonable.

The FSMT also concluded that paragraph 13(1) should not be limited to conduct **8.51** within the proceedings following a reference, and accordingly that it was entitled (where relevant) to take account of conduct which took place before the reference was made and the proceedings commenced. The FSMT concluded that the FSA decision in the *Baldwin* case was not unreasonable and it did not consider it would be right on the facts to award costs against the FSA on the basis of the criticisms of the investigation that preceded that decision. The FSMT also pointed out it did not wish it to be thought that it intended to lay down any general rule to the effect that no award of costs would be based on conduct prior to the FSA's decision, where the decision itself was reasonable and that there may very well be cases where the nature of such conduct and its significance in relation to the proceedings would justify such an award.

The Market Abuse Offences

The definition of market abuse in Part VIII FSMA and the impact of MAD on the market abuse regime

This section discusses the definition of behaviour that constitutes market abuse **8.52** under section 118 of FSMA, as amended to implement MAD. Paragraph 8.74 *et seq.* below will consider the prescribed behaviour types that constitute abusive behaviour and the 'safe harbours' which are available, together with a discussion of the guidance and evidential provisions issued by the FSA in the Code of Market Conduct ('COMC') and other exceptions and defences. This section will begin, however, by considering briefly the impact of the introduction of MAD on the market abuse regime.

---

[81] *Timothy Edward Baldwin and WRT Investments Ltd*, FSMT, Case 028, 5 April 2006.

The 'regular user' test at the heart of the pre-MAD market abuse regime

8.53   The types of behaviour covered by the pre-MAD market abuse regime related to three basic types of behaviour, namely:

(i)   misuse of information—behaviour based on information not generally available to market users;

(ii)   false or misleading impressions—behaviour giving a false or misleading impression as to the price of investments; and

(iii)   distortion—behaviour distorting the market.

The cornerstone of the regime was the 'regular user test', that is to say, that behaviour which would be likely to be regarded by a 'regular user' of the market as a failure on the part of the person or persons concerned to observe the standard of behaviour reasonably expected of a person in his or their positions in relation to the market. 'Regular user' was defined, in relation to a particular market, as 'a reasonable person who regularly deals on that market in investments of the kind in question'.[82] The FSA's guidance indicates that the regular user test was designed to import an objective element into the judgement of market behaviour, while retaining some subjective elements related to the markets in question.[83]

The FSMA market abuse regime following the implementation of the provisions of MAD

8.54   A number of key changes were introduced into the UK market abuse system as a result of the implementation of MAD in the UK on 1 July 2005.[84] In considering the introduction of MAD, HM Treasury and the FSA formulated the view that although the new MAD offences and the offences under the pre-MAD regime (the so-called 'legacy offences') conceptually covered very similar ground, their terms were not co-extensive (and indeed the general approach taken was different), and accordingly the MAD offences relating to insider dealing and market manipulation have in effect been superimposed onto the legacy offences. The pre-MAD 'legacy' offences therefore still exist, but will only apply where a person's conduct does not fall within any of the MAD behaviour types. The regular user test remains in place for the legacy offences, but not the new post-MAD offences (the view was taken that the 'regular user' test would be inconsistent with the approach taken by MAD). The post-MAD offences instead are assessed solely by consideration of the behaviour types set out and the specific safe harbours,

---

[82]   Definition now contained in FSMA, s 130A(3).

[83]   MAR 1.2.21G.

[84]   For a general discussion regarding the background to the introduction of MAD, see para 8.09 above.

exceptions, and defences, and guidance and evidential provisions set out in the legislation and the COMC.[85]

Sunset clause for the legacy offences

The two legacy offences were subject to a sunset date of 30 June 2008 - in other words, they were to cease to have effect on 30 June 2008 unless positive action was taken to retain them.[86] The Treasury committed to review the efficacy of the super-equivalent provisions to determine whether or not their retention as part of the UK market abuse regime was justified. The Treasury released a consultation paper in February 2008,[87] which recommended an extension of the sunset date of the super-equivalent provisions to 31 December 2009, pending the outcome of the 2008 European Commission ('EC') review of MAD. The Treasury considered that the evidence supporting the retention of the super-equivalences was finely balanced. According to the Treasury, the costs did not appear to be significant and, while the proven benefits were hard to quantify, proposed changes in the FSA's approach to enforcement might increase the use of and hence the demonstrable benefit of the super equivalences. The Treasury, however, considered that by having an extension, this would enable a wider consideration of the benefits of the super-equivalent provisions in the context of the forthcoming EC review and would minimise transition costs for industry.[88]

8.55

As part of the consultation, the Treasury gave an overview of the areas where the legacy regime was wider in its coverage than the post-MAD offences. These were, broadly, in its view that the concept of 'relevant information not generally available' ('RINGA') used in the legacy offence of misuse of information is wider in scope than 'inside information' used in the post-MAD offences of market abuse (insider dealing) and market advice (improper disclosure); that the post-MAD provisions required some specified positive action (eg dealing, effecting trade, disseminating information etc) whereas the super-equivalent provisions focus on 'behaviour' that might capture inaction; the post-MAD insider dealing provisions required the existence of an 'insider', as defined, but the legacy offence of misuse of information did not require an 'insider'; differences in the definitions of investments to which the provisions apply; and the different market coverage of the two

8.56

---

[85] See discussion at para 8.74 below.

[86] The 'legacy' offences were to remain in FSMA for a period of three years from the implementation of the MAD amendments, ie until 30 June 2008, after which date they would cease to have effect—FSMA, s 118(9).

[87] HM Treasury: 'FSMA market abuse regime: a review of the sunset clauses, a consultation' (February 2008).

[88] A sunset date of 31 December 2009 was introduced by the Financial Services and Markets Act (2000) (Market Abuse) Regulations 2008, SI.2008/1439.

sets of provisions. The paper also set out a number of specific examples, but criticism of some of these was subsequently expressed.[89]

8.57 As part of the consultation, the Treasury looked at the use made of the legacy offences post-MAD. No cases had been brought under the super-equivalent provisions since the introduction of the MAD offences, and the Treasury concluded that eight cases brought under the legacy offences pre-MAD would now fall within the MAD offences. Two cases may have included (although not solely relied on) adverse findings against what are now the super-equivalent provisions. The Treasury also indicated that other cases have been considered in this time under the super-equivalent provisions but not brought forward for evidential reasons and that there were also current investigations that relied on super-equivalent provisions.

The Code of Market Conduct

8.58 Under section 119(1) of FSMA, the FSA is required to prepare and issue a code containing such provisions as it considers will give appropriate guidance to those determining whether or not behaviour amounts to market abuse. This requirement has been satisfied in the form of the COMC, which is contained in Chapter 1 of the FSA's Market Conduct handbook (MAR). The structure of the COMC is based around each of the seven behaviour types now in section 118. It considers each type of behaviour and sets out descriptions of behaviour that, in the opinion of the FSA, do or do not amount to market abuse. In addition, the COMC sets out factors that, in the opinion of the FSA, are to be taken into account in determining whether or not behaviour amounts to market abuse.[90] It also sets out certain safe harbours which will apply.[91] In addition to those safe harbours set out in the COMC, there are a number of statutory exceptions in FSMA discussed further at para 8.157.[92] The COMC does not, however, exhaustively describe all types of behaviour that may or may not amount to market abuse. In particular, the FSA has stressed that the descriptions of behaviour which amount to market abuse should be read in the light of the elements specified by FSMA as making up the relevant type of market abuse and any relevant descriptions of behaviour which, in the opinion of the FSA, do not amount to market abuse.[93] The provisions of the COMC are designated with letter codes. Those relevant to the following discussion of the COMC are **E** (which indicates an evidential provision), **G** (which represents FSA guidance) and **C** (which indicates a safe harbour). The status of the

---

[89] See HM Treasury: 'FSMA Market Abuse Regime: Final Impact Assessment on the Sunset Clauses' (June 2008).

[90] MAR 1.1.5G.

[91] This derives from s 119(2).

[92] FSMA, ss 118(5)(a) and (b) and 120(1)(a) as explained at MAR 1.10. See para 8.157 below for a further discussion of these provisions.

[93] MAR 1.1.6G.

provision is a reflection of the weight attributed to it. An evidential statement (**E**) specifies descriptions of behaviour that, in the opinion of the FSA, amount to market abuse; and factors that, in the opinion of the FSA, are to be taken into account in determining whether or not behaviour amounts to market abuse. Evidential provisions are indicative in nature: they create rebuttable presumptions of compliance with or contravention of the binding rules to which they refer. By contrast, guidance (**G**) is used only to explain the implications of other provisions or to indicate possible means of compliance, but it is not binding on those to whom FSMA applies and nor does it have 'evidential' effect. Guidance is generally designed to throw light on a particular aspect of regulatory requirements. The existence of a safe harbour (**C**) is of particular importance to market participants as this is conclusive evidence that conduct falling within the safe harbour does not amount to market abuse.[94]

The COMC which existed under the pre-MAD regime underwent significant changes at the time of the introduction of MAD, partly to accommodate the new MAD offences and defences as discussed above, but also in part as a result of an exercise being undertaken by the FSA to simplify its rulebooks and related material. The FSA has indicated that the removal of material as part of this latter exercise was therefore not an indication that the former wording and guidance was incorrect, but simply that it did not need to be stated.[95] The effect, therefore, is that, other than to the extent inconsistent with MAD, guidance in the former COMC may still be indicative of the FSA's views and approach, although of course the relevance of this as a reference source will diminish over time. **8.59**

Other source material

There are a number of other sources of information on the market abuse regime. The FSA publishes an online periodical called *MarketWatch* which provides updates on the market conduct issues into which the FSA is looking.[96] This is by no means exclusively related to market abuse nor is it official guidance. It is stated to be primarily a news source—updating practitioners on recent or planned developments through brief summaries or highlighting successful instances of enforcement action—although it does appear to function as an informal channel for the **8.60**

---

[94] See Chapter 6 of the FSA's *Reader's guide: an introduction to the FSA Handbook*, available at <http://fsahandbook.info/FSA/pdf/rguide.pdf> for the full explanation of codes used in the FSA Handbook.

[95] Joint Treasury/FSA Consultation Paper: 'UK implementation of the EU Market Abuse Directive' (June 2004) paras 4.2–4.12.

[96] Available at <http://www.fsa.gov.uk/Pages/Library/Communication/NewsLetters/index. shtml>. The FSA also at one stage separately issued answers to Frequently Asked Questions on the market abuse regime. Following PS 124 (July 2002), the FAQs were added as an Annex to MAR1 and post-MAD they have been moved from MAR to an Appendix in *MarketWatch* issue 12. At the time of writing, 28 issues of *MarketWatch* have been published.

communication of the FSA's views. In addition, the FSA sporadically issues guidance or policy on a particular topic, for example the guidance that pre-hedging convertible bond issues would likely amount to market abuse.[97] So-called Level 3 guidance (as to which, see Chapter 3) is also produced by CESR as part of the process of assimilating practices among national regulators.

'Precedent Value'

8.61 It is also worth looking at the question of what value the decided cases under the market abuse regime to date have. In simple terms, this will depend on the type of decision, and, in the case of FSA decisions, the process adopted. These can be of two broad types. The first category is decisions made by the FSA itself following FSA processes and procedures. These can either result from full hearings of the RDC, or, in reality could be the result of a settlement reached with the FSA. Before changes introduced on 28 August 2007, the way in which a particular decision had been reached was not made clear in the Decision Notices, although it could often be gleaned from textual references or time frames referred to in the Decision Notices. Moreover, not only could the scope and effect of settled decisions be the result of negotiation and compromise (where commercial considerations no doubt come into play), but also the wording of Decision Notices itself, and this needs to be borne in mind when considering 'precedent value' of these decisions. After changes to the FSA enforcement procedure in 2007, decisions reached by settlement are concluded by the Settlement Decision Makers ('SDM') rather than the RDC, and decision notices refer to this specifically as well as the stage at which the particular matter was settled (reflected in the percentage of discount on penalties). The same process also applies to decisions made outside the context of the section 118 market abuse regime, for example decisions reached by the FSA under FSA rules or principles. Conversely, a decision of the RDC will have gone through the full FSA process and been determined on a full hearing.

8.62 The second category is hearings before the FSMT on a reference. As discussed further in Chapter 1, the FSMT operates independently from the FSA and its decisions are undertaken by way of a full rehearing. Following on comments made in the *Legal & General* decision, FSMT decisions, and also FSA Notices, reported decisions now also reflect the submissions made in order to reflect the fuller debate and conclusions drawn.

8.63 In this chapter, decisions are marked as being either FSA decisions or FSMT decisions and FSA decisions post 28 August 2007 are shown as either having been made by the SDM or RDC so the relative weight of the decisions can be gauged.

---

[97] PS 149: 'Market Abuse: Pre-Hedging convertible and exchangeable bond issues'.

Scope of the definition of market abuse in section 118

The definition of behaviour that constitutes market abuse is contained in section **8.64**
118 of FSMA. For conduct to be market abuse, it must relate to specified types of
investments (described at para 8.65 *et seq.*), fall within the stipulated territorial
scope (described at para 8.69 *et seq.*), and also fall within one of seven types of
behaviour (described at para 8.77 *et seq.*). Section 123(1) goes on to provide that
the FSA cannot impose a fine or, in effect, publish a censure where, having
considered any representation made to it in response to a warning notice, there are
reasonable grounds for it to be satisfied that the person in question believed on
reasonable grounds that this behaviour was not market abuse or he took all
reasonable precautions and exercised all due diligence to avoid behaving in a way
that would be.[98,99]

The 'qualifying investments' element

The first element of the market abuse definition is that the behaviour must **8.65**
occur in relation to one of the following sorts of qualifying investment,[100] namely
qualifying investments already admitted to trading on a prescribed market;[101] or
qualifying investments in respect of which a request for admission to trading on
such a market has been made. In the case of market abuse falling within the first two
types described below (market abuse (insider dealing) and market abuse (improper
disclosure)) the scope is extended to investments which are related investments in
relation to qualifying investments. A 'related investment', in relation to a qualifying
investment, means an investment whose price or value depends on the price or value
of the qualifying investment.[102] For these purposes, 'qualifying investments' means
transferable securities; units in collective investment undertakings; money-market

---

[98] This is discussed further at para 8.73.

[99] The s 123(1) defence has been discussed in a couple of cases. In the *Jabré* case (an RDC
decision), it was considered that although the compliance procedures operated by the firm in question may have been sufficient by the standards prevailing and expected in 2003 to protect the
firm from a general finding that its systems and controls were in breach of Principle 3 of the FSA's
Principles for Businesses ('a firm must take reasonable care to organise and control its affairs responsibly and effectively, with adequate risk management systems'), in a context where market abuse has
occurred, FSMA required a higher standard (that the firm should 'take all reasonable precautions
and exercise all due diligence to avoid . . .' engaging in market abuse). The FSA noted that there
were other steps which the firm could have taken and which were in place in some major firms at
the material time. In the *Davidson and Tatham* case, although it was found that no market abuse had
taken place, the FSMT observed that, on the facts of that case, there were reasonable grounds for
being satisfied that the applicants took all reasonable precautions and exercised all reasonable due
diligence to avoid behaving in a way which amount to market abuse or requiring or encouraging
another to engage in market abuse.

[100] FSMA, s 118(a).

[101] Discussed at para 8.68.

[102] FSMA, s 130A(3). At its most obvious, therefore, this would include derivatives referable to
qualifying investments. For example, in the *Shevlin* decision (*John Shevlin v FSA*, FSMT Case 060,

instruments; financial futures contracts; forward interest rate agreements; interest rate, currency, and equity swaps; options; derivatives on commodities; and any instrument admitted for trading on a regulated market in an EEA jurisdiction.[103]

8.66 It should also be noted that the scope of coverage is in effect extended in the case of the legacy offences. For these offences, behaviour that occurs in relation to anything that is the subject matter, or whose price or value is expressed by reference to the price or value of the qualifying investments, or occurs in relation to investments (whether or not they are qualifying investments) whose subject matter is the qualifying investments, is to be regarded as 'occurring in relation to qualifying investments'. To illustrate the differences, to use an example set out in the COMC, a fixed odds bet relating to a UK listed security would fall within the scope of the legacy offences but not the post-MAD offences.

8.67 According to the FSA, behaviour occuring prior to a request for admission to trading may potentially also be covered (relevant/indicative factors being where a person acts in relation to qualifying investments in respect of which a request for admission to trading is subsequently made, and where that behaviour continues to have an effect after the application has been made, or after admission to trading).[104]

8.68 The range of markets included within the definition of 'prescribed market', and therefore the scope of the market abuse regime, has also been modified post–MAD. Under the previous regime, market abuse was limited to behaviour occurring in relation to investments traded only on markets established under the rules of the UK recognised investment exchanges[105] (the LSE, LIFFE Administration and Management, ICE Futures, the LME, EDX, PLUS Markets plc (formerly OFEX), and SWX Europe Limited (formerly virt-x)).[106,107] MAD on the other hand applies to all regulated markets throughout the EEA.[108]

---

12 June 2008) (Type I (post-MAD) Insider Dealing),CFDs relating to shares traded on the LSE were confirmed to be 'related investments' for the purposes of section 118(1)(a)(iii) and section 130A.

[103] Art 1(3) of MAD.

[104] MAR 1.2.5E.

[105] This will therefore include AIM which is a market established under the rules of an RIE, namely the LSE.

[106] The FSA's list of recognised investment exchanges is available at <http://www.fsa.gov.uk/register/exchanges. do>.

[107] See the pre-MAD amendment versions of FSMA, s 118(3)(a) and Financial Services and Markets Act 2000 (Prescribed Markets and Qualifying Investments) Order 2001 ('the PMO'), art 4.

[108] Regulated markets are those markets listed by EEA jurisdiction regulators in accordance with Art 4(14) of the Markets in Financial Instruments Directive 2004/39/EC of 21 April 2004. The FSA presently lists EDX, ICE Futures Europe, LSE – Regulated Market, PLUS-listed Market, certain segments of SWX Europe, LIFFE and the London Metal Exchange. Prior to the introduction of MiFID, ICE Futures and the LME, which are commodity derivatives markets, had not been EU regulated markets but have since become so. For further details please see <http://www.fsa.gov.uk/register/exchanges.do>.

Territorial scope—where behaviour takes place

Under the territoriality provisions in FSMA,[109] the post-MAD market abuse **8.69** regime applies to behaviour only if it occurs in the UK, or if the behaviour, wherever it takes place, occurs in relation to qualifying investments which are admitted (or requested to be admitted) to trading on a prescribed market situated in, or operating in, the UK. In the case of market abuse (insider dealing) and market abuse (improper disclosure), this extends to related investments.[110] Under the arrangements set out in MAD, behaviour could therefore potentially be covered by the market abuse provisions operating in more than one EEA jurisdiction. For example, conduct undertaken in, say, Germany relating to shares listed on the LSE would constitute relevant behaviour for the purposes of the UK market abuse regime (as it occurs in relation to shares admitted to trading on a regulated market in the UK), as well as being relevant behaviour for the purposes of the German market abuse regime (as it is behaviour occurring within Germany relating to securities listed on an EEA regulated market). For a discussion of the coordination and cooperation which would apply between the UK and German authorities in such circumstances, see Chapter 9 at para 9.103.

The question of the territorial effect of the market abuse regime was discussed in **8.70** a preliminary hearing of the FSMT in the *Jabré* case.[111] The decision related to an earlier section 118(1) which referred to behaviour occurring 'in relation to the quality in investments "traded" on a prescribed market', which has since changed and so the detailed arguments are not particularly in point. However, the decision did contain the observation:

> the vice of insider dealing, and the reason why it was prohibited, was that it reduced confidence in the integrity and transparency of the market in the particular security which was being abused. The FSA had an interest in preventing market abuse that impacted on the market and its institutions because the abuse related to shares traded within the territory of its authority.

In that case, it was found that transactions undertaken on the Tokyo market in respect of shares which were also listed on the LSE did occur in relation to qualifying investments 'traded' on a prescribed market.

Vicarious liability

The extent to which a firm should be vicariously liable for market abuse offences **8.71** was also considered in the *Jabré* decision. In that case, the firm in question argued that it could not be held responsible for market abuse on the basis of vicarious

---

[109] FSMA, s 118A(1)(a) and (b).
[110] As to the extended scope for the legacy offences, see para 8.66 above.
[111] *Philippe Jabré v FSA*, FSMT Case 036, 2006—Decision on Market Abuse.

liability or the principles of 'attribution' (at the relevant time Jabré was an employee of the firm and held the title of 'Managing Director'; was a member of the firm's Management Committee (albeit that this was an informal committee); was one of three individuals on the firm's Investment Management Committee; and was responsible for managing six of the firm's funds including the fund to which the events in the case related). The FSA were satisfied that on the facts and having regards to the language and purpose of the market abuse provisions in FSMA, the firm could be liable for market abuse on the basis that Jabré's acts amounted to market abuse and were attributable to the firm. The FSA reached this conclusion having regard to, amongst other matters: Jabré's seniority and status within the firm; the fact that he clearly had authority to enter into the relevant transactions; the fact that within an agreed overall strategy his dealings were largely unsupervised and he exercised a large degree of autonomy.

The mental element

8.72 It is often said that market abuse is 'effects-based' and indeed that the absence of having to prove intention or recklessness will result in a more responsive and effective system of offences. It is true that there is no requirement in section 123 that the person who committed market abuse did so 'intentionally' or 'recklessly'. That is not to say, however, that the market abuse regime is without reference to the mental state of the person who is accused of market abuse. The mental state of such persons is referenced in four distinct ways:

(i) the availability of what is in effect a defence under section 123(2)(a) relating to the defendant's state of mind;

(ii) definitions of conduct that constitutes market abuse which refer (either directly or by implication) to a person's motive or knowledge;

(iii) statements made in the COMC which presuppose that a person's motive or knowledge may be relevant in certain circumstances; and

(iv) the FSA's policy on sanctioning market abuse.[112]

8.73 Looking at these in turn, according to section 123, the FSA may not impose a penalty on a person where, amongst other things, the FSA has reasonable grounds to be satisfied that 'he believed on reasonable grounds' that his behaviour did not constitute market abuse or 'requiring or encouraging'.[113] It has been argued that

---

[112] See the discussion by Swan, 'Market abuse regulation and energy trading', (2004) *IELTR* 4, 91–100, at 93. Note, however, that this discussion relates to the pre-MAD version of the COMC.

[113] FSMA, s 123(2)(a). Jain, 'Significance of mens rea in insider trading', (2004) *Comp Law* 25(5), 132–40, 'despite there being no express intent requirement, if the defendant can prove the required state of mind of either reasonable belief or due diligence being exercised by him, he will not be subjected to a penalty by the Financial Services Authority'. As to requiring and encouraging, see para 8.79.

this is a 'specified mental element to the offence'.[114] In addition, the state of mind of the defendant will also be considered when determining whether or not he committed one of the seven behaviour types under section 118 that constitute market abuse. Certain (but not all) of the behaviour types contain an explicit reference to the mental state of the defendant. For example, 'dissemination' under section 118(7) requires that the person disseminating false information 'knew or could reasonably be expected to have known' that the information was false or misleading. A subjective/objective test is also built in to 'manipulating transactions' under section 118(5) which requires that the behaviour be other than for legitimate reasons. This presupposes that the person (subjectively) has the reasons and that these (objectively) are legitimate.

More colour is given in the COMC.[115] The COMC begins by confirming the basic proposition that the definition of market abuse in section 118 'does not require the person engaging in the behaviour in question to have *intended* to commit market abuse'.[116] However, there are a number of situations in which the state of mind of the accused does come into play in the COMC. For example, in the context of market abuse (manipulating transactions), the fact that a person has an 'actuating purpose' to induce others to trade in a qualifying investment, or to position or move the price of a qualifying investment will, in the FSA's opinion, be indicative of an absence of 'legitimate reasons' for the transaction itself.[117] Conversely, the absence of such a purpose will be a relevant factor to consider, but is not in itself indicative of legitimate reasons. Similarly, the fact that a transaction was executed with the purpose of creating a false or misleading impression will be indicative of a lack of 'legitimate reasons' and the absence of such a purpose will be one of a number of relevant factors. The final way in which the state of mind of the defendant is relevant to the market abuse regime is that the FSA will consider the guilty party's state of mind when considering the sanction to impose. Under the FSA's enforcement policies, the FSA will take into account whether or not the breach was 'deliberate or reckless' when deciding whether or not to proceed against market abuse.[118]

The seven types of behaviour constituting market abuse

Once it is established that behaviour falling within the appropriate territorial scope has occurred in relation to relevant qualifying investments (or, where appropriate, related investments), it is necessary to ascertain whether the behaviour falls **8.74**

---

[114] Alcock, 'Market abuse—the new witchcraft?' (2001) *NLJ* 151/1398, Issue, 7001 (Sept).
[115] See para 8.58, for further discussion on the COMC.
[116] MAR 1.2.3G (emphasis added).
[117] See MAR 1.6.5E.
[118] DEPP 6.2.1G (1)(a). See also Chapter 6 at para 6.96.

within one of seven prescribed types of behaviour.[119] These seven behaviour types fall into two broad categories, namely behaviour which relates to the use of information, and behaviour which manipulates the market or creates a false or misleading impression.[120]

8.75 The provisions of Part VIII FSMA do not on the face of it require the person engaging in the relevant behaviour to have intended to carry out market abuse—it is sufficient that one of the behaviour types is present[121] (although for a discussion of the mental element built into the regime, see para 8.72 above). For all of the seven behaviour types, market abuse may be committed either by one person acting alone or by two or more persons acting jointly or in concert.[122]

8.76 Behaviour is stated to extend to both action and inaction.[123] That said, it would appear on closer analysis that this would apply only to the legacy offences. This would also seem to be supported by comments made in the Treasury review of the sunset clauses.[124] Section 118(1) states that market abuse is behaviour which occurs in relation to qualifying investments (etc) and which falls within any one or more of the seven behaviour types described at para 8.77 *et seq*. However, when these specific definitions of behaviour types are considered, it becomes apparent that there are real divergences in the drafting between the post-MAD offences and the legacy offences. The MAD offences all prescribe certain very narrowly defined types of action ('an insider deals or attempts to deal', 'an insider discloses inside information', 'effecting transactions or orders to trade', 'the dissemination of information', etc) rather than the broader concept of 'behaviour', capable of accommodating inaction, retained by the legacy offences.[125] It should be noted that the requiring and encouraging offence discussed at para 8.79 below may be committed by failing, or refraining from taking, any action. By contrast, under the

---

[119] FSMA, s 118(1)(b).

[120] Note that the legacy offences are due to expire on 31 December 2009 unless further extended. See para 8.55 *et seq*.

[121] MAR 1.2.3G.

[122] FSMA, s 118(1).

[123] FSMA, s 130A(3). This is elaborated on in an evidential provision in the COMC (MAR 1.2.6E.) which explains that, in the FSA's view, failure through inaction to discharge a legal or regulatory obligation would be indicative of relevant behaviour. Similar considerations will apply where a person who has created a reasonable expectation that he will act in a particular manner has failed to satisfy any duty or obligation which has arisen to inform persons that their expectations are not correct.

[124] HM Treasury: 'FSMA market abuse regime: a review of the sunset clauses, a consultation' (February 2008).

[125] HM Treasury's discussion of the regulatory impact of the various models for implementation of MAD (UK Implementation of the EU Market Abuse Directive, Annex B, Regulatory Impact Assessment) cites this as a key advantage for the retention of the legacy offences alongside MAD offences. The Treasury make it clear that in their opinion the MAD offences are drafted in such a way that inaction would not (in their example) constitute market manipulation under any of types 4–6 referred to at para 8.78, but it would be behaviour likely to give a regular user a false or misleading impression under legacy offence type 7.

criminal law insider dealing provisions, there is no scope for inaction to constitute the criminal offence at all (see discussion in Chapter 9, para 9.03).

Behaviour relating to the use of information

The first three behaviour types that constitute market abuse relate, broadly speak- **8.77** ing, to the use of information.[126] These are as follows:

- *Type 1—market abuse (insider dealing)*
  This applies where an insider deals, or attempts to deal, in a relevant qualifying investment or related investment on the basis of inside information relating to the investment in question.[127] The meaning of insider and inside information is discussed at paras 8.81 and 8.82 below.

- *Type 2—market abuse (improper disclosure)*
  This applies where an insider discloses inside information to another person otherwise than in the proper course of the exercise of his employment, profession, or duties.[128]

- *Type 3—market abuse (misuse of information) (legacy offence)*[129]
  This applies to behaviour which is neither market abuse (insider dealing) nor market abuse (improper disclosure) but rather based on information which is not generally available to those using the market but which, if available to a regular user of the market, would be, or would be likely to be, regarded by him as relevant when deciding the terms on which transactions in qualifying investments should be effected. The behaviour must also be likely to be regarded by a regular user of the market as a failure on the part of the person concerned to observe the standard of behaviour reasonably expected of a person in his position in relation to the market.

Behaviour relating to false or misleading impressions

Behaviour types 4 to 7 relate, broadly speaking, to transactions which are market **8.78** abuse as a result of a false or misleading impression being created or manipulation of the market occurring. These are as follows:

- *Type 4—market abuse (manipulating transactions)*
  This applies to effecting transactions or orders to trade (otherwise than for legitimate reasons and in conformity with accepted market practices[130] on the

---

[126] This regime is co-existent with the insider dealing regime in the CJA. See further Chapter 9, for a discussion of this.

[127] FSMA, s 118(2), as discussed at para 8.99 *et seq.* below.

[128] ibid, s 118(3), as discussed at para 8.126 below.

[129] ibid, s 118(4), as discussed at para 8.131 *et seq.* below. This provision is equivalent to the former s 118(2)(a) of FSMA under the pre-MAD regime.

[130] 'Accepted market practices' means practices that are reasonably expected in the financial market in question and are accepted by the FSA (or other competent EEA authority)—FSMA,

relevant market) which either give, or are likely to give, a false or misleading impression as to the supply of, or demand for, or as to the price of, one or more qualifying investments ('false or misleading impressions'), or alternatively secure the price of one or more such investments at an abnormal or artificial level ('price positioning').[131]

- *Type 5—market abuse (manipulating devices)*
  This applies to effecting transactions or orders to trade which employ fictitious devices or any other form of deception or contrivance.[132]

- *Type 6—market abuse (dissemination)*
  This type of behaviour applies to the dissemination of information by any means which gives, or is likely to give, a false or misleading impression as to a qualifying investment by a person who knew or could reasonably be expected to have known that the information was false or misleading.[133]

- *Type 7—market abuse (misleading behaviour and distortion) (legacy offence)*
  This applies to conduct which does not constitute market abuse (manipulating transactions), market abuse (manipulating devices), or market abuse (dissemination), but which is either likely to give a regular user of the market a false or misleading impression as to the supply of, demand for, or price or value of, qualifying investments or alternatively would be, or would be likely to be, regarded by a regular user of the market as behaviour that would distort, or would be likely to distort, the market in such an investment. In either case, the behaviour must be likely to be regarded by a regular user of the market as a failure on the part of the person concerned to observe the standard of behaviour reasonably expected of a person in his position in relation to the market.[134]

---

s 130A(3). In other words, there is a formal 'acceptance' requirement and market practices will therefore not automatically be 'accepted' for these purposes simply because they are commonplace or generally accepted within the market. Commission Directive 2004/72/EC implements sections of MAD as regards accepted market practices and sets out guidance in Arts 2 and 3 for the competent authorities of Member States to follow in evaluating market practices. CESR also publishes a 'master list' of the practices that are accepted by various EEA competent authorities: <http://www.cesr-eu.org/>.

[131] FSMA, s 118(5), as discussed at para 8.140 *et seq.*

[132] ibid, s 118(6), as discussed at para 8.148.

[133] ibid, s 118(7), as discussed at para 8.151 *et seq.*

[134] ibid, s 118(8) as discussed at para 8.153 below. This provision is equivalent to s 118(2)(b) and (c) of FSMA under the pre-MAD regime.

Requiring and encouraging

According to section 123(1)(b) of FSMA, a person will also be committing an **8.79** offence where the FSA is satisfied that that person, by taking or refraining from taking any action, has required or encouraged any other person or persons to engage in behaviour which, if engaged in by the first person, would amount to market abuse. The pre-MAD COMC contained extensive guidance on when behaviour would or would not be regarded as 'requiring or encouraging'. This guidance has not been replaced in the post-MAD COMC which contains only two examples of conduct that may constitute requiring or encouraging.[135]

Definitions for the purposes of the market abuse provisions concerning the use of information

The first two types of behaviour described above both relate to acts undertaken by **8.80** an 'insider' with respect to 'inside information'.

Insider

For the purposes of the market abuse provisions, the term 'insider' has a specific **8.81** meaning and is determined by the capacity or circumstances in which information is received (for example where information is received as part of a person's employment, profession, or duties).[136] Being an insider is not in itself necessarily offensive—it is simply a way of separating those to whom, from a policy perspective, the market abuse (insider dealing) and market abuse (improper disclosure)

---

[135] As to which, see MAR 1.2.23G, which limits itself to two fairly clear examples of behaviour which might constitute requiring or encouraging, namely: (a) a director of a company, while in possession of inside information, instructs an employee of that company to deal in qualifying investments or related investments in respect of which the information is inside information; and (b) a person recommends or advises a friend to engage in behaviour which, if he himself engaged in it, would amount to market abuse. See also para 8.59 *et seq.* for the background on the changes to the COMC. See also the *Harrison* case, FSA Final Notice to Steven Harrison, dated 8 September 2008.

[136] According to FSMA, s 118B, an 'insider' is any person who has 'inside information' as a result of membership of an administrative, management, or supervisory body of an issuer of qualifying investments; holding capital of an issuer of qualifying investments; having access to the information through the exercise of his employment, profession or duties; or criminal activities. An insider also extends to any person obtaining information by other means and which he knows, or could reasonably be expected to know, is inside information. According to MAR 1.2.8E, for these purposes, a person could be 'reasonably expected to know' that information in his possession is inside information where a normal and reasonable person in the position of that person would both (a) know that the person from whom he received it is an 'insider', and (b) know that it is inside information. Note that it is only in the latter category of insider that knowledge is relevant—for the other categories, the person concerned does not need to know that the information is inside information (MAR 1.2.9) (cf the position under the CJA offence discussed in Chapter 9 which requires knowledge).

offences potentially apply, from those to whom it should not (such as individuals acting in a private capacity innocently obtaining information which they do not know, or could not reasonably be expected to know, was inside information).

'Inside information'

8.82   The definition of 'inside information' differs according to whether or not the qualifying investments to which the behaviour relates are commodity derivatives.[137] In both cases, the information must be of a 'precise' nature,[138] and not generally available.[139] In the case of qualifying investments which are *not* commodity derivatives,[140] inside information is information which in addition relates to one or more issuers of the qualifying investments or to one or more of the qualifying investments; and would, if generally available, be likely to have a 'significant effect' on the price of the qualifying or related investments. This will be the case if and only if it is information of a kind which a reasonable investor would be likely to use as part of the basis of his investment decision).[141]

8.83   Where the qualifying investments are commodity derivatives, inside information is information relating directly or indirectly to one or more commodity derivatives which,[142] in addition to being of a 'precise' nature and not being generally available, users of markets on which the derivatives are traded would expect to

---

[137] According to MAR 1.2.17G, this is explained by the differences in the nature of information which is important to commodity derivatives markets.

[138] Information is to be regarded as being of a 'precise' nature for the purposes of the market abuse rules if it (a) indicates circumstances that exist or may reasonably be expected to come into existence or an event that has occurred or may reasonably be expected to occur, and (b) is specific enough to enable a conclusion to be drawn as to the possible effect of those circumstances or that event on the price of the qualifying investments or related investments—FSMA, s 118C(5).

[139] See the explanation at paras 8.86–8.87, as to when information is to be considered as 'generally available' for the market abuse rules.

[140] FSMA, s 118C(2).

[141] ibid, s 118C(6). Note also that the question of whether information is likely to have a significant effect on the price of issuers' shares, financial instruments, and related investments is dealt with in the context of the Disclosure Rules. Please see para 9.76 *et seq.* generally.

[142] ibid, s 118C(3). It would not appear to be relevant for the purposes of this definition whether or not the information would have a 'significant effect' on the price of qualifying or related investments. Note however that the European Securities Market Expert Group ('ESME') referred to the uncertainty of the definition in its 2008 report and the fact that the specific definition does not expressly state that information can only be inside information in relation to commodity derivatives if, were it to be made public it would be likely to have a significant effect on the prices of those derivatives (or related financial instruments), which it stated would, according to the ESME, be the preferred view. In support of this, ESME referred to Recital 16(2) MAD which contains a general statement that information is price-sensitive information, which supports the view that the specific definition of inside information relevant to derivatives on commodities should be regarded as a subset of that general definition, but also noted in contrast that MAD also provides for a specific definition of inside information in relation to persons charged with execution of client orders and which does expressly limit that definition to price-sensitive information. Part of ESME's advice is that this definition should be clarified.

receive in accordance with any accepted practices on those markets (ie information which is routinely made available to users of those markets or which is required to be disclosed by a statutory or market rule, contract, or market custom).[143]

Pending orders

An important change introduced into the post-MAD market abuse regime was **8.84** the proposition that 'in relation to a person charged with the execution of orders concerning qualifying investments or related investments' information relating to inside information will include information which has stipulated characteristics conveyed by a client relating to the client's pending orders.[144] This differs from the approach taken in the pre-MAD regime where (in the context of what is now the market abuse (misuse of information) offence), dealing or arranging activities undertaken on the basis of so-called 'trading information'[145] benefited from safe harbour treatment. In place of the trading information safe harbour, two new safe harbours relating to the 'dutiful execution of client orders' and the 'legitimate carrying on of the business of market makers etc' have been introduced. The practical implications of this change are discussed at para 8.121 *et seq*. below.

Section 118C(4) goes on to provide that inside information relating to a client's **8.85** pending orders must satisfy the criteria which apply to non-commodity derivatives (even though the definition applies to all qualifying investments, ie including commodity derivatives). In other words, in addition to being precise and not generally available, to fall within this section the information must relate to one or more issuers or one or more qualifying investments, and be likely to have a

---

The European Commission created ESME to look carefully at how the EU securities directives are applied in practice, determine whether or not they are delivering the intended results, and propose changes where necessary. This is a follow-up action to the White Paper on Financial Services Policy 2005–2010 (IP/05/1529) and is part of the Better Regulation agenda. The group is composed of practitioners and market participants who are directly affected by the EU legislative framework as well as by issues of contemporary relevance to the EU securities markets. ESME has three functions. Firstly, it assists the Commission in its analysis of the legal coherence of the EU securities framework. It aims to identify points of legal uncertainty which impair the functioning of securities markets from the perspective of the regulated community and users of these markets, and makes recommendations to the Commission accordingly. Secondly, it provides the Commission with input for the reports on the application of various provisions of the relevant directives. In addition, it analyses the economic impact of those directives. Finally, it provides technical advice in response to specific requests from the Commission—on issues of contemporary relevance in EU securities markets. Its advice is non-binding.

[143] ibid, s 118C(7).

[144] ibid, s 118C(4). A 'pending order' is where a person is approached by another in relation to a transaction and (a) the transaction is not immediately executed on an arm's length basis in response to a price quoted by that person; and (b) the person concerned has taken on a legal or regulatory obligation relating to the manner or timing of the execution of the transaction—MAR 1.2.16 E.

[145] For the definition of trading information, in the pre-MAD regime, see para 8.121 below.

significant effect on the price of those qualifying investments.[146] In this context, therefore (as distinct from the general definition of inside information as it applies to commodity derivatives), the likelihood of a significant effect on the market will be a requirement.[147]

FSA guidance and evidential provisions as to information that is not 'inside information' on the basis of whether information is 'generally available'

8.86   The FSA has identified a number of factors which are to be taken into account in determining whether or not information is 'generally available'. The presence of such factors would be indicative that the information would be regarded as being generally available.

8.87   The factors set out in the COMC are whether the information has been disclosed to a prescribed market through an RIS or has otherwise been disclosed in accordance with the rules of that market; whether the information is contained in records which are open to inspection by the public; whether the information is otherwise generally available, including through the Internet, or some other publication (including if it is only available on payment of a fee), or is derived from information which has been made public; whether the information can be obtained by observation by members of the public without infringing rights or obligations of privacy, property, or confidentiality;[148] or the extent to which the information can be obtained by analysing or developing other information which is generally available.[149] For the purpose of considering what constitutes generally available information, FSA guidance[150] indicates that it is not relevant that the information in question is only generally available *outside* of the UK.[151]

---

[146]   According to s 118C(6), information would be likely to have a significant effect on price if and only if it is information of a kind which a reasonable investor would be likely to use as part of the basis of his investment decisions.

[147]   This would seemingly apply in relation to client's pending orders in the context of commodity derivatives as the definition in s 118C(4) would apply to qualifying (and related) investments generally and in subsection (c) combines the elements of information relating directly to 'one or more issuers of qualifying investments' or 'one or more qualifying investments'. See also discussion at para 8.84.

[148]   The example given in MAR is where a passenger on a train passes a burning factory and calls his broker and tells him to sell shares in the factory's owner. In that instance, the passenger will be acting on information which is generally available, since it is information which has been obtained by legitimate means through observation of a public event.

[149]   MAR 1.2.12E. Whilst not identical, these factors follow fairly closely the non-exhaustive list of circumstances set out in the CJA where information is, or, in some cases, may be considered to be, made public—see s 58 of the CJA.

[150]   MAR 1.2.13E.

[151]   This again mirrors the guidance for the criminal regime which states that information may be treated as made public even though it is published only outside the UK. See s 58(3)(e) of the CJA.

Rumours

The issue of what constitutes 'generally available' information was discussed in **8.88** the *Arif Mohammed* case (a misuse of information case under the pre-MAD market abuse regime).[152] In that case, Mohammed argued that he had not traded on the basis of inside information because the sale of the particular division of the company in question was subject to widespread rumours. The FSMT held, however, that in order to hold that 'information' was available to the public, something 'precise in nature' is required. Rumours would not be sufficient for this.

The interrelation between rumours and information was also considered in the **8.89** *Jabré* case.

Precise Information

As mentioned in para 8.82, inside information is required to be 'of a precise **8.90** nature'. Information is precise if it indicates circumstances that exist or may reasonably be expected to come into existence or an event that has occurred (or may reasonably be expected to occur), and is specific enough to enable a conclusion to be drawn as to the possible effect of those circumstances or that event on the price of qualifying investments or related investments.[153]

In terms of the former, to take an example, in the *Jabré* case[154] the FSA also found **8.91** that even though Jabré may not have been told in terms that the investment bank in question had the mandate and may not have been told that the issue of securities by the Japanese bank in question would definitely be launched, or told when it would be launched, the information he was given did provide, 'with reasonable certainty, grounds to conclude' that 'possible future developments' would occur. As to the likely timing of the prospective issue, it was widespread in the market that the Central Bank of Japan had set a particular deadline for the improvement of the Tier 1 Ratios of the four major Japanese banks, which would have led any market participants to conclude that an issue of fresh capital of the kind canvassed could not be long delayed.

In terms of the second limb of the text, ie whether information is sufficiently **8.92** specific to enable a conclusion to be drawn on the possible effect or price, it is suggested that this would mean that most investors would draw the same conclusion as to the likely directional effect on price of the information, even if not the level.

---

[152] *Arif Mohammed v FSA*, FSMT Case 012, 29 March 2005.
[153] s 118C(5). In terms of the requirement relating to possible effect on price, see also the 'significant effect on price' requirement discussed at para 8.93.
[154] *Philippe Jabré v FSA*, FSMT Case 036, 10 July 2006.

Significant effect on price

8.93   The question of what would have a significant effect on price[155] was discussed in the recent *Woolworths* decision[156] albeit in the context of the Disclosure Rules and Listing Principles. This is discussed further at Chapter 9, para 9.79.

Analysis using expertise and resources

8.94   As is the case under CJA insider dealing, a key question to address is whether a professional investor in the market who is able to apply expertise and resources to investment analysis will be treated as having information which is not generally available to the market. The answer to this, according to guidance issued under the COMC,[157] is no. According to that guidance, it is not relevant that the observation or analysis is only achievable by a person with above average financial resources, expertise, or competence. Thus, for example, a professional investor who employs expert analysts, buys in investment research, or commissions external market research would still in principle be using information which was generally available, even though a private investor without such expertise or resources would not have the same level of information access or analysis. This has been confirmed by an FSA discussion paper on investment analysis, where the FSA conclude that: 'information which can be obtained by research and analysis conducted by, or on behalf of, users of a market is to be regarded for the purposes of this section as being generally available to them'[158] and thus would not be inside information. This is in line with the philosophy of the MAD, which states that research and estimates developed from publicly available data should not be regarded as inside information.[159]

Star analysts' reports

8.95   In the financial markets, there are a number of 'star analysts' whose reports on the prospects of particular issuers or their securities are so highly rated that the existence of a recommendation from such an analyst is enough in itself to cause a significant movement in the price of the securities in question. This therefore gives rise to the question whether knowledge of such a recommendation, prior to it becoming generally available, can be inside information. The report and recommendations contained in the report (prepared in the circumstances discussed at para 8.94 above) would not be inside information but the information that the

---

[155]   The question of whether the tests of inside information for disclosure purposes on the one hand and insider dealing offences on the other should be different generally is currently under discussion at the European level—see para 8.194 *et seq.*
[156]   FSA: Final Notice to Woolworths Group plc dated 11 June 2008. RDC hearing.
[157]   MAR 1.2.13E(2).
[158]   FSA DP 15: 'Investment research—Conflicts and other issues', at para 5.21.
[159]   MAD Recital 31.

report and recommendations have been prepared, but not yet released to the market, and knowledge of the recommendations made presumably could be inside information.

The position relating the distribution of research by analysts/investment firms **8.96** was considered in the FSA Decision relating to Roberto Casoni[160] although that decision related to Principle 3 of the FSA's Statement of Principles for Approved Persons. Casoni was a research analyst for an investment bank in London, and was involved in the approval process for the bank to initiate coverage on a particular Italian company. Casoni had prepared the research report, which contained a buy recommendation with a medium risk and a target price. Before the publication of the report, it was found that Casoni had selectively disclosed details of his valuation methodology, final recommendation, and the target price to certain clients and was found to have breached Principle 3.[161]

Guidance in the FSA's Conduct of Business Rules at the time (at COB 7.16.13G[162]) **8.97** made it clear that it was inappropriate for an employee (whether or not an investment analyst) to communicate the substance of any investment research, except those set out in the policy. The FSA stated that the rules relating to the fair distribution of research were fundamental to maintaining orderly markets. It was imperative that analysts were fully aware of the restrictions and acted in accordance with them. The FSA considered that, by selectively disseminating such information to clients ahead of publication, Casoni allowed those clients the opportunity to pre-empt the conclusions of the published research and thereby potentially influenced their investment decisions ahead of the rest of the market.

Market abuse offences that concern the use of information

The following paragraphs address the detailed provisions of the market abuse **8.98** offences relating to the use of information.[163]

---

[160] FSA Final Notice to Roberto Chiarion Casoni dated 20 March 2007. Note that the case was settled at an early stage (Stage 1 – 30%) discount under the FSA's Executive Settlement procedures and the penalty was therefore reduced from £75,000 to £52,500.

[161] On the facts, none of the recipients of the information traded in the shares of the company as a result of having received it. In reaching its decision, the FSA took into account the fact that Casoni did not have any intention of manipulating the company's share price nor did he obtain any financial gain from his misconduct. The FSA did not allege that *Casoni* had failed to comply with MAR 1.

[162] The current equivalent is COBS 12.2.11G.

[163] For the purposes of the following discussion, it is assumed that the behaviour relates to qualifying investments on prescribed markets, and that the requirements as to territorial scope are satisfied, as are the definitions of insider and inside information.

Market abuse (insider dealing)—Type 1

8.99   The key elements of the definition of 'insider dealing' are firstly that the insider must deal or attempt to deal, in qualifying or related investments, and secondly that the dealing, or attempt to deal, must be made *on the basis of* inside information.[164]

Types of conduct that fall within 'insider dealing'

8.100   The FSA has given a number of examples of situations that, in its opinion, fall within the definition of insider dealing and accordingly constitute market abuse.[165] The first of these is dealing on the basis of inside information which is not trading information. 'Trading information' means, broadly speaking, information concerning potential or executed transactions in investments.[166] It is to be noted that the converse is not necessarily the case, that is to say dealing on the basis of trading information will not automatically be outside the scope of market abuse.

8.101   The second example is so-called 'front-running' that is to say where an insider enters into a transaction for his own benefit, taking advantage of the anticipated impact on market price of an order which he is to carry out with or for another person. This proposition was introduced to the market abuse regime as a result of MAD, although this needs to be read in the context of the safe harbours relating to the 'dutiful execution of client orders' and the 'legitimate business of market makers etc' discussed at para 8.122 *et seq*. Prior to that, front running was not an offence per se under the pre-MAD regime (as a result of the pre-MAD 'trading information' safe harbour) although it would of course potentially give rise to a breach of FSA rules, principles, or statements of principle on the part of FSA authorised firms or approved persons. The difference in the post-MAD regime is that an analysis needs to be undertaken as to whether the behaviour in question is 'legitimate' or 'dutiful'.

8.102   The final example relates to an offeror or potential offeror, or a person acting for the offeror in the context of a takeover entering into a transaction in a qualifying investment, on the basis of inside information concerning the proposed bid that

---

[164] Note that the reference to 'dealing', required by MAD, is narrower than the 'behaviour' provided for in the pre-MAD 'misuse of information'. This was one of the reasons for the retention of the legacy offence of misuse of information. For a general discussion see para 8.54.

[165]   MAR 1.3.2E.

[166]   'Trading information' is defined in MAR as information that investments of a particular kind have been or are to be acquired or disposed of, or that their disposal is under consideration, or the subject of negotiation; that investments of a particular kind have been or are not to be acquired or disposed of; the quantity of investments acquired or disposed of or to be acquired or disposed of or whose acquisition or disposal is under consideration or the subject of negotiations; the price (or range of prices) at which investments have been or are to be acquired or disposed of or the price (or range of prices) at which investments whose acquisition or disposal is under consideration or the subject of negotiation may be acquired or disposed of; or the identity of the persons involved or likely to be involved in any capacity in an acquisition or disposal.

provides merely an economic exposure to movements in the price of the target company's shares (for example, a spread bet on the target company's share price).

Types of conduct that are not 'on the basis of' insider information

Safe harbour—implementing own intention to deal. MAR provides a safe **8.103** harbour clarifying the fairly self-evident proposition that a person's carrying out his own intention to deal will not in itself constitute market abuse.[167] This issue has come up in particular in the context of shareholder activism. In general terms, knowledge of a person's own activist intentions should not preclude that person from dealing, although knowledge of the intention of a number of shareholders could potentially do so, depending on the facts.[168]

Guidance relating to 'on the basis'. FSA guidance in the COMC sets out a **8.104** number of factors pointing to fairly self-evidently innocent circumstances which, in the FSA's opinion, should be taken into account in determining whether or not a person's behaviour is 'on the basis of' inside information.[169] If the criteria set out in these factors are met this would be an indication that the behaviour in question has not been undertaken 'on the basis of' inside information. These factors broadly speaking apply in circumstances where the person concerned is dealing to satisfy a legal or regulatory obligation which came into being before he possessed the relevant information,[170] or where the decision to deal or attempt to deal was made before the person possessed the relevant information; or in the case of an organisation, where none of the individuals in possession of the inside information had any involvement in, or influenced, the decision to deal. The latter proposition is restated in slightly different terms in the context of Chinese Walls—in the opinion of the FSA, a decision to deal by an organisation in circumstances where information is held behind Chinese Walls away from individuals who are involved in the decision to deal would not be taken 'on the basis of' inside information.

As a general proposition, it seems unlikely that contra-directional dealing (ie sell- **8.105** ing an investment where the inside information held by a person indicates that the price of the investment will rise (or vice versa)) would be dealing 'on the basis of' that information.

Material influence. The FSA has indicated that, in its opinion, a person's behav- **8.106** iour would be 'on the basis of' inside information where information is the reason for, or a material influence on, a decision to deal or attempt to deal.

---

[167] MAR 1.3.6.C.
[168] For further discussion, see *MarketWatch* 20.
[169] MAR 1.3.3E.
[170] It should be noted that in the pre-MAD market abuse regime equivalent provisions were expressed as safe harbours. However, in the Treasury's view, perpetuating these safe harbours would have been inconsistent with its obligations arising under MAD.

8.107 This approach was underlined in the *Bracken* finding (a finding under the misuse of information offence in the pre-MAD regime)[171] where Bracken's behaviour was deemed to be 'on the basis of' inside information because of the timeliness of his trading and the fact that he did not seek permission to trade under his employer's policy. The FSA concluded that this meant his decision to trade was 'materially influenced' by the inside information. In the *Arif Mohammed* case (a case relating to the pre-MAD misuse of information offence), the FSMT reiterated the message that for conduct to be *based on* inside information it must be one of the reasons for the dealing, but went further to say it need not be the only reason for the dealing.[172] In practice, this would mean that a person could fall within the market abuse (insider dealing) offence where he has both proper and improper motives for dealing. Although it does not necessarily follow from the above that a decision to deal or attempt to deal will not be taken to be 'on the basis of' information if it is immaterial, that would seem to be a common sense approach. Thus, if a professional investor were to thoroughly research a potential investment using myriad sources of publicly available information, and be inadvertently given a piece of incidental inside information which would in itself not have a material impact on its decision to deal, it would appear that this should not itself, in the context of wider research, constitute market abuse (insider dealing). This is sometimes referred to as the 'mosaic' or 'jigsaw' factor.

Prior decisions to deal and pre-existing strategies

8.108 The question of whether particular transactions were entered into on the basis of prior decisions, or pre-existing strategies, has been discussed in a number of cases.

8.109 In the *Parker* case,[173] Parker contended the transactions in question were hedging (in relation to share options, or shares, owned by Parker in the relevant company) and delta neutral strategies (straddles) (in relation to which the direction of movement in price of the shares was of less relevance, the greater relevance being that there was sufficient movement in the shares one way or another). Having looked at the evidence (which in broad terms showed a number of transactions and a change of direction occurring immediately prior to the announcements in question) it was concluded that Parker deliberately set out to profit from relevant information and could not bring himself within the then safe harbour which applied where a decision to deal was not influenced by the relevant information.

8.110 The RDC also considered the question of pre-existing trading patterns in the *Jabré* decision.[174] That decision related to the misuse of information legacy

---

[171] FSA Final Notice to Peter Bracken dated 7 July 2004.
[172] *Arif Mohammed v FSA*, FSMT Case 012, 29 March 2005.
[173] *James Parker v FSA*, FSMT Case 037, 18 August 2006.
[174] FSA Final Notice to Philippe Jabré and GLG Partners LP dated 1 August 2006.

offence as well as, in the case of Jabré personally, breaches of FSA Principle 2 (Due Skill, Care and Diligence) and 3 (Market Conduct) of the FSA's Statements of Principles for Approved Persons and, in the case of GLG, breach of Principle 5 (Market Conduct) of the FSA's Principles for Businesses. Jabré had been brought across a Chinese Wall (information barrier) by an investment bank as part of pre-marketing of a convertibles issue by a Japanese bank, SMFG, and had subsequently, prior to the announcement of the issue, shorted SMFG shares. It was again contended that the transactions in question were part of a pre-existing trading strategy. On the facts, Jabré believed, based on public information, that major Japanese banks were under pressure from the Bank of Japan to bring their Tier 1 Ratios back up towards internationally required standards. Accordingly, Jabré had started to borrow shares in the major Japanese banks and had subsequently started to short sell shares in SMFG.[175]

The FSA, however, considered stock borrowing of the kind in question to be a **8.111** preparation for a possible selling pattern, but not itself evidence that such selling had necessarily been decided on or would necessarily have occurred. It did not consider such stock borrowing to be evidence of a 'trading pattern', or that a single short trade convincingly provided a basis for a 'trading pattern'. Nor, in the absence of any definite orders to execute sales or trades at pre-determined market price levels which, it had also been contended, was a continuing strategy, did the FSA consider that the *ex post facto* assertion of an intention to sell or trade at a particular price level was in those circumstances sufficient evidence of a 'pre-existing trading pattern' to justify the short selling which occurred between Jabré's having been brought over the Chinese Wall and the public announcement by SMFG of whose intentions he had been given confidential and privileged advance information and which the FSA concluded was a material influence on the trades which followed. The FSA noted in particular the scale and repetitive pattern of the trades in question and the fact that immediately following the public announcement, one of the funds managed by Jabré executed further short sales.

The question of the basis for decisions was also considered in the FSA decision **8.112** in the *Shevlin* case.[176] In that case, Shevlin had also asserted that whilst he had made the contract for differences ('CFDs') trade to which the case related, he had traded on the basis of his own research, not inside information. Shevlin argued that the FSA had applied the wrong test in reaching its conclusions—he stated that the FSA had directly assessed his trading on the assumption that he was

---

[175] There was contested evidence as to whether or not Jabré had been told by the broker in a pre-marketing call relating to a proposed issue of convertible preference shares that he could 'maintain his existing trading pattern'.

[176] *John Shevlin v FSA*, FSMT Case 060, 12 June 2008.

a sophisticated investor by looking at expert evidence as to how trading should have been undertaken on the basis of the claimed trading philosophy and parameters, whereas he was merely an amateur trading on his own account on the basis of his own research. In the event, the FSA did not accept Shevlin's assertions that he based his trading on information obtained by research or analysis and that it was therefore based on information generally available. The FSA found, rather, from the weight of the circumstantial evidence surrounding this matter when it was considered as a whole, that it was based on inside information.

Review of decisions

8.113 The following looks at some of the decisions which illuminate the FSA's approach to the misuse of information and the sort of fact patterns that the FSA believes amount to insider dealing. Although most of these were cases under the 'misuse of information' offence contained in the pre-MAD market abuse regime, it is likely that these cases would now fit within the market abuse (insider dealing) offence in the current regime, were they to be brought today. Two cases have now been brought under the post-MAD insider dealing offence, namely the *Shevlin* case and the *Harrison* settlement, which are referred to below. Most of the cases relate to reasonably senior employees of listed companies who have received information as part of their employment, although one relates to information received by an auditor, and an IT technician having access to relevant emails. The *Jabré* case and the *Harrison* case relate to hedge fund managers who have been brought over the wall.

8.114 In the *Bracken*[177] case, the former Group Head of Communications at an LSE listed company was found guilty of insider dealing under the old section 118(2)(a) misuse of information offence.[178] Bracken had advance access to inside information regarding the disappointing trading prospects of the company. On the basis of this information, he engaged in short selling shares in the company shares in anticipation of the official announcements of the information. The *Bracken* case addressed the question of the standards expected of a regular user (in that case, a regular user of the LSE). The FSA noted that exploiting the sensitivity of available information and failing to comply with an employer's share dealing code both failed to meet the expected standard of behaviour.[179] The *Middlemiss*[180] case is a very similar decision to *Bracken*, albeit concerning the sale of shares actually

---

[177] *Bracken*, n 171 above.

[178] The former FSMA, s 118(2)(a) now the legacy offence of FSMA, s 118(4).

[179] *Bracken*, n 171 above, para 52.

[180] FSA Final Notice to Robert Middlemiss dated 10 February 2004. See also FSA Final Notice to Robin Mark Hutchings dated 13 December 2004 for a very similar example of misuse of information via dealing in shares on AIM (purchasing shares in a company before the announcement of takeover offer levels). The *Hutchings* case concerned dealing in shares subsequent to the disclosure censured in the *Smith* case referred to in para 8.128.

owned before a profit warning was made, rather than short selling. In this case, Robert Middlemiss, the company secretary at an AIM listed company, came into possession of a profit warning regarding the company and sold some of his own shareholding in the company before this news was announced to the market. In finding him guilty of market abuse (misuse of information) under the former section 118(2)(a), the FSA drew broadly comparable conclusions to *Bracken*. The FSA noted that the information Middlemiss possessed was a material influence on his decision to deal due to both the time of the dealing (at a time when he possessed non-public information as to the losses of a subsidiary) and the fact that he did not seek permission for the dealing.[181]

The *Davies*[182] case is a third FSA decision from 2004 on the misuse of informa- **8.115** tion, this time in relation to dealing ahead on what was then OFEX.[183] The facts of the case were that Davies was employed as an accountant in the financial division of a company and was given access to interim results that demonstrated that the company was returning to profitability. Davies purchased shares in the company, which he then sold for a profit once the information regarding the company was made public. In holding that this was market abuse under the former section 118(2)(a), the FSA stressed, similarly to the *Bracken* and *Middlemiss* cases, that the sensitivity of the information and the timeliness of the dealing were key elements of the abusive conduct.

The first market abuse case decided by the FSMT was the reference of *Arif* **8.116** *Mohammed*[184] of the FSA decision finding him guilty of market abuse under what was the section 118(2)(a) of FSMA. The importance of the case lies in the FSMT's broad approval of the approach taken by the FSA in the previous Final Notices and determining the standard of proof to be applied in market abuse decisions (see para 8.28). In that case, Mohammed, an auditor employed at PwC, was involved in auditing the accounts of a particular division of an LSE listed company. Mohammed purchased shares in the company at a time when he knew through his professional tasks that it was finalising a probable sale of the division. The FSMT upheld the FSA's decision that this dealing was market abuse on the basis of a misuse of information.

In another FSMT decision, the *Parker* case[185] Parker, who was a Chartered **8.117** Accountant employed by an LSE listed company as its credit risk and treasury

---

[181] *Middlemiss*, n 181 above, para 38(a)–(b).

[182] FSA Final Notice to Michael Davies dated 28 July 2004.

[183] The FSA has rejected the suggestion that action was brought against Davies only to demonstrate that the FSA would pursue market abuse on all markets, including on OFEX. 'OFEX referred the case to us and we had to investigate it. When we did so, we found market abuse' FSA spokeswoman quoted by Alex Davidson, 'Watch out for 'grey areas' of market abuse regime', *Complinet Securities and Banking News*, 9 August 2004. OFEX is no longer a prescribed market.

[184] *Arif Mohammed v FSA*, FSMT Case 012, 29 March 2005.

[185] *James Parker v FSA*, FSMT Case 037, 18 August 2006: pre-MAD regime.

manager, sold holdings of shares in his and his wife's names, adjusted spread bets he had previously made and placed new spread bets after learning that a possible takeover of the company by a much larger competitor had been abandoned, and that the company, for other reasons, was very likely to issue a profit warning within the next few days. It said that the information was not generally available, that Parker had relied on it, and that he did so in order to reduce or eliminate losses he would otherwise have suffered, and in order to gain by his spread betting, when (as in fact happened) the price of the company shares fell substantially following the publication of the profit warning.

8.118 In the *Malins* case,[186] the FSA found Jonathan Malins guilty of market abuse under the old section 118(2)(a) misuse of information legacy offence. The FSA considered that Malins had misused relevant information to buy shares in an AIM listed company of which he was the finance director, having bought 50,000 shares ahead of the announcement of a new share placing and 20,000 shares before the company's interim results. It is perhaps worth noting that Malins did not in fact sell his shares, but was found to have acted deliberately. Malins also made a presentation in the City without having checked or confirmed that the interim results announcement had been made (in the event, due to unforeseen circumstances, publication had been delayed by approximately one hour from the time such announcements are normally made). The financial penalty was stated to not only deprive Malins of potential gains he would have made but also to act as a powerful incentive to others to refrain from such abuse.

8.119 The first post-MAD market abuse (insider dealing) case was the *John Shevlin*[187] decision, where the FSA imposed a fine of £85,000. Shevlin was employed as an IT technician at an LSE listed company. On 10 January 2006, he established a short position in the company through a CFD, in effect betting that the share price would fall. The FSA found that the trade was made on the basis of inside information, obtained by improperly accessing confidential emails of certain senior executives of the company, which contained details of the key trading results and a draft announcement that the company had underperformed. Shevlin closed out his CFD position after the company announced its key trading results to the market, resulting in a profit.

8.120 A couple of cases have involved hedge fund managers given access to certain information having been brought across Chinese walls as part of pre-marketing or pricing exercises. In the *Jabré* case,[188] the FSA fined a hedge fund manager, GLG,

---

186 FSA Final Notice to Jonathan Malins dated 20 December 2005.

187 FSA Final Notice to John Shevlin dated 1 July 2008 RDC. The case had been referred to the FSMT but, after various delays and failure to comply with an 'unless order' issued by the FSMT, the reference was dismissed.

188 FSA Final Notice to Philippe Jabré and GLG Partners LP dated 1 August 2006.

and Philippe Jabré, a former managing director of the firm, £750,000 each for market abuse and breaching FSA principles. This case is discussed further at para 8.71. The second case, the *Harrison* case[189] (which was settled at stage 1) was a 'requiring and encouraging' case relating to the post-MAD insider dealing offence and focused on the issue of recognition of insider information. In that case, Harrison, an investment manager at a hedge fund management firm, was contacted by the investment bank arranging a refinancing of a French company in order to help ascertain the correct pricing and obtain other feedback on the specifics of the proposed refinancing (which involved the tender for certain of its existing bonds and the issue of new notes) which necessitated giving Harrison inside information. Subsequent to the call, Harrison arranged for a colleague to purchase existing bonds in the knowledge, according to the decision, that there was to be an imminent refinancing which would involve the company tendering for those bonds at a premium. The FSA accepted that Harrison did not consider at the time that the information was inside information, and that his behaviour was not deliberate, but failed to consider what should have been a clear and obvious risk that purchasing further bonds before the information was generally available would result in engaging in conduct that would amount to market abuse.

Market makers, dealers, and intermediaries

The trading information safe harbour under the pre-MAD regime.   A theme **8.121** that is common to the CJA insider dealing offence, and indeed both the pre- and post-MAD market abuse regimes, is the need to protect, through appropriate safeguards, the normal functioning of the professional marketplace. This applies particularly with respect to market makers, dealers and intermediaries, and those involved in the corporate finance sector where there is a risk that strictures relating to inside knowledge could be contrary to what is generally understood to be legitimate and common market practice. In the context of market makers, dealers, and intermediaries, as discussed at para 8.84, the 'trading information' safe harbour that existed under the pre-MAD market abuse regime[190] has not been carried forward to the post-MAD regime, and has been replaced by two safe harbours, the first relating to the 'dutiful execution of clients' orders', and the second relating to the 'legitimate carrying on of the business of market makers, etc'. These safe harbours are not co-extensive with the former trading information safe harbour under the pre-MAD regime; the trading information safe harbour was fairly clear

---

[189] FSA Final Notice to Steven Harrison dated 8 September 2008.

[190] Dealing or arranging deals did not amount to a 'misuse of information' solely because it was based on information as to that person's intention, or any other person's intention, to deal or arrange deals in relation to any qualifying investment, or information concerning transactions that had taken place (subject to certain carve-outs relating to takeover bids and certain primary market activity).

in its application. Under the post-MAD regime it is instead necessary to consider whether particular behaviour would fall within the dutiful execution and legitimate market making etc safe harbours; that is to say, whether that behaviour can properly be said to be 'dutiful' or 'legitimate'.

8.122 **The dutiful execution of client orders.** According to MAR 1.3.12C, the dutiful carrying out of, or arranging for the dutiful carrying out of, an order on behalf of another will not in itself amount to market abuse by the person carrying out that order.[191] This also applies where the person acts as portfolio manager. This safe harbour is amplified by guidance[192] which suggests that the dutiful execution carve-out will apply whether or not the person carrying out the order or the person for whom he is acting in fact possesses inside information. In other words, knowledge will not necessarily prevent execution from being dutiful, although a distinction is made between information which is trading information and that which is not—in the FSA's opinion, the fact that inside information is not limited to trading information would indicate that the behaviour is not the dutiful carrying out of an order on behalf of a client. It does not, however, necessarily follow that the converse is the case, that is, it does not necessarily follow that inside information limited to trading information will mean that behaviour will fall within the dutiful execution safe harbour, but it would seem to be the corollary that this would be the starting point. The key issue, therefore, is whether an intermediary's execution will in these circumstances be dutiful and the COMC sets out a number of factors which are, in the FSA's opinion, relevant in determining this question (the presence of these factors being indicative of dutiful execution). These in effect relate to what are either proper or acceptable standards in the market place, standards which can be enhanced through disclosure, pragmatic need (ie the need to facilitate effective execution), or what is *de minimis* (ie where the behaviour in question has no impact on price).

8.123 **Legitimate business of market makers, etc.** The second safe harbour applies to market makers and other persons lawfully dealing in qualifying investments or related investments on their own account ('market makers/dealers').[193] According to the safe harbour, the carrying on of the legitimate business of own account dealing by market makers/dealers (including entering into an agreement for the underwriting of an issue of financial instruments) will not in itself amount to market abuse

---

[191] This carve-out derives from wording found in Recital 18 to MAD.
[192] MAR 1.3.13G.
[193] MAD Recital 18 states that: 'the mere fact that market-makers, bodies authorised to act as counterparties, or persons authorised to execute orders on behalf of third parties with inside information confine themselves... to pursuing their legitimate business . . . should not in itself be deemed to constitute use of such information.'

(insider dealing).[194] The effect of this safe harbour should be to protect the business of market makers/dealers who have knowledge of client orders/executed transactions, and will take this information into account when, for example, making markets or determining when to hedge their exposure. There is, of course, a subtle but important distinction between the proper conduct of such business and abuse, say, through front running. The safe harbour accordingly tries to establish, by setting out relevant factors,[195] what would be legitimate in such circumstances and, in the same way as the 'dutiful execution' safe harbour,[196] does so by reference to matters such as what are proper or acceptable standards in the market place, standards which can be enhanced through disclosure, or what is *de minimis*. There is of course in practice likely to be an overlap between the 'dutiful execution' safe harbour and the 'legitimate business of market makers etc' safe harbour, particularly in the dual capacity markets. As with the 'dutiful execution' safe harbour, the fact that inside information is not limited to trading information will, in the FSA's opinion, be an indication that behaviour is not in pursuit of legitimate business.[197]

Corporate finance and takeovers

The market abuse regime creates a safe harbour for certain types of takeover or merger activities. The need for this is fairly self-explanatory as corporate finance houses undertaking activities on behalf of, say, an offeror for a listed target will by definition have information relating to the proposed offer. The safe harbour provides that in the context of a public takeover bid or merger, behaviour based on inside information relating to another company[198] for the purpose of gaining control of that company or proposing a merger with that company, does not in itself amount to market abuse.[199] The activities benefiting from the safe harbour include seeking irrevocable undertakings or expressions of support from the holders of securities in the target in relation to an offer or making arrangements in relation to an issue of securities which will be used as consideration or will be issued in order to fund the takeover or merger offer. This in turn includes arrangements for the underwriting or placing of those securities and any associated hedging arrangements by underwriters or placees which are proportionate to the

8.124

---

[194] According to guidance in MAR 1.3.7C, this safe harbour will apply even if the person concerned in fact possesses trading information which is inside information.

[195] MAR 1.3.10E.

[196] Although note that, whilst some of these factors are the same or similar, there are differences between the two sets of factors.

[197] MAR 1.3.9E.

[198] Guidance issued in the COMC clarifies that the information in question can be two-fold: firstly information relating to the offer or potential offer; and secondly information discovered during due diligence (MAR 1.3.18G). But note that as the CJA safe harbour is limited to market information (ie the equivalent of the first limb), stakebuilding on the basis of information in the second limb is effectively precluded.

[199] MAR 1.3.17C.

risks assumed. Making arrangements for any cash alternative to the offer is also included in the enumerated activities.

8.125　The COMC also goes on indicate that, in the FSA's opinion, relevant factors in determining whether a person's behaviour is for the purpose of his gaining control of the target or proposing a merger (and indicating that it is) are whether the transactions concerned are in the target company's shares (presumably as opposed to, say, CFDs referable to the company's shares) or whether the transactions concerned are for the sole purposes of gaining control or affecting that merger.

Market abuse (improper disclosure)—Type 2

8.126　The second behaviour type that constitutes market abuse is where an insider discloses inside information to another person otherwise than in the 'proper course' of the exercise of his employment, profession, or duties, irrespective of whether or not that information is used by someone else as the basis for dealing.[200] This definition of improper disclosure under the FSMA market abuse provisions is similar to the definition of the 'disclosure offence' under the CJA provisions, where it is a criminal offence for an insider to disclose inside information 'otherwise than in the *proper* performance of the functions of his employment, office or profession'.[201] In both cases, the definition of the wrongful conduct hinges on the propriety of a disclosure by a professional, etc, of inside information.

8.127　The FSA has indicated that it will take into account a range of factors to determine if disclosure was made in the 'proper course' of the exercise of his employment, profession, or duties. These factors, the presence of which are indicative that disclosure is made in the 'proper course', include whether the rules of a prescribed market, the FSA, or the Takeover Code permit the disclosure or whether the disclosure is accompanied by the imposition of confidentiality requirements upon the person to whom disclosure was made and is otherwise reasonable and for one of a number of stipulated purposes or in fulfilment of a legal obligation.[202] Although not specifically stated in the factors, an example of proper disclosure might be the disclosure of information to potential counterparties to a transaction solely for the purpose of broking a transaction where it would be normal market practice to do so, and to do so with those counterparties.

Examples of 'improper disclosure'

8.128　There have been no cases to date on market abuse (improper disclosure) although the *Smith* decision[203] (a case under the misuse of information heading in the

---

[200] FSMA, s 118(3).

[201] CJA, s 52(2)(b) discussed in Chapter 9, para 9.13 *et seq*.

[202] According to MAR 1.4.5E(2), these purposes include enabling the proper performance of employment and to facilitate giving advice or a commercial transaction.

[203] FSA Final Notice to Jason Smith dated 13 December 2004.

pre-MAD market abuse regime), if brought today, would be likely to be brought under the market abuse (improper disclosure) heading. In the *Smith* decision, Smith was found guilty of market abuse through the wrongful disclosure of information. On the facts of the case, Smith was employed as finance director and company secretary of a company whose shares were traded on AIM. As a result of his position, Smith knew that a takeover offer had been made for the company, and disclosed this information to his friend Robin Hutchings.[204] In holding that this disclosure was a misuse of information, the FSA stressed the impropriety of disclosures of inside information in a social context, ahead of the official disclosure of that information. In common with other cases, the FSA also stressed the need for propriety in handling sensitive information for the sake of market confidence. The FSA has also cited as an example of market abuse (improper disclosure) the selective briefing of analysts by directors of issuers or other persons who are persons discharging managerial responsibilities.[205] This again underlies the emphasis being placed on the concept of fair and equal access to information (see discussion at para 8.10 *et seq.*).

Safe harbours

The COMC sets out a number of safe harbours from the market abuse (improper disclosure) offence. These apply in respect of disclosures made to a government department, the Bank of England, the Competition Commission, the Takeover Panel, or any other regulatory body or authority for the purposes of fulfilling a legal or regulatory obligation[206] or otherwise to such a body in connection with the performance of the functions of that body.[207] **8.129**

There is also a safe harbour relating to the fulfilment of obligations under the Listing Rules, Prospectus Rules, and Disclosure and Transparency Rules or any similar regulatory obligation.[208] This would apply for example where inside information is disclosed as soon as possible (as required by the Disclosure Rules) or otherwise delayed in accordance with the 'legitimate interests' exception set out in the Disclosure Rules.[209] **8.130**

Market abuse (misuse of information)—Type 3 (legacy offence)

The third behaviour type that constitutes market abuse (and the final type falling within the scope of conduct connected to the use of information) is 'misuse of **8.131**

---

[204] The facts of this case mirror closely the example given at the new MAR 1.4.6G of a situation in which disclosure in a social context can constitute 'improper disclosure' for the purposes of the new s 118(3) offence.
[205] MAR 1.4.2E(2).
[206] MAR 1.4.3C(1).
[207] MAR 1.4.3C(2).
[208] MAR 1.4.4C.
[209] DTR 1.5.2R.

information'. This is a legacy offence and as such only applies to behaviour not falling within the market abuse (insider dealing) or (improper disclosure) behaviour types, but which otherwise involves the misuse of information as judged by the standard of a 'regular user'.[210] The two requirements for the 'misuse of information' are firstly that the behaviour must be based on information which is not generally available to those using the market but which, if available to a regular user of the market, would be, or would be likely to be, regarded by him as relevant when deciding the terms on which transactions in qualifying investments should be effected. The second requirement is that the behaviour must be likely to be regarded by a regular user of the market as a failure on the part of the person concerned to observe the standard of behaviour reasonably expected of a person in his position in relation to the market.[211]

8.132 According to evidential provisions in the COMC, relevant factors in determining whether information is to be considered as 'relevant information' (and which are indicative that it is) are: the extent to which the information is reliable; if the information is new or fresh information; whether the information provides grounds to conclude that a future event (which would trigger a disclosure requirement) will occur; or if there is no other material information available to inform users of the market.[212] The factors set out in para 8.86 *et seq*, relating to whether or not information is generally available, and when behaviour is 'based on' inside information, will also be relevant in the context of market abuse (misuse of information).

Examples of conduct which constitutes the 'misuse of information'

8.133 There are subtle distinctions between the coverage of market abuse (insider dealing) and (improper disclosure) on the one hand, and market abuse (misuse of information) on the other. The Treasury Consultation of the Sunset Clauses[213] referred for example to various circumstances in which it believed that the legacy offence of misuse of information could be wider than the post-MAD offences and pointed to the wider definition of 'relevant information', the lack of a price sensitivity test, and the lack of definition of 'insider'.

8.134 By way of illustration, a case which was determined under the pre-MAD misuse of information heading, and which might still be heard under that heading if it were brought today, would be the *Isaacs* case.[214] In this case, Isaacs visited the house of a friend who was an employee at an LSE listed company and came across

---

[210] See discussion at para 8.53.

[211] FSMA, s 118(4).

[212] MAR 1.5.6E.

[213] See para 8.55 *et seq*.

[214] FSA Final Notice to David Isaacs dated 28 February 2005. Note that, depending on the precise facts, other offences might also be in point. For example this type of behaviour might constitute 'contrivances' under market abuse (manipulating devices), although see para 8.148 for

copies of minutes which related to product development and expected profits. Isaacs then posted anonymous opinions relating to this information on an Internet bulletin board with the intention of thereby 'ramping up' the price of the shares and consequently the value of his own previously purchased shareholding and indeed shares bought subsequently. In holding that Isaacs' behaviour constituted market abuse, the FSA emphasised both his personal history as an 'experienced company executive and private investor', that the information had been obtained by 'dishonest and surreptitious means', and that the disclosure was motivated by 'a desire to "ramp up" the price' of the shares in question.[215] The FSA has also provided a number of examples of situations where the conduct concerned constitutes the 'misuse of information',[216] including, for example, informal, non-contractual icing (that is 'reserving') of qualifying investments by the manager of a proposed issue of convertible or exchangeable bonds, which are to be the subject of a public marketing effort, where this has the effect of withdrawing the qualifying investments from the lending market in such a way that other market participants are disadvantaged. This is predicated on the fact that market abuse (inside information) will only apply to dealings or attempts to deal, whereas market abuse (misuse of information) may in principle apply to behaviour (in this case, icing), falling short of dealing or attempts to deal.[217] Another example might be entering into a transaction covered by market abuse (misuse of information) but which was not a qualifying or relevant investment for the purposes of market abuse (inside information) where this was based on 'relevant information'. This might, for example, be the case where the transaction entered into was a fixed odds bet.[218]

Types of conduct that do not constitute the 'misuse of information'

The safe harbours applying to a person's own intention to deal, legitimate business of market making etc, dutiful execution of clients' orders, and relevant behaviour in the context of a public takeover bid or merger would apply equally in the case of market abuse (misuse of information).   **8.135**

The 'regular user' test

As discussed at para 8.54, market abuse (misuse of information) is a legacy offence and as such remains subject to the regular user test. The standards expected by a   **8.136**

---

discussion as to the interrelation between the contrivances on the one hand and transactions or orders on the other.

[215] ibid, paras 43–45.
[216] MAR 1.5.10E.
[217] MAR 1.5.10E(2).
[218] MAR 1.5.10E. FSA guidance at MAR 1.5.3G also indicates that behaviour could fall within the market abuse (misuse of information) offence where the information in question was relevant information but not inside information.

regular user have been considered in a number of market abuse decisions where the FSA has held that the defendant had failed to meet the regular user standard partly on the grounds that it had not complied with appropriate professional standards[219] (for example, in *Bracken* and *Middlemiss*, a failure to comply with share dealing codes imposed on the senior staff of listed companies). In *Arif Mohammed*, the FSMT held that Mohammed's failure to comply with the dealing rules applicable to auditors, while not amounting to market abuse per se, could reasonably be taken to indicate a failure to observe expected market standards.[220] In the *Parker* case[221] the FSMT also found that Parker's behaviour fell below the standard to be expected. He was professionally qualified and was employed by a listed company in a senior position of trust.

8.137   The FSA has also set out in the COMC a number of relevant (and, where present, indicative) factors when considering whether a regular user would reasonably expect relevant information to be disclosed to users of the market or to be announced, and as such whether the behaviour is likely to fall below the requisite standard. These factors refer to various disclosure requirements required by any legal or regulatory requirement[222] as well as information routinely made the subject of a public announcement even if not subject to any formal requirement (for example, changes to published credit ratings, changes to the constituents of an index, or information to be the subject of official announcements by government, central monetary or fiscal authorities, or regulatory bodies/exchanges). This in fact represents somewhat of a watering down of the 'disclosable' and 'announceable' requirements of earlier versions of the COMC, but still underlines the importance of these issues.

Flow chart—offences relating to the use and disclosure of information

8.138   The basic components involved in the offences relating to the use and disclosure of information (applicable to the non-commodity derivatives definition of inside information) are set out in Figure 8.1 by way of illustration.

---

[219] The COMC previously explicitly provided (MAR 1.2.3E(4) that the regular user was likely to consider the position of the person in question and the standards reasonably to be expected of that person at the time of the behaviour in the light of that person's experience, level of skill, and standard of knowledge.

[220] *Arif Mohammed v FSA*, FSMT Case 012, 29 March 2005, para 43.

[221] *James Parker v FSA*, FSMT Case 037, 18 August 2006.

[222] These include information required to be disseminated under the Listing Rules, Prospectus Rules, and Disclosure and Transparency Rules (or equivalents in the relevant jurisdiction), information required to be disseminated by the Takeover Code or SARs (or their equivalents) and information required to be disclosed by an issuer under the laws, rules, or regulations applying to the relevant market.

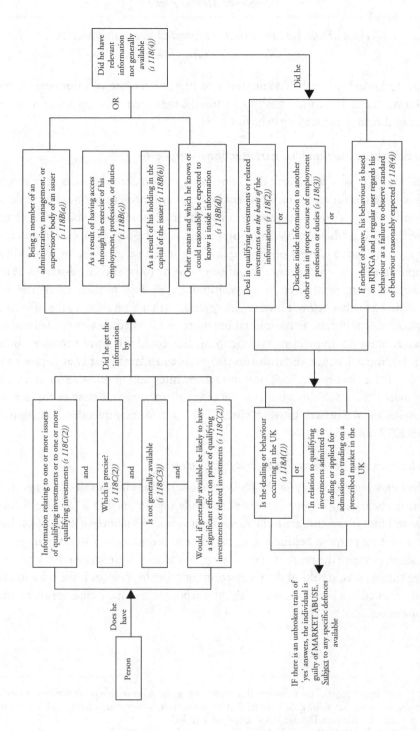

Figure 8.1 Market Abuse: Information Offences—Financial Services and Markets Act 2000

Types of market abuse that concern market manipulation
and false or misleading behaviour

8.139 Having looked at the behaviour types relating to the use of information, the
following considers conduct falling within the four behaviour types that relate to
manipulation or misleading behaviour.[223]

Market abuse (manipulating transactions)—Type 4

8.140 The fourth type of behaviour that constitutes market abuse consists of effecting
transactions or orders to trade (otherwise than for legitimate reasons and in conformity with accepted market practices on the relevant market) which give, or are
likely to give, a false or misleading impression as to the supply of, or demand for,
or as to the price of, one or more qualifying investments ('false or misleading
impressions'), or which secure the price of one or more such investments at an
abnormal or artificial level ('price positioning').[224] Both of these categories are
considered further below. However, a key factor is that both relate to the 'effecting
transactions or orders'. Behaviour falling short of this will therefore not fall within
market abuse (manipulating transactions), but could fall within market abuse
(misleading behaviour and distortion). This is considered further at para 8.153.
This offence does not in itself presuppose any intention or purpose (or at least is
not stated as such) although this is not to say that the mental state of the person
undertaking the behaviour will be irrelevant—see, for example, the discussion at
para 8.72 *et seq.*

Indications that behaviour is not for a legitimate reason

8.141 The following factors are, in the FSA's opinion, relevant in considering whether a
person's behaviour in entering into a manipulating transaction is for a legitimate
reason (and, if present, are indicative that it is not),[225] namely if the person has
an actuating purpose behind the transaction to induce others to trade in, or to
position or move the price of, a qualifying investment; if the person has another,
illegitimate, reason behind the transactions or order to trade; or if the transaction
was executed in a particular way with the purpose of creating a false or misleading
impression.

---

[223] For the purposes of the following discussion, it is again assumed that the other requirements
relating to the market abuse definition (ie that behaviour relates to relevant qualifying investments
on prescribed markets and geographical scope) are satisfied.

[224] FSMA, s 118(5). 'Accepted Market Practices' requires a process of formal approval and does
not simply refer to practices which are commonplace or generally considered to be acceptable—see
para 8.78.

[225] MAR 1.6.5E.

Indications that behaviour is for a legitimate reason

The COMC also sets out a number of relevant factors which, conversely, if present, **8.142** would be indicative that a person's reasons for entering into a manipulating transaction are legitimate.[226] These relate to the manner of execution (that is to say, whether the transaction complies with market rules as to the proper execution of transactions), whether the need for the market as a whole to operate fairly and efficiently has been taken into account, the nature of the transactions themselves (that is to say, the extent to which the transaction generally opens a new position, so creating, rather than removing, an exposure to market risk), and whether or not the transaction is pursuant to a prior legal or regulatory obligation owed to a third party.

Offences such as market abuse (manipulating transactions) point to a very difficult **8.143** debate, that is to say when transactions are manipulating, and when they are bona fide speculation or bona fide trading strategies. The FSA has tried to clarify this point by indicating that the purpose of the rules is not to find that market users have committed market abuse when they trade at times and in sizes most beneficial to them, as such behaviour improves the liquidity and efficiency of markets. Further, the FSA has indicated that the fact that prices are trading outside their normal range in the market does not necessarily mean that someone has engaged in price positioning, as high and low prices naturally result from the interplay of supply and demand.[227] The line can, however, be a very difficult one to draw.

The distinction can be illustrated by the *EBG and Potts* decision.[228] This case was **8.144** decided under the distorting the market in investments provision of the former section 118(2)(c) (and indeed was the only case under that heading) but, if brought today, could probably be brought under the market abuse (manipulating transactions) offence. In that case, Christopher Potts (head of market making at EBG) and EBG engaged in short-selling of shares in an AIM listed company. By the end of the short-selling process, EBG had established short positions in the company equal to 252 per cent of the issued share capital, with no prospect of settling these sales. Approximately 250 retail investors were adversely affected by this conduct and the LSE ultimately intervened to suspend trading in the AIM company's shares. The FSA provided a detailed analysis of why this behaviour constituted distortion:

> the normal market forces of supply, including sellers taking short positions, depends upon the reasonable expectation of market users that the selling party will be in a position to settle transactions in a timely fashion. If sellers cannot settle transactions in a timely fashion, or at all, because they have sold short beyond the level for which

---

[226] MAR 1.6.6E.

[227] MAR 1.6.7G–1.6.8G.

[228] FSA Final Notice to Evolution Beeson Gregory Limited and Christopher Potts dated 12 November 2004.

they have a reasonable settlement plan, then this will inevitably distort the market for those shares at the point of sale because the expectation of timely delivery on the part of investors who enter into that market and contract to buy shares will not be met.[229]

Accepted market practices

8.145 Transactions will not fall within the market abuse (manipulating transactions) offence to the extent they are in conformity with 'accepted market practices'.[230] As discussed at para 8.140, this is not simply a question of determining whether particular transactions are within acceptable market parameters, but rather pre-supposes that the practices be accepted by the FSA as complying with the factors to be taken into account by an EU competent authority when considering market practices. These factors include the level of transparency, the need to safeguard market forces, impact on liquidity, the risk inherent in the relevant practice, and the structural characteristics of the relevant market.[231] CESR maintains a pan-European list of accepted market practices.[232]

Types of conduct that fall within the definition of 'manipulating transactions' relating to false or misleading impressions

8.146 MAR sets out a number of examples of what, in the FSA's opinion, would consti-tute 'manipulating transactions' involving false or misleading impressions as to the supply of, demand for, or price of, qualifying investments, absent a legitimate reason.[233] These examples include transactions such as so-called 'wash trades' (ie transactions effected where there is no real assumption of market risk or change of beneficial ownership). Typically, this could be by way of a party (or parties acting in collusion or concert) simultaneously entering into purchase and sale transactions for the same security using different brokers in order to give the impression of liquidity, or increasing interest, in that security.[234] Another example

---

[229] ibid, para 37.

[230] 'Accepted market practices' means practices that are reasonably expected in the financial market in question and are accepted by the FSA (or other competent EEA authority)—FSMA, s 130A(3).

[231] Commission Directive 2004/72/EC implements sections of the MAD as regards accepted market practices and sets out guidance in Arts 2 and 3 for the competent authorities of Member States to follow in evaluating market practices.

[232] Available at <http://www.cesr-eu.org/>.

[233] MAR 1.6.2E. According to MAR 1.6.9E, the FSA will take into account a number of factors in determining whether a person's behaviour creates false or misleading impressions, including, broadly speaking, the extent to which orders to trade/transactions: (a) represent a significant pro-portion of the daily volume of transactions in the qualifying investment on the market concerned; (b) lead to a significant change in the price of an investment; (c) include position reversals in a short period; (d) are concentrated within a short time period and lead to a price change which is subse-quently reversed; (e) change the representation of the order book available to market participants and are then removed before being executed; and (f) are effected around the time at which reference prices are calculated and affect such calculations.

[234] MAR 1.6.3G states that a stock lending/borrowing or repo/reverse repo transaction, or another transaction involving the provision of collateral, do not constitute a wash trade under this provision.

cited is entering orders into an electronic trading system, at prices which are higher than the previous bid or lower than the previous offer, and withdrawing them before they are executed, in order to give a misleading impression that there is demand for or supply of the qualifying investment at that price.

Types of conduct that fall within the definition of 'manipulating transactions' relating to price positioning

As to price positioning, again the COMC sets out a number of examples illustrat- **8.147** ing what, in the FSA's opinion, would constitute 'manipulating transactions', absent a legitimate reason.[235] These include, for example, what is in effect corner- ing the market through a dominant position over the supply of or demand for a qualifying investment and 'abusive squeezes'[236] (which presupposes amongst other things that behaviour is entered into with the purpose of positioning at a distorted level the price at which others have to deliver, take delivery, or defer delivery to satisfy their obligations in relation to a qualifying investment). Another example cited is entering small orders into an electronic trading system, at prices which are higher than the previous bid or lower than the previous offer, in order to move the price of the qualifying investment.[237]

Market abuse (manipulating devices)—Type 5

The fifth behaviour type that constitutes market abuse is where a person's conduct **8.148** consists of effecting transactions or orders to trade which employ fictitious devices or any other form of deception or contrivance.[238] This would seem to presuppose

---

[235] MAR 1.6.4E. According to MAR 1.6.10E, the FSA will take into account the following factors when considering whether conduct amounts to price positioning, including the extent to which: (a) the person had an interest in the price of the investment; (b) the extent to which price volatility movements are outside the normal ranges; and (c) a person has successively and consist- ently increased or decreased his bid or offer for an investment.

[236] The FSA has specified a number of factors to be taken into account when deciding if a person has engaged in an abusive squeeze—MAR 1.6.11E. These factors are the extent to which: (a) a person is willing to relax his control or influence for the sake of an orderly market; (b) a person's activity risks causing settlement default by market users on a multilateral basis; (c) prices under the delivery mechanisms of the market diverge from the prices outside of those mechanisms; and (d) the immediate market compared to the forward market is unusually expensive or inexpensive.

[237] An example given by the FSA in MAR 1.6.15E is where a trader trades with himself by simul- taneously buying and selling the same qualifying investment to give the appearance of a legitimate transfer of title or risk at a price outside the normal trading range for the qualifying investment. The price of the qualifying investment is relevant to the calculation of the settlement value of an option. He does this while holding a position in the option. His purpose is to position the price of the quali- fying investment at a false, misleading, abnormal, or artificial level, making him a profit or avoiding a loss from the option. It is also interesting to consider whether an action could be brought under the s 397 misleading statements and practices offence in these circumstances. The acts in question would appear to have created a false or misleading market in the investment in question, but query whether any other party would have been 'induced' to enter into a transaction in such circumstances.

[238] FSMA, s 118(6). The FSA will take the following factors into account in determining whether a fictitious device or other form of contrivance has been used (and, if present, are indicative that it

some kind of deliberate act. The COMC again sets out a number of examples of conduct which, in the FSA's view, will constitute 'manipulating devices'.[239] The use of the word 'employed' would suggest there needs to be an interaction or link between the transaction or orders on the one hand, and the device, deception, or contrivance on the other, although the nature and extent of that relationship, whether in timing terms or otherwise, is not clear from the examples given. The examples include publicly voicing an opinion about a qualifying investment (or its issuer) and profiting subsequently from the impact of the opinion on positions held, without having simultaneously disclosed that conflict of interest to the public in a proper and effective way.[240] Other examples given include disseminating misleading positive information with a view to increasing the price of the investment in question ('pump and dump')[241] or, if the person disseminating the information has a short position, disseminating misleading negative information with a view to decreasing the price of the investment in question ('trash and cash').

8.149 Trash and cash schemes gained significant media coverage in March 2008 when HBOS plc (HBOS) was thought to have become a victim of false rumours spread by short-sellers.[242] The FSA launched an investigation into the HBOS rumours, but was unable to uncover evidence that the rumours were spread as part of a concerted attempted by individuals to profit by manipulating the share price.

8.150 Despite the FSA's failure to find any culprits, the FSA has confirmed that the FSA's Markets Division is currently carrying out a review of the systems and controls firms have in place to deal with market rumours. The press release of 1 August 2008, 'FSA concludes HBOS rumours investigation' FSA/PN/086/2008 also indicates the FSA's willingness to take a strong stance, and to pursue criminal prosecutions where possible:

> Market participants should, however, expect that our surveillance and investigation activity will continue at a high level of intensity. Where individuals or firms appear to have benefited following false or misleading rumours, we will require individuals and/or firms to provide immediate access to traders, information and trading strategies as well as to make available email, messaging and telephone records. Where there is evidence of market abuse then we will take enforcement—including criminal—action.

---

has) (a) if orders to trade are preceded or followed by the dissemination of false or misleading information by the person trading; or (b) if orders to trade are undertaken before or after the dissemination of research or recommendations which are erroneous, biased, or demonstrably influenced by the personal interest of the person trading. MAR 1.7.3E.

[239] MAR 1.7.2E.
[240] MAR 1.7.2E (1).
[241] MAR 1.7.2E(3).
[242] Various rumours had circulated to the effect that a British bank faced funding difficulties. Some identified HBOS by name. FSA, FSA concludes HBOS rumours investigation, 1 August 2008, FSA/PN/086/2008 (<http://www.fsa.gov.uk/pages/Library/Communication/PR/2008/086.shtml>).

Market abuse (dissemination)—Type 6

The sixth type of conduct that constitutes market abuse is behaviour which con- **8.151**
sists of the dissemination of information by any means which gives, or is likely to
give, a false or misleading impression as to a qualifying investment by a person
who knew or could reasonably be expected to have known that the information
was false or misleading.[243] As discussed at para 8.73, this offence carries both a
subjective element (that is to say, the knowledge of the person in question) and
an objective element (whether he could reasonably be expected to have that
knowledge). According to the COMC,[244] knowingly or recklessly spreading false
or misleading information about a qualifying investment through the media,
including in particular through an RIS or similar information channel, would, in
the FSA's opinion, fall under this heading, as would undertaking a course of conduct in order to give a false or misleading impression about a qualifying investment. Cited examples of behaviour which may constitute market abuse
(dissemination) are posting false or misleading information about the takeover of
a company whose shares are qualifying investments on an Internet chat room
knowing that information to be false or misleading, or where a person responsible
for the context of information to an RIS is reckless as to whether the information
submitted is false or misleading.[245] For the purposes of this provision, the dissemination of information by a journalist is to be assessed by taking into account the
codes governing the journalism profession, unless he derives any advantage or
profits from the dissemination of the information.[246] The suspected behaviour
relating to the HBOS rumours reported in media coverage[247] could potentially
have fallen under this category of market abuse, as well as under the manipulating
devices category.

Although there have to date been no cases under this offence, it is likely that the **8.152**
Shell case, if brought today, would be brought under the market abuse (dissemination) offence.[248] In that case, the FSA concluded that certain Shell entities were
guilty of market abuse through a dissemination of false or misleading information

---

[243] FSMA, s 118(7). According to MAR 1.8.4E, in the FSA's opinion, if a normal and reasonable
person would know or should have known that information was false or misleading, that indicates
that the person disseminating the information could reasonably be expected to have known the
same. However, if a person disseminating the false or misleading information could only know it
was false or misleading through access to information that was properly behind a Chinese Wall,
then, in the FSA's opinion, he is not taken to know that the information was so false or misleading.
MAR 1.8.5E.

[244] MAR 1.8.3E.

[245] Example provided at MAR 1.8.6E(2).

[246] FSMA, s 118A(4).

[247] See further discussion at para 8.149 *et seq.*

[248] FSA Final Notice to Shell Transport and Trading Company, plc and The Royal Dutch
Petroleum Company NV, dated 24 August 2004.

concerning announcements of their levels of hydrocarbon reserves. During the period 1998 to 2004, it was found that Shell regularly overstated its hydrocarbon levels in statements to the market, which the FSA held would be likely to give a false or misleading impression as to the price of UK listed Shell shares (as reserve levels are a key performance indicator for companies in the oil and gas industries).[249] In the judgment of the FSA, an average investor in listed shares on the FTSE-100 would not expect the information disclosed to the market concerning reserve levels to be false or misleading and Shell was therefore guilty of market abuse.[250] The evidential provision at MAR 1.8.4E indicates that if a normal and reasonable person would know or should have known that information was false or misleading, that indicates that the person disseminating the information could reasonably be expected to have known the same. Evidence in the *Shell* case suggested that it was known internally (or at least suspected) that the disclosed information was inaccurate. A number of decisions relating to inaccurate or misleading announcements have also been made under the Disclosure Rules—see discussion at para 8.174.

Market abuse (misleading behaviour and distortion)—Type 7 (legacy offence)

8.153 The seventh (and final) type of conduct that constitutes market abuse, as described at para 8.78 relates to both 'misleading behaviour' and 'distortion'. This is a legacy offence and as such catches behaviour only to the extent it does not fall within the other types of conduct relating to manipulation. To fall within this offence, the behaviour must be such as is likely to give a regular user of the market a false or misleading impression as to the supply of, demand for, or price or value of, qualifying investments. In terms of distortion, the behaviour must be such as would be, or would be likely to be, regarded by a regular user of the market as behaviour that would distort, or would be likely to distort, the market in such an investment. In both cases the behaviour must be likely to be regarded by a regular user of the market as a failure on the part of the person concerned to observe the 'standard of behaviour' reasonably expected of a person in his position in relation to the market.[251] The offence is based on behaviour generally rather than specifically behaviour relating to transactions, and is therefore wider than the equivalent MAD offences, given that the MAD covers simply 'transactions' and 'orders'. An example of behaviour which would, in the FSA's view, be market abuse under this heading, is the movement of physical commodity stocks or empty cargo ships where such movement creates the specified impression.[252]

---

[249] ibid, paras 61 and 69.

[250] ibid, para 64.

[251] FSMA, s 118(8). The regular user concept is explained at para 8.53

[252] MAR 1.9.2E. Note, however, CESR, 'Market Abuse Directives: Level 3—First Set of CESR guidance and information on the common operation of the Directive', which sets out various examples of types of practice which in the view of CESR members could potentially contravene the

By way of illustration, a finding of giving a false or misleading impression as to the **8.154** supply of or demand for particular investments was reached in the case of *Indigo and Bonnier*.[253] In that case, Bonnier (the managing partner of Indigo) made a number of statutory disclosures to an LSE listed company purporting to notify the company that Indigo had acquired an increasingly large shareholding in the company. In fact, Indigo had instead acquired CFDs with an investment bank relating to the company's shares, under the terms of which it was expressly stated that Indigo would not obtain ownership of the shares. The FSA held that these disclosures were likely to give regular users a false impression of the demand for the company's shares, as the impression was presented that shares had been acquired, where in fact only CFDs had been purchased.

According to the COMC, factors to take into account when determining if behav- **8.155** iour is likely to give a regular user a 'false or misleading impression' regarding qualifying investments[254] are the experience and knowledge of the users of the market in question; the structure of the market, including its reporting, notification, and transparency requirements; the legal and regulatory requirements of the market concerned; the identity and position of the person responsible for the behaviour which has been observed (if known); and the extent and nature of the visibility or disclosure of the person's activity. MAR sets out a number of factors relevant in determining whether behaviour creating a false or misleading impression or distorting the market has failed to meet the standard expected by a regular user.[255] These relate to the manner of execution (that is to say, whether the transaction complies with market rules as to the proper execution of transactions), whether or not the need for the market as a whole to operate fairly and efficiently has been taken into account, and whether or not the transaction is pursuant to a prior legal or regulatory obligation owed to a third party. These reiterate factors which, in the context of market abuse (manipulating transactions), are indicative of there being 'legitimate reasons',[256] but in the current context are stated to be factors which are relevant, rather than necessarily being indicative. Additional factors in the context of the 'regular user test' are the characteristics of the market in question, including the users and applicable rules and codes of conduct; the position of the person in question; and the standards reasonably to be expected of him in light of his experience, skill, and knowledge. Where an organisation has

---

prohibition on market manipulation, cites as an example of dissemination of false and misleading information (a post-MAD offence) the movement of physical commodity stocks to create a misleading impression as to the supply or demand for a commodity or the deliverable into a commodity futures contract.

[253] FSA Final Notice to Indigo Capital LLC and Robert Bonnier dated 21 December 2004.
[254] MAR 1.9.4E.
[255] MAR 1.9.5E.
[256] See para 8.142.

created a false or misleading impression, a relevant factor will also be whether the individuals responsible could only know they were likely to create a false or misleading impression if they had access to other information that was being held behind a Chinese Wall or similarly effective arrangements.

Short Selling Rules – MAR 1.9.2A E and MAR 1.9.2B R and MAR 1.9.2C, D & E

8.156   A key recent development has been the introduction of two sets of rules relating to short sales. The first of these required disclosure of 'significant' short positions created or increased while the issuer is pursuing a rights issue (Short Selling Rules). Under MAR 1.9.2A E, (introduced by the Short Selling Instrument 2008 (FSA 2008/30)), failure to give adequate disclosure that the holder has reached or exceeded a 'disclosable short position'[257] where: (1) that position relates, directly or indirectly, to securities which are the subject of a rights issue; and (2) the 'disclosable short position' is reached or exceeded during a rights issue period, is behaviour which, in the opinion of the FSA, is market abuse (misleading behaviour).[258] The Short Selling Rules were introduced at short notice, and without consultation, but according to the FSA were justified by the circumstances at the time:

> In current market conditions, there is increased potential for market abuse through short selling during rights issues. As a result, there has been severe volatility in the shares of companies conducting rights issues. This is potentially damaging not only to the issuers in question but also to confidence in the overall fairness and quality of the UK market. It can be particularly prejudicial to the interests of small investors. The problem is compounded by the length of time taken to complete rights issues.[259]

Subsequent to that, in the turmoil following the demise of Lehman Brothers, and the proposed takeover of HBOS by Lloyds TSB following the collapse in HBOS shares, further short selling rules were introduced by the Short Selling (No 2) Instrument 2008 (FSA 2008/50)) in MAR 1.9.2 C, D & E on 19 September 2008. These provisions (Short Selling No 2 Rules) in effect prohibited altogether the active creation or increase of net short positions in publicly quoted UK banks, UK insurers, or their parents by providing that such activity would, in the opinion of the FSA, be engaging in market abuse (misleading behaviour). The only exception

---

[257] A disclosable short position is a short position which represents an economic interest of 0.25% of the issued capital of a company.

[258] For the purposes of MAR 1.9.2A E, 'adequate disclosure' means disclosure made on an RIS by 3.30 pm the following business day (MAR 1.9.2B R).

[259] Generally, also see FSA: 'Financial Services Authority introduces disclosure regime for significant short positions in companies undertaking rights issues', 13 June 2008, FSA/PN/057/2008 (<http://www.fsa.gov.uk/pages/Library/Communication/PR/2008/057.shtml>) and 'Short Selling Instrument 2008—Frequently Asked Questions 20 June 2008 Update' (<http://www.fsa.gov.uk/pubs/other/Shortselling_faqs.pdf>).

to this relates to market makers. A short position, for the purposes of the Short Selling No 2 Rules, takes into account any form of economic interest in the shares of the company. In addition, the Short Selling No 2 Rules require daily disclosure of all net short positions in excess of 0.25% of the ordinary share capital of the relevant companies held at market close on the previous working day, by providing again that failure to disclose could, in the FSA's opinion, be market abuse. According to Hector Sants, Chief Executive of the FSA:

> While we still regard short selling as a legitimate investment technique in normal market conditions, the current extreme circumstances have given rise to disorderly markets. As a result, we have taken this decisive action, after careful consideration, to protect the fundamental integrity and quality of markets and to guard against further instability in the financial sector.

The Short Selling No 2 Rules are due to expire on 16 January 2009.

Statutory exceptions

As mentioned at para 8.58, FSMA provides a number of statutory exceptions **8.157** which state that particular behaviour does not amount to market abuse. These exceptions operate in addition to the safe harbours which apply in the COMC to particular types of market abuse. The first of these exceptions concerns behaviour which conforms with a rule which itself provides that conforming with the rule does not amount to market abuse.[260] MAR 1.10.2G explains that, where a person complies with the control of information rule concerning the establishment of Chinese Walls[261] for the purposes of withholding information from one part of a firm to another, or complies with those parts of the Disclosure Rules[262] relating to disclosures of information, such a person will not have committed market abuse. The purpose of these exceptions is to ensure that where a person complies with FSA rules on the use of information, such compliance will not amount to market abuse. The second of the statutory exceptions[263] states that compliance with the relevant provisions of the EC buy-back programmes and Stabilisation Regulation[264] will not amount to market abuse.[265] The final exception makes it clear that any

---

[260] FSMA, s 118A(5)(a).

[261] SYSC 10.2.2R(1).

[262] DTR 2, as discussed at para 8.11. The guidance at MAR 1.10.2 G(2) refers to those part of the Part 6 rules (namely the Disclosure Rules and Prospectus Rules) which relate to the timing, dissemination, or availability, content, and standard of care applicable to a disclosure, announcements, communication, or release of information.

[263] FSMA, s 118A(5)(b).

[264] Regulation 2273/2003, n 18 above, as implemented in the UK in MAR 1 Annex 1 (buy-backs) and MAR 2 (stabilisation).

[265] MAR 1.10.1G(1) confirms that conforming with Arts 3 to 6 of the EC Regulation and MAR 2 will not amount to market abuse.

behaviour conforming with a relevant rule of the Takeover Code or SARs[266] concerning the disclosure of information will not amount to market abuse.[267]

Principles-based Approach

8.158 The FSA also has the ability to take action against FSA authorised firms for breaches of FSA rules, (including the Principles for Businesses) or against FSA approved persons for breaches of the FSA's Statements of Principle and Code of Practice for Approved Persons. With reference to the Principles for Businesses, principles relating to acting with integrity (Principle 1), with due skill, care and diligence (Principle 2), and observing proper standards of market conduct (Principle 5) are particularly relevant in the context of market abuse, although note also that there have been a number of decisions where systems and controls issues have been brought into play by finding a breach of Principle 3 ('a firm must take reasonable care to organise and control its affairs responsibly and effectively, with adequate risk management systems'), an aspect on which increasing emphasis is being placed. Principles-based enforcement can be used in its own right (including in circumstances where behaviour does not necessarily fall within the market abuse offences) and in certain cases have featured in combination with market abuse offences.[268]

8.159 A number of high profile principles-based cases have emerged in recent years. In the *Citigroup* case, Citigroup Global Markets Limited ('CGML') executed a trading strategy on the European government bond markets which very broadly involved the firm building up and then rapidly exiting from very substantial long positions in European government bonds over a period of an hour, using specially configured technology. The trade caused a temporary disruption to the volumes of bonds quoted and traded on the MTS platform, a sharp drop in bond prices, and a temporary withdrawal by some participants from quoting on that platform. The FSA imposed a financial penalty consisting of the relinquishment of profits of £9,960,860 and an additional penalty of £4 million for breaching FSA Principles 2 and 3 by failing to conduct its business with due skill, care, and diligence and failing to control its business effectively.[269]

---

[266] The rules governing the substantial acquisition of shares issued by the Takeover Panel.

[267] MAR 1.10.4C (a safe harbour) which implements FSMA, s 120(1). The relevant rule must relate to the timing, dissemination, or availability of, content, and standard of care applicable to a disclosure, announcement, communication, or release of information, and be one listed in the table set out at MAR 1.10.5C. The behaviour must also be expressly required or expressly permitted by the rules in question (the associated notes being treated as part of the relevant rule for these purposes) and conform to any General Principles set out in the stipulated part of the Takeover Code relevant to that rule.

[268] See for example FSA Final Notice to Philippe Jabré dated 1 August 2005.

[269] FSA Final Notice to Citigroup Global Markets Limited dated 28 June 2005.

In terms of Principle 2 it was found in that in planning and authorising the **8.160** strategy, CGML did not have due regard to the inherent risks including the likely consequences the execution of the trading strategy could have for the efficient and orderly operation of the MTS platform and did not ensure that clear parameters for the size of the trade were understood, communicated, and reviewed. As to Principle 3, it was found that there was a failure within CGML to escalate the detailed trading strategy adequately and in advance to senior management, and a failure to consult with applicable control functions. Accordingly, insufficient weight and attention were given to the franchise risk to which the trading gave rise; the execution risk arising from, amongst other things, the use of a spreadsheet that was not fully testable; the market impact risk, (ie that the trade might have an adverse affect on price and on quotation levels on MTS and the effect that this might have on market confidence); and legal and regulatory risk resulting from the above. Secondly, it was found there were inadequate systems for the supervision of traders.

Another key example of the FSA's principles-based approach is the *Deutsche*[270] **8.161** case and the related decision concerning David Maslen, the bank's former Head of European Cash Trading. The *Deutsche* case arose from two separate transactions conducted by Deutsche Bank AG in 2004. The first transaction (the 'Scania' transaction) was in relation to a book build which involved Maslen. The Scania shares were listed on the Swedish Stock Exchange, which at the time was not a prescribed market. The provisions of MAR therefore did not apply to the Scania transaction. While being actively involved in the book build, the FSA found that Maslen gave instructions for proprietary trading which occurred at a sensitive time during the build, without notifying or seeking clearance from the Bank's compliance or senior management or checking the Bank's restricted list.

In addition, Deutsche had made a series of announcements to its Equity Sales **8.162** Force in London by means of an internal messaging system and various of the announcements were found to be incomplete, and/or inaccurate and/or failed to make appropriate disclosures or adequately consider all relevant issues. Further, the internal announcements stated that Deutsche would be reporting its holding to the Stockholm Stock Exchange prior to it actually doing so. As a result the contents of the announcements were disclosed by Equity Sales to some of the Deutsche's clients who had participated in the book build prior to it being disclosed by the Stockholm Exchange.

The second transaction related to a Swiss company, Cytos, listed on the Swiss **8.163** Exchange, whose share price was stabilised by a Zurich-based trader under instruction from Deutsche's London staff. The FSA's price stabilising rules did not apply to the Cytos transaction, but Deutsche decided that its internal procedures in

---

[270] FSA Final Notice to Deutsche Bank AG dated 10 April 2006 (SDM).

relation to price stabilisation, based on the FSA's stabilisation regime, should apply to the Cytos transactions. The FSA found that Deutsche did not ensure that the trader who conducted the stabilisation trades in Zurich understood and followed the internal procedures regarding stabilisation that Deutsche had intended to apply to the Cytos transaction nor escalate issues arising from the stabilisation exercise to compliance in a timely manner.

8.164 The FSA imposed a fine of £3,500,000 on Deutsche for breaching FSA Principle 5 (failing to observe proper standards of market conduct) and Principle 2 (failing to conduct its business with due skill, care, and diligence) in relation to the Scania transaction, a penalty of £500,000 in respect of breaches of Principle 2 in relation to the Cytos transaction and an additional amount of £2,363,643 in respect of the loss avoided by Deutsche in relation to the Scania transaction.[271] The FSA also imposed a financial penalty of £350,000 on David Maslen, for being knowingly concerned in the failure to observe proper standards of market conduct in the Scania transaction.[272]

8.165 A further example of principles-based enforcement was the *Pignatelli* case relating, as it was subsequently described, to 'outside information'. In that case, the FSA fined Sean Pignatelli £20,000 for breaches of Principles 2 (Due Skill, Care and Diligence) and 3 (Market Conduct) of the FSA's Statements of Principle for Approved Persons, for conduct relating to information which, as it turned out, was not in fact 'inside information'. Pignatelli, US equity salesman at an investment bank, had received an analyst's email concerning a particular company. The email was worded in such a way as to appear that it might have contained inside information about the company's prospects but it did not in fact contain inside information. The FSA found Pignatelli to be in breach of Principle 2 of the FSA's Statements of Principle for Approved Persons for failing to consider whether or not the email might have contained inside information and as a result, failing to escalate the matter as required by internal procedures. The FSA found Pignatelli to be in breach of Principle 3 of the FSA's Statements of Principle for Approved Persons, for subsequently relaying the information to the clients in a way that in the FSA's view gave the impression that it was inside information.

Discovering and Punishing Market Abuse

Suspicious transaction reporting

8.166 As part of the measures introduced by MAD aimed at combating insider dealing and market manipulation, a new, wide-ranging requirement was introduced,

---

[271] FSA Final Notice to Deutsche Bank AG dated 10 April 2006 (SDM).
[272] FSA Final Notice to David John Maslen dated 10 April 2006 (SDM).

namely the requirement to report suspicious transactions.[273] This sits alongside, but is different from, the reporting requirements under the Proceeds of Crime Act 2002 ('POCA'). The requirement set out in MAD is that, broadly speaking, any professional arranging transactions in financial instruments,[274] who reasonably suspects that a transaction constitutes market abuse, must notify the competent authority.[275] An EU Directive implementing aspects of MAD elaborated on this requirement, stating that investment firms and credit institutions:

> shall decide on a case-by-case basis whether there are reasonable grounds for suspecting that a transaction involves insider dealing or market manipulation . . . [and] shall be subject to the rules of notification.[276]

These EU requirements have been implemented in the UK via provisions in the FSA's Supervision Manual (SUP). The basic reporting rule is very similar to the wording in the EU directives, stating that:

> A firm which arranges or executes a transaction with or for a client in a qualifying investment admitted to trading on a prescribed market and which has reasonable grounds to suspect that the transaction might constitute market abuse must notify the FSA without delay.[277]

A similar elaboration to that described above applies to investment firms/credit institutions.[278] Further rules in SUP 15.10 describe the content and means of making the notification to the FSA and SUP 13 Annex 5 sets out a number of indicative examples of whether a transaction is suspicious.[279] Essentially, suspicious transaction reporting deputises to the market the requirement to monitor itself for abusive behaviour.

---

[273] Note that the obligation to report relates to transactions, not orders—see FSA *MarketWatch* Issue 12 June 2005.

[274] Note that the definition of financial instruments includes commodity derivatives.

[275] Art 6(9) of MAD.

[276] Art 7 of Commission Directive 2004/72/EC.

[277] SUP 15.10.2R.

[278] SUP 15.10.3R, based on the requirement of Art 7 of Commission Directive 2004/72/EC.

[279] These include the following examples that may indicate insider dealing: a client opens an account and immediately gives an order to conduct a significant transaction; a transaction is significantly out of line with the client's previous investment behaviour; a client specifically requests immediate execution of an order regardless of the price at which the order would be executed; there is unusual trading in the shares of a company before the announcement of price sensitive information relating to the company; or an employee's own account transaction is timed just before clients' transactions and related orders in the same financial instrument. The following are stated as examples of market manipulation: an order will, because of its size in relation to the market in that security, clearly have a significant impact on the supply of or demand for or the price or value of the security; a transaction appears to be seeking to modify the valuation of a position while not decreasing/increasing the size of that position; or a transaction appears to be seeking to bypass the trading safeguards of the market.

Appropriate reporting—practical issues

8.167 On a practical level, to enhance effective supervision, and indeed to avoid what could otherwise be considerable logistical problems, the FSA originally made it clear that it would not expect to receive purely defensive reports. In numerical terms, the FSA initially indicated that what it had in mind was, across the market, about 200 reports a year. By way of comparison the National Criminal Intelligence Service, the body to which reports were at the time made under POCA, received over 30,000 in the first year, over double that in the second year, and was at over 100,000 reports per year in the third year. The practical dilemma faced by firms has been how to manage their suspicious transaction reporting obligations. At the same time as wanting what would appear to be qualitative filtering of potentially reportable suspicious transactions, the FSA has indicated that the reporting requirement should be triggered by actual suspicion, and therefore does not need sophisticated systems and controls to administer, or dedicated resources. However, as mentioned above, the test set out in SUP 15.10.2 is having 'reasonable grounds to suspect' (an objective test), elaborated by guidance in SUP 15.10.4 (which suggests that there will need to be sufficient indications that an activity might constitute market abuse, which will include taking into account the perspective of other transactions or behaviour) which would suggest something more than this. As it transpired, the FSA found that they were receiving too few STRs and have undertaken a series of reviews and consultation to increase awareness and the need for appropriate systems and controls and training. For example, in 2006, the FSA carried out a thematic review of the suspicious transaction reporting regime, the STR Review 2006. In FSA *MarketWatch* 18,[280] the FSA stated that it regards suspicious transaction reports ('STRs') as a 'key intelligence asset', and emphasised that market practitioners need to be 'proactive in working' with the FSA in preventing market abuse. The FSA warned that they 'will identify firms which fail to submit STRs over time'. Importantly, the FSA detailed the core policies and processes which they hope to see at all firms, namely: initial/induction training on STRs and market abuse more generally; regular emails/newsletters/refresher training updating all relevant staff on key regulatory changes; extra detailed and continuous education of compliance staff; and some level of compliance checking of key staff's understanding of their obligations.

8.168 In FSA *MarketWatch* 26,[281] the FSA commented that from 1 July 2005 to 31 March 2008, it received over 700 STRs. The FSA noted that the:

> bulk of the STRs concerned possible insider dealing in the equity markets and we are now encouraging firms to consider whether there is more they can do to identify other types of market abuse and other types of market where abuse may be taking

---

[280] FSA *MarketWatch*, Issue 18, December 2006.
[281] FSA *MarketWatch*, Issue 26, April 2008.

place. We also encourage firms to report to us suspicious behaviour by other market participants, even if there is no regulatory requirement to do so.

In FSA MarketWatch 28,[282] the FSA noted that firms 'may be applying too high a test for what is "suspicious"', and confirmed that their suspicion:

> should not solely be linked to their perception of the actual or likely market impact from a trade but should also consider attempted manipulation regardless of the actual success. Firms should be able to define what they consider unusual based on their knowledge of the particular market, product or customer and tailor their approach accordingly to identify outliers in expected activity.

If firms are unclear as to whether to submit an STR, they can also contact the FSA's Market Conduct team to discuss the matter. In a recent consultation paper, it is noted that members of CESR have found STRs to be 'very useful and helpful in market abuse investigations'.[283] The paper consults on the criteria for determining the notifiable transactions, and the information which may be included in the notifications.

8.169 The FSA have also looked at particular market sectors. In FSA *MarketWatch* 28,[284] the FSA reported that it had made visits to a number of small firms that trade or facilitate trading in the UK exchange-traded commodities markets, with a threefold purpose: to review the market abuse controls in place; to increase dialogue to better understand the areas of greatest market abuse risk in commodity markets; and to raise the profile of the need to submit STRs in the commodity markets.[285]

Protected disclosures

8.170 FSMA contains an interpretative provision[286] that shields persons who have made 'protected disclosures' from breaching any market abuse provision concerning the disclosure of information. A disclosure of information must satisfy three conditions in order to be protected in this manner:

(i) the information must cause the person making the disclosure to know, suspect, or have reasonable grounds for suspecting that another person has engaged in market abuse;

(ii) the information came to the person making the disclosure in the course of his profession, trade, business, or employment; and

(iii) the disclosure is made to the FSA as soon as is practicable after the information comes to the attention of that person.

---

[282] FSA *MarketWatch*, Issue 28, June 2008.
[283] Consultation paper: 'Market Abuse Directive Level 3—Third set of CESR guidance and information on the common operation of the Directive to the market' (May 2008) see para 24.
[284] FSA *MarketWatch*, Issue 28, June 2008.
[285] FSA *MarketWatch*, Issue 28, June 2008.
[286] FSMA, s 131A.

The condition in (iii) will also be satisfied where an employee makes a disclosure to the nominated officer of his employer for receiving such disclosures. The practical impact of this provision is that where a person has made a disclosure either to the FSA or to his employer's nominated officer to report his suspicions that another person has engaged in market abuse, the person making the disclosure will not himself have committed market abuse, and so this provision is effectively a defence to market abuse.

Interrelation with reports to SOCA

8.171   As noted at para 8.166, the system of suspicious transaction reporting by MAD is in addition to, and to a degree overlaps with, the POCA reporting requirements. By way of illustration, insider dealing could constitute both a criminal offence under CJA insider dealing,[287] as well as being market abuse. Similarly, certain misleading statements and practices could constitute a criminal offence under section 397 of FSMA,[288] whilst at the same time constituting an offence under the market abuse regime. In circumstances involving both a suspicion of market abuse and a suspicion of the laundering of the proceeds of insider dealing, two reports would be required, one to the Serious Organised Crime Agency ('SOCA') and one to the FSA.[289]

8.172   Other than the reporting requirement itself, there are important differences between the two reporting regimes. Under the market abuse regime there is no process for obtaining clearance for participating in market abuse, and the restriction on tipping off simply requires that the fact that a report has been made should not be revealed to any person (particularly not the person that is the subject of the report or related persons).[290] Under POCA, a person asked to participate in what is suspected to be money laundering, is required to make a disclosure[291] and can proceed with the transaction (unless told not to by SOCA) and is under a requirement not to tip off the clients in such a way as might prejudice an investigation.[292] The FSA has also clarified that the market abuse reporting requirement applies to actual transactions, not orders to trade, although it has also said that if any firm voluntarily wishes to bring a suspicious order to the FSA's attention, it is welcome to do so.[293]

---

[287] The CJA insider dealing offence is discussed further in Chapter 9.
[288] The s 397, FSMA offence is discussed further in Chapter 9.
[289] FSA *MarketWatch*, Issue 12 (special edition) June 2005.
[290] SUP 15.10.9R.
[291] POCA, s 330.
[292] ibid, s 333.
[293] FSA *MarketWatch*, Issue 12 (special edition), June 2005.

Sanctions and enforcement policy

Decision to enforce sanctions under the market abuse offence rather than prosecute another criminal offence

As will be apparent from the preceding sections, in certain situations, suspicious **8.173** market misconduct may in principle constitute both market abuse and a breach of one of the criminal law offences (for example, misleading statements or practices, or insider dealing).[294] In the Enforcement Guide ('EG'), the FSA has issued guidelines on the factors that it will take into account in such situations when deciding whether to pursue a criminal prosecution rather than impose a sanction for market abuse.[295] These include the seriousness of the misconduct; whether there are victims who have suffered loss; the effect of the misconduct on the market; whether the person suspected of misconduct has been cooperative; and whether the misconduct involves dishonesty or an abuse of a position of authority or trust.[296] The FSA has commented that in the past, it has focused on the civil route, but now believes that the effective use of both the civil and criminal routes is critical to achieving its aims. According to the FSA:

> the civil route will continue to be used, [but] we are now, in recognition of the significant deterrent effect of custodial sentences, making more use of the criminal options available to us in appropriate . . . cases. We have also made it clear that we will be imposing increased financial penalties in cases we pursue through the civil route.

Interrelation with other enforcement powers

A number of cases and FSA decisions, all of which broadly concern 'misleading **8.174** announcements' by listed issuers,[297] illustrate the different approaches that the FSA may take with regard to enforcement action. At one end of the scale is the *AIT* decision,[298] in which two directors of AIT were found guilty of the criminal offence under section 397(1)(c) of FSMA of recklessly making false or misleading statements relating to a profit forecast, which relied on the existence of non-existent

---

[294] And indeed could potentially fall within certain other regulatory enforcement powers in certain circumstances—see discussion in Chapter 9.

[295] EG, paras 12.8(1)–(13).

[296] In the conviction of Asif Butt for insider dealing (see Chapter 9, para 9.39) Judge Elwen's sentencing drew attention to a breach of trust that was 'breathtaking in audacity'— indicating a criminal prosecution was appropriate under these guidelines.

[297] Note also the liability regime under s 90A, FSMA. HM Treasury proposals to extend the statutory regime, following on the Davies Report in 2007, are currently subject to consultation. In 2006, a new section 90A of FSMA established a statutory liability regime for misstatements to the market by issuers of securities admitted to trading on regulated markets, under which issuers should be liable for fraudulent misstatements in periodic disclosures under the Transparency Directive. For further details, see <http://www.hm-treasury.gov.uk/independent_reviews/davies_review/davies_review_index.cfm>.

[298] *R v Bailey and Rigby* [2005] EWCA Crim 3487.

lucrative contracts.[299] In the Final Notice against Shell,[300] on the other hand, the FSA concluded that Shell was guilty of civil market abuse through the dissemination of false or misleading information concerning announcements of its levels of hydrocarbon reserves. By contrast, cases of misleading announcements have been pursued as breaches of Listing Rule Requirements—see for example the *SFI* decision[301] where the FSA censured an issuer for breach of the rules relating to the accuracy of information announced to the market. The *Woolworths* decision[302] dealt with the position where information which the RDC decided should have been announced was not in fact announced. In that decision, the FSA fined Woolworths £350,000 for breaches of Disclosure Rule 2.2.1 and Listing Principle 4.

The FSA's power to impose penalties in cases of market abuse

8.175 According to section 123(1) of FSMA, if the FSA is satisfied that a person has either engaged in market abuse, or by taking or refraining from taking any action, has required or encouraged another person or persons to engage in behaviour which, if engaged in by the first person would amount to market abuse (generally referred to as 'requiring and encouraging'), it may impose one of two sanctions on the first person: either punish the first person with a penalty of such an amount that it considers appropriate,[303] or alternatively, it may publish a statement to the effect that that person has engaged in market abuse.[304] However, the FSA may not impose such a sanction on a person if there are 'reasonable grounds' for it to be satisfied that the person in question believed his behaviour did not fall within the scope of requiring and encouraging, or that he took all reasonable precautions and exercised all due diligence to avoid behaving in a way which fell within that scope.[305]

8.176 The FSA has provided guidance as to when it will publicise a breach rather than imposing a penalty. Broadly speaking, a penalty is seen as a more serious sanction and so a financial penalty will be favoured in cases where, for example, the firm has profited from its breach, the misconduct is of a serious nature, or the firm has

---

[299] As discussed further at Chapter 9, para 9.66.

[300] FSA Final Notice to Shell Transport and Trading Company plc and The Royal Dutch Petroleum Company NV dated 24 August 2004, as discussed at para 8.152. Note that the Final Notice also acknowledges that two Shell entities were in breach of the listing rules (they failed to take all reasonable care to ensure that announcements were not misleading, false, or deceptive and did not omit anything likely to affect the import of that information—para 70 of the Final Notice). However, the FSA chose not to penalise separately for this contravention on the basis that it was based on substantially the same facts as the market abuse findings.

[301] FSA Final Notice to SFI Group plc dated 11 December 2003.

[302] FSA Final Notice to Woolworths Group plc dated 11 June 2008.

[303] FSMA, s 123(1).

[304] ibid, s 123(3).

[305] ibid, s 123(2). See also discussion at para 8.73 above.

a poor disciplinary record.[306] Where the FSA decides to impose a penalty, the level
of that penalty is determined by the FSA on the basis of a number of factors set out
in the FSA's policy with respect to penalties,[307] namely the seriousness of the misconduct; the extent to which the market abuse was deliberate or reckless; the
financial resources of the person; the amount of profits accrued or loss avoided by
that person as a result of the market abuse; the person's conduct following the
market abuse; the person's disciplinary record and compliance history; and any
previous action taken by the FSA in respect of that person.[308] The FSA recently
confirmed that in 'setting fines, the guiding principle is that individuals or firms
should not benefit from misconduct and thus a financial penalty always includes
an element to cover the disgorgement of any potential profits or repayment of loss
avoided'.[309]

FSA's power to apply for restitution orders as a sanction for market abuse

In addition to the power to impose penalties for market abuse under section 123, **8.177**
the FSA may apply to court for a restitution order (in cases of market abuse (or
requiring and encouraging) where either profits accrued to a person as a result of
the abuse, or one or more persons suffered loss or have been adversely affected as
a result of the abuse).[310] The amount of the restitution order will be such sum as
appears to the court to be just having regard to the profits made or loss or adverse

---

[306] DEPP 6.4.2G.

[307] The FSA is required by FSMA, s 124 to issue a statement of its policy with respect to
the imposition of penalties for market abuse and the amount of those penalties. See generally
Chapter 6.

[308] DEPP 6.5.2G.

[309] 'Market Abuse Policy & Enforcement in the UK', speech by Sally Dewar, 22 May 2007. See
also DEPP 6.5.2G(6)(a).

[310] It is noted that the powers in ss 381 and 383 to apply to court for an injunction or restitution
order in cases of market abuse sit alongside the FSA's power to apply to court for an injunction or restitution order where a person has breached a 'relevant requirement' under FSMA (ss 380 and 382).
It must be considered whether the powers in ss 380 and 381 (injunctions) and ss 382 and 383 are
mutually exclusive. The answer to this will turn on the meaning of the phrase 'relevant requirement'.
This is defined as a requirement which is imposed by or under FSMA or a requirement imposed
by another Act the contravention of which would constitute a criminal offence (s 380(6)(a) and s
382(9)(a)). The better view is therefore that 'requirement' means (a) any positive step that FSMA
requires a person to take; or (b) any prohibition the contravention of which leads to criminal prosecution (in the sense that when one is prohibited from doing something there is a requirement not to
do it). The requirement not to commit market abuse is a requirement, but it is not a requirement the
contravention of which leads to criminal prosecution. Thus, a breach of the market abuse provisions
would not be a breach of a relevant requirement, and so the injunction or restitution order in ss 380
and 382 would not be available—only the alternatives in ss 381 and 383 would be. The existence of
the two sets of parallel provisions would seem to support this approach. For further discussion, see
Lomnicka, *The Financial Services and Markets Act: An Annotated Guide* (2002) at para 1–009.

By way of background under FSA 1986, s 61(1), the court had the power to impose an injunction or require restitution in respect to the contravention of certain specific, identified sections of
FSA 1986.

effect suffered (or both).[311] However, according to section 383(3) of FSMA (which mirrors the provisions of section 123(2) of FSMA, discussed at para 8.79) the court should not make a restitution order if it is satisfied that the person believed (on reasonable grounds) that his behaviour did not constitute market abuse or took reasonable precautions to avoid behaving in a way that constitutes market abuse (or requiring and encouraging).[312] In addition to this, the FSA has a separate power to require FSA authorised persons to make restitution in cases of market abuse (or requiring and encouraging)—a power that it is able to exercise without going to court.[313]

Injunctions in the cases of market abuse

8.178 The FSA may also apply to the court for an injunction where there is a reasonable likelihood that any person will engage in market abuse or where there is a reasonable likelihood that any market abuse that has occurred will continue or be repeated.[314] The court may also make an order requiring a person who is or has engaged in market abuse to take steps to remedy the abuse (or mitigate its effect), or to restrain a person who may be (or may have been) engaged in market abuse from disposing of or otherwise dealing with any of its assets which the court is satisfied he is reasonably likely to dispose of or otherwise deal with.

Enforcement policy

Approach

8.179 As to the FSA's overall approach to enforcement, Margaret Cole, as the then new director of FSA enforcement, adopted the theme of 'Bold and Resolute' for FSA enforcement in 2006.[315] The theme has evolved into the current theme of 'Credible Deterrence'. By 'Credible Deterrence', the FSA means 'using enforcement

---

[311] FSMA, s 383(4)–(5).
[312] ibid, s 383(3).
[313] ibid, s 384(5).
[314] ibid, s 381.
[315] Interestingly, in the *Jabré* reference to the FSMT (*Philippe Jabré v FSA*, FSMT Case 35, 10 July 2006 —Decision on Jurisdiction), the FSA, acting through its Enforcement Department, sought to persuade the FSMT that its own decision, reached by its own decision-making body (the RDC), was too lenient and could ask the FSMT to direct a more severe sanction. Philippe Jabré had referred to the FSMT a decision that he be fined for market abuse and for breaches of Principles 2 and 3 (this referral was subsequently withdrawn). The FSA however contended that the FSMT should in effect reopen an earlier issue and determine and consider the withdrawal of Jabré's approval or his prohibition. This issue had been raised in the FSA's Warning Notice but did not form part of the subsequent Decision Notice. The FSMT could consider the relevant evidence, and determine what was the appropriate action for the FSA to take in relation to the matter referred and found a determination of fitness and propriety, not addressed in a Decision Notice, could be part of the 'matter referred' to the FSMT.

strategically as a tool to change behaviour in the industry' so that wrongdoers 'realise that they face a real and tangible risk of being held to account and expect a significant penalty'.[316] In addressing the aim of the FSA, Margaret Cole commented as follows:

> I should make clear that our aim is to clean up the market, to change behaviour by making best use of all the powers—criminal, civil and administrative—that are available to us. If people have to go to prison for us to achieve that aim then that's what we are prepared to do. But sending people to prison isn't the aim in itself. [. . .] we intend to be bolder and more resolute about proceeding with market abuse and insider dealing cases so that we can actually bring about a change in the culture in the City. We've got to get all the market players to take this subject seriously.[317]

Margaret Cole also recently highlighted that the FSA's key priorities are: insider   **8.180**
dealing by City or business professionals who abuse positions of trust by misusing information legitimately passed to them for them to perform their jobs (for example, lawyers, accountants, brokers, and so on); repeat offenders—where the FSA suspects systematic trading on inside information; and cases where there is significant profit made or loss avoided. The FSA has also more recently increased its focus on the commodities area. At the same time, the FSA has pointed out that it keeps both its strategy and priorities under regular review.[318]

The FSA has also emphasised the importance of systems and controls, and train-   **8.181**
ing within firms, and the importance of suspicious transactions reports and in addition has emphasised the need for a collaborative approach involving dialogue on important matters and understanding new risk areas in order to agree priority areas of focus, and encouraging learning from good practice, whether identified by the industry or by FSA thematic work. According to the FSA:

> if the senior management of firms meet our expectations and can demonstrate that their firms have good systems and controls and are complying with them, we will not take enforcement action against the firm, but only against the individual, if an individual within a firm commits market abuse.[319]

Overview of effectiveness of the market abuse regime and trends in enforcement

The FSA acknowledge that the tougher approach is likely to mean that the   **8.182**
sanctioning process is more drawn out as civil cases seeking significant financial penalties or other sanctions against individuals are hard fought, and are rarely concluded in less than two years. The timetable for criminal prosecutions is

---

[316] FSA, 'Enforcement annual performance account 2007/08' at p 4.
[317] 'How Enforcement makes a difference', speech by Margaret Cole, 18 June 2008.
[318] 'The FSA's approach to insider dealing', speech by Margaret Cole, 4 October 2007.
[319] FSA *MarketWatch* Issue 26, April 2008.

similar—it is likely to take well over a year from laying an information (or 'charging') to a trial.

8.183 It is also worth looking at other recent, and proposed, developments in the FSA's approach in this context. Behind the scenes it would appear that the FSA has been laying the ground work to obtain a higher conversion rate: the enforcement division has overhauled its staff, and at the same time, has recruited criminal barristers and other lawyers to bolster its criminal fire power; the FSA's new IT system should significantly enhance monitoring of unusual market activity; the FSA is using bolder approaches to capture evidence. For example, despite objections, the FSA is persisting with it policy of cold calling traders and front desks and asking them to explain what they perceive as unusual trading. To preserve the admissibility of anything said on those calls for use in any future criminal trial, the calls are accompanied by a criminal caution. The FSA has stated that it 'found this to be a useful way of getting an individual's version of events on record at an early stage before recollections have dimmed';[320] suspicious transaction reporting has helped improve the quality of the FSA's information from the market; new call taping requirements in the FSA handbook should also, the FSA hopes, help preserve evidence, and, once the technology is good enough, these requirements are likely to be extended to mobile telephones.[321]

8.184 A perceived major impediment to previous prosecutions is in the process of being addressed, by giving accomplices sufficient incentive to give evidence. A consultation paper, 'Decision procedure and penalties manual and enforcement guide review 2008' published in May 2008, proposes a leniency scheme for suspects who assist in investigations into market abuse involving two or more individuals acting together. In practical terms, therefore, the FSA may wish to go for alternatives to criminal prosecution for those suspects who are prepared to come forward with evidence against other, more culpable, parties. Depending on the facts, the FSA might also agree a lower penalty, but as a minimum the FSA have indicated they would expect a cooperating witness to be stripped of the profits of his or her wrongdoing. The Government has also announced plans to give the FSA statutory powers to grant immunity from prosecution. The Attorney General has also recently issued proposals relating to a new plea negotiation system[322] which should improve the FSA's ability to build cases where there is a cooperating witness.

---

[320] FSA *MarketWatch*, Issue 26, April 2008.
[321] FSA publishes new rules on telephone recording, FSA/PN/017/2008, 3 March 2008 (<http://www.fsa.gov.uk/pages/Library/Communication/PR/2008/017.shtml>).
[322] The Attorney General (consultation paper), 'The Introduction of a Plea Negotiation Framework for Fraud Cases in England and Wales', 3 April 2008.

Enforcement of market abuse actions

Trends. The market abuse regime has to date[323] produced twenty-two civil mar- **8.185**
ket abuse decisions. As far as trends are concerned, having built up to a relatively
high concentration at the end of 2004 (with three market abuse Final Notices in
a month) the rate dropped off. In 2006, the FSA picked things up with five Final
Notices over the course of the year. In 2007, there was only one FSA Final Notice
(*Roberto Casoni*), and so far there has only been one FSA Final Notice in 2008
(*John Shevlin*). As discussed at Chapter 9, para 9.41 *et seq.*, the FSA has so far this
year launched three criminal prosecutions for insider dealing and indicated it has
31 market abuse cases in Wholesale Enforcement.[324] In each of the civil market
abuse cases since April 2003, financial sanctions have been imposed. In terms
of quantum, the lowest fine is £1,000, the highest is £17 million, and while
the FSA has sanctioned 16 individuals, only eight firms have been sanctioned.
Overall, there appear to be more enforcement actions against individuals or
senior management, in comparison to actions against firms. Indeed, the FSA
would now seem to conduct parallel investigations against a firm and an individual, whereas in the past the FSA would have investigated the firm before the
individual.

Overview of effectiveness to date. As mentioned in para 8.02 above, the **8.186**
market abuse regime was introduced as a result of perceived failures in obtaining
prosecutions under the criminal regime. It is therefore interesting to consider
whether the new regime has indeed achieved this objective, what lessons have
been learned in terms of enforcement, and what can be expected going forward.

Looking at this in the round, in the 12-year period from 1986 to 1997, there had **8.187**
been only 30 criminal market abuse prosecutions—and only 13, just over one a
year, were successful. By way of contrast, in the four or so years following the
introduction of the civil provisions (1 December 2001), the FSA successfully concluded 27 disciplinary actions for market abuse/misconduct and imposed total
financial sanctions of £40m. This figure probably put the position at its highest,
including listing rule sanctions, findings under Principle 5 of the FSA Principles,
and findings against both firms and individuals. For 'pure' market abuse, the
figure is more like 15 actions.

Between 2005 and 2007 the FSA started to experience difficulties in enforcement **8.188**
under the new civil regime, mainly because of the near criminal standard of proof
applied by the FSA in practice and the standards applied by them as discussed in

---

[323] August 2008.
[324] 'How Enforcement makes a difference', speech by Margaret Cole, 18 June 2008 (<http://
www.fsa.gov.uk/pages/Library/Communication/Speeches/2008/0618_mc.shtml>).

para 8.28 above.[325] At the same time, the FSA's own processes and procedures were subject to criticism by the FSMT in *Legal and General,* leading to a subsequent review and overhaul. Moreover, in terms of penalties, the FSMT also concluded that the penalties imposed by the FSA in one high profile case, (*Davidson and Tatham*) would have been too high in any event. That said, the FSMT in the subsequent *Parker* case did conclude that a slightly higher amount would be appropriate for the punitive element but concluded it should be slow to increase a penalty except in the case where the RDC has plainly misdirected itself and the penalty imposed fell substantially below a proper amount, since its doing so might otherwise act as a disincentive to the making of meritorious references.

8.189 In terms of practical impact, four years into the new civil regime, despite the profile the FSA had given market abuse, market behaviour appears to have deteriorated rather than improved. Analysis commissioned by the FSA itself in 2006 showed that there had been no improvement in market cleanliness following the introduction of the new market abuse regime. If anything, the FSA concluded that things seemed to be worse in 2004 (the year under analysis) than prior to the new civil regime coming into force in December 2001. In *MarketWatch* 26, the FSA confirmed that informed trading took place prior to 28.7 per cent of takeover announcements in 2007, up from 24 per cent in 2000.

8.190 In terms of output since the FSA determined to be 'bold and resolute' (see para 8.179 above), prior to 2008 (the *Shevlin* case) it is necessary to go back 16 months to March 2007 for the previous successful civil market conduct finding (the *Casoni* case).[326] The FSA's own report on enforcement activity also shows that in the enforcement year 1 April 2006–31 March 2007, 22 new market conduct cases were opened and 25 were closed. In that year three resulted in an FSA Final Notice. A year on, in the year 1 April 2007–31 March 2008, 24 new market conduct cases were opened and 19 closed—none resulted in a Final Notice.

8.191 **Outlook.**   In the meantime, as mentioned in para 8.179 above, the FSA has adopted an approach of 'credible deterrence' and has been laying the ground to obtain a higher conversion rate, both in infrastructure terms and other initiatives such as its leniency initiative and other developments.[327] It has also recognised

---

[325] See for example the *Davidson and Tatham* case and the *Baldwin* case. In the latter case, the FSMT overturned a decision by the FSA to fine Baldwin and WRT, an investment vehicle controlled by Baldwin, for market abuse. The FSA had imposed fines on Baldwin (of £25,000) and WRT (of £24,000) in relation to purchases of shares, following the alleged passing of inside information from the chief executive officer of the company in question to Baldwin by telephone conversation. The FSMT found in favour of Baldwin and WRT, concluding it found no evidence that the relevant telephone call had taken place. The FSMT was satisfied that WRT's trading had been innocently conducted.

[326] FSA: Final Notice to Roberto Casoni dated 20 March 2007.

[327] See para 8.184 with reference to statutory powers to grant immunity. In March 2008, following the HBOS share collapse on 19 March 2008 (see para 8.149 for further discussion) the Chancellor (Alistair Darling) announced that the FSA would be given the statutory power to grant immunity from prosecution to a whistleblower, typically a lesser actor, in return for hard witness evidence against other

that its credible deterrence approach will mean that cases will take longer to reach conclusion. It has also acknowledged that in the light of this and the inevitable lack of publicity as cases are progressed, it will need to establish 'a steady stream of cases—both criminal and civil'.[328]

The FSA has also so far this year launched three criminal prosecutions for insider **8.192** dealing amid considerable publicity and in addition to the 31 market abuse cases in Wholesale Enforcement. Also there have been various press reports relating to Winterflood Securities having received a fine in the region of £4 million from the FSA for market abuse which has been referred to the FSMT, although there is little information currently available on this.

European Developments

A number of initiatives are currently underway at the EU level which impact on **8.193** the area of market abuse. At the CESR level this has involved work to prepare ground for convergent implementation and application of the market abuse regime by ensuring that a common approach to the operation of the directive takes place throughout the EU amongst supervisors. Various analyses have been undertaken by CESR of the state of implementation as part of the review, as well as the continuing issuance of Level 3 Guidance.[329] At the same time, the EC is assessing the 'application of the Market Abuse Directive to commodity derivatives, exploring the desirability of further clarification of the regime or its extension as part of the general review of commodities derivatives being undertaken post MiFID'. Some of these are looked at below.

ESME report—market abuse EU legal framework and its implementation by Member States: a first evaluation—6 July 2007 [330]

The report concluded that although the market abuse legislation (directives, **8.194** regulations, and Level 3 guidelines) were an important achievement, some corrections were needed. The report pointed to a number of areas of concern. For example, the adoption of a single definition of 'inside information' at European level, applicable to both market abuse (under MAD) and disclosure

---

participants. See also 'Tripartite Authorities: Financial Stability and Depositor Protection: Further Consultation', July 2008.

[328] 'How Enforcement makes a difference', speech by Margaret Cole, 18 June 2008.

[329] See for example: CESR, 'Market Abuse Directive—Level 3—second set of guidance and information on the common operation of the Directive to the Market', July 2007.

[330] It should be noted that ESME's role is part of an overall process of analysis and recommendation, it is not in itself an executive body and its views are not determinative.

obligations, appeared to be at the heart of widespread inconsistencies of behaviour, the concern being that the definition could be too wide when it is used to determine when an issuer has a duty to disclose information to the public. There was also thought to be a need for better detailed European rules or for more effective CESR guidance on responding to market rumours and meetings amongst issuers, investors, and other stakeholders. The report also considered that refinements are needed to the regulation of insider lists and to make them more effective as their purpose has become more confused. Improvements are suggested to the legislation dealing with the disclosure of transactions by persons discharging managerial responsibilities and persons closely related to them—this has sometimes proved to be unnecessarily burdensome. Safe harbours and accepted market practices are also singled out as requiring some improvement as well as aspects of the buy-back and stabilisation regime. Many of these have since been, or are being, consulted on as part of the proposed third set of CESR Level 3 Guidance.

8.195 As far as commodity derivatives are concerned, the report states that the definition of inside information relating to commodity derivatives and the expanded meaning in the level 2 directive are too indefinite to create the necessary level of legal certainty for market participants as it was not clear under which circumstances market participants would expect to receive, in accordance with accepted market practices, the relevant inside information. The report believes a stricter and more stringent definition of inside information in respect of commodity derivatives should be introduced. The report suggests the definition should be harmonised with the definition of inside information and this would mean that information would only be inside information if all of the following conditions are fulfilled: the information refers to circumstances which are not publicly known (information of a precise nature which has not been made public); and the information relates directly or indirectly to one or more commodity derivatives (financial instruments); and the information refers to circumstances which exist or may reasonably be expected to come into existence; and these circumstances have, or are likely to have, a significant effect on the prices of those commodity derivatives. Significant effect on the prices of the commodity derivative should refer to information which a reasonable investor would be likely to use in his investment decision—the professional market participant rather than the private retail customer should be deemed to be the relevant reasonable investor. With reference to circumstances in which users of the markets would expect to receive information, only the second set of sub-tests (disclosure in accordance with legal and regulatory provisions etc) should be maintained as the 'routinely made available' test is quite difficult to determine.

8.196 In terms of market manipulation, it was considered advisable that an accepted practice for commodity derivative trading should in general be introduced: this would give more comfort to commodity trading market participants bearing in mind that where a commodity market is illiquid and immature manipulation as defined could easily be committed by the market participants without having the intention to manipulate the exchange or market price, who, for example, have to perform transactions for proper risk management purposes. This could also be the case for relatively liquid commodity derivative markets such as the power sector because the traded volumes by underlying commodity providers are regularly large. According to the report, this would not be a desirable effect for an emerging market and the liberalisation of the European energy markets.

HM Treasury and the FSA's discussion paper considering the European Commission review of commodity and exotic derivatives[331]

According to the discussion paper, the risk of improper conduct in commodity **8.197** derivatives markets resulting from information asymmetries was similar to those in other financial markets. However, it acknowledged there were specific issues in commodity derivatives markets related to the interplay between the commodity derivatives market and the market in the underlying commodity and points to the fact that these issues are reflected in the different definition of inside information in MAD which is incorporated in section 118C(3) of FSMA. The overall conclusion of the paper in the context of market abuse was that commodity derivatives markets were no less susceptible to improper conduct and other financial markets. This also applied in relation to market manipulation, which equally could be a feature of the commodities market. Given that the EC is to conduct a review of MAD in 2008, the conclusion of HM Treasury and the FSA was that that would be the appropriate forum in which to consider the various options.

Certain of these issues were also commented on in the May 2008 CESR/CEBS **8.198** report.[332]

Again, as far as market abuse issues were concerned, CESR/CEBS believed **8.199** that issues related to market abuse should be addressed in the EC's wider review of MAD.

---

[331] In HM Treasury and FSA, 'UK discussion paper on the commission's review of the financial regulatory frame work for Commodity and Exotic Derivatives' (December 2007).

[332] CESR/CEBS consultation paper on CESR's/CEBS's technical advice to the European Commission on the review of commodities business, 15 May 2008. CESR and CEBS are expected to deliver their final advice to the EC during autumn 2008.

ESME July 2008 Advice—commodity/exotic derivatives

8.200 The July 2008 ESME advice (in response to the mandate for advice given to it by the EC in the context of the review of the treatment of commodity/exotic derivatives)[333] also addresses the question on whether MAD properly addresses market integrity issues in the electricity, gas, and other commodity markets and if not, what suggestions would ESME have to mitigate any shortcomings.

8.201 In its advice, ESME has made various recommendations regarding definitional issues (for example the desirability of aligning the definition of commodity derivatives in MAD with those in MiFID but without broadening the scope of MAD to new kinds of instruments beyond its existing scope). Again, the advice picked up on issues relating to the common definition at EU level of insider information both for market abuse and disclosure purposes, as well as the practical problems in defining insider information and applying the insider dealer regime to the commodity and commodity derivatives business. ESME was of the view that that there was a need to further adapt the insider dealing regime to the needs of the commodity and commodity derivatives business.

8.202 The advice also recommends there should not be an extension of MAD beyond regulated markets to MTFs or to OTC markets or spot markets, and makes various recommendations with regard to transaction and position reporting (principally that regulated exchanges and MTFs are best placed to act as frontline regulators by monitoring positions of the market participants including where necessary reporting directly to and coordinating with regulators).

Electricity and gas markets

8.203 On 21 July 2008, CESR and the European Regulators' Group for Electricity and Gas ('ERGEG') published a consultation paper on market abuse issues relating to energy trading.[334] Again, the final advice will be produced in autumn 2008. In the consultation paper by ERGEG and CESR, the draft advice suggests the EC consider 'developing and evaluating proposals for a basic, tailor-made market abuse framework within the energy sector legislation for all electricity and gas products not covered by MAD, particularly in the physical markets and that the legal framework should address the abusive practices observed or potentially applied by market participants on electricity and gas markets, taking into account

---

[333] Mandate to ESME for advice: review under Arts 65(3)(a), (b), and (d) of MiFID and 48(2) of the CAD and proposed guidelines to be adopted under the Third Energy Package, 8 July 2008.

[334] Consultation Paper: CESR and ERGEG advice to the European Commission in the context of the Third Energy Package—Draft response to Question F.20—Market Abuse (July 2008) (Ref: CESR/08-509).

the specificities of the electricity and gas markets with regard to any misuse of information. CESR and ERGEG also call for the implementation of legally binding 'disclosure obligations comparable to Article 6 MAD in the energy sector regulations (bundling transparency obligations)'. The draft advice suggests that sector-specific disclosure obligations should oblige the relevant entities to disclose information likely to influence physical and/or derivatives markets prices in a timely manner and on a single platform.

9

INSIDER DEALING, MISLEADING STATEMENTS AND PRACTICES

Introduction

Having considered in Chapter 8 the civil market abuse offences brought in under **9.01** FSMA,[1] and revised following the implementation of MAD,[2] this chapter will consider the criminal offences of insider dealing under the Criminal Justice Act 1993 ('CJA') and misleading statements and practices under section 397 of FSMA, as well as considering briefly regulatory requirements relating to market misconduct. This chapter will then outline the roles of the various regulatory and prosecuting authorities with power to take action in respect of market misconduct and how these bodies interact.[3]

CJA Insider Dealing

The criminal law—insider dealing

Insider dealing first became a criminal offence within the UK in 1980.[4] Following **9.02** a revision of the Companies Act in 1985, the statutory basis for the offence was replaced by the Companies Securities (Insider Dealing) Act 1985. The introduction of new legislation in 1993 was prompted by the passage of the EU Directive on Insider Dealing,[5] and the current legislative provisions are contained in Part V of the CJA.

---

[1] The Financial Services and Markets Act 2000.
[2] Directive 2003/6/EC on insider dealing and market manipulation (market abuse).
[3] This Chapter does not however deal with the wider issues, such as common law offences or offences under the Fraud Act 2006.
[4] Companies Act 1980, ss 68–73.
[5] Council Directive EEC/89/592 of 13 November 1989 co-ordinating regulations on insider dealing (no longer in force).

Criminal Justice Act 1993, Part V

9.03   Section 52 of the CJA lays down the general prohibition of insider dealing, and this can be separated out into three distinct offences, namely the dealing offence,[6] the encouraging offence,[7] and the disclosure offence.[8] Section 53 sets out a number of general defences as well as providing for a number of special defences,[9] to which section 52 is subject. The remainder of Part V contains relatively lengthy provisions dedicated to the interpretation of the basic offences.

Territorial scope

9.04   In terms of territorial scope, section 62 requires that there is a link between the activities complained of and the UK.[10] Accordingly, an individual will not be guilty of the 'dealing offence' unless he was within the UK when he did any act constituting or forming part of the dealing, or the dealing took place on a market regulated by the UK, or the professional intermediary concerned was within the UK when he did any act constituting or forming part of the dealing. An individual will not be guilty of either the encouraging offence or the disclosure offence unless he was within the UK at the time of the disclosure/encouragement or the recipient or the disclosure/encouragement was within the UK.

The offences

9.05   The following sections consider each of the three discrete offences established under section 52 of the CJA.

The dealing offence—section 52(1)

9.06   An individual[11] who has 'information as an insider' will be guilty of the dealing offence where he deals in securities that are 'price-affected'[12] in relation to that information, either by acquisition or disposal of those securities on a regulated market, or through reliance on a 'professional intermediary', or by acting himself

---

6   CJA, s 52(1).

7   ibid, s 52(2)(a).

8   ibid, s 52(2)(b).

9   ibid, s 52(4) and Sched 1.

10   For a discussion of the territorial scope of insider dealing under the market abuse regime, see Chapter 8, para 8.69.

11   It should be noted that the CJA offences relate only to individuals, cf the FSMA market abuse regime.

12   'Price affected securities' are those which are affected by price-sensitive information (ie information which would, if it were to be made public, be likely to have a significant effect on the price of securities). For further discussion, see para 9.26 below.

as an intermediary.[13] To break this offence down into the constituent elements of a criminal offence, the *actus reus* can be identified as dealing in the manner described above. The *mens rea* of the offence would seem to be that the person dealing as an insider subjectively knows that he is in possession of inside information[14]—there is no requirement of intention or recklessness.[15]

'Securities'

For the purposes of the CJA, 'securities' means any security which is listed in **9.07** Schedule 2 of the CJA and which satisfies the conditions laid down by articles 4 to 8 of the Insider Dealing (Securities and Regulated Markets) Order 1994 ('IDO'). Schedule 2 lists the relevant securities as shares;[16] debt securities;[17] warrants;[18] depositary receipts;[19] options;[20] futures;[21] and contracts for differences ('CFDs').[22] Articles 4 to 8 of the IDO require that the security (or relevant right subsisting under a warrant, debt security, or depositary receipt) be officially listed in a State within the European Economic Area ('EEA') or be admitted to dealing on, or have its price quoted on or under, the rules of a regulated market. A 'regulated market' for the purposes of the CJA is any market established under the rules of one of the European investment exchanges listed in the Schedule to the IDO, and the former OFEX market (now PLUS Markets).[23]

---

[13] CJA, s 52(3).

[14] See CJA, s 57(1). See also Johnstone and Jones, *Investigations and Enforcements* (2001): guilt 'will depend on the view held by the person in possession of the information as to its "insiderness"' (para 1.89); and Jain, 'Significance of mens rea in insider trading', (2004) *Comp Law* 25(5), 132–40, at 136: 'if the accused does not have the requisite knowledge that the information is either inside information or that it is from an inside source, even if he deals in securities based on that information, he will not be held guilty of insider trading'.

[15] Traditionally, serious crimes require that the defendant intended to commit the relevant acts or was subjectively reckless as to their commission, although certain other offences require that the defendant 'knowingly' or 'dishonestly' carried out a particular commission. For example, the 'arrangements' offence under s 328(1) of POCA which states that: 'A person commits an offence if he enters into or becomes concerned in an arrangement which he knows or suspects facilitates (by whatever means) the acquisition, retention, use or control of criminal property by or on behalf of another person.' See also, for example, the offence of handling stolen goods under s 22(1) of the Theft Act 1968 which states that: 'A person handles stolen goods if (otherwise than in the course of the stealing) knowing or believing them to be stolen goods he dishonestly receives the goods, or dishonestly undertakes or assists in their retention, removal, disposal or realisation by or for the benefit of another person, or if he arranges to do so.'

[16] CJA, Sched 2 para 1.

[17] ibid, para 2.

[18] ibid, para 3.

[19] ibid, para 4.

[20] ibid, para 5.

[21] ibid, para 6.

[22] ibid, para 9.

[23] IDO, art 9. Contrast the definition of regulated market for the CJA purposes with the definition under the post-MAD version of FSMA (as discussed at Chapter 8, para 8.68). Under FSMA, 'regulated market' means those listed by EEA regulators in accordance with the Markets in Financial

'Dealing in securities'

9.08 Section 55 states that 'dealing' includes the acquisition or disposal of securities, either as principal or agent,[24] or the direct or indirect procurement[25] of an acquisition or disposal of securities by any other person (who is his agent, nominee, or any other person acting at his direction).[26] It goes on to establish that this includes any agreement to acquire[27] or dispose[28] of a security, or the entering into[29] or conclusion of[30] any contract which itself creates a security. The definition of dealing does not include abstaining from dealing, and therefore where a person decides not to deal on the basis of inside information, where he was previously intending to deal, this will not be caught by the CJA.[31]

'Professional intermediary'

9.09 The inclusion of the 'professional intermediary' provision within both the dealing offence and the encouraging offence is to ensure that those dealing otherwise than on the market itself are caught by the statutory provisions. A person is acting as a 'professional intermediary' where he carries on a business of acquiring or disposing of securities,[32] or he acts as an intermediary between persons dealing in securities[33] and he holds himself out to the public or any section of the public as willing to engage in any such business.[34] This business activity must not be merely incidental/occasional.[35] He will also be considered to be a professional intermediary where he is employed by such a person to carry out any such activity.[36]

The encouraging offence—section 52(2)(a)

9.10 An individual who has information as an insider will be guilty of the 'encouraging offence'[37] where he encourages another person to deal in price-affected securities,

---

Instruments Directive. The IDO at the time of writing still refers to OFEX, but that has since become PLUS Markets.

[24] CJA, s 55(1)(a).
[25] ibid, s 55(1)(b).
[26] ibid, s 55(4). This list is not exhaustive as to the circumstances in which one person may be regarded as procuring an acquisition or disposal of securities by another.
[27] ibid, s 55(2)(a).
[28] ibid, s 55(3)(a).
[29] ibid, s 55(2)(b).
[30] ibid, s 55(3)(b).
[31] Lomnicka, 'The New Insider Dealing Provisions: Criminal Justice Act 1993', Part V, (1994) *JBL MAR*, 173–88, at 177. For a discussion of the position under the FSMA market abuse regime, see Chapter 8 at para 8.76.
[32] CJA, s 59(2)(a).
[33] ibid, s 59(2)(b).
[34] ibid, s 59(1)(a).
[35] ibid, s 59(3).
[36] ibid, s 59(1)(b).
[37] ibid, s 52(2)(a).

knowing or having reasonable cause to know that the dealing would take place in the manner described in para 9.06.[38] The *actus reus* of this offence is encouraging another person to deal in price-affected securities in relation to that information. The *mens rea* of this offence is (similarly to the 'dealing' offence) the defendant's knowledge that he has information as an insider, and knowledge or reasonable cause to believe that dealing will take place as described above. It is important to note that the individual will be guilty of the offence whether or not the person encouraged realises that the securities are price-affected securities. It is also immaterial whether or not dealing actually takes place; the mere act of encouragement to trade is sufficient to amount to a criminal offence.

9.11 Although the CJA offences relate to the actions of individuals, the person encouraged does not need to be an individual. Thus where an individual has information as an insider, and encourages a company to deal in price-affected securities in relation to that information, he will also be guilty of the offence under section 52(2)(a).[39]

9.12 The CJA does not provide any interpretative guidance as to the meaning of the term 'encourage', and therefore it is left to the courts to decide on the facts of each individual case whether or not an activity amounts to encouraging.[40]

The 'disclosure' offence—section 52(2)(b)

9.13 An individual who has information as an insider will be guilty of the disclosure offence where he discloses that information to another person otherwise than in the proper performance of the functions of his employment, office, or profession.[41] Similarly to the other two insider dealing offences, the elements of the offence can be divided into the *actus reus* of disclosing this information otherwise than in the proper performance of the functions of an insider's employment office or profession. The *mens rea* is the test of whether the defendant has knowledge that the information in his possession is inside information.

Having 'inside information' as an 'insider'

9.14 For the purposes of the section 52 offences, an individual will only be guilty of insider dealing where he has information as an insider. A person will only be considered to have information as an insider if it is, and he knows it is, inside information,

---

[38] ibid, s 52(3).

[39] Band, 'Trustees and Insider Dealing: Part I', (2000) *PCB* 5, 293–303, at 301.

[40] Analogous guidance is given in MAR 1.2.23G(2) on the meaning of encouraging in the 'requiring or encouraging' provision under the FSMA market abuse regime: 'a person recommends or advises a friend to engage in behaviour . . .' The pre-MAD version of MAR 1.8 provided extensive guidance on the meaning of requiring or encouraging, but that guidance has now been deleted.

[41] CJA, s 52(2)(b).

and he has it, and knows that he has it, from an inside source.[42] It is therefore necessary to explore what is meant by the term 'inside information', and respectively, when a person will be considered to have received this information from an 'inside source'.

'Inside information'

Scope

9.15 Section 56(1) states that 'inside information' means information which:

    (i) relates to particular securities or to a particular issuer, or particular issuers, of securities (and not to securities generally or to issuers of securities generally);

    (ii) is specific or precise;

    (iii) has not been made public; and

    (iv) if it were made public would be likely to have a significant effect on the price[43] of any securities.[44]

The use of the term 'any' securities makes it clear that the disclosure does not need to affect the price of the particular securities about which the information is held—it is enough that the price of some other security is affected.

'Particular securities' and 'particular issuers of securities'

9.16 Further guidance is offered by section 60(4) which states that information is to be treated as relating to 'an issuer of securities' not only where it relates to the issuer

---

[42] ibid, s 57. This can be distinguished from the civil insider dealing offence where only one of the five categories of 'insider' requires there to be knowledge, or reasonable expectations of knowledge that information is 'inside information'. According to MAR 1.2.8E(1), one of the 'factors' to be taken into account in considering the question of reasonable expectation of knowledge (and an indication of it) is if a normal and reasonable person in the position of the person who has inside information would know or should have known that the person from whom he received it is an 'insider'. Note that in MAR 1.5.6E(1), for the purposes of market abuse (misuse of information), the extent to which information is reliable, including how near the person providing the information is, or appears to be, to the original source of that information is a 'factor' in determining whether a regular user would regard information as relevant, and are indications that he would.

[43] ibid, s 56(3) states that 'price includes value'.

[44] This test is similar to the definition of inside information (other than for commodity derivatives, and ignoring the elaboration in respect of pending orders) set out in the FSMA regime. That definition applies to information in relation to qualifying investments or related investments which is of a precise nature and which (a) is not generally available; (b) relates, directly or indirectly, to one or more issuers of the qualifying investments or to one or more of the qualifying investments; and (c) would, if generally available be likely to have a significant affect on the price of the qualifying investments or on the price of related investments. For these purposes, information is precise if it indicates circumstances that exist or may reasonably be expected to come into existence or an event that has occurred (or may reasonably be expected to occur) and is specific enough to enable a conclusion to drawn as to the possible effect of those circumstances or that event on the price of qualifying investments or related investments. Information would, according to s 118 regime, be likely to have a significant effect on price if and only if it is information of a kind which a reasonable investor would be likely to use as part of the basis of his investment decisions. See discussion in Chapter 8 at para 8.82.

company itself, but also where it may affect the company's business prospects. For example, an announcement which might affect business prospects within a particular sector would potentially be inside information without relating to any one company. It would also follow that information relating to one specific company which will have a significant effect on the market price of a different company would be caught.

The information itself can relate to more than one issuer, or the securities of **9.17** more than one issuer. This again would presuppose that information relating to a particular sector or group of companies could be caught. However, there is a limit on the type of information which will be caught, in that information relating to securities generally, or issuers generally, is excluded from the definition. For example, on this basis, information forecasting a general decline in the stock markets would not be considered to be inside information. It may be difficult in some circumstances to know where the line should be drawn between information which is to be considered general, and that which is specific to particular securities or their issuers, and this needs to be considered on a case by case basis.

'Specific' or 'precise'

The requirement that information be 'specific' or 'precise' would appear intended **9.18** to prevent generic information or rumour from being caught by the CJA provisions. However, it casts a wider net than was necessitated by the original Directive.[45] The CJA itself provides no interpretative guidance in relation to these terms, although it is possible to gain some insight as to their intended meaning from the parliamentary discussions which took place prior to its inception. According to the then Economic Secretary and Minister of State at HM Treasury, Mr Anthony Nelson, MP:

> if somebody were to say ... during a lunch, 'Our results will be much better than the market expects or knows,' that would not be precise. The person would not have disclosed what the results of the company were to be. However, it would certainly be specific, because he would be saying something about the company's results and making it pretty obvious that the information had not been made public ... It would be inside information because it would be specific.[46]

Again, the courts are left to consider whether or not this criterion has been satisfied by making an objective decision based on the evidence in each case. In *R v Cross*[47] it was held that knowledge that there was to be a placing of shares was

---

[45] Council Directive 89/592/EEC of 13 November 1989 co-ordinating regulations on insider dealing (no longer in force), Art 1 provides that information must be of a 'precise' nature.

[46] As cited by Alcock, 'Insider Dealing—How did we get here', (1994) *Comp Law* 15(3), 67–72, at 70.

[47] (1990) 91 Cr App R 115.

sufficiently specific, even though the defendant was not aware of the exact details of the placing.[48]

'Made public'

9.19 Guidance on determining when information can be regarded as having been 'made public' is outlined in section 58 of the CJA. This gives four non-exhaustive examples of circumstances in which information *will* be regarded as having been made public, and five examples of circumstances in which information *may* be regarded as having been made public. Section 58(2) states that information is made public if:

  (i)   it is published in accordance with the rules of a regulated market for the purpose of informing investors and their professional advisers;
  (ii) it is contained in records which are open to inspection by the public;
  (iii) it can be readily acquired by those likely to deal in any securities to which the information relates, or of an issuer to which the information relates; or
  (iv) it is derived from information which has been made public.

It would appear, in principle at least, that the use of the term 'published' in section 58(2)(a) may create an opportunity for those in possession of inside information to deal on the basis of that information as soon as the publication is made official, without strictly falling foul of the CJA legislation. Commentators have observed that, as the market effect of the information published will never be immediate, this potentially detracts from the purpose of the legislation in providing a level playing field for investors.[49]

9.20 Section 58 goes on to provide that information may be made public even though:

  (i)   it can be acquired only by persons exercising diligence or expertise;
  (ii) it is communicated to a section of the public and not to the public at large;
  (iii) it can be acquired only by observation;
  (iv) it is communicated only on payment of a fee; or
  (v)   it is published only outside the UK.

---

[48] The discussion as to whether information is precise is, however, made clearer in the context of the discussion under the FSMA market abuse regime. According to FSMA, s 118C(5), information is precise if it (a) indicates circumstances that may exist or may reasonably be expected to come into existence or an event that has occurred or may reasonably be expected to occur; and (b) is specific enough to enable a conclusion to be drawn as to the possible effect of those circumstances or that event on the price of qualifying investments or related instruments. There is also further discussion in the COMC MAR 1.2.10–1.2.16.

[49] For further commentary on this argument, see Ashe, 'Insiders at the Starting Blocks', (1993) *Comp Law* 14(8), 153–4. See also the example given in the Treasury consultation on the sunset clauses in the context of the civil market abuse regime Chapter 8, para 8.55 *et seq.*, although note that a number of the examples given have been criticised in practice.

Star analysts

In Chapter 8, consideration was given to whether a recommendation from a 'star **9.21**
analyst' which could in itself be enough to cause a significant movement in the
price of the securities in question, could constitute market abuse under the FSMA
market abuse regime. The first question, therefore, and one which prompted
debate both during the parliamentary processes that preceded the CJA and in the
academic discussion surrounding it, is whether the analyst's report itself could fall
within the scope of CJA insider dealing, to which the answer would seem to be
no.[50] Assuming the report itself has been derived wholly from publicly available
sources, information will be considered to be 'made public' (and therefore not
inside information).[51] The fact that some of the information used by the analyst
was derived from sources that make the information available only for a fee should
not necessarily affect this. Section 58(3)(d) makes it clear that such information
may still be treated as having been made public even though a fee is payable.
Similarly, a star analyst's expertise in producing the report should not affect
this conclusion as section 58(3)(a) states that information may be treated as made
public even where it is acquired only by persons 'exercising diligence or
experience'.

However, an interesting issue is whether a distinction can be drawn between the **9.22**
report itself (which would not be inside information on the basis of the above
analysis) and knowledge in the hands, say, of a fellow employee that a particular
recommendation that might have a significant effect on the share price was about
to be issued. It would seem that in this instance the knowledge of an impending
recommendation could be inside information—it would relate to a specific issuer,
be specific and precise, and not have been made public (the information that the
recommendation was impending would not in itself be derived from public information); the fellow employee would presumably be an insider[52] in that he would
know the impending recommendation would be inside information and in the

---

[50] This reflects parliamentary discussion at the time. See also Rider, Abrams, and Ashe, *Guide to
Financial Services Regulation*, (3rd edn, 1997) at para 609: 'This provision [s 58(2)(d)] was added
to placate analysts, who considered that despite the assurances of the government that this was
already implicit in the notion of public information, there was still some degree of uncertainty.
Thus, the superior insight of an insider will not be counted against him, if he uses it to derive insight
from information which is generally available.' Similarly, see Stallworthy, 'The United Kingdom's
new regime for the control of insider dealing', (1993) ICCLR 4(12), 448–53. In a broad discussion
paper on the regulation of investment analysts, the FSA itself concluded that: 'To the extent that the
research is derived from information made public, the research will not be inside information (CJA,
section 58).' See FSA DP 15, Investment research: Conflicts and other issues (July 2002) at 5.24.
[51] CJA, s 58(2)(d).
[52] See discussion at para 9.23 *et seq*.

example given would have received the knowledge directly or indirectly from a person who had access to information by virtue of his employment.[53]

As an 'insider'

9.23 For the purposes of the section 52 offences, information must be held as an 'insider'.

'Insider'

9.24 According to section 57(1) a person has information as an insider if and only if it is, and he knows that it is, inside information, and he has it, and knows that he has it, from an inside source. In order to determine whether someone is an insider the courts must apply a subjective test. The individual must have himself known both that the information was inside information and that the information came from an inside source. It is not enough that he ought to have known, or that a reasonable person would have known. However, Neha Jain argues that if a person deliberately closes his mind to the obvious, or fails to ask questions in circumstances where those questions are prompted, knowledge may be imputed.[54] Put another way, according to academic discussion, the test would appear to be whether the individual has consciously failed to question the unusual.[55]

'From an inside source'

9.25 Section 57(2) deals with the interpretation of the term 'from an inside source'. A person will have inside information from an inside source if he has it through being a director, employee, or shareholder of an issuer of securities, or having access to the information by virtue of his employment, office, or profession. He will also have information from an inside source if the direct or indirect source of his information is one of these persons. This catches two categories of 'insider': those who come into contact with the information directly through their vocation (often referred to as 'primary insiders'); and those who come into contact with the information through a primary insider (often referred to as 'tippees' or 'secondary insiders'). The latter category is particularly wide ranging, as a person could be a secondary insider irrespective of how long the chain of communication is and how he acquired the information, as long as the original source was a 'primary insider'.[56] There is no requirement that the individual seeks out the information. This is made clear by the wording of section 57(2) which simply talks of a person 'having' information.

---

[53] See also discussion in Chapter 8 at para 8.95.

[54] Jain, 'Significance of Mens Rea in Insider Trading' (2004) *Comp Law* 25(5), 132–40, at 136.

[55] Band, 'Trustees and Insider Dealing: Part 1' (2000) *PCB* 5, 293–303, at 293.

[56] Lomnicka, 'The New Insider Dealing Provisions: Criminal Justice Act 1993, Part V' (1994) *JBL* Mar, 173–88, at 176. Note however commentary in the Treasury consultation on the sunset clauses in the civil market regime Chapter 8, para 8.55 *et seq*. which discusses practical problems in proving information comes from an inside source where there are multiple levels of information transfer.

Price-affected securities—the dealing offence and the encouraging offence

Both the dealing offence and the encouraging offence relate to dealing in 'price-   **9.26**
affected securities'. 'Price-affected securities' are those which are affected by price-
sensitive information, and 'price-sensitive information' is defined as information
which would, if it were to be made public, be likely to have a significant effect on
the price of securities.[57] The CJA provides no clarification of what is meant by the
use of the word 'significant',[58] and in providing guidance to issuers on the dissemination of price-sensitive information the London Stock Exchange, the UK listing
authority at the time, commented that:

> It is not feasible to define any theoretical percentage movement in a share price which
> will make a piece of information price sensitive. Attempts at a precise definition of
> 'price-sensitive' are not possible, since it is generally necessary to take into account a
> number of factors specific to the particular case . . .[59]

Defences

Section 52(4) states that the offence has effect subject to the defences outlined in   **9.27**
section 53. The CJA provides both 'general' and 'special' defences.

General defences—section 53

No expectation of profit[60]

It is a defence to all three of the offences under section 52 for the defendant to   **9.28**
show that he did not at the time expect the insider dealing to result in profit (or
the avoidance of loss)[61] attributable to the fact that the information in question
was price-sensitive information.[62]

---

[57] CJA, s 56(2).

[58] Compare this to the FSMA market abuse regime where s 118C(4) stipulates that information
would be likely to have a significant effect on price if and only if it is information of a kind which a
reasonable investor would be likely to use as part of the basis of his investment decision. The FSA
guidance in the Disclosure Rules as to when an issuer of shares should consider that information
would have a significant effect on the price of financial instruments expresses this slightly differently. In that guidance, the FSA recommends that an issuer should 'assess whether the information
in question would be likely to be used by a reasonable investor as part of the basis of his investment
decisions and would therefore be likely to have a significant effect on the price of the issuer's financial
instruments'. For further discussion see para 9.76 *et seq*.

[59] 'Guidance on the Dissemination of Price Sensitive Information' (July 1996) para 4. (<http://
www.fsa.gov.uk/Pages/Library/Other_publications/UKLA/1996/index.shtml>). This guidance has
now, for the most part, been replaced by the DTRs.

[60] CJA, ss 53(1)(a), 53(2)(a), and 53(3)(b).

[61] ibid, s 53(6).

[62] See Blair, Allison, Morton, Richards-Carpenter, Walker, and Walmsley, *Banking and Financial
Services Regulation* (3rd edn, 2002), para 9.23: 'This [defence] would apply, for example, if the dealing was "against" the information.'

Wide disclosure[63]

9.29 It is a defence to both the dealing offence and the encouraging offence for the defendant to show that he believed on reasonable grounds that 'the information had been or would be disclosed widely enough to ensure that none of those taking part in the dealing would be prejudiced by not having the information'. This defence has been explained in a number of ways but it is possible to identify two broad strands in its interpretation, one which requires 'equivalence of information' in the disclosure, and the other which focuses more on finding a lack of prejudice in the scope of the disclosure.

9.30 The first of these strands of interpretation suggests that the requisite lack of prejudice is satisfied through the principle of 'equivalence of information'.[64] This turns on the idea that it does not matter if a person deals on the basis of inside information provided that all of the counterparties to the dealing are fully aware of the information. It has been suggested that:

> [t]he most obvious example of this defence is where the person with the information discloses it to another person and then enters into a dealing with that other person. For this reason, the defence is often referred to as the 'equality of information' defence.[65]

However, an alternative view is that the defence does not require all parties to the transaction to be in possession of the same information, as the statute merely stipulates that the defendant's belief must have been that the information was disclosed widely enough to ensure that no party to the transaction was prejudiced by their level of knowledge (it does not require every party to have the same degree of disclosure). A regularly cited example of this is an underwriting transaction. It is the nature of such transactions that different participants may have different levels of knowledge (for example, the issuer may know far more than a sub-underwriter about the underwriting) without the parties with less knowledge being prejudiced by their lack of knowledge.[66]

Immaterial information

9.31 It is also a defence to both the dealing offence and the encouraging offence for the defendant to show that he would have acted as he did even if he did not have

---

[63] ibid, s 53(1)(b) and s 53(2)(b).

[64] Stamp, Dawson, and Elliot, 'Insider Dealing', in *Practical Company Law and Corporate Transactions* (2004) 385–410, at 400 and see also Blair et al, n 62 above, at para 9.28.

[65] Blair et al, n 62 above.

[66] See for example Lomnicka, n 31 above, and Alcock, n 46 above. Lomnicka at 185 cites the defence as applying in an underwriting transaction where 'the issuer possessed information about the securities which was neither public nor known to all the underwriters'.

the information.[67] As a result of the broad scope of the section 52 offences, this defence is required to carve out a protection for those acting in good faith and in the ordinary course of their dealings. An example often cited is a liquidator who may be in the possession of inside information, but will be required to dispose of securities regardless of whether this information, if released, would have a significantly negative impact on the price of those securities. To take another example, a professional investor may have thoroughly researched a particular stock and made a decision to invest in that stock, on the basis of its own research analysis, when a piece of information is inadvertently disclosed to it by the management of the issuer in question.

No expectation of dealing

It is a defence to the disclosure offence if the defendant can show that he did not **9.32** at the time expect anyone to deal in the price-affected securities because of the disclosure. This is to be judged subjectively, and therefore an honest but unreasonable belief that no dealing would take place would be sufficient to amount to a defence on the basis that the person making the disclosure genuinely did not believe that persons would deal on the basis of this disclosure.[68]

Special defences—Schedule 1

Section 53(4) also provides for a number of 'special defences'. These are set out in **9.33** Schedule 1 to the CJA. These defences apply only in relation to the dealing offence and the encouraging offence. These defences are largely aimed at ensuring the proper functioning of professional market making, intermediary, and corporate finance activities.[69]

Market makers

A 'market maker' is provided with a special defence under Schedule 1 where he **9.34** can show that he was acting in good faith in the course of his business as such, or in the course of employment in such a business.[70] A market maker is someone who holds himself out as acting in compliance with the rules of a regulated market, or an approved organisation, as willing to acquire or dispose of securities, and is recognised as doing so under those rules.[71] For the purposes of this definition, the

---

[67] The equivalent discussion under the FSMA market abuse regime relates principally to whether the behaviour for market abuse (insider dealing) and market abuse (misuse of information) is 'on the basis of' the information under discussion, as to which, see Chapter 8, para 8.104 *et seq.*

[68] There is no equivalent to this defence under the market abuse (improper disclosure) offence discussed in Chapter 8 at para 8.126 *et seq.*

[69] For a discussion of the safe harbours in the FSMA market abuse regime relating to 'dutiful execution of clients' orders' and 'legitimate market making etc', see Chapter 8, para 8.122 *et seq.*

[70] CJA, Sched 1, para 1(1).

[71] ibid, s 1(2).

only body that presently has 'approved organisation' status from the Treasury is the International Capital Market Association ('ICMA').[72]

Market information

9.35 It is a defence for the defendant to show that the information he possessed was market information, and that it was reasonable for an individual in his position to have acted as he did despite having that information as an insider.[73] (Market information[74] is information relating to the acquisition or disposal of particular securities which a person may acquire through the course of his involvement in those dealings.) The CJA does not give direct guidance on what behaviour should be considered to be reasonable, but it does stipulate that in determining reasonableness, particular factors should be considered. These relate to the content of information, the circumstances in which the information was gained, and the capacity in which the person in question acted and now acts. It is likely that the courts would look at typical market practice as a means of guiding their judgement as to reasonableness.[75] It is also a defence for the defendant to show that he acted to facilitate an acquisition or disposal which was under consideration or negotiation, and that the information which he had as an insider was market information arising directly out of his involvement in the acquisition or disposal.[76]

---

[72] According to s 1(3) of Sched 1, an 'approved organisation' means an international securities self-regulating organisation ('ISSRO') approved by the Treasury under any relevant order under s 22 of the Financial Services and Markets Act 2000 (Regulated Activities) Order 2001 (the 'RAO'). Article 35 of the RAO makes provision for the Treasury to recognise ISSROs. ICMA was created in May 2005 out of the merger of the International Securities Market Association and the International Primary Market Association and is the self-regulatory organisation which represents both banks and investment firms that issue and deal in capital markets instruments.

[73] CJA, Sched 1, para 2(1).

[74] ibid, Sched 1, para 4 offers a full definition of the term 'market information', namely information consisting of one or more of the following facts: (a) that securities of a particular kind have been or are to be acquired or disposed of, or that their acquisition or disposal is under consideration or the subject of negotiation; (b) that securities of a particular kind have not been or are not to be acquired or disposed of; (c) the number of securities acquired or disposed of or to be acquired or disposed of or whose acquisition or disposal is under consideration or the subject of negotiation; (d) the price (or range of prices) at which the securities have been or are to be acquired or disposed of or the price (or range of prices) at which the securities whose acquisition or disposal is under consideration or the subject of negotiation may be acquired or disposed of; (e) the identity of the persons involved or likely to be involved in any capacity in an acquisition or disposal.

[75] For a discussion as to the 'trading information' safe harbour under the pre-MAD market abuse regime, and the safe harbour relating to the legitimate business of market makers/dealers and the dutiful execution of client orders under the current market abuse regime, see Chapter 8, para 8.121.

[76] CJA, Sched 1, s 3. For a discussion of takeover/corporate finance related provisions under the FSMA market abuse regime, see Chapter 8, para 8.124.

Price stabilisation

It is a defence for the defendant to show that he acted in conformity with either the **9.36** price stabilisation rules[77] as set out in the FSA Handbook[78] or the relevant provisions of Commission Regulation (EC) No 2273/2003 detailing exemptions for buy-back programmes and stabilisation of financial instruments.[79] These are the same rules as those that apply to the market abuse regime under section 118 of FSMA.

Penalties and prosecution

On summary conviction for an offence under section 52 of the CJA, the courts **9.37** may impose a fine not exceeding the statutory maximum, or imprisonment for a term not exceeding six months, or both.[80] On conviction on indictment, the courts have the power to impose a fine of any amount deemed appropriate, or to a term of imprisonment not exceeding seven years, or both.[81] The FSA's powers to apply to court to impose an injunction upon a person who is likely to, or has committed insider dealing and to require restitution in stipulated circumstances are discussed at para 9.54 below.

Key steps in proving CJA insider dealing

As discussed in Chapter 8, para 8.03, the perception has been that the CJA offence **9.38** has been inappropriate to or ineffective in capturing the complicated fact patterns of dealings in the financial markets. This in part relates to the difficulties faced by prosecutors in satisfying the higher burden of proof that will apply in respect of criminal proceedings,[82] and partly as a result of the multiple layers of facts or knowledge that need to be proved under the CJA offence.

Cases

The policy of the FSA in respect of criminal prosecutions is outlined in Chapter 8 **9.39** at para 8.173. To date, the only successful conviction for insider dealing under the

---

[77] FSMA, s 144(1).

[78] FSA Handbook Market Conduct Sourcebook ('MAR') sets out the price stabilisation rules in Chapter 2.

[79] Commission Regulation (EC) No 2273/2003 of 22 December 2003 implementing Directive 2003/6/EC of the European Parliament and of the Council as regards exemptions for buy-back programmes and stabilisation of financial instruments. See also Chapter 8, para 8.157, for the equivalent provisions in the market abuse regime.

[80] CJA, s 61(1)(a).

[81] ibid, s 61(1)(b).

[82] Although see commentary in Chapter 8, para 8.27 relating to the standard of proof required under the civil market abuse offences as a matter of practice.

CJA since the market abuse regime as brought in was the *Asif Butt* case.[83] Butt was a compliance officer at an investment bank and passed confidential information obtained through this position to a number of associates, who placed highly profitable spread-bets on the basis of the information. Butt and four of his associates were found guilty of conspiracy to insider deal by a jury in December 2004. The City of London Police have acknowledged that this is the first instance in which a prosecution for insider dealing has targeted spread-betting activities, and David Mayhew (the FSA's then acting head of enforcement) emphasised that the FSA continues to treat prosecutions for insider dealing as a serious matter: 'In the latter part of Butt's trial, the prosecution asked the FSA for an impact statement, and the judge referred to it extensively in his judgment. Our statement referred to the importance of insider dealing.'

9.40 Chapter 8 contains a discussion of the FSA's approach in deciding whether to pursue criminal or civil sanction as part of its 'credible deterrence' strategy. The practical manifestation of this is a number of criminal prosecutions for insider dealing by individuals which have been launched recently amid considerable publicity.

9.41 On 22 January 2008, the FSA launched its first criminal prosecution as prosecuting agency for insider dealing against former General Counsel of TTP Communications Christopher McQuoid and his father-in-law James Melbourne. The FSA's position is that on 30 May 2006, McQuoid and Melbourne, having received inside information which related to a proposed cash offer from Motorola Incorporated for the entire issued share capital of TTP Communications PLC, acquired 153,824 shares in TTP Communications PLC. Both McQuoid and Melbourne pleaded not guilty to the charges. The case is being heard at Southwark Crown Court and the trial is due to start on 23 February 2009. Both men are currently on bail.

9.42 On 24 July 2008, Malcolm Calvert, a former partner of Cazenove, appeared at City of Westminster Magistrates Court, accused of 12 charges of insider dealing between April 2003 and March 2005. The charges relate to trading in shares of several companies, all of which were involved in merger or takeover talks at the time Calvert traded. Calvert indicated a plea of not guilty and the magistrates declined jurisdiction. Proceedings have been adjourned and Calvert is currently on bail.

9.43 On 29 July 2008, it was reported that the FSA has also charged Matthew Uberoi and Neel Uberoi with 17 counts of insider dealing, in relation to 310,700 shares in a number of different companies, over a four-month period in 2006. It is not

---

[83] Unreported.

known at present how the defendants will plead to the charges. It has been reported that Matthew and Neel Uberoi subsequently requested the court to nullify the summons against them on the basis that the FSA did not follow the appropriate procedures by not obtaining the permission of the Director of Public Prosecutions ('DPP') or the Secretary of State to start proceedings for cases of insider dealing. The FSA argued that FSMA superseded the CJA and therefore no permission was required. The defendants' application was rejected, the court finding that it was the plain aim of Parliament in creating the FSA was to get it in the forefront of regulation, including, where necessary criminal proceedings.[84]

Also on 29 July 2008, the FSA publicly announced that it had arrested eight men **9.44**
and executed search warrants across London and the South East in connection with a major ongoing investigation into insider dealing rings. The operation involved 40 FSA staff, assisted by officers from City of London Police.[85] All eight men were released without being charged, although they have been bailed to return to a police station on a future date. Whether or not prosecutions or convictions follow from these arrests, the FSA has clearly proven its aggressive stance and willingness to take criminal action.

Flow chart

A flow chart illustrating the key components of the CJA insider dealing offence is **9.45**
set out at Figure 9.1 for ease of reference.

Misleading Statements and Practices

*Section 397 Financial Services and Markets Act 2000: misleading statements
and practices*

Section 397 of FSMA contains two criminal offences in relation to false and **9.46**
misleading statements and practices. These provisions re-enact the repealed section 47 of the Financial Services Act 1986 ('FSA 1986'), with a few drafting amendments. As noted in Chapter 8, at para 8.03, it was perceived by both academics and practitioners that the section 47 (now section 397 FSMA) offences

---

[84] M Herman and Emma Inkester 'FSA insider dealing cases proceed', Times Online, 23 September 2008, which also reports that an application was also made on behalf of Michael Calvert.

[85] FSA, 'Arrests made in major FSA insider dealing investigation' (<http://www.fsa.gov.uk/pages/Library/Communication/PR/2008/082.shtml>).

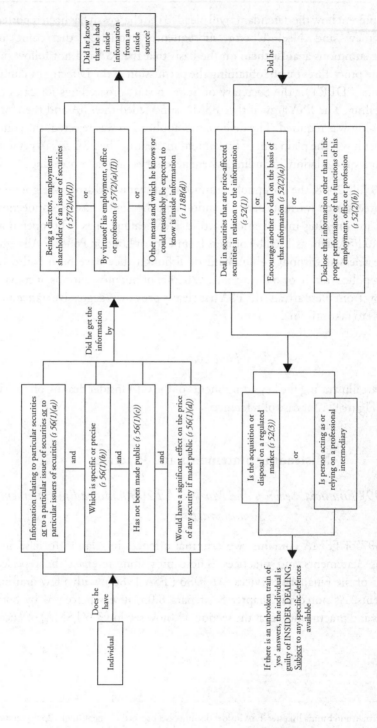

Figure 9.1 Insider dealing, Criminal Justice Act 1993, Part V

in themselves had proved unsuccessful at capturing misconduct occurring on the market. These failings led to the introduction of the civil market abuse regime, the coverage of which also includes various types of false or misleading statements and practices. This regime is discussed in further detail in Chapter 8.

Section 401 of FSMA gives the FSA the power to institute prosecutions for **9.47** offences under section 397 of FSMA (as part of the FSA's power under section 401 to institute prosecutions for offences under FSMA).[86] The Secretary of State has concurrent jurisdiction with the FSA to prosecute this offence, and this interaction is discussed at para 9.85 *et seq.*

Misleading statements

Sub-sections 397(1) and (2) of FSMA provide the first offence (misleading state- **9.48** ments). There are a number of elements to this. Firstly, for the offence to apply, a person must make a statement, promise, or forecast which he knows to be misleading, false, or deceptive in a material particular, or dishonestly conceal any material facts (whether in connection with a statement, promise, or forecast made by him or otherwise). Further, a person who is reckless (whether dishonestly or not) as to whether the statement made by him is misleading, false, or deceptive in a material particular also falls within the scope of section 397(1).[87] The second element requires the person making the statement, promise, or forecast, or concealing the facts, to have done so either *for the purpose* of inducing another person (whether or not the person to whom the statement, promise, or forecast is made) to do or refrain from doing certain acts, or to have been *reckless* as to whether the statement, promise, or forecast, or concealment, may have that effect. The acts to which the inducement must relate are entering or offering to enter into, or refraining from entering or offering to enter into, a relevant agreement, or exercising or refraining to exercise any rights conferred by a relevant investment.[88]

Defence

Section 397(4) of FSMA provides a defence to the misleading statements offence **9.49** if the relevant person can show that the statement, promise, or forecast was made in conformity with price stabilising rules, control of information rules,[89] or the

---

[86] The Director of Public Prosecutions may also initiate proceedings.

[87] A distinction was drawn in *R v Page, Holden, Dunning and Bradshaw* [1996] Crim LR 821 between (a) conspiracy to commit an offence under FSA 1986, s 47, for which no dishonesty is required as the reckless statement may be made dishonestly or otherwise; and (b) the offence of conspiracy to defraud for which dishonesty is required.

[88] As to the meaning of relevant investment and relevant agreement, see para 9.56.

[89] That is to say, rules made by the FSA in respect of the disclosure and use of information by an authorised person pursuant to the powers conferred by s 147 of FSMA. See, for example, the Senior

relevant provisions of Commission Regulation (EC) No 2273/2003 regarding exemptions for share buy-back programmes and stabilisation of financial instruments.[90] The 'price stabilising rules' are those made under section 144 of FSMA (ie in MAR) and the provisions of the Regulation are those in place to implement aspects of MAD concerning price stabilisation.

Territorial scope

9.50 For the first offence (misleading statements) to be committed, either:

   (i) the statement, promise or forecast must be made or arranged in or from the UK, or the facts must be concealed, or such concealment arranged, in or from the UK;

   (ii) the person on whom the inducement is intended to, or may, have effect is in the UK; or

   (iii) the agreement is or would be entered into or the rights are or would be exercised in the UK.[91]

Misleading practices

9.51 Section 397(3) provides the second offence (misleading practices). This applies to any person who does any act or engages in any course of conduct which creates a false or misleading impression as to the market in or the price or value of any relevant investments for the purpose of creating that impression, and of thereby inducing another person to acquire, dispose of, subscribe for, or underwrite those investments or to refrain from doing so or to exercise, or refrain from exercising, any rights conferred by those investments.

Defence

9.52 It is a defence to this second offence (misleading practices) if the relevant person can show that he reasonably believed that his act or conduct would not create a false or misleading impression or that he acted or engaged in the conduct for the purposes of stabilising the price of investments and in conformity with price stabilising rules, or in conformity with the same control of information rules and EU Regulation relating to share buy-back programmes and stabilisation of financial instruments[92] referred to in para 9.49.[93]

Management Arrangements Systems and Controls SYSC 10.2 for the rules regarding keeping information behind a Chinese Wall, as discussed at Chapter 8, para 8.155.

  [90] The range of acceptable conduct for these purposes was inserted by the Financial Services and Markets Act 2000 (Market Abuse) Regulations 2005, SI 2005/381.

  [91] FSMA, s 397(6).

  [92] Regulation 2273/2003.

  [93] FSMA, s 397(5).

Territorial scope

For the second offence (misleading practices) to be committed, the relevant act or **9.53** course of conduct must be done or engaged in the UK or the false or misleading impression must be created there.[94]

Sanctions

The maximum penalty for either offence is seven years' imprisonment or a fine, or **9.54** both. The sentencing policy of the court was considered in the Court of Appeal case of *R v Feld*.[95] In that case, the Court of Appeal held that, in addition to the factors set out in *R v Barrick*[96] the following non-exhaustive list would be relevant considerations for the sentencing judge: the amount involved and the manner in which the fraud is carried out; the period over which the fraud is carried out and the degree of persistence with which it is carried out; the position of the defendant within the company and his measure of control over it; any abuse of trust which is revealed; the consequences of the fraud; the effect on public confidence in the City and the integrity of commercial life; the loss to small investors, which will aggravate the fraud; the personal benefit derived by a defendant; the plea; and finally the age and character of the defendant. In addition to these sentencing powers, the FSA may also use its powers to apply to the court for an injunction or a restitution order[97] relating to offences under section 397. According to section 380, an injunction may be granted where there is a reasonable likelihood that any person will contravene a relevant requirement or that a contravention which has occurred will be continued or repeated. The court also has power to require a person who has contravened a relevant requirement, or who has been knowingly concerned in the contravention to take steps to remedy the contravention (or mitigate its effect) or to restrain him from dealing with his assets. According to section 382, the court may, on application of the FSA or the Treasury, make a restitution order if it is satisfied that a person has contravened a relevant requirement and either that profits have accrued to him as a result, or that one or more persons have suffered

---

[94] ibid, s 397(7).

[95] *R v Feld* [1999] 1 Cr App R (S) 1. This relates to FSA 1986, s 47, the precursor to FSMA, s 397.

[96] (1985) 7 Cr App R (S) 142. The factors stated in *Barrick* are: (a) the quality and degree of trust placed in the defendant; (b) the period over which the crimes were perpetrated; (c) the use to which the money dishonestly taken was put; (d) the effect upon the victim; (e) the impact of the offences on the public and public confidence; (f) the effect on fellow employees or partners; (g) the effect on the offender himself; (h) his own history; (i) those matters of mitigation special to himself such as illness, strain, and cooperation with the police.

[97] FSMA ss 380 (injunctions) and 382 (restitution orders) which apply in respect of contraventions of a relevant requirement. See Chapter 8 para 8.177 for a further discussion on this matter and in particular the meaning of 'relevant requirement'.

loss or have been otherwise adversely affected as a result of the contravention.[98] This power also applies in respect of persons knowingly concerned in the contravention. The amount of the restitution order will be such as appears to the court to be just having regard to the profits made or loss or adverse effect suffered (or both).

9.55 The FSA also has power to require FSA authorised persons who have contravened a relevant requirement to make restitution—a power that may be exercised without going to court. This power also applies in respect of authorised persons knowingly concerned in the contravention.[99] By way of illustration of the use of the equivalent powers under the FSA 1986,[100] in *Grant,*[101] both injunctive relief and a compensation order were granted against the defendants in connection with an unauthorised investment scheme under sections 6 and 61 of FSA 1986 and consequent misleading statements to the public contrary to section 47 FSA 1986 in advertisements.[102]

Relevant investments and relevant agreements

9.56 Both the misleading statements offence and the misleading practices offence apply in relation to 'relevant investments'. The inducement specified in the misleading statements offence refers in turn to 'relevant agreements'. 'Relevant investment' is defined[103] as an investment of a specified kind or one which falls within a prescribed class of investment, which includes:[104] deposits; rights under contracts of insurance; shares in a company; debentures; loan stock; bonds; government and public securities; warrants or other securities which give an entitlement to investments; certificates representing securities; units in a collective investment scheme; rights under a stakeholder pension scheme; options; futures; CFDs; participation in Lloyd's syndicates; loans secured on land and rights in investments, amongst others. 'Relevant agreement' is defined[105] as an agreement (i) the enter-

---

[98] See also discussion of compensation/clarification orders in the *AIT* case at para 9.66.

[99] FSMA, s 384(1).

[100] FSMA, s 61(1).

[101] *Secretary of State for Trade and Industry v Grant* [2000] WL 33122486 (Ch D) 15 September 2000.

[102] See also *Securities and Investments Board v Pantell SA (No 2)* [1991] 3 WLR 857 involving injunctive relief pursuant to s 61(1) of FSA 1986 relating to persons knowingly concerned in contraventions of s 47 of FSA 1986. Section 61(1) is broadly equivalent to s 380 of FSMA but related to specified provision rather than using the 'relevant requirement' definition.

[103] FSMA, s 397(10).

[104] ibid, s 397(14) states that 'specified' means as specified in an Order made by the Treasury for these purposes. The Financial Services and Markets Act 2000 (Misleading Statements and Practices) Order 2001, SI 2003/3645 is the relevant Order, arts 3 and 4 of which specify the kinds of activity and investment to which s 397(9) and (10), respectively, apply.

[105] ibid, s 397(9).

ing into or performance of which by either party constitutes an activity of a specified kind or one which falls within a specified class of activity; and (ii) which relates to a relevant investment (as defined above). For these purposes, an activity of a specified kind includes: accepting deposits; effecting and carrying out contracts of insurance; dealing in securities; arranging deals in investments; managing investments; safeguarding and administering investments; advising on investments; advising on syndicate participation at Lloyd's; sending dematerialised instructions; and establishing a collective investment scheme or stakeholder pension scheme, amongst others.

No civil law right of action under section 397 FSMA

The section 47 (now section 397 FSMA) offences do not give rise to a civil law **9.57** right of action for damages for breach of statutory duty actionable by those affected by the practices in question. The point was argued in the *Norwich Union* case[106] but rejected both at first instance and on appeal.

Effectiveness of the offences

Type of actions brought under FSA 1986, section 47

As discussed above, it was the perceived failure of the existing common law and **9.58** statutory offences (which included FSA 1986, section 47) to deal with particular types of market misconduct that led to the introduction of the civil market abuse regime in FSMA. Indeed, the significant burden of proving beyond reasonable doubt the criminal offences relating to misleading statements and practices, and the tests that have to be satisfied (for example, in the case of misleading statements, it is necessary to show knowledge, dishonest concealment, or recklessness as well as showing that the defendant had the necessary purpose or was reckless as to the effect) is illustrated by the small number of prosecutions reported.[107] The cases successfully prosecuted under FSA 1986, section 47 have tended for the most part to involve fairly clear cut cases.

For example, in *Chauhan*,[108] two defendants, the principal shareholder and man- **9.59** aging director of a company and the finance director of the company, pleaded guilty to engaging in a course of conduct which created a false or misleading impression of the market or in the price or value of investments. Their action,

---

[106] *Aldrich and others v Norwich Union Life Insurance Co Ltd; Norwich Union Life Insurance Society v Qureshi and others* [2000] Lloyd's Rep IR 1.

[107] Although see discussion at Chapter 8, para 8.27 of the standard of proof being applied in respect of the civil market abuse regime.

[108] *R v Chauhan and another* [2000] 2 Cr App R (S) 230.

which included backdating sales contracts, the creation of non-existing debts in the company's accounts, and inflating the value of the company's stock by removing plates to make machinery appear newer than it in fact was, had been undertaken in order to allow the company to proceed to flotation. The defendants received prison sentences of 18 months and five years (later reduced to four years on appeal) respectively.

9.60 In *Feld*,[109] the managing director of a company was found guilty of making misleading statements contrary to section 47. The company in question had issued a prospectus for a rights issue which contained statements intended to give a misleadingly favourable impression of the company's financial health. Forged documents were also supplied to the company's accountants and in support of a false profit announcement. The defendant was sentenced to six years' imprisonment for each of these counts of making a misleading statement, to run concurrently.[110]

9.61 In *Page*,[111] each of the defendants Page and Holden were convicted of three offences of recklessly making a misleading statement to induce entry into an investment agreement contrary to section 47(1)(b) of FSA 1986. The relevant statement was included in a brochure intended to be read by prospective investors in a fund and stated that 'funds placed with [the fund] are secured and guaranteed to the full amount designated overleaf, against mortgages on UK properties'. In fact, investments in the fund were shown to be not so secured. Page and Holden were sentenced to 30 months' imprisonment (reduced to nine months on appeal).

9.62 The case of *R v Stevens*[112] illustrates the difficulty in bringing successful prosecutions under these provisions. In this case, the Court of Appeal felt obliged to order a retrial of Stevens' conviction under section 47 of FSA 1986 due to inadequacies of the trial judge's summing up causing the defendant to have an unfair trial. The court held that:

> [t]he summing up is unclear in that it did not focus the jury's attention on the real issues the jury had to decide. It did not identify the false or misleading statement or statements. The result is that this court cannot be satisfied that all members of the jury, in reaching a verdict of guilty, were identifying the same statement or statements as being false or misleading.

9.63 The final case brought under section 47 FSA 1986, and which achieved a certain amount of notoriety the so-called 'City Slickers' case.[113] James Hipwell

---

[109] *R v Feld* [1999] 1 Cr App R (S) 1.

[110] The case was appealed on the basis of the length of the sentences determined by the court of first instance. On appeal the concurrent sentences of six years for the s 47 offence[s] were upheld, but the sentences for obtaining money by deception were reduced as the Court of Appeal decided on the facts that they should run concurrently, not consecutively.

[111] *R v Page, Holden, Dunning and Bradshaw* [1996] Crim LR 821.

[112] *R v Stevens*, transcript available at [2000] WL 1544599 (CA (Crim Div)) 12 October 2000.

[113] See the Court of Appeal decision, *R v Hipwell* [2007] All ER (D) 361 (Feb).

and a colleague, Anil Bhoyrul, were journalists who tipped various shares in the 'City Slickers' column in the *Daily Mirror* newspaper. They allegedly bought relevant investments which were to be tipped in the column and then sold them afterwards to make a profit. Hipwell, Bhoyrul and another were found guilty of conspiring to create a misleading impression of the value of the shares, in breach of section 47(2), FSA 1986. The judge at first instance ruled that if the position of a tipper is not disclosed at the time the tip is given, this was relevant to the evaluation and could mistakenly create a impression, irrespective of whether anyone was actually misled. The judge held that the misleading impression in this case did not rely on the mere non-disclosure of the tipper's position but the non-disclosure in the context of the pattern of trading, tone and content. James Hipwell's application to appeal was rejected by the Court of Appeal.

Interrelation with other offences and processes

A number of cases of FSA 1986, section 47 offences have also involved other alleged offences. In *R v Feld*,[114] a case which involved giving a misleadingly favourable impression of the financial health of a company undertaking a rights issue, as well as the production of forged documents which were given to the company's auditors, a prosecution was also brought under section 3 of the Forgery and Counterfeiting Act 1981. In *R v Page*,[115] one of the defendants was separately convicted of conspiracy to defraud. **9.64**

Section 47 prosecutions have also been used to assist with other processes. In *FSA v Lukka*,[116] a motion for judgment was granted in the absence of the defendant who had fled the country. He was accused of persuading investors to give him large amounts of money on the basis of false promises as to the profit they would make on the foreign exchange transactions in which he would invest the money on their behalf. Once this money had been transferred, he provided post-dated cheques as proof of the return the investors would receive. These cheques were not met. The evidence in relation to the alleged breach of section 47 of FSA 1986 was very strong, and the judge noted that the declaratory relief would be granted in order: **9.65**

  (i)   to assist domestic regulators in determining whether the defendant was a fit and proper person to be carrying on investment business;
 (ii)   to be of assistance in a subsequent consideration of any disqualification order;
(iii)   to assist any individual investors considering making a claim for compensation; and
 (iv)   to assist overseas regulators in determining whether the defendant should be authorised to provide services in their jurisdiction.

---

[114] n 109 above.
[115] n 111 above.
[116] *Financial Services Authority v Lukka* (Ch D, 23 April 1999).

AIT—the first prosecution under section 397

9.66   The first prosecution by the FSA under section 397 was *R v Rigby, Bailey and Rowley*[117] (known as the *AIT* case).[118] The three defendants, all former directors of AIT, were accused of both making a statement, promise, or forecast which they knew to be misleading, false, or deceptive (contrary to section 397(1)(a)) and recklessly making a statement, promise, or forecast which was misleading, false, or deceptive in a material particular (contrary to section 397(1)(c)). Rigby and Bailey were both convicted of the section 397(1)(c) offence and Rowley was acquitted on both counts. The conviction of Rigby and Bailey resulted from a statement issued by them in May 2002 that AIT's profits would meet the forecasts of £6.7 million for that year. This forecast depended on the existence of a number of contracts, which the jury accepted did not exist at the time the statement was made by Rigby and Bailey. The conclusion was therefore reached by the jury that the statement was 'misleading, false or deceptive in a material particular' because the contracts did not exist, and Rigby and Bailey were guilty of the section 397(1)(c) offence by virtue of their recklessness in affirming the profit forecast in those circumstances. It is noted, however, that the jury did not accept the FSA's case that any of the three defendants were guilty of the section 397(1)(a) offence. The FSA therefore failed to convince the jury that the defendants made a statement which they 'knew' to be misleading, false, or deceptive in a material particular.

9.67   Rigby and Bailey were guilty only of recklessness (not knowledge) in making the statement. The defendants were sentenced on 7 October 2005. Rigby was sentenced to three and a half years' imprisonment and was disqualified from acting as a company director for six years, and Bailey received a sentence of two years' imprisonment and was disqualified from being a company director for four years. Given that both were acquitted of the more serious offence under section 397(1)(a), the sentences were generally perceived to be harsher than anticipated. Following a hearing at the Court of Appeal on 20 December 2005, Rigby's sentence was reduced to 18 months and Bailey's sentence was reduced to nine months.[119]

9.68   Following the convictions, private and institutional investors who lost money after purchasing AIT shares on the basis of misleading information were invited by the FSA to apply to the court for compensation. Private investors applied for compensation totalling £18,716, while institutional investors (including pension

---

[117]   August 2005.

[118]   FSA/PN/091/2005, 18 August 2005.

[119]   FSA, 'Carl Rigby and Gareth Bailey—update' (<http://www.fsa.gov.uk/pages/Library/Communication/Statements/2005/rigby_bailey.shtml>); *R v Bailey (Gareth Scott)* [2006] 2 Cr App R (S) 36.

funds) applied for compensation totalling £1,262,736.[120] The court ordered that they should be paid in full, with one exception where the court ruled that their investment decision was not based on the misleading statements.

On 11 November 2005, Rigby was ordered to pay £208,796 in compensation to **9.69** investors, £381,273.97 by way of confiscation of assets, and £250,000 towards litigation costs incurred by the FSA. For Bailey, the judge ordered confiscation of £106,572.53 and compensation of £141,686. Rigby and Bailey both appealed against the confiscation orders, and Bailey appealed contingently against the compensation order.

With respect to the first ground of appeal, that the temporary and unrealised **9.70** increase in the value of Rigby's shares should not be taken into account as a benefit from the offences, the Court of Appeal held that there was 'no proper sense in which Rigby obtained a benefit or derived a pecuniary advantage'[121] (he had not sold any shares during the time when they had an inflated price—it was during a period when, by Stock Exchange rules, he was unable to sell his shares). With respect to the second ground of appeal, that the appellants' salaries and other emoluments earned after 2 May 2002 should not be taken into account as a benefit from the offence.[122] The Court of Appeal did not find a sufficient cause or link in the offences of which they were convicted and their continued employ- ment.[123] The Court of Appeal allowed the appeals and quashed the confiscation orders.

Other Regulatory Provisions Relating to Undesirable Market Conduct

Introduction

There are a number of other regulatory requirements relevant in the context **9.71** of undesirable market misconduct. Although not the primary focus of these chapters, these are outlined below for the sake of completeness.[124]

---

[120] FSA, 'Former AIT directors ordered to compensate investors', 11 November 2005, FSA/ PN/120/2005.

[121] *R v Rigby and another* [2006] 1 WLR 3067, para 17.

[122] The appellants continued to be employed after the statements, and indeed were retained during a transitional period whilst re-financing/re-structuring was undertaken and a new board brought in.

[123] ibid, para 21.

[124] As mentioned above, Chapters 8 and 9 do not however deal with common law or other offences, for example relating to the Fraud Act 2006.

Other requirements

FSA and exchange rules

9.72   Market misconduct may also fall within the ambit of the regulatory requirements. For example, misconduct by FSA regulated firms and approved persons, and by members of exchanges may be subject to sanctions under relevant FSA rules (including principles) and exchange rules respectively. This is discussed further in Chapter 8 at para 8.01. As to the scope of the FSA's Conduct of Business Sourcebook and related principles and statement of principle, see Chapters 12 and 13.

Listing Rules, Prospectus Rules, and the Disclosure and Transparency Rules

9.73   As mentioned in Chapter 8 at para 8.11 *et seq.*, there are provisions in the Disclosure Rules (which comprise three chapters of the Disclosure Rules and Transparency Rules ('DTR'))[125] which oblige 'issuers'[126] to comply with an additional layer of rules concerning the use, control, and disclosure of inside information.[127]

Sanctions for non-compliance with the Disclosure Rules

9.74   In terms of sanctions, the FSA may require the suspension of trading of a financial instrument. Such suspension does not relieve the issuer (or any persons discharging managerial responsibilities on behalf of the issuer, or any connected person of such person) from compliance with the Disclosure Rules. Once the matter causing suspension has been resolved, the FSA may nevertheless impose such conditions on the procedure for lifting the suspension as it considers appropriate.[128] In addition to the suspension of trading sanction, if the FSA considers that an issuer (or a person discharging managerial responsibilities, or a connected person) has breached any of the disclosure rules[129] it may, subject to the provisions of FSMA, impose on that person a financial penalty or publish a statement

---

[125]   DTR 2.2.

[126]   An issuer is any company or other legal person or undertaking (including a public sector issuer), any class of whose financial instruments: (a) have been admitted to trading on a regulated market; or (b) are the subject of an application for admission to trading on a regulated market; other than issuers who have not requested or approved admission of their financial instruments to trading on a regulated market—see FSA Legal Instrument 2005/16 Annex A which amends the FSA Glossary.

[127]   DTR 2.1.1G specifically acknowledges that the provisions of the Disclosure Rules overlap with ss 118 and 397 of FSMA and with Part V of the CJA. As far as s 118(1) of FSMA is concerned, if an issuer complies with the provisions of the Disclosure Rules, either by making disclosure of inside information as soon as possible (as required by the basic rule) or by delaying disclosure in accordance with the 'legitimate interests' exception, then such behaviour is a safe harbour from potential accusations that the disclosure constitutes market abuse under s 118(1) of FSMA.

[128]   DTR 1.4.1R–DTR 1.4.3R.

[129]   DTR 1.5.3G(1).

censuring that person.[130] The FSA's powers to impose penalties in this instance are a facet of its powers to impose penalties as competent authority under the listing regime.[131] In this context, it should be noted that the FSA may also bring enforcement proceedings against an issuer if it fails to take reasonable steps to establish and maintain adequate procedures, systems, and controls to enable it to comply with its obligations under the DTR.[132] This includes the rules relating to the disclosure of inside information.[133]

The basic rule on the disclosure of inside information

The basic requirement is that an issuer must disclose inside information to a **9.75** Regulatory Information Service ('RIS') as soon as possible,[134] subject to the 'delaying disclosure' exception set out at para 9.79. An issuer will be deemed to have complied with the basic rule if an event comes into existence but is not yet formalised and the issuer notifies an RIS as soon as is possible.[135] Additional guidance from the FSA allows issuers a short delay when faced with an unexpected or significant event, subject to the requirement to make an interim 'holding announcement' in some circumstances.[136] An issuer that has financial instruments admitted to trading or financial instruments listed on an overseas stock exchange

---

[130] For a discussion of actions taken for breaches of the Listing Rules in the pre-MAD regime, see Chapter 8 at para 8.174.

[131] FSMA, s 91(1)–(2).

[132] LR 7.1.

[133] ibid, 7.2.2(2).

[134] DTR 2.2.1R. Issuers operating an Internet site are obliged also to publish the inside information on such a website and it must remain there for a year—see the Rules at DTR 2.3. For the purposes of DTR 2.2.1R, inside information has the same meaning as in s 118C of FSMA (discussed at Chapter 8, para 8.82 *et seq*.), although DTR 2.2 considers various criteria that issuers may use in identifying inside information, DTR 2.2.4 for example states that in determining the likely price significance of information an issuer should assess whether the information in question would be likely to be used by a reasonable investor as part of the basis of his investment decision 'and would therefore be likely to have a significant effect on the price of the issuer's financial instruments' (the reasonable investor test) and in this respect see n 58. Further, there is an elaboration of the reasonable investor test (there is no equivalent in the COMC to these elaborations). For example, the DTRs indicate that there is no set figure (percentage change or otherwise) in determining what constitutes a significant effect – this will vary from issuer to issuer - and that a variety of factors such as the issuer's size, recent developments, market sentiment and the sector in which the issuer operates will come into play in ascertaining the significance of the information. Whilst not generally speaking prescriptive in terms of how the reasonable investor test will apply in this context, the DTRs do indicate that any assessment would need to take account of the anticipated impact of the information in light of the totality of the issuer's activities, the reliability of the source of the information, and other market variables likely to affect the relevant financial instruments. DTR 2.2.6 goes on to set out a non-exhaustive list of information which is likely to be considered relevant to a reasonable investor's decision. Note also DTR 2.2.2R (n 135).

[135] ibid, 2.2.2R, implementing the requirement of Art 2.

[136] ibid, 2.2.9G(2).

in other jurisdictions must ensure that the disclosure of inside information to the public is synchronised as closely as possible in all jurisdictions.[137]

9.76 The FSA recently fined Woolworths Group plc[138] £350,000 for breaches of Disclosure Rule 2.2.1 and Listing Principle 4 and also considered a number of issues raised in submission, including when information could be said to have a 'significant effect' on price for the purposes of the definition of 'inside information'. In that case, Woolworths contested, amongst other things, that the information in question (which it had not announced) would not have a 'significant effect' on the price of Woolworths' shares.

9.77 The facts as found were that Woolworths became aware of a variation to the terms of a major supply contract of one of its subsidiaries, which would reduce Woolworths' profits for the following year 2006/07 by an estimated £8 million. This was considered by the RDC to be inside information as it was likely to have a significant effect on Woolworths' share price and should therefore have been disclosed to the market as soon as possible.

9.78 The FSA was satisfied that 'likely to have a significant effect on price' had to be assessed against the test in section 118C(6) only, namely that information would be likely to have a significant effect on price if and only if it was information of a kind which a reasonable investor would be likely to use as part of the basis of his investment decisions, and that section 118C was not merely a set of factors to take into account, as had been contested. The FSA considered that whilst an analysis of actual price movement and the matters contributing to it could be relevant for certain purposes (eg the penalty) it was, in the FSA's view, the wrong approach to seek to analyse, as had been suggested, the amount of an actual fall that might be attributed to a particular piece of information in order to determine whether it was 'inside information'. This was, according to the RDC, entirely consistent with the guidance in the Disclosure Rules to the effect that there was no set percentage or other figure to determine whether there was a 'significant effect on price'. On the facts, the FSA was satisfied that the variation in question resulted in a profit reduction of more than 10 per cent and that that was, on any view, information of a type that a reasonable investor would be likely to use as a part of his investment decision. In this regard the decision would seem to indicate a reduced emphasis on the likely effect of the relevant information on the company's share price per se in the analysis of whether an announcement is required.

---

[137] ibid, 2.4 for the full Rules.
[138] FSA Final Notice to Woolworths Group plc dated 11 June 2008 [RDC hearing].

Exception from the basic rule allowing an issuer to delay disclosure

There is an exception to the basic disclosure rule, which allows an issuer to delay **9.79** disclosure of inside information to an RIS in order not to 'prejudice its legitimate interests', provided that:

(i) such omission would not be likely to mislead the public;
(ii) any person receiving the information owes the issuer a duty of confidentiality, regardless of whether such duty is based on law, regulations, articles of association, or contract; and
(iii) the issuer is able to ensure the confidentiality of that information.[139]

Two non-exhaustive examples of not prejudicing legitimate interests are then given by the FSA, such that non-disclosure is permissible firstly where negotiations concerning the future financial viability of the issuer would be threatened by disclosure (eg in a potential insolvency situation). The second example given is where the organisational structure of the issuer means that decisions need to be taken by more than one body within that issuer.[140] However, the issuer's ability to delay making disclosure to the RIS does not mean that the issuer is permitted to make disclosure to other persons. On the contrary, it is specifically stated in the Disclosure Rules that where an issuer makes selective disclosure of inside information to a third party, it must make immediate disclosure to an RIS.[141]

The requirements relating to the EU-based requirements to disclose 'inside infor- **9.80** mation', the definitions used, and the circumstances in which disclosure can be delayed were also discussed in the second set of CESR Level 3 Guidance—see discussion in Chapter 8, para 8.193.

Provisions relating to the control of insiders and inside information

As noted in Chapter 8 at para 8.12, in addition to the basic disclosure rule and **9.81** exceptions from that rule, the Disclosure Rules also impose rules on issuers relating to the control of insiders and inside information. For example, issuers are required to establish effective arrangements to deny access to inside information to persons other than those who require it for the exercise of their functions within the issuer,[142] and to have in place measures which enable public disclosure to be made via an RIS as soon as possible in case the issuer is not able to ensure the confidentiality of the relevant inside information.[143] Further, issuers are required

---

[139] DTR 2.5.1R, implementing Art 6(2) of MAD.
[140] ibid, 2.5.3R, implementing Art 3(1) of the MAD Implementing Directive 2003/124/EC.
[141] ibid, 2.5.6R, although guidance at DTR 2.5.7G permits disclosures to persons who owe the issuer a duty of confidentiality (eg its professional advisers).
[142] ibid, 2.6.1R.
[143] ibid, 2.6.2R.

to draw up and maintain lists of persons who have access to inside information.[144] There is also a set of rules which controls the notification by issuers to an RIS of transactions by certain officers of that issuer in financial instruments of the issuer. Persons discharging managerial responsibilities and their connected persons must notify the issuer in writing of the occurrence of all transactions conducted on their own account in the shares of the issuer, or derivatives, or any other financial instruments relating to those shares within four business days of the day on which the transaction occurred.[145] The issuer must in turn inform the RIS of any disclosure by such a person.[146] As discussed in Chapter 8 at para 8.11, issuers must also comply with 'listing principles', which include the principle that listed companies take reasonable steps to put in place systems and controls for complying with these obligations. The sanctions for a breach of these requirements would be the same as discussed above.

9.82 The FSA have also recently set out in *MarketWatch* 27 Principles of Good Practice for the Handling of Inside Information. This was produced by an industry working group comprised of market practitioners and relevant representative bodies. This followed up on the FSA's desire to consider ways to share good practice points with firms it did not regulate.

9.83 While the FSA fully supported the document, it is not an FSA document and the FSA say it will not be assessing firms' compliance against it. The main aim is that the work contributes to an overall heightened awareness of the ways to protect sensitive information.

The City Code on Takeovers and Mergers

9.84 The City Code on Takeovers and Mergers (the 'City Code') is a statutory set of rules which obliges market participants to act in accordance with certain rules on the procedure of making a takeover offer for a listed company. The Panel on Takeovers and Mergers (the Panel) is the UK regulatory body that issues and enforces the City Code on Takeovers and Mergers and oversees its daily application.[147] The Panel is able to investigate and punish breaches of the City Code (in the sense that the Panel may issue public censures or require other listed companies not to deal with 'blacklisted' firms).

---

[144] ibid, 2.8, implementing Art 6(3) of MAD. See also discussion in Chapter 8 at para 8.13.

[145] ibid, 3.1.2R.

[146] ibid, 3.1.4R(1)(a). The Rules are set out in full at DTR 3.1 and implement Art 6(4) of MAD. See also discussion in Chapter 8 at para 8.14.

[147] The Panel on Takeovers and Mergers was granted formal statutory powers pursuant to the implementation the Takeover Directive (2004/25/EC), which was implemented in the UK by Part 28 of the Companies Act 2006 on 20 May 2006.

Regulatory and Prosecuting Bodies

*Interaction between the various regulatory and prosecuting bodies
with powers relating to market misconduct*

Under the UK financial services regime, a number of bodies have the power to **9.85** investigate and take proceedings in respect of market misconduct. Again, the lack of clear and effective demarcation lines between the powers of these various bodies had historically given rise to considerable criticism. This section outlines the primary regulatory and prosecuting bodies and their various powers. It then considers the interaction between the prosecuting powers of these bodies and the FSA, as set out in the FSA's Guidelines on the interaction between prosecuting bodies[148] (the 'Prosecuting Guidelines'), and the arrangements that are now in place between the FSA and other regulatory bodies relating to the operation of regulatory investigations ('Operating Arrangements').[149]

Overview of the UK's prosecuting bodies

The following bodies all have responsibility for investigating or prosecuting **9.86** matters of market misconduct.

The FSA

The FSA take action, has the power to commence investigations and commence **9.87** prosecutions in any part of the UK regarding possible offences under section 118 of FSMA (market abuse); section 397 of FSMA (false or misleading statements or practices), and, except in Scotland, Part V of the CJA 1993 (insider dealing).[150]

---

[148] FSA Enforcement Guide ('EG') Annex 2G sets out the guidelines on investigation of cases of interest or concern to the FSA and other prosecuting and investigating agencies. See also EG 12.11 which states that guidelines have established a framework for cooperation in cases where one or more of these bodies also has an interest in prosecuting a matter that the FSA is considering for investigation. The Prosecuting Guidelines were previously set out in the FSA Handbook Enforcement manual Chapter 2 Annex 1G until 27 August 2007. The Enforcement manual ('ENF') and the Decision making manual ('DEC') were deleted and replaced by the Decision Procedure and Penalties manual ('DEPP') and a regulatory guide, the EG, as part of the FSA's work on simplifying the Handbook and promoting better regulation. The EG does not form part of the Handbook and comprises neither FSA rules nor guidance on the FSA rules.

[149] The FSA's Operating Arrangements for the coordination of investigations into market abuse are all available at <http://www.fsa.gov.uk/pages/About/What/financial_crime/market_abuse/library/index.shtml>

[150] The FSA's power to prosecute offences under FSMA is stated in s 401 of FSMA. The power to initiate prosecutions for criminal insider dealing under the CJA is contained in s 402(1)(a) of FSMA, which specifically excludes Scotland from the ambit of the FSA's prosecuting powers for CJA insider dealing. See also Chapter 8 at para 8.184.

9.88 In addition to this, of course, the FSA has a number of investigative and disciplinary powers relating to misconduct by firms and individuals regulated by it.

9.89 With reference to breach of DTRs as discussed at para 9.73 *et seq.*, powers in
respect of enforcement are also vested in the FSA.

9.90 The FSA also have powers in respect of the City Code as discussed at para 9.84.

The Department for Business, Enterprise & Regulatory Reform[151]

9.91 The Secretary of State of the Department for Business, Enterprise & Regulatory
Reform ('BERR') shares with the FSA a concurrent jurisdiction to investigate a
number of market misconduct matters. In practice, the BERR's role is primarily
an investigatory one, through the appointment of 'inspectors' or 'investigators'.[152]
However, the investigations may lead to prosecution by the BERR. For example,
Timothy Power is being prosecuted by the BERR whose precursor, the
Department for Trade and Industry ('DTI'), handled insider dealing prosecutions
until it started to share this role with the FSA from 2001. Timothy Power appeared
at Southwark Crown Court on 13 August 2008, accused of four counts of insider
dealing relating to his alleged activity during the sale of Belgo to Lonsdale Holdings
in 1997. Power denied all four counts of insider dealing, and was refused bail until
his trial, which was set for December 2008.[153] However, it would be more common for the BERR to disclose information to the FSA or other prosecutors to
allow them to take appropriate action.[154] Any enforcement action taken by the
BERR would ordinarily relate to corporate matters, for example orders for the
winding up of a company, or the disqualification of directors.[155]

---

[151] The Department for Business, Enterprise & Regulatory Reform ('BERR') was previously the
Department for Trade and Industry.

[152] The Secretary of State has the power to appoint an inspector where requested to do so by
a prescribed proportion of the members of a company, or where it appears that appointment is
necessary where circumstances suggest the company's affairs have been conducted for a fraudulent or unlawful purpose—ss 431–432 of the Companies Act 1985 (now amended by Companies
Act 2006) (it was these powers under which Ernest Saunders was investigated, see Chapter 8,
para 8.08). An investigator may be appointed by the Secretary of State to require the company to
produce documents or provide information, or to enter premises to investigate a company, under
s 447 of the Companies Act 1985, (as amended by the Companies (Audit, Investigations and
Community Enterprise) Act 2004) and s 448 (as amended by the Companies Act 2006). The DTI
published guidance on the amended provisions—DTI, 'A guide to the investigations provisions
introduced by the Act', January 2005.

[153] M Herman, 'Former Belgo boss faces insider dealing trial', Times Online, 14 August 2008.

[154] Disclosure is permitted under s 449(2) of the Companies Act 1985, as amended by the
Companies Act 2006 to such agencies and persons as are stated in Sched 15C, which includes the
Director of Public Prosecutions, a police constable, and the FSA.

[155] Prosecuting Guidelines, Appendix, para 2.2.

The Serious Fraud Office

The Serious Fraud Office ('SFO') is charged with the investigation of matters of **9.92** serious or complex fraud. Its remit overlaps with that of the FSA where the market misconduct could constitute serious fraud, with the SFO taking into account factors such as the financial value of any crime, the national interest, specialist knowledge required for the investigation, and any international dimension when determining whether to take action in a particular fraud case.[156]

Public prosecution bodies

The Crown Prosecution Service ('CPS') is the prosecuting body in England and **9.93** Wales in those cases of suspected misconduct where a criminal investigation has been initiated by the police (in Scotland prosecutions are initiated by the Crown Office and in Northern Ireland by the Public Prosecution Services ('PPS') for Northern Ireland).[157] There is a possibility of overlap with the FSA, especially in the area of fraud.[158]

Other powers of review, enquiry, and discipline

Whilst not prosecuting powers as such, the following powers are also relevant in **9.94** the context of market misconduct or market failings:

Treasury's powers of review and enquiry under FSMA

The Treasury has a statutory power to conduct investigations into serious failures **9.95** in the regulatory system, where, for instance, events have occurred which posed a grave risk to the financial system;[159] or which caused or could have caused damage to the holders of listed securities.[160] This is a power to conduct inquiries as a response to failings in the regulatory system, rather than a specific power to target market abuse, but large-scale events may in appropriate circumstances be such as to trigger an investigation.

Exchanges

As noted at para 9.72, exchanges in the UK will have various investigative and **9.96** disciplinary powers relating to misconduct by members or affecting the relevant exchange. The question of when misconduct should be considered by the FSA, and when by the exchanges, is discussed further at para 9.101.

---

[156] ibid, Appendix, para 3.3.
[157] The CPS, headed by the DPP, is the government department responsible for prosecuting criminal offences investigated by the police.
[158] Prosecuting Guidelines, Appendix, para 4.1.
[159] FSMA, s 14(2).
[160] ibid, s 14(3).

The Takeover Panel

9.97 As noted at para 9.84, the Panel can investigate and take action in respect of breaches of the City Code. There are a set of operating guidelines between the FSA and the Panel.[161]

The police

9.98 The police are responsible for the arrest of persons suspected of arrestable offences and in certain situations will assist the FSA with the investigation of market misconduct matters—such powers being most recently used in the FSA's arrests of eight men in connection with a major ongoing investigation into insider dealing rings.[162] There is a memorandum of understanding ('MOU') in place between the FSA and the police to assign responsibility in such instances.[163]

Interaction between the FSA and other prosecuting bodies

9.99 It is apparent from the foregoing discussion that there is potentially a significant overlap in the investigatory and prosecuting functions of a number of bodies and, as mentioned above, this had historically given rise to adverse criticism. To address this, in addition to the centralisation of certain powers on to the FSA which took place under FSMA, Prosecuting Guidelines have been introduced to enable the various agencies to determine which is responsible for pursuing a particular incident of market misconduct.[164]

The Prosecuting Guidelines

9.100 The Prosecuting Guidelines list firstly a number of situations which would 'tend' towards enforcement by the FSA being considered appropriate and then set out a number of factors which would tend towards action by another prosecuting body being appropriate. There is no prescribed number of these factors which must be satisfied in order to conclude which is the appropriate body to take action. Rather it is presupposed that this will be apparent after a comparison of these factors.

---

[161] Operating Guidelines between the Financial Services Authority and the Panel on Takeovers and Mergers on Market Misconduct (<http://www.fsa.gov.uk/pubs/other/operating_guidelines.pdf>).

[162] FSA, 'Arrests made in major FSA insider dealing investigation' (<http://www.fsa.gov.uk/pages/Library/Communication/PR/2008/082.shtml>); See para 9.44.

[163] MOU between the FSA and the Association of Chief Police Officers of England & Wales ('ACPO'), available at <http://www.fsa.gov.uk/pubs/mou/fsacolp.pdf>; brought into force in August 2005 to replace the former memorandum in place with the City of London Police.

[164] EG Annex 2 paras 3 to 7. The parties to the Prosecuting Guidelines are FSA, SFO, DTI, CPS (and therefore DPP), ACPO, Crown Office (for Scotland), PPS (for Northern Ireland), ACPO(S) (Scotland).

Interaction between the FSA and other bodies with regulatory powers

The FSA has entered into a number of operating arrangements with certain other **9.101** bodies which have a role in regulating the financial markets or taking regulatory action against suspected market misconduct. At present, there are such guidelines in place between the FSA and the Panel and arrangements with various recognised investment exchanges. The purpose of these operating arrangements is to determine those situations in which it would be appropriate for either the FSA or the other party to the operating arrangements to pursue suspicious conduct, where a particular matter may otherwise fall within both of their remits. In general, the recognised investment exchange will deal with misconduct that is limited to the exchange, where the perpetrators are all members, and where the exchange's powers are sufficient to deal with the matter, and the FSA will focus on cross-market abuse, abuse by persons who are not members of an exchange, and criminal activity.

Memorandum of Understanding with ACPO

As mentioned at para 9.98 above, there is an MOU in place between the FSA and **9.102** Association of Chief Police Officers of England & Wales ('ACPO'). The purpose of the MOU is to set out the agreed best practice for cooperation between the police and the FSA with regard to:

(i) the arrest of suspects where the FSA and the police have reasonable grounds to suspect that an individual has committed an arrestable offence,[165] and the FSA seeks the assistance of the police in questioning the suspect; or

(ii) a warrant obtained by the FSA where the FSA seeks the assistance of the police in connection with the execution of the warrant.[166]

The MOU sets out in considerable detail the procedures for this agreed cooperation to be implement ed in practice (paragraphs 4–13 of the MOU).

Interaction with overseas regulators under MAD

As discussed in Chapter 8,[167] directives such as MAD forming part of the EU **9.103** Financial Services Action Plan are predicated on the enhancement of cross-border business by the creation of harmonised standards. In the case of MAD, for example, this is illustrated by the territorial scope[168] of the offences envisaged by

---

[165] At the time of the MOU this was defined as an offence which has a punishment on conviction on indictment of a term of imprisonment of five years or greater.

[166] Para 3 of the MOU. The MOU also replaces the MOU that was in place between the FSA and the City of London Police.

[167] See Chapter 8, para 8.09.

[168] Discussed further at Chapter 8, para 8.69.

the directive. Thus, for example, offensive conduct undertaken in London relating to qualifying investments listed on a regulated market in Germany would in principle fall within the MAD determined market abuse regimes in both the UK and Germany. MAD addresses this by stating that it ought to be the authority of the State in which the abusive acts took place or, where acts affect securities listed on an exchange, the State in which the exchange is located.[169] The risk of double jeopardy (that is to say, in the example given above, that action will be taken both in the UK and Germany) is reduced to an extent by giving foreign regulators the right to refuse to take action if a 'final judgment' has already been delivered (Article 16(2)), although how this will work in practice remains to be seen.

9.104 As a general proposition, MAD also sets out detailed provisions for the cooperation expected between Member State regulators. The guiding principle in Article 16(1) is that these regulators 'shall co-operate with each other whenever necessary for the purpose of carrying out their duties'. The detail of the expected behaviour is set out in the remainder of Article 16, including information sharing, and making and responding to requests for an investigation to be carried out in another Member State.

---

[169] Art 16(3), although this does not seem to resolve the debate in particular. DEPP 6.2.21G states that where it is appropriate for both the FSA and an overseas or domestic regulatory authority or enforcement agency to take action, the FSA will work with the relevant authority to ensure that cases are dealt with efficiently and fairly, under operating arrangements in place (if any) between the FSA and the relevant authority.

10

MONEY LAUNDERING AND FINANCIAL CRIME[1]

What is Money Laundering?

The October 2004 UK anti-money laundering policy document[2] adopts a practical description of what constitutes money laundering. It is:

> a term generally used to describe the ways in which criminals process illegal or 'dirty' money derived from the proceeds of any illegal activity (e.g. the proceeds of drug-dealing, human trafficking, fraud, theft or tax evasion) through a succession of transfers and deals until the source of illegally acquired funds is obscured and the money takes on the appearance of legitimate or 'clean' funds or assets.

10.01

In the United Kingdom, the legal definition of money laundering is provided by the Terrorism Act 2000 and the Proceeds of Crime Act 2002 ('POCA'). The definition in those Acts is relied on by both the Money Laundering Regulations 2007[3] ('MLR 2007') and the FSA's Handbook.[4] In summary, the POCA definition provides that a person commits the offence of money laundering if he:

10.02

- conceals, disguises, converts, transfers or removes (from the United Kingdom) criminal property;
- enters into or becomes concerned in an arrangement which he knows or suspects, facilitates (by whatever means) the acquisition, retention, use, or control of criminal property by or on behalf of another person; or
- acquires, uses or has possession of criminal property.

The process of money laundering is considered to consist of three stages:

10.03

- placement;
- layering; and
- integration.

---

[1] The contributors to Chapter 10 were assisted by Lesley Wood, Norton Rose LLP.
[2] HM Treasury, Anti-Money Laundering Strategy (October 2004).
[3] The Money Laundering Regulations 2007, SI 2007/2157.
[4] SYSC section 6.3 (Financial crime).

Placement

10.04 In the initial stage of money laundering, the launderer places the cash generated from his criminal activity into the financial system or uses it to buy goods. This may be done by breaking up large amounts of cash into less conspicuous smaller sums and depositing them in a bank account or by purchasing negotiable financial instruments such as money orders or cheques. This process is sometimes referred to as 'smurfing', with the launderers employing a number of low-level criminals to make deposits at different branches of the same institution. It is at this stage of the laundering process that the 'dirty' funds are most easily identifiable. Given the fact that the laundered funds are most often held in cash form, launderers are generally considered to be most likely to target deposit-takers such as banks and building societies and suppliers of high value goods such as antique dealers.

Layering

10.05 Once the funds have entered the system, the second stage—layering—takes place. This is the stage where the dirty money is distanced from the original source. This is done by the launderer engaging in a series of transactions. These transactions will involve conversions or movements of the funds. As well as simple transfers between different accounts, the funds may be channelled through the purchase or sale of investments. Sometimes the layering stage is conducted cross-border with the launderer making use of accounts held in jurisdictions where anti-money laundering standards are low. The launderer may also disguise the transfers as payments for goods or services, thus giving them a legitimate appearance.

Integration

10.06 Once the original source of the funds has been obscured, the launderer moves on to the third and final stage: integration. Having successfully processed his criminal funds through placement and layering, the launderer is able to reintroduce them to the economy so they appear to be legitimate by converting them into legal business earnings through normal financial and commercial operations.

United Kingdom Policy Drivers

10.07 The Government Strategy Document[5] and the subsequent 'Financial Challenge to Crime and Terrorism' document[6] both make clear the UK Government's intention to combat money laundering. Fighting money laundering is not just seen as

---

[5] HM Treasury, Anti-Money Laundering Strategy (October 2004).
[6] HM Treasury (February 2007).

an end in itself, rather limiting the ability of criminals to launder the proceeds of criminal activity is seen as a vital part of the wider fight against criminal activity generally. Illegal arms sales, smuggling, and the activities of organised crime, such as drug trafficking and prostitution rings, can generate huge sums of money and lax financial markets and anti-money laundering standards will tend to attract criminal elements with consequences for law and order generally. The government's overriding goal is to protect its citizens and reduce the harm caused by crime and terrorism. Whilst finance is the lifeblood of criminal and terrorist networks, it is also one of their greatest vulnerabilities.

The Government's objectives are to use financial measures to: **10.08**

- deter crime and terrorism in the first place;
- detect the criminal or terrorist abuse of the financial system; and
- disrupt criminal and terrorist activity.

Given the pre-eminence of its financial markets, and their international nature,   **10.09**
the UK is an obvious target for money launderers. In recent years, Government policy has set great emphasis on restricting the ability of criminals, both domestic and international, to use the UK to launder funds. The importance of the financial markets to the wider UK economy cannot be overstated and, as a consequence, protecting and developing the reputation and standing of the UK as a financial centre is a major policy goal of all UK Governments, regardless of their political complexion. Whilst domestic criminal policy is largely driven by the Home Office and latterly by the Ministry of Justice, HM Treasury plays a major part in the development of anti-money laundering policy generally and leads Government negotiation of EU legislation in this area as well as developing and implementing specific domestic anti-money laundering legislation such as the MLR 2007.

HM Treasury was responsible for coordinating the implementation of the   **10.10**
Financial Services and Markets Act 2000 ('FSMA'). The importance of the fight against crime and the need to reduce the use by criminals of the UK's financial markets is expressly provided for in FSMA. The Act contains four regulatory objectives including section 6 which provides:

(1) The reduction of financial crime objective is: reducing the extent to which it is possible for a business carried on—
  (a) by a regulated person; or
  (b) in contravention of the general prohibition;
  to be used for a purpose connected with financial crime.

(2) In considering that objective the [Financial Services] Authority must, in particular, have regard to the desirability of—
  (a) regulated persons being aware of the risk of their businesses being used in connection with the commission of financial crime;
  (b) regulated persons taking appropriate measures (in relation to their administration and employment practices, the conduct of transactions by them

and otherwise) to prevent financial crime, facilitate its detection and monitor its incidence; and

    (c) regulated persons devoting adequate resources to the matters mentioned in paragraph (b).

  (3) 'Financial crime' includes any offence involving—

    (a) fraud or dishonesty;

    (b) misconduct in, or misuse of information relating to, a financial market; or

    (c) handling the proceeds of crime.

  (4) 'Offence' includes an act or omission which would be an offence if it had taken place in the United Kingdom.

  (5) 'Regulated person' means an authorised person, a recognised investment exchange or a recognised clearing house.

10.11 FSMA gives the Financial Services Authority ('the FSA') the power to make rules[7] and also the power to institute proceedings under Part V of the Criminal Justice Act 1993 (insider dealing) or regulations relating to money laundering.[8] The significance of the FSA's role in the fight against money laundering is underlined by the provision in FSMA of a specific power to the FSA to create money laundering rules at section 146.

The UK's Fight Against Money Laundering: The Policy Backdrop

10.12 Although the fight against money laundering has assumed greater prominence since the implementation of FSMA and the establishment of the FSA, anti-money laundering legislation has been in place for some time. The Money Laundering Regulations 1993[9] ('MLR 1993') which covered financial institutions implemented the First Money Laundering Directive ('1MLD'),[10] and came into effect in 1994. The MLR 1993 were developed as Government policy sought to extend the scope of regulation to other activities, such as money services businesses (including bureaux de change). However, the criminal offence of money laundering pre-dates the MLR 1993 (see, for example, the Criminal Justice Act 1988 and the Drug Trafficking Offences Act 1986).

10.13 Increasing concerns that those behind high profile terrorist acts had been heavily involved in money laundering in order to support their activities led to specific

---

    [7] FSMA, s 138.

    [8] ibid, s 402.

    [9] The Money Laundering Regulations 1993 (now repealed and substituted by the Money Laundering Regulations 2007).

    [10] Council Directive (EC) 91/308 on prevention of the use of the financial system for the purpose of money laundering [1991] OJ L166, P 0077–0083. Council Directive of 10 June on prevention of the use of the financial system for the purpose of money laundering (91/308/EEC) [1991] OJ L166, P 0077–0083.

legislation to deal with money laundering in the context of terrorism, (see, in particular, the Terrorism Act 2000 (as amended by the Anti-Terrorism, Crime and Security Act 2001).

International Nature of the Fight against Money Laundering

The international nature of the activities of money launderers has led to action **10.14** against the problem at supra-national level. The European Union ('EU') has implemented various pieces of legislation in an attempt to coordinate anti-money laundering activity within the EU. This legislation is discussed in detail at paras 10.35–10.81.

Concern about money laundering has been on the European policy agenda for **10.15** many years with the 1MLD reaching the European statute books in 1991. The policy background to the perceived need for EU level action on money laundering was restated in the European Commission Communication on Organised Crime and the Financial Sector dated April 2004[11] (the 'Communication on Organised Financial Crime'). The Communication on Organised Financial Crime notes that the fight against money laundering 'has been a top political priority of the European Union for a number of years, based on the need to protect the financial system from contamination and misuse, and to support efforts to combat organised crime in the financial sector'.

European legislators consider that the need to protect the financial system from **10.16** misuse and the desire to avoid Member States employing 'radically different measures' against money laundering, which could prejudice the proper functioning of the internal market, justify action at EU level. The recitals to 1MLD make it clear that one of the key drivers behind the directive was the desire to avoid Member States taking individual measures that could be inconsistent with the completion of a single European market.

The Financial Action Task Force

The international fight against money laundering has not been limited to the **10.17** European stage. In response to growing concerns regarding the development of money laundering, the Financial Action Task Force on Money Laundering[12] ('FATF') was set up by the G-7 summit in Paris in 1989. FATF was established expressly to develop an international response to what had become an international problem.

---

[11] Communication from the Commission to the Council and the European Parliament on the Organised Crime in the Financial Sector COM (2004) 262 Final, Brussels, 16.4.2004.
[12] The FATF website can be accessed at <http://www.fatf-gafi.org>.

10.18   FATF is an inter-governmental body and its members include countries that are home to the world's major financial centres. FATF states its purpose as being 'the development and promotion of policies, both at national and international levels, to combat money laundering and terrorist financing'. It considers itself to be 'a "policy-making body" which works to generate the necessary political will to bring about national legislative and regulatory reforms in these areas'.

10.19   Whilst FATF has been in existence since 1989, it does not have an unlimited life span; rather it reviews its mission every five years. The latest revised mandate for 2008–2012, having been agreed in April 2008, will only continue as long as it is considered by its Member States to have a viable role.

10.20   The founding members of FATF gave it the responsibility of examining money laundering techniques and trends, reviewing the action which had already been taken at a national or international level, and setting out the measures that still needed to be taken to combat money laundering.

10.21   FATF, since its establishment, has focused its work on three main activities:

   (i)   standard setting;
   (ii)   ensuring effective compliance with the standards; and
   (iii)   identifying money laundering and terrorist financing threats.

10.22   These activities remain at the core of the new mandate and FATF will build on this work and respond to new and emerging threats, such as proliferation financing and vulnerabilities in new technologies which could destabilise the international financial system.

10.23   The initial membership of FATF numbered 16 States but this has steadily expanded and as of spring 2008 there were 34 Member States.[13]

The 40 Recommendations

10.24   FATF has developed 40 Recommendations which set out minimum measures that national governments should take to implement effective anti-money laundering programmes. Since their initial drafting, the 40 Recommendations have been updated several times to reflect the evolution of anti-money laundering policies and best practice. The FATF website describes the 40 Recommendations as having been:

> . . . recognised, endorsed or adopted by many international bodies. The Recommendations are neither complex nor difficult, nor do they compromise the freedom to engage in legitimate transactions or threaten economic development. They set out

---

[13]   India and South Korea are 'observer members' and are expected to become members in due course.

the principles for action and allow countries a measure of flexibility in implementing these principles according to their particular circumstances and constitutional frameworks. Though not a binding international convention, many countries in the world have made a political commitment to combat money laundering by implementing the 40 Recommendations.

The 40 Recommendations have a broad scope and are detailed. The full text of the **10.25** 40 Recommendations and the accompanying interpretive notes can be accessed on the FATF website. The original form 40 Recommendations were given force at EU level by 1MLD and have been revised to take account of the changes in money laundering trends and to anticipate future threats. More recently the FATF has completed a thorough review and update of the Recommendations (2003) which continue to be the cornerstone of the current 3MLD.

Terrorist financing

The international community's concern with regard to terrorism has been reflected **10.26** in the development by FATF of nine Special Recommendations on Terrorist Financing. These Special Recommendations were published by FATF on 31 October 2001 and recognised that terrorists were increasingly relying on the international financial system both to fund terrorist activity and to launder funds obtained by terrorist organisations. FATF considers that the combination of the Special Recommendations and the 40 Recommendations has so far provided the right balance between giving the required stability to the FATF standards, whilst allowing for the necessary flexibility to respond to the changing nature of the threats faced. Maintaining this balance between stability and flexibility allows for more predictability and consistent implementation globally.

Identifying and responding to new threats

Globalisation has created potential new risks as criminals and terrorists seek to **10.27** penetrate the global financial system. The FATF intends to remain at the centre of international efforts to protect the integrity of the financial system and will respond to the significant new threats emerging which are related to, but may fall outside its core activities.

Proliferation financing is a current exa mple of an area where the FATF can add **10.28** value to the wider efforts of the international community.

FATF and the UK

The UK has been, and continues to be, an active member of FATF and held **10.29** the Presidency in 2007/8. The Financial Challenge to Crime and Terrorism document[14] emphasises the UK's commitment to FATF, and the Government's desire to continue to play a leading role in the work of FATF.

Non-co-operative countries and territories

10.30 FATF has also identified a number of jurisdictions which it considers have failed to establish and maintain proper anti-money laundering regulation. These jurisdictions are generally referred to as Non-co-operative Countries and Territories ('NCCTs'). The list of NCCTs is updated regularly and can be accessed on the FATF website.

10.31 As well as the activities of FATF, other public international bodies have sought to develop guidelines and principles for national supervisors of financial services firms to follow. Such initiatives include the Basel CDD paper,[15] IAIS Guidance Paper 5,[16] the Egmont Group, and the Wolfsberg Group.[17] IOSCO has also been active in the area of anti-money laundering generally.[18]

Law and Regulation

10.32 Most of the anti-money laundering legislation that impacts on the UK financial services sector finds its basis in EU legislation. To date, most of this legislation has taken the form of directives, although the EU has implemented FATF Special Recommendation 7 (information on the payer accompanying transfers of funds) by means of a European Regulation.[19]

Other Developments Driving EU Legislation

10.33 The Communication on Organised Financial Crime explored the need for future EU level policy initiatives. While some of these take the form of policy initiatives to encourage Member States to develop domestic capacity to combat identified

---

[14] HM Treasury, 'The Financial Challenge to Crime and Terrorism' (February 2007).

[15] Basel Committee on Banking Supervision's report on Customer Due Diligence for Banks issued in October 2001.

[16] Guidance Paper 5 'Anti-money Laundering and Combating the Financing of Terrorism' October 2004 is published by the International Association of Insurance Supervisors and can be accessed at <http://www.iaisweb.org/index.cfm?pageID=41>.

[17] The Wolfsberg Principles—Global Anti-Money Laundering Guidelines for Private Banking, Revised 1 May 2002

[18] See IOSCO website at <http://www.iosco.org/>.

[19] Regulation (EC) No 1781/2006 of the European Parliament and of the Council of 15 November 2006 on information on the payer accompanying transfers of funds.

money laundering risks, experience tends to indicate that such initiatives often lead to EU legislative action.

Some of the policy areas not now covered by the EU money laundering directives are: **10.34**

(a) Database of currency transactions
     The Communication on Organised Financial Crime discussed the feasibility of Member States establishing an electronic database of currency exchange transactions above a certain amount. The database would be available to the police and judicial authorities.

(b) Financial havens
     Consideration is being given to the adoption by the EU of legislation covering on-shore and off-shore financial centres and tax havens operating in Member States and their dependencies and a common EU policy towards financial centres and tax havens lying outside the EU.

(c) Underground banking
     The European Commission is concerned about the operation of underground banking and 'alternative remittance systems', which it considers are frequently used by criminals and terrorists for the international transfer of illegal funds. To combat the risks posed by such arrangements, the European Commission is participating in the establishment of an early warning system to promote information exchange and joint action to disrupt the unlawful international transfer of funds.

(d) Asset recovery bodies
     The Commission proposes the establishment of asset recovery bodies at national level and supports Europol's 'Asset seizure knowledge centre' to facilitate the identification of criminal assets in the course of major criminal investigations conducted by Member States.

(e) FIU-NET project
     This is designed to establish a fully operational computer network linking all Member States' financial intelligence units for the processing and exchange of financial information, including intelligence suspected to be associated with terror financing.

The First and Second Money Laundering Directives

FATF initially identified certain areas, which were vulnerable in the money laundering process and could, if monitored, assist in the fight against the money launderer. These were the entry of cash into the financial system, transfers to and from the financial system, and cross-border payments.   **10.35**

10.36 1MLD, which was based on the 1989 Banking Directive, originally concentrated on combating the laundering of the proceeds of drugs through the traditional financial sector and was published in the Official Journal in June 1991. It set out to ensure that money laundering was prohibited by requiring that financial institutions identify their customers when entering into a business relationship or when carrying out a one-off transaction above a certain value. Peripheral activities such as bureaux de change and money transmission agencies where excluded as well as the bulk of client accounts of lawyers and accountants.

10.37 Other features were the requirement for banks and financial institutions to report suspicious transactions to the authorities and the prohibition on 'tipping off', where a customer is advised that a report has been made. Banks were also required to provide training for their staff and establish internal systems and controls to prevent money laundering.

10.38 The limited scope of 1MLD was soon recognised as a weakness by European legislators and one of the key changes introduced by the Second Money Laundering Directive[20] ('2MLD') was the expansion of the range of criminal offences covered to 'serious crimes'. These included offences which may generate substantial proceeds and which are punishable by 'a severe sentence of imprisonment'.

10.39 2MLD also expanded the scope of persons captured from credit and financial institutions to persons carrying on other activities such as certain types of professional adviser, estate agents, and casinos. Article 6 provided that Member States are required to ensure that credit and financial institutions and their directors and employees 'cooperate fully with the authorities responsible for combating money laundering'. This captured a number of persons not previously subject to regulation and Article 6 was amended in part to reflect some of the consequences of this expansion of scope. For example, Article 6(3) expressly protected legal professional privilege.

10.40 Reporting obligations and the 'tipping off' provision were the subjects of much debate and, due to the differing structures of the professions between Member States, further legislation was required to clarify the position.

10.41 Implementation of 2MLD was uneven due to the accession of new Member States in May of 2004 and the failure of Greece and Italy to meet the June 2003 deadline.

10.42 Identification procedures under the two directives were broadly similar and were implemented in the UK by secondary legislation (originally the MLR 1993 and MLR 2003 and now by the MLR 2007). These requirements are examined below.

---

[20] Directive (EC) 2001/97 of the European Parliament and the Council amending Council Directive (EC) 91/308 on prevention of the use of the financial system for the purpose of money laundering [2001] OJ L344, P 0076–0082.

2MLD introduced an important concession. 1MLD provided that where the **10.43** customer was a credit or financial institution that was itself regulated by the directive there was no need to identify it for anti-money laundering purposes. 2MLD extended this concession to cover credit or financial institutions 'situated in a third country which imposes, in the opinion of the relevant Member [State], equivalent requirements to those laid down by [the directive]'.

The Third Money Laundering Directive

The Third Money Laundering Directive[21] ('3MLD') was adopted on 26 October **10.44** 2005. It reflected the belief among EU legislators that the substantial changes to the FATF 40+9 Recommendations, agreed in June 2003, should be implemented in a coordinated way at EU level and replaced the existing amended directive (ie 1MLD and 2MLD), to help ensure clarity. The directive confirms in Article 5 that it is a so-called 'minimum harmonisation' directive as it expressly permits Member States to implement super-equivalent anti-money laundering provisions.

In its original explanatory memorandum[22] the European Commission set out the **10.45** detailed policy aims of 3MLD and confirmed its view that the scope of the new directive should further widen the scope of anti-money laundering activity. For example, it suggested that the definition of money laundering should include terrorism to reflect the amended FATF 40 Recommendations. The definition of criminal activity was widened although this has no impact in the UK as Government policy has been to make any criminal activity a predicate to a money laundering offence. Other significant changes included the extension of the scope of regulation in 3MLD to capture life/investment insurance intermediaries and trust company service providers.

Customer due diligence

Articles 7 to 19 of 3MLD deal with customer due diligence ('CDD') procedures. **10.46** The provisions contained in these articles are more detailed than those in the previous money laundering directives. The directive introduces the concept of a risk-based approach at EU level for the first time, which, the European Commission notes in its commentary on the directive, reflects the requirement in the FATF 40 + 9 Recommendations.

---

[21] Directive 2005/60/EC of the European Parliament and of the Council dated 26 October 1995 on the prevention of the use of the financial system for the purpose of money laundering and terrorist financing.
[22] Document reference COM (2004) 448 Final 2004/0137 Brussels, 30.06.2004.

10.47   Article 7 of 3MLD requires Member States to ensure that firms complete the due diligence procedures before the establishment of a business relationship or the execution of a transaction. In other words, the directive acknowledges expressly that on occasion it may not be possible for a person falling within the scope of the directive to identify his customer before the relationship has started. The *quid pro quo* for this concession is that, where satisfactory information cannot be obtained, the relationship between the firm and its customer must be terminated.

10.48   Article 8 requires firms to apply due diligence procedures not only to new customers, but 'conducting ongoing monitoring of the business relationship including scrutiny of transactions undertaken throughout the course of that relationship'. This policy approach is familiar to UK firms subject to FSA regulation, as it is broadly similar to the UK regulator's 'monitoring customer activity' initiative.

Beneficial owner

10.49   Article 3(6) of 3MLD introduces a definition of 'beneficial owner'. This definition is far more detailed than anything that has been seen in previous money laundering directives and captures a 'natural person who ultimately owns or controls a legal entity through direct or indirect ownership or control over a sufficient percentage of shares or voting rights in that legal entity'. A percentage of 25 per cent plus one share is deemed sufficient to meet this criterion. Beneficial ownership is relevant not just for natural persons, but also for legal entities, trusts, and unincorporated associations. In each case the persons controlling the accounts need to be identified.

10.50   Where a legal entity is a holding company for the assets of another, it is important to know the beneficial owner of the assets and where the money came from to purchase them.

10.51   In the case of trusts, the situation is slightly different as the beneficial owner will probably be the person in whose favour the trust was created and it is the settlor that would need to be identified.

10.52   The approach of both the MLR 2007 and the FSA has been that, where an applicant for business/customer appears to be acting on behalf of another person, the firm should take reasonable steps to identify that other person as well. The Joint Money Laundering Steering Group Guidance Notes[23] ('JMLSG Guidance') stress that firms need to look behind an applicant for business/customer, especially if it is a corporate. However, the JMLSG Guidance suggests that generally identification evidence will only need to be obtained from shareholders that have an interest of 25 per cent.

---

[23] Joint Money Laundering Steering Group revised Guidance Notes 2007. Please see section on Joint Money Laundering Steering Group guidance notes at 10.240.

Simplified due diligence

The UK successfully argued the case that 3MLD should allow firms to reduce **10.53** customer due diligence checks in certain circumstances and also to rely on a third party for undertaking the customer due diligence measures. Article 11 allows institutions covered by the directive not to apply customer due diligence where the risk of money laundering is low.

The examples provided by Article 11 are where a firm deals with: credit or finan- **10.54** cial institutions from Member States; third countries that are subject to similar regulatory requirements; listed companies; beneficial owners of pooled accounts held by notaries and other independent legal professionals from the Member States or third countries subject to supervision of international requirements; and where the product offered has a low risk profile (such as life assurance with an annual premium of €1,000).

It is however still necessary to conduct ongoing monitoring of the business rela- **10.55** tionship and the relaxation of the identification requirement is not applicable where it is suspected that a transaction involves terrorism or money laundering.

Enhanced due diligence

In contrast to Article 11, Article 13 of 3MLD requires Member States to ensure **10.56** that firms carry out enhanced due diligence in situations where the risk of money laundering is perceived to be higher. Article 13 provides a non-exhaustive list of three such higher risk propositions: distance contracts; cross-frontier correspond-ent banking relationships; and where a firm is dealing with a politically exposed person ('PEP').

Article 13(6) of the directive requires Member States to ensure that persons cov- **10.57** ered by the directive:

> . . . pay special attention to any money laundering or terrorist financing threat that may arise from products or transactions that might favour anonymity, and take measures, if needed, to prevent their use in money laundering or terrorist financing purposes.

The European Commission has the power (in Article 40(1)(c)) to establish **10.58** detailed rules for identifying situations which represent a high risk of money laun-dering, assisted by the Committee on the Prevention of Money Laundering.

The risk-based provisions in Article 13 are broadly consistent with the UK policy **10.59** approach. The Treasury noted in its Consultation Document[24] that the UK already had provisions in the MLR 2003 that required firms to take account of the

---

[24] HM Treasury, Informal consultation on the Third EC Money Laundering Directive (May 2004).

higher risk of money laundering, however the risk-based approach established by the 3MLD includes examples of instances that are considered high risk. Further guidance on the risk-based approach can be found in the FATF Guidance on the Risk-Based Approach to Combating Money Laundering and Terrorist Financing[25] and the JMLSG Guidance.

Politically exposed persons

10.60 3MLD sets out the enhanced due diligence that is required when entering into transactions or business relationships with a PEP residing in another Member State or in a third country. Institutions and persons covered by the directive should:

(a) have appropriate risk-based procedures to determine whether the customer is a PEP;

(b) have senior management approval for establishing business relationships with such customers;

(c) take adequate measures to establish the source of wealth and source of funds that are involved in the business relationship or transaction;

(d) conduct enhanced ongoing monitoring of the business relationship.

10.61 Article 3(8) of the directive defines a PEP as:

> a natural person who is or has been entrusted with prominent public functions and immediate family members or persons known to be close associates of such persons.

10.62 The term is very general and is open to interpretation. The Swiss Federal Banking Commission defines a PEP as 'persons occupying an important public function' whilst the US inter-agency guidance defines these as a 'senior foreign political figure'.

10.63 Schedule 2(4) to the MLR 2007 sets out the examples of a PEP used in the UK, which are very wide and include members of supreme courts, or high-level judicial bodies, members of the board of central banks and members of supervisory bodies of state-owned enterprises. Generally, a PEP is a person whose current or former position can attract publicity beyond the borders of the country concerned and whose financial circumstances may be the subject of additional public interest.[26]

10.64 In the UK the objectives for identifying and performing enhanced due diligence were set out in a Treasury consultation document[27] which included to help and

---

[25] High-Level Principles and procedures (June 2007).
[26] Wolfsberg group FAQ 2007: 'How to define 'Politically Exposed Persons'.
[27] HM Treasury, 'Implementing the Third Money Laundering Directive' (January 2007).

protect national economies and to prevent the misappropriation of UK and international aid.

JMLSG Guidance[28] recommends that firms have appropriate risk-based proce- **10.65** dures for establishing whether a customer is a PEP and obtain appropriate senior management approval for establishing and maintaining business relationships with such customers. Reasonable measures should be taken to establish the source of funds and enhanced ongoing monitoring of the relationship should be conducted. It is also seen as important that specific training is given to staff in this area.

Performance by third parties

Article 14 of 3MLD provides that persons covered by the directive may rely on **10.66** third parties to perform the due diligence requirements in Article 8. However, this provision makes it clear that ultimate responsibility for the proper completion of the due diligence requirements of Article 8 rests with the person covered by the directive. In other words, it is possible to delegate the task of due diligence but not the legal responsibility. Article 15 provides that where a Member State permits that certain persons can be relied on in their own jurisdictions, they must also permit reliance on similar persons located in other Member States, with the exception of currency exchange offices and money transmission or remittance offices.

Article 15(1) and (2) taken together have the effect of permitting reliance on 'third **10.67** parties' located in countries outside the EU where anti-money laundering requirements meet certain specified criteria. Articles 16 and 18 list the requirements that must be met for reliance on the third party due diligence and provide that information requested by the third party in accordance with the Article 8 due diligence procedures, should be made available to the person to which the customer is being referred.

Article 19 provides that Articles 14 to 18 (inclusive) do not apply to an outsourc- **10.68** ing or agency relationship, where the effect of the arrangements between the outsourced service provider or agent and the principal are such that they are, in effect, to be regarded as part of the principal.

Reporting obligations

Section 1 of Chapter III of 3MLD covers reporting obligations. These provisions **10.69** have had little effect on the UK anti-money laundering regime, as the UK already has a financial intelligence unit ('FIU') established in the form of the Serious

---

[28] JMLSG Guidance, s 5.5.26–5.5.29.

Organised Crime Agency ('SOCA') (previously National Criminal Intelligence Service ('NCIS')). However, there has been much litigation in this area in the UK which is discussed further at paras 10.137–10.141. The MLR 2003 allowed professional legal advisers to be excused from reporting obligations if the information came to him in privileged circumstances. This was later extended to cover other relevant professional advisers.[29]

10.70 Article 23 allows regulated persons to designate their regulatory body as the first instance for reporting suspicious transactions and the regulatory body shall be responsible for forwarding the information to the FIU promptly and unfiltered.

10.71 Article 23 provides an exemption to the reporting requirements when notaries, independent legal professionals, auditors, external accountants, and tax advisors receive information in privileged circumstances.

10.72 Article 24 of 3MLD provides that persons covered by the directive should not carry out a transaction where they know or suspect that the transaction is related to money laundering. However, the second paragraph of Article 24 provides:

> where such a transaction is suspected of giving rise to money laundering or terrorist financing and where to refrain in such manner is impossible or is likely to frustrate efforts to pursue the beneficiaries of a suspected money laundering or terrorist financing operation, the institutions and persons concerned shall apprise the FIU immediately afterwards.

10.73 This provision can be contrasted with the defences in sections 327–329 POCA, which permits a person to continue with a transaction if he has 'appropriate consent' within the meaning of section 335 of POCA. As noted above, 3MLD is a minimum standards directive, and as long as it does not breach the principles of EU law, the UK Government can retain the current super-equivalent provisions of section 335 of POCA.

10.74 Section 2 of Chapter III of 3MLD covers the prohibition of disclosure of information. Article 28 creates a 'tipping off' provision, which has had little impact on financial services firms.

Record keeping

10.75 Chapter IV of 3MLD covers record keeping and statistical data. The basic requirement to keep records for five years does not differ from the previous directives. However, there are certain points to note. Article 31 of 3MLD obliges firms to instigate customer due diligence record keeping procedures in branches and

---

[29] By ss 2 and 3 of the Proceeds of Crime Act 2002 and Money Laundering Regulations 2003 (Amendment) Order 2006.

majority owned subsidiaries located in third countries that are 'at least equivalent to those set out in this directive'. In practice, many UK institutions previously employed this approach as a matter of good practice but it has had an impact on some firms. Moreover, if local laws prevent the firm applying the relevant EU standards, there is an obligation on firms to report this fact to the regulatory body in their home Member State.

There is also a requirement, in Article 32, that credit and financial institutions **10.76** put in place systems to enable them to cooperate with the national FIU and other authorities as to whether they maintain or have maintained a business relationship with a specified natural or legal person within the previous five years and details of that relationship.

Article 33 places an obligation on Member States to assess the effectiveness of **10.77** systems to combat money laundering and terrorist financing by producing a report containing the following statistics:

(a) the number of suspicious transaction reports made to its FIU;
(b) the number of cases investigated;
(c) the number of persons prosecuted for money laundering or terrorist financing offences; and
(d) value of assets frozen, seized, or confiscated.

Enforcement and implementing measures

Articles 34 to 39 (inclusive) of 3MLD cover matters such as firms' internal proce- **10.78** dures, training, and enforcement.

Article 34 requires that institutions and persons covered by 3MLD should estab- **10.79** lish policies and procedures of customer due diligence, reporting, internal control, risk assessment, risk management, compliance management, and communication. This built in the extra policies and procedures to cover the new risk-based approach to money laundering and terrorist financing and also meant that those covered by 3MLD have had to set up procedures to monitor their customers and transactions to maintain the required level of management information.

Article 40 of 3MLD provides the European Commission with a new power to **10.80** 'ensure uniform implementation of [the] directive'. Using the procedure provided by Article 38(2) the European Commission may adopt measures for the:

(a) clarification of the technical aspects of the definitions in Article (3)(2)(a) and (d), (6), (7), (8), (9), and (10);
(b) establishment of technical criteria for assessing whether situations represent a low risk of money laundering or terrorist financing as referred to in Article 11(2) and (5);

(c) establishment of technical criteria for assessing whether situations represent a high risk of money laundering or terrorist financing as referred to in Article 13;

(d) establishment of technical criteria for assessing whether, in accordance with Article 2(2), it is justified not to apply this directive to certain legal or natural persons carrying out financial activity on an occasional or very limited basis.

10.81 Although the directive is intended to be implemented uniformly throughout the EU, it is only at a high level that this uniformity can be achieved as each Member State will have its own FIU and detailed guidance on implementation. In fact, in June 2008 the Commission decided to take action against 15 Member States for failure to implement 3MLD into national law.

The European Regulation on FATF Special Recommendation 7

10.82 FATF Special Recommendation 7 provides:

> Countries should take measures to require financial institutions, including money remitters, to include accurate and meaningful originator information (name, address and account number) on funds transfers and related messages that are sent, and the information should remain with the transfer or related message through the payment chain. Countries should take measures to ensure that financial institutions, including money remitters, conduct enhanced scrutiny of and monitor for suspicious activity funds transfers which do not contain complete originator information (name, address and account number).

10.83 FATF countries agreed to implement Special Recommendation 7 by December 2006. This was implemented in Europe by Regulation EC 1781/2006 on 15 November 2006, which laid down rules on payer information accompanying transfers of funds. The Regulation applies to transfers of funds in any currency, which are sent or received by a payment service provider in a Member State.

10.84 There are some exclusions, payments made by credit or debit card for instance where the transaction has a unique identifier and can be traced back to the payer, payments made by mobile phone or any other digital or IT device, where funds are withdrawn from the payer's own account, or payments to public authorities for taxes, fines, or other levies.

10.85 Information on the payer is required, consisting of his name, address, and account number; where the payer does not have an account number the payment service provider must substitute a unique payment identifier to allow the payment to be traced back to the payer.

10.86 As with the MLR 2007 records of information on the payer must be kept for five years.

In the UK the Regulation was implemented by The Transfer of Funds (Information **10.87** on the Payer) Regulations 2007[30] and the offences are listed as failure to comply with the various articles of the EU Payments Regulation.

UK Legislation

Proceeds of Crime Act 2002

The Proceeds of Crime Act 2002 ('POCA') replaces previous UK anti-money **10.88** laundering legislation.

Section 1 of POCA established the Assets Recovery Agency ('ARA') which became **10.89** operational in February 2003 and with effect from 1 April 2008 was merged with SOCA.[31] POCA provides the SOCA with wide powers to investigate and recover assets. It provides five investigative tools for law enforcement agencies, all of these powers have the potential to be significant for financial services firms.

The powers are: **10.90**

- Production Order under section 345;
- Search and Seizure Warrant under section 352;
- Disclosure Warrant under section 357;
- Customer Information Order under section 363; and
- Account Monitoring Order under section 370.

Part 7 of POCA covers money laundering and makes it a criminal offence to: **10.91**

(a) (Section 327) conceal, disguise, convert, transfer or remove criminal property from the UK;
(b) (Section 328) enter into or become concerned in an arrangement which [a person] knows or suspects facilitates the acquisition, retention, use or control of criminal property by or on behalf of another person; or
(c) (Section 329) acquire, use or have possession of criminal property.

Section 340(11) of POCA extends the offence of money laundering to include **10.92** acts which constitute an attempt, conspiracy, or incitement to conceal, enter into or acquire as well as acts that constitute aiding, abetting, counselling, or procuring the commission of such activity. POCA also makes it an offence to do such an act outside the UK.

---

[30] SI 2007/3298 effective 15 December 2007
[31] Serious Crime Act 2007, s 74.

Criminal property/criminal conduct

10.93   The potential impact of these offences is wide as a consequence of the definition of criminal property and its relationship with the definition of criminal conduct.[32]

10.94   Property is criminal property if it:

- constitutes a person's benefit in whole or in part (including pecuniary and proprietary benefit) from criminal conduct; or
- represents such a benefit directly or indirectly, in whole or in part; and
- the alleged offender knows or suspects that it constitutes or represents such a benefit.

10.95   Criminal property[33] includes, but is not limited to:

- the proceeds of tax evasion;
- a benefit obtained through bribery and corruption (including both the receipt of a bribe and the income received from a contract obtained through bribery or the promise of a bribe);
- benefits obtained, or income received, through the operation of a criminal cartel; and
- benefits (in the form of saved costs) arising from a failure to comply with a regulatory requirement, where that failure is a criminal offence.

10.96   The original definition of criminal conduct in POCA was very wide. Conduct fell within the definition if it constituted an offence in any part of the United Kingdom or would have constituted an offence in any part of the United Kingdom if it had occurred there. In the much cited Spanish bull fighter example, it was suggested that a UK bank accepting a deposit from a Spanish citizen from his legitimate earnings (in Spain) as a bull fighter would be committing the offence of money laundering since bull fighting is illegal in the UK.

10.97   The scope of this definition was heavily criticised and despite initial scepticism the Government was persuaded to amend the principal money laundering offences in sections 327–329 of POCA and the offences of failure to disclose under sections 330–332 by section 102 of the Serious Organised Crime and Police Act 2005 ('SOCPA').

10.98   Section 102 of SOCPA introduces a new defence, which is available where:

(a) it is known or believed on reasonable grounds that the conduct occurred outside the UK;

(b) the conduct was not criminal in the country where it took place; and

(c) it is not of a description prescribed by the Secretary of State by Order.

---

[32] POCA, s 340(3).
[33] ibid, s 340(3).

It is of no consequence who carried out the conduct, who benefited from it or when the conduct occurred. POCA considers a person to have benefited from the conduct if he obtains property as a result of, or in connection with, the conduct concerned.

10.99

The UK definition of criminal conduct is wider than that set out in Article 3(4) of 3MLD which includes any kind of criminal involvement in the commission of a serious crime. Section 340(2) of POCA defines conduct as 'that which would have been an offence in any part of the UK', and has not been limited to serious offences but is applied to all crimes. Article 5 of 3MLD allows Member States to adopt or retain super-equivalent provisions to prevent money laundering and terrorist financing. In this area the UK legislation is said to be 'gold-plated' as it extends beyond the requirements of 3MLD.

10.100

The 'all crimes' approach allows UK money laundering legislation to be more flexible and dynamic and the initial crime is often referred to as the 'predicate offence'.

10.101

Reporting as a defence to a money laundering offence

Sections 327 (concealing etc), 328 (arrangements), and 329 (acquisition, use, and possession) of POCA provide that a person does not commit an offence if he makes a section 338 'authorised disclosure', had intended to make such a disclosure but had a reasonable excuse for not doing so, or the act concerned was done in relation to a function relating to the enforcement of relevant criminal law.

10.102

Section 338 of POCA provides that a disclosure is authorised if it is made to a constable, a customs officer, or to a person nominated by a person's employer to receive such disclosures. In the case of most financial services firms, the person so nominated will be the firm's money laundering reporting officer ('MLRO'). This section is subject to two conditions, one of which must be satisfied. The first condition is that the disclosure must be made prior to the person carrying out the act (ie concealing, entering into, acquiring etc). The second condition is that the disclosure was made after the act, but there is a good reason for failing to make disclosure prior to the act and the disclosure, when made, was made at the initiative of the person disclosing and as soon as it was practicable for him to make it.

10.103

Where a disclosure has been made a person may still commit a money laundering offence unless he has received 'appropriate consent'. Section 335 defines appropriate consent as:

10.104

(a) the consent of a nominated officer;
(b) the consent of a constable; or
(c) the consent of a customs officer.

10.105   A person will be treated as having been given appropriate consent if he has made an authorised disclosure and seven working days have elapsed and he has not received notice from a constable or customs officer that consent has been refused.

10.106   Where consent has been refused before the period of seven working days has elapsed, a person is treated as having received appropriate consent where a 31-day moratorium period has elapsed starting from the day on which the person received the refusal.

The regulated sector

10.107   Section 330 of POCA provides a separate offence of failure to disclose by a person in the regulated sector.

10.108   A person commits the offence of failure to disclose (sections 330–332) if three conditions are satisfied:

    (i)   if a person knows or suspects, or has reasonable grounds to know or suspect, that another is engaged in money laundering;

    (ii) if the information came to him in the course of business in the regulated sector; and

    (iii) if he does not make disclosure as soon as is practicable after the information came to him.

10.109   In deciding whether an offence has been committed, a court is required to consider any guidance issued by a supervisory authority or other body which has been approved by HM Treasury. The most recent version of the JMLSG Guidance was approved by HM Treasury on 18 December 2007.

10.110   Section 331 of POCA provides a separate offence of failure to report by a nominated officer in the regulated sector. This offence is subject to conditions that are similar to those that apply in section 330.

10.111   Part 1 of Schedule 9 to POCA (as amended[34]) sets out the scope of the regulated sector. Not all activities regulated by the FSA are captured by POCA (or the MLR 2007).

10.112   The activities which are caught are:

    (a) accepting deposits;

    (b) effecting or carrying out contracts of long-term insurance when carried on by a person who has received official authorisation pursuant to Article 4 or 51 of the Life Assurance Consolidation Directive;

    (c) dealing in investments as principal or as agent;

---

[34] The Proceeds of Crime Act 2002 (Business in the Regulated Sector and Supervisory Authorities) Order 2003 which came into force on 1 March 2004 aligns the definition of 'regulated sector' with that of 'relevant business' in the 2003 Regulations.

(d) arranging deals in investments;
(e) managing investments;
(f) safeguarding and administering investments;
(g) sending dematerialised instructions;
(h) establishing (and taking other steps in relation to) collective investment schemes;
(i) advising on investments; and
(j) issuing electronic money.

A business is not in the regulated sector to the extent that it engages in any of the following activities: **10.113**

(a) the issue of withdrawable share capital within the limit set by section 6 of the Industrial and Provident Societies Act 1965 (c 12) by a society registered under that Act;
(b) the acceptance of deposits from the public within the limit set by section 7(3) of that Act by such a society;
(c) the issue of withdrawable share capital within the limit set by section 6 of the Industrial and Provident Societies Act (Northern Ireland) 1969 (c 24 (NI)) by a society registered under that Act;
(d) the acceptance of deposits from the public within the limit set by section 7(3) of that Act by such a society;
(e) activities carried on by the Bank of England;
(f) any activity in respect of which an exemption order under section 38 of the Financial Services and Markets Act 2000 (c 8) has effect if it is carried on by a person who is for the time being specified in the order or falls within a class of persons so specified;
(g) the regulated activities of arranging deals in investments or advising on investments, in so far as the investment consists of rights under a regulated mortgage contract; or
(h) the regulated activities of dealing in investments as agent, arranging deals in investments, managing investments or advising on investments, in so far as the investment consists of rights under, or any right to or interest in, a contract of insurance which is not a qualifying contract of insurance.

The most notable absentee from the list of activities regulated by the FSA is general insurance. As yet this activity is not subject to specific financial services focused anti-money laundering legislation although a person active in the general insurance activities will of course be subject to the general criminal law provisions of POCA. **10.114**

Objective test

Both sections 330 and 331 of POCA apply an objective test of reasonable suspicion. This is in contrast to offences under section 328 (arrangements) which apply a subjective test. The implications for financial services staff and MLROs in the regulated sector are significant, as it means that they will be judged according to **10.115** the standard of the reasonable person carrying on their particular task. For MLROs in particular, this is likely to be quite a high standard.

Reporting by firms

10.116 Firms should make their money laundering disclosures to the SOCA. SOCA has published guidance notes on the practical aspects of making a disclosure in accordance with the requirements of POCA.[35]

Where consent is urgently needed

10.117 SOCA also operates a fast track reporting procedure where firms need appropriate consent to complete a transaction at short notice. This procedure generally requires a firm to complete a disclosure using the SAR Online[36] facility or where the firm has no access to these online facilities a fax can be used to submit a disclosure report to SOCA indicating that it requires it to be treated as a first track enquiry. Anecdotal evidence suggests that the procedure has functioned reasonably well to date.

Tipping off

10.118 Section 333A of POCA provides that a person commits an offence if:

- he discloses that he or another person has made a disclosure under Part 7—Money Laundering of information that came to him in the course of business in the regulated sector; and
- the disclosure is likely to prejudice an investigation that might be conducted following the disclosure;

or

- the person discloses that an investigation into allegations that an offence under Part 7 is being contemplated or carried out; and
- the disclosure is likely to prejudice that investigation; and
- the information on which the disclosure is based came to the person in the course of a business in the regulated sector.

10.119 A person convicted of an offence under this section can be subject to a fine or imprisonment of up to two years or both.

10.120 Defences to this offence can be found in sections 333B, 333C, and 333D[37] and allow disclosures to be made within an undertaking or group, between certain institutions, or in certain other situations where disclosures are permitted.

---

[35] The SOCA website can be accessed at <http://www.soca.gov.uk/>.
[36] <https://www.ukciu.gov.uk/saronline.aspx>.
[37] These new sections have been added by the Terrorism Act 2000 and Proceeds of Crime Act 2002 (Amendment) Regulations 2007.

Section 333B allows for disclosures within an undertaking or group and an **10.121**
offence is not committed if:

(a) an employee, officer or partner of an undertaking makes a disclosure to
    another employee, officer or partner of the same undertaking.
(b) a person makes a disclosure in respect of a credit or financial institution if:
    • the disclosure is to a credit or financial institution,
    • the institution to whom the disclosure is made is situated in the EEA State
      or in a country or territory imposing equivalent money laundering req-
      uirements, and
    • both the institution making the disclosure and the institution to whom it
      is made belong to the same group.
(c) A professional legal adviser or a relevant professional adviser makes a disclo-
    sure to another professional legal adviser or a relevant professional adviser
    and both parties carry on business in an EEA State or country or territory
    imposing equivalent money laundering requirements, and those persons
    perform their professional activities within different undertakings that share
    common ownership, management or control.

Section 333D allows disclosures between institutions, for example between credit **10.122**
institutions, financial institutions, professional legal advisers, and other relevant
professional advisers. An offence is not committed if the disclosure relates to:

• a client or former client of the institution or adviser making the disclosure
  and the institution or adviser to whom it is made;
• a transaction involving them both; or
• the provision of a service involving them both; or
• the purpose only of preventing an offence under Part 7 of POCA, the institution to whom the disclosure is made is situated in an EEA State or country or
  territory imposing equivalent money laundering requirements and the institutions or advisers are subject to equivalent duties of professional confidentiality
  and the protection of personal data.

Section 333D sets out other situations where a person does not commit an offence **10.123**
under section 333A if the disclosure is to a supervisory authority by virtue of the
MLR 2007 or for the purpose of detection, investigation, or prosecution
of a criminal offence or an investigation or enforcement of a court order under
POCA.

A professional legal adviser or other relevant professional adviser does not commit **10.124**
an offence if the disclosure is to the adviser's client and is made for the purposes
of dissuading the client from engaging in conduct amounting to an offence.

A person will also not commit an offence if he does not know or suspect that the **10.125**
disclosure is likely to have the effect of prejudicing an investigation.

Protected disclosures

10.126 Section 337 of POCA provides that disclosures made under POCA do not amount to a breach of any restriction on the disclosure of information, subject to three conditions being met:

(a) the information or matter being disclosed must have come to the person in the course of his trade, profession, business or employment;

(b) the information must either have caused the discloser to know or suspect, or to have reasonable grounds for knowing or suspecting, that another person is engaged in money laundering; and

(c) the disclosure must have been made to a constable, a customs officer or a nominated officer as soon as is practicable after the information or matter came to the discloser.

Penalties for breach of POCA

10.127 The maximum penalty for an offence of money laundering under POCA is 14 years' imprisonment and/or an unlimited fine. The maximum penalty for a person in the regulated sector who fails to make the required money laundering report, who commits a 'tipping off' offence, or who destroys or disposes of relevant documents is five years and/or an unlimited fine.

The Terrorism Act 2000 ('TA') (as amended by the Anti-terrorism, Crime and Security Act 2001)

10.128 Property, including money, is considered to be terrorist property[38] if it is likely to be used for the purposes of terrorism, or if it is the proceeds (directly or indirectly, wholly or partly) of the commission of an act of terrorism or of acts carried out for the purposes of terrorism. The important point to note is that whereas under PoCA only illegitimate funds (ie the proceeds of crime) are at issue it is quite possible for money which falls within the definition of terrorist property to have been obtained legitimately. For example, when an individual makes a payment

---

[38] Section 14(1) of the TA defines terrorist property as:

(a) money or other property which is likely to be used for the purposes of terrorism (including any resources of a proscribed organisation),

(b) proceeds of the commission of acts of terrorism, and

(c) proceeds of acts carried out for the purposes of terrorism.

(2) In subsection (1):

(a) a reference to proceeds of an act includes a reference to any property which wholly or partly, and directly or indirectly, represents the proceeds of the act (including payments or other rewards in connection with its commission), and

(b) the reference to an organisation's resources includes a reference to any money or other property which is applied or made available, or is to be applied or made available, for the use of the organisation.

from his salary to another who uses it for the purposes of terrorism that payment becomes terrorist property.

Section 15 of the TA outlaws fund-raising for the purposes of terrorism. Section 15(2) **10.129**
provides that a person commits an offence if 'he receives money or other property and intends that it should be used, or has reasonable cause to suspect that it may be used, for the purposes of terrorism'.

Section 16 provides that a person commits an offence if he uses money or other **10.130**
property for the purposes of terrorism. A person commits an offence if he possesses money or other property and intends that it should be used, or has reasonable cause to suspect that it may be used, for the purposes of terrorism.

Section 17 of the TA provides that an offence is committed if a person enters into or **10.131**
becomes concerned in an arrangement as a result of which money or other property is made available or is to be made available to another and he knows or has reasonable cause to suspect that it will or may be used for the purposes of terrorism.

Section 18 of the TA provides that a person is engaged in money laundering if **10.132**
he enters into or becomes concerned in an arrangement which facilitates the retention or control by, or on behalf of, another person of terrorist property by: concealment; removal from the jurisdiction; transfer to nominees; or in any other way. A person charged under section 18 has a defence if he can prove that he did not know and had no reasonable cause to suspect that the arrangement relates to terrorist property.

The TA contains similar reporting obligations as POCA. The Anti-terrorism, Crime **10.133**
and Security Act 2001 introduced a new section 21A of the TA whereby a person commits a criminal offence if he does not report the existence of criminal property where there are reasonable grounds for knowing or suspecting its existence.

Changes to POCA introduced by SOCPA

As mentioned above SOCPA introduced a defence to the principal money laun- **10.134**
dering offences where overseas conduct is legal under local law.

From 1 July 2005 SOCPA also implemented a *de minimis* threshold for deposit- **10.135**
takers. The secondary legislation[39] implementing these changes created a new section 339A in POCA, which sets the threshold amount at £250.

Section 104 of SOCPA amends the failure to disclose provisions in sections 330–332 **10.136**
of POCA, by inserting an additional condition that needs to be satisfied if the offences in those sections are to be committed. Under the amendment there is no

---

[39] Serious Organised Crime and Police Act 2005 (Commencement No 1, Transitional and Transitory Provisions) Order 2005.

need to report to SOCA where the identity of the culprit or the whereabouts of the property are unknown and there is no information that could assist in identifying the person or where the property is.

Case law and POCA

10.137 So far there has only been one significant judgment on the meaning of POCA. However there were a number under the previous legislation.[40] *Bowman v Fels*[41] reached the Court of Appeal as a result of county court litigation between two former cohabitees. As a result of information received by them prior to the county court hearing solicitors to one of the parties involved made an authorised disclosure (see section 338, POCA) to NCIS in accordance with the requirements of POCA. The reporting solicitors sought to adjourn the hearing as they considered that they were unlikely to receive appropriate consent from NCIS.

10.138 In a judgment given by Brooke LJ, the Court of Appeal held that the proper interpretation of section 328 of POCA was that it was not intended to cover or affect the ordinary conduct of litigation by legal professionals, which included any step taken by them in litigation from the issue of proceedings and the securing of injunctive relief or a freezing order up to its final disposal by judgment. Neither the European nor the UK legislature could have envisaged that any of these ordinary activities could fall within the scope of section 328. Such legal duties could not be considered to result in a person 'becoming concerned in an arrangement which . . . facilitates the acquisition, retention, use or control of criminal property'.[42]

10.139 Legal proceedings are a State-provided mechanism for the resolution of issues in accordance with the law. Every person has the right to a fair and public trial in the determination of his civil rights and duties, which was secured by Article 6 of the Convention for the Protection of Human Rights and Fundamental Freedoms. Parliament could not have intended that proceedings or steps taken by legal advisers with a view to determining or securing legal rights and remedies for their clients should involve them in the type of 'arrangements' envisaged by section 328 of POCA.

10.140 Under the Proceeds of Crime Act 2002 and the Money Laundering Regulations (Amendment) Order 2006[43] the defence for failure to disclose offences under section 330 POCA available to professional legal advisors was widened to include

---

[40] Namely the Criminal Justice Act 1988, s 93D cases which included *Bank of Scotland v A Ltd* [2001] EWCA Civ 52 and *P v P (Ancillary Relief: Proceeds of Crime)* [2003] EWHC 2260 (Fam).

[41] ibid, *Bowman v Fels* [2005] EWCA Civ 226 (CA).

[42] ibid, [100].

[43] SI 308/2006.

'relevant professional advisors' where information or other matters came to them in privileged circumstances.

Whilst in strict terms *Bowman v Fels* is primarily relevant to the legal profession[44] the case may have some application to financial services firms that are involved in court action where there are grounds to know or suspect (or reasonably suspect) that a party is involved in money laundering. **10.141**

The Money Laundering Regulations 2003

The MLR 2003[45] consolidated and expanded on existing anti-money laundering secondary legislation[46] and came into force on 1 April 2004. The MLR 2003 were the primary legislative tool for the UK's implementation of 1MLD and 2MLD. The activities captured by the MLR 2003 were wider than those originally caught by the MLR 1993 and reflected the increased scope of 2MLD. **10.142**

The aim of the MLR 2003 was to ensure that all relevant businesses had systems and procedures in place to identify and prevent money laundering, which was achieved by the recognition and reporting of suspicious transactions and the facilitation of the tracing of the proceeds of money laundering activities. Failure to comply was a criminal offence and prosecutions could be made by the Crown Prosecution Service or, where appropriate, the FSA. **10.143**

All persons carrying on a 'relevant business' were required to have appropriate measures in place to forestall and prevent money laundering. Specifically these procedures were to cover staff training, client identification, record keeping, and internal reporting. **10.144**

The Money Laundering Regulations 2007

The Money Laundering Regulations 2007 ('MLR 2007') were introduced on 15 December 2007 to implement 3MLD and replaced the MLR 2003 which were revoked. **10.145**

Application of the MLR 2007

Regulation 3 sets out those persons captured by the MLR 2007; these are referred to throughout the MLR 2007 as 'relevant persons'. **10.146**

---

[44] The significance of which is underlined by the fact that both the Law Society and the Bar Council intervened in the case.

[45] The Money Laundering Regulations 2003, SI 2003/3075.

[46] In particular the Money Laundering Regulations 1993.

10.147   Financial services that fall within the definition of relevant persons are the same in scope as those captured by POCA[47] and include the activities in the Annex to the Consolidated Banking Directive.[48]

---

[47] Regulation 3 provides that 'relevant persons' means:
   (a) credit institutions;
   (b) financial institutions;
   (c) auditors, insolvency practitioners, external accountants and tax advisers;
   (d) independent legal professionals;
   (e) trust or company service providers;
   (f) estate agents;
   (g) high value dealers;
   (h) casinos.
Where a 'credit institution' means;
   (a) a credit institution as defined in Article 4(1)(a) of the banking consolidation directive; or
   (b) a branch (within the meaning of Article 4(3) of that directive) located in an EEA state of an institution falling within sub-paragraph (a) (or an equivalent institution whose head office is located in a non-EEA state) wherever its head office is located,
when it accepts deposits or other repayable funds from the public or grants credits for its own account (within the meaning of the banking consolidation directive).
And a 'financial institution' means:
   (a) an undertaking, including a money service business, when it carries out one or more of the activities listed in points 2 to 12 and 14 of Annex 1 to the banking consolidation directive (the relevant text of which is set out in Schedule 1 to these Regulations), other than—
      (i) a credit institution;
      (ii) an undertaking whose only listed activity is trading for own account in one or more of the products listed in point 7 of Annex 1 to the banking consolidation directive where the undertaking does not have a customer,
and, for this purpose, 'customer' means a third party which is not a member of the same group as the undertaking;
   (b) an insurance company duly authorised in accordance with the life assurance consolidation directive, when it carries out activities covered by that directive;
   (c) a person whose regular occupation or business is the provision to other persons of an investment service or the performance of an investment activity on a professional basis, when providing or performing investment services or activities (within the meaning of the markets in financial instruments directive, other than a person falling within Article 2 of that directive;
   (d) a collective investment undertaking, when marketing or otherwise offering its units or shares;
   (e) an insurance intermediary as defined in Article 2(5) of Directive 2002/92/EC of the European Parliament and of the Council of 9th December 2002 on insurance mediation, with the exception of a tied insurance intermediary as mentioned in Article 2(7) of that Directive, when it acts in respect of contracts of long-term insurance within the meaning given by article 3(1) of, and Part II of Schedule 1 to, the Financial Services and Markets Act 2000 (Regulated Activities) Order 2001;
   (f) a branch located in an EEA state of a person referred to in sub-paragraphs (a) to (e) (or an equivalent person whose head office is located in a non-EEA state), wherever its head office is located, when carrying out any activity mentioned in sub-paragraphs (a) to (e);
   (g) the National Savings Bank;
   (h) the Director of Savings, when money is raised under the auspices of the Director under the National Loans Act 1968.

[48] Listed in Schedule 1, MLR 2007 and include:
   2. Lending including, inter alia: consumer credit, mortgage credit, factoring, with or without recourse, financing of commercial transactions (including forfeiting).
   3. Financial leasing.
   4. Money transmission services.
   5. Issuing and administering means of payment (eg credit cards, travellers' cheques and bankers' drafts).

Criminal offence

A person who is found guilty of contravening the regulations is liable to a fine and/ **10.148**
or imprisonment for up to two years. However, in deciding whether a person has
committed an offence the court handling the case is obliged to consider whether
the person concerned followed any relevant guidance:

(i) issued by a supervisory authority or other appropriate body;
(ii) approved by HM Treasury; and
(iii) published in a manner approved by HM Treasury.

An 'appropriate body' as described above is any body which regulates or is repre- **10.149**
sentative of any trade, profession, business, or employment carried on by the
alleged offender. In the context of financial services the JMLSG is a relevant body
and the Treasury has approved their 2007 guidance.

A person accused of an offence under the MLR 2007 will have a defence if he **10.150**
can show that he took all reasonable steps and exercised all due diligence to avoid
committing the offence.

Duty to identify

The duty to identify a customer has been the central obligation of anti-money **10.151**
laundering legislation since the introduction of the MLR 1993. The limitations
of heavy reliance on identification material are now well accepted and have led to
the development of wider CDD obligations and the requirement to monitor
transactions and the operation of customer accounts. Notwithstanding these
developments, the requirement to identify continues to form a major element,
perhaps the major element, of anti-money laundering obligations.

A relevant person is required to identify a person in four situations: **10.152**

(i) establishment of a business relationship; where a business relationship is
defined as a business, professional, or commercial relationship between a

---

6. Guarantees and commitments.
7. Trading for own account or for account of customers in:
   (a) money market instruments (cheques, bills, certificates of deposit, etc.);
   (b) foreign exchange;
   (c) financial futures and options;
   (d) exchange and interest-rate instruments; or
   (e) transferable securities.
8. Participation in securities issues and the provision of services related to such issues.
9. Advice to undertakings on capital structure, industrial strategy and related questions and advice as
   well as services relating to mergers and the purchase of undertakings.
10. Money broking.
11. Portfolio management and advice.
12. Safekeeping and administration of securities.
14. Safe custody services.

relevant person and a customer, which is expected by the relevant person at the time when the contact is established, to have an element of duration;

(ii) carrying out of an occasional transaction; where occasional transaction means a transaction (carried out other than as part of a business relationship) amounting to €15,000 or more, whether the transaction is carried out in a single operation or several operations which appear to be linked;

(iii) suspicion of money laundering or terrorist financing; or

(iv) where the relevant person has doubts of the veracity or adequacy of the documents, data, or information previously obtained for the purposes of identification or verification.

Offences committed by a body corporate

10.153   Regulation 47 has the effect of drawing individual officers of a body corporate into the criminal law regulatory net. If a firm commits an offence under the regulations and it can be shown that the offence was either committed with 'the consent or the connivance of an officer' or 'attributable to any neglect on his part', that individual officer will also be guilty of an offence.

10.154   In addition, partners in a partnership, officers in an unincorporated association, and members of a body corporate, who manage that body, are also liable to prosecution where the connivance or attribution tests have been met.

Identification procedures

10.155   Regulation 5 sets out the meaning of the CDD measures that a firm must follow. However, the detail regarding the form of the documentation that is required for identification and verification is set out in the JMLSG guidance.

10.156   Customer due diligence measures means;

(i) identifying the customer and verifying the customer's identity on the basis of documents, data or information obtained from a reliable and independent source;

(ii) identifying, where there is a beneficial owner who is not the customer, the beneficial owner and taking adequate measures, on a risk sensitive basis, to verify his identity so that the relevant person is satisfied that he knows who the beneficial owner is, including in the case of a legal person, trust, or similar legal arrangement, measures to understand the ownership and control structure of the person, trust, or arrangement; and

(iii) obtaining information on the purpose and intended nature of the business relationship.

10.157   Regulation 9 sets out the timing of the customer due diligence measures. A relevant person must verify the identity of the customer (and any beneficial owner) before the establishment of a business relationship or carrying out an occasional transaction. However, verification may be completed during the establishment of a business relationship if it is necessary to avoid interruption of the normal conduct of business and there is very little risk of money laundering. In these circumstances verification must be completed as soon as is practicable after contact is first established.

Identification in practical terms

In reality, the identification requirements provided in Regulation 5 are drafted at **10.158** a very high level. Regulation 5 does not attempt to distinguish between clients, other those who are obtained by distance means. In reality, firms will deal with many different types of client depending on the nature of their business. The UK anti-money laundering regime deals with this issue by passing the burden of setting out the detail of the identification process to the JMLSG Guidance. Chapter 5 of the JMLSG Guidance provides detailed guidance on identification requirements including the type of evidence that a firm should gather to verify the identity of its client.

Identification procedures should be risk-based

Regulation 7(3) requires the relevant person to determine the extent of CDD **10.159** measures on a risk-sensitive basis, depending on the type of customer, business relationship, product, or transaction.

The JMLSG Guidance emphasises the importance of employing a risk-based **10.160** approach to the identification of clients. Firms are required to carry out a risk assessment of their customers. A customer may present a higher money laundering risk for a number of reasons. Such reasons include the nature of the product, the nature of the client, the location of the client, and the level of contact that the firm has with the client. Firms should expect to be able to demonstrate that they have completed a risk assessment of their business and the types of clients they deal with.

Customer due diligence

Chapter 5 of the JMLSG Guidance refers to firms employing CDD procedures. **10.161** There is an important and subtle distinction between simple identification of a client at the start of a business relationship and CDD procedures. CDD is a wider obligation: it requires firms to get to know their customer and carry out ongoing monitoring of the business relationship.

The term 'ongoing monitoring' has been defined in Regulation 8 to ensure that **10.162** the obligations on the firm are clear and section 5.7 of the JMLSG Guidance sets out detailed guidance on what monitoring is and how it can be carried out.

The depth of this obligation will depend on the nature of the business, the relationship with the client, and the client itself. For example, a firm dealing on an ongoing basis with a corporate client may be expected to understand in detail the nature of the corporate's business, whereas a firm offering a simple savings product to a private customer, where the money laundering risk has been adjudged to be low, will in most cases need to understand less about its client.

Exceptions to the duty to identify

10.163 Regulation 4 introduces a number of exclusions to the MLR 2007 when persons are carrying out certain activities. However, none of these exclusions apply if a firm knows or suspects that a transaction involves money laundering. Also, as with all money laundering requirements, firms need to review the level of money laundering risk in their business on a risk-based analysis.

10.164 Regulation 13(2) provides that CDD measures set out in Regulation 7 do not apply where the customer is:

(a) a credit or financial institution which is subject to the requirements of the money laundering directive;

(b) a credit or financial institution (or equivalent institution) which—
- is situated in a non EEA state which imposes requirements equivalent to those laid down in the money laundering directive; and
- is supervised for compliance with those requirements;

(c) a company whose securities are listed on a regulated market subject to specified disclosure obligations;

(d) an independent legal professional and the product is in an account into which monies are pooled; or

(e) a public authority in the UK or one which fulfils certain criteria set out in the MLR 2007.

Long-term insurance

10.165 It is not necessary to identify where a person enters into a long-term insurance contract in connection with that person's contract of employment or occupation. To benefit from this exemption, the insurance contract concerned must not contain a surrender clause and should not be of a type that can be used as collateral for a loan. To qualify for the exemption, a single premium policy must be for a premium in excess of €2,500. If premiums are to be paid periodically, the total payable in any calendar year must not exceed €1,000.

Record-keeping, procedures, and training

10.166 Part 3 of the MLR 2007 covers record-keeping, procedures, and training. This section has been greatly expanded compared with the MLR 2003 and sets out detailed requirements.

Regulation 19 covers record-keeping and requires that copies of the customer's **10.167** identity are retained for a period of five years following the end of the business relationship or if an occasional transaction, five years from the completion of that transaction. Supporting records such as ongoing information and additional due diligence measures also need to be kept for the same five-year period.

Regulation 20 covers policies and procedures and sets out the risk-based policies **10.168** and procedures that should be adopted to cover:

(a) customer due diligence and ongoing monitoring;
(b) reporting;
(c) record-keeping;
(d) internal control;
(e) risk assessment and management; and
(f) the monitoring and management of compliance with, and the internal com-
      munication of, such policies and procedures,

in order to prevent activities related to money laundering and terrorist financing.

These policies should include monitoring of complex or unusually large transac- **10.169** tions and unusual patterns as well as determining whether a client is a PEP. The systems should enable a credit or financial institution to respond quickly and fully to requests and queries from the FSA or SOCA.

Regulation 21 provides that every relevant person must take appropriate measures **10.170** so that all relevant employees are:

(a) made aware of the law relating to money laundering and terrorist financing; and
(b) regularly given training in how to recognise and deal with transactions and other
      activities which may be related to money laundering or terrorist financing.

Chapter 7 of the JMLSG Guidance explores and develops the details of Part 3 of **10.171** the MLR 2007.

Appointed representatives

Where the firm is an appointed representative within the meaning of section 39(2) **10.172** of FSMA, it is the duty of its principal to ensure that the firm complies with the record-keeping requirements. If the appointed representative's principal fails to do this, he will be treated as having committed an offence under Regulation 20 of the MLR 2007 (failure to have systems etc to prevent money laundering).

Internal reporting procedures

Regulation 20 sets out the requirements applicable to a firm for internal reporting **10.173** procedures. A firm is required to nominate a person from within its organisation to receive money laundering disclosures from within the firm. The MLR 2007 refer to this individual as the nominated officer. In practice most firms use the term MLRO.

10.174 A firm must establish and maintain procedures so that any individual to whom information or other matter comes in the course of relevant business and which leads that individual to know or suspect, or have reasonable grounds for knowing or suspecting, that someone is engaged in money laundering, discloses such information or matter to the MLRO, or to a person authorised by the Director General of SOCA, as soon as practicable after it becomes known to him.

10.175 The firm must also ensure that once an individual makes a disclosure to the MLRO, he must consider the disclosure in the light of any available information that is available to the firm. In practice, this means that the MLRO has to be given wide access to information maintained by a firm. The firm is also obliged to ensure that the MLRO determines whether the disclosure and his/her further investigations, give rise to knowledge or suspicion, or reasonable grounds for knowledge or suspicion, that someone is engaged in money laundering.

10.176 Where the MLRO does so determine, the firm must ensure that he makes a report to SOCA or any other person authorised to receive disclosures by the Director General of SOCA.

10.177 Unsurprisingly, the requirement to have internal reporting procedures does not apply to sole traders who do not employ any staff or who do not act in association with any other person.

The FSA Anti-money Laundering Regime

10.178 FSMA established the basic framework of financial regulation in the UK and the FSA took over some of the work of the previous Self Regulating Organisations which were abolished under FSMA.

10.179 The FSA has its regulatory objectives set out by statute[49] and one of those objectives is the reduction of financial crime.

10.180 FSMA grants the FSA a specific power to make rules 'in relation to the prevention and detection of money laundering', whilst section 402(1)(b) of FSMA provides the FSA with a specific power to prosecute money laundering offences.[50]

10.181 There have been various consultation and discussion papers which have set out the FSA's approach to money laundering, the latest of which[51] sets out the FSA's approach to registering and supervising the relevant persons under the MLR 2007. This is a new role for the FSA which previously only concerned itself with

---

[49] FSMA 2000, ss 3–6.
[50] Not in Scotland.
[51] The FSA's new role under the Money Laundering Regulations 2007 dated September 2007.

regulated firms that were authorised under FSMA, such as banks, insurance companies, and financial advisers.

With effect from 15 December 2007 the FSA was given the responsibility of monitoring the anti-money laundering controls of businesses such as leasing companies, trade finance houses, and safe custody service providers and such persons will have to be included on the FSA register.   **10.182**

Risk-based regulation

The FSA's risk-based approach towards money laundering is consistent with its general risk-based approach to financial services regulation, the principles of which were set out at the FSA's inception.[52]   **10.183**

Initially, there was some uncertainty as to how a risk-based approach should be applied to money laundering regulation.   **10.184**

The FSA describes a risk-based approach as: **10.185**

> ... a management tool for developing and managing a firm's systems and controls. The risk-based system displays the following features that are essential for a regulatory regime that seeks to deliver value for money whilst at the same time disrupting those who seek to use the financial system for criminal purposes.

The FSA does not maintain a zero failure regime, as it considers that this would be disproportionate, but wants to see firms taking reasonable steps to identify and strengthen weaknesses in their systems and controls. Spending should be targeted at the weakest points in the system so that it makes it harder for criminals to use firms to launder money.   **10.186**

The risk-based approach recognises that much of the expertise in assessing risk lies within the firms themselves, as it is they who have the best knowledge and experience of their customers and products. Criminals themselves operate in a risk-based manner, constantly updating and changing their tactics to avoid detection. Firms need to be flexible and dynamic to keep up with the changing face of money laundering.   **10.187**

There will always be a requirement for firms to monitor their customer's activities, but specifics depend on the size and nature of the firm.   **10.188**

Identification and CDD should also be carried out on a risk sensitive basis, for example an elderly person opening a basic bank account is unlikely to require extensive procedures to identify them and the nature of the account usage, as long as sufficient monitoring procedures are in place.   **10.189**

---

[52] See, for example, 'Building the new regulator'—progress report 1 December 2000, Financial Services Authority.

10.190 Staff training is also an area where the requirements will vary depending on the size and nature of the firm. Customer contact staff for instance, will need training in spotting forged identity documents, whereas their managers will be looking at the overall anti-money laundering requirements and procedures that are necessary to address the risks they face.

10.191 The risk-based approach requires firms to be proactive in their approach in seeking out information regarding money laundering trends and threats from external sources as well as relying on their own experience.

Registered businesses

10.192 The registration of high value dealers and money service businesses was introduced under the MLR 2003 but the MLR 2007 added trust or company service providers to the list of persons required to be registered.

10.193 There are several bodies that are responsible for supervision including the FSA, which is the supervisory authority for:

- credit and financial institutions which are authorised persons:
- trust or company service providers that are authorised persons;
- annex I financial institutions (which excludes consumer credit financial institutions, money service businesses, and authorised persons);

and the Commissioners for HM Revenue and Customs ('the Commissioners'), which are the supervisory authority for:

- high value dealers;
- money service businesses that are not supervised by the FSA; trust or company service providers which are not supervised by the FSA, or one of the professional bodies listed in Schedule 3 to the MLR 2007;
- auditors, external accountants, and tax advisors that are not supervised by one of the bodies in Schedule 3 to the MLR 2007.

10.194 A 'money service business' means an undertaking which by way of business operates a currency exchange office, transmits money (or any representations of monetary value) by any means, or cashes cheques which are made payable to customers.

10.195 Other supervisory authorities include the Office of Fair Trading ('the OFT'), the Gambling Commission, the Department for Enterprise, Trade and Investment in Northern Ireland, and the professional bodies listed in Schedule 3 to the MLR 2007.

10.196 The supervisory authority is responsible for monitoring the relevant persons for whom it is the supervisory authority and must take the necessary measures to ensure that such persons comply with the MLR 2007.

Regulation 25 provides that the Commissioners must maintain registers of per- **10.197** sons who are required to be registered with them.

Under Regulation 27 an applicant for registration must provide such information **10.198** as the Commissioners may specify. Such information may be:

    (a) the applicant's name and (if different) the name of the business;
    (b) the nature of the business;
    (c) the name of the nominated officer (if any);
    (d) in relation to a money service business or trust or company service provider;
        (i) the name of any person who effectively directs or will direct the business and any beneficial owner of the business; and
        (ii) information needed by the Commissioners to decide whether they must refuse the application pursuant to Regulation 28 (fit and proper test).

The Commissioners may request additional information from applicants as they **10.199** reasonably consider necessary to enable them to determine the application. Where such additional information is requested, the applicant for registration must provide it within 21 days.

Where an applicant has provided information to the Commissioners in connec- **10.200** tion with an application for registration and there has been a change affecting any matter contained in the information or it becomes apparent to the applicant that any aspect of the information is inaccurate, the applicant must, within 30 days, provide details of the change or correct the inaccuracy.

The Commissioners must refuse to register an applicant as a money service **10.201** business or trust or company service provider if they are satisfied that the appli- cant, any person covered by Regulation 27(1)(d)(i), any beneficial owner, or nominated officer is not a fit and proper person. This fit and proper test require- ment has been introduced by the MLR 2007 and is designed to look at the persons owning and running the business, in much the same way as the approved persons in financial services firms are reviewed.

The fit and proper person test is set out in Regulation 28 and states that a person **10.202** is not a fit and proper person if he:

    (a) has been convicted of—
        (i) an offence under the Terrorism Act 2000;
        (ii) an offence under paragraph 7(2) or (3) of Schedule 3 to the Anti-Terrorism, Crime and Security Act 2001 (offences);
        (iii) an offence under the Terrorism Act 2006;
        (iv) an offence under Part 7 (money laundering) of, or listed in Schedule 2 (lifestyle offences: England and Wales),[53] 4 (lifestyle offences: Scotland) or 5 (lifestyle offences: Northern Ireland) to, the Proceeds of Crime Act 2002;

---

[53] These include offences such as drug trafficking, money laundering, directing terrorism, arms trafficking, counterfeiting etc.

(v) an offence under the Fraud Act 2006 or, in Scotland, the common law offence of fraud;

(vi) an offence under section 72(1), (3) or (8) of the Value Added Tax Act 1994 (offences); or

(vii) the common law offence of cheating the public revenue;

(b) has been adjudged bankrupt or sequestration of his estate has been awarded and (in either case) he has not been discharged;

(c) is subject to a disqualification order under the Company Directors Disqualification Act 1986;

(d) is or has been subject to a confiscation order under the Proceeds of Crime Act 2002;

(e) has consistently failed to comply with the requirements of these Regulations, the Money Laundering Regulations 2003 or the Money Laundering Regulations 2001;

(f) has consistently failed to comply with the requirements of regulation 2006/1781/ EC of the European Parliament and of the Council of 15 November 2006 on information on the payer accompanying the transfer of funds;

(g) has effectively directed a business which falls within sub-paragraph (e) or (f);

(h) is otherwise not a fit and proper person with regard to the risk of money laundering or terrorist financing.

10.203 The Commissioners may also refuse to register an applicant if any requirement as to registration (Regulation 27) or payment of fees (Regulation 35) has not been complied with or if any information supplied to them is false or misleading. The Commissioners have 45 days in which to accept or refuse a registration.

10.204 Regulation 30 provides that the Commissioners must cancel the registration of a money service business or trust or company service provider if they are satisfied that the person mentioned in Regulation 28 is not a fit and proper person. The Commissioners may also cancel a registration at any time if it appears to them that they would have grounds to refuse an application. Where the Commissioners cancel a registration, they must give notice of their decision. The person has a right to know the reasons for the decision and the fact that they have a right to require a review of the decision under Regulation 43 and a right of appeal under Regulation 44.

10.205 The MLR 2007 provide the Commissioners with certain powers including a power to enter premises and inspect information or currency found on the premises. Regulation 38(2) provides that the Commissioners may obtain an order requiring a relevant person to give them access to recorded information, to copy it, or to remove it from premises, subject in the latter case to certain specified procedures.

10.206 Registered firms differ from FSA authorised firms as they will only have their anti-money laundering systems and controls supervised by the FSA, whilst authorised firms are subject to regulation that covers many more aspects of their business.

Registered businesses, unlike authorised firms, do not have the need for a 'fit and proper' check on owners and managers.

Registered businesses will also not be members of the Financial Services **10.207** Compensation Scheme and customers will not be eligible for compensation if the business becomes insolvent. Customers who find themselves in dispute with a registered business will also not be able to approach the Financial Ombudsman Service to help seek a resolution.

Failure to register is an offence that potentially carries either a civil or criminal **10.208** sanction; however where a business performs an activity that would otherwise be required to be registered, on an occasional or very limited basis, then it will not need to register.

Part 4 of the MLR 2007 provides detail as to how a business is supervised and **10.209** registered. Regulation 23 lists the businesses which fall under the FSA's supervision and Regulations 32–35 set out the power to maintain registers, the requirement to be registered, applications for and cancellations of registration, and the costs of supervision.

Supervision

The FSA's risk-based approach to supervision means that it concentrates the **10.210** greatest resources where it perceives the risk to be greatest. The FSA expects firms to follow the same principle when designing their anti-money laundering systems and controls.

The FSA has said it will seek to identify which registered businesses are most **10.211** vulnerable to financial crime by requesting information from management about the business and its anti-money laundering procedures. The FSA may also use 'mystery shoppers' to observe adherence to the MLR 2007 and its staff may visit to meet senior management and examine documents.

Enforcement

The FSA also uses a risk-based approach when enforcing the MLR 2007. The **10.212** seriousness and nature of any breach is considered before a decision is made as to the appropriate action to take. Failures in anti-money laundering controls will not automatically result in disciplinary sanctions, although enforcement action is more likely where a firm has not put in place systems and controls to identify and mitigate risks.

The tools that are used for investigation and enforcement are the issuing of **10.213** written notices, the requirement of persons to attend interviews, and the use of search warrants to allow the police to enter premises, search, and take possession of documents.

10.214 The MLR 2007 allow a designated authority to impose 'appropriate' penalties on relevant persons who fail to comply with any requirement set out in them, where appropriate means effective, proportionate, and dissuasive. The FSA is one of the authorities that has been defined as a designated authority[54] and as such has been given wide-ranging powers. Officers of the FSA, including members of staff or its agents, have the power set out in Regulations 37–39 to:

- require information from, and the attendance of, relevant and connected persons;
- enter, inspect without a warrant etc; and
- enter premises under warrant.

Power to impose civil penalties

10.215 Regulation 42 of MLR 2007 gives the FSA as a designated authority the power to impose civil penalties in such amounts as it considers appropriate on a relevant person who fails to comply with the Regulations. The FSA must not impose a penalty where there are reasonable grounds for it to be satisfied that the person took all reasonable steps and exercised all due diligence to ensure that the requirements would be complied with.

10.216 When deciding whether a person has failed to comply with the Regulations the relevant authority must consider whether any relevant industry guidance has been followed.

10.217 The burden of proof for the civil offence is lower than that of a criminal offence, being on 'balance of probabilities' rather than 'beyond reasonable doubt'. Where the FSA decide to impose a penalty it must give the person notice of:

- their decision to impose a penalty and the amount;
- the reasons for imposing the penalty;
- the right to make representations to it within a specified period (not less than 28 days).

10.218 Appeals to a decision made by the FSA are directed to the Financial Services and Markets Tribunal.[55]

10.219 Detailed guidance of the FSA's powers under the MLR 2007 is set out in the draft amendments to the FSA's Enforcement Guide at sections 19.71–19.84.

---

[54] MLR 2007, reg 36.
[55] Established under s 132 of FSMA 2000.

It lists the powers given to the FSA under the MLR 2007 and confirms that the remit is extended to cover not only relevant authorised firms but also certain non-authorised firms.

The FSA has confirmed that where both the MLR 2007 and FSMA apply it will **10.220** discipline authorised firms using FSMA powers. Use of investigation powers will be limited to those cases where the FSA expects to take action under the MLR 2007, which will generally be to investigate civil breaches of the MLR 2007.

Criminal offences

Criminal offences are dealt with under Regulations 45–47 of the MLR 2007 **10.221** which state that where a person fails to comply with the requirements of the MLR 2007 they are guilty of an offence and can be liable to a fine or imprisonment up to a term not exceeding two years. As with the civil offences, the court must take into account whether any industry guidance has been followed and a person is not guilty of an offence if he has taken all reasonable steps and exercised all due diligence to avoid committing the offence.

Where an offence has been committed by a body corporate under Regulation 45, **10.222** and it can be shown that the offence has been committed with the consent or connivance of an officer of the body corporate or is attributable to any neglect on his part, the officer as well as the body corporate is guilty of an offence and liable to be punished accordingly.

Taking Money Laundering Seriously

The FSA takes its anti-money laundering role seriously and is active in developing **10.223** policy initiatives. It has produced a number of publications reviewing and commenting on the regulatory response to the problem of money laundering in financial services.

In line with a public commitment given by the FSA the Financial Crime Opera- **10.224** tions Team launched a major project aimed at establishing the extent to which a wide range of firms across the industry had adapted to the new FSA Handbook rules found in the Senior Management Arrangements, Systems and Controls Handbook ('SYSC') and the JMLSG Guidance.

The results were published in a review dated March 2008 which covered the **10.225** following areas:

(a) money laundering risk assessment;
(b) senior management responsibility;

529

(c) changes to AML policies and procedures;

(d) customer due diligence;

(e) enhanced due diligence;

(f) correspondent banking;

(g) monitoring customer activity; and

(h) staff awareness and training.

10.226 The report summarises key findings and includes observations of good practice adopted by firms, as well as some examples of poor practice. It recognises that smaller firms generally represent a lower risk without having fewer resources to devote to money laundering risk assessment and mitigation measures. One of the important points raised was the need for adequate staff training and not to treat reviewing AML policies and procedures as a one-off exercise.

FSA Rules Relating to Anti-money Laundering

10.227 The starting point for FSA regulated firms is the Principles for Businesses. Principles 1 (Integrity), 2 (Skill, care and diligence), and 3 (Management and control) have particular relevance. Firms should also pay due regard to their responsibilities under Principle 11 (Relations with regulators).

10.228 The FSA Money Laundering Handbook ('ML') has been deleted in its entirety and replaced with a new section in SYSC. One of the themes of FSA policy has been the key role of senior management in ensuring that firms are not used for the purposes of money laundering.

10.229 SYSC 3 looks at areas covered by systems and controls, and SYSC 3.2.6 looks at money laundering specifically. SYSC 6 deals with the areas of compliance, internal audit, and financial crime, and SYSC 6.3 deals with financial crime.

10.230 Rule 3.2.6 of SYSC requires firms to take reasonable care to establish and maintain effective systems and controls for compliance with the applicable requirements and standards under the regulatory system and for countering the risk that a firm might be used to further financial crime.

10.231 Guidance at SYSC 3.2.6 D provides:

> A firm may also have separate obligations to comply with relevant legal requirements, including the Terrorism Act 2000, the Proceeds of Crime Act 2002 and the Money Laundering Regulations.

10.232 In other words failure to comply with the requirements of POCA or the MLR 2007 would result in a breach of FSA rules.

FSA Enforcement

The FSA has in the past, been active in enforcing its systems and controls in **10.233** relation to compliance, financial crime, and money laundering. The FSA has sought to underline its clear policy goal that firms should take money laundering seriously. Assessment of firms' anti-money laundering ('AML') arrangements has been a major element of the FSA's ARROW visits to firms. More significantly, the FSA has taken enforcement action against a number of firms whose anti-money laundering arrangements have fallen below an acceptable standard. These actions have involved significant fines. In its Final Notice dated 9 December 2003, the FSA imposed a fine of £2,000,000 on Abbey National plc for failures in its AML arrangements.

The FSA has also shown itself willing to take action against firms that are incorpo- **10.234** rated and authorised in other EEA Member States. On 5 April 2004 the FSA imposed a fine of £150,000 on the London branch of Raiffeisen Zentralbank Österreich, for not updating its anti-money laundering and compliance manual promptly to reflect the introduction of new rules. Investment Services (UK) Limited was subject to a fine of £175,000 because it did not conduct its business with due care, skill, and diligence and for failing to control its business effectively in relation to AML systems and controls.

Themes from FSA Final Notices

Whilst there are hints in at least one of the cases that the FSA may have suspected **10.235** that money laundering had in fact taken place,[56] it is a notable feature of the actions taken by the FSA that they were not taken as a result of the identification of money laundering activity. Rather, the FSA decided to act because it had identified failings in the firms' anti-money laundering arrangements.

Also of significance, in some of the cases (see, for example, Abbey National plc) **10.236** the firm itself had identified the failings in its anti-money laundering arrange-ments and reported the matter to the FSA. Whilst this may, presumably, have reduced the level of the fine imposed, it did not persuade the FSA that it did not need to act.

---

[56] In the case of Abbey National plc at least part of the firm's failings related to lengthy reporting times for suspicious transactions to NCIS.

10.237   More than one of the FSA Final Notices refers to the role of senior management in anti-money laundering arrangements. The increase in emphasis on the role of senior management in anti-money laundering arrangements is a theme of recent FSA policy and was one of the drivers behind the redrafting of the JMLSG Guidance Notes.

10.238   The implementation of robust systems and controls is also important to FSA action. Whilst most of the Final Notices refer to breaches of specific provisions of the then FSA Money Laundering Rules, the Abbey National plc Final Notice also refers to breaches in rule 3.2.6 of SYSC. This emphasis on systems and controls is consistent with the development of the FSA's policy on money laundering prevention generally.

10.239   Finally, it seems clear from all the Final Notices issued by the FSA that the single biggest failing it has identified is the failure by the firms concerned to demonstrate that they took money laundering seriously.

The Joint Money Laundering Steering Group Guidance Notes

10.240   Both the MLR 2007 and the FSA Handbook cross refer to the JMLSG Guidance. The JMLSG has been publishing guidance since 1990. Initially, the guidance was part of a self-regulatory arrangement which involved of the Bank of England. However, following the introduction of the MLR 1993, the JMLSG was used to provide guidance on that secondary legislation. In its most recent version the JMLSG Guidance[57] was updated to provide guidance on the MLR 2007.

The status of the JMLSG Guidance Notes

10.241   Whilst the JMLSG Guidance is not formally part of the UK's anti-money laundering legislation it is important in legal terms. Section 330(8) of POCA and Regulation 42(3) of the MLR 2007 provide that a court must consider whether a person followed any relevant guidance issued by a supervisory body or other appropriate body that has been approved by HM Treasury and published in a manner most likely to bring it to the attention of those affected by it. Further, guidance in SYSC 3.2.6 provides that in assessing whether a breach of its rules on systems and controls against money laundering has occurred, the FSA will have regard to whether the firm has followed the relevant provisions of the JMLSG Guidance.

---

[57] *Prevention of Money Laundering—Guidance for the UK Financial Sector*, 2007 edition, Joint Money Laundering Steering Group Pinners Hall 105–108 Old Broad Street London EC2N 1EX.

The revised JMLSG Guidance

Following the extensive review of the JMLSG Guidance in 2006 and the introduction of the MLR 2007 the revised new format of JMLSG Guidance was launched in December 2007 and, in general, has been well received. Particular effort was made to improve the clarity of the guidance and provide a substantial amount of guidance and information that is relevant to non-retail providers of financial services. **10.242**

The JMLSG Guidance sets out the detail of a business's obligations under the MLR 2007 and is split into two parts. Part 1 contains generic guidance that applies to the UK financial services industry generally. Part 2 provides supplementary guidance for a number of specific sectors such as trade and asset finance and private equity. Some businesses will find that they do not yet have specific guidance relating to their industry, and the FSA is working to ensure that guidance is available to those sectors in due course. **10.243**

One of the key features of the new JMLSG Guidance is that it has been drafted to accommodate the regulatory emphasis on risk-based anti-money laundering regulation. **10.244**

JMLSG Guidance—Risk-based regulation

Chapter 4 of the JMLSG Guidance examines risk-based anti-money laundering regulation and looks at core obligations and actions required to be kept under regular review. **10.245**

The JMLSG Guidance sets out steps to assess the most cost effective and proportionate way to manage and mitigate money laundering and terrorist financing threats faced by firms. These are: **10.246**

- identifying money laundering and terrorist financing risks that are relevant to the firm;
- assessing the risks posed by the firm's particular:
  - customers
  - products
  - delivery channels
- identifying geographical areas of operation;
- designing and implementing controls to manage and mitigate these assessed risks;
- monitoring and improving the effective operation of these controls; and
- recording appropriately what has been done and why.

The JMLSG Guidance recognises that no system will be infallible, but the risk-based approach will balance the burden of the cost of these measures with a **10.247** realistic assessment of where the greatest dangers are that a firm will be used in connection with money laundering or terrorist financing. It focuses effort where it is needed and will have most impact.

10.248 A risk-based approach assists with the overall objective to prevent money laundering and terrorist financing in the following ways:

- recognises that the money laundering/terrorist financing threat to firms varies depending on customers, jurisdictions, products, and delivery channels;
- allows management to differentiate between their customers in a way that matches the risk to the particular business undertaken;
- allows senior management to apply its own approach to the firm's procedures, systems, and arrangements in particular circumstances; and
- helps to produce a more cost effective system.

Identifying and assessing the risks

10.249 Given the planning that is required to develop and implement risk-based anti-money laundering policies it is essential that senior management are fully committed to the process. As noted above, the FSA has criticised what it considers to be the failings of senior management in relation to money laundering. Not only must senior management be committed to the development of anti-money laundering policies, but they must communicate such commitment to all levels of their business. Senior management must decide on the appropriate approach in the light of their firm's structure.

10.250 The risk assessment process begins with identification and assessment of the risks involved in the business; a number of factors influencing these may be:

- customer product and activity profiles;
- distribution channels;
- complexity and volume of transactions;
- processes and systems; and
- operating environment.

10.251 In assessing the ability of their firm to be used for terrorist financing or money laundering, senior management should also ask themselves a number of questions, including, for example:

- What are the risks posed by the firm's customers, eg PEPs, complex business structures, and businesses involving large amounts of cash?
- What risk is posed by the customer's behaviour, eg no commercial rationale for the purchase of a product or service, requests for unusually large or complex transaction which has no apparent economic or legal purpose, unwillingness to divulge information regarding the transaction, and requests for undue levels of secrecy?

- How does the way the customer comes to the firm affect the risk, eg occasional transactions, introduced business or non face-to-face transactions? and
- What risk is posed by the products/services, eg can the product be used for money laundering or terrorist financing, do the products allow payments to third parties, do customers migrating from one product to another within the firm carry a risk?

Firms should not judge the level of risk solely on the nature of the customer, **10.252** product, delivery channel, or location. Where one of these categories carries a higher level of risk then the combination of the whole customer/product relationship should be viewed accordingly. Allowing a high risk customer to acquire a low risk product using standard verification appropriate to that product may lead to a requirement for further verification, particularly where the product is subsequently changed or the transactions have significantly changed in nature.

Design and implementation of controls

Once the firm has identified and assessed the potential risks to its business, senior **10.253** management must implement adequate controls to manage and mitigate those risks. In order to decide on the most appropriate and effective controls for the firm senior managers must ask themselves what the best procedures are to manage and mitigate these threats and risks in the most cost effective way.

Some examples of control processes can include: **10.254**

- introduction of a customer identification programme that varies procedures in a way that is appropriate to their assessed risk;
- requiring that the quality of verification evidence should be of a certain standard;
- obtaining, where appropriate, additional customer information; and
- monitoring customer transactions/activities.

To allow the firm to be able to identify suspicious transactions, some form of **10.255** monitoring of all transactions is necessary; procedures need to be set out as to the course of action to be taken when such transactions are identified.

Monitor and improve operation of control

The policies and procedures of the firm need to be kept under constant review. **10.256** An example picked up in the FSA's March 2008 Review of Firms' Implementation of a Risk-based Approach to Anti-Money Laundering ('AML') is the need to update AML policies and procedures.

In this paper the FSA found that large firms were well used to assessing the money **10.257** laundering risks in their business and responding appropriately. Medium-sized firms had carried out a gap analysis of existing policies against those outlined in the JMLSG Guidance and had made appropriate changes in client take-on, client monitoring, AML staff awareness and training, and senior management reporting. It was unclear whether this process was a one-off event or would be continuous. Small firms had reviewed the JMLSG Guidance and had made changes where appropriate, although not all said that they would carry out further reviews to ensure that they were still suitable for their business.

10.258 The JMLSG Guidance recommends that policies and procedures are kept under regular review. Aspects that firms should consider include:

- appropriate procedures to identify changes in customer characteristics, which come to light in the normal course of business;
- reviewing ways in which different products and services may be used for money laundering/terrorist financing purposes and how these ways may change, supported by typologies/law enforcement feedback, etc;
- adequacy of staff training and awareness;
- monitoring of compliance arrangements (such as internal audit/quality assurance processes or external review);
- the balance between technology-based and people-based systems;
- capturing appropriate management information;
- upward reporting and accountability;
- effectiveness of liaison with other parts of the firm; and
- effectiveness of the liaison with regulatory and law enforcement agencies.

10.259 Responses to the above and similar issues will enable the firm to tailor its policies and procedures on the prevention of money laundering and terrorist financing. Responses should be documented to allow the firm to demonstrate how it assesses its risks, implements systems and procedures, how it monitors and improves the effectiveness of systems and procedures, and the arrangements for reporting to senior management.

10.260 The risk-based approach to anti-money laundering is not a 'soft option'. Whilst it does enable firms to develop policies that are suited to the nature of the business that they carry on, the process of developing, implementing, and monitoring such policies is likely to make greater demands on a firm than the so-called 'box ticking' approach of anti-money laundering regulation.

10.261 Firms should also be aware that the regulatory regime is not an absolute risk-based regime. Although the implementation of 3MLD led to some relaxation of mandatory requirements, the basic anti-money laundering obligations are still retained. For example, the requirements on firms to identify customers and take and retain records of identification material remain in place. The risk-based regime is therefore characterised as a 'minimum standards plus' regime rather than a regime which permits firms to set their own minimum standards.

Judging firms against their own standards

Firms also need to be aware that where they have developed risk-based policies **10.262** that exceed the requirements of the legislation and FSA regulatory regime, it will be against these standards that the FSA will be likely to assess the effectiveness of their anti-money laundering procedures. A firm that fails to meet its own internal anti-money laundering standards may be censured by the FSA even where the firm has complied with the relevant legislation.

JMLSG Guidance—CDD

The MLR 2007 specify the CDD measures that must be carried out, and their **10.263** timing, as well as what actions must be taken if CDD measures are not carried out. The JMLSG Guidance looks in detail at the application of these measures and what is required to verify the identity of different types of customers.

The firm identifies its customer by obtaining certain information about that **10.264** customer and then verifying that information by comparing it to other documents, data, or information from an independent reliable source. Evidence of identity may take a number of forms and in respect of individuals the most common form of verification are so-called identity documents such as passports, identity cards, and photocard driving licences. Paragraphs 5.3.68–248 of the JMLSG Guidance go through the documents that are standard identification documents and what can be done if customers cannot provide these standard documents. It also looks at mitigation of risk of impersonation as identity theft is a growing problem in the UK and worldwide.

Paragraph 5.4 of the JMLSG Guidance describes where simplified due diligence **10.265** may be applicable and Paragraph 5.5 looks at the instances where enhanced due diligence is appropriate. Non face-to-face identification and verification are instances where enhanced due diligence procedures need to be applied. Transactions are increasingly being undertaken remotely, eg by Internet and telephone banking as well as online share dealing. Although these transactions do not appear to pose any greater risk than other non face-to-face transactions, such as applications submitted by post, there are other factors, which when taken together, increase the risks to businesses.

These other factors which increase the risks to business are: **10.266**

- ease of access to the facility, regardless of time and location;
- ease of making multiple fictitious applications without incurring extra cost or the risk of detection;
- absence of physical documents; and
- the speed of electronic transactions.

10.267   Where the customer has not been physically present, extra measures need to be taken to verify the customer's identity. For example, ensuring additional documentary evidence is provided or requiring that the first payment of the operation is carried out through a bank account in the customer's name. Detailed guidance is provided in Part II of the JMLSG Guidance which deals with each industry sector.

10.268   The extent of the extra information required will depend on the nature and characteristics of the product or service provided and the assessed money laundering risk presented by the customer.

10.269   Enhanced due diligence procedures must be carried out on PEPs and firms should also carry out checks to see whether individuals are listed on reports and databases on corruption risk published by specialised national, international, non-governmental, and commercial organisations. One such data base is the Transparency International Corruption Perceptions Index, which ranks approximately 150 countries according to their perceived level of corruption.

10.270   Any business relationship with PEP should be approved by senior management and on-going monitoring of the relationship performed. Firms should remember that new and existing customers may not initially meet the definition of a PEP but may subsequently become one. In this instance it is vital that firms keep up to date with public information regarding the possible change in status of its customers. As soon as an existing customer is identified as a PEP enhanced due diligence must be performed on that customer.

10.271   Paragraph 5.7 of the JMLSG Guidance looks at monitoring customer activity and describes the essentials of any system of monitoring. These are:

- flags to highlight transactions and/or activities for further examination;
- reports to be reviewed promptly by the right person(s); and
- the appropriate action to be taken on the findings of any further examination.

10.272   In designing monitoring arrangements it is important to take into account the frequency, volume, and size of transactions with customers, in the context of the assessed customer and product risk. The effectiveness of the monitoring system, automated or manual, will depend on the following:

- the quality of the parameters built into it which determine what alerts it makes; and
- the ability of the staff to assess and act appropriately.

10.273   The needs of each firm will be different and each system will vary according to the scale, nature, and complexity of its business.

JMLSG Guidance—Suspicious activities, reporting, and data protection

Under sections 330 and 331 of POCA and section 21A of TA persons in the **10.274** regulated sector are required to make a report in respect of information that comes to them within the course of a business in the regulated sector:

- where they know;
- where they suspect; or
- where they have reasonable grounds for knowing or suspecting

that a person is engaged in money laundering or terrorist financing. The JMLSG Guidance refers to this as 'grounds for knowledge or suspicion'.

Knowledge means actually knowing something is true. In a criminal court, it **10.275** must be proved that the individual in fact knew that a person was engaged in money laundering. Knowledge can also be inferred, so a failure to ask obvious questions may be relied upon by a jury to imply knowledge as in *R v Duff*[58] where the defendant 'wilfully and deliberately shut [his] eyes to the truth and has refrained from making proper enquiry' or as in *R v Griffiths*[59] 'closed your eyes to what would otherwise have been the clearest of evidence staring you in the face'.

Suspicion is more subjective and falls short of proof based on firm evidence. **10.276** Suspicion has been defined by the courts in *R v Da Silva*[60] as being the dictionary definition: 'an act of suspecting, the imagining of something without evidence or on slender evidence, inkling, mistrust . . .' and also as being 'beyond mere speculation and based on some foundation'.

A transaction that is unusual is not necessarily suspicious. Even customers with **10.277** stable and predictable transactions will have transactions which are unusual for them. Further enquiry may give a perfectly reasonable explanation for the transaction.

Where a member of staff of a firm knows facts or circumstances that, if known to **10.278** a reasonable person in a business subject to the MLR 2007, would have inferred knowledge or formed the suspicion that another person was engaged in money laundering then that member of staff should have reason to know or suspect money laundering. If he does not know or suspect money laundering then he fails the objective test and may be liable to prosecution. To defend against failure to meet this objective test, firms need to ensure that they can demonstrate that they took reasonable steps to identify the customer and understand the rationale behind the transaction in question.

---

[58] [2002] EWCA Crim 2117.
[59] [2006] EWCA Crim 2155.
[60] [2006] EWCA Crim 1654.

JMLSG—Record-keeping, procedures, and training

10.279 The JMLSG Guidance explores and develops the details of Part 3 of the MLR 2007 which deal with record-keeping, procedures, and training.

10.280 Chapter 7 of the JMLSG Guidance covers staff awareness, training, and alertness and sets out core obligations to relevant persons.

10.281 These core obligations state that:

- relevant employees should be:
  - made aware of the risks of money laundering and terrorist financing, the relevant legislation, and their obligations under that legislation;
  - made aware of the identity and responsibilities of the firm's nominated officer and MLRO;
    - trained in the firm's procedures on how to recognise and deal with potential money laundering or terrorist financing transactions or activity;
  - staff training should be given at regular intervals, and details recorded;
  - the MLRO is responsible for oversight of the firm's compliance with its requirements in respect of staff training; and
  - the relevant director or senior manager has overall responsibility for the establishment and maintenance of effective training arrangements.

10.282 A firm's employees are one of the most important tools in the fight against money laundering. Staff who are alert to the risks of money laundering/terrorist financing and are well trained in the identification of unusual activities or transactions are essential as even the best designed systems are ineffective if staff do not recognise what the data means or what to do with it.

10.283 The FSA sets outs in its Training and Competence Sourcebook ('TC') that the firm's commitments are that:

- its employees are competent;
- its employees remain competent for the work they do;
- its employees are appropriately supervised;
- its employees' competence is regularly reviewed; and
- the level of competence is appropriate to the nature of the business.

10.284 Staff should be trained on the firm's procedures and specifically how its products and services can be used as a vehicle for money laundering or terrorist financing, and the firms' procedures for managing this risk. Relevant persons should be trained in what they need to know in order to carry out their particular role. Paragraphs 7.25–7.33 set out how staff should be alert in specific situations.

10.285 Chapter 2 of the JMLSG Guidance sets out the legal and regulatory obligations with respect to internal controls. Firms are required to establish and maintain adequate and appropriate policies and procedures to forestall and prevent money laundering. They are also required to introduce appropriate controls to take account of the risks faced by the firm's business and maintain control and oversight over outsourced activities.

Chapter 8 of JMLSG looks at record-keeping and gives the details of what records **10.286** need to be kept and in what format they need to be stored. Usually the firm's records need to cover:

- customer information;
- transactions;
- internal and external suspicion reports;
- MLRO annual (and other) reports;
- information not acted upon;
- training and compliance monitoring; and
- information about the effectiveness of training.

As these documents need to be kept under review and may need to be produced **10.287** to a police officer quickly, they can be kept in different formats for ease of reference and storage. Original documentary evidence may be stored off site, but electronic, scanned, or microfiche copies must be easily accessible. Notwithstanding how the records are held the retention periods set out in MLR 2007 are the same.

Where there are ongoing investigations, records should be retained until the case **10.288** is closed. However, if a firm is not advised of an ongoing investigation following the reporting of a suspicious transaction, there is no requirement for it to retain its records for longer than the firm's record management policy specifies.

Overview

The UK has been a significant architect in the development of international **10.289** standards and underlining its policy aims to reduce the harm caused by crime and terrorism at home by the implementation of a package of measures which combine:

- solid legal foundations that outlaw the financing of terrorism and money laundering;
- financial safeguards applied by industry—backed up by law; supervision and guidance that help identify and trace illicit funds;
- measures to maximise the investigative and intelligence value of the financial information generated by criminals as they move through the financial system; and

- an armoury of measures to disrupt the flow of criminal or terrorist assets and hold those responsible to account.

10.290 The 'all crimes approach' of POCA provides for a single set of money laundering offences which apply to the proceeds of all crimes, unlike the previous legislation which tended to focus on targeting money derived from drugs trafficking. It also targets assets gained from the proceeds of a criminal lifestyle which can be recovered to break up criminal networks.

10.291 The role of the financial sector is to act as 'gatekeeper' preventing criminals from moving illicit money through the financial system. The verification of identity of customers and the reporting of suspicious activities are fundamental to this process. However there is increasing emphasis on monitoring transactions and the increasing sophistication of money launderers has placed greater demands on firms and their staff. This in turn has led to higher expectations in terms of staff training. The FSA enforces the high-level regulatory requirements in a risk-based way and expects firms under its supervision to have appropriate systems and controls in place to prevent money laundering.

10.292 Practical and enforceable guidance issued by the JMLSG and approved by HM Treasury has been updated to reflect the new money laundering legislation and is now set out in two very detailed sections. The first section covers the general money laundering procedures in great detail giving examples where appropriate for customer due diligence, senior management responsibility, and suspicious activities and reporting. The second section is specific detailed sectoral guidance to be read in addition to the general guidance.

APPENDIX I

Financial Services Authority Handbook (Extracts)

The Money Laundering Sourcebook ('ML') is revoked in its entirety. Guidance on the prevention of financial crime can be found in:

SENIOR MANAGEMENT ARRANGEMENTS, SYSTEMS AND CONTROLS WHO?

1.1.1 R . . .

(2A) for an *incoming Treaty firm* which has *permission* only for *cross border services* and which does not carry on *regulated activities* in the *United Kingdom*, SYSC 3.2.6AR to SYSC 3.2.6JG do not apply;

(3) for a *sole trader*:
  (a) SYSC 2 does not apply as long as he does not employ any *person* who is required to be approved under section 59 of the *Act* (Approval for particular arrangements);
  (b) SYSC 3.2.6IR does not apply if he has no *employees*;

(4) for a *UCITS qualifier*:
  (a) SYSC 2.1.1R and SYSC 2.1.2G do not apply;
  (b) SYSC 2.1.3R to SYSC 2.2.3G apply, but only in relation to allocation of the function in SYSC 2.1.3R(2) and only with respect to the activities in SYSC 1.1.4R;
  (c) SYSC 3 applies, but only with respect to the activities in SYSC 1.1.4R;

(5) for an *authorised professional firm* when carrying on *non-mainstream regulated activities* SYSC 3.2.6AR to SYSC 3.2.6JG do not apply.

What?

1.1.3 R SYSC 2 and SYSC 3 apply with respect to the carrying on of:

(1) *regulated activities*;
(2) activities that constitute *dealing in investments as principal*, disregarding the exclusion in article 15 of the *Regulated Activities Order* (Absence of holding out etc); and
(3) *ancillary activities* in relation to *designated investment business, home finance activity* and *insurance mediation activity*;

except that SYSC 3.2.6AR to SYSC 3.2.6JG do not apply as described in SYSC 1.1.3AR.

1.1.3A R SYSC 3.2.6AR to SYSC 3.2.6JG do not apply:

(1) with respect to the activities described in SYSC 1.1.3R(2) and (3); or
(2) in relation to the following *regulated activities*:
  (a) *general insurance business*;
  (b) *insurance mediation activity* in relation to a *general insurance contract* or *pure protection contract*;
  (c) *long-term insurance business* which is outside the *Consolidated Life Directive* (unless it is otherwise one of the *regulated activities* specified in this *rule*);
  (d) business relating to contracts which are within the *Regulated Activities Order* only because they fall within paragraph (e) of the definition of 'contract of insurance' in article 3 of that *Order*;

    (e)   (i) arranging, by *the Society of Lloyd's*, of deals in *general insurance contracts* written at Lloyd's; and

          (ii) *managing the underwriting capacity of a Lloyd's syndicate as a managing agent at Lloyd's*;

    (f) *mortgage mediation activity* and *administering a regulated mortgage contract*.

    (g) *home purchase mediation activity* and *administering a home purchase plan*; and

    (h) *reversion activity*.

1.1.4 R *SYSC* 2 and *SYSC* 3, except *SYSC* 3.2.6AR to *SYSC* 3.2.6JG, also apply with respect to the *communication* and *approval* of *financial promotions* which:

. . .

1.1.5 R *SYSC* 2 and *SYSC* 3, except *SYSC* 3.2.6AR to *SYSC* 3.2.6JG, also:

(1) apply with respect to the carrying on of *unregulated activities* in a *prudential context*; and

(2) take into account any activity of other members of a *group* of which the *firm* is a member.

Where?

. . .

1.1.9 R *SYSC* 2 and *SYSC* 3, except *SYSC* 3.2.6AR to *SYSC* 3.2.6JG, also apply in a *prudential context* to a *UK domestic firm* with respect to activities wherever they are carried on.

1.1.10 R *SYSC* 3, except *SYSC* 3.2.6AR to *SYSC* 3.2.6JG, also applies in a *prudential context* to an *overseas firm* (other than an *incoming EEA firm*, *incoming Treaty firm* or *UCITS qualifier*) with respect to activities wherever they are carried on.

. . .

Systems and controls in relation to compliance, financial crime and money laundering.

3.2.6 R A *firm* must take reasonable care to establish and maintain effective systems and controls for compliance with applicable requirements and standards under the *regulatory system* and for countering the risk that the *firm* might be used to further *financial crime*.

3.2.6A R A *firm* must ensure that these systems and controls:

(1) enable it to identify, assess, monitor and manage *money laundering* risk; and

(2) are comprehensive and proportionate to the nature, scale and complexity of its activities.

3.2.6B G 'Money laundering risk' is the risk that a *firm* may be used to further *money laundering*. Failure by a *firm* to manage this risk effectively will increase the risk to society of crime and terrorism.

3.2.6C R A *firm* must carry out regular assessments of the adequacy of these systems and controls to ensure that it continues to comply with *SYSC* 3.2.6AR.

3.2.6D G A *firm* may also have separate obligations to comply with relevant legal requirements, including the Terrorism Act 2000, the Proceeds of Crime Act 2002 and the *Money Laundering Regulations*. *SYSC* 3.2.6R to *SYSC* 3.2.6JG are not relevant for the purposes of regulation 3(3) of the *Money Laundering Regulations*, section 330(8) of the Proceeds of Crime Act 2002 or section 21A(6) of the Terrorism Act 2000.

3.2.6E G The *FSA*, when considering whether a breach of its *rules* on systems and controls against *money laundering* has occurred, will have regard to whether a *firm* has followed relevant provisions in guidance for the *UK* financial sector issued by the Joint Money Laundering Steering Group.

3.2.6F G In identifying its *money laundering* risk and in establishing the nature of these systems and controls, a *firm* should consider a range of factors, including:

(1) its customer, product and activity profiles;

(2) its distribution channels;

(3) the complexity and volume of its transactions;

(4) its processes and systems; and

(5) its operating environment.

3.2.6G G A *firm* should ensure that these systems and controls include:

(1) appropriate training for its employees in relation to *money laundering*;

(2) appropriate provision of information to its *governing body* and senior management, including a report at least annually by that *firm's money laundering reporting officer (MLRO)* on the operation and effectiveness of those systems and controls;

(3) appropriate documentation of its risk management policies and risk profile in relation to *money laundering*, including documentation of its application of those policies (see *SYSC* 3.2.20R to *SYSC* 3.2.22G);

(4) appropriate measures to ensure that *money laundering* risk is taken into account in its day-to-day operation, including in relation to:
   (a) the development of new products;
   (b) the taking-on of new customers; and
   (c) changes in its business profile; and

(5) appropriate measures to ensure that procedures for identification of new customers do not unreasonably deny access to its services to potential customers who cannot reasonably be expected to produce detailed evidence of identity.

3.2.6H R A *firm* must allocate to a *director* or *senior manager* (who may also be the *money laundering reporting officer*) overall responsibility within the *firm* for the establishment and maintenance of effective anti-*money laundering* systems and controls.

The money laundering reporting officer

3.2.6I R A *firm* must:

(1) appoint an individual as *MLRO*, with responsibility for oversight of its compliance with the *FSA's rules* on systems and controls against *money laundering*; and

(2) ensure that its *MLRO* has a level of authority and independence within the *firm* and access to resources and information sufficient to enable him to carry out that responsibility.

3.2.6J G The job of the *MLRO* within a *firm* is to act as the focal point for all activity within the *firm* relating to anti-*money laundering*. The *FSA* expects that a *firm's MLRO* will be based in the *United Kingdom*.

The compliance function

3.2.7 G (1) Depending on the nature, scale and complexity of its business, it may be appropriate for a *firm* to have a separate compliance function. The organisation and responsibilities of a compliance function should be documented. A compliance function should be staffed by an appropriate number of competent staff who are sufficiently independent to perform their duties objectively. It should be adequately resourced and should have unrestricted access to the *firm's* relevant records as well as ultimate recourse to its *governing body*.

APPENDIX II

Summary of UK Legislation

Proceeds of Crime Act 2002 (as amended)

1. The Proceeds of Crime Act 2002 ('POCA') consolidates and extends the existing UK legislation regarding money laundering. The legislation covers all crimes and any dealing in criminal property, with no exceptions and no de minimis. POCA:

- establishes the Assets Recovery Agency ('ARA'), to conduct an investigation to discover whether a person holds criminal assets and to recover the assets in question.
- creates five investigative powers for the law enforcement agencies:
  - a production order
  - a search and seizure warrant
  - a disclosure order
  - a customer information order
  - an account monitoring order
- establishes the following criminal offences:
  - a criminal offence to acquire, use, possess, conceal, disguise, convert, transfer or remove criminal property from the jurisdiction, or to enter into or become concerned in an arrangement to facilitate the acquisition, retention, use or control of criminal property by another person
  - a criminal offence for persons working in the regulated sector of failing to make a report where they have knowledge or suspicion of money laundering, or reasonable grounds for having knowledge or suspicion, that another person is laundering the proceeds of any criminal conduct, as soon as is reasonably practicable after the information came to their attention in the course of their regulated business activities.
  - Note: There are no provisions governing materiality or de minimis thresholds for having to report under POCA (although for deposit-taking firms, a transaction under £250 may be made without consent under certain circumstances—see paragraph 6.67).
  - a criminal offence for anyone to take any action likely to prejudice an investigation by informing (eg, tipping off) the person who is the subject of a suspicion report, or anybody else, that a disclosure has been made to a nominated officer or to SOCA, or that the police or customs authorities are carrying out or intending to carry out a money laundering investigation.
  - a criminal offence of destroying or disposing of documents which are relevant to an investigation.
  - a criminal offence by a firm of failing to comply with a requirement imposed on it under a customer information order, or in knowingly or recklessly making a statement in purported compliance with a customer information order that is false or misleading in a material particular.
- sets out maximum penalties:
  - for the offence of money laundering of 14 years' imprisonment and/or an unlimited fine.
  - Note: An offence is not committed if a person reports the property involved to the Serious Organised Crime Agency ('SOCA') or under approved internal arrangements, either before the prohibited act is carried out, or as soon afterwards as is reasonably practicable.
  - for failing to make a report of suspected money laundering, or for 'tipping off', of five years' imprisonment and/or an unlimited fine.

- for destroying or disposing of relevant documents of five years' imprisonment and/or an unlimited fine.

Terrorism Act 2000, and the Anti-terrorism, Crime and Security Act 2001

2. The Terrorism Act establishes a series of offences related to involvement in arrangements for facilitating, raising or using funds for terrorism purposes. The Act:

- makes it a criminal offence for any person not to report the existence of terrorist property where there are reasonable grounds for knowing or suspecting the existence of terrorist property
- makes it a criminal offence for anyone to take any action likely to prejudice an investigation by informing (ie tipping off) the person who is the subject of a suspicion report, or anybody else, that a disclosure has been made to a nominated officer or to SOCA, or that the police or customs authorities are carrying out or intending to carry out a terrorist financing investigation
- grants a power to the law enforcement agencies to make an account monitoring order, similar in scope to that introduced under POCA
- sets out the following penalties:
  - the maximum penalty for failure to report under the circumstances set out above is five years' imprisonment, and/or a fine.
  - the maximum penalty for the offence of actual money laundering is 14 years' imprisonment, and/or a fine.

3. A number of organisations have been proscribed under the Terrorism Act. The definition of terrorist property, involvement with which is an offence, includes resources of a proscribed organisation.

4. The Anti-terrorism, Crime and Security Act 2001 gives the authorities power to seize terrorist cash, to freeze terrorist assets and to direct firms in the regulated sector to provide the authorities with specified information on customers and their (terrorism-related) activities.

Money Laundering Regulations 2007

5. The Money Laundering Regulations 2007 specify arrangements which must be in place within firms within the scope of the Regulations, in order to prevent operations relating to money laundering or terrorist financing.

6. The ML Regulations apply, inter alia, to:
- The regulated activities of all financial sector firms, ie:
  - banks, building societies and other credit institutions;
  - individuals and firms engaging in regulated investment activities under FSMA;
  - issuers of electronic money;
  - insurance companies undertaking long-term life business, including the life business of Lloyd's of London;
  - bureaux de change, cheque encashment centres and money transmission services (money service businesses);
  - trust and company service providers;
  - casinos;
  - dealers in high-value goods (including auctioneers) who accept payment in cash of €15,000 or more (either single or linked transactions);
  - lawyers and accountants, when undertaking relevant business.

7. Persons within the scope of the ML Regulations are required to establish adequate and appropriate policies and procedures in order to prevent operations relating to money laundering or terrorist financing, covering:

- customer due diligence;
- reporting;
- record-keeping;
- internal control;
- risk assessment and management;

- compliance management; and
- communication.

8. The FSA may institute proceedings (other than in Scotland) for offences under prescribed regulations relating to money laundering. This power is not limited to firms or persons regulated by the FSA. Whether a breach of the ML Regulations has occurred is not dependent on whether money laundering has taken place: firms may be sanctioned for not having adequate AML/CTF systems. Failure to comply with any of the requirements of the ML Regulations constitutes an offence punishable by a maximum of two years' imprisonment, or a fine, or both.

FSA-Regulated Firms – the FSA Handbook

9. FSMA gives the FSA a statutory objective to reduce financial crime. In considering this objective, the FSA is required to have regard to the desirability of firms:

- Being aware of the risk of their businesses being used in connection with the commission of financial crime;
- Taking appropriate measures to prevent financial crime, facilitate its detection and monitor its incidence;
- Devoting adequate resources to that prevention, detection and monitoring.

10. Firms may only engage in a regulated activity in the UK if it is an authorised or exempt person. A person can become an authorised person as a result of: (a) being given a 'permission' by the FSA under Part IV of FSMA (known as a 'Part IV permission'); or (b) by qualifying for authorisation under FSMA itself. As an example of the latter, an EEA firm establishing a branch in, or providing cross-border services into, the UK can qualify for authorisation under FSMA Schedule 3 and, as a result, be given a permission; although such firms are, generally, authorised by their home state regulator, they are regulated by the FSA in connection with the regulated activities carried on in the UK.

11. A firm may only carry on regulated business in accordance with its permission. A firm with a Part IV permission may apply to the FSA to vary its permission, add or remove regulated activities, to limit these activities (for example, the types of client with or for whom the firm may carry on an activity) or to vary the requirements on the firm itself. Before giving or varying a Part IV permission, the FSA must ensure that the person/firm will satisfy and continue to satisfy the threshold conditions in relation to all of the regulated activities for which he has or will have permission. If a firm is failing, or is likely to fail, to satisfy the threshold conditions, the FSA may vary or cancel a firm's permission.

12. Threshold condition 5 (Suitability) requires the firm to satisfy the FSA that it is 'fit and proper' to have Part IV permission having regard to all the circumstances, including its connection with other persons, the range and nature of its proposed (or current) regulated activities and the overall need to be satisfied that its affairs are and will continue to be conducted soundly and prudently. Hence, the FSA 'will consider whether a firm is ready, willing and organised to comply, on a continuing basis, with the requirements and standards under the regulatory system which apply to the firm, or will apply to the firm, if it is granted Part IV permission, or a variation of its permission'. The FSA will also have regard to all relevant matters, whether arising in the UK or elsewhere. In particular, the FSA will consider whether a firm 'has in place systems and controls against money laundering of the sort described in SYSC 3.2.6 R to SYSC 3.2.6J G'. (COND 2.5.7G)

13. The FSA Handbook of rules and guidance contains high-level standards that apply, with some exceptions, to all FSA-regulated firms, (for example, the FSA Principles for Businesses, COND and SYSC) and to all approved persons (for example, the Statements of Principle and Code of Practice for Approved Persons). SYSC sets out particular rules relating to senior management

responsibilities, and for systems and controls processes. Some of these rules focus on the management and control of risk, and specifically require appropriate systems and controls over the management of money laundering risk.

14. In addition to prosecution powers under the Regulations, the FSA has a wide range of enforcement powers against authorised persons and approved persons for breaches of its Rules.

11

INTEGRATED PRUDENTIAL REGULATION

Background/History

Principle 4 in the FSA Principles for Businesses requires regulated firms to main- **11.01**
tain adequate financial resources. In short, firms must at all times maintain overall
financial resources adequate both as to amount and quality to ensure that there is
no significant risk that their liabilities cannot be met as they fall due.[1] In meeting
this obligation, firms are likewise required to satisfy the FSA's high-level requirements on systems and controls, that is Principle 2 'Care, skill and diligence',
Principle 3 'Management and control', and SYSC in their application to financial
risks.[2]

Prudential requirements address the risk that a regulated firm might not be able to **11.02**
meet its liabilities as they fall due. They include capital resources requirements,
liquidity requirements, limits on large or concentrated exposures and related systems, and controls requirements. The FSA's prudential requirements are risk-
based except for those applying to regulated firms whose limited activities mean
that they do not typically place themselves in debit with their customers. That is,
the requirements are based on a proxy or estimate of risk of inability to meet liabilities as they fall due. For these purposes risk is classified into credit risk, market
risk, liquidity risk, operational risk, insurance risk, concentration risk, residual
risk, securitisation risk, business risk, interest rate risk, pension obligation risk,
and group risk (as relevant to the firm, given the nature and scale of its business).[3]
GENPRU and the specialised sourcebooks mentioned below seek to harmonise
the prudential response to each of these risks across different types of regulated
firms in so far as this is consistent with the need to implement the different EU
directives that apply to the different types of regulated firms.

---

[1] See for example GENRU 1.2.26R.
[2] See in particular SYSC11 (liquidity risks), Chapters LM and LS of IPRU Bank and Chapter 5
of volume 1 of IPRU (BSOC).
[3] See GENPRU 1.2.30R.

The history of prudential standards

11.03   The move towards integrated prudential regulation began with the coming into force on 1 December 2001 (referred to in FSA-speak as the 'N2' date) of the main provisions of the Financial Services and Markets Act 2000 ('FSMA'). The FSA's initial objective was to streamline all prudential requirements in such a way as to provide a single cross-sectorally consistent set of prudential standards.[4] These were to be contained in the Integrated Prudential Sourcebook, setting out prudential standards for all firms. The advent of CRR[5] and MiFID[6] however forced the FSA to review its approach. The new prudential structure now applies the same or similar requirements across categories of firms but also provides dedicated sourcebooks for specialised firms. In order to see this structure in its proper setting it is helpful briefly to review the history of how, why, and when these prudential requirements were first created.

11.04   Prior to the creation of the FSA there were at least nine different regulatory authorities that were responsible for the prudential supervision of regulated firms. For example the Bank of England was responsible for banks but not building societies as responsibility for them fell to the Building Societies Commission. The Department of Trade and Industry (and briefly HM Treasury) was responsible for the prudential supervision of insurance companies, but not of friendly societies as responsibility for them fell to the Friendly Societies Commission. The Securities and Investments Board and the self-regulating organisations were responsible for other regulated financial firms. Each of these predecessor supervisory authorities was governed by different bodies of legislation and issued their own regulations, rules, or guidance under that legislation. They each drew on quite distinct and different regulatory traditions which had developed independently of each other, sometimes over many decades. For example prudential regulation for life insurance companies was first introduced in 1870 and the prudential regulatory rules that were in place for life insurance companies immediately prior to 1 December 2001 bore a closer resemblance to those that were first introduced in 1870 than those which applied for other financial services sectors.

11.05   The result of this separate development of the different regulatory traditions for the banks, building societies, insurance companies, friendly societies, and investment firms was a hotchpotch of different and often conflicting prudential regulations, rules, and guidance as between these different types of regulated firm. Until recently these differences between the prudential regulatory regimes for the different financial services sectors attracted little attention and even less criticism.

---

[4] See CP 'Integrated Prudential sourcebook' (published in June 2001).
[5] Capital Requirements Directive COM (2004) 486 Final of 14 July 2004. The directive was approved by the European Parliament in September 2005 and by the Council in October 2005.
[6] Council Directive (EC) 04/39 on markets and financial instruments (2004) OJ L145/1.

This lack of criticism reflected the traditional view that the different sectors each offered distinct products, in different marketing sectors, to satisfy different customer needs. As a result the focus of competition was within each financial services sector with little or no competition between the sectors. Also cross-ownership of one type of regulated firm (eg an insurance company) by another type of regulated firm (eg a bank) or of different types of regulated firms by the same holding company, although not unknown, was not typical, except perhaps for insurance groups also owning unit trust managers. Even where cross-ownership was in place the absence of group-consolidated prudential requirements lessened any pressure from such groups for a closer alignment of prudential standards across the different sectors.

However from the 1980s and 1990s onward things began to change. The traditional boundaries between the different financial services sectors began to be blurred by at least two distinct processes. First, risk transfer between the different financial services sectors, and indeed even to non-financial services firms, became easier. For example from the 1980s onward the transfer of credit risk from the banking sector via loan-book securitisation issues became more common and from the 1990s the use of credit derivatives for similar purposes also became more common. Also from the 1990s the transfer of insurance risk to the financial markets began to take place through insurance securitisations, finite reinsurance, and alternative risk transfer. Secondly the products themselves, especially within the savings markets, became less distinct. This was in part due to product development, for example the introduction in the 1970s and increasing prominence in the 1980s and 1990s of unit-linked life insurance blurred some of the traditional distinctions between life insurance savings products and those of the unit trust sector. However another factor was the withdrawal of tax incentives—such as life insurance premium relief in 1984—that applied to particular financial services products, and so until their withdrawal helped sustain product differences between the different financial services sectors. Also from the 1980s and 1990s onward mixed banking and insurance groups, also called bancassurance groups, became more common. This coincided with the introduction of group-consolidated supervision first for banking and financial groups in the late 1980s, then for insurance groups in the late 1990s, and finally for conglomerate groups at the start of the present decade. **11.06**

The Interim Prudential Sourcebooks

These trends in the 1980s and even more in the 1990s led to increasing criticism by regulated firms, market professionals, and even some customer groups of the continuing different prudential regimes that applied across the sectors. The Government's decision to create the Financial Services Authority ('FSA') as the single regulator was in part a response to the weight of this criticism of the existing arrangements. **11.07**

The FSA merged into itself the regulatory functions of the predecessor supervisors for the banks, building societies, insurance companies, friendly societies, and investment firms. It was not therefore surprising that the FSA took as one of its early priorities to replace the predecessor prudential regulations, rules, and guidance by a single cross-sectorally consistent, set of prudential standards. The guiding principle that the FSA set for itself was that 'like prudential risks should give rise to like prudential standards or requirements'. In addition the well-publicised difficulties that were being experienced in the UK with regulation of insurance companies, together with the perception that prudential standards for insurance companies were less well developed than the corresponding standards for banks, further increased the importance, and urgency, of prudential reform.

11.08   However, there were a number of reasons why the FSA quickly realised that this early priority would not necessarily be quickly achieved. First the pre-existing legislation under which the hotchpotch of pre-existing prudential standards had been put in place continued to operate. It was not until 1 December 2001 ('N2') that the main provisions of the Financial Services and Markets Act 2000 came into force including conferring on the FSA the power to make rules and issue guidance, and repealing the pre-existing legislation and the prudential and other regulations, rules, and guidance made under it.[7] Secondly, the sheer enormity of the task was sufficient to ensure it would take many years to complete. In addition at least initially very few people if any had sufficient cross-sectoral knowledge of the different prudential regimes to make informed policy choices as to the design of a new integrated regime. In particular a vast chasm of mutual misunderstanding and ignorance separated the banking and financial sectors on the one side and the insurance sector on the other side. Before informed policy choices could be made a process of mutual education both within the FSA and within the industry was needed. Thirdly, reform of prudential rules needed to take place within an international context. Prudential rules within the UK needed to implement, and be compliant with, both EU law and international standards. From 1999 onward the most important of those international standards, the Basel standard on capital adequacy, was being reviewed and revised. However the revision which would lead to the so-called Basel II standard was not expected at the time to be completed for a couple of years more. (In fact it took a little longer but this was not anticipated at the time.) This raised the unwelcome prospect that banks might be faced with two doses of fundamental reform in their prudential standards in rapid succession—first with the introduction of the Integrated Prudential Sourcebook and then a year or two later with the implementation of Basel II.

---

[7] FSMA 2000, s 138 (general rule making power), s 149 (evidential provisions), s 150 (actions for damages), s 156 (general supplementary power), s 157 (guidance), and s 316 (directions by the Authority).

As a result of the above three considerations the FSA took the decision not to **11.09** attempt to create the Integrated Prudential Sourcebook immediately at N2. The aim would be to create and bring into force those portions of the Integrated Prudential Sourcebook that did not derive from the Basel standards as quickly as reasonably practicable bearing in mind that fundamental change such as that envisaged in the creation of the Integrated Prudential Sourcebook would require an extended period of design and consultation. Those portions of the Integrated Prudential Sourcebook that fell within the scope of the Basel 2 standards were to be delayed until the time of implementation of those standards. This, however, left the problem of putting in place prudential standards in the interim, ie in the period from N2 until the Integrated Prudential Sourcebook was in place. The rulebooks, including the prudential rules, of the predecessor regulators, were due to disappear at N2.

The FSA consulted on how to deal with this problem when in November 1999 it **11.10** issued Consultation Paper 31. This consultation paper set out the FSA's proposed general approach to the use of its powers to enact rules and issue guidance to replace the prudential rules and regulations of the predecessor regulators. In particular it set out proposals to put in place Interim Prudential Sourcebooks. These Interim Prudential Sourcebooks were to come into force at N2, but were to be subsequently replaced by the Integrated Prudential Sourcebook as and when it was made. The aim of the Interim Prudential Sourcebooks was to re-enact with minimal change the prudential standards that were in force immediately prior to N2, and so to buy time to allow work on the Integrated Prudential Sourcebook to proceed.

The structure of the Interim Prudential Sourcebooks

The basic design principle for the Interim Prudential Sourcebooks was deter- **11.11** mined by their aim, that is in substance to reproduce the prudential standards that were in place immediately prior to N2 as then set out in the rules and regulations of the predecessor regulators. Change was to be kept to a minimum. In particular this meant that separate Interim Prudential Sourcebooks were needed to correspond to the separate rule books of the predecessor regulators. However a straight read-across from the predecessor rule books was not completely possible for two main reasons. First, rules enacted by, and guidance issued by, the FSA needed to conform to the requirements of FSMA. In particular this meant making a clear distinction between legally binding rules and non-binding guidance (which had not necessarily always been done in the material issued by the predecessor regulators). Secondly, the opportunity was taken to make some limited changes to achieve a very limited amount of harmonisation of standards across different sectors. In particular there was some limited harmonisation of standards as between banks and building societies.

Table 11.1

Interim Prudential Sourcebook (IPRU)	Type of firm to which it applies	Predecessor regulator 'rulebook'
IPRU(BANK)	Banks	Guidance notes issued by the Bank of England
IPRU(BSOC)	Building societies	Regulations made under the Building Societies Act and guidance issued by the Building Societies Commission.
IPRU(INS)	Insurance companies	Regulations made under the Insurance Companies Act and guidance issued by the Insurance Directorate of HM Treasury.
IPRU(FSOC)	Friendly societies	Regulations made under the Friendly Societies Act and guidance issued by the Friendly Societies Commission.
IPRU(INV)—Chapter 2	Professional firms	Prudential rules for investment business made by the professional bodies, eg accountants, lawyers, and actuaries.
IPRU(INV)—Chapters 3 & 10	Securities and investment firms	Rules and guidance issued by the self-regulating organisation, the Securities and Futures Association.
IPRU(INV)—Chapter 5	Investment management firms	Rules and guidance issued by the self-regulating organisation, the Investment Management Regulatory Organisation.
IPRU(INV)—Chapter 7	UCITS management firms	Rules and guidance issued by the self-regulating organisation, the Personal Investment Authority for ex-LAUTRO firms.
IPRU(INV)—Chapter 13	Personal investment firms	Rules and guidance issued by the self-regulating organisation, the Personal Investment Authority for these ex-FIMBRA firms.

11.12 The list of original Interim Prudential Sourcebooks is set out in Table 11.1. It is to be noted, however, that the Interim Prudential Sourcebook for Investment Firms was in reality a compendium of several predecessor rule books within which its different chapters in effect amounted to free-standing Interim Prudential Sourcebooks.

11.13 Chapters 4 and 8 of IPRU(INV) related to types of firm that were not subject to such detailed prudential regulation prior to N2. Chapter 4 referred to Lloyd's members agents. Prior to N2 advising on syndicate participations at Lloyd's was not a regulated activity. Chapter 8 applied to credit unions.

The Integrated Prudential Sourcebook

Problems in implementation

11.14 The Integrated Prudential Sourcebook was to be the single source of prudential standards for all types of regulated firm. The original design concept for the

Integrated Prudential Sourcebook was that of 'like prudential regulatory responses to like risks' across different types of regulated firm irrespective of the sector (eg banking or insurance) into which they fell.

The concept of like regulatory responses across sectors does not require that **11.15** prudential standards for, say, banks, investment banks, and insurance companies be identical. However, these different types of regulated firm operate according to different business models and within different legal, economic, and marketplace environments. In consequence they face different risks and therefore need at least some different regulatory responses.

Further, the FSA encountered a basic problem in applying the concept of like **11.16** regulatory responses to like risks. The prudential standards set by the FSA have to comply with, and implement, those set down in applicable EU directives. An EU directive is a legally binding text settled jointly by the EU Council of Ministers and the EU Parliament addressed to the EU Member States directing them to change their national laws to comply with the requirements set out in the directive. There was one set of EU directives that set out in some detail the prudential requirements that applied to credit institutions and financial firms, and another set of EU directives that set out the requirements that applied to insurance undertakings. There were still other sets of EU directives that applied to other types of firms. A full table of relevant directives is set out at Table 11.2 below. These different sets of EU directives limited the FSA's ability to apply like prudential regulatory responses to like prudential risks.

Despite these difficulties the FSA was able initially to implement in part its plan for **11.17** a streamlined cross-sectoral approach to prudential regulation for insurers, mortgage firms, and insurance intermediaries. These areas are now covered by MIPRU.[8] Initially (and reflecting its two-fold scope), the first part of Phase 1 came into force on 31 October 2004 for mortgage intermediation or lending. The second part of Phase 1 came into effect on 14 January 2005 for insurance intermediation.[9]

Prior thereto neither insurance mediation nor mortgage intermediation or lend- **11.18** ing were regulated activities. The prudential standards were therefore are entirely new and did not replace requirements of predecessor regimes or Interim Prudential Sourcebooks.

---

[8] See para 11.26 below.
[9] See the Insurance Mediation and Mortgage Mediation, Lending and Administration (Prudential Provisions) Instrument 2004 as amended by the Insurance Mediation and Mortgage Mediation, Lending and Administration (Miscellaneous Amendments) Instrument 2004 and the Child Trust Funds Instruments 2004.

Table 11.2

Type of regulated firm	EU directives
Banks, building societies, and investment firms, other than exempt so-called 'non-CAD' investment firms.	The Banking Consolidation Directive and Capital Adequacy Directive, which merged into the Capital Requirements Directive
Insurance companies, friendly societies, and Lloyd's	The First, Second, and Third Life and Non-life Directives as amended[10] and the Insurance Groups Directive
Unit trust managers	The UCITS directives
Insurance intermediaries	The Insurance Mediation Directive
Mortgage lenders and intermediaries	None
Non-CAD investment firms	None

The New Prudential Sourcebook Structure

11.19 The difficulties outlined above in paras 11.15 and 11.16 led the FSA to modify its plans for the creation of a single Integrated Prudential Sourcebook. Under the revised approach the FSA has sought to align EU prudential requirements with a 'copy-out' approach to the implementation of directives. Thus, directive text is copied out into the Handbook with additional guidance provided only where this is considered to be clearly justified. Prudential requirements for specialised firms have been made easier to navigate by introducing stand-alone dedicated sourcebooks.

11.20 GENPRU now contains the general prudential requirements broadly applying to banks, insurers, building societies, BIPRU investment firms, and groups containing such firms.[11] Key provisions now include the following rule requirements to:

- Maintain overall financial resources, including capital and liquidity resources, adequate as to both amount and quality, to ensure there is no significant risk that liabilities cannot be met as they fall due;[12]

- Have in place sound, effective, and complete processes, strategies, and systems to maintain financial resources adequate to cover the risks to which the firm is exposed;[13]

- Carry out stress tests and scenario analyses appropriate to the nature of major sources of risk (including the identification of realistic adverse circumstances

---

[10] For life insurance these directives have been consolidated into the Consolidated Life Directive.

[11] GENPRU 1.1.2.G.

[12] GENPRU 1.2.26R.

[13] GENPRU 1.2.30R.

and events in which the risk identified might crystallise and an estimation of the financial reserves that would be needed to meet the risks);[14]

- Make a written record of the major sources of risks identified and how they are to be dealt with and of the stress tests and scenario analyses carried out.[15]

In focusing both quantitatively and qualitatively on capital and liquidity resources **11.21** in the context of stress testing and scenario analyses the modern regime may reflect lessons learned from past failures in effective prudential regulation—such as exemplified by the Equitable Life debacle. Although these measures are important safeguards designed to secure investor protection breaches of these prudential rules do not give rise to a right of action by a private person for damages under section 150 of FSMA.[16]

Application to Lloyd's

Broadly the prudential requirements described above apply to both managing **11.22** agents and the Society of Lloyd's.[17] Thus, Lloyd's members taken together must maintain overall financial resources so as to be able to meet liabilities under contracts of insurance written at Lloyd's as they fall due.[18]

Capital resources requirement

Chapter 2 of GENPRU now contains the principal provisions dealing with the **11.23** calculation of capital resources requirements for BIPRU firms and insurers,[19] along with the definition of capital for this purpose.[20] Detailed treatment of these provisions is given elsewhere.[21] Their application is in broad terms extended to the Society of Lloyd's and its managing agents.[22]

The requirements for adequate capital resources are applied to financial conglom- **11.24** erates in accordance with provisions now found in GENPRU 3. Financial conglomerates may be identified in accordance with the decision tree in GENPRU 3, annex 4R.[23] The requirements extend to firms within the conglomerate.[24]

---

[14] GENPRU 1.2.42R.
[15] GENPRU 1.2.60R.
[16] GENPRU 1.4.1R.
[17] GENPRU 1.5.1R.
[18] GENPRU 1.5.7R.
[19] GENPRU 2.1.
[20] GENPRU 2.2.
[21] See Chapter 13.
[22] GENPRU 2.3.
[23] GENPRU 3.1.25R.
[24] GENPRU 3.1.6R.

Special rules apply to identifying and managing risk concentration and intra-group transactions in financial conglomerates headed by a mixed financial holding company.[25] Asset management companies within conglomerates likewise fall within the reach of these requirements.[26]

11.25   Departures from the prudential requirements discussed above give rise to notification requirements to the FSA. These are helpfully tabulated at GENPRU, Schedule 2.

MIPRU

11.26   MIPRU is the Prudential Sourcebook for Mortgage and Home Finance Firms and Insurance Intermediaries.[27] In addition to purely prudential requirements this sourcebook includes provisions imposing obligations on directors and senior managers to accept responsibility for the firm's conduct of insurance mediation activity.[28] This includes a duty to ensure those responsible for insurance mediation activity are possessed of the knowledge and ability necessary to perform their duties.[29] There are detailed requirements dealing with a firm's obligation to have appropriate professional indemnity insurance cover in place in respect of its activities,[30] although breach of the rules set out in MIPRU itself does not give rise to a right of action for damages by private persons.[31]

11.27   Chapter 4 of MIPRU contains the main provisions dealing with capital resources requirements for these types of firm. There is a general solvency requirement that the firm must be able to meet at all times its liabilities as they fall due.[32] In addition there is a requirement for the firm to maintain at all times capital resources equal to or in excess of specified levels.[33] These minimum requirements depend on whether the firm is carrying out mediation activity only,[34] home financing and home finance administration,[35] home finance administration only,[36] insurance mediation activity and home financing or home finance administration,[37] home finance mediation activity and home financing or home finance administration.[38]

---

[25] GENPRU 3.1.34R.
[26] GENPRU 3.1.39R.
[27] MIPRU 1.1.1G.
[28] MIPRU 2.2.1R.
[29] MIPRU 2.3.1R.
[30] MIPRU, Chapter 3.
[31] MIPRU 1.2.1R.
[32] MIPRU 4.2.1R.
[33] MIPRU 4.2.2R.
[34] MIPRU 4.2.11R.
[35] MIPRU 4.2.12R.
[36] MIPRU 4.2.18R.
[37] MIPRU 4.2.20R.
[38] MIPRU 4.2.21R.

There are detailed provisions dealing with recognition of income and the calculation of capital reserves.[39]

UPRU

UPRU is the Prudential Sourcebook for UCITS firms. Prudential requirements **11.28** applying to UCITS investment firms are set out elsewhere in the Prudential Sourcebook for Banks, Building Societies, and Investment Firms and in GENPRU.[40] The principal requirement is that any UCITS firm must ensure that it has at all times financial resources that equal or exceed specified financial resources requirements.[41] For this purpose detailed rules are set out governing the calculation of financial resources.[42] Breaches of these requirements do not however give rise to a right of action for private persons under s 150 of FSMA, 2000.[43]

IPRU(BANK)

As explained above,[44] the Integrated Prudential Sourcebook and with it the **11.29** Interim Prudential Sourcebook for Banks—IPRU(BANK)—have so far as banks are concerned been largely superseded by the provisions contained in GENPRU, parts of SYSC, and the Prudential Sourcebook for Banks, Building Societies and Investment Firms (BIPRU). The only parts of IPRU(BANK) that presently remain are those relating to liquidity requirements.[45] These are to be found in IPRU(BANK) LM (mismatch liquidity) and LS (sterling stock liquidity). These provisions are treated elsewhere in this work.[46]

IPRU(BSOC)

The content of this Interim Prudential Sourcebook has been largely redistributed **11.30** to GENPRU and BIPRU as far as it relates to solvency and capital requirements—and to the new Building Society's Regulatory Guide (BSOG) in relation to registration, transfers, and mergers. The only parts of IPRU(BSOC) that presently remain are those relating to financial risk management and liquidity requirements. These survive for the time being in sections 4 and 5 of IPRU(BSOC).

---

[39] MIPRU 4.3 and 4.4.
[40] UPRU 1.1.1R.
[41] UPRU 2.1.1R.
[42] UPRU 2.2.1R.
[43] UPRU, Schedule 5.
[44] Paras 11.15 and 11.16 above.
[45] IPRU(BANK) 2.
[46] Chapter 14.

IPRU(FSOC)

11.31 IPRU(FSOC) is the Prudential Sourcebook for Building Societies. The early sections of the sourcebook deal with the obligations of senior managers to ensure the business of the firm is conducted with integrity, skill, care, and diligence and is appropriately managed.[47] The mainstream requirements in respect of solvency margins and maintenance of adequate assets are set out in Chapter 4. A detailed account of these provisions is outside the scope of this general review of the prudential regulatory landscape.

Effective Prudential Regulation

11.32 Effective prudential regulation requires not only a framework of appropriate and robust rules but an equally robust and effective regulator to monitor and enforce them. As to the underlying framework, the UK regime, as with most international systems of prudential regulation, is built on an actuarial model, more particularly on a model of 'ruin theory'. This asserts that the purpose of regulation is to ensure that the probability of a financial undertaking succumbing to 'ruin' is below some given 'acceptable value'. In operating this model the regulator relies on one principal tool to achieve this aim, namely the imposition of a solvency margin intended to serve as a financial buffer. Various approaches are adopted such as the United States deployment of a 'risk-based capital' analysis or 'Financial Analysis and Surveillance Tracking'. The difficulty with these approaches is that their track record in predicting failure of a particular firm experiencing financial distress is poor. Studies of the use of these actuarial evaluations of the risk have shown them to be poor diagnostic and prognostic indicators.[48] In an illuminating critique of these issues Plantin and Rochet argue that part of the problem lies in the nature of long-term insurance risks inherent in the product itself. Premium income is collected generally well in advance of any obligation to settle a claim. They contend that this 'inversion of the production cycle' makes it easy for senior management of insurance companies to conceal difficulties.[49] The problem is exacerbated by any unwillingness on the part of the regulator to intervene in taking and imposing tough business decisions to cut losses at an early stage. This is in part a reflection

---

[47] Chapters 2 and 3, IPRU(FSOC).

[48] See Cummins, Harrington, and Klein, 'Solvency experience, risk-based capital and prompt corrective action in property-liability insurance' (Centre for Financial Institutions Working Paper 95-06), Wharton School Centre for Financial Institutions, University of Pennsylvania; Cummins, Grace and Phillips, 'Regulatory solvency prediction in property-liability insurance: risk-based capital, audit ratios and cash flow simulation' (1999) *Journal of Risk and Insurance* 66; Grace, Harrington and Klein, 'Risk-based capital standards and insurer solvency risk: an empirical analysis' (1993), paper presented to the American Risk and Insurance Association annual meeting in San Francisco, CA.

[49] *When Insurers go bust—an economic analysis of the role and design of Prudential Regulation*, Princeton University Press (2007)

of the fact that the regulator is a regulator and not a business operator. The model they advocate for prudential regulation of insurers rests on six primary principles:

(a) a requirement for a simple definition of prudential ratios derived from public accounts; 'double trigger regulation' in which once a solvency threshold requirement is breached regulatory intervention occurs, with a requirement for the firm to remedy the situation with an action plan, failing which the risks are to be transferred to an industry run guarantee fund;

(b) a clear agenda issued to the regulator accountable to Parliament; establishment of a guarantee fund to take over risks where insurers prove unable to implement a prompt recovery plan;

(c) a single accounting standard and prudential regulation focusing on primary insurance companies and insurance groups rather than assuming responsibility for supervision of the whole insurance production line.

The aim here is to invest the regulator with tough powers to transfer the business of a distressed insurer to an industry-run guarantee fund with a view to maximising policyholder recovery. The regime allows little room for conciliation or negotiation with senior management and so seeks to obviate the risk of the business continuing to be run in a manner that potentially increases the opportunity of policyholder losses.

11.33 It is interesting to observe that the problems of effective regulation discussed above may be seen in the collapse of Equitable Life and the difficulties experienced by it in managing policyholder claims on its with-profits fund. In March 2004 Lord Penrose's report to the Treasury into the collapse of this insurer was published. It included analysis and commentary on the Society's 'reserving' history so far as funding long-term insurance commitments was concerned. Lord Penrose recorded that prior to 1972 the Society had maintained an 'estate' ie a reserve fund out of which to 'smooth returns on invested premiums'.[50] In that year it had introduced a 'three call' system[51] which could have been prudently operated to preserve sufficient assets to meet policy values but for action taken in 1973 when equity markets fell. The 'estate' was then raided in order to maintain competitive and high bonus rates. As Penrose concluded:[52]

> Over the 1980's the Society maintained competitive levels of bonus allocation by cutting back on its general reserve until, by 1987 it had over allocated bonus so that its aggregate policy values on a realistic basis exceeded available assets.

---

[50] Report, chapter 4, para 4 and chapter 19, para 31.
[51] Report, chapter 3, para 14.
[52] Report, chapter 19, para 40.

He also noted that:[53]

> In 1990 the aggregate policy values estimated to policyholders were significantly higher than the assets available as a result of the allocations of that year. Thereafter the with profits assets of the Society were never in excess of or equal to aggregate with profits value including accrued terminal bonus.

11.34 The absence of any maintained estate was responsible for impairing if not completely disabling the Society's ability to deliver a 'smoothed return' on investments in its with-profits fund. Although from 1989 onwards the Society in its Key Features and other product literature offered investors a 'uniform smooth investment return allocated to accumulated policy values', the Penrose Report demonstrates clearly that no such policy was in fact discernibly operated. In dealing with the Society's 'smoothing technique' Lord Penrose stated:[54]

> A smoothing policy . . . would specify a projected target return, incorporating an assumed rate of growth; maximum deviation above and below the projection; and the duration of the cycle to achieve equilibrium between the projected and actual returns. In reality, such a policy would be unlikely to be realised over time and adjustments would be required to reflect experience. But it would be difficult to envisage any rational smoothing process that did not allow for the holding of surplus assets from time to time, during that phase of the cycle when actual returns exceeded projected returns, to balance periods when over allocation was necessary as against actual returns to support bonus allocation. . . . I have sought to demonstrate . . . the Society's free assets were eroded over the 1980's by the policies adopted until there was a net excess of policy values over available assets.

Further, he noted:[55]

> The most fundamental deficiency in the Society's attempt to smooth was in its approach to claims. Claims on average continued throughout the period of review [1989-2000] to be paid out in excess of their asset share leaving the enforced business to restore balance. Smoothing consequently was not applied at a claims level . . . consequently the Society became heavily dependent on unallocated investment earnings on new and enforced business in its attempts to restore fund balance

11.35 This is surely a classic illustration of senior management being offered the opportunity by a weak system of prudential regulation to take risks with policyholders' premiums designed to prop up a failing business model unchecked. Despite the prudential framework within which the Society operated it was able to present an inaccurate financial picture as a result of the use of certain accounting techniques. These were summarised by Lord Penrose in chapter 19 of the report.[56] In short, these enabled the Society to 'overvalue' its net premium valuation, 'undervalue' its

---

[53] ibid, para 48.
[54] Report, chapter 6, para 22.
[55] ibid, para 61.
[56] ibid, paras 50–55.

liabilities with the result of generating a perceived 'surplus'. Lord Penrose found for example that the Society had improperly applied a quasi-zillmer adjustment which had the effect of generating a non-existent surplus sum of approximately £1 billion; it relied on mortality factors which had not been updated, serving further to depress the real value of long-term liabilities; it supported its 'technical solvency' for regulatory purposes by issuing £350 million of subordinated debt, made extensive use of implicit profits adjustments, and had entered into a financial reinsurance agreement which did not materially transfer risk to the chosen underwriters. In reality, the Society was able to indulge in a degree of 'financial engineering' to appear to balance the books whilst hiding the true state of its financial condition and masking a deteriorating solvency position.

The findings and analysis of Lord Penrose serve to demonstrate how the Society **11.36** was able to 'duck and weave' around the prudential requirements that were meant to be governing the conduct of its business. They do not explain how Equitable Life was able to accomplish these accounting sleights of hand which robust monitoring and regulatory supervision ought to have detected and avoided. The latter issue was the subject of the Parliamentary Ombudsman Report by Anne Abrahams—*Equitable Life, a decade of regulatory failure* (published in July 2008). One of the key findings of the report related to the requirement for the Society each year to submit annual returns to the prudential regulators setting out detail about the business of the Society, its liabilities, the assets covering those liabilities, and its solvency position. The submission and scrutiny of those returns were the two prime mechanisms of prudential regulation relied upon by the prudential regulators. The report noted (at para. 5.13) that:

> The Society's returns for the years 1990 to 1993 raised certain issues about the approach that [it] was adopting to its business, which the scrutiny process was designed to highlight in order to enable the prudential regulators, acting with advice and assistance from GAD, to ascertain whether there was any need to raise and pursue those issues.

As to this process, her conclusion was:[57]

> That, with regard to the scrutiny of the Society's annual regulatory returns for the year ends for 1990 to 1993, GAD, in providing advice to the prudential regulators, failed to satisfy themselves that the way in which the Society had determined its liabilities and had sought to demonstrate that it had sufficient assets to cover those liabilities accorded with the requirements of the applicable Regulations . . . those regulators were unable to verify the solvency position of the Society as they were under a duty to do. The aspects in respect of which the Society's returns for these years raised questions which should have been identified, pursued and resolved [included the following] the valuation rate of interest used to discount the liabilities,

---

[57] See paras 5.14 to 5.18 of the Report.

which appeared to be imprudent and/or impermissible (discounting liabilities well below the guaranteed face value of policies); and the affordability and sustainability of the bonuses previously declared by the Society, which appeared to raise the expectations of the Society's policyholders which might not be met. . . . On the information before GAD, the Society's approach to discounting meant that a significant amount of any future surplus would be required simply to fund current guaranteed benefits. . . . This occurred in a situation in which GAD knew that the Society had informed its policyholders that, subject to smoothing, the additional returns they would receive by way of future bonus declarations would reflect the future investment performance of the with-profits fund. . . . In addition, serious questions arose from the information within the returns about whether the Society could afford the level of bonus it was paying and whether it could continue to pay out at that level.

11.37 This whole episode is a salutary illustration of prudential standards inadequately defined and ineffectively enforced. In identifying and responding to such deficiencies in prudential regulation in the past, however, it is fair to comment that the regulator has learned from the experience. The approach to prudential regulation described above and as now operated by the FSA involves a far more sophisticated appreciation of how financial risks can arise and impact businesses than has hitherto been the case. To this extent the regulatory landscape in this areas can be regarded as providing a much safer setting for the conduct of cross-sectoral investment activity than was formerly so. Nonetheless, as the recent experience of the 'credit crunch' demonstrates, however robust internal domestic regulatory regimes may be financial markets interact globally and face external challenges which call for coordinated international initiatives if market stability is to be maintained.

Part III

FINANCIAL SECTORS AND ACTIVITIES

12

INVESTMENT FIRMS—WHOLESALE SECTOR

Evolution

The evolution of investment firms' regulation has been, as is the case with most **12.01** modern forms of regulatory regime, an event-led process. This branch of financial services regulation is fascinating for a number of reasons, primarily because of the way in which securities products and trading methodologies have evolved through the years. Contemporary investment firms embrace technological developments in ways which pose constant challenges for regulators and for the firms themselves.

Increased global competition and the commoditisation of investment and other **12.02** products have contributed to a fast changing landscape which is perhaps at its most dynamic in the investment firms sector of financial services. Regulators are constantly challenged and have to constantly revise their rules, methods, and procedures. This has been markedly demonstrated by the failings exhibited by a large number of firms in the course of the still unfolding 'credit crunch'. At the same time, regulators in the UK, as elsewhere, have always been, and will no doubt continue to be, under-resourced in comparison with the leading investment firms. This partly explains the relatively recent shift by the UK regulatory authority to so-called 'risk-based regulation', which, in plain English, means concentrating regulatory efforts on those firms or sectors which are most likely to cause market destabilisation or to put at risk the objectives which the regulator is mandated to achieve. The FSA has also focused in recent times on honing its 'principles-based regulation'. Whilst this concept has obvious inherent attraction both for regulators and for regulated firms, its appeal has certainly lost some of its shine in light of the monumental losses incurred by certain investment firms pursuant to the sub-prime mortgage crisis and the associated lack of discipline that some firms seem to have suffered from.

12.03   In addition to this, the European Union ('EU') is polishing its most ambitious effort yet to consolidate regulation in the EU's financial markets. At the heart of this process are several directives which have changed the face of investment firms' regulation across the European Economic Area ('EEA'), which comprises the EU Member States, Norway, Iceland, and Liechtenstein. The most significant of these measures (in the non-prudential context) is the Markets in Financial Instruments Directive ('MiFID')[1] and its implementing measures—see paras 12.37 to 12.40.

12.04   As a prelude to a detailed review of the current position, there follows a brief historical overview of the evolution of investment firms' regulation so that readers are able to put the rest of this chapter in context.

The Anderson Report

12.05   On 9 March 1936, the Board of Trade appointed a committee chaired by Sir Alan Anderson to 'enquire into Fixed Trusts in all their aspects and to report what action, if any, is desirable . . . '. The committee reported in July 1936.[2] The terms of reference in fact extended not only to those collective investment schemes where the investments would be fixed for the life of the scheme, but also to collective investment schemes—as we know them today—which give investment managers scope for switching between different securities as they see fit or in accordance with a defined mandate.

12.06   The reason for the appointment of the committee was the occurrence of numerous cases of misleading advertisements and mis-selling of unit trusts to members of the public. Promoters of unit trusts, unlike those of companies, were at that time subject to no regulation at all. In a typical fashion, the committee advised against direct regulation of unit trusts in favour of reliance on self-regulation by then existing industry bodies. However, the committee did recommend that statutory provisions be introduced to regulate the marketing of units in such trusts by prescribing what information must be included in any public offering document.

12.07   The committee also proposed the registration of unit trusts' managers at Companies House (including the filing of specified documentation in connection with the trust), and recommended that managers of unit trusts should deposit a substantial amount of money with the Paymaster General (to be earmarked for the protection of unit-holders in the event of an adverse event). A further recommendation was that managers of unit trusts should be liable to pay

---

[1] Council Directive (EC) 04/39 on markets in financial instruments [2004] OJ L145/1.
[2] Fixed Trusts: Report of the Departmental Committee appointed by the Board of Trade (Cmd 5259, 1936).

compensation for any loss sustained by investors as a result of false statements in advertisements.

The Bodkin Report

Shortly after the report of the Anderson Committee, the Board of Trade appointed **12.08** a committee chaired by Sir Archibald Bodkin 'to consider the operations commonly known as share-pushing and share-hawking and other similar activities . . . and report what, if any, action is desirable'. The committee reported in July 1937.[3] The reason behind the appointment was the occurrence of an alarming number of fraud cases involving securities where, for example, members of the public were offered worthless securities or paid for securities they were offered only to find that the dealer absconded with the purchase price.

The committee was very reluctant to recommend the imposition of regulatory **12.09** requirements for fear of 'serious interference with [investment firms'] legitimate and useful activities'—but managed to overcome its reluctance. As a result, the committee's report became the first instance of a UK body expressing the rather obvious concern that there should be some type of mechanism to ensure that only persons of good character and with relevant expertise should be permitted to deal in securities. The committee recommended that anyone, other than a member of one of the then existing stock exchanges, who proposed to enter into the business of dealing in securities should be registered with a public authority, subject to satisfaction of certain conditions as to good repute and, significantly, should comply with prescribed conditions as to the conduct of that business. This was the first time rules of conduct for investment firms were referred to in official UK literature.

Prevention of Fraud (Investments) Acts 1939/1958

The recommendations of the Anderson Committee and the Bodkin Committee **12.10** formed the basis for the enactment of the Prevention of Fraud (Investments) Act 1939 ('PFA'), whose name alone tells us that it was never intended to be a comprehensive legislative measure to regulate investment firms. The PFA was a somewhat rushed attempt to get rid of a number of loopholes which facilitated the operation of dishonest firms to the detriment of mainly retail customers.

The PFA required, for the first time in the UK, that persons 'dealing in securities' **12.11** (as principal or agent) must obtain a licence prior to engaging in such activities.

---

[3] Share Pushing: Report of the Departmental Committee appointed by the Board of Trade (Cmd 5539, 1937).

This requirement applied both to firms and to individuals operating within firms. Breach of this requirement constituted a criminal offence. Members of the various Stock Exchanges (and persons acting on their behalf) were excluded from this requirement as it was deemed that their self-regulatory status was sufficient to ensure protection for investors. As a result of this limitation, the licence and conduct of business requirements made under the PFA applied to only a minority of the investment firms operating at the time.

12.12　Furthermore, with regard to transactions in securities with licensed or exempt persons the Board of Trade was empowered by the PFA to make 'rules for regulating the conduct of business by holders of licences'.[4] These rules covered, amongst other areas, classification of customers, forms of contracts to be used, and record-keeping requirements. Section 12 of the PFA provided the first explicit statutory provision directed at preventing fraudulent conduct intended to induce persons to invest in securities, a provision which forms the basis of what is now section 397 of the Financial Services and Markets Act 2000 ('FSMA'). (The enactment of the Prevention of Fraud (Investments) Act 1958 added little to the regime established by the PFA save for its conferring on the Board of Trade the power to appoint an inspector to investigate the affairs of unit trust schemes.)

Review of investor protection—the Gower Report

12.13　It was not until the late 1970s that the shortcomings of the PFA were exposed. The lifting of exchange control in 1979 and the increasingly international nature of the securities industry meant that the then rather patchy regulatory regime came under an enormous amount of pressure. At the same time there was a marked increase in the sophistication of investment firms and the products which they devised for their customers; products such as, for example, commodity derivatives were definitely not within the contemplation of those responsible for the drafting of the PFA. Also, while the PFA regulated dealers in securities, there was no explicit regulatory regime to cover investment advisers and investment managers, whose roles grew in prominence as the benefits of investing in securities though mutual funds became well known and appreciated by investors.

12.14　As is often the case with regulatory reform, the final triggers for changes to the PFA regime were specific problems in the market place, in this instance the rather spectacular collapse of Norton Warburg in February 1981 and the investigation into the affairs of senior executives of Halliday Simpson between 1978 and 1983.

---

[4]　PFA, s 7(1).

In 1981, Professor Jim Gower was entrusted, by the then Secretary of State for **12.15**
Trade, with the mammoth task of considering both the need for statutory protection of private and business investors in securities and other property, and the
need for statutory control of dealers in securities, investment consultants, and
investment managers.

Professor Gower reported to Parliament in January 1984[5] with his recommenda- **12.16**
tions. He had encountered unanimous dissatisfaction with the regime created
under the PFA and this resulted in the most far-reaching proposals ever made for
reform of the regulation of investment firms in the UK. The principles emanating
from this report (the Gower Report) still form the fundamental pillars of financial
services regulation to this day.

The Gower Report's recommendations advocated the establishment of a compre- **12.17**
hensive and self-contained statutory framework for regulation which was to be
based, so far as possible, on self-regulation subject to governmental supervision.
Self-regulation alone was found to be inadequate as a means of achieving the
objectives of financial services regulation. The Gower Report concluded that self-
regulation would only work with adequate and well-balanced supervision from
the Government. The Gower Report further recommended that the new statutory regime, the scope of which, as proposed, could, where necessary, be extended
with ease by the Department of Trade and Industry, should regulate a far wider
range of activities and investments (including contracts for commodity or financial futures or options) than had previously been the case.

Furthermore, all investment firms would require a licence. For members of self- **12.18**
regulatory agencies (which in turn comply with strict regulatory criteria) a licence
would be granted by virtue of membership. Alternatively, a licence could be
obtained directly from the relevant statutory body (which later became the
Securities and Investments Board).

The Gower Report also continued the trend of empowering the relevant statutory **12.19**
body to make rules for the conduct of business; investment firms, regulated by a
self-regulatory agency, would be bound by the rules to that effect issued by that
agency. One of the basic requirements for a self-regulatory agency would be its
ability to demonstrate that rules adopted by it for the regulation of conduct of
business would provide a minimum level of protection to investors 'in relation to
such matters as conflict of interest, disclosure of all sources of remuneration, recommendations unsupported by evidence or belief, information to be supplied to
clients, custody of clients' money and investments . . . '.[6]

---

[5] LCB Gower, 'Review of Investor Protection Report Part 1' (Cmnd 9125, HMSO, London,
1984–85) ('The Gower Report').
[6] The Gower Report, para 6.29.

12.20 One of the matters discussed at some length in the Gower Report was the need for rules addressing conflicts of interest.[7] It was clear to Professor Gower, as it is clear today (see paras 12.49 (Principle 8), and 12.146 to 12.149), that the tendency of investment firms to conduct a wide spectrum of activities and to contain multi-disciplinary sections significantly increases the risk of conflicts of interest arising without being accounted for. This issue continues to trouble investment firms, as can be seen from the various FSA revisions of the rules relating to the publication of investment research (now incorporating the requirements of MiFID), and the issue of securities.

12.21 The recommendations contained in the Gower Report were implemented by the Financial Services Act 1986 ('the FSA 1986'), which was the first piece of legislation in the UK to create a comprehensive regulatory framework for the regulation of all investment firms. This Act gave effect to (and took further) the recommendation of Professor Gower to rely, to a material extent, on self-regulating organisations and provided that they would be regulated by a statutory body, the Securities and Investments Board.

Investment Services Directive 1993

12.22 The coming into force, on 31 December 1995, of the Investment Services Directive 1993[8] ('ISD') marked a very significant step towards the removal, within the EEA, of trade barriers in the financial services field. The ISD facilitated the establishment by an EEA firm of branches in EEA Member States other than the one in which it was licensed, and the provision of cross-border services without the need to obtain a separate licence in each and every EEA Member State in which a firm might wish to set up a branch or into which it might wish to provide services (the principle of home Member State-led regulation).

12.23 Whilst the core idea behind the ISD was revolutionary by any standards, its practical operation proved to be less than satisfactory. First, the ISD was a minimum harmonisation measure. This means that Member States were left free to impose (potentially onerous) local requirements over and above those specified in the ISD. This was the result of a political compromise and is naturally counter-productive in the context of facilitating a truly level playing field across the EEA.

12.24 Secondly, the activities set out in the ISD as identifying what constitutes an 'investment firm' ('core activities') did not correspond to the 'regulated activities' under the FSMA. The result was an inevitable uncertainty in determining whether

---

[7] The Gower Report, para 6.30.
[8] Council Directive (EEC) 93/22 on investment services in the securities field [1993] OJ L141/27.

or not a firm which clearly engages or proposes to engage in a 'regulated activity' under the FSMA is also an investment firm under the ISD. Such a determination is critical because ISD firms are more rigorously regulated with regard to, amongst other things, capital requirements.

Thirdly, because the ISD had been rushed through the legislative process, the **12.25** activity of investment advice was not included as a core service and commodity derivatives were not included as financial instruments. One effect of this was that firms operating in the EEA and providing exclusively investment advisory services would not be subject to regulation under the ISD. These deficiencies, with the exception of the continued mismatch between regulated activities and core activities, have been remedied by the replacement of the ISD with the implementation of the MiFID (see paras 12.37 to 12.40) (art 4(4) of the Financial Services and Markets Act 2000 (Regulated Activities) Order 2001, SI 2001/544 ('RAO') provides for an 'override' of certain exclusions from the requirements to obtain authorisation for regulated activities where the relevant person is engaged in core investment services under MiFID).

Fourthly, there was very little detail in the ISD concerning the type of conduct of **12.26** business rules to which investment firms must be made subject. As a result, different EEA Member States had very different conduct of business rules for investment firms. This, for a large, internationally active investment firm, was very inconvenient. It required each of the national offices of such a firm to have different compliance strategies to deal with different rules and different regulators. This aspect of the ISD gave rise to many practical difficulties and justifiably featured regularly in trade associations' discussions with the EU Commission ('Commission') with regard to revision of the ISD.

In addition to this, Articles 17 and 18 of the ISD—which were the operative **12.27** Articles insofar as the freedom to provide cross-border services and to set up branches in other EEA Member States are concerned—were rather flimsily drafted (to accommodate a political compromise) to state that host Member States in relation to both the provision of cross-border services and the establishment of branches may stipulate 'rules of conduct, under which, in the interest of the general good, that business must be carried on [or with which providers of the investment service in question must comply] in the Host Member State'. The concept of 'general good' was not defined in the ISD. However, the European Court of Justice ('ECJ') has created substantial jurisprudence[9] concerning the interpretation of this concept, particularly in the context of insurance business.

---

[9] See, for example, *Gebhard* [I-1995] ECR I-4165. See also 'Freedom to provide services and the general good in the insurance sector', Commission Interpretative Communication (2000/C 43/03).

Accordingly, rules imposed in the interest of the general good must 'pursue an objective of the general good'. The ECJ has acknowledged, on an incremental basis, that the following areas (amongst others) fall within the scope of the general good: consumer protection; preservation of the good reputation of the national financial sector; prevention of fraud; and fairness of commercial transactions.

12.28 Additionally, any measure imposed in the interest of the 'general good' must be objectively necessary and proportionate to the objective pursued. Consequently, regulatory authorities in Member States acquired the power to impose conduct of business rules, the content of which may be completely unfamiliar to a firm from another State seeking to provide services into or set up a branch within the relevant Member State. This trend is now in the process of being reversed and the host Member State now has far less scope for imposing rules on firms which they do not principally regulate or more generally, which are inconsistent with the requirements of the common market directives (see para 12.54).

12.29 It would be surprising if that state of affairs did not result in cases where firms, no doubt inadvertently in many instances, failed to understand and thus to comply with the rules imposed by host Member States and where such non-compliance either went undetected or was tolerated by the home Member State regulator lest its own regulated firms' non-compliance was not tolerated in return when they offer their services or establish branches in other Member States.

Financial Services and Markets Act 2000

12.30 In May 1997, the Government announced its intention to overhaul the regulatory framework for financial services firms in the UK. The move was mainly a reaction to the well-established perception—unaffected by the coming into force of the Financial Services Act 1986—that the self-regulatory system had failed its intended beneficiaries. It was also clear that many firms with multi-disciplinary practices were regulated by numerous regulatory authorities with regard to different aspects of their financial services business. This was seen as inefficient and unduly burdensome on the firms concerned.

12.31 In July 1998, HM Treasury published a consultation document[10] in which it set out the case for reforming the regulation of financial services in the UK by consolidating a fragmented regulatory regime into the hands of a single, statutory 'super-regulator' which would regulate the insurance, banking, and investment sectors. The new regime was intended to simplify the authorisation process for financial services firms in the UK and the supervision and enforcement process for

---

[10] Financial Services and Markets Bill: A Consultation Document (July 1998).

the Financial Services Authority (FSA). In addition to the rationalisation of the powers and objectives of the FSA, the proposals included two new concepts.

First, the rather dated distinction between the restrictions on the issue of invest- **12.32** ment advertisements and the making of unsolicited calls was scrapped in favour of a more modern restriction on communicating financial promotions, a restriction which was intended to be media neutral in order to cope with the ever-changing methods through which financial services solicitations were being delivered. Secondly, the proposals contemplated a new market misconduct restriction to tackle market abuse. This civil regime was deemed appropriate in order to maintain orderly and efficient markets and tackle conduct which could also give rise to criminal offences (such as that of insider dealing)[11] but which proved difficult to prosecute. The FSMA, the implementing statute, came into force on 1 December 2001.

Whilst it is difficult to measure, certainly in the short term, the success of such a **12.33** radical statutory overhaul, it must be said that the reception given to the FSA was, at best, lukewarm. Initially, the large investment firms greeted with some degree of scepticism the ability of the FSA to consolidate efficiently and effectively a somewhat disparate group of regulatory organisations and deliver a more rational result. Subsequently, certain financial debacles, such as those concerning the decline of Equitable Life and of the Split-Capital Investment Trusts sector, have done little to inspire public confidence.

Additionally, the FSA was criticised by the Financial Services and Markets **12.34** Tribunal—in the course of dealing with an application by Legal & General—of lacking rigour and objectivity in its decision-making process with regard to pursuing enforcement actions. Subsequently, the then Prime Minister stated—in a speech to the Institute for Public Policy Research on 26 May 2005—that 'the Financial Services Authority ... is seen as hugely inhibiting of efficient business by perfectly respectable companies that have never defrauded anyone'.

Observations such as these must dismay the FSA as a regulator which undoubt- **12.35** edly faces immense challenges. The objectives of protecting consumers and clients while not imposing a disproportionate burden on the industry are in an inevitable and constant conflict with each other. Add to this a constant raft of EU directives under the EU Financial Services Action Plan ('FSAP')[12] to implement and the ever-increasing scope of regulation[13] and the FSA's task seems increasingly difficult.

---

[11] Part V, Criminal Justice Act 1993.
[12] This is the legislative framework for the reform and consolidation of EU financial services regulation which was agreed upon by the European Council in March 2000.
[13] The FSA now also regulates mortgage and general insurance intermediaries and it is possible that it will, in due course, be required to regulate credit providers under consumer credit legislation.

This toll is certainly not rendered any easier following the Northern Rock affair which has left the FSA in a rather shaken state.

12.36　Nonetheless, isolated events and sporadic criticism must be viewed in the context of the FSA's general operations. The FSA regulates thousands of firms conducting a wide range of differing businesses and does so on a very tight budget. Given the size of this task it may be unrealistic to expect a zero-failure environment not only for regulated firms but for the FSA itself.

Markets in Financial Instruments Directive

12.37　On 15 November 2000, the Commission issued a communication to the European Parliament and the Council of Europe setting out the case for reforming and upgrading the ISD. The reasons for the initiative behind MiFID had been visible to all participants in the EEA securities markets for some time (see paras 12.22 to 12.29).

12.38　The MiFID, which forms a fundamental pillar in the FSAP, seeks to address these concerns. It has introduced, for the first time, a truly comprehensive investment 'passport' enabling investment firms to offer their services across the EEA in compliance with a single set of rules. The provision of investment advice now constitutes a regulated activity across the EEA as is transacting business in commodity derivatives. The MiFID also deals with the regulation of all securities trading venues including investment firms that either match clients' orders or operate as a securities trading venue on an own account basis (see also para 12.169).

12.39　The finalisation of the MiFID was not free from controversy. In particular, there had been stiff resistance (particularly from the UK) to the introduction of pre-trade transparency obligations—the requirement to display a bid/offer spread which must be adhered to—on investment firms which systematically deal on their own account in the course of executing client orders outside regulated securities markets.

12.40　MiFID was implemented successfully in the UK on 30 November 2007, with the majority of provisions relevant to client-facing activities implemented via the FSA's Conduct of Business Rules ('COBS'). The scope of the MiFID is broad and encompasses all key aspects of business conduct. These necessitated substantively amended (or entirely new) provisions on client classification, inducements, best execution, suitability, appropriateness, and client solicitation/communication amongst others.

Rules of conduct

12.41　It is appropriate, before analysing the specific issues which arise, to attempt to clarify what is meant by an 'investment firm'. The term 'investment firm' is defined in the FSA Glossary. This definition identifies the type of firms which are the subject of this chapter, namely investment managers, investment banks, stockbrokers, and custodians operating in the wholesale markets. The MiFID has intensified the divide between 'buy' (eg investment managers) and 'sell' (eg investment banks) firms, principally through enhancement of the client order protections and liberation of securities trading venues (through abolition of the concentration rule). This chapter is concerned with the former aspect of regulation as it applies to 'sell' firms, but will clearly be of use to 'buy' firms as well.

These are firms which used to be regulated by the Securities and Futures Authority **12.42** ('SFA') and the Investment Management Regulatory Organisation ('IMRO') prior to December 2001, at which time the FSMA came into force.

The rules of conduct are of great importance as far as investment firms' day-to-day **12.43** activities are concerned. They may dictate or alter business practices and they therefore have a significant and direct impact on the way in which investment firms do business. The rules of conduct also indirectly affect the way in which firms receive remuneration for the services they provide and, therefore, their business models.

The concept of rules to regulate the conduct of investment firms was first **12.44** introduced in the Prevention of Fraud (Investments) Act 1939 (see paras 12.10 to 12.12). Many of the fundamental principles established by that Act remain with us to this day, including the types of customers with whom an investment firm may deal, forms of contracts which investment firms must use, and so on.

The current FSA Handbook's COBS is the result of an amalgamation of what **12.45** used to be three separate rule books prior to the coming into force of the FSMA, heavily revised and supplemented to implement the MiFID.

The analysis which follows deals with a selection of important and topical issues **12.46** but it is not a comprehensive description of COBS nor intended to be a substitute for COBS.

Principles for Businesses

There is value in setting out the FSA Principles for Businesses ('the Principles') at **12.47** this stage for two reasons. First, the Principles provide the fundamental pillars of the regulatory regime established by COBS. Secondly, COBS is substantially based on the Principles; in most cases, a rule within COBS (henceforth Rule or Rules) will constitute an elaboration of the application of a particular Principle to a particular set of circumstances. Consideration of the Principles is even more important as the FSA continues to pursue its Principles-led regulation, particularly enforcement.

12.48   There will be many instances where advice is sought from an investment firm as to a proposed course of conduct in relation to which there is no specific Rule. In such case, resort must first be had to the Principles so as to assess whether or not the conduct in question is likely to contravene one of the Principles. Many market participants find the difficulty with this approach is that there is no helpful definition of the material which is relevant in determining the precise scope of a particular Principle or its practical application. Accordingly, there is an element of substantial uncertainty on what constitutes valid evidence for compliance with the spirit or the letter of specific Principles.

12.49   These are the Principles.

1. A firm must conduct its business with integrity.
2. A firm must conduct its business with due skill, care and diligence.
3. A firm must take reasonable care to organise and control its affairs responsibly and effectively, with adequate risk management systems.
4. A firm must maintain adequate financial resources.
5. A firm must observe proper standards of market conduct.
6. A firm must pay due regard to the interests of its customers and treat them fairly.
7. A firm must pay due regard to the information needs of its clients, and communicate information to them in a way which is clear, fair, and not misleading.
8. A firm must manage conflicts of interest fairly, both between itself and its customers and between a customer and another client.
9. A firm must take reasonable care to ensure the suitability of its advice and discretionary decisions for any customer who is entitled to rely upon its judgement.
10. A firm must arrange adequate protection for clients' assets when it is responsible for them.
11. A firm must deal with its regulators in an open and cooperative way, and must disclose to the FSA appropriately anything relating to the firm of which the FSA would reasonably expect notice.

12.50   Some important points need to be made with regard to the application of the Principles to the activities of investment firms. The Principles distinguish between a 'client' and a 'customer'. A client is a reference to all and any persons to whom the firm provides its services. A 'customer' on the other hand denotes all of the firm's clients apart from those which are classified as 'eligible counterparties'. This important distinction, and the fine tuning of the distinction described in para 12.65, is pervasive and needs to be kept in mind whenever the effect of the Principles is in issue (see for example Principles 8, 9, and 10 in para 12.49).

The Principles do not solely apply to the UK activities of an investment firm. **12.51**
Principles 1, 2, 3, and 8 apply to international activities of investment firms but
only to the extent that a firm's financial resources or its ability to continue to be a
'fit and proper person' to conduct regulated activities (which is by no means an
easy determination!) may be affected. Principle 5 applies to international activities
of investment firms to the extent that a firm's conduct may impact on 'confidence
in the financial system operating in the United Kingdom'. Principle 11 applies
equally to firms' domestic and international activities.

Breaching a Principle exposes an investment firm to the risk of disciplinary action **12.52**
by the FSA which may, depending on the circumstances (including the magni-
tude of the breach), impose a financial penalty, publicly censure the firm, or, in
more extreme cases, vary or cancel the scope of a firm's permission to conduct
regulated activities (effectively barring a firm from one or more business lines).
There is now a substantial body of FSA enforcement cases where firms have been
disciplined on the basis of them breaching the Principles.

The regulation of investment firms across the EEA has been substantially har- **12.53**
monised by the MiFID. Investment firms across the EEA, upon transposition of
MiFID into domestic law,[14] now have a uniform set of conduct of business rules
by which they must abide. Whilst there remain super-equivalent provisions for
individual EEA States (for example, the UK rules on use of dealing commission
or the Solicitation Rules in France go beyond the remit of the MiFID), a minimum set of requirements has been established.

Scope of regulation

COBS applies to, amongst others, most firms which engage in designated invest- **12.54**
ment business. In this context, it is important to note that non-UK investment
firms which are regulated by the FSA pursuant to the EU single market directives[15] and operate through the passport regime[16]—whilst conducting business
through a branch in London—need, in general terms,[17] only comply with the
conduct of business regime as applied by the host State (UK). Prudential regulation (including organisational requirements) is, with very few exceptions, the
exclusive territory of the 'home State' regulator. The FSA's ability to impose rules
of conduct on firms for whom it is a 'host State' regulator was significantly limited

---

[14] The MiFID Implementing Regulation (1287/2006) is directly applicable without the need
for further action.

[15] Which in connection with investment firms mean primarily the MiFID.

[16] The regime entitling a firm established and authorised in one EEA Member State to provide
cross-border services and establish branches in other EEA Member States.

[17] As regards services provided in the jurisdiction of the branch (ie in this case in the UK).

when the MiFID was fully implemented in the UK. Broadly speaking, the rules of conduct apply to investment firms' activities which are conducted from an office in the UK (and therefore not to EEA firms providing cross-border services into the UK). The main exceptions concern (a) dealings concluded through branches of UK firms with persons from outside the territory of the branch (this is an unfortunate feature of the MiFID which is subject to a protocol procedure established by CESR in October 2007);[18] and (b) dealings with a UK client classified as either a 'retail client' or a 'professional client' (see para 12.65) from an office based outside the UK, in which circumstances the rules of conduct are subject to certain modifications in areas affected by the Distance Marketing Directive[19] and the Electronic Commerce Directive.[20]

Clients and Commissions

12.55 One of the cornerstones of any financial services regulatory system is that different types of clients should attract varying degrees of protection. This is, of course, to reflect the fact that certain clients are more sophisticated than others. Indeed, in the wholesale market certain clients may be more sophisticated than the provider of the service to them.

12.56 The rules of conduct are thus selective in their application depending on the type of client that the investment firm is serving. Client classification is essentially a mechanical process by which each client is placed by the investment firm concerned into one of three pre-determined classes. These are, in ascending order of sophistication, 'retail clients', "professional clients', and 'eligible counterparties'.

12.57 MiFID has brought substantial changes to the client classification rules. It has broadened the scope of the category of 'retail clients' (which, under the old regime, was the narrower conception of 'private customer'). Professional clients (which would have been classified as 'intermediate customers' before the MiFID implementation now attract a greater level of regulatory protection, by means of communications, best execution, appropriateness, suitability, and the requirement to provide further information concerning specific risk warnings (non-exhaustive list).

---

[18] CESR/07-672.
[19] Council Directive (EC) 02/65 concerning the distance marketing of consumer financial services [2002] OJ L271/16.
[20] Council Directive (EC) 00/31 on electronic commerce [2000] OJ L11/48.

Eligible counterparty business

Traditionally, the UK regulatory regime has always favoured self-regulation where **12.58** effective self-regulation can be achieved. This approach is reflected in a special 'light-touch' conduct of business regime (see para 12.71) which applies to investment firms conducting eligible counterparty business. The definition of the term 'eligible counterparty business' contains a number of elements. First, the regulated services and activities (and related ancillary activities)[21] must (in connection with the MiFID business) concern dealing in investments on own account, the execution of orders on behalf of clients or the reception, and transmission of orders. Secondly, the service or activity must be undertaken with or for a client classified as an 'eligible counterparty'.

The term 'eligible counterparty business' does not include, amongst others, the **12.59** following activities:

- approval by an investment firm of a financial promotion;[22]
- corporate finance business;
- safeguarding and administering investments (custody);
- investment management.

The consequences of a determination that part of an investment firm's business constitutes 'eligible counterparty business' is that only very few Rules apply to the conduct of such business.

Special conduct regimes

It is also to be noted that the application of the Rules is modified—in fact tailor- **12.60** made versions apply—in the context of professional firms, energy market participants, and oil market participants.

Senior management responsibilities

It can be agreed that the increased emphasis on senior management responsibili- **12.61** ties and accountability following the implementation of the FSMA has been (and continues to be) one of the most radical changes to have been made in the recent past to the UK financial services regulatory regime. This aspect of the regime operated by the FSA was born out of increased frustration at catastrophic events that occurred to UK regulated firms (eg Barings Bank) in which senior management

---

[21] Non-regulated activities which are closely related to the conduct of regulated activities.
[22] As defined in FSMA, s 21.

pleaded lack of direct supervisory control over the unit responsible for the calamitous activity.

12.62 The FSA's Senior Management Arrangements Systems and Controls Sourcebook ('SYSC') requires that an investment firm takes 'reasonable care to maintain a clear and appropriate apportionment of significant responsibilities among its directors and senior managers' and must appoint a person to manage its compliance with SYSC. The appointee (who must be either a director or a senior manager and for whom the FSA's prior approval is required) must assume the designated 'Controlled Function 8' of Apportionment and Oversight. It should be noted that this function is separate and distinct from a firm's compliance function. This escalation in the seniority of the personnel within an investment firm who can be made directly responsible for inadequate allocation of responsibilities and indirectly for problems which arise from such a failure led to some anxiety within investment firms. Nevertheless, this seemingly effective regulatory tool is now accepted as being responsible for some positive changes in the way investment firms' risk management structures have evolved in the last few years.

12.63 The principle of senior management responsibility has been supplemented by requirements to operate effective systems and controls which specifically (but not exclusively) include effective and safe delegation of managerial tasks, provision of timely and comprehensive information to management, and provisions for risk assessment and business continuity. The effectiveness of this aspect of the FSA's regime will depend on the extent to which, in practice, the FSA holds senior managers within investment firms accountable for their firm's conduct.[23]

Client classification

12.64 The significance of this topic must not be overlooked. Although mechanical, the task of classifying an investment firm's new clients is fundamentally important.[24] Investment firms frequently have their focus on a particular sector or sub-sector of clients. Thus, where a firm's strategy is to provide services to clients other than those classified under COBS as retail clients, its compliance policy and systems and controls will be framed accordingly. In such circumstances, it would be unsafe for the firm to accept retail clients as clients or, more generally, to take on new clients for which the firm does not have policies and systems which will ensure compliance with its regulatory obligations.

---

[23] See FSA Final Notice dated 10 April 2007 concerning Mr David Whistance.
[24] See COBS 3.

There are three categories of client under COBS (pursuant to the MiFID):   **12.65**

(a) retail client—in plain English this equates to 'the man in the street';
(b) professional client—a reference to a more sophisticated person;
(c) eligible counterparty—as its name implies, a client which is likely to be proficient in matters of investments (eg another investment firm).

The requirement to classify clients is to be satisfied by an investment firm *before* it   **12.66** conducts any investment business with or for them because otherwise it would not be able to establish what would constitute compliant conduct in relation to a particular client—as mentioned earlier (see para 12.56), the rules of conduct vary depending on what type of client the firm is dealing with. COBS requires a firm to notify a client of its status.

COBS, with regard to client classification, deals with a few cases in which it is not   **12.67** obvious whom an investment firm needs to classify (and indeed treat) as its client.

Agent as client

One such case is where the potential client acts as an agent and wishes to engage   **12.68** the services of an investment firm in that capacity. The general rule is that only the agent should be regarded as the firm's client provided that the arrangement involving the agency relationship is not intended to prevent the firm from having an obligation towards the agent's principal and complies with the Rule on agents as clients within COBS 2.4.3R. Nonetheless, this general rule can be overridden by the parties' agreement that the firm concerned would treat the principal as its only (or additional) 'client'.

In a pragmatic compromise, the client classification rules permit an investment   **12.69** firm to satisfy most of its obligations to communicate with its clients by communicating with the agent, with exceptions for certain required risk warnings, transaction confirmations, and the provision of periodic statements.[25]

There are a number of additional points which arise from the regulatory classifica-   **12.70** tion of an agent. First, the classification does not affect the general legal position in relation to an investment firm's duties to the principal. Secondly, investment firms are under anti-money laundering obligations (both under the rules of conduct and under the general law) to verify the identity of both the principal ('beneficial owner' as it is framed under the provisions of the Money Laundering Regulations 2007) and the agent. Thirdly, the FSA has provided guidance to the effect that the determination of who is an investment firm's client for regulatory

---

[25] COBS 2.4.3.

classification purposes should not affect the reality of the situation in so far as capital adequacy rules are concerned (in that the true identity of a firm's counterparty must be taken into account to reflect the true credit risk posed).

12.71 It is possible for an investment firm to classify one or more of its clients differently for different purposes. This facilitates the application of a light-touch regime (see para 12.58) where it is merited.

Terms of business

12.72 COBS requires that an investment firm must provide a retail client with its terms of business in good time before it provides services.[26]

12.73 COBS does not specify the minimum contents of a terms of business agreement which is largely dictated by an array of various mandatory disclosure and information requirements.[27] A firm's terms of business may take various forms so that 'low impact' customers do not need to bother with a long list of items which may not be relevant to their relationship with the firm. Thus, it is common for investment firms to have separate terms of business to cover investment management, custody, derivative transactions, and so on.

12.74 It must be noted in this context that although the FSA's requirements in relation to terms of business are not extensive, investment firms dedicate significant time and resources to ensure that their terms of business documents (for all categories of clients) are regularly updated and reflect the commercial reality of their relationships with their customers. Despite this, it is not uncommon in practice to encounter documentation prepared by firms, large and small, which is either legally incorrect or incompatible with other documents prepared by the firm or with the latest regulatory requirements. Given the pace of development in financial services regulation, an investment firm's terms of business need to be regularly reviewed, perhaps as frequently as monthly.

Inducements and dealing commission arrangements

12.75 The Rules concerning inducements and dealing commission are an elaboration of the FSA's Principles for Businesses on fair treatment of customers and the avoidance of conflicts of interest.

12.76 The new regime on inducements, as set out in the MiFID, is wider than any preceding regime and captures a very broad range of arrangements, some of which would

---

[26] COBS 8.1.1.
[27] See COBS 6.

certainly not have fallen within the ordinary conception of the term inducement. The substantial broadening of the regime was endorsed by the Committee of European Securities Regulators ('CESR') in its recommendations paper of May 2007.[28] The key changes brought about by the MiFID include the need for and format of disclosure and an absolute prohibition on certain inducements (such as trail commissions and commission overrides). These are expanded upon below.

Inducements

The MiFID[29] contains a wide-ranging prohibition on the receipt or payment by **12.77** investment firms of inducements in connection with the provision of investment and/or ancillary services to clients (other than eligible counterparties). In order to be allowed under the new regime, inducements paid to or received from third parties must be fully disclosed and designed to enhance the quality of service to the client.

The ISD did not contain specific rules on inducements. Article 11 provided prin- **12.78** ciples underlying conduct of business rules to be drawn up by EEA Member States. These included that investment firms should act honestly and fairly in conducting their business activities in the best interests of their clients, and that investment firms should try to avoid conflicts of interest and, where they cannot be avoided, to ensure that their clients are treated fairly.

FSA Principle for Businesses 1 requires a firm to conduct its business with integ- **12.79** rity. Principle 6 requires a firm to pay due regard to the interest of its customers and to treat them fairly. Previous FSA rules contained a prohibition on induce-ments. These prohibited a firm, or any person acting on its behalf, from offering, giving, soliciting or accepting an inducement, or directing or referring any actual or potential item of designated investment business to another person on its own initiative or on the instructions of an associate if it was likely to conflict to a mate-rial extent with any duty that the firm owes its customers in connection with designated investment business, or any duty which such a recipient firm owes to its customers. This requirement was supplemented by evidential provisions relat-ing to 'packaged products'. Specific additional requirements applied to firms relat-ing to the use of dealing commission, which continue to apply to firms as a super-equivalent provision notified to the Commission under Article 4(4) of the MiFID Implementing Directive.

---

[28] CESR/07-228b.
[29] The MiFID Article 19(1); Article 26 and Recital 39 of the MiFID Implementing Directive, as brought into the UK domestic regime through amendments to the FSA Handbook.

12.80 Article 26 of the MiFID Implementing Directive provides that the provision or receipt of inducements breaches Article 19(1) unless the conditions set out in Article 26 are satisfied.[30]

12.81 Article 26 applies to payment of any fee or commission or provision of any non-monetary benefit in relation to the provision of an investment and/or ancillary service to a client. Provision or receipt of a fee, commission, or non-monetary benefit (collectively a benefit) is prohibited unless it is one or more of the following:

(a) a benefit paid or provided to or by the client (or a person acting on behalf of the client);

(b) a benefit paid or provided to or by a third party (or a person acting on behalf of a third party), in relation to which the following conditions are satisfied:

(i) the existence, nature, and amount of the benefit or, where the amount cannot be ascertained, the method of calculating that amount, has been clearly disclosed to the client in a manner that is comprehensive, accurate, and understandable, prior to the provision of the relevant investment or ancillary services; and

(ii) the payment or provision of the benefit is designed to enhance the quality of the relevant service to the client and does not impair compliance with the firm's duty to act in the best interests of the client; or

(c) a 'proper fee' which enables or is necessary for the provision of investment services, such as custody costs, settlement and exchange fees, regulatory levies, or legal fees, and which, by its nature, cannot give rise to conflicts with the firm's duties to act honestly, fairly, and professionally in accordance with the best interests of its clients.

12.82 Instead of disclosing benefits paid to or received from a third party in accordance with Article 26(b)(i), firms may disclose the essential terms of the arrangements relating to the benefit, provided that they undertake to disclose further details at the request of the client and honour that undertaking.

12.83 Guidance on Article 26(b)(ii), states that where a firm provides investment advice or personal recommendations which are not biased as a result of the receipt of commission, then the advice or recommendation should be considered to enhance the quality of the investment advice to the client. The inducements

---

[30] Where, here and in later paragraphs reference is made to provisions in the MiFID as if they apply directly to firms and individuals, the reader is asked to accept that the provisions have been transposed into UK law.

requirements have been the subject of CESR recommendations.[31] These clarify certain issues raised through consultation:

- Article 26 applies to all benefits (including standard commissions or fees), not just those which may influence the actions of a firm. It also applies to benefits paid to or received by an entity in the same group as the firm;
- in considering whether a benefit is designed to enhance the quality of the relevant service for the purpose of Article 26(b)(ii), the following factors should be taken into account:
  - the type of service provided and any specific duties owed to the client in addition to those under Article 26;
  - the expected benefit to the client (which may be assessed at the level of the service, rather than on a client by client basis) and any expected benefit to the firm;
  - whether there will be any incentive for the firm to act other than in the best interests of the client and whether the incentive is likely to change the firm's behaviour;
  - the relationship between the firm and the third party paying or receiving the benefit;
  - the nature of the item, the circumstances in which it is paid or provided and whether any conditions attach to it;
- Recital 39, which relates solely to investment advice, does not prohibit payment or receipt of benefits to or from third parties in respect of non-advice based distribution models. This is because non-advice based distribution models benefits can be seen as being designed to enhance the quality of service by allowing an investment service to be provided over a wider range of financial instruments;
- disclosure under Article 26 of the 'essential terms' must provide adequate information to enable the investor to relate the disclosure to the particular service or product to which it relates and enable him to make an informed decision whether to proceed with the relevant service and whether to ask for full information—a purely generic disclosure is insufficient for these purposes;
- the list of types of fees set out in Article 26(c) is non-exhaustive as other items may also fall within the category of proper fees. In determining whether such other items fall within that category, it is particularly important to ascertain whether the item by its nature cannot give rise to conflicts with the firm's duties to the client;
- where a number of investment firms are involved in the distribution channel, each firm is obliged to comply with its obligation of disclosure to its clients.

---

[31] CESR/07-228b.

12.84 Establishing that benefits are designed to enhance the quality of service to a client is likely to prove particularly difficult in the case of distribution structures (other than those involving investment advice, which are effectively carved out from this requirement by virtue of Recital 39). It seems clear that commission overrides or other structures which cause the interests of the firm to be misaligned from those of the client are intended to be prohibited under Article 26.

12.85 Whilst CESR has provided some helpful commentary in connection with this determination (principally that the assessment may be conducted at the level of a class of customers) there are ample prevailing practices where it is very difficult to ascertain that the relevant fee or benefit has been 'designed' to provide any added value to the service provided by the firm. Trade associations continue to explore this topic with little success mainly due to the inconsistency that has emerged in firms' treatment of inducements. This state of affairs is not helped by the fact that certain EEA regulators have issued pronouncements on this topic which are feared to have created precedents limiting the available courses of actions for firms.

Dealing commission

12.86 The regulation of dealing commission (which is a subset of the MiFID inducement regime) is an example of the MiFID super-equivalence in the UK (which has been duly notified to the Commission by the UK).

12.87 The FSA completed a consultation process[32] with regard to proposals to reform the regime in connection with bundled brokerage[33] and soft commission arrangements.[34] The rules resulting from this consultation were published in July 2005.[35] The FSA review was triggered by a report commissioned by HM Treasury and conducted by Paul Myners on institutional investment in the UK. The Myners Report—Institutional Investment in the United Kingdom: A Review—identified certain weaknesses in the currently popular practices of bundled brokerage and soft commission arrangements, in that they may give rise to potential conflicts of interest for investment managers. The report also focused on the fact that whilst management fees are very much a focal point for institutional investors, bundled brokerage and soft commission arrangements allow fund managers to impose on

---

[32] The first Consultation Paper was published in April 2003 (CP176: 'Bundled Brokerage and Soft Commission Arrangements') and the final paper was published in March 2005 (CP05/5: 'Bundled Brokerage and Soft Commission Arrangements').

[33] The provision of services by securities brokers to investment managers which are additional to mere execution (such as investment research) and which are essentially paid for from the trading commission paid by investment managers.

[34] An arrangement involving securities brokers paying third party providers of services (other than execution services, eg computer terminal, hardware and software, dedicated telephone lines, etc) from the trading commission paid by investment managers.

[35] PS 05/9: 'Bundled brokerage and soft commission arrangements'.

their clients, in an indirect (and non-transparent) way, a charge for which it is difficult to ascertain a direct and exclusive benefit to the investor concerned. In fact, the report suggested, these practices enable fund managers to cut their operating expenses and in effect increase their management fees in an indirect way. The report recommended that fund managers should absorb the costs of dealing in securities in their entirety and charge an amount they deem appropriate to their clients.

Two fundamental problem areas were identified by the FSA in its own review. The **12.88** first of these is that bundled brokerage and soft commission practices are, at best, a mystery to investor clients. The opaque nature of these arrangements—as well as evidence from market research commissioned by the FSA—strongly suggests that fund managers have no incentive to be efficient or provide value for money to investors when negotiating terms of trading with securities brokers. These factors may also act as an obstacle for investment managers to comply fully with their 'best execution' obligation.[36]

The second area of concern is that the way in which some of these arrangements **12.89** are structured is such that the higher the volume of trading, the greater is the potential benefit for the fund manager concerned. This clearly gives rise to a conflict of interest; fund managers have an incentive to achieve a certain trading volume and potentially may over-trade. Furthermore, an investment manager's focus on achieving the best possible soft commission or bundled deal may clearly hinder its scrutiny of the quality and price of execution offered by securities brokers.

The first consultation paper (CP 176—see note 32) concluded that the regulatory regime which was applicable to soft commission and bundled brokerage arrange- **12.90** ments was inadequate and proposed changes on two counts. First, the services that can be bought under such arrangements should be limited to the purchase of execution[37] and research[38] services. Secondly, there should be imposed on fund managers a requirement to determine the cost of any services additional to trade execution which they buy with their customers' commission and to increase its customers' funds with a rebate of an equivalent amount.

The new rules applied to both soft commission and bundled brokerage arrangements, (which are in many ways one and the same thing), and are expected to add **12.91** a competitive edge to the market for services traditionally provided under such

---

[36] Which currently focuses on the achievement of the best price for the security concerned by reference to a benchmark.

[37] Services directly linked to arranging and finalising a transaction which arise from the point in time in which a decision to deal is taken by the fund manager until the transaction is finalised.

[38] Original material which involves analysis or manipulation of data and enabling the fund manager to reach a meaningful conclusion.

arrangements by forcing fund managers to look more closely at the value of such services.

12.92 The FSA proposals in CP176 attracted unprecedented industry feedback. This is understandable given that the proposed changes would require the commitment of substantial resources and thus need to be clearly justifiable in the light of the objective cost–benefit analysis to which the FSA is statutorily committed.[39] Industry participants also suggested that implementation of the FSA proposals would put them at a serious competitive disadvantage in the international arena.[40]

12.93 The latter suggestion prompted the FSA to commission an independent report from Deloitte which concluded, in general terms, that the FSA proposals were unlikely to have a significant impact on the competitive position of the UK fund management business. The report also supported earlier indications from the FSA that the potential savings to investment customers as a result of the proposals far outweigh the likely cost of implementation.

12.94 From the final FSA proposals on bundled brokerage and soft commissions (CP 05/5—see note 32), it appears that the FSA was persuaded in the course of the consultation that an industry-led solution could work as an effective alternative to the rebate proposal.

The current dealing commission regime

12.95 In order to implement the new rules, a new section was inserted into the FSA Rules.[41] As originally proposed, the scope of the rules' application was to be limited to shares and investments related to shares (eg they were not applicable to bond trading arrangements), but applied to UK investment management firms regardless of the client's location.

12.96 Additionally, the Rules require firms to provide their customers with periodic disclosure at least once a year[42] (unless the customer resides outside the UK and has waived this right or the firm reasonably concludes that a particular customer does not wish to receive this information). The disclosure should cover the percentage of soft commission out of the total commission paid by or at the direction of the firm, the value of goods or services received by the firm under soft commission arrangements as a percentage of the total commission paid by the firm, a summary of the goods or services received, a list of the brokers with whom the

---

[39] FSMA, s 2(3)(c).
[40] The FSA is also statutorily committed to maintaining the competitive position of the UK's financial services industry—FSMA, s 2(3)(e).
[41] COBS 11.6.
[42] COBS 11.6.18.

firm has soft commission arrangements, and an explanation of the firm's policy on soft commissions for the coming year.

Financial Promotions and Client Communications

One of the most notable changes introduced by the FSMA was the consolidation **12.97** of the previously applicable restrictions on the issue of investment advertisements and the making of unsolicited calls into a single restriction. This restricition is applicable to all media and carries a criminal sanction for contravention. The scope of this regime, created by section 21 of FSMA, is very much determined—as is frequently the case—by reference to exemptions which offer relief from compliance to the persons who may avail themselves of them.

Section 21 states that a financial promotion is a '[communication] in the course **12.98** of business [which is] an invitation or inducement to engage in investment activity . . . and which is capable of having an effect in the United Kingdom'. Two terms merit further analysis. First, an invitation or inducement to 'engage in investment activity' covers, broadly speaking, invitations or inducement to acquire, dispose of, or underwrite certain investments, or exercise rights conferred by such an investment for such purpose or for the purpose of converting it or receive or undertake an investment service such as managing certain investments.

Secondly, the phrase 'capable of having an effect in the United Kingdom', the **12.99** meaning of which has been clarified to only a limited extent in FSA Guidance, covers a potentially wide range of communications which include, but are not limited to, communications originating abroad with persons present in the UK. This is clearly unsatisfactory as the boundaries of what is a serious criminal offence remain uncertain. When the FSMA came into force some concerns were expressed about the financial promotion regime applying to a wide range of unintended situations, for example, a promotion which is ordinarily exempt as being made to an overseas person but which would result in that individual dealing through a foreign firm which would then execute the order on a UK investment exchange (this being the effect in the UK). As fanciful as this may sound, it is arguable that the financial promotion regime would apply in such circumstances.

The financial promotions restriction

Prior to the implementation of the MiFID, the financial promotions restriction **12.100** contained in section 21 of FSMA often did not apply to firms' promotional activities. The restriction in section 21 of FSMA did not apply where the relevant promotion was communicated (or formally approved) by a person who was authorised under the FSMA. The MiFID has had a big impact on the scope of the financial promotions regime (in addition to extending the ambit of regulation to any client communications). Certain of the carve-outs within the FSMA[43] are no longer compatible with the MiFID, and consequently a division has emerged between financial promotions which are caught by the MiFID and financial promotions which fall outside the MiFID (the latter category falling back upon the financial promotions regime under the FSMA). The result is an unwieldy regime which—in equal measures—begs for reform and is very difficult to interpret and apply in practice.

12.101 Where conducting the MiFID service or activity, communications with clients[44] (including financial promotions) are regulated by COBS,[45] whereas if the service or activity is non-MiFID, the financial promotions regime under the FSMA takes effect. The essence of the exercise is to ensure that investment firms are sufficiently diligent in ensuring that their communications with clients—principally in the UK—are clear, fair, and not misleading.

12.102 Under COBS 4, communications with clients in the course of the MiFID business, including financial promotions, are regulated on a mandatory basis. However, a number of exceptions apply, for example prospectuses drawn up and published in accordance with the EU Prospectus Directive[46](for which the firm is not responsible) by a third party are excluded from the remit of COBS 4.

12.103 There are other wider issues which investment firms must focus on when determining the desirability of selling securities comprised in a new issue directly to such individuals. Among the key concerns is the extent to which the investment firm (which typically acts as underwriter and is the initial purchaser of the securities) exposes itself to additional prospectus liability under English law. Increasing the circle of investors in the way described above may well increase the chances of a successful claim against an underwriter in the event of an omission or a misstatement in the prospectus, particularly in negligence where the extent of the duty of care may vary depending on the characteristics of the allegedly injured party.

12.104 There is ongoing uncertainty as to the extent to which a single communication can constitute a financial promotion and at the same time cause the relevant firm/ employee to be engaged in the regulated activity of giving investment advice. The MiFID has clarified this issue by refining the definition of a personal recommendation and applying the onerous suitability requirement only to such recommendations. The safe position to adopt is that when a communication contains a positive recommendation to acquire an investment it should be viewed as both a financial promotion and investment advice—but not necessarily a personal recommendation (and, potentially, a research recommendation).

---

[43] See FSMA (Financial Promotion) Order 2005.
[44] A term not including corporate finance and venture capital contacts.
[45] Conduct of Business Sourcebook, as found in the FSA Handbook.
[46] European Parliament and Council Directive (EC) 2003/71.

Communication rules

The following rules of conduct apply to investment firms when they communi- **12.105**
cate with clients.

(a) **Form and content**. Specific rules, which vary depending on the nature of the
promotion, regulate the required content of a communication. In this context, the principal types of promotion are: an ordinary written communication; a written communication which identifies and promotes a particular
investment or service (in which case the rules are very detailed); a direct offer
financial promotion (which takes the form of offering an investment or a
service to anyone responding to it and which specifies the manner of response,
such as including a tear-off slip); and an oral promotion. The topics covered
include presentation of comparisons, disclosure of risks, and past performance (a particularly sensitive topic).

(b) **Record keeping**. Written promotions (together with confirmation that the
promotions comply with the communication rules) must be kept by firms
and be readily accessible for inspection by the FSA. Such records must be kept
for at least three years and in some cases (including promotions involving
certain retail products), indefinitely.

(c) **Oral promotions**. There are special rules that apply where a promotion takes
the form of an interactive dialogue (eg a telephone conversation). Amongst
other things, these rules cover manner and timing of the calls and the proper
identification of the firm and the service or investment offered.

(d) **Direct offer financial promotions**. This category of financial promotion is
deemed the most worthy of regulatory scrutiny as it may result in the purchase of an investment or investment services without further action by the
promoting firm. The rules contain a detailed list of matters to be referred to
in the promotion, including numerous forms of risk warnings and statements
concerning taxation and charges.

(e) **Unregulated collective investment schemes**. Securities legislation in the UK
has historically[47] taken a strict approach to the regulation of collective investment schemes and particularly to the promotion of such schemes which are
not authorised by the FSA and therefore enjoy complete freedom to invest in any
asset in any manner (subject, where either the manager or the promoter is
regulated by the FSA, to the Principles for Businesses—see paras 12.47 to 12.53).

---

[47] One of the cornerstones of this approach can be traced to the Anderson Report (see paras
12.05 to 12.07).

The restriction concerning promotion by authorised persons of unregulated collective investment schemes[48] is twofold. Section 238 of FSMA provides that authorised persons (eg investment firms) must not communicate[49] an invitation or inducement to participate in an unregulated collective investment scheme, but a statutory instrument (the Exemption Order) made under the FSMA contains various exemptions from this restriction.[50] The most notable of these exemptions include those relating to investment professionals (article 14), to existing participants in an unregulated scheme (article 18) and to certified sophisticated investors (article 23).[51]

12.106 The FSMA provides for additional FSA rule-making powers in connection with permissible promotions (and approval of promotions) of unregulated collective investment schemes. These are contained in the financial promotions rules of conduct. A distinction must be drawn, however, with regard to promotions by investment firms of unregulated collective investment schemes pursuant to these two separate sets of exemptions. Where a proposed promotion is exempt under the Exemption Order, the relevant firm is, if engaging in the MiFID service or activity in the course of the promotion, subject to general rules of COBS4 and the Principles for Businesses.

Appropriateness

12.107 Investment firms which are subject to the MiFID but which do not provide investment advice or discretionary investment management services are required to assess the appropriateness of services and products which they provide to retail and professional clients. Investment firms may provide execution-only services without assessing appropriateness in relation to 'non-complex' financial instruments if certain conditions are met.

---

[48] A term which includes any collective investment scheme other than: a UK authorised unit trust (FSMA, s 242); a UK authorised Investment Company with Variable Capital (FSMA, s 262); an EEA UCITS scheme (FSMA, s 264); or a scheme recognised under special dispensation rules (FSMA, ss 270 and 272). For the purposes of promotion only, an FSA Qualified Investor Scheme, essentially an authorised scheme intended for certain non-retail investors, is regarded as an unregulated collective investment scheme.

[49] FSMA, s 240 prohibits investment firms from approving a financial promotion which they would be unable to communicate pursuant to the restriction set out in FSMA, s 238.

[50] The Financial Services and Markets Act 2000 (Promotion of Collective Investment Schemes) (Exemptions) Order 2001, SI 2001/1060.

[51] The exemption contained in art 23 is rarely used because a promoting firm cannot itself certify that a person to whom it wishes to issue a financial promotion is a sophisticated investor and because firms are in any event reluctant to provide such a certification because of the consequential risk of liability to such an investor when an investment performs badly.

The relevant rules are contained in COBS 10 and further helpful materials can be **12.108** found in the FSA-confirmed industry guidance, the MiFID Connect Guideline on Suitability and Appropriateness, and further FSA guidance.

The ISD requirements in this area were relatively unspecific. The ISD provided **12.109** that Member States were required to draw up a list of rules implementing the principles set out in the ISD, which included the principle that an investment firm must 'seek from its clients information regarding their financial situations, investment experience and objectives as regards the services requested' and must act 'in the best interests of its clients'. Before the MiFID, there was no obligation for an FSA-regulated investment firm to assess the appropriateness of a product or service in relation to any client where the firm was acting on an execution-only basis (ie where no investment advice was given or investment management undertaken).

An investment firm is required to assess the appropriateness of a product or service **12.110** (as described below) if:

- The transaction falls within the scope of the MiFID (ie it relates to a financial instrument which is within the scope of the MiFID, excluding, for example, a spot foreign exchange transaction unless it is an integral part of a transaction that falls within the MiFID).[52]

- The service does not include the provision of investment advice or portfolio management (if the service does include either of these, the relevant obligation is to assess 'suitability', rather than 'appropriateness' as to which see below).

- The service consists of receiving or transmitting orders, executing orders on behalf of clients dealing on own account, underwriting, or placing.

- The service is provided to a retail client or professional client.

- The firm is unable to or has not taken advantage of the carve-out in relation to non-complex financial instruments (discussed below).

The FSA has also applied the MiFID appropriateness test to certain non-MiFID **12.111** business so that for the MiFID firms the test also applies in respect of arranging or dealing in relation to a non-MiFID derivative or warrant with, or for, a retail client where the firm is aware or ought reasonably to be aware that the application or order is in response to a direct offer financial promotion.

Investment firms required to assess the appropriateness of a product or service are **12.112** required to ask their clients to provide information regarding their knowledge and experience in the relevant investment field so as to enable the investment firm to assess whether the investment service or product envisaged is appropriate for

---

[52] COBS 10.1.1.

the client.[53] Investment firms should determine, using this information, whether the relevant client (or potential client) 'has the necessary experience and knowledge in order to understand the risks involved in relation to the specific type of product or service offered or demanded'.[54] This is referred to as 'the appropriateness test'.

12.113 To meet the appropriateness test a firm must (to the extent appropriate to the nature of the client and the nature and extent of the service/product to be provided) obtain information on:

- The types of service, transaction, and investment with which the client is familiar.
- The nature, volume, and frequency of the client's transactions in investments and the period over which they have been carried out.
- The level of the client's education, profession, or relevant former profession.[55]

12.114 There is no need for investment firms to verify this information, unless they are aware (or ought to be aware) that the information is manifestly out of date, inaccurate, or incomplete. If, having carried out the appropriateness test, the investment firm determines that the product or service is not appropriate for the client, it must warn the client of this fact. If a client refuses to provide the information required to enable an investment firm to satisfy the appropriateness test, or provides insufficient information to enable it to do so, the investment firm will be able to provide the product/service without undertaking the appropriateness test, provided it has warned the client that it is therefore unable to determine whether the product or service to be provided is appropriate for it. However, the investment firm should ensure that the provision of required information by a client is encouraged.

12.115 If the client in question is classified as a professional client, the investment firm can assume that it has the necessary experience and knowledge to understand products or services in relation to which it is so classified.[56] The FSA has indicated that provided that a firm has categorised a professional client in line with the relevant requirements, it does not envisage it generally needing to obtain additional information from the client (or maintain additional records) for the purposes of the appropriateness test.

---

[53] COBS 10.2.1.
[54] COBS 10.2.1(2)(a).
[55] COBS 10.2.2.
[56] COBS 10.2.1.

A firm which provides services consisting solely of the execution and/or reception **12.116**
and transmission of client orders (with or without ancillary services) relating
to 'non-complex' financial instruments (see below) can provide such services
without carrying out the appropriateness test if:

- The service is provided at the initiative of the client. The recitals to the MiFID
  provide that this will be the case unless the client has asked for the service in
  response to a personalised communication to him containing an invitation or
  which is otherwise intended to influence the client in respect of that specific
  service/transaction. In other words, services provided in response to general
  marketing material will be 'provided at the initiative of the client'.

- The client has been clearly informed that in the provision of this service the firm
  is not required to undertake the appropriateness test, and the corresponding
  protections in the relevant conduct of business rules will not apply (this warning may be provided in a standardised format).

- The firm has complied with the applicable rules relating to conflicts of
  interest.[57]

MiFID specifies a number of instruments which are 'non-complex' for the pur- **12.117**
poses of the 'appropriateness test'. These are shares admitted to trading on a regulated market or equivalent third country market (a list of which is maintained by
the Commission on its website); money market instruments; bonds or other
forms of securitised debt (excluding those which embed a derivative); and UCITS
(undertakings for collective investment in transferable securities). The MiFID
Implementing Directive[58] sets out criteria for determining which other types of
financial instrument should be considered non-complex. These criteria include
the ability to realise the instrument at market price, the availability of comprehensive and understandable information about the instrument's characteristics, and
the lack of exposure to potential liability exceeding the cost of acquiring the instrument. Derivatives are expressly excluded from the category of non-complex financial instrument.

The effect of this carve-out is that only in relation to non-complex financial instru- **12.118**
ments can firms provide execution only services without having carried out the
appropriateness test.

The appropriateness test is less wide-ranging than the suitability test, which **12.119**
applies to firms providing investment advice or discretionary investment management services. The appropriateness test requires firms to assess whether the client
has the knowledge and experience necessary to understand the risks in relation to

---

[57] COBS 10.4.1.
[58] Commission Directive (EC) 2006/73 of 10 August 2006.

the specific type of product or service in question, whereas the suitability test also requires a firm to collect information about the client's financial situation and investment objectives. The regulatory consequences of the two tests are also different: while an investment firm is not allowed to provide an 'unsuitable' recommendation, it may provide a service which it considers as not 'appropriate', as long as the client is given the required warning.

12.120 Covered warrants, options, and contracts for differences are among the investments traded by retail clients that as complex financial instruments trigger appropriateness obligations. It should be noted, however, that all UCITS will be considered 'non-complex', irrespective of their underlying investment strategies, with the result that retail clients may be provided execution-only services relating to products with derivative exposures. In the case of non-UCITS collective investment schemes and funds, it is necessary to consider the extent to which the fund satisfies the specified criteria. The fact that a fund invests in derivatives, however, will not automatically make the fund itself 'complex' for the purposes of the appropriateness test.

12.121 The FSA has taken the view that bonds or other forms of securitised debt that embed a derivative are per se complex financial instruments. In relation to notes structured to return capital in full with regular 'interest' payments linked to the performance of an index, the FSA's understanding is that such notes are 'complex' instruments under MiFID because, although they may be structured as a bond and regarded as a form of debt security, they also involve features of a financial contract for differences (the MiFID derivative). The FSA acknowledged that each note will have to be considered separately to identify the derivative element and consider, among other things, its impact on risk profile and pricing.[59]

12.122 The Commission recognised that in many EEA Member States 'execution-only' markets were established in relation to financial instruments which do not qualify as non-complex under the MiFID. For this reason, Recital 59 to the MiFID Implementing Directive provides that where a client has engaged in a course of dealings involving a specific type of product or service before the MiFID came into effect, the investment firm can assume that such client has the necessary experience and knowledge to understand the risks involved in relation to such products or services. The recital also provides that the appropriateness test does not need to be applied in relation to each separate transaction in a course of dealings, provided that the assessment is made before the course of dealings commences.

---

[59] The boundary between complex or non-complex instruments is subject to further consideration in Europe and is included in the CESR MiFID Level 3 Workplan.

As regards the information which must be sought to support the appropriateness **12.123** test, firms can rely on information previously provided by clients, unless they are aware or ought to be aware that the information is manifestly out of date, inaccurate, or incomplete.

Advising customers

The activities of advising on securities (which may concern buying, selling, sub- **12.124** scribing for, or underwriting a security or exercising any right conferred by such security to buy, sell, subscribe for, or underwrite a security)[60] and selling securities are core activities for most investment firms. Although recent years have seen a proliferation of so-called 'execution-only' brokers (as to which see the appropriateness requirement set out above), most investment firms provide advisory as well as execution services in securities. It should be emphasised that the rules that relate to advising and selling now seek to protect retail and professional customers (although outside of eligible counterparty business, they apply to eligible counterparties as well). This is a marked change following the implementation of the MiFID as the previous position used to be that the bulk of the regulatory obligations either automatically did not apply to business with any client other than a retail client or were capable of being disapplied to such client base.

Suitability

The rules of conduct require that before an investment firm makes a personal **12.125** recommendation to a client or acts as a discretionary investment manager for such a client it must take appropriate steps to familiarise itself with the customer's personal characteristics, including his or her knowledge, risk appetite, and financial resources, so as to ensure that any recommendation which is made is suitable for the customer.

The MiFID contains 'know your customer' ('KYC') and suitability requirements **12.126** which apply when an investment firm provides investment advice or discretionary portfolio management. These requirements apply to both retail and (in more limited form) professional clients. The obligation will in practice extend to 'eligible counterparties' for whom investment advice or portfolio management services are provided as eligible counterparty status is only available in relation to dealing activities.

Article 11 of the ISD required Member States to have rules which implemented **12.127** specified principles. These principles did not include a suitability provision but

---

[60] Art 53 of the FSMA (Regulated Activities) Order 2001, SI 2001/544.

provided that a firm should act honestly and fairly and with due skill, care, and diligence in the best interests of clients and should seek from clients information about their financial situations, investment experience, and objectives. FSA Principle for Businesses 9 (Customers: relationships of trust) requires a firm to take reasonable care to ensure the suitability of its advice and discretionary decisions. This principle was amplified by conduct of business rules imposing KYC and suitability obligations. Prior to the implementation of the MiFID, these obligations only applied in relation to private customers. Specific additional suitability obligations applied in relation to 'packaged products' such as regulated funds, pensions advice, and broker funds and these have been maintained post MiFID.

12.128 The suitability obligation applies in relation to the provision of investment advice and portfolio management. These are both core services under the MiFID. Investment advice is defined as the *'provision of personal recommendations to a client, either upon its request or at the initiative of the investment firm, in respect of one or more transactions relating to financial instruments'*. The MiFID Implementing Directive provides that the recommendation must be made to a person in his capacity as an investor or potential investor, or as an agent of an investor or potential investor.[61] This means that certain advice given in connection with primary market transactions, corporate reorganisations, and other corporate finance transactions will not be caught.

12.129 In addition, the recommendation must be presented as suitable for the recipient or be based on a consideration of his circumstances and be to buy, sell, subscribe for, exchange, redeem, underwrite, or hold a particular financial instrument or exercise a right to buy, sell, etc a financial instrument. A recommendation is not a personal recommendation if it is issued exclusively through distribution channels or to the public.[62]

12.130 The recitals to the MiFID Implementing Directive seek to draw a distinction between personal recommendations—which trigger suitability obligations—and general recommendations which do not. This means that published research and marketing material are not subject to suitability (and an obligation to have performed KYC in relation to the recipients) but are subject to contents and presentation requirements. Furthermore, recipients who deal in response to a general promotion addressed to the public or a larger group or category of clients do not trigger the appropriateness obligation in relation to non-complex products.

12.131 The FSA has noted in consultation that it is therefore possible for a firm to provide information or opinions about markets, prices, and instruments to a professional

---

[61] Article 52 of the MiFID Implementing Directive.
[62] 'Distribution Channel' is defined in Directive (EC) 2003/125.

client without going as far as to provide a 'personal' recommendation to the client. It accepts that, in such a situation, the position of the firm will be reinforced if it makes it clear to the client that in providing the information it is not providing a recommendation. However, the FSA has cautioned that if it is clear from the circumstances that the firm is making a personal recommendation, a 'disclaimer' (eg to the effect that a recommendation is not being provided), whether in the terms of business, a notification, or otherwise, will have no effect. The FSA considers that a firm cannot contract out of the requirements applying to the provision of personal recommendations if that is what it has given but raises the question as to whether a 'disclaimer' statement can change the nature of the communication. It concludes that all the circumstances will have to be considered and that the proximity, prominence, and timeliness of such statements may have a bearing on this.[63]

The recitals to the MiFID Implementing Directive also provide that generic advice about a type of financial instrument is not investment advice and thus does not trigger the suitability obligation. However, if an investment firm presents such generic advice as suitable or based on a consideration of the client's circumstances and that is not the case, the firm is likely to be in breach of the MiFID, Article 19(1) which requires investment firms to act honestly, fairly, and professionally, or the MiFID, Article 19(2) which requires all information, including marketing communications, to be fair, clear, and not misleading.   **12.132**

Portfolio management means managing portfolios in accordance with mandates given by clients on a discretionary client-by-client basis where the portfolios include one or more financial instruments. For the purposes of the suitability provisions, a transaction entered into in the course of providing a portfolio management service amounts to a 'recommendation'. The MiFID Implementing Directive includes a recital to the effect that a request or advice/recommendation to alter the portfolio management mandate defining the manager's discretion should also be treated as a recommendation. The MiFID, Article 19(4) requires an investment firm, when providing investment advice or portfolio management to a client, to obtain the necessary information regarding a client's: **12.133**

- knowledge and experience in the investment field relevant to the specific type of product or service; and
- financial situation and investment objectives,

to enable the firm to make a suitable recommendation.

---

[63] See FSA CP 06/19.

12.134 This test is more onerous than the appropriateness test which requires a firm to assess knowledge and experience but not financial situation and objectives. Article 35 of the MiFID Implementing Directive provides criteria to be satisfied in relation to the 'necessary' information for the firm to be able to meet the suitability test. The information obtained must be that necessary for the firm to:

- understand the essential facts about the client;
- have a reasonable basis for believing that the recommendation/transaction:
  - meets the client's investment objectives;
  - is such that the client is able financially to bear any related investment risks; and
  - is such that the client has the necessary experience and knowledge in order to understand the risks involved.

12.135 In the case of a professional client, the MiFID Implementing Directive provides that the investment firm may assume that the client has the necessary experience and knowledge in relation to the products, transactions, and services for which he is so classified. In addition, where an investment firm provides investment advice to a per se professional client, the firm can assume that the client is able to bear any related investment risks consistent with his investment objectives.

12.136 The MiFID Implementing Directive gives examples of the information which should be obtained from a client in relation to his financial situation, investment objectives, knowledge, and experience. However, the MiFID is clear that this should only be collected 'to the extent appropriate to the nature of the client, the nature and extent of the service to be provided and the type of product or transaction envisaged, including their complexity and the risks involved'. The FSA considers that there is an irreducible minimum level of information without which it is not possible to provide a personal recommendation. However, it accepts that as long as it is consistent with the client's objectives and best interests, and understood by the parties, it is possible for a firm to focus the scope of its advice to suit the information the client wishes to disclose. For example, advice could be given in relation to just part of a client's portfolio if that is what the client wants or agrees to, and if sufficient level of information has been provided for suitability to be assessed in relation to that part of the portfolio (see FSA PS 07/6).

12.137 A firm is entitled to rely on the information provided by a client unless it is aware or ought to be aware that the information is manifestly out of date, inaccurate, or incomplete. If a firm does not obtain the relevant information it may not make a recommendation to the client. The FSA has provided guidance to the effect that this does not preclude the firm responding to the client's request for another service, for example, arranging a deal or dealing as agent but that the firm should ensure that it receives written confirmation of the client's instructions.[64]

The MiFID addresses the situation where a firm (A) receives an instruction on behalf of a client through the medium of another investment firm (B). In these circumstances, A can rely on information about the client provided by B (who will be responsible for its completeness and accuracy). In addition, B will remain responsible for the appropriateness for the client of any recommendations or advice provided.

12.138

A firm must retain records relating to suitability for a minimum of five years. The FSA has noted that records of the client information a firm obtains to assess suitability can include a firm's use of information it has already obtained for a different purpose, and that this may be particularly relevant for professional clients. The FSA recognises that, where possible, firms which provide personal recommendations to professional clients will wish to avoid having to re-establish (and record again) such a client's investment objectives in relation to each routine trading recommendation the firm makes concerning a plain vanilla instrument, if the client's commercial objectives are clear and the particular transaction does not raise additional considerations.[65]

12.139

It would be best practice for an investment firm which is subject to this regime to produce, on an annual basis, a form which requires a confirmation from each client concerning, at least, his or her financial standing, investment objectives, and risk appetite. This is likely to provide the firm with at least the starting point for a defence against regulatory claims of mis-selling and against potential civil claims.

12.140

Disclosure of charges, remuneration, and commission

There are specific rules of conduct within COBS requiring an investment firm to disclose (in a comprehensible form) to retail clients the basis or amount of all the firm's charges and of any other income which is receivable by the firm or its associates and is in any way attributable to business conducted for such clients. This disclosure is usually made in a firm's standard terms of business, but it is nevertheless very important for a firm's client-facing personnel to be reminded that if there is a transaction where the firm's remuneration does not correspond with the terms of business, then any discrepancies must be reported to the relevant client before the execution of the transaction or the provision of services. There are many more

12.141

---

[64] See FSA PS 07/2.
[65] See FSA PS 07/6.

detailed and prescriptive rules relating to the disclosure to retail clients of commissions in respect of packaged products.

Misconduct in securities offerings

12.142 In February 2003 the FSA published a Consultation Paper[66] in which it reviewed, amongst other matters, the extent to which UK investment firms had engaged in malpractices associated with the management of issues of securities. The FSA's efforts were in response to large-scale US investigations which concluded that certain investment firms had engaged in two particular types of misconduct.

12.143 The first type of misconduct[67] involved investment firms acting as underwriters in an Initial Public Offering ('IPO') of securities seeking to recapture profits made by their investor clients through charging unusually high commissions on unrelated transactions. The main concern in such circumstances is that the underwriting firm has a strong incentive to achieve a significant increase in the price of the security upon commencement of trading so that the profit of its investor clients is sufficient to cause them to agree to pay the high commissions.

12.144 The second type of misconduct[68] involved investment firms which were acting as underwriters in an IPO allocating the (highly desirable) securities to senior executive officers of potential or existing clients in return for past or future loyalty to the investment firm concerned.

12.145 These practices constituted a serious failure on the part of the relevant investment firms to manage their conflicts of interest effectively. In an IPO transaction, as in many other transactions involving the issue of securities, the investment firm's duty is first and foremost to the issuer. The practical problem within a multidisciplinary investment firm is that in the context of an IPO there is a constant tension between the firm's duties to its primary client (ie the issuer) and its desire to achieve the best possible outcome for its investor clients who essentially create the much sought-after demand for the securities which the firm promotes. It can be easily seen that such firms need very robust internal systems and controls to address potential conflicts of interest.

FSA guidance

12.146 Having conducted a limited survey of a number of selected investment firms, the FSA concluded that 'internal procedures and systems and controls to address the

---

[66] Consultation Paper 171: 'Conflicts of Interest: Investment Research and Issues of Securities'.
[67] Referred to as 'laddering'.
[68] Referred to as 'spinning'.

conflicts involved vary quite markedly between firms'. This implies, as the FSA stated elsewhere in the document, that no clear evidence of abusive practices was unveiled. Nevertheless, the FSA came to the view that it would be beneficial to set out, in guidance, some principles in relation to three specific areas: supervision and management of issues of securities, allocation of securities, and the determination of pricing.

The FSA guidance emphasises the fact that when dealing with issues of securities **12.147** on behalf of the issuer, an investment firm's primary duty is owed to the issuer client. Furthermore, the guidance states that firms must have in place appropriate systems, controls, and procedures concerning policies for allocation of securities in IPOs, and the determination of pricing and for securing the absence from this process of personnel from that part of the firm which serves investment clients.

Particular emphasis is placed on ensuring that investment firms have robust inter- **12.148** nal arrangements to ensure that the process of allocating securities is made by persons who exclusively serve the issuer client and take into account the issuer client's views. To preclude abuse involving an investment client's executives, investment firms are now required to delegate responsibility for allocating securi- ties to the firm's retail clients to senior managers. Firms are further reminded that allocations to a client should not be undertaken with a view to increasing the level of the firm's business with that client, the objective being to ensure that the alloca- tion process is more transparent and unlikely to yield results which conflict with the interests of the issuer client.

The FSA clarified in its guidance that the following practices would be deemed to **12.149** constitute a breach of its Principles for Businesses (as to which see paras 12.47 to 12.53):

- allocation of securities made as an inducement for the payment of excessive remuneration for unrelated services;
- allocation of securities to senior executives or officers of an existing or potential corporate finance client in exchange for future or past transaction mandates;
- allocation of securities which is expressly or implicitly conditional on receipt of orders for transactions in securities or the purchase of any other investment services.

Dealing in Securities

Reference is made in para 12.20 to the importance for investment firms of ade- **12.150** quately addressing any real or potential conflicts of interest that may arise in their businesses. As Professor Gower stated in his report, this area is one where '[the regulatory] aims . . . cannot be achieved in the absence of specific rules'. This is as true today as it was in 1984, and although the rules of conduct in the area of conflicts have traditionally been widely drafted with a view to allowing firms as many alternative ways as possible to deal with conflicts and potential conflicts of interest, this approach is now gradually being tightened up.

12.151　The rules on the management of conflicts of interest generally apply whenever an investment firm engages in investment services or activities (with or for all categories of clients).

Conflicts of interest

12.152　SYSC 10 sets out the principles which prohibit investment firms from engaging in a course of action which is likely to harm the interests of its clients including in the following circumstances that is if it:

- is likely to make a financial gain, or avoid a financial loss, at the expense of the client;

- has an interest in the outcome of a service provided to the client or of a transaction carried out on behalf of the client, which is distinct from the client's interest in that outcome;

- has a financial or other incentive to favour the interest of another client or group of clients over the interests of the client;

- carries on the same business as the client; or

- receives or will receive from a person other than the client an inducement in relation to a service provided to the client, in the form of monies, goods, or services, other than the standard commission or fee for that service.

12.153　SYSC 10 allows investment firms to conduct business in such circumstances only if they take one or more mitigating steps, such as establishing appropriate internal systems and procedures (Chinese Walls). Disclosure of a conflict is, under MiFID, a mitigating measure of last resort. Fundamentally, the purpose of disclosure to clients must be to inform them of the general policy of the firm on dealing with conflicts of interest and to inform them on a case by case basis of the existence of a conflict. In practice, most investment firms seek to bypass this approach by including a widely drafted clause in their terms of business to allow them to act in all possible situations despite an actual or potential conflict. This approach will not suffice to comply with the relevant rules. Disclosure will only be deemed acceptable where the circumstances dictate that no other mitigation method is relevant and the client is sufficiently sophisticated.

12.154　It is becoming increasingly clear that there will be situations where the relative bargaining powers of the parties, or the subject matter of the conflict, means that disclosure alone is not sufficient to ensure that the interests of customers are adequately protected (such as when an investment firm communicates investment research to its customers).

Other restrictions

Investment firms are also subject to the following restrictions when they engage in **12.155** investment activities with customers.

(a) **Churning and switching.**[69] Encouraging a customer to deal frequently in or switch an investment or an investment portfolio carries financial incentives for investment firms' securities dealers because they are commonly remunerated on an executed transaction basis. A series of transactions that are each suitable when viewed in isolation may be unsuitable if the recommendation or the decisions to trade are made with a frequency that is not in the best interests of the client. A firm should have regard to the client's agreed investment strategy in determining the frequency of transactions.

(b) **Customer order priority.** Where a securities dealer receives an execution order for a securities transactions from a customer the dealer might be tempted (especially where the order is a substantial one) to 'front-run' the customer, that is to place an order for the firm's own account before executing the customer's order so as to benefit from an anticipated increase/decrease in the price of the securities. The rules of conduct now specify that customers' orders must be executed fairly and in due turn. This Rule relates to both orders of customers and the firm and as between the orders of customers themselves.

(c) **Timely execution.** For reasons which are self explanatory, it is fundamentally important that securities brokers execute their customers' orders in a timely fashion so as to avoid any potential adverse impact from movements in the market. Thus, once an investment firm has received an order and agreed to execute it or has decided to execute an order in the exercise of a discretion, it must carry out the relevant order 'as soon as reasonably practicable'. There will be occasions, however, when it is in the customer's best interest for the firm to postpone execution of a securities transaction (eg where improved trading volumes in the security concerned is expected to better the terms on which the deal can be made). Timeliness is considered one of the execution factors, as delineated in COBS 11.2.

(d) **Aggregation and allocation.** It is common for securities dealers to aggregate clients' orders and own account orders. Here COBS 11.3.7 specifies that securities dealers adopt a detailed policy (which they must disclose to their

---

[69] See COBS.

customers) on the allocation of securities following aggregation. Allocation of securities following aggregate trading (whether or not the order has been completely filled) must be fair (which essentially means that as a general rule priority must be given to satisfying customers' orders first). Securities dealers are only permitted to aggregate clients' orders if to do so will not result in adverse consequences for the customers concerned.

(e) **Personal account dealing.**[70] These rules restrict the ability of investment firms' employees to engage in personal transactions in circumstances which may compromise the interests of the firms' customers—a rule which in practice applies to all clients. It is mandatory for investment firms to obtain a strict undertaking from their employees (which is incorporated into their contracts of employment), prior to the commencement of their employment, to comply with the firm's personal account dealing restrictions. The rules also require a firm to monitor—in practice, firms approve all such dealings—any personal transactions by employees and also by parties to whom the firm outsources the conduct of certain activities related to dealings or which provides exposure to confidential information. There are also specific restrictions placed by rules covering investment analysts who conduct personal transactions.

Best execution

12.156 Under the MiFID,[71] investment firms which execute client orders (whether as principal or as agent) in relation to financial instruments need to comply with detailed best execution requirements. In addition, firms which undertake portfolio management or receive and transmit orders on behalf of clients in relation to financial instruments will be subject to analogous requirements. Firms subject to the MiFID requirements (brokers, dealers, and asset managers) need to:

- put arrangements in place to comply with the best execution framework;
- produce and implement a best execution policy consistent with the new framework;
- provide appropriate information on the best execution policy to clients and obtain their consent to this policy; and

---

[70] COBS 11.7.
[71] The MiFID, Arts 14(3), 21, and 24(1) and Recital 33. The MiFID Implementing Directive, Arts 44, 45, and 46 and Recitals 66–76. Level 3: Best Execution under the MiFID Questions & Answers (CESR/07-320) (which includes the European Commission response to CESR questions on scope as an appendix); Best Execution under The MiFID Questions & Answers—Feedback Statement (CESR/07- 321).

- undertake continuous monitoring of compliance with the policy and update and notify clients of amendments to the policy.

Best execution is a key plank of investor protection under the MiFID. When pro- **12.157** viding investment services to their clients, investment firms are subject to a general obligation to act honestly, fairly, and professionally in accordance with the best interests of their clients.[72] Best execution elaborates on this obligation by focusing on the way client orders should be executed by an investment firm. This area is singled out due to the information asymmetry arising between the investment firm and the client—because clients generally have little access to (or ability to evaluate) pricing information, there is a danger that investment firms could take advantage of this information asymmetry and consequently treat customers unfairly.

A further driver of the best execution requirements under the MiFID is the loss of **12.158** the so-called concentration rule under the ISD, whereby EEA Member States may require retail order flow to be put through a regulated market. The loss of the concentration rule enables competition between trading venues and, in principle, lowers the cost of transacting financial instruments, but also gives rise to fragmentation concerns—in particular, the possibility that firms could fail to deal through a range of execution venues in a product, thereby depriving investors of access to the best price. The best execution requirement seeks to deal with this concern by mandating transparency on the part of firms as to the execution venues which they use.

The ISD did not specifically address best execution. Article 11 set out a series of **12.159** general principles which Member States were required to implement in domestic legislation and to apply in such a way as to take account of the professional nature of the client for whom the service is provided. These included principles that an investment firm should act honestly and fairly in conducting its business activities, and act with due skill, care, and diligence, in each case in the best interest of its clients and the integrity of the market.

The previous set of FSA rules required a firm executing a customer order in a des- **12.160** ignated investment to provide best execution, subject to certain exceptions. For the purposes of the previous requirements, a 'customer order' was an order to execute a transaction as agent (including a decision to execute a transaction in the exercise of discretion) for a customer, or any other order to a firm from a customer to execute a transaction in circumstances giving rise to duties similar to those arising on an order to execute a transaction as agent. The obligation did not apply

---

[72] MiFID, Art 19(1).

with respect to orders executed with or for clients which were classified as market counterparties.

12.161 In providing best execution, a firm was required to take reasonable care to ascertain the price which is the best available for the customer order in the relevant market at the time for transactions of the kind and size concerned, and execute the customer order at a price which is no less advantageous, unless the firm had taken reasonable steps to ensure that it would be in the customer's best interests not to do so. Execution of transactions traded on SETS (the London Stock Exchange order book for the most liquid equities) was generally deemed to constitute best execution for the purpose of the previous rules.

12.162 In providing best execution, a firm was required to disregard any charges or commissions made by it or its agents which are disclosed to the customer.

12.163 Firms were able to contract out of the obligation to provide best execution with clients classified under the previous regime as intermediate customers (other than certain pension funds). In practice, many firms did so. Accordingly, firms could (and frequently did) avoid providing best execution in the wholesale market.

12.164 Where a firm passed a customer order to a third party for execution, the firm could rely on the third party to provide best execution if it took reasonable care to ensure that the third party would do so. Portfolio managers simply relied on a contractual best execution obligation on the part of the brokers with which they dealt to discharge their best execution obligation.

12.165 By contrast the best execution obligation under the MiFID applies to three investment services undertaken with respect to financial instruments: execution of client orders, reception and transmission of orders on behalf of investors, and portfolio management. The expanded range of financial instruments caught by the MiFID means that the best execution obligation applies not only to securities market transactions but also with respect to commodity, credit, and other derivatives newly brought within the European regulatory regime.

12.166 There is a core obligation on investment firms to 'take all reasonable steps to obtain … the best possible result for their clients taking into account price, costs, speed, likelihood of execution and settlement, size, nature or any other consideration relevant to the execution of the order'.[73] Price, costs, speed, likelihood of execution and settlement, size, nature, and any other consideration are referred to as the factors.

12.167 The term 'best possible result' is not conclusively defined by the MiFID. However, where the client is a retail client the best possible result is to be determined in

---

[73] The MiFID Implementing Directive, Art 21.

terms of the total consideration, representing the price of the financial instrument and the costs related to execution, including all expenses incurred by the client directly related to the execution of the order.[74] These include execution venue fees, clearing and settlement fees, and any other fees paid to third parties involved in execution of the order. For the purpose of the best execution regime, the term 'execution venue' means a regulated market, an MTF, a systematic internaliser, or a market maker or other liquidity provider or an entity that performs a similar function in a non-EEA jurisdiction. The firm's own commissions and costs are to be taken into account when assessing best execution as between different execution venues.[75] Investment firms are also required not to structure their commissions in such a way as to discriminate unfairly between execution venues.

The requirement to include assessment of the firm's own commission when providing best execution represents a significant change from the previous FSA rules, which did not require the firm's own commissions to be taken into account, as long as they are disclosed. **12.168**

In respect of retail clients, total consideration (the price of the financial instrument less costs associated with execution on the relevant execution venue) is paramount—accordingly, speed, likelihood of execution and settlement, size, nature of the transaction, market impact, and implicit transaction costs should be given precedence over the immediate price and cost consideration 'only insofar as they are instrumental in delivering the best possible result in terms of the total consideration to the retail client'.[76] **12.169**

Accordingly, for retail orders it may be expected that the factors which are not related directly to costs will need to be subordinate to those which are. There is no such guidance in relation to execution for professional clients. **12.170**

The MiFID does not otherwise specify the relative importance of the factors to be taken into account for non-retail clients. Rather, it provides four sets of characteristics to be taken into account in determining the importance of the factors (referred to below as the characteristics). These are: **12.171**

• the client;
• the order;
• the financial instruments that are subject of the order; and
• the execution venues to which the order may be directed.

The importance of the factors will vary depending on the nature of the financial instrument—for example, likelihood of settlement will be a more significant **12.172**

---

[74] The MiFID Implementing Directive, Art 44.
[75] The MiFID Implementing Directive, Art 44(3).
[76] The MiFID Implementing Directive, Recital 67.

factor in respect of an OTC derivative carrying ongoing counterparty risk than in respect of a cash equity transaction. This lack of uniformity is recognised and it is considered that the obligation should be applied in a manner which takes into account the different circumstances associated with the execution of orders related to different types of instruments.[77] It will be for firms to determine how the factors are to be weighted across their different product lines.

12.173 The MiFID does not mandate the number of execution venues to be used by a firm in discharging its best execution obligations. However, Article 21(3), which sets out the requirement for an execution policy, states that a firm must deal on venues that enable it to obtain on a consistent basis the best possible result for the execution of client orders. Firms therefore need to engage their execution venues based on their determination of what constitutes the best possible result (including the weighting of the factors) in light of their client base and order flow in respect of any given product. The firm's resources are likely to be a relevant determination in this regard.

12.174 Article 45 of the MiFID Implementing Directive sets out the obligations of investment firms when undertaking portfolio management and reception and transmission of orders (RTO) on behalf of clients. Article 45(4) contains the same obligation—to take all reasonable steps to obtain the best possible results for their clients (and refers to the same factors and criteria as those detailed above). However, it is clear that the MiFID is not intended to duplicate effort between the firm undertaking reception and transmission of orders or portfolio management on the one hand, and the firm executing on the other hand.[78]

12.175 In addition, the focus of the best execution policy required under Article 45 is the choice of entities with which orders are placed or to which they are transferred for execution. A portfolio manager/RTO should determine that the entities it uses will enable it to comply with the overriding best execution requirement when placing an order with, or transmitting an order to, another entity for execution. A portfolio manager/RTO should review the execution arrangements of the entities it wishes to use to determine whether they will allow it to comply with its best execution requirements. This may include considering whether the entity is itself subject to Article 21 of the MiFID or will undertake by contract to comply with the MiFID best execution requirements.

12.176 However, when portfolio managers/RTOs execute their own decisions to deal/ orders directly with an execution venue, they are subject to Article 21 of MiFID (rather than Article 45 of the MiFID Implementing Directive). A portfolio

---

[77] The MiFID Implementing Directive, Recital 70.
[78] The MiFID Implementing Directive, Recital 75.

manager/RTO may produce a single best execution policy which covers both its order execution and portfolio management best execution obligations.

Article 21 excludes from the best execution obligation specific instructions **12.177** from a client. There is some doubt as to how far it will be feasible to argue that instructions from a client to transact are 'specific instructions' disapplying the obligation—see further discussion below.

Article 14(3) disapplies the obligation as between participants dealing on a regu- **12.178** lated market or MTF (although this does not affect any best execution obligations the participants may have to their clients for whom they trade on the regulated market or MTF).

Accordingly, the flexibility which used to be inherent in the ISD in enabling EEA **12.179** Member States to lift best execution obligations taking account of the professional nature of clients has been replaced by a harmonised and more prescriptive regime conferring best execution rights on all but a limited subset of institutional clients.

From a UK perspective, the ability to contract out of best execution has been **12.180** substantially removed. In addition, investment firms which solely receive and transmit orders or pass orders to third parties for execution are, for the first time, subject to the best execution requirement.

Investment firms subject to the best execution requirement must establish and **12.181** implement effective arrangements to ensure compliance with their obligations.[79] A written order execution policy must be established and implemented. The order execution policy must include, by class of instrument:

- the execution venues used to execute client orders (this must include at least those venues that deliver the best possible result on a consistent basis); and
- the factors affecting the choice of venue.[80]

The policy should set out the firm's strategy for determining best execution. It **12.182** should include an account of the relative importance, or process for determining the relative importance, placed on the factors when executing client orders and how the factors affect the choice of execution venues.[81] A single execution venue may be justified if a firm can show that it is able to obtain the best possible result on a consistent basis. A portfolio manager may include a single entity in its policy if this allows it to satisfy its overarching best execution obligation.

---

[79] COBS 11.2.14.
[80] COBS 11.2.15.
[81] COBS 11.2.7.

12.183   The policy must be reviewed annually and whenever a material change occurs which affects the ability of the firm to comply with the best execution requirement on a consistent basis using the venues set out in the policy.[82] In addition, the effectiveness of the policy must be monitored, including regular assessment of whether the execution venues included in the policy provide for the best possible result for the client or whether changes need to be made.

12.184   Investment firms which provide best execution are required to provide appropriate information to their clients on their order execution policy, and to obtain the prior consent of the client to it.[83] The policy must:

- specifically draw attention (and prior express consent must be obtained from the client) to the possibility of execution away from a regulated market or MTF (consent may be in the form of a general agreement);

- (for retail clients only) include an account of the relative importance the firm assigns to the factors, or the process by which the firm does so;

- list the execution venues on which the firm places specific reliance in meeting its best execution obligation; and

- include a warning that specific instructions from a client may prevent the firm from taking the steps that it has designed and implemented in its policy to give best execution.

12.185   Material changes to the policy must be notified to clients.

12.186   CESR acknowledges that 'prior consent' may, at least in some jurisdictions, be tacit and result from behaviour of the client such as the sending of an order to the firm after having received information on the firm's execution policy.

12.187   CESR[84] considers that 'prior express consent' for OTC order execution entails an actual demonstration of consent by the client (by written signature or equivalent means (electronic signature), by a click on a web page, or orally by telephone or in person, with appropriate record keeping). The express consent requirement is not regarded as applying in relation to financial instruments which are not admitted to trading on a regulated market or MTF.

12.188   Investment firms which execute client orders must be able to demonstrate to their clients, at their request, that they have executed orders in accordance with their policy. This requirement does not apply to portfolio management or reception and transmission of orders.

---

[82] COBS 11.2.28.
[83] COBS 11.2.23.
[84] CESR/07-321.

Best execution has been one of the most controversial areas of the MiFID. There **12.189** remain a number of areas of uncertainty around the scope of the regime. These largely relate to conceptual difficulties in applying best execution to principal (own account) dealing arrangements or to highly bespoke products.

There remains some difficulty in determining when the best execution require- **12.190** ment is intended to apply to principal dealers (ie firms which put their own capital at risk to trade). The MiFID contains countervailing indications in this respect: Recital 33 states that the best execution obligation 'should apply to the firm that owes contractual or agency duties to the client'. In circumstances where a firm makes prices (and risks its own capital), it may be argued that it may owe no such duties.

A related argument centres on the question of whether a principal dealer receives **12.191** 'client orders', on grounds that a request to trade in response to an offer to deal on risk by a firm does not constitute an order. As against each of these arguments, however, Recital 69 of the MiFID Implementing Directive states that dealing on own account with clients should be considered as the execution of client orders.

The Commission has now agreed an interpretation of the MiFID rejecting the **12.192** above approaches and focusing on the words 'on behalf of'. Under this interpreta- tion, firms which deal other than where they act on behalf of their clients do not have a best execution obligation. Whether a firm acts on behalf of a client when dealing as principal will be largely a question of fact. Generally, riskless principal dealings and orders worked by a firm will be executed on the client's behalf. The key issue will be whether the client legitimately relies on the firm to protect its interests.

As indicated above, a possible route to avoid the application of the best execution **12.193** obligation is to argue that particular instructions received are 'specific instruc- tions' from the client which the firm is following in executing the order. However, there is a prohibition on investment firms inducing or inviting specific instruc- tions from clients when the firm ought reasonably to know that an instruction to that effect is likely to prevent it from obtaining the best possible result for the client.[85] It also clarifies that when an investment firm executes an order following specific instructions from the client, it should be treated as having satisfied its best execution obligations only in respect of the part or aspect of the order to which the client instructions relate.

The Commission has sought to provide some clarification on the application of **12.194** the specific instruction provision in relation to customised products. It acknowl- edges that where the investment firm proposes to a client the elements of an OTC derivatives contract that would respond to the client's needs, it is more

---

[85] The MiFID Implementing Directive, Recital 68.

appropriate to characterise this as investment advice (triggering a suitability obligation) rather than best execution. However, it considers that the fact that the client specifies what he needs in terms of exposure and protection does not necessarily exclude the application of best execution. Where best execution applies because an order is executed on behalf of the customer, the identity of the instruments sought will be a matter of the information contained in the order rather than a question of specific instructions.

12.195 In the case of complex products, the Commission notes that best execution (when applicable) applies to the product as a whole and may be obtained even if best execution for each component, when considered in isolation, is not obtained.

12.196 CESR issued a consultation paper in February 2007[86] on best execution under the MiFID covering the following areas:

- the contents of the execution policy and arrangements;
- disclosure to clients;
- client consent;
- relationships between firms in chains of execution;
- review and monitoring; and
- quality of data.

12.197 In May 2007 CESR produced a feedback statement[87] summarising the most significant issues raised during the consultation and a Best Execution Q&A (to which the Commission interpretation referred to above is appended). Key issues addressed by the Q&A include the different obligations of investment firms executing orders directly with execution venues and portfolio managers and other firms which transmit or place orders with other entities for execution; the content of the best execution policy; the information about the policy which should be provided to clients; obtaining consent to the policy; and the distinction between reviewing and monitoring best execution arrangements.

12.198 The CESR Q&A is intended to explain CESR's views on how firms can comply with the MiFID which members of CESR can use on a voluntary basis in day-to-day supervision. It does not constitute European legislation and does not require national legislature action.

---

[86] CESR/07-321.
[87] ibid.

Investment Research

The provision of investment research[88] has been the subject of much debate in **12.199** regulatory circles since the US authorities unveiled irregularities in the way in which investment research was used to facilitate favourable results for certain investment firms (and their corporate finance clients) to the detriment of their investment clients. Investment analysts were heavily involved in marketing efforts in order to gain corporate finance mandates. This meant that their objectivity was compromised as they would be inclined to issue research (presented as being objective) which would favour the company concerned. Additionally, internal reporting structures within investment firms and investment analysts' remuneration structures were linked with the activities of corporate finance personnel which provided a further indication of the existence of a conflict of interest.

FSA consultation

In July 2002, the FSA issued a Discussion Paper concerning the state of invest- **12.200** ment research in the UK.[89] The summary conclusions were not encouraging. The paper produced evidence[90] which was difficult to reconcile with the premise that investment research was objective.

The paper identified as the main source of conflict for investment firms the prac- **12.201** tice of requiring research analysts to share their skills and knowledge in corporate finance deals as well as fulfilling their traditional role of providing research recommendations to the brokerage section of their firm. The result has been impaired integrity of investment research due to the desire to produce favourable results for corporate finance clients.

---

[88] The term 'investment research' is defined in the FSA Glossary (as derived from the MiFID) as research or other information recommending or suggesting an investment strategy, explicitly or implicitly, concerning one or several financial instruments or the issuers of financial instruments, including any opinion as to the present or future value or price of such instruments, intended for distribution channels or for the public, and in relation to which the following conditions are met:

(a) it is labelled or described as investment research or in similar terms, or is otherwise presented as an objective or independent explanation of the matters contained in the recommendation; and

(b) if the recommendation in question were to be made by an investment firm to a client, it would not constitute the provision of a personal recommendation.

[89] The publication of this Discussion Paper coincided with negotiations of the EU Market Abuse Directive which contains certain elements regulating the issue of research recommendations in relation to securities which are admitted to trading on an EEA Regulated Market or in respect of which an application for admission has been made.

[90] In the FSA's own words 'there is evidence that in certain cases analysts have compromised their integrity by issuing recommendations contrary to their own views'.

12.202 It was clear that the modern phenomenon of bringing research analysts closer to corporate finance clients was also liable to produce a negative effect on the willingness of analysts concerned to publish adverse research notes on their corporate clients. Corporate finance clients have shown throughout the years that they are willing to impose severe sanctions on investment firms and their analysts if they are not pleased with a particular research recommendation. These commercial issues are at the heart of the regulatory concerns as to the objectivity and integrity of investment research.

12.203 The paper also highlighted the significant impact that investment research was having on the price of the securities covered by the research. Some highly rated research analysts prove time and time again that their recommendations can mean doom or boom for the share price of the companies concerned. This gave regulators a wide mandate to address any actual and potential problems in this area due to its potential adverse effect on the integrity and orderly nature of the securities markets.

12.204 In July 2003, the FSA published Consultation Paper 171.[91] In the paper, the FSA advocated the strengthening of its regime to counteract any potential for abuse. As proposed this would take the form of more prescriptive guidance on how the FSA expects internal control structures to operate within investment firms in connection with investment research and on acceptable standards of analysts' conduct.

FSA guidance

12.205 Following further consultation,[92] the FSA published in March 2004 its rules and guidance in Policy Statement 04/6, which came into force on 1 July 2004. These are now incorporated into COBS 12. The following is a summary of the main provisions.

- Investment firms are required to establish a policy[93] for managing conflicts of interest (see SYSC 10.1.11) in the context of the publication of impartially presented investment research. The policy, which must be recorded and made available to clients, must identify conflicts of interest which might affect the impartiality of its investment research and must at least deal with the following matters: (a) supervision and management of investment analysts; (b) remuneration structure for investment analysts; (c) rules governing

---

[91] 'Conflicts of Interest: Investment research and issues of securities'.
[92] Consultation Paper 205: 'Conflicts of interest: Investment research and issues of securities' (October 2003).
[93] COBS 12.2.3.

investment analysts' activities other than the production of investment research (eg involvement in corporate finance transactions); (d) identification of persons who may comment on the content of investment research and the weight and force of such comments; (e) the timing and manner in which investment research should be communicated; and (f) disclosures for inclusion in investment research.

- It would generally not be appropriate for an individual with corporate finance responsibilities to be supervising or controlling investment analysts, making decisions on the subject matter or content of investment research, or deciding investment analysts' remuneration.[94]

- Whilst it is legitimate for investment firms to utilise the knowledge and information of investment analysts in corporate finance business, the participation of investment analysts in a marketing capacity (eg presentations to solicit corporate finance business) is likely to be inappropriate as it would give the impression of lack of impartiality in their investment research. Furthermore, the appearance of investment analysts in securities 'roadshows' (to promote interest in new issues of securities) is also noted as inappropriate.

- Investment firms must not give editorial control of investment research materials to persons within the firm whose role involves the representation of interests that could conflict with those of the target audience of the research and must not allow anyone other than the analyst concerned to provide final approval of the content of the investment research.[95]

- Investment firms are no longer allowed to engage in own account transactions in securities (and related securities) which are the subject matter of investment research (intended for circulation to the firm's clients) ahead of the publication of the research.[96] Such own account transactions are only permitted when the firm's clients have had 'a reasonable opportunity to act upon the research'. It is suggested that firms allow at least three working days from the time of the communication of the research before any own account transactions can be undertaken.

- Investment firms must prohibit analysts from undertaking personal account transactions in securities which are the subject matter of their investment research unless the transaction is in line with any current recommendation for which they are responsible or to enable them to meet prior obligations with the permission of the firm. FSA Guidance further provide that investment firms will be well advised to impose a voluntary restriction on their investment

---

[94] COBS 12.2.4.
[95] COBS 12.2.9.
[96] COBS 12.2.5.

analysts requiring them not to engage in personal account transactions at all or not to engage in personal account transactions in the sector which they cover.[97]

Market Abuse Directive

12.206 The EU Market Abuse Directive[98] introduced various requirements (mainly of disclosure) for investment firms which prepare or publish research recommendations. The term 'research recommendation' is defined more narrowly than the FSA Handbook term of 'investment research' mainly in that it only covers instruments which are listed on one or more EEA regulated markets or where an application for admission to trading of the relevant instrument is pending. In order for investment research to constitute a 'research recommendation' it must:

- recommend or suggest an investment strategy;
- express a particular investment recommendation; or
- express an opinion as to the present or future value or price of a security.

12.207 A short term investment recommendation originating from the sales or trading departments of an investment firm and which is not intended for wide circulation is excluded from the definition of 'research recommendation'. This is an important carve-out for more informal and frequent (sometimes daily) communications to a select group of clients (usually institutional clients).

12.208 The following is a summary of the obligations, as set out in COBS 12.4, of an investment firm under the Market Abuse Directive as they would apply to investment firms involved in the preparation of research recommendations.[99]

- Disclose interests or conflicts of interest concerning securities which are the subject matter of a research recommendation.[100] In particular, disclose any relationship and circumstances which could impair the objectivity of the recommendation. This includes: a major (exceeding five per cent) shareholding existing between the firm concerned (or its affiliates) and the relevant issuer; any other financial interests of the firm (or its affiliates) in the relevant issuer, where relevant; details of the firm's (or its affiliates') acting as lead manager or co-lead manager during the previous 12 months in respect of the relevant issuer's

---

[97] COBS 12.2.5A.

[98] Council Directive (EC) 03/6 on insider dealing and market manipulation (market abuse) [2003] OJ L 96/16.

[99] Where certain disclosure obligations are disproportionate to the length of a specific research recommendation, investment firms may include a reference in the body of the research to an easily accessible source providing such information (eg a link to a website).

[100] COBS 12.4.4.

securities or related derivatives, where relevant; and details of any agreements with the relevant issuer to provide investment banking services (insofar as this would not give rise to disclosure of confidential commercial information).

- Adhere to prescribed rules concerning the need for clear distinctions to be made between facts and estimates, interpretations, opinions and the like.[101]

- Ensure that the substance of recommendations can be substantiated as reasonable upon request by the FSA.[102]

- Indicate whether the issuer of the securities concerned has had an opportunity to review the recommendation and comment on it (if relevant).[103]

- Include any basis of valuation or methodology used to evaluate the issuer or the securities.[104]

- Where the substance of the recommendation differs to a material extent from a recommendation of the firm relating to the same security or issuer in the previous 12 months, this must be set out in a prominent manner.[105]

- Disclose the firm's internal systems and controls aimed at the prevention and avoidance of conflicts of interest in connection with research recommendations (including any 'Chinese Walls' arrangements).

- Additionally, investment firms must disclose in their research recommendations, on a quarterly basis, information concerning the proportion of all recommendations published during the relevant quarter that are 'buy', 'hold', or 'sell' and the proportion of securities in each of these categories issued by issuers which have been investment banking clients during the previous 12 months.

Dissemination of third party recommendations, whether altered or not, are generally treated as the relevant firm's own work for disclosure purposes and investment firms must treat such recommendations as if they had produced them themselves.   **12.209**

Clients' Assets

Investment firms are subject to strict rules—set out in a module of the FSA Handbook entitled 'Clients Assets' ('CASS')—concerning the way in which they hold assets (including cash) belonging to clients. The rules are intended to create an environment in which it is difficult for an investment firm to mix or mistake   **12.210**

---

[101] COBS 12.4.6(1)(a).
[102] COBS 12.4.6(1)(d).
[103] COBS 12.4.7(1)(a).
[104] COBS 12.4.7(1)(b).
[105] COBS 12.4.7(1)(f).

client assets with or for its own and to ensure that in the event of the firm's insolvency, the clients of the firm are in the best possible position as against any other creditors of the investment firm. It is clear, however, that whilst the rules seek to minimise any risk of loss to investment firms' clients they by no means guarantee that clients will not ultimately suffer loss.

12.211 MiFID had little impact on CASS,[106] although an important change was implemented in respect of professional clients. Whereas professional clients pre MiFID were able to opt out of the client money regime, under MiFID this ability to opt out has been removed and all professional clients will be covered by the client money regime (unless the relevant firm can make use of the extensive carve-outs from the definition of client money on which the FSA has provided liberal guidance).[107]

12.212 One of the main features of the rules is the requirement to inform clients (particularly vulnerable clients, eg retail clients) of the potential risk that they face as a result of the firm taking a particular course of action in relation to their assets. The clients' assets rules are divided into three parts: custody rules; collateral; client money.

Custody rules

12.213 The custody rules[108] apply to the regulated activity of safeguarding and administering investments.[109] Firms need to be aware that they are subject to the custody rules where they use a dedicated custodian unless the custodian is authorised as such under the FSMA or exempt for this purpose and has undertaken to the relevant clients to be responsible for the assets. The custody rules apply to any assets entrusted to the firm as long as they consist of regulated investments. Where the assets concerned include non-regulated investments, investment firms are entitled[110] to take a proportionate approach to the application of the custody rules to assets which are not regulated investments.

---

[106] It should, however, be noted that CASS has been sub-divided into parts which apply to the MiFID business and parts which apply to non-MiFID business. This distinction, for practical reasons, is expected to fade over time and the parts will eventually become a single set of rules.

[107] CASS 7.2 and CP 38, CP06/14 and CP 08/6 for recent guidance.

[108] A comprehensive analysis of the law and practice relating to custody of financial assets is outside the scope of this chapter which contains only a brief outline of the basic principles.

[109] (Regulated Activities) Order 2001, SI 2001/544, art 40.

[110] CASS 2.1.3.

Segregation and internal controls

The custody rules are designed to ensure that in the event of the insolvency of the **12.214**
firm concerned, assets belonging to the firm's clients do not form any part of the
pool of assets which are available for distribution to the firm's general (including
secured and unsecured) creditors. There is a large body of authorities concerning
which assets constitute part of an insolvent company's estate.[111] These authorities
establish that in order to exclude assets from an insolvent entity's estate, client
assets must be segregated from those belonging to the firm and this must be effectively recorded. As well as this, firms are also required to send to clients custody
statements indicating the assets which are held, at least on an annual basis, and to
conduct a periodical reconciliation of custody investments which are not held by
the firm.

The custody rules contain specific provisions in relation to the registration and **12.215**
recording of legal title to clients' investments which require firms to use one or
more of a number of alternative legal entities for this purpose, as appropriate eg a
nominee company or a custodian (and to provide, in certain circumstances, risk
warnings to affected clients).[112] Whilst it would be ideal for clients to have legal
title to their regulated investments, in practice this rarely happens. The reason for
this is that modern custody methods involve the use of nominee companies,
omnibus accounts, and specialised custodians (which may mean that a large
financial institution will delegate custody to an affiliate).

In addition, there are specific rules concerning retention of documents of title to **12.216**
regulated investments and the steps required before a custodian is appointed to
hold regulated investments of the firm's clients.[113]

Terms of business

COBS 6.1.7 contains a list of information which must be provided to a retail **12.217**
client as regards custody (which should be read in light of the requirements in
COBS 8 regarding client agreements). The custody terms may form part of
the firm's general terms of business or may be provided in a separate document as
soon as the firm expects to be providing custody services to the client. The objective is to inform clients of the manner in which their assets will be held by the firm
and, if relevant, any third parties which may have a role in the custody of those
assets.

---

[111] See eg *Re Kayford Ltd* [1975] 1 WLR 279.
[112] CASS 6.2.3.
[113] CASS 6.2.7.

12.218 The terms must include comprehensive risk disclosure provisions, particularly in respect of regulated investments held with third party custodians, and depositaries outside the UK which are subject to different legal and regulatory systems. Such arrangements frequently present complex questions of insolvency law and conflict of laws as to the level of protection afforded in the event of the third party's insolvency or the occurrence of other supervening events.

Custody

12.219 There are conflicting authorities[114] (and therefore the law is far from being settled) on the question of whether or not fungible securities held by a custodian are capable of forming the subject matter of a trust (the issue being lack of certainty as to the subject matter at any given time). Recognising this, the custody rules require an investment firm to have prior written consent from the client before it uses custody investments for its own account (whether for stock lending transactions or otherwise).

Stock lending

12.220 Where an investment firm engages in a stock lending transaction involving securities owned by clients, it must ensure that the borrower provides adequate collateral at the outset and is obliged to top up the collateral on a regular basis (otherwise the firm must provide for any shortfall).

Collateral

12.221 The term 'collateral' in this context denotes securities which are provided by clients effectively as security for their contingent obligations and which the firm may use (including by way of hypothecation) for the purposes of its business. Unless otherwise agreed, investment firms must monitor the collateral they hold for their clients and maintain appropriate records.

Client money

12.222 Investment firms' conduct in relation to monies placed by, or which are due to, their clients is subject, in the absence of an exemption, to a system of prescriptive rules concerning segregation and internal systems of controls (these rules being

---

[114] *Re Goldcorp Exchange Ltd* [1994] 2 All ER 806; *Hunter v Moss* [1994] 3 All ER 215, CA; *Re Harvard Securities (in liquidation)* [1997] 2 BCLC 369; *Re CA Pacific Finance Ltd (in liquidation)* [2000] 1 BCLC 494.

subsequently referred to as 'CMR'). Monies which qualify as 'client money' are (unless there is an exemption) subject to a statutory trust for the benefit of the relevant clients.[115]

By far the most significant exemption[116] from the application of the CMR is that relating to 'approved banks'. This reference includes all UK deposit-takers and means, in practical terms, that a UK bank may treat all monies which it receives in the course of conducting securities transactions with or for clients as deposits placed with the bank in the ordinary course of its business. **12.223**

Given that the relationship between a banker and a depositor is that of a debtor and a creditor,[117] the depositor ranks together with all other general creditors in the event of the bank's insolvency. Although it may be possible to negotiate with a particular bank to apply the CMR, as this would clearly be for the benefit of the client, most banks would not have the required administrative machinery to operate the CMR and would no doubt take a dim view of the client's perspective on their solvency! **12.224**

Operational issues

A firm which is subject to the CMR must segregate the firm's own monies from those of its clients and hold client monies in designated bank accounts. Monies should be paid into the designated client account without delay and in the case of an automated transfer system, directly into that account. **12.225**

There are further onerous requirements relating to dealing with mixed remittances, monitoring of client entitlements to monies, and the payment of interest. Investment firms should, in their terms of business for retail clients, set out the rate of interest payable on client monies because in the absence of such provisions they must pay retail clients all interest earned in respect of such monies. **12.226**

There are further restrictions on the type of banks with which the designated client accounts may be held. The starting position is that designated client accounts must only be opened with an 'approved bank'. For a UK-based bank account this means the Bank of England and any other OECD central bank, a UK deposit-taker, a UK building society, or an OECD supervised deposit-taker. For a bank account established anywhere else, an approved bank would mean any of the banks specified above, a bank which is regulated in the Isle of Man or the Channel Islands, a bank supervised by the South African Reserve Bank, or a regulated bank **12.227**

---

[115] CASS 4.2.3 (which is derived from the Client Asset Sourcebook Instrument 2003 made in the exercise of powers conferred by the FSMA).

[116] CASS 4.1.2.

[117] *Carr v Carr* (1811) 1 Mer 541n; 35 ER 799.

which is required to produce audited accounts, has minimum net assets of £5 million, and surplus revenue over expenditure over the last two financial years and whose annual audit report is not qualified.

12.228 However, a firm (other than a trustee firm) may open designated client accounts with a bank which is not an approved bank where the securities transactions concerned are subject to laws and regulations of a country outside the UK and if due to legal and regulatory requirements, it is impossible to hold client monies with an approved bank. In such case the firm must notify its clients (and obtain the consent of any retail clients) that client money will not be held with an approved bank, that different legal and insolvency systems would apply from that of the UK in the event of the bank's failure, and, if such is the case, that the bank insists on retaining a right of set-off in relation to the account. This requirement is best dealt with by a provision in a firm's standard terms of business.

12.229 When an investment firm opens designated client accounts with a bank (whether or not an approved bank) it must require the bank to acknowledge the special trust relationship which the firm has with its clients in relation to the monies deposited in the accounts. This is designed to ensure that all parties in the chain are aware of the firm's obligations as a trustee and (subject to what is said in the previous paragraph) that the funds may not be subject to set-off or counterclaims as they are not the property of the firm. Transfer of client monies to a third party (eg by way of transaction margin) does not discharge the firm from its general obligations under the CMR.

Trustees

12.230 Because of the nature of trustee firms, the CMR have limited application to such firms so as to avoid a conflict with the terms of the trust document. Consequently, the main obligation on trustee firms is to hold client money in accordance with the terms of the trust instrument and in any event separate from their own monies.[118]

Takeovers and Listing Rules

12.231 In the course of their business, investment firms may well become subject to the voluntary and regulatory regimes which apply to takeovers, to certain issues of equity securities, and to members of the London Stock Exchange.

---

[118] CASS 7.7.

Takeovers

The City Code on Takeovers and Mergers (the Code) is a code of conduct which **12.232** is designed to afford fair and equal treatment to shareholders in the context of a takeover. The Code is upheld and enforced by the Panel on Takeovers and Mergers (the Panel). Breaches of the Code may attract public censure and sanctions by the Panel and/or sanctions by the FSA (which formally endorses the Code and may, at the request of the Panel, take an enforcement action against a firm or any person within the firm who is approved by the FSA). The EU Directive on Takeover Bids[119] has introduced, for the first time, a statutory framework for the regulation of takeover activity in the UK. Under this framework, the Panel has additional powers to enforce compliance with the Code (including by ordering a person to pay compensation). Part 28 of the Companies Act 2006 implements the provisions of the Directive in the UK. Whilst the Code is primarily of interest to investment firms involved in corporate finance and investment management, it also has significant provisions which may affect, and should be familiar to, securities traders.

The Code applies to offers for public companies resident in the UK, Channel **12.233** Islands, and Isle of Man and a small proportion of private companies residing in such territories (most notably, a 'delisted' company which was listed within 10 years prior to the announcement of the offer). In the context of this chapter it is appropriate to mention only those provisions (rules) of the Code that directly affect investment firms.

Independence

Rule 3.1 of the Code requires that 'The board of the offeree company must obtain **12.234** competent independent advice on any offer and the substance of such advice must be made known to its shareholders'. The Code emphasises the importance of obtaining advice at an early stage of the engagement where the takeover involves offers that are initiated or backed by existing shareholders so as to ensure that independent advice is separate to any information made available by, or migrating from, the shareholders backing the takeover.

Rule 3.2 of the Code requires that 'the board of an offeror must obtain competent **12.235** independent advice on any offer when the offer being made is a reverse takeover (where the offer might necessitate an increase of more than 100 per cent of the offeror's issued voting share capital) or when the directors are faced with a conflict of interest. The substance of such advice must be made known to its shareholders.'

---

[119] Council Directive (EC) 04/25 on takeover bids (text with EEA relevance) [2004] 25 OJ L142/12.

An example of a conflict of interest for a director is where the director is a board member in both the offeree and the offeror companies.

12.236 The task for the advising firms is to operate effective systems and procedures in order to ensure that they are in fact independent for the purposes of advising in such circumstances. This must involve a rigorous review of all the aspects of the relationship that the relevant firm has with the parties involved in the transaction. For example, advisers may not be regarded as independent in relation to a party (and consequently may be precluded from advising such party) in circumstances where they have previously advised the opposite party (ie the offeree or offeror).

Prohibited dealings

12.237 The following rules are intended to prevent persons who take part in a takeover transaction from benefiting unfairly from their knowledge and are complementary to the general restrictions on insider dealing and market abuse.

12.238 Rule 4.1 of the Code requires that no person other than the offeror deals (or recommends others to deal) in securities of the offeree (including related derivatives) whilst in possession of price-sensitive information concerning an offer or a contemplated offer. This prohibition ends either upon termination of discussions concerning a possible offer or when the approach of the offeree or the offer itself is announced by the offeror.

12.239 Rule 4.2 of the Code imposes a restriction on the offeror and persons acting in concert with it[120] from selling any of the offeree's securities during an offer period except with the prior consent of the Panel and following a public notice that such sales would be made.

12.240 Rule 4.4 of the Code prohibits financial advisers and stockbrokers (other than exempt principal traders[121] and exempt fund managers[122]) to the offeree from doing the following:

- carrying out own-account or discretionary transactions in shares and related derivatives of the offeree;

---

[120] Briefly, persons who, pursuant to an agreement or understanding (formal or informal), actively cooperate, through the acquisition by any of them of shares in a company, to obtain or consolidate control of that company.

[121] A firm which is registered as a market-maker with the London Stock Exchange, or is accepted by the Panel as a market-maker, or is a London Stock Exchange member firm dealing as principal in order book securities, which is recognised by the Panel as an exempt principal trader for the purposes of the Code.

[122] A firm whose business involves discretionary investment management and is recognised by the Panel as an exempt fund manager for the purpose of the Code.

- providing a non-arm's length loan to assist a person to purchase such shares or derivatives;
- entering into an agreement requiring any person to retain, deal, or refrain from dealings in the offeree's 'relevant securities'.[123]

Disclosure of dealings

Disclosure of dealings in the offeror's relevant securities is only required if the offer involves the offeror's securities as part of the consideration. **12.241**

Rule 8.1 of the Code requires public disclosure of dealings in relevant securities by the offeror, the offeree, and any of their associates[124] (such as the parties' financial advisers) during the offer period. **12.242**

There are specific rules relating to the offeror, offeree, and associated parties where they act as discretionary fund managers and may engage in restricted transactions as part of that role. The guiding principle is that any such transaction must be disclosed to the public, but where an associate connected with the offeree or the offeror is an exempt fund manager (see n 117) such transactions, as a general rule, need only be privately disclosed to the Panel. Public disclosure is required, however, where the fund manager concerned owns or controls 5 per cent or more of the shares of either the offeror or the offeree. **12.243**

As regards non-discretionary management by an exempt fund manager which is an associate of the offeree or the offeror, disclosure of relevant dealings is to be made privately to the Panel. **12.244**

Dealings by 1 per cent shareholders

Rule 8.3 of the Code states that any person who owns or controls 1 per cent or more of any class of relevant securities of an offeror or of the offeree company (or who will do so as a result of further purchases) must publicly disclose any dealings in such securities during the offer period. In the context of derivative securities, disclosure of dealings is required where the person dealing owns or controls 1 per cent or more of the class of securities which is the subject of the option or to whose price the derivative is referenced. **12.245**

---

[123] Generally, securities of the offeree company being offered for or which carry voting rights, shares of the offeror, and any convertible and other securities having substantially the same rights (including options and other derivatives).

[124] Which covers all persons (whether or not acting in concert) who directly or indirectly own or deal in the shares of an offeror or offeree company and who have an interest or a potential interest in the outcome of the offer.

12.246 Investment management firms are treated for the purpose of this disclosure rule as the controllers of securities held for and on behalf of their clients for whom they undertake discretionary management. Furthermore, securities holdings should be consolidated within the group to calculate the level of control.

12.247 Exempt principal traders are not generally required to disclose information under Rules 8.1 and 8.3 of the Code with regard to their holdings of relevant securities as such disclosure is regarded as a disruption to their legitimate activities.

12.248 In note 10 to Rule 8 of the Code it is stated that securities dealers and banks dealing in relevant securities must be vigilant so as to ensure that their clients are aware of the disclosure obligations that apply to them. This requirement does not apply, however, to dealings where the total consideration within a seven-day period is less than £50,000.

12.249 The Code Committee of the Panel in 2005 published the results of its consultation on proposed amendments to the Code. The amended rules, which took effect on 7 November 2005, extended the scope of required disclosure to instances where a person has a derivative position such as a call option or a long derivative interest. The disclosure obligation arises where a person holds interest in relation to 1 per cent or more in any class of a relevant security of the offeree company (or, in the case of an exchange offer, of the offeror) or where a person would hold such a position as a result of a particular transaction. Thus, the Committee treats a person who has, or may have, a long economic exposure[125] to changes in the price of securities as interested in those securities.

Telephone campaigns

12.250 Campaigns conducted by financial advisers to solicit acceptance from shareholders must be handled by staff conversant with the requirements of the Code. Telephone campaigns can only be undertaken after an offer has been announced; there are strict rules regarding the secrecy of any offer prior to an announcement of a firm intention to make it. Information which is relayed to shareholders must conform to that which has already been published and continue to be accurate and up-to-date. Shareholders should not be put under undue pressure and must be encouraged to consult their professional advisers before making up their minds.

---

[125] eg the person will benefit economically if the price of that security goes up or has a right or option to acquire it or to call for its delivery.

Dealings by exempt principal traders

Rule 38 of the Code prohibits an exempt principal trader who is connected with **12.251** one of the parties, whether offeror or offeree, from transacting with the purpose of assisting that party. Additionally, an offeror (and any person acting in concert with it) must not deal as principal with a connected exempt principal trader in relevant securities of the offeree company during the offer period. The Code requires the offeror's financial advisers to ensure that their client complies with this requirement.

Dealings in relevant securities by an exempt principal trader connected with an **12.252** offeror or the offeree company should be aggregated and disclosed to an FSA designated Regulatory Information Service and the Panel following the date of the transaction.

Listing rules (sponsors)

The FSA (acting as the United Kingdom Listing Authority) sponsor regime **12.253** applies to certain London-listed issues of equity securities (eg initial public offerings and rights issues). Where the sponsor regime applies, the issuer must appoint an approved investment firm (the sponsor) to act as a key liaison point between the issuer and the FSA. The FSA recently took the opportunity to update its rules in relation to the sponsor regime.

The sponsor's primary role is to provide assurances to the FSA that the issuer has **12.254** met (and is well-placed to meet on a continuing basis) its obligations under the listing rules and assist the issuer in understanding and complying with the listing rules.

Investment firms seeking to be approved by the FSA as sponsors for the first time **12.255** must submit a formal application which includes details about the firm's capability and, more importantly, the competence and experience of its relevant employees.

FSA approval

In order to be approved as a sponsor by the FSA, an investment firm must dem- **12.256** onstrate that it is competent to perform the services envisaged by the listing rules and has adequate systems and controls to ensure that it can carry out such a role. The FSA has confirmed, informally, that firms with less than two experienced employees are unlikely to meet the required threshold of competence. The rules are prescriptive as to the type of an employee's experience that can be taken into account for this purpose.[126]

12.257 For the purposes of satisfying the systems and controls threshold, investment firms must establish effective reporting lines, adequately supervise employees engaging in transactions where they act as sponsors, effectively manage conflicts of interest, and maintain records of all matters in connection with their role as sponsor for the required period of six years.

12.258 It is possible, as was the case under the previous sponsor regime, for more than one investment firm to act as joint sponsor. In such case the obligations of each sponsor are absolute as if each sponsor were acting on a sole basis. However, one sponsor must be designated as taking the prime responsibility for communicating with the FSA.

Sponsors' obligations

12.259 An investment firm acting as a sponsor under the listing rules must ensure that it conducts a thorough risk analysis of the role and a compliance schedule to ensure that its obligations under the listing rules are fully complied with. An issue which tends to figure prominently is the extent to which sponsors expose themselves to suit by investors in cases where they fall short of their duties under the listing rules. A sponsor's general obligations are to:

- provide assurances, when required to do so by the FSA, that the responsibilities of the issuer under the listing rules have been met;
- guide the issuer in understanding and complying with the listing rules;
- deal with the FSA in an open and cooperative way;
- disclose to the FSA, in a timely manner, any material information relating to the sponsor's or the issuer's non-compliance with the listing rules (including the disclosure rules).

12.260 More specifically, in connection with a new applicant issuer, the sponsor is required to conduct a due diligence exercise (for which it may use external experts such as accountants and lawyers) before it submits documents for and on behalf of the issuer. The objective is to ensure that the documents (particularly the prospectus) comply with the listing rules, that the directors of the issuer have established procedures to comply with the listing rules (and with the disclosure rules) on an ongoing basis, to judge the financial position and prospects of the issuer, and to

---

[126] Experience should normally be demonstrated by the provision of relevant advice or services at least three times in the preceding 36 months and at least once in the preceding 12 months.

establish that the directors have a reasonable basis on which to make the required working capital statement under the listing rules.

The sponsor is also required to lodge a declaration with the FSA, once it lodges the final version of the prospectus, that the prospectus and other related disclosure to the FSA contain all matters that in the sponsor's reasonable opinion should be taken into account in considering the application for listing. **12.261**

13

INVESTMENT FIRMS—RETAIL SECTOR

Introduction

Traditionally the wares and labours of investment firms would have only been of **13.01**
interest to, and affordable by, the richest in society. Such individuals or families
might engage the services of stockbroker or investment manager in respect of their
portfolio of shares, corporate, and government bonds.[1] However in the twenty-
first century some of the most significant purchases by the typical, middle-income
citizen are financial products. Such an individual may have a large proportion of
his or her wealth tied up in securities, life insurance, collective investment schemes,
and other contracts for the purpose of saving, investment, property acquisition,
or pension provision.

Over the last three decades there has been major expansion of the retail invest- **13.02**
ment industry in the United Kingdom. It was the avowed intention of the
Conservative administrations of the 1980s and 1990s to create and promote a
property-owning, and in particular a share-owning, democracy. By the beginning
of the twenty-first century share ownership had trickled down from the richest in
society to embrace a significant proportion of the population. At the end of 1998
some 12 million UK citizens owned shares, some 27 per cent of the adult population. Whilst share-owning is not yet as widespread as in the United States of
America and some other Western countries, this still represents a considerable
extension.[2]

---

[1] See S Banner, *Anglo-American Securities Regulation—Cultural and Political Roots, 1690–1860*
(1998), p 24, discussing the rise of a securities market in late seventeenth century England: 'As the
secondary market in government debt and shares of businesses grew, the portion of the nation's total
wealth consisting of land and other tangible things gradually declined, replaced more and more by
mobile pieces of paper, representations of intangible fractions of a future stream of income. Within
a generation, contemporaries came to realise that an entirely new form of property had come into
existence.'
[2] In fact four countries have wider share ownership: Sweden (circa 50%); USA (40%); Denmark
(33%); and Australia (32%). Sources: ProShare (UK); London Stock Exchange; quoted in W Clarke,
How the City of London Works—An Introduction to its Financial Markets (5th edn, 1999), p 41. In 1992

13.03 Three factors have contributed to this. First, the wider prevalence of employee
share schemes. Secondly, the privatisation of formerly nationalised industries.
Thirdly, the introduction of Personal Equity Plans (or 'PEPs') as a tax-free shelter
for shares, in order to encourage saving and investment. From their introduction
in 1987 until 1998 some 15.5 million PEPs were sold.[3] In 1998 PEPs were replaced
by Individual Savings Accounts (or 'ISAs') as a vehicle for saving and
investments.

13.04 At the end of 2006 private individuals in the UK owned shares worth £239 billion.
Other significant holdings by insurance companies (£273 billion) and pension
funds (£236 billion) represented ways in which individuals indirectly participate
in the market for shares.[4]

13.05 The legal and regulatory environment has struggled to keep pace. Whilst the common law, in the general principles of private law, has the basic toolkit to determine
most issues that arise out of consumer financial services cases, it is only in a com-
paratively small number of cases in which the judiciary have had to grapple with
the issues thrown up by the modern mass market in retail investment products
and services. In 2008 Rix LJ in the Court of Appeal observed:

> It is a feature of our commercial law, robust, pragmatic and internationally respected
> as it may be, that it grew up in an age of commerce between merchants, when what
> we now think of as financial consumer contracts must have been relatively few in
> number, limited in their scope, and entered into by a small range of professional,
> mercantile and land-owning people. I speak of contracts outside ordinary sale of
> goods. Nowadays, however, huge numbers of consumers have pensions, make invest-
> ments, and enter into contracts of all kinds.[5]

His Lordship went on to observe that, for example, the principles of insurance
law, were developing (and were being developed by the Financial Ombudsman
Service, following in the footsteps of its predecessor, the Insurance Ombudsman)
to meet this rise in consumer transactions. However the task of setting the standards for financial professionals dealing with ordinary consumers has largely fallen
on the shoulders of the legislature, and the regulators and ombudsmen to whom

---

Page and Ferguson quoted a figure of 11 million, having risen from 3 million in 1979. So the main
growth had taken place during the first three Conservative administrations from 1979 to 1992: A
Page and R Ferguson, *Investor Protection* (1992), p 9.

[3] W Clarke, *How the City of London Works—An Introduction to its Financial Markets* (5th edn,
1999), p 41.

[4] W Clarke, *How the City of London Works—An Introduction to its Financial Markets* (7th edn,
2008), although this represented only 14% of the total market capitalisation, having fallen from
20% in 1994. Foreign investors accounted for £742 billion of shares.

[5] *R (on the application of Heather Moor & Edgecomb Ltd) v Financial Ombudsman Service* [2008]
EWCA Civ 642, para [87].

the task has been entrusted. Despite this (and that may be a charitable judgment) the experience of the last 20 years has been far from happy.

Between 1988 to 1994 it was estimated that between one million and two million **13.06** ordinary investors were sold the wrong type of pension. They were persuaded to opt out of, or not join, occupational pension schemes (with defined benefits) and instead take out an investment product-based pension. The latter involved greater exposure to risk, and fewer benefits than the occupational schemes. Such investors potentially faced a highly significant financial loss. The scale of the pension mis-selling scandal and its financial extent were unprecedented.[6] The final estimated bill for compensation exceeded £12 billion. What were the causes of mis-selling? Payment of salespersons by commission is a cause emphasised by many commentators. That may be an over-simplification. In the House of Lords in *Lloyds TSB General Insurance Holdings v Lloyds Bank Group Insurance Co Ltd*[7] Lord Hoffmann succinctly recorded the key factors (putting payment by commission into perspective): 'The underlying reasons for mis-selling were partly the method by which salesmen were paid but largely the inadequacy of the training and monitoring by the companies employing them.'[8]

Other significant scandals affecting the retail investment sector include a more **13.07** limited review of past business in respect of Free Standing Additional Voluntary Contributions ('FSAVCs') in respect of occupational schemes.[9] In respect of the almost equally time-consuming and costly (from the firms' perspective) mortgage endowment saga the regulators took a different tack, and rather than employ a general review of past business the PIA, and subsequently the FSA, required firms to write to consumers to warn them of the risk of under-performance of endowments used to finance house purchase, and (in effect) invite complaints of mis-selling.[10] The recent past has also seen the mis-selling of home income plans to vulnerable elderly consumers. Equitable Life, once the most respectable of mutual life insurers, imploded as a result of not being able to afford to honour its promised guaranteed annuity rates to retiring policyholders. Most recently split

---

[6] For detailed discussion of the saga see: G McMeel, 'The Consumer Dimension of Financial Services Law: Lessons from the Pension Mis-selling Scandal' [1999] *Company, Financial and Insolvency Law Review* 29; J Black and R Nobles, 'Personal Pensions Misselling: The Causes and Lessons of Regulatory Failure' (1998) 61 MLR 789; and G McMeel. 'Liability of Financial Advisers in the Wake of the Pension Mis-selling Scandal' (1997) 13 *Professional Negligence* 97.

[7] [2003] UKHL 48.

[8] Para [5].

[9] FSA and PIA, CP27, 'Free-standing Additional Voluntary Contributions' (August 1999); FSA and PIA, 'FSAVC Review—Model Guidance' (May 2000); FSA and PIA, 'FSAVC Review—Model Guidance Update' (March 2001); FSA and PIA, 'FSAVC Review—Model Guidance Update' (May 2001).

[10] FSA, 'Progress Report on Mortgage Endowments' (October 2000); FSA CP 75, 'Endowment Mortgage Complaints' (November 2000); FSA PS, 'Endowment Mortgage Complaints: Feedback on CP 75 and "Final Text"' (May 2001).

capital investment trusts and 'precipice bonds' or SCARPs have also attracted the appellation 'scandal'.

13.08 Probably as a result of the numerous scandals, stability of the regulatory environment has not been a feature of the landscape. Prior to the reforms associated with the Big Bang in the second half of the 1980s there was a rudimentary regime represented by the unambitiously-named Prevention of Fraud (Investments) Acts 1939 and 1958. Since the implementation of the Financial Services Act 1986 ('the 1986 Act') there have been four major phases of regulatory rules in respect of investor protection in the retail financial sector. First, under the 1986 Act, from its implementation on 29 April 1988 to 1 May 1994 there was the initial regime comprising the regulatory rules of various Self-regulatory Organisations ('SROs'), principally, for the retail sector, the Life Assurance and Unit Trust Regulatory Organisation ('LAUTRO')—broadly speaking the product providers—and the Financial Intermediaries, Managers and Brokers Regulatory Association ('FIMBRA'), representing the client-facing advisers and brokers. Secondly, under the same legislation, from 1994 to 2001, an amalgamated SRO, the Personal Investment Authority ('PIA') superseded LAUTRO and FIMBRA, but to a large extent adopted its predecessors' provisions in its own rulebook. Thirdly, under the Financial Services and Markets Act 2000 ('the 2000 Act') from 1 December 2001 ('N2') to October 2007, the Conduct of Business Sourcebook ('COB')[11] component of the Financial Services Authority ('FSA') Handbook of Rules and Guidance consolidated and superseded its various predecessor regulators' rulebooks for the conduct of investment business. After N2 COB was further amended on a number of fronts, including the depolarisation initiative and the reaction to the 'precipice bonds' or SCARPs scandal. In mid-2005 the FSA proposed fundamental changes to COB.[12] The main impetus came from the need to implement new European law—the Markets in Financial Instruments Directive ('MiFID')—with effect from 1 November 2007 and resulted in the new COBS component of the Handbook.[13] Accordingly in just over 20 years from the beginning of 1988 to 2008 there have been some five significant regulatory phases for investment firms.

---

[11] For discussion of the original version of COB see G McMeel and J Virgo, *Financial Advice and Financial Products—Law and Liability* (2001), ch 14.

[12] FSA CP 05/10, 'Reviewing the FSA Handbook—Money Laundering, Approved Persons, Training and Competence and Conduct of Business' (July 2005), chs 1 and 5; and Annex 5 which contained the proposed new structure for COBS.

[13] Directive (EC) 2004/39. See also Directive (EC) 2006/31: extending the time limit for the implementation of MiFID.

General Principles of Conduct for Investment Firms

When Professor Gower published his seminal report, *A Review of Investor* **13.09**
Protection, in 1984[14] he was explicit in setting out the underlying philosophy
behind his proposals. A value judgement had to be made as to the balance to be
struck between market freedom and investor protection. In Gower's view the
optimum degree of regulation 'should be no greater than is necessary to protect
reasonable people from being made fools of'.[15] Furthermore Gower believed it
was necessary to rationalise requirements for authorisation of those providing
investment services to ordinary investors and to deal with those who operated
outside the resulting framework: 'What is needed is a system which will help the
public identify the sheep and which will effectively curb the activities of the
goats.'[16]

The three pillars of the modern standard of behaviour required of a financial **13.10**
adviser are the obligations to know your client, to make suitable recommendations, and to provide an adequate understanding of risk. These are the principles
underlying the detailed requirements of the 'Conduct of Business' rules. The principles emerged from Gower's review of investor protection undertaken in the early
1980s. Professor Gower, speaking of the proposed requirements of: know your
customer, suitability and rules for the protection of clients' assets, together with
other proposed conduct of business rules, observed:

> Together they should go far to ensure the adequate protection of investors. I do not
> accept the criticism made in some quarters, that they are excessively 'legalistic' and
> will prove unduly restrictive. On the contrary, they seem to me to be a practical
> working-out of the gentlemanly ethics, on which the City has traditionally prided
> itself (even if all its members have not invariably lived up to them) that you should

---

[14] LCB Gower, *Review of Investor Protection: Part I*, Cmnd 9125 (1984) ('Gower'). Prior
to the report Professor Gower had issued a discussion paper: LCB Gower, 'Review of Investor
Protection—A Discussion Document' (January 1982). A Government White Paper followed the
first part of Professor Gower's report: Department of Trade and Industry, 'Financial Services in the
United Kingdom—A new framework for investor protection', Cmnd 9432 (1985) which to a large
extent adopted Professor Gower's recommendations in Part I of his Report. Subsequently the second
part of Professor Gower's Report was published: LCB Gower, 'Review of Investor Protection—Part
II', Cmnd 9125 (1985). For an account of the background and the main features of the resulting
system see L Gower, 'Big Bang and City Regulation' (1988) 51 *MLR* 1. Note also the view of Ford
and Kay, two economists, having observed that the regulatory structure for the financial industry
was designed by lawyers, that 'financial service regulation would benefit from the involvement
of fewer lawyers and more economists': C Ford and J Kay, 'Why Regulate Financial Services?' in
F Oditah (ed), *The Future for the Global Securities Market—Legal and Regulatory Aspects* (1996)
145, 146.
[15] LCB Gower, 'Review of Investor Protection: Part I', para 1.16.
[16] LCB Gower, 'Review of Investor Protection: Part I', para 1.10.

'do as you would be done by' and not do anything that you would not want found out.[17]

Information or advice?

13.11 In describing the Pensions Review in the context of a Professional Indemnity policy case—*J Rothschild Assurance plc v Collyear*[18]—Rix J (as he then was) described four elements of compliant advice:

> The assessment of compliance was to be addressed through four essential tests which reflected the regulatory regime: know your customer and suitability, understanding of risk, adequate information, and misleading statements.

It can be observed that Rix J lists both information-giving and advice provision, but a vexed topic is where the line is drawn between the two.

13.12 In the wake of the speech of Lord Hoffmann in the *South Australia Asset Management Corp v York Montague Ltd* (or the *SAAMCO* case), which concerned negligent valuations of commercial property, the information and advice dichotomy has been prominent in professional negligence cases. Accordingly whether a representative or intermediary of a financial services firm is under a duty only to provide accurate or adequate information, or whether he has a broader duty to advise as to the suitable course of conduct, is sometimes said to be one of the scope of duty of care or scope of the contractual retainer.[19] That does not take things much further forward in the retail investment context, where the line is between advised sales, where a full suitability regime applies, and 'execution only' transactions, where it is necessary that any information provided is clear, fair, and not misleading. Any suggestion of a personal recommendation as to the appropriate course of conduct is likely to push a particular case into the former category.

Know your customer

13.13 Adequate information is the key to complying with the exacting standards required by the modern law for a financial adviser. There are two distinct aspects to this. The first is encapsulated in the 'know your customer' principle. The customer's personal and financial circumstances, needs and priorities have to be ascertained and assessed. The extent of this investigation will depend on the task assumed.

---

[17] LCB Gower, 'Review of Investor Protection—Part II', Cmnd 9125 (1985), para 4.15.
[18] [1999] 1 Lloyd's Rep PN 6.
[19] *South Australia Asset Management Corp v York Montague Ltd ('SAAMCO')* [1997] AC 191. Compare the conclusion of the House of Lords in *Aneco Reinsurance Underwriting Ltd v Johnson & Higgins Ltd* [2001] UKHL 51, [2002] 1 Lloyd's Rep 157, [2001] 2 All ER (Comm) 929, [2002] PNLR 8 that in a particular transaction a reinsurance broker owed a duty to advise on whether to undertake a particular transaction, rather than a mere duty to provide information, and its impact on the remedy.

Furthermore, in appropriate cases the customer's attitude to risk may have to be evaluated.

Suitability

The second dimension to the information requirements on a financial adviser is **13.14** implicit in suitability: the adviser must investigate and evaluate the products and other financial arrangements available on the market. The range of providers and products may be circumscribed by the scope of business undertaken by a particular intermediary or provider. Obviously it will be much wider in the case of an independent as opposed to a tied or multi-tied intermediary. Nevertheless, an understanding of the available options is a *sine qua non* of compliant financial advice. The assessment of a suitable transaction or the identification of a suitable product is built on the foundations of the information obtained about both the customer and the marketplace.

'Best advice'

In respect of certain investment products (described as 'packaged products') a **13.15** separate obligation of 'best advice' was developed. This has its roots in the concept of suitability, but is distinct. Cranston says of 'best advice' that: 'this involves a prior, conscientious search for available services and then, in any particular transaction, recommending the service which is believed to be the best, or at least as good, as any other available, for that customer'.[20] However the 'best advice' appellation was inappropriate in the context of advice proffered by tied advisers of particular product providers or by multi-tied agents, who do not survey the whole of the market. Such advisers are limited to considering the products of one firm or marketing group, or a limited number of providers. In that context the superlative 'best' was necessarily confined to the available products of that particular firm or firms. Perhaps recognising this, the FSA in its implementation of the COB regime preserved the substance of the 'best advice' rules of its predecessor regulators, but no longer described them by that name. Furthermore, the rules were more clearly a subset of the suitability principle. In the wake of the implementation of MiFID the 'best advice' regime was eventually abandoned.

Customer's understanding of risk

At bottom the most appropriate advice concerning any proposed financial trans- **13.16** action is that which identifies and explains the risks attending it. The requirement to ensure that the customer has an adequate understanding of the risks involved is a distinct requirement to the firm's investigation into the customer's appetite for,

---

[20] R Cranston, *Principles of Banking Law* (1997), pp 223–4.

or aversion to, risk pursuant to the 'know your customer' and 'suitability' rules. An appropriate approach to risk might deal with a number of factors which can be separated out:

- Risk to capital: is there a risk that the original sum deposited or invested will not be returned in full? If so what is the extent of that risk? A return of capital is usually the hallmark of a deposit, but endowment policies and now some bond products promise the preservation of initial capital.

- Risk in relation to return: how is the return to be generated on the saving or investment? Is this fixed or does it depend upon some person's discretion?

- Insolvency risk: the risk that the product provider or an intermediary may be unable to perform or perform in full.

- Fraud risk: the risk that the product provider or an intermediary may be the perpetrator or the victim of some fraudulent activity which affects their ability to perform.

The first two are usually the focus of financial advice cases. For example, in the recent concern about 'precipice bonds' or 'SCARPS' the concern was often that the risk to capital was not sufficiently highlighted or explained. Similarly the Equitable Life collapse and the subsequent scrutiny of 'with profits' life business have revealed that the discretionary basis of returns on investment was not always sufficiently highlighted. On occasion the latter two have been important. The Financial Services Compensation Scheme is designed to provide for insolvency risk, which often entails some coverage for fraud risk.

The New Conduct Of Business Sourcebook ('COBS')

COBS: General issues

The hinterland to COBS: previous conduct of business regimes

13.17 The introduction of detailed prescriptive rules for the investment sector was a significant element of the reforms launched by the Financial Services Act 1986, and implemented in 1988. Accordingly 2008 marked the end of the second decade of the investment conduct of business regime. The first phase from 1988 to 1994 was implemented through the rulebooks of the Self-Regulatory Organisations for the retail investment sector, the Life Assurance and Unit Trust Regulatory Organisation ('LAUTRO') and the Financial Intermediaries and Brokers Regulatory Association ('FIMBRA'), albeit that the overall regulator the Securities and Investments Board ('SIB'), the previous incarnation of the FSA, laid down certain minimum standards. From 1994 to 2001 these rulebooks were superseded by that of the merged Personal Investment Authority ('PIA'), but its rules largely replicated those of its predecessors.

The immediate hinterland of COBS was the FSA's original Conduct of Business **13.18**
Sourcebook ('COB') which applied between 2001 and 2007. COB was more
obviously the product of domestic UK concerns, periodically spawning new rules
or even whole new chapters to address current mis-selling crises ('SCARPS') or
other regulatory concerns (with profits contracts or stakeholder products). In
contrast, COBS is much more obviously the fruit of European-inspired reform
(albeit the UK influence on the EU measure is often significant). Where appropriate in discussing COBS, it is helpful to identify points of departure from its
predecessor, COB.

What the original FSA COB replaced

Launched on 1 December 2001, the original FSA Conduct of Business Sourcebook **13.19**
('COB') replaced miscellaneous provisions, from both legislative and other
sources:

(i) the FSA (formerly Securities and Investments Board ('SIB')) rules;

(ii) the Investment Management Regulatory Organisation ('IMRO') rules;

(iii) the Securities and Futures Authority ('SFA') rules;

(iv) the Personal Investment Authority ('PIA') rules (encompassing the adopted
rules of PIA's predecessor bodies: the Life Assurance and Unit Trust Regulatory
Organisation ('LAUTRO') and the Financial Intermediaries and Brokers
Regulatory Association ('FIMBRA'));

(v) the London Code of Conduct—the Bank of England code for principals and
broking firms in the wholesale market;

(vi) miscellaneous provisions of the Insurance Companies Act 1982, the Banking
Act 1987, and the Building Societies Act 1986.[21]

These provisions migrated to COB, and now the equivalent regime is to be found
in COBS.

The Markets in Financial Instruments Directive

The motivation, or perhaps the necessity, for the FSA to revisit and replace COB **13.20**
is in order for the UK to implement the Markets in Financial Instruments Directive
('MiFID').[22] It is one of the most significant measures to emerge from the Financial
Services Action Plan ('FSAP'). This Directive replaces and extends the Investment

---

[21] FSA CP 45a, 'The Conduct of Business Sourcebook' (February 2000), para 2.11.
[22] Directive (EC) 2004/39. For the background see: FSA CP 05/10, 'Reviewing the FSA
Handbook—Money Laundering, Approved Persons, Training and Competence and Conduct of
Business' (July 2005), chs 1 and 5. See also FSA, 'Planning for MiFID' (November 2005).

Services Directive ('ISD'),[23] implemented in 1995, which was the backdrop to the original COB and its predecessors. Previously Article 11 of the ISD merely required domestic regulators to impose conduct of business rules on incoming firms, but left the detail a matter for domestic implementation. MiFID is far more prescriptive.[24] MiFID had to be implemented by 1 November 2007.[25]

The EC implementing measures

13.21 The principal Markets in Financial Instruments Directive (EC) 2004/39 of the European Parliament and Council ('MiFID')[26] is supplemented by 'Level 2' implementing measures in accordance with the structure implemented by the FSAP. The secondary measures comprise Commission Regulation (EC) 1287/2006 ('the MiFID Regulation') and Commission Directive (EC) 2006/73 ('the MiFID Implementing Directive').

UK implementing legislation

13.22 MiFID has required changes to UK primary and secondary legislation, albeit the changes have all been achieved through secondary legislation. The main UK domestic legislative measures implementing MiFID are:[27]

- the Financial Services and Markets Act 2000 (Regulated Activities)(Amendment No 3) Order 2006;[28]

- the Financial Services and Markets Act 2000 (Markets in Financial Instruments) Regulations 2007;[29]

- the Financial Services and Markets Act 2000 (Markets in Financial Instruments) (Modification of Powers) Regulations 2006;[30]

- the Financial Services and Markets Act 2000 (Appointed Representatives) (Amendment) Regulations 2006;[31]

- the Financial Services and Markets Act 2000 (Exemption) (Amendment) Order 2007.[32]

---

[23] Directive (EEC) 93/22.
[24] For an overall cost-benefit analysis see FSA, 'The overall impact of MiFID' (November 2006).
[25] Directive (EC) 2006/31: extending the time limit for the implementation of MiFID.
[26] Directive (EC) 2004/39.
[27] See PERG 13 Annex 4.
[28] SI 2006/3384, including amending the RAO to add a new regulated activity of operating a multilateral trading facility (art 25D).
[29] SI 2007/126.
[30] SI 2006/2975.
[31] SI 2006/3414.
[32] SI 2007/125. There is also a separate 'Explanatory Memorandum' in relation to SI 2007/126, SI 2006/3384, SI 2006/2975, SI 2006/3414, SI 2007/125, and the other MiFID implementing measures.

FSA implementation

The FSA has implemented MiFID by extensive revision to its Handbook, most **13.23**
importantly the complete deletion of COB and its replacement by COBS. (The
additional 'S' is important for accurate citation.) These changes came into force
on 1 November 2007, implemented by the FSA, The Conduct of Business
Sourcebook Instrument 2007.[33] Other changes affect the structure of the remainder of the Handbook and the location of the material. For example, the material
on conflicts of interest[34] has now migrated to SYSC.[35] Conversely ECO is no
longer a separate handbook, but is now integrated in COBS. The Inter-professional
Conduct Code (MAR 3) has also been deleted from the Handbook in the wake of
MiFID.[36] PERG 13 now contains detailed guidance on the scope and application
of MiFID with regard to firms, services, and products.

Matters have not rested there because the FSA has launched a Retail Distribution **13.24**
Review ('RDR')[37] and also a review of its Basic Advice Regime, with new proposals anticipated in late 2008.

The consultation process

Much ink was spilt on the consultation process leading up to the FSA's implemen- **13.25**
tation of MiFID. An attempt has been made to improve both the navigability
and overall effectiveness of the regime. The FSA has insisted that the predecessor
COB rules had improved standards of consumer protection, but conceded that
'mis-selling and mis-buying still happen too often'.[38]

The main consultation documents were: **13.26**

- FSA DP 06/3, *Implementing MiFID's best execution requirements* (May 2006)
  ('FSA DP 06/3');

- FSA CP 06/14, *Implementing MiFID for Firms and Markets* (July 2006) ('FSA
  CP 06/14');[39]

- FSA CP 06/19, *Reforming Conduct of Business Regulation (including proposals for
  implementing relevant provisions of the Markets in Financial Instruments Directive,
  and related changes in SYSC, DISP, TC, SUP and other Handbook modules)*
  (October 2006) ('FSA CP 06/19');

---

[33] See also FSA, Glossary (Conduct of Business and Other Sourcebooks) Instrument 2007.
[34] Previously in COB 7.1.
[35] SYSC 10.
[36] See FSA CP 06/19, paras 7.102–7.108; FSA PS 07/6, paras 7.9–7.12.
[37] FSA DP 07/1, 'A Review of Retail Distribution' (June 2007). For detailed discussion see
below.
[38] FSA CP 06/19, para 2.6.
[39] See also FSA, 'Implementing MiFID's Client Categorisation requirements' (August 2006),
which is not strictly a consultation paper.

- FSA CP 06/20, *Financial promotion and other communications (Including draft Handbook text for NEWCOB 4 and 5)*(October 2006) ('FSA CP 06/20').[40]

13.27 The principal policy statement documents were:

- FSA PS 07/2, *Implementing the Markets in Financial Instruments Directive (MiFID)—Feedback on: CP 06/14—Implementing MiFID for Firms and Markets (July 2006); CP06/19—Reforming Conduct of Business Regulation (October 2006) [and] Financial promotion and other communications (October 2006)*(January 2007) ('FSA PS 07/2');

- FSA PS 07/6, *Reforming Conduct of Business Regulation—Feedback on CP06/19—Reforming Conduct of Business Regulation (October 2006) and Financial promotion and other communications (October 2006)*(May 2007) ('FSA PS 07/6');

- FSA PS 07/14, *Reforming Conduct of Business Regulation—Final feedback on CP06/19* (July 2007) ('FSA PS 07/14');

- FSA PS 07/15, *Best Execution—Feedback on DP 06/3 and CP06/19 (part)* (August 2007) ('FSA PS 07/15').[41]

Method of implementation: 'intelligent copy-out'

13.28 Given the need to implement EU requirements accurately the FSA has characterised its approach as one based on 'intelligent copy-out' of the text of the relevant directives. This is part of the FSA's approach to financial services directives generally, and it now clearly labels all rules which are derived from EU measures.[42] Some have found the modified phrase 'unintelligent cop-out' irresistible, but it is difficult to see what wriggle room the FSA has in many instances, especially in the light of the approach of the European Commission and the Court of Justice to implementation of Directives.

13.29 It is also intended that COBS should be a significant step in the FSA's move towards more principles-based regulation and higher level rules. This includes less reliance on detailed guidance and, in the opinion of the FSA, the deletion of material it considered to be 'redundant, superfluous or obselete'.[43]

Status of FSA rules in COBS: rights of action and discipline

13.30 Broadly speaking the FSA Handbook is made up of three main types of provisions: rules, evidential provisions, and guidance. FSA rules are made under

---

[40] See also FSA CP 07/9, 'Conduct of Business regime: non-MiFID deferred matters (including proposals for Telephone Recording)' (May 2007).

[41] See also for future development: FSA DP 07/1, 'A Review of Retail Distribution' (June 2007), launching the FSA's Retail Distribution Review ('RDR').

[42] FSA CP 06/19, paras 1.19 and 2.11.

[43] FSA PS 07/6, para 1.9.

delegated powers in the 2000 Act. Accordingly they are statutory rules, as is evidenced by the fact that they are potentially actionable by a private person pursuant to section 150[44] or may be the basis for disciplinary action by the FSA against firms under sections 205 or 206, or for other measures under the 2000 Act.

Prior to the implementation of COB in 2001 the FSA decided that a right of **13.31** action should be available to a private person in respect of *any* rule within it.[45] This was despite doubts expressed by some respondents to the consultation exercise about the utility of private claims, given the comparative rarity of actions brought under section 62 of the Financial Services Act 1986.[46] However despite the claim for breach of statutory duty only appearing in a handful of reported cases, the existence of the statutory claim was the basis of internal complaints handling and ombudsman redress in millions of cases.

The FSA has continued the same policy in the wake of MiFID and has given the **13.32** right to bring an action for breach of statutory duty to private persons for any breach of any of the rules in COBS.[47]

FSA rules must (ultimately) be construed by reference to ordinary principles of **13.33** statutory construction. However, given that many of the rules implement EU measures, and that each rule now explicitly cites the relevant article of the relevant measure, it is likely that the courts may go straight to the relevant directive should any point of construction arise.

FSA requirements which go beyond MiFID

The FSA has decided to retain a number of existing Conduct of Business Rules **13.34** which apply to MiFID firms which go beyond the requirements of MiFID. Such additional requirements can only be retained or imposed in 'exceptional cases' where they are 'objectively justified and proportionate to address specific risks to investor protection or to market integrity' which are not addressed by the MiFID regime. Such measures must also satisfy one of two conditions: (a) it addresses specific risks arising out of the market structure of the Member State; or (b) the measure addresses risks which emerge or become evident after MiFID applies, and is not addressed by other EC measures.[48] Such measures must be notified and justified to the European Commission under Article 4 of the MiFID Implementing

---

[44] Replacing ss 62 and 62A of the 1986 Act.
[45] For the background see: FSA CP 45a, 'The Conduct of Business Sourcebook' (February 2000) ('FSA CP 45a'), para 4.9; and FSA PS 45, 'Conduct of Business Sourcebook—Feedback on consultation and 'final text' and consultation on supplementary rules' (February 2001) ('FSA PS 45'), para 3.46.
[46] FSA PS 45, para 3.47.
[47] COBS Sched 5. See FSA CP 07/9, 'Conduct of Business regime: non-MiFID deferred matters (including proposals for Telephone Recording)' (May 2007), ch 18.
[48] MiFID Implementing Directive, (Commission Directive (EC) 2006/73), Art 4(1).

Directive.[49] Such national additional requirements raise the spectre of 'super-equivalence'[50] (or some call it 'gold-plating' of regulation).

13.35 The measures which the FSA has notified to the EU Commission and which the latter body has agreed are consistent with the criteria in Article 4 of the MiFID Implementing Directive include:

- the rules governing the way firms can describe the scope of their advice (in the wake of depolarisation) and the conditions that have to be met before an adviser can describe himself as 'independent';
- the provision of a simplified prospectus or key features document;
- the disclosure of actual commission or equivalent in the sale of packaged products;
- the use of dealing commission.[51]

Other notifications have been withdrawn, either because the proposal has been abandoned or because it is agreed that notification is not necessary because the measures are only an elaboration of MiFID, and not in addition to it.[52]

The contents of COBS

13.36 In July 2005 the FSA first published its outline plan for the reform of the investment conduct of business regime.[53] The proposed structure was further refined during the consultation process.[54] The final chapter structure is:

1 Application
2 Conduct of business obligations
3 Client categorisation
4 Communicating with clients, including financial promotion
5 Distance communications
6 Information about the firm, its services and remuneration
7 Insurance mediation
8 Client agreements
9 Suitability (including basic advice)
10 Appropriateness (for non-advised services)

---

[49] MiFID Implementing Directive, (Commission Directive (EC) 2006/73), Art 4(3).
[50] FSA CP 06/19, paras 2.13–2.16.
[51] FSA CP 06/19, para 2.14; FSA PS 07/14, paras 1.5–1.13.
[52] FSA PS 07/14, para 1.9.
[53] FSA CP 05/10, 'Reviewing the FSA Handbook—Money Laundering, Approved Persons, Training and Competence and Conduct of Business' (July 2005), chs 1 and 5; and Annex 5 which contained the proposed new structure for COBS (or NEWCOB as it was often described in the consultation process).
[54] FSA CP 06/19, ch 3 and Table 2: Structure of NEWCOB; FSA PS 07/6, para 4.6 and Table: Structure of NEWCOB.

11 Dealing and managing
12 Investment research
13 Preparing product information
14 Providing product information to clients
15 Cancellation
16 Reporting information to clients
17 Claims handling for long-term care insurance
18 Specialist regimes
19 Pensions: supplementary provisions
20 With-profits
21 Permitted links for long-term insurance business
22 Schedules

Scope and application

Scope

The predecessor rulebook COB prima facie applied to all regulated activities and, **13.37** to some extent to non-regulated activities undertaken by firms. However, in reality most of the provisions were expressly targeted at a subset of regulated activities which fall within the definition of 'designated investment business'. Briefly stated, the Conduct of Business Rules were generally not applicable to deposit, mortgage, and general insurance business.[55]

In its first consultation on the original COB the FSA announced that it intended **13.38** that generally 'designated investment business equated with what was previously "investment business" for the purposes of the Financial Services Act 1986'.[56] It therefore aimed to exclude deposit-taking, general insurance, and pure protection policies.[57] 'Designated investment' and 'designated investment business' were defined in detail in the Handbook Glossary by reference to regulated investments and regulated activities in the Financial Services and Markets Act 2000 (Regulated Activities) Order ('RAO 2001') which were carried on by way of business.[58]

These definitions continue to be important in the post-MiFID world of **13.39** COBS, as they still provide the definition for the application of the FSA's conduct

---

[55] MCOB and ICOBS were the components concerned with mortgages and general insurance respectively.

[56] FSA CP 45a, 'The Conduct of Business Rules' (February 2000) ('FSA CP 45a'), para 2.10.

[57] For definitions of 'deposit', 'deposit-taking firm', 'general insurance contract', and 'pure protection contract' see the Handbook Glossary.

[58] Handbook Glossary. For the background see: FSA PS 45, 'Conduct of Business Sourcebook— Feedback on consultation and 'final text' and consultation on supplementary rules' (February 2001) (Interim glossary for COB); FSA CP 45a, para 2.9.

of business regime for investment firms which often has a wider scope than required by MiFID. The scope of MiFID is narrower than the FSA's concept of 'designated investment business'. The Handbook Glossary continues to define 'designated investments' and 'designated investment business' by reference to the RAO. These concepts were the traditional territory of the FSA's COB regime, and often provide the scope of COBS. In addition the Handbook Glossary now also defines 'MiFID business', and 'equivalent third country business'.

13.40 'MiFID business' is defined by reference to 'investment services and activities' and 'ancillary services'. The former are defined by reference to MiFID itself: any of the services and activities listed in Section A of Annex I to MiFID relating to any financial instrument, that is:

(a) reception and transmission of orders in relation to one or more financial instruments;
(b) execution of orders on behalf of clients;
(c) dealing on own account;
(d) portfolio management;
(e) the making of a personal recommendation;
(f) underwriting of financial instruments and/or placing of financial instruments on a firm commitment basis;
(g) placing of financial instruments without a firm commitment basis;
(h) operation of multilateral trading facilities.[59]

'Ancillary services' are also defined by reference to the list in the directive.[60]

13.41 Broadly speaking the FSA has generally found it easier to apply the MiFID requirements to 'designated investment business', whether it is MiFID business or not. Although these are exceptions in many cases MiFID-inspired rules are being applied to non-MiFID business. Consultation is also ongoing as to the approach to specialist regimes, including corporate finance business (to the extent to which such business is outside MiFID) with further new rules anticipated in 2008.[61]

Application

13.42 COBS 1 contains the rules explaining which rules apply to which firms.[62] The basic rule applies COBS to firms carrying out specified activities from an

---

[59] Handbook Glossary: MiFID Art 4(1) and (2) and the list in Annex I section A.
[60] MiFID Annex I section B.
[61] FSA CP 07/9, 'Conduct of Business regime: non-MiFID deferred matters (including proposals for Telephone Recording)' (May 2007).
[62] For the background see: FSA CP 06/19, ch 5; FSA PS 07/6, ch 5.

establishment maintained by it or its appointed representative in the UK. The activities are:

(a) accepting deposits;
(b) designated investment business;
(c) long-term insurance business in relation to life policies.

It also extends to activities connected with them.[63] Therefore ancillary non-MiFID business may be caught.

The basic rule is then substantially modified by a detailed table.[64] This limits the scope of certain COBS obligations where the business is MiFID or equivalent third party business with an eligible counterparty.[65] However the modification does not extend to the suitability regime in COBS 9.[66]

13.43

Territorial application

COBS applies to UK-authorised firms operating in the UK and throughout the EEA in accordance with the principle of home State regulation. The rule of basic application is further modified so that its territorial scope is compatible with European law.[67] Therefore the general principle of home State regulation implemented by MiFID, the Distance Marketing of Consumer Financial Services Directive,[68] Electronic Commerce Directive,[69] and other EU measures is respected, and detailed guidance is provided on this.[70] COBS also applies to the branches of financial services providers from so-called 'third countries', that is non-UK or non-EEA firms, which are operating in the UK.[71]

13.44

General conduct of business obligations

COBS 2 contains rules which apply to all designated investment business, comprising general requirements, inducements, and provision of services through another firm.[72]

13.45

The client's best interests rule

A new MiFID-inspired rule requires that a firm must act 'honestly, fairly and professionally in accordance with the best interests of its client'. This applies to all

13.46

---

[63] COBS 1.1.1R.
[64] COBS 1.1.2R and COBS 1 Annex 1 R.
[65] COBS 1 Annex 1 R, Part 1.
[66] This omission is intentional: FSA PS 07/6, para 5.10.
[67] COBS 1 Annex 1 R, Part 2, para 1.1R. This rule overrides every rule in COBS.
[68] 2002/65/EC.
[69] 2000/31/EC.
[70] COBS 1 Annex 1 R, Part 3. See also PERG 13.
[71] FSA CP 06/19, para 1.1.5.
[72] For the background see: FSA CP 06/19, ch 6; FSA PS 07/6, ch 6; FSA PS 07/14, ch 2.

retail clients and all clients engaged in MiFID or equivalent third country business.[73] Unlike the similar existing FSA Principle 6 (treating customers fairly), this rule will be actionable by private persons in accordance with section 150 of the 2000 Act.[74]

Exclusion of liability

13.47 In the original version of the Handbook, COB 2.5 prevented an authorised person from excluding or limiting any duty or liability it has to customers (private, intermediate, and in relation to distance contracts, retail) which it has under the regulatory system.[75] In relation to private customers, firms were required not to attempt to exclude any other duty or liability 'unless it is reasonable to do so'.[76] In the process of implementing MiFID, initially the FSA proposed removing the rules formerly in COB 2.5,[77] but after consultation the FSA has retained a more limited requirement that in relation to designated investment business a firm must not in a communication to a client seek to exclude or restrict any obligation imposed under the regulatory system.[78] Guidance also refers to the general legal restrictions on other duties or liabilities which would otherwise arise.[79]

Inducements

13.48 COBS 2.3 contains a more stringent regime on inducements and indirect benefits than any previous regulatory regime. It is based on an 'intelligent copy-out' of the relevant MiFID provision. The net result is a full disclosure of third party commission regime. It is also now necessary that any fee, commission, or non-monetary benefit where this is paid or provided to or by a third party 'must be designed to enhance the quality of the relevant service to the client'.[80] In accordance with guidance from the Committee of European Securities Regulators ('CESR') a firm will be able to comply with its obligations on inducements so long as it discloses the essential arrangements relating to any fee, commission, or non-monetary benefit in summary form and undertakes to give further disclosure on request, and honours that undertaking.[81] The regime also extends to packaged products which fall outside the scope of MiFID.[82]

---

[73] COBS 2.1.1R. MiFID Art 19(1).
[74] Compare FSA PS 07/6, para 6.4.
[75] COB 2.5.3R.
[76] COB 2.5.3R, in effect applying a regime akin to the Unfair Contract Terms Act 1977.
[77] FSA CP 06/19, paras 6.55–6.67.
[78] COBS 2.1.2R. See FSA PS 07/6, para 6.7.
[79] COBS 2.1.3G, citing the Unfair Terms in Consumer Contracts Regulations 1999.
[80] MiFID Implementing Directive, Art 26(b)(ii), fleshing out MiFID, Art 19(1).
[81] COBS 2.3.1R and 2.3.2R. See FSA PS 07/14, ch 2.
[82] FSA PS 07/14, para 2.6. The remainder of COBS 2.3 contains detailed guidance and evidential provisions in the context of inducements and packaged products.

Agent as client

Previously under COB[83] an investment firm which received instructions from **13.49** another firm on behalf of a client was entitled to treat the firm as the client and therefore not be subject to the (probably more stringent) rules affecting a deal with the underlying client. A corresponding rule, consistent with MiFID, is now to found in COBS.[84]

Client categorisation

One of the most significant changes from the compliance perspective is COBS 3 **13.50** which contains the new MiFID-based regime for classification of clients,[85] abandoning the FSA's own somewhat complicated three-category regime of COB (private customer, intermediate customer, market counterparty).[86]

The two principal categories of client under MiFID are retail client and profes- **13.51** sional client. In addition, in some contexts a third category of 'eligible counterparty' ('ECP') is recognised. The categories are intended to target different levels of regulatory protection. Clients are entitled to 'step up' or 'step down' in order to obtain additional or less stringent protection. Unlike the regime in COB, under MiFID firms must notify clients of this ability and the consequences of so acting.[87] Overall the FSA anticipates that there will be more persons classified as 'retail clients' under COBS than there were persons labelled 'private customers' under COB.[88]

Rules in COBS 3.2 define who is the client and deal with issues of trusteeeship **13.52** and agency. A 'retail client' is defined negatively as one who is neither a professional client nor an eligible counterparty.[89] The definition of 'professional client' is elaborate, divides into 'per se professional clients' and 'elective professional clients', and is based on the EU measures. It includes entities required to be authorised in the financial market and other large undertakings.[90] A similarly elaborate definition based on MiFID is provided for 'eligible counterparty'.[91] COBS 3.7 makes provision for 'stepping up' or providing clients with a higher degree of protection than their usual classification.

---

[83] COB 4.1.5R.
[84] COBS 2.4.3R. See MiFID, Art 20.
[85] For the background see: FSA, 'Implementing MiFID's Client Categorisation requirements' (August 2006); FSA CP 06/19, ch 7; FSA PS 07/6, ch 7.
[86] Previously COB 4.1.
[87] COBS 3.3.1R.
[88] FSA, 'Implementing MiFID's Client Categorisation requirements' (August 2006), para 1.09.
[89] COBS 3.4.1R.
[90] COBS 3.5.1R. MiFID, Annex II.
[91] COBS 3.6.1R. MiFID, Art 24.

Communication with clients and financial promotion

13.53 COBS 4 contains the rules on client communication and on financial promotion.[92] The chapter applies generally to firms communicating with or communicating or approving a financial promotion in connection with designated investment business with a retail client.[93]

Territorial scope

13.54 The territorial scope of COBS 4 is determined in accordance with the general application rule.[94] In addition, it applies to the communication of a financial promotion to a person inside the UK and (subject to some qualifications) the communication of a cold call to a person outside the UK.[95] A 'cold call' according to the Handbook Glossary is an unsolicited real-time communication as defined in article 8 of FPO 2005.

13.55 The reference to the 'general application rule' ensures COBS 4 is modified in line with the 'home State' principle of the EU law.

The fair, clear, and not misleading rule

13.56 A very general rule provides that a 'firm must ensure that a communication or financial promotion is fair, clear and not misleading'.[96] This differs from the old COB rule on 'clear, fair and not misleading' communications[97] not just in the inversion of the first two adjectives, but also, more importantly, in the move to a strict liability standard, rather than the 'reasonable steps' required by the previous regime. The FSA has acknowledged that this imposes a higher standard and could have an impact on firms in that, whilst FSA Principle 7 could always have been the basis of disciplinary action, it was not actionable by private persons. In contrast, the new strict COBS rule will be actionable in accordance with the policy decision to apply section 150 of the 2000 Act to all rules in COBS.[98]

Financial promotions

13.57 The statutory background to COBS 4 is the basic financial promotion restriction in section 21 of the 2000 Act and the various exemptions found in the Financial Services and Markets Act 2000 (Financial Promotion) Order 2005 (the 'Financial

---

[92] For the background see: FSA CP 06/20; FSA PS 07/6, ch 26.

[93] COBS 4.1.1R. There are exceptions for qualifying credits, certain home finance schemes, and unregulated collective investment schemes.

[94] The 'general application rule' is defined in the Handbook Glossary. COBS 1.1.1R and COBS 1.1.2R.

[95] COBS 4.1.8R.

[96] COBS 4.2.1R. Exclusions include 'non-retail communications' which are directed at recipients who are professional clients or ECPs. See also MiFID, Art 19(2).

[97] Previously COB 2.1.

[98] FSA, PS 07/6, paras 26.9 and 26.10.

Promotion Order' or 'FPO 2005').[99] In this context, where we are concerned with regulated firms dealing with the retail sector the relevant rules to be complied with are to be found in COBS 4. Failure to comply with the regime may expose an authorised firm to private action or disciplinary sanction.

The regulator's approach to financial promotions[100]

The FSA has issued various documents on the financial promotion regime for regulated firms and has increasingly focused on this issue since N2.[101] Given **13.58** the perceived role of misleading financial promotions in mis-selling cases and the potential for consumer detriment, the FSA decided in 2004 to increase the resources allocated to financial promotions.[102] Accordingly it created a specialist Financial Promotions department in April 2004, with about 30 staff.[103] Overall the FSA's approach to this topic forms part of its overall retail strategy of 'Treating Customers Fairly' ('TCF'), based on FSA Principle 6[104] and FSA Principle 7.[105]

Financial promotions and disciplinary action

This greater focus on advertising can be illustrated by the FSA's enforcement activity,[106] which has focused on misleading financial promotions over recent **13.59** years. For example:

- DBS Financial Management plc was fined £100,000 in March 2003 for a misleading direct offer advertisement in the form of a brochure distributed in national newspapers;[107]

- Berkeley Jacobs Financial Services Ltd was fined £175,000 in February 2004 in respect of 'pension unlocking', including a finding that there had been misleading financial promotions;[108]

---

[99] Financial Services and Markets Act 2000 (Financial Promotion) Order 2005, SI 2005/1529 ('FPO 2005') came into force on 1 July 2005. It supersedes the original Financial Services and Markets Act 2000 (Financial Promotion) Order 2001, SI 2001/1335 ('FPO 2001'), (as amended by eight prior instruments). FPO 2005 revokes and re-enacts FPO 2001, with some further amendments. It preserves the original numbering. For the background to FPO 2001 see: HM Treasury, 'Financial Promotion: Third Consultation Document; Financial Promotion of Collective Investment Schemes—First Consultation' (October 2000).

[100] eg FSA, 'Financial Promotions: taking stock and moving forward' (February 2005).

[101] FSA, 'The FSA's regulatory approach to financial promotions' (April 2002).

[102] FSA, 'Business Plan 2004/5' (2004), 23.

[103] FSA, 'Financial Promotions: taking stock and moving forward' (February 2005), 5.

[104] ibid, 3. From the second half of 2005 the FSA issued quarterly bulletins for investment firms (subject to COB 3).

[105] FSA, 'Financial Promotions: Progress update and future direction' (August 2006), 4.

[106] FSA, 'Financial Promotions: taking stock and moving forward' (February 2005), 7–8.

[107] FSA, Final Notice (24 March 2003).

[108] FSA, Final Notice (11 February 2004).

- Hargreaves Lansdown Asset Management Ltd was fined £300,000 in June 2004 in relation to the marketing of split-capital investment trusts by direct offer advertisements which described the 'splits' as having a 'lower equity risk' rating;[109]

- David M Aaron (Personal Financial Planners) Ltd had its permission cancelled under section 45 in August 2004 because of failure to meet the threshold conditions arising out of the marketing and mis-selling of 'precipice bonds' or SCARPS;[110]

- Cantor Index was fined £70,000 for a misleading campaign on spread-betting and contracts;[111]

- Axa Sun Life was fined £500,000 for misleading promotions in respect of various endowment policies which downplayed risks and contained misleading comparative information;[112]

- Hemscott Investment Analysis was fined £50,000 for a promotion using the headline 'We even make a bear market all soft & cuddly', and picturing a teddy bear, which has held not to be fair and balanced;[113]

- City Index was fined £36,000 for misleading campaign on spread-betting and contracts for differences;[114]

- Courtover Investment Management Ltd was fined £20,000 in April 2005 for issuing a misleading promotion for unlisted shares in a property investment company as a free supplement in national newspapers which conveyed the impression that the offer had been approved under FSMA 2000;[115]

- Kings (a firm) was fined £60,000 in October 2005 in relation to misleading promotions in relation to 'pension unlocking';[116]

- The Ancient Order of Foresters Friendly Society Ltd was fined £55,000 in August 2006 for failing to ensure appropriate risk warnings were included in television commercials starring Stephanie Cole aimed at older consumers and for failing to ensure direct offer marketing material was clear, fair, and not misleading;[117]

---

[109] FSA, Final Notice (2 June 2004).
[110] FSA, Final Notice (25 August 2004).
[111] FSA, Final Notice (30 December 2004).
[112] FSA, Final Notice (21 December 2004).
[113] FSA, Final Notice (13 January 2005). The FSA made much of the failure of the firm to follow its approach in FSA, 'The FSA's regulatory approach to financial promotions' (April 2002), stressing that the firm was aware of this publication (para 1.9 of the Final Notice).
[114] FSA, Final Notice (23 March 2005).
[115] FSA, Final Notice (29 April 2005).
[116] FSA, Final Notice (8 November 2005).
[117] FSA, Final Notice (23 August 2006).

• Mortgageland Ltd was disciplined by censure under section 205 of the 2000 Act in May 2008 for, amongst other rule breaches, failing to ensure its financial promotions were clear, fair, and not misleading and failing to ensure the promotions were approved by a person with sufficient expertise.[118]

As the outcome of full disciplinary action, these cases represent only the tip of the iceberg of the FSA's, and in particular its Financial Promotions team's, activities in relation to financial promotions in respect of its regulated community. Much work has been done on areas of concern such as 'splits', 'precipice bonds', or 'SCARPS' and 'pension unlocking' (which allows access to pension benefits for ready money, but with considerable detriments).

General COBS Rules on financial promotions

Financial promotions should be clearly identifiable as such.[119] The basic rule in COBS 4.5 for investment firms dealing with retail clients is that: **13.60**

(a) information must include the name of the firm;
(b) information should be accurate, and in particular should not emphasise the benefits of any service or product without giving a fair and prominent indication of relevant risks;
(c) the information is understandable by the average member of the target audience;
(d) the information should not disguise, diminish, or obscure important items, statements, or warnings.[120]

Further rules copy out the MiFID Implementing Directive's rules on comparative information,[121] the requirement that any reference to the fiscal implications of any investment must carry a warning that tax rules may change,[122] and requiring consistency in communications.[123]

Past, simulated past, and future performance

COBS 4.6 contains the rules on past performance, simulated past, and future performance. The basic rule on past performance requires that such information is not the most prominent feature of the communication, is based on five years' previous performance (where available or the whole period if shorter), and must contain a prominent warning in the familiar terms, that it is not a reliable **13.61**

---

[118] FSA, Final Notice (21May 2008).
[119] COBS 4.3.1R, with exceptions including 'image advertising'. MiFID, Art 19(2), second sentence.
[120] COBS 4.5.2R. MiFID Implementing Directive, Art 27(2), developing MiFID, Art 19(1).
[121] COBS 4.5.6R. MiFID Implementing Directive, Art 27(3), developing MiFID, Art 19(1).
[122] COBS 4.5.7R. MiFID Implementing Directive, Art 27(7), developing MiFID, Art 19(1).
[123] COBS 4.5.8R. MiFID Implementing Directive, Art 29(7), developing MiFID, Art 19(3).

indicator of future results.[124] Further detailed guidance carries over some old FSA material for particular products.[125] Further rules provide for simulated past[126] and future[127] performance.

Direct offer financial promotions

13.62 Provision is made as to which of the client communication rules must be observed in the case of direct offer financial promotions to retail clients.[128]

Cold calling

13.63 Since the introduction of the Financial Services Act 1986 the practice of unsolicited communications or 'cold-calling' retail customers has been the subject of a general prohibition. The basic provision in COB was that unsolicited real-time financial promotions were prohibited.[129]

13.64 The restrictions on 'cold calling' retail clients and other communications which are not in writing are now to be found in COBS 4.8.[130]

Principal conduct of business rules for retail firms

Distance communications

13.65 COBS 5 now consolidates the conduct of business regime arising out of the Distance Marketing of Consumer Financial Services Directive[131] and the Electronic Commerce Directive,[132] replacing rules previously found in COB and in the separate ECO Sourcebook, the latter of which has now been deleted.[133]

Information about the firm, its services, and remuneration

13.66 The detailed disclosure regime concerning provision of information by firms is to be found in COBS 6.[134]

13.67 Article 19(3) of MiFID requires appropriate information to be provided in appropriate form about an investment firm and its services, and its costs and charges. COBS 6.1 contains the MiFID-inspired rules in detail which a firm must provide

---

[124] COBS 4.6.2R. MiFID Implementing Directive, Art 27(4), developing MiFID, Art 19(1).
[125] COBS 4.6.3G–4.6.5G.
[126] COBS 4.6.6R. MiFID Implementing Directive, Art 27(5), developing MiFID, Art 19(1).
[127] COBS 4.6.7R. MiFID Implementing Directive, Art 27(6), developing MiFID, Art 19(1).
[128] COBS 4.7.1R.
[129] COB 3.10.3R.
[130] COBS 4.8.1R and COBS 4.8.3R.
[131] 2002/65/EC. See COBS 5.1.1R–5.1.17R and COBS 5 Annex 1R and Annex 2R.
[132] 2000/31/EC. See COBS 5.2.1R–5.2.9R.
[133] For the background see: FSA CP 06/20 ch 10; FSA PS 07/6, ch 8.
[134] For the background see: FSA CP 06/20 ch 11; FSA PS 07/6, ch 9; FSA PS 07/14, ch 3.

before conducting business, including rules where the firm undertakes the activity of safeguarding client assets.[135]

Of particular interest in the new COBS 6.1 is the rule requiring the firm to dis- **13.68** close to retail clients the total price to be paid by the client in respect of an investment or service, including all related fees, commissions, charges, and expenses.[136] The general rule on the timing of such disclosure is that it must be disclosed in good time before the firm starts to render the service. Only in cases of services effected by distance communication at the request of the client may such information be delayed until immediately after starting to perform, but only where the firm is unable to comply because of those circumstances.[137]

COBS 6.2 contains the rules introduced in the wake of depolarisation, including **13.69** the continuing requirement for firms to disclose the breadth of the firm's ability to give personal recommendations, whether from the whole of the market, limited to several product providers, or limited to one product provider. This was one of the main points on which the FSA felt it necessary to notify the European Commission under Article 4 of the MiFID Implementing Directive that it was going beyond the scope of EU measures.[138]

The rules apply to personal recommendations to retail clients to buy a packaged **13.70** product.[139] A firm cannot hold itself out as a whole of market adviser unless it provides personal recommendations on all types of personal pension schemes, including SIPPs.[140] A firm cannot hold itself out as 'independent' unless it provides personal recommendations to the client on packaged products from the whole of the market *and* offers the client the option of fee-based advice.[141]

COBS 6.3 and 6.4 provide further detailed rules for disclosure by firms in relation **13.71** to its services, fees, and commissions in respect of packaged products. Despite originally proposing to retain the two principal documents implementing its disclosure regime—the 'Menu' and the 'Initial Disclosure Document' ('IDD')—introduced in the wake of depolarisation,[142] the FSA ultimately decided to give firms the option as to how to comply with the MiFID-based information rules. The Menu and the IDD continue in the form of guidance as a safe harbour, so that

---

[135] COBS 6.1.1R–6.1.17G. MiFID Implementing Directive, Arts 29–32, developing MiFID, Art 19(3).

[136] COBS 6.1.9R. MiFID Implementing Directive, Art 33, developing MiFID, Art 19(3).

[137] COBS 6.1.11R.

[138] FSA CP 06/19, para 2.14; FSA PS 07/14, paras 1.5–1.13.

[139] COBS 6.2.1R.

[140] COBS 6.2.10R.

[141] COBS 6.2.15R. See also COBS 6.2.16R.

[142] See FSA CP 06/19, paras 11.1–11.25.

firms who continue to use them can be sure they have satisfied the MiFID requirements.[143]

Excessive charges

13.72 The old COB 5.6 conferred on the FSA a power to regulate excessive charging by firms. One consequence of the implementation of MiFID was a reconsideration of whether these rules were necessary, as no corresponding regime exists in the EU measures. Rather the emphasis is on the compulsory disclosure of total cost. Following consultation on not carrying these rules forward in NEWCOB,[144] the FSA has decided to delete the excessive charges rules. It had never used them or taken enforcement action in respect of them. The FSA is content not to act as a price regulator.[145]

Insurance mediation

13.73 COBS 7 implements for investment firms in a revised form (based on 'intelligent copy-out') the requirements of the separate EU measure on insurance intermediaries, the Insurance Mediation Directive ('IMD'). The rules set out in detail the information which an insurance intermediary must generally provide when doing business with a client.[146]

Client agreements

13.74 The rules formerly found in COB 4.2 are replaced by the rules in COBS 8.[147] Firms must provide to new retail clients both a written basic agreement setting out the essential rights and obligations of the firm and the client (effectively the existing 'Terms of Business' requirement).[148] In addition, firms must in general provide the written terms of that agreement in good time before a retail client becomes bound by any agreement. Only in cases of services effected by distance communication at the request of the client may such information be delayed until immediately after starting to perform, but only where the firm is unable to comply because of those circumstances.[149]

Client assets and client money

13.75 FSA Principle 10 states: 'A *firm* must arrange adequate protection for *clients*' assets when it is responsible for them.' Section 139 of the 2000 Act provides that rules

---

[143] See FSA PS 07/14, paras 3.8–3.17. For the guidance see COBS 6.3.3G.

[144] See FSA CP 06/19, paras 11.51–11.59.

[145] FSA PS 07/6, paras 9.11–9.15.

[146] Directive (EC) 2002/92. For the background see: FSA CP 06/20 ch 12; FSA PS 07/6, ch 10.

[147] For the background see: FSA CP 06/20 ch 13; FSA PS 07/6, ch 11.

[148] COBS 8.1.2R. It applies to 'designated investment business' but excepting 'advising on investments'. MiFID Implementing Directive, Art 33.

[149] COBS 8.1.3R. MiFID Implementing Directive, Art 29.

can be made which ensure client money is held in trust (or in Scotland as agent). The rules concerning client assets and money are found outside of COBS, in a separate component of the Handbook. Prior to the implementation of MiFID, the FSA's Client Assets Rules ('CASS') provided for the handling of client assets[150] and for a statutory trust for client money, creating a fiduciary relationship and priority for the customer on insolvency of the firm.[151] However professional firms could opt out of the protective rules on client money.[152] These chapters—CASS 2 and 4—still apply to designated investment business which is not MiFID business. In the wake of the implementation of MiFID[153] two new chapters in CASS—chapters 5 and 7—establish rules (with effect from 1 November 2007) in relation to MiFID business for the safeguarding of client assets (the custody rules) and imposing a statutory trust for client money, creating a fiduciary relationship and priority for the customer on insolvency of the firm.[154] There is no professional firm opt-out from the client money trust regime, because the FSA considered it to be incompatible with the directive.

Suitability (including basic advice)

The important rules on the suitability of advice or portfolio management services **13.76** are now to be found in COBS 9.[155] Previously the rules on 'know your customer' ('KYC') and suitability were found in COB 5. With the implementation of MiFID the FSA decided to use the EU standards as the basis of its suitability regime in COBS. Accordingly the MiFID standard would be applied to all advisory and discretionary transactions previously covered by COB 5, including products which fall outside of the scope of MiFID, such as life and pensions contracts and other 'packaged products'. Similarly, where dealing with a retail client the standards would be applied to MiFID and non-MiFID firms (which may include IFAs, who do not hold client money).[156] The KYC and suitability requirement are spelt out economically in Article 19(4) of MiFID:

> When providing investment advice or portfolio management the investment firm shall obtain the necessary information regarding the client's or the potential client's knowledge and experience in the investment field relevant to the specific type of product or service, his financial situation and his investment objectives so as to enable

---

[150] CASS 2.

[151] CASS 4.2.3R (non-MiFID). Detailed rules for segregation of client money are provided in CASS 4.3.

[152] CASS 4.1.9R.

[153] MiFID, Art 13(7) and (8) and MiFID Implementing Directive, Arts 16t–20. For the background to the post-MiFID FSA CASS rules: see FSA CP 06/14 chs 9 and 10 and FSA PS 07/2 ch 8.

[154] CASS 7.7.2R. For definition of 'client money' see CASS 7.2.

[155] For the background see: FSA CP 06/20 ch 14; FSA PS 07/6, ch 12.

[156] See FSA CP 06/20, para 14.2–14.11.

the firm to recommend to the client or potential client the investment services or financial instruments that are suitable for him.

That is the basis for all domestic regulation in this field, albeit further prescriptive detail is provided by the MiFID Implementing Directive.[157]

13.77 Application. COBS 9 applies to personal recommendations in relation to a designated investment[158] and to firms which manage investments.[159] In respect of non-MiFID business it applies to dealings with retail clients and where the firm is managing the business of an occupational pension scheme, stakeholder pension scheme, or personal pension scheme.[160]

13.78 'Know your customer'. The new COBS rule on KYC provides:

(1) A firm must obtain from the client such information as is necessary for the firm to understand the essential facts about him and have a reasonable basis for believing, giving due consideration to the nature and extent of the service provided, that the specific transaction to be recommended, or entered into in the course of managing:

   (a) meets his investment objectives;

   (b) is such that he is able financially to bear any related investment risks consistent with his investment objectives; and

   (c) is such that he has the necessary experience and knowledge in order to understand the risks involved in the transaction or in the management of his portfolio.

(2) The information regarding the investment objectives of a client must include, where relevant, information on the length of time for which he wishes to hold the investment, his preferences regarding risk taking, his risk profile, and the purposes of the investment.

(3) The information regarding the financial situation of a client must include, where relevant, information on the source and extent of his regular income, his assets, including liquid assets, investments and real property, and his regular financial commitments.[161]

---

[157] MiFID Implementing Directive, Arts 35, 37 and 52. See also Recitals 57 and 58.

[158] COBS 9.1.1R. But firms can choose to give basic advice in respect of 'stakeholder products' under the regime in COB 9.6.

[159] COBS 9.1.3R.

[160] COBS 9.1.4R. A special rule provides for only IMD-required rules to apply to personal recommendations of life policies to professional clients.

[161] COBS 9.2.2R. See MiFID Implementing Directive, Art 35(1), (3), and (4). For professional clients the firm is entitled to assume the client has the necessary knowledge and experience: COBS 9.2.8R. See MiFID Implementing Directive, Art 35(2). There is a discrete rule for small friendly societies: COBS 9.2.9R.

Further provision is made as to the information which must be sought:

> The information regarding a client's knowledge and experience in the investment field includes, to the extent appropriate to the nature of the client, the nature and extent of the service to be provided and the type of product or transaction envisaged, including their complexity and the risks involved, information on:
>
> (1) the types of service, transaction and designated investment with which the client is familiar;
> (2) the nature, volume, frequency of the client's transactions in designated investments and the period over which they have been carried out;
> (3) the level of education, profession or relevant former profession of the client.[162]

Echoing a curious requirement of the MiFID Implementing Directive, a rule **13.79** insists that a firm must not encourage the client *not* to provide this information.[163] A firm must not make a personal recommendation or make a decision to trade if it does obtain the necessary information to assess suitability.[164] This goes somewhat further than the predecessor rules on 'reticent clients'. Nevertheless a firm is entitled to rely on what its client says, unless it is 'manifestly out of date, inaccurate or incomplete'.[165]

The suitability rule

The new MiFID inspired 'suitability' rule provides: **13.80**

(1) A firm must take reasonable steps to ensure that a personal recommendation, or a decision to trade, is suitable for its client.
(2) When making the personal recommendation or managing his investments, the firm must obtain the necessary information regarding the client's:
   (a) knowledge and experience in the investment field relevant to the specific type of designated investment or service;
   (b) financial situation; and
   (c) investment objectives;

   so as to enable the firm to make the recommendation, or take the decision, which is suitable for him.[166]

The FSA has carried forward as guidance, based on Recital 57 of the MiFID **13.81** Implementing Directive, a provision that unsuitability may arise from the risks of an investment, the type of transaction, the characteristics of the order, or the fre-

---

[162] COBS 9.2.3R. See MiFID Implementing Directive, Art 37(1).
[163] COBS 9.2.4R. See MiFID Implementing Directive, Art 37(2).
[164] COBS 9.2.6R. See MiFID Implementing Directive, Art 35(5). This Article refers to the information required under Art 19(4) of MiFID itself, rather than the more elaborated version in the MiFID Implementing Directive. See also COBS 9.2.7G.
[165] COBS 9.2.5R. See MiFID Implementing Directive, Art 37(3).
[166] COBS 9.2.1R. See MiFID Implementing Directive, Art 19(4) and IMD, Art 12(2).

quency of the trading.[167] The latter point is reinforced by specific guidance on 'churning and switching'.[168] There is also guidance on the sensitive topic of income withdrawals and short-term annuities.[169]

13.82 **Suitability reports.**   Article 19(8) of MiFID entitles clients to 'adequate reports on the service provided' by firms, and the costs associated with services and transactions. This has led the FSA to modify its traditional requirement of a 'suitability letter'.[170] The new rules appear in COBS 9.4. This is intended by the FSA to be a 'simplified and less prescriptive form' of the previous 'suitability letter' regime,[171] and the change in terminology from 'letter' to 'report' should not be understood as suggesting the contrary. It is inspired by the MiFID language, already quoted. The FSA has also withdrawn its notification to the EU Commission on the basis that its rules go no further than MiFID requires.[172]

13.83 **Abandonment of 'most suitable' standard for packaged products.**   The FSA has not maintained the 'most suitable' standard for recommendations about packaged products from the range on which the adviser can advise. This is the final death-knell for so-called 'best advice'. The FSA believes that other rules, such as the client's best interests rule and the disclosure regime, will achieve the aim of the predecessor rules.[173]

13.84 **Basic advice in respect of stakeholder products.**   This regime was previously found in COB 5A. MiFID does not recognise the concept of 'basic advice', therefore this recent initiative is carried forward in a truncated fashion. Only non-MiFID firms can offer basic advice in relation to all stakeholder products and any firm can offer basic advice in relation to stakeholder products which fall outside the scope of MiFID.[174] The detailed rules are now to be found in COBS 6.9.[175] Having invested much time and energy in this project, the FSA was reluctant to abandon it wholesale, despite the poor take-up in the marketplace. Accordingly it has launched a further review—the Basic Advice Review, to run alongside its Retail Distribution Review—to consider the future of the regime, which is expected to report in the second half of 2008.[176]

---

[167] COBS 9.3.1G.

[168] COBS 9.3.2G. See FSA CP 06/20, para 14.11.

[169] COBS 9.3.3G. See FSA PS 07/6, para 12.12.

[170] See FSA CP 06/20, para 14.16; FSA PS 07/6, paras 12.13–12.20; FSA PS 07/14, ch 4.

[171] See FSA PS 07/14, para 4.2.

[172] See FSA PS 07/14, para 4.4.

[173] See FSA CP 06/20, para 14.10; FSA PS 07/6, para 12.12.

[174] See: FSA CP 06/20, paras 14.27–14.39; FSA PS 07/6, paras 12.21–12.28; FSA PS 07/14, paras 3.22 and 3.23.

[175] COBS 6.9.1–6.9.20R.

[176] See: FSA CP 06/20, paras 14.36 and 14.38; FSA PS 07/6, paras 12.27–12.28.

Appropriateness (for non-advised services)

MiFID introduces a new and, for UK practitioners, unfamiliar standard of 'appro-   **13.85**
priateness' for non-advisory services. The rules are contained in COBS 10.[177] The
essential background is MiFID itself. Having concisely defined the 'KYC' and
suitability rules for personal recommendations and portfolio management in
Article 19(4), the directive next addresses investment services which fall outside
the scope of the preceding paragraph in Article 19(5). Whereas previously UK
regulation drew a sharp line between those transactions (advisory and discretionary portfolio management) where a suitability regime applied and 'execution only'
transactions, MiFID recognises a distinct 'appropriateness' standard. For those
transactions which fall within Article 19(5) the firm must carry out a form of
KYC. It must ask:

> the client or potential client to provide information regarding his knowledge
> and experience in the investment field relevant to the specific type of product or
> service offered or demanded so as to enable the investment firm to assess whether
> the investment service or product envisaged is appropriate for the client.

If the firm concludes the investment is not appropriate it must warn the (poten-   **13.86**
tial) client, albeit it may do so in a standardised format. Where the (potential)
client elects to provide no information or inadequate information the firm must
warn the client that it is unable to judge the appropriateness of the service or
product for him the (potential) client, albeit it may do so in a standardised format.
The MiFID Implementing Directive provides that a firm is entitled to assume
that a professional client has the necessary knowledge and experience.[178]

Accordingly the 'appropriateness' standard is more negative in its approach, in   **13.87**
contrast to the positive duty imposed by the suitability regime. Nevertheless this
new standard, with its associated warnings, tilts the balance of responsibility as to
the client's interests, requiring more of investment firms than under the predecessor COB regime, where 'execution only' transactions were commonplace, especially in the context of responses to direct offer financial promotions.

Given its novelty, the FSA has only implemented the 'appropriateness' regime for   **13.88**
the MiFID business in respect of which it has no choice, and has not for now
extended it to retail business generally. Nevertheless its implementation will be a
significant new regulatory burden for firms who previously undertook significant
'direct offer' sales business or 'execution only' business in relation to affected products.[179] The basic MiFID rules are copied out in COBS 10.2 and 10.3.

---

[177] For the background see: FSA CP 06/20 ch 15; FSA PS 07/6, ch 13.
[178] MiFID Implementing Directive, Art 36.
[179] See FSA CP 06/20, para 15.7; FSA PS 07/6, para 13.9. For the scope of COBS 10, see COBS
10.1.1R–COBS 10.1.3R.

'Execution only' business

13.89 Where a firm claimed to act for a customer on an 'execution only' basis it was on the understanding that it was not required to carry out any investigation into the customer's personal and financial circumstances. Accordingly the stringent suit-abllility regime did not apply. However the FSA has always been suspicious of claims that transactions with private customers were 'execution only' and in COB issued guidance that even the provision of 'limited' advice will lift a transaction out of that category.[180] It is often claimed in mis-selling cases that advisers had acted on an execution only basis in deals arranged on behalf of ordinary, often unsophisticated, investors. Such claims were intended to relieve the adviser of the full rigour of the Conduct of Business Rules. However such claims have been treated with scepticism by the FOS and the courts.[181] It seems similar scepticism exists at European level, albeit in a more extreme form. One of the most important changes resulting from the introduction of MiFID is a severe reduction of the occasions on which a firm can deal on an execution only basis.[182]

13.90 The last vestiges of 'execution only' business derive from MiFID, Article 19(6) which permits services that 'only consist of execution and/or the reception and transmission of client orders' where all of four conditions are met:

(1) the services relate to 'non-complex financial instruments', which include shares traded on regulated markets, bonds and UCITS;[183]
(2) the service is provided at the initiative of the (potential) client;
(3) the (potential) client is warned (in a standardised format if preferred) that the suitability regime does not apply and the protection of the Conduct of Business Rules is inapplicable;
(4) the firm complies with the conflict of interest rules in MiFID, Article 18.[184]

These provisions are implemented by COBS 10.4,[185] with further provision, based on Recital 59 of the MiFID Implementing Directive, that the exercise need not be carried out where a course of dealings is undertaken, save on the first occasion,[186] and that clients who had undertaken such a course of dealing prior to 1 November 2007 can be presumed to have the necessary knowledge and experi-ence.[187] Given the novelty of the regime the FSA has provided further guidance on the appropriateness regime in COBS 10.5 and 10.6.

---

[180] See the previous guidance at COB 5.2.2G and COB 5.2.3G.
[181] See for example *Loosemore v Financial Concepts* [2001] Lloyd's Rep PN 235.
[182] FSA, 'Planning for MiFID' (November 2005), p 13.
[183] The definition is further developed in MiFID Implementing Directive, Art 38.
[184] MiFID, Art 19(6).
[185] COBS 10.4.1R.
[186] COBS 10.4.2R.
[187] COBS 10.4.3R.

Product information and explanation of risk

Preparing and providing product information to clients comprise respectively **13.91**
COBS 13 and COBS 14. The latter is also the location for the important rules on
clients' understanding of risk.[188] These rules supersede the old general rule about
customers' understanding of risk in COB 5.4, and the new regime covers products
such as SCARPs, albeit any product-specific warnings have been deleted. The new
regime is a more general requirement for the disclosure of risks affecting investments, based on an 'intelligent copy-out' of MiFID Implementing Directive,
Article 31.

COBS 14.3 applies to MiFID business and the following regulated activities **13.92**
when carried on for a retail client:

- making a personal recommendation about a designated investment;
- managing designated investments;
- arranging (bringing about) or executing a deal in a warrant or a derivative;
- engaging in stock lending activity.[189]

The principal rule provides: **13.93**

A firm must provide a client with a general description of the nature and risks of
designated investments, taking into account, in particular, the client's categorisation
as a retail client or a professional client. That description must:

(1) explain the nature of the specific type of designated investment concerned, as
    well as the risks particular to that specific type of designated investment, in suf-
    ficient detail to enable the client to take investment decisions on an informed
    basis; and
(2) include, where relevant to the specific type of designated investment concerned
    and the status and level of knowledge of the client, the following elements:
    (a) the risks associated with that type of designated investment including an
        explanation of leverage and its effects and the risk of losing the entire
        investment;
    (b) the volatility of the price of designated investments and any limitations on
        the available market for such investments;
    (c) the fact that an investor might assume, as a result of transactions in such
        designated investments, financial commitments and other additional obli-
        gations, including contingent liabilities, additional to the cost of acquiring
        the designated investments; and
    (d) any margin requirements or similar obligations, applicable to designated
        investments of that type.[190]

---

[188] For the background see: FSA CP 06/19 chs 18 and 19; FSA PS 07/6, chs 16 and 17; FSA PS
07/14, chs 6 and 7. On understanding of risk see FSA CP 06/19 paras 19.21–19.31; FSA PS 07/6,
ch 17.
[189] COBS 14.3.1R.
[190] COBS 14.3.2R. MiFID Implementing Directive, Art 31(1) and (2).See also COBS 14.3.4R
(two or more investments) and COBS 14.3.5R (third party guarantees) implementing the remainder of Art 31.

Usually the information must be provided 'in good time' before business is done.[191] Furthermore clients must be kept up to date with any material change in the information provided.[192]

13.94 COBS 16 provides further rules on reporting information to clients.[193]

Cancellation rights

13.95 The rules on the customer's right to cancel (where applicable) are now to be found in COBS 15.[194]

Specialist rules on pensions and with profits

13.96 Special rules are maintained with regard to pensions advice[195] and in relation to with profits policies.[196]

Case Law on Retail Investment Business

13.97 Whilst the overwhelming majority of consumer claims arising out of retail investment business have been resolved through the mechanisms of internal complaints-handling by firms or by the Financial Ombudsman Service and its predecessors, there have been a handful of significant decided cases, which provide important explorations of the applicable common law principles. It is noteworthy that these cases all concern non-linear relationships, where there is either an indirect loss suffered on the consumer side, or there are a number of parties on the industry side, and the respective responsibilities have to be explored.[197]

Gorham v British Telecommunications

13.98 Many financial products confer potential benefits upon persons other than the immediate recipient of the advice. This is especially so in respect of life insurance

---

[191] COBS 14.3.9R. MiFID Implementing Directive, Art 29(2) and (5).
[192] COBS 14.3.10R. MiFID Implementing Directive, Art 29(6).
[193] For the background see: FSA CP 06/20 ch 21; FSA PS 07/6, ch 19.
[194] For the background see: FSA CP 06/20 ch 20; FSA PS 07/6, ch 18.
[195] COBS 19. For the background see: FSA CP 06/20 ch 25; FSA PS 07/6, ch 22.
[196] COBS 20. For the background see: FSA CP 06/20 ch 24; FSA PS 07/6, ch 23.
[197] See also *Investors Compensation Scheme Ltd v West Bromwich Building Society* [1999] Lloyd's Rep PN 496, where a building society was held to be a joint tortfeasor with a firm of independent financial advisers in marketing unsuitable home income plans, and the initial skirmish in *Financial Services Compensation Scheme Ltd v Abbey National Treasury Services Ltd* [2008] EWHC 1897 (Ch), where it is alleged by the FSCS that Abbey collaborated in the development and production of SCARPS products.

and pension provision contracts. Accordingly the question is posed whether a duty is owed directly to the ultimate beneficiaries to take reasonable care in providing information or advice to the customer. Suppose a life company mis-sells a personal pension plan ('PPP') to an employee who was entitled to membership of an occupational pension scheme ('OPS') which was more suitable for his financial needs. The OPS included valuable benefits in the shape of a death-in-service benefit and spouse's pension which were not afforded by the PPP. This was the context of pension mis-selling.

In the House of Lords in *Lloyds TSB General Insurance Holdings v Lloyds Bank* **13.99**
Group Insurance Co Ltd[198] Lord Hoffmann observed:

> Whether it was in the interests of an employee to leave his employer's occupational scheme and commit his future to a personal scheme was often a difficult question. A fully informed decision required the employee to be aware of the respective risks, costs and benefits of the choices open to him. Much depended upon his personal and family circumstances. The LAUTRO Code of Conduct required a sales representative to make a detailed analysis in order to give the investor what was compendiously called 'best advice' on all relevant aspects of the decision. It imposed a positive duty upon the salesman (who was usually paid commission on the schemes which he sold) to advise the employee against giving up his rights under the occupational scheme unless he honestly thought it was in the employee's best interests to do so.[199]

Suppose further that the employee died before it was discovered that the life com- **13.100**
pany had proffered incorrect advice. In principle it seems appropriate that the life company should owe a direct duty to the employee's dependants who were the foreseeable victims if the company broke its duty with respect to the advice provided and that was acted upon by the employee. The analogy with the leading negligence case of *White v Jones*[200] appears irresistible.

In *Gorham v British Telecommunications plc*[201] the problem of what is sometimes **13.101**
described as transferred loss arose in the financial services context. An employee of BT was entitled to membership of that company's OPS. He was wrongly advised by Standard Life that he should not join that scheme and instead enter into a PPP. This he did. The OPS provided significantly better benefits in the event of the early death of the employee. Sadly this occurred, raising the question of whether the employee's widow and surviving children had any direct claim against the life company. The Court of Appeal unanimously held that a cause of action did vest

---

[198] [2003] UKHL 48.

[199] Para [4]. See similarly Lord Hobhouse at para [36].

[200] [1995] 2 AC 207 (HL): (solicitor liability to disappointed beneficiaries of negligently prepared will).

[201] [2000] 1 WLR 2129; noted G McMeel [2001] *LMCLQ* 321.

in the disappointed dependants, applying the principles in *White v Jones* by analogy. In the view of Pill LJ:

> [T]he present situation is identical to that in *White v Jones*. Mr Gorham intended to create a benefit for his wife and children in the event of his pre-deceasing them. Under the BT scheme they would benefit substantially in that event.[202]

13.102 The fact that there was a detailed regulatory scheme did not preclude the court from recognising a duty of care on general principles, given that the regulatory code was silent on the rights of beneficiaries. The detailed facts militated strongly in favour of this solution. The adviser had completed a fact find on behalf of both partners, and both signed it. The identified priorities for the couple made pre-eminent 'provision for family'. The possibility of life insurance for Mrs Gorham was canvassed, but not ultimately pursued.

13.103 Sir Murray Stuart-Smith was therefore prepared to go further:

> In a sense the case is even stronger than *White v Jones* because Mrs Gorham suffered a real loss; the premiums are paid out of what might be regarded as the family income, and her loss is a reduced pension. The beneficiary in *White v Jones* merely lost a windfall.[203]

Alone of the members of the Court of Appeal Sir Murray was concerned about problems posed where there might be a conflict of interest between the customer and his dependants. However he regarded these as borderline factual problems, which should not deter the court from recognising a claim in clear cases such as the instant one.

13.104 In contrast, Schiemann LJ saw no position of conflict: '[T]he assumption of responsibility to beneficiaries in cases such as the present does not operate to widen the scope of the duty but merely to widen the number of those who can sue in respect of any breach.'[204]

13.105 Some guidance can also be found in *Gorham v British Telecommunications plc*[205] on the relationship between the statutory rules and the common law. The Court of Appeal rejected a submission that the detailed statutory scheme for investor protection created by the Financial Services Act 1986 precluded the court from developing a common law tortious claim that went beyond the statutory code. Whilst primarily concerned with the existence of a duty of care for a third party

---

[202] ibid, 2140.
[203] ibid, 2144.
[204] ibid, 2146.
[205] [2000] 1 WLR 2129.

beneficiary, some of the observations made by the court also bear on the appropriate standard of liability. Pill LJ observed:

> Had Parliament not intervened, remedies for the abuses which existed in this field would almost certainly have been developed by the courts. The courts now do so in the context, and with the benefit of, rules and codes of practice laid down by those concerned with the maintenance of proper standards. The courts can be expected to attach considerable weight to the content of the codes drafted in these circumstances but are not excluded from making their own assessment of a situation.[206]

13.106 In the particular context of a dependants' claim the court was not bound by the Conduct of Business Rules, as they did not expressly address the question.

Seymour v Ockwell

13.107 The leading case in the financial services context on the duties owed by those other than the immediate adviser, such as product providers or intermediate distributors, is now the recent case of *Seymour v Caroline Ockwell & Co (a firm)*.[207] Mr and Mrs Seymour sold their family farm in Wiltshire yielding net proceeds of about £1.4 million. They were looking for a low risk temporary home for their money which could provide an income in the meantime as they intended to reinvest some of the proceeds into a new business within three years in order to benefit from rollover relief from capital gains tax ('CGT'). They approached a friend ('CO') who traded as a sole practitioner independent financial adviser, and who was also their accountant, for advice. CO in turn approached a representative of Zurich IFA Ltd ('ZIFA') (which was part of the Zurich/Allied Dunbar group) for help. ZIFA acted as a marketing wing, providing information to financial advisers about the group's products. Ultimately an investment of £500,000 was made by the Seymours in an investment comprising (a) a 'wrapper bond' life insurance product provided by an Allied Dunbar subsidiary in the Isle of Man which was recommended, and held within that wrapper (b) a fund operated by Imperial Consolidated (a company based in the Bahamas) called the 'Alpha + Fixed Income Fund' ('the Fund'). Imperial Consolidated and the Fund collapsed amid allegations of fraud causing the Seymours (and many other UK and overeas investors) to lose all their money. It is a significant feature of the case that the Seymours were not privy to the communications between the ZIFA representative and CO, and they did not know of these exchanges.[208] At one meeting the ZIFA representative gave to CO a brochure prepared by Imperial Consolidated in relation to the Fund and said that the Fund could be held in the Allied Dunbar wrapper bond. The key

---

[206] ibid, 2141.
[207] [2005] EWHC 1137 (QB), [2005] PNLR 758 (Bristol Mercantile Court).
[208] ibid, para [145].

feature of the Fund was said to be that it offered 100 per cent guaranteed capital with guaranteed annual return of 15 per cent. Two oral representations were held to have been made by the ZIFA representative to CO. First, in response to a specific question by CO as to the status of Imperial Consolidated it was stated that ZIFA or a Zurich group company would have 'gone through their books'. Secondly, that the Fund was being 'marketed by Imperial Consolidated as a low risk fund'. [209] Whilst CO did her own research, including contacting a representative of the Fund, in substance those representations were repeated to the Seymours. At the time that the Seymours were completing their investment, and during a 'cooling off period', doubts were circulating about Imperial Consolidated. An internal Zurich memorandum dated 15 January 2001 stated that there were causes for concern and that no new business should be transacted with Imperial Consolidated.[210] This was never communicated to either CO or the Seymours. The judge held that had CO seen the memorandum she would have taken steps and that had the Seymours seen it they would have reversed their investment.[211] In July 2002 Imperial Consolidated collapsed and the Seymours lost the whole of their investment in the Fund.

13.108 First, the Seymours brought claims against the IFA and CO, as First Defendant, for negligence and breaches of sections 62 and 76 of the Financial Services Act 1986 ('the 1986 Act.'). Secondly, the Seymours added a claim against ZIFA as Second Defendant for negligence and also for breach of section 76 of the 1986 Act. Thirdly, CO claimed under CPR Part 20 against ZIFA for an indemnity in the event of her being held liable to the Seymours (or for contribution in the event of their both being liable to the Seymours). In the outcome in the first claim CO was held to be negligent and in breach of sections 62 and 76 of the 1986 Act and therefore liable for the full value of the Seymours' lost investment. The Seymours were unsuccessful in their argument that ZIFA owed them a direct duty of care, and also in the argument based on section 76 of the 1986 Act, which generally prohibited the promotion of unregulated collective investment schemes. In the Part 20 claim CO was successful in arguing that ZIFA should indemnify her to the extent of 66% of the lost capital claim by the Seymours.

13.109 HHJ Havelock-Allen QC treated the allegation that ZIFA, as in effect 'product provider',[212] owed a duty of care directly to the Seymours as investors as an instance of a novel duty of care situation, and refused to take the step of imposing such a

---

[209] ibid, para [24]. There was a conflict of evidence. CO understood ZIFA were saying the Fund was low risk. The judge accepted the ZIFA representative's evidence but added: 'the distinction would in all probability have been lost on Miss Ockwell'.

[210] ibid, paras [51]–[52].

[211] ibid, para [54].

[212] ibid, paras [30] and [152].

duty which would cut across contractual and statutory responsibilities. With regard to the claim by CO against ZIFA

HHJ Havelock-Allen QC held:

> It is unprofitable to consider whether the positive misstatements made by Mrs Clarke [the ZIFA representative] constituted advice or information. I am quite satisfied that Mrs Clarke owed a duty of care in making them . . . In my judgment the three important statements about risk and investor protection were made negligently and ZIFA is liable to Miss Ockwell for the consequences of that negligence.[213]

Further there was a continuing duty to provide the IFA with information about the investment in certain circumstances:

13.110

> . . . there are undoubtedly circumstances where a duty to speak does arise and where a failure to do so can and does give rise to liability. The obvious circumstance is where something has been previously said or done which, if not corrected or qualified in the light of subsequent information or events, may appear false or misleading. If the original statement was in the nature of a continuing representation, in the sense of being one which was still likely to be relied upon by the representee, the representor is under a duty to speak and to correct information which will become false or misleading if he remains silent.[214]

The 'unexplained failure' to communicate the contents of ZIFA's 15 January 2001 memorandum to CO whilst the Seymours were still in the 'cooling off' period was an 'exemplar of circumstances which gave rise to a duty to speak' and there was accordingly a further breach. CO was entitled to know in those circumstances that ZIFA had information that the Fund was no longer regarded as low risk and suitable for inclusion within the Allied Dunbar wrapper bond. Accordingly on the particular facts of that case the responsibility of provider and adviser was split 66 per cent to 33 per cent.

13.111

Walker v Scottish Equitable

The case of *Seymour v Ockwell* can be usefully contrasted with the recent decision of *Walker v Inter-Alliance Group plc (in administration) and Scottish Equitable plc*.[215] Whilst in the former case there was no allegation that the investors met or had any direct dealings with the product provider's representatives, in the latter a representative of Scottish Equitable ('SE') attended the crucial meetings alongside the IFA and was ultimately held to have provided investment advice direct to the underlying client.

13.112

Mr Walker had been a director and senior manager of a major construction company, and a member of its defined benefits occupational pension scheme ('OPS'),

13.113

---

213 ibid, para [153].
214 ibid, para [155].
215 [2007] EWHC 1858 (Ch).

which would have entitled him, after many years' service, to: a pension based on two-thirds of his final salary; an inflation-linked pension; a five-year guarantee in the event of early death; and a 50 per cent widow's pension. Nevertheless following meetings attended by both his IFA (a representative of the First Defendant) and a representative of SE, Mr Walker executed a pension transfer in the sum of £1.2 million to an SE product, called 'Retirement Control', which was a deferred phased retirement and income drawdown scheme. Whilst the SE scheme was more flexible, it was not guaranteed and it was a money purchase scheme which depended on the future performance of underlying investment funds.

13.114   Mr Boakes was the representative of SE who attended the meetings, initially in 1999, and later in January 2001, when Mr Walker actually retired. Mr Boakes was a broker consultant who was described as a 'retirement options specialist'. Nevertheless at trial it was common ground that Mr Boakes was prohibited both by the regulatory code and by SE's own compliance manual from proffering any investment advice at the meetings which he attended.

13.115   Subsequently, dissatisfied with the SE product, Mr Walker initiated proceedings against the IFA for breach of contract and negligence and against SE for breach of statutory duty (section 62 of the Financial Services Act 1986) and negligence. The IFA went into administration and the trial was solely concerned with the liability of SE, the Second Defendant. Mr Walker complained about maladministration of the SE product and about the performance of the SE investment manager. However his principal contention was that he should never have been advised to effect the pension transfer in the first place. The SE scheme was fundamentally unsuitable for someone with his cautious attitude to risk. In contrast, as Henderson J recorded: 'With the benefit of hindsight the Taylor Woodrow [Mr Walker's employers] scheme represents the gold standard of pension provision that is unlikely to be matched, let alone surpassed, in the foreseeable future.'[216]

13.116   SE's defence was that no advice was ever proffered by its representative and the decision is largely fact- and evidence-based. There was no dispute in principle that if advice was proffered it would have been a breach by SE's representative of the requirement not to provide investment advice, because it offended the policy of polarisation.[217] SE could, of course, have chosen to give advice on its own products, but had decided not to employ a direct sales force, so accordingly none of its representatives were authorised to provide investment advice.[218] It could be added that the joint representations of IFA and life office representative would have

---

[216]   ibid, para [6].

[217]   ibid, para [18]: citing PIA Rule 1.2.2(5)(a) requiring members not to exceed the business for which the PIA had granted authorisation. See also para [20]: citing breach of PIA rules 4.2.1 and 4.2.4.

[218]   ibid, para [25].

offended the regulatory policy in any event given that a representative of one firm would have been operating in tandem with a supposedly independent adviser.

Overall the Judge preferred the factual evidence of Mr Walker as to what happened **13.117** in the meetings. He commented that: 'Mr Boakes' attitude to compliance matters was at times rather cavalier.'[219] Henderson J recorded that the issue for him to decide was whether SE through its representative gave investment advice within the meaning of the Financial Services Act 1986, Schedule 1 paragraph 15 at the meetings which he attended. The judge decided that Mr Boakes' repeated statements of what he would do in the situation of Mr Walker was investment advice.[220] Furthermore, he was satisfied that the SE representative had in fact taken the lead in the meetings in explaining the relative merits of the OPS and SE's income drawdown scheme. Henderson J rejected a submission that the statements were too vague or ambiguous to constitute investment advice. Henderson J stated:

> It seems to me that the concept of investment advice is broad enough to include any communication with the client which, in the particular context in which it is given, goes beyond the mere provision of information and is objectively likely to influence the client's decision whether or not to undertake the transaction in question. If that, or something like it, is the correct test, I have no doubt that Mr Boakes' statements to Mr Walker constituted investment advice, even if the precise words that he used cannot now be reconstructed.[221]

On causation, Henderson J was also satisfied that if Mr Boakes had not so advised, **13.118** Mr Walker would have remained a member of the OPS.[222]

Retail Distribution Review

Over the last few years the FSA has been examining the retail investment industry **13.119** and its modes of delivering its products and services to consumers as part of the Retail Distribution Review ('RDR').[223] One starting-part for the review was concern over how the regulatory framework placed the responsibility for advice squarely on the shoulders of the direct or immediate adviser. However it was obvious that there had been repeated failures by small, often small high street, financial advisers to deliver in practice the high standards laid down. Until recently save where a direct sales force or appointed representatives have been employed, product providers, which are often substantial organisations responsible for product

---

[219] ibid, para [72].

[220] ibid, para [96].

[221] ibid, para [97]. That is somewhat broader than the statutory definition of investment advice which is limited to advice on a 'particular investment': Regulated Activities Order 2001, art 53.

[222] ibid, para [104].

[223] FSA DP 07/1, 'A Review of Retail Distribution' (June 2007).

design and marketing, have largely been able to absolve themselves from the consequences of the delivery of unsatisfactory products at high street level from an IFA supposedly at arm's length from the provider. In the light of *Seymour v Caroline Ockwell & Co (a firm)*[224] (discussed above) the respective responsibilities of product providers and intermediaries were reviewed by the FSA issues as part of its Treating Customers Fairly ('TCF') theme-based work.[225] In a speech in September 2005 by John Tiner, then FSA Chief Executive, he stated:

> Over the next year we will be carrying out further analysis to clarify the division of responsibilities between product producers and product distributors. In particular, we will consider the implications of the High Court case, Seymour vs. Ockwell, in which it was held that a marketing company must share liability to the end consumer with an adviser. We will review the extent to which product providers can abrogate their responsibility for products, particularly when their performance may be highly susceptible to variability in different market environments. Irrespective of the outcome of this analysis, firms would be well advised to think carefully about different advisers' abilities [to] understand and explain product features. Time taken to consider properly the distribution of products by their manufacturers will go a long way towards mitigating the risk of the products ending up in the hands of consumers for whom they are not suitable.[226]

13.120 This led in part to a new Regulatory Guide giving an indication of regulatory expectations in respect of the Responsibilities of Providers and Distributors for the Fair Treatment of Customers, ('RPPD'), issued as guidance under section 157 of the 2000 Act.

13.121 In June 2007 the principal Discussion Paper on the RDR was published,[227] and it was originally intended to provide full feedback in October 2008. However in August 2008[228] the FSA announced that it would be November 2008 before any full feedback statement would be published, principally in the wake of the appointment of Jon Pain as managing director of retail markets at the FSA. It can also be observed that the original Discussion Paper attracted some 888 responses, and obviously prompted some significant further thinking at the FSA, as evidenced by an Interim Report,[229] which is the most up-to-date perspective available at the time of writing. The original Discussion Paper pointed out that although the retail investment sector had been regulated for two decades numerous features of the industry—complex charging structures, heavy reliance of commission-based advisers, poor quality advice going undetected for many years, and the limited

---

[224] [2005] EWHC 1137 (QB), [2005] PNLR 758 (Bristol Mercantile Court).

[225] See generally FSA, 'Treating customers fairly—building on progress' (July 2005).

[226] FSA SP 'Asset management: current challenges and the hedge funds debate' (19 September 2005). See also FSA, 'Treating customers fairly—building on progress' (July 2005), para 6.16.

[227] FSA DP 07/1, 'A Review of Retail Distribution' (June 2007).

[228] FSA Press Release, 7 August 2008.

[229] FSA, 'Retail Distribution Review—Interim Report' (April 2008).

training of advisers—suggested an inefficient market. It favoured, effectively, a class-based system of 'professional financial planning' for high-income consumers and more basic 'primary advice' for the rest. The latter regime might include a watering-down of the suitability regime.[230] It was not difficult to foresee that both European standards required by MiFID and other Directives, not to say the common law standard of care, might pose obstacles for this project.[231]

In April 2008 the Interim Report,[232] perhaps driven by the relatively large con- **13.122** sultative response (presumably industry-led[233]), the FSA conceded that there was a consensus amongst respondents that its original proposals were too complex and appeared sympathetic to consultees' calls for a 'simpler landscape' with a clear distinction between 'advice' and 'sales'. It now favoured only one species of adviser, coupled with a 'step-change in the standards required of advisers'. All would be independent, whole of market advisers whose remuneration was set without product provider input. Professional or educational standards would be increased. In contrast, 'sales' would be strictly non-advised, in the form of either execution only or guided sales in the context of wider government initiatives to promote more saving and investment. Again it is easy to foresee significant obstacles ahead of this anticipated terrain, from both European and domestic legal constraints. Furthermore, the long-standing lack of clarity in the consumer financial services context between giving advice and providing information does not look capable of swift resolution,[234] and the widespread incidence of supposedly 'execution only' transactions in the earlier pensions and endowment mis-sales episodes should not be forgotten. In addition, in this Interim Report, as a first step, the FSA exhorts product providers to drop out of their traditional role of remunerating advisers, and regulated firms generally are prodded in the direction of common professional standards. As indicated above, it will be near the end of 2008 before the FSA provides full feedback,[235] and further into the future before any steps are taken to implement the RDR.

---

[230] FSA DP 07/1, 'A Review of Retail Distribution' (June 2007), para 22.

[231] FSA DP 07/1, 'A Review of Retail Distribution' (June 2007), paras 5.32 to 5.35.

[232] FSA, 'Retail Distribution Review—Interim Report' (April 2008).

[233] As suggested by calls for a 'long stop' limitation period for complaints, a well-known industry concern brought into sharp relief by the endowment mortgage complaints saga.

[234] FSA, 'Retail Distribution Review—Interim Report' (April 2008), para 4.9.

[235] FSA Press Release, 7 August 2008.

14

BANKS AND BANKING

Introduction

Banks are subject to the new integrated regulatory regime under FSMA. While **14.01** much of this reflected the earlier supervisory practice applied by the Bank of England under the Banking Acts 1979 and 1987, a number of substantial new initiatives have been developed over time. Banks operating in the UK are required to be authorised (FSMA, section 19(1)) and hold permission to carry on deposit taking business (FSMA, section 21(1) and Schedule 2). Responsibility for banking supervision was transferred from the Bank of England to the FSA under the Bank of England Act 1998 (section 21(a)) in summer 1998 (N1). The FSA also assumed responsibility for building societies and other financial institutions under FSMA with effect from 1 December 2001 (N2). Both banking and building society business now fall within the definition of deposit-taking which is included as a regulated activity for the purposes of FSMA (FSMA, section 22 and Schedule 2). The effect of this has been to extend the earlier definition of investment business as set out in Schedule 1 to the Financial Services Act 1986 to include deposit taking (as well as insurance business and Lloyd's of London syndicates) as regulated activities for the purposes of FSMA.

The statutory regime for the regulation of banks and banking business had been **14.02** introduced under the Banking Act 1979 which gave effect to the requirement in the European First Banking Directive for all Member countries to establish a formal system of authorisation and supervision for banking business. The original provisions set out in the 1979 Act were subsequently amended in 1987 following a government White Paper into the conduct of banking supervision by the Bank of England. The regime was further amended during the early 1990s following the collapse of BCCI and then Barings. This resulted in the production of a new consolidated Guide to Supervisory Policy which restated all of the earlier Bank of England non-statutory papers that applied to banking activity and bank supervision. Following the conferral of full operational and policy autonomy with regard to the conduct of monetary policy on the Bank of England in 1997, it was decided to transfer bank supervision to the FSA. This was considered necessary to avoid any future crises, such as in connection with BCCI and Barings, which could potentially undermine the ability or credibility of the Bank in the conduct of its monetary activities. It was only following the decision to transfer bank supervision to the FSA that the new integrated regulatory regime was extended to include all other key financial sectors and markets within the UK in addition to banking and investment services.[1] A number of further amendments have also been proposed more recently following the liquidity crisis at Northern Rock and its subsequent acquisition by the Treasury in February 2008.[2]

14.03 Building societies are regulated in a parallel manner due to the common deposit taking function involved.[3] Building society supervision was conducted by the Building Societies Commission under the Building Societies Act 1986. This provided for a parallel regime to that set up under the Banking Act 1987, although adjusted to reflect the property secured nature of the main lending conducted. The provisions set out in the Building Societies Commission rule book were continued on an interim basis following N2 under the Interim Prudential Sourcebook for building societies ('IPRU(BSOC)') with most of these provisions being replaced by the new integrated general provisions in GENPRU and prudential requirements for deposit-taking institutions (banks and building societies) and investment firms in BIPRU.[4] The earlier constitutional provisions contained in IPRU(BSOC) have been moved to a new Building Societies Regulatory Guide ('BSOG'). The earlier liquidity provisions on mismatch liquidity ('LM') and sterling stock liquidity ('LS') contained in volume 2 of IPRU(BANK) will be continued on an interim basis pending further revision following the most recent credit crisis.

14.04 As regulated entities, banks (and building societies) have to comply with all relevant provisions set out in the FSA's Handbook of Rules and Guidance. These include the general standards set out in Block 1 including, in particular, the Principles for Businesses ('PRIN'), the senior management arrangements, systems and controls ('SYCS'), the threshold conditions ('COND'), the statements of principle for approved persons ('FIT'), and the code of conduct for approved persons ('APER'). They previously had to comply with the interim prudential measures for banks ('IPRU(BANK)' and building societies 'IPRU(BSOC)') although these have now been replaced by the new rules contained in the restructured Prudential Standards Block 2 of the Handbook including General Application and Group Risk requirements ('GENPRU') and Banking and Investment Firms ('BIPRU'). They are also subject to the requirements on money laundering which were set out in a separate sourcebook ('ML') but are now dealt

---

[1] Chapter 1, paras 1.08–1.10.
[2] Chapter 1, paras 1.151–1.180; and paras 14.22–14.24 and 14.220–14.240.
[3] Chapter 15.
[4] Paras 14.141–14.183 and 14.184–14.219 and Chapter 11.

with under the revised provisions in SYSC and the three sets of process provisions previously contained in Authorisation ('AUTH'), Supervision ('SUP'), and Enforcement ('ENF'). Banks now use one of the portals in the separate 'application pack' section of the website replacing AUTH with ENF having been superseded by the Enforcement Guide ('EG') in the new final 9 of the Handbook.[5] Banks are also now subject to the new Supervisory Enhancement Programme ('SEP') set up following the Northern Rock crisis.[6] The integrated redress provisions set out in Block 5 will also apply including Complaints ('DISP') and Compensation ('COMP') with the right to make complaints against the FSA ('COAF'). They may also be subject to some of the other more particular sourcebooks to the extent relevant such as administering collective investment schemes ('COLL' which replaced 'CIS').

While it had been intended to bring the new single Prudential Sourcebook ('PRU') **14.05** into effect during 2005, this was not possible due to the extended consultation required on the revised capital standards produced by the Basel Committee on Banking Supervision under its new Capital Accord (Basel II) and parallel European measures under the Capital Requirements Directive ('CRD'). These replace the earlier rules set out in the 1988 Capital Accord (Basel I) and European Own Funds Directive and Solvency Ratio Directive for banks and Capital Adequacy Directive for securities firms.[7] Basel II and the CRD create a new framework for calculating credit risk capital cover based on the three pillars of revised minimum standards, supervisory review, and enhanced market discipline. The European measures were to be implemented in the UK under the final provisions set out in the PRU although the PRU has since been replaced by a number of separate sub-sourcebooks which include in the banking area General Application and Group Risk requirements ('GENPRU') and Banking and Investment Firms ('BIPRU').[8]

The extended regime for banks and building societies also includes measures **14.06** adopted with regard to mortgage advice and general insurance sales.[9] These were not transferred to the FSA directly as with its other functions but represent new or extended regulatory areas considered necessary to protect the interests of consumers. The Government had announced that the FSA would be required to adopt measures in connection with the provision of mortgage advice and general insurance sales and that these will fall within the scope of the new regime set up under FSMA. The new requirements have since been included within a new Conduct of Business Sourcebook and additional special Handbook Guides in the revised

---

[5] Paras 14.45 and 14.71–14.74 and Chapter 6.
[6] Paras 14.86 and 14.230.
[7] Paras 14.184–14.190 and 14.191–14.219.
[8] Paras 14.184–14.190 and 14.191–14.219.
[9] Chapters 15 and 16.

Block 8 of the FSA's Handbook of Rules and Guidance.[10] These new regimes came into effect in October 2004 and January 2005 (N3). The responsibilities of the FSA have been further extended to cover all personal pension schemes including self-invested personal pensions ('SIPPS') from April 2007 and connected travel insurance ('CTI') which is sold with holiday or other related travel firms and holiday providers from 1 January 2009.[11] All of this represents a further extension and refinement of the integrated regulatory regime for financial services and markets set up under FSMA in the UK.

14.07   The purpose of this chapter is to consider the background to and development of UK banking supervision. The traditional nature of bank supervision and the role and function of the Bank of England are reviewed. Earlier and more recent crises in UK banking markets are noted and the circumstances surrounding the transfer of responsibility for bank supervision from the Bank to the FSA referred to. The main provisions contained in the Bank of England Act 1998 are outlined. The relevant sections of FSMA are then considered in further detail with the principal parts of the FSA's Handbook of Rules and Guidance that are relevant to banks. This includes, in particular, the Supervision manual ('SUP') and earlier Interim Prudential Sourcebook for banks ('IPRU(BANK)') as well as the final measures contained in General Application and Group Risk requirements ('GENPRU') and Banking and Investment Firms ('BIPRU') as part of the single Integrated Sourcebook. Relevant supporting international and European bank measures are also referred to. The circumstances surrounding the forced assistance of Northern Rock and its subsequent acquisition by the Treasury as well the principal regulatory lessons to be learnt in the banking area are also assessed. Building societies and mortgage regulation as well as insurance sales are dealt with the following Chapters 15 and 16.

UK Banking Supervision

14.08   UK bank supervision has traditionally been conducted on an informal basis. Historically, bank supervision refers to the general oversight of the banking and financial markets in the UK as conducted by the Bank of England as one part of its more general central bank functions. Supervision can be distinguished from regulation which refers to the imposition of specific legal, secondary, or

---

[10] These consist of the Mortgages and Home Finance Conduct of Business Sourcebook ('MCOB') in Block 3 and Handbook Guides in Block 8 on Small Mortgage and Insurance Intermediaries General Rules (('MIGI'), Mortgage Intermediaries ('MOGI'), and Insurance Intermediaries ('GIGI')).

[11] Chapter 1, para 1.113 and Chapter 11.

administrative obligations on financial institutions.[12] Formal statutory regulation was only introduced in the UK under the Banking Act 1979 following the UK's accession to the then European Economic Community (EEC) and the coming into effect of the 1977 First Banking Directive in 1979.

Bank of England

A formal statutory framework for the regulation of the banking markets was only **14.09** created in 1979. Until then, the Bank of England had monitored the efficiency and stability of the banking and financial markets in the UK on an informal basis.[13] Bank supervision was, in particular, regarded as a necessary part of the lender of last resort support role within the financial system.[14] The Bank would manage the amount of liquidity in the banking system on a daily basis especially through its operations in the primary money market (or discount market) and provide emergency assistance to particular institutions in the event that credit or other financial difficulties arose.

This lender of last resort role is regarded as being particularly necessary in the bank- **14.10** ing sector due to the inherently unstable nature of the financial risks involved with banks funding medium to long-term loans through sight or demand deposits. This creates an essential maturity mismatch or maturity transformation within the banking system. Banks maintain a necessary reserve of approximately one third of their deposit base in a liquid form to cover possible withdrawal demands. In the event that this is exhausted due to unexpected withdrawals or a run on the bank, it will have to obtain funds from other financial institutions failing which it will approach the central bank for emergency assistance. The Bank of England's lender of last resort role was confirmed at the end of the nineteenth century following the first Barings crisis in 1890.

While the Bank of England has informally monitored the daily operations of the **14.11** markets, this process had become more structured as its ability to collect statistical and reporting information from banks has evolved during the twentieth century. The collection of increasingly detailed data in connection with all of the main activities of banks allowed the Bank to monitor market activity on an increasingly more sophisticated and accurate basis. The collection of market information was

---

[12] GA Walker, *International Banking Regulation—Law, Policy and Practice* (2001) Introduction (n 1).

[13] H Thornton, *An Enquiry into the Nature and Effects of the Paper Credit of Great Britain* (1802); and W Bagehot, *Lombard Street* (1873). On the history of the Bank of England, see, W Marston Acres, *The Bank of England from Within* (1931); Sir John Clapham, *The Bank of England 1797–1914* (1944); RS Sayers, *The Bank of England 1891–1944* (1976); and J Fforde, *The Bank of England and Public Policy 1941–1958* (1992).

[14] GA Walker (n 12 above), ch 3 (n 51).

then supplemented through formal and informal meetings and contact with senior bank staff, with the Bank being able to advise institutions on an individual basis of any concerns that arose and to issuance guidance or recommendations as appropriate. This process of informal direction given by the Bank to particular institutions came to be known to as 'moral suasion'.[15] This, in particular, referred to the market or moral authority of the Bank which historically commanded sufficient weight that individual institutions would always act on any recommendations or directions made. The supporting or implied threat was always, of course, that daily liquidity assistance or emergency support may be withheld in the event that a bank failed to comply with the directions given.

Overseas banks and secondary banking crisis

14.12 The non-statutory based nature of the system of bank supervision that emerged was characterised by the personal contact, flexibility, and judgement or discretion-based nature of the oversight exercised and with the most minimum and then only implied threat of sanction. This system proved sufficiently effective to allow the Bank of England to monitor and control the London and UK markets until the early 1970s.

14.13 The informal and individual contact nature of this system began to break down with the large influx of overseas banks into London during the end of the 1960s and early 1970s. By 1973 and 1974, the Bank was forced to reconsider the nature of its traditional supervisory function and activities. Following a crisis in the secondary banking markets in 1972 and 1973, the Bank had to organise a 'lifeboat' operation to support a number of financial institutions that were threatened with closure.

14.14 Following this, the Bank set up the first formal Banking Supervision Department rather than continue with this function being carried on by the Discount Office. A formal prudential (rather than purely statistical) return was introduced to allow Bank staff to assess individual banks' capital and financial positions more accurately. While bank supervision was already becoming a more formal process within the Bank, the need to establish a formal licensing or authorisation system only became necessary with the coming into effect of the European First Banking Directive in 1979 which required that a formal licensing system was a set up. The Banking Act 1979 was accordingly enacted to establish a statutory framework for bank supervision within the UK, although much of the traditional nature

---

[15] JJ Norton, 'The Bank of England's Lament: the Struggle to Maintain the Traditional Supervisory Practices of "Moral Suasion"' in Norton (ed), *Bank Regulation and Supervision in the 1990s* (1991), ch 2; and G Penn and Wadstone, *Banking Supervision* (2000), ch 1.

of the earlier informal practices developed by the Bank of England was continued in connection with the daily operation of the supervision conducted.

Banking Act 1979

The Banking Act 1979 introduced a formal definition of deposit taking business **14.15** and imposed a general prohibition on the conduct of such activities unless licensed to do so under the Act. A general distinction was nevertheless drawn between recognised banks and licensed deposit-takers. This reflected the perceived market or reputational distinction that existed between the larger more established banks and new lending institutions that had grown up during the late 1960s and 1970s. The Bank was given legal power to issue and to restrict bank licences and to issue directions as well as to require information to be provided by banks and to conduct investigations as required. Controls were introduced on the use of banking names and descriptions. A formal appeals procedure was created and provision included for the establishment of a deposit protection support scheme. Statutory restrictions were placed on the exchange of confidential information except under prescribed channels (or gateways).

As part of this new more formal supervisory process and in response to the changes **14.16** that were taking place within the banking markets, the Bank of England issued a number of supervisory papers during the late 1970s and 1980s on such matters as foreign exchange currency management, capital adequacy, and liquidity. The objective was to attempt to identify relevant best market practice in each of these areas at that time and to set this out in the form of recommended guidelines with which banks would be expected to comply. There was no legal obligation imposed on banks to comply with these measures as such, although the Bank had power to restrict or revoke a licence where they failed to continue to satisfy the threshold conditions set out in Schedule 2 to the Banking Act (then Schedule 3 to the 1987 Act and now Schedule 6 to FSMA).

Johnson Matthey and the Banking Act 1987

Despite the improvements adopted in the conduct of supervisory practice, the **14.17** Bank's intervention in the markets was questioned especially following the Johnson Matthey crisis in autumn 1984. The Bank was again compelled to rescue a major financial institution through the provision of a £150 million guarantee to Johnson Matthey. The shares in Johnson Matthey were also purchased which effectively nationalised the institution. The Bank of England had insisted that the intervention was necessary to avoid a potential threat to the stability of the markets as Johnson Matthey was involved in the daily fixing of the price of gold within the London gold market.

14.18 Following a further government White Paper, the Banking 1987 was enacted.[16] This abolished the earlier two-tier system of recognition for banks and licensed deposit-takers and strengthened the authorisation criteria set out in Schedule 3 to the Act. The powers of the Bank to revoke or restrict licences and issue directions were revised and a new Board of Banking Supervision established. The role of auditors was strengthened to investigate and confirm the accuracy and validity of prudential information provided and systems and controls maintained within banks, as well as to report suspicious transactions to the Bank.

BCCI and Barings

14.19 Further steps were again taken to improve the conduct of UK bank supervision following the collapse of the Bank of Credit and Commerce International ('BCCI') in July 1991.[17] BCCI had been closed in a coordinated response arranged between all of the major supervisory authorities in the countries within which it operated. The closure was led by the Bank of England following the confirmation of fraud in the UK. Although no statutory changes to bank supervision were given effect to, a number of internal corrections were adopted at the time by the Bank.

14.20 The nature of the supervision effected was further reconsidered following the collapse of Barings in February 1995.[18] Barings had to be purchased by ING after it had suffered £650 million of trading losses through the activities of a financial derivatives subsidiary in Singapore under the management of Nick Leeson. Following the scandal, a report was commissioned by the Bank of England from Arthur Andersen which made a number of recommendations that were given full effect to by the Bank.[19] These included the adoption of a new supervision by risk framework referred to as RATE (Risk Assessment, Tools of Supervision, Evaluation).[20] All of the Bank's earlier supervisory papers were restated in a consolidated Guide to Supervisory Policy which was issued in two volumes in 1998. The function and structure of the Bank of England more generally was considered by a Treasury and Civil Service Select Committee report in 1993/1994.

---

[16] 'Banking Supervision' (Cmnd 9695) of 17 December 1985. See also 'Report of the Committee Set up to Consider the Question of Banking Supervision' (Cmnd 9550, 1985).

[17] Lord Justice Bingham, 'Inquiry into the Supervision of the Bank of Credit and Commerce International' (22 October 1992).

[18] Board of Banking Supervision, 'Inquiry into the circumstances of the Collapse of Barings', HC (1994–95) 673.

[19] Arthur Andersen, 'Findings and Recommendations of the review of Supervision and Surveillance' (July 1996).

[20] Bank of England, 'A Risk Based Approach to Supervision (the RATE framework)' (March 1997); 'A Risk Based Approach to the Supervision of Non-EEA Banks (the SCALE framework)' (July 1997); and 'A Risk Based Approach to Supervising Foreign Exchange and Other Market Risks' (July 1997). See 'Bank of England, A Risk Based Approach to Bank Supervision (the RATE Framework)' (May 1998).

The internal organisation of the Bank was subsequently then divided into a separate Monetary Stability wing and Financial Stability wing in July 1994.[21]

Responsibility for bank supervision was then formally transferred from the Bank **14.21** of England to the FSA under the Bank of England Act 1998. This was considered necessary partly to insulate the conduct of monetary policy by the Bank from potential difficulties arising in the conduct of bank supervision and, in particular, the possibility of further crises such as with BCCI or more recently Barings. While the Bank of England had historically always claimed that it considered it necessary to maintain an essential link between bank supervision and the provision of lender of last resort support to the financial system, this policy was reversed following the conferral of full policy and operational autonomy in respect of the conduct of monetary policy on the Bank. Bank supervision was then to be conducted by the FSA under the Banking Act 1987 between the coming into effect of the Bank of England Act 1998 in summer 1998 ('N1') and the coming into effect of FSMA in December 2001 ('N2'). Since then, deposit taking has been included as a regulated activity for the purposes of FSMA and banking included within the new integrated regulatory regime created under the Act.

Northern Rock

The most significant recent event in UK banking was the liquidity crisis faced **14.22** by Northern Rock and its subsequent acquisition by the Treasury in February 2008. Northern Rock was forced to approach the Bank of England for financial assistance following the drying up of credit on national and international inter-bank markets in August 2007. The public announcement of these difficulties led to the first major run on a UK financial institution since Overend Gurney in 1866.[22] Northern Rock was nevertheless solvent and backed by a Bank of England facility and the Financial Services Compensation Scheme (FSCS) although depositors were still concerned with the delays that may arise in obtaining funds and possible limits on recovery after the first £31,700 and then £35,000.[23]

---

[21] Treasury and Civil Service Select Committee Report: 'The Role of the Bank of England', HC (1993–94) 98; and 'Reorganisation of the Bank of England' Press Notice, July 1994.

[22] GA Walker, 'Northern Rock Falls' (2008) *Bankers' Law*, Vol 2, No 2, 4–12. See also GA Walker, 'The Deconstruction of Financial Risk' (2008) *Palgrave Journal of Banking Regulation* (October) 1, 2; and GA Walker, 'Credit Crisis—Regulatory and Financial Systems Reform' (2007) *Butterworths JIBL* (November) 567–72; and GA Walker, 'Sub-prime Loans, Inter-Bank Markets and Financial Support' (2007) *The Company Lawyer* (November) 22–5. See also Walker, 'Credit Contraction, Financial Collapse and Global Recession' *Butterworths JIBL* (January 2009) 5–10; and Walker, 'Credit Crisis, Bretton Woods II and A New Global Response' *Butterworths JIBL* (February 2009). See Chapter 1, paras 1.151–1.180.

[23] Eligible claimants were entitled under the FSA's compensation sourcebook COMP managed by the FSCS up to £31,700 being 100% of the first £2,000 and 90% of the following £33,000 in each account. This was subsequently raised to 100% of the first £35,000 of each claim with effect

14.23 After a series of unsuccessful private bids to acquire Northern Rock which included a preferred bid by the Virgin Group, the bank was taken into public control under the Banking (Special Provisions) Act 2008 which was enacted for this purpose on 21 February 2008. The Act allows the Treasury to make orders relating to the transfer of securities issued by an authorised deposit-taking institution (or a building society) as well as with regard to the property, rights, and liabilities of such an institution.[24] A number of other official reports have also been issued in this area and, in particular, by the key Tripartite Authorities—the FSA, the Treasury, and the Bank of England—which attempt to identify the principal regulatory lessons to be learned from the crisis and to make necessary revisions to the current statutory framework and supervisory practice.[25] Implementing legislation was expected in October 2008 with a new Banking Bill that would, inter alia, replace the temporary provisions contained in the Banking (Special Provisions) Act 2008. The difficulties at Northern Rock nevertheless only represented one part of the larger damage caused by the credit crisis in global markets following the original sub-prime mortgage scandal in the US.[26]

14.24 The initial credit contraction in the money markets beginning in August 2007 then erupted into a full financial crisis during September 2008. This followed the announced losses at the giant US mortgage providers Federal National Mortgage Association ('Fannie Mae') and Federal Home Loan Mortgage Corporation ('Freddie Mac') and the decision by the US Treasury to provide over US$85bn in support for the troubled lenders as well as to bail out the largest insurance company American International General ('AIG'). The Treasury had nevertheless decided not to support the third largest Wall Street investment bank, Lehman Brothers, which was forced into Chapter 11 insolvency protection in September 2008. This led to the collapse in the share price of many financial institutions in the US and the UK and elsewhere as earlier concerns with market liquidity shifted to solvency. Following successive collapses in the share prices of Halifax Bank of Scotland (HBOS) and the Royal Bank of Scotland Group (RBS) in the UK, the Government announced a three-part rescue package based on a £50m recapitalisation of the major banks and an increase in the amount of the Special Lending Scheme ('SLS') made available by the Bank of England from £100m to £200m with a separate guarantee facility on money market lending for up to three years at commercial rates. This was intended to stabilise the financial system and to reactivate the money markets. The UK model was subsequently adopted in

---

from 1 October 2007. This was raised to £50,000 in October 2008 with a possible further increase to £100,000 although this has not been given effect.

[24] Paras 14.231–14.234.
[25] Paras 14.228–14.230.
[26] Paras 14.221–14.225.

a number of other countries following earlier EU resistance with parts of the recapitalisation package also being incorporated into the US$700bn US Troubled Asset Recovery Programme ('TARP').

Bank of England Act 1998

The Bank of England Act 1998 revised the constitution and duties of the Court **14.25** of Directors of the Bank of England and contains new provisions with regard to the funding, accounts, and profits of the Bank. The establishment of the Monetary Policy Committee is confirmed and a formal statutory basis for the conduct of monetary policy conferred. Responsibility for bank supervision under the Banking Act 1987 was transferred to the FSA as well as the Bank's functions under the Banking Coordination (Second Council Directive) Regulations 1992 and the Building Societies Act, as well as section 43 of the Financial Services Act 1986 and the Investment Services Regulations 1985 (section 171 of the Companies Act 1989). The gilt registration function of the National Savings Stock Register was transferred to the Bank to create a brokerage service for gilt registration with the amendment of section 27 of the Companies Act 1989 with regard to bearer securities. Further amendments were proposed to the institutional structure and statutory function of the Bank following the Northern Rock crisis.[27]

Constitution and regulation

The Court of Directors of the Bank was continued although a second Deputy **14.26** Governor was to be appointed. Schedule 1 contains provision with regard to the offices of the Governor, Deputy Governors, and Directors, and the procedures and proceedings of the court. These replace the provisions previously set out in the Bank of England's Charter of 1696. The functions of the court are stated to be to manage the Bank's affairs including determining the objectives and strategy required to ensure the effective discharge of its functions and the most efficient use of its resources. Certain functions may be delegated to a non-executive sub-committee of the court with an annual report being produced which is to include the role of the sub-committee, financial information, and directors' remuneration rates. The Report is to be laid before Parliament and published. Additional provisions are included with regard to the custody and use of the Bank's seal.

---

[27] Chapter 1, paras 1.151–1.180 and paras 14.226–14.227.

Financial arrangements

14.27   The Act contains further provisions concerning the maintenance of cash ratio deposits which did not formally operate on a statutory basis before (Schedule 2). A written notice is to be issued to banks specifying the amounts to be deposited calculated having regard to the liability base of the institution concerned. Sterling and foreign currency liabilities may be specified by the Treasury by order with the requirements being subject to a penalty payment in lieu of deposit. The Bank is required to keep proper accounts and records including an annual statement of accounts consisting of its balance sheet and profit and loss accounts. The Bank is to pay the Treasury an amount equal to 25 per cent of the Banks' net profits from its previous financial year or such other sum as the Treasury and Bank may agree. Failing agreement, payment is to be made in two instalments equal to 50 per cent of the Bank's post-tax profits from the previous year. These replace the earlier provisions set out in the Bank of England Act 1946.

Transfer of functions

14.28   The Bank's functions with regard to the supervision of banks are transferred under section 21(a). The Bank's functions in connection with listing settlement arrangements under section 171 of the Companies Act 1989 are transferred under section 21(b) and (c). Schedule 4 contains supplementary provisions with regard to the transfer of functions. These include guaranteeing the legal validity of all previous activities and transactions.

Additional provisions

14.29   Miscellaneous and general provisions are set out in Part IV. These include exempting transactions between listed money market institutions and the Treasury, empowering the Treasury to close the National Savings Stock Register with regard to gilts, issuance of regulations in respect of the purchase and sale of government stock and bonds through the Bank, extending the Treasury's power to make regulations in respect of the dematerialisation of securities applicable to bearer securities, and amendments to the restrictions on the disclosure of information contained in the Banking Act 1987. The schedules contain further provisions concerning the Court of Directors, cash ratio deposits and bank supervision fees, the Monetary Policy Committee, and supplementary and consequential amendments related to the transfer of function as well as revised restrictions on the disclosure of information. These arrangements have since been further amended following the Northern Rock crisis.[28]

---

[28]   Chapter 1, paras 1.151–14.180 and paras 14.228–14.230.

Financial Services and Markets

The statutory basis for UK bank supervision is FSMA 2000. Banks have been **14.30** subject to the general prohibition set out in FSMA, section 19(1) since N2 which requires that they are either authorised or exempt. They must also hold the relevant permission under section 20(1) and comply with the restrictions on the issuance of financial promotions under section 21(1) and (2) of FSMA. Deposit-taking and deposits are included as regulated activities and investments under Schedule 2 of FSMA and the Financial Services (Regulated Activities) Order (as amended).[29]

Banks are subject to the Handbook of Rules and Guidance issued by the FSA **14.31** (under sections 138 and 157 of FSMA) in the conduct of their activities. This requires compliance with all of the high-level standards in Block 1, the prudential standards in Block 2 applicable to banks (GENPRU and BIPRU) with the residual liquidity rules in IPRU(BAN). Authorisation is dealt with under the separate application pack section of the website, Supervision under SUP in Block 4, and Enforcement under EG in Block 9 with complaints and compensation redress provisions in Block 5.

The main obligations with regard to capital and financial requirements as well **14.32** as internal systems and controls are set out in GENPRU and BIPRU which replaced the earlier interim measures in IPRU(BANK) apart from liquidity. The final prudential provisions have come into effect in stages with the revised capital adequacy standards produced by the Basel Committee on Banking Supervision on Basel II[30] which were given effect to in the EU under the Capital Requirements Directive ('CRD').[31]

General prohibition

A person cannot carry on a regulated activity in the UK (or purport to do so) **14.33** unless it is an authorised or exempt person under the general prohibition (section 19(1) and (2) of FSMA. A person who contravenes the general prohibition commits an authorisation offence (section 23(2)) and is liable for up to six months in prison (on summary conviction) or two years (on indictment) or a fine or both (section 23(1)(a) and (b)). It is a defence to show that the person took all reasonable precautions and exercised all due diligence to avoid committing the offence (section 23(3)).

---

[29] Financial Services and Markets Act 2000 (Regulated Activities) Order 2001, SI 2001/544 as amended.
[30] Paras 14.145–14.159.
[31] Paras 14.160–14.170.

14.34 An agreement made by or through an unauthorised person is unenforceable against the other party who is entitled to recover the property or money transferred and compensation for any loss sustained (sections 26(1) and (2) and 27(1) and (2)). The amount of compensation is as agreed between the parties or as determined by the court (section 28(2)). Where money has been received by a person without authorisation or exemption and the depositor is not entitled under the agreement to recover the amount deposited without delay, he may apply to the court for an order directing repayment (section 29). The order will be made unless the court is satisfied that it would not be just and equitable for the money deposited to be returned having regard to whether the deposit taker reasonably believed that he was not in contravention of the general prohibition (section 29(3) and (4)).

14.35 An activity is a regulated activity for the purposes of FSMA if it is of a specified kind carried on by way of business and relates to investments of a specified kind or is of a specified kind and relates to property of any kind (section 22(1)(a) and (b)). Specified means by order of the Treasury with the detailed definitions of investments and regulated activities and investments being set out in the RAO (as amended).

14.36 The RAO follows the earlier deposit taking definitions included within sections 5 and 6 of the Banking Act 1987. Accepting deposits is an activity of a specified kind if money received by way of deposit is lent to others or any other activity of the acceptor is financed wholly or to a material extent out of the capital of or interest on money received by way of deposit (RAO, article 5(1)(a) and (b)). Deposit means a sum of money paid on terms under which it is to be repaid, with or without interest or premium, and either on demand or at a time or in circumstances agreed by or on behalf of the person making the payment and the person receiving it, and which is not referable to the provision of property (other than currency) or services or the giving of security (article 5(2)(a) and (b)).

14.37 Money is paid on terms which are referable to the provision of property or services or the giving of security if (and only if) it is paid by way of advance or part payment under a contract for the sale, hire, or other provision of property or services and is repayable only in the event that the property or services is or are not in fact sold, hired, or otherwise provided (article 3(a)). This includes money paid by way of security for the performance of a contract or by way of security in respect of loss that may result from the non-performance of the contract or is otherwise paid by way of security for the delivery up or return of any property whether in a particular state of repair or otherwise (article 5(3)(a) and (b)).

14.38 Deposits are included as specified investments for the purposes of FSMA (RAO, article 74). Certain payments are nevertheless excluded. These include sums paid by exempt or other persons such as the Bank of England, the central bank of an

EEA State or the European Central Bank, another bank or insurance company, a local authority, and the main international financial institutions (article 6(1)(a)). Businesses consisting wholly or to a significant extent of the lending of money are excluded and payments between group companies or close relatives (article 6(1) (b),(c), and (d)). Sums received by solicitors and persons authorised to deal in investments and payments in consideration of the issue of debt securities are excluded (articles 7, 8, and 9).

Activities must also be carried on by way of business (section 20(1)). Under the **14.39** Carrying on of Regulated Activities by Way of Business Order 2001,[32] a person accepting deposits is not to be regarded as doing so by way of business unless he holds himself out as accepting the deposits on a day-to-day basis and provided that he does not only accept them on particular occasions whether or not involving the issue of any securities (article 2(1)(a) and (b)). In determining whether deposits are accepted only on particular occasions, regard is to be had to the frequency of those occasions and to any characteristics distinguishing them from each other (article 2(2)). This follows the earlier extended definition of deposit taking under sections 5 and 6 of the Banking Act 1987.

A number of institutions are separately exempt from the general prohibition **14.40** under the Financial Services Exemptions Order 2001.[33] Exempt persons include the Bank of England, the central bank of any EEA State, and the main international financial institutions as well as municipal banks, local authorities, charities, industrial and provident societies, and student loan companies. This replaces the earlier regulations issued under the Banking Act 1987.

Permission

FSMA creates a dual authorisation and permission regime. An authorised person **14.41** can only carry on a regulated activity (or purport to do so) in accordance with the permission given to him by the FSA under Part IV or any other provision of the Act (section 20(1)(a) and (b)). Breach of the permission requirement is liable to administrative penalty such as a fine or censure, or restriction or withdrawal of an existing permission. Contravention does not constitute an offence and transactions are not void or unenforceable (section 20(2)(a) and (b)). No separate right of action for breach of statutory duty arises except in prescribed cases

---

[32] Financial Services and Markets Act 2000 (Carrying On Regulated Activities by Way of Business) Order 2001, SI 2001/1177 as amended.
[33] Financial Services and Markets Act 2000 (Exemption) Order 2001, SI 2001/1201 as amended.

(section 22(2)(c) and (3)).[34] The significance of the permission requirement is that banks must be both authorised (under section 31(1)) and hold the relevant permission to carry on the particular regulated activity (including deposit-taking) intended to be engaged in the UK.

14.42   Banks do not apply for authorisation directly. They are automatically authorised once they obtain a Part IV permission (section 31(1)(a)). Institutions will then generally apply for permission to carry on deposit-taking activity (under section 41 of FSMA) after which they will become authorised for the purposes of section 19(1) (under section 31(1)). Accepting deposits may only be carried on by a body corporate or partnership (paragraph 2(a) and (b), Schedule 6 to FSMA).

14.43   The FSA will grant permission to carry on one or more regulated activities where it is satisfied that the institution complies with and will continue to comply with the threshold conditions set out in Schedule 6 to FSMA (section 41(1) and (2)). Schedule 6 generally requires that institutions have appropriate legal status, a head or registered office in the UK, and have no close links that may prevent the effective supervision of the institution. They must have adequate resources and be judged fit and proper to carry on the activities concerned (paragraphs 1 to 5, Schedule 6 to FSMA). These restate the earlier Schedule 3 conditions set out in the Banking Act 1987 although restricted only to include the main market entry components. The more specific continuing requirements with regard to ongoing prudential obligations are now given effect to under the FSA's Handbook of Rules and Guidance and, in particular, GENPRU and BIPRU supported by the Supervision (SUP) process manual and Enforcement Guide ('EG').

14.44   The FSA may grant the permission applied for either in full or in part and subject to such conditions or requirements as may be considered appropriate (sections 42(2) and 43(1)). Permission or any requirement imposed may be extended or cancelled on request (section 44(1)) or on the FSA's initiative (section 45(1)). Permission may be varied following the acquisition or control of a UK authorised person (section 46(2)) or in response to an overseas regulator's request (section 47(1)). Asset requirements may be imposed which prohibit the disposal of an institution's assets or require that the assets are to be held in trust (section 48(2)). Connected relationships are to be considered in granting, varying, or cancelling a Part IV permission (section 49(1)). Additional procedural requirements are included within FSMA (sections 51 to 54) with applicants having a right to refer any decisions to the Financial Services and Markets Tribunal (section 55(1)). Authorised persons aggrieved by the FSA's exercise of its powers to vary

---

[34] On breach of statutory duty, see *X (Minors) v Bedfordshire County Council* [1995] AC 633, HL. See generally Freshfields Bruckhaus Deringer, *Financial Services Investigations and Enforcement* (2001), paras 10.23–10.24 and 10.27–10.48.

permission or impose or vary a requirement may also refer the case to the Tribunal (section 55(1)).

Authorisation

Authorisation is automatically conferred under FSMA where a person holds a **14.45** Part IV permission to carry on one or more regulated activities (section 31(1)(a)). EEA firms holding passport rights under any of the main European financial directives and exercising rights under the European Community Treaty are also exempt (section 31(1)(b) and (c) and Schedules 3 and 4 to FSMA).[35] A person is also authorised where this is otherwise provided for under the Act (section 31(1)(d)).

European firms may either exercise passport rights under Schedule 3 or Treaty **14.46** rights under Schedule 4 FSMA. Passport rights apply with regard to 'single market directives' which include the First and Second Banking Directive (now the Banking Consolidation Directive), the insurance directives, and the Investment Services Directive (now the Markets in Financial Instruments Directive).[36] An EEA right means the entitlement to establish a branch or provide services in another EEA State in accordance with the European Community Treaty and subject to the conditions set out in the relevant single market directive.[37]

EEA firms are required to satisfy the establishment or service conditions to become **14.47** authorised.[38] The establishment conditions reflect the requirements set out in the main financial directives that have to be complied with by firms wishing to exercise branching rights in another Member State under the particular measure. These include the provision of notice to the FSA from the home country competent authority (referred to as a consent notice) with the firm being advised of any applicable conditions that it has to comply with within two months of receipt of the notice.[39]

The service conditions only require that notice is given to the home State regula- **14.48** tor (a notice of intention) and that the FSA is provided with a notice (a regulator's notice) from the home authority containing such information as may be prescribed.[40] The FSA must prepare for the firm's supervision and notify it of any applicable provisions within two months of receipt of the notice. Permission is then automatically conferred on European firms that have qualified for authorisation

---

[35] Treaty refers to European Community Treaty, FSMA, s 417(1).
[36] FSMA, Sched 3, para 1.
[37] ibid, Sched 3, para 7.
[38] ibid, Sched 3, para 12(1) and (2).
[39] ibid, Sched 3, para 13(1)(a), (b), and (c).
[40] ibid, Sched 3, para 14(1)(a) and (b).

under paragraph 12 of Schedule 3 to FSMA equivalent to the terms set out in the consent notice, regulator's notice, or notice of intention.[41]

14.49 UK firms wishing to exercise passport rights in other EEA countries are required to notify the FSA which will send a consent notice to the host State regulator. The firm will have to comply with any notified conditions.[42] The FSA may nevertheless refuse to issue a consent notice provided that the firm concerned is served with a warning notice and then a decision notice with the firm having the right to refer the matter to the Tribunal.[43] A notice of intention must also be served on the FSA where a UK firm wishes to provide services in another EEA State.[44] A UK firm may be fined where it breaches these procedural requirements.[45] Regulations may be issued by the Treasury in connection with the exercise of EEA rights.[46]

14.50 European firms may qualify separately for Treaty rights where their head office is situated in an EEA State other than the UK (its home State), and it is recognised as a national of that State and satisfies certain authorisation conditions.[47] The firm must have been authorised in its home State to carry on a particular permitted activity and the laws of the home State provide for equivalent protection or satisfy relevant Community requirements relating to the carrying on of the activity. The firm must also have no EEA right under Schedule 3 and the home State regulator must have informed the FSA in writing.[48] Provisions are considered to be equivalent where they afford consumers protection which is, at least, equivalent to that provided by or under FSMA with regard to the particular activity considered. Permission is again automatically conferred on Treaty firms where they qualify for authorisation under Schedule 4.[49]

14.51 The effect of section 31 and Schedules 3 and 4 of FSMA is to treat European firms exercising either passport or Treaty rights as being automatically authorised and holding equivalent permission for the particular activity (or activities) for which they are already licensed to carry on and which also constitute regulated activities for the purposes of FSMA. Such firms will then not have to comply

---

[41] FSMA, Sched 3, paras 12 and 15(1) and (2).
[42] ibid, Sched 3, para 19(1), (2), (4) and (5).
[43] ibid, Sched 3, para 19(8) and (12).
[44] ibid, Sched 3, para 20(1).
[45] ibid, Sched 3, para 21(1) and (2).
[46] ibid, Sched 3, para 22(1). Financial Services (EEA Passport Rights) Regulations SI 2001/1376 and SI 2001/2510 as amended.
[47] FSMA, Sched 4, paras 1, 2, and 3.
[48] ibid, Sched 4, para 3(1).
[49] ibid, Sched 4, para 4(1).

with the Part IV application procedures although they will be subject to the separate notification conditions provided for under Schedules 3 and 4. The FSA is nevertheless entitled to inform European firms of the relevant UK requirements that will apply with regard to the conduct of the activity concerned. This will generally involve most of the ongoing regulatory obligations imposed under the Handbook of Rules and Guidance apart from initial authorisation and ongoing capital and related systems and controls obligations. Each Member State within the Community may impose equivalent continuing regulatory obligations on banks where this can be justified as being in the general good under the banking and other financial directives.

Promotions

Banks issuing financial promotions have to comply with the separate require- **14.52** ments set out in section 21 of FSMA. This prohibits the communication of an invitation or inducement to engage in an investment activity unless this is issued by an authorised person or the content of the communication has been approved by an authorised person (section 21(1) and (2)). Engaging in an investment activity means entering (or offering to enter) into an agreement involving a controlled activity or exercising any rights conferred by a controlled investment to acquire, dispose of, underwrite, or convert a controlled investment. A controlled activity is an activity of a specified kind and which relates to an investment of a specified kind with a controlled investment also being as specified. A controlled investment generally corresponds with the specified investments set out in FSMA, Schedule 2.

Exemptions to the restriction on the issuance of financial promotions are included **14.53** within the Financial Promotions Order and in the Conduct of Business Sourcebook (COBS) within the FSA Handbook. Exemptions within the FPO include generic promotions, promotions to investment professionals, overseas recipients, one-off communications, promotions to certified high net worth individuals, certified sophisticated investors, and high net worth companies. Additional exemptions are provided for within the COBS 3 of the Handbook although only from the rules themselves.

Breach of the restriction on promotions constitutes an offence liable to six months **14.54** in prison (on summary conviction) and to two years in prison (on indictment) or a fine or both (section 20(1)(a) and (b)). It is a defence to show that the person believed on reasonable grounds that the content of the communication had been prepared or approved by an authorised person or that all reasonable precautions had been taken or the person had exercised all due diligence to avoid committing the offence (section 25(2)(a) and (b)).

Approved persons

14.55 In addition to being authorised and holding the relevant permission, banks must ensure that they comply with the approval requirements imposed under FSMA with regard to key management and personnel. Every authorised person is required to take reasonable care to ensure that no person carries on a controlled function unless the performance of the function by that person has been approved by the FSA (section 59(1) of FSMA). A controlled function means as specified in the FSA's rules (section 59(3)) and generally includes significant influence functions, customer functions, and property functions (section 59(5), (6), and (7)).[50]

14.56 Applications for approval are to be in such manner as the FSA may direct and contain such information as may reasonably be required (section 60(2)). The FSA must be satisfied that the candidate is a fit and proper person to perform the function (or functions) to which the application relates (section 61(2)). Approval may be withdrawn where the person fails to continue to satisfy the fit and proper standard (section 63(1)). Notice must be given where the FSA proposes or decides to refuse an application to the applicant and all other interested parties (section 62(2), (3), and (5)). Decisions to refuse an application or withdraw approval are referable to the Financial Services and Markets Tribunal (sections 62(4)) and 63(6)).

Approved functions

14.57 The list of approved functions is set out in the FSA Handbook. This expands the significant influence functions, customer, and property functions referred to in FSMA. This basic classification is also extended under the Supervision Manual (SUP) to include allocation and apportionment functions, compliance functions, money laundering reporting functions, EEA investment business oversight functions (if applicable), and appointed actuary functions (where applicable).[51]

Significant influence functions

14.58 Significant influence functions include governing body functions, required control functions, and management functions, as well as significant management functions in relation to business and controls and certain temporary and emergency functions.

14.59 Governing body functions include the director of a company or a holding company, non-executive director, chief executive officer, and partner or limited partner.

---

[50] Chapter 6 and paras 14.57–14.63.
[51] Paras 14.123–14.125.

Required functions consist of director or other senior member responsible for apportionment and oversight, director or senior manager responsible for investment business compliance, money laundering reporting officer (MLRO), and appointed actuary (with regard to insurance companies).

Management functions include the members of senior management reporting **14.60** to the governing body in relation to the financial affairs of the firm, the setting and controlling of risk exposures, and internal audit.

Certain functions are covered where equivalent activities are carried on by manag- **14.61** ers to the specified activities conducted by the governing body. These include investment services related functions (such as head of equities or other product division), other business areas apart from specified investments (such as personal or corporate lending or credit card issuances), insurance underwriting, finance related functions (such as acting as the chief corporate treasurer), and responsibility for back office functions. Where persons carry out any such functions on a temporary or emergency basis for more than eight weeks within a 12-month period they have to be separately approved.

Dealing with customer functions

Dealing with customer functions include life and pension advisers, life and pen- **14.62** sion advisers acting under supervision, pension transfer advisers, investment advisers, investment advisers acting under supervision, corporate finance advisers, advisers to underwriting members of Lloyd's, customers' trading advisers, and investment management functions.

Property functions

Property functions include persons dealing or arranging deals on behalf of cus- **14.63** tomers and discretionary fund management.

Code of conduct

The FSA may issue statements of principle with respect to the conduct expected **14.64** of approved persons (section 64(1)). Where the FSA issues statements of principle, it must also issue a code of practice to assist in determining whether or not a person's conduct complies with the principles issued (section 64(2)). The FSA is required to consult on the production of the code of conduct of approved persons (section 65(1)). These principles are set out in the APER section within the Block 1 High-Level Standards of the Handbook.

The first four principles apply to all controlled functions with the last three to **14.65** significant influence functions:

(a) an approved person must act with integrity in carrying out controlled functions;

(b) an approved person must act with due skill, care, and diligence in carrying out controlled functions;

(c) an approved person must observe proper standards of market conduct in carrying out controlled functions;

(d) an approved person must deal with the FSA and other regulators in an open and cooperative manner and disclose appropriately any information that would reasonably be expected;

(e) an approved person performing a significant influence function must take reasonable steps to ensure that the business of the firm for which he is responsible is organised so that it can be controlled effectively;

(f) an approved person performing a significant influence function must exercise due skill, care, and diligence in managing the business of the firm for which he is responsible in the controlled function; and

(g) an approved person performing a significant influence function must take reasonable steps to ensure that the business of the firm for which he is responsible complies with the regulatory requirements imposed on that business.

14.66 The FSA may take action against an approved person who is considered guilty of misconduct and it is appropriate to proceed (section 66(1)). Misconduct includes failing to comply with any of the statements of principle specified or the person has knowingly assisted in other breaches by an authorised person of any requirement imposed under FSMA (section 66(2)). The FSA may impose a financial penalty or publish a statement of misconduct subject to a limitation period of two years from the date the FSA became aware of the misconduct (section 66(3) and (4)). A copy of any statement of misconduct must be sent to the person concerned (section 68). Disciplinary action is subject to the issuance of warning and decision notices with final decisions being referable to the Financial Services and Markets Tribunal (section 67).

14.67 The FSA is required to issue a separate statement of policy with regard to the imposition of fines against approved persons subject to appropriate consultation (sections 69(1) and 70(1)). The FSA may additionally impose a prohibition order on any individual not considered to be fit and proper to perform functions in relation to a regulated activity carried on by an authorised person (section 56(1)). Private parties who suffer loss as a result of breach of the approved persons requirement or a prohibition order may proceed in action for breach of statutory duty (section 71(1)). This remedy may also be available to non-private persons in certain prescribed circumstances (section 71(2)). This parallels the more general action from damages available under section 150 of FSMA for breach of statutory duty.[52]

---

[52] Chapter 7.

Handbook of Rules and Guidance

The obligations with which banks have to comply on a continuing basis are set **14.68**
out in the FSA's Handbook of Rules and Guidance issued under sections 138 and
157 of FSMA. The effect of the Handbook is to create a rules-based regulatory
regime rather than one with the detailed regulatory provisions being set out in a
statutory form. The advantage of this is flexibility and speed of amendment
in response to changes in market structure and practice. Although the corresponding disadvantages are possibly of accessibility and complexity, the FSA has
attempted to ensure maximum transparency within its consultation processes in
preparing all of the separate sections that make up the Handbook. Final rules
and guidance are also made available in hardcopy, CD ROM, and Handbook
online formats to ensure that all interested parties have full, timely, and cost effective access to all relevant provisions.

The FSA has separately tried to ensure that the Handbook is as easy to follow as **14.69**
possible. Certain stylistic formats have been adopted including marking in the
margins to the text rules as 'R', guidance with 'G', and other evidential provisions
with the letter 'E'. Regular contents listings are included as well as a supporting
glossary of terms. Earlier preparatory and consultation documents are also made
available in the archive sections on the website. The FSA has nevertheless remained
sensitive to concerns with regard to complexity and continues to attempt to
simplify Handbook provisions whenever possible.

Banks and other deposits-takers will generally have to comply with the author- **14.70**
isation requirements set out in the application pack section of the website (previously the Authorisation Manual ('AUTH')) and then the High-Level Standards
set out in Block 1 and continuing prudential obligations with regard to capital
and controls contained in the Integrated Prudential Sourcebook applicable to
banks (GENPRU and BIPRU) in Block 2. They are also subject to oversight
and reporting requirements contained in the Supervision Manual ('SUP') and
will have to comply with any investigation or verification requests and sanctions
imposed under the Enforcement Guide ('EG'). Each of these provisions are
considered in further detail in the following sections.

Bank authorisation

Banks must initially be authorised to carry on their activities (under section 19(1) **14.71**
of FSMA). Deposits and deposit taking are included within the definitions of
investments and regulated activities referred to in Schedule 2 and in the RAO.[53]

---

[53] Paras 14.35–14.38.

Rather than apply for authorisation directly, banks will submit an application for Part IV permission to conduct deposit taking business (section 40(1)) and will then automatically become authorised for the purposes of the Act (section 30(1)(a)).[54]

14.72 An application for permission will be granted if the financial institution satisfies the threshold conditions set out in Schedule 6 of FSMA. These are generally concerned with legal status, location, close links, adequate resources, and suitability. Relevant procedural requirements were set out in AUTH within the Block 4 process section of the Handbook which essentially consisted of guidance rather than rules to which the relevant application forms are attached. As a large number of different types of firms have to apply for relevant permission under FSMA, the FSA has created a special 'application pack' section on its website, firms can 'build their own' applications using up to six portals depending upon the type of business involved.[55]

14.73 Banks are generally required to complete and submit a corporate application to obtain permission to conduct regulated activities and a series of individual applications for approved persons and controllers. The purpose of the application documentation is to provide the FSA with all necessary information in connection with the applicant's business plans, management and organisational structure, outsourcing arrangements, financial budgets and projections, systems, compliance procedures and documentation, senior management and staffing numbers, and controls and close links.

14.74 The revised application pack generally includes a Core Details Form (with a business-specific supplement), a Regulatory Business Plan (with a business-specific supplement), Personnel details and Compliance arrangements with separate individual forms, Owners and Influencers, and supporting documents as well as a Change of Legal Status application pack for firms that wish to amend their permission.[56] The relevant application fee will also be paid. Decisions are taken in accordance with the procedures set out in DEPP with applicants having the right to make representations with the decision being taken by the RDC.

Part IV permission

14.75 Where an application has been accepted, the firm will be advised of the activities that it may carry on including any specified limitations or requirements where applicable. The grant of the Part IV permission will take effect from the specified date, although this may differ from the business commencement date set out

---

[54] Paras 14.41–14.44 and 14.45–14.51.
[55] Chapter 6, para 6.23.
[56] Chapter 6, paras 6.25–6.55.

in the applicant's regulatory business plan. The FSA may vary or revoke the permission where the applicant has not carried on a regulated activity for which it has a Part IV permission for 12 months including commencing to do so (section 45(1) of FSMA). Any significant changes in particulars must be notified to the FSA subsequently.

High-level standards

All regulated persons are subject to the high-level standards set out in Block 1 of the FSA's Handbook of Rules and Guidance. This sets out the general principles and standards with which all regulated firms are expected to comply in the conduct of their regulated activities. These accordingly constitute a set of absolute minimum standards of good practice expected by the FSA from all financial institutions and across all sectors. These apply to firms, senior management, and other approved persons, and include such matters as integrity, skill, care, and diligence, financial, and market and client interests. Many enforcement decisions including the imposition of financial penalties are most often based on breach of the high-level standards rather particular regulatory rules or obligations.   **14.76**

Principles for Businesses ('PRIN')

The Principles for Businesses ('PRIN') contain a statement of 11 fundamental obligations with which all regulated institutions are expected to comply. These develop the main aspects of the fit and proper standard referred to in the threshold condition 5 (suitability). Firms are expected to comply with the Principles at all times. This is considered critical in applications for permission under Part IV of the Act and any breach will involve the possible withdrawal or restriction of permission on the basis that the firm is no longer fit and proper.   **14.77**

Senior Management Arrangements, Systems, and Controls ('SYSC')

Senior Management Arrangements, Systems, and Controls ('SYSC') sets out the main requirements governing senior management responsibility and control systems. The purpose is to encourage banks' directors and senior managers to take appropriate responsibility for the banks' arrangements on matters likely to be of interest to the FSA and to encourage banks to assign responsibility for effective and responsible organisation to specific directors and senior managers.   **14.78**

The money laundering provisions previously contained in the Money Laundering Sourcebook have since been restated as general principles within SYSC and the sourcebook cancelled.[57] A new common platform regime has also been created   **14.79**

---

[57] Chapter 10. See also GA Walker, 'Money Laundering' in *Encyclopaedia of Banking Law* (Butterworths, 6 Volume Looseleaf) Division A.

for firms subject to the EU CRD and MiFID[58] with both directives containing provisions concerning management and internal systems and controls standards. Seven new chapters were to be added to SYSC to create the new common platform regime which would take effect from 1 November 2007 following implementation of MiFID. The following new measures apply to common platform firms:

(a) Chapter 4: General Organisational Requirements (including business continuity);
(b) Chapter 5: Employees, Agents and other Relevant Persons (including senior management requirements);
(c) Chapter 6: Compliance (including internal audit);
(d) Chapter 7: Risk Controls (including certain CRD risk-specific material);
(e) Chapter 8: Outsourcing;
(f) Chapter 9: Record-keeping; and
(g) Chapter 10: Conflicts of Interest.

Threshold Conditions ('COND')

14.80 Threshold Conditions ('COND') develops the threshold conditions set out in Schedule 6 of FSMA with which firms have to comply to be granted Part IV permission (section 41(2) of FSMA) and to continue to comply with to retain that permission (section 45(1)(a))). The threshold conditions generally relate to legal status, location of offices, close links, adequate resources, and suitability. The meaning and content of each of these conditions is expanded in COND.

Statements of Principle and Code of Practice for Approved Person ('APER')

14.81 The FSA's requirements with regard to approved persons are developed in the Statements of Principle and Code of Practice (both contained in APER) and in the fit and proper tests for approved persons ('FIT').[59] APER is issued under section 64 of FSMA which allows the FSA to issue statements of principle with regard to the conduct expected of approved persons within financial firms with such statements being supported by a code of practice for the purpose of assisting determine whether a person's conduct complies with the principles set.

14.82 The Statements of Principle for Approved Persons are set out in section 2 of APER. General and specific guidance is provided under the Code of Practice sections 3 and 4. Further direction is provided with regard to record keeping requirements (Schedule 1), notification requirements (Schedule 2), fees and other

---

[58] Chapter 3 and paras 14.160–14.170.
[59] Paras 14.55–14.63.

required payments (Schedule 3), powers exercised (Schedule 4), rights of action for damages (Schedule 2), and waiver (Schedule 6).

Fit and Proper Test for Approved Persons ('FIT')

The criteria to be taken into account in assessing whether an individual is fit and **14.83** proper to conduct a particular controlled function is set out in the Fit and Proper Test for Approved Persons ('FIT'). This applies to applicants and approved persons. The FSA will generally have regard to honesty, integrity and reputation, competence and capability, and financial soundness. In making assessments with regard to honesty, integrity, and reputation, the FSA will have regard to a number of matters including convictions, civil settlements, previous investigations or disciplinary proceedings, regulatory action, complaints, insolvency, professional discipline, censure or suspension, fiduciary infractions, director `disqualifications, and previous honesty and cooperation with regulatory authorities. In examining competence and capability, the FSA will have regard to whether the person satisfies the relevant requirements of the FSA's Training and Competence Sourcebook ('TC') with regard to the specific controlled function concerned and whether the person has demonstrated by experience and training that he or she is able to perform the control function.

General Provisions ('GEN')

Matters that apply across the Handbook as a whole are set out in the General **14.84** Provisions ('GEN'). These are considered by their nature not to be suitable to be set out in any particular manual or sourcebook. These include necessary or useful material relevant to all modules such as transitional arrangements, provisions that apply to all authorised persons, guidance on interpreting the Handbook, and FSA fees.

Banking Supervision

Bank supervision is generally concerned with ensuring that banks conduct them- **14.85** selves in accordance with agreed or established standards of best market practice. For this purpose, they have initially to be authorised (or licensed) to enter the market. They must then carry on their activities in compliance with a series of prescribed regulatory obligations or best market practices governing such matters as liquidity and capital, internal control systems, and management suitability and oversight. They may be subject to sanction or discipline in the event that they breach any relevant requirements which may include the imposition of financial penalties or restrictions on the scope of the licence to carry on banking activities.

14.86   The core functions of licensing, continuing oversight, and sanction were governed by the three process manuals set out in Block 3 of the FSA Handbook of Rules and Guidance. Market entry was dealt with under AUTH and now the application portals are subject to the general threshold conditions set out in Schedule 6 to FSMA (and COND). Oversight is governed by SUP which sets out the continuing information and reporting obligations that banks and other financial firms have to comply. Sanctions are applied under the Enforcement Guide ('EG' previously 'ENF') which clarifies the range of powers available to the FSA under FSMA. The core supervisory obligations imposed under SUP are expected to be revised to give effect to the new Supervisory Enhancement Programme ('SEP') set up following the crisis at Northern Rock bank.[60]

14.87   The particular regulatory obligations that banks have to satisfy with regard to such matters as capital, liquidity, and internal controls are set out in the Integrated Prudential Sourcebook sections applicable to banks (GENPRU and BIPRU) although their application and compliance is supported by the Authorisation, Supervision, and Enforcement Manuals. The particular obligations imposed will also be further revised over time with the coming into effect of the Final Integrated Sourcebook ('PRU') with some consequential amendments also being possible to the three process manuals.

14.88   UK bank supervision was previously conducted by the Bank of England under the Banking Acts 1979 and 1987 until responsibility in this regard was transferred to the FSA under the Bank of England Act 1998.[61] The FSA initially carried out its bank supervision under the transferred powers conferred under the 1998 Act until the coming into effect of FSMA on 1 December 2001 (N2).

14.89   UK bank supervision has generally been conducted on the basis of five general processes or practices. Banks are initially required to provide continuing information through the submission of regular prudential returns in respect of both their individual (solo) and group (consolidated) activities. This is in addition to the general information provided under annual accounts or company law returns. The information produced is discussed in meetings between the senior management within the bank and relevant supervisory staff. The purpose of these meetings is to clarify and expand the paper submissions made. These can either be conducted on a bilateral basis or trilateral basis with the bank's accountants or auditors also in attendance.

14.90   The supervisory authorities may conduct on-site visits to confirm or verify particular matters and have a general power to require documents or other informa-

---

[60]   Paras 14.04 and 14.230.
[61]   Para 14.21 and paras 14.25–14.29.

tion to be provided. Separate reports may be commissioned from special parties such as the bank's accountants or auditors in connection with such matters as the quality of internal systems and controls. These more informal possesses are supported by a range of enforcement powers which may include the conduct of formal investigations if necessary or to access premises or to call for documents to be provided or persons interviewed. This will, in turn, be supported by a range of formal sanctions including the imposition of penalties, prohibitions, or other actions against individuals (including bankruptcy), restriction or withdrawal of permission, and ultimately the winding up of institutions.

The manner in which these information and other confirmatory powers are **14.91** exercised in practice is now set out in the Supervision Manual ('SUP'). This contains provisions concerning all of the separate processes referred to including information reporting and requests, meetings, on-site visits, reports and investigations, and formal disciplinary action. All of this is expanded in the individual chapters within SUP. The FSA's general approach to supervision is set out in SUP 1. This outlines the FSA's risk-based approach to supervision, the use of impact and probability factors, and lead regulation. Information gathering is dealt with under SUP 2 with special provisions concerning auditors (SUP 3), actuaries (SUP 4), and reports commissioned by skilled persons (SUP 5). Applications to vary or cancel Part IV permission are provided for (SUP 6) with additional measures included in connection with individual requirements (SUP 7), waiver and modification of rules (SUP 8), and individual guidance (SUP 9).

Provisions are also included with regard to particular categories of persons. These **14.92** include approved persons (SUP 10), controllers and close links (SUP 11), appointed representatives (SUP 12), and passport rights by UK firms and incoming EU firms (SUP 13 and 14). Notifications are considered (SUP 15) with reporting requirements (SUP 16) and transaction reporting (SUP 17). Additional guidance is provided with regard to business transfers (SUP 18) and Commodity Futures Trading Commission exemptions (SUP 18).

Supervisory approach (SUP 1)

SUP 1 contains introductory and more general provisions concerning application **14.93** and purpose, content, risk-based approach, supervisory tools, and lead supervision. SUP 1 applies to every firm although its effects are limited with regard to investment companies with variable capital ('ICVCs'). The statutory basis is paragraph 6(1) Schedule 1 of FSMA which requires the FSA to maintain arrangements designed to enable it to determine whether persons on whom requirements are imposed by or under the Act are complying with them (SUP 1.1.2G). In designing these arrangements, the FSA has had regard to its regulatory objectives (section 2(2) of FSMA) and the principles of supervision or good regulation (section 2(3) of FSMA). In so doing, the FSA has considered the need to reinforce the responsibility of management but to do so in a proportionate and appropriate manner (SUP 1.1.4G). SUP sets out the relationship between the FSA and authorised persons which are referred to as 'firms' for the purposes of the Handbook (SUP 1.2.1G). This will generally include matters of continuing relevance following authorisation under AUTH although the more specific regulatory obligations to be complied with are imposed under other parts of the Handbook.

Risk-based supervision

14.94 In carrying out its supervision, the FSA generally adopts a risk-based approach. The purpose of this is to focus its resources on the mitigation of risks to its regulatory objectives and to use its resources in the most efficient and economic way (SUP 1.3.1G). Its approach to risk assessment is then based on the extent to which firms create risks to the FSA's regulatory objectives having regard to the impact and probability of such exposures arising. For this purpose, supervision by risk refers to the threat to the FSA's statutory objectives. The term can also be used to refer to the particular type of risk involved (such as credit risk, market risk, or interest rate risk). This is the manner in which it was originally used as part of the Bank of England's RATE framework which was adopted in the mid-1990s following the Arthur Andersen Report.[62] The adoption of a cumulative or aggregation approach with regard to each of the main financial exposures is now referred to as 'risk-by-risk' supervision which will be followed under the Integrated Prudential Sourcebook (PRU) as it comes into full effect.

Impact and probability assessment

14.95 The FSA has been developing a new regulatory approach and supporting operating framework since its creation in 1997.[63] This is, in particular, based on applying a standard risk assessment process across all activities which involves assessing the risks posed by a firm against a number of impact and probability factors on both an initial and a continuing basis. This is now expanded in the Supervision Manual (SUP 1.3.2G). The impact of a firm is assessed by reference to a range of factors derived from the FSA's regulatory objectives. These include the degree to which the exposures related to the firm could damage market confidence, the extent to which the firm may undermine public understanding, the

---

[62] Para 14.20 and (nn 18, 19 and 20). See also Chapter 1, paras 1.120—1.121 and 1.122–1.123.
[63] Chapter 1, paras 1.121–1.123. See FSA, 'A new regulator for the new millennium' (January 2000); FSA: 'Building the New Regulator—Progress Report' (December 2001); and FSA, 'Building the New Regulator—Progress Report 2' (February 2002); and FSA, 'The FSA's Risk-Based Approach' (November 2006).

extent to which consumers may be adversely affected, and the possible incidence and materiality of any criminal activity with which the firm may be involved (SUP 1.3.3G).

This probability is assessed having regard to 'risk groups' which are stated to be discrete sources of risks corresponding with the regulatory objectives. These relate to the firm's strategy, business risk, financial soundness, nature of the customers involved, supporting internal systems and controls, and organisation within the firm (SUP 1.3.4G). These impact and probability assessments are combined to create an overall judgement of the firm's priority for the FSA and the nature of the relationship which the FSA will have with the firm in terms of regulatory intervention or otherwise (SUP 1.3.5G). This is reflected in the client classification system adopted.[64] The particular choice of supervisory approach will also be affected by three other more general considerations. These consist of the level of confidence in the information on which the assessment is based, the quality of the home regulatory regime applicable, and any anticipated material changes in the impact and probability factors adopted (SUP 1.3.6G). **14.96**

Assessment process

Five main steps in the risk assessment process are identified within SUP. These consist of a preliminary assessment of the firm's potential impact on the regulatory objectives, a probability assessment, use of a validation panel for peer review of risk grading and resource allocation, informing the firm of the risk assessment selected and any remedial action required, and subsequent continuing review of the risk assessment made as necessary (SUP 1.3.8G). The FSA considers it important that firms understand the evaluation process to create the necessary incentives to raise standards and maximise the success of the supervisory arrangements in place (SUP 1.3.9G). The FSA will advise the firm of the risk assessment and provide a programme of action intended to correct any material defects identified (SUP 1.3.10G). **14.97**

Supervisory relationship

The relationships between the FSA and regulated institutions can be divided into five main types. These consist of confirming continuing satisfaction with the threshold conditions, baseline monitoring to ensure that firms comply with regulatory requirements on an ongoing basis, sectoral reviews and thematic work to assess market and risk trends, preparation of risk mitigation programmes **14.98**

---

[64] See also GA Walker, 'Deposit Taking and Banking Supervision' in Blair, Allison, Morton, Richards-Carpenter, Walker and Walmsley, *Banking and Financial Services Regulation* (Butterworths, 3rd edn, 2002) ch 6, paras 6.04 and 6.84–6.100.

for specific firms, and response work in connection with particular identified threats (SUP 1.3.11G). The mixture of these relationships will vary with the firm's risk categorisation (SUP 1.3.12G).

Tools of supervision

14.99 The FSA may rely on one or more of a number of tools of supervision to correct identified risks to its regulatory objectives. The FSA distinguishes between diagnostic, monitoring, preventative, and remedial tools (SUP 1.4.1G). Diagnostic measures are designed to identify, assess, and measure risks. Monitoring options follow the development of identified risks wherever these may arise. Preventative responses limit or reduce perceived risks and prevent crystallisation or aggravation. Remedial measures respond to risks following occurrence. Particular tools may serve more than one purpose and may or may not involve a direct relationship with the particular firm concerned.

14.100 The main supervisory tools include desk-based reviews, liaison with other agencies or regulators, management meetings or representative meetings, on-site inspections, reviews and analysis of periodic returns and notifications, past business reviews, transaction monitoring, and use of auditors and skilled persons (SUP 1.4.5G). Specific risks may also be dealt with through a number of additional tools including making recommendations for preventative or remedial action, providing individual guidance, imposing requirements, or varying a firm's permission (SUP 1.4.6G). The main supervisory tools listed in SUP reflect the traditional techniques used to conduct bank supervision in the UK although reformulated for use within a larger integrated system set up for the oversight of all financial services and markets. This extended range of supervisory tools also includes some corrective responses such as issuing recommendations, guidance, requirements, and permission short of formal enforcement action.

Lead supervision

14.101 Firms that are part of larger groups are also subject to lead supervision. The FSA has developed appropriate arrangements for the supervision of banking and financial groups to be monitored on a more efficient and effective basis with a coordinated approach being adopted where more than one supervisory contact may be involved within the FSA. This then assists the FSA to coordinate monitoring and responses (SUP 1.5.1 and 2G). The FSA appoints a lead supervisor for any group which has more than one supervisory contact at the FSA with the choice of supervisor being based principally on the dominant business conducted within the group (SUP 1.5.3G).

14.102 The lead supervisor has three main responsibilities. The supervisor is to produce an overall assessment of the group which consists of an examination of the strengths and weaknesses of the business of the group and each of the firms within the group as well as a risk assessment of the group as a whole. The supervisor directs the supervisory programme to be adopted with a coordinated supervisory programme being developed consisting of a single risk-based supervision plan for the group as a whole. The lead supervisor also acts as the central point of contact for the group within the FSA to avoid duplication and regulatory overlap (SUP 1.5.4G).

Lead supervision was initially considered in the UK as part of a new policy to **14.103** govern the relationships between the separate regulatory authorities involved with complex groups before any integrated regulatory regime was set up under FSMA.[65] The identification of a primary point of contact and central manager has subsequently been internalised within the integrated regulatory structure set up within the FSA. Lead supervision has also been discussed at the international level especially through the work of the Joint Forum on Financial Conglomerates. An outline paper was produced in 1998 which attempts to set out the core responsibilities of a possible lead regulator for internationally active financial groups. This was of some value although generally of only limited effect in practice due to the need for national authorities to retain full legal and operational responsibility for the oversight of the activities of institutions authorised within their jurisdiction.[66]

Information (SUP 2)

SUP 2 contains rules and guidance concerning the collection of information **14.104** from firms for supervisory purposes. Cooperation between firms and the FSA is necessary to allow it to discharge its responsibility to monitor compliance. SUP 2 is issued under the FSA's statutory obligation to ensure compliance (FSMA, Schedule 1, para 6(1)) and the obligation to cooperate with other regulators (section 354 of FSMA). Firms are required to deal with regulators in an open and cooperative manner and to disclose anything of which the FSA would reasonably expect notice (PRIN 11 and SUP 2.2 and 2.3). SUP also develops a number of the statutory powers conferred on the FSA to collect information (section 165 and ENF 2), commission reports from skilled persons (section 166 and SUP 5), appoint investigators (sections 167, 160, and 169 and ENF 2), and apply for warrants to enter premises (section 176 and ENF 2).

Firms may be required to provide information to the FSA. The FSA may con- **14.105** duct visits, hold meetings with staff at the FSA's offices or elsewhere, and request

---

[65] See Walker (n 12), ch 4.
[66] Walker (n 12), ch 3.

information or documents including by telephone, during meetings or in writing and by electronic communication (SUP 2.3.1G). Meetings or access can only be requested during reasonable business hours and on reasonable notice. The FSA expects firms to make themselves readily available and provide reasonable access to all records, files, tapes, or computer systems or facilities as may be reasonably requested (SUP 2.3.3(1) and (2)G). Firms may be required to produce any specified material as reasonably asked for, print information in the firm's possession or control, permit the copying of documents or other material, and answer truthfully, fully, and promptly all reasonable questions or inquiries (SUP 2.3.3(3), (4), (5), and (6)G).

14.106   The FSA and its agents must be allowed access during reasonable business hours to any of a firm's premises which obligation is extended to its agents, suppliers under material outsourcing arrangements, and appointed representatives (SUP R 2.3.5(1) and (2)). Outsourcers must deal with the FSA in an open and co-operative manner (SUP R 2.3.7). While the FSA will generally only seek information from firms directly, it may approach outsourcers as appropriate (SUP 2.3.10G). Firms may be required to provide information on behalf of another regulator including the Takeover Panel or an overseas authority. Information may be disclosed subject to banking confidentiality and legal privilege. The FSA may carry out 'mystery shopping' and other programme or focus visits to obtain information concerning suspect practices (SUP 2.2.1–5G).

14.107   Firms are liable to sanction for breach of SUP or PRIN 11. This includes any disciplinary measures under Part XIV of FSMA although breach is not a criminal offence nor contempt (section 177 of FSMA). Supervisory information is subject to bank confidentiality (section 175(5) of FSMA) and may not be disclosed unless a relevant exception applies or consent is available.[67]

Auditors (SUP 3)

14.108   The role and function of auditors is developed in SUP 3. This includes appointment rules (SUP 3.3), minimum qualifications (SUP 3.4), and the rights and duties of auditors (SUP 3.5–10). The statutory basis for these provisions is sections 340 to 346 of FSMA.

14.109   Firms may be required to appoint an auditor if they are not already under an obligation to do so and the FSA may issue rules requiring authorised persons to

---

[67] FSMA, s 349(1) and the Financial Services and Markets Act 2000 (Disclosure of Confidential Information) Regulations 2001, SI 2001/218. See also Financial Services and Markets Act 2000 (Disclosure of Confidential Information) (Amendment) Regulations 2001, SI 2001/3437 and Financial Services and Markets Act 2000 (Disclosure of Confidential Information) (Amendment (No 2)) Regulations 2001, SI 2001/3624.

produce periodic financial reports and have them reported on by an auditor (section 340(1) and (2) of FSMA). Auditors may be made subject to such duties as the FSA may specify. Further directions may be given with regard to the manner and time of appointment, notification requirements, remuneration and terms of office, removal, and resignation (section 340(4) of FSMA). It is an offence to provide false or misleading information to an auditor (section 346) and auditors may be disqualified where they have failed to comply with any duty imposed under the Act (section 345(1)).

Auditors have a statutory right of access to books, accounts and vouchers, and to **14.110** ask for any information or explanation as may be required (section 341(1)). Auditors are immune from an action in damages where they have disclosed to the FSA any matter or opinion in good faith and reasonably believed to be relevant to the FSA's functions (section 342(3)). The circumstances in which auditors may communicate matters with the FSA are developed in Treasury regulations (issued under section 342(5)). The FSA is to be separately notified where an auditor has been removed from office, resigns before the expiry of term, or is not reappointed (section 344).

Bank auditors are subject to the provisions set out in SUP. This includes appli- **14.111** cation (SUP 3.1), purpose (SUP 3.2), appointment (SUP 3.3), qualifications (SUP 3.4), independence (SUP 3.5), firm's cooperation with auditors (SUP 3.6), notifications (SUP 3.7), and cooperation (SUP 3.8). Auditors are expressly required to cooperate with the FSA in the discharge of its functions, provide any skilled person with all assistance as may be reasonably required, act in an independent manner, take reasonable steps to satisfy themselves that they are free from any conflicts of interest, notify the FSA without delay of removal, resignation, or loss of reappointment, and notify the FSA of any matter that ought to be drawn to its attention or that there is no such matter (SUP R 3.8.2–12).

Actuaries (SUP 4)

The statutory provisions with regard to actuaries are developed in SUP 4. These **14.112** are based on Part XXII of FSMA and generally only apply to insurers or friendly societies that carry on long-term insurance business. These are generally inapplicable to banks.

Skilled persons report (SUP 5)

The requirements with regard to the appointment of skilled persons are now set **14.113** out under Part XI FSMA as developed in SUP 5. These replace the earlier section 39 reports provided for under the Banking Act 1987. The FSA is given statutory power to require reports to be prepared for any authorised person, member of a firm's group, a partnership of which it is a member, or any such person provided that it was carrying on business at the relevant time (section 166(2)) Reports may be requested on any matter as may reasonably be required in connection with the exercise of the FSA's functions under the Act (section 166(1)). The report may be in such form as may be specified and is to be conducted by persons nominated or approved by the FSA with the necessary relevant skills (section 166(4)).

14.114 The provisions set out in SUP 5 apply to every firm (SUP R 5.1.1). Reports may be commissioned for diagnostic or reporting and preventative or remedial purposes (SUP 5.2.1G). Reports are generally to be requested for information purposes, as part of a risk mitigation programme, in response to a specific event, or for the provision of expert advice. Appointment and reporting procedures are specified (SUP 5 5.4 and Annex 2) with additional provisions concerning the duties of skilled persons and confidentiality and legal privilege (SUP 5.5 and 5.6).

Part IV permission, variation, or cancellation (SUP 6)

14.115 Applicable procedures for the variation or cancellation of a Part IV permission are dealt with under SUP 6. SUP 6 contains specific provisions with regard to applications (SUP 6.1), statutory basis (SUP 6.2), variation (SUP 6.3), cancellation (SUP 6.4), and ending authorisation (SUP 6.5). Relevant procedures are summarised in SUP 6 Annexes 1, 2, and 3 with additional guidance on firm's winding down their business in SUP Annex 4.

14.116 Applications are generally considered on an individual basis having regard to all relevant information in the specific case. Applications for the variation of an existing permission are made under section 44(1) and cancellations under section 44(2) (SUP 6.2.3 and 6.4.1G). Applications are made in writing and considered by the firm's supervision team. An application for cancellation may be refused where the interests of consumers or potential consumers may be adversely affected or it would otherwise be desirable in the interests of depositors for the application to be refused (section 44(4) and SUP 6.4.2G).

Individual requirements (SUP 7)

14.117 Requirements may be imposed on a firm's permission to carry on a regulated activity under section 45 of FSMA and SUP 7. Specific requirements may be considered where a firm is not in full compliance with all threshold conditions such as with regard to relevant systems and controls. Firms may, for example, be required to maintain higher capital ratios or be subject to certain geographic or product restrictions. Relevant criteria are set out in SUP 7.3. Individual requirements may also be used for enforcement purposes (SUP 7.2.3 and ENF 3).

Waiver and modification of rules (SUP 8)

The waiver or modification of the application of particular rules is provided for **14.118** under section 148(2) of FSMA. This is developed in SUP 9. Rules may also be waived with regard to collective investment schemes under section 250. The main rules that may be waived or modified are listed in section 148(1) and include auditors and actuaries rules (section 340), financial promotion rules (section 145), money laundering rules (section 146), and general rules (section 138) (other measures covered include control of information rules, insurance business rules, and price stabilising rules).

Applications for waiver must be in writing (SUP 8.3.3G). Decisions are gener- **14.119** ally made within 20 business days of receipt with reasons for refusal being given (SUP 8.3.5 and 7G). Additional provisions are included with regard to reliance (SUP 8.4), notification or changes in circumstances (SUP 8.5), publication (SUP 8.6), variations (SUP 8.7), revocation (SUP 8.8), and decision-making (SUP 8.9). The relevant procedures are summarised in SUP 8 Annex 1.

Individual guidance (SUP 9)

Individual guidance may be provided with regard to the activities of specific firms **14.120** (section 157(2), FSMA). General guidance may also be issued under the Act and guidance provided with regard to a particular class of regulated persons (section 157(1) and (3)). Compliance is required with the relevant consultation requirements set out in section 155 (section 157(3)).

Firms may apply to the FSA for individual guidance as to how rules and gen- **14.121** eral guidance set out in the Handbook apply to their activities (SUP 9.1.3G). Applications may be made in writing or orally. Guidance may, for example, be requested with regard to the amount of financial resources including individual capital ratios (SUP 9.3.2G). Firms are considered to have complied with the relevant rules where they act in accordance with the guidance provided (SUP 9.4.1G). Further guidance may be requested where circumstances have changed (SUP 9.4.3G).

The FSA may publish its guidance (section 157(4)(a)). It may offer copies of **14.122** its guidance for sale at a reasonable price and make a reasonable charge in response to requests for individual guidance (section 157(4)(b) and (c)).

Approved persons (SUP 10)

Additional rules and guidance are provided with regard to approved persons **14.123** under SUP 10. Regulated entities are required to apply for prior approval from the FSA in connection with any person carrying on a controlled function (section 69(1) of FSMA).[68] An earlier registration system had operated under the self-regulatory regime set up under the FSA 1986 although this has since been extended under the provisions contained in Part V, FSMA and the FSA Handbook. The effect of this is to create a parallel assessment and approvals system for individuals carrying on regulated functions as well as firms themselves.

14.124 SUP 10 contains specific provision with regard to application (SUP 10.1), purpose (SUP 10.2), statutory base (SUP 10.3), specified functions (SUP 10.4), and the main controlled functions (SUP 10.5–10). Additional provisions are included with regard to procedures and forms (SUP 10.11), applications (SUP 10.12), changes to an approved person's details (SUP 10.13), and frequently asked questions (SUP 10.14 and Annex 1G). Relevant procedures are summarised in SUP 10.1 Annex 3G.

14.125 The relevant forms attached to SUP include Application to perform controlled functions under the approved persons regime (SUP 10 Annex 4D), Notice to withdraw an application to perform controlled functions (SUP 10 Annex 4R), Notice to cease to perform controlled functions (SUP 10 Annex 5R), Notification of changes in personal information or application details (SUP 10 Annex 7R), and internal transfer of an approved person (SUP 10 Annex 8G).

Controllers and close links (SUP 11)

14.126 Guidance with regard to the exercise of the FSA's powers with regard to controllers and close links is outlined in SUP 11. Any person proposing to acquire, increase, or reduce a controlling interest in an authorised person must notify the FSA under section 178(1) of FSMA. A person acquires control where they own or can exercise or control the exercise of 10 per cent or more of the shares in the company or exercise a significant influence over the management of the company or its parent (section 179(2)). The acquirer refers to the acquirer or any of its associates or the acquirer and any of its associates. Increases or reductions in control refer to any alteration in holdings up to 10 per cent, from 10 per cent to below 20 per cent, from 20 per cent to below 33 per cent, from 33 per cent to below 50 per cent and 50 per cent or more (sections 180(2) and 181(2)). The FSA must be notified of the change in control in writing and is required either to approve it or serve a warning notice within three months (sections 182(1) and 183(1)). Approvals are to be notified without delay subject only to such conditions as may be considered appropriate (sections 184(1) and 185(1)).

---

[68] Paras 14.57–14.63.

Acquirers must generally be fit and proper persons to exercise control and the **14.127**
interests of consumers must not otherwise be threatened (section 186(2)(a)
and (b)). A warning and decision notice must be served where the FSA is not satisfied that the approval requirements have been made (sections 187(1) and 188(1)).
Decision notices may be referred to the Financial Services and Markets Tribunal
(section 187(4)). A restriction notice may be served where shares have been
improperly acquired which may include restrictions on transfer, exercise of voting
rights, further acquisitions, or payments on liquidation (section 189(2)).
Corresponding notices of reductions in control must also be provided (section
190(1), (2), and (3)). Offences are dealt with under section 191 with the Treasury
having power to issue regulations under section 192.

These statutory provisions are developed in SUP 11. This includes guidance **14.128**
with regard to the FSA's powers (SUP 11.2), relevant requirements (SUP 11.3
and 4), notification forms (SUP 11.5), and subsequent notification requirements
(SUP 11.6). The approval procedures for acquisition or increase in control are
provided for (SUP 11.7) with changes in circumstances of existing controllers
(SUP 11.8) and changes in close links (SUP 11.9). Relevant procedures are
summarised in SUP 11 Annex 3G.

Appointed representatives (SUP 12)

SUP 12 contains guidance on the application of section 39 of FSMA under **14.129**
which appointed representatives may be exempt from the general prohibition
under section 19(1). Specific provision is included with regard to firm responsibility (SUP 12.3), appointment requirements (SUP 12.4), required terms of
contracts (SUP 12.5), continuing obligations (SUP 12.6), notification requirements (SUP 12.7), termination of appointment (SUP 12.8), and record keeping
(SUP 12.9). Assessments of the financial position of appointed representatives
and their fitness and proprietary are included within Annexes 1 and 2.

The rules governing the operation of the appointed representatives regime has **14.130**
since been relaxed with the introduction of the new polarisation regime with
effect during 2005. Financial advisers must now act as either tied appointed representatives, fully independent financial advisers, or multi-tied agents. This will
not apply with regard to pure banking activities although it may be relevant where
banks sell insurance and other financial products.

Passport rights (SUP 13)

The exercise of passport rights by UK firms is dealt with under SUP 13 and incom- **14.131**
ing EEA firms under SUP 14. SUP 13 applies with regard to the establishment
of a first branch or the provision of services in another EEA country or revising

existing arrangements (SUP 13.1.5 and 13.1.6G). The provisions apply to UK firms that are authorised persons under FSMA as well as to wholly owned subsidiaries of credit institutions capable of exercising the right of establishment or services under the Banking Consolidation Directive (SUP 13.2.1G).

14.132 Guidance is provided with regard to the establishment of a branch in another EEA State (SUP 13.3), the provision of cross-border services (SUP 13.4), notices of intention (SUP 13.5), changes to branches (SUP 13.6), changes to cross-border services (SUP 13.7), changes of details (SUP 13.8), application (SUP 13.9), applicable provisions (SUP 13.10), record keeping (SUP 13.11), and further information (SUP 13.12). Details of the relevant information to be provided are expanded in Annexes 1, 2, and 3.

Incoming firms (SUP 14)

14.133 Incoming EEA firms are authorised under section 31(1) of FSMA to exercise passport rights under the main European financial directives or Treaty rights directly.[69] While the authorisation issued is dealt with under AUTH, relevant notification procedures for EEA firms are set out in SUP 13 for outgoing firms and SUP 14 for incoming firms.

14.134 SUP 14 applies to incoming EEA firms that have already established a branch or are already providing cross-border services into the UK. Guidance is provided for firms that wish to change the details of a branch or the services provided or cancel their qualification for authorisation (SUP 14.1.1 and 4G). Additional guidance is provided with regard to changes in branch details (SUP 14.2) and cross-border services (SUP 14.3), notices (SUP 14.4), variation of top-up permission (SUP 14.5), cancellation of authorisation (SUP 14.6), and top-up permission (SUP 14.7) and further guidance (SUP 14.8).

Notifications (SUP 15)

14.135 Supervisory information provision under the Handbook is generally dealt with in SUP 15, 16, and 17. General notifications are made under SUP 15 with reporting requirements in SUP 16 and transaction reporting for specific firms in SUP 17. Firms are generally required to cooperate with regulators and provide any information relating to their activities which the FSA would reasonably expect to be provided with (PRIN 11). The FSA considers that this applies to regulated and

---

[69] This also includes collective investment schemes under the European UCITS Directive 85/611. On European Financial Services, see generally Chapter 3 and on Collective Investment Schemes, Chapter 17. See also GA Walker, *European Banking Law—Policy and Programme Construction* (British Institute of International Comparative and Commercial Law (BIICCL), London, 2006).

unregulated activities including group activities. This will include such matters as proposed restructurings, reorganisation or business expansions, and any significant failure of a firm's systems and controls or any action that would result in a material change in its capital adequacy or solvency position (SUP 15.3.8G).

A number of rules are included within SUP 15 concerning notification. These **14.136** include any matters having a serious regulatory impact, breaches of rules or any other FSA requirements, and civil, criminal, or disciplinary proceedings against the firm or fraud, errors, or other irregularities and any insolvency, bankruptcy, or winding up (SUP R 15.3.1–11). Reasonable advance notice of certain other matters must also be provided including change of name, change of address, change in legal status, and any changes with regard to supervisory authority (SUP R 15.5.1–7). Overseas firms are required to notify any change of position of global chief executive, any person with purely strategic responsibility for UK operations, and any two or more persons that effectively direct a bank's business (SUP R 15.4.1). This is necessary as such persons would otherwise fall outside the FSA's reporting requirements. Firms must also take all reasonable steps to ensure that the information provided is factually accurate and complete (SUP R 15.6.1).

The FSA must be notified immediately if any false, misleading, or incomplete **14.137** or inaccurate information has been provided or information has changed in a material respect. Updated information must be provided as soon as reasonably practicable (SUP R 15.6.4 and 5). Additional guidance is provided with regard to the form and method of notification (SUP 15.7), notification in respect of particular products or services (SUP 15.8), and adjustments for incoming Treaty firms that do not have top-up permission (SUP 15 Annex 1).

Reporting requirements (SUP 16)

SUP 16 sets out the general reporting requirements with which firms have to **14.138** comply on a continuing basis. This includes general reporting conditions (SUP 16.3), annual reports on controllers (SUP 16.4), annual close links reports (SUP 16.5), as well as compliance reports (SUP 16.6), and financial reports (SUP 16.7). A number of additional rules are included with regard to such matters as the timing and contents of reports and on the separate individual reports required. Banks must generally submit a list of all overseas regulators for each legal entity in the firm's group and an organigram which sets out all authorised entities within the group within six months after the firm's accounting reference date (SUP R 16.6.4 and 5). Financial reports must be submitted either annually, quarterly, or half-yearly in accordance with the relevant due dates (SUP R 16.7.7). Supervisory reports are to be submitted to the line manager within the FSA with other statistical returns being submitted to the Bank of England (SUP R 16.7.13).

Transaction reporting (SUP 17)

14.139 SUP 17 contains rules and guidance concerning the submission of transaction reports in connection with particular securities and related derivatives activities. Such reports were required under Article 20 of the European Investment Services Directive ('ISD') and given effect to in the UK under the earlier rule books of the SFA, PIA, and IMRO.

14.140 SUP 17 imposes a general obligation to make transaction reports subject to certain specific exemptions (SUP 17.4). Reportable transactions are listed (SUP 17.5), transaction reports provided (SUP 17.6), and reporting procedures specified (SUP 17.7). The annexes contain additional information with regard to relevant exchanges, mandatory fields for reporting systems, manual transaction reporting, market identified codes, and relevant regulated markets.

Integrated Prudential Regulation

14.141 The earlier regulatory requirements imposed under the Interim Prudential Sourcebook IPRU(BANK) were to be replaced by a single set of integrated prudential provisions. One of the underlying objectives within the new regulatory regime was to create a common set of prudential requirements for all financial firms. This would require that they maintain adequate financial resources as well as proper systems and controls at all times irrespective of the particular type and range of activities carried on although within a single overall regulatory and supervisory framework.

14.142 The core difficulty that arises is that distinct underlying financial risks are involved in each of the main sectors which require differentiated treatment. It was for this reason that the original supervision by risk policy adopted by the FSA was extended to include a 'risk-by-risk' approach in the new Prudential Sourcebook. This was to be dealt with by a separate chapter being included on each of the main sources of exposure identified, although still within a single common approach or methodology and integrated set of rules. The six key risks initially identified for this purpose were credit risk, market risk, insurance risk, liquidity risk, operational risk, and group risk. Financial firms would then be required to comply with the separate chapters to the extent that their activities involved any of the particular types of exposure covered.

14.143 This process of designing and building the new single Integrated Prudential Sourcebook was originally referred to as the 'PSB'. It was subsequently confirmed that the new sourcebook to be included within the Handbook would be designated the 'PRU'. The FSA then confirmed that separate sub-sourcebooks would be issued in each of the main sector areas covered. This was considered necessary, in particular, to reflect the structure and content of the main recent European directives that had been adopted in each sector area and that had to be separately implemented in the UK. The timetable for the PRU and each of the sub-sourcebooks coming into effect had also had to be extended to correspond with the dates agreed for the coming into effect of the relevant European and supporting international Basel II standards on which they are based.[70]

A number of separate sub-sourcebooks have since been produced within the new **14.144** Prudential Standards Block 2 of the Handbook with a revised set of common provisions applicable to all firms (GENPRU) and dedicated requirements for banks and investment firms (BIPRU). Additional specialised sourcebooks have then been issued in respect of insurance and Lloyd's managing agents (INSPRU), unit trust managers and UCITS firms (UPRU), and mortgage and insurance mediation firms (MIPRU) with the earlier interim rules continued in respect of investment firms not subject to the CRD (INVPRU) and other residual friendly societies (FPRU).

Basel II and Basel III

The capital rules incorporated within the PRU were necessary to give effect to **14.145** the revised framework agreed by the Basel Committee on Banking Supervision under its new Basel II Accord.[71] These revised capital measures were prepared between June 1999 and June 2004. The Committee had issued an initial consultation document on capital revision in June 1999 which was supplemented by the publication of a number of separate component papers in January 2001. Following the comments received, a further consultation document was issued with a number of further calibration exercises being conducted through industry-based quantitative impact studies ('QIS'). The revised capital rules were then produced in June 2004 subject to some final adjustments under a QIS 5 to be conducted during 2005/2006. The new framework was to come into full effect between 2007 and 2009 in all participating countries.

The Basel II framework is stated to be based on three pillars. These consist of a **14.146** revised set of minimum capital requirements (Pillar 1), a new supervisory review process (Pillar 2), and enhanced market discipline through mandatory market disclosure (Pillar 3). Pillar 1 includes a revised set of minimum capital requirements in respect of credit risk, an amended market risk charge, and a new operational risk charge. Basel III refers to the proposed further amendment of

---

[70] See FSA CP 2005/3, 'Strengthening capital standards' (2005); FSA CP 189, 'Report and First Consultation on the Implementation of the New Basel and EU Capital Adequacy Standards'; and FSA DP 13, 'UK implementation of the New Basel and the New Capital Adequacy Standards'.

[71] Walker (n 12 above), 'Capital Supplement'.

the Basel II provisions although no express provisions have yet been issued in this regard.[72]

14.147 The current minimum charge introduced under the 1988 Capital Accord has been retained within the revised standardised approach, although this been made more risk sensitive through the use of external credit rating agency scores rather than the earlier simple risk bands or buckets. Bank loans are generally classified depending upon whether they are with OECD government or central banks borrowing in their own currencies, OECD government or central bank borrowing in other currencies, secured borrowers, or other commercial borrowers. Each is then assigned a risk grading which approximates with the underlying credit risk involved (the possibility of non-payment of interest during term or repayment of principal on maturity). The main risk factors used are 0 per cent (cash or OECD debt) or 10 per cent or 20 per cent (domestic public sector entities), 20 per cent (non-OECD or development banks), 50 per cent (secured borrowing), and 100 per cent (commercial and private sector claims).

14.148 Off-balance sheet items (such as guarantees and other credit substitutes as well as performance and bid bonds and sale and repurchase agreements (repos)) are multiplied by specified conversion factors (either 20 per cent, 50 per cent, or 100 per cent) to create on-balance sheet credit equivalent amounts. The same general credit risk factors are then applied depending on the nature of the borrower. The total exposure in each risk category is multiplied by the amount of the loans outstanding at any time and then aggregated to produce a total risk adjusted asset figure for the loan book of the bank. This must be covered by, at least, 8 per cent of available capital as defined. Tier 1 capital (4 per cent) is essentially made up of paid-up share capital or disclosed reserves and Tier 2 (the other 4 per cent) undisclosed reserves, asset revaluation reserves, general provisions, hybrid instruments or five-year subordinated debt (but only up to one quarter (2 per cent) of the total 8 per cent).

14.149 Under Basel II, the earlier simple bucket system (0 per cent, 20 per cent, 50 per cent, or 100 per cent) is to be replaced by a series of more sophisticated gradings based on external credit rating agency figures for the individual borrowers involved. This should allow the process to be considerably more accurate provided that necessary external rating information is available. The rating agencies themselves have to be approved as eligible having regard to a set of assessment criteria provided (which include objectivity, independence, international access and transparency, disclosure, resources, and credibility).

---

[72] Paras 14.158–14.159.

Security related risks continue to be dealt with under the terms of the Basel **14.150** Committee's January 1996 Market Risk Amendment. This provides for the use of a number of options to be made available in respect of the calculation of general and specific risk on interest rate debt (bond) and equity positions. Separate charges are imposed in respect of settlement delays, foreign exchange, and commodities with a system of allowances being available against underwriting exposures. This cumulative (building block) approach generally follows that developed under the European Capital Adequacy Directive ('CAD').

With regard to market exposures, interest rate risk-specific risk is either assigned **14.151** a 0, 0.25 per cent, 1 per cent, 1.60 per cent, or 8 per cent charge depending upon whether it is government, qualifying, or other general interest rate risk. General risk may be calculated on either a maturity basis (10 per cent to 150 per cent of weighted matched positions) or a duration-based approach (or 2 per cent to 150 per cent of matched duration). Specific equity position is essentially 4 per cent of the gross amount subject to a 2 per cent per cent concession if it is well diversified and liquid. General equity position risk is 8 per cent of the net position. The foreign exchange charge is 8 per cent of the total net foreign exchange position in excess of 2 per cent of capital. Commodity related risks may be calculated on a simplified, maturity ladder, or models basis.

The main market risk charges may alternatively be calculated on an internal mod- **14.152** els basis subject to certain qualitative and quantitative standards. Qualitative standards include independent risk control, regular back testing, full involvement of the board of directors and senior management, integrated internal risk measurement models, internal trading and exposure limits, routine and rigorous stress testing, a compliance documented set of internal policies, and regular independent review. Quantitative requirements include use of a daily value-at-risk ('VAR') calculation, a 99 per cent (1 tailed) confidence interval, a 10-day holding interval, a one-year historical observation period, updated data sets every three years and a supervisory safety multiplier of three. The particular risk model selected must also be subject to stress testing and external validation procedures. These options have been continued under Basel II.

The new capital framework includes a new charge in respect of operational risk. **14.153** This is designed to cover losses arising as a result of fraud, personnel, or other systems or controls failures. Although not calculated in the same manner as other financial risks having regard to the particular exposures concerned (such as credit, market, or liquidity risk), larger banks have been setting aside amounts of capital against operational risk failures for some time. The Basel Committee accordingly decided to extend this to create an additional general charge included within the new minimum requirements imposed under Pillar 1.

14.154 With Basel II, the operational risk charge may either be calculated on a basic indicator approach (a fixed percentage of the factor selected of gross income), a standardised approach (using distinct business units and lines with a beta factor being applied), and an advanced measurement approach (using a separate exposure indicator ('EI'), probability of loss event ('PE'), and expected loss ('EL')). The new basic operational risk charge is estimated to be equivalent to approximately 20 per cent of total capital. While bank charges should fall under the more sensitive credit risk approach followed under the rest of Pillar 1, in practice this will generally be more than offset by the new operational risk charge imposed with no overall reduction in capital levels or costs.

14.155 Two further internal ratings-based approaches ('IRB') were also to be made available in respect of credit risk under Pillar 1 of Basel II. This can operate on either a foundation or an advanced basis which uses a number of additional factors including probability of default ('PD'), loss given default ('LGD'), and exposure at default (the 'EAD'). Effective maturity ('M') and expected loss ('EL') are also used in connection with retail exposures. Banks are generally to be allowed to use their own internal measures of PD in estimating credit risk under the foundation approach. This will be extended under the advanced approach to include the LGD and EAD. The factors which banks do not supply themselves are subject to supervisory estimates. These IRB approaches do not, however, allow for the use of full credit risk modelling at this stage (as under the Market Risk Amendment or CRD in respect of trading book charges) although this may be reconsidered over time under the further Basel III revisions as models become more sophisticated and more reliable historical data becomes available.

14.156 Pillar 2 of Basel II consists of a new supervisory review process. This imposes an express obligation on national supervisory authorities to confirm the adequacy of banks' internal control systems to measure and manage their capital exposures. This is based on four general components including maintaining an effective capital assessment process, a new supervisory obligation to review systems and strategies, use of supplementary capital amounts (such as the trigger and target ratios used in the UK), and supervisory intervention or correction in appropriate cases.

14.157 This Pillar 2 supervisory review is further strengthened under Pillar 3 enhanced market discipline. This operates on the basis of the mandatory disclosure of information concerning banks' capital policies and practices. These are divided into core and supplementary disclosures with the information to be provided set out in a series of templates included within the Basel II framework documents. The objective is to facilitate the additional or parallel supervision of bank activities by the markets themselves with banks becoming subject to market discipline, in particular, either through increases in lending premia or share price falls.

Basel III refers to the ongoing revision and update work that has been undertaken **14.158** since Basel II. The same process occurred with Basel I as the authorities knew at the time of agreement and adoption in 1988 that a number of residual issues remained (such as with regard to the underlying simplicity of the model and the absence of any market risk controls under Basel I) with further work being carried out immediately. This, in particular, led to the adoption of the Basel Market Risk Amendment in 1996 and with the later Basel II amendments which reflect the continuing nature of these processes and successes.

Further changes are then expected in due course under Basel III with regard **14.159** to such matters as agreement on new measurement approaches to credit risk, the treatment of diversification effects, the assessment of complex counterparty credit risks, the treatment of interest rate risk, and firm approaches to validation of internal capital assessments.[73] The key revisions will to a large extent be based on the increased use of internal risk management data and systems within banks including credit (as opposed to market) risk modelling as at present and new focus on interest and other risks in addition to core credit, market, and operational risk under Basel II. The underlying objective will be to achieve a closer approximation of internal economic and regulatory capital within banks which should, in turn, make them more efficient at the same time as better risk managed and more stable. Much of this work on capital regulation will now be further reviewed following the global credit crisis in 2007 and 2008 at the same time as other key initiatives brought forward on liquidity risk management.[74]

Capital Requirements Directive

The Basel Committee capital standards have been adopted within Europe subject **14.160** to certain revision and amendment under the European Capital Requirements Directive ('CRD').[75] The draft directive was issued for comment on 14 June 2004 in parallel with the Basel Committee final agreement documents and subsequently agreed in autumn 2005.

The objective of the CRD is to ensure the common application across Europe **14.161** of the new international capital standards agreed by the Basel Committee under

---

[73] See, for example, L Balthazar, *From Basel I to Basel 3: the Integration of State-of-the-Art Risk Modeling in Banking Regulation* (Palgrave, 2006).

[74] See, for example, Basel Committee on Banking Supervision, 'Liquidity Risk: Management and Supervisory Challenges' (February 2008); and Basel Committee, 'Principles for Sound Liquidity Risk Management and Supervision' (September 2008).

[75] Capital Requirements Directive COM (2004) 486 final of 14 July 2004 ('CRD'). The Directive was approved by the European Parliament in September 2005 and by the Council in October 2005.

its Basel II framework. This should more closely align financial risks with capital support and enhance consumer protection, reinforce financial stability, and increase the competitiveness of the European financial industry. The CRD will replace the earlier Own Funds Directive ('OFD') (EC) 89/299 of 17 April 1989 and the Solvency Ratio Directive ('SRD') (EC) 89/647 of 18 December 1989 as consolidated under the Banking Directive (EC) 2000/12 of 20 March 2000 in respect of banks and the Capital Adequacy Directive (EC) 93/6 of 15 March 1993 in respect of investment funds.

14.162 The earlier capital regime was considered to be inadequate with the crude estimates of credit risk provided, the scope for capital avoidance or arbitrage, lack of recognition of effective risk mitigation, gaps in the risks covered (including specifically operational risk), absence of any obligation on the part of supervisors to assess the risk profile or capability of financial institutions, lack of any supervisory cooperation, and requirements for proper market disclosures as well as inflexibility in the overall regulatory framework imposed. Capital requirements and financial risks would then continue to be misaligned resulting in limited effectiveness of the prudential rules and increased risk to consumers of financial instability. A number of risks would be omitted while the most recent and most effective risk management techniques would not have been properly encouraged and recognised with firms conducting overseas business being significantly disadvantaged as against other institutions due to the disproportionate regulatory burdens imposed.

14.163 Following agreement on the Basel II rules, it was considered necessary to agree a corresponding package of measures that could be given effect to across Europe although sufficiently differentiated to create an effective new capital regime for the whole of the single marketplace and for all institutions operating within it. An appropriate degree of variation had to be included for less complex institutions, although without resulting in an inferior or 'second class' perception or condition. A number of significant modifications had to be incorporated to allow the new measures to apply to both credit institutions and investment services providers. Sufficient flexibility had to be provided to ensure that the new framework could respond to changes in market and supervisory innovation. The Commission has also tried to make the text more user friendly with increased simplification and less prescription while nevertheless retaining the existing options and alternative approaches available as firms proceed from simpler to more complex calculation systems.

14.164 The legal basis for the directive is Article 47(2) of the EC Treaty which allows for measures to be adopted supporting the achievement of the Internal Market in financial services. A directive (rather than a regulation or decision) was considered to be the most appropriate instrument, although a 're-casting technique' is adopted under the Institutional Agreement 2002/C 77/01. This allows substantive amendments to be made to existing legislation without the need for any new self-standing amending directive. This is considered more appropriate in reducing complexity and increasing accessibility and comprehensibility. Some non-substantive amendments may nevertheless be made to improve the structure, layout, and drafting of relevant provisions. The general content of the new measures are set out in the explanatory memoranda attached to the CRD. A correspondence table was provided in the earlier consultation document produced on 1 July 2003.

Some new definitions are incorporated within the CRD to clarify the meaning **14.165** and relevance of certain concepts (Article 4). The obligation of credit institutions to maintain effective internal risk management systems are strengthened (Article 22). Some amendments are incorporated to the existing definition of own funds especially in connection with the modified approach to expected loss although these are stated not to be substantial (Articles 56 to 677). Credit institutions are to continue to hold adequate own funds on an ongoing basis but expressly required to state the minimum level of those funds (Articles 68 to 75). The existing solvency regime requirements for credit risk are replaced by the new standardised approach (Articles 78 to 83) and internal ratings-based approaches (Articles 84 to 89). New provisions are included on risk mitigation (Articles 90 to 93) with harmonised rules for securitisation activities and investments (Articles 94 to 101). Supporting technical provisions are set out in Annex VI.

The new Basel proposals on operational risk are incorporated (Articles 102 to **14.166** 105). This allows for the three different methodologies to be used consisting of either the basic indicator (Article 103), the standardised (Article 104), or the advanced measurement approaches (Article 105). The existing large exposures rules are amended in response to the extended recognition of credit risk mitigation provided for (Articles 106 to 119). Second Pillar supervisory review is provided for (under Articles 123 to 124) with improved coordination and cooperation between national supervisor agencies (Articles 125 to 143). Minimum disclosure requirements are imposed (Article 144) to enhance convergence of implementation and transparency with the new full Pillar 3 disclosure requirements being included (Articles 145 to 149). Additional technical provisions are provided for under Annex XII. The CRD also extends the technical areas that may be amended under the flexible revision procedure provided for under Directive (EC) 2000/12, in particular, with the distinction between core and technical rules with many of the more detailed provisions being included in the annexes to allow for their separate quick revision (Article 150).

Equivalent revisions were made to the Directive (EEC) 93/6 (CAD) in respect of **14.167** the capital adequacy obligations of investment firms and credit institutions in relation to their securities activities. These include provisions dealing with scope (Article 2), definitions (Article 3), trading book capital (Article 11), and minimal market risk requirement (Articles 18 and 20). Further amendments are made with regard to large exposures (Article 28), valuation of positions for reporting purposes (Article 33), consolidation (Article 22), risk management and capital assessment (Article 34), supervision (Article 37), and amendment (Article 42).

14.168 The Basel II Pillar 2 requirements are dealt with under the new 'supervisory review process' rules in the CRD. This is intended to ensure that firms hold adequate capital consistent with their risk profile and strategy subject to external supervisory review and assessment. This will be given effect to in the UK through an Internal Capital Adequacy Assessment Process ('ICAAP') supported by an external Supervisory Review and Evaluation Process ('SREP'). High-level guidance is being developed by European Committee of Banking Supervisors ('ECBS'). The content of the ECBS consultation paper was issued in January 2005.

14.169 The FSA conducted a number of exercises to determine to how to apply the ICAAP and SREP in practice. The FSA confirmed that Pillar 2 would not be automatically additive with the effect that higher charges will not arise in all cases. Firms would nevertheless be expected to operate above the minimum Pillar 1 requirements set and to hold sufficient additional capital to cover all risks involved with their activities at all times. Firms were expected to be responsible for assessing their own internal capital needs which will form part of the evaluation process conducted by supervisors. Senior management had to be fully involved in the Pillar 2 process. While some larger firms had already been looking towards developing an economic capital model, the FSA accepted that this would not be appropriate for all firms. Smaller firms may be able to rely on their basic Pillar 1 methodology provided that this covers all relevant risks.[76]

14.170 The Pillar 3 disclosures would generally be given effect to through revisions to many banks' existing disclosure practices as provided for under SUP and BIPRU. Firms would be expected to integrate Pillars 1, 2, and 3 with Pillar 3 being based on the firm's Pillar 1 compliance.

Prudential Sourcebook

14.171 IPRU(BANK) was originally to be replaced by the provisions set out in the Integrated Prudential Sourcebook.[77] The FSA originally consulted on the proposed Interim Prudential Sourcebook in Consultation Paper 27 in June 2001. Provisional draft rules and guidance were set out in Annex C to CP 97 with separate commentary on the main sections in Part II. A number of further papers were

---

[76] K Hale, 'The FSA's strategic view of regulation of the banking sector' address before the British Bankers Association, 16 February 2005.
[77] Chapter 11.

subsequently issued with more expected to follow on such issues as implementation of the European CRD and MiFID in the UK.

In designing the final sourcebook, the FSA had to include appropriate **14.172** provisions to deal with the different exposures that arise in each of the separate financial sectors. For this purpose, a risk-by-risk approach was adopted which amplifies and extends the more general supervision by risk system adopted within the new regime constructed by the FSA. As a number of distinct financial risks can be identified within any financial system, the FSA has decided that the core exposures involved are credit risk, market risk, and insurance risk as well as liquidity risk, operational risk and group risk. A six-part framework was accordingly adopted.

The proposed Integrated Sourcebook was originally to be divided into eight sepa- **14.173** rate modules with two general sections on application and general requirements (PRAG) and capital (PRCA).[78] Six further chapters were to be included on credit risk (PRCR), market risk (PRMR), liquidity risk (PRLR), operational risk (PROR), insurance risk (PRIR), and group risk (PRGR). Each module would have been divided into a number of separate chapters with a glossary of definitions also being provided. The credit risk (PRCR) would have included separate chapters on credit risk systems and controls, credit risk in the trading book, counterparty risk in the trading book, provisioning, concentration risk, collateral (credit and counterparty risk), netting (credit and counterparty risk), securitisation, credit derivatives risk, and credit risk in insurance funds. The market risk module ('PRMR') was to include market risk systems and controls, interest rate risk capital component, equity risk capital component, commodity risk capital component, securities underwriting, foreign-exchange risk, options risk, collective investment schemes, and traded endowment policies as well as use of CAD 1 models, value-at-risk models, market risk in insurance funds, and derivatives in insurance funds. Operational risk ('PROR') was to include operational risk systems and controls, outsourcing, and professional indemnity insurance.

The original approach was subsequently revised to refer to the Integrated Pru- **14.174** dential Sourcebook as the PRU. This was then to be divided into eight and then

---

[78] FSA, Integrated Prudential Sourcebook (June 2001), Consultation Paper 97; and FSA, Integrated Prudential Sourcebook, Annex C: Draft Rules and Guidance (June 2001), Consultation Paper 97a. See also FSA, Integrated Prudential Sourcebook—timetable for implementation (November 2001), Consultation Paper 115. Two subsequent consultation papers were then released in 2002 with a Policy Statement in October 2003. FSA, 'Liquidity Risk in the Integrated Prudential Sourcebook—Systems and controls chapter' (March 2002) Consultation Paper 128; and FSA, 'Operational risk systems and controls' (June 2002) Consultation Paper 142; and FSA, 'Integrated Prudential Sourcebook—Near-final text on prudential risks systems and controls' (October 2003). On early policy approach, see FSA, 'The FSA's approach to setting prudential standards' (1999), CP 31.

nine chapters. These consisted of application and general requirements (PRU 1), capital (PRU 2), credit risk (PRU 3), market risk (PRU 4), liquidity (PRU 5), operational risk (PRU 6), insurance risk (PRU 7), and group risk (PRU 8) with a further Integrated Prudential Sourcebook chapter being added (PRU 9). Relevant transitional provisions were set out in PRU TP 1 with six further schedules. Almost final text was released in October 2003.[79]

14.175 The FSA announced during 2004 that a further restructuring was to be considered in light of the implementation obligations imposed under the European CRD of 14 July 2004 which would substantially amend the Banking Consolidation Directive (EC) 2000/12 and the CAD (EC) 93/6. The prudential and systems and controls material in the Handbook would be revised to make them more accessible to specialised firms and to improve navigability although the idea of grouping material by risk would be retained. This was also considered desirable to align more closely the structure of the PRU with the FSA's 'copy-out' approach to European implementation and avoid unnecessary 'super-equivalence' or complex drafting in non-scope areas. With its copy-out approach to implementation, the FSA will restate relevant EU measures with more additional (super-equivalent) obligations only being added where this is considered necessary to secure its statutory objectives or to clarify the operation or application of relevant rules. A more general correspondence and comparability of relevant requirements should also be achieved between UK and European measures.

14.176 The FSA issued a further policy statement on Strengthening Capital Standards 2 in July 2006 (CP06/3).[80] This followed two earlier consultation papers on restructuring the Handbook and common platform firms (CP06/10 and CP06/09) and a following feedback statement in July 2006 (PS06/6).[81] The core provisions on the revision of the capital regime were set out in PS06/6 which included specific chapters on each of the main capital tranches in CP06/3. This dealt with the clarity and accessibility of copy-out rules, key policy decisions and updates, status of the material produced by the Committee of European Banking Supervisors ('CEBS'), individual guidance, international implementation, and outstanding issues. The FSA was committed to the adoption of a copy-out approach to UK implementation with only limited super-equivalence and sufficient flexibility where necessary. The clarity and accessibility of the text would be dealt with through extended guidance and navigational tables and worked examples with

---

[79] FSA, 'Integrated Prudential Sourcebook—Near-final text on prudential risks systems and controls' (October 2003).

[80] FSA CP06/3, 'Strengthening Capital Standards 2' (July 2006).

[81] FSA CP06/10, 'Strengthening Capital Standards—Restructuring the Handbook' (May 2006); FSA CP06/09, 'Organisational Systems and Controls—Common Platform for Firms' (May 2006); and FSA PS06/6, 'Strengthening Capital Standards Figures 2—Feedback on CP06/3' (July 2006).

personal handbooks being provided containing dedicated sets of relevant provisions. Personal handbooks would be issued in response to ten specific questions concerning firms' business activities.

Certain difficulties remained with regard to the operation of provisions based on **14.177** effective home host relations and, in particular, with regard to firms adopting an advanced approach under Pillar 1 in more than one jurisdiction and the operation of Pillar 2 with regard to international groups. Guidelines had been produced by the CEBS with further recommendations being issued by the Basel Accord Implementation Group ('AIG') for non-EEA countries. A series of 'regulatory colleges' had also been set up to allow authorities to work together effectively and to limit duplication of activity.

A number of industry groups had been set up to assist the FSA in implementing **14.178** the new capital provisions within the UK and, in particular, preparing relevant measures. A Basel/CRD Implementation Advisory Group ('BIAG') was established with representatives from the FSA, the Treasury and Bank of England as well as trade associations and regulated firms to discuss strategic objectives, implementation review, and exchange of information and timetable issues. A number of other groups were also set up including the Banks and Investment Firms Commodity Standing Group ('BIFCOM'), the Capital and Groups Standing Group ('CGSG'), the Commodity Standing Group ('COMSG'), the Covered Bond Standing Group ('CBSG'), the Credit Risk Mitigation Standing Group ('CRMSG'), the Credit Risk Standing Group ('CRSG'), the Market Risk and Trading Books Standing Group ('MRTSG'), the Operational Risk Standing Group ('ORSG'), the Pillar Two Standing Group ('PTSG'), and the Securitisation Standing Group ('SSG').[82]

Following this work, the final Integrated Prudential Sourcebook has since been **14.179** divided into a number of separate sub-sourcebooks. This consists of a revised set of common provisions applicable to all firms ('GENPRU') with separate requirements for banks and investment firms ('BIPRU') and insurance and Lloyd's managing agents ('INSPRU') as well as unit trust managers and UCITS firms ('UPRU') and mortgage and insurance mediation firms ('MIPRU'). Investment firms not subject to the CRD were to be dealt with under INVPRU with other residual friendly societies in FPRU. The provisions on financial groups (originally contained in PRU 8.4) have been moved to GENPRU 3.1.).

Banks and investment firms are now subject to the provisions contained in **14.180** GENPRU, BIPRU, and the revised post-MIFID SYSC. Advanced capital measures

---

[82] The composition and mandate of each group are dealt with on the FSA website <http://www. fsa.gov.uk/>.

came into effect on 1 January 2008 although firms had the option of complying with IPRU(Bank) during 2007 or adopting the revised standard provisions contained in BIPRU subject to certain exceptions. The liquidity provisions within IPRU(Bank) were continued on a provisional basis until revised measures could be agreed at the international and European levels with the issue being further reconsidered following the Northern Rock crisis. This applies with regard to the provisions on mismatch liquidity ('LM') and sterling stock liquidity ('LS') in volume 2 of IPRU(Bank).[83]

14.181 Building societies are also subject to GENPRU, BIPRU, and the revised SYSC although the constitutional provisions within volume 2 of IPRU(BSOC) have been retained and reissued in the form of a separate Regulatory Guide. A new common platform regime was created for firms subject to both the EU CRD and MiFID with effect from 1 November 2007 on implementation of MiFID. Seven new chapters have been inserted within SYSC for common platform firms which expand the general management and internal systems and controls requirements set out in PRIN 3. (Firms must take reasonable care to organise and control their affairs responsibly and effectively with adequate risk management systems.[84]) IPRU(INV) would continue in effect for firms not subject to BIPRU.

14.182 These are important provisions which will allow the completion of the construction of a more coordinated but still not fully integrated Handbook of Rules and Guidance in the UK. A single set of relevant prudential obligations was to have been provided for all types of financial firms. A common risk-based methodology has been adopted although adjusted to reflect the separate and distinct underlying exposures involved. The principal compromise that has been made to the use of the original risk-by-risk approach has been to divide the final sourcebook into a number of separate sub-sourcebooks to reflect the individual categories of financial institutions used under the European financial directives rather than operate on a purely risk basis. This is, in turn, necessary to give effect to the copy-out implementation approach adopted and to simplify transparency and accessibility of relevant measures within the UK.

14.183 The residual gap that remains is with regard to liquidity rather than capital controls.[85] The fallout from the credit crisis in 2007 and 2008 revealed the importance of liquidity and funding risk and the dependence of banks and other financial institutions on stable and effective inter-bank markets.[86] Parallel progress will be needed in these areas before any complete new regime will have been created.

---

[83] FSA DP24, 'Liquidity Risk in the Integrated Prudential Sourcebook: A Quantitative Framework' (2006); and CP06/10.

[84] Chapter 5.

[85] Para 14.159 and (nn 74 and 83).

[86] Paras 14.220–14.240.

General Prudential Sourcebook (GENPRU)

The general provisions applicable to banks, building societies, BIPRU invest- **14.184**
ment firms, insurers, and groups containing such firms are now set out in
GENPRU which came into effect on 1 January 2007. This restates many of the
earlier provisions contained in the Integrated Prudential Sourcebook (PRU)
including financial resources, risk identification and assessment, minimum
capital resources, and the definition of capital including relevant deductions and
other risks.[87]

GENPRU 1 is concerned with the identification and assessment of risks that **14.185**
may undermine the ability of firms to cover their liabilities as they fall due, how
those risks are dealt with, and the amount and nature of the financial resources
considered necessary to do so. Adequate financial resources and systems and
controls are stated to be necessary for the effective management of prudential risk
(GENPRU 1.2.12). Firms must maintain at all times overall financial resources
(including capital and liquidity resources) that are adequate both as to amount
and quality to ensure that there is no significant risk that their liabilities cannot
be met as they fall due (GENPRU 1.2.26R).

Firms must have sound, effective, and complete processes, strategies, and systems **14.186**
to assess and maintain on an ongoing basis the amounts, types, and distribution
of financial resources, capital resources, and internal capital required to cover all
relevant risk including credit risk, market risk, liquidity risk, operational risk,
insurance risk, concentration risk, residual risk, securitisation risk, business risk,
interest rate risk, and pension obligation risk to the extent relevant (GENPRU
1.2.30R). Pillar 2 processes, strategies, and systems must be comprehensive and
proportionate to the nature, scale, and complexity of a firm's activities (GENPRU
1.2.35R). Firms must also carry out stress tests and scenario analysis appropriate
to the nature of each major source of risk (GENPRU 1.2.42R).

GENPRU 2.2. contains the revised provisions on the definition and measure- **14.187**
ment of capital. Firms must maintain at all times capital resources equal to or in
excess of their variable capital requirement (GENPRU 2.1.40R). This is the
aggregate of the credit risk capital requirement, market risk capital requirement,
and operational risk market requirement for banks and building societies and
full scope BIPRU investment firms (GENPRU 2.1.45R). Firms must also maintain on an initial and continuing basis capital resources equal to or in excess
of their Base Capital Resources Requirement (GENPRU 2.1.41 and 42R).
This includes Tier 1 capital, upper and lower Tier 2 capital, Tier 3 capital for

---

[87] Para 14.174.

investment firms, non-standard capital instruments and capital deductions, as well as limits and applications (GENPRU 2.2.9G–2.2.276).

14.188 Core Tier 1 capital includes permanent share capital, profit and loss account and other reserves, share premium account, externally verified interim net profits, eligible partnership capital, eligible LLP members' capital, and sole trader capital with other Tier 1 capital consisting of perpetual non-cumulative preference shares. Upper Tier 2 capital consists of perpetual cumulative preference shares, perpetual subordinated debt, perpetual subordinated securities, revaluation reserves, general/collective provisions and surplus provisions with lower Tier 2 being made up of fixed term preference shares, long-term (five-year) subordinated debt, and fixed term subordinated securities. Upper Tier 3 capital consists of short-term (two-year) subordinated debt for investment firms and lower Tier 3 capital net interim trading book profits. Innovative Tier 1 capital has also been included for building societies and investment firms.

14.189 Required deductions from Tier 1 capital are investments in own shares, intangible assets, excess drawings over profits for partnerships and limited liability partnerships, and net losses on equities held in the for sale asset category. Deductions from total Tier 1 and Tier 2 include qualifying holdings, material holdings, expected loss amounts and other negative amounts, securitisation positions, reciprocal cross-holdings, investments in subsidiary undertakings, and participations not already deducted as well as connected lending of a capital nature. Excess trading book position and free deliveries are to be deducted from total capital. Summary tables are provided in the Annexes to GENPRU 2.

14.190 BIPRU firms are also required to comply with the provisions on individual capital adequacy (BIPRU 2.2), common provisions (BIPRU 4.3), group risk and consolidation (BIPRU 8), concentration risk requirements (BIPRU 10), and settlement and counter party risk (BIPRU 14). Financial conglomerates are now dealt with under GENPRU 3.

Prudential Sourcebook (BIPRU)

14.191 The revised capital and financial provisions for banks, building societies, and investment firms are set out in BIPRU. BIPRU is made up of 14 sections with additional transitional provisions and schedules. These consist of application (BIPRU 1), capital (BIPRU 2), standardised credit risk (BIPRU 3), the IRB approach (BIPRU 4), credit risk mitigation (BIPRU 5), operational risk (BIPRU 6), market risk (BIPRU 7), group risk consolidation (BIPRU 8), securitisation (BIPRU 9), concentration risk requirements (BIPRU 10), disclosure under Pillar 3 (BIPRU 11), counter party risk exposure for financial derivatives, securities financing and loan settlement transactions (BIPRU 13), and settlement and counterparty risk (BIPRU 14). BIPRU 12 is to follow. Complex transitional provisions apply with regard to the application of GENPRU and BIPRU. These are available on the FSA website.

Application—BIPRU 1

BIPRU applies to banks, building societies, BIPRU investment firms, and groups containing such firms. Each chapter of BIPRU is separately applied. BIPRU applies to a firm in relation to the whole of its business except where a particular provision otherwise provides. BIPRU 1 includes provisions concerning the definition of the trading book (BIPRU 1.2), special provisions on advanced approaches (1.3) and the disapplication of a right of action for breach under s 150 of FSMA (1.4). **14.192**

Capital—BIPRU 2

BIPRU contains rules and guidance concerning solo consolidation (2.1), internal capital adequacy standards (2.2), and interest rate risk in the non-trading book (2.3). Firms must incorporate in the calculation of their main Pillar 1 rules (and concentration risk requirement under BIPRU 10) each subsidiary undertaking to which any solo consolidation waiver applies except with regard to the base capital resources requirement. Firms must treat themselves and each such subsidiary as a single undertaking. **14.193**

BIPRU 2.2 provides for the operation of the internal capital adequacy assessment process (ICAAP) and the supervisory review and evaluation process or SREP. Firms must carry out regular assessments of the amounts, types, and distribution of financial resources, capital resources, and internal capital considered adequate to cover the nature and level of the risks to which they are exposed under the ICAAP. Where a firm is a member of a group, it should base its ICAAP on the consolidated financial position of the group. The firm should ensure that its ICAAP is the responsibility of its governing body, reported to the governing body, and forms an integral part of its management process and decision-making culture. The FSA will review the firm's ICAAP (and any IRB stress tests) as part of its SREP. **14.194**

The purpose of the SREP is to allow the FSA to review the arrangements, strategies, and processes and mechanisms implemented by the firm to comply with GENPRU, BIPRU, and SYSC and any other requirements imposed under the regulatory system. It will also determine whether such arrangements ensure a sound management and coverage of the risks concerned and require the firm **14.195** where necessary to take any additional actions or steps to address any failures identified. The FSA may give firms individual capital guidance including a statement of the amount and quality of capital the FSA considers that the firm requires to comply with its overall financial adequacy requirement. BIPRU 2.2 contains further guidance on the risks covered within the ICAAP.

14.196 Separate provisions are included concerning interest rate risk in the non-trading book. This may apply with regard to risks relating to the mismatch or repricing of assets and liabilities and off-balance sheet short and long positions, risks arising from hedging exposures under different conditions, risks relating to transaction uncertainties and risks from consumers redeeming fixed rate products as market rates change. Firms must carry out an evaluation of their exposures to interest rates arising from their non-trading activities. This must include the effect of a sudden and unexpected parallel change in the interest rates of 200 basis points in both directions with the FSA being notified where the economic value of the firm may decline by more than 20 per cent of its capital resources in the event of such an event. Additional conditions apply with regard to more complex firms with firms being required to maintain written records of their assessments. The FSA will periodically review whether the level of shock referred to is appropriate in light of changing circumstances and the general level of interest rates and volatility.

Standardised Credit Risk Approach—BIPRU 3

14.197 BIPRU contains the revised provisions concerning the minimum capital requirements to be held under the standardised approach to credit risk contained in Basel II Pillar 1 and the CRD. This generally applies the earlier minimum 8 per cent capital adequacy regime subject to amendment to make this more risk-sensitive and responsive. The minimum 8 per cent of total risk weighted exposure amounts is retained as the core credit risk capital component. Greater risk sensitivity is nevertheless created through the use of external credit ratings. Firms are required to assign their credit exposures across 16 classes and apply more risk-sensitive weightings to each ranging from 0 per cent to 150 per cent depending upon the perceived credit quality of the counterparty.

14.198 Separate provisions apply with regard to central governments and central banks, regional governments and local authorities, administrative bodies and non-commercial undertakings, multilateral development banks, international organisations, financial institutions, corporate bodies, retail exposures, real estate property, past-due items, regulatory high-risk categories, covered bonds, securitisation positions, short-term claims on institutions and corporates, collective investment undertakings and other items. Relevant risk weights are set out in BIPRU 3.4. Firms that only have incidental credit risk exposures may use the 'simplified standardised approach' which does not use external credit risk weightings.

Firms can also apply a single risk weight to all exposures in each class as under the previous regime. Rating agency assessments are dealt with under BIPRU 3.6 and off-balance sheets items in BIPRU 3.7.

IRB Approach—BIPRU 4

The Basel/CRD internal ratings-based ('IRB') approach is implemented under **14.199** BIPRU 4. Capital requirements are based on a firm's internal estimates of certain parameters which are as specified in the BCD. Exposures are divided into a number of distinct classes (with special rules for purchased receivables). The foundation IRB approach is available for sovereign, institution, and corporate exposure classes using a firm's own estimates of probability of default ('PD'). Advanced IRB approaches allow firms to use their own estimates of loss given default ('LGD') and supporting conversion factors. Firms use own estimates of PD (LGD) and conversion factors for retail exposures. Two approaches based on market-based measures or own estimates of PD only can be used in connection with equity exposures. A separate sub-class of specialised lending exposures applies in connection with corporate exposures. BIPRU 4 contains specific provisions with regard to high-level material (4.2), common provisions (4.3), corporates, institutions, and sovereigns (4.4), standardised lending exposures (4.5), retail exposures (4.6), equity exposures (4.7), purchased receivables (4.8), securitisation (4.9), and credit risk mitigation (4.10).

Credit Risk Mitigation—BIPRU 5

BIPRU 5 implements the provisions concerning the recognition of techniques **14.200** used to reduce the credit risk associated with a particular exposure. The credit risk mitigation ('CRM') rules allow firms to hold lower capital under either the standardised or IRB approaches. CRM can be achieved either through the use of funded or unfunded protection. Funded protection applies with regard to the taking of rights over assets or reducing liabilities in the event that the borrower does not pay (such as under a mortgage) with unfunded protection being provided by third parties (such as under a guarantee or insurance policy). CRM techniques include netting, collateral, guarantees, and credit derivatives. BIPRU 5 generally applies to firms relying on the standardised approach with BIPRU 4.10 being used for IRB approaches.

Certain high-level principles have to be considered to ensure that a particular **14.201** type of CRM can provide sufficiently effective protection against credit risk. The main principles of credit risk mitigation are set out in BIPRU 5.2. BIPRU contains additional provisions concerning on-balance sheet netting (5.3), financial collateral (5.4), other funded credit risk mitigation including deposits and life insurance policies or other purchased instruments and credit linked notes (5.5), master netting agreements (5.6), unfunded credit protection (5.7), maturity mismatches (5.8), and CRM combinations (5.9).

Operational Risk—BIPRU 6

14.202 The new operational risk regime created under Basel II is applied under BIPRU 6. Firms are required to hold capital to cover operational risk losses and maintain appropriate systems and controls to manage operational risk and explain how the operational risk capital requirement ('ORCR') is calculated. Firms can generally either use a basic indicator approach, standardised approach, or advanced measurement approach ('AMA'). The ORCR under the basic indicator approach is stated to be equal to 15 per cent of the relevant indicator as defined. Firms must divide their activities into a number of business lines under the standardised approach (including corporate finance, trading and sales, retail brokerage, commercial banking, retail banking, payment and settlement, agency services, and asset management). Firms must satisfy certain general risk management standards imposed under SYSC as well as additional qualitative and quantitative standards to be able to make use of the AMA approach to operational risk. The AMA must produce a practical and appropriate 99.9 per cent confidence level, produce sufficiently robust overall model outputs, and be reviewed on an ongoing basis.

Market Risk—BIPRU 7

14.203 BIPRU 7 reapplies the market risk rules originally developed in the Basel Committee 1996 Market Risk Amendment and EU CAD. These were previously contained in IPRU(BANK) and IPRU(INV) Chapter 10. The earlier provisions are generally restated with additional measures on collective investment undertakings ('CIUs'), interest rate specific risk treatments and the modelling of default risk under value-at-risk ('VAR') models.

14.204 The rules generally impose capital requirements on interest rate related instruments (bonds and debentures), equities, and CIUs in the trading book and foreign exchange risk and commodities risk across the firm. Firms are required to mark-to-market ('MTM') their positions daily. Firms can either adopt a standard 'building block' or internal models-based approach to the calculation of their minimum capital requirements. Under the standard rules, identical or similar long and short positions are netted with a percentage capital haircut or position risk addition ('PRA') being calculated on a percentage basis. The haircut varies with the risks involved. Interest rate and equity exposures are divided into general risk (market factors) and specific risk (individual issuer) components. Specific rules are imposed with regard to interest rate risk (BIPRU 7.2), equities (7.3), commodities (7.4), foreign exchange (7.5), options (7.6), CIUs (7.7), and credit derivatives (7.11). Firms can also use more sophisticated 'CAD 1 models' including interest rate pre-processing models (to net positions within certain maturity bands before applying the standard rules for general interest rate risk) and options aggregation models (to recognise hedging within options portfolios). The CAD 1 rules and guidance are contained in BIPRU 7.9.

Firms can separately apply for waivers to use VAR models. The firms have to comply with specific quantitative and qualitative minimum criteria (BIPRU 7.10). Separate provisions apply with regard to underwriting commitments (BIPRU 7.8). Valuation is dealt with in GENPRU 1.3 and trading book positions in BIPRU 1.2.   **14.205**

Group Risk—BIPRU 8

Group capital resources and resource requirements are imposed with regard to larger financial groups. The detailed rules and guidance on consolidated capital requirements for BIPRU firms and groups are contained in BIPRU 8. This applies with regard to UK consolidation groups, non-EEA sub-groups and parent financial holding companies. These implement the relevant provisions contained in the BCD and CAD. This replaces IPRU(BANK) consolidated supervision and IPRU(INV) Chapter 14. Firms not subject to consolidated supervision under BIPRU 8 may still be subject to IPRU(INV) Chapter 14 such as commodities firms under an Article 48(2) CRD exemption. Diagrams (decision trees) are provided to identify relevant groups.   **14.206**

Some new elements are included within the rules. The CRD provisions apply consolidation at each Member State level rather than only to the ultimate parent firm within the EEA. A non-EEA sub-group exists where a subsidiary BIPRU firm or its parent (where it is a financial holding company (FHC)) has a subsidiary or participation in an institution, financial institution, or asset management company established outside the EEA. Groups that contain only limited licence or limited activity investment firms are exempt subject to minimum conditions. Groups that do not contain credit institutions or investment firms dealing on own account are not subject to consolidated operational risk requirements. Firms can include requirements calculated using non-EEA regulations provided that they are deemed to be equivalent to the CRD rules. A list of equivalent measures is provided in BIPRU 8 Annex 6R. This includes those used in the USA, Australia, Canada, Switzerland, Japan, South Africa, Hong Kong, Singapore, India, and Korea measures governing market risk, credit risk, and operational risk.   **14.207**

The application of the consolidation provisions is dealt with under GENPRU 1.3. Financial conglomerates are covered in GENPRU 3.1 with banking and investment   **14.208** services groups headed by a non-EEA parent undertaking in GENPRU 3.2. Embedded waivers (including groups) are dealt with under BIPRU 1.3 and consolidated Pillar 3 requirements under BIPRU 11.

Securitisation—BIPRU 9

14.209 New securitisation measures are provided for under BIPRU 9. This replaces the securitisation and asset transfer provisions in IPRU(BANK) Chapter SE and IPRU(BSOC). This includes specific rules dealing with exposures to tranched positions arising under a securitisation.

14.210 Firms must calculate the risk weight exposure amounts for securitisation positions under BIPRU 9. Firms must apply the securitisation framework to determine regulatory capital requirements on exposures arising from traditional and synthetic securitisations or similar structures that contain equivalent features. Traditional securitisation involves the economic transfer of exposures to a special purpose entity ('SPE') which issues new securities following a full transfer of ownership with securities not representing payment obligations of the originator. Synthetic securitisations provide for the tranching of risk through the use of credit derivatives or guarantees with the exposure pool not being removed from the balance sheet of the originator. Firms must look to the economic substance of a transaction to determine whether the securitisation framework is applicable for the purposes of determining regulatory capital.

14.211 The securitisation rules apply both with regard to whether the capital position of the originator can be reduced in some way as well as that of firms holding relevant securitisation positions. Different results may apply in each case. Securitisation positions include loans, liquidity facilities, and counterparty exposures under derivative positions.

14.212 Specific provisions apply with regard to originators. The originator is either the originator of the underlying exposures that are securitised or the securitisation. A sponsor of an asset-backed commercial paper ('ABCP') conduit is generally not considered an originator unless the sponsor is economically the same. The provisions impose three operational requirements with regard to effective risk transfer, significant risk transfer, and the absence of implicit support.

14.213 Securitisation recognition may be achieved under either a standardised or internal ratings base (IRB) approach. This is dependent on the Pillar 1 minimum capital requirement applied with regard to the underlying portfolio of securitised exposures. Under the standardised method, the risk weighted asset amount of a securitised exposure is calculated by multiplying the amount of the position by a specified risk weight (varying from 20 per cent, 50 per cent, 100 per cent, 350 per cent, and 1250 per cent). Special rules apply with regard to unrated securitisation positions. The IRB approach uses three potential calculations with a ratings-based approach ('RBA'), internal assessment approach ('IAA'), and supervisory formula method (SF). Ratings are similar to the standardised approach although the tables are more sophisticated and include a granularity element. IAA only applies to ABCP programme exposures and is generally concerned with liquidity facilities and credit enhancement. A firm's internal assessment process is mapped against an external credit assessment institution ('ECAI'). SF applies with regard to non-rated exposures with five inputs being used. Special rules apply with regard to securitisations containing early amortisation provisions.

Concentration Risk—BIPRU 10

BIPRU 10 applies with regard to large exposures and concentration risk capital **14.214** component ('CNCOM'). Large exposures may threaten the financial position of a firm through increased counterparty risk. Various limits are imposed following relevant EU requirements. These include a 25 per cent ceiling on exposures to the same counterparty and an 800 per cent total limit with regard to non-trading book items. A 500 per cent limit is imposed on exposures to the same counterparty for up to 10 business days on trading book items. A 600 per cent limit applies with regard to exposures held for over 10 days. Special rules apply with regard to the application of these provisions to integrated groups ('UKIGs') and wider integrated groups ('WIGs'). The IG rules are relevant to parents or subsidiary companies within a larger financial group with one or more exposures to each other. The measures apply on a solo and consolidated basis.

Disclosure—BIPRU 11

New disclosure requirements are imposed under BIPRU 11 which give effect to **14.215** the Basel Committee and CRD Pillar 3 obligations. The disclosure provisions apply with regard to individual firms, EEA parent institutions, significant subsidiaries of EEA parent institutions or firms controlled by an EEA parent financial holding company, and a significant subsidiary of an EEA parent financial holding company. Specific measures apply with regard to information to be disclosed, frequency and verification, technical criteria on disclosure and content (including risk management objectives and policies, capital resources, credit risk and dilution risk, credit and market risk disclosures, interest rate risk, and securitisation), and IRB and credit risk mitigation disclosure.

Counterparty Risk—BIPRU 13

Counterparty risk is concerned with default before final settlement on a tran- **14.216** saction. Trading book exposures are covered by the counterparty rules with non-trading book transactions being dealt with under the credit risk provisions. While traditional credit risk can be assessed at the time the transaction is entered into, the potential exposure under a financial derivative or securities financing transaction ('SFT') may vary over the life of the transaction. An assessment is accordingly made of both the mark-to-market ('MTM') value and potential future exposure ('PFE'). Counterparty exposures are calculated on a position-by-position basis unless a legally enforceable netting agreement applies. Firms may use either an MTM method, standardised method, or internal model method. Only the MTM option was previously available.

14.217 Under the MTM option, the exposure is calculated as the MTM plus the PFE with the PFE being determined as a percentage of the notional value of the contract which varies having regard to product and maturity. The standardised method is more risk-sensitive with exposures being classified (or bucketed). An effective expected positive exposure (effective EPE) is calculated under the internal model approach. Specified quantitative and qualitative minimum criteria again apply before waivers are granted to use internal models and SFTs.

Unsettled Transactions and Free Deliveries—BIPRU 14

14.218 BIPRU 14 contains the capital requirements with regard to unsettled transactions and free deliveries. Unsettled transactions are those dealt with through a delivery versus payment DVP system providing for the simultaneous exchange of securities for cash with the specific transaction not settling. The loss is the difference between the transaction value at the agreed settlement price and current market price. Free deliveries arise where one party has paid for securities before receiving them or delivered securities before receiving payment. The potential loss is the full amount of the cash paid or securities delivered. The rules then apply with regard to transactions that have been confirmed but not settled. The rules do not apply with regard to repos, securities and commodities borrowing or lending, long settlement transactions, or one-way cash payments due under OTC derivative transactions.

14.219 The provisions with regard to unsettled transactions are generally the same as under the earlier rules with some minor amendments. Firms have a five-day grace period where no charge applies with capital being calculated on the basis of a percentage of the difference between the agreed settlement price and current market value up to 48 days after which the full difference applies. Under the free delivery rules, firms must deduct the full value of the transaction from their capital resources after five days following the due settlement date although greater flexibility is applied with the use of either a standardised or IRB approach.

Northern Rock

The relative stability of the new integrated system of financial regulation set up   **14.220**
under FSMA has been most substantially tested with the liquidity crisis in the
inter-bank market beginning in August 2007 and the funding difficulties this
caused at Northern Rock in September 2007 which led to its later acquisition by
the Treasury in February 2008.[88] Following the credit tightening that had occurred
in many of the principal inter-bank markets across the world in August 2007,
Northern Rock was forced to ask for liquidity support from the Bank of England
which was agreed on 14 September 2007. The Government had initially confirmed that it would prefer a private market solution to the problems at Northern
Rock and various private sector bids were considered for its acquisition during
autumn 2007. Following the Treasury's rejection of the remaining bids by the
Virgin Group and a private management team in February 2008, the Government
announced that it would take Northern Rock 'into public ownership' on Sunday
17 February 2008. While Northern Rock had only limited direct exposure to
the US sub-prime crisis that had caused the larger credit crisis in global markets
during summer 2007, its low deposit base and wholesale funding business model
had meant that it was unable to borrow sufficient continuing funds in the market
with the credit tightening that had occurred.

Credit crisis

The credit crisis began with concerns of default in the US sub-prime mortgage   **14.221**
market with almost two-thirds of a US$12t market being reported to have been
used to support securitised instruments sold in the asset-backed securities sector.
These included collateralised debt obligations ('CDOs') which were used to
trade separate tranches of underlying securitised sub-prime debt with many
of these being purchased by structured investment vehicles ('SIVs') or bank
'conduits' that had been set up on an off-balance sheet basis to invest in high yield
products such as CDOs and other structured instruments including credit linked

---

[88] GA Walker, 'Northern Rock Falls' (2008) *Bankers' Law* Vol 2, No 2, 4–12 (n 22). See also
GA Walker, 'The Deconstruction of Financial Risk' (2008) *Palgrave Journal of Banking Regulation*
(October) 1, 2; and GA Walker, 'Credit Crisis—Regulatory and Financial Systems Reform' (2007)
Butterworths JIBL (November) 567–72; and GA Walker, 'Sub-prime Loans, Inter-Bank Markets
and Financial Support' (2007) *The Company Lawyer* (November) 22–25 (n 22). See also Walker,
'Credit Contraction, Financial Collapse and Global Recession' *Butterworths JIBL* (January 2009)
5–10; and Walker, 'Credit Crisis, Bretton Woods II and A New Global Response' *Butterworths JIBL*
(February 2009). See also Chapter 1, paras 1.151–1.180.

notes ('CLNs').[89] These instruments had been created as part of a larger process of the securitisation and 'deconstruction' of financial risk with the transfer of debt and credit from loan to securities markets and then with the further breaking up and separate trading of the individual risk components created within this new debt.[90]

14.222 Difficulties in the US sub-prime mortgage market had arisen as this had been unregulated at the federal level with up to one quarter of the loans granted being expected to go into default and with a huge number of early fixed rate mortgages having to be reset with new adjustable rate policies. This was blamed on the sales practices of aggressive unregulated brokers and the use of self-certification by many borrowers as well as the questionable provision of credit by banks and other financial institutions to fund these commitments. The problems within the US sub-prime markets spread elsewhere as two-thirds of this sub-prime debt had been securitised. This securitised debt was then incorporated into larger structured products including principally CDOs which were sold across the globe to major financial institutions including through their SIVs and conduits as well as to hedge funds and other investors. The debt was attractive as the returns were generous, with the quality of the debt having been overrated by the rating agencies involved who had been paid by the debt issuing companies concerned.

14.223 The value of this debt began to collapse in summer 2007 with evidence of underlying default in the sub-prime sector and with many major banking and securities groups having to write off substantial losses.[91] This led to an immediate drying up of credit in the main domestic and international inter-bank markets as banks decided to hoard cash and became increasingly reluctant to deal with counterparties with unknown structured product losses. Total losses in connection with the sub-prime crisis were initially estimated to be in excess of £100bn and then increased to £500bn. This also led to separate difficulties in related markets such as the mono-line insurance market in the US which was valued at US$2.3t and with other losses being suffered at individual institutions such as Société Générale which lost US$7.2bn (£3.1bn or €4.9bn) through its trader Jerôme Kerviel. Evan Dolley at one of the largest global commodity brokerages, MN Global, lost US$141bn in unauthorised wheat trades. Bear Stearns also had to write off US$3.2bn in CDO related losses which led to its subsequent

---

[89] GA Walker, 'Sub-prime loans, inter-bank markets and financial support' (n 22); and GA Walker, 'Credit crisis: regulatory and financial systems reform' (n 22) 568.

[90] GA Walker, 'The deconstruction of financial risk' (n 22) 1–2.

[91] Initial figures announced included: UBS US$13.5bn, City Group US$11bn, Morgan Stanley US$9.4bn, Merrill Lynch US$8bn, HSBC US$3.4bn, Bear Stearns US$3.2bn, Deutschebank US$3.2bn, Bank of America US$3bn, Barclays US$2.6bn, and Royal Bank of Scotland US$2.6bn.

acquisition by J P Morgan Chase in March 2008 under a support facility organised through the Federal Reserve Board.

The Federal Reserve Board and European Central Bank ('ECB') had attempted to **14.224** support the markets by injecting liquidity following the drying up of inter-bank credits on 9 August 2007. The ECB made available €95bn (US$131bn) on 9 August (more than after the terrorist attacks on 11 September 2001) and a further €61bn on 10 August. The Federal Reserve injected US$24bn and then US$38bn with the central banks in Canada, Japan, and Australia following. The US discount rate was cut by 0.5 per cent on 17 August and then again on 31 October and 11 December 2007.

The major world central banks agreed to a further coordinated injection of **14.225** US$100bn in the short-term inter-bank markets on 13 December 2007. The Federal Reserve intervened on 7 March and 11 March 2008 under its Term Auction Facility ('TAF') which had been set up the previous December. A new Term Securities Lending Facility ('TSLF') was also created on 11 March 2008 to allow primary dealers (rather than banks) to borrow up to US$200bn of Treasury securities for 28 days against lesser quality bond collateral. While the Bank of England had initially been more cautious than other central banks, it announced a series of auctions on 19 September 2007 although none of the funds available was taken up due to the perceived stigma attached.

Northern Rock

The major UK casualty from the credit tightening was Northern Rock which was **14.226** forced to accept emergency funding from the Bank of England on 14 September 2007. The Northern Rock Building Society had originally been set up in 1965 following the merger of the Northern Counties Permanent Building Society (established in 1850) and the Rock Building Society (set up in 1865). The society was demutualised and converted into a bank in 1997, with a Northern Rock Foundation having been set up in 1986 to carry out local community and charity work. Northern Rock became one of the five top mortgage lenders in the UK although it was heavily dependent on wholesale mortgage securitisation with only 22.4 per cent of its lending being covered by retail deposits. The bank accordingly became unable to borrow following the contraction of credit on the inter-bank markets in August 2007 with a further proposed securitisation that autumn having to be postponed. Northern Rock had minimal direct exposure to the US sub-prime market and US CDO market although it was caught out on the drying up of wholesale inter-bank funding due to its high wholesale funding-based business model.

Emergency liquidity support was agreed with the Bank of England on 14 **14.227** September 2007 although a run on the bank's deposits persisted through 15 and

16 September. A statement was issued by the Treasury on 17 September confirming that all of the bank's then existing deposits would be covered. This was extended on 20 September to cover all existing accounts, new money into existing accounts and reopened accounts, as well as unsecured wholesale borrowing. All new retail deposits were also covered under a further announcement on 9 October. These Treasury support announcements represented a considerable extension of traditional lender of last resort ('LLR') funding in the UK.[92] A new financing package was then announced on 21 January 2008 under which the Bank of England's loan of £25m would in effect be securitised with a Treasury guarantee.

Regulatory response

14.228 The circumstances surrounding the crisis at Northern Rock were considered by the House of Commons Treasury Committee in an initial report on 'The Run on the Rock' on 26 January 2008 (HC56-1). An exploratory discussion paper on *Banking Reform: Protecting Depositors* was issued by the Bank of England, FSA, and Treasury as the 'Tripartite Authorities' in October 2007. This was followed by a more formal consultation document on *Financial Stability and Depositor Protection: Strengthening the Framework* on 30 January 2008.[93] Under this paper, regulatory reform would be based on the five key objectives of strengthening the financial system, reducing the likelihood of banks failing, limiting the impact of collapse, developing effective compensation arrangements, and strengthening the Bank of England and securing improved coordination between the authorities.[94]

14.229 The FSA had commissioned a separate internal audit which published its results on 26 March 2008. This confirmed that there had been a lack of sufficient supervisory engagement with the bank with the supervisory team having, in particular, not followed up rigorously enough with management on increased business model vulnerability arising through changing market conditions. There had been a lack of adequate oversight and review by FSA line management on the quality, intensity, and rigour of the bank's supervision. There had been inadequate specific

---

[92] GA Walker 'Credit Crisis—Regulatory and Financial Systems Reform' (n 22); and GA Walker, 'Sub-prime Loans, Inter-Bank Markets and Financial Support' (n 22).

[93] HM Treasury, Bank of England, and FSA, 'Banking Reform—Protecting Depositors: a Discussion Paper' (October 2007); and HM Treasury, Bank of England, and FSA, 'Financial Stability and Depositor Protection: Strengthening the Framework' (January 2008) Cm 7308. See also Bank of England, HM Treasury, and FSA, 'Financial Stability and Depositor Protection: Further Consultation' (July 2008) Cm 7436; Bank of England, HM Treasury, and FSA, 'Financial Stability and Depositor Protection: Special Resolution Regime' (July 2008); and HM Treasury, 'Financial Stability and Depositor Protection: Cross-Border Challenges' (September 2008).

[94] For comment, GA Walker, 'Northern Rock Falls' (n 22) 5–6.

resources assigned to supervising the bank and a lack of intensity by the FSA in ensuring that all available risk information was properly utilised to inform its supervisory actions.

A number of high-level recommendations were made. The engagement of FSA **14.230** senior management would be increased in high impact firms. There would be increased rigour in day-to-day supervision with an increased focus on prudential supervision (including liquidity and stress testing) as well as improvements in the use of information and intelligence in supervision. There would be corresponding improvements in the quality and resourcing of financial and sectoral analysis, a strengthening of supervisory resources, and an increased level of firm supervision oversight. The principal result was to create a new Supervisory Enhancement Programme ('SEP') to strengthen the overall supervisory process which also incorporated other changes that were already being given effect to. Seven general high-level recommendations were made with 10 specific Recommended Actions. FSA Chief Executive, Hector Sants, agreed to implement the improvements in an FSA response statement which included further specific enhancements with regard to culture and people, organisation, process, and technology.

Treasury acquisition

It was separately announced on 17 February 2008 that Northern Rock would be **14.231** taken into public ownership after the private bids tendered were rejected by the Treasury on the advice of Goldman Sachs. The deadline for private offer bids had been 16 November 2007 with the preferred bid having been made by the Virgin Group and two others from Olivant and a private management group. Virgin had offered £1.3bn of equity with £11bn of the Bank of England loan to have been repaid immediately and the balance cancelled by 2010. Virgin had been pressed to pay more for the government guarantee and to issue equity warrants although it considered that it could only offer £300m in total and £500m in the event of Northern Rock's recovery.[95]

The Bill to acquire Northern Rock had already been prepared and was introduced **14.232** to the House of Commons on 19 February 2008 within two days of the acquisition announcement and received Royal Assent on 21 February 2008. This allowed the Treasury to make an order in specified circumstances relating to the transfer of securities issued by an authorised deposit-taking institution (or a building society) as well as with regard to the property, rights, and liabilities of such an institution. The Act applies to 'authorised deposit-takers' which covers any UK undertaking

---

[95] For comment, GA Walker, 'Northern Rock Falls' (n 22) 7.

that holds permission to accept deposits under Part 4 of FSMA 2000 (s 1(1)). This will include banks and building societies.

14.233   The Treasury is given power to transfer securities or property, rights, and liabilities where this is considered desirable for one of two stated purposes (s 2(1)(a) and (b)). This applies with regard to (a) maintaining the stability of the UK financial system in circumstances where the Treasury considers that there would otherwise be a serious threat to its stability or (b) to protect the public interest where financial assistance has already been provided by the Treasury to the institution for the purpose of maintaining the stability of the UK financial system (s 2(2)(a) and (b)). Financial assistance covers both funding provided by the Bank of England or guarantee arrangements by the Treasury either with or without the involvement of the bank (s 2(3)(a) and (b)). Treasury orders only last for one year although the powers confirmed may be re-exercised within the year (s 2(8) and (9)) with relevant orders being provided for under Schedules 1 and 2.

14.234   The Treasury may transfer securities and property (under ss 3 and 6) with securities being transferred either to the Bank of England, a nominee of the Treasury, a company wholly owned by the Bank or the Treasury or another body corporate (s 3(1)(a)–(d)). Any subscription rights in the institution or any subsidiary undertakings may be cancelled (s 4(2)) with the Treasury being required to determine how compensation will be payable to shareholders or other persons holding relevant rights (s 5(1) and (2)). Compensation is to be valued without reference to the financial assistance provided (s 5(4)). Similar provisions apply with regard to the transfer of property, rights, and liabilities of any authorised deposit-taker.

Financial stability

14.235   A further consultation document was issued by the Tripartite Authorities on 1 July 2008 on *Financial Stability and Depositor Protection*.[96] This develops the material contained in the earlier consultation documents and anticipates draft legislation to follow in autumn 2008. The Chancellor of the Exchequer noted that no system of regulation could or should prevent the failure of every institution although the authorities had to do everything possible to prevent problems that could create a wider threat to stability. The challenge was then to ensure that the authorities could act quickly and decisively when necessary to support financial institutions with all necessary powers being conferred. The original integrated model set up under FSMA would be strengthened with the FSA being responsible for individual institutions and the Bank of England for the stability of

---

[96] Bank of England, HM Treasury, and FSA, 'Financial Stability and Depositor Protection: Further Consultation' (July 2008) Cm 7436.

the financial system as a whole. Each would nevertheless be provided with further additional powers and improved coordination facilitated.[97]

The report refers to the conditions in financial markets following the US sub- **14.236** prime mortgage crisis during the second half of 2007. The paper refers to the separate report prepared by the Financial Stability Forum on *Enhancing Market and Institutional Resilience* in April 2008.[98] This contained five principal recommendations on the strengthening of the prudential oversight of capital, liquidity and risk management, enhanced transparency and valuation, improvements in the role and use of credit ratings, the strengthening of authorities' responsiveness to risks, and establishing effective arrangements for dealing with stress in the financial system. These had been endorsed by the G-7 Finance Ministers with a commitment to their rapid implementation with priority actions being secured within 100 days. A number of the key observations and recommendations contained in the FSF report were restated in the July 2008 Tripartite report.

The report refers to the need to support Northern Rock in the UK and the enact- **14.237** ment of the Banking (Special Provisions) Act 2008 as well as the main findings of the FSA audit report. The special liquidity arrangements set up by central banks are referred to including a Bank of England's extended three-month repo (sale and repurchase) open market operations ('OMOs') facility in March and April 2008 and the Special Liquidity Scheme (SLS) opened in April 2008 to allow banks to swap high quality mortgage-backed and other securities for UK Treasury bills for a limited period and subject to appropriate haircuts (deductions). The authorities remained committed to the five key policy objectives set out in the January consultation paper.[99] A series of specific recommendations are then set out in connection with each of the key objectives of strengthening the stability and resilience of the financial system (Chapter 2), reducing the likelihood of banks facing difficulties (Chapter 3) and the impact of banks in difficulty (Chapter 4), as well as providing effective compensation (Chapter 5) and strengthening the Bank of England and tripartite coordination (Chapter 6). Proposed implementing legislation was to be produced in autumn 2008.

This was an important, although to a large extent anticipated, set of key recom- **14.238** mendations. The paper borrowed substantially from other official documents including principally the FSF April 2008 report and especially in connection with stability and resilience proposals. The paper also continues the earlier policy

---

[97] Chapter 1, paras 1.134–1.150 and 1.151–1.180.
[98] FSF, 'Enhancing Market and Institutional Resilience' (April 2008) Report to the G-7 Finance Ministers.
[99] Para 1.22.

framework of stability, bank failure, impact, compensation, and institutional revision referred to in the Tripartite Authorities' earlier consultation documents.

14.239 The most significant concrete proposal was possibly the Special Resolution Regime ('SRR') responsibility for which was to be assigned to the Bank rather than the FSA. It has to be accepted that while the Bank must be involved in the trigger decisions, day-to-day management of restructurings would almost certainly have been dealt with more efficiently within the FSA. It may nevertheless have been that the Bank wished to have a more active and direct involvement in the process although it has to be accepted that new personnel and expertise will have to be developed within the Bank for this purpose. One of the most welcome recommendations was to allow the Bank to make available emergency assistance without disclosure, disruption, or penalty. The compensation arrangements are also more balanced with the Government accepting industry objections to mandatory pre-funding at this stage. The compromise position was to grant the FSCS a reserve power in this regard. Institutional revision should always have been centred on an improved MOU which more clearly set out the role and function of each of the principal authorities concerned. These constitute useful but by no means revolutionary new measures in UK banking and financial regulation and financial stability protection more generally.

14.240 These regulatory initiatives would be further supported by the market support announcements made by the UK Government in October 2008 following the worsening of the global credit crisis.[100] This followed the US Treasury's refusal to bail out Lehman Brothers but support Fannie Mae and Freddie Mac as well as AIG. Following a further collapse in bank stock prices in the UK, the Treasury confirmed that it would make available up to £50m to recapitalise the major UK banks and building societies with the Bank of England's SLS being increased to £200m and with credit guarantees being provided on inter-bank lending for up to three years. This coordinated package was sufficient to slow the collapse in the prices of financial shares with the stock markets then immediately shifting their attention from the financial crisis to the impending recession. The UK combined support model was subsequently adopted by other EU countries and elsewhere across the globe which included the incorporation of a US$250bn recapitalisation element into the US$700bn TARP scheme. Work continued on money market reform within the UK while other initiatives were taken forward at the EU level and with further proposals for a new 'Bretton Woods II' international financial architecture being considered at the special G20 conferences in Washington in November 2008 and in London in April 2009.

---

[100] See para 14.24 and Chapter 1, para 1.151.

15

HOME FINANCE TRANSACTIONS

One of the main purchases during an individual's life is residential property. This **15.01** means that the stability of the home finance sector of the financial services industry is a particularly important challenge for the sector itself and for its regulators. Some years ago, the sector was the more or less exclusive preserve of building societies, but the market has been opened up to wider competition, and a substantial percentage of residential mortgages is now granted by banks. The building society sector has shrunk in size, because of this competition and because some of the larger building societies have converted themselves from the mutual structure and have become, or have merged with, banks.

The purposes of this chapter are two. One is to outline the main distinctive ele- **15.02** ments of the regulation of building societies in their capacity as lenders. The second is to give an account of the regime for the regulation of home finance transactions, which includes lending on mortgage secured on domestic property, home purchase business, and home reversion business.

Supervision and Regulation of Building Societies

Since building societies are essentially funded from retail or wholesale deposits, **15.03** they are basically deposit-takers and are regulated in the same manner as banks. Much of the content of Chapter 14 above accordingly applies to building societies. This chapter therefore deals only with the aspects of building societies that differ from the regime for banks.

These differences are attributable to two main causes. First, the historical develop- **15.04** ment of building societies has been different to that for banks. Mutuality, still today one of the distinguishing marks of the movement, is the main feature here. And, secondly, Parliament's decision to create a regime for regulation of mortgage business inevitably meant that the reforms had to apply to building societies themselves, since the grant of a mortgage did not always involve an external intermediary.

Building societies before FSMA

15.05 Building societies are important providers of financial savings and loan services, especially in the residential property market. Building societies are mutual organisations, or incorporated bodies that raise funds principally from shareholders and members. Those funds were, until recently, used exclusively to advance amounts secured on land for residential use. Since the coming into effect of the Building Societies Act 1986 and more particularly the Building Societies Act 1996, building societies have been able to carry on a number of additional financial services. They were also allowed to convert into banks using a simplified transfer procedure, the first major institution to do so being the Abbey National in 1989.

15.06 The first building society in the UK was set up by Richard Ketley in Birmingham in 1775.[1] This was the first mutual fund set up for this purpose although other alternative forms of financing had been set up earlier. In Scotland, the decision was taken to use an early savings bank model with the first society being the Glasgow and West of Scotland Savings, Investment and Building Society in 1808.

15.07 The original societies were referred to as terminating societies as they would be closed down once all of their original members had been provided with proper accommodation. The first permanent societies were the Chesham in 1845 and the Scarborough in 1846. The permanent societies soon began to focus on lending for the purchase of properties rather than for building them. Early growth was nevertheless limited due to the preference for savings to be placed with friendly societies. Early commercial banks were not commonly used as they required an initial deposit of at least £10 and paid little or no interest (except in Scotland) which restricted their use to the wealthier members of society. The earlier building societies thus tended to be used by skilled or higher paid workers who could afford to purchase their own homes.

15.08 Statutory oversight was introduced in 1836 and provided a friendly societies model for supervision and control. Following a series of complaints including governance difficulties and excessive charging, supervision was transferred to the Chief Registrar of Friendly Societies under the Building Societies Act 1874. This Act established the basic conditions under which building societies would be operated for over 100 years; it confirmed their mutual status and legal personality with members' liability limited to amounts outstanding on their mortgages or otherwise owed. Monies were raised through members' subscriptions and used to

---

[1] Mr Ketley had been the landlord of the Golden Cross Inn, Snow Hill, Birmingham. For the development of the movement, see generally, M Boddy, *The Building Societies* (1980); D McKillop and C Ferguson, *Building Societies: Structure, Performance and Change* (1993), ch 2, and G Davies, *Building Societies and their Branches—A Regional Economic Survey* (1981).

advance loans secured on freehold or leasehold property. Mergers were permitted with the consent of three-quarters of members holding two-thirds of the total value of shares issued. Later amending statutes required the provision of more complete information and the auditing and certification of annual accounts.

The immediate post-war period was characterised by an expansion in the rental **15.09** market under the new Labour government although private property ownership was subsequently promoted by later Conservative governments. Home owner- ship rose to 43 per cent by 1961. While the total amount advanced by societies continued to grow, the number of societies and branches contracted as a result of mergers and business transfers. Banks were first allowed to enter the residential mortgage market in the early 1980s closely followed by insurance companies and other financial institutions. Bank penetration in the market initially rose from 26 per cent to 36 per cent but then fell to 25 per cent by 1987.

Building societies were not immune from the deregulation of the UK financial **15.10** system, advocated by the Wilson Committee, which took place in the 1980s.[2] The Building Societies Act 1986 enabled societies to retain their mutual status or to convert into bodies corporate through a simplified procedure, and permitted the range of their activities to be considerably extended to include the provision of current accounts and the sale of life assurance and unit trusts to members. The Building Societies Act 1986 created a new statutory framework for the supervi- sion and regulation of building societies, including the establishment of the Building Societies Commission, an Ombudsman, and an Investor Protection Board; in this way the legislation in this sector accurately predicted what was to follow in 2000 for the financial services world as a whole.

Further freedom of action was conferred on building societies by legislation at the **15.11** tail end of the Conservative administration in 1996.

Building societies under FSMA

The Building Societies Commission has been abolished. Building societies are **15.12** now subject to regulation under FSMA. The regulatory aspects of the Building Societies Act 1986 were repealed with effect from 1 December 2001, but the other provisions of that Act remained in effect. The content and effect of these remain- ing provisions is explained in the FSA's Building Societies Regulatory Guide ('BSOG'). They are mainly constitutional in nature and include such matters

---

[2] See the report by John Spalding to the Council of the Building Societies Association on The Future Constitution and Powers of Building Societies (January 1983) and the Final Report in 1984.

as principal purpose, annual accounts, governance, membership, meetings and voting arrangements, and mergers and transfers. Accordingly some of the FSMA provisions which apply elsewhere do not have any effect for building societies. An example is accounts,[3] and another is business transfers, where Part VII of FSMA is restricted to banks and insurance companies, and the special arrangements for building societies remain.[4]

15.13 Building societies are subject to the general prohibition (FSMA, s 19(1)) and the permission requirement (FSMA, s 20(1)). Building societies are required to comply with all of the relevant provisions of the FSA's Handbook of Rules and Guidance. This includes the High-Level Standards, Prudential Standards (including in particular the General Prudential Sourcebook ('GENPRU'), the Prudential Sourcebook for Banks, Building Societies and Investment Firms ('BIPRU'), and Business Standards. BIPRU (amongst other components of the FSA Handbook) has replaced the earlier rule book of the Building Societies Commission and the FSA Interim Prudential Sourcebook for Building Societies ('IPRU(BSOC)'), which survives only as a repository for a small number of residual prudential provisions.

15.14 Volume 2 of IPRU(BSOC) was principally concerned with constitutional matters. The material that it contained has now been replicated or replaced by guidance in BSOG. The main subjects covered are the statutory provisions in the Building Societies Act 1986 (and supporting regulations) about:

(a) access to the building society's Register of Members with relevant request procedures;

(b) merger procedures; and

(c) transfer procedures.

---

[3] See BSOG 1.4.1G: every building society is required (by s 71 of the 1986 Act) to keep accounting records which: (1) explain its transactions; (2) disclose, with reasonable accuracy and promptness, the state of its business at any time; and (3) enable the directors and the society to properly discharge their respective duties under the 1986 Act and article 4 of the Regulation of the European Parliament and of the Council of 19th July 2002 on the application of international accounting standards (1606/2002/EC) ('the IAS Regulations') if applicable.

[4] See BSOG 2 (Merger Procedures) and BSOG 3 (Transfer Procedures): Members' approval by ordinary resolution is required where a society proposes to acquire or transfer a relevant business either directly or through a subsidiary. This is necessary with regard to acquisitions or transfers where the activity does not involve lending on residential property or the acquisition or establishment would cost 15 per cent more of the society's own funds. Mergers or business transfers are permitted subject to special resolution of members and the borrowers of the society. Building societies can be dissolved on a three-quarters vote of all of the members holding two-thirds of the shares. Winding-up is by special resolution of members or by the court on specified grounds.

The Regulation of Home Finance Transactions

Regulated mortgage business

The previous edition of this work includes (at paras 13.17 to 13.31) an account of **15.15**
the development of the policy thinking by which, from 31 October 2004, the
Financial Services Authority became responsible for the authorisation and supervision of certain activities connected with lending on mortgage. FSA regulation of
mortgage business rests on FSMA, s 22(1), read with Schedule 2, Part 2, paragraph 23. That combination of provisions brings within the scope of regulation
rights under any contract under which (a) a person provides another with credit;
and (b) the obligation of the borrower to repay is secured on land. 'Credit' is
defined widely, to include any cash loan or other financial accommodation and
'cash' defined to include money in any form.[5] The RAO definition of a 'regulated
mortgage contract'[6] follows Schedule 2 in its wide ambit but specifies that what is
regulated is borrowing secured by 'a first legal mortgage on land'. The FSA's principal guidance on the scope of the mortgage regime is in PERG 4 (Guidance on
regulated activities connected with mortgages).

The wide range of transactions caught by this definition can be illustrated by an **15.16**
example: if a bank issues a secured bank guarantee or performance bond in favour
of its customer, that is potentially a regulated mortgage contract, because the customer will be indebted to the bank if the bank performs under the guarantee.[7]
More obviously, other types of secured loan are also potentially regulated mortgage contracts, including secured overdraft facilities and secured bridging loans.[8]

To reduce the width of the definition, all but consumer borrowing in relation to **15.17**
domestic property is excluded from regulation. That is achieved by specifying that
in addition to the specific features of a mortgage (borrowing secured on land, as
above) a regulated mortgage contract must also have three more general features:

(a) A regulated mortgage contract is a contract between an individual (or a
    trustee[9] for an individual beneficiary) and a person (the 'lender') who carries
    on that activity 'by way of business'.[10]

---

[5] FSMA, Sched 2, Part 2, para 23(2) and (3).
[6] RAO, art 61(3)(a)(ii).
[7] PERG 4.4.1AG(2).
[8] PERG 4.4.11G.
[9] RAO, art 61(3)(a)(i).
[10] An activity is not a regulated activity unless it is carried on by way of business in the UK.

(b) A regulated mortgage contract must be secured on land[11] in the UK (other than timeshare accommodation[12]).

(c) There is an 'occupancy requirement': the individual borrower (or a related person) must use or intend to use at least 40 per cent of that land as a dwelling, or in connection with a dwelling.[13] A 'related person' is a close relative (grandparent, parent, sibling, child, or grandchild), or partner (spouse, civil partner, partner in fact).[14]

15.18 The combination of these features has the result that, for example, loans to companies secured on company property will not be regulated mortgaged contracts. But loans to individual sole traders or to partners may be, if the loans are secured on residential property.[15]

15.19 If the borrower is a trustee, then the existence of these features is tested by reference to the actions, intentions, and relationships of an individual beneficiary of the trust.[16] All the features must be present at the time the transaction is entered into.[17] If they are all present, the contract is and remains a regulated mortgage contract. If the contract is subsequently amended so that one of the features is no longer present, the contract will still be a regulated mortgage contract. The corollary is also true: a contract cannot become a regulated mortgage contract by subsequent variation.[18] That produces certainty because it means that fine judgments are not required about whether variations might lead to a change in regulatory status. But there may nevertheless, it seems, be difficult questions of degree as to whether a contract has been varied (no change in status) or replaced (status assessed afresh at the time of replacement).[19]

15.20 Because the 'occupancy requirement' imposes an arbitrary 40 per cent threshold it can occasionally produce odd results. But, for the most part it is relatively straightforward in its effect as the following examples show:

(a) The large garden of a residential property will most likely be used 'in connection with' the dwelling.

(b) Loans to purchase farmland that are secured on that land are unlikely to be regulated mortgage contracts. First, because the proportion of the land destined for use as or in connection with a dwelling (the farm house and garden)

---

[11] RAO, art 61(3)(a)(ii).
[12] As defined in the Timeshare Act 1992.
[13] RAO, art 61(3)(a)(iii).
[14] ibid, art 61(4)(c).
[15] PERG 4.4.2G.
[16] RAO, art 61(3)(a)(iii).
[17] ibid, art 61(3).
[18] PERG 4.4.3G.
[19] PERG 4.4.4G.

is probably less than 40 per cent of the total. Second, because the FSA does not regard farmland as 'used in connection with' the farmhouse.[20]

(c) 'Buy to let' mortgages secured on the rental property are generally not regulated mortgage contracts. But they may be in some cases. For example a mortgage to purchase a property to be leased to a 'connected person' (the flat purchased for the borrower's son or daughter at university), or a mortgage to purchase a property that the borrower intends ultimately to use as a dwelling (the cottage by the sea, purchased in anticipation of retirement, but leased out in the meantime) will both be regulated mortgage contracts.[21]

15.21 A person acting by way of business in the UK might (unless he is otherwise exempt) carry on one of six regulated activities in relation to a regulated mortgage contract:[22]

(a) arranging (bringing about) regulated mortgage contracts;[23]
(b) making arrangements with a view to regulated mortgage contracts;[24]
(c) advising on regulated mortgage contracts;[25]
(d) entering into a regulated mortgage contract as lender;[26]
(e) administering a regulated mortgage contract, where that contract was entered into by way of business after 31 October 2004;[27] and
(f) agreeing to carry on any of the above.[28]

15.22 As always with FSA rules, terminology is important, so it is worth keeping in mind the following definitions and collective nouns extracted from the glossary to the Handbook:

(a) A regulated mortgage contract is a subset of '*home finance transaction*'.
(b) Collectively, all the regulated activities in paragraph 15.21 are '*regulated mortgage activities*' and a subset of '*home finance activities*'.
(c) The regulated activities of arranging, making arrangements with a view to, and advising on a regulated mortgage contract are collectively defined as '*mortgage mediation activities*'. A person that has (or ought to have) permission

---

[20] PERG 4.4.7G.
[21] PERG 4.4.8G.
[22] PERG 4.3.1G.
[23] RAO, art 25A(1).
[24] ibid, art 25A(2).
[25] ibid, art 53A.
[26] ibid, art 61(1).
[27] ibid, art 61(2).
[28] ibid, art 64. The FSA's view (in the context of insurance mediation, at least) is that the art 64 regulated activity concerns 'the entering into of a legally binding agreement to provide the services to which the agreement relates' (see PERG 5.9.1G). Accordingly, a lender or provider should not be carrying on a regulated activity under RAO art 64 merely because it makes an offer to lend or participate in the arrangements.

to carry on any of these activities is a '*mortgage intermediary*' and its activities are a subset of '*home finance mediation activity*'. That means the firm is also a '*home finance intermediary*'.

(d) A person that has (or ought to have) permission to arrange or make arrangements with a view to a regulated mortgage contract is a '*mortgage arranger*' and also a mortgage intermediary and a '*home finance arranger*'.

(e) A person that has (or ought to have) permission to advise on regulated mortgage contracts is a '*mortgage adviser*' and also a mortgage intermediary and a '*home finance adviser*'.

(f) A person that has (or ought to have) permission to enter into a regulated mortgage contract is a '*mortgage lender*' and its activities are a subset of '*home finance providing activity*' or '*home financing*'. That means the firm is also a '*home finance provider*'.

(g) A person that has (or ought to have) permission to administer a regulated mortgage contract is a '*mortgage administrator*' and its activities are a subset of '*administering a home finance transaction*'. That means the firm is also a '*home finance administrator*'.

15.23 Terminological overload aside, the overall result is that there is a good analogy between the range of regulated activities relating to insurance and to regulated mortgage business. In each case, pre-contract broking or producing activities are regulated (arranging deals or making arrangements for deals in the contract or plan, or advising on it), as is the activity of lending or insuring as principal, and the post-contract activity of administering the contract.

15.24 Each activity identified in para 15.21 above is subject to exemptions, the detail of which can be found in the RAO and in PERG 4. For present purposes, however, it is useful to note the following limitations and extensions to the scope of regulated mortgage activities:

(a) Mortgage mediation activities are regulated only if the services comprised in those activities are provided to a borrower. Services provided only to a lender are not regulated.

(b) The rider to the definition of mortgage administration (in para 15.21(e), above) has the effect that administering a contract is not a regulated activity if the lender was a private lender, not acting by way of business.

(c) A person cannot carry on the regulated activity of arranging or advising unless he does so by way of business. But the 'By Way of Business Order'[29] goes further:

> A person is not to be regarded as carrying on by way of business [mortgage mediation activity] unless he carries on the business of engaging in that activity.[30]

---

[29] Financial Services and Markets Act 2000 (Carrying on Regulated Activities by Way of Business) Order 2001, SI 2001/1177.
[30] ibid, art 3A.

The FSA's interpretation is that 'this is a narrower test than that of carrying on regulated activities by way of business (as required by [FSMA s.] 22...), as it requires the regulated activities to represent the carrying on of a business in their own right.'[31]

Pressure to extend the scope of regulation

The regime for regulated mortgage activities came under pressure from two devel- **15.25**
opments. First, from the growth of 'equity release transactions' driven by substantial rises in the value of domestic property. These schemes allow a home owner to release some of the capital value in his home by selling some of his interest in it, while retaining the right to occupy the property. Schemes based on 'lifetime mortgages'[32] were already regulated because they included a regulated mortgage contract. But 'home reversion schemes', under which a home owner sells outright an interest in his property, but on condition that he remains entitled to occupy the property, were not caught except to the extent that the transaction included a regulated financial services product, such as a bond or a contract of insurance.[33]

Second, from the need to accommodate Islamic finance arrangements within the **15.26**
regulatory structure. Some of these are regulated mortgage contracts, for example Murabaha arrangements, under which an institution buys and re-sells a home to a consumer, accepting payment of the price over a long period. Others were not regulated, including Ijara and Diminishing Musharaka products, under which a provider buys a property and a consumer agrees to purchase it (or an increasing interest in it) over time or at the end of an agreed period, combined with a right (under a lease) to occupy the part of the property that the consumer does not own.[34]

The process of extending the regulatory regime began in December 2005, when **15.27**
the Regulation of Financial Services (Land Transactions) Act 2005 came into force. That Act (by amendment to FSMA) specified a new class of investment in relation to which a person might carry on a regulated activity:

> ...rights under any arrangement for the provision of finance under which the person providing the finance either ... acquires a major interest in land from the person to whom the finance is provided, or ... disposes of a major interest in land to that person.[35]

---

[31] PERG 2.3.2G(2).

[32] Under which a home owner borrows money on mortgage, but on terms that interest is rolled up and repayable only at the end of the mortgage term.

[33] See, for example, *Investors Compensation Scheme Ltd v West Bromwich Building Society* [1998] 1 WLR 896 (HL).

[34] HM Treasury, 'Secondary legislation for the regulation of Home Reversion and Home Purchase Plans: A consultation' (March 2006), p 6.

[35] FSMA, Sched 2, Part 2 para 23A (Other finance arrangements involving land).

15.28 The RAO was then amended[36] to include the detailed specification of two new home finance products, to sit alongside the regulated mortgage contract: the home reversion plan and the home purchase plan. The policy intention was as far as possible to create a level playing field, on which, from 6 April 2007, the existing and new 'home finance transactions'[37] would be treated equally. As a result, the amendments to the RAO closely followed the model used for the regulated mortgage contract. The FSA's principal guidance on the scope of the regime for regulated home purchase plans and regulated home reversion plans is in PERG 14 (Guidance on home reversion and home purchase activities).

Home reversion plans and home purchase plans

15.29 Under a 'regulated home reversion plan'[38] the provider buys a qualifying interest in land (for example, in England a freehold or leasehold estate)[39] from an individual seller, who remains entitled to occupy the land for at least 20 years, or until he enters a care home or dies.[40]

15.30 Under a 'regulated home purchase plan'[41] the provider buys a qualifying interest in land. An individual purchaser is entitled to occupy the land and agrees to buy the provider's interest over the course of, or at the end of, a specified period. If the provider's interest is an undivided share, it must be held on trust for the provider and the individual purchaser as beneficial tenants in common.

15.31 Neither a home reversion plan nor a home purchase plan will be regulated unless in addition to exhibiting these specific characteristics it also exhibits three more general characteristics which limit the scope of regulation to consumer transactions in residential land. These general characteristics are very similar to the general characteristics of a regulated mortgage contract outlined in para 15.17, above, but with some variation:

    (a) Each activity must be performed under an arrangement (comprised in one or more instruments or agreements) between an individual (or a trustee[42] for an individual beneficiary) and a person (the 'provider') who carries on that

---

[36] By the Financial Services and Markets Act 2000 (Regulated Activities) (Amendment) (No 2) Order 2006, SI 2006/2383.

[37] The portmanteau term, covering activities relating to regulated mortgage contracts, regulated home reversion plans, and regulated home purchase plans. See para 15.22 above and 15.34 below.

[38] RAO, art 63B(3).

[39] ibid, art 63B(4)(a).

[40] ibid, art 63B(4)(d).

[41] ibid, art 63F(3).

[42] ibid, art 63B(3)(a)(i) (home reversion plans); and art 63F(3)(a)(i) (home purchase plans).

activity 'by way of business'. Except for the reference to 'arrangements'[43] that is the same as for regulated mortgage contracts.

(b) A regulated arrangement or 'plan' must relate to land or an interest in land[44] in the UK (other than timeshare accommodation[45]). That is essentially the same as for regulated mortgage contracts.

(c) There is an 'occupancy requirement': the individual participant in the plan (or a related person[46]) must be entitled (and intend) to use at least 40 per cent of that land as a dwelling, or in connection with a dwelling.[47] This requirement is the same as for a regulated mortgage contract, except that the individual must in the case of a home reversion plan or home purchase plan be 'entitled' to occupy the home. 'Related person' is defined as for the borrower under a regulated mortgage contract (see para 15.17(c), above). It seems logical that the FSA's guidance on the operation of the occupancy test in relation to regulated mortgage contracts[48] should apply *mutatis mutandis* in this context also, though the guidance does not say so.

If the participant in the plan is a trustee, then the existence of these features is tested by reference to the actions, intentions, and relationships of an individual beneficiary of the trust.[49] All the features must be present at the time the transaction is entered into.[50] If they are all present, the plan is and remains a regulated home reversion plan or home purchase plan. If the plan is subsequently amended so that one of the features is no longer present, the plan will still be a regulated home reversion plan or home purchase plan. The corollary is also true: a plan cannot become a regulated home reversion plan or home purchase plan by later amendment.[51]   **15.32**

A person acting by way of business in the UK might (unless he is otherwise exempt) carry on one of six regulated activities in relation to home reversion plans or home purchase plans.[52]   **15.33**

---

[43] The same terminology is used elsewhere in the legislation, for example in FSMA, s 235 (Collective investment schemes).

[44] RAO, art 63B(3)(a)(i) (home reversion plans); and art 63F(3)(a)(i) (home purchase plans).

[45] As defined in the Timeshare Act 1992.

[46] RAO, art 63B(4)(c) (home reversion plans); and art 63F(4) (home purchase plans).

[47] ibid, art 63B(3)(a)(ii) (home reversion plans); and art 63F(3)(a)(iv) (home purchase plans).

[48] In PERG 4.4.6G to 4.4.9G.

[49] RAO, art 63B(3)(a)(ii) (home reversion plans); and art 63F(3)(a)(iv) (home purchase plans).

[50] ibid, art 63B(3) (home reversion plans); and art 63F(3) (home purchase plans).

[51] The FSA has not published guidance to this effect, but see HM Treasury, 'Secondary legislation for the regulation of Home Reversion and Home Purchase Plans: A consultation' (March 2006): home reversion plans (para 3.6) and home purchase plans (para 3.21).

[52] PERG 14.2.

(a) Arranging (bringing about) home reversion plans[53] or home purchase plans;[54]

(b) Making arrangements with a view to home reversion plans[55] or home purchase plans;[56]

(c) Advising on home reversion plans[57] or home purchase plans;[58]

(d) Entering into home reversion plans[59] or home purchase plans[60] as provider;

(e) Administering home reversion plans[61] or home purchase plans;[62] and

(f) Agreeing to carry on any of the above.[63]

15.34 As indicated in para 15.22 above, terminology is important:

(a) A home reversion plan or home purchase plan is subset of '*home finance transaction*'.

(b) Collectively, all the regulated activities in para 15.33 are '*reversion activities*' or '*home purchase activities*' and a subset of '*home finance activities*'.

(c) The regulated activities of arranging, making arrangements with a view to and advising on a home reversion plan or home purchase plan are collectively defined as '*reversion mediation activity*' or '*home purchase mediation activity*'. A person that has (or ought to have) permission to carry on any of these activities is a '*reversion intermediary*' or '*home purchase intermediary*' and its activities are a subset of '*home finance mediation activity*'. That means the firm is also a '*home finance intermediary*'.

(d) A person that has (or ought to have) permission to arrange or make arrangements with a view to a home reversion plan or home purchase plan is a '*reversion arranger*' or a '*home purchase arranger*' and also a reversion intermediary or home purchase intermediary and a '*home finance arranger*'.

(e) A person that has (or ought to have) permission to advise on a home reversion plan or home purchase plan is a '*reversion adviser*' or a '*home purchase adviser*' and also a reversion intermediary or home purchase intermediary and a '*home finance adviser*'.

---

[53] RAO art 25B(1).
[54] ibid, art 25C(1).
[55] ibid, art 25B(2).
[56] ibid, art 25C(2).
[57] ibid, art 53B.
[58] ibid, art 53A.
[59] ibid, art 63B.
[60] ibid, art 63F.
[61] ibid, art 63B.
[62] ibid, art 63F.
[63] ibid, art 64. See n 28, above.

(f) A person that has (or ought to have) permission to enter into a home reversion plan or home purchase plan is a *'reversion provider'* or a *'home purchase provider'* and its activities are a subset of *'home finance providing activity'* or *'home financing'*. That means the firm is also a *'home finance provider'*.

(g) The consumer or trustee participant in the plan is the *'reversion occupier'* or *'home purchaser'*.

(h) A person that has (or ought to have) permission to administer a home reversion plan or home purchase plan is a *'reversion administrator'* or a *'home purchase administrator'* and its activities are a subset of *'administering a home finance transaction'*. That means the firm is also a *'home finance administrator'*.

(i) Collectively, lifetime mortgages (see para 15.25, above) and home reversion plans are *'equity release transactions'*.

The range of regulated activities is, therefore, essentially the same as for regulated **15.35** mortgage activities, and as in that case, each activity identified in para 15.33 is subject to exemptions, the detail of which can be found in the RAO and in PERG 14.

Unlike the mortgage (and home purchase plan) market, a significant part of **15.36** the home reversion market is made up of private investors acting as the reversion provider.[64] This is reflected in two ways in the FSA's rules:

(a) Mortgage mediation activities and home purchase mediation activities are only regulated activities if provided to the borrower[65] or to the home purchaser[66] respectively. However, reversion mediation activities are regulated when provided to what the RAO calls the reversion seller (but the FSA calls the reversion occupier), and also when provided to the reversion provider.[67] This is because of the significant number of private investors (ie consumers) who enter into home reversion plans as reversion providers.

(b) Mortgage administration is a regulated activity only where the mortgage was entered into by way of business after the commencement of regulation (see para 15.21(e), above). However, reversion administration is a regulated activity whether or not the plan was entered into by way of business before the commencement of regulation.[68] This is because private investors (acting as

---

[64] Explanatory Memorandum to the Financial Services and Markets Act 2000 (Regulated Activities) (Amendment) (No 2) Order 2006, SI 2006/2383, prepared by HM Treasury.
[65] See para 15.24(a), above.
[66] RAO, art 25C(1) and 53C(1).
[67] ibid, arts 25B and 53B.
[68] ibid, art 63B(2).

reversion providers) are unlikely to enter into home reversion plans by way of business. However as these plans are administered by professional reversion administrators for the life of the plan (which can be a significant length of time), the policy intention is to catch continuing administration activities.

15.37   A person cannot carry on the regulated activity of advising or arranging unless he does so by way of business. But, as with regulated mortgage contracts (see para 15.24(c), above), the 'By Way of Business Order'[69] goes further:

> A person is not to be regarded as carrying on by way of business [reversion mediation activity or home purchase mediation activity] unless he carries on the business of engaging in that activity.[70]

The FSA's interpretation is that 'this is a narrower test than that of carrying on regulated activities by way of business (as required by [FSMA s.] 22 . . .), as it requires the regulated activities to represent the carrying on of a business in their own right'.[71]

Hybrid home finance products

15.38   Hybrid products that share features of home purchase plans and regulated mortgage contracts are treated as home purchase plans.[72]

The requirement for home finance providers to use authorised intermediaries

15.39   A firm with permission to carry on home financing (ie a mortgage lender, reversion provider, or home purchaser provider) must not use, or propose to use, the services of another person consisting of home finance mediation activity unless that intermediary is authorised, is an exempt person, is an exempt professional firm, or is not carrying on on his activity in the UK.[73]

15.40   That requirement is contained in chapter 5 of the FSA Prudential Sourcebook applicable to home finance business ('MIPRU', on which see para 15.43 *et seq.*, below). Guidance indicates that MIPRU 5 is intended to have the effect that if there is a chain of intermediaries between the provider and the borrower, reversion

---

[69] Financial Services and Markets Act 2000 (Carrying on Regulated Activities by way of Business) Order 2001, SI 2001/1177.

[70] ibid, art 3B (home reversion plans) and art 3C (home purchase plans).

[71] PERG 2.3.2G(2).

[72] RAO, art 61(3), rider to the definition of a regulated mortgage contract: 'such a [regulated mortgage contract] is not a regulated mortgage contract if it is a regulated home purchase plan'. See also rider to PERG 4.4.1G.

[73] MIPRU 5.2.1R and 5.2.2R.

occupier or home purchaser, all the UK intermediaries in the chain must be authorised:

> To avoid the loss of protection where an intermediary itself uses the services of an unauthorised person this chapter also ensures that each person in the chain of those providing services is authorised.[74]

But it is difficult to see how that result is achieved since the chapter applies only to **15.41** firms which have permission for home financing (that is, providers of home finance transactions, see the hierarchy of glossary definitions in para 15.34, above) The FSA indicates that it regards a firm as 'using' the services of

> *in particular*, its immediate counterparty (typically the intermediary that passed the business to the firm) and of all other persons who have been granted the right or authority *directly by the firm* to enter into a home finance transaction.[75] (Emphasis added)

But that offers little assistance as it is consistent with the application of MIPRU 5 **15.42** only to immediate counterparties and not to intermediaries lower down the chain.[76]

Prudential requirements for home finance firms

Most firms regulated by the FSA must hold capital resources (broadly, net assets **15.43** of a specified minimum quality) or other financial resources in excess of a capital resources requirement set out in the FSA Handbook. The precise content of these capital or 'prudential' requirements varies for different types of firm and for the combination of business that the firm carries on. The starting point to determine the prudential requirements applicable to a firm that carries on home finance activities is the FSA's Prudential Sourcebook for Mortgage and Home Finance Firms and Insurance Intermediaries ('MIPRU'). Broadly, MIPRU operates by applying to the firms within its scope a combination of requirements to hold professional indemnity insurance (which apply to home finance intermediaries) and capital requirements (which apply to all firms carrying on home finance activities). The capital requirements and insurance requirements are interlinked (for example because capital requirements rise as the excess applicable to a firm's professional indemnity insurance increases and because both capital and insurance requirements increase as the firm's annual income increases). The capital

---

[74] MIPRU 5.1.2G.
[75] MIPRU 5.2.1A G.
[76] The result would be different if MIPRU 5 applied to firms with permission to carry on 'home finance activities', since that encompasses both home finance providers and home finance intermediaries. Complexity has its perils, for the FSA as much as for regulated firms.

requirements are proportioned to reflect the volume of the firm's business and are higher if the firm holds client assets or client money.

Professional indemnity insurance requirements for home finance mediation firms

15.44   MIPRU 3 requires that (subject to one exception in para 15.46, below), unless a home finance intermediary has net tangible assets of more than a specified minimum amount, it must carry professional indemnity insurance of appropriate quality.[77]

15.45   That insurance must[78] provide:

(a)   cover in respect of claims for which a firm may be liable as a result of the conduct of itself, its employees and its appointed representatives (acting within the scope of their appointment);

(b)   a specified minimum limit of indemnity per year, usually proportioned to the firm's annual income;

(c)   an excess no higher than a specified amount. The permitted excess is higher if the firm holds client money or client assets, reflecting the greater risk to which the firm is exposed. A firm may hold a contract of insurance that imposes a larger excess, but it must then hold a specified amount of additional capital;[79]

(d)   appropriate cover in respect of legal defence costs;

(e)   continuous cover in respect of claims arising from work carried out from the date on which the firm was given permission to carry on home finance mediation activity; and

(f)   cover in respect of Ombudsman awards made against the firm.

15.46   A firm need not hold professional indemnity insurance if it has the benefit of a 'comparable guarantee' from another authorised person with a specified minimum level of financial resources. A comparable guarantee is a written agreement on terms at least equal to those in the contract of professional indemnity insurance that would otherwise be required, provided to finance the claims that might arise as a result of a breach by the firm of its duties under the regulatory system or the civil law.[80]

---

[77] MIPRU 3.1.1R.
[78] MIPRU 3.2.4R.
[79] MIPRU 3.2.14R.
[80] MIPRU 3.1.1R.

Capital requirements

Not all firms that carry on home finance activities have their capital requirements **15.47**
set in MIPRU. A bank, building society, solo consolidated subsidiary of a bank or
a building society, insurer, or friendly society that carries on home finance activity
is subject to the capital requirements set in the Prudential Sourcebook that applies
specifically to firms of that type.[81] Similarly, MIPRU does not apply to a firm with
a permission limited to designated investment business,[82] or authorised professional firms whose home finance activities are incidental to the practice of their
profession.[83]

Credit unions cannot carry on home purchase activities or reversion activities[84] **15.48**
but may carry on mortgage lending activities, mortgage administration activities,
or mortgage mediation activities. Small credit unions (assets and number of members below a specified minimum threshold)[85] and credit unions that have permission for mortgage lending activity or mortgage administration activity, but not for
insurance or mortgage mediation activity, have their capital requirements set by
the FSA's Credit Unions Sourcebook ('CRED').[86]

Capital requirements for firms to which MIPRU applies

MIPRU 4 requires a firm to meet, on a continuing basis, a basic solvency require- **15.49**
ment (the firm must at all times ensure that it is able to meet its liabilities as they
fall due[87]) and a minimum capital resources requirement (the firm must at all
times maintain capital resources equal to or in excess of its relevant capital resources
requirement[88]). Unless a rule requires otherwise, the firm must (in determining
whether or not it meets these requirements) recognise an asset or liability, and
measure its amount, in accordance with the accounting principles that apply to
the firm in preparing its annual financial statements.[89] MIPRU 4.3 specifies how
a firm's annual income is to be calculated, in order to determine both the limits of
the required professional indemnity insurance (if the firm carries on home finance
mediation activities) and as a component of the calculation of a firm's capital
resource requirement. MIPRU 4.4 contains rules which specify which assets and

---

[81] MIPRU 4.1.4R.
[82] MIPRU 4.1.6R.
[83] MIPRU 4.1.10R.
[84] MIPRU 4.1.9G.
[85] MIPRU 4.1.8R.
[86] MIPRU 4.1.8R.
[87] MIPRU 4.2.1R.
[88] MIPRU 4.2.2R.
[89] MIPRU 4.2.3R.

other items are eligible to contribute to a firm's capital resources, and which items must be deducted.

15.50 The structure underlying MIPRU 4 is that the capital resources requirement for a home finance firm varies according to the particular home finance activity (or combination of home finance activities) that it carries on. MIPRU 4.2.10R sets out the most common combinations in a table, with cross references to the particular rules specifying the capital requirement applicable to that activity or combination of activities. In general the capital resource requirement is the sum of a fixed minimum amount and a percentage of a specified measure of the volume of the firm's activity or its size (commonly annual income). There are also specific additions or deductions to reflect particular risks or features of certain activities combinations of activities.

15.51 There are three deviations from this general approach:

(a) If a firm carries on regulated activities that include designated investment business, the capital resources requirement is the higher of that imposed by MIPRU or the specific Prudential Sourcebook that applies to its activities.[90]

(b) A credit union to which MIPRU applies (see para 15.48, above) has its capital requirement set as the higher of the MIPRU requirement in respect of its mediation activities (disregarding its activities that are not mediation), or the requirement imposed by the Credit Unions Sourcebook ('CRED'), or (if it has permission to carry on designated investment business and is approved to provide Child Trust Funds) the requirement imposed under chapter 8 of the Interim Prudential Sourcebook for Investment Firms.[91]

(c) Social housing firms (wholly-owned subsidiaries of local authorities or registered social landlords that carry on non-profit regulated activities in connection with housing) that carry on only home financing (that is, the activity of providing mortgages, home reversion plans, or home purchase plans) or home financing administration activities, have a minimal capital requirement: their net tangible assets must be greater than zero.[92] That concession ceases to apply if the firm takes up mediation activities.[93]

Conduct of Business requirements for home finance firms

15.52 The relevant requirements are set out in the Mortgage and Home Finance: Conduct of Business Sourcebook ('MCOB') which applies to the communication

---

[90] MIPRU 4.2.5R.
[91] MIPRU 4.2.6R.
[92] MIPRU 4.2.7R.
[93] MIPRU 4.2.8G.

or approval of a financial promotion of qualifying credit,[94] of a home purchase plan or of a home reversion plan[95] and to every phase of the life-cycle of a home finance transaction.

Business customers

There is an important adjustment to the way MCOB operates in relation to busi- **15.53** ness loans secured on domestic property. The general position (see para 15.17, above) is that loans secured on property used exclusively for business purposes are not regulated mortgage contracts, because the occupancy requirement (at least 40 per cent of the property must be used or intended to be used as a dwelling) is not met. But, of course, loans taken out for business purposes may be secured on domestic property that meets the occupancy requirement. In that case MCOB applies if the loan is for the purposes of a business which has a group annual turn-over of less than a specified amount (£1 million at the time of writing). Information in the annual report and accounts of the business, or its business plan, should be a sufficient basis for determining its turnover. The firm may also rely on other information provided by the customer about the annual turnover of the business, unless, taking a 'common sense view', there is reason to doubt it.[96]

If the property, the purpose of the loan, and the size of the business are such that **15.54** MCOB does apply, then the firm has the option of either complying with MCOB in its unmodified form, or of complying with it as modified by a set of 'tailored provisions' for business loans, located throughout MCOB.[97] In general, the effect of the tailored provisions is to reduce the burden on the firm, although some additional requirements apply if the firm opts to rely on the tailored provisions.

There is guidance to the effect that whether a regulated mortgage contract is for a **15.55** business purpose is a matter of fact to be determined by a firm depending on the individual circumstances of each case. In the FSA's opinion, a regulated mortgage contract secured, for example, on the borrower's own home, but used to finance the purchase of a single buy-to-let property will not be for a business purpose.[98] That suggests that notions of continuity and regularity that are relevant to deter-mine whether a firm carries on an activity 'by way of business' under FSMA

---

[94] Credit offered by a person who enters into or administers regulated mortgage contracts and secured on land. Qualifying credit thus includes, but also goes beyond credit provided by way of a regulated mortgage contract.

[95] MCOB 3 sets out particular requirements relating to the financial promotion of qualifying credit and home reversion plans.

[96] MCOB 1.2.6G.

[97] MCOB 1.2.3R.

[98] MCOB 1.2.5R(2).

generally,[99] should be relevant also in determining whether a loan is for a business purposes.

Pre-contractual arrangements made by a home finance provider

15.56 Generally, a person who participates in a transaction as a principal does not also carry on the regulated activity of arranging that transaction, or making arrangements with a view to that transaction.[100] That is replicated for home finance transactions by RAO, article 28A. So, for example, when the general position applies, a mortgage lender that carries on the regulated activity of entering into a regulated mortgage contract as lender, does not also carry on a mortgage mediation activity, even if it arranges the loan using its own staff.

15.57 But that is not the position in relation to home finance providers under MCOB. Their activities which would be arranging but for RAO, article 28A are treated as if they were regulated activities.[101] The result is that MCOB applies to those activities.

Responsible lending

15.58 MCOB 11 imposes novel requirements on mortgage lenders and home purchase providers. The intention is to ensure that a customer is not exploited by a firm that lends in circumstances where the customer is 'self-evidently unable to repay through income and yet [has] no alternative means of repayment'.[102] In pursuit of that policy a firm is required to be able to demonstrate that, in deciding to make an advance or further advance to the customer, it took into account the customer's ability to repay the loan.

15.59 The firm may rely on the customer's self-certification of income only if appropriate, having regard to the interests of the customer, and where the firm has no reasonable grounds for doubting the information provided. Guidance indicates that it may be appropriate for the firm to accept self-certification for a range of reasons, including an established payment history, where proof of income is not readily available because of the nature of the customer's employment, or where the customer has a deadline for entering into the contract (for example, where a regulated mortgage contract is taken out to fund the purchase of a property at auction), so

---

99 See for example PERG 2.3 (The business element).
100 RAO art 28.
101 MCOB 1.2.12R.
102 MCOB 11.2.1R(1).

that there is insufficient time for the firm to complete 'its usual enquiries'.[103] Overall, the tenor of the rules and guidance is that there is a fairly wide margin of discretion available to firms in deciding whether a customer can repay. It will, however, be relatively easy to conclude with hindsight that, for example, a person was 'self-evidently unable to pay'. Robust processes and a well-documented decision are likely to be the best defence against retrospective judgements of that kind.

Two specific requirements apply to mortgage lenders. First, a mortgage lender is **15.60** required to make and keep an adequate record to show that it took the customer's ability to pay into account.[104] Second, a mortgage lender must put in place, record, and operate in accordance with, a written policy setting out the factors it will take into account in assessing a customer's ability to repay.[105] Guidance indicates that the assumption underlying that policy should normally be that loans will be repaid from the customer's actual or reasonably anticipated income.[106] Although these provisions are expressed to apply to mortgage lenders alone, in practice all firms to which MCOB 11 applies are likely to benefit from formulating and applying a policy and keeping records, as the means of demonstrating that they reached an appropriate decision as to the customer's ability to repay, in the circumstances prevailing at the time and given the information then available.

Advising and selling

MCOB 2.4 contains a 'reminder' in the form of guidance that firms are required **15.61** to have due regard to customers' interests and treat them fairly (FSA Principle for Businesses 6) and to pay due regard to the information needs of their customers and communicate with them in a way that is fair, clear, and not misleading (FSA Principle for Businesses 7).[107] MCOB 4 imposes general advising and selling standards for mortgage lenders, mortgage intermediaries, home purchase providers, and home purchase intermediaries. The standards are intended to ensure that the customer is adequately informed of the scope of home finance transactions available to him and that, where advice is given, it is suitable for the customer.

---

[103] MCOB 11.3.3G.
[104] MCOB 11.3.1R(2).
[105] MCOB 11 3.4R.
[106] MCOB 11.3.5G.
[107] The guidance is framed as a warning to avoid high pressure selling practices in relation to regulated mortgage contracts and home reversions plans; for example, practices that (a) commit customers (or lead customers to believe that they are committed) to any regulated mortgage contract or home reversion plan before they have been able to consider the illustration and offer document; or (b) give customers a misleading impression that a particular deal is not available after a certain date, unless that really is the case.

15.62   The application of MCOB 4 to reversion providers and reversion intermediaries is modified by MCOB 8, which imposes advising and selling standards for equity release products. MCOB 2.7 and 2.8 impose additional requirements where sales are made by electronic media, distance communications, or e-commerce (although these are not exhaustive of the requirements relevant to distance selling and e-commerce, which appear throughout MCOB).

Disclosure

15.63   MCOB 5 imposes pre-application disclosure requirements on mortgage lenders, mortgage intermediaries, home purchase providers, and home purchase intermediaries. These are intended to ensure that, before a customer submits an application for a home finance product, he is supplied with information that makes clear the price that he will be required to pay for that product, and (in relation to a regulated mortgage business), the features of the product including any linked deposits and linked borrowing.

15.64   MCOB 6 imposes pre-offer disclosure requirements on mortgage lenders and home purchase providers. These are intended to ensure that a customer receives a clear offer document to enable him to check the features and price of the home finance transaction before he enters into it.

15.65   MCOB 7 imposes disclosure requirements that bite at the start of the contract and after sale. These apply to mortgage lenders, mortgage intermediaries, mortgage administrators, home purchase providers, home purchase intermediaries, and home purchase administrators. They are intended to ensure that:

(a) a customer is supplied with information at the start of a regulated mortgage contract to enable him to check that the regulated mortgage contract has been set up in accordance with his requirements and to notify him of the first and subsequent payments;

(b) when the firm provides subsequent services to the customer, such as a further advance, rate switch, or addition or removal of a party to a regulated mortgage contract, the customer is provided with an illustration to make clear the price and features associated with that variation;

(c) a customer is supplied with information that enables him to check the payments and charges on a home finance transaction, to keep track of the transactions on, and the features of, a home finance transaction and stay informed of material changes.

15.66   The application of MCOB 5, 6, and 7 to mortgage lenders, mortgage intermediaries, mortgage administrators, reversion providers, reversion intermediaries, and reversion administrators is modified by MCOB 9, which imposes product disclosure standards for equity release products.

Charges

MCOB 12 imposes requirements on all home finance firms, intended to supple- **15.67**
ment the disclosure requirements outlined in paras 15.63 to 15.65, above (many
of which are concerned with disclosure of the price of a home finance product), by
preventing firms from imposing unfair and excessive charges. The level of charges
under a financial services product is not usually a matter for regulation. Indeed in
some cases (as under the Insurance Directives) the regulator is prevented from
imposing systematic controls on the price or form of a product. MCOB 12 is
intended to address four specific instances in which charges are, in the FSA's view,
likely to be unfair:

(a) the charges imposed on a customer seeking to terminate a regulated mortgage
     contract before the end of the term of the contract do not reflect the cost of
     termination to the firm;
(b) the charges imposed on a customer in payment difficulties are not based upon
     the costs incurred by the firm;
(c) the charges (including rates of interest) imposed on a customer under a regu-
     lated mortgage contract or home reversion plan are excessive and contrary to
     the customer's interests; and
(d) the charges made to a customer in connection with a regulated mortgage
     contract or home reversion plan are excessive.[108]

Arrears and repossessions

MCOB 13 imposes requirements on mortgage lenders, mortgage administrators, **15.68**
home purchase providers, and home purchase administrators in their administration of a home finance transaction and their administration of any unpaid amount
due to the home finance provider following the sale of the property after reposses-
sion. These requirements set out the information and services that the firm is
required to provide to a customer who has payment difficulties or faces a shortfall,
or is otherwise in breach of a home purchase plan. The requirements include that
the firm must put in place and operate a written policy (approved by its governing
body) to ensure that such customers are treated fairly;[109] provide the customer
with information about the extent of the arrears, any likely charges, and the possible consequences if the shortfall is not cleared;[110] and refrain from putting pressure on a the customer through excessive telephone calls or correspondence or by
contact at an unreasonable hour.[111] Where the firm administers a repossessed

---

[108] MCOB 12.2.1G.
[109] MCOB 13.3.1R.
[110] For example, MCOB 13.4.
[111] MCOB 13.5.3R.

property, it must ensure that it markets the property as soon as possible and obtains

> the best price that might reasonably be paid, taking account of factors such as market conditions as well as the continuing increase in the amount owed by the customer.[112]

15.69 If the firm proposes to recover a sale shortfall it must ensure that the customer is notified of its intention within six years (five in Scotland).[113]

Post-contract charges and arrears

15.70 A particular feature of the provisions against excessive charges and in relation to arrears and repossessions (in MCOB 15 and 16) is that many of them continue to apply to activities that occur after a regulated mortgage contract or a home purchase plan has come to an end following the sale of a repossessed property, or after a home reversion plan has come to an end for any reason.

---

[112] MCOB 13.6.1R.
[113] MCOB 13.6.4R.

16

INSURANCE REGULATION

Introduction

This chapter looks at insurance regulation; it covers the regulation of insurers **16.01** and of intermediaries which deal with insurance products. This introduction is followed by five sections—History and Background (para 16.07 *et seq.*); European Union Law (para 16.23 *et seq.*); UK Law and Regulation—the Legislation (para 16.73 *et seq.*); UK Law and Regulation—the FSA Handbook (para 16.151 *et seq.*); and UK Law and Regulation—FOS and FSCS (para 16.345 *et seq.*). There is extensive EU legislation concerning insurers and insurance intermediaries. EU legislation dictates the structure and much of the detail of the UK regime and domestic law and regulation often has to be interpreted in the light of EU requirements.

Terminology and categorisation

Insurance is categorised in a variety of different ways under EU legislation and UK **16.02** regulation. It is important to have an overview of how this terminology is used; some of the key terms are therefore considered below.

European legislation for insurers deals separately with non-life insurance and life **16.03** insurance (see para 16.23 *et seq.* below). These correspond to 'general insurance' and 'long-term insurance' in the UK regime. Most insurers are authorised for one but not the other; those which underwrite both are referred to as composite insurers. Life/long-term and non-life/general are each broken down into 'classes of insurance' (see paras 16.39 and 16.40 below).

Under UK regulation of sales and mediation, there are a variety of defined categories **16.04** of insurance used in the Regulated Activities Order[1] and in the FSA Glossary

---

[1] Financial Services and Markets Act 2000 (Regulated Activities), Order 2001, SI 2001/544 (as amended) (the 'RAO').

and Handbook. A 'qualifying contract of insurance' is defined in article 3(1) of the RAO;[2] very broadly, it is a long-term insurance which is neither reinsurance nor a pure protection policy.[3] It includes insurance with an 'investment element' such as 'with-profits' insurance or unit linked contracts and annuities. A pure protection policy (a defined term in the FSA Glossary) includes certain term life and permanent health contracts. Under the RAO, rights under a qualifying contract of insurance constitute 'contractually based investments' and rights under any contract of insurance constitute 'relevant investments'. 'Designated investments' (defined in the FSA Glossary) include contractually based investments which are 'life policies' (a separately defined term with a different meaning to the EU term 'life insurance') and long-term care insurance contracts[4] which are pure protection contracts (long-term care insurance sales are regulated under the FSA's Conduct of Business Rules ('COBS'), ie as an investment product). 'Non-investment insurance' is other kinds of insurance, ie all general insurance and pure protection (long-term) insurance other than long-term care insurance.

16.05 A further distinction in EU legislation (also used in the UK regime) is between insurance of 'mass risks' and 'large risks'. Mass risks are all risks other than large risks. Large risks are defined as contracts of insurance covering the following risks:

(a) railway rolling stock, aircraft, ships (sea, lake, river, and canal vessels), goods in transit, aircraft liability, and liability of ships (sea, lake, river, and canal vessels);

---

[2] A 'qualifying contract of insurance' (as defined at art 3, RAO) means a contract of long-term insurance which is not (a) a reinsurance contract; nor (b) a contract in respect of which the following conditions are met: (i) the benefits under the contract are payable only on death or in respect of incapacity due to injury, sickness, or infirmity; (ii) the contract has no surrender value, or the consideration consists of a single premium and the surrender value does not exceed that premium; and (iii) the contract makes no provision for its conversion or extension in a manner which would result in it ceasing to comply with any of the above conditions. This definition was amended in 2007 to remove a further condition that 'the contract provides that benefits are payable on death (other than death due to an accident) only where the death occurs within 10 years of the date on which the life of the person in question was first insured under the contract, or where the death occurs before that person attains a specified age not exceeding 70 years'. This definition was amended in order to remove some contracts of long-term insurance (such as whole of life policies) from the definition of a qualifying contract of insurance so that they would fall under the less stringent regulation of ICOBS.

[3] A 'pure protection policy' is one falling under (b) in n 2 above.

[4] Long-term care insurance contract is defined in the FSA Glossary as a long-term insurance contract which: (a) provides (or would at the policyholder's option) or is sold or held out as providing, benefits that are payable or provided if the policyholder's health deteriorates to the extent that he cannot live independently without assistance, and that is not expected to change; and (b) the benefits under the contract are capable of being paid for periodically for all or part of the period that the policyholder cannot live without assistance; where 'benefits' are services, accommodation, or goods necessary or desirable for the continuing care of the policyholder because he cannot live independently without assistance.

(b) credit and suretyship where the policyholder is engaged professionally in an industrial or commercial activity or in one of the liberal professions and the risks relate to such activity; and

(c) land vehicles (other than railway, rolling stock), fire and natural forces, other damage to property, motor vehicle liability, general liability, and miscellaneous financial loss, in so far as the policyholder exceeds the limits of at least two of the following three criteria:

    (i) balance sheet total: €6.2 million;

    (ii) net turnover: €12.8 million;

    (iii) average number of employees during the financial year: 250.[5]

The expression 'direct insurance' is used in EU legislation to distinguish insurance (of **16.06** the original risk) from reinsurance and retrocession (taken out by an insurer or reinsurer). 'Direct selling', on the other hand, is used to describe the situation where an insurer sells directly to the policyholder without an intermediary being involved.

History and Background

Insurers

Prior to FSMA, UK insurers (general and long-term[6]) were subject to authorisa- **16.07** tion under the Insurance Companies Act 1982 (ICA). This legislation reflected the initial EU directives and developed as further EU insurance legislation was adopted. The ICA was focused on prudential regulation, particularly the solvency regime. The Department of Trade and Industry ('DTI') (ie a government department) was responsible for authorising and regulating insurers under the ICA. The detailed requirements were set out in statutory instruments which were supplemented by circular letters and notices from the DTI.

Financial Services Act 1986

Concerns about the UK investment market led to the Gower Report[7] and to the **16.08** Financial Services Act 1986 ('FSA 1986'). This established the Securities and

---

[5] FSA Glossary definition of 'contracts of large risks'. Also defined in the Second Council Directive (EEC) 88/357 on the coordination of laws, regulations and administrative provisions relating to direct insurance other than life assurance and laying down provisions to facilitate the effective exercise of freedom to provide services and amending Directive (EEC) 73/239[1988] OJ L172/1 (the 'Second Non-life Directive').

[6] See the explanation of 'general' and 'long-term' at paras 16.03–16.04.

[7] Review of Investor Protection Report by LCB Gower: Presented to Parliament by Secretary for Trade and Industry (January 1984).

Investments Board (SIB)[8] and a number of self-regulating organisations ('SROs')[9] and recognised professional bodies ('RPBs').[10] Intermediaries dealing with investment insurance[11] (or other investment products) had to be a member of an SRO/RPB, be directly regulated by SIB or appointed as an appointed representative (of an authorised firm which took responsibility for their representative). Insurers providing these insurance products were also subject to the FSA 1986 and had to be dual authorised under this act as well as the ICA.[12] They were prudentially regulated by the DTI, whilst their sales of relevant products were regulated under the FSA 1986 and under the rules of SIB/LAUTRO/PIA.

Intermediaries and brokers

16.09 A statutory regime for the regulation of 'insurance brokers' operated in the UK for over 20 years.[13] The effect of the Insurance Brokers (Registration) Act 1977 ('IBRA')[14] was that insurance intermediaries could only use the title 'broker' if they were registered under that Act with the Insurance Brokers Registration Council ('IBRC').[15] This was described as regulation 'by title'; an intermediary could avoid registration and the related requirements simply by avoiding the use of 'broker' and describing himself as an advisor or consultant. Those that did register were subject to a Code of Conduct and other requirements established in statutory instruments including a disciplinary regime.[16] The effect of the legislation was to divide general insurance mediation between, on the one hand, regulated brokers and, on the other hand, intermediaries or agents which operated outside statutory regulation. A broker was regulated on the basis that he acted as the agent of the insured, independent of insurers, and offering access to a sufficiently wide range of insurers. This was broadly similar to the concept of an insurance broker in EU legislation (including the terminology used in the VAT Directives) and in other Member States, many of which, like the UK, regulated brokers but not insurers' agents. It was a requirement that all 'Lloyd's brokers' (ie those able to place insurance at Lloyd's) be registered with the IBRC;

---

[8] FSA 1986, Sched 9, para 8.
[9] ibid, s 8(1).
[10] ibid, s 16(1) and 17(1).
[11] ie qualifying contracts of insurance.
[12] Part 1, Sched 1, para 10 and 28(1)(d) of the FSA 1986; s 2(1) and 3(2) of the ICA.
[13] Insurance Brokers (Registration) Act 1977, ss 1 and 2.
[14] IBRA was introduced as a Private Members Bill.
[15] IBRA, s 1.
[16] ibid, ss. 10, 11, 13, 14–19.

these brokers were subject to dual regulation by Lloyd's, for example, under Lloyd's Brokers Bye-Law, and by IBRC under the IBRA and related requirements.[17]

As noted above, the FSA 1986 introduced an authorisation requirement for inter-   **16.10**
mediaries selling investment insurance. This prohibited a firm from selling, arranging sales, or advising on such products unless the intermediary was directly authorised by SIB or a member of an SRO/RPB (such as LAUTRO, FIMBRA, and PIA). The regime included SIB's 10 Principles[18] and included detailed Conduct of Business Rules in common with other investment products, as well as rules covering discipline, complaints and dispute resolution, client money, invest-ment advertisements, and an Investors Compensation Scheme. Within the insur-ance industry, the modern compliance function first evolved in this sector. One particular feature of the regime was 'polarisation'. Prompted by a variety of con-cerns, including a lack of transparency about the role of intermediaries, SIB's rules (and those of the SROs) split intermediaries selling investment insurance to the public into two 'polarised' sectors. An intermediary had either to be 'independent' acting for and advising the customer, offering a choice of products drawn from all providers generally (like a 'broker' under IBRA) or it was restricted to acting as a tied agent selling only the products of the particular company or group which it represented.[19] This has been a contentious and much discussed feature of the UK investment market; it was a classic example of restrictive regulation (it prohibited multi-tying and prevented intermediaries offering products from a limited range of providers) and attracted the critical attention of the Office of Fair Trading ('OFT') acting under its competition powers.[20] The polarisation regime survived the migration to FSA regulation, but was abolished in 2004. Intermediaries are now free to offer, and advise upon, products from a limited range of providers (or to offer a 'whole of market' service or to represent a single provider). More recently, the possibility of a new form of polarisation has arisen during FSA's Retail Distribution Review. In this context, FSA has suggested restricting the ability of firms to provide advice unless they provide a 'whole of market service' and are remunerated without traditional 'commission' determined by the product provider.

The IBRA and FSA left a considerable gap in the regulation of insurance interme-   **16.11**
diaries; intermediaries selling general and other non-investment insurance[21]

---

[17] ibid, ss 2 and 3; ss 2 and 3(3) of Lloyd's Brokers Byelaw No 5 of 1988 revoked on 6 December 2000 by Byelaw No 17 of 2000 and revoked on 1 December 2004 by Lloyd's Brokers Byelaw No 7 of 2004.
[18] Volume I SIB Rules and Regulations: Statements of Principle.
[19] Volume I, Chapter III SIB Rules and Regulations: Conduct of Business Rule 4.
[20] 'The Rules on the Polarisation of Investment Advice' A report by the Director General of Fair Trading August 1999 (OFT 264).
[21] See explanation of 'general' and 'non-investment insurance' at paras 16.03–16.04.

fell outside regulation if they avoided describing themselves as a 'broker'. The Association of British Insurers ('ABI') had been formed in 1985 as the principal UK trade body for insurers. It published two codes for general and for long-term insurance.[22]

16.12   A particular feature of the ABI codes was the distinction between independent intermediaries on the one hand (which acted for the insured like an insurance 'broker') and agents which were restricted to offering the products of a limited number of insurers (the basic limit was six). A number of insurers set up an independent monitoring programme (outsourced to a firm of accountants) to monitor compliance with the ABI code by subscribing intermediaries. Independent intermediaries were required to maintain professional indemnity insurance. Firms operating under the code were given certificates to display.[23]

16.13   In July 1998, the Government announced the repeal of IBRA, having concluded that a system of statutory regulation which applied only to those general insurance intermediaries using the title 'broker' was no longer appropriate.[24] This paved the way for the industry to establish a new body, the General Insurance Standards Council ('GISC') which commenced regulation in July 2000. GISC was established outside any statutory authority but with the apparent support of the Government. It was established as a 'voluntary' regulator of general insurance sales by both insurers and intermediaries. Lloyd's dismantled most of its regime for the regulation of Lloyd's brokers which all became members of GISC. The regime was also intended to replace the ABI code on general insurance. Many insurers and intermediaries joined, but plans to achieve full industry coverage were thwarted, initially by the new competition law procedures[25] and more finally by adoption of the Insurance Mediation Directive[26] and the Government's decision not to make GISC a competent authority under it.

16.14   The GISC rulebook was based on two codes of conduct; one for private customers (an individual acting for non-business purposes) and another for commercial customers. It included financial requirements for intermediaries (principally rules requiring the use of insurance bank accounts ('IBAs') to segregate monies held for clients and insurers) and the maintenance of professional indemnity insurance, a monitoring, enforcement, and disciplinary regime similar to the FSA model and

---

[22]   ABI Codes of Practice on 'General Insurance Sales' and 'Long Term Insurance Sales'.
[23]   ibid.
[24]   IBRA was repealed on 30 April 2001 by ss 416(1)(c), 432(3), and Sched 22 of FSMA.
[25]   The OFT clearance of the GISC rulebook and its proposed rule F42 to prevent insurers dealing with non-GISC intermediaries was the subject of appeals to the Competition Commission Appeals Tribunal which overturned the OFT's decision and referred the rulebook for consideration under the procedure for exemption of anti-competitive agreements.
[26]   Council Directive (EC) 2002/92 on insurance mediation [2003] OJ L009/3 (the 'IMD').

specific codes which were developed for areas of particular concern.[27] One example was the GISC Private Medical Code[28] which dealt with the sale of private medical insurance to individuals. The GISC rules maintained the previous practice of intermediaries mixing insurer and client monies in their IBAs and (in some cases) of deducting commission from the IBA when it was 'earned' on placement, even though the premium had not yet been received.[29] It also excluded secondary intermediaries (those selling insurance as an ancillary activity) from IBA requirements. There were other 'voluntary' bodies involved with insurance intermediary regulation prior to the regime introduced under FSMA, for example, the Institute of Insurance Brokers ('IIB') and the Association of British Travel Agents ('ABTA') (in relation to travel insurance sold by its members). Whilst ABTA retained a role in respect of sales excluded from FSMA, FSA regulation of general insurance intermediaries commenced on 14 January 2005[30] and GISC ceased its operations.

Financial Services and Markets Act 2000[31]

Both the ICA and FSA 1986 were repealed and replaced by the regulatory regime **16.15** introduced by FSMA which came into effect on 1 December 2001 (a date known as N2). (The responsibilities of the DTI under the ICA had already passed to HM Treasury and day-to-day operations were taken over by the FSA before FSMA came into full effect.) The FSA was therefore responsible for the authorisation of all insurers (general and long-term) and for the detailed regulation of designated investment insurance sales (ie sales of long-term insurance which constituted designated investments). The insurance regime introduced by FSMA, however, was considerably wider; in particular it included a new regime for the regulation of the Lloyd's insurance market, ie the Society of Lloyd's, its members, the managing agents which underwrite insurance on their behalf, as well as members' agents and advisors. The new Financial Promotions Regime under FSMA (which extended the investment advertisement regime under the 1986 Act) covered all forms of insurance including general insurance.

At that stage the regulation of the sales and administration of general and pure **16.16** protection insurance products[32] was limited, broadly, to the financial promotions regime and limited provisions applicable to insurers, such as those reflecting the

---

[27] General Insurance Standards Council Rule Book: Private Customer Code C and Commercial Code D; Practice Requirement G1 Financial Requirements.

[28] General Insurance Standards Council Rule Book: Section E-Code Practice Requirement E2 Private Medical Insurance.

[29] General Insurance Standards Council Rule Book: Practice Requirement G1 Financial Requirements.

[30] For further information in relation to the regulation of travel insurance, see paras 16.135 and 16.196.

[31] Referred to as 'FSMA'.

[32] See the explanation of 'general' and 'pure protection insurance products' in paras 16.03–16.04.

requirements in the First,[33] Second,[34] and Third[35] Life Directives (which were later consolidated)[36] and the First,[37] Second, and Third[38] Non-life Directives.[39] The application of the FSA's Sourcebook Principles for Businesses ('PRIN') to general insurers was limited to reflect the definition of regulated activities which did not include the sale and administration of general or pure protection insurance products[40] by authorised insurers (or intermediaries).

16.17   For about four years (from 2000 to 2004) many general insurers were members of GISC and followed the GISC rulebook. In January 2005, GISC ceased its operations and its insurer members became subject to broader FSA regulation covering the sale and administration of non-investment insurance products.

16.18   At the time the IMD was adopted, the Government announced that the FSA would be the sole authority for the registration of insurance intermediaries. The FSA regime under FSMA was extended by amending the secondary legislation and the FSA Handbook. This involved:

- extending the perimeter of the section 19 prohibition to bring mediation of general and protection products (non-investment insurance) into regulation;

- new FSA rulebooks (or chapters) for non-investment insurance business such as Insurance: Conduct of Business,[41] Client Assets 5,[42] and Integrated Prudential Sourcebook 9;[43]

- a large number of amendments to other secondary legislation and to existing rulebooks of the FSA Handbook.

---

[33] First Council Directive (EEC) 79/267 on coordination of laws, regulations and administrative provisions relating to the taking-up and pursuit of the business of direct life assurance (as amended) [1979] OJ L63/1 (the 'First Life Directive').

[34] Council Directive (EEC) 90/619 on coordination of laws, regulations, and administrative provisions relating to direct life assurance, laying down provisions to facilitate the effective exercise of freedom to provide services and amending Directive (EEC) 79/267 [1990] OJ L330/50 (the 'Second Life Directive').

[35] Council Directive (EEC) 92/96 on coordination of laws, regulations, and administrative provisions relating to direct life assurance and amending Directives (EEC) 79/267 and 90/619 (as amended) [1992] OJ L311/1 (the 'Third Life Directive').

[36] Council Directive (EC) 2002/83 concerning life assurance [2002] OJ L345/1 (known as the Consolidated Life Directive, 'CLD').

[37] First Council Directive (EEC) 73/239 on the coordination of laws, regulations, and administrative provisions relating to the taking up and pursuit of the business of direct insurance other than life insurance [1973] OJ L228/3 (the First Non-life Directive').

[38] Council Directive (EEC) 92/49 on the coordination of laws, regulations, and administrative provisions relating to direct insurance other than life assurance and amending Directives (EEC) 73/239 and 88/357 [1992] OJ L228/1 (the 'Third Non-life Directive').

[39] The three non-life directives are collectively referred to as '3NLD'.

[40] ibid.

[41] ICOB, now ICOBS.

[42] CASS 5.

[43] PRU 9, now MIPRU.

The changes went well beyond the requirements of the IMD (which only related **16.19** to intermediaries), reflecting the decision to introduce more comprehensive regulation of the sale and administration of all insurance products for both insurers and intermediaries. As a result:

- the new regulated activities for non-investment insurance applied to insurers (as well as intermediaries), authorised insurers had to apply for new mediation permissions, and the ICOB rulebook regulated insurers as product providers and as sellers of insurance; and

- intermediaries were subject to various aspects of the FSA regime which went beyond the IMD such as the FSA's high-level standards and its various initiatives based on PRIN (see para 16.158 *et seq.* below) and the approved persons regime.

The extension to regulation took effect on 14 January 2005 (a date known as **16.20** NGI). A large number of intermediaries and brokers had to apply for FSA authorisation (a much greater number than all the authorised firms before NGI). Most applied before the 14 July 2004 deadline, but late in the day a system of interim authorisation was adopted to allow firms to apply at any time before NGI.

The present regulatory regime under FSMA is described in the other chapters of **16.21** this book; for insurers it brought a single more broadly based system of regulation with detailed rules and high-level standards. This extremely flexible and comprehensive structure (and its extension to all intermediaries at NGI) has enabled the FSA to change fundamentally both the style and policy agenda for the regulation of insurance.

At the time the FSA took over the regulation of insurers under FSMA, it submitted **16.22** a report to HM Treasury on 'The Future Regulation of Insurance'.[44] This report, promoted by the problems of Equitable Life, was followed by a further progress report in October 2002 from John Tiner (then managing director of Consumer, Investment and Insurance at the FSA).[45] The Tiner Project made the reform of insurance regulation a key priority for the FSA. The reports had three policy objectives—'securing a fair deal for consumers', 'firms that are soundly managed and have adequate financial resources', and 'smarter regulation of insurance'.[46] It was at this stage that the Government announced that FSA regulation would be extended to include the sales and administration of general/non-investment insurance.

---

[44] 'The future regulation of insurance'. Report submitted by the Board of the Financial Services Authority to the Economic Secretary to the Treasury (November 2001) in response to 'The regulation of Equitable Life: an independent report' Ronnie Baird (September 2001).

[45] 'The future regulation of insurance: a progress report' (October 2002) which responded to 'The Equitable Life Inquiry' Lord Penrose (2002).

[46] 'The future regulation of insurance'. Report submitted by the Board of the Financial Services Authority to the Economic Secretary to the Treasury (November 2001).

The reform of policy which followed the Tiner Project was much broader than the original issues arising from Equitable Life and with-profits policies. It led to (amongst other things) the reform of financial regulation of insurers as described at para 16.267 *et seq.* below.

European Union Law

16.23   EU law in the insurance field is critical to the domestic regulatory regime. In addition to the single passport system for cross-border business, it provides the framework for insurer and intermediary regulation and detailed requirements in many key areas such as solvency. There is now EU legislation in almost all areas of insurance regulation. An understanding of EU insurance law is critical because so much of the domestic regime implements or reflects EU requirements and concepts. Although one refers to EU legislation, the insurance and single market directives apply to the 30 States of the EEA,[47] including the new accession States.[48]

16.24   Switzerland is not a member of the EEA, but there are bilateral arrangements for mutual recognition of insurers in relation to direct insurance other than life (ie general)[49] between the EU and Switzerland.[50] The Channel Islands and the Isle of Man are not part of the EU or EEA for these purposes. There are special arrangements dealing with insurers established and authorised in Gibraltar.[51]

16.25   EU legislation deals separately with insurers and intermediaries. Intermediary regulation is dealt with under the IMD, whilst the main legislation covering direct insurers is dealt with under:

- the CLD (which replaced and consolidated the First, Second, and Third Life Directives); and

---

[47] EEA States: Iceland, Liechtenstein, Norway, and the 27 EU States, namely Austria, Belgium, Bulgaria, Cyprus, the Czech Republic, Denmark, Estonia, Finland, France, Germany, Greece, Hungary, Ireland, Italy, Latvia, Lithuania, Luxembourg, Malta, the Netherlands, Poland, Portugal, Romania, Slovakia, Slovenia, Spain, Sweden, and the United Kingdom.

[48] Accession States which joined on 1 May 2004: Cyprus, Czech Republic, Estonia, Hungary, Latvia, Lithuania, Malta, Poland, Slovakia, and Slovenia. Accession States which joined the EU on 1 January 2007: Bulgaria and Romania.

[49] See the explanation of 'life' and 'general' in paras 16.03–16.04.

[50] Council Regulation (EEC) 91/2155 Provisions of the Agreement between the EEC and the Swiss Confederation [1991] OJ L205/1; Council Decision (EEC) 91/370 Conclusion of the Agreement between the EEC and the Swiss Confederation [1991] OJ L205/2; Council Directive (EEC) 91/371 Implementation of the Agreement between the EEC and the Swiss Confederation [1991] OJ L205/40; Council Decision (EC) 01/776 Switzerland Joint Committee Decision No 1/2001 amending annexes and protocols [2001] OJ L205/37.

[51] For further detail, please see the Financial Services and Markets Act 2000 (Gibraltar) Order 2001, SI 2001/3084. For EU purposes, Gibraltar forms part of the UK, but there are domestic arrangements under UK and Gibraltar law to enable 'passporting' between Gibraltar and the UK.

- the 3NLD (ie the First, Second and Third Non-life Directives, which have not yet been consolidated).

The CLD and the 3NLD only apply to insurers who undertake direct business; they do not apply to specialist or 'pure' reinsurers. However, with the adoption of the Reinsurance Directive[52] the authorisation and single licence regime was extended to pure reinsurers (see para 16.51 *et seq.* below). **16.26**

As part of the Solvency II project, the insurance directives will be consolidated into a single framework directive (for details, see para 16.310 *et seq.* below). **16.27**

Insurers and reinsurers

Direct insurers—CLD and 3NLD

Unlike investment services, the single licence regime for insurers has emerged in stages. The CLD and the 3NLD apply to insurers that undertake 'direct' business (until implementation of the RID (see para 16.51 below), there was no EU requirement for a specialist or 'pure' reinsurer to be authorised; in the UK 'pure' reinsurers were required to be authorised and were subject to solvency and capital requirements, but some Member States either had no authorisation requirement at all or had only a light regulatory regime). **16.28**

The First Life Directive and the First Non-life Directive established a common authorisation requirement for insurers. The directives introduced common basic authorisation procedures and requirements including harmonised solvency margins (so that the home Member State regulator was solely responsible for the insurer's solvency in respect of its entire business). Insurers had a right to establish branches in other Member States but this was subject to local or host State authorisation and local regulation of technical reserves. **16.29**

Following the European Court of Justice decision in the German Co-Insurance case,[53] freedom of services for insurers was introduced in the Second Life and Non-life Directives (see the explanation of 'services' business at para 16.42 *et seq.* under the heading 'Passporting and cross-border business'). This reflected the findings in the German Co-Insurance decision that (i) a requirement for a foreign insurer from another Member State to be established (ie to have a local branch) in the host State contravened the Treaty, (ii) that a requirement for local authorisation for services business was, in principle, contrary to the Treaty, and (iii) that a requirement for local authorisation, for some types of policyholder, was not **16.30**

---

[52] Council Directive (EC) 05/68/EC on reinsurance and amending Council Directives (EEC) 73/239, 92/49 as well as Directives (EC)98/78 and 02/83 [2005] OJ L323/1 (the 'RID').
[53] Case 205/84 *Commission v Federal Republic of Germany* [1987].

justified even without further harmonisation. The second directives therefore introduced limited freedom of services enabling insurers to conduct cross-border business without a separate authorisation in the host State. For non-life (general), this freedom was restricted to 'large' risks (see the explanation of large risks in para 16.05 above); for life, it only applied to group and employment related life policies and those taken out (with the foreign insurer) on the consumer's own initiative.

16.31 The third generation of directives introduced the full single licence system or European 'passport'. This removed dual authorisation completely; an insurer's home State authorisation covered all services business and any branches established in other States. Critical to this development was the harmonisation of technical reserves (to enable home State authorities to regulate the reserves for business written by branches in other States); the Insurance Accounts Directive,[54] adopted at the same time as the Third Non-life Directive, was an important part of this harmonisation.

Key aspects of the CLD and 3NLD regimes

16.32 The directives require all direct insurers to be authorised and set out common standards and procedures for the authorisation process and for prudential supervision, particularly in relation to solvency, including the solvency margin, technical reserves, and admissible capital.

Solvency requirements and the minimum guarantee fund

16.33 Over and above technical reserves, the insurers must have what the directives describe as a 'supplementary reserve' or 'solvency margin'. This is the amount by which an insurer's assets exceed foreseeable liabilities and are free to provide against business fluctuations. There must be an adequate solvency margin in respect of the insurer's entire business.

16.34 For non-life business, the solvency margin requirement is the greater of two sums calculated by reference to premiums on the one hand and claims on the other. Regardless of the amount set by the solvency margin calculation (which may be small during the initial stages of establishment), the margin cannot fall below the minimum guarantee fund requirements.

16.35 The original solvency regime for insurers was updated by the Solvency I Directives.[55] This made some relatively minor amendments and was an interim

---

[54] Council Directive (EEC) 91/674 on the annual accounts and consolidated accounts of insurance undertakings [1991] OJ L374/7.

[55] Council Directive (EC) 02/12 amending Council Directive (EEC) 79/267 as regards the solvency margin requirements for life assurance undertakings [2002] OJ L77/11; Council Directive

measure pending a more fundamental review of the solvency regime for insurers known as Solvency II (see para 16.310 *et seq.* below).

Special characteristics of authorised insurers

The CLD and the 3NLD both require insurers to limit their 'objects to the busi- **16.36** ness of insurance and operations arising directly therefrom to the exclusion of all other commercial business'.[56] This is incorporated in the UK in INSPRU 1.5.14.[57] Unlike a firm conducting mediation or providing investment services, an insurer must be a specialist insurance entity. You cannot conduct the business of an insurer as a secondary activity. A company cannot therefore apply for authorisation to write insurance as an ancillary activity nor can authorised insurers conduct unrelated business (although a subsidiary or group company may be able to do so).

Under the directives, the only types of private sector entity which can be author- **16.37** ised in the UK as an insurer are a body corporate (other than a limited liability partnership), a registered friendly society, or a member of Lloyd's.[58]

The directives do not define insurance or the essential elements of a contract of **16.38** insurance nor do they harmonise insurance contract law. The idea of a directive on insurance contract law has been considered but not adopted (see further at para 16.89 *et seq.* below).

The directives divide life and non-life insurance into different classes; an insurer **16.39** must be authorised in respect of each class it underwrites (subject to certain provisions on ancillary risks). The classes are reflected in Schedule 1 to the RAO[59] (albeit in slightly different terms). The classes of non-life (general) insurance are:

   (i) Accident (section 1)
  (ii) Sickness (section 2)
 (iii) Land vehicles (section 3)
 (iv) Railway rolling stock (section 4)
  (v) Aircraft (section 5)
 (vi) Ships (section 6)
 (vii) Goods in transit (section 7)
(viii) Fire and natural forces (section 8)
 (ix) Other damage to property (section 9)

(EC) 02/13 amending Council Directive (EEC) 73/239 as regards the solvency margin requirements for non-life insurance undertakings [2002] OJ L77/17 (the 'Solvency I Directives').

[56] CLD, Art 6.1(b); the Third Non-life Directive, Art 8.1(b).

[57] Previously in the Interim Prudential Sourcebook for Insurers (IPRU(INS)) 1.3.(1)R and (in a slightly different form) at section 16 of the ICA.

[58] Art 8(1) of the First Non-life Directive; Art 8(1) of the First Life Directive as repealed by Art 6(1) of CLD. COND 2.1.

[59] RAO, Sched 1, Part 1 paras 1 and 18 and Part 2 IX.

  (x) Motor vehicle liability (section 10)
 (xi) Aircraft liability (section 11)
(xii) Liability for/of ships (section 12)
(xiii) General liability (section 13)
(xiv) Credit (section 14)
 (xv) Suretyship (in the RAO this includes fidelity, performance, administration, bail and custom bonds and similar contracts of guarantee if the provider is not carrying on a banking business; it is not merely incidental to some other business carried on by the person effecting it; and it is effected in return for the payment of one or more premiums (section 15))
(xvi) Miscellaneous financial loss (section 16)
(xvii) Legal expenses (section 17)
(xviii) Assistance (section 18).

16.40 For life (long-term) insurance, the classes are.

  I Life and annuity
 II Marriage and birth
III Limited long term
 IV Permanent health (which is excluded for non-life)
  V Tontines
 VI Capital redemption contracts
VII Pension fund management (by insurers)
VIII Collective insurance
 IX Social insurance.

16.41 Class VII is peculiar in that it relates to an activity unrelated to a contract of insurance; it reflects the extension of a life office's permitted/authorised business to include the management of group pension funds.

Passporting and cross-border business

16.42 As is the case with other single market directives, the single licence means that insurers and reinsurers (see para 16.51 *et seq.* below) are effectively authorised to write insurance business across the EEA. However, there are mandatory procedural requirements before an insurer can start, for the first time, to write business in a Member State (a host State) other than the State of its registration and authorisation (home State).

16.43 The CLD and the 3NLD provide rules to determine where insurance business is to be regarded as being conducted for passporting purposes.[60] For life business it is the Member State where the policyholder has his/her habitual residence or, in

---

[60] CLD, Art 1(g)–(h); the Third Non-life Directive, Art 1(e).

the case of a company insured, the location of the relevant office/branch (the State of commitment). For non-life business this depends on the location of the risk which is (in summary):

- property insurance—location of property;
- vehicle insurance—place of registration;
- place of purchase for short-term travel policy;
- other policies—habitual residence/company branch (as for State of commitment above).

As well as determining the State of the risk or commitment, it is also necessary to determine the location of the insurer's establishment which is underwriting the insurance. If the risk is located in the home State, there is no 'passporting' involved. If the establishment is in the home State and the risk in another, a service notification to the host State must have been completed. If the State of the establishment is not the home State, a branch notification for that State must have been completed. If that branch underwrites risks in another State, a service notification for that State is also required. The European Commission has published its view of when the use or involvement of a local intermediary or agent will be regarded as constituting a local branch of the insurer.[61]   **16.44**

The process for exercise of the passport to establish a branch of an insurer in another Member State is much more onerous than for services business or for the branch of an intermediary (see paras 16.336 to 16.339 below).   **16.45**

General good and the review of policy terms/premium rates

The CLD and the 3NLD expressly forbid any prior or systematic substantive control of insurance policies and documents;[62] Member States should long ago have abandoned the previously widespread practice of controlling policy terms and premium scales/rates in this way. There are some limited exceptions; for example it is permissible for regulators to require the terms of compulsory insurance to be notified.   **16.46**

More broadly, the CLD and the 3NLD permit various host State regulation subject to the general good—for example in relation to the operations of a local branch of an insurer or in relation to laws on insurance policies or advertising. The case law on the 'general good' in the context of insurance is considered in some detail by the Commission in its interpretative Communication.[63]   **16.47**

---

[61] Part I, Commission Interpretative Communication: Freedom to provide services and the general good in the insurance sector, Brussels 02/02/2000 C (1999) 5046 P.

[62] CLD, Art 45; Third Non-life Directive, Arts 29 and 39.

[63] Commission Interpretative Communication (EC) 43/03: Freedom to provide services and the general good in the insurance sector [2000] OJ C043/5.

Applicable law

16.48 The CLD and the 3NLD contain provisions dealing with the ability of Member States to require that their law is the applicable law for an insurance contract[64] (see para 16.80 *et seq.* below which refers to the applicable regime from a UK perspective—the UK allows a greater freedom of choice than some Member States). It is now recognised that the ability of Member States, such as France, to require insurers from other Member States to write their insurance policies under French law (when the policyholder is a French national in France) is a significant barrier to cross-border business (see further at para 16.93 *et seq.* below).

Information for policyholders

16.49 The Directives set out certain information requirements for policyholders; these are implemented in the UK through the FSA's Conduct of Business Rules (now COBs) (see para 16.195 *et seq.* below).

16.50 The CLD and the 3NLD also deal with:

- transfer of policies 'en bloc' under portfolio or insurance business transfers (in the UK, these are Part VII transfers or transfers relating to Lloyd's business under section 323 of FSMA);[65]
- cancellation rights in relation to life (long-term) policies;[66]
- transparency in group structures to ensure effective supervision[67] (the post-BCCI directive amendments).

Reinsurers—The Reinsurance Directive[68]

Background

16.51 The 1964 directive on the abolition of restrictions on the freedom of establishment and freedom to provide services in respect of reinsurance and retrocession[69] was one of the first pieces of EU insurance legislation. It prohibited the discrimination against incoming reinsurers, but it did not require Member States to authorise or regulate 'pure' reinsurers (ie insurers which only underwrite reinsurance and

---

[64] CLD, Art 32; Third Non-life Directive, Art 31.

[65] CLD, Arts 14 and 53; Third Non-life Directive, Arts 12 and 53.

[66] CLD, Art 35.

[67] Council Directive (EC) 95/26 amending Directives (EEC) 77/780 and 89/646 in the field of credit institutions, Directives (EEC) 73/239 and 92/49 in the field of non-life insurance, Council Directives 79/267/EEC and 92/96/EEC in the field of life assurance, Council Directive (EEC) 93/22 in the field of investment firms, and Directive (EEC) 85/611 in the field of undertakings for collective investment in transferable securities ('UCITS'), with a view to reinforcing prudential supervision [1995] OJ L168/7.

[68] See n 52 above.

[69] Council Directive (EEC) 64/225 on the abolition of restrictions on freedom of establishment and freedom to provide services in respect of reinsurance and retrocession [1964] OJ 56/878.

retrocession, and which do not underwrite any 'direct' insurance and which therefore fall outside the CLD and the 3NLD). Member States were therefore free either to regulate pure reinsurers or not, as they saw fit. Some States did not regulate pure reinsurers at all or adopted a very light touch regime, whereas others (such as the UK) regulated them in much the same way as direct insurers.

The lack of harmonisation and a 'single passport' for pure reinsurers was not **16.52** initially a major concern, partly because reinsurance was already an international business, and direct insurers faced greater cross-border barriers.

The RID was adopted in December 2005, and was due to be implemented by **16.53** December 2007. The legislation:

(i) harmonised the authorisation and regulation (principally prudential regulation such as solvency) of pure reinsurers; and
(ii) introduced the single passport system for pure reinsurers.

It aimed to improve consumer protection (because EU direct insurers would be **16.54** better protected by their reinsurance arrangements with EU pure reinsurers and this would indirectly benefit the policyholders of the direct insurer), cross-border operation, and hence competition. It was also envisaged that a harmonised EU regime might assist in trade negotiations with the US, particularly in the context of onerous US collateral requirements in relation to foreign reinsurers.

Authorisation and solvency

Like direct insurers, the directive requires authorisation of pure reinsurers and **16.55** imposes conditions such as the form of reinsurance undertakings, close links and controllers, and a scheme of operations. There is a limitation on activities, but this is a little broader than that for direct or primary insurers (see para 16.156 below).

The RID introduces a harmonised solvency regime based on the Solvency I regime **16.56** for direct non-life insurers, although it is recognised that this will change with the introduction of Solvency II.

The single passport system and home State authorisation for the entire EEA **16.57** apply for both cross-border services business and for branches in other EEA States. The RID does not mirror the procedural requirements for cross-border notifications in the regime for direct insurers. As with direct insurers, pure reinsurers incorporated outside the EEA are subject to separate authorisation in each EEA State.

Collateralisation

The RID improved the position of EU pure reinsurers by amending the CLD and **16.58** the 3NLD to restrict some collateral requirements imposed on direct insurers in relation to their reinsurance.

Other provisions

16.59 The RID also:

(i) defines 'finite' reinsurance and permits Member States to regulate it;[70]

(ii) introduces Insurance Special Purpose Vehicles ('ISPVs'),[71] which are defined as SPVs that accept risks from insurers/reinsurers and are funded by debt issuance (or other financing) subordinated to the SPVs' reinsurance obligations. ISPVs can be authorised, if a Member State so permits, without compliance with RID requirements (but under appropriate domestic procedures and requirements);

(iii) completes the system for EU wide portfolio transfers.[72]

Other EU insurance legislation

16.60 There is further EU legislation adopted or proposed in the following areas:

- Motor insurance (the five generations of directives dealing with compulsory motor insurance).[73]

- Insurers Winding-Up Directive,[74] which came into force on 15 April 2003.

- Insurance Committees—establishing the European Insurance and Occupational Pensions Committee ('EIOPC') and extending the Lamfalussy Process to insurance with the creation of the Committee of European Insurance and Occupational Pension Supervisors ('CEIOPS').[75]

- Co-insurance,[76] legal expenses insurance,[77] accounting,[78] and exchange of information with third countries.[79]

---

[70] RID, Art 2.1(q) and Art 45.

[71] ibid, Art 2.1(p) and Art 46.

[72] ibid, Art 18.

[73] Council Directive (EC) 2005/14 amending Council Directives (EEC) 72/166, 84/5, 88/357 and 90/232 and Directive (EC) 2000/26 relating to insurance against civil liability in respect of use of motor vehicles [2005] OJ L149/14.

[74] Council Directive (EC) 2001/17 on the reorganisation and winding-up of insurance undertakings [2001] OJ L110/28.

[75] Commission Decision (EC) 04/9 of 5 November 2003 establishing the European Insurance and Occupational Pensions Committee [2004] OJ L003/34, as amended by Regulation (EC) No 1882/2003, Directive 2005/1/EC and Directive (EC) 2008/21; Commission Decision (EC) of 5 November 2003 establishing the Committee of European Insurance and Occupational Pensions [2004] OJ L003/30.

[76] Council Directive (EEC) 78/473 on the coordination of laws, regulations and administrative provisions relating to Community co-insurance [1978] OJ L151/25.

[77] Council Directive (EEC) 87/344 on the coordination of laws, regulations, and administrative provisions relating to legal expenses insurance [1987] OJ L185/77.

[78] Council Directive (EEC) 91/674 on annual and consolidated accounts of insurance undertakings [1991] OJ L374/7; Council Directive (EEC) 78/660 on annual accounts of certain types of companies [1978] OJ L222/11; Directive (EEC) 83/349 Seventh Council Directive—Consolidated accounts [1983] OJ L193/1.

[79] Council Directive (EC) 00/64 amending Council Directives (EEC) 85/611, 92/49, 92/96, 93/22 as regards exchange of information with third countries [2000] OJ L290/27.

- Mergers and Acquisitions in the financial services sector.[80] Member States must implement the directive by 21 March 2009.[81]

- Solvency and financial supervision (see para 16.265 *et seq.* below).

- Amendments to the Third Non-life Directive concerning tourist assistance, credit insurance, and suretyship insurance.[82]

- Insurance Guarantee Scheme—Unlike credit institutions and investment services, there is currently no EU legislation requiring or regulating compensation schemes to protect policyholders when insurers become insolvent. In response to calls for harmonised rules on guarantee schemes across the EU, the European Commission appointed a consultancy firm (Oxera) to carry out a detailed assessment of the current situation. Oxera's report was published in early 2008. Between May 2008 and July 2008 the Commission subsequently carried out a consultation in relation to insurance guarantee schemes. As at the date of writing, the Commission was currently considering the responses received and will issue its response in due course.

- Money Laundering Directives—three directives which include identification requirements for certain life business.[83]

- Distance Marketing Directive[84]—this applies to insurance contracts and insurance mediation contracts with consumers and is implemented in the UK, in relation to insurance, through ICOBS, and the Financial Services (Distance Marketing) Regulations 2004, SI 2004/2095. It prohibits unsolicited services and requires, for distance contracts, the provision of information to consumers (normally in good time prior to the conclusion of the contract) and gives cancellation rights (long-term insurance contracts—including face-to-face sales—were already subject to cancellation under the 3LD).

---

[80] Council Directive (EC) 2007/44 amending Council Directive (EEC) 92/49 and Directives (EC) 2002/83, 2004/39, 2005/68 and 2006/48 as regards procedural rules and evaluation criteria for the prudential assessment of acquisitions and increase of holdings in the financial sector [2007] OJ L247/1.

[81] HM Treasury issued a discussion paper in September 2006 on the proposed directive.

[82] Council Directive (EEC) 84/641 amending, particularly as regards tourist assistance, the First Directive (EEC) 73/239 on the coordination of laws, regulations, and administrative provisions relating to the taking-up and pursuit of the business of direct insurance other than life assurance [1984] OJ L339/21.

[83] Council Directive (EEC) 91/308 on the prevention of the use of the financial system for the purpose of money laundering [1991] OJ L166/77; Council Directive (EC) 01/97 amending Directive (EEC) 91/308 on prevention of the use of the financial system for the purpose of money laundering [2001] OJ L344/76; Council Directive (EC) 04/0137 (COD) on the prevention of the use of the financial system for the purpose of money laundering and terrorist financing will update and consolidate these directives.

[84] Council Directive (EC) 02/65 concerning the distance marketing of consumer financial services and amending Council Directive (EEC) 90/619 and Directives (EC) 97/7 and 98/27 [2002] OJ L271/16 (the 'DMD').

- E-Commerce Directive[85]—The ECD is designed to remove potential restrictions on e-commerce across the EU. The ECD applies to the provision of services (to businesses and consumers) by means of electronic equipment (and therefore has a wide application which includes some areas of insurance business). The ECD removes restrictions on the cross-border provision of services by electronic means, introducing a 'country of origin' approach to regulation.[86] Member States must therefore impose their requirements on the outward provision of such services and lift them from inward providers. Insurance is one of the few areas where 'derogations' are available to allow host States to apply their advertising rules in the 'general good' under CLD and 3NLD.[87]

Insurance intermediaries

Pre-IMD measures

16.61 Prior to the IMD, there were two EU measures dealing with insurance intermediaries. These were the Insurance Agents and Brokers Directive of 1976[88] and the subsequent Commission Recommendation of 1991 (the 'Recommendation').[89] The Directive was intended as a transitional measure pending mutual recognition of qualifications and was very limited in scope. It required those Member States which imposed qualification or experience requirements to recognise experience in other Member States. The Recommendation was not binding on Member States and envisaged the introduction of a more comprehensive system of compulsory registration and professional competence requirements. Both measures focused on the activities of professionals rather than firms and distinguished between independent brokers (as registered in the UK under the IBRA—see para 16.09 *et seq.* above) and agents of insurers.

The IMD

16.62 The IMD was adopted in 2002. This was a binding directive which replaced the two previous measures and introduced an EEA wide registration requirement for intermediaries with the single or 'European' passport.

---

[85] Council Directive (EC) 00/31 on certain legal aspects of information society services, in particular electronic commerce, in the Internal Market [2000] OJ L178/1 (the 'ECD').

[86] This approach means that Member States must impose their requirements on the outward provision of the relevant services, but must not impose them for inward service providers.

[87] Member States which have adopted the derogations may continue to impose their existing requirements on the inward provision of services, but in accordance with the ECD, they will not be able to impose their domestic requirements on the outward provision of services falling with the scope of the ECD. Instead, the country of destination's requirements (if any) will apply. See ICOBS 1 Annex 1 8.4 for further information.

[88] Council Directive (EEC) 77/92 on measures to facilitate the effective exercise of freedom of establishment and freedom to provide services in respect of the activities of insurance agents and brokers [1977] OJ L26/14.

[89] Commission Recommendation (EEC) 92/48 on insurance intermediaries [1991] OJ L019/32.

The IMD definition of intermediary is not limited to the concepts, in the earlier **16.63** legislation, of brokers and insurers' agents. It can apply to a company (as well as self-employed individuals). It is based on five mediation activities (see paras 16.119 to 16.136 below) where these relate to direct insurance contracts or reinsurance or retrocession contracts. It does not apply to the mediation of risks located outside the EEA nor to authorised EEA insurers or their employees.

There is no requirement for an insurance intermediary to be a specialist company **16.64** (as with insurers); insurance mediation is often conducted as a secondary or ancillary activity. Indeed, a firm may be authorised as a credit institution under the Banking Consolidation Directive[90] (or as an investment firm under the Markets in Financial Instruments Directive[91]) and, at the same time, it can be registered as an insurance intermediary under the IMD; such a firm can 'passport' under both directives.

The IMD introduced a 'registration' requirement (unlike the insurance, banking, **16.65** and investment firms legislation, the IMD refers to 'registration' rather than 'authorisation'). In the UK, insurance intermediaries are 'registered' with the FSA through authorisation under FSMA or, in the case of appointed representatives, by registration with the FSA following their appointment (see paras 16.143 to 16.148 below). There are exclusions for certain introducers and those dealing with 'connected contracts' (see paras 16.122 to 16.136 below in relation to article 72B and 72C of the RAO, and para 16.197 *et seq.* below in relation to the relevant ICOBS requirements).

There are minimum professional requirements for intermediaries concerning **16.66** knowledge and ability and good repute, professional indemnity insurance, and the protection of customers (against the failure of intermediaries to transfer premiums to insurers or to pay claims or premium refunds to customers). In this last area, Member States are given the choice of four measures under Article 4(4):

(a) provisions (in law or contract) whereby payment by the customer to the intermediary is treated as payment to the insurer (and payment by the insurer to the intermediary is not treated as payment to the customer);
(b) capital requirements with a minimum of 4 per cent of annual premiums received or €15,000, if greater;
(c) segregated client accounts; and
(d) a guarantee fund.

---

[90] Council Directive (EC) 06/48 relating to the taking up and pursuit of the business of credit institutions [2006] OJ L177/1 (the 'BCD').
[91] Council Directive (EC) 04/39 on Markets in Financial Instruments, amending Council Directives (EEC) 85/611 and 93/6 and Directive (EC) 2000/12 and repealing Council Directive (EEC) 93/22 [2004] OJ L245/1 ('MiFID').

16.67   The UK has adopted measures in all four areas but for directive compliance it relies on a mixture of the rules under Article 4(4)(a) and (c). The IMD is unusual in allowing Member States a choice of measures within a single licence/mutual recognition system. It appears that there is some scope for conflict, although the intention is that home State rules will apply.

16.68   The passporting process is relatively simple even in the case of a branch with a maximum two-month waiting period from notification. The directive makes special provision for Member States to waive the right to receive notifications in respect of incoming firms.

16.69   There are requirements for intermediaries to provide their customers with information about their regulatory status and the service they provide as well as a demands and needs statement (these do not apply to large risks[92] or reinsurance mediation). These requirements are reflected within the FSA's Conduct of Business Rules (see para 16.197 *et seq.* below in relation to ICOBS).

16.70   As the IMD does not apply to authorised EEA insurers, the demands and needs requirement does not apply to direct sales. However, insurers must be prohibited, under home State regulation, from using the mediation services of unregistered intermediaries—a provision incorporated in MIPRU 5.2 (see paras 16.334 to 16.335 below).

16.71   Unlike the CLD and the 3NLD, IMD does not define what amounts to 'cross border' or 'services' business (which requires a notification and potentially brings 'host' State's general good rules into play). Mediation by, say, a UK intermediary, may involve a variety of different contacts or potential links with other Member States—such as the location of the risk, the location of the policyholder, the location of the insurer, the location of a producing broker in relation to the placing broker and vice versa, or the location at which mediation or placing activities take place. CEIOPS has considered these issues and advocated a combined test, namely that an intermediary would be carrying on business on a freedom of services basis if it intends to supply a policyholder established in a Member State different from the one where the intermediary is established, with an insurance contract relating to a risk situated in a Member State different from the one where the intermediary is established. CEIOPS members considered this proposal to be the most workable solution, but there is currently no indication as to whether and how such a proposal might be adopted.[93]

---

[92] See the explanation of 'large risks' in para 16.05.
[93] The reasoning was that this proposal takes into consideration the intention of the intermediary provided in Art 6 of the IMD. This definition creates no artificial barriers for existing mediation activities and it minimises the administrative burden; the protection of the consumer is guaranteed

Various aspects of the IMD were criticised, particularly when the scope of IMD **16.72** requirements became clear at the time of implementation. For example, the FSA has expressed concern that the scope of the IMD is too broad and questioned whether the activity of introducing insurance business should be regulated. CEIOPS has also considered problems with the IMD and potential amendments.[94] In the UK, there was also a gradual recognition that some of the gold-plating introduced at NGI was unnecessary (see para 16.208 *et seq.* below). The original idea was that the Commission would conduct a substantive review of the IMD followed by amending legislation to correct the various problems that had been identified. The impetus behind the review has, however, faded, and it now seems unlikely that amending legislation will emerge in the near future.

Competition issues

Block exemption for the insurance sector

In the competition law field, there is some specific sectoral legislation dealing with **16.73** insurance. The general prohibition on anti-competitive agreements and practices is applicable to insurance but there is a block exemption for certain agreements and practices relating to insurance (a new exemption[95] came into force in April 2003; this replaced the previous block exemption introduced in 1992).[96] The block exemption regulation allows, subject to various conditions and limitations, certain types of cooperation agreements between insurance companies.

The regulation is unusual in providing an exemption on a sectoral basis. It deals **16.74** with the following types of agreement:

- joint calculations of risks and joint studies on future risks;
- the establishment of non-binding standard policy conditions;
- the establishment and management of insurance pools; and
- the testing and acceptance of security equipment.

The block exemption provides automatic exemption for those agreements that **16.75** come within its scope. If an agreement falls outside of the block exemption this

since it is based on the decision of the consumer to request the services of an intermediary operating in another Member State.

[94] CEIOPS' Report on the Implementation of the Insurance Mediation Directive's Key Provisions—March 2007; CEIOPS' Survey on proposals for amending the IMD and Luxembourg Protocol—March 2008.

[95] Commission Regulation (EC) 358/2003 on the application of Art 81(3) of the Treaty to certain categories of agreements, decisions and concerted practices in the insurance sector [2003] OJ L53/8.

[96] Commission Regulation (EEC) 3932/92 on the application of Art 85(3) of the Treaty to certain categories of agreements, decisions and concerted practices in the insurance sector [1992] OJ L398/7.

does not necessarily mean that the agreement will infringe the EU rules on competition. The agreement may not infringe competition rules or it may satisfy the generic criteria for exemption. The exemption is also important in the context of the Competition Act 1998 as compliance with an EU block exemption provides a 'parallel' exemption under the 1998 Act.

16.76 The Block Exemption Regulation expires on 31 March 2010; the Commission has expressed doubts about continuing the exemptions in their present terms and has consulted on the terms of any renewal.

Regulation and competition law overlap—the Commission's sectoral inquiry into business insurance

16.77 There is a considerable overlap and inter-play between insurance regulation and competition, or anti-trust, issues. This can be seen at an EU level in the Commission's recent report on business insurance.[97] Despite being a competition inquiry conducted by the Directorate General for Competition, the Commission's report looked at conflicts of interest in the insurance sector, particularly insurer bias deriving from intermediary remuneration structures and, for SME clients, the lack of commission disclosure. These are all also regulatory issues which concern insurance regulators; FSA's approach is considered at para 16.151 *et seq.* below. The Commission raised a number of other concerns about competition and considered various aspects of subscription insurance markets such as the London Market; these included the traditional arrangements for, and respective roles of, a 'lead' underwriter and 'following' underwriters. The Commission considered the use of standard insurance policy wordings or clauses; it was critical, from a competition perspective, of various practices used to align other terms amongst the different underwriters of a risk, particularly the use of 'best terms and conditions' clauses. Another overlap in competition and insurance regulation can be seen in recent developments concerning payment protection insurance (see para 16.166 below).

UK Law and Regulation—The Legislation

16.78 In the next sections we look at how the legislation and FSA Handbook, described in outline in earlier chapters, apply to insurers and insurance intermediaries. Paragraph 16.80 *et seq.* deal mainly with the legislation, contracts of insurance and regulated activities, financial promotions, appointed representatives, and other

---

[97] Sector Inquiry under Article 17 of Regulation (EC) No 1/2003 on business insurance (Final Report) (SEC (2007) 1231).

issues; and para 16.151 *et seq.* with parts of the FSA Handbook (namely COND,[98] PRIN,[99] SYSC,[100] ICOBS, CASS, GENPRU,[101] INSPRU,[102] MIPRU,[103] TC[104]). In the final section, we look at the Financial Ombudsman Scheme ('FOS') under DISP[105] and the Financial Services Compensation Scheme ('FSCS') under COMP.[106]

As explained in para 16.07 *et seq.*, since NGI, insurers and insurance intermediar- **16.79** ies have been subject to broadly based regulation under FSMA and the FSA Handbook. This includes general/non-life and non-investment insurance as well as long-term/life and investment insurance; it covers underwriting as well as sales and administration (such as claims handling) by insurers and intermediaries and the Lloyd's market.

Contracts of insurance

There is no comprehensive statutory definition (in EU or UK legislation) to **16.80** determine whether a contract amounts to a contract of insurance. (The issue had received surprisingly little attention in a regulatory context until FSA decided to consult on draft guidance, although the courts have had to determine the issue in relation to various specific contracts which were the subject of litigation.) The question is important in a variety of contexts including tax and regulation.

The definition of insurance in the context of the regulatory perimeter and regu- **16.81** lated activities under the RAO is considered below at para 16.97 *et seq.*; there are particular aspects which are dealt with in the statutory provisions but the funda-mental issue of what does or does not constitute a contract of insurance is consid-ered in the FSA's guidance and is based on the case law. These are considered by FSA, in the context of regulation under FSMA.

FSA Guidance: what constitutes a contract of insurance

The FSA published a Consultation Paper[107] which outlined principles to be used **16.82** in the identification of insurance contracts; the guidance was then adopted in the

---

[98] FSA Sourcebook: Threshold Conditions.
[99] FSA Sourcebook: Principles For Businesses.
[100] FSA Sourcebook: Senior Management Arrangements, Systems and Controls.
[101] FSA Sourcebook: General Prudential Sourcebook.
[102] FSA Sourcebook: Prudential Sourcebook for Insurers.
[103] FSA Sourcebook: Prudential Sourcebook for Mortgage and Home Finance Firms, and Insurance Intermediaries.
[104] FSA Sourcebook: Training and Competence.
[105] FSA Sourcebook: Dispute Resolution: Complaints.
[106] FSA Sourcebook: Dispute Resolution: Compensation.
[107] FSA CP150: 'Financial Services Authority: The Authorisation Manual: Consultation on Draft Guidance on the identification of contracts of insurance'.

Authorisation Sourcebook Appendix 6 and is now contained in the Perimeter Guidance Manual ('PERG').[108] Feedback on the Consultation Paper was mixed. Some parties supported the guidance while others remarked that attempting to give guidance on this matter was undesirable in light of the small quantity of often contradictory or ambiguous case law.[109]

16.83 The FSA has stressed that it considers each case on its own merits.[110] The principles outlined are to be used as guidance only.[111] In line with case law, the FSA view is that the substance of the contract prevails over its form.[112] The agreed starting point is the definition in *Prudential v Commissioners of Inland Revenue*,[113] but there has been other more recent case law which is also considered by the FSA.[114] If case law is unclear the FSA will interpret and apply the law in a way that is consistent with the purpose of the FSA's statutory objectives.[115]

16.84 FSA summarises the description of an insurance contract as an enforceable contract under which a 'provider' undertakes:

- in consideration of one or more payments;
- to pay money or provide a corresponding benefit (including in some cases services to be paid for by the provider) to a 'recipient';
- in response to a defined event the occurrence of which is uncertain (either as to when it will occur or as to whether it will occur at all) and adverse to the interests of the recipient.[116]

16.85 Additionally the FSA will use the following guidelines:

- Substance over form. The FSA regards the substance of the contract, in particular the substance of the provider's obligation, to be more important than its form in determining whether it is a contract of insurance.[117]
- One cannot rely on the contract having a dominant purpose other than insurance, or the relatively small element of insurance within it, to conclude that it is not a contract of insurance. The FSA simply requires the presence of

---

[108] FSA Statutory Instrument 2004/58: Identification of Contracts of Insurance; amending AUTH Appendix 6 and now reflected in PERG 6.

[109] FSA PS04/19: 'Financial Services Authority: The identification of contracts of insurance: Feedback on CP150 and made text'.

[110] PERG 6.4.3G.

[111] PERG 6.4.1; 6.4.2G.

[112] PERG 6.5.4(1)G citing *Fuji Finance Inc v Aetna Life Insurance Co Ltd* [1997] Ch 173 (CA).

[113] PERG 6.5.1G.

[114] *Department of Trade and Industry v St Christopher's Motorist Association Ltd* [1974] 1 WLR 99, [1974] 1 All ER 395; *Medical Defence Union v Department of Trade* [1980] Ch 82, [1979] 2 WLR 686.

[115] PERG 6.5.3G.

[116] PERG 6.3.4G.

[117] PERG 6.5.4(3)G.

an insurance obligation undertaken by the provider—it need not be substantial, nor does it need to form a significant part of the provider's business.[118]

- Providers must be obliged to provide a benefit. Contracts where a provider has an absolute discretion as to whether any benefit is provided are not contracts of insurance, even if the provider has never exercised this discretion to deny the benefit.[119]

- There must be an 'assumption' or 'transfer of risk', this is considered an important descriptive feature of contracts of insurance and the FSA has derived its meaning largely from case law.[120] The 'assumption of risk' or 'transfer of risk' can be seen as an 'enforceable obligation to respond to the occurrence of some uncertain event'. Transfer of risk is not viewed as the same thing as the insurer's risk of profit or loss from insurance business.[121]

- Contracts that constitute a simple payment for services (where the payment is related to cost) are not insurance contracts. Factors considered are the amount and timing of the payments made by the insured.[122] Where the provider simply undertakes to provide periodic maintenance of goods/facilities irrespective of any events occurring,[123] or where in consideration for an initial payment a provider undertakes to provide services on the condition that they are to be paid at the commercial rate,[124] a contract of insurance is unlikely to be involved.

- Consideration in a contract of insurance does not need to be a distinct or discrete premium. Consideration may either be part of some other payment or be provided in a non-monetary form.[125]

Other factors influencing the FSA's determination of whether a contract of insurance exists include: how the amount payable by the recipient is calculated,[126] whether the risk is 'pure' or 'speculative',[127] whether the contract is actually described as insurance,[128] and in some cases the existence of terms inconsistent with obligations of good faith.[129] FSA refers to the general position that a contract **16.86**

---

[118] PERG 6.6.7(2)(3)G.
[119] PERG 6.6.1G.
[120] PERG 6.6.2G.
[121] PERG 6.6.2(1),(2),(3),(4)G.
[122] PERG 6.6.3G.
[123] PERG 6.6.4G.
[124] PERG 6.6.5G.
[125] PERG 6.6.6G.
[126] PERG 6.6.8(1)G.
[127] PERG 6.6.8(2)G.
[128] PERG 6.6.8(3)G.
[129] PERG 6.6.8(4)G.

of insurance[130] need not be in writing although there are exceptions such as marine insurance[131] and guarantee insurance.[132]

'Finite' or financial reinsurance

16.87 In the FSA's original consultation[133] the FSA defined financial engineering as 'an umbrella term for certain types of arrangements used by insurance firms for financing or regulatory reporting purposes, or both. These arrangements are used to improve, or sometimes to smooth, reported profits or to improve the reported balance sheet position.'[134] Financial engineering was recognised as a valid method of strengthening an insurer's solvency and of recognising and reporting economic reality. However, it should be properly constructed and applied and must involve genuine and material risk transfer to an unconnected third party. It was noted that financial engineering could obscure the financial condition of an insurer, thereby misleading consumers, investors, and regulators, which would breach several requirements of the FSA. The FSA Handbook now has specific provisions designed to ensure sufficient transparency in financial returns regarding financial reinsurance agreements.[135] The RID[136] specifically allows Member States to regulate finite reinsurance[137] (including the use of mandatory contractual provisions, accounting and risk management controls, and solvency requirements).

16.88 Some reinsurance contracts may ultimately involve limited or questionable risk transfer. One test to determine whether there has been a significant transfer of risk for accounting purposes is the 10/10 rule; there is significant risk transfer only if there is at least a 10 per cent chance of losing a value equal to 10 per cent of the premium paid. If the transfer of risk is not significant, then it is not treated as reinsurance. The legal test for the existence of a contract of insurance is clearly different to tests that determine the appropriate accounting treatment; a contract which fails the accounting tests may still, as a matter of law, constitute a contract of insurance.

---

[130] PERG 6.5.4(4).

[131] Marine Insurance Act 1906, s 22.

[132] Statute of Frauds 1677, s 4.

[133] FSA CP144: 'A new regulatory approach to insurance firms' use of financial engineering'.

[134] ibid, s 3.

[135] FSA CP05/14: Quarterly Consultation (No 6); SYSC 17.1.34A and IPRU (INS) 9.32A and 9.32B.

[136] See n 52. EEA States will generally have two years from when published in the Official Journal for implementation into national law.

[137] Art 2(1)(q) defines finite reinsurance as 'Reinsurance under which the explicit maximum economic risk transferred, arising both from a significant underwriting risk and from a timing risk transfer, exceeds the premium over the lifetime of the contract, by a limited but significant amount, together with at least one of the following two features: (i) explicit and material consideration of the time value of money; (ii) contractual provisions to moderate the balance of economic experience between the parties over time to achieve the target risk transfer'.

Insurance contract law and regulation

There have been discussions about possible European legislation to harmonise **16.89**
insurance contract law, but the area remains unharmonised.[138] There are, however, European rules relating to applicable law, jurisdiction, and unfair terms
which are relevant to insurance contracts.[139] In addition, we also consider below
the domestic legislation concerning third party rights which is also relevant to
insurance contracts.

Unfair Terms in Consumer Contracts Regulations 1999

The Unfair Terms in Consumer Contract Regulations 1999[140] ('UTCC Regulations') **16.90**
apply to contracts of insurance where the contracting insured is a 'consumer'.[141]
Those terms in insurance contracts defining risk, including exclusions, relate to
the 'definition of the main subject matter of the contract' and fall outside the 'fairness obligation' if they are written in plain intelligible language;[142] this also applies
to exclusions that define the cover provided. Other provisions in an insurance
contract, which do not define risk, or any term not in plain intelligible language,
are subject to the full regulations; a term will be considered unfair if 'contrary to
the requirement of good faith it causes a significant imbalance in the parties' rights
and obligations arising under the contract, to the detriment of the consumer'.[143]
A term which is unfair cannot be enforced or relied upon against the consumer.[144]

Under the UTCC Regulations the FSA (as well as the OFT) is a qualifying body **16.91**
which may apply for injunctions against unfair terms.[145] The FSA's approach to the
use of its powers in relation to the Regulations[146] is captured in the FSA Unfair

---

[138] See for example the recent Commission report of 25 July 2007 (The Second Progress Report
on the Common Frame of Reference [COM (2007) 447]—Not published in the Official Journal).

[139] For example, the Common Frame of Reference ('CFR') is a long-term project which aims
at providing the European Legislators (Commission, Council and European Parliament) with a
'toolbox' or a handbook to be used for the revision of existing and the preparation of new legislation
in the area of contract law. This toolbox could contain fundamental principles of contract law, definitions of key concepts and model provisions. In the area of consumer contract law the preparatory
work for the CFR of the researchers and of stakeholders has already served as a starting point for the
Green Paper on the Review of the Consumer Acquis, adopted by the Commission on 8 February
2007.

[140] Unfair Terms in Consumer Contract Regulations 1999, SI 1999/2083, replacing SI 1994/
3159 and implementing Council Directive (EEC) 93/13 on Unfair Terms in Consumer Contracts
[1993] OJ L95/29.

[141] Unlike the Unfair Contract Terms Act 1977, which did not apply to 'contracts of insurance'.

[142] Reg 6(2) of the UTCC Regulations.

[143] Reg 5(1) of the UTCC Regulations.

[144] Reg 4(1) of the UTCC Regulations.

[145] The Unfair Terms in Consumer Contracts Regulations 1999, Regulation 12; the FSA became
a Qualifying Body under the Regulations on May 2001 giving the FSA powers to challenge the use
of unfair terms in standard form consumer contracts.

[146] As discussed in FSA CP148: The FSA's approach to the use of its powers under the Unfair
Terms in Consumer Contracts Regulations 1999.

Contract Terms Regulatory Guide ('UNFCOG'). The FSA may consider the fairness of a contract following a complaint from a consumer or on its own initiative.[147] If the FSA after first expressing its concern and inviting comments from the firm in question remains of the view that a term is unfair it will normally ask the firm to undertake to stop including the term in new contracts and stop relying on it in contracts which have been concluded.[148] This may have a major impact if the term is important and has been used in a large number of consumer contracts.

Contracts (Rights of Third Parties) Act 1999

16.92 This Act removed the difficulties arising from the English law of 'privity of contract'; it assists third party insureds to claim under a contract of insurance to which they were not a party. Under the Act a third party may in his own right enforce a contract term provided (a) the contract expressly so provides or (b) the term purports to confer a benefit on the third party.[149] The Act also gives the third party similar rights to those of the contracting party, for example the right not to have contract terms varied without its consent. However, parties to a contract are able to exclude the operation of this Act in part or completely. For this reason insurers often insert an exclusion of the Act in a wide range of insurance contracts.[150] Separate legislation deals with the rights of certain victims where the responsible person is insured but becomes insolvent.[151]

Applicable law

16.93 The determination of the correct applicable law of an insurance contract is an important feature of the insurance; it is also a regulatory issue. The relevant European law is to be found in

- The Rome Convention, which applies to risks located outside the EEA and to reinsurance (and retrocession) contracts; and
- CLD and 3NLD, which apply, respectively, to life and non-life direct insurance of risks located within the EEA.

---

[147] UNFCOG 1.4.1.

[148] UNFCOG 1.3.4.

[149] Sections (1)(1) (b) and (2) of the Contracts (Rights of Third Parties) Act 1999.

[150] This act does not apply in Scotland. Policies written under Scots law will be subject to the doctrine of *jus quaesitum tertio* which provides that third party rights cannot be excluded. Such rights are enforceable subject to certain conditions being met. The Third Parties (Rights against Insurers) Act 1930 does apply in Scotland.

[151] The Third Parties (Rights Against Insurers) Act 1930 confers on third parties rights against insurers of third-party risks in the event of the insured becoming insolvent (and in certain other events). The act was put in place to deal with situations where an insured had caused damage or personal injury and then becomes bankrupt. In such circumstances, the insured's right to claim on his insurance is transferred by the act to the victim, allowing him to claim directly on the insured's insurance and obtain the proceeds of that insurance.

CLD and 3NLD contain detailed rules to determine, in a variety of different situations, which Member State's law applies and whether there is any choice of law and, if so what choice is available to the parties. These provisions enable Member States, if they so wish, to require, for example, that an insurance contract taken out by an individual who is a French resident and national in relation to a mass risk located in France with an insurer in the UK, must be a policy written under French law; this ensures that the policyholder is buying a contract to which French insurance law applies and not one written under, say English law which may be unfamiliar to the French consumer. The UK and some other Member States, however, allow choice of law; so a French insurer can sell a French law policy to a UK consumer. This European structure for choice of law is implemented, in respect of UK insurers, in the Financial Services and Markets Act 2000 (Law Applicable to Contracts of Insurance) Regulations 2001 which effectively applies all the different choice of law positions of each Member State under 3NLD and CLD. There are disclosure, or product information, requirements relating to choice of law in both directives and these are reflected in ICOBS chapter 5 (see para 16.197 et *seq.* below). **16.94**

For reinsurance of all risks and for direct insurance of non-EEA risks, the Rome Convention applies; this is implemented in the UK in the Contracts (Applicable Law) Act 1990.[152] Both regimes also address the issue of the extent to which the mandatory rules of a Member State will apply notwithstanding that the parties have chosen a law of another Member State. There is increasing recognition that the need to develop a different policy under the local law of a Member State which does not permit choice of law is a significant barrier to cross-border trade. **16.95**

Jurisdiction

EC Council Regulation No 44/2001, as implemented in the UK by the Civil Jurisdiction and Judgments Order 2001[153] which supersedes the Brussels Convention, provides the rules for determining allocation and for the enforcement of judgments between all Member States except Denmark.[154] Regulation 44/2001 sets out the basis for jurisdiction[155] (including domicile) and includes **16.96**

---

[152] The Rome Convention is due to be replaced by the Rome I Regulation in 2009.

[153] Civil Jurisdiction and Judgment Order 2001, SI 2001/3929.

[154] Council Regulation (EC) 01/44 on jurisdiction and the recognition and enforcement of judgments in civil and commercial matters [2001] OJ L307; these regulations do not apply to Denmark, but the Commission extended the provisions of these regulations by parallel agreements between Denmark and the Member States. The parallel agreements, which entered into force on 1 July 2007, contains various provisions to ensure uniform interpretation by the courts of the Member States and Denmark, and acceptance by Denmark of any future amendments to these regulations.

[155] Council Regulation (EC) 01/44 on jurisdiction and the recognition and enforcement of judgments in civil and commercial matters [2001] OJ L307, Arts 2, 3, 5, 6.

special rules with regard to jurisdiction for insurance matters.[156] For example, it is not possible for an EEA insurer of a mass risk[157] to exclude the right of an EEA policyholder or insured to sue the insurer in the courts of the Member State where the policyholder is domiciled.

Regulated activities[158]

16.97   The definition, or 'perimeter', of regulated activities is important in various contexts. In particular, it defines the key elements in determining, for activities relating to insurance contracts, whether the prohibition under section 19, FSMA applies and whether authorisation (or exemption) is required. Regulated activities are defined in the RAO; additional elements relevant to the section 19 prohibition are set out as follows:

- the 'By Way of Business' order under section 22 of FSMA;
- section 418 of FSMA (relevant to territorial scope);
- the definition of policyholder in article 3 of the Financial Services and Markets Act 2000 (Meaning of 'Policy' and 'Policyholder') Order 2001, SI 2001/2361.

16.98   The definition of regulated activities is also important to authorised firms (and their appointed representatives):

- in relation to the Part IV permission they hold; a firm can only conduct those regulated activities for which it holds a permission;
- the scope of requirements in the FSA Handbook relates to regulated activities (although some requirements have broader application).

16.99   The scope of the financial promotion regime is, however, based on a separate definition of controlled investments, activities, and exemptions in the FPO (see paras 16.139 to 16.142) There are differences between the scope of the FPO regime and the section 19 'perimeter' that are relevant to insurance.

By way of business and remuneration

16.100   Under section 22 of FSMA, an activity will not be a regulated activity unless it is carried on 'By Way of Business'. For the main activity of insurers (effecting and carrying out contracts of insurance under article 10 of the RAO), there is no further statutory amendment or definition of the requirement in section 22. The narrower test (for investment business—see article 3 of the By Way of Business

---

[156] Council Regulation (EC) 01/44 on jurisdiction and the recognition and enforcement of judgments in civil and commercial matters [2001] OJ L307, S 3, Arts 8–13.

[157] See para 16.05 above.

[158] The RAO; PERG 2; HM Treasury consultation document: 'Financial Services and Markets Act Regulated Activities—Second Consultation Document' (October 2002).

Order)[159] of carrying on 'the business of engaging in' regulated activities does not apply. In most cases it will be clear that a commercial entity conducting an article 10 activity will be doing so 'by way of business' and will require authorisation. (The position is similar to that under the ICA, which referred to 'carrying on insurance business'.)

For insurance mediation activities, the activities must be conducted by way of business (section 22) and also must be taken up or pursued 'for remuneration'. (Again the 'engaging' test for investment business does not apply.) The second limb reflects the definition of an insurance intermediary in the IMD and was introduced at NGI.   **16.101**

Some intermediaries could fall outside the section 19 perimeter if they receive no remuneration for their mediation activities. However, the concept of remuneration is interpreted very broadly by the FSA[160] and includes direct or indirect remuneration which may be a benefit other than commission from the insurer or fees paid by the customer. For example, it may include remuneration earned through enhanced sales of another product sold with the insurance.   **16.102**

The adoption of the 'remuneration' element of the IMD has also been used by the FSA, in some contexts, to focus on the recitals to the IMD which refer to pursuing mediation activities 'for third parties' for remuneration. In the context of companies which arrange or purchase insurance for other companies in the group, the FSA has concluded that the activity may fall outside the IMD and the section 19 perimeter, on the basis that the other group companies do not constitute third parties (even though the expression is not adopted in the UK legislation and only appears in a recital to the IMD).   **16.103**

In the United Kingdom

The question of whether or not an activity is conducted in the UK (and may therefore require authorisation under FSMA) is not comprehensively defined in FSMA or related statutory instruments. There are, however, various situations where an activity is deemed to be carried on in the UK under section 418 of FSMA.   **16.104**

For example, an activity carried on from a UK establishment maintained by a foreign firm is carried on in the UK. The activities of an EEA branch of a UK insurer or insurance intermediary are deemed to be conducted in the UK. This extends the section 19 prohibition and FSA regulation to the activities of the overseas branch.   **16.105**

---

[159] The Financial Services and Markets Act 2000 (Carrying on Regulated Activities by Way of Business) Order 2001, SI 2002/1177 as amended.
[160] PERG 5.4.8G.

16.106   For non-EEA insurers not authorised in the UK (essentially those established and operating outside the EEA), it is possible to underwrite risks located in the UK without breaching the section 19 prohibition. Unlike other countries, there is no prohibition on insuring risks located in the UK (and in contrast to the use of the 'location of risks' rules for the EU insurance passport regime—see below). However all article 10 activities, both effecting/concluding and carrying out the contract of insurance (such as paying claims), must take place entirely outside the UK/EEA. Where an intermediary or agent in the UK is involved, this may result in an article 10 activity being conducted in the UK with the result that the insurer breaches the section 19 prohibition. Great care is required if an unauthorised foreign insurer is to underwrite a UK risk with a UK insured. There is an absolute prohibition on the marketing of certain life policies of foreign insurers (see para 16.142 below); the separate prohibition on financial promotions will also need to be considered (see para 16.139 *et seq.* below).

Location rules for UK and EEA authorised firms

16.107   The location test for determining whether non-EEA intermediaries require UK authorisation depends on the activity they are conducting. The FSA's guidance distinguishes between, for example, advice (where the location of the customer or client is critical) and arranging (the location where the arrangement takes place is critical) and dealing (which depends on the contractual mechanics and place of acceptance). However, the position will often depend on the application of the overseas persons exclusion in article 72 of the RAO (but this is not available for insurers in relation to the article 10 activities). This may be available where the intermediary does not have a permanent place of business in the UK and it deals only with or through authorised (or exempt) firms such as UK authorised insurers (including the Lloyd's market) or brokers. A further part of the exclusion can cover services (eg advice) provided to UK customers where the business resulted from a legitimate approach (ie where there was no breach of the financial promotion's regime—see paras 16.139 to 16.142).

16.108   Finally, whilst article 10 applies irrespective of the location of the risk, mediation of non-EEA 'large' risks[161] (even within the UK) is not regulated.

16.109   UK and other EEA insurers and intermediaries are authorised for the entire EEA but location is still important in determining whether passport notifications are required and which Member State's rules apply. In this context, the location of the risk is the critical test for determining in which Member State an article 10 activity is being conducted (see paras 16.42 to 16.45) under the single passport system

---

[161]   Art 72D of the RAO. See the explanation of 'large risks' in para 16.05.

as it applies to general insurance (see further at paras 16.53 to 16.55 in relation to the distinction between branch and services business).

The test for mediation activities is different. For EEA intermediaries there are no **16.110** strict rules (as there are for EEA insurers above) to determine in which Member State an activity is taking place under the single passport system. As explained at para 16.71 above, under the IMD there is no definition of what constitutes carrying on mediation in another Member State and CEIOPS has formulated certain proposals.

The regulated activities relating to insurance

The structure of the RAO is explained in Chapters 1 and 2. There are 10 activities **16.111** relating to insurance (three of which are specific to the Lloyd's Market) defined by a complex series of definitions of activities, investments, and exclusions (specific to an activity or general).

Under the RAO the mediation activities apply to 'relevant investments' which **16.112** include 'rights under a contract of insurance' rather than merely 'a contract of insurance' (the expression used in the IMD). This means, for example, that mediating in relation to rights under an existing insurance contract is a regulated activity; this covers fresh investments under a life policy or additional coverage added during the term of an existing general insurance policy. Regulated mediation therefore arises not only in relation to a new policy (eg at renewal) but also during the term of the policy. For investment/qualifying contracts of insurance, but not for general/pure protection/non-investment insurance, there is an additional specified investment of 'rights to, or interests in'. This extends the scope of regulated mediation for this type of insurance (see further below).[162]

In addition, the RAO expressly includes various contracts as contracts of insur- **16.113** ance, reflecting the provisions of CLD and 3NLD and the different classes of insurance (see para 16.39 *et seq.* above). These include annuities, tontines and, in certain circumstances, fidelity, performance, administration, bail and custom bonds and similar contracts of guarantee (see 'suretyship' at para 16.39 above).

Effecting and carrying out

Article 10 of the RAO sets out the regulated activity for insurance underwriting **16.114** as an insurer (and replaced the 'carrying on of insurance business' test in the ICA). It covers 'direct' insurance, reinsurance, and retrocession. There are two separate activities—'effecting' and 'carrying out' contracts of insurance. The former covers

---

[162] See the explanation of 'life policy', 'investment/qualifying contracts of insurance', 'general/ pure protection/non-investment insurance' in paras 16.03–16.04.

entering into insurance contracts and the latter covers the performance of the contract, such as paying claims. In both cases there is a qualification in that this must be 'as principal'; so neither an underwriting agent nor a claims agent falls within this definition. If an insurer is in run-off, it is still conducting an article 10 activity as it is carrying out (although not effecting) contracts of insurance.

16.115 For this purpose the RAO lists the classes of insurance, reflecting the classes in the CLD and the 3NLD[163] (see paras 16.39 to 16.41 above). An insurer's Part IV permission specifies the different classes it is permitted to underwrite; it must therefore apply to amend its permission if it wishes to underwrite a different class of business.

16.116 Two activities, which otherwise constitute the effecting or carrying out of contracts of insurance, are expressly excluded:

- in circumstances specified in article 11 of the RAO, the activities of an EEA firm where participating in a community co-insurance operation other than as leading insurer; and

- in circumstances specified in article 12 of the RAO, activities that are carried out in connection with the provision of on-the-spot accident or breakdown assistance for cars and other vehicles.

16.117 The special provisions relating to underwriting in the Lloyd's market are considered below (see para 16.137 *et seq.* below). An article 10 activity is conducted by 'members' (and not by the Society or by members' agents or managing agents) but currently there is no requirement for members to apply for FSA authorisation.

Dealing as principal

16.118 There is a further regulated activity which concerns dealing as principal. Article 14 of the RAO covers buying, selling, or underwriting contractually based investments which include rights under, or rights to or interests in, qualifying contracts of insurance.[164] This reflects the equivalent provision in the FSA 1986 which extended regulation to principal transactions in rights under existing contracts of insurance (as well as fresh contracts) and to indirect interests in (or rights to) rights under, as principal, contracts of insurance. This covers various activities of life offices and of those who buy or sell indirect rights and interests in qualifying insurance contracts, eg those buying and selling the entitlement to payments under an endowment policy (sometimes referred to as 'traded' endowments).

---

[163] The 18 classes of general insurance and nine classes of long-term insurance in Sched 1 of the RAO are supplemented by additional definitions in art 3(1) including fidelity, performance, and other bonds and similar contracts of insurance where these are not effected by a banking business, are not incidental to another business, and a premium is paid.

[164] See the explanation of 'qualifying contracts of insurance' in para 16.04.

Mediation activities[165]

Prior to the IMD, whilst the RAO covered the underwriting of all forms of insur- **16.119**
ance under article 10, mediation activities were only regulated in relation to qualifying contracts of insurance. To implement the IMD the RAO needed to be
extended to bring the mediation of general insurance and pure protection long-
term insurance within the perimeter of regulated activities. Certain changes were
also required to the scope of pre-NGI mediation activities relating to qualifying
insurance contracts.[166]

The RAO amendments for NGI did not adopt the IMD definitions directly. **16.120**
Instead it used the existing breakdown of dealing as agent, arranging, and advising
(an activity not directly referred to in the IMD definition) but added the new
IMD activity of 'assisting'. Existing exclusions had to be amended, for example
where they did not mirror the IMD. For this reason a number of RAO exclusions[167] are now not available or are limited in relation to insurance.

The mediation activities are: **16.121**

(a) dealing in investments as agent (article 21);
(b) arranging (bringing about) deals in investments (article 25(1));
(c) making arrangements with a view to transactions in investments (article 25(2));
(d) assisting in the administration and performance of a contract of insurance
    (article 39A);
(e) advising on investments (article 53);
(f) agreeing to carry on a regulated activity in (a) to (e) (article 64).

The additional activities relating to the Lloyd's market are considered below.

Activities and exclusions

The RAO was also amended to apply the regulated mediation activities to insurers **16.122**
in relation to their 'mediation' of their own general and pure protection insurance
contracts. This was not required by the IMD (and was 'super-equivalent'); it

---

[165] The Financial Services and Markets Act 2000 (Regulated Activities) (Amendment) (No 2)
Order 2003, SI 2003/1476; PERG, FSA PS04/1, 'Insurance selling and administration and other
miscellaneous amendments—Feedback on CP187 and made text'; FSA CP187, 'Insurance selling and administration and other miscellaneous amendments'; FSA CP160, 'Insurance selling
and administration—the FSA's high-level approach to regulation'; HM Treasury Consultation
Document: Regulating Insurance Mediation (21 October 2002) and Summary of consultation
feedback and HM Treasury decisions.
[166] See the explanation of 'qualifying contracts of insurance', 'general insurance', 'pure protection', 'non-investment insurance' in paras 16.03–16.04.
[167] These exclusions include art 22 (dealing as agent with or through authorised persons), art 29
(arranging deals with or through authorised persons), art 68 (in connection with the sale of goods
and supply of services), art 69 (groups and joint enterprises), and art 70 (in connection with the sale
of a body corporate) of the RAO.

underpinned the broader policy objective of regulating the sale and administration of these products by insurers (as well as intermediaries) as reflected, for example, in the application of ICOBS (see para 16.197 *et seq.* below).

16.123 Under the RAO, the noun to which mediation activities apply is 'rights under a contract of insurance'. As already noted, this extends regulation to include the mediation of additional coverage added during the term of an existing policy. In relation to qualifying contracts of insurance it extends to indirect rights and beneficial interests (eg in relation to the trading of interests in an endowment policy in the second hand market). The RAO therefore extends mediation regulation beyond the scope of the IMD.

16.124 **The activities.** The three activities of dealing as agent, arranging, and advising relate to 'buying' and 'selling' which are broadly defined to include acquiring insurance rights (or interests where relevant) for valuable consideration and surrendering, assigning, and converting—in each case for valuable consideration. This is wider than the IMD.

16.125 **Dealing as agent.** This covers the contractual activity of buying or selling as agent and covers, for example, intermediaries which hold a binding authority to conclude contracts of insurance (or otherwise sell rights under such contracts) as agent of the insurer. It also applies where the intermediary, such as a broker, concludes a contract of insurance as agent of the insured.

16.126 **Arranging.** This covers two separate activities; in essence, making general arrangements for someone to buy or sell insurance, or making arrangements which bring about a specific insurance transaction. The first activity may apply to introducing customers to an intermediary or insurer (although a distinction can be drawn between introducing and some purely passive display of insurance marketing materials). The second limb covers activities closer to the conclusion of the insurance contract, for example negotiating or assisting the insured to complete the application and deliver it to the insurer. For insurance, this activity is relevant even where the arranger will be a party to the insurance contract (or will conclude it as agent); so it covers insurers in relation to their own products. The party contracting with the insurer will also be arranging except where it is, or will be, the sole policyholder. So the purchase/conclusion of insurance by the policyholder can involve 'arranging' if other parties have rights under the policy, for example as 'insureds'.

16.127 The definition of policyholder for this purpose is 'the person who for the time being is the legal holder of the policy, including any person to whom, under the policy, a sum is due, a periodic payment is payable or any other benefit is to be provided or to whom such a sum, payment or benefit is contingently due, payable or to be provided'.[168]

---

[168] The Financial Services and Markets Act 2000 (Meaning of 'Policy' and 'Policyholder') Order 2001, SI 2001/2361.

A policyholder can therefore be 'arranging' in relation to the rights of other **16.128** insureds. In some cases this activity, on its own, may fail the 'by way of business/ remuneration test' but it may apply in other cases, for example where one lender takes out insurance covering other lenders under a syndicated loan.

Article 72C implements an IMD exclusion for introducing or the 'provision of **16.129** information on an incidental basis'.[169] It only covers the provision of information incidental and complementary to a business which does not otherwise involve regulated activities. (It does not cover activities such as assisting in the completion of application forms or forwarding them to insurers; it only covers the flow of information down the chain.) The classic example is a vet, who does no more than passively display marketing materials for pet insurance, for example by drawing a client's attention to the product and handing out or mailing the insurer's market- ing material (but where no advice is given and where the pet owner is left to com- plete the application form and return it to the insurer). The introducer, in this case, the vet, can be remunerated for introductions made and still remain within this exclusion.

There are other exclusions including those relating to very limited activities which **16.130** simply enable parties to communicate (article 27) and for money lenders arrang- ing transactions in connection with lending on the security of insurance contracts (but see paras 16.135 to 16.136 below).

The FSA's view is that the article 33 exemption for introducing is unlikely to apply **16.131** to introductions for general insurance.

Advising. The article 53 activity relates to advice on the merits of buying and sell- **16.132** ing insurance. It does not cover generic advice about the need to disclose material information to insurers or about the benefits of insurance or about the strength of an insurer or the merits of a broker, if the advice in all cases is unrelated to, and not given in the context of, a particular product; it is also possible to construct a deci- sion tree for insurance sales whereby information is solicited from the customer in order to select a particular product to offer but without the process amounting to the regulated activity of advising. The FSA gives detailed guidance on this issue,[170] which is important in the context of whether suitability obligations will apply. Subtle distinctions often have to be drawn between the mere provision of infor- mation and the provision of information in circumstances which will constitute advice.

There are a number of exclusions relating to the periodical publications, broad- **16.133** casts, and websites (article 54 of the RAO)—see FSA's guidance in PERG 7 which

---

[169] IMD, Art 2(4) (see n 22).
[170] PERG 5.8.15G.

explains the arrangements for applying to the FSA for a certificate that this exclusion applies.

16.134 **Assisting in the administration and performance of a contract of insurance.** This activity, in article 39A, reflects the IMD wording and was a new activity added at NGI. It brings claims handling for insureds/policyholders into regulation but it does not apply to agents appointed to handle claims for certain insurers (or expert appraisal or loss adjusting for insurers)—see article 39B. The scope of the activity is uncertain; the FSA offers certain guidance without reaching any firm conclusions on the precise 'perimeter'.[171]

16.135 **General exclusions.** There are various exclusions that can apply to more than one activity. Certain exclusions (including article 30 referred to above) are subject to an IMD override,[172] ie if directive mediation is being conducted the domestic exclusion does not apply. Article 72B reflects the IMD exclusion for connected contracts modified to reflect the UK Government's decision to regulate connected contracts in the motor trade. This is relevant to those selling non-motor goods who sell certain complimentary insurances against breakdown, loss, or damage to the goods. There are a number of detailed conditions which must be satisfied. Following NGI, this was also relevant to travel agents and tour operators selling certain travel policies linked to travel booked with them. The IMD requires the sale of general insurance (including stand-alone travel insurance) by intermediaries to be regulated. However, the sale of connected travel insurance ('CTI') (ie travel insurance sold alongside a holiday or other related travel by, for example, travel firms) is exempt. When the UK implemented the IMD, it adopted a CTI exclusion. However, there were concerns about mis-selling of CTI by travel agents and tour operators and it was therefore decided to bring this area into FSMA regulation.[173] With effect from 1 January 2009, tour operators and travel agents will not be able to rely upon the CTI exclusion in IMD; in order to sell, advise, or conduct other regulated activities in relation to CTI, they will have to be authorised or appointed as an appointed representative and will have to follow FSA's rules and requirements (see para 16.201 *et seq.* below).

16.136 The IMD does not cover the mediation of non-EEA risks (eg a London broker placing insurance at Lloyd's for a UK owner of property in the United States—see location of risk rules in section above). However, in the RAO, the exclusion at

---

[171] PERG 2.8.7G and 5.7.7G.

[172] Art 4(4A) of the RAO (as amended) applicable to arts 30, 66, and 67.

[173] For further information, please see FSA CP07/22 and PS08/04 ('Regulating Connected Travel Insurance') and the Financial Services and Markets Act 2000 (Regulated Activities) (Amendment) (No. 2) Order 2007, SI 2007/3510.

article 72D only applies to large (non-EEA) risks[174]—so the mediation of mass non-EEA risks is regulated under the RAO (although this falls outside the IMD).

The Lloyd's market activities

The specific Lloyd's related activities in the RAO are: **16.137**

 (i)   arranging (bringing about) deals in the underwriting capacity of a Lloyd's syndicate or membership of a Lloyd's syndicate (article 25(1));[175]
 (ii) making arrangements with a view to transactions in the underwriting capacity of a Lloyd's syndicate or membership of a Lloyd's syndicate (article 25(2));[176]
 (iii) advising on syndicate participation at Lloyd's, that is advising a person to become, or continue, or cease to be, a member of a particular syndicate (article 56)[177]—this activity is undertaken by members' agents;
 (iv) managing the underwriting capacity of a Lloyd's syndicate as a managing agent at Lloyd's (article 57)[178]—this activity is unique to managing agents;
 (v)   arranging deals in contracts of insurance written at Lloyd's, that is arranging by the Society of Lloyd's of deals in contracts of insurance written at Lloyd's (article 58)—this activity is unique to the Society of Lloyd's.

The regulation of the Lloyd's market is considered further in para 16.341 *et seq*. below.   **16.138**

Other aspects of insurance legislation

Financial promotions

At N2, section 21 of FSMA (which imposes a restriction on the communication   **16.139**
of financial promotions unless an authorised person makes the communication or an authorised person has approved the content of the financial promotion) and the Financial Services and Markets Act 2000 (Financial Promotions) Order[179] came into force. These replaced the three sets of regulation under FSA 1986 and under the banking and insurance legislation. The regime deals with real time and

---

[174] See the explanation of 'large risks' in para 16.05.
[175] This regulated activity may be carried on in connection with the following specified investments: underwriting capacity of a Lloyd's syndicate (art 86(1)), membership of a Lloyd's syndicate (art 86(2)), rights to or interests in investments (art 89) in so far as they relate to underwriting capacity of a Lloyd's syndicate, or membership of a Lloyd's syndicate.
[176] ibid.
[177] This regulated activity may be carried on in connection with membership of a Lloyd's syndicate (art 86(2)).
[178] This regulated activity may be carried on in connection with underwriting capacity of a Lloyd's syndicate (art 86(1)).
[179] Financial Services and Markets Act 2000 (Financial Promotion) Order 2001, SI 2001/1335, since replaced by the Financial Services and Markets Act 2000 (Financial Promotion) Order 2005, SI 2005/1529 (the 'FPO').

non-real time promotions. The section 21 'perimeter' is different to the section 19 regulated activities perimeter; it is defined by reference to controlled activities and investments in the FPO. Detailed guidance on the scope of the financial promotions regime is set out in PERG 8. Although not appreciated by everyone at the time, promotions concerning all types of insurance were subject to the section 21 prohibition from N2. In the case of non-investment insurance[180] (general and pure protection), for which mediation fell outside the section 19 perimeter until NGI, there are several important exceptions which cover the following:

- a generic promotion which does not identify the insurer (or any person carrying on a controlled activity); the promotion can identify the intermediary as non-investment insurance mediation is not a controlled activity (article 17 of the FPO);
- a non-real time communication concerning relevant insurance (ie broadly, non-investment insurance) which contains the following information (article 24):
  - the full name of the insurance undertaking;
  - the country or territory in which the insurance undertaking is incorporated (described as such);
  - if different from the above, the country or territory in which the insurance undertaking's principal place of business is situated (described as such);
  - whether or not the insurance undertaking is regulated in respect of its insurance business;
  - if the insurance undertaking is regulated, the name of the regulator in its principal place of business or, if there is more than one regulator, the name of the prudential regulator;
  - whether any transaction to which the non-investment financial promotion relates would be covered by a dispute resolution scheme or compensation scheme, if so identifying each such scheme;
- reinsurance and large risks[181] (article 25); and
- real time communications (article 26).

16.140 These exemptions were not removed at NGI, reflecting the Government's decision not to extend the section 21 regime to promotions concerning mediation services for non-investment insurance.

16.141 The FSMA gives the FSA separate powers to make rules on financial promotions; these are set out in COBS 3 and ICOBS 3. The rules in ICOBS relating to financial promotions and communications to customers are explained at para 16.212 *et seq.* below. In addition, there are also high-level requirements in the FSA's Principles for Businesses, including Principle 6 (firms must pay due regard to the interests of its customers and treat them fairly) and Principle 7 (communications to the customer must be clear, fair, and not misleading)—see further at para 16.158 below.

---

[180] See the explanation of 'non-investment insurance' in para 16.04.
[181] See the explanation of 'large risks' in para 16.05.

The prohibition on the promotion of foreign life policies

The effect of article 10 of the FPO and COB 3.13.1 is to prohibit absolutely (even **16.142** by an authorised intermediary) the promotion of life policies except, broadly, those of UK and EEA authorised insurers and those of life offices authorised in Jersey, Guernsey, the Isle of Man, or the states of Pennsylvania and Iowa.

Appointed representatives

The appointed representative regime applies to the mediation of investment and **16.143** non-investment insurance. An appointed representative conducting insurance mediation cannot commence its mediation activities until its name is entered on the record of insurance intermediaries (ie registered on the FSA Register) and if it ceases to be so registered, it can no longer carry on such activities (this reflects the IMD requirement for an insurance intermediary to be registered); a provision to this effect must be included in the agreement appointing the appointed representative.

An appointed representative cannot conduct various regulated activities includ- **16.144** ing the following insurance activities:

- article 10 (effecting and carrying out contracts of insurance);
- article 14 (dealing as principal);
- article 21 (dealing as agent in relation to qualifying contracts of insurance or long-term care insurance);
- article 25 (arranging transactions in the underwriting capacity of a Lloyd's syndicate or in the membership of a Lloyd's syndicate);
- article 56 (advice on syndicate participation at Lloyd's), article 57 (managing the underwriting capacity of a Lloyd's syndicate, article 58 (arranging by the Society of Lloyd's).

Either an authorised insurer or an authorised insurance intermediary can appoint **16.145** an appointed representative to conduct insurance mediation (but only within the scope of the principal's Part IV permission).

The requirements of section 39 of FSMA, the Appointed Representative **16.146** Regulations[182] and the FSA Handbook apply including:

- the appointed representative must have a contract with an authorised person (the 'principal') permitting the appointed representative to carry on business of a prescribed description[183] (see above);

---

[182] The Financial Services and Markets Act 2000 (Appointed Representative) Regulations 2001, SI 2001/1217 (as amended).
[183] The Financial Services and Markets Act 2000 (Appointed Representative) Regulations 2001, SI 2001/1217 (as amended) stipulate the type of business which appointed representatives may carry out (if permitted to do so by their principals).

- the principal must have accepted responsibility in writing for those prescribed activities of the appointed representative;

- the appointed representative is exempt (from authorisation) only in relation to the carrying on of those regulated activities for which the principal has accepted responsibility (and cannot therefore carry on any other regulated activities unless under another appointed representative appointment);

- the principal of the appointed representative is responsible, to the same extent as if he had expressly permitted it, for anything done or omitted by the appointed representative in carrying on the business for which he has accepted responsibility.

16.147 A firm which is authorised under FSMA cannot be an appointed representative. This applies where the firm is directly authorised by the FSA for any activities, even for activities unrelated to insurance. The FSA's Supervision Sourcebook 12 ('SUP') contains rules and guidance relating to the appointed representative agreement/relationship. Some of the restrictions on appointed representatives that are worth noting are as follows. All firms carrying on insurance mediation activity, including principals of appointed representatives, must establish in relation to any appointed representative that a reasonable proportion of the persons within its management structure and all other persons directly responsible for insurance mediation activity demonstrate the knowledge and ability necessary for the performance of their duties and are of good repute—see para 16.331.[184] Appointed representatives are generally restricted to one principal (although a firm can have multiple principals from the same group in respect of some types of investment products).[185] There are no restrictions on the number of principals an appointed representative may have in relation to non-investment insurance contracts. If an appointed representative has more than one principal, a multiple principal agreement between the principals will be required.[186]

16.148 An introducer appointed representative is an appointed representative appointed by a firm whose scope of appointment is limited to effecting introductions and distributing non-real time financial promotions. An introducer appointed representative must enter into an agreement with its principal (similar to an appointed representative agreement) and broadly similar rules apply to an introducer

---

[184] MIPRU 2.3.1R; MIPRU 2.3.3R; SUP 12.4.8R.

[185] SUP 12.4.5BG; SUP 12.5.6AR; SUP 12.5.6BG.

[186] SUP 12.4.5BR to SUP 12.4.5GG. As part of its initial consultation on the implementation of the IMD, the FSA proposed that an appointed representative should be able to have one principal for 'substitutable product categories' but in the end decided that there would be no restriction on the number of principals and no rule preventing the sale of substitutable products for different insurers in the non-investment insurance market. It concluded that the risks of consumer detriment in this market could be appropriately addressed through multiple principal agreements and the FSA's wider rules on the sale and administration of non-investment insurance products.

appointed representative as to an appointed representative. One exception is that an introducer appointed representative does not need to have any approved persons registered with the FSA.[187]

Section 397

Section 397 contains an important criminal offence relating to misleading state- **16.149** ments and practices. At NGI, this was extended to non-investment insurance, so that a criminal offence may be involved where:

- misleading statements are made in the course of selling insurance;
- material facts are dishonestly concealed;
- a false or misleading impression is given as to the market in, or price of, insurance.

Part VII Transfers[188]

Part VII of FSMA, reflecting the EU legislation, provides for the approval of **16.150** insurance business transfer schemes. There are special provisions for transfers involving Lloyd's.[189] Subject to FSA and court approval, it is possible to transfer obligations under insurance contracts from one insurer to another which means that primary liability under the insurance policies (forming part of the business transferred) is transferred to the transferee and, for practical purposes, the policyholders are thereafter treated as if their contracts had always been with the transferee. Schemes must be approved by the court under section 111. The Financial Services and Markets Act 2000 (Control of Business Transfers)(Requirements on Applicants) Regulations 2001 also apply and detailed FSA guidance is set out in SUP 18. These provisions now take into account the RID.

---

[187] See SUP 10.1.16R and SUP12.

[188] Schemes of Arrangement: Insolvent and solvent insurers can also enter into schemes of arrangement under Part 26 of the Companies Act 2006. The essence of the procedure is a three stage approval process; first an application is made to the court by the company or its members or creditors for the court to give directions for a meeting or meetings of members or creditors (or any class of members or creditors) to be convened; at the second stage the members or creditors must approve the proposal by the requisite majority, namely a majority in number representing not less than 75% in value of those who attend and vote, in person or by proxy; at the third stage the court must sanction the scheme. Although schemes of arrangement for insurance companies are nothing new (many of the early cases on schemes relate to insurance companies, particularly insolvent life insurance companies) they enjoyed a renaissance in the 1990s as a legal framework to enable insolvent non-life insurance companies to effect an orderly run-off of the remaining business, permitting them to continue as nearly as possible in the same way, subject only to agreed claims being paid in part only, rather than paid in full.

[189] The definition of an insurance business transfer scheme at s 105 of FSMA includes transfers from members of Lloyd's to reflect the effect of the Financial Services and Markets Act 2000 (Control of Transfers of Business Done at Lloyd's) Order 2001, SI 2001/3626.

UK Regulation—the FSA Handbook

Introduction

16.151 Authorised insurers and insurance intermediaries (and their appointed represent-atives) are subject to many of the rulebooks and other sourcebooks/manuals which make up the FSA Handbook. It is not possible to review all of these but this sec-tion highlights some of the important ways in which these rulebooks impact insurance; it deals, in particular, with the rules for non-investment insurance.

16.152 One of the difficulties, for smaller intermediaries which conduct general insurance mediation as an ancillary activity, is the complexity of the FSA Handbook structure, particularly the different scope of application of the different rulebooks, including high-level standards and other rulebooks which contain general FSA requirements; non-investment intermediaries, which were previously members of GISC, previ-ously operated under a single rulebook for their type of business. For some firms, the complexity of the different scope rules for each rulebook and for individual chapters within them, can be quite daunting. Chapter 1 of ICOBS is an example of scope rules which are extremely difficult to apply (see paras 16.200 to16.207 below).

Insurance chains

16.153 The sale of non-investment insurance often involves, in addition to the insurer, 'chains' of intermediaries introducing, selling, placing insurance, and in the claims process. It is important to have a clear understanding of how the different FSA rulebooks apply to each of the chain participants. For example, ICOBS imposes obligations on the insurer, as the product provider; it places separate obligations on the firm which deals with the customer (ie the purchasing policy-holder) which may be the insurer in the case of a direct sale where no intermediary is involved. ICOBS does not apply to a 'wholesale' intermediary (such as a placing broker). However, 'wholesale' mediation is a regulated activity and it is subject to the FSA's high-level standards as is other mediation falling outside of ICOBS such as the broking of reinsurance. CASS 5 (client money) is concerned with clients (rather than the customers/policyholders), so it does apply to wholesale broking (and may or may not apply to the broking of reinsurance depending on the elec-tions made by the individual firm).

Threshold Conditions for authorisation (COND)

16.154 To gain, and retain, the status of an authorised person, an applicant must satisfy and continue to satisfy Threshold Conditions[190]—these relate to legal status,

---

[190] FSMA, Sched 6.

location of offices, close links, adequate resources, and suitability,[191] and are set out in COND.

For the regulated activity of effecting and/or carrying out of contracts of insurance, the person (ie the insurer) applying for authorisation must be a body corporate (other than a limited liability partnership) or a registered friendly society.[192] A member of Lloyd's can also apply,[193] but there is currently no need for a member to be authorised (see para 16.137).   **16.155**

For an insurer to be authorised in the UK, it must have its head office and registered office in the UK. As noted in the section on European Union Law, this reflects CLD and 3NLD. INSPRU 1.5.13[194] prohibits an insurer (other than a pure reinsurer) from carrying out activities 'other than insurance business and activities directly arising from that business'. A pure reinsurer must not carry on any business other than the business of reinsurance and related operations. The regime for the prior approval of controllers is described in Chapter 6. For insurers the initial threshold for a controller is 10 per cent.   **16.156**

For insurance intermediaries there is no prescribed legal form; the applicant may be a company, limited liability partnership, individual, sole trader, or partnership. For insurance intermediaries formed in the UK the registered office or, if it has no registered office, the head office must be in the UK.[195] The controller threshold, which is higher than for other firms, is 20 per cent. As already noted, intermediaries may conduct insurance mediation as a secondary activity (for example a bank) or a tertiary activity (for example a retailer acting as a creditor broker and promoting payment protection insurance).   **16.157**

Principles for Businesses ('PRIN') and current issues in insurance

The Principles for Businesses ('PRIN') are a general statement of the fundamental obligations that govern all authorised firms. PRIN is considered in Chapter 5 above; some further aspects relating to insurance are considered below.   **16.158**

Principles-based regulation

In summary, the Principles require an insurer or intermediary to: **16.159**

• Conduct its business with integrity and with due skill, care, and diligence;

---

[191] COND 2.

[192] Some friendly societies are covered by the EU insurance directives; others, known as small friendly societies, are not (FREN contains guidance to these latter firms on applicable provisions of the FSA Handbook).

[193] FSMA, Sched 6 para 1(1).

[194] This rule replaced PRU 7.6.13 which had replaced IPRU(INS) 1.3(1) which had replaced s 16 of the Insurance Companies Act 1982.

[195] COND 2.2.1.

- Take reasonable care to organise and control its affairs responsibly and effectively, with adequate risk management systems;
- Maintain adequate financial resources;
- Observe proper standards of market conduct;
- Pay due regard to the interests of customers and treat them fairly;
- Communicate with clients in a way which is clear, fair, and not misleading;
- Manage conflicts of interest fairly;
- Take reasonable care to ensure suitability of advice and discretionary decisions;
- Arrange adequate protection for clients' assets when it is responsible for them; and
- Deal with its regulators in an open and cooperative way and keep them informed.

16.160   The FSA's enforcement actions are almost invariably founded on breaches of Principles, rather than merely on breaches of detailed rules. In recent years, the FSA has shifted its approach further away from a rules-based system of regulation to outcome-focused principles-based regulation or 'PBR' (see Chapter 5). Increasingly, rather than adopting a comprehensive set of detailed rules, the FSA provides firms with guidance, such as statements of good and poor practice and case studies illustrating ways in which firms have successfully met its requirements. The FSA is also intending to make greater use of industry codes and guidelines. Firms must place greater focus on interpretation of and adherence to the spirit of the Principles, as opposed to adherence to the letter of detailed and prescriptive rules.

16.161   In theory, PBR allows firms greater flexibility to interpret the principles in a way that will best reflect their particular risks and challenges inherent in their business. However, firms will still have to be able to demonstrate to the FSA that the approach they have adopted satisfies each of the relevant principles. Each firm has to evaluate the practical implications of applying these very broadly expressed requirements to its particular business, products, and services. Some examples of PBR in the insurance sector are considered below.

Treating customers fairly

16.162   Principle 6 states 'A firm must pay due regard to the interests of its customers and treat them fairly.' Based on this Principle, FSA has developed a new, and additional, layer of regulation called 'Treating Customers Fairly' or 'TCF'. In the insurance sector, this now extends across retail supply chains in both the general and life sectors; (FSA had originally used the TCF initiative to focus on 'with-profits' insurance and the treatment of life policy customers after the point of sale).

16.163   TCF represents a significant regulatory burden both in terms of the customer outcomes and also in relation to the internal processes of insurers and intermediaries; yet FSA has not adopted any formal rules, consistent with its PBR approach, but has instead relied upon threats of action under the existing provisions of its high-level standards. It set an interim deadline in March 2008 and a final deadline of December 2008 for firms to demonstrate that senior management had embedded 'TCF' in the firm's internal processes and culture including management information systems and systems to measure their TCF performance.[196] The initiative is supported by a diverse range of materials which FSA has published indicating the results of TCF related research and areas of concern. The FSA has emphasised the need for insurers and intermediaries to address TCF at each stage of the product life-cycle including:[197]

- product/distributor interface;[198]
- product design and information;
- identifying target markets;
- marketing and promoting the product;
- claims handling;[199]
- sales and advice;[200]
- the remuneration of sales forces and advisers;
- after sales information;
- complaints handling;
- linked sales.[201]

The FSA considers that 'fairness' represents a series of values including the following: **16.164**

- honesty and integrity;
- disclosure of relevant information in an understandable way;
- fulfilling legitimate expectations;
- consistency of action;
- reasonableness;
- competence and diligence.

---

[196] At the time of writing, there is some confusion as to whether the FSA will fully pursue its original plans for TCF—'FSA update on the Treating Customers Fairly initiative and the December deadline (November 2008)'; and 'Speech by Sarah Wilson: FSA Treating Customers Fairly—Making it Happen Roadshow ICAEW Financial Services Faculty (18 November 2008).

[197] 'Treating Customers Fairly: progress update' (June 2008); Speech by Sarah Wilson: 'Treating Customers Fairly—a continuing priority' (12 February 2008); 'Treating customers fairly—towards fair outcomes for consumers' (July 2006); FSA DP7, 'Treating customers fairly after the point of sale'.

[198] Highlighted in 'Treating Customers Fairly, Progress and Next Steps—July 2005' as key areas for the insurance industry.

[199] ibid.

[200] ibid.

[201] ibid.

16.165   As part of the TCF initiative, the FSA looked at the responsibilities of providers
and distributors for the fair treatment of customers.[202] In September 2006, the
FSA published a discussion paper,[203] which set out the FSA's view of the respective
regulatory responsibilities of providers and distributors in relation to TCF, and
included an overarching statement of responsibilities for providers and distributors and sector-specific case studies. This led to a 'Regulatory Guide'[204] which the
FSA published to assist firms meet their TCF obligations.

16.166   The FSA's current action on payment protection insurance ('PPI') is an example
of how it applies TCF and Principle 6. As a result of its recent investigations, following thematic reviews, the FSA concluded that PPI was being widely mis-sold
and that products were, in some cases, being structured in a way that breached
Principle 6. The FSA therefore brought enforcement action against some firms.
To a large extent the FSA relied upon PRIN as the basis for enforcement action
against firms. A similar approach is taken by the FOS (see para 16.350 *et seq.*
below) and a large number of complaints have been upheld without the need to
establish breaches of the FSA's Conduct of Business Rules. Firms may have complied with the detailed requirements of ICOB(S), but nonetheless they had not
satisfied the requirements of Principle 6 to treat their customers fairly. Some firms
are concerned that this approach enables the regulator to impose standards on
insurance sales after the event, at a time when the FSA has realised, in hindsight,
that its rules had not addressed customer detriment it is now concerned about. The
FSA also imposed new and additional requirements for future sales of PPI as part
of its new Conduct of Business Rules in ICOBS (see para 16.197 *et seq.* below).
The Competition Commission will soon be announcing remedies to address competition concerns; these may involve radical changes to the distribution of PPI.

Contract certainty

16.167   At the time of NGI, the FSA had widespread concerns about the lack of 'contract
certainty' in the non-investment insurance sector. It has attacked a 'deal now,
detail later'[205] culture, which posed a risk to the FSA's objectives. In the London
Market, traditional market mechanics (primarily relating to subscription risks)
caused particular difficulties. Alarmingly from the FSA's perspective, the precise
terms of an insurance contract might be uncertain at the time of the placing
and could remain so after inception and for a considerable time thereafter.

---

[202] See FSA DP06/4.

[203] See also feedback in FSA PS07/11.

[204] See FSA PS07/11 (Responsibilities of providers and distributors for the fair treatment of
customers). See also the FSA's guide, 'The Responsibilities of Providers and Distributors for the Fair
Treatment of Customers', published July 2007.

[205] John Tiner, FSA Chief Executive, in a speech at the LeBoeuf, Lamb, Greene & MacRae
Symposium in New York.

Indeed, some insureds (and insurers) had found that when a claim was made, there was still no policy in existence and no agreed record of the full terms of the contract of insurance.

The implication was that firms had tolerated substantial operational risk and poor **16.168** protection for their clients and had found it easier to pay the cost of 'clearing up the mess' after the event, rather than investing in systems and training to mitigate the risk up front. This area is another example of how the FSA can require substantial changes in market practice without adopting any rules, simply by using PRIN and the threat of more prescriptive regulation. Various parts of PRIN are relevant to this issue; for example Principle 5 requires firms to observe proper standards of market conduct. The FSA had threatened prescriptive measures and specific regulation unless the market adequately addresses its concerns. This prompted a major programme within the London Market and substantial 'contract certainty' projects at individual firms. This led to changes in the market process and infrastructure, which were part of a general modernisation of the market and a move to more electronic-based documentation, including electronic or 'e-slips'. In particular, the slip accepted by underwriters must now have the full contract terms and clauses of the insurance contract attached or referenced.

Conflicts of interest[206]

General and FSA

FSA Principle 8 provides that a firm must manage conflicts of interest fairly, both **16.169** between itself and its customers and between a customer and another client.[207] The effective management of conflicts of interest within the insurance industry is a particular concern of the FSA.[208]

The FSA accepts that some conflicts of interest are 'endemic and unavoidable'[209] **16.170** but firms must have effective systems to identify conflicts, to manage them fairly, and to ensure the firm is not in breach of the general law applicable to agents and fiduciaries.[210]

Conflicts in the insurance sector

This is an important issue for insurance intermediaries and brokers. Brokers have **16.171** fiduciary obligations which often conflict with their own interests or duties owed

---

[206] On conflicts of interest more generally see FSA Principle 8.
[207] In addition, FSA Principle 6 provides that a firm must pay due regard to the interests of its customers and treat them fairly.
[208] FSA, *Annual Report 2004/05*.
[209] 'Delivering more transparent and flexible financial markets': a speech by Callum McCarthy made on 30 September 2004.
[210] See for example the FSA's Dear CEO Letter on conflict of interest dated 18 November 2005.

to another client or customer (see below). Insurance brokers frequently provide services to both insurers and insureds, which may lead to conflicts of interest. Examples of such conflicts include:

- an intermediary holding a binding authority from a particular insurer to conclude contracts of insurance and yet also advising clients on policies from a range of insurers;
- an intermediary assisting insureds in making claims and yet also assisting the insurer, even to the point of having authority to settle claims;
- an intermediary providing services to insurers relating to the insurance policies of its insured clients, such as administration and line slip services;
- a broker placing insurance and related reinsurance;
- a broker negotiates its commission with an insurer or obtains payments from an insurer which increase by reference to the volume of business the broker places with that insurer.

The remuneration of insurance brokers, conflicts, and commission disclosure

16.172 Over recent years, the FSA has raised particular concerns in relation to the remuneration of brokers, as remuneration structures may pose conflicts between the broker and its client (see above), and may involve a breach of the duties under the general law relating to fiduciary and agents.

16.173 **Fiduciaries and agents.** The general law on agents and fiduciaries applies to many insurance intermediaries such as brokers which cannot make a 'secret profit' and should not put themselves in a position where their own interests conflict with the duties they owe to their principals. They will be liable to account for any secret profits. In certain circumstances and by way of exception, insurance brokers who are not remunerated by fees paid by their client are entitled to agree with insurers and to retain a commission within market rates. In other cases it may be necessary for an intermediary to obtain its client's consent in order to retain a commission or for other forms of remuneration paid to it by insurers.

16.174 Recent case law has clarified that if the intermediary is to be entitled to retain commission, in the context of a client who has paid a fee, there must be informed consent from the client, and not merely knowledge of the possibility that the profit may be made.[211] In all cases an agent or fiduciary is obliged on request to disclose the remuneration and other benefits received as a result of his acting on the principal's behalf. This covers all remuneration: commissions, fees, profit shares, etc.[212]

---

[211] *Hurstanger Ltd v Wilson* [2007] EWCA Civ 299.
[212] ibid.

The Spitzer Investigation. The FSA is not alone in its concerns in relation to these **16.175** issues. Conflicts of interest in the insurance sector which were previously regarded as normal market practice have now come under regulatory scrutiny across the US and the EU, particularly those relating to remuneration structures.[213] The investigations by Eliot Spitzer[214] in the US focused attention on the conflicts of interests posed by various forms of remuneration paid by insurers to brokers and other intermediaries, notably contingent commissions, volume overriders, and profit commissions. As a result, several international intermediaries have adjusted their operating models to the extent that they now voluntarily disclose commission information to their clients and have steered away from aligning their remuneration with the profits of the insurers with whom they deal.

The Competition Commission insurance sector inquiry. Following the Spitzer **16.176** investigations the European Competition Commission undertook a sector inquiry into business insurance that sought to identify anti-competitive practices and distortions of competition.[215] When considering the distribution of business insurance through intermediaries, the Commission identified the tendency for brokers to act as advisors to their clients and as distribution channels to insurers as a potential source of conflict. In particular, fair competition was undermined by various practices aimed at inciting brokers to place business with particular insurers, often without complete, clear, or understandable disclosure to the client. The Commission found that the potential for conflicts of interest is highest where a broker is acting under a delegated authority for an insurer regarding their own insurance clients.

Current position in the UK

The FSA is currently concerned not only about the lack of transparency in com- **16.177** mission information (both regarding the client-facing intermediary and others further down the chain), but also the fact that clients are not always aware of the extent to which an intermediary searches the market when acting on their behalf, nor the extent to which an intermediary acts on behalf of the client as opposed to the insurer. The FSA considers that all this information should be clear and accurate, easily accessible, and presented in way that facilitates comparisons across the market and over time, and that its current rules do not ensure these outcomes.[216]

---

[213] See below at para 16.187; for the FSA's approach to such conflicts see *General Insurance Newsletter* (Issue 5—March 2005), available on the FSA's website.
[214] 'Spitzer Complaint'; *People of the State of New York v Marsh & McLennan Companies, Inc, and Marsh, Inc* No 04403342 (Sup Ct New York County, 14 Oct 2004).
[215] Sector Inquiry under Article 17 of Regulation (EC) No 1/2003 on business insurance (Final Report) (SEC (2007) 1231).
[216] FSA DP 08/02, 'Transparency, disclosure and conflicts of interest in the commercial insurance market'.

16.178 The FSA's treatment of these types of conflicts is underpinned by the FSA's high-level principles 1, 6, and 7, and, in particular, 8, which requires a firm to manage conflicts of interest fairly. Case law has also had an influence on the current regime (see para 16.175).

16.179 **ICOBS Rules.** There are specific rules in ICOBS dealing with remuneration which gives rise to a conflict and to conflicts in claims handling (see para 16.226 *et seq.* below).

16.180 **Rules on Commission Disclosure.** While prior disclosure of fees is mandatory under ICOBS 4.3.1R, there are no requirements for own-initiative prior disclosure of commission. ICOBS 4.4 (commission disclosure to customers) gives commercial customers enhanced rights to require commission disclosure. This is an unusual rule in that it gives commercial consumers rights that were not given to consumers. The effect of ICOBS 4.4.1 is to give commercial customers enhanced rights to require disclosure (i) even where the intermediary is not acting on their behalf (as an agent or fiduciary) and (ii) including remuneration received by the intermediary's associates. Disclosure is required in 'cash terms'. The rule does not address the disclosure of commission retained throughout the insurance chain. FSA felt it was necessary to remind authorised firms of their obligations in relation to commission disclosure in its 'Dear CEO' letter of December 2006.

16.181 **Rules on Inducements.** The FSA gives guidance under ICOBS 2.3.1G on the accepting and offering of inducements (see para 16.215 et *seq.*). It requires a firm to take reasonable steps to ensure that it does not offer or accept inducements or direct business to any person if it is likely to conflict to a material extent with any duty that the firm or the recipient owes to its customers in connection with insurance mediation activities. This rule can apply to remuneration, commission, or benefits in kind paid to individual sales staff and from one company to another. The guidance may be breached both by an insurer who pays, and a broker who receives, an inappropriate form of remuneration.

Future developments in the UK

16.182 The FSA issued a discussion paper in March 2008[217] which aims to identify how best to ensure that commercial insurance customers are appropriately protected and to ensure that this market operates in an efficient, orderly, and fair manner. The FSA outlines three potential solutions:

(i) More rigorous supervision and enforcement of the existing rules referred to above;

---

[217] ibid.

(ii) Enhanced 'on-request regime' (ie introduce measures designed to improve the transparency and comparability of disclosure requirements);

(iii) Mandatory commission disclosure.

Whichever route is taken will need to be supported by improved conflict manage-ment processes. **16.183**

The FSA has not ruled out the possibility of a solution in the form of guidance issued by industry bodies such as the London Market Insurance Brokers' Committee (the 'LMBC') and the British Insurance Brokers' Association (the 'BIBA'). The LMBC has produced draft guidance that focuses on commission disclosure requirements, conflicts management, and the capacity in which an intermediary is acting. **16.184**

The FSA also notes that the current status disclosure rule under ICOBS 4.1.2R does not require any formal disclosure of whom the intermediary acts for, and in what capacity. The current rule regarding disclosure of the scope of an intermediary's service under ICOBS 4.1.6R, whilst requiring an initial disclosure of the basis on which it advises, does not go as far as requiring the intermediary to inform its client of the number of quotes it obtains, or their criteria for selecting any shortlist of preferred insurers, and the frequency of this selection process. **16.185**

The FSA's current review of retail distribution (known as RDR)[218] may also be indicative of the future regulatory regime policy relating to advisors, although the scope of the review is limited to investment insurance and does not extend to general insurance, a market that the FSA acknowledges has distinct features. In particular, the FSA has shown interest in creating a regime in which all advisers would be independent, would receive remuneration determined without the input of the product provider, and would recommend products from across the whole market as standard. **16.186**

Systems and Controls in relation to conflicts

Firms conducting insurance activities are subject to the general requirements under the FSA's Systems and Controls[219] (and see para 16.192 *et seq.* below about potential further rules in this area) rules to: **16.187**

(1) Apportion significant responsibilities among senior executives, including for monitoring and managing conflicts;

(2) Have appropriate systems and controls, especially where conflicts exist, and establish an effective compliance system to help manage those conflicts; and

---

[218] FSA, 'Retail Distribution Review—Interim Report' (April 2008).

[219] See SYSC 2, PRIN, and the FSA's CEO letter on Conflicts of Interest dated 18 November 2005.

(3) Have an appropriate flow of management information, including information about the incidence and management of conflicts.

Senior Management Arrangements and Systems and Controls ('SYSC')

16.188 FSA's Senior Management Arrangements, Systems and Controls Sourcebook ('SYSC') and the related regime for the prior approval and individual regulation of approved persons under APER is covered in Chapter 5. Two of the FSA's fundamental themes are to ensure that firms have adequate systems and controls in place, and to hold senior management responsible for ensuring that all business operations are conducted within the regulatory framework.[220] These obligations derive from Principle 3 in PRIN and are reflected in the extensive SYSC requirements that apply to firms.

16.189 There are extensive systems requirements for insurers in GENPRU, INSPRU (see para 16.269 *et seq*. below), and in SYSC.

16.190 Some applicable SYSC requirements are general high-level requirements which apply to all firms including insurance intermediaries, some are specific requirements for insurers. The applicable SYSC requirements are—

    (i) 2 (Senior management arrangements);
    (ii) 3 (Systems and controls);
    (iii) 11 (Liquidity risk systems and controls);
    (iv) 12 (Group risk systems and controls requirements);
    (v) 13 (Operational risk systems and controls);
    (vi) 14 (Prudential risk management and associated systems and controls);
    (vii) 15 (Credit risk management systems and controls);
    (viii) 16 (Market risk management systems and controls);
    (ix) 17 (Insurance risk systems and controls); and
    (x) 18 (Guidance on Public Interest Disclosure Act: Whistle blowing).

16.191 These requirements include, for example, the establishment and maintenance of systems and controls, in relation to the management of operational risk—ie the risk of loss, resulting from inadequate or failed internal processes, people and systems, or from external events. They also include requirements relating to insurance risk (ie the risk as an underwriter of insurance policies that the quantum, timing, or frequency of claims will not be as expected) including, for example, the aggregation of risk and the need for a written policy setting out an insurer's risk appetite and how it identifies, measures, monitors, and controls that risk.

---

[220] FSA Principle 3; SYSC 2.1.1R and 3.1.1R.

Systems and controls and the possible extension of the common platform requirements

The common platform (ie those rules contained within SYSC 4-10) includes **16.192**
rules specifically dealing with conflicts[221] such as:

(i) The requirement for a written conflicts policy;[222]

(ii) The requirement to take all reasonable steps to identify conflicts and prevent them;[223] and

(iii) The requirement to clearly disclose the general nature and/or sources of conflicts of interest to a client before undertaking business for that client.[224]

The common platform does not currently apply to insurers or insurance intermedi- **16.193**
aries. However, the FSA is considering extending the scope of some of its more
prescriptive common platform requirements[225] to firms which are currently outside
of the common platform, such as insurance intermediaries (but not insurers).[226]

The FSA will consider whether and how to expand the scope of its Systems and **16.194**
Controls rules in relation to insurers as part of its work on the Solvency II Directive,
which is planned to take place in 2009.

Business standards

Conduct of Business Rules—insurance investment products (COBS)

Broadly speaking, COBS applies to regulated activities which fall within the defi- **16.195**
nition of designated investment business[227] and long-term care insurance contracts.[228] It no longer has any application to non-investment insurance and was
amended at NGI to reflect changes required by IMD and DMD.[229]

---

[221] SYSC 10.

[222] SYSC 10.1.10R.

[223] SYSC 10.1.3R.

[224] SYSC 10.1.8R.

[225] The FSA's common platform requirements in SYSC implement the general organisational
requirements of MiFID. These include the requirement to have a formal conflicts policy—see
SYSC 10.1.9 and Recital 27 of Council Directive (EC) 04/39 on markets in financial instruments
amending Council Directives (EEC) 85/611 and 93/6 and Directive (EC) 2000/12 of the European
Parliament and of the Council and repealing Council Directive (EEC) 93/22 OJ L145/1.

[226] FSA CP07/23: 'Organisational systems and controls—extending the common platform';
FSA PS08/9, 'Organisational systems and controls—extending the common platform—Feedback
on CP07/23 and final rules'. At the time of writing, the FSA's proposals to extend the common
platform requirements to non-scope firms (includes insurance intermediaries but not insurers) are
due to be implemented into the FSA Handbook mainly as guidance on 1 April 2009.

[227] COBS 1.1. See the explanation of the 'designated investment' in para 16.04.

[228] See the explanation of 'long-term care insurance contracts' in para 16.04.

[229] Council Directive (EC) 02/65 on distance marketing of consumer financial services [2002]
OJ L271/16.

16.196 COBS is considered in more detail in Chapter 12. The COBS chapters specifically dealing with insurance include: chapter 7 (Insurance mediation), chapter 20
(With-profits), and chapter 17 (Claims handling for long-term care insurance).

Conduct of Business Rules—non-investment insurance (ICOBS)

16.197 It is not possible to cover all the detailed rules in ICOBS; the following paragraphs
highlight, in broad terms, some of the more important provisions.

16.198 The application and scope rules for ICOBS (principally in chapter 1 of ICOBS)
are complex, sometimes more so than the obligations themselves. This is partly to
cope with the difficulty of implementing provisions contained in a number of EU
directives[230] and the different cross-border regimes which they establish.

16.199 ICOBS replaced the original ICOB rules which had been introduced in 2005
(when the FSA took on the regulation of general insurance sales as part of the UK's
implementation of IMD). The new sourcebook took effect on 5 January 2008
subject to a transitional regime which enabled firms to continue to operate under
ICOB until 6 July 2008.

Scope and EU implementation

16.200 ICOBS applies to the sale and administration of non-investment insurance; these
are general insurance and pure protection contracts (other than long-term care
contracts). Pure protection contracts are those long-term contracts which do not
fall within the definition of qualifying contracts of insurance (and therefore of
relevant investments) under the RAO. ICOBS does not therefore apply to insurance products regulated under COBS or where an election for COBS regulation
of a pure protection product has been made by the firm in question. Certain long-
term life products (such as some whole of life contracts) were switched to regulation under ICOBS (instead of COBS) in 2007.[231]

16.201 The FSA has consulted on the regulatory regime and rules for those selling connected travel insurance ('CTI'). The new regime will come into effect on 1 January
2009 when CTI activities will become regulated. ICOBS will apply to CTI.

---

[230] The IMD (see n 28), in respect of non-investment insurance contracts; the DMD (Council
Directive (EC) 02/65 on distance marketing of consumer financial services [2002] OJ L271/16), in
respect of non-investment insurance contracts and distance non-investment mediation contracts;
the CLD (see n 36) in respect of cancellation rights and information requirements relating to non-
investment insurance contracts which are pure protection contracts; the Third NLD (see n 50);
and the Fourth Motor Insurance Directive (Council Directive (EC) 00/26 on the approximation
of the laws of the Member States relating to insurance against civil liability in respect of the use of
motor vehicles and amending Council Directives (EEC) 73/239 and 88/357 [2000] OJ L181/65),
in respect of claims made by an EEA resident arising from a motor accident in the EEA but outside
his country of residence.
[231] See n 2 above.

Like standalone insurance, CTI is not subject to the additional requirements for higher risk or protection products (see para 16.212 *et seq*. below); indeed certain other ICOBS requirements that apply to standalone travel insurance do not apply to CTI. This disapplication is possible in relation to ICOBS provisions implementing IMD because CTI falls outside the scope of that directive.[232]

ICOBS does not apply to reinsurance of any kind. It has limited application to **16.202** 'large risks' (although it recites the broader application of Principle 7); generally the mediation rules do not apply to large risks unless the risk is located in the EEA and the customer is a consumer.

ICOBS applies to business conducted from a UK establishment but it contains an **16.203** EEA territorial scope rule which modifies this principle (see para. 16.207 below).

ICOBS does not apply to a 'wholesale' intermediary (such as a placing broker) **16.204** which is not in contact with the end customer.

ICOBS rules (on the production of product information and claims handling) **16.205** apply to insurers as product providers; insurers which sell direct without an intermediary are also subject to some (but not all) of the selling rules (such as the obligation to provide the product information to the customer).

ICOBS rules implement various requirements in different EU directives; these **16.206** include the directives on Insurance Mediation, Distance Marketing, E-commerce, Consolidated Life and Non-life. These rules (and domestic requirements in these areas) are subject to different cross-border regimes which determine whether, for example, home or host State rules apply.

The scope rules are therefore extremely complex, although superficially they **16.207** appear simpler than the previous scope rules in ICOB because FSA has adopted (as it has in COBS) an 'EEA territorial scope rule'. This rule states that the scope provisions in ICOBS are deemed to be overridden to the extent required by EU law (which is left unspecified and as to which the FSA may be uncertain); this leaves the reader to interpret EU law and apply or disapply ICOBS provisions accordingly! The benefit from the FSA's point of view is that FSA rules cannot be criticised for incorrect implementation of EU requirements.

Differential requirements and the changes from ICOB

The FSA carried out a review of ICOB and consulted on the new rules during **16.208** 2007 against a general recognition that, in many respects, IMD implementation was seen to be overly prescriptive. Some of this reflected shortcomings in the

---

[232] See FSA CP07/22 and PS08/04 ('Regulating Connected Travel Insurance') and the Financial Services and Markets Act 2000 (Regulated Activities) (Amendment) (No 2) Order 2007, SI 2007/3510.

IMD which the UK could not rectify, but some shortcomings in ICOB reflected unnecessary gold-plating and additional UK regulation.[233]

16.209   ICOBS is considerably shorter than the previous rulebook, reflecting the general move to lighter touch and more principle-based regulation. ICOB had applied to insurers in two distinct ways—as product providers and where they sold directly without an intermediary in the chain. ICOBS continued a process of cutting back the application of selling rules (such as status disclosure and demands and needs statements) to insurers (which was possible because the European requirements of IMD did not apply to insurers).

16.210   In contrast with the recognition that some ICOB provisions were unnecessary to remedy market failure for most products, FSA concluded that tougher regulation was required for certain products. ICOBS therefore imposes additional obligations in relation to 'pure protection contracts' and 'payment protection contracts' for consumers.

16.211   ICOBS is concerned with policyholders ie those entitled to make a claim under a policy. In the context of insurance sales, many of the rules apply only to the person buying the insurance. These are split into 'consumers' and non-consumers referred to as 'commercial customers' (which includes those who are acting in both capacities).

Communications, financial promotions, and distance communications (ICOBS 2.2 and 3)

16.212   There are high-level requirements (clear, fair, and not misleading) for all promotions and for all communications to a customer or other policyholder. There are some further limited provisions (for example, in relation to pricing claims) for promotions which are not covered by one of the various exemptions in the FPO.

16.213   For distance marketing to consumers (within the DMD), a variety of directive requirements are applicable under ICOBS 3. These include the regulation of oral and written marketing, the provision of prescribed pre and post contract information and documents, requirements for telephone sales, and a prohibition in relation to unsolicited services.

16.214   There are separate rules concerning insurance business conducted from the UK under the E-Commerce Directive.[234]

---

[233] FSA CP07/11, 'Insurance selling and administration—proposed amendments to the Insurance: Conduct of Business Sourcebook'.

[234] Council Directive (EC) 00/31 on certain legal aspects of information society services, in particular electronic commerce, in the Internal Market [2000] OJ L178/1.

Inducements and information about the firm, its services,
and remuneration (ICOBS 2.3 and 4)[235]

ICOBS 4.1 implements IMD provisions; it requires intermediaries (but not direct **16.215**
selling insurers) to give 'status disclosure' comprising certain specified information about the firm and information about the type of service it will provide
(whether advised or non-advised service, whether a full market service is provided
or a limited range, and whether the intermediary is tied by an exclusivity obligation to an insurer). This must be given before the sale and may be required at
renewal or amendment of a policy. Guidance is given on the use of 'panels' in order
to provide a service which can be described as 'whole of market'.

The information must be given in a durable medium unless the customer requests **16.216**
it orally or cover is required immediately. Telephone sales are governed by the
distance marketing rules. There are also requirements for the prior disclosure of all
fees (ie charges other than premiums) and for commission disclosure on request
to commercial customers (see further at para 16.172 *et seq.* above and para 17.180
in particular). A standard form 'initial disclosure document' can be used for status
and fee disclosure.

There are additional requirements for the sale of payment protection and pure **16.217**
protection contracts to consumers. Intermediaries have to provide additional
information about the limits of the service they will be providing which will
include, in the case of a non-advised sale, explaining orally to the customer that he
is responsible for determining whether the policy meets his demands and needs.
Insurers (when selling direct) must give status information and confirm whether
they will be giving a personal recommendation.

Identifying client needs and advising (ICOBS 5)

The distinction in the ICOB rules between advised and non-advised sales has **16.218**
been watered down to some extent. The new rules contain additional obligations
in relation to non-advised sales. The suitability requirement applies to any advice
which a customer is entitled to rely upon its judgement; there are additional
obligations for payment protection and pure protection contracts.

The IMD requirements for demands and needs statements applies to both advised **16.219**
and non-advised sales by an intermediary and are extended to direct sales by
insurers of payment protection and pure protection contracts to consumers. For
non-advised sales there is helpful guidance as to how the different ways in which
these statements can be given during the sales process; for example it might be

---

[235] See para 16.181 above for further discussion of ICOBS 2.3.1 concerning inducements and
para 16.180 for further discussion of ICOBS 4.

included in product documentation, an application form, or a key features document.

16.220 In addition, there are general obligations applicable to non-advised sales by insurers and intermediaries; for example they are required to take reasonable steps to ensure that the customer only buys a policy under which he is eligible to claim benefits. There are additional requirements in relation to sales of payment protection insurance.

Preparation and provision of product information (ICOBS 6)

16.221 The rules draw a distinction between the responsibility for producing product information, which normally falls on the insurer, and for the provision of the information which normally falls on the intermediary arranging the sale or, in the case of a direct sale, on the insurer. There are a variety of situations (including various cross-border scenarios) where the responsibilities may differ.

16.222 There are specific information requirements for pre-contract information for general insurance (from the Third Non-life Directive and also relating to cancellation) and pre-contact and post-contract information (ie mid-term changes) for pure protection and payment protection contracts (the former includes the requirements of the CLD). The additional requirements include obligations in relation to oral sales, the provision of a policy summary, and significant regulation of the way in which price information for payment protection policies is provided (with a distinction between policies for revolving and non-revolving credit).

16.223 The general requirements applicable to all polices do not require the use of a policy summary but these, and a key features document, can be used to meet the general requirements. The basic rule requires reasonable steps to ensure a customer is given appropriate information (including price information) about a policy in good time and in a comprehensible form so that the customer can make an informed decision; these obligations extend post sale to mid-term changes and to renewals. Guidance under Principle 7 requires evidence of cover to be provided promptly after inception and that in the case of group policies information should be provided for the customer to pass on to each policyholder. For insurance sold as a secondary product with goods or other services, there is a requirement to disclose the premium separately from any other prices and whether the purchase of the insurance is compulsory.

Cancellation (ICOBS 7)

16.224 A consumer has the right to cancel pure protection and payment protection contracts within 30 days and the right to cancel any other contract of insurance within 14 days. This implements the requirements of the CLD and the DMD but extends cancellation to all general insurance sales including those made face to face. There are a variety of exceptions which either reflect directive exceptions or relate to sales outside those directives.

The rule also stipulates the start of the cancellation period, how the right is exercised, and the effects of cancellation. **16.225**

Claims handling (ICOBS 8)

The final chapter of ICOBS deals with claims handling. There are rules which impose general requirements on insurers in relation to all claims and extend to claims by a policyholder who was not the original customer on the sale of the policy. These requirements include restrictions, originally taken from ABI codes, which restrict the ability of the insurer to reject claims from a consumer where the insurer would be entitled to do so under the general law on account of certain non-disclosures. **16.226**

There are additional requirements in relation to the handling of claims under motor vehicle liability policies including (Fourth) Motor Insurance Directive requirements for a claims representative in each Member State. **16.227**

Finally there is guidance under Principle 8 on the conflicts of interest which may arise for insurance intermediaries (or insurers handling claims on another insurer's policy). In some situations, an intermediary will be unable to act for both an insurer and the policyholder. **16.228**

Client money[236]

The Client Money Sourcebook ('CASS') sets out the rules for dealing with client money. It is divided into five chapters dealing with scope/application ('CASS 1'); custody ('CASS 2'); collateral ('CASS 3'); client money and mandates: designated investment business ('CASS 4'); client money and mandates: insurance mediation activity ('CASS 5'). **16.229**

In this section we look at some of the key elements of CASS 5. This contains the rules introduced at NGI for non-investment insurance mediation and which are **16.230**

---

[236] FSA CP174, 'Prudential and other requirements for mortgage firms and insurance intermediaries'; FSA PS174, 'Prudential and other requirements for mortgage firms and insurance intermediaries: feedback on CP174 and "near final text"'; FSA CP04/13, 'Quarterly consultation (No 1)'; FSA Handbook notice 29; FSA Handbook notice 38; Insurance Mediation and Mortgage Mediation, Lending and Administration (Prudential Provisions) Instrument 2004 (2004/1): Client Assets Sourcebook (Amendment No 2) Instrument 2004 (2004/92); Guide to the FSA Handbook for Small Mortgage and Insurance Intermediaries Part III; FSA Frequently Asked Questions; FSA letter to CEOs of all general insurance intermediaries supervised within the FSA's wholesale unit, dated 20 July 2005.

part of UK compliance with Article 4(4) of the IMD. During the consultations on CASS 5, two key issues emerged:

(i) the practice of the London Market of paying premiums (or claims) out of a broker's insurance bank account ('IBA') before the client had paid the premium to them (and the payment of claims out of the IBA before the insurer had paid). This necessitated the development of non-statutory client bank accounts referred to below;

(ii) the handling of insurer monies—the lack of clear documentation and clarity concerning the basis on which premium/claims monies were held by inter-mediaries in their IBAs (ie whether the monies were held for clients/insureds or for insurers), the implication of intermediaries acting as agents under a binding authority in relation to related premium and claims monies and the IMD/FSMA requirements that client money bank accounts protect monies held for customers, whereas IBAs were used to 'co-mingle' insurer monies and client money.

Scope of CASS 5

16.231 **Which firms does it apply to?** As stated above, CASS 5 applied to an intermediary (not an insurer acting as such) which receives or holds money in the course of or in connection with insurance mediation activity.[237] Insurance intermediaries can also elect to treat monies relating to reinsurance under the client money rules. The election must be in respect of all the firm's reinsurance business.[238] It can also elect to treat monies relating to large risks[239] situated outside the EEA in the same way; again it must apply to all such business. Absent an election, these monies fall out-side CASS 5. A firm which mediates in relation to both investment and non-in-vestment insurance may elect to operate entirely under the CASS 4 rules for designated investment business.[240] The CASS 5 rules are intended to apply to UK registered firms on a home State basis across the EEA.

16.232 **Who is a client?** A client is any person with or for whom the intermediary con-ducts or intends to conduct insurance mediation activities. A client includes:

- a potential client;
- a client of an appointed representative of an intermediary with or for whom the appointed representative acts or intends to act in the course of business for which the intermediary has accepted responsibility.[241]

---

[237] CASS 5.1.1R.

[238] CASS 5.1.1R(3).

[239] See the explanation of 'large risks' in para 16.05.

[240] See the explanation of 'non-investment insurance' and 'designated investment business' in paras 16.03–16.04.

[241] FSA Glossary.

A policyholder/insured may be a client. An insurer will be a client,[242] if it agrees to become one (see below, para 16.215 *et seq*.). An insurance intermediary can be the client of another insurance intermediary, for example in the following chain the retail producing broker is the client of the wholesale placing broker: **16.233**

Policy holder $\rightarrow$ 'Retail'producing broker $\rightarrow$ 'Wholesale' placing broker

$\rightarrow$ Insurer

IBA versus client money bank account. The new 'client bank accounts' intro-   **16.234**
duced by the FSA under CASS 5 are significantly different from the pre-14 January 2005 IBAs, for example those operated under GISC. The key differences can be summarised as follows.

- The accounts are trust accounts. 'Client monies' must be held on trust (or as agent in relation to Scotland) in a segregated bank account that cannot be used to reimburse other creditors if the intermediary becomes insolvent.[243]

- Client money bank accounts are directed at protecting policyholders and customers not insurers. IBAs under GISC were intended to separate monies held for insurers and insured from the monies of the intermediary.

- Firms which conduct insurance mediation activity only as a secondary activity must operate client bank accounts (unlike the position under GISC).

- Only 'received' commission can be withdrawn from a client bank account.

An intermediary cannot remove commission from the client bank account until   **16.235**
the client has paid the premium (an IBA under GISC rules could be operated so that the intermediary could deduct commission from the IBA even where the relevant premium had not been paid).

Review of the Client Assets Sourcebook

The FSA issued a Consultation paper in March 2008 entitled 'Review of the   **16.236**
Client Assets sourcebook' in which it indicated that it would consult on CASS 5 (insurance mediation activity) during the first quarter of 2009. The objective of the review is to create a common client-money platform by incorporating the client money rules for general insurance intermediaries into a single client money chapter within CASS. Another objective is to implement a more principle-based approach to CASS provisions where appropriate.

---

[242] CASS 5.1.1R.
[243] CASS 5.3, 5.4.

16.237 An intermediary must hold client money in a segregated bank account on a statutory or non-statutory trust basis.[244] Statutory and non-statutory trust client bank accounts can be operated side by side.[245]

16.238 A **statutory account** is a bank account with individual client ledgers, but with no cross-lending between each client ledger.[246] These accounts (like those under CASS 4) are governed by the statutory trust established under section 139(1) of FSMA.

16.239 A **non-statutory account** is a bank account where one client's money may be used to pay the premium/claim of another client, ie to allow an intermediary to pay a premium which has not yet been received from the client out of the client bank account (to the insurer) and to pay premium refunds/claims monies which have not yet been received from the insurer.[247] Under a non-statutory trust an intermediary can also make use of a 'letter of credit' (see para 16.264 below).[248]

16.240 Non-statutory trusts are subject to more detailed rules on systems and controls. An intermediary must also execute a formal trust deed (or the equivalent in Scotland) in line with CASS 5 requirements to establish the trust and set out its terms.[249] It must also obtain the informed consent of the client.[250]

Operating segregated accounts

16.241 **Paying client money into the client bank account.** The main obligation is to segregate client money.

16.242 If an intermediary is liable to pay money to a client, it must as soon as possible, and no later than one business day after the money is due and payable:

- pay it into a client bank account as soon as practicable. The FSA expects that in most circumstances this will be the next business day after receipt;[251] or
- pay it to, or to the order of, the client.

16.243 **Mixed remittance.** Mixed remittance can be paid into client bank accounts provided the money which is not client money or has ceased to be client money is withdrawn from the client bank account as soon as is reasonably practicable

---

[244] ibid.
[245] CASS 5.4.2R.
[246] CASS 5.3.
[247] CASS 5.4.1G.
[248] CASS 5.4.8R(2).
[249] CASS 5.4.7R.
[250] CASS 5.4.4R(5).
[251] CASS 5.5.5R and 5.5.6G.

(and no later than 25 business days) after remittance is cleared in the account (or, if earlier, when the firm performs the client money calculation in accordance with CASS 5.5.63(1)).[252]

For intermediaries unable to identify remittance transactions, if there is any doubt the money should be treated as client money while the intermediary takes steps to match the remittance as soon as practicable.[253] **16.244**

Interest. There are specific requirements in relation to retail customers, relating to interest on client money (eg, there is a requirement for an explanation of and, where necessary, the client's informed consent to treatment of interest).[254] Where a client is entitled to interest, it must be treated as client money. **16.245**

Withdrawal of commission. CASS prohibits an intermediary from removing commission from the client bank account until the client or premium finance provider firm has paid the premium to it (ie the bank account must be operated on a 'commission received' basis and not on a 'commission earned' basis (see para 16.235 above)). The commission may only be withdrawn from the client bank account at the point at which it is due to the firm for its own account. Until then the commission will remain client money.[255] **16.246**

Where an intermediary's terms of business with its client *and* its terms of business with the insurer set out when the commission element will become due, the withdrawal of commission must be consistent with this. Commission can be withdrawn before the intermediary pays the premium to the insurance company if the intermediary has received the premium from the client or premium finance firm and the insurance company's terms of business allow this. **16.247**

If the commission becomes due immediately upon receipt of the premium from the client, the premium must be treated as mixed remittance (see para 16.243 above). **16.248**

If the insurance company's terms of business do not specify a time for withdrawal of commission, then the intermediary may assume that commission is due on receipt of the premium from the client.[256] **16.249**

When a client pays premiums to an intermediary in instalments, then in most cases, the commission must also be withdrawn from the client bank account in **16.250**

---

[252] CASS 5.5.16R(2).
[253] CASS 5.5.17G(4).
[254] CASS 5.5.30R.
[255] CASS 5.5.16R.
[256] Guide to the FSA Handbook for Small Mortgage and Insurance Intermediaries, Part III, para 2.4.7.

instalments. The withdrawal must also comply with the intermediary's terms of business with both client and insurer.[257]

16.251 **Paying money out of the client bank account to an insurer.** If it is a statutory account the intermediary cannot meet the client's premium obligation to the insurer unless it is funded, ie that the client has already paid the monies to the intermediary.[258] If it is a non-statutory account a client's premium obligation can be met from the pool of client money held for the intermediary's other clients before the client pays the premium to the intermediary.

16.252 **Paying money out of the client bank account to another intermediary.** An intermediary may allow another person, such as another broker, to hold or control client money, but only if:

- the intermediary transfers the client money for the purpose of a transaction for a client through or with that person; and
- in the case of a retail customer that customer has been notified (whether through a client agreement, terms of business, or otherwise in writing) that the client money may be transferred to another person.[259]

16.253 When a firm transfers a premium to a third party, it will not automatically discharge its duties to its client as trustee. Therefore, if the intermediary pays a premium to a third party firm, the premium will remain client money of the intermediary until it is paid to the insurer. The premium will also be client money of the third party firm, held on behalf of the intermediary, until it is paid to the insurer. However, if the money is held at any time by a firm which is an agent of the insurer, the premium then becomes the insurer's money.

16.254 Where the money remains client money of the intermediary, the intermediary must use appropriate skill, care, and judgement when transferring monies to third parties[260] and track the payments in the chain for the purposes of performing its own client money calculation and reconciliation which will include monies held by third parties.

Insurer monies—acting as agent of insurers, client money, and subordination

16.255 Under CASS 5, the intermediary may have one of three relationships with an insurer. These may vary between individual risks.

16.256 Providing the intermediary is not operating a binding authority for the relevant business, the intermediary may receive and hold the money as agent of its client

---

257 CASS 5.5.17G(3).
258 CASS 5.3.3G(2).
259 CASS 5.5.34R.
260 CASS 5.5.81G.

and not for the insurer. In this situation, the money received/held by the intermediary is held for the client and is, therefore, client money which must be held in a client bank account. Payments of premium by the client to the intermediary do not discharge the debt due to the insurer—this occurs when the intermediary pays the insurer (or its agent). Money paid by the insurer to the intermediary constitutes payment by the insurer to the client or ultimate policyholder.

The intermediary may act as agent of the insurer to receive/hold premiums and to hold premiums refund/claims monies.[261] This is compulsory if the intermediary has a binding authority agreement with the insurer in relation to the relevant business.[262] In this situation, premiums paid by the client to the intermediary are a payment to the insurer (through its agent). This is sometimes referred to as a risk transfer because in this situation it is the insurer which bears the risk of the intermediary becoming insolvent. Money paid to the intermediary by its client or by the insurer (within this agency) is insurer money and, unless the necessary agreements for co-mingling are in place, cannot be paid/held in the client bank account, ie it must be held in other bank accounts of the intermediary (either office accounts or non-FSA/specific insurer accounts). **16.257**

There are specific requirements for an agency agreement between intermediary and insurer in these circumstances, and requirements to inform relevant clients of the arrangement.[263] (These requirements reflect Article 4.4(a) of the IMD as distinct from the provisions requiring segregated client accounts for customer's money under Article 4.4(c) of the IMD.) **16.258**

When the intermediary acts as an agent of an insurer in receiving/holding monies, the insurer may agree with the intermediary that the insurer's money may be co-mingled in the intermediary's client bank account.[264] This situation is then as described above except that money received/held as agent of the insurer may be held in the client bank account as if the insurer were a client of the intermediary. **16.259**

To co-mingle, an intermediary must obtain the insurer's written agreement that the monies may be treated as client money and its written consent and acceptance that its interest under the trust is subordinated to the intermediary's 'true' clients.[265] **16.260**

Appointed representatives

An appointed representative cannot operate its own client bank account. It may, however, receive money as agent of the insurer (see para 16.257 *et seq.*). Alternatively it can accept client money under one of three procedures in accordance with the **16.261**

---

[261] CASS 5.2.
[262] CASS 5.2.3R.
[263] ibid.
[264] CASS 5.1.5AR.
[265] ibid.

relevant CASS requirements. The options are (i) the money is paid directly into the principal's client bank account,[266] (ii) 'immediate segregation' which involves forwarding the funds to the principal to arrive within three business days,[267] or (iii) 'periodic segregation' under which the principal maintains a balance in its client bank account equivalent to the estimated amount of client money held by the appointed representative (subject to reconciliation against the actual amount held on a periodic basis).[268]

Reconciliation, insurance debtors, and letters of credit

16.262 Under CASS 5, intermediaries are required to carry out a client money calculation and reconciliation.[269]

16.263 The client money calculation requires an intermediary to calculate—at least every 25 business days—the amount of money which ought to be segregated in its client bank account(s) (and at third parties) to meet its obligations to its clients.[270] This is done by comparing the client money resource with the client money requirement. Any shortfall or surplus should be rectified by the end of the day on which the calculation is performed.[271]

16.264 There are two methods permitted for the client money calculation—a cash-based method and an accruals method.[272] Under the accruals method (which includes insurance creditors and debtors), the intermediary is required to value debts on a prudent and consistent basis.[273] If the client bank account is a non-statutory trust, the intermediary can make use of a 'letter of credit'[274] provided by an approved bank to satisfy a shortfall in the intermediary's client money resource when compared to its client money requirement.[275]

Prudential standards—insurers[276]

16.265 The Prudential requirements in the FSA Handbook are concerned with financial resources, capital solvency, and related systems requirements, particularly for risk mitigation. Broader requirements relating to systems and controls are set out in

---

[266] CASS 5.5.19R.
[267] ibid.
[268] CASS 5.5.23R.
[269] CASS 5.5.62G–5.5.77R.
[270] CASS 5.5.63R.
[271] ibid.
[272] CASS 5.5.66R and 5.5.68R.
[273] CASS 5.5.65R(3)(a).
[274] CASS 5.4.8R(2).
[275] ibid.
[276] This section looks mainly at the position of 'directive' insurers authorised under the CLD or 3NLD. It does not address the variations and different prudential requirements for other risk

SYSC (see para 16.188 *et seq.* above) (within 'High-level' standards). This section looks briefly at the current financial regime for insurers in the FSA Handbook and the Solvency II initiative and then at the financial regime for insurance intermediaries.

Background to the current UK regime

The current EU minimum requirements are set out in the CLD, the 3NLD, and the RID; these were subject to relatively minor amendments under the Solvency I Directives, which came into effect in 2004.[277] For many years UK solvency requirements were based on the EU regime, although insurers were frequently required by the FSA to maintain higher levels of capital or a higher 'solvency ratio'. This reflected the view that the EU requirements were generally set too low; there is also general recognition that the whole structure of the solvency ratio regime was out of date and needed to be replaced. **16.266**

It was clear that the project, named Solvency II, of developing a modern financial regime for insurers, and securing political agreement across Europe, would take many years. In the UK the Tiner Project (see para 16.22 above) had identified reform as a priority and FSA therefore decided not to wait for EU agreement on Solvency II and to develop and implement its own updated regime. This would meet the historic EU minimum requirements as updated under Solvency I (which still applied) but would include a more modern, sophisticated, and demanding regime which anticipated, in very broad terms, many of the approaches which would emerge in Solvency II. **16.267**

This new regime was initially introduced in the Integrated Prudential Sourcebook (PRU) section of the Handbook but is now found in the General Prudential Sourcebook (GENPRU) and the Prudential Sourcebook for Insurers (INSPRU). **16.268**

The UK regime—GENPRU and INSPRU[278]

The three pillars

In broad terms, the UK regime for insurers and the emerging Solvency II regime are risk-based and reflect some aspects of the modern financial regime for banks, **16.269**

---

carriers such as reinsurers, captives, ISPVs, mutuals, composites, non-directive insurers, and the Lloyd's market.

[277] Council Directive (EC) 2002/12/EC amending Council Directive (EEC) 79/267 as regards the solvency margin requirements for life assurance undertakings [2002] OJ L77/11; and Council Directive (EC) 2002/13 amending Council Directive (EEC) 73/239 as regards the solvency margin requirements for non-life insurance undertakings [2002] OJ L77/17.

[278] The FSA's General Prudential Sourcebook for Banks, Building Societies, Insurers and Investment Firms and the Prudential Sourcebook for Insurers.

particularly under the Basel II accord (see Chapter 14). This is based on the three pillars of:

(1) Minimum capital requirements
(2) Supervisory review
(3) Public transparency and market discipline

16.270 GENPRU contains requirements both for banks and investment firms (subject to the Capital Requirements Directive) and insurers;[279] it reflects the move towards common elements across the sectors, for example, with a similar approach to 'tiered' capital. (This is a different technique to the current insurance directives, which are based on deducting foreseeable liabilities from total assets but the same result can be reached using under the alternative approach.)

16.271 GENPRU 2 sets out the calculation of an insurer's capital resources requirements (CRR) and its admissible forms of capital and how the amounts or values of capital, assets, and liabilities are to be determined. These reflect the minimum requirements of the CLD, the RID, and the 3NLD; in addition the firm is required to make its own assessment of its capital needs and this assessment and the process and systems by which it is made are reviewed by the FSA are explained below in relation to 'Individual capital assessment'.

Pillar 1—minimum capital rule

16.272 An insurer must maintain at all times capital resources ('CR') equal to or in excess of its capital resources requirement (CRR).[280] The CRR represents a cushion of free capital over and above all liabilities (after technical provisions for all liabilities which will arise on insurance underwritten and allowances for other risks).

16.273 **Capital Resources.** CR is the sum of the 'Total Capital' and, if a waiver has been granted, of 'other capital resources'. CR is the sum of various capital components calculated according to various tiers/types (ie components) of capital as follows:

(i) Tier 1 capital—
  • Core Tier 1 capital components (eg permanent share capital, share premium account and externally verified interim net profits);
  • Perpetual non-cumulative preference shares; and
  • Innovative Tier 1 capital.
(ii) Tier 2 capital—
  • Upper Tier 2 (permanent cumulative preference shares, perpetual subordinated debt, and perpetual subordinated securities); and

---

[279] GENPRU 1.1.2G.
[280] GENPRU 2.1.13R.

- Lower Tier 2 (fixed term preference shares, long-term subordinated debt, and fixed term subordinated debt).

(iii) Other capital resources (unpaid share capital and implicit items).

Various requirements and limitations apply to different capital components. Deductions are made from each component and deductions and positive adjustments made to the totals and sub-totals as follows:

(a) From Tier 1 capital—investments in own shares, intangible assets, and negative valuation differences.

(b) Positive adjustment to the total for related undertakings which are regulated.

(c) Deductions from the total for
- inadmissible assets;[281]
- assets in excess of market risk and counterparty limits in INSPRU 2.1.22 R (see para 16.295 below);
- related undertakings.

The full capital resources calculation is as follows:[282]

16.274

Table 16.1

Type of capital	Stage
Core Tier 1 capital	(A)
Permanent share capital	
Profit and loss account and other reserves (taking into account interim net losses)	
Share premium account	
Externally verified interim net profits	
Positive valuation differences	
Fund for future appropriations	
Perpetual non-cumulative preference shares	(B)
Perpetual non-cumulative preference shares	
Innovative Tier 1 capital	(C)
Innovative Tier 1 instruments	
Total Tier 1 capital before deductions = A+B+C	(D)
Deductions from Tier 1 capital	(E)
Investments in own shares	
Intangible assets	
Amounts deducted from technical provisions for discounting and other negative valuations differences	

---

[281] Inadmissible assets—any asset (except where held to cover property linked or index linked liabilities) other than the list of admissible assets (investments (eg shares, loans, debt securities, land and approved derivatives, quasi-derivative, and stock lending transactions that satisfies certain conditions—see para 16.290 below), debts and claims (eg debts owed by reinsurers including reinsurers shares of technical provisions), deposits and debts owed by ceding undertakings, debts owed by policyholders and intermediaries) and other assets (eg tangible fixed assets and cash). FSA can grant waivers for the inclusion within limits of Implicit items under the CLD (which are economic reserves within long-term insurance provisions relating to future profits, zillmerisation, and hidden reserves).

[282] This is taken from GENPRU 2 Annex 1.

Table 16.1 *Cont.*

Type of capital	Stage
Total Tier 1 capital after deductions = D–E	(F)
Upper Tier 2 capital	(G)
Perpetual cumulative preference shares	
Perpetual subordinated debt	
Perpetual subordinated securities	
Lower Tier 2 capital	(H)
Fixed term preference shares	
Long-term subordinated debt	
Fixed term subordinated securities	
Total Tier 2 capital = G+H	(I)
Positive adjustments for related undertakings	(J)
Related undertakings that are regulated related undertakings (other than insurance undertakings)	
Total capital after positive adjustments for insurance undertakings but before deductions = F + I + J	(K)
Deductions from total capital	(L)
Inadmissible assets	
Assets in excess of market risk and counterparty limits	
Related undertakings that are ancillary services undertakings	
Negative adjustments for related undertakings that are regulated related undertakings (other than insurance undertakings)	
Total capital after deductions = K + L	(M)
Other capital resources*	(N)
Unpaid share capital or, in the case of a mutual, unpaid initial funds and calls for supplementary contributions	
Implicit items	
Total capital resources after deductions = M + N	(O)

*Items in section (N) of the table can be included in capital resources if subject to a waiver under s 148 FSMA.

There are various limits on the use of different forms of capital. These include the requirement that Tier 1 capital must represent at least half, and innovative Tier 1 capital must represent no more than 15 per cent, of total Tier 1 capital after deductions (GENPRU 2.2.29 and 2.2.30).

16.275 **Capital Resources Requirement.** The CRR of an insurer is the MCR (Minimum Capital Requirement) or, if the insurer is a realistic basis life firm (ie a firm which has with profits liabilities above a threshold), the higher of the MCR and the Enhanced Capital Requirement for long-term business ('ECRLT').[283]

---

[283] GENPRU 2.1.18R.

MCR[284] is the higher of:

- the base capital resources requirement ('BCRR') for general /long-term insurance; and
- the general/long-term insurance capital requirement plus, for long-term insurers which are regulatory basis only life firms (ie those which are not realistic basis life firms and which are not subject to an ECRLT), the resilience capital requirement[285] (calculated in accordance with INSPRU 3.1.9G to 3.1.26R) (the RCR).

  (a) The BCRR is €2·2 million for general business and €3·2 million for long-term business (or other amounts depending on the type of insurer).[286]

  (b) The general insurance capital requirement ('GICR')[287] is the highest of:

    - the premiums amount[288] which is 18 per cent of gross adjusted premiums (which is the higher of the gross written and gross earned premiums as calculated and adjusted under INSPRU 1.1.56) less 2 per cent of the excess over €53·1 million multiplied by the reinsurance ratio (which is based on the ratio of net claims to gross claims over three years);
    - the claims amount[289] which is 26 per cent of the gross adjusted claims (as calculated and adjusted under INSPRU 1.1.57) amount less 3 per cent of the excess over €37·2 million multiplied by the reinsurance ratio; and
    - the brought forward amount.[290]

  (c) The long-term insurance capital requirement ('LTICR')[291] is the sum of the:

    - insurance death risk capital component;
    - insurance health risk and life protection reinsurance capital component;
    - insurance expense risk capital component; and
    - insurance market risk capital component (based on adjusted mathematical reserves).

  (d) The ECRLT is the sum of the LTCIR and the with-profits insurance capital requirement (calculated in accordance with the extensive and detailed rules and guidance at INSPRU 1.3).

Overall financial adequacy rule

The 'overall financial adequacy rule' ('OFAR') requires an insurer, at all times, to maintain overall financial resources, including capital resources and liquidity **16.276**

---

[284] GENPRU 2.1.24R.
[285] GENPRU 2.1.25R.
[286] GENPRU 2.1.30R.
[287] GENPRU 2.1.34R.
[288] INSPRU 1.1.45R.
[289] INSPRU 1.1.47R.
[290] INSPRU 1.1.51R.
[291] GENPRU 2.1.36R.

resources, which are adequate, both as to amount and quality, to ensure there is no significant risk that its liabilities will not be met as they fall due.[292] This is supported by the 'Overall Pillar 2 rule'.

Overall Pillar 2 rule[293]

16.277 The Overall Pillar 2 rule requires systems to assess and ensure sufficient resources are maintained based on a risk assessment. Key aspects of this rule are:

(a) It covers financial, capital and internal capital.

(b) The assessment covers the amount, type and distribution of those resources.

(c) The risk to be assessed is the risk of a failure to comply with:
   (i) OFAR and
   (ii) CRR.

(d) Risks to be identified and managed include credit, market, liquidity, operational, insurance, and other risks.

(e) Both the assessment and the process/systems used must be reviewed regularly.

16.278 **Scenario and stress testing.** As part of the Overall Pillar 2 rule, the general scenario and stress testing rule requires an insurer, for each of the major risks, to carry out stress tests and scenario analysis.[294] There is related additional guidance which explains the use of these forward looking analysis techniques to anticipate possible losses that might occur, if an identifiable risk crystallises, in order to test the adequacy of overall financial resources. Such analyses can provide a better understanding of the vulnerabilities that an insurer faces under extreme conditions for three purposes:[295]

- quantification of capital required on a 'what if' basis;
- review of risk model outputs particularly for non-linear effects of risk aggregation; and
- to explore sensitivities in longer term business plans and how capital needs may change over time.

16.279 There is further guidance on the use of stress tests and scenario analysis in relation to individual capital assessment (which involves higher confidence levels than the once in 25 years start point in this rule) and SYSC 11 relating to liquidity risk systems and controls.

---

[292] GENPRU 1.2.26R.
[293] GENPRU 1.2.30R.
[294] GENPRU 1.2.42R.
[295] GENPRU 1.2.66G.

Individual capital adequacy and assessment[296]

This is an additional regime which insurers must follow as part of the GENPRU   **16.280**
1.2 requirements relating to the assessment of risks to OFAR (it is therefore separate from the assessment of risk to CRR which is another part of Overall Pillar 2
rule—see above). Key aspects are:

(a) Individual capital assessment ('ICA') is risk-based assessment reflecting the
higher level requirements of OFAR.
(b) The ICA is focused on the capital elements of the OFAR; so a firm must first
consider whether capital is an appropriate mitigant for risks identified and
then consider the quality and amount of the capital it holds.
(c) INSPRU 7.1 sets out detailed requirements for an insurer to follow when
conducting an ICA.
(d) FSA assess whether the CRR—ie the minimum requirements of Pillar 1
derived from the CRR calculations above eg the claims and premium-based
calculations of the GICR—are sufficient for the individual firm in question.
In doing so, FSA considers/reviews—
   (i) the firm's own assessment of its capital needs ('ICA');[297]
   (ii) the process and systems used in the ICA;[298] and
   (iii) where relevant, the ECRGI (see para 16.283 below) will be a key part of
       the review.

Assessments that assets exceed liabilities over different time periods and confidence
levels[299]—

(i) benchmark of confidence level of 99.5 per cent over one year;
(ii) assessment according to firm's own model but detailed guidance given and
subject to FSA review.

After review of a firm's ICA, related information (such as ARROW risk assess-   **16.281**
ment) and other factors, such as the firm's wider risk management, the FSA gives
feedback and gives the firm individual capital guidance ('ICG') with reasons why
any capital add-ons identified were applicable. If an insurer does not accept this
guidance, it must inform FSA and the issues will normally be resolved through
analysis and discussion but ultimately FSA can vary an insurer's permission to
require the additional capital.[300]

The ICA may also be important in any application for a waiver from CRR   **16.282**
elements that are not directive requirements.

---

[296] Contained in INSPRU ch 7.
[297] INSPRU 7.1.
[298] ibid.
[299] INSPRU 7.1.42R *et seq.*
[300] INSPRU 7.1.91G *et seq.*

16.283 Enhanced capital requirement for general insurance ('ECRGI'). There is a rule requirement to calculate (but no absolute rule to meet) the ECRGI calculated in accordance with INSPRU 1.1.72 *et seq*. Key aspects of this requirement are:

(a) ECRGI is an indicative measure of the capital resources that an insurer may need to hold based on risk-sensitive calculations applied to its business profile and is used by the FSA as a benchmark for its consideration of the appropriateness of the firm's own capital assessment.

   (i) ECRGI is the sum of the
   - asset-related capital requirement (in accordance with INSPRU 2.2.10R *et seq*. which involves applying a stipulated ECR asset related capital charge factor (percentage of value) to specified assets and producing the total figure);
   - insurance related capital requirement ('IRCR'); and
   - the firm's equalisation provisions.

   (ii) IRCR addresses risk of adverse movements in a firm's liabilities, ie volatility in claims and technical provisions resulting from a wide range of sources both in relation to assets and insurance liabilities and of premiums from particular business not being sufficient to fund liabilities arising. It is calculated by multiplying the value of net written premiums and technical provisions in respect of each class of business by prescribed capital charge factors and adding these together.

   (iii) Additional market risk provisions relating to the assumed rate of interest used in calculating the present value of general insurance liabilities are contained in the insurance accounts rules and are outlined at INSPRU 3.1.27G.

(b) ECRGI assumes that the firm's business is well diversified and well managed, with good matching and controls and stable with no large, unusual, or high risk transactions; if this is not the case the ICA is likely to produce a higher capital requirement.

Reserves (technical provisions) and matching[301]

16.284 **Technical provisions** are on balance sheet provisions for liabilities under insurance contracts (and are therefore deducted from a firm's resources before CR, etc is calculated).[302]

16.285 For general insurance, these are established according to the general accounting rules applied by GENPRU (see para 16.290 below) and take into account the

---

[301] See INSPRU chapter 1.
[302] INSPRU 1.1.

expected ultimate outcome of claims including those not yet incurred and related expenses. It includes provisions for:

- outstanding claims,
- unearned premiums,
- unexpired risk, and
- equalisation provision (for which there are specific rules in INSPRU 1.4 for credit and non-credit equalisation provisions)—an allowance for smoothing claims for volatile claims (in business such as property, marine and aviation, nuclear, credit insurance and certain non-proportional reinsurance treaty business).

There are restrictions on discounting (ie discounting for the time value of money) **16.286** in order to protect against uncertainty in the timing of claims.[303]

For long-term insurance, in addition to provisions for liabilities that have fallen **16.287** due under general accounting standards, there are mathematical reserves calculated in accordance with the rules and guidance of INSPRU 1.2 and with due regard to generally accepted accounting practice—

(a) These are the main components of technical provisions for long-term business. They are a minimum and so alternative methods and assumptions may be used, subject to certain requirements and that these produce reserves equal to or greater than the INSPRU methodology.

(b) INSPRU 1.2 deals with—
    (i) the best valuation method;
    (ii) methods and assumptions;
    (iii) margins for adverse deviation;
    (iv) valuation of individual contracts;
    (v) negative mathematical reserves;
    (vi) avoidance of future valuation strain;
    (vii) cash flows to be valued; and
    (viii) valuation assumptions—detailed rules and guidance—on valuation rates of interest, future premiums, expenses, mortality and morbidity options, persistency assumptions, and reinsurance.

There are additional rules and guidance on the methodology to be used in relation to long-term insurance liabilities at INSPRU 3.1.28R to 3.1.48G.

Credit for Reinsurance. INSPRU 1.1.19 only allows credit for reinsurance based **16.288** on genuine risk transfer which is effective in all circumstances. This extends to analogous non-reinsurance financing arrangements and reinsurance with an ISPV

---

[303] INSPRU 1.1.14G.

(insurance special purpose vehicle). Guidance is given on the factors which will determine the effectiveness of risk transfer for these purposes (eg the legal enforce-ability in all relevant jurisdictions of the agreements and the potential impact of termination rights).

16.289 Credit make be taken in various different ways:

(a) Treating the reinsurer's share of technical provisions as an admissible asset.

(b) Reducing the solvency requirement in accordance with the deduction for reinsurance allowed in the calculation of the GICR.

(c) Bringing into account receivables under the contract when valuing cash flows under prospective valuation of mathematical reserves.

(d) See also credit risk in relation to reinsurance (see para 16.296 below).

16.290 Admissible assets[304] must be held to a value of at least—

  (i) technical provisions; and

 (ii) other general/long-term insurance liabilities.

    (a) For long-term business, the rules apply at a fund level for each with prof-its fund. There are additional requirements for a realistic basis life firm in this context.

    (b) Long-term assets must be held in a separate fund under INSPRU 1.5 (internal contagion risk).

Admissible assets must be localised ie generally held in an EEA State and must match liabilities in terms of—[305]

(a) safety, yield, and marketability;

(b) diversification and adequate spread;

(c) being of sufficient amount, appropriate currency, and term to ensure cash inflows from those assets will meet expected cash flows from the firm's insur-ance liabilities as they fall due. This permits some currency mismatching if sufficient excess assets are held. The level of mismatching is further restricted by INSPRU 3.1.52 *et seq.* which is based on an 80 per cent matching.

There is a prohibition on writing long-term business unless the firm is able to establish the necessary technical provisions, hold the admissible assets required, and meet the OFAR.

Accounting and valuation

16.291 The rules and guidance on how, when applying GENPRU and INSPRU, insurers should recognise and value assets, liabilities, exposures, and other items, are set out in GENPRU 1.3.

---

304 INSPRU 1.1.20R *et seq.*
305 INSPRU 1.1.34R *et seq.*

These include compliance with applicable requirements such as the insurance **16.292** accounts rules, Financial Reporting Standards and Statements of Recommended Accounting Practice and international accounting standards, and the Companies Acts.

Credit risk and related limits[306]

Overall limitation of credit risk.[307] An insurer must restrict its counterparty expo- **16.293** sures (including reinsurer exposures) and asset exposures to prudent levels and ensure that those exposures are adequately diversified. It can only take account of loss mitigation techniques (rights on default—set-off, collateral, charges—and third party rights, ie guarantees and credit insurance/derivatives—and reinsurance related rights—eg back up reinsurance such as 'top and drop' reinsurance), if it has good reason to believe they will be effective, which may require legal opinions.

Large exposure limits.[308] An insurer must limit counterparty or asset exposure **16.294** (but excluding re-insurance exposures and exposures to approved credit institu- tions) to a single counterparty/group or an assets/class, so that if a total default occurs, it will not become unable to meet its liabilities as they fall due.

Market risk and counterparty limits. Where a firm has assets in excess of market **16.295** risk and counterparty limits, as specified in INSPRU 2.1.22(3), a firm must deduct the excess from its assets as valued under GENPRU—this is a deduction from capital when calculating the CR (see para 16.273(c) second bullet above).

Large exposure calculation for reinsurance exposures.[309] Various obligations **16.296** arise if a reinsurance exposure to a reinsurer or group of closely related reinsurers is reasonably likely to exceed 100 per cent of the insurer's CR; these include noti- fication to FSA and the need to demonstrate how the reinsurance exposure is being safely managed. In addition there is an evidential provision restricting rein- surance concentration and credit risk—gross earned premiums paid to a reinsurer or reinsurer group are restricted to the higher of £4 million or 20 per cent of the firm's projected gross earned premiums for that financial year.

Market risk[310]

This is addressed in various ways, including: **16.297**

(i) the CCR—see para 16.275 above;
(ii) currency risk requirements—matching requirements described above and the requirements for cover to be held for a contract for the purchase or sale of foreign currency; and

---

[306] INSPRU 2.1.
[307] INSPRU 2.1.8R.
[308] INSPRU 2.1.20R.
[309] INSPRU 2.1.23R *et seq.*
[310] See INSPRU chapter 3.

(iii) requirements, for long-term business, to hold assets for coverage of property-linked liabilities and index-linked liabilities.

16.298 **Derivatives in insurance.** A derivative or quasi-derivative is approved (and so no deduction is required as an inadmissible asset and also in the context of permitted links) if it is:

(a) held for efficient portfolio management;

(b) covered; and

(c) on/under the rules of a regulated market or is off-market with an approved counterparty and on approved terms and capable of valuation.

Detailed rules and guidance are set out in INSPRU 3.2.

Other risk management—liquidity and operational risk

16.299 INSPRU contains additional detailed requirements for insurers for the management of liquidity ('INSPRU 4') and operational risk ('INSPRU 5').

16.300 In addition to the above provisions in GENPRU and INSPRU, there are extensive systems and controls requirements in SYSC (see para 16.188 above).

Internal contagion risk

16.301 The requirements in INSPRU 1.5 address internal contagion risks including risks from a firm carrying on:

(a) insurance and non-insurance risks;

(b) two or more different types of insurance;

(c) insurance activities of non-EEA insurers from offices or branches both within and outside the UK.

16.302 Insurers are prohibited from carrying on any commercial activity other than insurance business and activities directly arising from that business (see para 16.156 above). It must also limit, manage, and control its non-insurance activities so that there is no significant risk arising that it may be unable to meet its liabilities as they fall due. Financial penalties imposed by FSA cannot be paid from the long-term fund. There are specific requirements for property-linked funds.

16.303 Composites cannot use long-term insurance assets to meet general insurance liabilities (and these assets must be separately identified and maintained) and those assets are separated from shareholders' funds.

16.304 FSA cannot grant permission for a newly authorised composite or an existing insurer to become a composite (subject to certain limited exceptions).

16.305 There are requirements for certain non-EEA insurers relating to their worldwide financial resources and a UK (or EEA) MCR; there are also requirements for the localisation of assets and the deposit of assets as security.

Groups

Insurance groups. INSPRU 6 implements the Insurance Groups Directive **16.306** ('IGD') as amended by the Financial Groups Directive (and the RID). It contains the sectoral rules for insurance groups, insurance conglomerates, and insurers with participating interests in other insurers.

The requirements include: **16.307**

(a) INSPRU 6.1.8—The calculation of the group capital resources ('GCR') and the group capital resources requirement ('GCRR') for the ultimate insurance parent undertaking and (if different) the ultimate EEA insurance parent undertaking and for an insurer itself if, for example, it has a subsidiary which is an insurer or the insurer has a participation in another insurer. This reflects the IGD soft requirement. The GCRR is the sum of the individual CRRs of the relevant group companies.

(b) INSPRU 6.1.9—An insurer, as mentioned above, must maintain Tier 1 capital resources and Tier 2 capital resources, so that the insurer's GCR are equal to or exceed its GCRR (this is an adjusted solo calculation—it addresses potential double gearing).

(c) INSPRU 6.1.15—An insurer's CR are of such an amount that the GCR of its ultimate EEA insurance parent undertaking is equal to or exceeds the GCRR for that undertaking. This is a 'hard' requirement for an insurer to hold sufficient capital resources so that the group capital resources, are at least equal to the group capital resources requirement, which goes beyond the soft IGD requirement in (a) above. In addition, the adequacy of group capital resources is assessed by the insurer and by FSA and the insurer will carry out an assessment of the adequacy of their financial resources under the OFAR, the Overall Pillar 2 rule and GENPRU 1.2.39R. This will be reviewed by FSA and it may provide individual guidance on the amount and quality of capital resources and as to the appropriateness of the group capital resources requirement and group capital resources and FSA may give individual guidance on the capital resources a firm should hold in this context.

Cross sector/financial conglomerate groups. There are separate requirements **16.308** for financial conglomerates and mixed financial holding companies. Chapter 3 of GENPRU on cross-sector groups implements the Financial Groups Directive.

Financial reporting

Most of the old Interim Prudential Sourcebook for insurers ('IPRU(INS)') has **16.309** been replaced by INSPRU and GENPRU but there are still extensive requirements in IPRU(INS) relating to financial reporting by insurers.

Solvency II

16.310 The two main objectives of the new legislation are:

- to consolidate EU legislation on insurance; and
- to introduce modern prudential regulation of insurers across the EU.

Current status

16.311 Solvency II is a framework Lamfalussy-style directive which aims to create a harmonised system for risk-based prudential regulation. The European Commission published a proposal framework directive on 10 July 2007[311] and its slightly amended version in February 2008.[312] The proposed text of the Level 1 directive consolidates, with minor amendments, most of the existing insurance and reinsurance directives and it is anticipated that the final text will be agreed by the European Council and the European Parliament by the end of 2008.

16.312 The provisions in the Level 1 directive will be additionally supplemented by more detailed Level 2 implementation measures drawn up in accordance with the Lamfalussy process. At the moment, the Committee of European Insurance and Occupational Pensions Supervisors ('CEIOPS'), which is composed of authorities from Member States including the FSA, is drafting advice on Level 2 implementing measures and has conducted a number of quantitative impact studies ('QIS') to investigate whether the proposed requirements are necessary and appropriate. The third QIS was completed in 2007 with the final report published in November 2007. The fourth QIS began in April and ended in July 2008. CEIOPS is still finalising its findings following the fourth QIS and once it develops its final advice it will send it to the European Insurance and Occupational Pensions Committee ('EIOPC') and the European Commission.

16.313 As the Level 1 framework directive is still a draft, the Level 2 measures are still being developed, and the new regime does not come into force until 2012, what follows is a brief overview of the proposed legislation rather than a detailed consideration of the many issues currently being considered in relation to the various Solvency II texts and the consultations, calls for evidence, and quantative impact studies.

Scope and consolidation

16.314 The framework directive will apply to all life and non-life insurance undertakings and to reinsurance undertakings. It will consolidate and replace the main insurance directives—the CLD, the 3NLD, and the RID and related directives (14 in total

---

[311] Proposal for a Directive of the European Parliament and of the Council on the taking-up and pursuit of the business of Insurance and Reinsurance (SOLVENCY II) 2007/0143 (COD).

[312] Amended Proposal for a Directive of the European Parliament and of the Council on the taking-up and pursuit of the business of Insurance and Reinsurance (SOLVENCY II) 2007/0143 (COD).

including those relating to insurance groups, winding up of insurance undertakings, legal expenses, tourist assistance, and co-insurance). It does not consolidate the motor vehicle directives nor does it change the regime applicable to financial conglomerates. The text of the existing directives has been amended by a large number of amendments and deletions, but these are not intended to be of a substantive nature, except for those relating to the new solvency regime.

The new solvency provisions are principles-based and adopt the Lamfalussy structure; the main framework directive gives implementing powers to the Commission, which is assisted by EIOPC; the national regulators, in the form of CEIOPS, have a major role including responding to mandates from the Commission.   **16.315**

The new solvency regime

As already mentioned, Solvency II is based on the three pillars of: **16.316**

- Pillar 1—minimum capital requirements (harmonised standards for the valuation of assets and liabilities, and the calculation of capital requirements);
- Pillar 2—supervisory review process (to help ensure that insurers have good monitoring and management of risks, and adequate capital); and
- Pillar 3—market discipline and disclosure (requirements that allow capital adequacy to be compared across institutions).

Under the existing EU regime, insurers are subject to requirements relating to technical provisions and a regulatory capital requirement. The main solvency requirement is the Required Minimum Margin ('RMM') although this is subject to an absolute minimum—the Minimum Guarantee Fund ('MGF').   **16.317**

As explained above, the UK has already anticipated some of the broad approaches in Solvency II with the introduction of requirements over and above the current EU requirements in the insurance directives and Solvency I;[313] these include tiered approach to capital resources in common with the Basel rules for banks, Pillar 2 requirements, individual capital assessment (including a 'soft' Enhanced Capital Requirement calculation for general insurers), FSA review of ICAs, and ICG from FSA.   **16.318**

Solvency II capital requirements will be based on: **16.319**

- a Minimum Capital Requirement (MCR)—the minimum level of regulatory capital;
- a Solvency Capital Requirement (SCR)—a risk-based level of regulatory capital;
- adjusted SCR—SCR including any supplemental capital requirement determined through the Pillar 2 supervisory review.

---

[313] The latest material from UK authorities at the time of writing includes: FSA FS08/4, 'Review of the interaction of our solo and group capital requirements—Feedback on DP07/5'; and HMT's 'Solvency II: a partial Impact Assessment' (June 2008).

16.320 The SCR is a more flexible and risk-sensitive analysis that the MCR; an insurer will either use a standard formula to determine its SCR or it can use its own internal model. The use of an internal model will have to be approved by the regulator according to criteria. Failure to maintain the SCR (which will be higher than the MCR) represents the first regulatory intervention point.

16.321 Insurers will be subject to broad Pillar 2 requirements in relation to risk management including an Own Risk and Solvency Assessment ('ORSA'). This will include a Supervisory Review Process ('SRP') which may result in supplementary capital requirements within an adjusted SCR. Adjusted SCRs may be less common than ICG under the current UK regime.

16.322 Pillar 3 requirements provide for an enhanced regime for the publication and disclosure of information about the insurer's regulatory capital position. The may extend to the amount of the SCR (and any enhanced SCR) and any non-compliance with it; currently in the UK the ICG/ECR is not published and there are concerns about the publication of the SCR information because it may then effectively replace the MCR as the absolute minimum and any non-compliance could cause a run on the insurer.

16.323 One of the most important and controversial areas relates to the supervision of groups. The industry and the UK favour a regime which would enhance the role of the group supervisor, ie the supervisor in the EEA State which was the main country of the group. The original idea was that the SCR would only have to be met at the group level, so other insurers in the group in other States would only have to meet the MCR on a solo basis under the rules of that State. This would mean that the insurance group could deal with its group regulator (and not have to deal with various regulators in different countries with split responsibilities) in relation to SCR, internal model approvals, and any Adjusted SCR. It would also mean that full account could be taken of diversification across the group, contagion risks, and intra-group capital and reinsurance arrangements. It appears, however, that this principle is being watered down in order to get consensus among Member States; it seems likely that the SCR may, potentially, be applicable at EU group, national sub-group, and solo levels. However, the group regulator will have an enhanced role, for example in relation to internal model approval.

16.324 Under Solvency II, capital will be divided into three tiers (reflecting the Basel approach for banks) with further sub-divisions. For example ancillary elements (as distinct from basic elements) in Tiers 2 and 3 can only be used with regulatory approval. Letters of credit will be included for the first time. Technical provisions (ie the reserves for insurance liabilities which must be held before capital is measured) will be based on a current exit value (the expected payment to secure an immediate transfer to another insurer) and will include a margin in addition to this estimate of liabilities.

Prudential standards—insurance intermediaries

Capital resources

The capital requirements for insurance intermediaries are set out in MIPRU 4.2.   **16.325**
These apply to an FSA authorised firm which carries on insurance mediation
activities. They do not apply to various firms, including a Lloyd's managing agent,
a bank, building society, a solo consolidated subsidiary of a bank or building society, an insurer or a friendly society, or a firm which carries on designated investment business only. For firms carrying on designated investment business the
higher of MIPRU 4.2 or IPRU(INV) applies.[314] (MIPRU 4.2 does not reflect the
capital requirements for insurance intermediaries in the IMD because the UK
chose other means to implement Article 4.4 of the IMD on the basis that the IMD
capital requirements were unnecessarily high.)[315] The capital resources requirements ('CRR') for insurance intermediaries are as follows:

* For a firm which does not hold client money or other client assets in relation to
  insurance mediation activity it is the higher of £5,000 and 2.5 per cent of the
  annual income from its insurance mediation activity.

* For a firm which holds client money or other client assets in relation to insurance mediation activity it is the higher of £10,000 and 5 per cent of the annual
  income from its insurance mediation activity.

The CRR is calculated by reference to insurance income; so a 'secondary' interme-   **16.326**
diary with large non-insurance income and small insurance income would have a
relatively small CRR. However, the firm's capital resources are calculated by reference to the intermediary's entire business and assets. Losses of the non-insurance
business may therefore lead to a breach of the FSA's requirements and a need for
additional capital to maintain capital resources in excess of the CRR.

Professional indemnity insurance[316]

The professional indemnity requirements in MIPRU 3 apply to insurance and   **16.327**
reinsurance intermediaries only and not to insurers or managing agents.[317]
MIPRU 3.2 requires FSA authorised insurance intermediaries to take out and

---

[314] MIPRU 4.2.5.

[315] IMD, Art 4(4)(b). As noted at para 16.67 above, it is unusual to give Member States a choice
of this kind.

[316] For original consultation in this regard please see FSA PS174, 'Prudential and other requirements for mortgage firms and insurance intermediaries—Feedback on FSA CP174 and 'near
final' text'; FSA CP174, 'Prudential and other requirements for mortgage firms and insurance
intermediaries'.

[317] MIPRU 3 does not apply to an insurer, a managing agent, a firm to which IPRU(INV)
13.1.4(1) applies or an exempt CAD firm to which IPRU(INV) 9.2.5 applies (MIPRU 3.1.1(5)).

maintain professional indemnity insurance which covers its insurance mediation activity from the date of authorisation and which:[318]

(i) provides a minimum level of cover of €1 million for each single claim and €1.5 million or, if higher, 10 per cent of annual income in aggregate (up to €30 million);

(ii) (for firms with the ability to hold client money) provides an excess which is less than the higher of £5,000 and 3 per cent of annual income (subject to a higher excess where additional capital is held up to a maximum of £200,000);

(iii) covers claims for which the firm may be liable as a result of its own conduct or the conduct of its employees and/or its appointed representatives (acting within the scope of their appointment as the firm's appointed representatives in performing insurance mediation activity);

(iv) covers Financial Ombudsman awards made against the firm in connection with its insurance mediation activity; and

(v) covers costs of legal assistance in relation to clauses (iii) and (iv) above.

16.328 'Annual income' is the annual income given in the firm's most recent annual financial statement from insurance mediation activities, ie all brokerage, fees, commissions, and other related income due to the firm in respect of or in relation to those activities. Annual income includes amounts due to appointed representatives in respect of insurance mediation activities for which the firm has accepted responsibility.

16.329 In relation to insurance mediation activity, the professional indemnity insurance described above is not required by a firm if it can obtain a 'comparable guarantee'[319] from another authorised person with net tangible assets of more than £10 million. Where there is another authorised person with net tangible assets of more than £10 million within the group of the relevant firm, then the guarantee must come from that person.

Other requirements

Competence—MIPRU 2.3 and TC

16.330 In this section we look at the application of TC, MIPRU 2.2, and MIPRU 2.3 to insurers and insurance intermediaries.

16.331 MIPRU 2.3.1 R (which implements Article 4(2) of the IMD and applies to intermediaries) imposes general requirements relating to knowledge and ability and

---

[318] MIPRU 3.2.4R; MIPRU 3.2.12R.
[319] MIPRU 3.1.1R.

good repute to the firm's management and staff involved in insurance. This requirement extends to insurance intermediaries' appointed representatives.[320]

In addition, the FSA's approved persons regime requires persons performing con- **16.332**
trolled functions such as senior managers and directors (including non-executive directors) and certain advisers to be individually registered as 'approved persons'. For insurers and insurance intermediaries carrying on insurance mediation activities in relation to non-investment insurance contracts the relevant control-led functions are governing functions, required functions (the apportionment and oversight function is the only relevant applicable function), systems and con-trols functions, and significant management functions, as appropriate. For sec-ondary insurance intermediaries the only relevant function is the apportionment and oversight function (so only one approved person is required). MIPRU 2.2.1 provides that an insurance intermediary must allocate the responsibility for the firm's insurance mediation activity to a director or senior manager. All firms there-fore have to have at least one individual who is individually regulated by the FSA and subject to the FSA's Statements of Principle and Code of Practice for approved persons as set out in APER. For all other FSA authorised firms there are customer functions (eg investment adviser function). The customer functions have no application to non-investment insurance business but do apply to designated investment business. SUP 4 requires a number of firms, including all long-term insurers, to appoint an actuary which must be an approved person.

TC 1 imposes general, high-level commitments[321] to training and competence **16.333**
which apply to every firm—including insurers and insurance intermediaries. TC 2 contains detailed rules and guidance applicable to certain activities carried out by regulated firms.[322] The application of TC 1 and TC 2 to designated invest-ment is explained in Chapter 12. TC applies to employees of insurers or interme-diaries who give advice on non-investment insurance business for a consumer.

Use of unregistered intermediaries—MIPRU 5

The purpose of MIPRU 5 is to implement Article 3.6 of the IMD in relation to **16.334**
insurance undertakings.

---

[320] In determining a person's knowledge and ability, the firm should have regard to whether the person has demonstrated by experience and training that he is or will be able to perform duties related to the firm's insurance mediation activity and satisfies the FSA's training and competence requirements. In considering a person's 'good repute' a firm must ensure that the person has not been convicted of any serious criminal offences linked to crimes against property or other crimes related to financial activities (other than spent convictions under the Rehabilitation of Offenders Act 1974 or any other national equivalent), and has not been adjudged bankrupt unless the bankruptcy has been discharged.
[321] TC 1.
[322] TC 2.

16.335   MIPRU 5.2.1–5.2.2[323] requires insurers to ensure that, in relation to a person whose insurance mediation services they are using, that person has either permission to carry on such activities (ie a Part IV permission from the FSA) or is exempt—(such as an appointed representative) or is a registered insurance intermediary in another EEA State or does not carry on these activities in the EEA. This can be confirmed, for example, by checking the FSA register if the person is a UK incorporated entity or is resident in the UK or by checking the relevant register of that person's home State regulator, if it is a non-UK based person.

Cross-border business

EEA insurers and intermediaries

16.336   Overseas firms may become authorised in the UK under FSMA by:

- exercising single market directive rights;
- exercising treaty rights; or
- applying to the FSA for authorisation.

16.337   For EEA firms which have single market directive rights (including insurers under CLD, 3NLD, reinsurers under RID, and insurance intermediaries under the IMD), the use of the 'passport procedure' is compulsory for activities falling within the scope of the relevant directive. The different procedural requirements for insurers and insurance intermediaries are set out in Schedule 3 to FSMA and in the FSA Handbook at SUP Chapter 13A. Notifications are made to the home State regulator and then passed on to the FSA.[324]

16.338   An EEA firm which is not covered by a single market directive[325] or which is conducting an activity outside the scope of a directive may have treaty rights based on its home State authorisation and home State regulatory regime where it affords

---

[323] For original consultation in this regard see FSA CP174: 'Prudential and other requirements for mortgage firms and insurance intermediaries'; FSA PS174: 'Prudential and other requirements for mortgage firms and insurance intermediaries—Feedback on CP174 and "near final" text'.

[324] General requirements set out in Sched 3 paras 19 and 20 of FSMA. In order to qualify for rights to establish a branch or provide services into the UK the insurer must be an 'EEA firm' set out in Sched 3 para 5 to FSMA and SUP 13A.2.1; SUP 13A.3.1. General conditions for establishing a branch: Sched 3 paras 12–13 to FSMA: SUP 13A.4.1. General conditions for provision of services: Sched 3, paras 12–14 to FSMA: SUP 13A.5.3. Consent notice requirements for establishing a branch: given in CLD and First Non-life Directive. Consent notice requirements for provision of services: reg 3(3) of the Financial Services and Markets Act (EEA Passport Rights) Regulations 2001.

[325] Before the implementation of the RID, Treaty rights were potentially relevant to 'pure' reinsurers which then fell outside the Single Market Directives. Where the home State already required such reinsurers to be authorised and equivalence could be demonstrated, Treaty rights could be exercised. Pure reinsurers however, can now 'passport' under the RID and do not need to rely on Treaty rights.

equivalent protection to the UK regime. The procedure for exercising treaty rights is set out in Schedule 4 of FSMA and in SUP Chapter 13A.[326]

UK insurers and intermediaries

A firm applying for authorisation as an insurer or intermediary will effectively **16.339** exercise passport rights (services and branch) as part of its application to the FSA. Thereafter it will need to follow the procedure in Schedule 3 of FSMA and SUP 13 before undertaking (for the first time) services business or establishing a branch in a Member State. These procedures and the timetables reflect the directive requirements. Notifications are made to the FSA. The notification for the establishment of a branch of an insurer requires much more information; minimal information is required for intermediary notifications, even for establishing a branch.[327]

Appointed representatives

An appointed representative undertaking insurance mediation is regarded as a **16.340** registered intermediary under the IMD (see para 16.143 above). It is therefore able to exercise the IMD passport (on a services or branch basis). Under SUP 13, the representative cannot give the requisite notification directly to the FSA; the notification must be made by the principal (ie the authorised insurer or intermediary) which has appointed the representative.[328] It is not entirely clear how appointed representative status operates in all the other Member States; appointed representatives cannot 'passport' under any of the other single market directives.

The regulation of the Lloyd's insurance market

The structure of the Lloyd's market is unusual; regulation of Lloyd's has evolved **16.341** since the difficulties which it experienced and the subsequent market reforms in the 1990s. EU legislation recognises 'the Association of Underwriters known as Lloyd's' as a form of permissible insurance undertaking but does not generally make specific provision for the unusual structure of Lloyd's. It is therefore the responsibility of the UK to ensure that the regulation of Lloyd's satisfies the requirements of the EU insurance directives (and there have been challenges in the past as to whether the UK has correctly implemented the European legislation as it applies to Lloyd's).

---

[326] Sched 4, para 3(1) to FSMA: SUP 13A.3.4; SUP 13A.3.5; SUP 13A.3.6; SUP 13A.3.7.

[327] Notification requirements for intermediaries (contrast with requirements for insurers in n 3 above): EEA Firms passporting in: SUP 13A.4.2; SUP 13A.4.4; SUP 13A.5.3; SUP 13A.5.4; UK Firms passporting out: SUP 13.3.2A; SUP 13.3.4(1); SUP 13.3.5(1)(c); SUP 13.4.2(3); SUP 13.4.3(4); SUP 13.4.4(2A).

[328] SUP 13.3.2B; SUP 13.4.2A.

16.342   A full review of the complex structure of Lloyd's and the regulatory regime that applies to it under FSMA and the Lloyd's Acts falls outside the scope of this book. This section however gives a brief overview.

16.343   The key participants or entities are:

- the Society of Lloyd's;
- members of Lloyd's—individual members and corporate members which accept risks and contract as insurers via a syndicate;
- managing agents (which effectively act as agents for syndicates of members);
- members' advisers—corporate advisers and managing agents (who advise members);
- Lloyd's brokers;
- the Council of Lloyd's (which is the governing body of the Society and which has various roles under the Lloyd's legislation); and
- the franchise board (to which certain functions have been delegated, and which impose requirements on individual Lloyd's market participants in the interests of the 'franchise' as a whole).

16.344   The most unusual feature of Lloyd's is its hybrid role—part insurance undertaking and part insurance market (with competing underwriters within it insuring different risks). The EU legislation treats the Society of Lloyd's (or the Association of Underwriters) as an insurance undertaking; indeed, the Society is authorised under FSMA. All policies underwritten at Lloyd's are supported by the 'Central Fund' which all members are liable to pay into and which will be available to pay claims on a policy if a member which underwrote that policy becomes insolvent. This is very different from the so-called 'company market' in London where insurance companies do not guarantee each other's solvency. In many respects, however, Lloyd's does operate as a market (rather than a single underwriter) with underwriters competing for business. Individual risks are not underwritten by the Society; they are underwritten by a member or particular members (grouped together in a syndicate). There are other unusual aspects to Lloyd's; for example, mediating on the transfer of underwriting capacity at Lloyd's is a regulated activity under FSMA (see para 16.111 *et seq.* above). Another complexity was that previously, Lloyd's operated its accounting on a three-year rather than an annual basis.

16.345   The structure of Lloyd's has therefore represented something of a challenge in terms of regulation. The different mechanics by which regulation (both EU and domestic) is applied to market participants is somewhat complex. The general trend has been to increase FSA supervision and oversight and to reduce freestanding 'self-regulation' within the market.

16.346   Lloyd's brokers, managing agents, members' advisers, and the Society of Lloyd's itself conduct regulated activities under FSMA and are authorised; the members themselves do not need to be authorised to underwrite business at Lloyd's. Section 316 of FSMA provides that the general prohibition or a 'core provision'[329] only applies to the carrying on of an insurance market activity by a member of the Society, if the FSA so directs. The FSA has not directed that members need to be authorised.

The FSA has, however, directed that certain core provisions apply (for example the compulsory jurisdiction of the FOS under section 266 of FSMA), and, in relation to financial requirements, directions have been given concerning the central fund and the application of GENPRU in order to require members to maintain adequate financial resources (directions are given under section 318 and are marked in the margin of the FSA Handbook with the letter 'D'). FSA requirements are applied to the Lloyd's market in various other ways. For example, Chapter 8 of INSPRU (see para 16.269 *et seq.* above) contains general provisions applying INSPRU and GENPRU to Lloyd's.[330] In relation to certain requirements applied to insurers, the Society is required to manage members' funds, central assets, and to supervise the insurance business carried on by each member, so as to achieve the same effect as the requirements have as applied to an authorised firm. Some requirements are applied to managing agents in the same way in relation to their management of syndicate assets and of the insurance business carried on by the members of the syndicate through that syndicate. There are also special requirements relating to Lloyd's, including requirements for the capacity transfer market, the central fund, future underwriting members, risk management, reinsurance to close and trust funds. Managing agents are also treated as a proxy for the insurer under ICOBS (see para 16.205 et seq. above) and therefore generally have to comply with the ICOBS rules applicable to insurers. **16.347**

For Conduct of Business Rules, Lloyd's brokers are regulated directly by the FSA and are subject to exactly the same FSA requirements and rules as non-Lloyd's brokers (see the background to the regulation of Lloyd's at para 16.341 et seq. above). **16.348**

At the time of writing, the Lloyds Act 1982 is being amended to remove the general requirement (already subject to a variety of exemptions) that managing agents only accept insurance business from or through a Lloyd's broker. The Legislation Reform (Lloyd's) Order 2008 will also remove the previous prohibition on certain links between managing agents and Lloyd's brokers. **16.349**

---

[329] The core provisions are FSMA Parts V, X, XI, XII, XIV, XV, XVI, XXII, and XXIV, ss 384–386 and Part XXVI (s 317, FSMA).

[330] There was previously a separate sourcebook: 'Lloyd's (LLD)' but this was replaced at the end of 2006.

UK Regulation—FOS and the FSCS

The Financial Ombudsman Service

16.350 The Financial Ombudsman Service ('FOS') is covered in Chapter 7. The work of the FOS is divided into different areas, one of which deals with complaints (by eligible complainants) involving insurance. (The Insurance Ombudsman Bureau ('IOB'), along with several other financial services ombudsman schemes, was incorporated to form the FOS at N2.) The jurisdiction of the FOS is divided into compulsory[331] and voluntary[332] jurisdictions. Voluntary jurisdiction covers firms which are not covered by the compulsory jurisdiction, but choose to participate in the FOS scheme by contractual agreement with the FOS.[333]

16.351 UK authorised insurers and insurance intermediaries and UK branches of EEA insurers and intermediaries are subject to the FOS's compulsory jurisdiction (which includes responsibility for complaints concerning their appointed representatives). Pre–NGI, insurance intermediaries and brokers selling general insurance contracts could agree to come under the voluntary jurisdiction of the FOS. Under the GISC rules, in the absence of FOS voluntary jurisdiction, intermediaries were generally subject to GISC's dispute resolution scheme for complaints relating to general insurance contracts.

16.352 An important feature of the FOS regime is that it allows eligible complainants to pursue a complaint at no cost to themselves. In addition, the FOS will determine a complaint by reference to what is, in its opinion, fair and reasonable in all the circumstances of the case. Importantly, the FOS is not bound by the law; it is required only to take account of the law and will determine what, in its opinion, were the applicable standards at the time. The FOS may make awards for policyholders against either insurers or intermediaries, and its jurisdiction can pre-date FSA regulation. For example, where an intermediary was a member of the old GISC regime prior to 14 January 2005, the FOS can make an award against that firm in relation to a sale which took place before FSA regulation of the sale of general insurance began. This has been particularly relevant recently in the context of complaints about the sales of payment protection insurance.

16.353 The FOS is in a position to see industry or product-specific issues arising from the complaints it receives across a number of firms. As a result, the FOS may decide to refer an issue to the 'wider implications process' where it considers there to be a new issue which affects a large number of customers or firms, the financial

---

[331] FSMA, s 226.
[332] ibid, s 227.
[333] DISP 4.

integrity of a firm, the interpretation of FSA rules or guidance, or a common industry practice. (The FOS may also consider the implications in any one case to be of sufficient importance that the FSA's attention should be drawn to it.)

The significance of the wider implications process is that the FSA becomes **16.354** involved and, if it considers it appropriate to do so, the FSA may ask the Treasury to authorise an industry-wide review under section 404 of FSMA. Under section 404 of FSMA, the Treasury has the power to authorise the FSA to establish a scheme for reviewing past business if it is satisfied that there is evidence suggesting that there has been widespread or regular failure on the part of authorised firms to comply with the rules relating to a particular kind of activity and, as a result, private persons have suffered loss in respect of which authorised firms are liable to make payments. Firms are required to comply with such a scheme in order to establish the nature and extent of the failure, the liability of the firms, and the amounts payable by way of compensation.

The Financial Services Compensation Scheme

The Financial Services Compensation Scheme[334] ('FSCS') was established under **16.355** FSMA and provides compensation to eligible claimants where authorised persons (or appointed representatives, but not necessarily EEA firms)[335] fail.[336] (see further at Chapter 7). The FSCS replaced the previous regime under the Policyholders Protection Acts 1975 and 1997. As well as paying compensation, the FSCS also has the power to replace long-term insurance cover. The previous separate schemes within the FSCS for insurers, deposit-takers, and investment firms have effectively been merged, so that there is now potential cross-funding in terms of levy liabilities.

The rules governing the operation of the FSCS are set out in COMP (see Chapter **16.356** 7 above). As mentioned at para 16.60 bullet point 8 above, there is currently no EU legislation requiring or regulating compensation schemes to protect policyholders when insurers become insolvent (whereas for credit institutions and investment firms there is EU legislation which is implemented in the UK through COMP). The Commission is now working on proposals and has published working papers.[337]

---

[334] FSMA, s 213(10).
[335] ibid, s 213(1).
[336] ibid, s 213.
[337] Working paper MARKT/2534/05.

17

Introduction

Investment funds and collective investment schemes

Investment funds,[1] where participants pool financial resources and abdicate man- **17.01** agement decisions to others, invite particular regulatory treatment. FSMA imposes a special regulatory regime on those funds that fall within its wide defini- tion of 'collective investment scheme' (or CIS).[2] In particular, the Act restricts the promotion of such schemes and regulates various other activities in relation to them.[3] This chapter therefore devotes some space to an examination of the defini- tion of a CIS before considering that regime. It will be seen that the definition of CIS covers almost all types of investment funds with the exception of: schemes that take the form of a body corporate other than that of an 'open-ended invest- ment company' ('OEIC'—again as defined in FSMA[4]) or of a limited liability partnership ('LLP').[5] Hence investment companies[6] and investment trusts[7] are not covered, the rationale being that company law and the Listing Rules[8] provide adequate protection. This exclusion was called into question by the 'Splits' saga,[9] but the response was a tightening of, inter alia, the Listing Rules[10] applicable to them rather than a withdrawal of the exclusion.

---

[1] For a comparison between the position in the UK and US, see Spangler, *The Law of Private Investment Funds* (2008).

[2] See para 17.08 *et seq* below.

[3] See para 17.124 *et seq* below.

[4] See para 17.61 *et seq* below.

[5] See para 17.52 below.

[6] Within Companies Act 2006, s 833.

[7] See Income Taxes Act 2007, ss 276–277.

[8] See Chapter 18, below.

[9] Examined in the FSA's publications: (i) 'Split Capital Closed-Ended Funds' (DP10, Dec 2001), (ii) 'Split Capital Investment Trusts ("Splits")' (PS, May 2002).

[10] And Conduct of Business Rules applicable to FSA authorised persons, preceded by FSA CP164, 'Investment Companies (including Investment Trusts): Proposed Changes to the Listing Rules and Conduct of Business Rules' (January 2003).

17.02 Although it was the rise of the unit trust in the 1930s that prompted the first regulatory intervention in the UK,[11] the Financial Services Act 1986 first defined 'collective investment scheme'[12] widely and introduced a comprehensive regulatory regime for all such schemes. That approach has been followed in FSMA, which re-adopted that definition almost verbatim.

The European dimension and OEICs

The UCITS Directives

17.03 One of the first EC (as it then was) 'single market' initiatives was the attempt to create a single market for open-ended retail investment funds—or rather UCITS, an acronym for 'undertakings for collective investment in transferable securities'. As a result of the UCITS Directive[13] Member States had to adopt harmonised rules regulating such UCITSs, their management companies, and how units were promoted to the public. In particular, UCITSs must have both a 'depositary' safeguarding the assets and a separate management company with circumscribed powers of investment and borrowing, and investors must have access to detailed information about the scheme. The UCITS Directive then provides the management company with a 'single market passport', enabling it to market the UCITS elsewhere in the EEA, after giving due notice to the home and host regulators, and only needing to comply with the host State's marketing rules and to maintain certain facilities for investors in that State.[14] The UCITS Directive has been amended, most recently[15] by the so-called 'Product Directive'[16] and the 'Management Directive',[17] the revised regime being known as UCITS III.[18] Most notably, UCITSs

---

[11] The Prevention of Fraud (Investments) Act 1939, replaced by the 1958 Act of the same name. For a study of the unit trust, see Kam Fan Sin, *The Legal Nature of the Unit Trust* (1997).

[12] The definition reflected the US case of *SEC v W J Howey Co* (1946) 328 US 293; 66 S CT 1100; 90 L Ed 2d 1244 where the definition of 'security' in the (US) Securities Act of 1933, s 2(1) was said to connote four characteristics: (a) the investment of money (b) in a common enterprise (c) with an expectation of profits (d) solely from the efforts of others. See also Arden LJ in *FSA v Fradley and Woodward* [2005] EWCA Civ 1183, [3]: 'at the heart of the [CIS] concept is the requirement for the sharing of profit or income by participants who do not have day-to-day control over the management of the property'.

[13] Directive 85/611/EEC, [1985] OJ L 375/03, as subsequently amended, see below.

[14] See the Commission Interpretative Communication on the respective powers retained by the Home Member State and the Host Member State in the marketing of UCITS pursuant to Section VIII of the UCITS Directive (Com (2007) 112).

[15] See also the previous amendments made by Directive 88/220 [1988] OJ L100/31 and Directive 95/26 [1995] OJ L168/07.

[16] Directive 2001/108 [2002] OJ L41/35.

[17] Directive 2001/107 [2002] OJ L41/20.

[18] It came into force on 13 February 2004. See Rouch and Smith 'The UCITS Directive and the Single European Funds Market: A Case Review', [2005] JIBLR 251.

can now invest in a wider range of investments than 'transferable securities' (including certain units in other funds, money market instruments, deposits, and derivatives). Thus the term 'UCITS' (in referring to funds investing in 'transferable securities') is no longer entirely apposite to describe these funds—although the name is probably too well entrenched to be abandoned. A major overhaul of the UCITS Directive is likely, at the earliest by mid-2011.[19]

As will be noted below, the UCITS regime is implemented by FSMA and the FSA **17.04** Handbook. As a result, provision is made for the automatic 'recognition' (after notification) of UCITSs constituted and regulated in other EEA Member States so that they may be marketed in the same way as domestic authorised funds.[20] And UK schemes that satisfy the UCITS Directive requirements are similarly able to market elsewhere in the EEA.[21]

UK Open-Ended Investment Companies (OEICs)

The advent of the UCITS Directive provided the final impetus for the introduc- **17.05** tion in the UK of open-ended investment companies ('OEICs').[22] The creation of OEICs was not possible under the then existing UK company law, as the capital maintenance doctrine restricted the extent to which registered companies could be 'open-ended' in buying or redeeming their own shares. Nor was there any particular need for such investment vehicles domestically, as the unit trust was available. However, the open-ended corporate vehicle is the usual form taken by retail investment funds elsewhere, especially in Europe[23] where the trust is largely an unknown concept. Hence the arguments for legislative change to enable a UK form of OEIC to be established became overwhelming in the face of fears that the unfamiliarity of the unit trust would put it at a competitive disadvantage in the single market and beyond.

As the introduction of OEICs could be regarded as an aspect of the implementa- **17.06** tion of the UCITS Directive, the requisite (substantial) legislative changes were initially effected by Regulations made under the European Communities

---

[19] See (i) The Green Paper on the enhancement of the EU Framework for Investment Funds (COM (2005) 314, final), 12 July 2005; (ii) The White Paper on enhancing the Single Market Framework for Investment Funds (COM (2006) 686, final), 15 November 2006; (iii) Proposal for new UCITS Directive (COM (2008) 458/3), 16 July 2008.

[20] See paras 17.108 and 17.137 below.

[21] See paras 17.88 and 17.97.

[22] See Lomnicka, 'Open-ended Investment Companies—A new bottle for old wine' in EB Rider, *The Corporate Dimension* (1998).

[23] For example, the SICAV (société d'investissement à capital variable).

Act 1972.[24] However, this was a short-term expedient because those Regulations could only provide for OEICs (in fact termed 'investment companies with variable capital'—ICVCs—the name still used for a UK OEIC)[25] that satisfied the directive and hence that could only invest in a narrower category of investments than retail domestic unit trusts. The enactment of FSMA presented the opportunity of placing UK OEICs on the same legislative footing as domestic unit trusts. This was done, not by incorporating the OEIC provisions into the statute itself alongside the unit trust provisions, but by conferring wide powers on the Treasury to issue new OEIC Regulations.[26] Thus the regime for UK OEICs remains in a statutory instrument.

Basic Definitions

General

17.07 Both FSMA and the FSA Handbook Glossary contain (sometimes very detailed) definitions of the terms used in CIS regulation. The FSA Handbook on the whole adopts the FSMA definitions[27] but often expands them and adds new terminology of its own. This section will consider the FSMA definitions of three basic terms.

Definition of 'Collective Investment Scheme' (CIS): FSMA, section 235

The core definition

General

17.08 The term 'collective investment scheme' (or CIS) is defined in section 235 of FSMA.[28] The core statutory definition is very wide, so provision is made for the Treasury to narrow it by Order.[29] Each element of the core definition will be discussed, followed by a consideration of the Treasury CIS Order. The definition has been the subject of judicial consideration in two cases: *The Russell-Cooke Trust*

---

[24] s 2(2), see the Open-ended Investment Companies (Investment Companies with Variable Capital) Regulations 1996, SI 1996/2827.

[25] See para 17.96 below.

[26] See FSMA, s 262 and the Open-ended Investment Company Regulations 2001, SI 2001/1228, as amended, considered in para 17.97 below. For Northern Ireland, see the Open-ended Investment Company Regulations (Northern Ireland) 2004, SR 2004/335.

[27] But note that although the term 'depositary' is inapplicable to unit trust schemes when used in the Act (see s 237(2)—the 'trustee' being the term used in the context of unit trusts) in the FSA Handbook it covers the trustee of a unit trust scheme.

[28] It replaces, and is in almost identical terms to, the Financial Services and Markets Act 1986, s 75.

[29] s 235(5), see further, below.

Company v Elliot, (*The Russell-Cooke Trust Company*)[30] and *The Financial Services Authority v Fradley* (*Fradley*).[31]

'Arrangements'

The definition requires there to be 'arrangements' with certain characteristics. **17.09**
The term 'arrangements' is one with wide connotations[32] and therefore the scheme
may take any form or combination of forms. It may be corporate—although
companies other than OEICs and LLPs are excluded from the definition by the
Treasury CIS Order.[33] The arrangements may take the form of or include a trust
and hence unit trusts are covered. The arrangements may also be contractual and
hence partnerships are covered. In *The Russell-Cooke Trust Company* Laddie J
regarded the term 'arrangements' in the CIS definition as covering all the steps
undertaken, including the preliminary steps of placing investors' funds in a common account, and considered all the steps as a whole, seeing 'no justification for
dividing these arrangements into discrete parts'.

The core definition has no territorial limitation and thus where the 'arrangements' **17.10**
are made is irrelevant. However, the FSMA regulatory regime is territorially limited[34]
and therefore only activities 'in the UK' in relation to CISs are caught by it.

'With respect to property'

The 'arrangements' must be 'with respect to property of any description, includ- **17.11**
ing money'. Thus the underlying property may take any form. In particular, it
need not comprise 'specified investments' or even 'investments' as defined by
FSMA.[35] This point was confirmed in *The Russell-Cooke Trust Company* where the
underlying property was loans secured on land.[36] Normally, the contributions of

---

[30] 2001 WL 753378, on the identically worded Financial Services Act 1986, s 75, applied by
Lindsay J in *The Russell-Cooke Trust Co v Prentis* [2002] EWHC 2227 (Ch).

[31] [2005] EWCA 1183, noted by Omoyele (2007) 28 *Company Lawyer* 245. See also the subsequent proceedings for recovery of monies from the protagonists, for distribution to investors, noted
in the FSA's Press Release of 8 August 2008.

[32] See *Re Basic British Slag's Application* [1963] 1 WLR 727 (on 'arrangement' in the Restrictive
Trade Practices Act 1956, s 6(3)), recently applied in *Office of Fair Trading v Lloyds TSB Bank plc*
[2006] EWCA 268 in interpreting 'arrangements' in Consumer Credit Act 1974, s 187. In *FSA
v Fradley and Woodward* [2005] EWCA Civ 1183, Arden LJ at [33] referred to the discussion of
'arrangements' in the companies legislation in *Re Duckwari plc* [1999] Ch 235, 260, but declined to
discuss the width of the term in the s 235 context.

[33] See para 17.52 below.

[34] See para 17.124 and n 348 below.

[35] See s 22.

[36] Although rights under certain mortgages are now 'specified investments' (see the RAO,
art 88) this was not the case when *The Russell-Cooke Trust Company* was decided and, in any event,
the mortgages in that case would not have been 'specified investments'.

the participants will be used to acquire the underlying property, but it was con-firmed in *Fradley* that the 'property' may be the contributions themselves.[37]

17.12 However, the type of property involved may be important when it comes to the Treasury CIS Order exemptions, as some only apply in relation to arrangements if the property comprises certain types of assets (often certain 'specified investments').[38]

'Purpose or effect'

17.13 The 'arrangements' must satisfy a number of conditions. **First**, they must have a certain 'purpose or effect'. 'Purpose' suggests some subjective motive and looks to the intended effect—although it does not matter whether it is achieved or not. The alternative word 'effect' has purely objective connotations and looks to the actual result achieved. Thus the 'arrangements' must be intended to or must achieve a certain objective.

17.14 **Second**, the 'purpose or effect' of those arrangements must be 'to enable persons taking part in [them] (whether by becoming owners of the property or any part of it or otherwise)' to achieve the requisite objective. Such persons are termed 'par-ticipants'.[39] There are no restrictions on the way in which such persons may par-ticipate; the definition mentions the possibility that they may become owners of the property, or part of it, but then uses the general 'or otherwise'. Thus the con-ferment of purely contractual rights on 'participants' will suffice.

17.15 The use of the plural 'persons' makes it clear that a CIS must have more than one participant. After all, the definition pertains to 'collective' investment. This was confirmed by Laddie J in *The Russell-Cooke Trust Company*, although he held that as long as there was some initial commingling of contributions, the fact that funds representing the contribution of one investor were in fact used to invest in one iden-tifiable item of property (a particular mortgage secured on land) did not preclude a CIS arising: the contributions from a number of persons had been pooled for the purpose of communal investment, even though in fact one person's contribution was expended on one, identifiable item.[40] However, as long as the 'purpose or effect'

---

[37] The scheme was a CIS even though the contributions were used to place bets—which (at the time), being void gaming contracts, were held not to be 'property'. There was no appeal on this point from the first instance decision ([2004] EWHC 3008).

[38] See, especially, paras 1, 2, 3, 5, 8 of the Treasury CIS Order, considered below at paras 17.26–28, 17.32 and 17.35 below.

[39] FSMA, s 235(2). See further, para 17.53 below.

[40] But if, from the outset, the intention is that all the contributions be subsequently separate out and expended on one item of property per contributor, then a CIS would probably not arise in that (i) s 235(3), see below, would be unlikely to be satisfied, and (ii) in any event, the 'common account' exclusion in the Treasury CIS Order (SI 2001/1062, art 6, see para 17.33, below) would be likely to apply.

is that there is to be more than one participant, a CIS arises as soon as the first contribution is made.[41]

Third, the required 'purpose or effect' is again expressed in wide terms with a **17.16** number of (somewhat confusing) alternatives.[42] Its essence is the participation in profits or income arising from the underlying property. It may be broken down as follows. It is to enable the participants: either 'to participate in' or '[to] receive' either (a) 'profits or income' or (b) 'sums paid out of profits or income', in both cases those profits or income 'arising from the acquisition, holding, management or disposal of the property'. Thus the arrangements must envisage (or achieve) 'profits or income' (a phrase covering the alternatives of capital appreciation or revenue production), such profit or income arising from at least one of the following activities: the acquisition, holding, management, or disposal of the underlying property. This list is broad enough to cover any activity (and non-activity: 'holding') in relation to the underlying property. Moreover, the 'purpose or effect' of the arrangements must be for the participants either to 'participate in' or 'receive' that profit or income or sums paid out of the profit or income.

Section 235(2): No 'day-to-day control'

The essence of a CIS—and the reason why it is subject to special regulatory atten- **17.17** tion—is that participants abdicate control over their contributions to others.[43] Hence the participants must not have 'day-to-day control' over the 'management' of the property, although they may have 'the right to be consulted or to give directions'.[44] This requirement poses a number of difficulties. First, clearly the line between 'giving directions' and having 'day-to-day control' is not always easy to draw. As the intention is to include in the definition of CIS those schemes where the participants have surrendered control over their property to others, it would seem that 'day-to-day' control connotes actual, continuous control over the management of the property. Hence it seems clear that the term 'day-to-day' is not to be taken literally. Thus directions, which are not given daily but merely periodically, may still constitute 'day-to-day' control. On the other hand, some power to 'give directions' (such as shareholders usually have over directors by special resolution) does not take the arrangements out of the definition of CIS; it is only when that power is so extensive as to constitute effective control, that this condition ceases

---

[41] And see the future tense 'to participate in . . .', noted in para 17.21 below.

[42] The wording contains eight 'or's.

[43] But a participant who delegates 'day-to-day' control to an agent that is *independent of the operator* still retains 'day-to-day' control through his agent: confirmed in *FSA v Fradley and Woodward* [2005] EWCA Civ 1183, [46].

[44] FSMA, s 235(2).

to be satisfied. The issue therefore resolves itself into a difficult question of degree.[45] The FSA gives some guidance on how it interprets this requirement in the context of property investment clubs and schemes.[46]

17.18 Second, it is enough if *some* of the participants do not have 'day-to-day' control, as the gist of a CIS is the protection of those delegating managerial control to others. Thus this condition is not satisfied only if *all* the participants have 'day-to-day' control, as only then can it be said that 'those persons' (that is, all the participants) have day to 'day-to-day control'.[47] It follows that a limited partnership (under the Limited Partnerships Act 1907) satisfies this condition in that the limited partners leave management to the general partner. It also follows that if there are numerous participants (unless, perhaps, there is some system of majority voting on 'day-to-day' decisions with each participant having the opportunity to control decision-making if he can convince the others of his point of view) then this condition will necessarily be fulfilled.

17.19 Third, it seems clear that a court will look beyond the documentation and consider how the scheme operates in practice. As an Australian judge put it in relation to a similar requirement under Australian legislation, the regulatory regime 'would be easily defeated if the court felt obliged to rely solely upon a strict view of the legal rights and duties created by the documentation and was required to ignore the realities of the scheme as it is designed to operate in practice'.[48]

17.20 Fourth, it will be recalled that the definition of a CIS envisages arrangements, not only involving the 'management' of the property but alternatively the 'acquisition, holding [or] disposal' of property. Normally any arrangements with respect to property will reserve to those holding the property some powers of management, but if the nature of the arrangements is that custodians merely *hold* the property without more, there will be no 'management' and hence no question of any 'day-to-day' control over management.

17.21 Finally, the condition talks of 'the persons who are to participate' having no 'day-to-day control'. The use of the future tense indicates that the issue must be tested at the outset. As Laddie J said in *The Russell Cooke Trust Company*: 'it is relevant to consider not just what happens when the investment is in place but also whether

---

[45] The point was left open in *FSA v Fradley and Woodward* [2005] EWCA Civ 1183 [50]: 'it is not necessary to consider how regularly a client must actually exercise control for his control to constitute "day-to-day control" for the purposes of section 235(2)'.

[46] See its Handbook, PERG 11, especially FAQ 6–FAQ 11.

[47] See *The Russell-Cooke Trust Co*, confirmed in *FSA v Fradley and Woodward* [2005] EWCA Civ 1183.

[48] *Enviro Systems Renewable Resources Pty Ltd v ASIC* (2001) ACSR 762, per Marin J. The documents gave 'day to day' control to investors but in practice they were not expected to and did not exercise these rights. See (to the same effect) the FSA Handbook, PERG 11, FAQ 10.

the necessary control function is shouldered by those who *will be* contributing. Therefore the way the investment is promoted is relevant.'

Section 235(3): 'Pooling' and/or 'management as a whole'

The arrangements must have one or other or both of the characteristics set out in   **17.22**
section 235(3): either pooling[49] and/or 'management as a whole'.[50]

The 'pooling' alternative requires the participants' contributions *and* 'the profits or   **17.23**
income out of which payments are to be made' to be 'pooled'. Thus the contributions of the participants and the resulting profits or income must be aggregated.[51]
Subsection (4) provides for the case where there is pooling only in relation to separate parts of the property. Such arrangements are only to be considered as *one* CIS if the participants are entitled to exchange their rights in one part for rights in another part. Otherwise (presumably) the distinct, pooled parts may be separate CISs.

The second alternative (or cumulative) characteristic is that the property must be   **17.24**
'managed as a whole' by or on behalf of the 'operator' (a term partially defined, in relation only to unit trust schemes and open-ended investment companies).[52]
Two of the exemptions in the Treasury CIS Order apply (in certain circumstances) only if this alternative (and not 'pooling') is present.[53]

Exemptions

General

The section 235 core definition of a 'collective investment scheme' is an all-inclu-   **17.25**
sive one, which catches a wide variety of schemes for collective investment. Not all such schemes merit the regulatory treatment accorded to 'collective investment schemes' and hence the Treasury is given the power, by Order, to fine-tune the definition by excluding various types of arrangement[54] and arrangements in certain circumstances.[55] The relevant Order is the Financial Services and Markets Act 2000 (Collective Investment Schemes) Order 2001 (the Treasury CIS Order),[56]

---

[49] FSMA, s 235(3)(a).
[50] ibid, s 235(3)(b).
[51] This condition was held satisfied in *FSA v Fradley and Woodward* [2005] EWCA Civ 1183 where the participants' contributions were paid into a single bank account albeit in circumstances where the money was held on trust and each contribution identified.
[52] See para 17.59 below.
[53] FSMA, Sched, paras 1 and 2, see paras 17.26 and 17.27 below.
[54] ibid, s 235(5)(b).
[55] ibid, (5)(a).
[56] SI 2001/1062, as amended by SI 2001/3650, art 2; SI 2005/57; SI 2005/2114, Sched 16(1), para 3; SI 2006/1969, art 8(3); SI 2006/3384, art 36(2); SI 2007/800, art 2(2); SI 2008/1641, art 2; SI 2008/1813, art 2. Although s 235(5) enables the Treasury to decide which situations are regulated

and its Schedule lists 21 categories of 'arrangements not amounting to' a CIS. These exemptions either relate to schemes which are otherwise adequately regulated,[57] or cover cases where it was felt unnecessary to extend CIS regulation to the arrangements at issue.[58]

Paragraph 1: Individual Investment Management Arrangements

17.26   Schemes such as ISAs (Individual Savings Accounts) and their predecessors PEPs (Private Equity Plans) may satisfy the core CIS definition in that investment is undertaken in accordance with an overall policy applicable to all accounts. Hence, although there is no 'pooling', the 'management as a whole' alternative is likely to be satisfied.[59] Paragraph 1 excludes such arrangements if they satisfy three conditions. First, the property must comprise certain 'specified investments' only,[60] for example, shares, debt securities, or units in certain CISs.[61] Second, each participant must be entitled to 'part' of that property and to withdraw it at any time.[62] Third, as far as the 'pooling' and/or 'management as a whole' condition is concerned, there must be no 'pooling' and the 'management as a whole' alternative must only be satisfied because the 'parts' attributable to each participant are not bought and sold separately (except where a person becomes or ceases to be a participant).

Paragraph 2: Enterprise Initiative Schemes

17.27   In order to encourage investment in new businesses, the Income Taxes Act 2007, Part 5 (previously the Income and Corporation Taxes Act 1988, Part VII, Chapter III) gives income tax relief to individuals when they buy shares in certain new companies (the so-called 'Enterprise Investment Scheme'). To encourage collective investment in such shares, paragraph 2 excludes from the definition of a CIS certain arrangements which constitute a 'complying fund',[63] that term meaning arrangements where the operator will invest in shares which qualify for tax relief

---

by the Act and which are not, the Order is not subject to the affirmative resolution procedure for statutory instruments.

[57] See especially paras 1, 3, 13, 16–21. It is expected that those *Sukuks* that are CISs (see para 17.124, below) will be exempted and regulated in the same way as their non-*Shari'a* equivalents (see the Consultation Paper on the legislative framework for the regulation of alternative finance investment bonds (Sukuk) issued by HMT and the FSA in December 2008.

[58] See especially paras 2, 4–12, 14–15.

[59] See s 235(2), paras 17.22 and 17.24 above.

[60] ie those specified in FSMA 2000 (Regulated Activities) Order 2001, SI 2001/544, as amended (the RAO), arts 76–80 or contracts of long term insurance: para 1(a)(i), (iii).

[61] ie units in AUTs (see para 17.88, below), recognised schemes (see para 17.105, below), or shares in any OEIC (see para 17.61 *et seq.* below): para 1(a)(ii).

[62] Presumably this requirement would still be satisfied even if withdrawal requires the payment of a (reasonable) fee and/or entails a short delay to complete formalities.

[63] Treasury CIS Order Sched, para 2(1)(b).

(in relation to each participant's individual circumstances) under those tax provisions and where the minimum contribution of each participant is not less than £2,000.[64] For the exemption to apply a number of further conditions are laid down,[65] in particular each participant must be entitled to part of the property and to withdraw it after a certain period.[66]

Paragraph 3: Pure deposit-based schemes

If the whole amount of a participant's contribution is a 'deposit', for the purposes **17.28** of FSMA,[67] and this is accepted either by an authorised person with permission to accept deposits or by an exempt person (in relation to such an activity), then any arrangements with respect to those deposits which might otherwise fall within the CIS definition are exempted.

Paragraph 4: Schemes not operated by way of business

The core CIS definition does not have a 'business' element. Thus even family or **17.29** private arrangements may fall within it. As the FSMA regulatory regime is generally only concerned with activities in the business context,[68] paragraph 4 exempts from the CIS definition arrangements 'operated otherwise than by way of business'. This echoes the wording of FSMA, section 22 which requires regulated activities to be 'carried on by way of business', a narrower concept than 'in the course of business' which is used in relation to financial promotion in section 21.[69]

The word 'business' occurs in many legal contexts and has been called an 'etymo- **17.30** logical chameleon' by Lord Diplock.[70] It is notoriously difficult to decide if activity is done 'by way of business' in that this usually depends on balancing a number of factors (none of which is conclusive), in particular profit motive and regularity.[71] A particularly wide meaning was given to the phrase as it occurred in the predecessor to FSMA, section 412(2)(a)[72] ('entered into . . . by way of business') by

---

[64] ibid, para 2(2)(b).

[65] ibid, para 2(1)(a), (c), (d).

[66] ibid, para 2(1)(c). The period depends on the type of shares involved.

[67] RAO, art 5. See further paras 14.36–38 above.

[68] See s 21 (financial promotion 'in the course of business') and s 22 (regulated activities 'carried on by way of business'). See further, paras 17.126, 17.131.

[69] The s 22 phrase has been the subject of a clarificatory Treasury Order (FSMA 2000 (Carrying on Regulated Activity by Way of Business) Order 2001, SI 2001/1177, as amended by SI 2003/1475, art 25; SI 2003/1476, art 18; 2005/922; SI 2006/1969, art 9; SI 2006/2383, art 29; SI 2006/3384, art 37, made under s 419) but this is (in terms) inapplicable.

[70] In *Town Investments Ltd v Department of the Environment* [1978] AC 359 at 383C.

[71] The FSA has given very tentative guidance on the meaning of the phrase in s 22 in its FSA Handbook, PERG 2.3. See further the discussion in *The Encyclopedia of Financial Services Law*, para 2A–851.

[72] FSA 1986, s 63.

Hobhouse J in *Morgan Grenfell & Co v Welwyn Hatfield DC*.[73] In the context of deciding if the exemption from the gaming laws in that provision applied to swaps contracts, he saw 'no reason to put a narrow meaning on the word "business"' and said 'it should not be given a technical construction but rather one which conformed to what in ordinary parlance would be described as a business transaction as opposed to something personal or casual'. Moreover, he added that a 'one-off' scheme could still be regarded as operated 'by way of business' even though the term 'business' has been construed as requiring some repetition.[74] Thus Hobhouse J added that the 'frequency with which the relevant type of transaction is entered into ... can be no more than a guide ... it is equally possible that the very first time [a person] enters into such a contact it is doing so by way of business'. Similarly, 'business' does not always connote a profit or commercial motive.[75]

17.31 It would appear that a similarly wide interpretation would be appropriate in the context of paragraph 4, as the regulatory policy seems merely to exclude those private arrangements that do not merit regulation. Thus paragraph 4 would be apt to exclude family arrangements for collective investment and 'private' investment clubs or syndicates operated by groups of friends or colleagues.

Paragraph 5: Debt issues

17.32 Paragraph 5[76] is a very complex provision that excludes certain arrangements in securitisations under which the rights of the participants are (only) one type of certain debt instruments either issued by a single issuer or arising under swap arrangements (as defined).

Paragraph 6: Common accounts

17.33 Arrangements under which money is held 'in a common account' on the understanding that it is to be applied either (i) 'in making payments to' the participant, or (ii) 'in satisfaction of sums owed to him', or (iii) 'in the acquisition of property for him or the provision of services to him' are excluded by paragraph 6. Obvious examples would be clients' accounts. This exemption, in particular the scope of the three alternative 'uses' of the money, was considered both in *The Russell-Cooke Trust Company* and *Fradley*. In the former case Laddie J held that the use of the

---

[73] [1995] 1 All ER 1.

[74] See *Smith v Anderson* (1880) 15 Ch D 247, at 277–8, but the phrase there was 'carrying on business'. See *GE Capital Bank Ltd v Rushton* [2005] EWCA Civ 1556: purchase of a number of vehicles as a 'one-off' transaction but as a 'business venture' did constitute the 'carrying on of business' for the purposes of the Hire-Purchase Act 1964, s 29(2).

[75] *Rolls v Miller* (1884) 27 Ch D 71 at 81: business means 'anything which is an occupation as distinguished from a pleasure—anything which is an occupation or duty which requires attention'.

[76] As amended by SI 2006/3384, art 36(2).

singular in the three alternative uses of the money was deliberate and therefore the exemption did not apply where the money in the common account was paid out on behalf of more than one contributor towards a common investment. In *Fradley* the money was applied in placing bets for the participant and it was held that this did not fall within any of the three 'uses'.[77]

Paragraph 7: Certain funds relating to leasehold property

The Landlord and Tenant Act 1987, section 42(1) requires sums paid into a sink- **17.34** ing fund by way of service charges by tenants to be held on trust first to defray the costs and thereafter for the contributors. In this way the tenant-contributors have an equitable claim to the fund that prevails over the payee's creditors should the payee become insolvent. By virtue of paragraph 7[78] such a statutory trust is not a CIS. This exemption has now been extended to a similar 'designated account' of a scheme administrator under a 'tenancy deposit scheme' within the meaning of the Housing Act 2004, section 212(2).

Paragraph 8: Certain employee share schemes

Paragraph 8[79] sets out the standard definition of an 'employee share scheme' and **17.35** exempts such a scheme from being a CIS. For many years it has been government policy to encourage employees to participate in the shareholding of their employer. For example, activities carried on in connection with 'employee share schemes' are excluded from the definition of 'regulated activities' by the RAO,[80] and the promotion of employee share schemes is outside the financial promotion restriction.[81] Paragraph 8 adds to that special treatment and removes a disincentive for employers to establish and operate such schemes by taking them out of CIS regulation.

Paragraph 9: Schemes entered into for commercial purposes wholly or mainly related to existing business[82]

This exemption is sometimes referred to as the 'joint venture' or 'existing business' **17.36** exemption as it operates to exempt certain collective investment 'wholly or mainly

---

[77] In particular a bet was neither 'property' nor a provision of 'services' within (iii): see [2004] EWHC 3008 (a point not further considered on appeal: [2005] EWCA 1183).

[78] As substituted by SI 2007/800, art 2(2) to add the reference to the Housing Act 2004. Para 7 was previously amended by SI 2005/57 so as to extend the exemption to trust funds that would be within the 1978 Act, s 42 but for the landlord being exempt under s 58.

[79] As amended by SI 2005/2114, Sched 16(1) para 3.

[80] ie FSMA 2000 (Regulated Activities) Order 2001, SI 2001/544, as amended, art 71.

[81] FSMA 2000 (Financial Promotion) Order 2005, SI 2005/1529 (the FPO), art 60.

[82] A new para 9 was substituted on 15 July 2008 by SI 2008/1641 and was amended by SI 2008/1813. Previously, a new para 9(1)(a) was substituted on 1 December 2001 by SI 2001/3650.

for commercial purposes related to' existing (non-investment) businesses. It is a widely used exemption and has been amended on a number of occasions, resulting in a complex provision.[83]

17.37   Broadly speaking, in order for the exemption to apply, two conditions need to be fulfilled in relation to *each*[84] of the participants. The first is that they each must 'carry on a business other than the business of engaging in' one of the investment business-type of 'specified activities' in the RAO.[85] It is clear that the various exclusions applicable to each of those types of 'specified activities' in the RAO are relevant in deciding if a participant carries on that 'specified activity' for the purposes of this exclusion.[86] Moreover, the non-investment business must be an *existing* business: this first condition is not satisfied where the participant *will* carry on the business by virtue of being a participant in the arrangements.[87] However, that non-investment business need not be the same kind of business in relation to each participant. Moreover, it does not matter if a participant, as well as carrying on a non-investment business, *also* carries on an investment business.[88]

17.38   The second condition is that each participant must enter 'into the arrangements for commercial purposes wholly or mainly related' to that business. Thus the collective arrangements must be wholly or mainly[89] related to that existing non-investment business. An example would be property developers who collectively invest in a further property development or manufacturers who collectively invest in raw materials.

See the similar 'joint enterprise' exclusion (from 'regulated activity') for 'participators in a joint enterprise' where the 'transaction is entered into for the purposes of or in connection with that enterprise' in RAO, art 69.

[83]   See the provisions in para 9(1) for arrangements made before the latest version of para 9 came into force (on 15 July 2008). In particular, participants may (unanimously) elect (irrevocably and in writing) to take advantage of the relaxations in the new provision.

[84]   See para 9(4).

[85]   ie in relation to certain investments: dealing as principal (art 14) or agent (art 21), arranging deals (arts 25 and 25D), managing (art 37), safeguarding and administering (art 40), sending dematerialised instructions (art 45), as well as establishing etc a CIS (art 51), establishing etc a stakeholder pension (art 52), and advising (art 53). Agreeing to undertake any of these activities (apart from that in art 51) is also covered (art 64).

[86]   The various exclusions determine what is and what is not within the relevant articles setting out the 'specified activity' (see RAO, art 4(3)). Thus the activity is not 'specified by' the relevant article if it falls within a relevant exclusion. Elsewhere (eg RAO, art 4(4)(b)) where the exclusions are not to be taken into account, this is made clear explicitly. And see para 14(b) (in relation to exclusions to 'specified investments'), considered at para 17.44 below. For a contrary view, see E Perry, *The Financial Services and Markets Act: A Practical Legal Guide* (2001) para 12.12.

[87]   Para 9(5)(i) —a clarification not present (but implicit) in the predecessor to this provision in the FSA 1986.

[88]   This has now been made explicit in para 9(5)(a).

[89]   A qualification added in the new para 9 inserted by SI 2008/1641.

The latest version of this paragraph has introduced a relaxation in order to facilitate **17.39** participation by SPVs that (being especially established for the purpose of any arrangements) do not satisfy the 'existing business' requirement. Thus SVPs[90] that only have as their members persons who would satisfy those two conditions[91] do not need to carry on an 'existing business' as long as they do not carry on those investment business type of 'specified activities' mention above.[92] A further innovation is that if the exemption in paragraph 9 otherwise applies, all[93] the participants may nevertheless agree in writing that the exemption does not apply.[94]

Paragraph 10: Group schemes

Arrangements between companies in the same group are exempted. Thus if each **17.40** of the participants in the 'arrangements' is a body corporate in the same 'group' (as defined in FSMA, s 421)[95] then the arrangements do not constitute a CIS. Consequently, members of the same group may pool resources for investment without the arrangements being regulated as CISs.

Paragraph 11: Franchise arrangements

'Franchise arrangements'—which are defined broadly as arrangements conferring **17.41** the right to exploit intellectual property (such as a trademark or design) or the goodwill attached to it[96]—are exempted from the definition of a CIS. This is potentially a wide exemption which is likely to be interpreted narrowly so that the right to exploit is the predominant purpose of the arrangements (otherwise they would not be 'franchise arrangements'), so that the mere inclusion of a right of exploitation of (say) a trademark in a scheme with a wider purpose would not bring it within the exemption.

Paragraph 12: Trading schemes

Arrangements providing for the payment of incentives for recruitment to schemes **17.42** may constitute CISs if the funds used to pay those incentives are pooled and/or managed as whole pending their distribution. Paragraph 12 operates to exclude

---

[90] viz.: a body corporate, unincorporated association, partnership, or corporate trustee (para 9(5)(b)).

[91] See paras 17.37 and 17.38 above.

[92] See n 85, above.

[93] The election must be unanimous.

[94] Para 9(3)—and see para 9(7) (election unaffected by subsequent change in participants or later agreement). There are certain tax advantages to a scheme being a CIS, hence it is sometimes the desire of participants that the exemption does not apply.

[95] Which (as amended by SI 2008/948) in turn refers to Companies Act 2006 (and equivalent Northern Irish legislation) and the Building Societies Act 1986.

[96] Treasury CIS Order, art 2(1).

such arrangements where the financial incentives are wholly or mainly funded out of the contributions of other participants.

Paragraph 13: Timeshare schemes

17.43 'Timeshare rights'—as defined by the Timeshare Act 1992, section 1—are already regulated under that Act. Therefore, if arrangements confer such rights on participants, those arrangements do not constitute a CIS.

Paragraph 14: Other schemes relating to use or enjoyment of property

17.44 Paragraph 14 broadens the 'timeshare' exclusion to cover arrangements over both real and personal property satisfying two conditions. The first is that their 'predominant purpose' must be to 'enable the participants to share in the use or enjoyment' of property or to make that use or enjoyment available gratuitously to others.[97] Although the terms 'use or enjoy' might imply that only tangible property is covered, the second condition, in excluding certain intangible property, confirms that even intangible property (for example, intellectual property but see the exemption in paragraph 11, above) can be 'used or enjoyed'. The second condition states that the property must not 'consist of' currency and must not 'consist of or include' any 'investment' specified by the RAO (ignoring any exclusions).[98] Thus collective rights in any property (apart from that excluded by the second condition) where the predominant (not necessarily the 'sole') purpose is that the participants 'use or enjoy' it or allow others to do so without payment, do not constitute a CIS.

Paragraph 15: Schemes involving the issue of certificates representing investments

17.45 The term 'certificates representing securities' is shorthand for one type of 'specified investment' in the RAO: certificates or other instruments (defined to mean a record in any form)[99] conferring rights (contractual or property) over equity or debt securities.[100] Examples are depository receipts. Paragraph 15 exempts from the definition of CIS, arrangements where the rights of the participants are such investments. Although the RAO definition of 'certificates representing securities' is potentially very wide in referring to 'instruments' which confer 'contractual or proprietary rights' over equity or debt securities held by another, it was held in the *The Russell-Cooke Trust Company* that it did not cover mere documentary evidence of rights in a scheme but only covered securities and similar choses in action.

---

[97] Para 14(a).
[98] Para 14(b). This refers to the RAO, Part III, which is the Part that lists the specified investments.
[99] RAO, art 3(1).
[100] ibid, art 80.

Thus the exemption did not apply when participants were issued with a 'Certificate of Mortgage Investment' which (together with other documents) set out their entitlements. This did not fall within the RAO definition because 'if the investor wants to recover his fund he must either sue in contract or under the declaration of trust . . . he cannot bring an action on the basis of the Certificate of Mortgage'.

Paragraph 16: Clearing services

This exemption covers clearing services operated either by an authorised person,[101] **17.46** or a recognised clearing house,[102] or a recognised investment exchange.[103] Such regulatory control as is desirable in these situations can already be exercised by the FSA in its capacity as regulator of authorised persons and recognised clearing houses and exchanges.

Paragraph 17: Contracts of insurance

If an arrangement falls within the definition of 'contract of insurance' set out in **17.47** the RAO,[104] then it is exempted from the definition of a CIS as insurance has its own regulatory treatment under FSMA.

Paragraph 18: Funeral Plan Contracts[105]

Providing 'funeral plan contracts', as defined in the RAO[106] is a 'regulated activity' **17.48** unless the plans are protected by insurance or trust arrangements.[107] Thus such plans are already subject to regulation and no doubt on that basis are excluded from the definition of a CIS.

Paragraph 19: Individual pension accounts; Paragraph 20: Occupational and personal pension schemes

These two paragraphs exclude various arrangements for pension provision from **17.49** the CIS definition as these are already subject to regulation under the pension schemes legislation.

---

[101] FSMA, s 31.
[102] ibid, s 285.
[103] ibid.
[104] See the Treasury CIS Order, art 2(1) cross-referring to RAO, art 3(1). This does not answer the vexed question of what is 'insurance', an issue on which the FSA gives Guidance in its Handbook, PERG 6.
[105] A new para 18 was substituted by SI 2001/3650, art 2(3).
[106] See the Treasury CIS Order, art 2(1) cross-referring to RAO, art 59.
[107] RAO, art 60.

17.50   First, paragraph 19 exempts 'individual pension accounts', which are defined as accounts which satisfy strict conditions,[108] including strict criteria as to investment. Thus they may generally only be invested in 'safe' investments such as units in regulated collective investment schemes.[109] Second, paragraph 20 exempts 'occupational pension schemes' and 'personal pension schemes',[110] both as defined in (and regulated under) the Pension Schemes Act 1993.[111]

Paragraph 21: Bodies Corporate[112]

17.51   Most bodies corporate fall within the core definition of a CIS in FSMA, section 235.[113] They generally constitute 'arrangements with respect to property' (the share capital raised by the issue of shares and then used in the company's business) which enable participants (the shareholders) to participate in profits arising from the management of the property by the directors of the company. Shareholders generally do not have 'day-to-day' control and the participants' contributions are pooled and the scheme property is managed 'as a whole' by the directors.[114]

17.52   However, paragraph 21 excludes *all* bodies corporate—wherever constituted[115]— from the definition of CIS apart from two categories: OEICs (open-ended investment companies) as defined by FSMA[116] and LLCs (limited liability companies).[117] Thus a corporate body can only be a CIS if it is either an OEIC or an LLC. In particular, closed-ended corporations, such as UK investment companies and investment trusts[118] that invest in other companies' securities are not CISs.

---

[108] Treasury CIS Order, art 2(1) cross-referring to the definition in the Personal Pension Schemes (Restriction on Discretion to Approve) (Permitted Investments) Regulations 2001, 2001/117, reg 4.

[109] See para 17.84 below.

[110] But not a 'personal pension unit trust' (meaning an AUT of the kind mentioned in the Personal Pension Schemes (Appropriate Schemes) Regulations 1997, SI 1997/470, Sched 1, Part 1: see Treasury CIS Order, art 2(1)) which is or comprises feeder funds.

[111] Treasury CIS Order, art 2(1).

[112] A new para 21 was substituted on 1 December 2001 by SI 2001/3650, art 2(4).

[113] See para 17.08 *et seq*, above.

[114] Moreover, each corporation is a single CIS as its property will be one pooled fund and hence s 236(4) (pooling in relation to separate parts of the property) will not be relevant: see FSA Handbook, PERG 9.2.4.6G.

[115] See the definition in FSMA, s 417(1). Thus, for example, Dublin-based Exchange Traded Funds ('ETFs') are not CISs.

[116] See para 17.61 *et seq*. below.

[117] These are not defined but may be established in the UK under the Limited Liability Partnerships Act 2000.

[118] See para 17.01 above.

Other general CIS definitions

Participant

The term 'participant' is frequently used in the CIS statutory provisions[119] yet a **17.53** definition of the term is not listed either in the special CIS definition section (section 237) or in the general FSMA definition section (section 417(1)). However, it is 'defined' in a rather oblique way in section 235(2), which sets out the lack of 'day-to-day control' requirement,[120] by the addition of the bracketed word '("participants")' after the reference to 'persons who are to participate'. Moreover, section 235(3) then refers to the 'contributions of the participants' being pooled. Therefore it is clear that 'participant' has the natural meaning of the investor[121] in the scheme, that is, the person who takes part in the arrangements by making contributions to the scheme property.[122] The use of the future tense in section 235(2) ('persons who are to participate') makes it clear that, where relevant, potential investors in the scheme as well as actual investors are covered by the term.

The FSA Handbook Glossary does define 'participant' for the purposes of that **17.54** document as 'a person who participates in a' CIS. That definition begins with the words '(in accordance with section 235(2) of the Act)', suggesting that the meaning of the term in FSMA is the same. However, the FSA Handbook definition uses the present not the future tense and thus, in terms, does not cover future investors in the scheme.

The FSA Handbook also contains provision in relation to certain types of partici- **17.55** pants: 'unitholders' and 'shareholders'. Broadly speaking, a unitholder is the person entered in the register in relation to that unit[123] or if a unit is represented by a Bearer Certificate[124] then the 'unitholder' is the holder of that Certificate. The term 'shareholder' is specific to an ICVC[125] and has a similar meaning, noted in the discussion of ICVCs below.

Unit

Although the term 'unit' seems most appropriate to the unit trust context, in both **17.56** FSMA and the FSA Handbook it is the general term which denotes 'the rights or

---

[119] See ss 237, 238, 243, 247, 248, 250, 254, 257, 264, 272, 279, 281, 283, 284.

[120] See para 17.17 above.

[121] The definition of an OEIC in s 236(3) (considered further in para 17.66 *et seq.* below) talks of a 'reasonable [potential] investor' where it could have used the term 'participant' but perhaps the former phrase was regarded as clearer in that (corporate) context.

[122] See also s 238(11), which refers to 'participant (within the meaning given by section 235(2))'.

[123] See para 17.56 below.

[124] As further defined in the FSA Handbook Glossary.

[125] See para 17.96 below. There is a separate meaning given to 'shareholder' for the purposes of the DTR Module of the Handbook.

interests (however described) of the participants in' *any* CIS.[126] Thus, for the purposes of the regulatory provisions, shares in an OEIC and contractual rights in a purely contractual CIS, well as units in a unit trust scheme, are all 'units' in the CIS.

Depositary; operator

17.57   CISs very frequently vest the scheme property in one person for safekeeping and then designate another to manage the property. Indeed, such a division of responsibility is necessary in order to obtain an authorisation order for the scheme from the FSA.[127]

17.58   FSMA defines 'depositary' as the person to whom the scheme property is 'entrusted for safekeeping' but expressly states that the definition is inapplicable to unit trust schemes.[128] This is because the more precise term 'trustee' is used in FSMA to denote the corresponding person in a unit trust scheme context. However, as noted below,[129] the FSA Handbook uses the term 'depositary' in relation to *all* CISs, including unit trust schemes, and hence the trustee of a unit trust scheme is a 'depositary' for the purposes of the FSA Handbook.

17.59   The term 'operator' is only defined in FSMA in relation to two categories of CISs: unit trust schemes with separate trustees and OEICs.[130] In relation to the former, if there is a separate trustee, it means the manager whilst in relation to the latter, it means the company itself (even if another person manages its property on its behalf).

17.60   However, the FSA Handbook contains a comprehensive definition of that term in relation to all CISs. For the purposes of the Enforcement Guide in the FSA Handbook,[131] as far as unit trust schemes and OEICs are concerned, the FSA Handbook definition of 'operator' is broadly consistent with the FSMA definition.[132] For the purposes of the rest of the Handbook the definition of 'operator' varies with the type of CIS at issue but the default definition[133] is 'any person who,

---

[126]   s 237(2).

[127]   See paras 17.90 and 17.101. It is a requirement for a UCITS scheme under the UCITS Directive, see para 17.03 above. It is not an explicit requirement for ss 270 or 272 'recognised schemes' (see paras 17.111 and 17.114 below).

[128]   s 237(2).

[129]   Para 17.81.

[130]   s 237(2). And see the discussion in 'Operating a Collective Investment Scheme', Financial Markets Law Committee, Issue 86, (July 2008).

[131]   See para 17.146 *et seq.* below.

[132]   See paras 17.76 and 17.83 below. But if an OEIC within the UCITS Directive (see para 17.03, above) has appointed a manager, it is that manager.

[133]   For an AUT (see para 17.88, below) it is the 'manager' (as further defined in the Glossary); for an ICVC (see para 17.96, below) it is that company or 'if applicable' the ACT (for the ACT, see para 17.98, below); for an OEIC within the UCITS Directive (see para 17.03 above) that has appointed

under the constitution or founding arrangements of the scheme, is responsible for the management of the property held for or within the scheme'.

Definition of Open-Ended Investment Company (OEIC): FSMA, section 236

General

The term 'open-ended investment company' ('OEIC') is also defined in FSMA **17.61** (in section 236) and therefore also has a distinct meaning. The statutory definition may be (but has not yet been) altered by Treasury Order.[134] Unlike the core CIS definition, that is almost a verbatim transcription of the corresponding provision in the Financial Services Act 1986, the FSMA definition of an OEIC differs from the predecessor provision,[135] attempting to clarify some of the difficulties of interpretation that the old definition gave rise to. Nevertheless, the definition is still a difficult one to apply and therefore extensive guidance is provided in the FSA Handbook.[136] An OEIC is the only type of body corporate (other than an LLP) that can be a CIS[137] and hence it is important to draw the line between OEICs and other corporations. The issue only arises in relation to overseas open-ended investment companies as any such UK company necessarily falls within the definition.[138]

In order to fall within the statutory definition of an 'open-ended investment com- **17.62** pany', the body corporate must be a 'collective investment scheme' that satisfies two further conditions.[139] Thus before considering those two conditions, the CIS definition must be applied.[140] As noted above, most corporations will be CISs unless they fall within one of the exclusions in the Treasury CIS Order.[141] However, the exclusion in paragraph 21 of that Order must clearly be disregarded at this stage, as this excludes all bodies corporate except OEICs (and LLPs) and hence the decision of whether a company is an OEIC needs to be made before paragraph 21 can be applied.

---

a manager, it is that manager; for other OEICs it is that company or 'if applicable' whoever has management responsibilities under the constitution; for a unit trust scheme with a separate manager, it is the manager;

[134] s 236(5).
[135] FSA 1986, s 75(8).
[136] In PERG 9.
[137] See para 17.52 above.
[138] See para 17.96 below. This is because the only form of UK OEIC that may be established is an ICVC.
[139] s 236(1).
[140] See para 17.08 *et seq*, above.
[141] See para 17.51 *et seq*.

17.63 The two conditions that a CIS has to fulfil for it to be an OEIC are termed 'the property condition' and 'the investment condition'. Their effect is that, broadly speaking, an OEIC is a corporate vehicle for collective investment whose property is managed so that risk is spread and where most or all of its shares can be realised, typically through redemption or repurchase, on a 'net-asset value' basis within a reasonable period. It will be seen that the status of a corporation—whether it is an OEIC or not—may change from time to time, depending on how the way it operates is perceived by a 'reasonable' potential 'investor'.[142]

The property condition: section 236(2)[143]

17.64 The so-called 'property condition' requires that the scheme property is both owned beneficially[144] by a body corporate and is managed by (or on behalf of) that body corporate so that investment risk is spread[145] and its shareholders[146] obtain the benefits of that management.[147] As the term 'body corporate' covers both domestic and overseas companies,[148] it is clear that the term 'open-ended investment company' is not confined to domestic schemes.[149] According to general principles, whether an arrangement gives rise to a 'body corporate' is a matter for the law of the place where the arrangement takes place.[150] If it does, it will be for the law of the relevant part of the UK in which the question arises to decide if that body corporate is an OEIC within section 236.[151]

17.65 The property condition requires a spread of investment risk and therefore companies that merely hold one or a very narrow category of assets cannot be OEICs. However, nothing is said about the level of risk, merely that the risk (however high or low) is 'spread'.[152] Moreover, this condition requires the active management of those assets. It is therefore not enough that the company merely holds assets in the expectation that they will increase in value. It should be noted that for the

---

[142] Confirmed in PERG 9.11.1G, FAQ 2 and PERG 9.7.5G.
[143] See PERG 9.5G.
[144] If it is held by the company on trust, a unit trust may arise, see para 17.78 *et seq* below.
[145] FSMA, s 236(2)(a).
[146] ibid, s 236(2)(b) uses the more general term 'members'.
[147] ibid, s 236(2)(b).
[148] ibid, s 417(1).
[149] Indeed, as noted above in para 17.61, whether the definition is satisfied is, in practice, only an issue in the case of overseas companies.
[150] Dicey & Morris on the *Conflict of Laws* (14th edn, 2006) para 30.001 *et seq.*
[151] PERG 9.3.6G. This is also in accordance with the general principle that the words of a UK statute are to be interpreted according to the law of the relevant part of the UK. It is therefore irrelevant whether the overseas applicable law of the place of constitution regards the body corporate as an open-ended investment company or not.
[152] PERG 9.5.5G.

purposes of the Act,[153] the 'operator' of an OEIC is always the company itself, even if it employs a manager to 'operate' the scheme and manage its assets on its behalf.

The investment condition: section 236(3)[154]

General

The investment condition has two aspects, both referable to the assessment that a **17.66** 'reasonable' potential 'investor' would make as regards the scheme. The FSA Guidance contains a very full discussion of this condition. It makes a number of general points. The first is that, as the condition needs to be satisfied 'in relation to' the company, it is the 'overall impression' that is critical. Therefore the condition 'should not be applied rigidly in relation to specific events such as particular issues of shares or securities or in relation to particular points in time'.[155] The second point is that if shares with different rights are issued, they all need not satisfy the condition as long as 'the overall balance between those that do and those that do not is strongly in favour of those that do'.[156] As regards the 'reasonable investor', the FSA takes the view that the term 'investor' connotes a person with some knowledge of collective investment and the proposed underlying property[157] Moreover, as the condition is worded in terms of the assessment that such a person 'would, if he were to participate' make, it is focused on assessments before participation. It follows that if the scheme changes significantly, so that the investment condition becomes, or is no longer, satisfied, the scheme can change throughout its life into an OEIC or into a non-OEIC (and hence not a CIS)[158] and vice versa.[159]

Realisation within a reasonable period

The first aspect of the investment condition[160] (called the 'expectation test' in the **17.67** FSA Guidance)[161] is that the 'reasonable investor' would:

> expect that he would be able to realise, within a period appearing to him reasonable, his investment in the scheme represented, at any given time, by the value of

---

[153] See the definition of 'operator' in s 237(2), noted in para 17.76 below. Who the 'operator' is for the purposes of the FSA Handbook depends on the context: see para 17.77 below.

[154] PERG 9.6G–9.9G.

[155] PERG 9.6.3G. However, the OEIC's status may change over time: see PERG 9.11.1G FAQ.2, noted above and below.

[156] PERG 9.6.4G. See also PERG 9.8.8G and 9.11.1G FAQ 5. But they will all be 'units' in a CIS, even the ones that are irredeemable.

[157] PERG 9.7.2G. If an investment is targeted at investors with particular characteristics, the 'reasonable investor' is to be assumed to have those characteristics: ibid.

[158] As the only type of corporate CIS possible is an OIEC (or an LLP): see para 21.

[159] see n 142.

[160] FSMA, s 236(3)(a).

[161] PERG 9.6.2G.

the body corporate's shares or securities. Thus, in essence, the 'reasonable investor', when contemplating investing in the scheme, must anticipate that he will be able to realise his investment within a reasonable (to him) period. In making that assessment a number of factors will be relevant, including the terms on which the securities are issued, the company's constitution, any representations as to policy, and how that policy is implemented in practice.[162]

17.68 A number of issues arise. There need not be an actual *entitlement* so to realise the investment; an expectation to be able to do so is enough. So if, in practice, the scheme regularly redeems or repurchases its securities or has a declared policy to that effect, this aspect of the condition is likely to be satisfied[163] at least until that practice or policy changes. Such realisation will usually occur either through redemption or resale to the company—although redemption or resale under certain statutory provisions[164] permitting the reduction of share capital does not amount to realisation for this purpose. Because of the second aspect of the 'investment condition' (which requires realisation on a net-asset value basis) considered below, the possibility of realisation through sale on an exchange, in itself, will not be enough.[165] It seems clear[166] that 'realise' means convert into money and therefore an expectation that the securities will be exchanged for other securities will not suffice—unless those securities themselves can be 'realised', the whole process taking place within a 'reasonable period'.

17.69 As the requisite expectation is to be able to realise 'within a period appearing to' the 'reasonable investor' to be 'reasonable', there is no need for *immediate* realisation to be available. Thus an expectation that redemption or repurchase will occur periodically suffices as long as a 'reasonable investor' would regard the intervals between the occasions as 'reasonable'. This will depend on the liquidity of the underlying scheme property; the greater the illiquidity, the longer the period that would be likely to be regarded as 'reasonable'.[167] The FSA takes the view that redemption or repurchase every six months 'would generally be too long to be a reasonable period for a liquid securities fund'[168] but that an *initial* period, during which it is not possible to realise the investment would necessarily not preclude

---

[162] See PERG 9.8.5G and 9.8.8G.

[163] PERG 9.8.5G.

[164] Listed in s 236(4) and reflecting (in relation to the UK and other EEA States) the maintenance of capital requirements of Directive (EEC) 77/91 (the Second Company Law Directive). See PERG 9.6.5G. Hence so-called 'closed-ended' investment trusts which redeem/repurchase their shares under these provisions are not OEICs (confirmed in PERG 9.11.1G FAQ7).

[165] See below and PERG 9.8.3G; 9.9.4G–9.9.6G.

[166] See PERG 9.8.2G.

[167] See PERG 9.8.9(7)G.

[168] PERG 9.11.1G FAQ 8.

the scheme being an OEIC.[169] It seems clear that the participant's *whole* investment needs to be realisable within a reasonable period, although it is enough that it can be realised in stages—as long as realisation of the whole contribution can take place within a 'reasonable period'.[170]

Realisation on 'net-asset value' basis

The second aspect of the investment condition[171] (called the 'satisfaction test' in the FSA Guidance)[172] is that the 'reasonable investor' must 'be satisfied that his investment would be realised on a basis calculated wholly or mainly by reference' to the net-asset value. The use of the verb 'satisfied'—in contrast to 'expects' in the first aspect of the condition—indicates a higher threshold, requiring him to be convinced that this is the case, rather than merely expect that this will be so. The FSA Guidance states that 'satisfy' connotes 'justifiable grounds on which the reasonable investor could form a view'.[173]

17.70

This aspect of the condition will not be fulfilled if realisation is to occur through a secondary market, as the market price of the securities (determined by the laws of supply and demand) may not exactly reflect the net-asset value of the company's property, unless the company undertakes to take steps (such as intervening in the market) to ensure that the price of its securities is based on the net-asset value.[174] On the other hand, if the company undertakes that it will redeem or repurchase its shares or arranges for some other person to undertake to purchase its shares, on a net-asset value basis, then the condition is likely to be fulfilled.[175] Some flexibility is introduced by the phrase 'wholly or mainly', so that minor departures from the net-assert value basis (for example, by the deduction of redemption charges)[176] are not fatal, as long as the net-asset value is the 'main' basis of realisation.

17.71

Other OEIC definitions

'Participants' in OEICs

In FSMA and FSA Handbook terminology, the shareholder or other securities holder in an OEIC is the 'participant' in the CIS that is the OEIC.[177] However, for

17.72

---

[169] PERG 9.11.1G FAQ 9.
[170] PERG 9.8.4G.
[171] FSMA, s 236(3)(b).
[172] PERG 9.6.2G.
[173] PERG 9.9.3G.
[174] PERG 9.9.3(3)G; 9.9.4G–9.9.6G.
[175] PERG 9.9.3(2)(a)G.
[176] PERG 9.9.7G.
[177] See para 17.53 above.

the purposes of the OEIC definition, FSMA uses the alternative terms 'reasonable investor' and (a term appropriate to the corporate context) 'member', rather than referring to 'participant'. Nevertheless, for the purposes of applying the FSMA regime, it is clear that the securities holders are the 'participants'.

17.73 The FSA Handbook, whilst in essence[178] giving the term 'participant' the same meaning as in FSMA, also contains a definition of the term 'shareholder' in relation to ICVCs.[179] If a share is represented by a Bearer Certificate[180] then the 'shareholder' is the holder of that certificate. Otherwise the 'shareholder' is the person entered on the share register in relation to the share.

Unit

17.74 In both FSMA and the FSA Handbook, the shares or securities in an OEIC are referred to as 'units'—the general term used to denote the rights of the participants in any CIS.[181]

Depositary; operator

17.75 For the purposes of both FSMA and the FSA Handbook, the 'depositary' in relation to an OEIC is the person to whom the scheme property is 'entrusted for safekeeping'.[182]

17.76 The 'operator' of an OEIC has a less obvious meaning. FSMA states that it means the company itself.[183] This is even if the OEIC engages another person to manage its property on its behalf. Hence for the purpose of applying the FSMA provisions,[184] the OEIC is still the 'operator'.

17.77 The FSA Handbook definition is more qualified and depends on the types of OEIC and which parts of the Handbook are in issue. In the case of an OEIC within the UCITS Directive which has appointed a person to manage 'the scheme', it always means that manager. Otherwise a distinction needs to be drawn between the use of the term 'operator' in the Enforcement Guide (EG)[185] and elsewhere in the Handbook. In EG the 'operator' is the company. Elsewhere it is either the

---

[178] Although, as noted above in para 17.53, the present, not future, tense is used.

[179] For ICVCs, see para 17.96 below. There is also a definition of 'shareholder' in the Glossary in relation to the DTR Module.

[180] As further defined in the FSA Handbook Glossary.

[181] See para 17.56 above.

[182] FSMA, s 237(2); FSA Handbook Glossary—although in the Glossary, in relation to an ICVC (see para 17.96, below) such a person must also have been 'appointed for the purpose' in accordance with the OEIC Regulations (see para 17.97 below).

[183] FSMA, s 237(2).

[184] eg FSMA, Sched 5 para 1(1), see further nn 275 and 374 below.

[185] See 17.146 *et seq.* below.

company 'or, if applicable' the ACD in the case of an ICVC[186] and 'any person who, under the constitution or founding arrangements of the scheme, is responsible for the management of the property held for or within the scheme' in the case of other OEICs.

'Unit trust scheme'

General

A 'unit trust scheme' is defined in section 237(1) of FSMA as a CIS 'under which **17.78** the property is held on trust for the participants'. Thus in deciding if a 'unit trust scheme' arises, the first question to ask is whether the arrangements satisfy the definition of a CIS.[187] If so, the second question is whether the scheme property is held 'on trust' for the participants.

Other unit trust definitions

Participant

In FSMA and FSA Handbook terminology, the unitholder in a unit trust scheme **17.79** is the 'participant' in the scheme[188]

Unit

The general term used in FSMA and the FSA Handbook to denote a participant's **17.80** interest in *any* CIS—a 'unit'—has been taken from the unit trust context.[189] Hence, naturally, the beneficial interest of a participant in a unit trust scheme, as declared in the trust deed (his unit, as it is usually known), is a 'unit' for the purposes of the regulatory regime.

Trustee/depositary; operator

Unsurprisingly, in FSMA the 'trustee' of a unit trust scheme is defined as the per- **17.81** son holding the property on trust and the 'operator' in relation to a unit trust scheme with a separate trustee is defined as 'the manager'.[190]

---

[186] See para 17.98.

[187] See para 17.08 *et seq*. above.

[188] See para 17.53 above. Note also the FSA Handbook term 'unitholder', which is not confined to unit trusts (as 'unit' refers to participatory rights in *all* CISs).

[189] s 237(2). See para 17.56 above.

[190] s 237(2). For an argument that the manager of a unit trust is functionally (and so for the purposes of liability) a 'trustee', see A Hudson, *Law of Investment Entities* (2000) p 207. Cf Kam Fan Sin, n 11 above.

17.82 The FSA Handbook terminology is less simple. It uses the generic term 'deposi-tary' to cover persons to whom the CIS property is 'entrusted for safekeeping' and makes it clear that this covers the trustee of a unit trust scheme.[191] Therefore as far as the application of the FSA Handbook is concerned, the provisions applicable to 'depositaries' apply to unit trust scheme trustees. Confusingly, although the term 'depositary' is defined in identical terms in FSMA, that definition is stated not to apply to a unit trust scheme. Thus in FSMA (and secondary legislation made under it) 'depositary' does not cover the trustee of a unit trust scheme whilst in the FSA Handbook it does.

17.83 The FSA Handbook also uses, and defines, the term 'operator' but in relation to *all* CISs. Curiously, in relation to unit trust schemes, it does not refer to the FSMA definition but starts afresh. However, the Handbook definition does not appear to alter—but merely slightly to expand on—the FSMA definition. In essence, it defines the operator as the person designated by the trust deed as having manage-ment of the property.[192] Thus (unlike the term 'depositary'), the term 'operator' in relation to unit trust schemes essentially has the same meaning in both FSMA and the FSA Handbook.

Regulatory Categorisation of CISs

Introduction: the terminology

17.84 A number of different terms are used to cover different categories of CISs in both FSMA and the FSA Handbook. For the purposes of regulation there are four main categories of CISs:

(1) (UK) authorised unit trust schemes or AUTs;
(2) (UK) authorised open-ended investment companies ('OEICs'), (termed 'invest-ment companies with variable capital' or 'ICVCs' in the FSA Handbook);
(3) (Overseas) recognised schemes, of which there are three sub-categories:
    (i) section 264 EEA (UCITS) schemes,
    (ii) section 270 schemes authorised in 'designated' countries or territories;
    (iii) section 272 individually recognised overseas schemes;
(4) Other (*unregulated*) CISs.

---

[191] FSA Handbook Glossary, definition of 'depositary', see (b) and (c) thereof.
[192] There are separate provisions for AUTs (the operator is the 'manager' who is defined as the firm that is the manager in accordance with the trust deed) and other unit trust schemes (if there is a sepa-rate trustee, the operator is the person with responsibility for management under the trust deed).

The FSA Handbook, as well as introducing the acronym 'ICVC' to denoted **17.85** UK-authorised OEICs, uses a number of other terms to cover various categories of CIS. It uses the term '*authorised fund*' to cover the first two categories of UK CISs (that is, both AUTs and ICVCs), the epithet 'authorised' denoting that the FSA has made an 'authorisation order' in respect of the scheme.[193] Authorised funds are subdivided into three categories for the promotion purposes: '*UCITS schemes*', '*non-UCITS retail schemes*', and '*qualified investor schemes*' (QISs). As its name suggests, a 'UCITS scheme' is either an AUT or an ICVC that has a 'single market passport' under the UCITS Directive so it may be marketed, without further authorisation requirements, throughout the single market.[194] All other authorised funds are termed 'non-UCITS schemes'. However, these are divided into 'non-UCITS retail schemes' and QISs. A QIS is a type of authorised fund that can only be promoted to the same limited audience as unregulated schemes.[195] A 'non-UCITS retail scheme' is an authorised fund which does not comply with the UCITS Directive and may be promoted to the general public in the UK (hence 'non-UCITS *retail* scheme').

The FSA Handbook uses the more general term '*regulated collective investment* **17.86** *scheme*' to cover the first three categories of scheme listed above (that is, (1) AUTs, (2) ICVCs, and (3) 'recognised schemes'), the epithet term 'regulated' denoting that the constitution and operation of these schemes are subject to detailed regulation either by the FSA itself (in relation to the 'authorised funds' within (1) and (2)) or the overseas regulator (in relation to the 'recognised schemes' within (3)).

The term '*unregulated collective investment scheme*' is used in the FSA Handbook **17.87** to refer to the fourth, residual category which covers all CISs other than regulated schemes, whether UK or overseas. They are 'unregulated' in the sense that the schemes themselves do not need to comply with the detailed requirements which 'regulated' schemes have to satisfy. However, the term 'unregulated' should not be taken to indicate that FSMA has no application to them. As will be explained below,[196] the Act generally precludes such CISs being promoted to the public and its regime applies to persons involved in them.

---

[193] See paras 17.88 (AUT) and 17.96 (ICVC).
[194] See para 17.03 above.
[195] See further, paras 17.137 and 17.144 below.
[196] See para 17.124 *et seq.* below.

(UK) Authorised unit trust schemes (AUTs)

General

17.88 Authorised unit trust schemes or 'AUTs' are defined in FSMA as 'unit trust schemes'[197] that are authorised by virtue of the conferment of an 'authorisation order' by the FSA. FSMA contains the regulatory framework for AUTs, including the conferment of powers on the FSA to impose detailed regulatory requirements,[198] with the COLL Module of the FSA Handbook containing most of that detail.[199] The regulatory requirements reflect the EC UCITS Directive and hence enable AUTs to become 'UCITS schemes',[200] with the single market passport. However, as noted above,[201] AUTs may adopt wider investment and borrowing powers and hence be 'non-UCITS retail schemes' or even QISs.

Requirements for an 'authorisation order'

17.89 The basic requirements for obtaining an authorisation order from the FSA are set out in FSMA, section 243 and may be divided into three categories. These are amplified in the COLL Module of the FSA Handbook.[202]

17.90 First, there are the requirements imposed by the section itself.[203] The manager[204] and trustee, who must both be 'authorised persons' with permission to act as manager and trustee respectively,[205] must be independent of each other[206] and must each be a body corporate incorporated either in the UK or another EEA State and have their affairs administered in the country in which they are incorporated, with a place of business in the UK.[207] The scheme's name must not be 'undesirable or

---

[197] See para 17.78 *et seq.* above.

[198] See especially, Part XVIII, Ch III.

[199] See para 17.143 below and note para 17.142. COLL imposes most of these requirements on 'authorised funds' and hence (in so far as possible) treats AUTs and ICVCs together.

[200] See para 17.03 above. Section 246 enables the FSA to issue a certificate that the AUT complies with the UCITS Directive.

[201] Para 17.85.

[202] See para 17.143 below.

[203] s 243(1)(a) and see subss (4)–(11). The FSA must be 'satisfied' that these are fulfilled.

[204] The term 'manager' is not defined in the Act but the term is self-explanatory, FSMA merely stating that the 'manager' of a unit trust scheme is the 'operator' for the purposes of the Act: s 237(2).

[205] s 243(7). See further, para 17.125 below.

[206] s 243(4). COLL 6.9.2G–6.95G contains Guidance from the FSA on how it interprets 'independence'.

[207] s 243(5). However if the manager is incorporated in another EEA State then the scheme must not be one that qualifies for recognition under s 264 (see para 17.108 *et seq.* below, as EC law—in particular the UCITS Directive (see para 17.03 above)—requires the 'home' EEA State to authorise and the UK 'host' State to recognise that authorisation without being able to impose any further authorisation requirements itself): subs (6).

misleading':[208] and 'the purposes of the scheme must be reasonably capable of being successfully' effected.[209] Finally, the participants must be able to withdraw their contributions at a price reflecting the net-asset worth of the scheme.[210] The second main requirement is that the scheme must comply with the requirements of the FSA's 'trust scheme rules',[211] noted below, which are in the COLL Module.

The third requirement is a formal one: the FSA must have received (a) a copy of the **17.91** trust deed and (b) a solicitor's certificate stating that the scheme complies with the trust deed contents requirements of section 243 and the trust scheme rules.[212]

The AUT regulatory regime

As noted above, FSMA sets out the regulatory framework and, as well as provi- **17.92** sions concerning the determination of applications for 'authorisation orders',[213] it confers powers on the FSA to make two types of rules in relation to AUTS: 'trust scheme rules'[214] and 'scheme particular rules'.[215] These may be found in the COLL Module of the FSA Handbook. Provisions in both sets of rules may be waived or modified on request.[216]

'Trust scheme rules' concern the constitution, management, and operation of **17.93** AUTs.[217] In particular they regulate the contents of the trust deed itself,[218] dealing with the legal position of the various parties, regulating the powers, duties, rights, and liabilities of both the manager and trustee,[219] as well as the rights and duties of the participants.[220] Thus they regulate the investment and borrowing powers of

---

[208] s 243(8). COLL 6.9.9G contains FSA guidance on misleading names.

[209] s 243(9).

[210] s 243(10). This requirement is regarded as fulfilled if the scheme obliges the manager 'to ensure' (for example, by trading himself) that the participant can sell his units on an investment exchange (not necessarily an exchange recognised under s 285) at such a price.

[211] s 243(1)(b). The FSA must be 'satisfied' that these are fulfilled, see para 17.93 below.

[212] s 243(1)(c). Any subsequent proposal to alter the scheme, which involves a change in the trust deed, must also be accompanied by such a solicitor's certificate: s 251(2).

[213] ss 244 (determination), 245 (procedure when refusing), 251–252 (alterations to schemes and changes of manager and trustee), 256 (request for revocation of authorisation order).

[214] s 247.

[215] s 248.

[216] s 250: but in respect of (a) persons to whom they apply or (b) the scheme itself.

[217] s 247(1)(a), including their winding up (subs (1)(d)).

[218] s 247(3).

[219] s 247(1)(b). See also s 253, reflecting Arts 9, 16 of the UCITS Directive, which renders void any exemption clause in the trust deed which purports to exempt either the manager or trustee from negligence liability. Although the trust scheme rules could have included such a prohibition, it was considered desirable to place the prohibition in the Act itself.

[220] s 247(1)(c).

AUTs[221] and the redemption rights of the participants.[222] The rules are stated to be binding on the parties (the manager, trustee, and participants) 'independently of the contents of the trust deed'[223] and hence in the unlikely case[224] of the deed contradicting the rules, the rules will prevail.

17.94   The 'scheme particular rules'[225] require the manager of an AUT to produce and publish an information document resembling a share prospectus ('scheme particulars')[226] and to produce revisions of it when circumstances change.[227] As equivalent requirements are imposed on ICVCs by the OEIC Regulations,[228] where the corresponding document is a true share prospectus (as the 'units' in an OEIC are, of course, 'shares' in the OEIC), and as one set of these requirements (in relation to both AUTs and ICVCs) are imposed by the FSA, the relevant provisions of the COLL Module, refer to the document generically as a 'prospectus'. The rules impose liability to pay compensation for misleading particulars, similar to that which may arise in relation to a misleading share prospectus,[229] and the rules do not affect any common law liability that may otherwise arise—for example in tort (or delict) or contract[230] as a result of misrepresentations in the scheme particulars. As will be noted below,[231] FSMA also enables the FSA to make rules corresponding to scheme particular rules in relation to operators of overseas schemes recognised under section 270 (schemes from designated countries) or section 272 (individually recognised schemes) but not operators of section 264 (EEA (UCITSs)) recognised schemes.

17.95   FSMA also confers extensive powers of investigation (common to all CISs)[232] and powers of intervention (specific to AUTs and ICVCs) in relation to AUTs when things go wrong, for example when there is a breach of the statutory requirements or FSA rules, or where intervention is in the interests of participants. The FSA's

---

[221] s 247(2)(d).

[222] s 247(2)(a).

[223] s 247(4). This further provides that, in the case of the participants (only) the rules have effect as if contained in the deed. Thus when a participant wishes to rely on the rules, he may treat them as if they were provisions in the deed itself.

[224] A solicitor will have certified that the deed complies with the trust rules: see s 243(1)(c).

[225] In COLL 4.

[226] s 248(1). See subs (2) (definition of 'scheme particulars').

[227] s 248(3)–(4).

[228] See para 17.97 below.

[229] s 248(5).

[230] s 248(7). See Kam Fan Sin, n 11 above, 81, citing *Graham Australia Pty Ltd v Corporate West Management Pty Ltd* (1990) 1 ACSR 682, 687 holding that the unit trust particulars are the basis of a contract between the unit holders and manager.

[231] See paras 17.110, 17.113, and 17.120.

[232] s 284—except ICVCs as corresponding powers are conferred by the OEIC Regulations, reg 30.

less drastic power of intervention is to issue 'directions'[233] requiring that the issue or redemption, or both, of units cease[234] or that the scheme be wound up.[235] Moreover, the FSA may apply to court for an order removing and replacing the manager or trustee, or both, or removing either or both and for the appointment of an authorised person to wind up the scheme.[236] It also may revoke the AUT's authorisation order,[237] but has said[238] it will only do so after the AUT has been wound up and the scheme property has been distributed to the participants.

(UK) Authorised open-ended investment companies (ICVCs)

General

The general definition of 'an open-ended investment company' ('OEIC') has **17.96** been discussed above.[239] OEICs are a relatively new phenomenon in the UK and the only OEICs that can be established are those that obtain an 'authorisation order' from the FSA. Although FSMA calls such schemes 'authorised open-ended investment companies', the FSA Handbook uses the term 'ICVCs' (short for 'investment companies with variable capital').

Whilst the regulatory framework for AUTs is in FSMA, the corresponding provi- **17.97** sions for ICVCs are in the OEIC Regulations 2001,[240] made by the Treasury under FSMA, section 262. Further detailed requirements (imposed under powers conferred by the OIEC regulations on the FSA for the purposes of regulating ICVCs) are contained, together with the corresponding AUT provisions, in the COLL Sourcebook of the FSA Handbook. ICVCs, like AUTs may become 'UCITS schemes' or may adopt wider investment and borrowing powers and become 'non-UCITS retail schemes' or QISs.[241]

An ICVC is constituted by an 'instrument of incorporation' (corresponding to a **17.98** trust deed in the case of an AUT) and it must have at least one director. If there is only one director, that director must be a body corporate with permission to act

---

[233] s 257. See FSA Handbook, EG 14.1–14.5. Contravention of the direction is civilly actionable by persons suffering loss: s 257(5) cross-referring to s 150. For the procedure, see ss 259–261.
[234] s 257(2)(a): this direction is addressed to the manager.
[235] s 257(2)(b): this direction is addressed to the manager and trustee.
[236] s 258. See FSA Handbook, EG 14.1–14.5.
[237] s 254. See FSA Handbook, EG 14.1–14.5.
[238] See FSA Handbook, EG 14.5.
[239] See para 17.61 *et seq.*
[240] SI 2001/1228, as amended by SI 2001/3755, SI 2003/2066, SI 2005/923, and SI 2007/1973. For Northern Ireland, see the Open-ended Investment Company Regulations (Northern Ireland) 2004, SR 2004/335.
[241] See para 17.85 above.

as a director of an ICVC[242] and is termed (by the FSA Handbook) the 'authorised corporate director' (the 'ACD'). Corresponding to the trustee of an AUT, there must also be a 'depositary' to take responsibility for the safekeeping of the scheme property[243]

17.99 Although, as will be noted below, in essence the regulatory regime for AUTs and ICVCs is very similar, there are differences stemming from the fact that an ICVC is a corporation—with a separate legal existence. It acquires its corporate status when the FSA confers an authorisation order.[244] ICVCs have their own 'Corporate Code' which is set out in the OEIC Regulations[245] and they are entered on a Register kept by the FSA.[246] The Code is a modification of the corresponding provisions in the Companies Act 1985[247] applicable to ordinary registered companies.

Requirements for an 'authorisation order'

17.100 The basic requirements for obtaining an authorisation order are set out in the OEIC Regulations[248] and are very similar to those for AUTs but reflect the fact that an OEIC is a separate legal entity, with an ACD[249] instead of an AUT 'manager' and with a 'depositary' instead of an AUT 'trustee'.

17.101 The ACD and depositary, who must both be 'authorised persons' with permission to act as ACD and depositary respectively,[250] must be independent of each other.[251] The depositary must be a body corporate incorporated either in the UK or another EEA State and have its affairs administered in the country in which it is incorporated, with a place of business in the UK.[252] The ICVC must have its head office in England, Wales, or Scotland[253] and will, of course, be incorporated there (under the OEIC Regulations). The ICVCs name must not be 'undesirable or misleading',[254] and 'the aims of the company must be reasonably capable of being

---

[242] OIEC Regulations, reg 15(6).

[243] Reg 5 and Sched 1. As noted above (para 17.58), the FSA Handbook uses the term 'depositary' to cover both the depositary of an ICVC and a trustee of an AUT.

[244] OEIC Regulations, reg 3.

[245] Regs 34–70.

[246] Reg 4. See OEIC Regulations Part IV. The FSA performs various 'registrar' functions.

[247] Since replaced by the Companies Act 2006.

[248] OIEC Regulations reg 15 and see Part IV.

[249] For the 'ACD', see para 17.98, above.

[250] OIEC Regulations reg 15(6) (ACD) and 15(8)(d) (depositary). If the OEIC has more than one director, they must be 'fit and proper' (reg 15(5)) with appropriate combined expertise (reg 15(7)).

[251] Reg 15(8)(f): the depositary must be independent of both the directors and company. COLL 6.9.2G–6.9.6G contains Guidance from the FSA on how the FSA interprets 'independence'.

[252] Reg 15(8)(a)–(c).

[253] Reg 15(3).

[254] Reg 15(9). And see the 'company law' provisions as to names in regs 18 (FSA as Registrar's approval), reg 19 (prohibition of certain names), and reg 20 (Registrar's index of names). COLL 6.9.9G contains FSA guidance on misleading names.

achieved'.[255] Finally, the participants must be able to withdraw their contributions (ie realise their shares) at a price reflecting the net-asset worth of the scheme.[256]

The other requirements for an authorisation order are also very similar to those **17.102** that AUTs have to satisfy. Thus there is the general requirement to comply with the OEIC Regulations and FSA rules[257] (which are mainly in the COLL Module),and the need to provide the FSA with the requisite documents including (a) the instrument of incorporation, and (b) a solicitor's certificate stating that the instrument complies with OEIC Regulations.[258]

The ICVC regulatory regime

In setting out the regulatory framework, the OEIC Regulations make provision as **17.103** to the determination of applications for 'authorisation orders'.[259] In addition, the regulations extend the FSA's power (under FSMA in relation to AUTs)[260] to make 'trust scheme rules' and 'scheme particular rules' in relation to ICVCs.[261] And provision is made (adapting the relevant FSMA sections) for the modification or waiver of these rules on request.[262] For more details of these rules see the discussion on AUTs above.[263]

ICVCs are not subject to the extensive powers of investigation in relation to CISs **17.104** in general, conferred on the FSA by FSMA[264] However correspondingly wide powers are conferred on the FSA by the OEIC Regulations.[265] Similarly, those Regulations confer corresponding powers of intervention in relation to ICVCs when things go wrong. Thus the FSA may issue 'directions' requiring that the issue or redemption, or both, of shares cease or that the ICVC be wound up.[266] Moreover, the FSA may apply to court for an order removing and replacing any

---

[255] Reg 15(10)—the wording is slightly different to the corresponding provision in relation to AUTs (see para 17.90, above).

[256] Reg 15(11) either by redemption or repurchase, or sale on an exchange.

[257] Reg 15(1)(a).

[258] Reg 14.

[259] See reg 12 (application), reg 13 (particulars of directors), reg 14 (determination), reg 16 (procedure when refusing), regs 21–22 (alterations to schemes and changes of manager and trustee), regs 23–24 (request for revocation of authorisation order).

[260] See s 247 (trust scheme rules) and s 248 (scheme particular rules), considered at paras 17.93 and 17.94 above.

[261] Reg 6. As noted above, one set of rules is made for 'authorised funds', ie AUTs and ICVCs.

[262] Reg 7.

[263] Para 17.92 *et seq.*

[264] s 284—see subs (1)(c), although curiously the FSA Handbook EG 3.11 seems to assume that s 284 applies to all CISs.

[265] Reg 30.

[266] Reg 25. Again (see n 233), contravention is civilly actionable by persons suffering loss: reg 25(2) cross-referring to s 150. For the procedure, see regs 27–29.

director or the depositary, or both, or removing either or both and for the appointment of an authorised person to wind up the scheme.[267] Finally, the FSA may revoke the ICVC's authorisation order,[268] this time the Regulations making it clear that, before revocation, the FSA must ensure that steps have been taken to secure the winding up of the ICVC.[269]

(Overseas) Recognised CISs

General

17.105 Whilst the term 'authorised' when used in relation to AUTs or OEICs (or rather, ICVCs)[270] connotes a CIS that is established in the UK and that has an 'authorisation order' from the FSA, the term 'recognised' when used in relation to a CIS connotes a CIS constituted *outside* the UK but 'recognised' in the UK by virtue of one of three provisions: section 264 or 270 or 272. In essence, those provisions apply to those CISs that are regarded as sufficiently regulated in their home jurisdictions to be treated—primarily for the purposes of promotion to the public—as if they were UK AUTs or ICVCs.

17.106 Recognised status is sought for overseas schemes so that they may be promoted to the public in the UK. However, recognition brings with it a degree of regulatory oversight by the FSA, which varies depending on the category of 'recognised scheme'. Common to all recognised schemes is the requirement, imposed by the FSA under powers conferred by FSMA, section 283 and contained in the COLL Module,[271] that they maintain certain 'facilities' at a place of business in the UK[272] so that UK investors may readily obtain information about the scheme, be able to redeem their units in it and complain to it. Moreover, recognised schemes are subject to the FSA's extensive investigation powers over all CISs.[273]

17.107 The three categories of recognised scheme will now be considered. The UK is constrained in the extent to which it can exercise regulatory powers over the first category—the EEA (UCITS) recognised schemes—by EC law and this is reflected in the limited regulatory power the FSA has over them.

---

[267] Reg 26.

[268] Reg 23.

[269] Reg 23(3). There is no corresponding provision (in relation to AUTs) in s 254, but see FSA Handbook, EG 14.5, noted at n 238 above.

[270] See paras 17.88 and 17.96 above.

[271] COLL 9.4, see further, para 17.143, below.

[272] See COLL 9.4.6R: either the operator's principal place of business in the UK or an alternative 'convenient' address (which, in the case of a s 272 scheme where the operator is not an authorised person, must be the principal place of business of the authorised person who is the representative of the operator).

[273] See FSMA, s 284(1)(b).

EEA (UCITS) schemes: FSMA, section 264

General

The first category of 'recognised' CIS covers those authorised in other EEA **17.108** Member States and complying with the UCITS Directive.[274] As noted above, these have a 'single market passport' enabling them to be marketed, without the need for further authorisation, throughout the EEA single market. The FSMA, section 264 makes provision for such CISs, conferring on them 'recognised' CIS status. Moreover, again in compliance with EC obligations, the operator, trustee, or depositary of such a scheme (being authorised in the home Member State) is automatically an 'authorised person' under FSMA[275] in so far as it acts as such.[276]

In order to be recognised under section 264, a CIS must be 'constituted in another **17.109** EEA State' and satisfy requirements set out in Treasury Regulations.[277] The requirements in the Regulations[278] are that the CIS falls within the UCITS Directive, as amended. The term 'constituted in another EEA State' is defined[279] so that, in essence, the CIS must involve a company incorporated under the law of another EEA Member State: the CIS must either be an OEIC incorporated in that Member State or be managed by a company incorporated in that Member State (in which case it must also be 'constituted'—whether under contract or trust law—under that law). In addition, before the scheme can acquire 'recognised' status under section 264, its 'operator'[280] must give the FSA at least two months' notice of how the scheme is intended to be marketed in the UK.[281] In accordance with the UCITS Directive,[282] the FSA then has two months to consider if the marketing method complies with UK law. If it decides that it does not, the FSA may serve a notice to that effect.[283] The service of such a notice of objection by the

---

[274] See para 17.03 above.

[275] FSMA, s 31(1)(d) and Sched 5, para 1(1),(2). See further, para 17.126 below. As the 'operator' of an OEIC is always the OEIC itself (see s 237(2)), if the CIS is an OEIC, it will therefore be an 'authorised person' under these provisions. The FSA Handbook calls such persons 'UCITS qualifiers'.

[276] Sched 5, para 2(1).

[277] s 264(1)(a).

[278] The FSMA 2000 (Collective Investment Schemes Constituted in Other EEA States) Regulations 2001, SI 2001/2383, as amended by SI 2003/2066 (implementing UCITS III, see para 17.03 above).

[279] s 264(5).

[280] Partially defined in s 237(2). If the scheme is neither an OEIC nor a unit trust scheme (and hence s 237(2) does not apply), presumably the 'operator' is the manager of the scheme.

[281] s 264(1)(b) and see COLL 9.2.2G. See s 264(3) and COLL 9.2.1 for the requisite contents of the notice, including a certificate from the home State regulators that the scheme enjoys marketing rights under EC law. (As regards UK AUTs and ICVCs, the FSA has power under s 246 and OEIC Regulations reg 17 (respectively) to issue such a certificate should they wish the market in other EEA States.)

[282] Art 46.

[283] s 264(2): on (a) the 'operator' and (b) the home State regulators. For the contents of the notice, see s 264(4). See also s 265 (representations and reference to the Financial Services and Markets Tribunal).

FSA precludes the scheme from being 'recognised'.[284] Once the scheme is recognised, the operator may, by 'written notice' to the FSA cause the scheme to cease to be recognised.[285]

FSA powers

17.110 The division of regulatory responsibilities between the home and host regulators under the UCITS Directive[286] is reflected in FSMA, which therefore confers limited powers on the FSA in relation to section 264 recognised schemes. First, all the FSA rules are disapplied in relation to such schemes[287] (as the schemes are subject to corresponding rules in their host State), except for the financial promotion rules,[288] and the rules as to facilities and information mentioned above.[289] Second, the only sanction the FSA has over such schemes is to issue a direction (of limited duration)[290] suspending the exemption which the scheme enjoys from the general restriction on the promotion of CISs,[291] if the operator breaches the financial promotion rules.[292] As it is the home State regulator that has primary disciplinary responsibility, notice of the direction must be given to it.[293] In addition (as this is consistent with EC law), the provision giving the FSA extensive investigation powers over CISs applies to section 264 recognised schemes in relation to their UK activities.[294]

**Schemes authorised in 'designated countries or territories':
FSMA, section 270**

General

17.111 The FSMA, section 270 makes provision for the second category of 'recognised' CIS: certain CISs managed and authorised[295] in a country or territory 'designated'

---

[284] s 264(2).

[285] s 264(6)–(7). In accordance with EC law (see below) the FSA has no power to terminate such a scheme's recognition of its own accord. But see s 251 (suspension of promotion) also noted below.

[286] See para 17.03 and n13

[287] s 266.

[288] Made under s 145 and in the FSA Handbook in COBS 4. See the UCITS Directive (n 13), Art 44 applying the 'host' State promotion rules.

[289] See para 17.106 above—made under s 283(1). Section 283(2) (notice from FSA requiring information to be included in promotions) also applies to s 264 recognised schemes. See the UCITS Directive (n 13), Art 45.

[290] s 267(3).

[291] See s 238, considered in para 17.137 below.

[292] s 267. For the procedure, see s 268–270.

[293] s 268(3)(b). And see FSA Handbook, EG 14.10 where the FSA confirms that it will ask the home State regulators 'to take such action . . . as will resolve the FSA's concerns'.

[294] s 284(1)(b).

[295] It seems clear from the wording of s 270(1) that the management of the scheme must occur in the same (designated) country in which it is authorised.

by Treasury Order. The section sets out the circumstances when the Treasury may make such an Order (after consultation with the FSA)[296]—in essence where it is satisfied both that the country's law (and practice) affords UK investors 'at least equivalent' protection to that under UK law in relation to 'comparable' authorised schemes,[297] and that their regulators cooperate with the FSA.[298] This is in contrast to the test under section 272 (see below, in relation to individually recognised schemes), which merely requires 'adequate' protection, presumably because it was thought appropriate to have a more exacting test in the case of the 'blanket recognition' conferred under section 270. The Treasury has made such Orders in respect of:[299] Guernsey, Jersey, the Isle of Man, and Bermuda.

The section also sets out the procedure that must be followed before a CIS from **17.112** such a 'designated' country or territory becomes a 'recognised scheme'. Thus the 'operator'[300] must give the FSA written notice[301] that he wishes his scheme to be recognised and the FSA has two months to respond.[302] Unless the FSA serves a 'warning notice'[303] that it proposes to refuse recognition within the two months, the scheme becomes recognised unless the FSA has given earlier approval.[304]

FSA powers

The powers of the FSA under section 283 to require all recognised schemes to **17.113** maintain certain 'facilities' at a place of business in the UK and its extensive investigation powers in relation to all CISs—including 'recognised' schemes[305]— under section 284 have already been noted.[306] In addition, the FSA has further powers over both section 270 (and section 272) schemes. First, it may make rules, corresponding to the 'scheme particular rules' in relation to AUTs[307] and ICVCs,[308]

---

[296] The Treasury must ask the FSA for a Report on the criteria for designation (s 270(5)(b)), the FSA must provide such a Report (s 270(5)(b)), and the Treasury must 'have regard' to the Report (s 270(5)(c)).

[297] s 270(2)(a). ie AUTs and/or ICVCs: see s 270(4).

[298] s 270(2)(b).

[299] See the FSMA 2000 (Transitional Provisions) (Authorised Persons) Order 2001, SI 2001/2636, art 67: scheme recognised under FSA 1986, s 87 (the predecessor to FSMA, s 270) are automatically treated as recognised under s 270. See now the FSMA 2000 (CIS) (Designated Countries and Territories) Order 2003, SI 2003/1181 (covering Guernsey, Jersey, and the Isle of Man).

[300] Partially defined in s 237(2). If the scheme is neither an OEIC nor a unit trust scheme (and hence s 237(2) does not apply), presumably the 'operator' is the manager of the scheme.

[301] For the contents, see s 270(6) and COLL 9.3.

[302] s 270(1)(c),(d).

[303] See FSMA, s 387.

[304] s 270(1)(d).

[305] See especially s 284(1)(b).

[306] See para 17.106 above.

[307] Under s 248, see para 17.94 above.

[308] Under OEIC Regulations, reg 6, see para 17.103 above.

for such recognised schemes.[309] Second, the FSA has powers of intervention if things go wrong. Thus the FSA may revoke recognition[310] and it may also issue 'directions' suspending recognition.[311] Alternatively, the FSA may decide to refer the matter to the relevant home regulator.[312]

Individually recognised overseas schemes: FSMA, section 272

General

17.114   FSMA, section 272 makes provision for the third category of 'recognised' CIS, enabling the FSA to recognise overseas schemes on an individual basis. This is a residual category in that it only applies to schemes that do not qualify for recognition under either section 264 (schemes from other EEA Member States)[313] or section 270 (schemes from Treasury 'designated' countries or territories).[314] The FSA has a discretion to make an order recognising such a scheme if it 'appears to' the FSA that certain requirements—some formal, some requiring judgement as to their 'adequacy' to be taken—are satisfied. Very few schemes have sought recognition under this head.

17.115   Bearing in mind that the main consequence of obtaining 'recognised' status is that the scheme may be promoted in the same way as UK AUTs or ICVCs (and schemes recognised under sections 270 and 272), clearly the essence of these requirements is that such individually recognised schemes are as 'safe' for retail investors as other 'regulated' schemes. Of the requirements, which will be summarised below, the crucial one is that 'adequate' protection is afforded to participants. As noted above, this requirement is less exacting than the 'at least equivalent' protection precondition for a country or territory to be designated under section 270. As also suggested above, it was probably thought appropriate that the test could be less strict for individual recognition. However, there is no guidance in FSMA on how the FSA is to judge adequacy. In particular, there is no express requirement that the FSA look to 'comparable' UK authorised schemes[315] nor that it look to the law and *practice* of the overseas regulatory regime.[316]

---

[309] s 278. See COLL 9.3.2R and 9.3.3R (information in and preparation and maintenance of prospectus).

[310] Under s 279 (and see s 280 for the procedure). See EG 14.9 and para 17.150 below.

[311] s 281 (and see s 282 for the procedure). See EG 14.9 and para 17.150 below.

[312] See FSA Handbook, EG 14.10 and para 17.150 below.

[313] See para 17.107 *et seq*. above.

[314] See para 17.111 *et seq*. above.

[315] s 272(5) only makes 'comparable authorised schemes' relevant to other issues (whether the constitution and management are 'adequate' (s 272(3)), and whether powers and duties of operator and (if any) trustee or depositary are 'adequate' (s 272(4))).

[316] Made explicit in s 270, see para 17.111, above.

There are a number of formal requirements. First, the scheme must either be an **17.116**
OEIC[317] or the 'operator'[318] must be a body corporate.[319] Second, the operator
and trustee or depositary (if any) must either, if an authorised person under the Act,
have permission to act as such or, if not an authorised person, be a 'fit and proper
person' to so act.[320] Third, the participants must be entitled (although not necessarily on demand)[321] to have their units redeemed (or to sell their units on an
investment exchange)[322] at a price related to the net-asset value of the scheme.[323]

There then follow a number of factors requiring the FSA to exercise judgement of **17.117**
their 'adequacy'. In particular, as noted above, 'adequate' protection must be
afforded to participants in the scheme.[324] The 'arrangements' for the scheme's
'constitution and management' must be 'adequate'.[325] Finally, the 'powers and
duties' of the operator and (if any) trustee or depositary must be 'adequate'.[326] In
judging adequacy in the last two (but not first) cases, the FSA must 'have regard'
to (a) any rule of law and (b) any matter which is or could be subject to rules applicable to 'comparable' authorised UK schemes.[327]

Finally, there are three further requirements. Thus the operator and trustee or **17.118**
depositary (if any) must be 'able and willing' to cooperate with the FSA. The name
of the scheme must not be 'undesirable or misleading'[328] and the purposes of the
schemes must be 'reasonably capable of being successfully carried into effect'.[329]

FSMA also sets out the procedure, which must be followed by a CIS that wishes **17.119**
to obtain individual recognition under section 272. The 'operator'[330] must make

---

[317] As defined in s 236, see para 17.61 *et seq.* above.
[318] Partially defined in s 237(2). If the scheme is neither an OEIC nor a unit trust scheme (and
hence s 237(2) does not apply), presumably the 'operator' is the manager of the scheme.
[319] s 272(7).
[320] s 272(8), (9). Section 273 sets out the matters, which the FSA 'may' take into account in
deciding if they are 'fit and proper'. 'Operators' (see n 318 above) and trustees/depositaries will
not need to be 'authorised persons' if they do not carry on 'regulated activities' in the UK: see para
17.126 below.
[321] s 272(15). But if the CIS is an OEIC, note that s 236(3)(a) (realisation within 'reasonable'
period, considered further in para 17.67 above) will be satisfied.
[322] s 272(14).
[323] s 272(13). Again, if the CIS is an OEIC, note that s 236(3)(b), considered further in para
17.70 above, will be satisfied.
[324] s 272(2).
[325] s 272(3). And note the formal requirements as to form, status of operator, and (if any) trustee
or depositary and redemption of units considered above.
[326] s 272(4).
[327] s 272(5).
[328] s 272(11), cf the same requirement for AUTs (s 243(8), para 17.90 above) and ICVCs (OEIC
Regulations, reg 15(9), para 17.101 above).
[329] s 272(9), cf the same requirement for AUTs (s 243(9), para 17.90 above) and ICVCs (OEIC
Regulations, reg 15(10), para 17.101 above).
[330] A term only partially defined in s 237(2), see n 318 above.

the application[331] and the FSA has six months to respond.[332] Moreover, once recognised, the operator must notify the FSA of alterations of the scheme, its operator, trustee, or depositary.[333]

FSA powers

17.120 The power of the FSA under section 283 to require all recognised schemes to maintain certain 'facilities' at a place of business in the UK and its extensive investigation powers in relation to all CISs—including 'recognised' schemes—under section 284 have already been noted,[334] as have the FSA's further powers over both section 272 (and section 270) schemes.[335] These are the FSA's power to make rules, corresponding to the 'scheme particular rules' in relation to AUTs and ICVCs, for such schemes[336] and its powers of intervention if things go wrong. Thus the FSA may revoke recognition[337] and it may also issue 'directions' suspending recognition.[338] Alternatively, the FSA may decide to refer the matter to the relevant home regulator.[339]

'Unregulated' CISs

17.121 The CISs so far considered, the UK 'authorised funds', and the overseas 'recognised schemes', all have to fulfil detailed requirements as to their constitution and operation. CISs not satisfying these requirements may be established, but they suffer from the disadvantage that generally they cannot be promoted to the general public.[340] Thus 'unregulated schemes' are created in order to enable groups of investors to undertake collective investment, unconstrained by FSA regulation as far as constitution and operation is concerned. To that extent they are 'unregulated', although those establishing and operating those schemes in the UK are

---

[331] Under s 274 which is in similar terms to s 242 (application for AUT authorisation order). See also COLL 9.3.

[332] s 275—again similar to s 242 in relation to AUTs. See s 276 (procedure when refusing an application).

[333] s 272.

[334] See para 17.106 above.

[335] See para 17.113 above.

[336] s 278. See COLL 9.3.2R and 9.3.3R (information in and preparation and maintenance of prospectus).

[337] Under s 279 (and see s 280 for the procedure). See FSA Handbook, EG 14.9 and para 17.150 below.

[338] s 281 (and see s 282 for the procedure). See FSA Handbook, EG 14.9 and para 17.150 below.

[339] See EG 14.10 and para 17.150 below.

[340] ss 21 and 238. See n 406.

certainly subject to the FSMA regulatory regime in general. In particular, as well as being unable to promote the scheme to the public, their managers need to be authorised persons[341] and in so far as they (and the depositaries, if any) are authorised persons, they are subject to the FSA Handbook.[342]

Some so-called 'hedge funds',[343] funds that invite contributions of a significant **17.122** size and adopt sophisticated investment strategies, are structured as 'unregulated' CISs, usually entailing contractual arrangements and/or offshore OEICs. Other examples of unregulated CISs are 'private equity' or 'venture capital' funds providing funds for new business. These are often limited partnerships,[344] the general partner being the operator and the limited partners are the other 'participants'. Examples of unregulated CISs set up as unit trusts are Enterprise Zone Property Unit Trusts ('EZPUTs').[345] Moreover, many offshore funds, for example US mutual funds, are also 'unregulated' CISs. *Sukuks*—investment vehicles structured so as to be *Shari'a* compliant—may also be 'unregulated' CISs, but it is proposed that they be exempted from that definition and regulated in accordance with their economic substance, rather than legal form.[346]

However, as noted above, *any* arrangement for collective investment is potentially **17.123** a CIS and hence may constitute an 'unregulated' CIS. In consequence, care must be taken when establishing schemes that involve the pooling of contributions and/or collective management in order to generate profits or income, as an unregulated CIS may, inadvertently, arise.[347] If those involved are not 'authorised persons' then serious consequences may follow, as the next section will now consider.

---

[341] As they carry on the regulated activity of managing investments (RAO, art 37) or advising (RAO, art 53): See 'FSA DP 05/4' (n 343), para 2.49.

[342] See para 17.141 *et seq*. below.

[343] See the FSA discussion papers (i) DP 05/4, 'Hedge Funds: A discussion of risk and regulatory engagement' (June 2005) ('FSA DP 05/4') and the related Feedback Statement (FS06/2), March 2006, (ii) DP 05/03, 'Wider range retail investment products: consumer protection in a rapidly changing world' (June 2005) and the related Feedback Statement (FS 06/3), March 2006 and (iii) DP16, 'Hedge Funds and the FSA' (August 2002) and the related Feedback Statement, March 2003. See also 'Private Equity: A discussion of risk and regulatory engagement' (November 2006, DP 06/6) and the related Feedback Statement (FS 07/3), June 2007.

[344] Under the Limited Partnership Act 1907.

[345] See *Ball v Banner & others* [2000] WL 824097 (CA, Civ Div).

[346] See the Consultation Paper on the legislative framework for the regulation of alternative finance investment bonds (Sukuk) issued by HMT and the FSA in December 2008.

[347] See the *The Russell-Cooke Trust Co* and *Fradley* cases, noted in para 17.08 above where CISs were found to have been inadvertently created. Ostrich farms and some so-called 'land banking' companies are other examples of CISs that were eventually shut down at the instigation of the FSA.

Application of FSMA to CISs

General

17.124 FSMA 2000 uses two key provisions to regulate financial services activities and their promotion. The first is the so-called 'general prohibition' in section 19 which precludes anyone other than an 'authorised person' or 'exempt person' from carrying on 'regulated activity' in the UK.[348] The second is the so-called 'financial promotion restriction' in section 21, which restricts the promotion of 'investment activity'. Thus the scope of the terms 'regulated activity' and 'investment activity' determines the scope of regulation and is achieved by Treasury Order: the Regulated Activities Order (the 'RAO')[349] and the Financial Promotion Order (the 'FPO'),[350] respectively. These Orders define 'regulated activity' and 'investment activity' respectively. How these terms catch involvement in and the promotion of a CIS is explained below. Breaching section 19 or 21 has serious consequences. Contraventions of the sections are criminal offences,[351] consequent agreements are unenforceable,[352] and the FSA has power to apply to court for injunctive orders[353] and orders requiring the payment of compensation and/or the 'disgorgement' of profits.[354]

17.125 It is important at the outset to distinguish the status of an 'authorised person' from that of an 'authorised fund'. As noted above, the latter term refers to an AUT or ICVC, that is, a CIS that has the benefit of an FSA 'authorisation order'.[355] An 'authorised person' is usually (but by no means invariably)[356] a person who has a 'Part IV permission' from the FSA to undertake one or more categories of regulated activity.[357]

---

[348] There is limited guidance on the meaning of 'in the UK' in s 418. In *FSA v Fradley and Woodward* [2005] EWCA Civ 1183, Arden LJ held that 'it is sufficient if the activities which [take] place in this jurisdiction [are] a significant part of the business activity of running the CIS'; hence in that case where (i) the operator had an accommodation address and bank account in the UK and (ii) many participants were UK residents, it did not matter that the operator had moved his operations outside the UK.

[349] FSMA 2000 (Regulated Activities) Order 2001, SI 2001/544, as extensively amended.

[350] FSMA 2000 (Financial Promotion) Order 2005, SI 2005/1529, as amended, replacing SI 2001/1335, as amended.

[351] See FSMA, ss 23 and 25, respectively.

[352] See FSMA, ss 26–28 and 30, respectively.

[353] See FSMA, s 380.

[354] See FSMA, s 382.

[355] See para 17.84.

[356] See FSMA, s 31(b)–(d) for the other categories of 'authorised person' and note Sched 5, para 17.128 below.

[357] As also noted above, in order to obtain an 'authorisation order' the manager/ACD and trustee/depositary of the AUT/ICVC (respectively) need to be 'authorised persons'.

Section 19: Regulated activity

The RAO renders each of the three functions of establishing, operating, and winding up a CIS, if done 'by way of business',[358] a 'regulated activity'.[359] Thus only authorised (or exempt) persons[360] are permitted to set up, run, and wind up a CIS by way of business. Moreover, acting in certain specific CIS capacities 'by way of business' is also a regulated activity: acting as trustee of an AUT,[361] acting as the 'depositary' of an OEIC, and as the sole director of an OEIC.[362]

17.126

Less obviously, the RAO renders other activities in relation to CISs 'regulated activities'. Participatory rights in CISs— 'units' in FSMA terminology[363]—are one of the so-called 'specified investments' in the RAO[364] with the result that various activities 'by way of business' in relation to such 'units' are also 'regulated activities'. Thus dealing in units as principal[365] or agent,[366] arranging deals in units,[367] managing assets belonging to another which include units,[368] safeguarding and administering such assets (or arranging for others to do so),[369] and advising on the merits of investment in particular units[370] are all 'regulated activities'. Many of these activities will be undertaken by those actually operating the CIS involved, but other persons, for example those merely advising on or arranging investment in the CISs, may be caught by these more general provisions and will require authorised (or exempt) person status in order to undertake them.

17.127

---

[358] The meaning of which is considered in paras 17.29 – 17.31 above.

[359] RAO, art 51(1)(a).

[360] As noted above, FSMA, Sched 5 confers automatic 'authorised person' status on (i) the operator, trustee, or depositary of a s 264 (ie an EEA (UCITS)) recognised scheme (see para 17.108) and (ii) on an ICVC (see para 17.128).

[361] RAO, art 51(1)(b). Section 243(7) requires a trustee of an AUT to be an 'authorised person': see para 17.88 above.

[362] RAO, art 51(1)(c). OEIC Regulations, reg 15 requires the depositary and ACD of an ICVC to be an 'authorised person': see para 17.101 above.

[363] See para 17.56 above.

[364] RAO, art 81. They fall within the term 'security' (see RAO, art 3(1)). Moreover, 'any right to or interest in' a unit is itself a 'specified investment' and 'security': RAO, art 89.

[365] ibid, art 14, and note the specific exclusion in art 15, and more general exclusions in arts 66(1), 68–72A.

[366] ibid, art 21, and note the specific exclusion in art 22, and more general exclusions in arts 67–72E.

[367] ibid, art 25, and note the specific exclusions in arts 26–29,32,33 and more general exclusions in arts 66(2)–72E.

[368] ibid, art 37, and note the specific exclusion in art 38, and more general exclusions in arts 66(3), 68, 69, 72A, 72C, 72E.

[369] ibid, art 40, and note the specific exclusions in arts 41–43 and more general exclusions in arts 66–69, 71, 72A, 72C, 72E.

[370] ibid, art 53, and note the specific exclusion in art 54 and more general exclusions in arts 66–70, 72–72A, 72B, 72D, 72E.

17.128 An OEIC is a legal person and therefore if it (as opposed to its manager or depositary)[371] undertakes any 'regulated activity' in the UK it will need to be an 'authorised person'. An ICVC—the only type of OIEC which can be established in the UK—is automatically an 'authorised person',[372] but OEICs from abroad that conduct regulated activities in the UK will need to obtain the requisite permission from the FSA. However, an OEIC from another EEA Member State that is recognised under s 264[373] is (in accordance with UK obligations under the UCITS Directive) also automatically an 'authorised person'.[374]

Restrictions on financial promotion

General

17.129 Two provisions of FSMA are relevant to the promotion of CISs: the more general section 21, and the specific (to CISs) section 238. These two provisions have a number of common features.

17.130 First, they are both expressed in terms of restricting the 'communicat[ion of] an invitation or inducement',[375] the word 'communicate' being stated to include 'causing a communication to be made'.[376] Thus they cover every form of making information known ('communicate' or 'causing a communication') as long as there is a promotional element ('invitation or inducement'). Second, they confer power on the Treasury to exempt certain communications from the restriction, by Order.[377] Third, the territorial scope is similar in that there is no statutory territorial limitation apart from a provision that communications originating outside the UK are only caught if they are 'capable of having an effect in the UK'.[378] Thus the restrictions apply to both 'inward' and 'outward' communications, although in practice the relevant Treasury Orders make specific (similar) provision in this respect, for example ensuring that the territorial scope is consistent with the Electronic Commerce Directive.[379]

---

[371] See n 362 above: acting as depositary or sole director of an OEIC is a 'regulated activity'.

[372] Sched 5, para 1(3).

[373] See para 17.108, above.

[374] See Sched 5, para 1(1): the 'operator' of such a scheme is an authorised person and the operator of an OEIC is the OEIC itself (see s 237(2)). See also n 275.

[375] ss 21(1), 238(1).

[376] ss 21(13); 238(9).

[377] ss 21(5),(6); 238(6),(7). The Orders made, which contain similar exemptions, are noted below. The FPO (see para 17.124, n 350) is the relevant Order made under s 21.

[378] ss 21(3); 238(3). These subsections may be (but have not been) repealed by Treasury Order: s 21(7); s 238(8).

[379] Directive No 2000/31/EC, [2000] OJ L178/1—which generally adopts a 'country of origin' approach to the regulation of electronic communications within the EEA.

Section 21: The general financial promotion restriction

Section 21 imposes a general financial promotion restriction. Apart from so-called **17.131** 'exempt communications', which are set out in the FPO,[380] essentially section 21 requires the involvement of authorised persons in all financial promotions 'in the course of business'.[381] Thus, 'exempt communications' apart, the only financial promotions that are permitted are those communicated *by* authorised persons or those whose contents have been *approved by* authorised persons. The FSA Handbook, in its COBS Module, then regulates the communication and approval of promotions by authorised persons.[382]

The way in which the financial promotion restriction, and the FPO made under **17.132** it, catch the promotion of units in a CIS is rather complex but similar to the way in which the RAO catches the various activities in relation to such units. Section 21 restricts the promotion of 'investment activity' which is defined in terms of 'controlled activity' and 'controlled investments', as specified in the FPO. These two concepts are generally similar to 'specified activity' and 'specified investments' in the RAO, but they are of slightly different scope to reflect the slightly different reach of the general prohibition in section 19 (defined in terms of 'regulated activity') on the one hand and the financial promotion restriction in section 21 (defined in terms of 'investment activity') on the other. In particular, although 'units' in CISs (as well as being 'specified investments' in the RAO) are also 'controlled investments'[383] in the FPO, establishing, operating, or winding up a CIS (although a 'regulated activity') is not a 'controlled activity' in the FPO.[384] The result is that promoting the buying (or selling) of units is caught.[385] Moreover, as dealing in units as principal or agent,[386] arranging deals in units,[387] managing assets belonging to another which include units,[388] safeguarding and administering such assets (or arranging for others to do so),[389] and advising on the merits of

---

[380] See para 17.124 above.

[381] A wider concept than 'by way of business', the term used in s 22 (and considered in paras 17.29–17.31 above).

[382] In COBS 4, see para 17.151 below.

[383] FPO, Sched 1, para 19. They fall within the term 'security' (see ibid, para 28(c)). Moreover, 'any right to or interest in' a unit is itself a 'specified investment' and 'security': ibid, para 27.

[384] As there is no need to control the promotion of these activities themselves (as they are undertaken by professionals), as opposed to the promotion of units (ie participation) in them.

[385] By s 21(8)(b): 'exercising any rights conferred by a controlled investment to acquire, dispose of, underwrite or convert a controlled investment'. And see s 21(8)(a) (n 391, below): as a result of the wide meaning given to 'buying' and 'selling' in FPO, Sched 1 para 28, this would also fall within s 21(8)(a) as the promotion of 'dealing'.

[386] FPO, Sched 1 para 3(1).

[387] ibid, Sched 1 para 4.

[388] ibid, Sched 1 para 5.

[389] ibid, Sched 1 para 6.

investment in particular units[390] are all 'controlled activities', promoting any of these activities[391] is also caught by the financial promotion restriction.

17.133 The FPO, as well as defining the scope of the financial promotion restriction, also sets outs which financial promotions are exempt from it. For these purposes, the FPO divides communications first into 'real time' and 'non-real time'[392] communications and then subdivides 'real time' communications into 'solicited' and 'unsolicited'[393] communications. Unsurprisingly, the largest number of exemptions applies to 'non-real time' communications, whilst the least apply to 'unsolicited real time'. This list of 'exempt communications' is very long. As well as covering the more obvious situations, such as non-specific ('generic') communications,[394] communications by 'mere conduits',[395] and communication to 'investment professionals'[396] the FPO also refines the territorial application of the financial promotion restriction.[397] Moreover, there are specific exemptions for 'non-real time' and 'solicited real time' communications by operators of sections 270 and 272 recognised schemes[398] to their participants and by OEICs to certain of their creditors or members.[399] There are also more general exemptions in favour of 'certified high net worth individuals'[400] and 'sophisticated investors'.[401]

Sections 238 and 240: Additional CIS promotion restriction

General

17.134 Section 238 imposes a further promotion restriction in relation to CISs on authorised persons, with the aim of ensuring that generally only 'regulated schemes' are promoted to the general public.[402] The section is confined, in terms, to authorised persons because persons who are not authorised (or exempt) are caught by the

---

[390] ibid, Sched 1 para 7.

[391] To be precise, the promotion of 'entering or offering to enter into an agreement the making or performance of which by either party constitutes a controlled activity' s 21(1),(8)(a).

[392] Defined in FPO, art 7. 'Real time' are those 'made in the course of a personal visit, telephone conversation or other interactive dialogue' whilst 'non-real time' are those which are not 'real time'.

[393] Defined in FPO, art 8.

[394] FPO, art 17, ie those not identifying a *particular* product.

[395] ibid, art 18, ie by those who have no control over the content but merely transmit the communication.

[396] ibid, art 19, a term which includes authorised persons, exempt persons, governments, local authorities, international organisations.

[397] See especially FPO, arts 12, 20B, 30–33.

[398] See paras 17.111 *et seq.* and 17,114 *et seq.* above.

[399] FPO, arts 40, 44.

[400] FPO, art 48—and see art 49 (high net worth companies etc).

[401] FPO, art 50, 50A ('self-certified sophisticated investors') and art 51 (associations of high net worth or sophisticated investors).

[402] FSA Handbook, PERG 8.20G contains (limited) guidance on this provision.

general financial promotion restriction in section 21 discussed above.[403] As the promotion restriction in section 21 is inapplicable, not only to communications by authorised persons but also to communications where the contents have been 'approved' by an authorised person, section 240 precludes an authorised person approving a CIS communication if they would have been precluded by section 238 from making (or causing the making) of the communication themselves.

Contravention by an authorised person of section 238 or 240 constitutes a 'breach **17.135** of a requirement imposed' by FSMA and thus enables the FSA to exercise its usual powers of discipline[404] and, if necessary, of applying to court for injunctive and/or compensation and/or disgorgement orders.[405] Moreover, section 150 applies[406] to confer a right of action on a private person who suffers loss as a result of the contravention.[407]

Section 238 begins with a general blanket prohibition on authorised persons pro- **17.136** moting participation in *any* CIS.[408] However, there are a number of exceptions.[409] But it should be noted that in so far as the exceptions apply to permit authorised persons to promote (and approve the promotion) of certain schemes, those persons will be subject to the FSA Handbook,[410] in undertaking that promotion (or approval).

Exceptions

Section 238(3): 'Safe' collective investment schemes.[411] Section 238(3) excludes **17.137** from the blanket restriction on the promotion of CISs, three categories of schemes: AUTs,[412] ICVCs,[413] and recognised schemes.[414] It will be recalled that the first two categories are FSA-authorised schemes (so-called 'authorised funds' in its

---

[403] See para 17.131 *et seq.*

[404] ie public censure (FSMA, s 205), the imposition of a penalty (FSMA, s 206) or even variation or cancellation of permission (FSMA, s 45).

[405] See ss 380, 382.

[406] s 241, see (on the similar provision in the Financial Services Act 1986), *Seymour v Ockwell* [2005] EWHC 1137.

[407] See further s 150 and the FSMA 2000 (Rights of Action) Regulations 2001, SI 2001/2256 made thereunder, defining 'private person' and extending the right of action to certain other persons.

[408] s 238(1). Section 238(11) confirms that 'participate' means becoming a 'participant (within the meaning given by section 235(2)) in the scheme'.

[409] The exemption in relation to 'single property schemes' in s 239 is not considered as the requisite regulations have not been made by the Treasury.

[410] In particular, COBS 4, see para 17.151 below.

[411] See the FSA Guidance in its Handbook, PERG.8.20.

[412] See para 17.88 *et seq.* above.

[413] See para 17.96 *et seq.* above. Section 238(3)(b) calls these schemes 'constituted by an authorised' OEIC but, as noted above (see para 17.86), these are termed 'ICVCs' by the FSA in its Handbook.

[414] See para 17.105 *et seq.* above.

Handbook) and the last covers overseas schemes that are similarly heavily regulated by their overseas regulators. It follows that only such 'regulated schemes' (using the FSA term, which covers authorised funds and recognised schemes)[415] may be promoted (or their promotion approved) by authorised persons to the public at large. However, as also noted above,[416] there is one type of 'authorised fund', a 'qualified investor scheme' (so-called 'QISs'—intended for particular non-retail investors) which is treated by the FSA Handbook as an unregulated scheme as far promotion is concerned.

17.138 **Section 238(5): Limited promotion under FSA rules.** The FSA is given the power to make rules permitting the promotion of certain unregulated CISs 'otherwise than to the general public'.[417] These rules, which also apply to allow the promotion of 'qualified investor schemes' (QISs),[418] are contained in COBS 4.12 (and the Annex thereto) of the FSA Handbook. The Annex is in the form of a table, the left-hand column of which categorises the potential recipients of the promotion and the right hand column then sets out what type of CISs may be promoted to such recipients.

17.139 The Annex provides that *any* CIS may be promoted by authorised persons to a number of recipients, for example an 'eligible counterparty' or 'professional client'[419] (as defined in the FSA Handbook Glossary) or 'exempt person' (other than an appointed representative)[420] in the context of their exemption.[421] An authorised person may also promote *any* CIS to certain customers[422] if he has taken 'reasonable steps to ensure that investment in the . . . scheme is suitable'.[423] A more limited range of CISs may be promoted to other persons. For example, if a person is already a participant in an unregulated CIS or QIS then that scheme or another scheme 'whose underlying property and risk profile are both substantially similar'[424] may be promoted to them.[425]

17.140 **Section 238(6): Exemptions in Treasury Order.** Just as the FPO exempts certain communications ('exempt communications') from the general financial promotion

---

[415] See para 17.86 above.
[416] See para 17.85 above.
[417] The phrase 'promotion otherwise than to the general public' is stated to include promotion designed to reduce 'the risk of participation by persons for whom participation would be unsuitable': s 238(10).
[418] See para 17.85 above.
[419] COBS 4 Annex, Category 7.
[420] As defined in FSMA, s 39.
[421] COBS 4 Annex, Category 6.
[422] 'Established' or 'newly accepted' customer, as defined: see COBS 4 Annex, Notes 2 and 3.
[423] COBS 4 Annex, Category 2.
[424] See COBS 4 Annex, Note 1 for an amplification of what this means.
[425] COBS 4 Annex, Category 1.

restriction in section 21,[426] a corresponding Order has been made by the Treasury[427] exempting communications in similar[428] circumstances from the CIS financial promotion restriction in section 238(1). The result is that (as section 238(1) does not apply in those circumstances) authorised persons are able to promote CISs in similar circumstances as unauthorised persons are able to promote CISs without the approval of an authorised person.

FSA Handbook

Introduction

Many parts of the FSA Handbook are applicable to CISs and reference has been made to the relevant provisions throughout this chapter. Some parts are of particular relevance to CISs (in particular, their operators and depositaries) whilst others apply more generally by virtue of the relevant persons being 'authorised persons' (or 'firms', using the FSA terminology). OEICs are, of course, separate legal entities and therefore, if they are 'authorised persons', they will be subject to the Handbook and the powers of the FSA over such 'firms'. This is necessarily the case with ICVCs[429] and OEICs from other Member States recognised under section 264,[430] as these are automatically granted 'authorised persons' status. Other overseas OEICs, who carry on regulated activity in the UK[431] and therefore who obtain 'authorised person' status,[432] will similarly be subject to the FSA's regulatory jurisdiction. **17.141**

One of the Sourcebooks in Block 5 of the Handbook is specifically dedicated to 'regulated collective investment schemes': the COLL module.[433] **17.142**

---

[426] See para 17.131 above.

[427] FSMA 2000 (Promotion of CISs) (Exemptions) Order 2001, SI 2001/1060 as amended by SI 2002/1310, SI 2002/2157, SI 2003/2067, SI 2005/270, SI 2005/1532, made under s 238(6) and (7).

[428] But not identical. Compare the differences in formal requirements for the 'high net worth' exemptions in FPO, art 48 and the FSMA 2000 (Promotion of CISs) (Exemptions) Order 2001, art 21.

[429] Sched 5, para 1(3): see para 17.96 *et seq.* above. However, the only part of the COBS Module applicable to ICVCs is the financial promotion rules: see FSA Handbook, COBS 18.9.1.

[430] Sched 5, para 1(1) (the OEIC being the 'operator' under s 237(2): see nn 275 and 374 above).

[431] See para 17.126 above.

[432] See ibid. If they do not obtain authorised person status they will be in breach of the general prohibition, see para 17.124 above.

[433] Before 13 February 2007, there was an older version: the 'CIS' Module. See also the Collective Investment Scheme Information Guide (COLLG)—one of the Guides at the end of the FSA Handbook.

Regulated collective investment schemes

The COLL Module

17.143   The COLL Module is primarily concerned with the regulation of 'authorised funds': UK AUTs and ICVCs.[434] As its focus is the schemes themselves, it also has one chapter on overseas 'recognised schemes' containing the details of the notification procedures which these schemes need to undertake in order to obtain 'recognised scheme' status[435] and the rules as to the facilities which such schemes must provide for UK investors.[436] COLL also contains a final chapter on fees payable in connection with the FSA's functions over all these regulated schemes.[437] Thus, in essence, COLL deals with those schemes that may be promoted to the general public by authorised persons.[438]

17.144   As far as authorised funds are concerned, the regulatory distinctions noted above are reflected in how COLL is subdivided. The principal sub-division is between schemes ('retail schemes'—a term not used in COLL)[439] which may be marketed to the general public and 'qualified investor schemes' ('QISs') which can only be marketed to a more limited audience. COLL 2 applies to both categories and deals with applications to become 'authorised funds' and then, depending on whether the fund is a retail scheme or a QIS, COLL 3 to COLL 7 or COLL 8 contain the product regulation details. Unsurprisingly, the restrictions as to, for example, investment and borrowing powers and the running of the scheme are much greater for retail schemes. The focus of the regulation of QISs in COLL 8 is disclosure.

17.145   Retail schemes are themselves subdivided into 'UCITS' and 'non-UCITS retail' schemes.[440] Special provision is made for the latter[441] which, as their name suggests, do not comply with the UCITS Directive[442] as far as investment and borrowing powers are concerned and hence do not benefit from the single passport enabling them to be marketed, without further authorisation, throughout the EEA. However, being non-QIS authorised funds, they may of course be marketed to the public in the UK by authorised persons.

---

[434]   See paras 17.84–17.104 above.

[435]   For recognised schemes, see para 17.105 *et seq.* above. See COLL 9.2 (for s 264 schemes) and COLL 9.3 (for ss 270 and 272 schemes).

[436]   COLL 9.4.

[437]   COLL 10.

[438]   s 238(1), (3). See para 17.137 above.

[439]   But used in COLLG, see n 433, above. As noted below, the term 'non-UCITS retail scheme' is defined in the Glossary and used in COLL.

[440]   See paras 17.03 and 17.85 above.

[441]   COLL 5.6.

[442]   See para 17.03 and n 13, above.

FSA enforcement powers

The FSA Handbook, in its final 'Regulatory Guides' Block, contains a special **17.146**
'Enforcement Guide': EG.[443] EG has a special chapter, EG 14, dealing with the
FSA's powers of intervention over 'regulated collective investment schemes':
AUTs, ICVCs, and overseas 'recognised schemes'.[444] An earlier, more general,
chapter on information gathering and investigation powers, EG 3, also briefly
mentions the wide power statutory power the FSA has to investigate *all*[445] CISs
under FSMA, section 284. Reflecting the different powers that the FSA has in
relation to the three categories of scheme (AUTs, ICVCs, and recognised schemes)
separate provision is made for each.

EG begins with the statutory powers that the FSA has under FSMA over AUTs, **17.147**
which are noted above:[446] under section 254 to revoke the authorisation order
otherwise than by consent; under section 257 to give directions to the manager and
trustee; and under section 258 to apply to court for the removal of the manager
and/or trustee and either their replacement or the appointment of a person to wind
up the scheme. It explains the FSA's policy in relation to these powers, in particular
listing (non-exhaustive) 'relevant factors' it will take into account when deciding
whether to invoke the powers.[447] The FSA also explains how it will choose between
these powers—and other powers it has against the trustee or manager (as authorised persons).[448] Thus it will only revoke the authorisation order after requiring the
winding up of the AUT to ensure that participants receive their entitlements.

EG 14.6 deals with the statutory powers that the FSA has under the OEIC **17.148**
Regulations over ICVCs, which are very similar to the powers it has over AUTs.
As noted above,[449] these powers are: under regulation 23 to revoke the authorisation order otherwise than by consent; under regulation 25 to give directions; and
under regulation 26 to apply to court for the removal of any director and/or
depositary and either their replacement or the appointment of a person to wind
up the company. However, ICVCs differ from AUTs in that, being legal entities,
they are themselves given automatic 'authorised person' status.[450] Hence an ICVC
is subject to the additional disciplinary powers (of public censure[451] and the

---

[443] Replacing the old 'ENF' Module.
[444] See paras 17.84–17.120, above.
[445] This is the only statutory power applicable to *all* (regulated and unregulated) CISs—except
ICVCs (over which corresponding powers are given by OEIC Regulations, reg 30). Curiously there
is no mention of this corresponding ICVC power.
[446] Para 17.95.
[447] EG 14.1.
[448] In EG 14.2–14.5.
[449] Para 17.104.
[450] See Sched 5, para 1(3), noted at para 17.141 and n 429 above.
[451] FSMA, s 205, see EG 7.

imposition of financial penalties)[452] that the FSA has over authorised persons. Otherwise, the FSA confirms that its policy as to the exercise of its powers over ICVCs is the same as that in relation to AUTs

17.149 The rest of EG reflects the different statutory powers the FSA has over EEA (UCITS) recognised schemes[453] and other (sections 270 and 272) recognised schemes,[454] noted above.[455] Again, it sets out the different powers and articulates its policy in relation to them. As regards the former, the FSA confirms that it will liaise with the regulators of the relevant EEA Member State as these have the primary responsibility for discipline under the UCITS Directive.[456]

17.150 As well as these special powers over CISs themselves, the FSA also has its usual disciplinary powers over those involved in CISs who are 'authorised persons' and its usual powers to enforce breaches by non-authorised persons of the general prohibition in section 19 and breaches of the financial promotion restriction in section 21.[457]

Collective investment schemes in general

General

17.151 As noted above,[458] only 'authorised persons' may undertake various activities in relation to *any* CISs and such 'authorised persons' (or 'firms') will be subject to the FSA Handbook in general. For example, establishing, operating, or winding up *any* CIS can only be done by authorised persons and once these persons have become 'authorised persons', the relevant parts of the rest of the Handbook will apply in the usual way, in particular the PRIN, SYSC, APER, COBS, DEPP, and CASS Modules. The COBS Module is also of particular relevance—the rules on promotion in COB4 have been noted above[459]—but it is modified in its application to 'operators' and 'depositaries' of CIS, as will now be discussed.

---

[452] FSMA, s 206, see EG 7.
[453] s 267: to suspend promotion: see EG 14.7–14.8.
[454] s 279 (revocation of recognition) and s 267 (directions): see EG 14.9–14.10.
[455] Paras 17.111 (s 267), 17.113 (s 279), and 17.120 (s 267).
[456] EG 14.8.
[457] See para 17.126: the special CIS financial promotion restriction in s 238 is only imposed on authorised persons, see para 17.134 above.
[458] Para 17.126.
[459] See para 17.131.

COBS Module

Special provision is made in the COBs Sourcebook for 'operators'[460] and 'deposi-   **17.152**
taries'[461] of *all* (both regulated and unregulated) CISs.

COB 18.5 is a special chapter applicable to 'operators' of all CISs. The term 'oper-   **17.153**
ator' is defined to cover, in essence, the person who manages the scheme property.[462] The chapter has three purposes.[463] The first is to disapply parts of the COBS
Module in relation to operators when undertaking 'scheme management activity'
(defined[464] to mean managing the scheme property but excluding holding client
money, and safeguarding and administering investments), in the light of the other
parts of the Handbook which apply to them, in particular the COLL Module for
operators of 'regulated schemes' and the rest of COB 18.5 for operators of 'unregulated schemes'.[465] Second, it modifies some of those COBS rules which still
apply in such cases.[466] For example, obligations in relation to 'customers' or 'clients' generally apply in relation to the CIS itself.[467] Third, it contains some special
rules applicable to operators of 'unregulated collective investment schemes'.[468]
Operators of 'regulated schemes' are, of course, subject to more onerous requirements in the COLL Module. Thus, in relation to operators of unregulated
schemes, the exceptions to the 'best execution' rule in COBS 11.2 are modified[469]
and requirements are imposed as to scheme documents[470] and periodic statements
to participants.[471]

---

[460] COBS 18.5.
[461] COBS 18.7, which list those provisions of COBS that apply to a depositary when not covered
by MiFID (see Chapter 21 below).
[462] In the FSA Glossary definition, see para 17.59 above. He must be an authorised person: see
para 17.126 and as such is, of course, subject to COBS.
[463] As explained in the older (now replaced by COBS) version of the Module in COB 10.1.5G.
[464] In the FSA Handbook Glossary.
[465] COBS 18.5.2R.
[466] See ibid and COBS 18.5.3R.
[467] COBS 18.5.3(1) but see (2) (unregulated scheme).
[468] COBS 18.5.4–18.5.18.
[469] COBS 18.5.4R.
[470] In particular, those that are 'retail customers', see COBS 18.5.5R–18.5.10E.
[471] COBS 18.5.11R–18.5.18E.

18

LISTING AND PUBLIC OFFERS

The Listing Review and Implementation of Related Directives in the UK

Background

For many years the London Stock Exchange ('LSE') was the competent authority **18.01** for the admission of securities to listing and the subsequent admission of those securities to trading. The role of competent authority for listing was transferred to the FSA in May 2000 in advance of the introduction of the Financial Services and Markets Act 2000. The structure of the listing regime has been altered significantly due to the domestic implementation of European directives. The Prospectus Directive[1] and Market Abuse Directive[2] were implemented domestically in the UK on 1 July 2005 as part of the Listing Review. The subsequent implementation of the Transparency Directive[3] (January 2007), Statutory Audit Directive,[4] and Company Reporting Directive[5] (June 2008) has also had an impact on the structure of the regime. This chapter describes the current arrangements for listing following those changes and also an intervening listing review conducted by the FSA during 2005. This chapter also discusses the possible changes to the regime in light of an as yet uncompleted FSA policy review.

The Prospectus Directive regulates offers of transferable securities to the public **18.02** and/or when securities are admitted to trading on a regulated market. The Market Abuse Directive applies to issuers who have requested or approved admission of their securities to a regulated market based in the UK and to persons discharging managerial responsibility in those issuers and their associates. This extends the

---

[1] Directive 2003/71/EC.
[2] Directive 2003/6/EC.
[3] Directive 2004/109/EC.
[4] Directive 2006/43/EC.
[5] Directive 2006/46/EC.

powers, obligations, and regulatory reach of the FSA (as Competent Authority under Part VI of FSMA) well beyond listed issuers.

18.03 The result of the Listing Review consultations was a new sourcebook comprising the Listing Rules, the disclosure rules (now Disclosure and Transparency Rules), and the Prospectus Rules which came into force on 1 July 2005.

18.04 Since 2005, the UK and global markets have been subject to a number of challenges. In response to the continued evolution of global markets, and the resulting concerns raised about the potential for confusion between the various segments of the listing regime, the FSA has published Discussion Paper 08/1 which reviews the structure of the listing regime in the context of the continuously evolving EU legislative structure.

18.05 Each segment of the listing regime is distinct in terms of regulatory oversight and applicable standards. However, the primary listing, secondary listing, and Global Depositary Receipts ('GDR') segments all relate to similar instruments and some market participants have expressed concern about the potential for confusion between these segments.[6]

18.06 The primary listing segment is the 'premium brand' of the Official List, and is subject to super-equivalent standards over and above the minimum requirements of the EU directives. These super-equivalent standards relate to: the UK Combined Code; related party transactions; class tests; sponsors; pre-emption rights; the requirement for a clean working capital statement; and a three-year track record of earnings. The secondary listing and GDR segments are subject to directive minimum standards only. However, all three segments are loosely referred to as a 'London listing', and there is concern that some market participants may not appreciate the differing levels of regulatory quality attributable to each of these segments.

18.07 The primary listing segment itself also provides different standards to issuers based on their country of incorporation. UK incorporated companies with a primary listing must 'Comply or Explain' against the UK Combined Code, whereas non-UK incorporated companies with a primary listing must merely disclose whether or not they comply with the corporate governance regime applicable in their country of incorporation. Further, the Listing Rules relating to pre-emption rights are taken from UK company legislation and as such do not apply to non-UK incorporated companies holding a primary listing. DP 08/1 therefore re-opens the debate on whether it is still sensible for the UK market to apply

---

[6] DP 08/1: 'Structure of the Listing Regime: Review' (January 2008), p 33.

differing standards to issuers based on their geographical location and differing domestic requirements. This debate must now be conducted in the context of a UK capital market which enjoys increasing participation from overseas companies.

In order to improve clarity between segments, the DP sets out two options and a **18.08** series of sub-options as to how the regime may be segmented and labelled in order to clarify the regulatory oversight applicable in each segment.

a) Option 1: A single listing segment for equity securities—the 'premium brand' of the official list with 'super-equivalent standards' (currently known as the primary listing of equity securities). Secondary listing and the listing of GDRs would be removed from the Official List but the FSA would continue to have regulatory oversight over the approval of prospectuses and these securities, as they would continue to be admitted to trading on a regulated market.[7]

b) Option 2: The status quo of the existing two-tier structure with modernised labels—A tiered regime for equity securities—Two listing segments consisting of (a) the premium brand with 'super-equivalent' standards as described above and (b) what is currently known as secondary listing where the standards are directive minimum but only open to overseas companies together with the listing of GDRs.[8]

Regardless of which option is chosen the DP proposes to re-label the existing segments, distinguishing two tiers of securities. 'Tier 1' would be the label for primary equity securities, and 'Tier 2' would be the label for all other listed segments. The FSA has said that it intends to produce a feedback statement in the third quarter of 2008.

The Listing Rules contain rules and guidance for issuers of securities admitted **18.09** (or seeking admission) to the Official List. These rules focus on eligibility for listing, the continuing obligations of listed issuers (other than those obligations contained in the disclosure rules), and sponsors. The Listing Rules apply higher (or super-equivalent) standards to issuers of primary listed shares than those set out in the EU directives. In relation to secondary listed issuers of shares and issuers of other types of securities the regulatory regime has been generally pared back to directive standards.

In light of ongoing discussions regarding how the UK implements EU legislation **18.10** and the strong preference of industry to avoid 'gold-plating' or super-equivalent implementation of directives it is interesting to see that a significant majority

---

[7] DP 08/1: 'Structure of Listing Regime: Review' (January 2008) p 34.
[8] ibid, p 37.

of respondents to listing related consultations continue to support 'gold-plating' or super-equivalent provisions imposing higher standards than those required by the European directives.

18.11   As a result of this the Listing Rules provide:

(i)   a primary listing regime based on demanding eligibility criteria and exacting standards of continuing obligations, underpinned by high-level principles;

(ii)   rules for secondary listed issuers, debt issuers, and issuers of certificates representing securities (eg Global Depositary Receipts) based on directive standards with minimal additions (this approach provides an alternative to the primary listing regime for issuers seeking to list and investors seeking to invest in London. It is based on appropriate EU standards, embracing the Prospectus Directive passport and pan-EU aspects of the EU directives, but without the additional primary listed requirements);

(iii)   a sponsor regime for primary listed issuers which sets out what is expected of sponsors and reflects the high standards of performance and behaviour for which the sponsor regime is known; and

(iv)   a framework which enables a choice for issuers of, and investors in, debt and specialist securities between a regulated market and the Professional Securities Market ('PSM') according to what best suits their situation.

18.12   Issuers whose securities are admitted to a regulated market, including listed issuers, are also subject to, and derive their continuing obligations from, the Prospectus Rules (also known as PR for the purposes of rule references), derived from the Prospectus Directive ('PD'), and the Disclosure and Transparency Rules, derived from the Market Abuse and Transparency Directives as well as Part VI of FSMA.

Structure and format

18.13   In amending Part VI of FSMA, HM Treasury has provided that the FSA is the competent authority not only for Official Listing but also for the Prospectus Rules and the Disclosure and Transparency Rules (FSMA, s 73A). In discharging its functions as competent authority for Part VI of FSMA the FSA continues to use the UK Listing Authority or UKLA name (PR 1.1.2G).

18.14   In discharging its functions under Part VI of FSMA the UK Listing Authority must have regard to the factors set out in section 73 of FSMA rather than the regulatory objectives relevant to the FSA, set out in section 2 of FSMA (see section 73(2) and Schedule 7 of FSMA). The factors are:

(i)   the need to use its [the competent authority's] resources in the most efficient and economic way;

(ii) the principle that a burden or restriction which is imposed on a person should be proportionate to the benefits, considered in general terms, which are expected to arise from the imposition of that burden or restriction;

(iii) the desirability of facilitating innovation in respect of listed securities and in respect of financial instruments which have otherwise been admitted to trading on a regulated market or for which a request for admission to trading on such a market has been made;

(iv) the international character of capital markets and the desirability of maintaining the competitive position of the UK;

(v) the need to minimise the adverse effects on competition of anything done in the discharge of those functions; and

(vi) the desirability of facilitating competition in relation to listed securities and in respect of financial instruments which have otherwise been admitted to trading on a regulated market or for which a request for admission to trading on such a market has been made.

18.15 One of the significant structural differences which emerges from the implementation of the Prospectus Directive and the Market Abuse Directive (as it affects issuers of securities) and the consequential amendments to Part VI of FSMA is that, from 1 July 2005 onwards, the UK Listing Authority has assumed certain legal and regulatory responsibilities for a wider group of issuers other than listed issuers. The UK Listing Authority has powers under Part VI of FSMA (section 73A) to make:

(i) rules in relation to issuers who are listed on (or are seeking admission to) the Official List (Listing Rules);

(ii) rules in relation to issuers who have financial instruments admitted to trading on a regulated market in the UK; and 'persons discharging managerial responsibilities' and their 'connected persons' (disclosure rules); and

(iii) rules in relation to those who are seeking admission of securities to trading on a regulated market; or offering securities to the public in the UK (Prospectus Rules).

Section 73A also gives the UKLA the power to make the transparency rules and corporate governance rules.

18.16 To reflect this structure, the FSA deleted the UKLA Sourcebook (Listing Rules and Guidance Manual) and created a new Block of the Handbook. This new block contains three new modules, based on the old listing material. These modules (under the collective Block name of 'Listing, Prospectus and Disclosure') comprise:

(a) **The Listing Rules** which contain rules and guidance for issuers of securities admitted (or seeking admission) to the Official List. These rules focus on eligibility for listing, the continuing obligations of listed issuers (other than those obligations contained in the Disclosure and Transparency Rules), and sponsors;

(b) **The Prospectus Rules** which contain the rules, regulations, and guidance outlining circumstances in which a prospectus is required and what that prospectus must contain;

(c) **The Disclosure and Transparency Rules,** themselves consisting of:

(i) **The Disclosure Rules** which contain rules and guidance in relation to the publication and control of 'inside information', insider lists, and the disclosure of transactions by persons discharging managerial responsibilities and their connected persons;

(ii) **The Transparency Rules** which contain rules and guidance in relation to continuing financial reporting, the disclosure of major shareholdings, information that issuers must provide to holders of their securities, and wider access to information about issuers and their securities; and

(iii) **The Corporate Governance Rules** which contain the rules and guidance in relation to audit committees and the corporate governance statements of listed companies.

18.17 The Listing, Prospectus, Disclosure, and Transparency Block now form part of the FSA Handbook. As well as seeking to simplify and modernise the listing regime the existing rules were put into Handbook style. The most visible manifestation of this is that pertinent guidance now appears next to the rule rather than in a separate guidance manual. The elements of the old rules and guidance which dealt with appeal, procedural, or enforcement matters are now located within the appropriate parts of the FSA Handbook such as the Decision Procedure and Penalties manual ('DEPP'), or Supervision Manual ('SUP').

18.18 Issuers who are secondary listed or issue other types of securities other than shares face a reduced regulatory burden as a result of the FSA's decision to remove super-equivalence and generally rely on directive standards. The UK Listing Authority was keen to explain its approach generally and, specifically, in CP 05/7. In particular it has highlighted some of the areas which may give rise to complex boundary issues, for example where matters may fall to be treated differently under the Listing Rules and the Prospectus Rules. Historically eligibtility for listing and the nature and extent of the disclosure in a set of listing particulars shared a very close relationship. For example, a competent person's report, additional disclosure, or even quarterly reporting for some would be required for certain specific issuers to satisfy concerns when an issuer did not have a three-year revenue earning track record. As the Prospectus Directive is a maximum harmonisation directive, as regards prospectus contents, the home competent authority cannot impose additional disclosure obligations on issuers. As a result of this, it is possible that:

(a) a security could be treated as equity under the Prospectus Rules but, for Listing Rules purposes, fall within the specialist securities regime and be treated as debt for the purposes of the Professional Securities Market ('PSM') (LR4) and LR17—eg convertible bonds issued by the issuer of the underlying shares;

(b) an issuer may now be required to make a working capital statement in a prospectus even though there is no eligibility requirement which requires the working capital position to be clean (ie venture capital trusts (LR 16), and, in a limited sense, banks and other regulated entities (LR 6.1.18)); or

(c) an issuer may be able to seek a primary or secondary listing without being required to produce a prospectus (specifically if it can rely on PR 1.2.3(8) and produce a summary document only).

The Listing Rules, Prospectus Rules, and Disclosure and Transparency Rules, represent three stand-alone and distinct bodies of regulation. Each has its own scope, powers, rules, waiver provisions, fee structure, and administrative procedures. All three rulebooks will apply to listed issuers, except in the limited circumstances when an issuer seeks to list specialist debt securities under LR4 on the PSM. In relation to the various segments in the regime, the nature of the prospectus disclosure required will depend on whether the securities fall within the PD definition of equity securities in each case or non-equity securities and the applicability of the various disclosure building blocks. **18.19**

Offers to the public and prospectuses

Introduction

The aims of the Prospectus Directive were to enhance investor protection through the production of high quality prospectuses and to improve the efficiency of the internal market through the issue of a single approved prospectus which will be valid across the EU. It was one of the first two proposals for directives (the other being the Market Abuse Directive) under the new 'Lamfalussy' format endorsed at the Stockholm European Council distinguishing framework principles from implementing technical details. The Prospectus Directive introduces the concept of a pan-EU passport for issuers. This means that once a prospectus had been approved by the home competent authority of the issuer it will be accepted in other EU jurisdictions for the purposes of any offer of securities to the public and/or admission to trading on a regulated market. **18.20**

The Prospectus Directive[9] deleted large swathes of the Consolidated Admissions and Reporting Directive ('CARD'),[10] specifically those aspects which governed **18.21**

---

[9] Art 27, Prospectus Directive.
[10] Directive (EC) 2001/34.

listing particulars and public offer prospectuses. Important elements of CARD do remain including the ability for the competent authority to impose additional obligations (such as class tests or eligibility requirements) on listed issuers. Part VI of FSMA has been amended to reflect this, and provides for the domestic implementation of the Prospectus Directive and the aspects of the Market Abuse and Transparency Directives which apply to issuers.

18.22 The Prospectus Directive is a maximum harmonisation directive in relation to the form and content of prospectuses. This means that, unlike the position in relation to other directives, such the Market Abuse Directive, Member States cannot impose obligations which go beyond those set out in the directive and accompanying regulations.

18.23 Implementation of the Prospectus Directive requires all prospectuses required under the Prospectus Rules to be approved by the competent authority (the UK Listing Authority in the UK).

When a prospectus is required

18.24 A prospectus may be required to be published under the Prospectus Directive when an offer of securities is made to the public and/or when securities are admitted to trading on a regulated market.

18.25 The public offer definition and exemptions are dealt with first and then the admission to trading on a regulated market provisions in the following paragraphs. To establish whether a public offer is being made and, if so, whether such offer requires a prospectus, issuers and practitioners should establish whether the securities in question are within the scope of the provisions. If the securities are transferable securities (other than those set out in Schedule 11A of FSMA and PR 1.2.2) it is likely the provisions will apply. Having established the question of scope the next question is whether the proposed offer or transaction falls within the definition of public offer (FSMA, section 102B). On the basis that most offers of securities or transactions involving the purchase or subscription of securities will, under the Prospectus Directive, amount to a public offer the next question is whether the offer is exempt (FSMA, section 86). A prospectus will be required to be published if the securities are within scope, the offer is caught under the definition in section 102B of FSMA, and the offer is not an exempt offer. A similar, but separate process will be required to analyse the applicability of the admission to trading limb contained in section 85(2) of FSMA.

18.26 The UK Listing Authority has retained the requirement for issuers to produce listing particulars in the limited circumstances set out in LR4. The provisions relating to listing particulars have been retained to cater for situations where an issuer is seeking to admit securities to listing in circumstances where no prospectus is required (specifically that there is no public offer and the market to which the securities are being admitted is not a regulated market). An issuer of specialist securities[11] seeking admission of its securities to this market will be required to produce listing particulars and have them approved by the UK Listing Authority. Consequently, the Professional Securities Market (PSM) was established. The PSM is a non-regulated market operated by the LSE for specialist securities. PSM securities are admitted to the Official List. At present, over 550 debt securities are admitted to the PSM.[12]

Offers of transferable securities to the public

The Prospectus Directive provides a pan-European definition of offer of transfer-able securities to the public. This is designed to encourage common interpretation across the EU so that an identical issue is not a public offer in one jurisdiction and a private placement in another. However, to achieve this aim of producing a politically acceptable definition of offer of securities to the public with pan-European reach, the Prospectus Directive has settled on a definition which has been criticised for being both broad and lacking in detail. As can be seen from the extract from the Prospectus Directive below, the definition can be construed to apply to any communication which enables an investor to subscribe or buy securities. It also extends to any subsequent resale of securities by a person when the original offer was the subject of one or more of the exemptions.[13] The reference to an offer of securities *for the first time*[14] which was a feature of the domestic regime which preceded the Prospectus Directive, was superseded by the resale provisions.

18.27

The definition of offer of transferable securities to the public is

18.28

> a communication to persons in any form and by any means, presenting sufficient information on the terms of the offer and the securities to be offered, so as to enable an investor to decide to purchase or subscribe to these securities. This definition shall also be applicable to the placing of securities through financial intermediaries.[15]

This was implemented domestically in section 102B of FSMA. In implementing this aspect of the Prospectus Directive HM Treasury acknowledged that agreeing a pan-European definition had 'proved challenging' and that the definition is '... capable of a wide variety of interpretations and is potentially ambiguous'.[16]

18.29

---

[11] 'Securities which because of their nature are normally bought and traded by a limited number of investors who are particularly knowledgeable in investment matters'—LR Appendix 1—Relevant Definitions.

[12] Herbert Smith, *A Practical Guide to the UK Listing Regime*.

[13] Art 3(2), Prospectus Directive.

[14] Para 4(1), The Public Offers of Securities Regulations 1995, SI 1995/1537 (POSR).

[15] Art 2 1(d), Prospectus Directive.

[16] Para 4.10, HM Treasury 'UK implementation of the Prospectus Directive 2003/71/EC—October 2004'.

They have clarified that the definition of offer, particularly the communication aspect of the definition, does not apply to communications in connection with trading on a regulated market, a multilateral trading facility, or a prescribed market under section 130A of FSMA (any market which is prescribed for the purposes of the offence of market abuse under Part VIII of FSMA).[17] The clear policy aim here is to provide clarification to ensure that genuine market transactions and the offer of prices through screens are not caught through the wide definition agreed in the Prospectus Directive.

18.30 The domestic implementation clarifies that, for domestic purposes, the definition of offer is limited to the UK.[18] This means that offers of securities to overseas persons will not amount to an offer under FSMA, although clearly domestic law in the jurisdiction in question will be relevant.

18.31 The wide definition of offer of transferable securities to the public means that many transactions will now fall within the definition and the issuer and/or offeror, as appropriate, will need to consider carefully if an exemption is available to determine whether a prospectus needs to be published. For the purposes of the Prospectus Rules an offer which falls within the definition set out in section 102B of FSMA will always amount to an offer of transferable securities to the public. If one of the exemptions applies the transaction will still amount to an offer of transferable securities to the public, but one which does not require the publication of a prospectus. This construct, which differs from the historic UK position under the POSR where, if an exemption applied, the transaction did not amount to an offer, is relevant to the equality of treatment provision contained in PR 5.6.1. It could also be relevant in determining the home competent authority for overseas issuers.[19]

18.32 A takeover transaction undertaken by way of Scheme of Arrangement under Part 26 of the Companies Act 2006 should not amount to a public offer. As stated above, it will be for issuers or offerors to establish whether they are making a public offer which requires the publication of a prospectus. The UK Listing Authority noted in its publication *List!* that in its view a takeover, involving the issue of transferable securities, effected by way of a statutory scheme of arrangement under Part 26 of the Companies Act 2006, should not fall within the definition of public offer. The common view among practitioners is that the issue of new securities pursuant to a scheme of arrangement under Part 26 of the Companies Act 2006 should not fall within the definition of public offer. The analysis is that there is no offer which enables investors to buy or subscribe for

---

[17] FSMA, s 102B(5).
[18] ibid, s 102B(2).
[19] Art 2(1)(m) and (n), Prospectus Directive.

securities but rather there is a court procedure under which members and creditors, as appropriate, are asked to vote on and approve an arrangement. This is a matter of law, and, ultimately for the courts to decide. The UK Listing Authority is inclined to agree with this view. It should be noted that a prospectus will be required to be produced if the transaction which is the subject of the scheme of arrangement involves the admission of shares to a regulated market unless one of the exemptions contained in PR 1.2.3 applies. As with the previous listing rules, if the issuer is listed, the requirement to seek shareholder approval under LR 10 or LR 11 also may apply to the transaction in question.

As well as the exemptions which relieve an issuer or offeror of the obligation to **18.33** publish a prospectus (FSMA, section 86 and PR 1.2.2) FSMA[20] sets out certain types of transferable securities which are outside the scope of the offer definition. Clearly this will be so if the security in question is not transferable and does not meet the definition set out in section 102A(3) of FSMA. Article 4(18) of MiFID[21] defines Transferable Securities as:

> those classes of securities which are negotiable on the capital market, with the exception of instruments of payment, such as:
> (a) shares in companies and other securities equivalent to shares in companies, partnerships or other entities, and depositary receipts in respect of shares;
> (b) bonds or other forms of securitised debt, including depositary receipts in respect of such securities; and
> (c) any other securities giving the right to acquire or sell any such transferable securities or giving rise to a cash settlement determined by reference to transferable securities, currencies, interest rates or yields, commodities or other indices or measures.

The MiFID definition applies to classes of securities which are negotiable on **18.34** a capital market. This has been interpreted to include, for example, loan notes if the notes are constituted on a basis which makes them freely transferable. The position in relation to securities which have limited transfer rights (such as between spouses or to group companies) has been interpreted to take such securities outside the scope of the definition. The UKLA has stated in its *List!* Publication (issue 10, June 2005) that the grant of an option under an employee share option scheme should not fall within the definition as the security is not a transferable security. The exercise of the option and issue of ordinary shares should not amount to a public offer. The EU Commission and Committee of European Securities Regulators (CESR) now share this analysis.[22]

---

[20] FSMA, s 85(5) and Sched 11A.
[21] Directive (EC) 2004/39.
[22] CESR: 'Frequently asked questions regarding Prospectuses: Common positions agreed by CESR members'. Question 5, September 2007.

18.35 Section 85(1) of FSMA sets out the prohibition on offering transferable securities to the public without an approved prospectus in the UK. In particular section 85(5) of FSMA makes it clear that the prohibition contained in section 85(1) of FSMA does not apply to transferable securities listed in Schedule 11A to FSMA or other transferable securities specified in the Prospectus Rules. PR 1.2.2 sets out the forms of transferable securities to which the prohibition in section 85(1) of FSMA does not apply. Schedule 11A sets out the types of issuers exempted from the public offer regime under the Prospectus Directive (including EEA State issuers, etc). It also implements Article 1(2)(h) of the Prospectus Directive which states that the Prospectus Directive shall not apply to offers of less than 2,500,000.[23]

18.36 Under the now revoked POSR (as defined in n 14 above) public offers in excess of £100,000 required a prospectus to be prepared and filed at Companies House. The domestic implementing legislation for the Prospectus Directive revoked the POSR in their entirety. Following consultation, HM Treasury decided that it would not introduce a statutory domestic regime for offers below €2,500,000.

18.37 There is a potentially odd interplay between the provisions of Article 1(2)(h) of the Prospectus Directive (referred to in para 18.35 above) and the exemption from the requirement to produce a prospectus contained in section 86(1)(e) of FSMA (which implements Article (3)(2)(e) of the Prospectus Directive) and which states that no prospectus is required for offers with a total consideration of less than €100,000. As Article 1(2)(h) of the Prospectus Directive effectively takes offers below €2,500,000 out of scope of the directive (and the domestic regime) this appears to be the more pertinent provision.

Exempt offers to the public

18.38 There are a number of exemptions from the requirement to publish a prospectus for certain types of offer set out in section 86 of FSMA. These are similar but not identical to the exemptions which were previously found in POSR. Specifically the number of persons to whom the offer can be made or directed without the requirement for a prospectus has been increased from fewer than 50 to fewer than 100. A person does not contravene the prohibition contained in section 85 of FSMA if:

(a) the offer is made to or directed at qualified investors only;

(b) the offer is made to or directed at fewer than 100 persons, other than qualified investors, per EEA State;

---

[23] FSMA, Sched 11A, Part 2, para 9.

(c) the minimum consideration which may be paid by any person is at least €50,000;
(d) the transferable securities being offered are denominated in amount of at least €50,000; or
(e) the total consideration for the transferable securities being offered cannot exceed €100,000.[24]

Qualified investors

The definition of qualified investor is set out in section 86(7) of FSMA which implements Article 2(1)(e) of the Prospectus Directive. Under Article 2(1)(e) a qualified investor is defined to include: **18.39**

(a) entities authorised or regulated to operate in the financial markets and entities not so authorised or regulated whose corporate purpose is solely to invest in securities;
(b) organisations such as national and regional governments, central banks, and the International Monetary Fund;
(c) legal entities which are not small or medium-sized enterprises;
(d) natural persons or small and medium enterprises who ask to be considered as qualified investors.

The FSA is required to establish and maintain a qualified investors register **18.40** under section 87R of FSMA. Any person or entity who does not meet the criteria referred to in sub-paragraphs (a) to (c) above cannot be treated as a qualified investor unless such person or entity is entered on the register, even if they meet the criteria to entitle them to be entered on the register. PR 5.4 provides further detail on the requirements and procedures in relation to the qualified investors register.

For an individual the person may not be entered on the register unless: **18.41**

(a) he is resident in the UK; and
(b) he meets two of the following criteria:
   (i) he has carried out transactions of a significant size on securities markets on an average frequency of at least 10 per quarter over the previous four quarters;
   (ii) his portfolio size exceeds €0.5 million;
   (iii) the investor works or has worked, for at least one year, in the financial sector in a professional position which requires knowledge of securities investment.[25]

---

[24] FSMA, s 86(1).
[25] FSMA, s 87R(2).

18.42   A company may not be entered on the register unless:

(a) it is a small or medium enterprise within the definition of the Prospectus
Directive. This means it has to meet two of the following criteria:

(i)   average number of employees of less than 250;

(ii)   total balance sheet not exceeding €43,000,000; or

(iii)   annual net turnover not exceeding €50,000,000.

(b) it has its registered office in the UK.

18.43   Following its consultation the UK Listing Authority has determined that, because
persons seeking to be entered on the register will be financially sophisticated,
persons will be able to self-certify that they meet the criteria rather than requiring professional verification that they meet such criteria. This approach reflects
the new approach of HM Treasury in relation to certified high net worth
individuals and sophisticated investors under the financial promotion regime.[26]
The registration forms are available on the FSA website and make it abundantly
clear that any person seeking to be entered on the register is giving up the
opportunity to receive both the information and protection provided by a
prospectus.

18.44   The underlying aim of providing the qualified investor register under the Prospectus Directive was to benefit potential issuers in the capital raising process. It
is not designed for the benefit of those willing to be entered on the register.
Accordingly the register will be made available to all issuers. Persons seeking to be
entered on the register will be required to provide name and contact details to
the FSA. The name, but not contact details, will be made available to an issuer
which requests access to the list.

18.45   During the domestic consultation, concern was expressed to the UK Listing
Authority and HM Treasury that one of the effects of the Prospectus Directive was
to alter the existing practice by which securities are placed with discretionary
private client brokers. Under POSR an offer to a broker was treated as being
an exempt offer as it is to a single person 'whose ordinary activities involve
them acquiring investments . . . (as principal or agent) for the purposes of their
business'.[27] It was not clear whether, under the Prospectus Directive, particularly the reference to the fact that the placement of securities through financial
intermediaries should require the publication of a prospectus,[28] such behaviour
would be viewed as an offer to the discretionary broker or to its underlying clients.

---

[26] Arts 48 and 50 respectively of The Financial Services and Markets Act 2000 (Financial
Promotion) Order 2005, SI 2005/1529.

[27] Art 7(2) (a), Public Offers of Securities Regulations 1995, SI 1995/1537.

[28] Art 3(2), Prospectus Directive.

This was clarified by HM Treasury through amendments to Part VI of FSMA. These provide that if a client engages a private client broker (or other person falling with Article 2.1(e)(1) of the Prospectus Directive) and such person can exercise full discretion on behalf of the underlying client then the offer should be considered to be made only to a single qualified investor. The practical effect of this should be that many public offers, particularly those by issuers whose securities are admitted to AIM and OFEX, will not require an approved prospectus to be published.

Less than 100 persons

As explained above this extends the similar exemption contained in POSR from **18.46** 50 to 100 persons. On a pan-European basis the definition also makes it clear that the 100 persons exemption applies per Member State. On this basis it should be possible to offer to less than 100 persons in any number of EEA jurisdictions without requiring a prospectus to be approved. This exemption clearly stands separately from the qualified investors exemption ensuring that issuers can offer in the UK to any number of qualified investors and up to another 100 persons (not being qualified investors).

Offers to trustees of a trust, members of a partnership in a capacity as such, or two **18.47** or more persons jointly should be treated as an offer to a single person.[29]

Minimum consideration/denomination

Setting the minimum denomination and consideration to be paid under the **18.48** offer at 50,000 means that wealthy or sophisticated persons partaking in such an offer are deemed not to require the information and protections afforded by a prospectus.

Total consideration less than €100,000

As discussed in para 18.37 above the relevance of this provision is open to question **18.49** in light of the provision contained in Schedule 11A of FSMA which takes offers below €2,500,000 out of scope. One effect of this provision could be that, if HM Treasury did ever decide to introduce a domestic public offer regime for offers below €2,500,000 this regime could not be applied to offers below €100,000. CESR has indicated that this exemption will apply to free share awards.[30]

---

[29] FSMA, s 86(3).
[30] CESR: 'Frequently asked questions regarding Prospectuses: Common positions agreed by CESR members', Question 6, July 2006.

Exempt securities—offers of securities to the public

18.50 PR 1.2.2 implements section 85(5)(b) of FSMA and states that the prohibition contained within section 85(1) of FSMA does not apply to offers of transferable securities of the following types:

(a) shares issued in substitution for shares of the same class provided the issue does not increase the issued share capital;

(b) transferable securities offered in connection with a takeover or merger if an equivalent document is made available;

(c) shares allotted free of charge to existing shareholders and dividends paid out in the form of shares of the same class as the shares in respect of which the dividend is paid. This exemption is available so long as a document containing information on the number and nature of the shares and the reasons for and details of the offer are made available;

(d) securities offered allotted or to be allotted to existing or former directors or employees by their employer or an affiliated undertaking which has securities admitted to trading on a regulated market. This exemption is only available where a document containing information on the number and nature of the securities and the reasons for and details of the offer are made available.

Equivalent documents

18.51 The exemption in relation to equivalent documents reflects a CARD provision which was implemented through 5.23A of the pre 1 July 2005 Listing Rules applicable only to the admission of listed securities for listed issuers. Historically, the rules under POSR (now revoked) contained an exemption from the requirement to publish a prospectus in the case of securities issued pursuant to a takeover offer. UK non-listed issuers are now required to prepare prospectuses or equivalent documents in relation to securities exchange offers. Market practice and the approach of the UK Listing Authority had ensured that listed issuers had almost exclusively produced listing particulars rather than equivalent documents under the Listing Rules prior to PD implementation.

18.52 The UK Listing Authority follows a similar approach in relation to equivalent documents under the Prospectus Directive. This means that in order for the UK Listing Authority to determine whether the document is equivalent to a prospectus, they intend to apply the full vetting process to the document. There will be a degree of discretion about what will be acceptable as being equivalent, but it is nevertheless limited. It is perhaps also worth pointing out that whereas a prospectus benefits from the passporting provisions under the Prospectus Directive, there are no similar provisions for such equivalent documents. This means that it may be open to any 'host' competent authority to challenge such a document as not being equivalent. Importantly there is no obligation to publish supplementary prospectuses for an equivalent document which means that withdrawal rights as provided for under section 87Q of FSMA will not be introduced.

Securities allotted to existing or former employees or directors

There is an inconsistency between this exemption under the public offer limb **18.53** when compared to the similar exemption under the admission to trading limb. The UK Listing Authority has provided its own view on how this ambiguity can be dealt with in issue 10 of *List!*. This states that:

> We wish to clarify how PR1.2.2R(5) (see Article 4(1)(e) of the PD) should be interpreted. We believe that it should be read and interpreted in the same manner as the corresponding exemption in PR1.2.3(6), So, the employer **or** the affiliated undertaking must have securities trading on a regulated market. This means that the exemption applies if an employee of a subsidiary of an issuer is incentivised through the grant of listed securities in the capital of the issuer.

The practical effect of this interpretation is that employees of subsidiary or hold- **18.54** ing companies will be entitled to participate in share plans as long as a member of the group has shares admitted to trading on a regulated market.

It is not clear from the wording of the exemption whether the transferable securi- **18.55** ties offered to employees or directors need to be of the same class as the transferable securities which are admitted to trading on a regulated market. The words '. . . of the same class . . .' appear in the corresponding exemption contained in PR 1.2.3(6) for admission to trading on a regulated market but are notably absent from the PR 1.2.2(5) exemption. In any event issuers whose securities are not admitted to trading on a regulated market, such as issuers whose shares are admitted to trading on AIM, will not be able to benefit from this exemption.

The above exemption is only applicable to offers of transferable securities. **18.56** The grant of an option under an employee share option scheme should fall outside the scope of the Prospectus Directive as it would not be expected to constitute a transferable security (as defined). The UK Listing Authority has confirmed in issue 10 of *List!* that in its view it:

> would not expect the grant of an option under an employee share option scheme to involve a security which is negotiable on the capital markets and hence subject to the provisions of the Prospectus Directive. It would be unlikely that the exercise of the employee share option would amount to a public offer.

Admission to trading on a regulated market

As referred to above there is a second prospectus related prohibition contained **18.57** within section 85 of FSMA. Section 85(2) of FSMA provides that it is unlawful to request the admission of transferable securities to a regulated market in the UK unless an approved prospectus has been made available.

18.58 The obligation to publish a prospectus and the exemptions in the circumstances set out in section 85(2) of FSMA represent distinct and separate obligations on issuers. Issuers are required to consider the requirements of both the public offer limb and the admission to trading limb in order to establish if a prospectus is required. It is possible for a listed issuer (as well as any other issuer whose securities are admitted to trading on a regulated market) to issue securities which fall within the 10 per cent exemption contained in PR 1.2.3(1) and so do not require a prospectus but nevertheless under the admission limb amounts to a public offer and so requires a prospectus.

18.59 The Prospectus Directive and FSMA impose the requirement to publish a prospectus on those persons seeking admission of securities to a regulated market. The list of regulated markets can be found at <http://www.fsa.gov.uk/register/exchanges.do>.

18.60 The emerging EU framework places emphasis on the concept of the regulated market and the importance of these markets throughout the EU. The Prospectus Directive, Market Abuse Directive, and Transparency Directive make only passing reference to the concept of listing. These directives bite on listed issuers because the listed markets operated by the LSE also happen to be regulated markets. Under the MiFID markets which are not regulated, markets will be known as multi-lateral trading facilities or MTFs. The directives which relate to securities regulation and which regulate the solvency requirements for pension funds and certain other asset managers focus on the regulated market.

18.61 Section 85(2) of FSMA sets out the prohibition on requesting admission of transferable securities to trading on a regulated market situated in the UK without an approved prospectus. In particular section 85(6) of FSMA makes it clear that the prohibition contained in section 85(2) of FSMA does not apply to transferable securities listed in Part I of Schedule 11A to FSMA or other transferable securities specified in the Prospectus Rules. PR 1.2.3 sets out the forms of transferable securities to which the prohibition in section 85(2) of FSMA does not apply. Part I of Schedule 11A sets out the types of issuers exempted from the admission to trading prospectus regime under the Prospectus Directive (including EEA State issuers, etc). The exemptions which fall outside Part I of Schedule 11A to FSMA (particularly the sub €2,500,000 exemption)[31] do not apply to requests for admission but only to public offers.

---

[31] FSMA, Sched 11A, Part 2, para 9.

Exempt securities—admission to trading on a regulated market

The exemptions from the requirement to publish a prospectus in relation to **18.62** the admission to trading limb are similar but not identical to the public offer exemptions. PR 1.2.3 implements section 85(6)(b) of FSMA and states that the prohibition contained within section 85(2) FSMA does not apply to admission to trading of transferable securities of the following types:

(a) shares representing, over a 12-month period, less than 10 per cent of the number of shares of the same class already admitted to trading;

(b) shares issued in substitution for shares of the same class provided the issue does not increase the issued share capital;

(c) transferable securities offered in connection with a takeover or merger if an equivalent document is made available;

(d) shares allotted free of charge to existing shareholders and dividends paid out in the form of shares of the same class as the shares in respect of which the dividend is paid if a document containing information on the number and nature of the shares and the reasons for and details of the offer are made available;

(e) securities offered, allotted, or to be allotted to existing or former directors or employees by their employer or an affiliated undertaking which has securities of the same class admitted to trading on a regulated market if a document containing information on the number and nature of the securities and the reasons for and details of the offer are made available;

(f) shares resulting from the conversion or exchange of other transferable securities; or

(g) transferable securities already admitted to trading on another regulated market.

10 per cent exemption

This exemption is similar to the previous CARD exemption although there are a **18.63** number of important differences. For example, the 10 per cent limit is applied over a rolling 12-month period. So, any shares admitted over the previous 12 months not covered by any other exemption would count towards the 10 per cent. It is irrelevant whether these admissions relate to one or more transactions.

The UK Listing Authority has stated in issue 10 of *List!* that in calculating the **18.64** 10 per cent, their approach will be to discount any securities that have benefited from the application of another exemption from the requirement to produce a prospectus. So, for example, shares admitted under the employee share exemption would be disregarded for the calculation of the 10 per cent limit. This approach is justified on the grounds that to do otherwise would have the odd result that if the employee share admission were done prior to the admission of a further 10 per cent it would be included—resulting in the need for a prospectus for the subsequent 10 per cent tranche—whereas if it were done after the 10 per cent admission, it would be covered by its own exemption and no prospectus would be required for either case.

18.65 The period for calculation is a rolling 12-month look back on any given date when it is proposed to issue and admit securities. Due to difficulties in trying to apply the rule to issues before 1 July 2005, the UK Listing Authority proposed not to apply the provision retrospectively to shares issued before 1 July 2005.

18.66 The following example is provided in issue 10 of *List!* and is designed to help practical interpretation of the provisions:

> A company has 150 shares in issue on 1 June 2008. It has a further 10 shares admitted on 25th June 2008 under the current 10% exemption. These shares are disregarded for the purposes of any later calculation to establish whether a prospectus is required after 1 July.
>
> The company issues a further 20 shares to employees (covered by the relevant admission to trading exemption) after three months (ie after implementation of the PD). There is a further issue of 10 shares placed with institutions (hence covered by the public offer exemption) six months later. The calculation determining the application of the 10% exemption is 10/180 i.e. this transaction would be covered by the 10% exemption. We can ignore the employee shares in the numerator as they are covered by another exemption.
>
> A further placement of 8 shares occurs 1 month later as a fundraising for the acquisition of A. The calculation is now 18/190 ie this latest issue is still covered by the 10% exemption. The numerator includes all shares issued in the relevant time period not benefiting from an exemption. As with our current approach the denominator is increased as a result of previous issues.
>
> A further placement of 2 shares occurs 1 month later as a fundraising for unconnected acquisition of B. The calculation is now 20/198, which is >10% so a prospectus will be required in this final case.

Equivalent documents/ securities allotted to existing or former employees or directors

18.67 The provisions explained in paras 18.50 and 18.51 above are equally relevant to the production of equivalent documents in the case of admissions to a regulated market and issues of securities to existing or former employees or directors.

Shares resulting from the conversion or exchange of other transferable securities

18.68 The UK Listing Authority has clarified its approach to PR 1.2.3(7) (Article 4(2) (g) of the Prospectus Directive) in issue 16 of *List!* Whilst the shares arising from the conversion or exchange must be of a class which is already admitted to trading, on a literal reading of the Prospectus Directive text, there seems to be no express requirement that the securities which are being converted or exchanged must themselves have been previously admitted to trading or the subject of a prospectus.[32] This literal interpretation[33] would, however, result in the strange position that anyone wishing to admit shares under a placing need merely interpose a convertible security as an artificial intermediate step, and thereby avoid the need to produce a prospectus. However, the UK Listing Authority has suggested[34] that it will take enforcement action or cancel the transactions in cases where the issuer appears to be abusing the exemption, ie interposing an artificial convertible to avoid the production of a prospectus.

Transferable securities already admitted to trading on a regulated market

PR 1.2.3(8) provides a new exemption which was designed to allow investment or stock exchanges to admit securities of an issuer to a platform for trading without the consent of the issuer. It can also be used by issuers already admitted in one Member State to seek admission in another Member State with minimal documentary requirements.   **18.69**

The conditions under PR 1.2.3(8) are: **18.70**

(a) the transferable securities, or securities of the same class have been admitted to a regulated market for more than 18 months;

(b) if the transferable securities were first admitted after 31 December 2003 the admission was associated with the publication of an approved prospectus;

(c) except where (b) applies, if the transferable securities were admitted after 30 June 1983 listing particulars were approved;

(d) the ongoing obligations for trading on that market have been complied with;

(e) the person requesting admission makes a summary document available in the language of the Member State where admission is sought;

(f) the summary document is made available in the manner set out in Article 14 of the Prospectus Directive;

(g) the contents of the summary document comply with Article 5(2) of the Prospectus Directive and state where the most recent prospectus can be obtained and where the financial information on the issuer is available.

---

[32] The convertible or exchangeable was required to be listed under 5.27 of the pre-1 July 2005 Listing Rules.

[33] In issue 16 of *List!*, the UKLA supported this position (modifying its position as set out in issues 10 and 11 of *List!*).

[34] Issue 16 of *List!*.

18.71 The summary document is required to contain at least the information required in a summary in relation to a prospectus.[35] The document is not a summary nor is it a prospectus. There is no statutory responsibility regime for a summary document.

Drawing up the prospectus

18.72 **Format of prospectus.**   The Prospectus Directive provides that a prospectus can be drawn up as a single document or as separate documents[36] comprising:

(a) a registration document which contains information relating to the issuer;
(b) a securities note which provides details of the securities to be offered or admitted;
(c) a summary which conveys the essential characteristics and risks associated with the issuer and securities.

The registration document accompanied by the securities note, updated if applicable, and the summary together constitute a valid prospectus. Issuers are able to file a registration document, which is valid for up to 12 months. They can then, subject to the obligation to update the registration note in PR2.2.5, file a securities note and summary when they plan to offer or issue the securities.

18.73 In earlier drafts of the Prospectus Directive the registration document concept reflected the current US approach, and the intention was to require such a document to be filed annually. This approach was sensibly abandoned before the directive was finalised, but the concept of a tripartite prospectus remains. It is not clear whether the tripartite prospectus will be well used, particularly by equity issuers. It may well be preferred by certain issuers of non-equity securities as the registration document can be updated via the securities note and has to be so updated in the event of a material change or recent development. There is a view that using the tripartite document, rather than a base prospectus and final terms, may render an issuer less likely to fall within the supplementary prospectus requirements. This may be preferable depending on the effect the introduction of withdrawal rights may have.

18.74 The summary is designed to convey briefly and in non-technical language the essential characteristics and risks associated with the issuer and transferable securities to which the prospectus relates. A summary is required for prospectuses in relation all transferable securities except non-equity securities with a denomination of at least €50,000. The summary should normally be no more than 2,500 words.[37] The UK Listing Authority has commented on its approach to this provision in issue 10 of *List!*. From a policy perspective the UK Listing Authority

---

[35] Art 5(2), Prospectus Directive and PR 1.2.4.
[36] Art 5(3), Prospectus Directive and PR 2.2.1.
[37] PR 2.1.5 (derived from Recital 21 of the Prospectus Directive).

consider that the requirement to produce a compact and comprehensible overview is useful and they intend to apply this guideline on the number of words reasonably strictly and so would normally expect summaries to be no more than 2,500 words. However, there will be circumstances when, due to the particularly complex nature of the issuer or the securities, this limit would make it very difficult, if not impossible, to explain reasonably the 'essential characteristics and risks associated with the issuer and the securities'. In such circumstance they would be prepared to allow summaries to be slightly longer than 2,500 words.

An issuer can, in relation to certain non-equity transferable securities, produce a **18.75** prospectus which comprises a base prospectus containing all the information concerning the issuer and the transferable securities. The final terms, detailing the criteria and/or conditions or, in the case of price, the maximum price, can then be added to the base prospectus to make the document a valid prospectus. However under PR 2.2.8 the requirement for an issuer to publish a supplementary prospectus subsists during the currency of the base prospectus (maximum 12 months). The fact that the publication of a supplementary prospectus would trigger withdrawal rights may be relevant to any decision to follow solely the base prospectus/final terms structure.

The prospectus is required to include the following parts in the following order: **18.76**

(a) table of contents;
(b) summary;
(c) risk factors; and
(d) other information required by the schedules and the building blocks.[38]

The order set out above is prescribed by law. However there does not appear to be any impediment on following the above order but interleaving the parts with other additional information. For example in the case of a combined prospectus and class 1 circular an issuer could place the chairman's letter between, say, the summary and the risk factors and still be in compliance with the obligations. An issuer is not required to comply with the order set out in the schedules and building blocks so long as a checklist is provided.[39]

The contents of prospectuses are now prescribed by EU law in the PD Regula- **18.77** tion[40] which is directly applicable in the UK. The UK Listing Authority has copied the content requirements out into the Prospectus Rules for ease of reference and use by stakeholders. In determining whether the rules have been

---

[38] Art 25.1, Prospectus Directive.
[39] Art 25.4, Prospectus Directive.
[40] Regulation 809/2004 of the European Commission.

complied with the UK Listing Authority will take into account whether an issuer has complied with the CESR recommendations.[41]

18.78 A prospectus shall be drawn up by using one or a combination of the following schedules and building blocks set out in Articles 4 to 20, according to the combinations for various types of securities provided for in Article 21.

18.79 A prospectus shall contain the information items required in Annexes I to XVII depending on the type of issuer and securities involved, provided for in the schedules and building blocks set out in Articles 4 to 20. A competent authority shall not request that a prospectus contains information items which are not included in Annexes I to XVII.

18.80 In order to ensure conformity with the obligation referred to in section 87A(2) of the Act, the FSA when approving a prospectus in accordance with section 87A of the Act, may require that the information provided by the issuer, the offeror, or the person asking for admission to trading on a regulated market be completed for each of the information items, on a case-by-case basis.

18.81 Information may be incorporated in the prospectus by reference to one or more previously or simultaneously published documents that have been approved by the FSA or filed with or notified to it in accordance with the Prospectus Directive or Titles IV and V of CARD. The rules governing statutory responsibility for prospectus are set out in PR 5.

18.82 In particular under paragraph (1), information may be incorporated by reference to information filed under PR 5.2 (annual information update).[42]

18.83 Information under Titles IV and V of CARD that may be incorporated by reference includes, for example, instruments of incorporation or statutes of a company, annual accounts, and annual reports, equivalent information made available to markets in the UK, half yearly reports, listing particulars, and supplementary listing particulars.

18.84 Information incorporated by reference must be the latest available to the issuer, offeror, or person requesting admission. The summary must not incorporate information by reference.[43]

General contents of prospectus

18.85 Section 87A(2), (3), and (4) of FSMA provides for the general contents of prospectuses. A prospectus is required to contain the necessary information to

---

[41] PR 1.1.8.
[42] Art 11.1, Prospectus Directive.
[43] Art 11.1, Prospectus Directive.

enable investors to make an informed assessment of the assets and liabilities, financial position, profits and losses, and prospects of the issuer of the transferable securities and of any guarantor; and the rights attaching to the transferable securities. In addition the necessary information must be presented in a form which is comprehensible and easy to analyse.

Responsibility

The rules in PR 5.5 specify in accordance with section 84(1)(d) of the Act and for the purposes of Part 6 of the Act, the persons responsible for a prospectus. The UK Listing Authority conducted an abbreviated consultation into these rules. Following their consultation exercise on PD implementation, HM Treasury decided that it would be more appropriate to provide the UK Listing Authority with a rule-making power to establish the persons responsible for prospectuses rather than deal with this through legislation. This allows a greater degree of flexibility, as the regime is not embedded in statute, and is in keeping with the general policy of giving the UK Listing Authority rule-making powers under a statutory framework. **18.86**

The UK Listing Authority used both POSR and the Listing Particulars regime as the basis for the new rules. The policy approach has generally been to replicate as closely as possible the existing regimes. The Prospectus Directive does not specifically state who should take statutory responsibility for prospectuses. But Article 6 of the PD does impose an obligation on Member States to ensure that statutory responsibility applies to at least 'the issuer or its administrative, management or supervisory bodies, the offeror, the person asking for admission to trading on a regulated market or the guarantor, as the case may be'. Within these parameters Member States therefore have the ability to determine who should take statutory responsibility for prospectuses. **18.87**

The rules only require the directors or proposed directors of an issuer to accept responsibility if the securities are equity shares. This would not apply to non-equity securities or convertible or exchangeable securities. **18.88**

The previous listing particulars carve out in relation to takeovers has not been carried forward.[44] These provisions currently allow issuers to exclude themselves from responsibility in relation to information on a target which is included in a set of listing particulars. As referred to above Article 6 of the PD requires that at least the issuer must be responsible for the *whole* of a prospectus. It will be possible for the target and target directors to take responsibility, in addition to the issuer and its directors, in takeover and acquisition situations, but they will not be able **18.89**

---

[44] The Financial Services and Markets Act 2000 (Official Listing of Securities) Regulations 2001, SI 2001/2956, reg 7.

to take responsibility *instead* of the issuer and its directors. The approach in relation to responsibility for prospectuses will therefore be more closely aligned with the domestic class 1 circular regime for listed issuers, where the directors of the issuer are required to take responsibility for all the information in the document.

18.90 In relation to equity shares the following are responsible:

(a) the issuer of the transferable securities;

(b) if the issuer is a body corporate:

 (i) each person who is a director of that body corporate when the prospectus is published; and

 (ii) each person who has authorised himself to be named, and is named, in the prospectus as a director or as having agreed to become a director of that body corporate either immediately or at a future time;

(c) each person who accepts, and is stated in the prospectus as accepting, responsibility for the prospectus;

(d) in relation to an offer:

 (i) the offeror, if this is not the issuer; and

 (ii) if the offeror is a body corporate and is not the issuer, each person who is a director of the body corporate when the prospectus is published;

(e) in relation to a request for the admission to trading of transferable securities:

 (i) the person requesting admission, if this is not the issuer; and

 (ii) if the person requesting admission is a body corporate and is not the issuer, each person who is a director of the body corporate when the prospectus is published; and

(f) each person not falling within any of the previous paragraphs who has authorised the contents of the prospectus.

PR 5.5.7 (offeror not responsible in certain circumstances) continues the current carve-out available to offerors of securities in the event that the issuer takes responsibility for and draws up a prospectus and the offeror makes the offer in association with the issuer. This should cover standard IPO situations.

Advertisements, supplementary prospectuses, and withdrawal rights

18.91 The definition of advertisement in the PD Regulation[45] and Prospectus Rules is wide. It covers announcements relating to a specific offer or admission aiming specifically to promote the potential subscription or acquisition of securities. PR 3.3.2 provides that advertisements must not be issued unless:

(a) it states that a prospectus has been or will be published and indicates where investors are, or will be, able to obtain it;

---

[45] Regulation 809/2004 of the European Commission.

(b) it is clearly recognisable as an advertisement;

(c) information in the advertisement is not inaccurate, or misleading; and

(d) information in the advertisement is consistent with the information contained in the prospectus, if already published, or with the information required to be in the prospectus, if the prospectus is published afterwards.[46]

The UK Listing Authority clarified, in PR 3.3.2 that an advertisement should **18.92** also contain a bold and prominent statement to the effect that it is not a prospectus but an advertisement and investors should not subscribe for any securities referred to in the advertisement except on the basis of information in the prospectus. In issue 12 of *List!*, the FSA explains that in practice this would mean having a heading inserted on the front page of the document titled 'Advertisement' followed closely by the warning required by PR 3.3.3G and any other statement that is stipulated by PR 3.3.2R(1).

It is anticipated that issuers may seek to issue a pathfinder prospectus under **18.93** the advertisement regime. This would enable initial public offerings to be conducted on a similar basis and timetable as previously. Advertisements will require approval as a financial promotion under section 21 of FSMA as they are specifically carved out of the Article 70 exemption (promotions included in listing particulars, etc).[47] The FSA has given guidance to the effect that they are likely to regard a pathfinder as an advertisement relating to a public offer in situations where it is sent exclusively to institutional placees prior to a proposed offer (no admission to trading) being made to the public.[48]

A supplementary prospectus is required if, during the relevant period, there **18.94** arises or is noted a significant new factor, material mistake, or inaccuracy relating to the information contained in the prospectus.[49] Section 87G of FSMA governs the relevant period during which an issuer must submit a supplementary prospectus.

Section 87G(3) of FSMA sets out the relevant period when a supplementary **18.95** prospectus may be required. The relevant period begins when the prospectus is approved and ends with the closure of the offer or when trading begins. The Prospectus Directive and statute are silent as to whether it should be the earlier, or later, of the closure of the offer or admission. The favoured interpretation appears to be that it should be the later of the closure of the offer or admission

---

[46] Arts 15.1, 15.2, and 15.3 of Prospectus Directive.

[47] The Financial Services and Markets Act 2000 (Financial Promotion) Order 2005, art 70.

[48] Issue 12 of *List!*.

[49] FSMA, s 87G(1).

as the public offer and admission to trading aspects of the Prospectus Directive are generally separate and stand-alone provisions and obligations.

18.96 FSMA contains withdrawal rights for investors in the following circumstances (see section 87Q):

(a) if a person agrees to buy or subscribe for transferable securities in circumstances where the final offer price or the amount of transferable securities to be offered to the public is not included in the prospectus, he may withdraw his acceptance before the end of the withdrawal period specified in section 87Q(2); and

(b) if a supplementary prospectus has been published (as required by section 87G) and, prior to the publication, he agreed to buy or subscribe for transferable securities to which it relates, he may withdraw his acceptance before the end of the period of two working days beginning with the first working day after the date on which the supplementary prospectus was published.

18.97 A person who has agreed to buy or subscribe transferable securities prior to the publication of the supplementary prospectus may withdraw within two working days beginning on the day the supplementary prospectus is published.[50]

18.98 Under Rule 34 of the Takeover Code, an acceptor is only entitled to withdraw his acceptance from the date which is 21 days after the first closing date of the initial offer if the offer has not by such date become or been declared unconditional as to acceptances (ie from day 42 if the bid has a normal timetable). This right of withdrawal is then exercisable until the earlier of (a) the time that the offer becomes or is declared unconditional as to acceptances, and (b) the final time for lodgement of acceptances which can be taken into account in accordance with Rule 31.6 (ie normally before 1 pm on day 60 if the bid has a normal timetable). No withdrawals are normally permitted after the offer has become or been declared unconditional as to acceptances (other than if an offeree protection condition is invoked or if a competitive situation arises) on the basis that a bidder should be allowed to go unconditional (which it may do at 50 per cent) in the knowledge that it will not thereafter lose statutory control of the target company.

18.99 The Takeover Panel issued a public statement[51] to address concerns in this area in relation to Takeover Code transactions. The Panel states that it has received legal advice that the new FSMA provisions can be interpreted as meaning that the period for withdrawal by an acceptor of an offer ends once the offer has become

---

[50] FSMA, s 87Q(4).
[51] Takeover Panel Statement 2005/29.

or been declared wholly unconditional and the relevant securities have been unconditionally allotted to the acceptor—ie wholly unconditional bids could not be re-opened through the exercise of withdrawal rights, provided unconditional allotments of the consideration securities have been made. Additionally the Panel has also received legal advice that section 87Q(4) of FSMA does not apply to the issue of new securities in the context of a scheme of arrangement under Part 26 of the Companies Act 2006 or if the new securities are offered by means of an 'equivalent document', rather than a prospectus (see para 18.32). An equivalent document is one which is regarded by the FSA as containing information equivalent to a prospectus. This is on all fours with the views on Schemes of Arrangement and equivalent documents of the UK Listing Authority contained in issue 10 of *List!*.

The UK Listing Authority has confirmed in issue 11 of *List!* that they consider   **18.100**
that the withdrawal rights conferred by section 87Q(4) of FSMA do not apply in relation to any investor whose agreement to buy or subscribe for securities has become wholly unconditional including for this purpose the unconditional allotment of the securities. Section 87Q(4) of FSMA refers to the situation where a person has 'agreed to buy or subscribe' and only permits the withdrawal of an acceptance. This should not apply once the securities have been unconditionally allotted to the acceptor.

Disclosure Rules

General

The Disclosure and Transparency Rules ('DTR') contain detailed stand alone   **18.101**
rules derived from the Market Abuse Directive, Transparency Directive, and Company Reporting Directive. The disclosure rules (derived from the Market Abuse Directive) are contained in DTR 2 and DTR 3 and apply to issuers who have requested or approved admission of their securities to a regulated market based in the UK and to persons discharging managerial responsibility in those issuers and their associates. This extends the application of the rules beyond listed issuers. However, it is worth noting that the regime set out in DTR2 does not extend to financial instruments (including derivatives) which are issued by another party.

Disclosure of inside information

There are a number of key issues under the new disclosure regime. The starting   **18.102**
point is to establish whether an issuer is in possession of inside information. If so the question is whether the disclosure can be delayed. If disclosure can be delayed issuers can consider selective disclosure.

18.103   DTR 2.2.1 requires inside information to be disclosed as soon as possible. Inside information is defined in section 118C of FSMA and is information of a precise nature which:

(a) is not generally available;

(b) relates to one or more issuers of qualifying investments; and

(c) would be likely to have a significant impact on the price of the qualifying investments.

18.104   DTR 2.2.3G to DTR 2.2.8G provide detailed guidance to assist issuers in identifying inside information. In particular, DTR 2.2.6G specifies the types of information which are likely to be relevant in making this assessment and these are derived directly from the existing Listing Rules. In establishing whether a piece of information amounts to inside information issuers should, in particular, carefully consider the limits of the test which require the information to be both precise (see section 118C(5) of FSMA) and price-sensitive (including the reasonable investor test aspects).

18.105   Information may be commercially sensitive but this does not mean it meets the test for inside information. If an issuer has inside information, it should consider whether an immediate announcement is required or whether the issuer can delay disclosure. DTR 2.2.9G(2) provides guidance on the use of a holding announcement when an issuer is faced with an unexpected and significant event which requires a short delay to clarify the situation prior to making a regular disclosure to the market. If the information does not amount to inside information, the Disclosure and Transparency Rules are not relevant and the issuer is not constrained under the Disclosure and Transparency Rules in how it deals with that information.

18.106   In issue 16 of *List!* the FSA emphasised that in determining when to announce updates in performance, DTR 2.2 does not set materiality thresholds, and that there is no specific figure (percentage change or otherwise) that can be set for any issuer when determining what constitutes a 'significant effect' on the price of the financial instruments, as this will vary from issuer to issuer. This FSA newsletter goes on to state that the FSA is aware that some market participants inappropriately consider 10 per cent as a threshold for impact on the price of an issuers financial instruments. The FSA made reference to this guidance in deciding to take action against Woolworths group plc in June 2008. Woolworths was fined £350,000 due to its failure to identify inside information and subsequently disclose this information to the market in a timely manner, creating a false market in its shares which breached DTR 2.2.1 and Listing Principle 4. In reaching this decision, the FSA rejected Woolworths' representation that a share price fall of 10 per cent or more attributable to the particular piece of information is needed for there to have been a 'significant effect on price' from that piece of information.[52]

DTR 2.7 provides guidance on dealing with rumours. There is a possibility that **18.107** the knowledge which an issuer has that a particular piece of information or story is false could, in very limited circumstances, amount to inside information. The guidance given in DTR 2.7.3(G) makes it clear that the knowledge that a rumour is false is unlikely to amount to inside information and, even if it did, the issuer would usually be able to delay disclosure, often indefinitely. The more accurate a rumour, the more likely it is that there has been a breach of confidentiality and that disclosure is required as soon as possible. DTR 2.7.2(G) gives additional guidance on this point and reinforces the importance of maintaining the confidentiality of inside information.

Delaying disclosure

An issuer may delay disclosure of inside information in the limited circum- **18.108** stances set out in DTR 2.5. The market understands that the disclosure of inside information can be delayed in appropriate circumstances and that such delay in disclosure will normally be limited to impending developments or matters in the course of negotiation. Issuers should be careful to distinguish between an event which gives rise to inside information (eg the loss of an important contract) that requires disclosure as soon as possible under DTR 2.2.1R and subsequent events (eg attempts to renegotiate the contract) that may benefit from the delay provisions (DTR 2.5.4G (1)).

An issuer must disclose the inside information as soon as possible if it is not able **18.109** to ensure the confidentiality of the information (DTR 2.6.2R).

Selective disclosure

Where an issuer is delaying disclosure of inside information in accordance with **18.110** the Disclosure and Transparency Rules it can selectively disclose the information to persons who owe the issuer a duty of confidentiality and have a valid reason to receive the information. The list of persons who fall into this category set out in DTR 2.5.7G is not exhaustive.

Insider lists and senior managers

The basic requirement is for an issuer to draw up a list of employees and persons **18.111** acting on its behalf who have access to inside information. The list is not a list of

---

[52] FSA, Final Notice, Woolworths Group plc, para 5.3 (June 2008).

persons who actually have inside information but those who have access to the information—this is an important matter for issuers to consider in deciding who should be on the list.

18.112   Guidance provides a practical approach for issuers who are responsible for ensuring that insider lists cover not only their own employees but also persons acting on the issuer's behalf or account, namely advisers. The guidance is designed to provide a practical solution for issuers and clarifies that it is not necessary for an issuer to maintain a list of all the individuals working for another firm or company acting on its behalf or account where it has:

(a) recorded the name of the principal contact(s) at that firm or company;

(b) made effective arrangements, which are likely to be based in contract, for that firm or company to maintain its own list of employees, both working on behalf of the issuer and with access to inside information on it; and

(c) made effective arrangements for that firm or company to provide a copy to the issuer of its list as soon as possible upon request.

18.113   For advisers, a person needs to meet a two-stage test to be included on the insider list in DTR 2.8.8G. Persons need both to be acting for the issuer and have access to inside information to be included on the list.

18.114   DTR 3.1.2R requires persons discharging managerial responsibility and persons connected to such persons (as defined in section 96B(1) of FSMA) to disclose all transactions conducted on their own account in the shares or derivatives or financial instruments relating to shares, to the issuer within four days of the transaction. This information must then, in turn, be notified to a Regulatory Information Service (DTR 2.1.4 R(1)).

18.115   DTR3 replaces the Companies Act 1985, section 324 regime, and applies to any issuer incorporated in the United Kingdom whose financial instruments are admitted to trading on a regulated market or for whose financial instruments a request for admission to trading on a regulated market in the United Kingdom has been made (DTR 1.1.1 R(2)). DTR3 also applies to non-EEA issuers that are required to file with the FSA annual information in relation to shares in line with Article 10 of the Prospective Directive.[53]

18.116   DTR3 does not clarify what is meant by 'own account' in relation to director dealings. In issue 11 of *List!* the FSA provides the following principles which suggest when a transaction by a person discharging managerial responsibilities ('PDMR') is 'on own account':

(a) a transaction which is the result of an action taken by a PDMR or otherwise undertaken with their consent;

---

[53] Issue 11 of *List!*.

(b) a transaction whose beneficiaries are mainly PDMRs; and

(c) transactions having a material impact on a PDMR's interest in an issuer.

Each transaction should be considered on its own facts to assess if it was conducted 'on own account'.

Issuers should be aware that non-compliance with certain elements of the **18.117** DTR rules may also have the following legal consequences over and above the punishment for regulatory breach:

(a) Under section 397 of FSMA, it is a criminal offence to make an intentionally misleading or reckless statement, promise or forecast or dishonestly conceal any material facts for the purpose of inducing another person to buy or sell or exercise any rights conferred by a relevant investment.

(b) Under sections 2 and 3 of the Fraud Act 2006 it is a criminal offence either to make false representations or to fail to disclose information when there is a legal duty to do so.

(c) Under the market abuse regime set out in Part VIII of FSMA. Market abuse offences include: insider dealing, improper disclosure, misuse of information, manipulating transactions, manipulating devices, dissemination; distortion and misleading behaviour—each of which may have application to elements of the DTR rules.

There may also be implications under Part V of the Criminal Justice Act 1993 relating to inside information (See Chapter 9 above). (It is a criminal offence to transact in securities that are price-sensitive to that information; encourage another person to deal in securities that are price-sensitive to that information; or improperly disclose inside information.)

With specific regard to insider dealing, the FSA has re-iterated their intention **18.118** to exercise their powers as a criminal prosecutor.[54] This shift in strategy is in accordance with their view that the risk of a custodial sentence associated with a criminal prosecution will act as a stronger deterrent than the regime created under FSMA. Consistent with this more aggressive stance, the FSA has also stated that they are prepared to use immunity agreements and plea bargaining in order to secure convictions. The FSA already has the common law power to grant immunity from prosecution by applying the public interest limb of the Code for Crown Prosecutors. In addition, the Chancellor has announced that

---

[54] Speech by Margaret Cole (FSA Director of Enforcement) to European Policy Forum, 4 April 2008.

the FSA will be added to the list of specified prosecutors,[55] effectively giving the FSA the power to grant such immunity on a statutory basis under SOCPA.

Transparency Rules

18.119 The Transparency Directive[56] ('TD') harmonises the requirements to disclose information about issuers whose securities are admitted to trading on a regulated market and serves to replace and update areas of the CARD. The TD requires regulated market issuers to produce periodic financial reports and shareholders in such companies to disclose major shareholdings. In addition, the TD deals with the mechanisms for disseminating and storing such information. The FSA's approach to implementing this 'minimum harmonisation' directive was to implement the directive minimum provisions, and to retain super-equivalent provisions only if they could be clearly justified in terms of cost to benefit, and where they were strongly supported by both issuers and investors.

18.120 Amendments to Part 6 of FSMA (made by Part 43 of the Companies Act 2006) together with the FSA's Transparency Obligations Directive (Disclosure and Transparency Rules) Instrument 2006 served to implement the TD in the United Kingdom. The changes were primarily reflected in the FSA's transparency rules, which were included into the Disclosure Rules Sourcebook to become the Disclosure and Transparency Rules Sourcebook (DTR). Three new chapters were added to the DTR Sourcebook on periodic financial reporting (chapter 4), vote holder and issuer notifications (chapter 5), and continuing obligations and access to information (chapter 6).

Periodic financial reporting

18.121 An objective of the TD is to improve the quality, quantity, and timeliness of periodic financial information for investors. To this end, the TD sets out the financial reporting requirements applicable to issuers on a regulated market. The pre-existing financial reporting requirements for listed issuers were set out in LR9. Although similar to the TD requirements, the LR rules set out less prescriptive content requirements, longer deadlines for production, and covered a less comprehensive range of periodic reporting.

18.122 A copy-out approach was taken to implement the requirements of the TD, resulting in the creation of DTR 4. Elements of the Listing Rules that were equivalent to TD requirements were deleted; however, some elements of the old LR9 regime were retained, effectively 'gold-plating' the directive requirements. These super-equivalent financial reporting requirements relate to corporate

---

[55] As at the date of writing, this statutory power had not yet been granted by the Treasury.
[56] Directive (EC) 2004/109.

governance and directors' remuneration disclosures in the Annual Financial Report of Listed companies.

The new financial reporting regime applicable to listed companies is now a combination of requirements derived from the Companies Act, Listing Rules, Disclosure and Transparency Rules, and International Financial Reporting Standards (IFRS). This new regime is implemented from January 2007 for companies with a financial year commencing on or after 20 January 2007. **18.123**

DTR4 requires listed companies to produce an Annual Financial Report, Half-yearly Report, and Interim Management Statements. It also sets out the responsibility statements, content requirements, and publication deadlines for each report, together with the partial exemptions available to issuers of debt, convertible securities, GDRs, and non-EEA issuers. **18.124**

The regime no longer requires companies to issue preliminary statements of their annual results. However, companies are likely to continue to publish preliminary results. **18.125**

In order to implement Article 7 of the Transparency Directive, a statutory civil liability regime has been imposed for periodic financial information published under the provisions made implementing the TD. The regime is set out in section 90A, and applies to all companies with securities admitted to trading on a regulated market in the UK. The regime also applies to companies admitted to trading on an overseas regulated market if the UK is that company's home Member State. **18.126**

The regime applies to information contained in the Annual Financial Report, Half-yearly Report, and Interim Management Statements in addition to preliminary statements made in advance of the Annual Financial Report. **18.127**

Section 90A(3) provides that an issuer will be liable to pay compensation to a person who has purchased securities in the company and suffered a loss as a result of any untrue or misleading statement in or omission from publications to which section 90(A) applies. **18.128**

It is important to note that the current regime will not protect a person who suffers a loss as a result of holding or selling securities on the basis of incorrect or incomplete information contained in the relevant reports. Further, a company will only be liable if a director knew that the statement was untrue or misleading, was reckless as to whether it was reckless or misleading, or knew the omission to be dishonest concealment of material fact. The regime restricts liability to third parties to the company itself, although the directors involved in the misstatement/omissions may be held liable to the company. **18.129**

The scope of the current regime is restricted to periodic disclosures under the TD and preliminary statements. The regime does not apply to announcements **18.130** made to the market by way of a Regulated Information Service or ad hoc disclosures of inside information under the provisions of the Market Abuse Directive. This narrow scope has been the focus of a recent review conducted by HM Treasury (conducted by Professor Paul Davies QC). The key proposals in this review include extending the narrow scope of the current regime to include:[57]

(a) issuers with securities admitted to trading on a UK multilateral trading facility.

(b) issuers with securities admitted to trading on an EEA regulated market or MTF, provided they have a registered office in the UK or the UK is their home State under the TD.

(c) a wider range of ad hoc and periodic disclosures to markets.

(d) to permit sellers, as well as buyers, of securities to recover losses

(e) allow recovery of losses resulting from dishonest delay of disclosure.

Responses to the consultation are expected in 2008.

18.131 This regime should also be considered in light of the Companies Act 2006 (CA 2006) provisions relating to directors. Section 463 of CA 2006 imposes personal liability in certain circumstances on a director of a UK company for losses suffered by the company as a result of certain misleading statements contained in the Annual Financial Report. In addition, in instances where a company elects not to take action against a director in relation to losses suffered, shareholders may pursue a derivative action under CA 2006, sections 260 to 264 in order to force the company to do so.[58] Finally, under section 501 of CA 2006, the director will, under certain circumstances, commit a criminal offence if he or she knowingly or recklessly makes misleading, false, or deceptive representations to the company's external auditors.

Vote holder and issuer notification

18.132 The TD provisions relating to the disclosure of major shareholdings were implemented in the UK through sections 89A to 89L of FSMA and DTR 5. These new provisions replace the regime set out in sections 198 to 220 of the Companies Act 1985, with responsibility for monitoring and enforcement of the Notification Rules transferring from the Department of Trade and Industry to the FSA.

18.133 Under the repealed CA 1985 regime, notifications were triggered by 'interests in shares'. In contrast, the DTR 5 requirements relate to control over voting rights

---

[57] HM Treasury, 'Extension of the statutory regime for issuer liability'.
[58] Herbert Smith, *A Practical Guide to the UK Listing Regime*.

attached to shares. The scope of the disclosure regime has also been changed by the new rules. The repealed section 198 regime did not apply to an interest held in any overseas companies. The new DTR 5 regime applies to all companies whose shares are admitted to trading on a regulated market for whom the UK is the home Member State. The regime also applies to UK companies incorporated under section 1(3) of the Companies Act 1985 with shares admitted to trading on a prescribed market (including LIFFE, AIM, and PLUS).

DTR 5.1.2 states that a person must notify the issuer of the percentage of its **18.134** voting rights he holds as shareholder or through his direct or indirect holding of qualifying financial instruments if, as a result of an acquisition, disposal, or change in the breakdown if the voting rights, percentage of those voting rights:

(i) reaches, exceeds, or falls below 3%, 4%, 5%, 6%, 7%, 8%, 9%, 10%, and each 1% threshold thereafter (in the case of a UK issuer); or
(ii) reaches, exceeds or falls below 5%, 10%, 15%, 20%, 25%, 30%, 50% and 75% (in the case of a non-UK issuer).

as a result of an acquisition, disposal, or events changing the breakdown of voting rights in the issuer.

DTR 5 follows the provisions and definitions of the TD, and is therefore refer- **18.135** enced to direct and indirect control of voting rights attaching to a share. Consequently, major positions in contracts for difference ('CFDs') generally fall outside the scope of DTR 5, unless the contracts explicitly gave access to the voting rights attached to shares held as a hedge by the CFD writer. However, in CP 07/20 the FSA has concluded that the DTR 5 regime should be extended to require disclosure of substantial economic interests in shares held through derivatives such as CFDs. The consultation paper proposed two options for increased disclosure, a more targeted disclosure regime (option 2 in the CP), and a general disclosure regime requiring disclosure of all CFDs over 5 per cent (option 3). The FSA ultimately decided to implement a general disclosure regime of long CFD positions based on option 3 in the consultation paper.

DTR 5.1.3 provides exemptions from the general notification requirements **18.136** potentially available to custodians and nominees, market makers, credit institutions, and shares acquired for settlement purposes or held as collateral.

Continuing obligations and access to information

DTR 6 contains detailed provisions relating to the dissemination of regulated **18.137** information. This chapter also includes a number of continuing obligations to work alongside those set out in LR9 and applies to issuers admitted to trading on a regulated market.

DTR 6.1 sets out detailed information requirements aimed at ensuring that **18.138** all shareholders are treated equally in terms of access to information, and the exercise of their voting rights. These provisions are aimed at existing shareholders, the FSA, and the market and are set out as follows:

(a) provision of information relating to proposed amendments to constitution (DTR 6.1.2);

(b) equality of treatment (DTR 6.1.3);

(c) exercise of rights by holders (DTR 6.1.4);

(d) exercise of rights by proxy (DTR 6.1.5);

(e) appointment of a financial agent (DTR 6.1.6);

(f) electronic communications (DTR 6.1.7);

(g) information about changes in rights attaching to securities (DTR 6.1.9);

(h) information about meetings, issue of new shares and payment of dividends – share issuers (DTR 6.1.12);

(i) information about meetings and payment of interest – debt security issuers (DTR 6.1.14);

(j) non-EEA states exemption (DTR 6.1.16);

(k) regional and local authority exemption (DTR 6.1.18);

(l) exemption for issuers of convertible securities, preference shares, and depository receipts (DTR 6.1.19).

18.139 The rules make it clear that all regulated information disclosed under this chapter must be filed simultaneously with the FSA (DTR 6.2.2 R). The rules also detail the language requirements for issuers with securities admitted to trading in more than one EEA State.

18.140 The new DTR 6 operates alongside the CA 2006 provisions relating to issuers using 'electronic means' to communicate with equity and debt holders. The CA 2006 and the DTR 6 were brought into force simultaneously and it is understood that the CA 2006 is to take precedence over DTR 6 in situations where both apply.[59] CA 2006 provides that the communication of documents via 'electronic means' is permissible provided that security measures are in place and 'consent' has been obtained prior to its application. The consent obtained must be in writing, and identification arrangements must be put in place so that those persons entitled to exercise voting rights are effectively informed (DTR 6.1.8 R(3)). The decision to use electronic means to communicate with shareholders or debt securities holders must be taken in general meeting (DTR 6.1.8 R(1)), and the use of electronic means must not depend on the location of the seat of residence of the recipient (DTR 6.1.8 R(2)).

---

[59] Herbert Smith, *A Practical Guide to the UK Listing Regime*, p 255.

Corporate governance

DTR 7 was introduced in order to implement the corporate governance state- **18.141**
ment requirement of the Company Reporting Directive[60] and the audit committee requirement of the Statutory Audit Directive.[61] These rules will apply in
relation to financial years commencing on or after 29 June 2008.

DTR 7.1 contains the requirement for companies whose securities have been **18.142**
admitted to trading on a regulated market to have an audit committee which
contains at least one member who is independent and at least one member who
is competent in accounting and/or auditing.[62] Such companies are also required
to base any proposal to appoint a statutory auditor on a recommendation from
the audit committee. In addition, these companies should make a statement
available to the public disclosing which body carries out the functions required
by DTR 7.1.3 R (audit committee in most cases) and how it is composed. It is
important to note that much of DTR 7.1 overlaps with requirements laid down
in the Combined Code. The FSA have therefore added DTR 7.1.7 to make
it clear that in their view, compliance with provisions A.1.2, C.3.1, C.3.2, and
C.3.3 of the Combined Code will result in compliance with DTR 7.1.1 R to
DTR 7.1.5 R.

DTR 7.2 applies to an issuer whose securities are admitted to trading and which **18.143**
is a company within the meaning of section 1(1) of the Companies Act 2006
(DTR 1B.1.5 R). DTR 7.2 requires issuers to which this section applies to include
a corporate governance statement as a specific statement in its directors' report,
and goes on to list content requirements for this statement. Several parts of
this new rule overlap with the pre-existing governance rules in place for UK companies with a primary equity listing, specifically the LR 9.8.6 requirements to
'comply or explain' against the UK Combined Code on Corporate Governance.

After consultation, the FSA decided to retain and modify the 'comply or explain' **18.144**
rule (LR 9.8.6R) to sit alongside the new DTR 7.2. LR 9.8.6R(5) has been
modified to reduce 'boilerplate disclosures' so that a company to whom the rule
applies will only need to report on compliance against the main principles set
out in section 1 of the Combined Code, as opposed to reporting on the whole
of section 1 of the Code. In relation to the DTR 7.2.7 requirement for the
corporate governance statement to contain a description of the composition and
operations of the issuer's various governance bodies, DTR 7.2.8 now clarifies the

---

[60] Directive (EC) 2006/46.
[61] Directive (EC) 2006/43.
[62] The requirement for independence and competence in accounting and/or auditing may be
satisfied by the same member.

FSA's view that compliance with provisions A.1.1, A.1.2, A.4.6, B.2.1, and C.3.3 of the Combined Code satisfy the requirements of DTR 7.2.7.

Listing Rules

General

18.145 The FSA, acting through the UK Listing Authority is the UK's competent authority for the regulation of the admission of securities to the Official List.[63] As competent authority, the FSA is responsible for maintaining the Official List and for admitting to listing the securities covered by Part VI of FSMA. The FSA are empowered by section 73A of FSMA to make rules through the UKLA governing the admission to listing, the enforcement of those obligations, and suspension and cancellation of listing.[64] These rules, which also contain the overarching Listing Principles are collectively known as the Listing Rules.

18.146 There are currently five[65] listing segments on the Official List: primary listing of equity; secondary listing of equity; listing of Global Depository Receipts ('GDRs'); listing of Debt; and listing of Securitised Derivatives ('SDs'). Segments are differentiated by the level of regulatory burden attached, both in terms of standards and oversight.

18.147 In terms of equity securities or certificates representing such securities, a UK incorporated company that seeks admission to the FSA's Official List must apply for a primary listing. However, a non-UK incorporated company (including an EEA company) which seeks a listing of such securities is offered the choice of three segments: primary listing, secondary listing, or alternatively a listing of GDRs. The Securitised Derivative and Debt segments are available to all companies, regardless of their country of incorporation.

18.148 A primary listing of equity securities is the 'premium brand' of the Official List to which additional requirements, otherwise known as 'super-equivalent'[66] requirements, apply. All other listing segments are based on 'directive-minimum'[67] standards only—ie the minimum standards which EU legislation requires the FSA to impose on all securities trading on a regulated market and/or offered to the public.

---

[63] s 72 of FSMA.
[64] FSA Discussion Paper 08/1: 'A review of the structure of the Listing Regime'.
[65] Official Listing here excludes Investment Entities.
[66] These are requirements over and above the 'directive-minimum' requirements which may be found in the Listing Rules.
[67] These are requirements derived either from CARD, PD, TD, or MAD.

This structure was put in place in 2005, following consultations in which a sig-   **18.149**
nificant majority of respondents supported 'gold-plating' or super-equivalent
provisions imposing higher standards than those required by the European directives in this way.

Primary listed equity securities

An issuer of equity securities who complies in full with the obligations set out in   **18.150**
LR6 to LR13 is a primary listed issuer. The definition of equity securities includes
convertible bonds issued by the issuer of the underlying shares. However, issuers
of such securities are also able to list under LR14 (Secondary Listing), or, if they
are specialist securities, under either LR4 (PSM), or LR17 (Debt Securities).

A primary listed issuer of equity securities should consider: **18.151**

(a) eligibility—an issuer will be required to comply with the relevant require-
    ments of LR2 and LR6;
(b) sponsors—a sponsor is required to assess and provide assurances, generally
    and specifically in relation to issuer's eligibility under LR8;
(c) continuing obligations—an issuer will be required to comply with the
    Disclosure and Transparency Rules, the continuing aspects of the Prospectus
    Rules (eg PR 5.2—Annual Information Update) and LR7, LR9, LR10,
    LR11, LR12, and LR13;
(d) general—an issuer will be subject to LR1, LR2, LR3, and LR5.

If an issuer is admitted to trading on a regulated market anywhere in the EEA   **18.152**
or has a UK secondary listing, that issuer will still be treated as new applicant if
it seeks a primary listing. This does not mean that the issuer will be required to
produce listing particulars under LR4 and it may only need to produce minimal
documentation under the Prospectus Rules. However it will still be required
to satisfy the eligibility criteria set out in LR6 (such as the three-year revenue
earning track record and clean working capital requirement) and a sponsor will be
required to undertake the work and provide the requisite assurances under LR8
(such as those required for the working capital position and in relation to systems
and controls).

An important distinction should be drawn between the primary listing regime   **18.153**
applicable to overseas incorporated companies and that for companies incorporated in the UK. Although all companies with a primary listing of equities are
required to adhere to the super-equivalent provisions set by the FSA, LR9 sets
different standards for overseas and UK incorporated companies with regard to
the following:

(a) UK incorporated companies are required to state in the annual report whether
    the company complies with the Combined Code and provide an explanation

for any areas of non-compliance. Overseas companies are not subject to this 'Comply or Explain' requirement against the UK Combined Code, but are instead required to disclose whether or not they comply with the corporate governance regime in their country of incorporation. Overseas companies are then required to disclose the significant ways in which their actual corporate governance practices differ from those set out in the Combined Code.

(b) UK incorporated companies are required to offer pre-emption rights to existing shareholders. This requirement is derived from UK company legislation, and as such does not apply to companies incorporated outside the United Kingdom.

The FSA accept that the rules as they currently stand may be a source of uncertainty and confusion in the market. As a result, the FSA have indicated in DP08/1 their intention to revisit the issue of whether it is sensible for the UK market to treat companies differently based on geographical location and differing domestic requirements.

Warrants and options

18.154 As well as meeting the definition of equity securities LR 2.2.14 makes it clear that warrants and options over shares are treated as if the issue were a share issue. Warrant and option holders do not benefit from the right to vote under the class test and related party regimes.

Secondary listed equity securities

18.155 An overseas issuer (that is a non-UK issuer) seeking a secondary listing of its equity securities can, instead of seeking a primary listing, comply with the reduced obligations set out in LR14 to establish its eligibility and continuing obligations. LR14 has the effect of carving overseas issuers of equity securities out of the super-equivalent provisions in LR6 to LR13. LR14 now provides a standalone list of requirements for secondary listed overseas issuers of equity securities. LR14 sets out those parts of LR2, LR6, and LR9 which are relevant to secondary listed overseas issuers. To list under LR14 an issuer must be an overseas issuer; it is not possible for UK issuers to list under LR14. Despite the fact that the rules use the shorthand of 'secondary listed' LR14 issuers are not required to have a listing or trading facility elsewhere. LR14 now reflects a standard similar to that required by the directives, without significant embellishment, and provides a suitable market for those seeking to passport into the UK as well as those with a listing or trading facility elsewhere who are looking for exposure to the London market.

Debt securities

LR17 takes a similar approach to LR14 and spells out the eligibility and continu- **18.156** ing obligations regime for debt issuers, both specialist and retail. The obligations generally represent the directive standards, without significant embellishment, and are very closely aligned to the old Chapter 23 continuing obligations req- uirements for issuers of specialist securities. The obligations in relation to retail debt are now closely aligned to the directive standards and the specialist regime.

Specialist securities

Issuers of specialist securities can list under LR17 if they want their securities **18.157** admitted to a regulated market or under LR4 if they want to have their securities admitted to the PSM. The document contents and continuing obligations for both regimes are very similar. The key difference is that the minimum disclosure requirements for issuers seeking to admit under LR4 to the PSM will be limited to the PD wholesale building blocks whatever the denomination of the security. Convertible and exchangeable securities can be specialist securities.

Global depository receipts

A key feature of the evolution of the UK capital markets since 2005 has been the **18.158** substantial growth in GDR issuance in the UK. GDRs are transferable securities which represent ownership of a given number of a foreign company's equity issued on behalf of a company by a depository bank. Issuers of GDRs have the choice of listing under LR18 if they want their shares admitted to trading on a regulated market (the London Stock Exchange) or under LR4 if they want their shares admitted to the PSM (non-regulated market).

The Listing Rules applicable to GDRs exclude the super-equivalent require- **18.159** ments of LR6–LR12, including eligibility requirements such as a three-year track record and continuing obligations such as class tests. In addition, the shares which underlie the certificates are not required to be admitted to trading.

LR18 also requires the depository to be a suitably authorised and regulated finan- **18.160** cial institution acceptable to the FSA.

The Prospectus Rules require an issuer to publish a prospectus regarding the **18.161** GDRs if they are to be admitted to trading on an EU regulated market and/or if they are being offered to the public. Consequently, where a prospectus is not required under the Prospective Directive and the issuer is seeking admission to listing on the PSM, LR4 mandates the preparation of listing particulars in relation to the GDR issue. Conversely, a listing under LR18 will require the prep- aration of a prospectus in relation to the GDR issue. Regardless of the regime selected, any prospectus or listing particulars must be approved by the FSA's Global Debt Group.

18.162   The continuing obligations of the GDR issuer will also be determined by the market in which the securities are admitted, with LR18 issuers expected to comply with all of the continuing obligations of the DTRs. This is in contrast to PSM issuers who are expected to comply with DTR2 (disclosure and control of inside information) and DTR 6.3 (dissemination of inside information).

Securitised derivatives

18.163   Securitised derivatives ('SDs') are derivative financial instruments which are sold to retail investors and include covered warrants, options, and contracts for difference. Issuers of SDs will list under LR19 if they want their securities admitted to a regulated market. These issuers will also be expected to meet the requirements of LR2. However, as with specialist securities, issuers are permitted to list under LR4 if they intend to have their securities admitted to the PSM.

Convertible and exchangeable securities

18.164   An issuer of convertible securities will, depending on the nature of the securities and the status of the issuer, be able to select what kind of regime they wish to list under. For the purposes of the Listing Rules equity securities are defined to include equity shares and securities which are convertible into equity shares. The UK Listing Authority has interpreted the Listing Rules definition of equity securities to include securities issued by the issuer of the underlying shares (ie convertible bonds) but exclude securities convertible into third party underlying shares (ie exchangeable bonds).

18.165   This means that issuers of convertibles can list under the full super-equivalent regime in LR6 to LR13 or under LR14 (if they are an overseas issuer and meet the criteria). If the securities are specialist securities they can also list under LR4 or LR17.

18.166   Issuers of securities exchangeable into underlying securities issued by a third party are treated as debt securities and can, if they are specialist securities, list under LR4 or, whether or not they are specialist securities, list under LR17. In general the UK Listing Authority approach to convertibles and exchangeables, as set out in LR 2.2.12, has been to ensure that the underlying security is admitted to a market and that there is sufficient information on the underlying security to allow security holders to value the convertible bond. Holders of listed convertible or exchangeable securities, where the underlying security is also listed, benefit from certain anti-dilution protections set out in LR12.

Listing Principles

The Listing Principles are designed to ensure adherence to the spirit—as well as the letter—of the rules in the interests of promoting a fair and orderly market. The Listing Principles are intended to inform the interpretation of the rules and to reflect the existing obligations of all primary listed issuers. They are based on recognised standards of corporate governance. In policy terms, the Listing Principles are not intended to apply different standards and processes to issuers than are expected under the previous rules. The UK Listing Authority policy position and cost benefit analysis are based on the firm belief that well-managed listed companies would already satisfy the Listing Principles. Issuers who currently comply with the rules and have systems and controls in place to enable them to comply with the rules will be able to comply with the Listing Principles without significant additional cost. The introduction of Listing Principles should not have required issuers to produce long and detailed compliance manuals. **18.167**

The Listing Principles are set out below. **18.168**

Principle 1	A listed company must take reasonable steps to enable its directors to understand their responsibilities and obligations as directors.
Principle 2	A listed company must take reasonable steps to establish and maintain adequate procedures, systems, and controls to enable it to comply with its obligations.
Principle 3	A listed company must act with integrity towards holders and potential holders of its listed equity securities.
Principle 4	A listed company must communicate information to holders and potential holders of its listed equity securities in such a way as to avoid the creation or continuation of a false market in such listed equity securities.
Principle 5	A listed company must ensure that it treats all holders of the same class of its listed equity securities that are in the same position equally in respect of the rights attaching to such listed equity securities.
Principle 6	A listed company must deal with the FSA in an open and cooperative manner.

Listing Principles 2 and 4 have engendered most debate. The UK Listing Authority considers that Listing Principle 4 is an important element of the Listing Principles. Reflecting the fundamental obligations of listed issuers, the Listing Principles would be incomplete without an overarching and high-level principle that sets a high standard for market communications by issuers, as investors are entitled **18.169** to expect a high standard of responsibility and care. Listing Principle 4 is not designed to overlay or duplicate well regulated areas of market communication such as DTR2 or elements of sections 118 (false and misleading impressions) and 397 (misleading statements and practices) of FSMA. Listing Principle 4 is designed to remind issuers, at a high level, that accurate and timely communication with the market is an important part of the UK regulatory regime. It is not intended to cut across or change existing rules relating to disclosure. The UK Listing Authority spent some time crafting appropriate language to deal with unfounded market rumour in the disclosure rules and the listing principles do not go beyond or require more than the detailed rules. In particular it does not require an issuer to prevent inappropriate market reaction as this would extend the listing principle to matters outside an issuer's control.

18.170 Further guidance was provided in the final rules to allay concerns regarding Principle 4. The additional guidance to LR7 makes it clear that the Listing Principles should be interpreted in accordance with the underlying rules and guidance, and that they are designed to assist issuers in identifying their obligations and responsibilities under the rules and guidance. The Listing Principles should be interpreted together with the relevant rules and guidance which underpin them. This guidance is designed to provide comfort to issuers that the Listing Principles do not expand the scope or application of the rules and guidance, particularly in the case of Principle 4 where the disclosure rules provide detailed regulatory provisions.

18.171 Additional guidance was also provided in the final rules in relation to Principle 2. Listing Principles 1 and 2 reflect basic obligations of issuers to take reasonable steps to enable directors to understand their obligations under the Listing Rules and disclosure rules, and establish and maintain systems and controls to enable the issuer to comply with such rules.

18.172 In order to provide a framework for the systems and controls principle, additional guidance was provided which makes it clear that the focus of Listing Principle 2 is on:

(a) the timely identification, escalation, consideration, and, if necessary, disclosure of inside information to the market; and

(b) identification of situations where a circular is required, particularly in relation to class 1 transactions and related party matters.

Issuers should be able to identify, assess, and, if necessary, make disclosures of inside information in a timely manner. Whilst it may be appropriate to convene formal board meetings to discuss time critical matters, issuers should have procedures in place to ensure that the consideration of such issues can happen quickly. This guidance should be helpful in relation to Listing Principle 4 as well.

Like the other Listing Principles, Listing Principle 2 is limited in its application to the Listing Rules and disclosure rules. It does not extend to matters outside the Listing Rules or disclosure rules, such as the internal control requirements of the Combined Code (The Turnbull Guidance). The sophistication and complexity of the systems and controls required will, as now, obviously depend on the nature of the issuer and its business.

Another area of debate has centred on the fact that Listing Principles are enforce-   **18.173**
able as rules. This means that a regulatory enforcement action can brought for breach of principle alone against an issuer and against a director who is knowingly concerned with such breach. The UK Listing Authority has been at pains to play down the practical effect of this. The Listing Principles are designed for regulatory and not enforcement purposes. In enforcing the Listing Principles, the UK Listing Authority will need to demonstrate that an issuer has been at fault. They have stated publicly that they will exercise such enforcement powers reasonably and on a proportionate basis. Most disciplinary cases are likely to be based on breaches of particular rules. However, the Listing Principles will be available to use against a minority of issuers who deliberately circumvent the rules. Listing Principles 1 and 2, being the two principles with which issuers are required to take active steps to comply, incorporate the concept of reasonableness. This objective standard is the safeguard to ensure that standards are not imposed retrospectively in respect of the Principles.

Eligibility

The basic CARD derived eligibility requirements which apply to all securities can   **18.174**
be found in LR2. These included provisions such as the free transferability and, for shares only, the free float requirements. LR6 contains the super-equivalent eligibility requirements for primary listed equity issuers, including the requirement for a three-year track record, a clean working capital position, and the control of assets requirement.

At the time of the listing review, the UK Listing Authority proposed removing   **18.175**
certain eligibility requirements for the initial admission of equity securities to the Official List that are super-equivalent to the CARD requirements. These proposals included moving from a requirement for a three-year revenue earning track record to the requirement for three years of accounts. Following consultation they decided to retain the requirement for primary listed issuers to demonstrate a three-year revenue earning track record and the modified eligibility criteria for mineral companies, scientific research-based companies, investment entities, and venture capital trusts. The specific requirements for Innovative High Growth Companies and the little used Strategic Investment Companies have been removed. Issuers who do not fall within the specific issuer exemptions will be

required to seek a modification in the terms on LR 6.1.15. This guidance shows the factors to be taken into account in deciding whether to waive the three-year revenue earning track record.

Sponsors

18.176   The sponsor regime is a super-equivalent regime imposed on the primary listing segment only. The statuatory basis for the regime is set out in section 88(1) of FSMA which permits the FSA, acting as competent authority for listing: to make rules requiring a listed company to make arrangements with a sponsor to provide services to the company; for the FSA to approve firms as sponsors; and to impose requirements on sponsors. This is a separate approval and regulatory framework from the authorised persons regime which the FSA operate in relation to regulated activities.[68]

18.177   A sponsor is required to provide any service, guidance, or advice on the rules with due care and skill. This is the general standard expected of sponsors and is not one of strict liability. Rules (such as LR 8.3.3) require sponsors to provide comfort to make it clear that the sponsor is expected to come to a reasonable opinion, after having made due and careful enquiry.

18.178   In terms of the nature of the assurances provided by sponsors, the rules split out the requirements for new applicants, existing listed issuers undertaking a fundraising, and existing listed issuers undertaking a transaction. These rules make it clear that the nature of the assurances required in relation to existing issuers, subject to the full rigour of a continuing obligations regime, should be less onerous than those required for new applicants. For new applicants the focus is on the importance of procedures generally (LR 8.4.2(4)) and specifically in relation to the financial position of the group. The requirement at LR 8.4.2(3) requires sponsors to be clear that procedures are in place to enable compliance on an ongoing basis. The requirement means that sponsors are required at the date of admission to be satisfied that the issuer has in place the ability to comply on a continuous basis. It is clearly not an ongoing sponsor obligation. For existing listed issuers undertaking a major transaction the sponsor must be satisfied that the transaction will not have an adverse impact on the issuer's ability to comply with the Listing Rules or the Disclosure and Transparency Rules (LR 8.4.11(2))—effectively a negative assurance for which the focus is procedures. As a result of this, and because the Listing Principles by their nature are not objectively verifiable (except Listing Principles 1 and 2), sponsors will not be required to provide specific assurance on the issuer's ability to comply, on an ongoing basis, with the Listing Principles.

---

[68] CP 08/5: 'Sponsor regime—a targeted review' (March 2008).

In March 2008, the FSA published a Consultation Paper on proposed amend- **18.179** ments to the Sponsor regime (CP 08/5 'Sponsor regime—a targeted review'). The consultation sought to reform LR8 to ensure that it would remain practical and reflect good market practice. Issue 18 of *List!* summarises the key proposals of the consultation paper as follows:

(a) to clarify the scope of the sponsor Principles in LR 8.3;
(b) to remove use of the suitably experienced employee (SEE) to demonstrate competence (part of the approval criteria for sponsors) and replace it with a firm-wide approach to sponsor competence;
(c) to modernise the FSA's approach to sponsor independence by focusing on procedures for identifying and managing conflicts; and
(d) to revise guidance as to what will generally be accepted as appropriate systems and controls for sponsors.

In July 2008, the FSA published CP 08/12 (Quarterly consultation No 17) which **18.180** proposed additional amendments to those set out in CP 08/5. The FSA proposes that the Listing Rules be amended as follows:[69]

(a) to require an issuer to appoint a sponsor that satisfies the requirement to be independent (proposed LR 8.2.4);
(b) to give the UKLA the ability to require a sponsor to disclose information to the UKLA that it reasonably requires (proposed LR 8.7.1A); and
(c) to make the appointment of an independent sponsor an approval condition for a circular (proposed LR 13.2.8A).

The amendment to LR8 inserts a rule that was erroneously omitted from the revised Listing Rules at the time of the Listing Review. The effect of the proposed changes to LR8 and LR13 would be to create an obligation on the issuer itself to ensure that the sponsor is independent. The Listing Rules as they currently stand place an obligation on the sponsor alone to ensure its independence.

Market participants have been asked to consider the amendments proposed to **18.181** the regime in CP 08/5 and CP 08/12 as a whole, and comment accordingly.

---

[69] CP08/12: Quarterly Consultation (No 17) (July 2008).

19

ISLAMIC FINANCIAL SERVICES

Introduction

Islamic finance firms

Firms that offer Islamic financial services ('IFFs') are established on the principle **19.01** that there should be no separation between temporal and religious matters. Compliance with the *Shari'a* is the governing law for all aspects of a practising Muslim's life, including financial and business transactions. Recognising that, under the *Shari'a*, money does not have a time-value separate from the value of goods that are exchanged through the use of money, IFFs embrace the principle of sharing profit and loss and reject interest as a cost for accepting and lending money. Within these constraints, IFFs offer various services, including: (a) Islamic commercial banking, where the IFF manages client money using *Shari'a* compliant accounts, arranges and makes loans to clients using *Shari'a* compliant contracts, advises on and arranges *Shari'a* compliant corporate and project finance structures, and offers other banking services such as money transfer services; (b) Islamic wealth and asset management, where the IFF uses investment vehicles, structured in a *Shari'a* compliant manner, to make *Shari'a* compliant investments, avoiding investments in, for example, conventional financial institutions or alcohol related businesses, which are *Haram* or Islamically unacceptable; (c) Islamic insurance, where the IFF uses a *Shari'a* compliant form of mutual insurance, to offer general or life and family insurance; and (d) social services, where the IFF makes loans, where it only requires the borrower to repay an amount equal to that borrowed, or pays *Zakat*.[1] In practice, a firm will offer Islamic financial services as a full IFF, whereby its entire business is dedicated to offering *Shari'a* compliant services and products, or offer Islamic financial services through an 'Islamic Window', whereby a part of the firm's business is dedicated to offering *Shari'a* compliant

---

[1] *Zakat* is a charitable tax. See Ayub, *Understanding Islamic Finance* (Wiley, 2007), p 495 and Ghuddah et al, *Islamic Finance Qualification* (ESA and SII, 2007), p 12.

services and products.[2] In either case, the firm will appoint a *Shari'a* Supervisory Board ('SSB') entrusted with the duty of directing, reviewing, and supervising the firm's activities in order to ensure that they comply with the *Shari'a*.[3]

The scope and limits of Islamic finance regulation

19.02 The growth in IFFs has resulted in financial services regulators in various jurisdictions, including the United Kingdom, adopting special regimes for the regulation of IFFs, or adapting their existing regimes.[4]

19.03 Despite the special nature of the services which an IFF offers, it is still a financial services provider that participates in the financial services industry and, generally, poses the same risks as a non-IFF. For this reason, a financial service regulator's primary objective in regulating an IFF remains the same as those for regulating a conventional, ie non-Islamic finance firm.[5] Similarly, like the users of non-*Shari'a* compliant financial services, the desire for favourable borrowing terms and positive investment returns drives the consumers of *Shari'a* compliant services. The Islamic nature of a financial service may be a necessary condition for a practising Muslim's decision to use the service. However, it is not a sufficient condition.

19.04 The scope of Islamic finance regulation may also have a bearing on the limits of the role that a financial services regulator plays or should play in the context of Islamic finance; in particular, its role in ensuring that a service or investment, offered by an IFF, is *Shari'a* compliant. The main question in this regard is: 'what role should a secular regulator play in determining standards which are religious in nature?' In this respect, there are two basic models: a *substantive* model and a *formal* model.

19.05 On a substantive model of Islamic finance regulation, a regulator uses its powers to identify or determine the *Shari'a* standards against which an IFF must measure its services and products—if a service or product does not comply with those standards, the IFF may not offer that service or product or hold it out as *Shari'a* compliant. The regulator determines the substance of the *Shari'a* compliant outcome: the regulator's own scholars, or other scholars identified by the regulator, are responsible for ruling on the standards with which the services or investments

---

[2] Islamic Windows are discussed in para 19.64 *et seq*.below.

[3] SSBs are discussed in para 19.68 *et seq*.below.

[4] In this chapter, regimes other than that in the United Kingdom are mentioned or discussed. Where the location of any regulatory or legal regime is not mentioned, the reader should assume that the reference is to the regime in the UK.

[5] In the UK, these include the maintenance of confidence in the financial system and securing an appropriate degree of protection for the consumers of financial services. See FSMA, s 2(2) read together with FSMA, s 3(1) and (2) and FSMA, s 5(1) and (2), respectively. See para 1.48 above.

offered by an IFF must comply for the IFF to hold them out as *Shari'a* compliant. Aspects of the regulation of *Shari'a* compliant securities in Malaysia incorporate the substantive model. As part of the Malaysian Islamic Capital Market, the Securities Commission has its own *Shari'a* Advisory Council.[6] The Council was given the mandate to ensure that the running of the Islamic Capital Market complies with *Shari'a* principles.[7] The substantive model has the advantage that the standardisation of particular Islamic finance requirements, which the substantive model seeks to achieve, enhances liquidity by reducing the costs which the originators of investments have to incur on a case-by-case basis to ensure that the investments are *Shari'a* compliant. Enhancing liquidity is hardly at odds with a financial regulator's objectives.[8]

On a formal model of Islamic finance regulation, a regulator uses its powers to **19.06** identify the standards, with which an IFF's systems and procedures must comply in order for the IFF to determine the *Shari'a* standards for its services and products services and products—if the process for ensuring that a service or product is *Shari'a* compliant does not comply with those standards, the IFF may not offer that service or product or hold it out as *Shari'a* compliant. The regulator determines the form or manner in which an IFF must achieve a *Shari'a* compliant outcome rather than the substance of that outcome. On this model, the *Shari'a* scholars appointed by an IFF, rather than those appointed by the regulator, are responsible for ruling on the standards with which the service or investment offered by an IFF must comply for the IFF to hold them out as *Shari'a* compliant. In the Dubai International Financial Centre (DIFC), the Dubai Financial Services Authority (DFSA) has adopted specific rules governing the processes which it expects IFFs to implement in order to ensure *Shari'a* compliant outcomes and has summed up its role as a "*Shari'a* Systems Regulator" not a "*Shari'a* Regulator".[9] The formal model has the advantage for a regulator, charged primarily with the protection of investors' financial welfare rather than their spiritual welfare in that it prevents a regulator from entering an arena, in which it might otherwise feel

---

[6] The Commission established the Council in 1996 under s 18 of the Securities Commission Act 1993.

[7] The Council advises the Commission on all matters related to the comprehensive development of the Islamic Capital Market, and functions as a reference centre for issues related to the Islamic Capital Market. The members of the Council consist of Islamic scholars/jurists and Islamic finance experts. The Council advises on and publishes lists of products which, in its view, are *Shari'a* compliant (see <http://www.sc.com>).

[8] Industry bodies may have a role in creating a 'third way' between the formal and substantive models. For example, the joint efforts of the International Swaps and Derivatives Association and the International Islamic Financial Market to develop a *Shari'a* compliant Master Agreement offer a path to standardisation with the attendant cost reduction benefits (see <http://www.isda.org>).

[9] *Islamic Finance Regulation in the IFC*, DFSA Leaflet 2, 2008, <http://www.dfsa.ae>. (See also Henderson 'Limiting the Regulation of Islamic Finance: Lessons from Dubai' (2007) LFMR (1) 213.)

uncomfortable, and leaves the regulator to regulate systems and controls, something with which the regulator is familiar.[10]

The regulation of IFFs in the United Kingdom

19.07 There is currently no dedicated regime in the UK for regulating IFFs. Instead the FSA is able to regulate IFFs under the general powers, which Parliament has granted it under FSMA. In a 2007 Discussion Paper, *Islamic Finance in the UK: Regulation and Challenges*,[11] the FSA set out the risks and challenges for IFFs and the regulation of IFFs, highlighting the issues for Islamic finance in the retail market and Islamic finance in the wholesale market and the scope for expansion in these markets, mentioning specifically *Takaful*, complex products, hedge funds, EU passporting, and government initiatives.[12] The 2007 Discussion Paper is also a useful reference in that it casts light on the FSA's approach to the regulation of IFFs, which it set out as follows:

> All financial institutions authorised by the FSA and operating in the UK, or seeking to do so, are subject to the same standards. This is true regardless of their country of origin, the sectors in which they wish to specialise, or their religious principles. This approach is fully consistent with FSMA's six Principles of Good Regulation, in particular, facilitating innovation and avoiding unnecessary barriers to entry or expansion within the financial markets. There is, therefore, a 'level playing field' in dealing with applications from conventional and Islamic firms. The FSA is happy to see Islamic finance develop in the UK, but it would not be appropriate, nor would it be legally possible, to vary its standards for one particular type of institution. This was clearly articulated by Sir Howard Davies in his speech in Bahrain in September 2003. The FSA's approach can be summed up as 'no obstacles, but no special favours'.[13]

19.08 The FSA's approach to regulating IFFs, therefore, rests on the principle of non-discrimination or equal treatment which has a bearing, particularly in the context of the FSA's and Treasury's regulatory classification and treatment of the products and services which IFFs offer.[14] In this respect, the FSA's approach does not fall within the substantive model discussed above:[15] the FSA does not have its own

---

[10] An important question for a regulator: 'what if an IFF follows a regulator's systems and procedures requirements but achieves an outcome which is not *Shari'a* compliant?' It is submitted that, on a proper application of the formal model, the regulator would not be able to intervene unless it could show that the relevant decision of the *Shari'a* Supervisory Board was so irrational or contrary to the *Shari'a* that no rational SSB adhering properly to the Regulator's could have reached the decision. In this respect, a regulator would be applying a review standard similar to that which a court would use in judicial review proceedings avoiding so-called 'merits review'.

[11] 'Islamic Finance in the UK', FSA Discussion Paper, November 2007.

[12] ibid, pp 16 *et seq*.

[13] ibid, p 11.

[14] This is discussed in para 19.76 *et seq*. below.

[15] See para 19.05 above.

Shari'a scholars who might rule on whether a particular product or service is *Shari'a* compliant and has stated: 'The FSA is, however, a secular and not a religious regulator. It would not be appropriate, even if it were possible, for the FSA to judge between different interpretations of *Shari'a* law.'[16] However, its approach does not fall squarely within the formal model, in that it does not prescribe the procedures or expressly identify the standards to which it would expect an IFF to adhere before the IFF could hold out its services or products as *Shari'a* compliant. Instead, its approach could be said to be a risk-based approach whereby it seeks to treat IFFs in the same manner as it would conventional firms, taking into consideration the risk which an IFF poses, within a general regulatory framework which is sufficiently flexible to allow the FSA to regulate IFFs in this manner.

The FSA has authorised IFFs that offer wholesale and retail banking services, **19.09** IFFs that carry on investment business and IFFs that carry on insurance business and these IFFs are subject to FSA oversight and control.[17] The FSA's regulation of IFFs must be seen in the context of the UK Government's commitment to entrench London as a leading centre for Islamic finance in the world and to ensure that all British citizens can participate in the financial system, regardless of faith.[18]

The regulation of Islamic capital markets

The FSA in its capacity as the UK Listing Authority is responsible for the listing **19.10** of *Shari'a* compliant securities, such as *Sukuk*, in the UK. At present there is no Islamic exchange, per se, in the UK. However, the London Stock Exchange, for example, has listed *Sukuk*.[19] The listing and public offer of *Shari'a* compliant securities in the UK is discussed below;[20] the regulation of Islamic securities exchanges, generally, is discussed in chapter 15 of *Financial Markets and Exchanges Law*, the companion volume to this work.

The Treasury has also shown an interest in *Shari'a* compliant securities, consulting **19.11** in November 2007 on the merits of the Government becoming an issuer of *Shari'a*

---

[16] 'Islamic Finance in the UK', see n 11.

[17] The activities of IFFs have also been subject to the jurisdiction of the courts. For example, in *Riyad Bank and others v Ahli Bank (UK) plc* [2006] EWCA Civ 780, the Court of Appeal held that the defendant's Islamic investment banking unit owed a duty of care in tort to ensure that it properly valued certain leases which comprised part of the investments made by a *Shari'a* compliant fund established by the claimants.

[18] See HM Treasury, 'Government Sterling Sukuk Issuance: a Response to the Consultation', p 3 which can be found at <http://www.hm-treasury.gov.uk>.

[19] See <http://www.londonstockexchange.com>.

[20] See para 19.113.

compliant financial instruments.[21] It published a response to the Consultation in June 2008.[22] The result of the Consultation was, inter alia, proposed amendments to the Finance Bill plus an examination of the application of Stamp Duty Land Tax, Value Added Tax, and the settlement of *Sukuk* within CREST.[23] The regulatory regime for *Sukuk* was also highlighted.

International regulatory bodies

19.12 In addition to the establishment of standards for IFFs at a national level, international bodies have been established to set and develop regulatory and *Shari'a* standards for IFFs. The two most significant bodies, insofar as certain national regulators rely on their standards to regulate IFFs, are: the Accounting and Auditing Organisation for Islamic Financial Institutions ('AAOIFI'); and the Islamic Financial Services Board ('IFSB').

19.13 AAOIFI is an Islamic international autonomous not-for-profit corporate body that determines accounting, auditing, governance, ethics, and *Shari'a* standards for Islamic financial institutions and the industry.[24] At the time of writing, AAOIFI has issued 22 accounting standards, five auditing standards, four AAOIFI Governance Standards, two ethics standards, and the 18 AAOIFI *Shari'a* Standards issued in 2004, which set out the standards to which the services and products identified in the AAOIFI *Shari'a* Standards have to adhere.

19.14 The IFSB serves as an international standard setting body of regulatory and supervisory agencies focusing on the soundness and stability of the Islamic financial services industry. The IFSB's work complements that of the Basel Committee on Banking Supervision, International Organisation of Securities Commissions, and the International Association of Insurance Supervisors. At the time of writing, the IFSB has issued guiding principles for risk management for IFFs, capital adequacy standards for IFFs, and guiding principles of corporate governance.[25]

19.15 In addition to AAOIFI and the IFSB, various other international institutions support the Islamic finance industry. These include: the International Islamic Financial Market, established to facilitate international secondary trading of Islamic capital market instruments and enhance cooperation between Islamic financial institutions globally;[26] the General Council for Islamic Banks and

---

[21] See HM Treasury, '8 Issuance: a Consultation', which can be found at <http://www.hm-treasury.gov.uk>.

[22] See 'Government Sterling Sukuk Issuance: a Response to the Consultation', n 18.

[23] ibid.

[24] See <http://www.aaiofi.com>.

[25] See <http://www.ifsb.org>.

[26] See <http://www.iffm.com>.

Financial Institutions, established to promote Islamic financial institutions and disseminate rules and concepts relevant to Islamic finance; and the International Islamic Rating Agency, established to provide credit ratings for Islamic finance institutions.[27]

Islamic finance regulation in other jurisdictions

Islamic finance is regulated in other jurisdictions under special regimes for IFFs or as part of the regime for regulating firms, generally. An examination of other jurisdictions is beyond the scope of this work; however the following Middle East regimes are worth mentioning because their regulatory laws and rules are similar to those in the United Kingdom and the relevant laws and regulations are available in English: **19.16**

- Bahrain, where the Central Bank of Bahrain ('CBB') regulates IFFs under the Central Bank of Bahrain and Financial Institutions Law 2006 and has, inter alia, a dedicated Rulebook for Islamic Banks, special rules for *Takaful* and *Retakaful* providers, and those offering *Shari'a* compliant collective investment schemes.[28]

- The DIFC, where the DFSA regulates IFFs and firms offering *Shari'a* compliant financial services through an 'Islamic Window' under the Law Regulating Islamic Financial Business, DIFC Law No 13 of 2004, and has, inter alia, special rules governing IFFS, *Shari'a* compliant markets and exchanges, and those offering *Shari'a* compliant collective investment funds.

- The Qatar Financial Centre, where the Qatar Financial Centre Regulatory Authority ('QFCRA') regulates IFFs and firms offering *Shari'a* compliant financial services through an 'Islamic Window' under the Qatar Financial Centre Law 2005 and has, inter alia, an Islamic Finance Rulebook and special rules that govern *Shari'a* compliant collective investment funds.[29]

In addition, Malaysia is a useful comparative source as a Far East jurisdiction both for understanding the regulation of Islamic banks and Islamic capital markets. In Malaysia, the Bank Negrasa Malaysia ('BNM') regulates those institutions offering banking products in Malaysia under the Islamic Banking Act 1983, including the Malaysia International Islamic Financial Centre, and has its own *Shari'a* Advisory Council;[30] and the Securities Commission of Malaysia ('MSC') regulates Islamic capital markets and those offering Islamic securities under the Capital   **19.17**

---

[27] See <http://www.iirating.com>.
[28] See <http://www.cbb.gov.bh>.
[29] See <http://www.qfcra.com>.
[30] See <http://www.bnm.gov.my> and <http://www.mifc.com>.

Markets and Services Act 2007, including the Malaysia International Islamic Financial Centre, and has its own *Shari'a* Advisory Council.[31]

The legal effect of international standards

19.18 In the same way that neither the Basel Committee's recommendations nor the EU directives have direct effect on any particular firm, the standards set down by AAOIFI or the IFSB should not have direct effect on any IFI. This is not to say, however, that the FSA could not implement the AAOIFI and IFSB standards through rules via FSMA, s 138. In this respect, the following examples should be noted:

• In Bahrain, as part of its duty under 'Principle of Business 10—Management, Systems and Controls', the CBB requires an Islamic bank to comply with all AAOIFI issued accounting standards as well as the *Shari'a* pronouncements issued by the *Shari'a* Board of AAOIFI.[32]

• In the DIFC, the DFSA requires a SSB to carry on its internal *Shari'a* review in accordance with AAOFI Governance Standard for Islamic Financial Institutions No 2.[33]

19.19 In the absence of binding legal effect, the various AAOIFI and IFSB standards are useful as a guide which points to best practices for IFFs and serve as examples of the application of regulatory rules in an Islamic finance context. As such, compliance with these standards would not, as a matter of law, serve as a defence to FSA enforcement action or establish a legitimate expectation for an IFF that the FSA would not take action against it. They could, however, help an IFF demonstrate that it had not, as a matter of fact, breached an FSA rule or standard. For example, an IFF's compliance with the relevant AAOIFI guidelines for SSBs could help it demonstrate that, as a matter of fact, it had complied with its duties under PRIN to take reasonable care to organise and control its affairs responsibly and effectively, with adequate risk management systems.[34]

Shari'a Principles

Introduction

19.20 Any examination of the regulation of an IFF would be incomplete without some understanding of the *Shari'a* principles that govern the IFF's business.

---

[31] See <http://www.sc.com.my>.
[32] CBB Rulebook, Volume 2: *Islamic Banks, The Principles*, Rule PBB-1.1.10.
[33] DFSA Rulebook: *Islamic Finance Module*, Rule 5.2.1.
[34] PRIN 2.1.1 R.

For the purposes of this chapter, the *Shari'a* may be viewed as divine law which   **19.21**
embodies all aspects of the Islamic faith, including its beliefs and practices.[35]

Sources and authorities

The primary source of the *Shari'a* is the Holy *Qur'an*—divine law revealed to the   **19.22**
Holy Prophet (PBUH).[36] The *Sunna* of the Holy Prophet (PBUH), supplement
the Holy *Qur'an* as a primary source of the *Shari'a*. The *Sunna* can be divided
between: the *Hadith* or sayings of the Holy Prophet (PBUH); the acts of the Holy
Prophet (PBUH); and the silence or tacit approval of the Holy Prophet (PBUH).
The following are secondary sources of *Shari'a*: *Ijma'a*—the consensus of the
Islamic community; *Qiyas*—the application of accepted principles by analogy to
new cases; and *Ijtihad*—the opinions and interpretations of Islamic jurists on a
particular issue.[37]

There are four *Sunni* Muslim schools of thought on *Shari'a* interpretation: *Hanafi*,   **19.23**
Hanbali, *Maliki*, and *Shaafi'i*, and the *Shia* Muslim school of thought: *Jaafari*.
These five schools all base their *Fatawa*[38] on the Holy *Qur'an* but interpret it and
the other *Shari'a* sources differently.[39] In addition, the Islamic *Fiqh* Academy,
which is based in the Kingdom of Saudi Arabia and includes members from most
Islamic countries, meets periodically to debate contemporary matters and issue
resolutions.[40]

The main Shari'a *principles relevant to Islamic finance*

The prohibition on *Riba*

Riba, means literally, an excess or increase. In the context of Islamic finance, it   **19.24**
includes an increase in the principal repayable to the lender in a loan transaction,
an increase in a debt, or an increase in value attributed to one part of an exchange
transaction, which accrues to the lender/creditor or a party to exchange without

---

[35] For an overview of Islam and the *Shari'a* see Ruthven, *Islam: a Very Short Introduction* (OUP, 1997).

[36] The designation PBUH stands for "Peace Be Upon Him" and is used whenever reference is made to the Holy Prophet.

[37] See further Ayub, n 1, pp 21–2 and Ghuddah et al, n 1, pp 4–6.

[38] The plural of *Fatwa*—a religious decree or edict.

[39] For example, Ayub, n 1, p 146 reports that while jurists from the *Hanbali* school accept as *Shari'a* compliant the *Arbun* contract, discussed in para 19.49 below, jurists from the other schools do not because it involves *Gharar*, risk taking and the taking of money without any consideration in return.

[40] See <http://www.fiqhacademy.org.sa>.

an equivalent increase in value or recompense to the other party. There are two types of *Riba*: *Riba Al-Nasiah* and *Riba Al-Fadl*.

- *Riba Al-Nasiah* means an increase due to delay, or due to exchange not being immediate. It includes, for example, lending money on the understanding that the borrower will return to the lender, at the end of the period, the amount originally lent together with an increase on it, in consideration of the lender having granted him time to pay. The charging, paying, and witnessing of interest, in all modern banking transactions, falls under *Riba Al-Nasiah*.

- *Riba Al-Fadl* is relevant in the context of an exchange or sale of goods and addresses the situation where there is an exchange of high quality goods with low quality goods. It relates to *Ribawi* goods, ie monetary units and items sold by weight and/or by measure such as gold, silver, paper currencies, and edible goods like wheat, rice, barley, dates, salt.

19.25 The prohibition on *Riba* was the subject of the decision of *Shariat* Appellate Bench of the Supreme Court of Pakistan in 2000 invalidating various banking and financial laws.[41] The Court held at paragraph 245 that:

> Any additional amount over the principal in a contract of loan or debt is the *Riba* prohibited by the Holy Qur'an in several verses. The Holy Prophet (PBUH) has also termed the following transactions as *Riba*:
> 1. A transaction of money for money of the same denomination where the quantity on both sides is not equal, either in a spot transaction or in a transaction based on deferred payment.
> 2. A barter transaction between two weighable or measurable commodities of the same kind, where the quantity on both sides is not equal, or where the delivery from any one side is deferred.
> 3. A barter transaction between two different weighable or measurable commodities where delivery from one side is deferred.

19.26 The purpose of an obligation to pay interest or the debtor's ability to pay interest made no difference to the analysis. The court held, at paragraph 245 that:

> ... there is no difference between different types of loan, so far as the prohibition of *Riba* is concerned. It also does not make any difference whether the additional amount stipulated over the principal loan or debt is small or large. It is, therefore, held that all the prevailing forms of interest, either in banking transactions or in private transactions do fall within the definition of '*Riba*'. Similarly, any interest stipulated in the government borrowings, acquired from domestic or foreign sources, is *Riba* and clearly prohibited by the Holy Qur'an.[42]

---

[41] See <http://www.albagh.net/Islamic_economics_riba_judgment.shtml> for the text of the *Riba* case.

[42] For a discussion of the prohibition on *Riba*, see Ayub, n 1, pp 44–57; Ghuddah et al, n 1, pp 29–30.

The prohibition on *Gharar*

Gharar means, literally, uncertainty, hazard, or risk. It refers to an element of **19.27** excessive uncertainty or mere speculative risk in any business or contract. It includes, for example, uncertainty about the subject of a contract or its price. *Gharar* is prohibited because it may lead to undue loss to one party and unjustified enrichment of another. Gambling is a form of *Gharar* because the gambler is ignorant of the result of the gamble. Selling goods without allowing the buyer to properly examine the goods is also a kind of *Gharar*. Further examples of *Gharar* are: selling goods that the seller is unable to deliver; selling known or unknown goods against an unknown price, such as selling the contents of a sealed box without exact information about its contents; selling goods without proper description; selling goods without specifying the price, such as selling at the 'going price'.

The prohibition on *Gharar* was considered in the context of spot and forward **19.28** foreign exchange contracts in a case that came before the Court of Cassation in Abu Dhabi, one of the United Arab Emirates, in 1996.[43] The court invalidated the contracts for two reasons. First because they amounted to contracts of 'competition' within the meaning of article 1012 of the United Arab Emirates Civil Code, Federal Law (2) of 1987, which is part of Chapter IV governing 'Contracts of *Gharar*'. Second, because they were contrary to the principles of *Shari'a*. Article 1012 states (in translation) that: 'A competition (for reward) is a contract whereby one person is obliged to pay a sum of money or gives some other thing by way of agreed recompense to a person who succeeds in achieving the object specified in the contract.' The court held that:

> The intention of both parties was to generate profit from the fluctuation of the various currencies. They would not know the result of their speculation until the transactions were closed. When the subject of a transaction is not assessed or known to either party and is based partially on luck, it is very misleading. They become, according to Articles 1012 and 1014 of the Code, illegal bets.[44]

The prohibition on *Maisir* or *Qimar*

The words *Maisir* and *Qimar* are used interchangeably to refer to games of chance. **19.29** *Maisir* refers to easily available wealth or the acquisition of wealth by chance,

---

[43] Abu Dhabi Court of Cassation Judgment No 158&208/18 reported in Price and Tamimi, *United Arab Emirates Court of Cassation Judgments 1989–1997* (Kluwer Law International, 1998) p 23.

[44] Price and Tamimi, n 43, p 25. The Abu Dhabi Court of Cassation reached the same conclusion but for different reasons in Judgment No 197/19 dated 21 February 1999 reported in Price and Tamimi, *United Arab Emirates Court of Cassation Judgments 1998-2003* (Brill, 2005), p 27. For a discussion of the prohibition on *Gharar*, see Ayub, n 1, pp 57–61 and Ghuddah et al, n 1, pp 31–2.

whether or not at the expense of another. *Qimar* means a game of chance—in which one participant gains at the cost of another.

19.30 *Maisir* and *Qimar* appear also to have played a part in the reasoning of the Abu Dhabi Court in the 1996 decision on the compatibility with the *Shari'a* of foreign exchange spot and forward contracts, referred to above:[45]

> As regards the appeal filed by the Defendant, the Court of Cassation held that according to Articles 1012 and 1014 of the Code, speculation in foreign currency transactions is illegal as the transactions are normally carried out for a consideration which is never delivered and the only interest both parties have is in the profits generating from the speculation. Such transactions cannot be sanctioned by the UAE Courts.[46]

Islamic business ethics and norms

19.31 In addition to the three primary prohibitions above, the *Shari'a* includes a set of principles that provide a basic framework for the conduct of economic activities in general, and financial and commercial transactions in particular. The Holy *Qur'an* and the *Sunna* refer to a number of norms and principles which govern the rights and obligations of parties to a contract. Principles of justice, mutual help, free consent, and honesty on the part of the parties to a contract, avoiding fraud, misrepresentation, and negation of injustice or exploitation provide grounds for valid contracts.[47]

Prohibited investments

19.32 Islamic investment management and fund management must operate without making investments that may be prohibited or *Haram*. Prohibited investments include investments in the following industries: insurance; banking (including all banks and organisations principally active in conventional finance); alcohol (including producers, distributors, sellers, and businesses deriving substantial income from transactions in alcohol). As a result, supermarkets, airlines, and hotels, also being at risk of exclusion:

- pork—producers, distributors, and meat stores. Businesses that handle pork products, such as restaurants and supermarkets are also at risk of exclusion);
- defence (including businesses which derive substantial income from defence and munitions);

---

[45] See para 19.28.
[46] Price and Tamimi, n 43, p 24. For further discussion of the prohibition on *Maisir*, see Ayub, n 1, pp 61–4.
[47] For further discussion of Islamic business ethics, see Ayub, n 1, pp 64–70 and Ghuddah et al, n 1, pp 26–9.

- gambling (including casinos, hotels, and other companies involved with gambling, such as bookmakers); and
- entertainment (including business involved with adult entertainment).[48]

The enforceability of Shari'a *in the English courts*

In *Shamil Bank of Bahrain EC v Beximo Pharmaceuticals*,[49] the Court of Appeal **19.33** considered the enforceability of a contract containing the following choice of law clause: 'Subject to the principles of the Glorious *Shariah* [sic], this Agreement shall be governed and construed in accordance with the laws on England.' The defendants denied liability under the contract and associated contracts on the basis that: (a) on a true construction of the governing law clause, the contracts were only enforceable insofar as they were valid and enforceable both in accordance with the English law and the *Shari'a*; and (b) the contracts were unenforceable under the *Shari'a*.

The Court rejected the defendants' contention holding that English law alone was **19.34** the proper law of the contract because: (a) the Rome Convention only contemplates the choice of law of a country—it was not applicable to a choice between the law of a country and a non-national system of law; (b) the incorporation of foreign law only applies where the parties have sufficiently identified specific provisions—the general reference to *Shari'a* in this case and not to 'basic rules' was insufficient for this purpose; (c) reference to *Shari'a* was intended merely to reflect the religious principles which the parties held themselves out as doing business, rather than a system of law intended to trump the application of English law to the contracts.

The *Shamil Bank* judgment appears to leave it open to the parties to a contract to **19.35** specify the *Shari'a* as the contract's governing law provided that the parties specify the particular *Shari'a* rules that should govern the contract. In this respect, however, there is uncertainty: would it be necessary or sufficient for the relevant clause to identify the particular school of thought on *Shari'a* interpretation?[50] Would it be necessary to specify the particular rules that apply, eg the prohibition on *Riba* and, if so, would this necessarily exclude the other rules not expressly identified, including rules of interpretation? The position remains unclear.

---

[48] See Ghuddah et al, n 1, pp 158–61.

[49] [2004] EWCA Civ 19.

[50] Cf Abu Dhabi Court of Cassation Judgment No 9/19 reported in Price and Tamimi, n 43 in which the court held that a clause in the United Arab Emirates Penal Code No 3 of 1987 stating that 'Islamic law should be applied to all crimes specified by Divine Command and to the payment of blood money' did not specify the school of Islamic jurisprudence to be followed. It was, therefore, in the judge's discretion to interpret the clause in accordance with whatever principles were in the best interests of the community.

19.36 Nevertheless, Potter LJ's remarks about *Shari'a* in an English court are noteworthy:

> . . . so far as the 'principles of . . . *Shari'a*' are concerned, it was indeed the evidence of both experts that there are indeed areas of considerable controversy and difficulty arising not only from the need to translate into propositions of modern law texts which centuries ago were set out as religious and moral codes, but because of the existence of a variety of schools of thought which the Court may have to concern itself with in any given case before reaching a conclusion upon the principle or rule in dispute. The fact that there may be a general consensus on the proscription of *Riba* and the essentials of a valid *Morabaha* [sic] agreement does no more than indicate that, if the *Shariah* [sic], law proviso were sufficient to incorporate the principles of *Shariah* [sic] law into the parties' agreements, the defendants would have been likely to succeed. However, since I would hold that the proviso is plainly inadequate for that purpose, the validity of the contract and the defendants' obligations thereunder fall to be decided according to English law.[51]

19.37 His Lordship seems to suggest that an English court would enforce an agreement where the parties had properly agreed that the *Shari'a* would be the sole law governing that agreement. The parties would, however, need to lead expert evidence to prove the contents of the *Shari'a*.

Shari'a Compliant Financial Products and Services

Techniques for developing Shari'a *compliant products and services*

19.38 In order to avoid breaching the prohibitions referred to above,[52] IFFs have developed various financing techniques for ensuring that the services and products that they offer are *Shari'a* compliant. These may be grouped into the following broad categories:

- money acceptance arrangements, used by IFFs for offering *Shari'a* compliant deposit products;

- deferred payment arrangements, used by IFFs for offering *Shari'a* compliant asset financing products;

- profit-sharing arrangements, used by IFFs for offering *Shari'a* compliant equity participation products;

- capital market arrangements, used by IFFs for offering *Shari'a* compliant products capable of being listed on an exchange; and

- mutual assistance arrangements, used by IFFs for offering *Shari'a* compliant insurance products.

---

[51] Para 55 of the *Shamil Bank* judgment.
[52] See paras 19.24 to 19.32.

The arrangements may be used in combination. For example an IFF could: use deferred payment or profit sharing arrangements to create products capable of being listed on an exchange, as in the case of *Sukuk*; or offer a *Shari'a* compliant investment fund which employs deferred payment arrangements, such as a *Murabaha*, to make investments; use deferred payment arrangements to create a *Shari'a* compliant risk mitigation product as in the case of a *Shari'a* compliant currency swap.[53] The arrangements, together with some miscellaneous arrangements and contracts, are discussed below.[54]

Money acceptance arrangements[55]

Al Wadi'a—an agreement for an IFF's safe-keeping of *Amana*, deposits held on trust, where the IFF: (a) does not seek profit from the depositor; (b) has no liability to the depositor unless caused by the IFF's breach of duty; and (c) is liable to pay back the full amount deposited with the IFF.[56]   **19.39**

Qard—an agreement whereby a lender transfers ownership in property, including money, to a borrower on the condition that the borrower will pay back the property on demand. In the case of monies deposited with an IFF, the IFF would be the borrower and the depositor the lender. To be *Shari'a* compliant, only the principal is repayable.[57]   **19.40**

Deferred payment arrangements

Ijara—a contract of lease whereby the owner (A) of an asset (the Leased Property) transfers the right to use and enjoy the Leased Property to B for a predetermined period in exchange for a predetermined rental. The Leased Property must be such that B's use of it does not consume it or change its form. In this way, A retains the risk related to the Leased Property in return for the reward in the form of the rental. *Ijara Muntania Bittamleek* is a type of *Ijara*, which ends with transfer of the Leased Property to B.[58]   **19.41**

---

[53] *Shari'a* compliant derivatives are discussed in para 19.99 below.

[54] Para 19.39 *et seq*. A detailed discussion of the Islamic finance arrangements is beyond the scope of this work. Moreover, the arrangements referred to in para 19.39 *et seq*.below are not exhaustive but merely set out those likely to be the most relevant in the context of the regulation of Islamic finance. For further discussion of various Islamic finance arrangements, see Hainsworth 'Islamic Financial Institutions and Islamic Finance' in Blair et al, *Encyclopaedia of Banking Law*, (Lexis Nexis, 2008) para 4.

[55] IFFs may also use profit-sharing financing arrangements, such as *Mudaraba*, as the primary means for accepting and holding monies. The regulatory treatment of money acceptance arrangements is discussed in para 19.76 below.

[56] See further Ayub, n 1, pp 188–91 and Ghuddah et al, n 1, pp 33–4.

[57] See further Ayub, n 1, pp 162–3.

[58] See further *AAOIFI Shari'a Standards* (2004), pp 135–58, Ayub, n 1, pp 279–305 and Ghuddah et al, n 1, pp 76–8. For capital adequacy purposes, the IFSB Capital Adequacy Standard

19.42 *Murabaha*—a contract of sale, in which the seller (A) agrees to sell *Shari'a* compliant goods to the buyer (B) for a purchase price equal to the cost of the goods plus a profit mark-up. Under a *Murabaha*, A delivers the goods to B on the date of the contract but B pays the purchase price at a future date. There are two types of sale under a *Murabaha*: (a) the IFF purchases the goods from A and makes them available to B without B making any prior promise to buy the goods from the IFF; (b) the IFF purchases the goods from A and makes them available to B who promises to buy the goods from the IFF—a '*Murabaha* for the Purchase Orderer'.[59] A and B might execute the *Murabaha* contract in conjunction with a second or 'Parallel *Murabaha*' contract, whereby B, as buyer under the first *Murabaha* contract, agrees to sell goods with the same specifications as the goods under the first *Murabaha* contract. Under *Shari'a* rules, A, as buyer under the second *Murabaha* contract, cannot buy back from B the same goods which A sold to B under the first *Murabaha* contract.[60] An example of parallel *Murabaha* arrangements arises in the context of a *Shari'a* compliant profit rate swap where the parties may wish to replicate the cash flows under an interest rate swap in a manner that is *Shari'a* compliant by using a parallel *Murabaha* structure: (a) under the first *Murabaha*, A agrees to purchase a specified commodity from B for a cost price of GBP 1,000,000 plus a mark-up based, inter alia, on a fixed rate; (b) under the second *Murabaha*, B agrees to purchase a specified commodity from A for a cost price of GBP 1,000,000 plus a mark-up based, inter alia, on a floating rate calculated by reference to an index, such as LIBOR. By (a) having the deferred payments under both *Murabaha* arrangements fall on the same date and (b) achieving a net settlement of the offsetting deferred payments, A and B swap a fixed and floating payment flows on a notional of GBP 1,000,000.

19.43 *Istisna'a*—a forward sale contract where a buyer of *Shari'a* compliant goods (A) asks the seller (B) to manufacture the goods according to the A's specifications using B's materials at a predetermined price for delivery upon completing the manufacture of the goods. An *Istisna'a* contract is often executed in conjunction with a second or 'Parallel *Istisna'a*' contract, whereby A, the buyer of the goods under the first *Istisna'a* contract, agrees to sell goods to B with the same product specifications as the goods specified in the first *Istisna'a* contract. Under *Shari'a*

---

for Institutions (Other than Insurance Institutions) Offering Only Islamic Financial Services (2005) ('the IFSB CAS') distinguishes between *Ijara* arrangements and *Ijara Muntania Bittamleek* arrangements. The IFSB CAS are discussed below.

   [59] See further *AAOIFI Shari'a Standards* (2004), pp 109–34, Ayub, n 1, pp 213–39 and Ghuddah et al, n 1, pp 68–74. Finance Act 2005, s 47 deals with the taxation of *Murabaha* which is described under the heading of 'alternative finance arrangements: purchase and re-sale'. For capital adequacy purposes, the IFSB CAS distinguishes between *Murabaha* arrangements and *Murabaha* for the Purchase Orderer arrangements.

   [60] See further *AAOIFI Shari'a Standards* (2004), pp 159–74, Ayub, n 1, pp 241–63 and Ghuddah et al, n 1, pp 79–82. For capital adequacy purposes, the IFSB CAS distinguishes between *Salam* arrangements and Parallel *Salam* arrangements.

rules, A, as buyer under the second *Istisna'a* contract, cannot buy back from B the same goods which A sold to B under the first *Istisna'a* contract.[61]

Salam—a forward sale contract in which a buyer (B) pays seller (A) for specified **19.44** *Shari'a* compliant goods which A or its agent will deliver to B at a future date. Under a *Salam* contract, B pays the full purchase price for the goods on the date of the contract or within a subsequent period, which the SSB that approves the *Salam* arrangements, deems appropriate. A and B might execute the *Salam* contract in conjunction with a second or 'Parallel *Salam*' contract, whereby B, as buyer under the first *Salam* contract, agrees to sell goods with the same specifications as the goods as that in the first *Salam* contract. Under *Shari'a* rules, A, as buyer under the second *Salam* contract, cannot buy back from B the same goods which A sold to B under the first *Salam* contract.[62]

Profit sharing arrangements

Mudaraba[63]—an arrangement whereby investment account holders, the *Rab Al* **19.45** *Mal*, provide funds to a manager, the *Mudarib*, who uses its management expertise to manage the funds. The *Rab Al Mal* and the *Mudarib* share in the profits on a pre-agreed basis with the *Rab Al Mal* bearing the risk of any loss and the *Mudarib* being liable for any loss only as a result of its misconduct, negligence or breach of any conditions governing the *Mudaraba*. The *Mudarib* can offer the *Mudaraba* on a *restricted* basis, where the *Rab Al Mal* allow the *Mudarib* to make investments subject to specified investment restrictions such as type of instrument, sector, or country exposures, or on an *unrestricted* basis, where the *Rab Al Mal* allow the *Mudarib* to invest the funds freely, subject, of course, to the requirement that the funds are not invested in a manner that may be *Haram*.[64]

Musharaka—a partnership agreement between two parties A and B, with B usu- **19.46** ally being an IFF, who both provide capital towards the financing of a project. A and B share any profits on a pre-agreed basis but losses are shared on the basis of equity participation. A and B manage the project. A and B have a right to forgo

---

[61] See further *AAOIFI Shari'a Standards* (2004), pp 175–95, Ayub, n 1, pp 263–77 and Ghuddah et al, n 1, pp 83–5. For capital adequacy purposes, the IFSB CAS distinguish between *Istisna'a* arrangements and Parallel *Istisna'a* arrangements.

[62] See further *AAOIFI Shari'a Standards* (2004), pp 159–74, Ayub, n 1, pp 241–63 and Ghuddah et al, n 1, pp 79–82. For capital adequacy purposes, the IFSB CAS distinguishes between *Salam* arrangements and Parallel *Salam* arrangements.

[63] *Mudaraba* are also known as 'Profit Sharing Investment Accounts' ('PSIAs'). The operation of PSIAs is discussed in para 19.83 *et seq*. below.

[64] See further *AAOIFI Shari'a Standards* (2004), pp 227–45, Ayub, n 1, pp 320–8 and Ghuddah et al, n 1, pp 62–4. Finance Act 2005, s 49 deals with the taxation of *Mudaraba* which is described under the heading of 'alternative finance arrangements: deposit'. The regulatory treatment of *Mudaraba* is discussed in para 19.83 *et seq*. below.

the right of management/work in favour of each other or another person. There are two main forms of *Musharaka:* Permanent *Musharaka,* whereby the participation shares remain the same, and Diminishing *Musharaka,* whereby one party, usually the IFF, gradually transfers its share until the other becomes owner.[65]

Capital market arrangements

19.47 *Sukuk*[66]—certificates of equal value representing undivided shares in ownership of tangible assets, the right to use and enjoy property, and services.[67] *Sukuk* are capable of being classified in different ways. One system of classification distinguishes between asset-based *Sukuk,* where the underlying assets are governed by *Salam, Istisna'a,* or *Ijara* contracts giving predictable returns, and equity-based assets, where the underlying assets are governed by *Musharaka* or *Mudaraba* contracts giving returns based on profit and loss.[68] Another system of classification identifies the following categories: asset-backed *Sukuk* where investors take risk on an identified pool of assets, similar to the position under a conventional, non-*Shari'a* compliant, securitisation; asset-based *Sukuk* where the *Sukuk* originator enters into a binding promise or purchase undertaking by the *Sukuk* originator where investors take risk on the creditworthiness of the *Sukuk* originator, similar to the position under a conventional bond issue; and 'pass through' *Sukuk* where a separate issuing entity purchases the underlying assets from the originator, packages them as a pool of assets, and acts as issuer of the *Sukuk.*[69]

Mutual assistance arrangements

19.48 *Shari'a* scholars take the view that commercial insurance is unlawful due to the involvement of *Riba, Gharar, Qimar,* and *Maisir* and the invalid transfer of risk from the insured to the insurer. Their view is that, as a whole, insurance business contains elements of temptation and cheating and is incompatible with natural

---

[65] See further *AAOIFI Shari'a Standards* (2004), pp 196–226, Ayub, n 1, pp 312–20 and Ghuddah et al, n 1, pp 64–8. The Finance Act 2005, s 47A deals with the taxation of Diminishing *Musharaka,* which is described under the heading of 'alternative finance arrangements: diminishing shared ownership'. For capital adequacy purposes, the IFSB CAS distinguishes between *Musharaka* arrangements and Diminishing *Musharaka* arrangements. The regulatory treatment of *Musharaka* is discussed in para 91 further below.

[66] '*Sukuk*' is the plural of '*Sak*' which is the Arabic translation of 'certificate'.

[67] See further *AAOIFI Shari'a Standards* (2004), pp 280–307, Ayub, n 1, pp 389–415, Ghuddah et al, n 1, pp 175–94. The Finance Act 2005, s 48A deals with the taxation of *Sukuk,* which are described as 'alternative finance arrangements: alternative finance investment bonds'. The regulatory treatment of *Sukuk* is discussed in para 19.93 *et seq.*below.

[68] See the IFSB CAS, chapter C7.

[69] See 'IFSB Capital Adequacy Requirements for Sukuk Securitisations and Real Estate Investment', Exposure Draft, December 2007 (IFSB *Sukuk* CAR), para 9.

and ethical methods of earning money. *Takaful* is an Islamic insurance contract based on the principle of *Ta'awon* or mutual assistance. *Takaful* embodies shared responsibility, common benefit, and mutual solidarity. Every policyholder pays his subscription in order to assist other policyholders who need assistance. *Takaful* incorporates the concept of *Tabarru* or donation. A *Takaful* policyholder agrees to relinquish, as *Tabarru*, the whole or a certain proportion of his *Takaful* contributions that he undertakes to pay, therefore enabling him to fulfil his obligation of mutual help should any of his fellow *Takaful* participants suffer a defined loss. There are two basic types of *Takaful*: general *Takaful*—an alternative to general insurance—and family *Takaful*—an alternative to life insurance. In addition, IFFs may offer *Retakaful* as an alternative to reinsurance. A *Takaful* company operates as a trustee or a manager on the basis of *Wakala* or *Mudaraba*. The operator and the participants contribute to the *Takaful* fund. Claims are paid from the fund and the participants share the underwriting surplus or deficit.[70]

Some miscellaneous arrangements

Arbun—a down payment sale with the condition that if the buyer: (a) takes the **19.49** commodity, which is the subject of the sale, the down payment will become part of the selling price; (b) does not purchase the commodity, the buyer will forfeit the down payment. *Arbun* is similar to a covered call option in that the buyer has the option to confirm or rescind the purchase.[71]

Hamish Jiddyya—a refundable security deposit taken by a lender prior to estab- **19.50** lishing a contract which carries a limited recourse to the extent of the lender's loss if the borrower fails to honour a binding promise to purchase or to lease the asset against which the lender has made a loan.[72]

Tawarruq—an adaptation of the *Murabaha* whereby a purchaser buys a commod- **19.51** ity on credit and sells it immediately at spot value to a third party with the objective of generating cash.[73]

Wa'ad—a unilateral promise whereby the promisor binds himself to do some- **19.52** thing for the promisee.[74]

Wakala—an agency agreement whereby an investor appoints a manager, the **19.53** *Wakil*, as his agent. The *Wakala* is a means by which an IFF can hold and invest

---

[70] See further Ayub, n 1, pp 418–31 and Ghuddah et al, n 1, pp 195–212.
[71] See further Ayub, n 1, p 116.
[72] ibid.
[73] See further Ayub, n 1, pp 349–51 and Ghuddah et al, n 1, pp 75–6.
[74] See further Ayub, n 1, pp 114–16. *Shari'a* scholars do not agree whether the *Wa'ad* creates a legally binding obligation.

monies on a client's behalf—the *Wakalatul Istitmar*. The *Wakalatul Istitmar* may be contrasted with the *Mudaraba* in that the investor alone shares any profit or loss, with the *Wakil* getting a fixed management fee, whereas, in the case of a *Mudaraba*, both the *Rab Al Mal* and the *Mudarib* share any profits.[75]

19.54 *Waqf*—the retention of property for the benefit of a charitable or humanitarian objective whereby the person creating the *Waqf* transfers ownership of property to the *Waqf* in perpetuity. The *Waqf* property cannot be sold but the *Waqf* manager can assign the use and enjoyment of the property to identified beneficiaries. The *Waqf* may be used the basis for *Takaful*, in the same way as *Mudaraba* or *Wakala*.[76]

The Authorisation of IFFs

A non-discriminatory regime

19.55 At the time of writing, the FSA has authorised five wholly Islamic banks and one Islamic insurance company. The FSA has stated that all financial institutions that it regulates are subject to the same standards. IFFs are therefore subject to the same authorisation requirements as other firms.[77] An IFF seeking to become FSA authorised would need permission to carry on the same regulated activities as a conventional firm and its permission would, generally, relate to the same specified investments as a conventional firm, eg an IFF could carry on the regulated activity of 'arranging deals in investments'[78] albeit that the investments in question would be *Shari'a* compliant investments.[79] IFFs may nevertheless require special consideration in certain areas: the FSA highlights the role of the SSB, the regulatory definition of certain products, and financial promotion as special areas that need to be considered.[80]

AAOIFI standards as best practice guidelines for establishing an IFF

19.56 The FSA does not prescribe any special requirements for IFFs. However, as set out above, an IFF's compliance with the AAOIFI or IFSB standards could help

---

[75] See further Ayub, n 1, pp 347–9 and Ghuddah et al, n 1, p 45. The Finance Act 2005, s 49 deals with the taxation of *Wakala* which is described under the heading 'alternative finance arrangements: profit share agency'.

[76] See further Ayub, n 1, pp 423–5.

[77] 'Islamic Finance in the UK', n 11, pp 11–13.

[78] RAO, art 25.

[79] See the definition of 'arranging deals in on *Shari'a* compliant financial instruments' in the CBB Rulebook, Volume 2: *Islamic Banks, Licensing Requirements*, LR-1.3.37, the wording of which is similar to RAO, art 25.

[80] 'Islamic Finance in the UK', n 11, p 11.

demonstrate that the IFF had not, as a matter of fact, breached a FSA rule or standard.[81] Moreover, an IFF's failure or inability to put in place internal systems and controls that adhere to internationally recognised or developing standards could have damaging commercial consequences, irrespective of any express or implied regulatory duty to follow such standards. In this respect, AAOIFI's *Shari'a* Standard for Conversion of a Conventional Bank to an Islamic Bank[82] sets out useful standards to guide an IFF establishing itself in a manner that would enable it to hold itself out as an IFF.[83] In this respect the following standards are noteworthy:

- *Providing Financial Services in Permissible Ways*—in providing banking services, it is not permissible for [an IFF] to receive interest as compensation for services rendered. It is a requirement that an Islamic alternative be worked out, such as treatment of uncovered documentary credits through *Murabaha* to the purchase orderer [sic], *Musharaka* or *Mudaraba* in accordance with the rules of *Shari'a*. It is not permissible to take a commission for providing a mere facility. However, the commission may be linked to expenses incurred for the execution of the credit facility accordingly.[84]

- *The Mobilisation of Funds*—[An IFF] must confine itself to permissible operations for acquiring the necessary funds to operate or to meet its liabilities. Examples of such operations are:

  - The shareholders may increase their share capital in order to increase the [IFF's] capital and provide a basis for attracting investment accounts and current accounts.
  - Issuance of Islamic certificates such as *Mudaraba, Musharaka* or *Ijara* certificates within the parameters of *Shari'a*.
  - Concluding *Salam* contracts whereby the [IFF] acts in the capacity of a supplier, or *Istisna'a* contracts whereby the [IFF] acts in the capacity of a manufacturer or builder with the condition that the contract price of the *Istisna'a* is paid to the [IFF] in advance, although the deferment of payment of the price in *Istisna'a* is allowed by *Shari'a*.
  - Concluding a sale-and-leaseback deal by selling some of the assets of the [IFF] for liquidity and leasing them back by means of an *Ijara* contract. The transaction must take into account the *Shari'a* standards on *Ijara* and *Ijara Muntania Bittamleek* whereby the contract of sale must be independent from

---

[81] See para 19.19 above.

[82] AAOIFI *Shari'a* Standard No 6.

[83] Although compliance with this and other AAOIFI standards would not of itself demonstrate to the FSA that an IFF should be FSA authorised or would not operate as a 'safe harbour' from FSA enforcement action, compliance with such standards would, to the extent that produces the same outcomes as relevant FSA standards, help demonstrate compliance with the relevant FSA standards.

[84] *AAOIFI Shari'a Standard No 6*, para 5.

the contract of lease, ie the two contracts must remain separate from each other.[85]

- Concluding *Tawarruq* deals in line with *Shari'a* principles by buying a commodity on a deferred payment basis and selling it to a third party, other than the previous seller, for immediate payment.[86]

- *The Disposal of Impermissible Earnings*—Any interest and other non-permissible earnings should be channelled to charity. It is not permissible for the [IFF] to use this money, directly or indirectly, for its own benefit. Examples of charitable channels include, among others, training people other than the staff of the bank, funding research, providing relief equipment, financial and technical assistance for Islamic countries or Islamic scientific, academic institutions, schools, anything to do with spreading Islamic knowledge, and similar channels. The charity money must go to these channels in accordance with the resolutions of the [SSB] of the [IFF].[87]

- *Zakat Obligations*[88]—... [IFFs] must take into account that they are obliged to pay *Zakat* even if the revenues and the money earned are impermissible because the shareholders are obliged in the first place to dispose of all accrued interest and impermissible earnings. So, the payment of *Zakat* is part of the obligation to dispose of impermissible earnings and interest.[89]

Prudential standards for IFFs

19.57 On the basis that the FSA's regime is a non-discriminatory regime, its rules governing capital adequacy and other prudential requirements should apply to IFFs. The FSA identify 'an *Ijara* mortgage is an example of an exposure described in BIPRU 3.4.58 R'[90] to which its general risk weighting rules apply.[91] The FSA does not set out any further guidelines for IFFs, notwithstanding the fact that the special nature of the arrangements which an IFF puts in place, to ensure that it conducts its business in a *Shari'a* compliant manner, may give rise to unique types of risk which the FSA's prudential regime requires the IFF to address. To assist an IFF in managing such risks, the standards developed by the IFSB are useful but only insofar as they provide non-binding guidance. However, as set out above,

---

[85] See paras 19.40 to 19.42 above.
[86] ibid, para 6/2.
[87] ibid, para 10/2.
[88] *Zakat* is a charitable tax. See n 1.
[89] ibid, para 11.
[90] BIPRU 3.4.59 R.
[91] BIPRU 3.4.58 R which governs the risk weighting which a firm should attach to an exposure which it has to a tenant under a property leasing transaction concerning residential property under which the firm is the lessor and the tenant has an option to purchase.

compliance with the IFSB standards would not, as a matter of law, serve as a defence to FSA enforcement action or establish a legitimate expectation for an IFF that the FSA would not take action against it.[92]

The IFSB Capital Adequacy Standard for Institutions (Other than Insurance **19.58** **Institutions) Offering Only Islamic Financial Services, 2005 (IFSB CAS).** The IFSB CAS deals with capital adequacy requirements for IFFs.[93] The IFSB describe the IFSB CAS as based primarily on Pillar 1 of the Basel II recommendations.[94] The IFSB CAS is intended to apply to non-insurance institutions offering only Islamic financial services however the IFSB indicates that the IFSB CAS may also be applied to conventional firms operating 'Islamic Windows'.[95]

The IFSB CAS sets out the minimum capital adequacy requirements for both **19.59** credit risk and market risk exposures arising from an IFF's holding of the following financial instruments: *Murabaha* and *Murabaha* for the Purchase Orderer; *Salam* and Parallel *Salam*; *Istisna* and Parallel *Istisna*; *Ijara* and *Ijara Munatahia Bittamleek*; *Musharaka* and Diminishing *Musharaka*; *Mudaraba*; and *Sukuk* held as investments in the IFF's non-trading book (the *Shari'a* Compliant Instruments Standards).[96] The IFSB CAS also provides guidance on operational risk (the Operational Risk Standards) and sets out capital adequacy requirements for Profit Sharing Invest Accounts.[97]

The IFSB CAS sets out Capital Adequacy Ratio ('CAR') formulae for IFFs based **19.60** on the definition of eligible regulatory capital and risk weighted assets (calculated by reference to credit risk and market risk exposures identified in the *Shari'a* Compliant Instruments Standards) and operational risk identified in the Operational Risk Standards.[98] The IFSB CAS identifies the minimum capital adequacy requirements for IFFs as a CAR of not lower than eight per cent for total capital.[99]

---

[92] See para 19.19.

[93] In Bahrain, the CBB implemented the IFSB CAS in January 2008. See CBB Rulebook, Volume 2: *Islamic Banks, Capital Adequacy*—<http://www.cbb.gov.bh>.

[94] IFSB CAS, paras 3 and 4. The IFSB CAS do not address the requirements covered by Pillar Two (Supervisory Review Process) and Pillar Three (Market Discipline) of Basel II as the IFS plans to deal with these in separate standards. (See IFSB CAS, para 5.)

[95] IFSB CAS, par 6. Islamic Windows are discussed in para 19.64 *et seq.*below.

[96] IFSB CAS, ss C.1 to C.7. In December 2007, the IFSB published the IFSB *Sukuk* CAR, n 114, to address caporal adequacy for requirements for *Sukuk* securitisations and real estate investments, which the IFSB CAS do not currently address.

[97] IFSB CAS, ss B.3 and B.4, respectively. Profit Sharing Investment Accounts are discussed below.

[98] IFSB CAS, paras 13 to 14 and Appendix A.

[99] IFSB CAS, para 16. In calculating capital adequacy ratios, the IFSB recommends that regulatory capital as the numerator be calculated in relation to the total risk weighted assets as the denominator. The total of the risk weighted assets is determined by multiplying the capital requirements for

19.61 The IFSB CAS identifies credit risk exposures in connection with accounts receivable in *Murabaha* contracts, counterparty risk in *Salam* contracts, accounts receivable and counterparty risk in *Istisna* contracts and lease payments receivable in *Ijara* contracts, capital impairment risk in *Musharaka* and *Mudaraba* contracts, and *Sukuk* held to maturity in the IFF's banking book.[100] The IFSB recommend that an IFF take the following into consideration in assigning risk weightings to the relevant contracts: the credit ratings of a debtor, counterparty, or other obligor or a security based on an external credit assessment; credit risk mitigation arrangements, which may include *Hamish Jiddiyya*, *Arbun* contracts, third party guarantees, assets pledged as collateral in a *Shari'a* compliant manner, or leased assets; and specific provisions made for the overdue portion of accounts receivable or lease payments receivable.[101]

19.62 The IFSB CAS identifies market risk exposures in connection with the risk of losses in on- and off-balance sheet positions arising from movements in market price and includes equity position risks in the IFF's trading book and market risk, which includes specific and general market risk, on trading positions in *Sukuk*; foreign exchange risk; and commodities and inventory risk.[102]

19.63 **The Disclosures to Promote Transparency and Market Discipline for Institutions Offering Islamic Financial Services, 2007 ('IFSB PTMDS').** The IFSB PTMDS sets out the standards for IFFs in making disclosures and builds on Pillar Three of the Basel II recommendations. It sets out: financial and risk disclosure principles;[103] disclosure requirements for investment account holders, including those for restricted and unrestricted accounts;[104] retail investor-oriented disclosures for investment account holders;[105] risk management, risk exposures, and risk mitigation, including provisions governing credit risk, liquidity risk, market risk, operational risk, rate of return risk, displaced commercial risk, and contract-specific risk;[106] general governance and *Shari'a* governance disclosures;[107] and the treatment of 'Islamic Windows'.[108]

---

market risk and operational risk by 12.5 to convert into risk-weighted equivalent assets and adding the resulting figures to the sum of the risk weighted assets computed for credit risk. (IFSB CAS, para 17.) This approach is consistent with BIPRU 3.1.5 R.

[100] IFSB CAS, s B.2, generally, and IFSB CAS ss C.1 to C.7, which go into detail for each contract. The IFSB are looking to supplement the standards for *Sukuk* with the IFSB

[101] IFSB CAS, para 20 *et seq*. An IFF would need to test these against the requirements in BIPRU 5.2.

[102] IFSB CAS, s B.3, generally, and IFSB CAS, ss C.1 to C.7, which go into detail for each contract.

[103] IFSB PTMDS, s 2.

[104] IFSB PMTDS, s 3.

[105] IFSB PMTDS, s 4.

[106] IFSB PMTDS, s 5.

[107] IFSB PMTDS, s 6.

[108] IFSB PMTDS, s 7. Islamic Windows are discussed in para 19.64 *et seq*. below.

The 'Islamic Window'[109]

In jurisdictions, such as the DIFC, regulators allow firms, which are not IFFs, to **19.64** offer *Shari'a* compliant products and services without the need to apply to become full IFFs.[110] Firms achieve this by operating an 'Islamic Window', ie a part of the firm's business through which the firm can offer *Shari'a* compliant products and services.

As it does for IFFs, AAOIFI emphasises the importance of a *Shari'a* Supervisory **19.65** Board and, where a firm chooses not to have a SSB, the need to disclose the fact:[111]

Institutions offering Islamic financial services shall declare that such services are in compliance with *Shari'a* requirements, and are therefore required to: (a) appoint a [SSB] which shall present a *Shari'a* report; and (b) implement the Governance Standards issued by AAOIFI that relate to the [SSB].

In the exceptional cases where the institution does not appoint a [SSB], which shall be with the approval of the regulatory and supervisory bodies, the institution shall disclose the following: (a) reasons for not appointing a [SSB]; (b) how the institution shall comply with *Shari'a* rules and principles in implementing the financial services it offers; (c) the body that approves the services offered in (b) above.[112]

In addition to the importance of the SSB, AAOIFI highlights the need for a **19.66** firm to ensure that it keeps its Islamic business separate from its non-Islamic business:

(a) Institutions shall disclose whether or not they commingle funds relating to Islamic financial services with funds relating to conventional financial services.

(b) Institutions shall disclose, in detail, the sources and applications of funds mobilised and invested by their Islamic financial services and the sources of funds used to cover a deficit if it occurs.

(c) Institutions shall disclose any revenues or expenditures prohibited by *Shari'a* rules and principles related to funds mobilised according to *Shari'a* rules and principles, and the disposition of any such revenues. The latter shall be determined by the [SSB].

(d) Institutions shall disclose any reserves deducted from the funds mobilised according to *Shari'a* rules and principles, the purposes of such reserves and to whom these reserves shall revert in case the activities, in respect of which such reserves were deducted, have ceased.

(e) Institutions shall disclose the percentage amount of the funds relating to Islamic financial services in comparison to the percentage amount of funds relating to conventional financial services.

---

[109] For further discussion of Islamic Windows, see 'Islamic Financial Institutions and Islamic Finance', n 54, para 47 *et seq*.

[110] See the Law Regulating Islamic Financial Business, DIFC Law No 13 of 2004, as amended, Arts 9, 11, and 12 and Henderson 'Limiting the Regulation of Islamic Finance', n 9, p 215.

[111] SSBs are discussed in para 19.68 *et seq*.below.

[112] ibid, para 6.

(f) The disclosure requirements stated in Financial Accounting Standard No. (1) General Presentation and Disclosure in the Financial Statements of Islamic Banks and Financial Institutions should be observed.[113]

19.67 As is the case with IFFs, the FSA does not prescribe any special requirements for a firm wishing to operate an Islamic Window and has stated that it does not expect operations conducted by conventional firms through an Islamic Window to require separate permissions on the assumption that the firm has authorisation; the question will be whether additional permission is required. If a new branch is established to operate as the Islamic Window, the branch will require both authorisation and permission.[114] However, as is the case with an IFF, a firm's failure or inability to put in place internal systems and controls that adhere to internationally recognised or developing standards for the operation of an Islamic Window could have damaging commercial consequences, irrespective of any express or implied regulatory duty to follow such standards. In this regard, AAOIFI has set out a standard for Islamic Financial Services Offered by Conventional Financial Institutions.[115] However, as set out above, compliance with the IFSB standards would not, as a matter of law, serve as a defence to FSA enforcement action or establish a legitimate expectation for an IFF that the FSA would not take action against it.[116]

The *Shari'a* Supervisory Board

Introduction

19.68 The FSA identifies the role of the SSB as one that the FSA has to consider in examining an IFF's activities.[117] The FSA does not impose any express requirements on IFFs with respect to SSBs but has described the key features of SSB scholars as ensuring *Shari'a* compliance in all an IFF's products and transactions, examining a new product or transaction and, if satisfied that it is *Shari'a* compliant, issuing its approval.[118]

19.69 AAOIFI defines a SSB as follows:

A *Shari'a* Supervisory Board is an independent body of specialised jurists in *Fiqh Almuámaiat* (Islamic commercial jurisprudence). However, the *Shari'a* supervisory

---

[113] ibid, para 7.
[114] 'Islamic Finance in the UK', n 11, p 10.
[115] AAOIFI Financial Accounting Standard No 18.
[116] See para 19.19 above.
[117] 'Islamic Finance in the UK', n 11, p 13. See also Hainsworth, 'Governance Rules for Islamic Financial Institutions: the New Frontier', (2007) 22 *JIBFL* 515 and Aldohini 'Islamic Banking Challenges Modern Governance: the Dilemma of the *Shari'a* Supervisory Board' (2008) *Company Lawyer* 156.
[118] 'Islamic Finance in the UK', n 11, p 13.

board may include a member other than those specialised in *Figh Almuámaiat*, but who should be an expert in the field of Islamic financial institutions and with knowledge of *Figh Almuámaiat*. The *Shari'a* Supervisory Board is entrusted with the duty of directing, reviewing and supervising the activities of the Islamic financial institution in order to ensure that they are in compliance with Islamic *Shari'a* Rules and Principles. The *Fatawa*, and rulings of the *Shari'a* Supervisory Board shall be binding on the Islamic financial institution.[119]

The regulation of an IFF's SSB

As discussed above, the FSA has indicated that, it would not be appropriate to judge between different interpretations of the *Shari'a* made by SSBs.[120] The FSA does not, therefore, seek to regulate the substance of an SSB's activities. The FSA has indicated, however, that it would expect to know, from an operational and a financial perspective, exactly what role an SSB will play in an IFF and, in particular, whether and how the SSB affects the running of the IFF.[121]   **19.70**

In its application to become FSA authorised, an IFF would need to indicate to the FSA whether the members of the IFF's SSB were intended to play an executive role or an advisory role.[122]   **19.71**

Where, the SSB members were intended to play an executive role: **19.72**

* The IFF would need to apply to the FSA for each member to be an approved person. The candidate SSB member would need to satisfy the requirements set out in the FSA"s Handbook of rules and guidance relevant to approved persons, including the requirements as to competence and capability.[123] In this regard, the FSA would expect each candidate SSB member to have relevant experience.[124]

* An SSB typically plays an active role in an IFF's day-to-day operations. For that reason the role of each member of the SSB in the IFF would be more likely to resemble the role of an executive director than a non-executive director. The IFF would also need to demonstrate that, where a SSB member was also a

---

[119] AAOIFI Governance Standard for Islamic Financial Institutions No 1, para 2. The IFSB echoes the final requirement by recommending that IFFs comply with the rulings of the IFF's SSB. (See Guiding Principles on Corporate Governance for Institutions Offering Only Islamic Financial Services, December 2006, Principle 3.2.) It is submitted that this requirement would need to be read subject to the IFF's duty not comply with the rule or ruling of any national regulator to which it was subject.

[120] 'Islamic Finance in the UK', n 11, p 13.

[121] ibid.

[122] ibid.

[123] FIT 2.2.

[124] 'Islamic Finance in the UK', n 11, p 13.

member of another IFF's SSB, this would not give rise to a conflict of interest.[125]

19.73 Where the SSB members are intended to play more of an advisory role, then the IFF would not need to apply for each member to be an approved person.[126] There is no FSA controlled function of 'member of a SSB'. The SSB members' competence should, however, be relevant in assessing whether an IFF is fit and proper to be FSA authorised. Other jurisdictions take a different approach. For example, in Bahrain membership of an SSB is controlled function.[127]

Compliance with AAOIFI Governance Standards to demonstrate compliance with senior management systems and controls requirements?

19.74 In Bahrain, the CBB takes a similar approach to the FSA in that it does not seek to regulate the substance of an SSB's activities. The CBB does, however, regulate the manner in which a SSB carries on its activities. Every IFF regulated by the CBB must establish an independent SSB complying with AAOIFI's Governance Standards for Islamic Financial Institutions, No 1 and No 2. That requirement is a component of CBB 'Principle for Businesses 10—Management, Systems and Controls', the text of which is similar to that of FSA Principle for Businesses 3.[128] The CBB also requires every IFF to have a separate *Shari'a* review function to verify the SSB's compliance with the AAOIFI's Governance Standards. The review function must itself comply with AAOIFI's Governance Standards for Islamic Financial Institutions, No 3 and must be part of the IFF's internal audit function.[129] Although the FSA, unlike the CBB, has not imposed any express requirements or sought to determine standards with respect to the manner in which a SSB carries out its functions, such standards could be relevant in the context of the

---

[125] ibid. The FSA indicates that it would be difficult to justify multiple memberships of SSBs of different IFFs because of significant conflicts of interest. The FSA highlights the fact that this would put further constraints on an industry already facing a shortage of *Shari'a* scholars with suitable skills.

[126] This turns on the issue of whether in issuing their *Fatwa*, it could be said that the SSB members were not carrying on the regulated activity of 'advising on investments'.

[127] CBB Rulebook, Volume 2: *Islamic Banks, High Level Controls*, HC-2.1.2.

[128] 'Islamic bank licensees' board of directors and *Shari'a* Boards (where applicable) and management must take reasonable care to ensure that their affairs are managed effectively and responsibly, with appropriate systems and controls in relation to the size and complexity of their operations. Islamic bank licensees' systems and controls, as far as reasonably practical, must be sufficient to manage the level of risk inherent in their business and ensure compliance with the CBB Rulebook. In particular, the CBB requires that banks comply with AAOIFI issued accounting standards as well as *Shari'a* pronouncements issued by the *Shari'a* Board of AAOIFI.' CBB Rulebook, Volume 2: *Islamic Banks, High Level Controls*, HC-1.3.15.

[129] CBB Rulebook, Volume 2: *Islamic Banks, High Level Controls*, HC-1.3.16.

FSA's regulation of an IFF's senior management systems and controls. In this respect, AAOIFI's Governance Standards could serve as a useful guide for an IFF seeking to determine appropriate standards for the functioning of its SSB.

AAOIFI recommends, amongst other things, that: **19.75**

- Every IFF should have a SSB appointed by the shareholders in their annual general meeting upon the recommendation of the board of directors; the IFF should properly document the SSB's appointment and fix its remuneration; the SSB should consist of at least three members none of whom should be directors or significant shareholders of the IFF; any SSB member's dismissal should be subject to the approval of the IFF's shareholders in a general meeting; and the SSB should prepare a written report.[130]

- Every IFF should ensure that its SSB undertakes a 'Shari'a Review', ie an examination of an IFF's compliance with the *Shari'a*. AAOIFI sets out standards and provides guidance to assist IFF's SSB in performing its *Shari'a* Reviews but emphasises that the *Shari'a* Review does not relieve the IFF's management of their duties to ensure that the IFF undertakes all its transactions in accordance with the *Shari'a*. AAOIFI also sets out detailed requirements with respect to: the *Shari'a* Review procedures; quality assurance; and the report which the SSB should prepare upon completion of the *Shari'a Review*.[131]

- Every IFF should ensure that it appoints personnel to undertake an 'Internal *Shari'a* Review' to ensure that the IFF's management discharge their responsibilities in relation to the implementation of the *Shari'a* rules and principles as determined by the IFF's SSB. Unlike the *Shari'a* Review, the SSB does not undertake the Internal *Shari'a* Review. Instead, the IFF must entrust the Internal *Shari'a* Review to IFF personnel who should not have any executive authority or responsibility for the activities which they review and should enjoy a status within the IFF not lower than that of the IFF's internal audit or control department. The IFF Internal *Shari'a* Review should receive IFF management's full and continuous support. AAOIFI also sets out detailed requirements with respect to: the staffing and supervision of the Internal *Shari'a* Review function; a code of ethics for staff; staff knowledge, skills and experience; continuing education and training; due professional care; scope of work; performance of the review, including examining and evaluating Internal *Shari'a* Review information, reporting and follow up; management of the Review process; quality assurance; and the elements of an effective Internal *Shari'a* Review.[132]

---

[130] See AAOIFI Governance Standard for Islamic Financial Institutions No 1, para 3 *et seq.*

[131] See AAOIFI Governance Standard for Islamic Financial Institutions No 2.

[132] See AAOIFI Governance Standard for Islamic Financial Institutions No 3. AAOIFI also sets out its recommendations for audit and governance committees responsible for overseeing an IFF's financial reporting. (See AAOIFI Governance Standard for Islamic Financial Institutions No 4.)

The Regulatory Classification of *Shari'a* Compliant Products and Services

CIS regulation and Shari'a *compliant arrangements*

19.76 Although the FSA did not identify Collective Investment Schemes ('CIS') regulation as a general issue in the context of Islamic finance, confining its discussion of the impact of CIS regulation in the context of *Sukuk*,[133] the impact of CIS regulation on the regulatory classification of *Shari'a* compliant arrangements cannot be overlooked. The issue is particularly acute in light of: (a) the broad definition of CIS in FSMA;[134] (b) the principles of mutual cooperation, one of the general principles of Islamic business ethics and norms;[135] (c) the sharing of profits which underpins arrangements such as *Mudaraba* and *Musharaka*.

19.77 FSMA defines a CIS as follows:

> (1) . . . any arrangements with respect to property of any description, including money, the purpose or effect of which is to enable persons taking part in the arrangements (whether by becoming owners of the property or any part of it or otherwise) to participate in or receive profits or income arising from the acquisition, holding, management or disposal of the property or sums paid out of such profits or income.
>
> (2) The arrangements must be such that the persons who are to participate ('participants') do not have day-to-day control over the management of the property, whether or not they have the right to be consulted or to give directions.
>
> (3) The arrangements must also have either or both of the following characteristics—
>   (a) the contributions of the participants and the profits or income out of which payments are to be made to them are pooled;
>   (b) the property is managed as a whole by or on behalf of the operator of the scheme.
>
> (4) If arrangements provide for such pooling as is mentioned in subsection (3)(a) in relation to separate parts of the property, the arrangements are not to be regarded as constituting a single collective investment scheme unless the participants are entitled to exchange rights in one part for rights in another.[136]

19.78 Acknowledging the definition's breadth, FSMA empowers the Treasury to provide, by order, that arrangements do not amount to a collective investment scheme (a) in specified circumstances; or (b) if the arrangements fall within a specified category of arrangement.[137] The relevant Treasury Order in this regard is the

---

[133] 'Islamic Finance in the UK', n 11, p 25.
[134] FSMA, s 235.
[135] See further Ayub, n 1, p 68.
[136] FSMA, s 235. For discussion see paras 17.07–17.24 above.
[137] FSMA, s 235(5).

Financial Services and Markets 2000 (Collective Investment Schemes) Order 2001 (the Treasury CIS Order)[138] and its Schedule lists 21 categories of 'arrangement not amounting to' a CIS.[139]

The classification of an arrangement as a CIS means that those establishing and operating the arrangement would need to be FSA authorised.[140] Moreover, anyone wanting to promote the arrangement to the public would be unable to do so because the arrangement would be an 'unregulated CIS'.[141] Finally, persons appointed to manage the arrangement would need to be a FSA authorised.[142] **19.79**

As set out further below,[143] the regulatory definition of a *Shari'a* compliant product as a specified investment, other than a unit in a CIS, may place it outside the scope of the CIS regime because it falls within a CIS Treasury Order exclusion. Generally, the person looking to avail himself of a relevant CIS Treasury Order exclusion would need to be FSA authorised: in order to carry on business with respect to the specified investment that allowed the person to benefit from the exclusion, the person would need to be FSA authorised with respect to that investment. However, as mentioned above, a product's classification as an unregulated CIS could limit the scope of anyone's marketing efforts with respect to that product and the person would find himself subject to parts of the FSA Handbook which it would otherwise prefer to avoid.[144] Moreover, some entities, such as the issuers or originators of *Sukuk*, might want to avoid FSA authorisation altogether. Therefore, the issue of classification as a CIS should be one that anyone offering a *Shari'a* compliant investment based on money acceptance arrangements, profit sharing arrangements, capital market arrangements, mutual assistance arrangements, or some miscellaneous arrangements will need to consider as a threshold issue.[145] In this respect, it is perhaps important to note that, where an IFF seeks to argue that the particular product which it seeks to offer should not require it to seek FSA authorisation to carry on a particular regulated activity, such as accepting deposits, it could nevertheless find itself becoming regulated as a CIS. The application of the CIS regime to various investments is considered in the discussion of the particular investments below.[146] **19.80**

---

[138] SI 2001/1062, as amended.

[139] For discussion see paras 17.25–17.52 above.

[140] As they carry on the regulated activity of establishing, etc a collective investment scheme (RAO, art 51).

[141] See FSMA, s 238 and the discussion in paras 17.134–17.140 above.

[142] As they carry on the regulated activity of managing investments (RAO, art 37) or advising (RAO, art 53. See further, paras 17.121–17.124 above.

[143] See para 19.82.

[144] For discussion of the sections of the FSA Handbook relevant to a CIS, see paras 17.141-17.145 above.

[145] The issue should not generally arise in the context of deferred payment techniques.

[146] See para 19.81 *et seq*.

Money acceptance arrangements as 'deposits'

19.81 The RAO[147] defines a 'deposit' as a 'sum of money paid on terms under which it will be repaid, with or without interest or premium, and either on demand or at a time or in circumstances agreed by or on behalf of the person making the payment and the person receiving it; and which are referable to the provision of property (other than currency) or services or the giving of security'.[148] The RAO, therefore, captures money acceptance arrangements designed to avoid the charging of interest, such as the *Al Wadi'a* or *Qard*, structured such that the IFF is the borrower, referred to above, or any other interest free deposit account. On the basis that the IFF sought to mobilise any funds accepted in order to lend the money to others or to finance its own activities, the FSA would need to authorise an IFF looking to offer clients products or facilities which involved the IFF accepting and holding money on an interest-free basis by way of business.

19.82 For the purposes of excluding an *Al Wadi'a* or *Qard* from the CIS definition, their definition as a deposit within the meaning of the RAO is important because paragraph 3 of the Schedule to the Treasury CIS Order excludes 'pure deposit-based schemes' from the definition of a CIS.[149]

Profit sharing investment accounts as 'deposits'

19.83 Unlike, for example, the DIFC, in the UK there is no regulated activity of 'operating a Profit Sharing Investment Account' ('PSIA') and neither the Treasury nor the FSA has expressly identified a 'PSIA' as a specified investment,[150] although its general characteristics would cause it fall within the definition of a CIS.[151] The FSA identifies the main issue in its authorisation of the Islamic Bank of Britain ('IBB'), the UK's first wholly Islamic retail bank, as the definition of deposit insofar as the IBB originally proposed a *Mudaraba*, a type of PSIA.[152] As set out above, under a *Mudaraba*, the *Rab Al Mal*, as the account holders, and the *Mudarib*, normally an IFF as manager, share in the profits on a pre-agreed basis with the *Rab Al Mal* bearing the risk of any loss and the *Mudarib* being liable for any loss only as a result of its misconduct, negligence, or breach of any conditions governing the *Mudaraba*. For the FSA, this was inconsistent with the definition of 'deposit' under the RAO, which requires capital certainty because a fundamental characteristic of a *Shari'a* compliant 'deposit' is that the 'depositor' should take some risk

---

[147] FSMA (Regulated Activities) Order 2001 (SI 2001/544) as amended.
[148] See RAO, art 5(2).
[149] For discussion, see para 17.28 above.
[150] See DFSA Rulebook: *General Module*, rule 2.2.2 and rule 2.21.
[151] This is discussed in para 19.85 below.
[152] 'Islamic Finance in the UK', n 11, p 14.

on the underlying asset in which the 'deposit-taker' invests the money deposited with it.[153] The same concern would arise where a PSIA was structured as a *Wakala*.[154]

The FSA and IBB adopted a solution whereby, legally, depositors under a **19.84** *Mudaraba* would be entitled to full payment, thereby satisfying the RAO requirements and enjoying the protection offered with respect to a 'protected deposit'.[155] However, account holders would have the right to turn down the deposit protection on religious grounds and choose instead to be repaid under the risk sharing and formula under the PSIA.[156] The same approach should be acceptable in the context of a PSIA structured as a *Wakala*.

The classification of PSIAs as deposits within the meaning of the RAO excludes **19.85** them from the definition of a CIS on the basis that they are pure deposit-based schemes within the meaning of the paragraph 3 of the Schedule to the Treasury CIS Order.[157] Discussing the authorisation of IBB and the treatment of PSIAs as deposits, the FSA suggests that this may not necessarily be appropriate in other contexts.[158] This suggests that it would not be always be appropriate for the FSA to treat a PSIA or PSIA type product as a 'deposit' for authorisation purposes. Even if this were the case, a PSIA, whether structured as a *Mudaraba* or a *Wakala*, has characteristics which would bring it within the FSMA definition of a CIS.[159] Ultimately, the IFF and the FSA will need to determine which category of specified investment most accurately captures the commercial nature of the product or service that the IFF wishes to offer.[160] In practice, it may be that the IFF applies for FSA authorisation both to accept deposits and to operate a CIS. Irrespective of how the FSA chooses to classify a PSIA, an IFF's operation of a PSIA may have certain conduct of business consequences for the IFF.[161]

---

[153] ibid. See, also, FSA Briefing Note BNO 16/06.

[154] As set out in para 19.53 above, the *Wakala* may be contrasted with the *Mudaraba* in that the investor alone shares any profit or loss, with the *Waki*, the manager under a *Wakala* getting a fixed management fee, whereas, in the case of a *Mudaraba*, both the *Rab Al Mal* and the *Mudarib* share any profits or losses.

[155] See COMP 5.3.1R and para 7.150 above.

[156] 'Islamic Finance in the UK', n 11, p 14. See also the Finance Act 2005, s 49 which describes *Mudaraba* arrangements as 'alternative finance arrangements: deposits'.

[157] For discussion, see para 17.25 above.

[158] 'Islamic Finance in the UK', n 11, p 14.

[159] FSMA, s. 235. In the DIFC, for example, the DFSA's CIF Rules (CIR), rule 4 excludes a PSIA from the definition of 'collective investment fund' (CIF). The definition of CIF in art 15 of the DIFC Collective Investment Fund Law, DIFC Law No 1 of 2006 is almost identical to the definition of CIS in FSMA, s 235 and the list of exclusions the CIR, rule 4 similar to those in the Treasury CIS Order. Depending on its structure, a PSIA could fall within the 'individual investment management arrangements' in the Treasury CIS Order, para 1. (See para 17.26 above.)

[160] The FSA suggest this in 'Islamic Finance in the UK', n 11, p 14.

[161] These are discussed in para 19.111 below.

Islamic mortgages[162]

19.86 In 2007, the Treasury amended the RAO to include two new types of home financing arrangements: the 'home purchase plan' ('HPP') and the 'home reversion plan'.[163] The amendment was designed to capture *Ijara* home financing arrangement under the definition of HPP to 'ensure a level regulatory playing field within the equity release market and within the *Sharia* [sic] compliant home financing market'.[164] *Ijara* arrangements do not fall within the definition of 'regulated mortgage contract'[165] because, as discussed above, ownership of the property financed under an *Ijara* remains with the IFF offering finance for the term of the *Ijara* and not with the person selling the property. As set out below,[166] the HPP definition brings *Ijara* and other financing services and products, where ownership of the property remains with the IFF, within the RAO's scope.

19.87 The RAO identifies entering into a regulated HPP as home purchase provider as a specified kind of activity.[167] It defines an HHP as:

> An arrangement comprised in one or more instruments or agreements, in relation to which the following conditions are met at the time it is entered into: (i) the arrangement is one under which a person (the 'home purchase provider') buys a qualifying interest or an undivided share of a qualifying interest in land (other than timeshare accommodation) in the United Kingdom; (ii) where an undivided share of a qualifying interest in land is bought, the interest is held on trust for the home purchase provider and the individual or trustees mentioned in . . . (iii) below as beneficial tenants in common; (iii) the arrangement provides for the obligation of an individual or trustees (the 'home purchaser') to buy the interest bought by the home purchase provider over the course of or at the end of a specified period; and (iv) the home purchaser (if he is an individual) or an individual who is a beneficiary of the trust (if the home purchaser is a trustee), or a related person, is entitled under the arrangement to occupy at least 40% of the land in question as or in connection with a dwelling during that period, and intends to do so.[168]

19.88 An IFF would need to determine whether a particular *Shari'a* compliant home financing product had the characteristics of a HPP and if so ensure that the FSA authorised it to carry on the regulated activity of entering into an HPP as home purchase provider or administering an HPP. In this respect, an *Ijara* or Diminishing

---

[162] See Patient 'Islamic Finance in the UK Consumer Sector' (2008) *JIBLR* 9 and Hainsworth, 'Islamic Financial Institutions and Islamic Finance', n 54, para 77(iv) and paras 91 *et seq.*

[163] FSMA (Regulated Activities) (Amendment) (No 2) Order 2006, SI 2006/2383.

[164] See 'Secondary Legislation for the Regulation of Home Reversion and Home Purchase Plans: a Consultation', March 2006, para 3.1.

[165] See RAO, art 61 and Chapter 13 above.

[166] See paras 19.87 *et seq.*

[167] RAO, art 63F(1). 'Administering' an HHP is also a specified activity. (See RAO, art 63F(2) and (3)(b).) See also the FSA guidance on HPPs in PERG 14.4.

[168] RAO, art 63F(3).

Musharaka arrangement should fall within the definition of an HPP.[169] However, a *Murabaha* arrangement should not because it does not involve a homeowner buying the property from the IFF on deferred payment terms and would be classified as 'regulated mortgage contract'.[170] To offer a full range of Islamic mortgage services and products, an IFF would, therefore, need to apply to the FSA for authorisation to carry on activities both with respect to HPPs and regulated mortgage contracts.

The regulatory classification of other financing arrangements

On their face, the deferred payment contracts such as *Istisna'a*, which involves a   **19.89** forward sale contract, or *Salam*, which involves immediate payment for goods with deferred delivery fall within the RAO definition of a 'future', defined as 'rights under a contract for the sale of a commodity or property of any other description under which delivery is to be made at a future date and at a price agreed on when the contract is made'.[171] In both cases, however, the parties and their advisers would need to ask whether the contracts were entered into for 'investment purposes' or 'contractual purposes'. If the parties can show that a contract is made for commercial purposes, it will not be a 'future'.[172] In this respect, article 84 of the RAO states:

(3) A contract is to be regarded as made for investment purposes if it is made or traded on a recognised investment exchange, or is made otherwise than on a recognised investment exchange but is expressed to be as traded on such an exchange or on the same terms as those on which an equivalent contract would be made on such an exchange.

(4) A contract not falling within paragraph (3) is to be regarded as made for commercial purposes if under the terms of the contract delivery is to be made within seven days, unless it can be shown that there existed an understanding that (notwithstanding the express terms of the contract) delivery would not be made within seven days.

(5) The following are indications that a contract not falling within paragraph (3) or (4) is made for commercial purposes and the absence of them is an indication that it is made for investment purposes—
  (a) one or more of the parties is a producer of the commodity or other property, or uses it in his business;
  (b) the seller delivers or intends to deliver the property or the purchaser takes or intends to take delivery of it.

---

[169] See PERG 14.2, Q2.

[170] RAO, art 61(3). See PERG 14.4, Q25.

[171] RAO, art 84(1).

[172] RAO, art 84(2) which states: 'There are excluded from [art 84(1)] rights under any contract which is made for commercial and not investment purposes.'

(6) It is an indication that a contract is made for commercial purposes that the price, the lot, the delivery date or other terms are determined by the parties for the purposes of the particular contract and not by reference (or not solely by reference) to regularly published prices, to standard lots of delivery dates or to standard terms.

19.90 The fact that, for *Istisna'a* and *Salam* arrangements to be valid under the *Shari'a*, the parties must intend to make and take physical delivery of the assets subject to the arrangements, is an indicator that the contracts are made for a commercial purpose.[173] Under an *Istisna'a* arrangement, the fact that one party is the manufacturer of the assets which are delivered upon completion, thereby using it in its business, may also be an indicator that the contracts are made for a commercial purpose.[174] The fact that under both *Istisna'a* and *Salam* arrangements, generally, the contract terms are individually negotiated and the parties determine the price and delivery date, as opposed to determining them by reference to a regularly published price, standard lots or delivery, or to standard terms, will indicate that the contracts are made for a commercial purpose.[175] In practice, it may be that the IFF applies for FSA authorisation to carry on regulated activities with respect to futures where it wishes to offer *Istisna'a* or *Salam* products or services.

19.91 As set out above, a PSIA could fall within the definition of a CIS. Other profit-sharing arrangements, such as the *Musharaka*, could also fall within the CIS definition depending on how the parties structure them. On its face, a *Musharaka* should satisfy: (a) the 'arrangements', 'property', and 'purpose or effect' conditions in FSMA, section 235(1);[176] and (b) the 'pooling' or 'management as a whole' condition in FSMA, section 235(3).[177] The question of whether any participant in the *Musharaka* relinquishes 'day-to-day control' within the meaning of FSMA, section 235(2) will, however, be one of fact.[178] Where the 'management' of a *Musharaka* or Diminishing *Musharaka* arrangement, for example, in the context of trade financing,[179] may be an activity that is undertaken jointly by the IFF and client, it may be possible for the parties to a *Musharaka* to argue that 'day-to-day control' remains with both parties and, therefore, the arrangement is not a CIS.

---

[173] RAO, art 84(5)(a). The intention to make and take physical delivery is determined at the time that the contract is made. See *CR Sugar Trading Ltd (in administration) v China National Sugar & Alcohol Group* [2003] EWHC 79 (Comm), para 39.

[174] RAO, art 84(5)(b). The parties will have to determine this by reference to the specific facts: an entity that is in the business of purchasing and selling a commodity cannot be said to use that commodity in its business. See *CR Sugar Trading Ltd (in administration) v China National Sugar & Alcohol Group*, n 173, para 21.

[175] RAO, art 84(6).

[176] See para 17.09 *et seq.* above.

[177] See para 17.22 *et seq.* above.

[178] See para 17.17 *et seq.* above.

[179] See Ayub, n 1, pp 332–43.

Alternatively, a particular arrangement could fall within the 'schemes entered into for commercial investment purposes related to existing business' exclusion, depending on its structure.[180] Finally, it is difficult to identify a relevant exclusion in the CIS Treasury Order which would exclude *Musharaka*. Again, in practice, it may be that the IFF applies for FSA authorisation to operate a CIS to give it the most freedom possible to structure and offer *Shari'a* compliant financing arrangements.

Sukuk

Because *Sukuk* originators seek to avoid the interest bearing structures, *Sukuk* **19.92** have different legal structures from conventional debt instruments. As set out above, *Sukuk* can have different structures capable of being classified in various ways. Potentially, this makes it difficult to classify them in a uniform, 'one-size-fits-all' both in the context of any FSA authorisation and for listing purposes.

On their face, most *Sukuk* arrangements fall within the CIS definition in FSMA, **19.93** section 235: (a) the *Sukuk* certificate holders participate in or receive profits or income arising from the assets on which the *Sukuk* are based; (b) the *Sukuk* certificate holders do not have day-to-day control of the assets; (c) the *Sukuk* certificate holders' contributions are pooled in order to investment in the property, eg purchase the property; and (d) the property is managed by the operator of the vehicle, which has purchased the property, or is delegated to a third party, possibly the original owner of the property.[181]

Therefore, in the absence of a relevant Treasury CIS exemption, the FSA could **19.94** treat a *Sukuk* vehicle established in the UK as a CIS and require the *Sukuk* manager to be FSA authorised to establish, operate, and wind up a CIS.[182] Moreover, since it is unlikely that *Sukuk* could be structured as units in an 'authorised fund',[183] the FSA would classify them as units in an 'unregulated CIS' which, as discussed above, has the disadvantage that generally they cannot be promoted to the public.[184]

---

[180] See para 17.36 above.

[181] See Henderson 'Testing the Water' (2007) ILFR, September <http//:www.iflr.com>; 'Islamic Finance in the UK', n 11, p 25; and 'Consultation on the legislative framework for the regulation of sukuk' at p 10 which can be found at <http://www.hm-treasury.gov.uk> (the '*Sukuk* Consultation').

[182] See, 'Islamic Finance in the UK', n 11, p 26, and the *Sukuk* consultation, n 181, p11.

[183] See para 17.84 *et seq*.above.

[184] The classification of *Sukuk* as units may also have an impact in the context of the purchase or offer to purchase *Sukuk* in order to stabilise their price after a primary or secondary offering (Stabilisation). Those performing Stabilisation activities with respect to *Sukuk* may be unable comply with EU Regulation (EC) 2273/2003 (Buy-back and Stabilisation Regulations) because the Buy-back and Stabilisation Regulations govern 'relevant securities', which the Buy-back and Stabilisation Regulations define as 'transferable securities', within the meaning of Directive (EC) 2001/34 (ISD).

19.95 *Sukuk* are, however, typically structured to have the same economic characteristics as conventional debt instruments albeit in a *Shari'a* compliant manner. Treating *Sukuk* as units in a CIS would mean treating *Sukuk* issuers differently from the issuers of conventional debt instruments, thereby (a) placing them at a competitive disadvantage and (b) ignoring the economic reality of *Sukuk* where the risks and rewards are equivalent to conventional debt instruments.[185] One approach is to exclude *Sukuk*, which are economically equivalent to debt securities, could therefore be excluded from the definition of units in a CIS by bringing *Sukuk* within the RAO definition of 'instruments acknowledging indebtedness'[186] and the 'Debt Issues' exclusion in the Treasury CIS Order[187] by focusing on their economic effect and risk characteristics.[188]

19.96 An alternative approach would be to create a category of specified investment and make it subject to the 'Debt Issues' exclusion. This is the approach suggested in the *Sukuk* Consultation, which creates a type of investment known as an 'alternative finance investment bond' ('AIF'). An AIF has the following characteristics:

(a) it must provide for a bond-holder to pay capital a bond-issuer;

(b) it must identify assets, or a class of assets, which the bond-issuer will acquire for the purpose of generating income or gains directly or indirectly;

(c) it must specify a period at the end of which it ceases to have effect ('the bond term');

(d) the bond-issuer must undertake to repay the capital ('the redemption payment') to the bond-holder during or at the end of the bond-term (whether or not in installments), and to pay to the bond-holder other payments on one or

---

Although this includes 'bonds and other forms of securitised debt' (see Title 1, Art 1, (4)), it does not include units. It would, not therefore by able to perform Stabilisation in accordance with MAR 2.2.1R which provides a 'safe harbour' from market abuse proceedings (see MAR 2.2.3R). MAR 2.2.5G may offer relief. It states that 'the mere fact that stabilisation does not conform with the provisions in the Buy-back and Stabilisation Regulations or with MAR 2.2.1R(2) will not of itself mean that the behaviour constitutes markets abuse'. This should be read in light of the definition of 'financial instruments' in section C of Directive (EC) 2004/39 (MiFID), which includes 'units in collective investment undertakings' (see para (3)).

[185] See Henderson 'Testing the Water', n 181 and 'Government Sterling Sukuk Issuance: a Response to the Consultation', n 18, p 29. For taxation purposes, the Finance Act 2005, s 48B(5) states expressly that *Sukuk* or 'alternative investment bonds', as *Sukuk* are described, are to be treated differently from, inter alia, a unit trust scheme for the purposes of the Taxation of Chargeable Gains Act 1992.

[186] RAO, art 77.

[187] The 'Debt Issues' exclusion in the CIS Treasury Order is discussed at para 17.32 above. The consequence of the manner in which the Treasury CIS Order excludes *Sukuk* is that *Sukuk* would need to be treated as 'specified investments' for RAO purposes and anyone carrying on a regulated activity with respect to *Sukuk* would require FSA authorisation with respect to 'debentures' to avoid breaching the General Prohibition (FSMA, s 21). An issuer should, however, be able to rely on the exclusion in art 18, RAO for a company issuing its own securities.

[188] See Henderson 'Testing the Water', n 181.

more occasions during or at the end of the bond term; the amount of the additional payments must not exceed an amount which would be a reasonable commercial return on a loan of the capital;

and the AIF must be listed on a recognised investment exchange.[189]

A definition based on the 'alternative finance investment bond' would cover arrangements that replicated the circumstances in which a person subscribed for a conventional listed debt security from which they received a return that included interest and other amounts of redemption. The definition would not, however, cover *Sukuk* where the risks and rewards under the *Sukuk* were not equivalent to a conventional bond.[190]   **19.97**

The consequence of designating *Sukuk* as specified investments for RAO purposes, whether expressly or by necessary implication, is that anyone carrying on a regulated activity with respect to *Sukuk* would require FSA authorisation to avoid breaching the General Prohibition.[191] In the context of an entity looking to carry on activities by way of business with respect to *Sukuk*, this would not be an unfair result and, indeed, the principle of non-discrimination would require it. For the issuers and originators of *Sukuk*, however, an exclusion, similar to that in the RAO,[192] that excluding a company's issue of its own debentures from the RAO definition of 'dealing in investments as principal'[193] would be necessary. It would seem unfair to exclude *Sukuk* issuers and originators from the CIS regime only to have them fall within the regime for dealing in investments as principal, which would also require authorisation.[194]   **19.98**

---

[189] The *Sukuk* Consultation, n 181, p 25. The Finance Act 2005, s 48A an alternative finance investment bond, which is economically equivalent to a conventional debt security, in same the way as a conventional debt security for both income and corporation tax purposes.

[190] The definition is also focused on *Sukuk* which are *asset-based*, where investors take risk on the creditworthiness of the *Sukuk* originator; it does not include *Sukuk* which are *asset-backed*, where investors take risk on an identified pool of assets and would, therefore, not apply to a *Shari'a* compliant securitisation. It is, however, arguable that a *Shari'a* compliant securitisation would generally be closer in structure to conventional securitisation than *Sukuk* would be to conventional debt instruments: the payments under each would, generally, be determined by reference to a fixed asset or pool of fixed assets. *Sukuk* under a *Shari'a* compliant securitisation should, therefore, enjoy the exclusions afforded securities under a conventional securitisation. In any event, the principle of non-discrimination would render it unfair to require the parties to a *Shari'a* compliant securitisation to become FSA authorised where the parties to a conventional securitisation were not. The distinction between asset-based and asset-backed *Sukuk* is also important in the context of the categorisation for listing purposes, which is discussed in para 19.113 below.

[191] FSMA, s 21.

[192] RAO, art 18.

[193] RAO, art 14.

[194] See Henderson 'Testing the Water' n 181, the *Sukuk* Consultation, n 181, p 11 and 'Government Sterling Sukuk Issuance: a Response to the Consultation', n 18, pp 29 to 30. In the DIFC, the DFSA excludes *Sukuk* from the definition of collective investment fund in Article 15 of the Collective Investment Fund Law, DIFC Law No. 1 of 2006. DFSA Rulebook: *Offered Collective Investment Rules*, Rule CIR 2.3.9 states: 'Arrangements do not, for the purposes of Article 15 of the

Shari'a *compliant derivatives*[195]

19.99   As set out above, the *Shari'a* does not permit conventional derivatives because they may infringe the prohibitions on *Gharar* and *Maisir* or *Quimar*.[196] However, IFFs may offer *Shari'a* compliant products which have a derivative effect. For example, IFFs can create put and call options using *Arbun* contracts,[197] futures or forwards using *Salam* contracts,[198] and contracts for differences combining *Murabaha* and *Wa'ad*,[199] whereby the parties enter into purchase undertakings that replicate the two-way cash flows that one would encounter under a conventional contract for differences. In addition, IFFs may offer foreign currency trading services in accordance with 'AAOIFI *Shari'a* Standard No 1—Trading in Currencies'.[200] In all cases, the products and services will be structured so as to include the sale or purchase of physical commodities.[201] Insofar as these *Shari'a* compliant products and services have a derivative effect, an IFF that wished to offer these services by way of business in the UK would need to be FSA authorised to undertake regulated activities relating to commodity futures, commodity options on commodity futures, contracts for differences, futures, options, rights to or interests in contractually based investments, and rolling spot forex contracts.[202]

Takaful

19.100   The RAO defines a 'contract of insurance' in very broad terms.[203] The FSA summarises the description of an insurance contract as an enforceable contract under

---

Law, amount to a Collective Investment Fund if the arrangements are arrangements under which the rights or interests of the participants are evidenced by *Sukuk* certificates where the holders of the certificates are entitled to rely on the credit worthiness of: (a) the issuer of the *Sukuk* certificates; or (b) any other Person who has assumed obligations under the *Sukuk* certificates, for obtaining their rights and benefits arising under the certificates.' The DFSA's exclusion focuses on *Sukuk* which are *asset-based*, where investors take risk on the creditworthiness of the *Sukuk* originator; it does not include *Sukuk* which are *asset-backed*, where investors take risk on an identified pool of assets. It also acknowledges the fact that in a *Sukuk* structure, the issuer may not also be the originator and, therefore, the creditworthiness on which investors will rely is not necessarily that of the issuer of the *Sukuk*.

[195] See further Hainsworth 'Islamic Financial Institutions and Islamic Finance', n 54, para 35 *et seq*. and Naumowicz and Atkinson 'Close-out Netting and *Shariah*-compliant Derivatives' (2007) 22 JBIFL 245.

[196] See paras 19.28 and 19.30 above.

[197] See para 19.49 above. There is, however, debate as to the validity of the *Arbun* as a mechanism for creating an option. (See Ayub, n 1, pp 145 and 116.)

[198] See para 19.44 above.

[199] See paras 19.42 and 19.52 above.

[200] *AAOIFI Shari'a Standards* (2004–5), p 1 *et seq*. See Ghuddah et al, n 1, pp 45–9.

[201] See the example of a Shari'a compliant swap discussed in the context of *Murabaha* in para 19.42 above.

[202] See, for example, details of the FSA permission for European Islamic Investment Bank Plc (438537) published on the FSA Register (<http://www.fsa.gov.uk>).

[203] RAO, art 3(1). See para 16.04 *et seq*. above.

which a 'provider' undertakes: (a) in consideration of one or more payments; (b) to pay money or provide a corresponding benefit to a 'recipient'; (c) in response to a defined event the occurrence of which is uncertain and adverse to the interests of the recipient.[204] The characteristics of *Takaful*, as discussed above, suggest that a *Takaful* contract would generally fall within the definition of 'a qualifying contract of insurance': in this respect, the FSA emphasis on substance over form is noteworthy.[205] However the analysis does not stop there: insofar as an IFF used *Mudaraba* or *Wakala* arrangements to offer *Takaful*, it is likely the FSA would require it to be authorised to accept deposits.[206] Therefore, an IFF that wished to offer *Takaful* products, would need to be FSA authorised and have permission to effect or carry out contracts as principal, limited to the appropriate classes of insurance set out in the Third Non-life Directive[207] and Schedule 1 to the RAO,[208] or the types of life insurance identified in the Third Life Directive[209] and Schedule 2 to the RAO, as appropriate.[210]

For the purposes of excluding *Takaful* from the CIS definition, their definition as **19.101** a qualifying contract of insurance within the meaning of the RAO is important because paragraph 17 of the Schedule to the Treasury CIS Order excludes 'contracts of insurance' from the definition of a CIS.[211]

Regulating an IFF's Conduct of Business

Introduction

On the basis that the FSA operates a non-discriminatory regime, IFFs will be **19.102** subject to the same conduct of business requirements as conventional firms according to the type of services which the IFFs offer, eg wholesale or retail investment business, banking business, or insurance business. The mortgage regime under MCOB is currently the only regime with some special provisions for IFFs that offer HPPs and is discussed below.[212] However, the FSA has indicated that financial promotion and disclosure requirements for IFFs is an area of

---

[204] PERG 6.3.4G.

[205] See PERG 6.5.4(3)G.

[206] See, for example, details of the FSA permission for Principle Insurance Company Limited (467853) published on the FSA Register (<http://www.fsa.gov.uk>).

[207] Council Directive (EEC) 92/49. See paras 16.23 *et seq.* above.

[208] See, the details of the FSA permission for Principle Insurance Company Limited, n 181 above.

[209] Council Directive (EEC) 92/96. See paras 16.23 *et seq.* above.

[210] See, the details of the FSA permission for Principle Insurance Company Limited, n 181 above. For discussion of the regulated activities relating to insurance, see para 14.90 *et seq.* above.

[211] For discussion, see para 17.47 above.

[212] See para 19.108 *et seq.*

particular interest.[213] In addition, the issue of suitability and the extent to which an IFF's duties with respect to its client may extend to ensuring that a product is in fact *Shari'a* compliant is also an area worthy of discussion. Finally, the experience in other jurisdictions with respect to the treatment of PSIAs provides a useful guide to the issues which an FSA regulated IFF may need to address in order to comply with the FSA Principles for Businesses.[214]

Financial promotion and disclosure

19.103 The FSA identify two features of *Shari'a* compliant products and services which reinforce the need for IFFs to ensure that risks are appropriately disclosed in the context of the duty of an IFF under Principle 7 to ensure that its communications are 'clear, fair and not misleading':[215] (a) the novelty of *Shari'a* compliant products and services and the fact that they differ from conventional products and services;[216] and (b) the relative inexperience of the users of *Shari'a* compliant products and services.[217]

19.104 The issue of clear communications may have an important commercial role to play for an IFF that wishes to sell its services or products to customers looking for *Shari'a* compliant services and products where an IFF would, in practice, need to point to facts to demonstrate that the products and services which it offers are *Shari'a* compliant. In this respect, the disclosures surrounding the systems and controls, which an IFF has put in place to ensure that its products and services are *Shari'a* compliant, assume a central position in an IFF's conduct of its business. Although the FSA does not state it, the need for an IFF to disclose to customers the systems and controls, ie the *Shari'a* scholars, which it has in place to ensure *Shari'a* compliance could be viewed as a necessary component of an IFF's duty to communicate sufficient information about the IFF's products and services to enable a customer to decide whether the products and services satisfy the customer's own *Shari'a* requirements. Without the FSA's own scholars, or other scholars identified by the regulator, the judgement of whom a customer could

---

[213] 'Islamic Finance in the UK', n 11, p 11.

[214] See also the CBB's special requirements for *Takaful* and *Retakaful* firms set out in CBB Rulebook, Volume 3: *Insurance*, Chapter CA-8.

[215] See PRIN 2.2.1.

[216] This implies that investors could confuse a *Shari'a* compliant product or service for a conventional product or service and assume that the *Shari'a* compliant product or service had the same or similar features and, therefore, same or similar risk profile as the conventional product or service.

[217] This seems to imply that the scarcity of *Shari'a* compliant products and services, until recently, means that, by definition, the number of inexperienced users of such products or services is far less than the users of conventional products and services. It fails to take into account the possibility that Muslims might use conventional products and services. 'Islamic Finance in the UK', n 11, p 14.

assess, the customer must be put in the best position possible to assess the effectiveness and credentials of the IFF's *Shari'a* scholars.[218]

The full disclosure approach is that taken, for example, in the DIFC where the **19.105** DFSA sets out a single requirement for an IFF with respect to the marketing and promotion of *Shari'a* compliant products and services: before an IFF communicates any marketing material to a person, it must ensure that, in addition to the information that a conventional firm must include in any marketing material, the IFF must ensure that the material governing *Shari'a* compliant products or services state which SSB has reviewed the products or services.[219]

Another example of such disclosure, albeit more comprehensive, is that under the **19.106** Saudi Arabia Capital Market Authority Investment Fund Regulations which require the manager of an investment fund established in Saudi Arabia which is 'stated to be operated in accordance with the principles of *Shari'a*' to disclose: '(a) the identity and qualifications of the *Shari'a* committee members; (b) whether those members are compensated for their advice and the nature and source of any compensation provided; and (c) the criteria used to determine the eligibility of investments for the investment fund'.[220]

The suitability of Shari'a *compliant investments*

The FSA requires a firm that carries on designated investment business to take **19.107** reasonable steps to ensure that a 'personal recommendation' or a decision to trade, is suitable for the firm's client.[221] The question for an IFF is whether this duty includes the duty to ensure that a designated investment is *Shari'a* compliant. The FSA defines a 'personal recommendation' by reference to the regulated activity of 'advising on investments', ie advice on the merits of, inter alia, buying a designated investment.[222] In this context, there is an argument to say that, where a person carries on the activity of 'advising on investments' which are *Shari'a* compliant, the regulatory definition assumes or presupposes the *Shari'a* compliant nature of the investments and does not include it within the scope of the definition

---

[218] This is consistent with the principle of public awareness in FSMA, s 4 and the need for the users of *Shari'a* compliant products and services to understand the nature of those products and whether the relevant *Shari'a* scholars and their methods for issuing the necessary *Fatawa* satisfy the conscience of the individual user of the product or service in question.

[219] See the DFSA Rulebook: *Islamic Finance Module*, Rule 6.1.5 and Henderson 'Limiting the Regulation of Islamic Finance', n 9, p 217.

[220] Annex 1. The official translation is contained at <http://www.cma.org.sa>.

[221] COBS 9.2.1R.

[222] See RAO, art 53.

of advising.[223] Against this is the requirement on a firm to obtain from its client such information as is necessary for the firm to understand the essential facts about the client and have a reasonable basis for believing, giving due consideration to the nature and extent of the service provided, that the specific transaction to be recommended, or entered into in the course of managing, inter alia, meets the client's investment objectives.[224] Even if an IFF's duties to ensure that a designated investment is suitable extend to the requirement to ensure that the investment is *Shari'a* compliant, that duty should be no greater than the duty that the FSA would impose on it with respect to ensuring *Shari'a* compliance, ie that the IFF or another IFF has subjected the investment to SSB scrutiny and the SSB has issued the appropriate *Fatwa*.[225]

Special considerations for IFFs offering Islamic mortgages[226]

19.108 The regime for those firms that offer mortgages under MCOB applies to IFFs that offer HPPs.[227] However, MCOB contains special provisions for IFFs. The FSA described the effect of its regulation of IFFs that offer HPPs as follows: 'It allows us to deliver a level consumer protection playing field with products designed for similar purposes. It also builds on the work that we have already done in the field of Islamic financial services, to improve consumer access to these products.'[228]

19.109 The special requirements for IFFs under MCOB include the requirement that an IFF ensure that the interests of its customer under an HPP are protected to a reasonable standard.[229] It also requires an IFF to pay due regard to the interests of its customer and treat him fairly when drafting or amending the terms of, or imposing obligations or exercising rights or discretions under an HPP.[230]

---

[223] This is the approach which the CBB takes in defining 'advising on *Shari'a* compliant financial instruments', the wording of which is similar to RAO, art 53. (See CBB Rulebook, Volume 2: *Islamic Banks*, Rule LR-1.3.45.)

[224] COBS 9.2.2R.

[225] Ultimately the issue should be one of contract determined by the precise nature of the service that the IFF, like any other firm, offers. (See *JP Morgan Chase Bank and others v Springwell Navigation Corp* [2008] EWHC 1186.)

[226] See also Patient 'Islamic Finance in the UK Consumer Sector', n 162, p 9.

[227] MCOB 1.2.1R.

[228] See FSA/PN041/2006, which accompanied FSA CP 06/08 'The Regulation of Home Reversion and Home Purchase Plans'.

[229] MCOB 2.6A.1R. For discussion of the protection of customer interests in the context of early redemption, see Hainsworth 'Islamic Financial Institutions and Islamic Finance', n 54, para 95 *et seq.*

[230] MCOB 2.6A.8R.

MCOB prohibits an IFF firm entering into a HPP transaction or agreeing to do **19.110**
so with a customer unless the customer has submitted an application for the particular HPP.[231] MCOB requires the IFF to provide its customer with an appropriate financial information statement for an HPP before the customer submits an
application for the HPP and without due delay when the IFF makes a personal
recommendation to the customer to enter into an HPP (unless the personal recommendation is made by telephone, in which case an IFF must ensure the financial statement is or has been provided as soon as practicable after the telephone
call); the IFF provides written information that is specific to the amount of finance
to be provided on a particular plan; or the customer requests written information
from the IFF that is specific to the amount of finance to be provided on a particular HPP, unless the IFF does not wish to do business with the customer.[232] MCOB
sets out the requirements for the format and content of the financial information
statement.[233] An IFF must ensure that its customer has had a reasonable opportunity to consider the financial information statement and risks and features statement before committing the customer to an application.[234]

Special considerations for IFFs offering PSIAs

The FSA does not set out any specific requirements for IFFs that offer PSIAs, **19.111**
either by way of *Mudaraba* arrangements or *Wakala* arrangements. The operation
of PSIAs, however, offers special challenges for an IFF because the IFF has to balance properly the interests of the PSIA holders against those of the IFF as PSIA
manager. In this respect, there is a potential conflict of interest between PSIA and
an IFF's shareholders as higher dividend payments to the shareholders may be at
the expense of profits that would otherwise accrue to the PSIA holders. In Bahrain,
for example, in its 'Principles of Business' for Islamic Banks, the CBB requires an
Islamic bank licensee's management: (a) as part of their duties to observe high
standards of integrity and fair dealing under 'Principle 1—Integrity', to 'safeguard
not only the interests of the shareholders of the bank but also those of the PSIA
holders';[235] and (b) as part of their duties to identify, prevent, or manage conflicts
of interest under 'Principle 2—Conflicts of Interest', to 'bear in mind the interests
of shareholders and PSIA holders'.[236] There is no reason why the same considerations would not arise for IFFs under the FSA Principles for Businesses governing

---

[231] MCOB 5.3.1R.
[232] MCOB 5.8.1R.
[233] See MCOB 5.8.4R *et seq.*
[234] MCOB 5.8.11R.
[235] CBB Rulebook, Volume 2: *Islamic Banks*, Rule PB-1.1.1.
[236] CBB Rulebook, Volume 2: *Islamic Banks*, Rule PB-1.1.2.

the same subjects in Principles 1 and 8, respectively, as well as its duty to treat customers fairly under 'Principle 6—Customer's Interests'.[237]

19.112 The CBB also requires Islamic banks to insert minimum terms and conditions in PSIA contracts and a statement of policies and procedures to safeguard the interests of PSIA holders and a policy dealing with the following: (a) the basis for allocation of profit or loss to the PSIA; (b) a policy for making provisions and reserves against assets and equity for PSIAs and to whom these provisions and reserves revert in case of write-back or recovery;[238] (c) a policy on the priority for investment of own funds and those of unrestricted PSIA holders; and (d) the basis for allocating expenses to the PSIA.[239]

The Listing and Public Offer of *Shari'a* Compliant Securities

The classification of Sukuk

19.113 The classification of *Sukuk* under the RAO would not necessarily determine how they would be classified for listing purposes.[240] In practice, the UKLA assesses the *Sukuk* structures in relation to the underlying assets, examining such factors as the on/off balance sheet nature of the assets and the nature of the cash flows that the assets generate. Currently, the Listing Rules and Prospectus Rules would appear to give the FSA the ability to treat *Sukuk* in a manner consistent with the economic substance and underlying risk without the need for a specific definition of *Sukuk* for listing purposes.[241]

---

[237] See para s 5.16 *et seq*.76 above.

[238] IFSB CAS, section B.4 sets out the requirements for PSIAs to make adequate capital adequacy provisions for its PSIAs. Paragraph 76 deals with the concept of 'displaced commercial risk' which it defines as 'the risk arising from assets managed on behalf of [PSIA holders] which are effectively transferred to the [IFF's] own capital because the [IFF] follows the practice of foregoing part or all of its *Mudarib* share of profits on such funds, when it considers this necessary as a result of commercial pressure in order to increase the return that would otherwise be payable to the PSIA holder'. The CBB, DFSA, and QFCRA set out special prudential and capital adequacy requirements for PSIA holders.

[239] CBB Rulebook, Volume 2: *Islamic Banks, Business and Market Conduct Module*, Rule BC-7.1. The CBB must agree the statement.

[240] In this respect, the position in Saudi Arabia is noteworthy. In its Glossary of Defined Terms used in the Regulations and Rules of the Capital Market Authority, the Capital Market Authority sates that 'the definition of "share" includes every instrument having the characteristics of equity, including *Sukuk*'. (The official translation is contained at <http://www.cma.org.sa>.) However in practice, *Sukuk* are listed on the debt list of the *Tadawul*, the Saudi Arabia stock exchange. (See <http://www.tadawul.com.sa>.)

[241] See 'Islamic Finance in the UK', n 11, p 26.

The UKLA have been able to classify asset-based *Sukuk* where investors take risk **19.114** on the creditworthiness of the *Sukuk* originator as 'debt securities', ie debentures, debenture stock, loan stock, bonds, certificates of deposit, or any other instrument creating or acknowledging indebtedness, for the purposes of the Listing Rules subject to appropriate additional information requirements.[242] If the performance of the *Sukuk* is directly related to the performance of an underlying asset, ie asset-backed *Sukuk* where investors take risk on an identified pool of assets as opposed to taking risk on the creditworthiness of the *Sukuk* originator, then the UKLA is likely to treat them as 'asset-backed securities'.[243]

Disclosure standards

With respect to disclosure standards, the UKLA does not impose any special **19.115** requirements. The extent to which it can be said that the details of how an issuer or originator can say that particular *Sukuk* are *Shari'a* compliant should form part of the information which investors and their professional advisers would reasonably require and reasonably expect to find in a prospectus, in order to make any investment decision,[244] is an open question. However, in, for example, the DIFC, the DFSA requires the issuer of securities, which are held out as being *Shari'a* compliant, to disclose details of: (a) the members of the SSB appointed by the issuer who have undertaken a review of the securities; and (b) details of the qualifications and experience of each of the SSB members.[245] Although there is no express requirement under the PR or any other relevant UKLA or FSA rule for the issuer or originator of *Sukuk* to disclose details of the SSB that approved the *Sukuk*, commercial considerations may, in any event, drive the issuer or originator to do so.[246]

---

[242] ibid. LR 17 and PR Appendix 3 govern the listing requirements and disclosure requirements for debt securities, respectively. See para 16.128 above. At the time of writing (September 2008), the UKLA has treated all *Sukuk* listed in the UK as guaranteed debt.

[243] The Prospectus Directive Regulation (No 2004/809/EC) defines 'asset-backed securities' as securities which: (a) represent an interest in assets, including any rights intended to assure servicing, or the receipt or timeliness of receipts by holders of assets of amounts payable thereunder; or (b) are secured by assets and the terms of which provide for payments which relate to payments or reasonable projections of payments calculated by reference to identified or identifiable assets. LR 17 also governs the listing of asset-backed securities but the disclosure requirements under PR Appendix 3 differ. The capital adequacy requirements in BIPRU 9 would apply to an IFF and any other firm with exposures under a *Shari'a* compliant securitisation.

[244] FSMA, s 80(1).

[245] DFSA Rulebook: *Offered Securities Module*, Rule OSR A1.1.1, para 25.

[246] The issues are the same as those discussed in the context of financial promotion and disclosure in para 19.103 *et seq.*above.

Continuing obligations

19.116 The UKLA does not impose any special continuing obligations for *Sukuk* issuers in addition to those for the issuers of conventional securities. The continuing obligations relevant to issuers of debt securities or asset-backed securities should also apply to issuers of *Sukuk*.[247]

---

[247] The continuing obligations do not, however, apply to the originator in *Sukuk* tractions. *Sukuk* transactions commonly use a Special Purpose Vehicle ('SPV') to issue the *Sukuk* and the continuing obligations apply to the SPV rather than the originator. The regime is, therefore, less burdensome for the originator of a *Sukuk* as compared to a conventional debt instrument and may be an area for amendment.

INDEX